# Goldmine

# PROMO RECORD
## & CD PRICE GUIDE

### 2nd Edition

## Fred Heggeness
### Edited by Tim Neely

Published by

**krause
publications**

700 E. State Street • Iola, WI  54990-0001
Telephone: 715/445-2214

Please call or write for our free catalog of music publications.
Our toll-free number to place an order or obtain a free catalog is 800-258-0929
or please use our regular business telephone 715-445-2214
for editorial comment and further information.

Library of Congress Catalog Number: 95-77314
ISBN: 0-87341-634-1
Printed in the United States of America

PROMO RECORD AND CD PRICE GUIDE

# CONTENTS

# Introduction to the 2nd Edition

Regular readers of *Goldmine* magazine know this, but many buyers of the first edition of this book may not: Fred Heggeness, the author of the book, died in 1997 after a bout with cancer. He knew he was dying, so when Krause Publications opted to print a second edition of the *Promo Record & CD Price Guide*, he tried to add as many listings as he possibly could. Many readers contacted him with praise and corrections; he also continued to research the pricing right up until the end.

Krause Publications has purchased the rights to the two books of his that we published, and as long as there is interest in continuing them, we will do so. (The other one is the *Goldmine Country Western Record & CD Price Guide*.)

For this edition, as Fred had done so much work on it before his death, we felt it best to tinker and not to do a major overhaul. We have left his name on the cover of the book as the author, with myself as the editor.

My primary job was to make the additions and changes he scribbled and pasted in his marking copy of the first edition. Sometimes it wasn't easy, but I think we've accounted for everything. Also, we have added several thousand listings contained in the *Goldmine* database that were not in Fred's first edition. Finally, we've significantly beefed up listings of promotional CD singles by collectible artists. Many of these are fetching more than their stock copy equivalents – if there was one at all. We feel that, in the future, promo CD singles of songs that are not released to the general public as singles will escalate in value, especially as non-singles will be allowed to chart on the *Billboard* Hot 100 effective Dec. 5, 1998.

## What's new?

The biggest difference between the second edition and the first is in how the listings are arranged. We hope this will make things easier to find. It also will make it easier to find out what we've missed and what you need to help us with.

Within each artist's listings, we have first segregated the "regular" promos from the radio shows, which Fred had done already. But we've broken it down farther. Within each section, we sort by format – 45s, albums, compact discs, reel-to-reel tapes. And finally, we've arranged the listings alphabetically by title within each format.

We've deleted the abbreviations for the different types of music. Some may lament this passing, but we found that some artists can't easily be classified. And we don't do this in any of our other general price guides.

We've altered what was the most confusing part of the first edition – the listings of soundtracks and various artists collections. They now have been moved from the artists listings into their own section in the back.

Thanks to a reader of the first edition, we've also added a small write-up on what may be the first promo 45 ever. You'll find that just before the listings start.

And finally, in keeping with Fred's notes, we've raised and lowered values where appropriate. In general, regular promos were more likely to go up, while radio shows were more likely to stay the same or go down.

## What is a "promo," anyway?

This is a good time to remind the reader: All records, tapes and compact discs listed in this book are PROMOS.

A "promo," short for "promotional," is a copy of a recording not meant for the general public, but instead to promote an artist, album, label or type of music. A synonym for "promo" is "demo," short for "demonstration"; this is the more common term in the United Kingdom, whereas "promo" is the more common term in the United States.

In contrast, a "stock copy" of a record/CD is the kind you find for sale at most stores – it's pressed for the public and meant to be sold.

For the most part, the labels on promo copies are different than stock copy labels. In most cases, this means that a record's label is white. If it's not white, then it's usually a different shade than regular stock copies. Also, most of them will have words such as "Audition Copy," "Demonstration – Not for Sale," "Promotion Copy," "For Promotion Only, Not for Sale" or words to this effect, and these words will be part of the label typeface.

Most promos are pressed in limited numbers before the stock copies of the same items. Thus they often boast higher fidelity and are true "first editions."

Promos present a fascinating collecting focus, but they also represent a legal gray area. Simply, promos are marked as such because the artists earn no royalties from them; in fact, more often than not the record companies deduct the cost of these items from an artist's future royalties. Many more recent "designate promos" (more on which later) have dire warnings in gold letters that claim that the record company retains the ownership of the item and that it "must be returned on demand of recording company" (the common warning on Time Warner product).

For all intents and purposes, this is hogwash. Music magazines and radio stations receive hundreds of promos a month, most of which they will never use. Some are used as contest prizes; others are distributed in-house; still others end up given to charity or thrown away. The logistical nightmare of recalling all the promos of a particular release make it almost impossible that it would ever happen. Nonetheless, at least one label (Mobile Fidelity) has recalled a promo it found "defective." And most labels do have a list of the places they send promos.

In 1988, Warner Bros. sent a cease-and-desist letter to a prominent Pennsylvania dealer who was selling promotional CD singles of a then-current Warner release. Nonetheless, he continues to sell promos to this day. Once a promo reaches the secondary market (record collectors), there's nothing the record companies can do to stop the sales of these items for whatever the market will bear.

They can better police the distribution of the promos by cutting off supply to known sellers and disciplining their own employees who sell to collectors' shops. But what the major record companies REALLY need to do to slow down the sale of promotional items is very simple: Make everything they distribute promotionally available for sale to the public as well! If a label sends a single to radio, release it to the public. If it releases an EP of the new songs on a box set, release the same sampler to the public. If it releases remixes of a song that are better than the album version, release those remixes to stores. If it packages a new album in an elaborate radio-only package, issue the same packaging to the public. Until that day (don't hold your breath), promos will remain collectible.

## What is a "designate promo"?

We mentioned this term in the last section; now we'll explain.

A "designate promo," basically, is a stock copy labeled to look like a promo. It is identical to the copies sold in stores except for a sticker, notch, hole or rubber stamp on the cover that "designates" the item as a promotional copy. In more recent years, with the advent of bar coding, most of the time the bar code is defaced so that it cannot be read by a scanner. By doing so, a label can send out a promo any time it wants to take a stock copy and designate it as such.

With only a few exceptions (Elvis Presley comes to mind), gold-stamped "designate promos" are worth at most 10 percent more that the regular stock copy. Ones with a notch or hole are worth less than stock copies.

An exception is certain "audiophile pressings," such as the Warner family's use of "Quiex II" vinyl in the early to middle 1980s. The labels are the same as stock copies, but the covers of these always have a sticker noting the use of the different vinyl. Those always are more valuable than their stock copy counterparts. Otherwise, this book basically ignores "designate promos."

## What is a "Jukebox LLP"?

This is a term you'll see frequently in the listings. The letters "LLP" refer to "Little LP," which was a brand name for some of these records, most of which have a separate number in addition to the record company's own number.

Through the 1960s and until about 1974, some jukeboxes were set up to play small-holed 33 1/3 records in addition to playing 45s. To take advantage, many record companies created abridged versions (four to six tracks) of a current album; these were not sold to the public, but were distributed only to the jukebox trade. Most of these came with either hard or soft covers, usually a two-color copy of the album cover and with a blank back. They also had title strips that could be used in the jukebox.

As most of these ended up in jukeboxes, they are often found in poor to fair condition. Surprisingly, though, you still see copies with all the pieces intact, even the title strips, still sealed in shrink wrap. Many of these are undervalued in comparison to their rarity.

Stereo singles were also pressed for jukeboxes, often 33 1/3 rpm with a small center hole. These compact singles often were in sets of five records, 10 songs, and are rarely found all together (again, these were played heavily).

Since 1992, there has been another form of jukebox record: the regular 45. Those that have come out through Capitol-EMI's special markets division are even marked "For Jukeboxes Only!" Few of these are pressed in quantities of more than 10,000, making them extremely rare compared to popular 45s of the 1960s, 1970s and 1980s. However, in contrast to the LLPs, these are made available for purchase by the general public anywhere that 45s are still available, so these technically are not promos. Nonetheless, several of them are listed in here.

## What are some other types of promos?

Movie ad discs were pressed for theaters to give to radio stations for creation of radio ads. Many were pressed in numbers around one thousand. Most of them were thrown away by either the radio station or theater. Each disc has from one to six ads, 10 to 60 seconds each. Most are 45 rpm format, some are 10- or 12-inch discs. All are rare and some feature the Beatles (Help!), Elvis (Roustabout, etc.) and other top collectible artists.

PSA spots are public service radio commercials featuring major movie, sports and music stars donating time for free public service advertising. Discs range from one to twenty cuts, ten to sixty seconds each. "What's It All About" is a five-minute public service show with interviews and music from a major recording artist. Most of these shows are collectible, on 45 rpm format and are listed in this book.

By the way, this book does not attempt to document the vast quantities of promotional items that are not recordings. For that kind of material, we refer you to the *Goldmine Price Guide to Rock 'n' Roll Memorabilia* by Mark Allen Baker.

## For the purposes of this book, what is a "radio show"?

This isn't as stupid a question as it sounds. Consider the following story:

When I was a teenager, I discovered the radio program "American Top 40." This was a godsend for a chart junkie like myself: I didn't have to search out *Billboard* magazine, which was hard to find in those days, to know what was on the national charts; I could get it right off my radio! It seemed to be on most stations at about the same time – Sunday evenings.

Early in my listening career, I won a radio station contest: If you guessed the No. 1 song that week, you won the countdown. I assumed this meant that I won 40 45s with that week's biggest hits on them. Imagine my surprise when the package came and it contained a box marked "American Top 40"! This was the actual program that I had listened to! At first I was disappointed that I still had to buy those 45s, but not for long. I even entered and won the contest again a few months later and added another AT 40 broadcast to the collection.

Today, most of the syndicated shows you hear on the radio (other examples include the "King Biscuit Flower Hour," "The Beatle Years" and "American Country Countdown," and there are dozens more) are sent to the subscribing radio station on compact discs. Before the advent of CDs, they came on records. Sometimes, they come on reel-to-reel tapes. This gives the station the freedom to air the show when it wants to. Of course, it creates a collectible as well; most radio shows are pressed in editions of 1,000 or fewer. And while they are supposed to be destroyed or returned after airing, many are not. Some are given away, as the station that aired "American Top 40" did.

"American Top 40" may be among the most famous of all radio shows (there's even an independent web site that pays tribute to it), but it's not the most collectible.

Below are six levels of radio show collectibility. This list does not take into consideration the pressing number and/or rarity of the show. Level 1 is the most collectible, down to the less collectible at Level 6. Examples of each type are listed.

**Level 1: Live concert** (King Biscuit Flower Hour, In Concert, Superstar Concert, and the most collectible of all radio shows, the BBC Transcription Disc)

**Level 2: Music and interviews with live or unreleased material** (Up Close, High Voltage, NBC Source, The Lost Lennon Tapes)

**Level 3: Music and interviews on one act without rare material** (Off the Record, Here's to Veterans, Robert W. Morgan Special of the Week, Innerview)

**Level 4: Music and interviews on many acts** (World of Rock, Nightbird & Company, Rock Roll & Remember, Solid Gold Scrapbook)

**Level 5: Countdown shows** (American Top 40, The National Music Survey, Rick Dees' Weekly Top 40, American Country Countdown)

**Level 6: Famous DJ shows, usually sponsored by a branch of the military** (Wolfman Jack, Billy Pearl, Lawrence Welk, Sounds of Solid Gold)

Add to the information above the rarity of the record, the demand of the artist, the format of music, and the location and time of the live concert, and you've got the range of value.

## Why only one price listed? And why can't I get that for my promos?

One price listing was Fred's thing, and as we said earlier, we largely left the formatting the way he did it.

That one price, by the way, is a Near Mint value. That means essentially new, no wear, played only once or twice at the most, not off center, no label damage like writing or a sticker, no scuffs or scratches. This is a clean pressing. It's possible for a record to be unplayed but not mint if it's off center or a poor pressing that has surface noise when it is played, or if the cover has damage.

Also, the price represents the HIGHEST amount you might expect to pay for that record or that you might get for that record/CD if you sold it to a person willing to pay the HIGHEST price. Most dealers would only pay 25 to 50 percent for your mint product because they have to make a profit to stay in business. If the item is not mint condition, its value diminishes significantly. When buying or selling it is always wise to check around since you may be able to get a better price somewhere else.

## Why is a value range listed for most radio shows?

Simply, radio show collecting is a limited market with fluctuating prices. In general, these items haven't been bought and sold enough to establish a stable price. The collector's market for them tends to be dominated by a handful of dealers who sell mostly radio shows, so if one of them gets a surplus, the price can drop significantly overnight. Prices can rise overnight if an artist becomes suddenly popular and a dealer is caught short.

Also, radio shows are quite rare and have great investment potential, which is another reason for the price range.

## How do I grade my stuff, anyway?

When it comes to records, and how much you'll get for them, remember this above all:

Condition is (almost) everything!

Yes, it's possible to get a high price for a beat-up record, if it's exceptionally rare. But for common material, if it's not in at least Very Good condition – and preferably closer to Near Mint – you won't get many buyers. Or at least you won't the second time around. So accurately grading your discs is important, whether you're selling your records to a dealer or selling them to another collector.

**Visual or play grading?** In an ideal world, every record would be played before it is graded. But the time involved makes it impractical for most dealers, and anyway, it's rare that you get a chance to hear a record before you buy through the mail. Some advertisers play-grade everything and say so. But unless otherwise noted, records are visually graded.

**How to grade.** Look at everything about a record -- its playing surface, its label, its edges -- under a strong light. Then, based on your overall impression, give it a grade based on the following criteria:

**Mint (M):** Absolutely perfect in every way -- certainly never played, possibly even still sealed. (More on still sealed under "Other considerations.") Should be used sparingly as a grade, if at all.

**Near Mint (NM or M-):** A nearly perfect record. Many dealers won't give a grade higher than this, implying (perhaps correctly) that no record is ever truly perfect.

The record should show no obvious signs of wear. A 45 RPM or EP sleeve should have no more than the most minor defects, such as almost invisible ring wear or other signs of slight handling.

An LP jacket should have no creases, folds, seam splits or any other noticeable similar defect. No cut-out holes, either. And of course, the same should be true of any other inserts, such as posters, lyric sleeves and the like.

Basically, an LP in Near Mint condition looks as if you just got it home from a new record store and removed the shrink wrap.

Near Mint is the highest price listed in all *Goldmine* price guides. Anything that exceeds this grade, in the opinion of both buyer and seller, is worth significantly more than the highest *Goldmine* book value.

**Very Good Plus (VG+):** Generally worth 50 percent of the Near Mint value.

A Very Good Plus record will show some signs that it was played and otherwise handled by a previous owner who took good care of it.

Record surfaces may show some slight signs of wear and may have slight scuffs or very light scratches that don't affect one's listening experience. Slight warps that do not affect the sound are OK.

The label may have some ring wear or discoloration, but it should be barely noticeable. The center hole will not have been misshapen by repeated play.

Picture sleeves and LP inner sleeves will have some slight ring wear, lightly turned-up corners, or a slight seam split. An LP jacket may have slight signs of wear also and may be marred by a cut-out hole, indentation or corner indicating it was taken out of print and sold at a discount.

In general, if not for a couple minor things wrong with it, this would be Near Mint. All but the most mint-crazy collectors will find a Very Good Plus record highly acceptable.

A synonym used by some collectors and dealers for "Very Good Plus" is "Excellent."

**Very Good (VG):** Generally worth 25 percent of the Near Mint value.

Many of the defects found in a VG+ record will be more pronounced in a VG disc.

Surface noise will be evident upon playing, especially in soft passages and during a song's intro and fade, but will not overpower the music otherwise. Groove wear will start to be noticeable, as will light scratches (deep enough to feel with a fingernail) that will affect the sound.

Labels may be marred by writing, or have tape or stickers (or their residue) attached. The same will be true of picture sleeves or LP covers. However, it will not have all of these problems at the same time, only two or three of them.

**Good (G), Good Plus (G+):** Generally worth 10-15 percent of the Near Mint value.

Good does not mean Bad! A record in Good or Good Plus condition can be put onto a turntable and will play through without skipping. But it will have significant surface noise and scratches and visible groove wear (on a styrene record, the groove will be starting to turn white).

A jacket or sleeve will have seam splits, especially at the bottom or on the spine. Tape, writing, ring wear or other defects will start to overwhelm the object.

If it's a common item, you'll probably find another copy in better shape eventually. Pass it up. But if it's something you have been seeking for years, and the price is right, get it... but keep looking to upgrade.

**Poor (P), Fair (F):** Generally worth 0-5 percent of the Near Mint price.

The record is cracked, badly warped, and won't play through without skipping or repeating. The picture sleeve is water damaged, split on all three seams and heavily marred by wear and writing. The LP jacket barely keeps the LP inside it. Inner sleeves are fully seam split, crinkled, and written upon.

Except for impossibly rare records otherwise unattainable, records in this condition should be bought or sold for no more than a few cents each.

**Other grading considerations.** Most dealers give a separate grade to the record and its sleeve or cover. In an ad, a record's grade is listed first, followed by that of the sleeve or jacket.

With **Still Sealed (SS)** records, let the buyer beware, unless it's a U.S. pressing from the last 10-15 years or so. It's too easy to re-seal one. Yes, some legitimately never-opened LPs from the 1960s still exist. But if you're looking for a specific pressing, the only way you can know for sure is to open the record. Also, European imports are not factory-sealed, so if you see them advertised as sealed, someone other than the plant of manufacture sealed them.

## How do I make sense of the listings?

First, the artist is in bold. Underneath many of the artists are italicized notes. Fred liked to list solo acts from a group under the group unless there were simply too many to list that way (for example, the Beatles), so he mentions who else is included and under what other listings you might find related material. Following that are some general value comments about an artist's more common promo records and CDs.

## What's with all the general comments instead of individual listings?

Space. At some point, we'd like to list as many of the white label or different label promos (NOT designate promos) as possible for each artist in the book. But with only 496 pages, we had to trim somewhere. Thus all the designations such as "Warner Bros. promo 45s $3 each." In the future, we'd like to decrease the number of listings like this.

## OK, now what?

Below the general comments are individual listings. The regular promos in 12-inch single, 45, LP, cassette, compact disc, and reel-to-reel tape are listed first, in that order, followed by radio show listings. They are listed alphabetically by title. Also listed, when known for radio shows, is month and year of broadcast.

The next column is the year of release.

The next column has the label and number or the syndicator (in the case of a radio show). A number in parentheses after this listing is the number of records, tapes or discs in the complete set.

Finally, we list the Near Mint value for the items.

Underneath many of the items is a comment about the item above it, italicized and in parentheses.

## Where do I find promos?

Almost anywhere you can buy used records and CDs, you can find promos. If you're fortunate and have contacts in the recording industry, such as with radio or entertainment media, you might get some that way.

Record conventions are a good source, especially for lower-priced items such as common 45s and CD singles.

Collector's magazines such as *Goldmine* are excellent sources for promos also. And an increasingly important source is the Internet, both from auction sites and dealers who have set up shop on the World Wide Web.

The places you won't find promos are the mall music stores and the electronics shops that use music as a loss leader. Once in a while, though, a chain like Best Buy will have an exclusive item that you can't buy, but can get as a bonus with the purchase of a given CD. So it doesn't hurt to check their ads. Best Buy had a Paul McCartney CD in 1997 and a Jimi Hendrix 45 in 1998 that were not available at any other primary-market store.

Happy hunting and have fun!

## Oh yes. I've got something that should be in the book but isn't. How do I let you know?

Simple. Just contact the editor. Address correspondence with corrections, additions, etc. to:

Tim Neely
Goldmine Promo Record & CD Price Guide, 2nd Edition
700 E. State St.
Iola, WI 54945;
or call (715) 445-4612, extension 782 during regular Central Time business hours;
or e-mail neelyt@krause.com.

## Acknowledgments

First, I'd like to thank Fred Heggeness for his work on the book. He and I were kindred spirits; if we had been able to do so, we could have talked collectible records all day. I wish I'd been able to get to know him better.

Also, thanks to Greg Loescher, editor of *Goldmine;* Don Gulbrandsen of the Krause Publications book department; the KP proofreading department; and the KP book production staff, especially Patsy Morrison, for their assistance in getting this done. Also, thanks to Gretchen Dahl and Lauren Borth for helping with input of corrections and additions. Two former Krause employees, Deborah Faupel and Melissa Warden, got the first edition in good enough shape so that it was, without too much difficulty, able to be transferred to the KP records database.

Of course, thanks go out to the many contributors who added listings for the second edition. Unfortunately, Fred didn't leave notes as to who contributed what, or if he did, I couldn't find them. So if you wrote Fred in Minnesota and your additions/corrections are in here, pat yourself on the back. We are grateful. A special thanks to John Wren for the information and tape on the "first promo 45."

Finally, thanks to all of you who wrote with comments, positive or negative, about the first edition. We've read your letters and we hope you like this edition as much, if not more, than the first.

Tim Neely
Iola, WI
November 1998

# Special Report: The First Promo 45?

The pictured RCA Victor 45, the "Whirl-Away Demonstration Record," may have been the first 45 rpm record ever made especially for promotional purposes. We're not prepared to say it definitely was, but the evidence is certainly convincing.

In the spring of 1949, RCA Victor introduced its new 45 rpm single and record changer, both as a replacement to the more fragile 78 rpm record and as a competitor to Columbia's new 33 1/3 "Microgroove" albums and singles. The 45 failed in its competition with albums, but succeeded in displacing 78s within 10 years. Despite sometimes stiff competition, the 45 remained the preferred singles medium until the late 1980s, and many still prefer it today.

To introduce this new record, RCA created a custom display for record stores. It consisted of a rotating, elevated carousel, which had seven different color threads hanging from it, one each for the seven different colors of records that RCA planned to produce. (These colored threads were black for pop, cerise [orange] for blues, green for country, red for classical, blue for light classics, yellow for children's, sky blue for international.) The base of the display was a 45 rpm turntable that played the "Whirl-Away Demonstration Record" over and over as the carousel rotat-

ed above it. It was named for the famous horse Whirlaway, winner of the Triple Crown of thoroughbred racing in 1941.

When the promotion was over, RCA Victor's representatives took back the displays, including the record, presumably to be thrown out. We don't know if any of the displays, or even a photo of one, survives today. But the record does.

John Wren of Philadelphia talks about the man from whom he bought this unusual item: "(He was) a retired record store owner. He told me that the record had gotten a little scratched during the promotion so the RCA rep gave him a new copy without picking up the old one." It then was stashed away in a box, not to be re-discovered until Wren met the former store owner many years later.

So what is on the record? It promotes the new RCA Victor 45 record and changer, using snippets from some of the first 45s. The segments include part of Vaughn Monroe's then-current hit, "Riders in the Sky," and Eddy Arnold's "Bouquet of Roses," the latter of which was released on 45 as RCA Victor 48-0001. It's an interesting artifact of the time. Has anyone else ever seen one?

| Title | Yr | Label, Number | NM $ |
|---|---|---|---|

# A

## A-HA
### 12-Inch Singles
| | | | |
|---|---|---|---|
| TAKE ON ME (4:46)/TAKE ON ME (3:46) | 1985 | Warner Bros. PRO-A-2291 | 8 |
| TRAIN OF THOUGHT (same on both sides) | 1985 | Warner Bros. PRO-A-2370 | 8 |

## ABBA
*Atlantic promo 45s $5; Polydor promo 45s by Agnetha $3; Atlantic promo 45s by Frida $3; Atlantic solo 12" promo singles $10 each; any US promo CDs $6-$8*
### 12-Inch Singles
| | | | |
|---|---|---|---|
| LAY ALL YOUR LOVE ON ME | 1980 | Disconet | 30 |
| *(Promo-only release)* | | | |

### 45s
| | | | |
|---|---|---|---|
| BANG-A-BOOMERANG  Svenne & Lotta (Swedish) | 1976 | Morningstar 507 | 12 |
| *(Produced by Benny & Bjorn)* | | | |
| HAPPY NEW YEAR | 1980 | Atlantic PR 380 | 12 |
| *(Stereo/Mono version, promo only)* | | | |
| HAPPY NEW YEAR | 1980 | Atlantic PR 390 | 12 |
| *(One-sided promo)* | | | |
| TAKE A CHANCE ON ME | 1978 | (Atlantic) No label | 15 |
| *(Pre-pressing, limited to radio stations, white label, 3:25 version)* | | | |

### Albums
| | | | |
|---|---|---|---|
| A COLLECTION OF HITS | 1982 | Atlantic PR 432 | 30 |
| *(Promo-only release)* | | | |
| ABBA | 1978 | Atlantic PR 300 | 30 |
| *(Promo-only release)* | | | |
| THE ABBA SPECIAL | 1983 | Atlantic PR 436 | 50 |
| *(Promo-only release)* | | | |

### RADIO SHOWS
### Albums
| | | | |
|---|---|---|---|
| BBC TRANSCRIPTION DISC  Live concert | 1980 | BBC Transcription | 300-750 |
| *(Live concert)* | | | |
| NIGHTBIRD & COMPANY (Nov 74) | 1974 | U. S. Army Reserve (2 LP) | 40-75 |
| *(Music and interviews)* | | | |
| ROBERT W. MORGAN SPECIAL OF THE WEEK (June 81) | 1981 | Watermark 812 | 40-75 |
| *(Music and interviews)* | | | |

## ABC
*Mercury promo singles $4 each*
### 12-Inch Singles
| | | | |
|---|---|---|---|
| BE NEAR ME (same on both sides) | 1985 | Mercury PRO 371 | 8 |
| HOW TO BE A ZILLIONAIRE (4 versions) | 1985 | Mercury PRO 397 | 8 |

### 45s
| | | | |
|---|---|---|---|
| THE NIGHT YOU MURDERED LOVE | 1987 | Mercury PRO 546-7 | 10 |

### RADIO SHOWS
### Albums
| | | | |
|---|---|---|---|
| KING BISCUIT FLOWER HOUR (May 83) w/Ultravox | 1983 | DIR (2) | 50-75 |

## ABDUL, PAULA
*Virgin promo singles $3 each*
### Compact Discs
| | | | |
|---|---|---|---|
| SPELLBOUND | 1991 | Virgin | 30 |
| *(Promo-only release)* | | | |

### RADIO SHOWS
### Compact Discs
| | | | |
|---|---|---|---|
| THE PAULA ABDUL STORY (Jan 90) Profile | 1990 | Unistar | 15-25 |
| *(Show repeated June and Nov 91)* | | | |

## AC/DC
*Atco promo 45s $4 each; Atlantic and Atco promo LPs $10 each; Atlantic 12" promo singles $10 each*
### 12-Inch Singles
| | | | |
|---|---|---|---|
| LIVE IN GERMANY | 1980 | Atlantic | 25 |
| *(Promo 12" single)* | | | |

### 45s
| | | | |
|---|---|---|---|
| GUNS FOR HIRE | 198? | Atlantic 89774 | 10 |

### Albums
| | | | |
|---|---|---|---|
| FLICK OF THE SWITCH INTERVIEW ALBUM | 1983 | Atlantic PR 562 | 40 |
| LIVE AT THE ATLANTIC STUDIOS | 1977 | Atlantic LAAS-001 | 60 |
| *(This album has been counterfeited)* | | | |

### RADIO SHOWS
### Albums
| | | | |
|---|---|---|---|
| BBC TRANSCRIPTION SERVICE  Live concert | 1980 | BBC | 300-500 |
| *(Very rare concert)* | | | |
| HIGH VOLTAGE Various artists | 1993 | Westwood One (2) | 25-50 |
| *(Includes live segment featuring AC/DC)* | | | |
| OFF THE RECORD | 1990 | Westwood One (2) | 10-25 |
| *(Music and interviews)* | | | |
| SOURCE SPECIAL (July 82) | 1982 | NBC Radio (3) | 50-75 |
| *(Profile, some live material)* | | | |

### Compact Discs
| | | | |
|---|---|---|---|
| BBC CLASSIC TRACK (Apr 91) | 1991 | Westwood One | 15-25 |
| *(Repeated in Apr 92 and Nov 93)* | | | |
| IN CONCERT (Jan 94) w/Urge Overkill | 1994 | Westwood One (2) | 40-75 |
| *(Live concert)* | | | |

| Title | Yr | Label, Number | NM $ |
|---|---|---|---|
| IN CONCERT (May 93) | 1993 | Westwood One (2) | 40-75 |
| *(Live concert)* | | | |
| IN THE STUDIO Profile of an album | 1990 | Album Network | 15-25 |
| *(Music and interviews)* | | | |
| SUPERSTAR CONCERT (Feb 95) | 1995 | Westwood One (2) | 30-60 |
| *(Live concert)* | | | |
| UP CLOSE | 1990 | Media America | 30-60 |
| *(Music and interviews, repeated in 1993)* | | | |

## ACUFF, ROY

*Columbia promo 45s $10 each; Hickory 45s $4 each; Elektra 45s $3 each; Other MGM and Capitol promo LPs $20-30 each*

**45s**

| | | | |
|---|---|---|---|
| ONCE MORE | 1958 | Hickory 1073 | 10 |
| *(White promo label)* | | | |

**7-Inch Extended Plays**

| | | | |
|---|---|---|---|
| KING OF COUNTRY MUSIC | 196? | Hickory H LPM 109 | 50 |
| *(Black label promo, six songs from LP 109)* | | | |

**Albums**

| | | | |
|---|---|---|---|
| FAVORITE HYMNS | 1958 | MGM 3707 | 50 |
| *(Yellow promo label)* | | | |
| INTERVIEW WITH ROY ACUFF (Oct 78) Joe Smith | 1978 | Elektra 10-1-78 | 25 |
| *(Radio only, interviews)* | | | |
| SONGS OF THE SMOKEY MOUNTAINS | 1963 | Capitol 2103 | 30 |
| *(Yellow promo label)* | | | |

**RADIO SHOWS**

**16-Inch Transcriptions**

| | | | |
|---|---|---|---|
| JUBILEE USA  Various artists | 195? | | 40-75 |
| *(Live show with guests, Roy is host of this show)* | | | |
| LEATHERNECK JAMBOREE  Various artists | 195? | U. S. Armed Forces | 40-50 |
| *(Music and interviews)* | | | |
| U. S. ARMY BAND (40s and 50s) Various artists | 194? | U. S. Army | 40-75 |
| *(Live music and interviews)* | | | |

**Albums**

| | | | |
|---|---|---|---|
| GRAND OL' OPRY  WSM Radio Presents | 196? | WSM Radio | 40-75 |
| *(Music and interviews)* | | | |

## ADAM AND THE ANTS

**12-Inch Singles**

| | | | |
|---|---|---|---|
| LOS RANCHEROS/PHYSICAL | 1980 | Epic AS 973 | 12 |

**45s**

| | | | |
|---|---|---|---|
| STAND AND DELIVER/BEAT MY GUEST | 1981 | Epic AE7 1236 | 10 |
| *(with promo picture sleeve)* | | | |

**Albums**

| | | | |
|---|---|---|---|
| ADAM AND THE ANTS | 1981 | Epic AE 1331 | 10 |
| *(Five-song promo-only sampler)* | | | |

## ADAMS, BRYAN

*ElectroSOUND and Monarch test pressing 45s $8 each; there are two picture sleeves for A&M 8651; A&M promo 45s $3 each*

**45s**

| | | | |
|---|---|---|---|
| CUTS LIKE A KNIFE | 1983 | (no label) | 15 |
| *(White label test pressing)* | | | |
| HEAVEN | 1985 | Electrosound | 15 |
| *(White label test pressing)* | | | |
| RUN TO YOU | 1984 | Electrosound | 15 |
| *(White label test pressing)* | | | |
| THIS TIME | 1984 | Monarch | 15 |
| *(White label test pressing)* | | | |

**RADIO SHOWS**

**Albums**

| | | | |
|---|---|---|---|
| BBC ROCK HOUR | 1984 | London Wavelength | 25-35 |
| *(Live concert)* | | | |
| HOT ROCKS (Dec 85) | 1985 | United Stations (2) | 20-30 |
| *(Box set, music and interviews)* | | | |
| IN CONCERT  Live concert | 1982 | Westwood One (2) | 75-100 |
| *(With U2)* | | | |
| IN CONCERT (Jan 83) Live concert | 1983 | Westwood One (2) | 40-75 |
| *(With Toronto)* | | | |
| INNERVIEW | 198? | Innerview | 10-20 |
| *(Music and interviews)* | | | |
| KING BISCUIT FLOWER HOUR | 1987 | DIR (2) | 20-40 |
| *(Live concert)* | | | |
| KING BISCUIT FLOWER HOUR (Feb 84) w/Graham Parker | 1984 | DIR (2) | 25-50 |
| *(Live concert)* | | | |
| PROFILE '86 | 1986 | NBC Radio (3) | 15-30 |
| *(Music and interviews)* | | | |
| SUPERSTAR CONCERT | 1988 | Westwood One (3) | 25-50 |
| *(Live concert, repeated)* | | | |

**Compact Discs**

| | | | |
|---|---|---|---|
| ALBUM NETWORK | 1996 | (2) | 50-100 |
| *(Live concert)* | | | |
| BBC CLASSIC TRACKS (June 94) | 1994 | Westwood One | 15-25 |
| *(Various classic live tracks)* | | | |
| IN CONCERT (July 92) | 1992 | Westwood One (2) | 25-50 |
| *(Live concert)* | | | |
| IN THE STUDIO Profile of an album | 199? | Album Network | 10-20 |
| *(Music and interviews)* | | | |

| Title | Yr | Label, Number | NM $ |
|---|---|---|---|
| KING BISCUIT FLOWER HOUR (Nov 93) | 1993 | DIR | 25-50 |
| *(Live concert)* | | | |
| KING BISCUIT FLOWER HOUR (Oct 92) w/Tom Cochrane | 1992 | DIR | 20-45 |
| *(Live concert)* | | | |
| SUPERSTAR CONCERT (Nov 93) | 1993 | Westwood One (2) | 25-50 |
| *(Live concert, repeated)* | | | |

### ADAMS, NICK
*Star of the TV series The Rebel.*
**45s**

| JOHNNY YUMA, THE REBEL | 1960 | Mercury 71607 | 10 |
|---|---|---|---|
| *(White label, "The Rebel" theme song)* | | | |

### ADAMSKI
**12-Inch Singles**

| KILLER (2 versions) | 1990 | MCA 18443 | 8 |
|---|---|---|---|

### ADDERLEY, CANNONBALL
**Albums**

| BIG MAN SAMPLER | 1975 | Fantasy FSP 2 | 20 |
|---|---|---|---|

### ADVENTURERS, THE
**45s**

| ROCK & ROLL UPRISING | 1961 | Columbia 42227 | 40 |
|---|---|---|---|
| *(White promo label)* | | | |

### AEROSMITH
*Columbia and Geffen 12" promo singles worth $10 each*
**Albums**

| PURE GOLD FROM R & R'S GOLDEN BOYS | 1976 | Columbia A3S-187 (3) | 50 |
|---|---|---|---|
| *(Promo box of three previously released LPs)* | | | |
| THE FIRST DECADE | 1980 | Columbia NNO (8) | 125 |
| *(Promo 8-record set)* | | | |

**Compact Discs**

| DUDE Promo-only 3" CD single | 1988 | Geffen | 25 |
|---|---|---|---|
| *(More common 5" version worth $3)* | | | |
| PUMP Single CD issued in leather case | 1992 | Geffen | 25 |
| *(Most of the value is for the leather case)* | | | |

**RADIO SHOWS**
**Albums**

| HIGH VOLTAGE (Feb 89) Various artists | 1989 | Westwood One (2) | 10-20 |
|---|---|---|---|
| *(Music and interviews)* | | | |
| IN CONCERT (June 86) Live concert | 1986 | Westwood One (2) | 10-20 |
| *(With Eddie Money)* | | | |
| INNERVIEW with Joe Perry and Steve Tyler | 1976 | Innerview Series 12 | 40-75 |
| *(Brown marble vinyl)* | | | |
| INNERVIEW with Joe Perry and Steve Tyler | 1976 | Innerview Series 12 | 30-60 |
| *(Green marble vinyl)* | | | |
| INNERVIEW with Joe Perry and Steve Tyler | 1976 | Innerview Series 12 | 15-30 |
| *(Black vinyl)* | | | |
| METALSHOP (Dec 91) Special Aerosmith show | 1991 | MJI 413 (2) | 10-20 |
| *(Repeat versions on reel or vinyl)* | | | |
| OFF THE RECORD | 199? | Westwood One (2) | 5-15 |
| *(Music and interviews, repeated)* | | | |
| PROFILES IN ROCK (Apr 80) | 1980 | | 15-25 |
| *(Music and interview)* | | | |
| SUPERSTAR CONCERT | 1989 | Westwood One (3) | 10-20 |
| *(Live concert)* | | | |
| THE LEGEND OF AEROSMITH (Jan 89) Profile | 1989 | NBC Radio (4) | 5-10 |
| *(Music and interviews)* | | | |
| UP CLOSE | 1988 | MCA Radio (2) | 20-40 |
| *(Repeated in 1989 and 1993)* | | | |

**Compact Discs**

| 4th OF JULY SPECIAL (July 92) | 1992 | Westwood One (4) | 20-30 |
|---|---|---|---|
| *(Music and interviews)* | | | |
| BBC CLASSIC TRACKS (Jan 95) | 1995 | Westwood One | 5-15 |
| *(Various classic live tracks)* | | | |
| BBC CLASSIC TRACKS (Oct 93) | 1993 | Westwood One | 5-15 |
| *(Various classic live tracks)* | | | |
| DREAM ON (May 91) Memorial Day Concert | 1991 | Westwood One (3) | 15-25 |
| *(Music and interviews)* | | | |
| GET A GRIP ON YOURSELF (May 93) | 1993 | (2) | 20-40 |
| *(Music and interviews)* | | | |
| IN THE STUDIO Profile of an album | 199? | Album Network | 10-15 |
| *(Music and interviews)* | | | |
| KING BISCUIT FLOWER HOUR (Aug 88) Live concert | 1988 | DIR | 10-25 |
| *(With Thin Lizzy)* | | | |
| KING BISCUIT FLOWER HOUR (Oct 89) Live concert | 1989 | DIR | 10-20 |
| *(With Billy Squier)* | | | |
| KING BISCUIT FLOWER HOUR (Sept 90) | 1990 | DIR | 10-20 |
| *(Live concert)* | | | |
| MASTERS OF ROCK (Dec 90) | 1990 | Radio Ventures (2) | 15-25 |
| *(Music and interviews)* | | | |
| STORY OF AEROSMITH (Sept 90) Profile | 1990 | Unistar | 10-20 |
| *(Music and interviews)* | | | |

| Title | Yr | Label, Number | NM $ |
|---|---|---|---|
| SUPERSTAR CONCERT | 1990 | Westwood One (2) | 10-25 |
| *(Repeated in Feb 1994)* | | | |
| THE AEROSMITH STORY (Jan 92) | 1992 | Unistar (3) | 10-20 |
| *(Music and interviews)* | | | |
| UP CLOSE (Feb 95) | 1995 | Media America (2) | 15-25 |
| *(Mostly music and interviews)* | | | |
| **Reel-to-Reel Tapes** | | | |
| KING BISCUIT FLOWER HOUR (July 78) Live concert | 1978 | DIR/ABC (2) | 25-50 |
| *(On reel-to-reel, live with Ted Nugent)* | | | |

**AFGHAN WHIGS**
**RADIO SHOWS**
**Compact Discs**

| ON THE EDGE (Jan 94+) Live concert | 1994 | | 10-15 |
|---|---|---|---|

**AFTER THE FIRE**
**12-Inch Singles**

| DANCING IN THE SHADOWS/ONE RULE FOR YOU | 1983 | Epic AE 1678 | 8 |
|---|---|---|---|

**AIR SUPPLY**
*Arista promo 45s worth $2 each*
**45s**

| MAKING LOVE OUT OF NOTHING AT ALL | 1983 | Arista AS 1-9056 | 10 |
|---|---|---|---|
| THE RIVER CRIED (by Russell Hitchcock) | 1987 | no label or title or artist | 10 |
| *("Mystery Record" with special title sleeve)* | | | |

**RADIO SHOWS**
**Albums**

| ROBERT W. MORGAN SPECIAL OF THE WEEK (July 81) | 1981 | Watermark | 25-40 |
|---|---|---|---|
| *(Repeated)* | | | |
| STAR SESSION | 1982 | DIR (3) | 25-50 |
| *(Rare live concert)* | | | |
| STARTRAK PROFILE | 1985 | Westwood One (2) | 15-25 |
| *(Music and interviews)* | | | |

**ALABAMA**
*Other RCA Victor promo 45s $2 each*
**12-Inch Singles**

| GREEN RIVER  Green vinyl, yellow label | 1982 | RCA Victor 13205 | 20 |
|---|---|---|---|
| *(12" singles issued in printed clear plastic cover)* | | | |

**45s**

| CHRISTMAS IN DIXIE | 1982 | RCA JB-13358 | 15 |
|---|---|---|---|
| *(Red vinyl promo, green label)* | | | |
| FIRE IN THE NIGHT Blue vinyl | 1984 | RCA 13926 | 12 |
| *(Silver promo label)* | | | |
| I WANNA BE WITH YOU TONIGHT  Yellow vinyl | 1982 | Sun 1173 | 25 |
| *(Standard version and edited version)* | | | |
| I WANNA COME OVER  Color vinyl promo | 1979 | MDJ 7906 | 18 |
| *(Multi-colored stock and promo label)* | | | |
| MOUNTAIN MUSIC Green vinyl | 1981 | RCA Victor 13019 | 12 |
| *(Brown promo label)* | | | |
| PASS IT ON  Includes 12-second PSA | 1990 | RCA Victor 2519 | 10 |
| *(Picture sleeve includes PSA script and Not for Sale)* | | | |
| TAR TOP  Promo-only picture sleeve | 1987 | RCA 5222 | 10 |
| *(Record is black vinyl, red promo label)* | | | |
| TOUCH ME WHEN WE'RE DANCING With insert | 1986 | RCA 5003 | 10 |
| *(Gold promo label, black vinyl, must include insert)* | | | |

**Albums**

| OPEN END INTERVIEW WITH ALABAMA | 1988 | RCA 9574-1-RDJ | 30 |
|---|---|---|---|
| *(Promo-only release)* | | | |
| STARS White promo label | 1982 | Sun 148 | Unknown |
| *(If this LP exists, it is very rare, probably promo only, and contains the same material as Plantation 44.)* | | | |
| WILD COUNTRY  Promo version of above | 1981 | Plantation 44 | 50-75 |
| *(Quickly recalled and removed from stock)* | | | |

**RADIO SHOWS**
**Albums**

| AUSTIN ENCORE Live concert | 1988 | Mainstreet Broadcast | 15-25 |
|---|---|---|---|
| *(With Johnny Rodriguez)* | | | |
| LIVE AT GILLEY'S (May 88) Live concert | 1988 | Westwood One | 20-35 |
| *(With Loretta Lynn)* | | | |
| LIVE AT GILLEY'S (Sept 83) | 1983 | Westwood One | 20-35 |
| *(Live concert)* | | | |
| THE ALABAMA STORY (June 83) Box set | 1983 | United Stations (3) | 10-20 |
| *(Profile, interviews and music)* | | | |
| THE SILVER EAGLE | 1981 | DIR (3) | 40-75 |
| *(Live concert with Charlie McClain)* | | | |
| THE SILVER EAGLE | 1981 | DIR (3) | 40-75 |
| *(Live concert with Razzy Bailey)* | | | |
| THE SILVER EAGLE (Apr 82) Alabama in concert | 1982 | DIR (3) | 40-75 |
| *(Live concert, repeated)* | | | |
| TRIPLE (June 83) Box set radio show | 1983 | Mutual Radio (3) | 20 |
| *(Profiles, with Janie Fricke and Ricky Skaggs)* | | | |

**Compact Discs**

| SUMMER COUNTRY CONCERT | 1996 | (2) | 50 |
|---|---|---|---|
| *(Lari White, John Anderson, Lorrie Morgan, Aaron Tippin)* | | | |
| WESTWOOD ONE SPECIAL (Nov 94) Profile | 1994 | Westwood One (3) | 20-40 |
| *(Once Upon A Lifetime music and interviews)* | | | |

| Title | Yr | Label, Number | NM $ |
|---|---|---|---|

**ALAIMO, STEVE**
*ABC Paramount promo 45s $3; ABC Paramount promo LPs $15*
**7-Inch Extended Plays**

| | | | |
|---|---|---|---|
| DON'T CRY/CRY | 196? | Checker EP-5135 | 15 |
| *(White promo label, from LP 2986)* | | | |
| WHERE THE ACTION IS  Issued in hard cover | 196? | ABC 531 | 25 |
| *(Jukebox promo)* | | | |

**ALARM, THE**
*Other IRS promo 45s $4 each; other IRS promo 12" singles $6 each*
**12-Inch Singles**

| | | | |
|---|---|---|---|
| ABSOLUTE REALITY/MAJORITY/REASON 36 | 1986 | I.R.S. L33-17108 | 12 |
| PRESENCE OF LOVE (same on both sides) | 1987 | I.R.S. L33-17474 | 6 |
| RAIN IN THE SUMMERTIME (edit) (same on both sides) | 1987 | I.R.S. L33-17406 | 7 |
| SIXTY EIGHT GUNS (same on both sides) | 1984 | I.R.S. 70971 | 8 |
| SOLD ME DOWN THE RIVER/BLACK SUN/HOW THE MIGHTY FALL | 1989 | I.R.S. L33-8927 | 6 |
| SPIRIT OF '76 (edit)/SPIRIT OF '76 (AOR edit) | 1985 | I.R.S. L33-17080 | 10 |
| STRENGTH (edit) (same on both sides) | 1985 | I.R.S. 4986 | 8 |
| STRENGTH (edit)/STRENGTH (album version) | 1985 | I.R.S. L33-17043 | 10 |
| STRENGTH (edit)/STRENGTH (extended) | 1985 | I.R.S. L33-17068 | 8 |
| THE DECEIVER/HOWLING WIND | 1984 | I.R.S. 70975 | 10 |

**45s**

| | | | |
|---|---|---|---|
| UNSAFE BUILDING/RAIN | 1989 | I.R.S. (# unknown) | 8 |
| *"I.R.S. Final Vinyl" promo release; B-side by Water Walk; numbered sleeve* | | | |

**RADIO SHOWS**
**Albums**

| | | | |
|---|---|---|---|
| BBC TRANSCRIPTION SERVICE Live concert | 1984 | BBC | 100-150 |
| *(Very rare concert)* | | | |
| IN CONCERT | 1988 | Westwood One (2) | 25-40 |
| *(Live concert)* | | | |
| IN CONCERT (Dec 85) With X | 1985 | Westwood One (2) | 50-100 |
| *(Live concert)* | | | |
| IN CONCERT (Nov 84) With Talk Talk | 1984 | Westwood One (2) | 50-100 |
| *(Live concert)* | | | |
| IN CONCERT (Nov 86) Live concert | 1986 | Westwood One (2) | 125-200 |
| *(With R.E.M.)* | | | |

**ALBERT, EDDIE**
**45s**

| | | | |
|---|---|---|---|
| EDGAR GUEST'S ON GOING HOME FOR CHRISTMAS/(B-side unknown) | 195? | Cadence ZTSP 66814 | 10 |

**ALDA, ALEX**
**45s**

| | | | |
|---|---|---|---|
| LITTLE PONY (one-sided) | 1961 | Topix 6007 | 100 |
| *(Actually Nick Massi of the Four Seasons)* | | | |

**ALICE IN CHAINS**
**12-Inch Singles**

| | | | |
|---|---|---|---|
| WE DIE YOUNG/IT AIN'T LIKE THAT/KILLING YOURSELF | 1990 | Columbia CAS 2095 | 12 |

**45s**

| | | | |
|---|---|---|---|
| BLEED THE FREAK/PUT YOU DOWN | 1991 | (Columbia) CS7-04013 | 25 |
| *(White label with no label name)* | | | |

**Albums**

| | | | |
|---|---|---|---|
| JAR OF FLIES/SAP | 1995 | Columbia C2 57804 (2) | 25 |
| *(Vinyl promo with timing strip; stock copies also exist at $15)* | | | |
| WE DIE YOUNG | 1990 | Columbia CAS 2192 | 20 |
| *(Five-song promo-only EP from the Facelift LP)* | | | |

**RADIO SHOWS**
**Albums**

| | | | |
|---|---|---|---|
| METALSHOP (Apr 92) Various artists | 1992 | MJI 428 (2) | 15-35 |
| *(Live segment of music and interview show)* | | | |

**Compact Discs**

| | | | |
|---|---|---|---|
| IN CONCERT (Dec 96) | 1996 | | 20-40 |
| ON THE EDGE (Apr 94) | 1994 | Westwood One | 10-20 |
| *(Music and interviews)* | | | |

**ALLAN, DAVIE**
*Tower label promos $6 each*
**45s**

| | | | |
|---|---|---|---|
| APACHE '65 | 1965 | Sidewalk 1 | 20 |

**ALLEN, BILL**
**45s**

| | | | |
|---|---|---|---|
| PLEASE GIVE ME SOMETHING  Cream-colored label | 1959 | Imperial 5500 | 75 |

**ALLEN, DAVE**
**Albums**

| | | | |
|---|---|---|---|
| INTERCHORDS | 1987 | Epic 2782 | 15 |

**ALLEN, DEBORAH**
**45s**

| | | | |
|---|---|---|---|
| ROCKIN' LITTLE CHRISTMAS (same on both sides) | 1984 | RCA Victor JK-13904 | 4 |

| Title | Yr | Label, Number | NM $ |
|---|---|---|---|
| **ALLMAN BROTHERS BAND, THE** | | | |
| *Includes listings for Gregg Allman, Duane Allman, The Hour Glass. Hour Glass and Liberty 45s $8; other label promo 45s $4 each* | | | |
| **45s** | | | |
| MORNING DEW | 1972 | Bold Records | 20 |
| *(Red vinyl promo single)* | | | |
| POWER OF LOVE Hour Glass | 1967 | Liberty 56029 | 15 |
| *(Cream-colored promo label)* | | | |
| **7-Inch Extended Plays** | | | |
| BEGINNINGS Jukebox LLP | 1973 | Atlantic 805 | 18 |
| *(Issued with a hard cover)* | | | |
| BROTHERS AND SISTERS Jukebox LLP | 1973 | Capricorn 229 (Cap 0111) | 20 |
| *(Issued with a paper cover)* | | | |
| LAID BACK Jukebox LLP | 1973 | Capricorn 0116 | 20 |
| *(From a Gregg Allman LP)* | | | |
| **Albums** | | | |
| DUANE ALLMAN DIALOGS | 1972 | Capricorn PRO 545 | 100 |
| *(Promo-only release)* | | | |
| **Compact Discs** | | | |
| ACOUSTIC EVENING Eight tracks by Allmans | 1993 | Epic CD | 75 |
| *(Also eight tracks by the Indigo Girls)* | | | |
| **RADIO SHOWS** | | | |
| **Albums** | | | |
| A NIGHT ON THE ROAD Live concert | 1982 | ABC Radio (3) | 50-100 |
| *(Issued in box with scripts and time clock)* | | | |
| IN CONCERT  Allman Brothers | 1988 | Westwood One (2) | 20-40 |
| *(Live concert)* | | | |
| IN CONCERT (Oct 90) Allman Brothers | 1990 | Westwood One (2) | 20-40 |
| *(Live concert, repeated)* | | | |
| INNERVIEW Allman Brothers | 197? | Innerview | 10-20 |
| *(Music and interviews)* | | | |
| KING BISCUIT FLOWER HOUR Allman Brothers | 1981 | DIR/ABC (2) | 25-50 |
| *(Live concert)* | | | |
| OFF THE RECORD Allman Brothers | 1989 | Westwood One (2) | 10-15 |
| *(Music and interviews)* | | | |
| ROCK AROUND THE WORLD (June 77) | 1977 | RATW | 75-125 |
| *(Live concert)* | | | |
| SOURCE SPECIAL (Nov 81) Allman Brothers | 1981 | NBC Source (3) | 25-50 |
| *(Music and interviews)* | | | |
| SUPERGROUPS Allman Brothers | 1979 | DIR (3) | 75-125 |
| *(Live concert)* | | | |
| SUPERSTAR CONCERT Allman Brothers | 1990 | Westwood One (3) | 20-40 |
| *(Live concert, box set, repeated)* | | | |
| THE ALLMAN BROTHERS STORY | 1990 | Unistar (3) | 10-20 |
| TOYOTA PRESENTS Gregg Allman | 197? | Toyota Presents (2) | 25-50 |
| *(This very rare series features Greg Allman)* | | | |
| WORLD OF ROCK (Aug 89) Greg Allman | 1989 | DIR (2) | 15-25 |
| *(Allman is co-host, music and interviews)* | | | |
| **Compact Discs** | | | |
| ALBUM NETWORK SPECIAL (Aug 94) Allman Brothers | 1994 | Album Network (2) | 20-40 |
| *(Music and interviews)* | | | |
| CRY OF LOVE IN CONCERT (Jan 94) Allman Brothers | 1994 | (2) | 20-35 |
| *(Music and interviews)* | | | |
| GLOBAL SATELLITE SPECIAL | 1992 | Global Satellite (3) | 20-40 |
| *(Repeated later the same year)* | | | |
| IN CONCERT (Oct 94) New Allman Band | 1994 | Westwood One | 25-40 |
| *(Live concert, repeated)* | | | |
| IN THE STUDIO Profile of an album | 199? | Album Network | 10-15 |
| *(Music and interviews)* | | | |
| KING BISCUIT FLOWER HOUR (Dec 90) Allman Brothers | 1990 | DIR | 20-30 |
| *(Live concert, repeated)* | | | |
| KING BISCUIT FLOWER HOUR (July 89) | 1989 | DIR (2) | 40-60 |
| *(Live concert, two shows)* | | | |
| KING BISCUIT FLOWER HOUR (Mar 92) Greg Allman | 1992 | DIR | 20-30 |
| *(Live concert)* | | | |
| KING BISCUIT FLOWER HOUR (Nov 87) with/C,S & N | 1987 | DIR | 20-30 |
| *(Live concert)* | | | |
| KING BISCUIT FLOWER HOUR (Nov 94) Greg Allman | 1994 | DIR | 20-30 |
| *(Live concert with Warren Hayns)* | | | |
| KING BISCUIT FLOWER HOUR Allman Brothers | 1987 | DIR | 20-30 |
| *(Live concert)* | | | |
| KING BISCUIT FLOWER HOUR Gregg Allman | 1987 | DIR | 20-30 |
| *(Live concert)* | | | |
| OFF THE RECORD Allman Brothers | 1991 | Westwood One | 10-15 |
| *(Music and interviews)* | | | |
| ROCK AT THE CORE Various artists | 1989 | Rock Core (3) | 25-60 |
| *(Music and interviews)* | | | |
| ROCK STARS (July 89) Allman Brothers | 1989 | Radio Today (2) | 20-40 |
| *(Earlier live tracks)* | | | |
| SUPERSTAR CONCERT  Allman Brothers | 1993 | Westwood One (2) | 20-40 |
| *(Live concert, repeated Dec 94)* | | | |
| UP CLOSE Allman Brothers | 1989 | Media America (4) | 20-40 |
| *(Mostly music and interviews)* | | | |
| UP CLOSE Gregg Allman | 1988 | Media America (2) | 20-40 |
| *(Mostly music and interviews)* | | | |

| Title | Yr | Label, Number | NM $ |
|---|---|---|---|

**ALLSUP, TOMMY**
*From the Crickets. Reprise promo 45s $5 each.*
**Albums**

| | | | |
|---|---|---|---|
| TOMMY ALLSUP White promo label | 1965 | Reprise 6182 | 60 |

**ALPERT, DORE**
**45s**

| | | | |
|---|---|---|---|
| TELL IT TO THE BIRDS | 1962 | Dot 16396 | 15 |

**ALPERT, HERB**
*Jukebox LLPs $2 each; A&M promo singles $1 each*
**12-Inch Singles**

| | | | |
|---|---|---|---|
| RISE Red vinyl | 1979 | A&M 12078 | 12 |

*(Promo 12" single)*
**45s**

| | | | |
|---|---|---|---|
| HERB ALPERT  Red vinyl | 1966 | Rowe AMI 1004-A | 15 |

*(Record is about 30 seconds long)*

| | | | |
|---|---|---|---|
| THE TRIAL  Herb B. Lou and The Legal Eagles | 1958 | Arch 1607 | 25 |

*(White promo label)*
**RADIO SHOWS**
**Albums**

| | | | |
|---|---|---|---|
| THE BEST FROM HERB ALPERT & THE TIJUANA BRASS | 196? | A&M LP-9004 | 15 |

*(Promo-only compilation)*

| | | | |
|---|---|---|---|
| FOR CHRISTMAS SEALS | 1968 | | 20 |

*(Four shows, one with Alpert)*

**ALPHAVILLE**
**12-Inch Singles**

| | | | |
|---|---|---|---|
| RED ROSE (Remix) (same on both sides) | 1986 | Atlantic 1005 | 5 |
| ROMEOS (4 mixes) | 1989 | Atlantic 1318 | 8 |
| ROMEOS (edit)/Romeos (LP) | 1989 | Atlantic 2682 | 8 |
| THE JET SET (2 versions) | 1985 | Atlantic 842 | 10 |
| THE MYSTERIES OF LOVE (3 versions) | 1989 | Atlantic 1456 | 5 |

**ALTERED IMAGES**
**12-Inch Singles**

| | | | |
|---|---|---|---|
| HAPPY BIRTHDAY (long & short)/I COULD BE HAPPY (long & short) | 1982 | Portrait AS 1417 | 8 |

**AMBROSIA**
**45s**

| | | | |
|---|---|---|---|
| HOLDIN' ON TO YESTERDAY | 1975 | Label unknown | 10 |
| MAGICAL MYSTERY TOUR | 1976 | Columbia | 10 |
| NICE NICE VERY NICE | 197? | (Hand written label) | 10 |

*(Above three are test pressings)*

**AMERICA**
*Warner Brothers and Capitol promo 45s $3 each*
**RADIO SHOWS**
**Albums**

| | | | |
|---|---|---|---|
| PROFILE | 1983 | Westwood One (2) | 25-50 |

*(Music and interviews)*

| | | | |
|---|---|---|---|
| STAR SESSION (Sept 82) | 1982 | DIR (3) | 200-350 |

*(Live concert)*

**AMERICAN SPRING**
*Marilyn Wilson of the Honeys; Produced by Brian Wilson*
**45s**

| | | | |
|---|---|---|---|
| GOOD TIME  Spring | 1972 | United Artists 50907 | 40 |

*(Brown promo label)*

| | | | |
|---|---|---|---|
| NOW THAT EVERYTHING'S BEEN SAID Spring | 1971 | United Artists 50848 | 25 |

*(Brown promo label)*

| | | | |
|---|---|---|---|
| SHYIN' AWAY | 1973 | Columbia 45834 | 40 |

*(Promo record and stock picture sleeve, members of the Beach Boys and Honeys)*

**AMES BROTHERS, THE**
*RCA Victor and Coral promo 45s $3*
**45s**

| | | | |
|---|---|---|---|
| I COULDN'T SLEEP A WINK LAST NIGHT | 1958 | RCA Victor NNO | 10 |

*(Promo-only release)*

| | | | |
|---|---|---|---|
| THE NAUGHTY LADY OF SHADY LANE | 195? | US Army Recruiting | 10 |
| THE NAUGHTY LADY OF SHADY LANE  White promo label | 1955 | RCA Victor 5897 | 25 |

*(Biggest pop hit)*
**7-Inch Extended Plays**

| | | | |
|---|---|---|---|
| PLATTER PARTY WITH THE AMES BROTHERS Six songs | 1958 | RCA Victor SP45-48 | 15 |

*(For French's Mustard, issued with paper picture cover)*

| | | | |
|---|---|---|---|
| SING A SONG OF SANTA CLAUS/WINTER'S HERE AGAIN// | 195? | Coral 83010 | 15 |
| LET'S HAVE AN OLD FASHIONED CHRISTMAS/I'VE GOT THE CHRISTMAS SPIRIT | | | |

*(B-side by Don Cornell)*
**RADIO SHOWS**
**16-Inch Transcriptions**

| | | | |
|---|---|---|---|
| TREASURY DEPARTMENT (50s) Public Service series | 195? | U. S. Treasury Dept | 10-25 |

*(The Ames Brothers are host of this show)*

| Title | Yr | Label, Number | NM $ |
|---|---|---|---|
| **AMES, ED** | | | |
| **45s** | | | |
| LET IT SNOW! LET IT SNOW! LET IT SNOW! | 1968 | RCA SP-45-188 | 8 |
| *(Promo only, yellow label)* | | | |
| **AMOS 'N' ANDY** | | | |
| **45s** | | | |
| THE LORD'S PRAYER/LITTLE BITTY BABY | 1962 | Columbia 42623 | 8 |
| **AMOS, DANIEL** | | | |
| **78s** | | | |
| ON THE LINE  Blue/white vinyl promo 78rpm | 1980 | Solid Rock 207 | 40 |
| *(Promo-only release with cardboard jacket, produced by Larry Norman)* | | | |
| **AMOS, TORI** | | | |
| **12-Inch Singles** | | | |
| THE BIG PICTURE | 1988 | Atlantic | 40 |
| *(Issued with a picture cover)* | | | |
| **45s** | | | |
| COOL ON YOUR ISLAND | 1988 | Atlantic 89021 | 10 |
| *(Blue promo label)* | | | |
| THE BIG PICTURE | 1988 | Atlantic 89086 | 12 |
| *(Blue promo label)* | | | |
| **Albums** | | | |
| Y KANT TORI READ | 1988 | Atlantic | 100 |
| *(Designate promo with cut-out notch; stock copies with no notch worth more)* | | | |
| **Compact Discs** | | | |
| TEA WITH THE WAITRESS Includes inserts | 1992 | MCA PR5498 | 25 |
| *(Interviews and music)* | | | |
| **RADIO SHOWS** | | | |
| **Compact Discs** | | | |
| IN CONCERT Live concert | 1993 | Westwood One | 125-200 |
| *(Live concert)* | | | |
| IN CONCERT-NU ROCK (Aug 93) Live concert | 1993 | Westwood One | 295 |
| *(Live concert)* | | | |
| ON THE EDGE | 1996 | | 40 |
| *(With Nada Surf and Reacharound)* | | | |
| ON THE EDGE (Mar 94) | 1994 | Westwood One | 50-75 |
| *(With three live acoustic tracks by Sarah McLachlan)* | | | |
| ON THE EDGE (Sept 94) | 1994 | | 45 |
| *(With Sugar and Gigolo Aunts)* | | | |
| ON THE EDGE | 1996 | | 50 |
| *(With Seven Mary Three)* | | | |
| RUNDGREN-DIFFERENCE (Feb 96) | 1996 | (2) | 105 |
| *(Music and interviews with live tracks; Melissa Etheridge, Rusted Root, etc.)* | | | |
| **Digital Audio Tapes** | | | |
| SPIN SESSION (Dec 96) | 1996 | | 200-300 |
| *(Two live songs)* | | | |
| **ANDERSON, BILL** | | | |
| *Decca promo 45s $1 each; Decca promo LPs $3 each* | | | |
| **45s** | | | |
| 1965 MARCH OF DIMES  Sings "Still" | 1965 | March of Dimes 5501 | 20 |
| *(PSA programming, 4:24 version)* | | | |
| CITY LIGHTS  Rare promo version | 1958 | TNT 9015 | 50 |
| *(Rockabilly version of his original song)* | | | |
| **Albums** | | | |
| BILL ANDERSON SINGS COUNTRY SONGS | 1962 | Decca 4192 | 25 |
| *(Pink promo label)* | | | |
| COUNTRY & WESTERN DRUMMERS Production aids | 1960 | Sesac 159/160 | 30 |
| *(Also features Roy Drusky and Darrell McCall)* | | | |
| THE BILL ANDERSON STORY | 1969 | Decca 7198 (2) | 25 |
| *(White promo labels)* | | | |
| **RADIO SHOWS** | | | |
| **Albums** | | | |
| CHRISTMAS WITH... | 196? | Diamond Productions | 10-20 |
| *(Originals have green label, music and interviews)* | | | |
| GRAND OL' OPRY  Various artists | 196? | WSM Radio | 10-20 |
| *(Music and interviews)* | | | |
| HOOTENAVY  Various artists | 196? | U. S. Navy | 10-20 |
| *(Music and interviews)* | | | |
| **ANDERSON, JOHN** | | | |
| *Colored vinyl promo 45s $5 each* | | | |
| **RADIO SHOWS** | | | |
| **Albums** | | | |
| AMERICAN EAGLE (July 86) | 1986 | DIR | 10-20 |
| *(Live concert)* | | | |
| LIVE FROM GILLEY'S (Dec 86) | 1986 | Westwood One | 10-20 |
| *(Live concert)* | | | |
| **Compact Discs** | | | |
| SUMMER CONCERT SERIES (July 94) Live concert | 1994 | | 30-60 |
| *(With Boy Howdy)* | | | |

| Title | Yr | Label, Number | NM $ |
|-------|-----|---------------|------|

**ANDERSON, JON**
*Also see A/B/W/H; Vangelis; Yes. Polydor promo 45s $4 each*
**45s**

| Title | Yr | Label, Number | NM $ |
|-------|-----|---------------|------|
| HEART OF THE MATTER (same on both sides) | 1981 | Atlantic 3795 | 5 |
| *(May be promo only)* | | | |
| SOME ARE BORN (same on both sides) | 1980 | Atlantic 3774 | 5 |
| *(May be promo only)* | | | |
| SURRENDER (same on both sides) | 1982 | Atlantic 4054 | 5 |
| *(May be promo only)* | | | |

**RADIO SHOWS**
**Albums**

| Title | Yr | Label, Number | NM $ |
|-------|-----|---------------|------|
| KING BISCUIT FLOWER HOUR (Sept 82) Live concert | 1982 | DIR | 150-175 |
| *(With Animotion)* | | | |

**ANDERSON, LAURIE**
**12-Inch Singles**

| Title | Yr | Label, Number | NM $ |
|-------|-----|---------------|------|
| EXCELLENT BIRDS/SHARKEY'S DAY/SHARKEY'S NIGHT + 1 | 1984 | Warner Bros. PRO-A-2123 | 6 |
| IN OUR SLEEP (3 versions)/POISON (3 versions) | 1995 | Warner Bros. PRO-A-7508 | 10 |
| LANGUAGE IS A VIRUS (same on both sides) | 1986 | Warner Bros. PRO-A-2465 | 7 |

**Albums**

| Title | Yr | Label, Number | NM $ |
|-------|-----|---------------|------|
| HOME OF THE BRAVE INTERVIEW | 1986 | Warner Bros. WBMS-134-2 | 30 |
| *(Part of the Warner Bros. Music Show series)* | | | |
| MISTER HEARTBREAK | 1984 | Warner Bros. 25077 | 12 |
| *(Quiex II audiophile pressing)* | | | |
| SELECTIONS FROM UNITED STATES LIVE | 1984 | Warner Bros. PRO-A-2229 | 12 |

**ANDERSON, LIZ**
**45s**

| Title | Yr | Label, Number | NM $ |
|-------|-----|---------------|------|
| CHRISTOPHER THE CHRISTMAS SEAL (same on both sides) | 196? | Hobby House CSA-1 | 8 |
| THE SPIRIT OF CHRISTMAS/Promos | 196? | RCA Victor 659G-2446 | 10 |

**ANDERSON, LYNN**
*Chart promo 45s $2 each; Columbia promo 45s $1 each; Columbia LLPs $5 each*
**45s**

| Title | Yr | Label, Number | NM $ |
|-------|-----|---------------|------|
| DING-A-LING THE CHRISTMAS BELL | 1970 | Columbia AE7 1010 | 10 |
| *(Special Christmas Seals record; different than the stock copy picture sleeve)* | | | |
| FROSTY THE SNOWMAN  Promo only | 1972 | Columbia AE7 1056 | 10 |
| LISTEN TO A COUNTRY SONG Promo only | 1970 | Columbia AE7 1052 | 12 |
| *(Medley of songs from the LP)* | | | |

**7-Inch Extended Plays**

| Title | Yr | Label, Number | NM $ |
|-------|-----|---------------|------|
| THE BEST OF LYNN ANDERSON  Jukebox LLP | 1969 | Chart 7-1009 | 15 |
| *(Six songs, issued in hard cover)* | | | |
| THE FRANK JONES INTERVIEW | 1970 | Columbia AE7 1024 | 10 |
| *(Promo-only release)* | | | |

**ANDERSON/BRUFORD/WAKEMAN/HOWE**
**Compact Discs**

| Title | Yr | Label, Number | NM $ |
|-------|-----|---------------|------|
| ABWH | 1989 | Arista 90126 | 25 |
| *(Nine-track CD promo-only release)* | | | |

**RADIO SHOWS**
**Albums**

| Title | Yr | Label, Number | NM $ |
|-------|-----|---------------|------|
| OFF THE RECORD | 199? | Westwood One (2) | 10-25 |
| *(Music and interviews)* | | | |
| ROCK STARS (Aug 89) | 1989 | Westwood One (2) | 20-30 |
| *(Yes material)* | | | |
| WORLD OF ROCK (Aug 89) | 1989 | DIR (2) | 10-20 |
| *(Music and interviews)* | | | |

**Compact Discs**

| Title | Yr | Label, Number | NM $ |
|-------|-----|---------------|------|
| KING BISCUIT FLOWER HOUR (Dec 94) ABWH | 1994 | DIR | 20-40 |
| *(Live concert)  See Yes* | | | |
| KING BISCUIT FLOWER HOUR (Sept 90) | 1990 | DIR | 20-30 |
| *(Recorded live in California in 1978)* | | | |
| UP CLOSE | 1989 | Media America (4) | 20-30 |
| *(Profile of Yes)* | | | |

**ANGEL**
**45s**

| Title | Yr | Label, Number | NM $ |
|-------|-----|---------------|------|
| THE CHRISTMAS SONG | 1978 | Casablanca NB 903 DJ | 10 |
| *(Promo only with Winter Song on other side)* | | | |

**ANIMALS, THE**
*The Original Animals on Jet/UA promos $3-5; Other MGM yellow promo label LPs $25 each; MGM white promo label LPs $10-15 each; Other promo yellow label MGM 45s $8-12 each; IRS promo 45s $5 each; Alan Price promo 45s Warner $4 each; Eric Burdon Band on Capitol $5 each*
**45s**

| Title | Yr | Label, Number | NM $ |
|-------|-----|---------------|------|
| BABY, LET ME TAKE YOU HOME | 1964 | MGM 13242 | 25 |
| *(Yellow promo label)* | | | |
| BOOM BOOM | 1964 | MGM 13298 | 15 |
| *(Yellow promo label, stock picture sleeve worth $25)* | | | |
| BRING IT ON HOME TO ME | 1965 | MGM 13339 | 12 |
| *(Yellow promo label, stock picture sleeve worth $25)* | | | |
| DON'T LET ME BE MISUNDERSTOOD | 1965 | MGM 13311 | 15 |
| *(Yellow promo label)* | | | |
| HOUSE OF THE RISING SUN | 1964 | MGM 13264 | 25 |
| *(Yellow promo label, stock picture sleeve worth $25)* | | | |

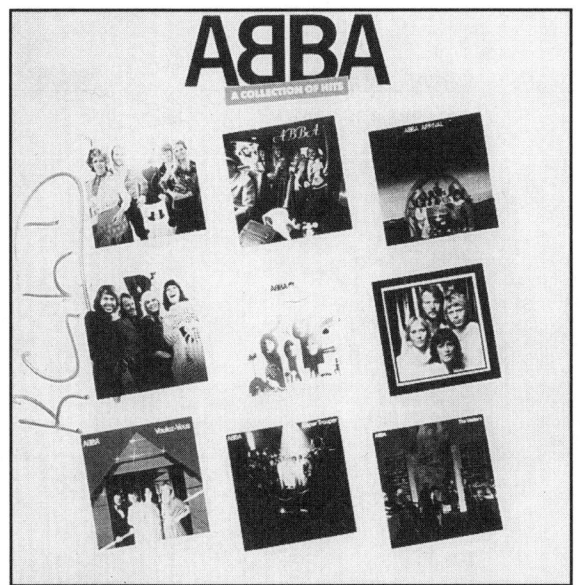
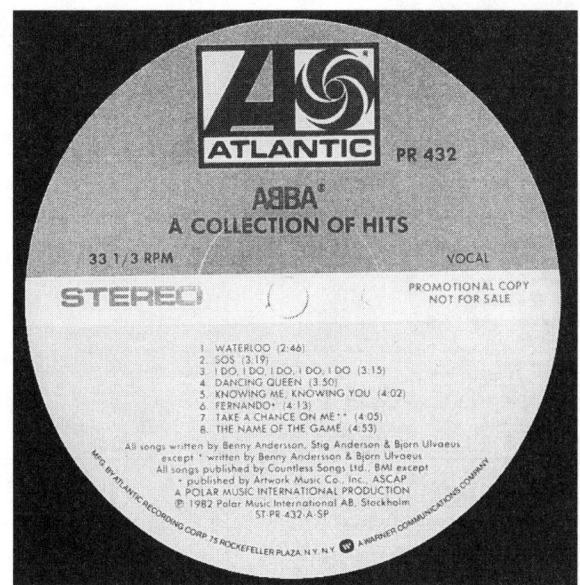

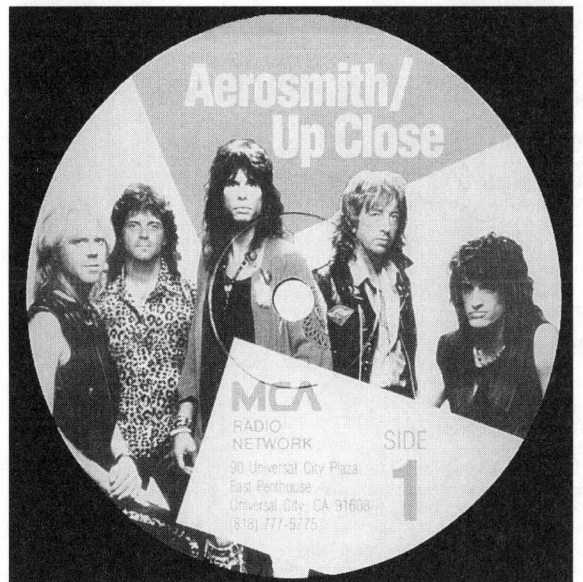
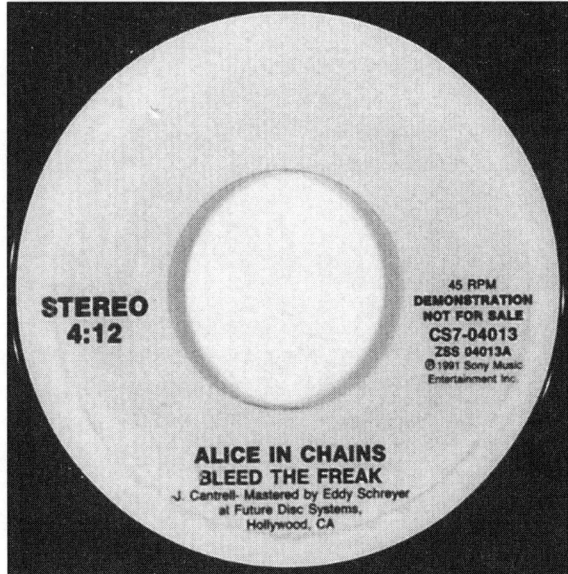

(Top row) The front cover and Side 1 label for the ABBA promo album *A Collection of Hits*, their only career-spanning retrospective on one record. (Center row) Two radio shows featuring Aerosmith from different times in their career. The one at left is an Innerview show from 1976, when "Dream On" was re-released to become a hit single; the Up Close is from 1988, during their comeback. (Bottom left) An unusual promo 45 from Alice in Chains from 1990, it has no label name on it but is, based on the typeface, a Columbia product. (Bottom right) An unusual radio-show appearance for the group America from their brief 1982 "You Can Do Magic" comeback era.

| Title | Yr | Label, Number | NM $ |
|---|---|---|---|
| I'M CRYING | 1964 | MGM 13274 | 20 |
| *(Yellow promo label, stock picture sleeve worth $25)* | | | |
| MGM CELEBRITY SCENE Promo 5 singles box set | 1967 | MGM CS 11-5 | 18 ea |
| *(Yellow promo labels, box set, complete $100)* | | | |
| **Albums** | | | |
| ANIMAL TRACKS | 1965 | MGM E-4305 | 150 |
| *(Yellow label promo)* | | | |
| ANIMALISM | 1966 | MGM E-4414 | 100 |
| *(Yellow label promo)* | | | |
| ANIMALIZATION | 1966 | MGM E-4384 | 100 |
| *(Yellow label promo)* | | | |
| THE ANIMALS | 1964 | MGM E-4264 | 100 |
| *(Yellow label promo)* | | | |
| THE ANIMALS ON TOUR | 1965 | MGM E-4281 | 100 |
| *(Yellow label promo)* | | | |
| THE BEST OF THE ANIMALS | 1966 | MGM E-4324 | 80 |
| *Yellow label promo* | | | |
| **RADIO SHOWS** | | | |
| **45s** | | | |
| WHAT'S IT ALL ABOUT (Apr 77) Eric Burdon Band | 1977 | W. I. A. A. 259 | 20 |
| *(Profiles several Burdon-related groups)* | | | |
| **Albums** | | | |
| KING BISCUIT FLOWER HOUR (Jan 84) | 1984 | DIR (2) | 30-45 |
| *(With Clarence Clemons)* | | | |
| LEGENDS OF ROCK (Oct 89) The Animals | 1989 | NBC Radio (2) | 10-20 |
| *(Music and interviews)* | | | |
| **Compact Discs** | | | |
| BBC CLASSIC TRACK (Oct 90) The Animals | 1990 | Westwood One | 10-25 |
| *(Music and interviews)  (SEE ERIC BURDON BAND; WAR)* | | | |
| KING BISCUIT FLOWER HOUR (May 91) Live concert | 1991 | DIR | 25-40 |
| *(With Mitch Ryder)* | | | |

## ANIMOTION
*Mercury promo 45s worth $3 each*

| Title | Yr | Label, Number | NM $ |
|---|---|---|---|
| **12-Inch Singles** | | | |
| I ENGINEER (same on both sides) | 1986 | Casablanca PRO 403 | 7 |
| OBSESSION (7")/LET HIM GO (Dub) | 1984 | Mercury PRO 353 | 10 |
| **RADIO SHOWS** | | | |
| **Albums** | | | |
| KING BISCUIT FLOWER HOUR (Sept 82) Live concert | 1982 | DIR | 150-175 |
| *(With Jon Anderson)* | | | |

## ANKA, PAUL
*ABC Paramount promo 45s after 9900 $10-$15 each; RCA Victor white label promo 45s $4; Other label 45s $2 each; Other ABC Paramount promo LPs $15 each*

| Title | Yr | Label, Number | NM $ |
|---|---|---|---|
| **45s** | | | |
| DIANA White promo label | 1957 | ABC Paramount 9831 | 25 |
| *(Biggest selling single)* | | | |
| I CONFESS  White promo label | 1956 | RPM 499 | 40 |
| *(Promo RPM singles more common than stock copies)* | | | |
| I CONFESS White promo label | 1956 | RPM 472 | 50 |
| *(First Anka recording)* | | | |
| I LOVE YOU, BABY White promo label | 1958 | ABC Paramount 9855 | 20 |
| *(Hard to find in any format)* | | | |
| SHARE THE LOVE White promo label | 1958 | ABC Paramount 104 | 50 |
| *(Promo only, not released to the public)* | | | |
| THE TEEN COMMANDMENTS White promo label | 1958 | ABC Paramount 9974 | 30 |
| *(With George Hamilton IV, Johnny Nash and Anka)* | | | |
| WHAT YOU'VE DONE TO ME  By Micki Marlo | 1957 | ABC Paramount 9841 | 30 |
| *(Anka does background vocal)* | | | |
| YOU ARE MY DESTINY White promo label | 1958 | ABC Paramount 9880 | 18 |
| *(Anka's second charted hit single)* | | | |
| **7-Inch Extended Plays** | | | |
| LET'S SIT THIS ONE OUT  Jukebox LLP | 1968 | RCA Victor 2575 | 20 |
| *(Issued with a hard cover)* | | | |
| OUR MAN AROUND THE WORLD Jukebox LLP | 1968 | RCA Victor 2614 | 20 |
| *(Issued with a hard cover)* | | | |
| PAUL ANKA GOLD  Jukebox LLP | 1972 | ABC 273 (3704) | 15 |
| *(Issued with a paper cover)* | | | |
| PAUL ANKA GOLD  Jukebox LLP | 1974 | Sire (ABC) 273 | 15 |
| *(Issued with paper cover)* | | | |
| **Albums** | | | |
| MY HEART SINGS | 1959 | ABC Paramount 296 | 60 |
| *(White promo label)* | | | |
| PAUL ANKA | 1957 | ABC Paramount 240 | 75 |
| *(White promo label)* | | | |
| SOLID GOLD SCRAPBOOK (July 89) | 1989 | United Stations | 10-20 |
| *(Music and interviews from 7LP set)* | | | |

## ANN-MARGRET
*RCA Victor promo 45s $5 each*

| Title | Yr | Label, Number | NM $ |
|---|---|---|---|
| **7-Inch Extended Plays** | | | |
| BEAUTY AND THE BEARD  Jukebox LLP | 1970 | RCA Victor 2690 | 20 |
| *(Issued with a hard cover, with Al Hirt)* | | | |

| Title | Yr | Label, Number | NM $ |
|-------|----|----|------|

**ANNETTE**
*Buena Vista promo 45s $15 each; Promo LPs by Annette $50-100 each*
**45s**

| | | | |
|-------|----|----|------|
| GOLD DOUBLOONS AND PIECES OF EIGHT | 1958 | Disneyland 114 | 40 |
| *(White promo label)* | | | |
| HAPPY GLOW | 1965 | Disneyland 786 | 35 |
| *(White promo label)* | | | |
| HOW WILL I KNOW MY LOVE | 1958 | Disneyland 102 | 30 |
| *(White promo label, stock picture sleeve worth $50)* | | | |
| I CAN'T DO THE SUM | 1961 | Disneyland 722 | 40 |
| *(White promo label)* | | | |
| MEETIN' AT THE MALT SHOP | 1958 | Disneyland 105 | 40 |
| *(White promo label, stock picture sleeve worth $100)* | | | |
| TALL PAUL | 1958 | Disneyland 118 | 25 |
| *(White promo label)* | | | |
| **Albums** | | | |
| MERLIN JONES Movie spots and interview | 1963 | Buena Vista 2567-70 | 250 |

**ANOTHER BAD CREATION**
**Albums**

| | | | |
|-------|----|----|------|
| IT AIN'T WHAT U WEAR, IT'S HOW U PLAY IT | 1993 | Motown 37463 6363-1 | 15 |
| *(Vinyl is promo only; in black company sleeve)* | | | |

**ANOTHER GIRL**
**45s**

| | | | |
|-------|----|----|------|
| GROWING GOLD/HOLIDAY | 1996 | RCA RDAB 64699-7 | 5 |

**ANT, ADAM**
**12-Inch Singles**

| | | | |
|-------|----|----|------|
| FRIEND OR FOE/DESPERATE BUT NOT SERIOUS | 1983 | Epic AE 1593 | 10 |
| HELLO I LOVE YOU/DESPERATE BUT NOT SERIOUS/GOODY TWO SHOES | 1982 | Epic AE 1556 | 10 |
| ROUGH STUFF (4 mixes) | 1990 | MCA 18436 | 6 |
| ROUGH STUFF (alternative mix)/ROUGH STUFF (alternative dub) | 1990 | MCA 18466 | 7 |

**ANTHONY, RAYBURN**
**45s**

| | | | |
|-------|----|----|------|
| ALICE BLUE GOWN | 1963 | Sun 333 | 30 |

**ANTHRAX**
**RADIO SHOWS**
**Albums**

| | | | |
|-------|----|----|------|
| HIGH VOLTAGE (Oct 89) | 1989 | Westwood One (2) | 25-50 |
| *(Live segment features Anthrax)* | | | |
| METALSHOP (May 89) Special Anthrax show | 1989 | MJI (2) | 10-20 |
| *(Live segments)* | | | |

**APPICE, CARMEN**
*See Vanilla Fudge.*
**RADIO SHOWS**
**Albums**

| | | | |
|-------|----|----|------|
| KING BISCUIT FLOWER HOUR (Mar 82) Live concert | 1982 | DIR (2) | 25-50 |

**APRIL WINE**
**RADIO SHOWS**
**Albums**

| | | | |
|-------|----|----|------|
| KING BISCUIT FLOWER HOUR (June 81) Live concert | 1981 | DIR (2) | 20-40 |
| *(With the Cars)* | | | |
| KING BISCUIT FLOWER HOUR (Mar 81) Live concert | 1981 | DIR (2) | 20-40 |
| *(With the Michael Stanley Band)* | | | |
| KING BISCUIT FLOWER HOUR (Sept 85) | 1985 | DIR (2) | 20-40 |
| *(Live concert, with Saga)* | | | |
| NBC SOURCE (May 82) | 1982 | NBC Radio (2) | 40-75 |
| *(Live concert)* | | | |

**ARC ANGELS**
**RADIO SHOWS**
**Compact Discs**

| | | | |
|-------|----|----|------|
| IN CONCERT (Mar 93+) | 1993 | Westwood One (2) | 20-45 |
| OFF THE RECORD (July 92+) | 1992 | Westwood One | 20-30 |
| *(With Sass Jordan)* | | | |

**ARCHIES, THE**
*Kirshner promo 45s $8*
**Albums**

| | | | |
|-------|----|----|------|
| EVERYTHING'S ARCHIE BOX | 1969 | Calendar (no #) | 100 |
| *(Box with LP, photos, press kit and buttons)* | | | |

**ARGENT**
*Rod Argent; other Epic promo 45s $5 each*
**45s**

| | | | |
|-------|----|----|------|
| GOD GAVE ROCK AND ROLL TO YOU  Argent | 1973 | Epic 10972 | 10 |
| *(Orange promo label)* | | | |
| **Albums** | | | |
| ARGENT | 1969 | Epic 26525 | 25 |
| *(White promo label)* | | | |

| Title | Yr | Label, Number | NM $ |
|-------|-----|---------------|------|
| RING OF HANDS | 1970 | Epic 30128 | 20 |
| *(White promo label)* | | | |
| **RADIO SHOWS** | | | |
| **Albums** | | | |
| BBC TRANSCRIPTION SERVICE Live concert | 1972 | BBC | 125-250 |
| *(Rare show in a very rare series)* | | | |
| **Compact Discs** | | | |
| KING BISCUIT FLOWER HOUR (July 88) Live concert | 1988 | DIR | 20-50 |
| *(With Mott the Hoople)* | | | |
| | | | |
| **ARMATRADING, JOAN** | | | |
| **45s** | | | |
| CALL ME NAMES (same on both sides) | 1983 | A&M 2564 | 5 |
| *Stock copies do not exist* | | | |
| **7-Inch Extended Plays** | | | |
| FREE JOAN ARMATRADING | 1980 | A&M SP-2391 | 10 |
| **RADIO SHOWS** | | | |
| **Albums** | | | |
| BBC TRANSCRIPTION DISC  Live concert | 1977 | BBC Transcription | 150-300 |
| *(Very rare show in a rare series)* | | | |
| | | | |
| **ARMSTRONG, LOUIS** | | | |
| *Decca promo 45s $4; Other label promo 45s $2; Decca promo LPs $15; Other label promo LPs $5* | | | |
| **45s** | | | |
| CULTURAL EXCHANGE Promo only | 1959 | Columbia NNO | 10 |
| *(Matrix JZSP 58120)* | | | |
| HERE IS MY HEART FOR CHRISTMAS/HIS FATHER WORE LONG HAIR | 1970 | Amsterdam 85017 | 10 |
| **7-Inch Extended Plays** | | | |
| HELLO, DOLLY Six-song jukebox EP | 196? | Kapp 3364 | 15 |
| *(Issued with hard cover)* | | | |
| HELLO, DOLLY Six-song jukebox EP | 197? | Decca LLP 162 | 10 |
| *(Cover credits Kapp Records #3364, issued w/paper sleeve, not the same songs as Kapp 3364)* | | | |
| | | | |
| **ARNOLD, EDDY** | | | |
| *Promo RCA 78s and 45s worth $2-$5 each; RCA jukebox stereo singles are worth $5 each; RCA colored vinyl promo singles worth $5 each; RCA jukebox LLPs worth $8 each* | | | |
| **45s** | | | |
| ARE YOU BEHAVIN'? PSA spots by Arnold | 1983 | NR 14951 | 10 |
| HIGH BLOOD PRESSURE PSA spots by Arnold | 1982 | NR 14128 | 10 |
| *(Reissued in 1983, NR 14344)* | | | |
| I'LL HOLD YOU IN MY HEART  U.S.A.F. PSA | 1957 | U.S.A.F. 42 | 15 |
| *(Music in the Air series)* | | | |
| MARY CARTER PAINTS Radio jingles, yellow label | 1968 | Mary Carter 1421 | 25 |
| *(Includes Eddy Arnold jingle)* | | | |
| NEW WORLD IN THE MORNING | 197? | RCA Victor SP 227 | 10 |
| *(White promo label, promo only)* | | | |
| NEW YEAR'S GREETINGS  12 cuts, one by Arnold | 1963 | RCA Victor SP 128 | 20 |
| *(Also Christmas greetings from RCA artists)* | | | |
| THE FABULOUS 45 11 cuts, one by Arnold | 1956 | RCA Victor SPD-21 | 20 |
| *(Introduction to the 45 rpm record by RCA)* | | | |
| **7-Inch Extended Plays** | | | |
| DO YOU LOVE ME  EP promo-only single | 1957 | RCA Victor 6842 (DJ-88) | 15 |
| *(Jaye P. Morgan on other side)* | | | |
| POP SHOPPER | 195? | RCA SPC-7-13 (3) | 15 |
| *(With Arnold)* | | | |
| THE BALLAD OF WES TANCRED EP promo-only single | 1957 | RCA Victor 6699 (DJ-14) | 15 |
| *(Different artist on other side)* | | | |
| **Albums** | | | |
| CHRISTMAS WITH EDDY ARNOLD | 1971 | RCA Victor PRS 346 | 50 |
| *(White promo label, promo-only release)* | | | |
| **RADIO SHOWS** | | | |
| **16-Inch Transcriptions** | | | |
| COUNTRY MUSIC TIME  15-minute PSA show | 1955 | Country Music 70 | 15-30 |
| *(Music and interviews)* | | | |
| JUBILEE USA (40s & 50s) Public service show | 194? | PSA | 15-30 |
| *(Host of this show, music and interviews)* | | | |
| MARCH OF DIMES  Public service show | 1954 | March/Dimes 5436 | 15-40 |
| *(Music and interviews)* | | | |
| NAVY HOEDOWN (50s) Public service show | 195? | U. S. Navy #43 | 15-40 |
| *(Music and interviews)* | | | |
| **Albums** | | | |
| CHRISTMAS IS... (60s) Radio show | 196? | Diamond 502 | 10-25 |
| *(Original shows have green label)* | | | |
| EDDY ARNOLD TIME (60s) series of 5-minute shows | 196? | U. S. Dept Health | 15-25 |
| *(Over 40 records in series, music and interviews)* | | | |
| | | | |
| **ART OF NOISE** | | | |
| **12-Inch Singles** | | | |
| CLOSE (TO THE EDIT) (2 versions)/BEATBOX (Diversion 1) | 1984 | Island 744 | 7 |
| E.F.L./ONE EARTH/ODE TO DON JUAN/A DAY AT THE RACES | 1987 | China VAS 2841 | 6 |
| PETER GUNN (Long)/PETER GUNN (Short) | 1986 | China VAS 2327 | 6 |
| *(With Duane Eddy)* | | | |
| **45s** | | | |
| BEAT BOX ISLAND | 198? | Island PR595 | 10 |
| *(Special radio re-edit with generic promo paper sleeve)* | | | |

| Title | Yr | Label, Number | NM $ |
|---|---|---|---|
| **ARTISTICS, THE** | | | |
| **Albums** | | | |
| I'M GONNA MISS YOU | 1960 | Brunswick 54123 | 25 |
| *(Brunswick promo label)* | | | |
| THE ARTICULATE ARTISTICS | 1961 | Brunswick 54139 | 25 |
| *(Brunswick promo label)* | | | |
| WHAT HAPPENED | 1961 | Brunswick 54153 | 20 |
| *(Brunswick promo label)* | | | |
| | | | |
| **ARTISTS UNITED AGAINST APARTHEID** | | | |
| **12-Inch Singles** | | | |
| SUN CITY (Rock Version)/SILVER AND GOLD | 1985 | Manhattan SPRO 9544/5 | 10 |
| *(B-side is a Bono song, later recorded by U2)* | | | |
| **Albums** | | | |
| VOICES OF SUN CITY | 1985 | Manhattan SPRO-9538 | 35 |
| *(Promo album of interviews with participants)* | | | |
| | | | |
| **ASH, DANIEL** | | | |
| **RADIO SHOWS** | | | |
| **Compact Discs** | | | |
| ON THE EDGE (Feb 93) | 1993 | Westwood One | 10-20 |
| *(Daniel Ash & Sugar)* | | | |
| | | | |
| **ASIA** | | | |
| *Also see Yes. Geffen promo 45s $2 each* | | | |
| **Albums** | | | |
| ALPHA | 1983 | Geffen GHS 4008 | 20 |
| *Promo on Quiex II vinyl* | | | |
| ASIA | 1982 | Geffen GHS 2008 | 20 |
| *Promo on Quiex II vinyl* | | | |
| **RADIO SHOWS** | | | |
| **Albums** | | | |
| BBC ROCK HOUR (Sept 82) | 1982 | London Wavelength | 20-40 |
| *(Live concert)* | | | |
| INNERVIEW Profile | 1976 | Innerview | 20-40 |
| *(Music and interviews)* | | | |
| SOURCE SPECIAL (Aug 83) | 1983 | NBC Radio (2) | 20-40 |
| *(Mostly music and interviews)* | | | |
| SUPERSTAR CONCERT (June 84) | 1984 | Westwood One (3) | 40-100 |
| *(Live concert, repeated)* | | | |
| **Compact Discs** | | | |
| IN THE STUDIO (Sept 90) Profile of an album | 1990 | Album Network | 10-20 |
| *(Music and interviews)* | | | |
| | | | |
| **ASLEEP AT THE WHEEL** | | | |
| *Epic and Capitol promo 45s $3 each* | | | |
| **RADIO SHOWS** | | | |
| **Albums** | | | |
| AUSTIN ENCORE | 1988 | Mainstreet | 25-40 |
| *(Live concert)*  Entertainment | | | |
| LIVE AT GILLEY'S  Live concert | 1988 | Westwood One | 20-40 |
| *(Repeated)* | | | |
| | | | |
| **ASTAIRE, FRED** | | | |
| **45s** | | | |
| ONCE A YEAR NIGHT (same on both sides) | 1979 | DC 201 | 6 |
| | | | |
| **ASTLEY, RICK** | | | |
| *RCA Victor promo 45s $2 each* | | | |
| **RADIO SHOWS** | | | |
| **Albums** | | | |
| THE RICK ASTLEY STORY (Mar 89) Profile | 1989 | Unistar | 10-20 |
| *(Music and interviews)* | | | |
| | | | |
| **ASTRONAUTS, THE** | | | |
| *RCA Victor promo 45s $6 each* | | | |
| **7-Inch Extended Plays** | | | |
| BEAT! Jukebox LLP | 1963 | RCA Victor 1203 | 35 |
| *(Issued with a hard cover)* | | | |
| SURFIN' WITH THE ASTRONAUTS Jukebox LLP | 1963 | RCA Victor 1128 | 40 |
| *(Issued with a hard cover)* | | | |
| **Albums** | | | |
| ROCKIN' WITH THE ASTRONAUTS | 1965 | RCA Victor PRM-183 | 30 |
| *(Special products release)* | | | |
| | | | |
| **ASTROS, THE** | | | |
| **45s** | | | |
| LITTLE OSCAR THE ASTRODEER/SILENT NIGHT | 196? | Party-Time 4591 | 8 |
| | | | |
| **ATKINS, CHET** | | | |
| *RCA Victor promo 45s $2-$5 each; Other Sesac EPs $30 each; RCA Victor jukebox LLPs $6 each* | | | |
| **45s** | | | |
| EAST TENNESSEE CHRISTMAS/WINTER WONDERLAND | 1983 | Columbia AE7 1776 | 10 |
| **7-Inch Extended Plays** | | | |
| IS ANYTHING BETTER THAN THIS/BOOGIE FOR CECIL/ | 1974 | RCA Victor DJEO-0278 | 20 |

| Title | Yr | Label, Number | NM $ |
|---|---|---|---|
| MUTUAL ADMIRATION/DOWN SOUTH BLUES | | | |
| *(Yellow label, with promo picture cover, from "The Atkins/Travis Traveling Show"* | | | |
| MR. ATKINS, IF YOU PLEASE  Promo-only EP | 1959 | SESAC 13 | 40 |
| NO GREATER LOVE Promo-only EP | 1959 | SESAC 48 | 35 |
| *(With Faron Young, promo-only release)* | | | |
| **Albums** | | | |
| 25TH ANNIVERSARY TRIBUTES AND ANNOUNCEMENTS | 1972 | RCA SP-AT25 | 25-40 |
| *(One-sided, white label, in plain white cover with timing strip. Has greetings for Chet by 21 RCA artists)* | | | |
| SAILS/MY SONG | 1987 | Columbia CS7-02712 | 10 |
| *(7-inch 33 1/3, small center hole, normal Columbia label with "Demonstration Not for Sale" on label, with promo sleeve)* | | | |
| SPATS 'N' HATS/ALISHA | 1986 | Columbia CS7 2355 | 10 |
| *(WLP 7-inch 33 1/3 small center hole, with promo picture sleeve)* | | | |
| **RADIO SHOWS** | | | |
| **16-Inch Transcriptions** | | | |
| LEATHERNECK JAMBOREE (50s) Public service show | 195? | Leatherneck 19 | 20-65 |
| *(Music and interviews)* | | | |
| NAVY HOEDOWN (40s & 50s) Public service show | 194? | U. S. Navy #35 | 15-40 |
| *(Music and interviews)* | | | |
| **Albums** | | | |
| CHRISTMAS WITH... (60s) Radio show | 196? | Diamond 514 | 15-30 |
| *(Original copies have green label)* | | | |
| U.S. AIR FORCE COUNTRY MUSIC TIME | 1981 | Program #738 | 15-25 |
| *(Interview with Chet and songs, flip is by Steve Wariner)* | | | |

## ATLANTA RHYTHM SECTION
**RADIO SHOWS**
**Albums**

| Title | Yr | Label, Number | NM $ |
|---|---|---|---|
| A NIGHT ON THE ROAD | 1981 | ABC Radio (3) | 25-50 |
| *(Music and interviews)* | | | |
| BBC ROCK HOUR (Nov 81) | 1981 | London Wavelength | 50-60 |
| *(Live concert)* | | | |

## ATLANTIC STARR
**RADIO SHOWS**
**Compact Discs**

| Title | Yr | Label, Number | NM $ |
|---|---|---|---|
| STORY OF ATLANTIC STARR (Apr 92) Profile | 1992 | Unistar | 10-20 |
| *(Music and interviews)* | | | |

## ATOMIC ROOSTER
**RADIO SHOWS**
**Albums**

| Title | Yr | Label, Number | NM $ |
|---|---|---|---|
| BBC TRANSCRIPTION SERVICE  Live concert | 1972 | BBC | 100-150 |
| *(With Roxy Music)* | | | |

## ATTILA
*Epic promo 45s $8 each*
**Albums**

| Title | Yr | Label, Number | NM $ |
|---|---|---|---|
| ATTILA  White promo label | 1970 | Epic 30030 | 50 |
| *(Featuring Billy Joel)* | | | |

## AUDREY
**45s**

| Title | Yr | Label, Number | NM $ |
|---|---|---|---|
| DEAR ELVIS Promo version is 3:21 on both sides) | 1956 | Plus 104 | 40 |
| *(Green print on white label)* | | | |

## AUSTIN, GENE
**RADIO SHOWS**
**16-Inch Transcriptions**

| Title | Yr | Label, Number | NM $ |
|---|---|---|---|
| TREASURY DEPARTMENT (40s & 50s) Public service show | 194? | Treasury Department | 10-20 |
| *(Music and interviews)* | | | |

## AUSTIN, SIL
**7-Inch Extended Plays**

| Title | Yr | Label, Number | NM $ |
|---|---|---|---|
| SLOW WALK ROCK | 1958 | Mercury MEP-19 | 25 |

## AUSTRALIA
**RADIO SHOWS**
**Compact Discs**

| Title | Yr | Label, Number | NM $ |
|---|---|---|---|
| AUSTRALIA (May 94) Live concert | 1994 | (3) | 60-100 |
| *(From live pay-for-view television special of Nov 93)* | | | |

## AUTOGRAPH
**RADIO SHOWS**
**Albums**

| Title | Yr | Label, Number | NM $ |
|---|---|---|---|
| KING BISCUIT FLOWER HOUR (Feb 85) Live concert | 1985 | DIR (2) | 20-40 |
| *(With Zebra)* | | | |

## AUTRY, GENE
*Promo Columbia 78s $10, Columbia promo 45s $4; Promo Republic 45s $6; Country Crossroads radio shows $15*
**45s**

| Title | Yr | Label, Number | NM $ |
|---|---|---|---|
| RUDOLPH, THE RED-NOSED REINDEER | 1959 | Columbia | 15 |
| *Special 10th anniversary promo of the song, white label, no number, flip is the same song performed by the Ray Conniff Singers)* | | | |
| RUDOLPH, THE RED-NOSED REINDEER Reissue series | 1970 | Columbia 33165 | 10 |
| *(Red and black promo label, issued with picture sleeve, not available with the stock copy)* | | | |

| Title | Yr | Label, Number | NM $ |
|---|---|---|---|
| **7-Inch Extended Plays** | | | |
| SANTA'S HIT PARADE Columbia Record Club | 1958 | Columbia D-17 | 15 |
| *(Test record, mailed to club members, with paper picture sleeve)* | | | |
| **Albums** | | | |
| GENE AUTRY'S GREATEST HITS | 1961 | Columbia 1575 | 25 |
| *(White promo label)* | | | |
| **RADIO SHOWS** | | | |
| **Albums** | | | |
| COUNTRY CROSSROADS (Dec 81) Special Christmas Show | 1981 | S. Baptists 52-81 | 10-25 |
| *(There were several Crossroads shows w/Autry)* | | | |
| MELODY RANCH RADIO SHOW | 197? | Murray Hill 897296 (4) | 40 |
| *(Not actually a release for radio stations)* | | | |
| | | | |
| **AVALON, FRANKIE** | | | |
| *Chancellor white label promo 45s $15; Promo 45s on other labels $2* | | | |
| **45s** | | | |
| CHRISTMAS HOLIDAY  Promo-only release | 1958 | Chancellor 45FX-1 | 35 |
| *(White label promo)* | | | |
| CHRISTMAS HOLIDAY | 196? | Chancellor FX-1 | 25 |
| *(This version is black label)* | | | |
| DEDE DINAH | 1958 | Chancellor 1011 | 25 |
| *(White promo label)* | | | |
| FRANKIE AVALON Jukebox set of five singles | 196? | Chancellor 5022 | 55 |
| *(Issued in brown printed pack with color insert)* | | | |
| SHY GUY/TOO YOUNG | 1959 | Chancellor G-1 | 40 |
| *(Promo-only record made for "Acnecare")* | | | |
| SHY GUY/TOO YOUNG Promo-only picture sleeve | 1958 | Chancellor C-1 | 50 |
| *(Issued with the record for Acnecare)* | | | |
| TRUMPET SORRENTO | 1954 | "X" 0026 | 50 |
| *(White promo label)* | | | |
| **Albums** | | | |
| FABIAN AND AVALON | 1960 | Chancellor 5009 | 40 |
| *(White promo label)* | | | |
| FRANKIE AVALON | 1958 | Chancellor 5001 | 75 |
| *(White promo label)* | | | |
| SWINGIN' ON A RAINBOW | 1959 | Chancellor 5004 | 45 |
| *(White promo label, issued in a paper sleeve)* | | | |
| THE YOUNG FRANKIE AVALON | 1959 | Chancellor 5002 | 60 |
| *(White promo label)* | | | |
| YOUNG AND IN LOVE | 1960 | Chancellor 69801 | 50 |
| *(White promo label)* | | | |
| | | | |
| **AVERAGE WHITE BAND** | | | |
| *Atlantic promo 45s $3 each* | | | |
| **45s** | | | |
| WHEN WILL YOU BE MINE (same on both sides) | 1979 | Atlantic 3614 | 4 |
| *(May be promo only)* | | | |
| **RADIO SHOWS** | | | |
| **Albums** | | | |
| BBC TRANSCRIPTION DISC  Live concert | 1974 | BBC Transcription | 150-300 |
| *(Very rare series)* | | | |
| NIGHTBIRD AND COMPANY (Mar 75) Music and interview | 1975 | U. S. Army (2) | 10-30 |
| *(Three other guests have their own shows)* | | | |
| TOYOTA PRESENTS  Live concert | 197? | Toyota (2) | 15-30 |
| *(Rare live concert series)* | | | |
| **Reel-to-Reel Tapes** | | | |
| BBC ROCK HOUR | 1978 | London Wavelength | 50-100 |
| *(Live music and interviews)* | | | |
| BBC ROCK HOUR | 1979 | London Wavelength | 40-75 |
| *(Live music and interviews)* | | | |
| | | | |
| **AVERN, HARVEY, BAND** | | | |
| **45s** | | | |
| LET'S GET IT TOGETHER THIS CHRISTMAS/CHRISTMAS SONG | 19?? | Fania 551 | 4 |
| | | | |
| **AXTON, HOYT** | | | |
| *A&M promo 45s $3 each* | | | |
| **45s** | | | |
| WHAT'S IT ALL ABOUT (July 79) Public service show | 1979 | W. I. A. A. 482 | 18 |
| *(Flip side features Roxy Music)* | | | |
| **RADIO SHOWS** | | | |
| **Albums** | | | |
| COUNTRY COOKIN' Various artists | 1975 | Army Reserve (2) | 10-30 |
| *(Other artists, Wanda Jackson, Tom T. Hall and Freddy Weller)* | | | |
| LIVE FROM GILLEY'S (Sept 84) Live concert | 1984 | Westwood One | 15-30 |
| | | | |
| **AZTEC CAMERA** | | | |
| **12-Inch Singles** | | | |
| DEEP AND WIDE AND TALL/DEEP AND WIDE AND TALL (Edit) | 1987 | Sire PRO-A-2848 | 8 |
| GOOD MORNING BRITAIN (6 versions) | 1990 | Sire PRO-A-4517 | 8 |
| SOMEWHERE IN MY HEART (2 versions)/RODDY FRAME INTERVIEW | 1988 | Sire PRO-A-3160 | 8 |
| SOMEWHERE IN MY HEART (Alternate Mix)/same (Remix) | 1988 | Sire PRO-A-3232 | 8 |

| Title | Yr | Label, Number | NM $ |
|---|---|---|---|

# B

## B-52'S, THE
*Warner promo 45s $4 each; Warner promo 12" singles $10 each*
### 12-Inch Singles

| Title | Yr | Label, Number | NM $ |
|---|---|---|---|
| GIVE ME BACK MY MAN/STROBE LIGHT | 1980 | Warner Bros. PRO-A-927 | 12 |
| LEGAL TENDER/WHAMMY KISS/FUTURE GENERATION | 1983 | Warner Bros. PRO-A-2045 | 10 |
| MESOPOTAMIA/DEEP SLEEP/CAKE | 1982 | Warner Bros. PRO-A-1016 | 12 |
| PRIVATE IDAHO/PARTY OUT OF BOUNDS (Instrumental) | 1979 | Warner Bros. PRO-A-890 | 12 |
| REVOLUTION EARTH (4 versions) | 1992 | Reprise PRO-A-5852 | 8 |

### RADIO SHOWS
#### Compact Discs

| Title | Yr | Label, Number | NM $ |
|---|---|---|---|
| ON THE EDGE (Nov 92) | 1992 | Westwood One | 20-30 |

*(Music and interviews)*

## BABY GRAND
*Early version of The Hooters.*
### 45s

| Title | Yr | Label, Number | NM $ |
|---|---|---|---|
| ALL NIGHT LONG (same on both sides) | 1979 | Arista 0394 | 5 |

*(May be promo only)*

## BABYS, THE
*Chrysalis white promo label 45s $3 each; Also see John Waite*
### RADIO SHOWS
#### Albums

| Title | Yr | Label, Number | NM $ |
|---|---|---|---|
| INNERVIEW (70s) Music and interview | 197? | Innerview | 25-35 |
| *(This show was repeated)* | | | |
| KING BISCUIT FLOWER HOUR (Mar 80) | 1980 | DIR/ABC (2) | 60-100 |
| *(Live concert)* | | | |
| KING BISCUIT FLOWER HOUR (Mar 80) Live concert | 1980 | DIR/ABC (2) | 75-125 |
| *(In concert with Blue Oyster Cult)* | | | |
| SUPERSTAR RADIO NETWORK PRESENTS THE BABYS LIVE | 1977 | Chyrsalis CHS-4-DJ | 10 |

## BACHMAN-TURNER OVERDRIVE
*Other Mercury 45s $5 each*
### 45s

| Title | Yr | Label, Number | NM $ |
|---|---|---|---|
| DOWN THE ROAD (same on both sides) | 1978 | Mercury DJ-549 | 10 |
| *(Promo-only release)* | | | |
| DOWN TO THE LINE (stereo/mono) | 1975 | Mercury DJ-438 | 10 |
| *(Promo-only release)* | | | |
| LOOKIN' OUT FOR #1 (long/short) | 1975 | Mercury DJ-449 | 10 |
| *(Promo-only release)* | | | |
| TAKE IT LIKE A MAN (long/short) | 1975 | Mercury DJ-446 | 12 |
| *(Promo-only release)* | | | |

### RADIO SHOWS
#### Albums

| Title | Yr | Label, Number | NM $ |
|---|---|---|---|
| CAPTURED LIVE (Sept 84) | 1984 | RKO (2) | 100-150 |
| *(Live concert)* | | | |
| TOYOTA PRESENTS Music and interview | 197? | Toyota (2) | 25-40 |
| *(Profile of the group)* | | | |

#### Compact Discs

| Title | Yr | Label, Number | NM $ |
|---|---|---|---|
| IN THE STUDIO (Oct 89) Profile of an album | 1989 | Album Network | 10-15 |
| *(Music and interviews)* | | | |

## BACKBEAT BAND
### Albums

| Title | Yr | Label, Number | NM $ |
|---|---|---|---|
| BACKBEAT (Original Soundtrack) | 1994 | Virgin SPRO-14124 | 15 |
| *(Green vinyl in plastic sleeve)* | | | |

## BAD COMPANY
*Includes Paul Rodgers. Atlantic company promo labels $3-5 each*
### 45s

| Title | Yr | Label, Number | NM $ |
|---|---|---|---|
| THIS TELL IT LIKE IT IS (same on both sides) | 1986 | Atlantic 89355 | 4 |
| *(May be promo only)* | | | |

### RADIO SHOWS
#### Albums

| Title | Yr | Label, Number | NM $ |
|---|---|---|---|
| IN CONCERT (May 89) Live concert | 1989 | Westwood One (2) | 25-50 |
| *(With White Lion)* | | | |
| LEGENDS OF ROCK (Sept 87) Profile | 1987 | NBC Radio (2) | 20-30 |
| *(Music and interview)* | | | |
| LONDON PROFILE (Nov 88) Paul Rodgers | 1988 | | 15-25 |
| *(Music and interview)* | | | |
| NBC SOURCE (May 83) Profile of an album | 1983 | NBC Radio (3) | 30-40 |
| *(Music and interview)* | | | |
| OFF THE RECORD Profile | 1990 | Westwood One (2) | 10-15 |
| *(Music and interview)* | | | |
| ROCK STARS (Nov 88) Profile, music and interview | 1988 | DIR (2) | 15-25 |
| *(Some live material)* | | | |
| SUPERSTAR CONCERT (Sept 91) Live concert | 1991 | Westwood One (3) | 25-40 |
| *(Vinyl version of the show, repeated several times)* | | | |
| TIMOTHY WHITE SESSIONS (Oct 88) Profile | 1988 | Westwood One (2) | 20-30 |
| *(Music and interview)* | | | |

| Title | Yr | Label, Number | NM $ |
|---|---|---|---|
| **Compact Discs** | | | |
| ALBUM NETWORK SPECIAL | 1996 | Album Network (2) | 50-100 |
| *(Live concert material)* | | | |
| BBC CLASSIC TRACKS (Oct 93) Profile | 1993 | London Wavelength | 10-20 |
| *(Music and interview, repeated several times)* | | | |
| ELECTRIC LADYLAND (Dec 92) Live concert | 1992 | | 75-100 |
| *(Rare concert material)* | | | |
| OFF THE RECORD (May 93) Profile | 1993 | Westwood One | 15-20 |
| *(Music and interview)* | | | |
| SUPERSTAR CONCERT (Mar 93) Live concert | 1993 | Westwood One | 30-50 |
| *(Also featured: Free & the Firm)* | | | |
| UP CLOSE Music and interview | 1991 | Media America (2) | 30-40 |
| *(Some live material)* | | | |

## BAD ENGLISH
*Epic promo singles worth $3; See Paul Carrack*

**RADIO SHOWS**

| | | | |
|---|---|---|---|
| **Albums** | | | |
| OFF THE RECORD (Oct 91) Music and interview | 1991 | Westwood One (2) | 10-15 |
| *(Music and interviews)* | | | |

## BADFINGER
*Apple 45s with star $8; Warner Brothers promo 45s $4; Other label promos worth $4 each*

| **45s** | | | |
|---|---|---|---|
| APPLE OF MY EYE (mono/stereo) | 1973 | Apple P-1864 | 25 |
| *(Must have the "P" prefix)* | | | |
| BABY BLUE/FLYING | 1972 | Apple 1844 | 120 |
| *White label* | | | |
| COME AND GET IT Apple promo label | 1970 | Apple P-1815 | 50 |
| *(Must have the "P" prefix)* | | | |
| DAY AFTER DAY/MONEY | 1971 | Apple 1841 | 120 |
| *White label* | | | |
| NO MATTER WHAT Apple promo label | 1970 | Apple P-1822 | 50 |
| *(Must have the "P" prefix)* | | | |
| WHAT'S IT ALL ABOUT (Nov 79) Public service show | 1979 | W. I. A. A. 499 | 50 |
| *(With Tommy Evans and Joey Molland, flip is Jennifer Warnes)* | | | |

**RADIO SHOWS**

| **Albums** | | | |
|---|---|---|---|
| BBC TRANSCRIPTION DISC  Live concert | 1973 | BBC Transcription | 700-800 |
| *(With Thin Lizzy)* | | | |
| IN CONCERT (Feb 91) Live concert | 1991 | Westwood One (2) | 100-150 |
| *(In concert with Queen)* | | | |

## BAEZ, JOAN
*Vanguard promo 45s $4 each; A&M promo 45s $3 each; A&M promo LPs $5 each*

| **45s** | | | |
|---|---|---|---|
| DEPORTEE | 1968 | Vanguard VSQ-6 | 10 |
| *(Small center hole)* | | | |
| THE NIGHT THEY DROVE OLD DIXIE DOWN (3:25 version) | 1971 | Vanguard | 15 |
| *(Mono test pressing)* | | | |
| **7-Inch Extended Plays** | | | |
| JOAN BAEZ IN CONCERT Jukebox LLP | 1968 | Vanguard 2123 | 20 |
| *(Issued with a hard cover)* | | | |
| **Albums** | | | |
| RADIO AIRPLAY ALBUM | 1976 | A&M 8375 | 15 |
| *(Sample cuts from several LPs)* | | | |

**RADIO SHOWS**

| **Albums** | | | |
|---|---|---|---|
| BBC TRANSCRIPTION DISC | 1978 | BBC Transcription | 200-400 |
| *(Live concert and possible only live radio show in this, one of the most rare and desirable series in collecting)* | | | |
| **Reel-to-Reel Tapes** | | | |
| COLUMBIA RECORDS RADIO HOUR (Sept 95) | 1995 | (2) | 50-100 |
| *(Live concert material; with James McMurtry)* | | | |
| KING BISCUIT FLOWER HOUR (July 76) Live concert | 1976 | DIR/ABC (2) | 100-150 |
| *(Very rare)* | | | |

## BAILEY, RAZZY
*Aquarian label promos $5 each; RCA Victor and MCA promo 45s $2 each; RCA Victor and MCA color vinyl promos $7 each; SOA colored vinyl promos $4 each*

**RADIO SHOWS**

| **Albums** | | | |
|---|---|---|---|
| COUNTRY SESSIONS (80s) Music and interview | 198? | NBC Radio | 10-15 |
| *(Bailey is guest host on a weekly series)* | | | |
| SILVER EAGLE (Apr 83) | 1983 | Westwood One (3) | 15-20 |
| *(Live concert)* | | | |

## BAJA MARIMBA BAND, THE

| **45s** | | | |
|---|---|---|---|
| THE 12 DAYS OF CHRISTMAS/MY FAVORITE THINGS | 1968 | A&M XMAS 1 | 12 |
| *(B-side by We Five)* | | | |

## BALIN, MARTY
*Also see Jefferson Airplane; Jefferson Starship.*

| **Albums** | | | |
|---|---|---|---|
| BALIN | 1981 | EMI America SPRO-9673 | 20 |
| *Red vinyl* | | | |

| **Title** | **Yr** | **Label, Number** | **NM $** |
|---|---|---|---|
| **BALLARD, HANK, AND THE MIDNIGHTERS** | | | |
| *King promo 45s $15* | | | |
| | | | |
| **BALLEW, JIM** | | | |
| **45s** | | | |
| HOLY IS THE DAY/HOLY IS THE DAY (Instrumental) | 19?? | Wynn-Ballew (no #) | 3 |
| | | | |
| **BALTIMORA** | | | |
| **12-Inch Singles** | | | |
| LIVING IN THE BACKGROUND (3 versions) | 1985 | Manhattan SPRO 9636/7 | 6 |
| | | | |
| **BAMBAATAA, AFRIKA, AND THE SOUL SONIC FORCE** | | | |
| **45s** | | | |
| RECKLESS (same on both sides) | 1988 | Capitol 44163 | 3 |
| *(With UB40)* | | | |
| | | | |
| **BANANARAMA** | | | |
| *London promo 45s worth $4* | | | |
| **12-Inch Singles** | | | |
| (HE WAS) REALLY SAYIN' SOMETHIN' (same on both sides) | 1982 | London PRO 221 | 10 |
| NA NA HEY HEY (KISS HIM GOODBYE) (2 versions) | 1983 | London PRO 240 | 8 |
| **RADIO SHOWS** | | | |
| **Albums** | | | |
| BANANARAMA SPECIAL (May 88) Profile | 1988 | Unistar (2) | 10-20 |
| *(Music and interviews)* | | | |
| | | | |
| **BAND, THE** | | | |
| *Lead singer Robbie Robertson; Capitol promo 45s $5 each* | | | |
| **Albums** | | | |
| THE LAST WALTZ SAMPLER | 1978 | Warner Bros. PRO-A-737 | 20 |
| *(Edited version of the stock copy)* | | | |
| **RADIO SHOWS** | | | |
| **Compact Discs** | | | |
| IN THE STUDIO (Sept 88) | 1988 | Album Network | 15-25 |
| *(Profile of an album)* | | | |
| KING BISCUIT FLOWER HOUR (Apr 91) | 1991 | DIR | 30-50 |
| *(With Blues Traveler)* | | | |
| KING BISCUIT FLOWER HOUR (Mar 88) | 1988 | DIR | 30-50 |
| *(Live concert)* | | | |
| UP CLOSE | 1994 | Media America (2) | 25-50 |
| *(Music and interviews)* | | | |
| | | | |
| **BANDY, MOE** | | | |
| *Columbia promo 45s $2 each* | | | |
| **RADIO SHOWS** | | | |
| AMERICAN EAGLE (Jan 87) Live material | 1987 | Westwood One | 10-15 |
| *(With Joe Stampley, Moe & Joe)* | | | |
| COUNTRY SESSIONS (70s) Profile | 197? | | 10-15 |
| *(Music and interview)* | | | |
| LIVE AT GILLEY'S (Oct 88) Live concert | 1988 | Westwood One | 10-15 |
| SILVER EAGLE (June 84) Live concert | 1984 | DIR (3) | 15-25 |
| *(Entire concert)* | | | |
| | | | |
| **BANGLES** | | | |
| *Columbia promo 45s $2 each; Columbia promo picture sleeves $1 each* | | | |
| **12-Inch Singles** | | | |
| GOING DOWN TO LIVERPOOL (same on both sides) | 1984 | Columbia AS 1939 | 12 |
| HAZY SHADE OF WINTER (with intro)/ (without intro) | 1987 | Def Jam CAS 2857 | 8 |
| HERO TAKES A FALL (same on both sides) | 1984 | Columbia AS 1883 | 12 |
| IF SHE KNEW WHAT SHE WANTS (same on both sides) | 1986 | Columbia CAS 2334 | 10 |
| MANIC MONDAY (same on both sides) | 1986 | Columbia CAS 2249 | 12 |
| THE REAL WORLD (same on both sides) | 1983 | Faulty Products DJ 1000 | 15 |
| WALK LIKE AN EGYPTIAN (same on both sides) | 1986 | Columbia CAS 2453 | 8 |
| **45s** | | | |
| HERO TAKES A FALL  Promo picture sleeve | 1984 | Columbia 04479 | 10 |
| *(Price includes promo record with sleeve)* | | | |
| **Albums** | | | |
| INTERCHORDS | 1986 | Columbia CAS 2270 | 20 |
| *(Promo-only interview album)* | | | |
| **Compact Discs** | | | |
| EVERYTHING Promo-only sampler picture disc | 1989 | Columbia | 40 |
| **RADIO SHOWS** | | | |
| **Albums** | | | |
| BANGLES SPECIAL (June 89) Profile | 1989 | Unistar | 10-20 |
| *(Music and interview)* | | | |
| | | | |
| **BANKS, TONY** | | | |
| *Of Genesis* | | | |
| **45s** | | | |
| FOR AWHILE | 1979 | Charisma 3503 | 10 |
| THIS IS LOVE (same on both sides) | 1983 | Atlantic 89820 | 4 |
| *(May be promo only)* | | | |

| Title | Yr | Label, Number | NM $ |
|---|---|---|---|

**BARCLAY JAMES HARVEST**
*German rock band; MCA promo 45s $5 each*
**RADIO SHOWS**
**Albums**

| | | | |
|---|---|---|---|
| BBC TRANSCRIPTION DISC Live concert | 1973 | BBC Transcription | 75-125 |

*(Very rare show)*

**BARE, BOBBY**
*Blue label Fraternity promo singles $25 each; White label Fraternity promo singles $30 each; Capitol white label promos $15 each; RCA white label promos $3-4 each; Mercury white label promos $3 each; Mercury white label LPs $5 each*
**45s**

| | | | |
|---|---|---|---|
| EDUCATED ROCK AND ROLL White promo label | 1959 | Fraternity 846 | 35 |

*(Label credits Bill Parsons but recording is actually Bare)*

| | | | |
|---|---|---|---|
| THE ALL AMERICAN BOY White promo label | 1959 | Fraternity 835 | 40 |

*(Label credits Bill Parsons but recording is actually Bare)*

| | | | |
|---|---|---|---|
| WHAT'S IT ALL ABOUT (Jan 79) Public service show | 1979 | W. I. A. A. 459 | 20 |

*(Flip side is Gino Vannelli)*
**7-Inch Extended Plays**

| | | | |
|---|---|---|---|
| WHAT AM I GONNA DO White promo label | 1972 | Mercury MEPL-16 | 10 |

*(Four-song promo EP)*
**RADIO SHOWS**
**Albums**

| | | | |
|---|---|---|---|
| AMERICAN EAGLE (Oct 86) | 1986 | Westwood One | 10-15 |

*(Live concert, repeated)*

| | | | |
|---|---|---|---|
| LIVE AT GILLEY'S (Apr 83) | 1983 | Westwood One | 10-15 |

*(Profile and live music)*

| | | | |
|---|---|---|---|
| SILVER EAGLE (Jan 87) | 1987 | Westwood One (3) | 15-20 |

*(Live concert)*

**BARRY, LEN**
*Of the Dovells. Decca promo 45s $8 each; Decca pink label promo LPs $20 each; Other promo label 45s $4-8 each*
**7-Inch Extended Plays**

| | | | |
|---|---|---|---|
| 1-2-3 Jukebox LLP | 1966 | Decca 74720 | 20 |

*(Issued with a hard cover)*

**BARTHOLOMEW, DAVE**
*Other promo 45s $15*
**45s**

| | | | |
|---|---|---|---|
| MY DING-A-LING | 1952 | King 4544 | 100 |

*(Promo colored vinyl version)*

| | | | |
|---|---|---|---|
| MY DING-A-LING Black vinyl | 1952 | King 4544 | 50 |

*(Number one record by Chuck Berry)*

| | | | |
|---|---|---|---|
| THE REST OF MY LIFE | 1952 | Imperial 5210 | 40 |

*(Cream-colored promo label)*

| | | | |
|---|---|---|---|
| TRA-LA-LA | 1963 | Decca 48216 | 80 |

*(Pink promo label)*

**BASIL, TONI**
**12-Inch Singles**

| | | | |
|---|---|---|---|
| NOBODY/ROCK ON | 1983 | Chrysalis AS 1615 | 6 |

**BATORS, STIV**
**45s**

| | | | |
|---|---|---|---|
| NOT THAT WAY ANYMORE/CIRCUMSTANTIAL EVIDENCE | 1979 | Bomp! X-128 | 15 |

**BATTIN, SKIP**
*Ex-member of the Byrds.*
**45s**

| | | | |
|---|---|---|---|
| BALLAD OF DICK CLARK (mono/stereo) | 1973 | Signpost 70010 | 6 |

*(May be promo only)*

**BAY CITY ROLLERS**
*Bell promo 45s $4 each; Arista promo 45s $3 each*
**45s**

| | | | |
|---|---|---|---|
| WHAT'S IT ALL ABOUT (May 77) Public service show | 1977 | W. I. A. A. 372 | 15 |

*(Flip side features David Gates)*

**BE-BOP DELUXE**
**Albums**

| | | | |
|---|---|---|---|
| BE-BOP'S BIGGEST | 1978 | Harvest SPRO-8531 | 30 |

*(Promo-only compilation)*

| | | | |
|---|---|---|---|
| SUNBURST FINISH | 1975 | Capitol SPRO-8486 | 25 |

*(Specially banded version for radio)*

**BEACH BOYS, THE**
*Also see California Music. Critique promo 45s duets w/Little Richard $5 each; Reprise LP white labels $25-30 each; Columbia promo 45 and sleeve duet (04726) $8 each; FBI label promo 45s $5 each; Capitol jukebox 45s (green vinyl) $5 each; Capitol jukebox 45s (black vinyl) $3 each; Elektra promo 45s $5; Columbia and Caribou promo LPs $15 each and Carl Wilson promo LPs; Columbia promo 45s by Carl Wilson (Caribou) and Mike Love on Boardwalk, Dennis Wilson on Columbia all $4 each*
**12-Inch Singles**

| | | | |
|---|---|---|---|
| CALIFORNIA DREAMIN' | 1986 | Capitol SPRO-9796 | 25 |

*(Promo-only 12" single with title cover)*

| | | | |
|---|---|---|---|
| GETCHA BACK | 1985 | Caribou ZAS 2008 | 20 |

*(Promo-only 12-inch, says "Demonstration Not for Sale")*

| | | | |
|---|---|---|---|
| HERE COMES THE NIGHT | 1979 | Caribou 9028 | 15 |

*(Gray promo label, promo only)*

| Title | Yr | Label, Number | NM $ |
|-------|----|----|------|
| HERE COMES THE NIGHT | 1979 | Caribou 9029 | 12 |
| *(White promo label)* | | | |
| HERE COMES THE NIGHT Special promo-only release | 1979 | Caribou AS 557 | 50 |
| *(Record is blue vinyl)* | | | |
| HERE COMES THE NIGHT Special promo-only release | 1979 | Caribou AS 557 | 100 |
| *(Record is blue vinyl and AUTOGRAPHED!)* | | | |
| **45s** | | | |
| ADD SOME MUSIC TO YOUR DAY | 1970 | Reprise 0894 | 18 |
| *(White promo label)* | | | |
| BARBARA ANN | 1975 | Capitol 4110 | 10 |
| *(White promo label)* | | | |
| BLUEBIRDS OVER THE MOUNTAIN | 1968 | Capitol P-2360 | 20 |
| *(Green promo label)* | | | |
| BREAK AWAY | 1969 | Capitol 2530 | 18 |
| *(Green promo label)* | | | |
| CALIFORNIA DREAMIN' | 1986 | Capitol 5630 | 12 |
| *(White promo label)* | | | |
| CALIFORNIA SAGA | 1973 | Reprise 1156 | 18 |
| *(White promo label, mono/stereo versions)* | | | |
| CHILD OF WINTER | 1974 | Reprise 1321 | 40 |
| *(Brown promo label)* | | | |
| COME AND GET IT Tri-Five | 1962 | Danmark 2400 | 100 |
| *(Brian, Carl and Dennis Wilson)* | | | |
| COME GO WITH ME | 1981 | Caribou 02633 | 10 |
| *(White promo label)* | | | |
| COOL COOL WATER | 1970 | Reprise 0998 | 75 |
| *(White promo label, "Forever" on flip)* | | | |
| COOL COOL WATER | 1970 | Reprise 0998 | 50 |
| *(White promo label, same song on each side)* | | | |
| COTTON FIELDS | 1970 | Capitol 2765 | 20 |
| *(Green promo label)* | | | |
| DANCE, DANCE, DANCE  Starline reissue | 1967 | Capitol P-6105 | 25 |
| *(Green promo label)* | | | |
| DARLIN' | 1967 | Capitol P-2068 | 25 |
| *(Green promo label)* | | | |
| DO IT AGAIN | 1968 | Capitol P-2239 | 20 |
| *(Green promo label)* | | | |
| DON'T WORRY BABY | 1988 | Capitol P-B-44297 | 10 |
| *(Everly Brothers with the Beach Boys; with stock title sleeve)* | | | |
| FRIENDS | 1968 | Capitol P-2160 | 25 |
| *(Green promo label)* | | | |
| FUN, FUN, FUN  Starline reissue | 1967 | Capitol P-6016 | 25 |
| *(Green promo label)* | | | |
| FUN, FUN, FUN  Starline reissue | 1975 | Capitol P-6106 | 10 |
| *(Promo label)* | | | |
| GETCHA BACK | 1985 | Caribou 04913 | 12 |
| *(Promo record and promo sleeve)* | | | |
| GETTIN' HUNGRY | 1967 | Brother 1002 | 25 |
| *(Brown promo label)* | | | |
| GOIN' ON | 1980 | Caribou 9032 | 10 |
| *(White promo label)* | | | |
| GOOD TIMIN' | 1979 | Caribou 9029 | 10 |
| *(White promo label, mono/stereo)* | | | |
| GRADUATION DAY | 1976 | Capitol 4334 | 10 |
| *(White promo label)* | | | |
| HERE COMES THE NIGHT | 1979 | Caribou 9026 | 10 |
| *(White promo label, mono/stereo)* | | | |
| HEROES & VILLAINS | 1967 | Brother 1001 | 30 |
| *(Brown promo label, stock picture sleeve with  Capitol number 5826, worth over $500)* | | | |
| HONKIN' DOWN THE HIGHWAY | 1977 | Reprise 1389 | 10 |
| *(Brown promo label)* | | | |
| I CAN HEAR MUSIC | 1969 | Capitol P-2432 | 18 |
| *(Green promo label)* | | | |
| I CAN HEAR MUSIC | 1974 | Reprise 1310 | 18 |
| *(Brown promo label)* | | | |
| IT'S A BEAUTIFUL DAY | 1979 | Caribou 9031 | 10 |
| *(White promo label)* | | | |
| IT'S GETTIN' LATE | 1985 | Caribou 05433 | 12 |
| *(Promo record and promo sleeve)* | | | |
| IT'S OK | 1976 | Reprise 1368 | 10 |
| *(Brown promo label)* | | | |
| LADY LYNDA | 1979 | Caribou 9030 | 10 |
| *(White promo label, mono/stereo)* | | | |
| LITTLE HONDA | 1975 | Capitol 4093 | 10 |
| *(White promo label)* | | | |
| LIVIN' WITH A HEARTACHE | 1980 | Caribou 9033 | 10 |
| *(White promo label)* | | | |
| LONG PROMISED ROAD | 1971 | Reprise 1015 | 18 |
| *(White promo label, "Deirdre" on flip)* | | | |
| LONG PROMISED ROAD | 1971 | Reprise 1047 | 25 |
| *(White promo label, mono/stereo versions)* | | | |
| MARCELLA | 1972 | Reprise 1101 | 20 |
| *(Promo label, mono/stereo versions)* | | | |
| PEGGY SUE | 1978 | Reprise 1394 | 10 |
| *(Brown promo label)* | | | |
| ROCK 'N' ROLL TO THE RESCUE | 1986 | Capitol 5595 | 10 |
| *(White promo label)* | | | |

| Title | Yr | Label, Number | NM $ |
|---|---|---|---|
| ROCK AND ROLL MUSIC | 1976 | Reprise 1354 | 10 |
| (Brown promo label) | | | |
| SAIL ON SAILOR | 1973 | Reprise 1138 | 18 |
| (Brown promo label) | | | |
| SAIL ON SAILOR | 1975 | Reprise PRO 557 | 100 |
| (Promo-only release) | | | |
| SAIL ON SAILOR | 1975 | Reprise 1325 | 15 |
| (Brown promo label) | | | |
| SALT LAKE CITY Special products release | 1965 | Capitol PRO 2937 | 200 |
| (Promo-only release) | | | |
| SCHOOL DAY | 1981 | Caribou 9034 | 300 |
| (Promo-only release) | | | |
| SHE BELIEVES IN LOVE | 1985 | Caribou 05624 | 12 |
| (Promo record and promo sleeve) | | | |
| SLIP ON THROUGH | 1970 | Reprise 0929 | 15 |
| (White promo label) | | | |
| SOMEWHERE NEAR JAPAN | 1989 | Capitol 7PRO-79841 | 100 |
| (Vinyl is promo only) | | | |
| SPIRIT OF AMERICA KFWB record release | 1963 | Capitol Custom | 1,000 |
| (Promo-only release and promo sleeve) | | | |
| STILL CRUISIN' | 1989 | Capitol 7PRO-79789 | 100 |
| (Promo-only release) | | | |
| SUMMERTIME PROMO SPOTS  Radio ads | 1970 | Warner PRO 422 | 50 |
| (Promo-only release) | | | |
| SURF'S UP | 1971 | Reprise 1058 | 40 |
| (White promo label) | | | |
| SURFER GIRL Starline reissue | 1967 | Capitol P-6107 | 25 |
| (Green promo label) | | | |
| SURFER GIRL  Starline reissue | 1975 | Capitol P-6107 | 10 |
| (Promo label) | | | |
| THE SURFER MOON Bob and Sheri | 1963 | Safari 101 | 1,500 |
| (White promo label) | | | |
| SURFIN' | 1961 | Candix 301 | 300 |
| (Candix promo label) | | | |
| SURFIN' USA | 1974 | Capitol 3924 | 10 |
| (White promo label) | | | |
| SUSIE CINCINNATI | 1976 | Reprise 1375 | 10 |
| (Brown promo label) | | | |
| TEARS IN THE MORNING | 1970 | Reprise 0957 | 15 |
| (White promo label) | | | |
| THINGS ARE CHANGING w/The Blossoms | 1965 | E.E.O.C. | 400 |
| (7" 33rpm radio ads with cardboard black/white cover, price is for record and cover) | | | |
| VOTE '72  Radio ads "Get Out and Vote!" | 1972 | Warner Brothers PRO 534 | 50 |
| (Promo-only release) | | | |
| WHAT'S IT ALL ABOUT  Public service show | 1976 | W. I. A. A. 1790 | 100 |
| (Flip side features the Rolling Stones) | | | |
| WHAT'S IT ALL ABOUT (Nov 78) Public service show | 1978 | W. I. A. A. 450 | 75 |
| (Flip side features Dr. Hook) | | | |
| WHAT'S IT ALL ABOUT (Sept 81) Public service show | 1981 | W. I. A. A. 594 | 75 |
| (Flip side features Barbara Mandrell) | | | |
| WILD HONEY | 1967 | Capitol P-2028 | 30 |
| (Green promo label) | | | |
| WOULDN'T IT BE NICE | 1971 | ODE 66016 | 30 |
| (Black and white promo label, mono/stereo  versions) | | | |
| WOULDN'T IT BE NICE | 1975 | Reprise 1336 | 12 |
| (Brown promo label) | | | |
| YOU NEED A MESS OF HELP TO STAND ALONE/CUDDLE UP | 1972 | Reprise 1091 | 20 |
| (Promo label, mono/stereo versions, WLP 7-inch) | | | |
| **7-Inch Extended Plays** | | | |
| BEACH BOYS PARTY | 1965 | Capitol PRO 2993 | 1,000 |
| (Promo-only release) | | | |
| BRIAN WILSON INTRODUCES SELECTIONS FROM | 1964 | Capitol PRO 2754 | 1,000 |
| BEACH BOYS CONCERT | | | |
| (Promo-only EP) | | | |
| GIRLS ON THE BEACH | 1964 | Capitol (no #) | Unknown |
| (Little information known) | | | |
| MT. VERNON AND FAIRWAY  White promo label | 1972 | Reprise 2118 | 10 |
| (Included with the promo Holland LP) | | | |
| RADIO SPOTS BACKING TRACKS FOR BEACH BOYS IN CONCERT | 1973 | Brother PRO 881 | 225 |
| (Promo-only EP) | | | |
| RIVER SONG Dennis Wilson | 1977 | Columbia AE7-1128 | 12 |
| (Various-artists record, includes two others) | | | |
| ROCK SHOP DEMO DISC | 197? | Syndicated | 40 |
| (Promo-only record) | | | |
| SHUT DOWN, VOL. 2 Jukebox LLP | 1968 | Capitol 2027 | 250 |
| (Issued with a hard cover) | | | |
| SUNFLOWER Radio ads | 1970 | Reprise PRO-422 | 250 |
| (Promo-only ads for the LP) | | | |
| SURFER GIRL Jukebox LLP | 1968 | Capitol 1981 | 250 |
| (Issued with a hard cover) | | | |
| TEN LITTLE INDIANS  Ray Anthony on flip | 1963 | Capitol PRO 2186 | 1,500 |
| (Promo-only EP, issued with a cardboard cover) | | | |
| THE BEACH BOYS RADIO SPECIAL | 1976 | Reprise (no #) | 30 |
| (Promo only, music and interviews) | | | |
| THE BEACH BOYS TODAY  Jukebox LLP | 1968 | Capitol 2269 | 250 |
| (Issued with a hard cover) | | | |

| Title | Yr | Label, Number | NM $ |
|---|---|---|---|
| THE BEST OF THE BEACH BOYS  Jukebox LLP | 1968 | Capitol 2545 | 200 |
| *(Issued with a paper cover, #189)* | | | |
| THE BEST OF THE BEACH BOYS Jukebox LLP | 1972 | Capitol LLP-189 | 40 |
| *(Issued with a paper sleeve)* | | | |
| WURLITZER DANCE MUSIC  10-record jukebox EP set | 1965 | Columbia (10) | 100 |
| *(Price is for all 10 discs)* | | | |
| **Albums** | | | |
| AMERICATHON Soundtrack LP Various artists | 1979 | Lorimar (Columbia) 36174 | 10 |
| *(One cut by the Beach Boys, this promo is rare)* | | | |
| BEACH BOYS CONCERT | 1964 | Capitol PRO 2754 | 300 |
| *(Promo-only release)* | | | |
| THE BEACH BOYS IN CONCERT | 1973 | Brother/Reprise 2RS 6484 | 40 |
| *(White label promo)* | | | |
| BEACH BOYS INTERVIEW FOR KEEPING THE SUMMER ALIVE | 1980 | Caribou 1024 | 40 |
| *(Profile and interview for the LP)* | | | |
| BIG SURFIN' SOUNDS Various artists | 1963 | Capitol PRO 2396 | 40 |
| *(Including the Beach Boys)* | | | |
| BIG SURFIN' SOUNDS Various artists | 1964 | Capitol PRO 2658 | 40 |
| *(Includes the Beach Boys)* | | | |
| CAPITOL DISC JOCKEY ALBUM (60s) Various artists | 196? | Capitol SPROS | 10-20 |
| *(These LPs with special covers were released each month from Capitol for radio stations, price is for LPs with one or two Beach Boys cuts)* | | | |
| CAPITOL DISC JOCKEY ALBUM (Oct 67) Various artists | 1967 | Capitol SPRO 4404/4405 | 25 |
| *(Includes two tracks by Murry Wilson, father of three Beach Boys and well-known writer/producer)* | | | |
| CAPITOL STUDIES OPEN HOUSE SAMPLER | 1977 | Capitol PRO 101 | 150 |
| *(Another Capitol promo series for a Beach Boys LP)* | | | |
| CARL AND THE PASSIONS "SO TOUGH"/PET SOUNDS | 1972 | Brother/Reprise 2MS 2083 | 50 |
| *(White label promo)* | | | |
| CRAWDADDY INTERVIEW | 1977 | Crawdaddy Magazine | 75 |
| *(Beach Boys profile interviews)* | | | |
| EXCERPTS FROM GREAT NEW RELEASES... VARIOUS | 1963 | Capitol PRO 2377 | 50 |
| *(Promo only, includes Shut Down)* | | | |
| GREAT NEW RELEASES... Various artists | 1964 | Capitol PRO 2686 | 25 |
| *(Includes "I Get Around," other LPs in the series also worth $25 each if Beach Boys have at least one track)* | | | |
| HOLLAND | 1973 | Brother/Reprise MS 2118 | 40 |
| *(White label promo; includes bonus white-label promo EP, "Mount Vernon and Fairway," in picture sleeve, taped to back cover)* | | | |
| HOLLAND | 1973 | Brother/Reprise MS 2118 | 500 |
| *(Test pressing with "We Got Love," deleted from promos and stock copies)* | | | |
| HOT ROD MUSIC ON CAPITOL  Various artists | 1964 | Capitol PRO 2480 | 40 |
| *(Includes the Beach Boys)* | | | |
| KEEPIN' THE SUMMER ALIVE | 1980 | Caribou FZ 36283 | 15 |
| *(White label promo)* | | | |
| L.A. (LIGHT ALBUM) | 1979 | Caribou JZ 35752 | 15 |
| *(White label promo)* | | | |
| MENU (70s) SAMPLER LPS FROM WARNER BROTHERS | 197? | Warner PRO 474 (2) | 10 |
| *(Several 2LP sampler sets from Warner/Reprise that feature one or two Beach Boys cuts)* | | | |
| MUSIC FOR EVERY EAR | 1977 | Columbia AS 384 | 25 |
| *(With custom cover, contains "River Song" and "You and I" by Dennis Wilson)* | | | |
| PROGRAMMING AIDS FROM CAPITOL | 1965 | Capitol PRO 2744 | 40 |
| *(Various artists including Beach boys)* | | | |
| SILVER PLATTER SERVICE (Oct 64) Interviews with Brian Wilson | 1964 | Capitol PRO 3123 | 75-100 |
| *(Interviews with Brian Wilson)* | | | |
| SILVER PLATTER SERVICE (Dec 64) Christmas special | 1964 | Capitol PRO 3133 | 250-500 |
| *(The entire program is Beach Boys)* | | | |
| SILVER PLATTER SERVICE (Sept 67) Interviews w/Brian | 1967 | Capitol PRO 3266 | 75-100 |
| *(Interviews with Brian Wilson)* | | | |
| SUMMERTIME BLUES | 1970 | Sears SPG 608 | 100 |
| *(Available from Sears)* | | | |
| SUNFLOWER | 1970 | Brother/Reprise RS-6382 | 50 |
| *(White label promo)* | | | |
| SURF'S UP | 1971 | Brother/Reprise RS 6453 | 40 |
| *(White label promo)* | | | |
| YULESVILLE | 1987 | Warner Bros. PRO-A-2896 | 30 |
| *(Red vinyl, contains Christmas greetings from Brian Wilson, Madonna, George Harrison)* | | | |
| **Compact Discs** | | | |
| STILL CRUISIN' | 1989 | Capitol DPRO-79735 | 10 |
| *(Promo-only compact disc)* | | | |
| THIRTY YEARS OF THE BEACH BOYS (90s) 29 tracks | 1992 | Capitol | 40 |
| *(Selections from "Good Vibrations")* | | | |
| **RADIO SHOWS** | | | |
| **Albums** | | | |
| 4TH OF JULY SUMMER BEACH PARTY (June 84) | 1984 | United Stations (3) | 75-100 |
| *(Box set, includes music by Jan & Dean, The Motels)* | | | |
| BBC TRANSCRIPTION DISC (80s) Live show | 198? | BBC Transcription (6) | 1,000-1,500 |
| *(Very rare)* | | | |
| BEACH BOYS 25TH ANNIVERSARY SHOW | 1987 | Creative Radio (3) | 75-100 |
| *(Music and interviews)* | | | |
| BEACH BOYS SILVER ANNIVERSARY SPECIAL (July 86) | 1986 | United Stations (3) | 50-75 |
| *(Box set, music and interviews)* | | | |
| BEACH BOYS SUMMER PARTY (July 88) | 1988 | Westwood One (3) | 50-75 |
| *(Music and interview)* | | | |
| DICK CLARK PRESENTS BEACH BOYS (May 81) Profile | 1981 | Mutual Broadcasting (3) | 100-150 |
| *(Memorial Day box set)* | | | |
| DICK CLARK PRESENTS BEACH BOYS (May 82) Profile | 1982 | Mutual Broadcasting (3) | 100-150 |
| *(Memorial Day box set, different cover)* | | | |
| GOOD VIBRATIONS FROM LONDON w/Mike Love | 197? | M. M. #79 | 50-75 |
| *(Music and interviews)* | | | |

| Title | Yr | Label, Number | NM $ |
|---|---|---|---|
| HERE'S TO VETERANS The Beach Boys | 1962 | V. A. #866 | 500-1,250 |
| *(Music and interviews)* | | | |
| HERE'S TO VETERANS The Beach Boys | 1964 | V. A. #1015 | 300-1,000 |
| *(Music and interviews)* | | | |
| INNERVIEW  Host is Jim Ladd | 1976 | Series 1, Show 6 | 75-100 |
| *(Music and interview)* | | | |
| LEGENDS OF ROCK (Dec 89) BEACH BOYS PROFILE | 1989 | NBC Source (2) | 25-50 |
| *(Music and interview)* | | | |
| LOOKING BACK WITH LOVE | 1981 | Surf City Radio (3) | 100-150 |
| *(Music and interview)* | | | |
| NATIONAL MUSIC SURVEY (80s) Various artists | 198? | Mutual Broadcasting (3) | 20-30 |
| *(Music and interviews)* | | | |
| NIGHTBIRD & COMPANY (Nov 76) Various artists | 1976 | Army Reserve #289 (2) | 100-150 |
| *(Beach Boys show is music and interviews)* | | | |
| PIONEERS IN MUSIC (Mar 86) The Beach Boys | 1986 | DIR (2) | 50-75 |
| *(Music and interview profile)* | | | |
| PIONEERS IN ROCK (Mar 86) | 1986 | DIR Show 35 (2) | 50-120 |
| *(Music and interviews)* | | | |
| ROBERT W. MORGAN | 1978 | Watermark | 50-100 |
| *(Music and interview, rare show, this show was repeated Aug. 79)* | | | |
| ROCK ROLL & REMEMBER (80s) Various artists | 198? | United Stations (4) | 25-40 |
| *(Collectible Beach Boys shows in this series, music and interviews)* | | | |
| ROCK ROLL & REMEMBER (Sept 88) | 1988 | United Stations (4) | 40-50 |
| *(Members of the group are co-hosts of the show)* | | | |
| ROCK SHOPPE-THE BEACH YEARS | 1976 | (6) | 125-150 |
| *(with Jan & Dean, Dick Dale, Surfaris and others, music and interviews)* | | | |
| ROYALTY OF ROCK Beach Boys profile | 1982 | (2) | 30-45 |
| *(Music and interviews)* | | | |
| SOLID GOLD SCRAPBOOK (80s) THE BEACH BOYS | 198? | United Stations | 10-25 |
| *(One 60-minute show from a set of five, there are several surf/sixties/Beach Boys, etc. theme shows that are music and interview)* | | | |
| SOUNDTRACK FIVE  The Beach Boys | 1962 | V. A. #10 (10-inch LP) | 300-1,000 |
| *(Music and interviews)* | | | |
| STARTRACK PROFILE (Aug 85) The Beach Boys | 1985 | Unistar (2) | 50-75 |
| *(Music and interviews)* | | | |
| THE BEACH BOYS (Apr 90) BEACH BOYS PROFILE | 1990 | Unistar (4) | 50-75 |
| *(Music and interview)* | | | |
| THE BEACH BOYS STORY | 1989 | United Stations (4) | 50-75 |
| *(Music and interview)* | | | |
| TIMOTHY WHITE SESSIONS (July 88) | 1988 | Album Network (2) | 50-100 |
| *(Music and interview)* | | | |
| TWENTY YEARS OF GOOD VIBRATIONS (May 81) | 1981 | Surf City Radio (3) | 100-150 |
| *(Music and interview)* | | | |
| UPDATE (Dec 74) | 1974 | Army Reserve #281 | 75-125 |
| *(Music and interviews)* | | | |
| VOICES OF VISTA | 1968 | VISTA | 100-200 |
| *(Music and interviews)* | | | |
| **Compact Discs** | | | |
| 30TH ANNIVERSARY SPECIAL Music and interview | 1992 | Westwood One (3) | 50-100 |
| *(Material from previous WWI shows)* | | | |
| END OF SUMMER SPECIAL (Aug 93) | 1993 | Westwood One (3) | 50-100 |
| *(Music and interview)* | | | |
| **Reel-to-Reel Tapes** | | | |
| BBC SPECIAL (80s) The Beach Boys | 198? | London Wavelength (6) | 300-500 |
| *(Music and interviews on six 7" reels)* | | | |

## BEACH, BILL
*Other promo 45s $10-$20*
### 45s

| PEG PANTS  White label | 1956 | King 4940 | 75 |
|---|---|---|---|

## BEASTIE BOYS
### 12-Inch Singles

| GET IT TOGETHER (8 versions) | 1994 | Capitol SPRO 79269/70 | 12 |
|---|---|---|---|
| PROFESSOR BOOTY (same on both sides) | 1992 | Capitol SPRO 79226 | 12 |
| SURE SHOT (10 versions) | 1994 | Capitol SPRO 79412 | 15 |

### Albums

| HIP HOP SAMPLER | 1994 | Capitol SPRO 79461 | 50 |
|---|---|---|---|
| *(Promo-only compilation of remixes and things)* | | | |

## BEAT FARMERS
### 12-Inch Singles

| DARK LIGHT (same on both sides) | 1987 | MCA 17356 | 6 |
|---|---|---|---|
| DECEIVER (same on both sides) | 1986 | MCA 17788 | 5 |
| HOLLYWOOD HILLS (same on both sides) | 1987 | Curb/MCA 17401 | 6 |
| KEY TO THE WORLD/MAKE IT LAST | 1987 | MCA 17457 | 5 |
| RIVERSIDE (same on both sides) | 1986 | MCA 17127 | 7 |
| THE GIRL I ALMOST MARRIED (same on both sides) | 1989 | MCA 17906 | 7 |

### RADIO SHOWS
### Albums

| IN CONCERT (Nov 87) Live concert | 1987 | Westwood One (2) | 25-50 |
|---|---|---|---|
| *(With the Insiders)* | | | |

## BEAT RODEO
### 12-Inch Singles

| NEW LOVE (same on both sides) | 198? | I.R.S. 17241 | 8 |
|---|---|---|---|

| **Title** | **Yr** | **Label, Number** | **NM $** |
|---|---|---|---|

**BEATLES, THE**

*Also see George Harrison; John Lennon; Paul McCartney; Ringo Starr; Capitol promo 45s not listed $8 each; Apple singles including reissues with star on label $15 each (Not legal promos, these records were used as promo copies); Capitol jukebox black vinyl 45s, purple label $4 each; Capitol jukebox colored vinyl 45s, purple label $5 each*

**12-Inch Singles**

| Title | Yr | Label, Number | NM $ |
|---|---|---|---|
| THE BEATLES' MOVIE MEDLEY | 1982 | Capitol SPRO-9758 | 50 |
| *(With custom title cover)* | | | |
| MERRY CHRISTMAS AND HAPPY NEW YEAR | 1965 | (no label) (no #) | 500 |
| *(Promo item from KYA Radio, San Francisco; B-side is blank)* | | | |

**45s**

| Title | Yr | Label, Number | NM $ |
|---|---|---|---|
| AIN'T SHE SWEET "Vocal by John Lennon" | 1964 | Atco 6308 | 400 |
| *(All-white promo label)* | | | |
| ALL YOU NEED IS LOVE | 1967 | Capitol P-5964 | 300 |
| *(Green promo label, prefix "P" with number)* | | | |
| ANNA | 1964 | Vee Jay Spec. DJ-8 | 15,000 |
| *(Fewer than five copies known)* | | | |
| CHRISTMAS 1964 FLEXI-DISC | 1964 | | 350 |
| *(From the Beatles Fan Club)* | | | |
| CHRISTMAS 1965 FLEXI-DISC | 1965 | | 250 |
| *(From the Beatles Fan Club)* | | | |
| CHRISTMAS 1966 FLEXI-DISC | 1966 | | 175 |
| *(From the Beatles Fan Club)* | | | |
| CHRISTMAS 1967 FLEXI-DISC | 1967 | | 175 |
| *(From the Beatles Fan Club)* | | | |
| CHRISTMAS 1968 FLEXI-DISC | 1968 | | 150 |
| *(From the Beatles Fan Club)* | | | |
| CHRISTMAS 1969 FLEXI-DISC | 1969 | | 100 |
| *(From the Beatles Fan Club)* | | | |
| CHRISTMAS COLLECTION | 197? | Capitol (7) | 60 |
| *(Limited pressing, seven 7" picture discs)* | | | |
| CRYING, WAITING, HOPING/TAKE GOOD CARE OF MY BABY | 1983 | Backstage 1155 | 25 |
| DIALOGUE FROM THE BEATLES' MOTION PICTURE "LET IT BE" | 1970 | Apple Promo-1970 | 60 |
| *(White promo label, one-sided record)* | | | |
| DO YOU WANT TO KNOW A SECRET | 1964 | Vee Jay 587 | 600 |
| *(White promo label)* | | | |
| FROM ME TO YOU | 1963 | Vee Jay 522 | 500 |
| *(White promo label)* | | | |
| GET BACK | 1969 | Americom 335 | 1,000 |
| *(Unusual and rare 4" flexi-disc)* | | | |
| GET BACK One-sided record | 1969 | Capitol 2490 | 175 |
| *(Small center hole, orange label)* | | | |
| GET BACK One-sided record | 1969 | Apple 2490 | 175 |
| *(Small center hole)* | | | |
| GIRL | 1977 | Capitol P-4506 | 75 |
| *(Promo sleeve for unreleased single)* | | | |
| GIRL Mono/stereo | 1977 | Capitol P-4506 | 200 |
| *(Promo-only, black vinyl, custom label)* | | | |
| GOT TO GET YOU INTO MY LIFE Mono/stereo | 1976 | Capitol P-4274 | 15 |
| *(White promo label)* | | | |
| A HARD DAY'S NIGHT George Martin | 1964 | United Artists 750 | 125 |
| *(White promo label)* | | | |
| A HARD DAY'S NIGHT Open End Interview | 1964 | United Artists UAEP 10029 | 1500 |
| *(Small center hole)* | | | |
| A HARD DAY'S NIGHT Theatre Lobby Spot | 1964 | United Artists SP-2357 | 1500 |
| *(Small center hole)* | | | |
| HELLO GOODBYE | 1967 | Capitol P-2056 | 300 |
| *(Green promo label, prefix "P" with number)* | | | |
| HELTER SKELTER Mono/stereo | 1976 | Capitol P-4274 | 40 |
| *(White promo label)* | | | |
| HEY JUDE | 1969 | Americom 2276 | 450 |
| *(Unusual and rare 4" flexi-disc)* | | | |
| HEY JUDE One-sided record | 1968 | Capitol 2276 | 175 |
| *(Small hole, orange label, very rare)* | | | |
| I WANT TO HOLD YOUR HAND | 1984 | Capitol PRO-9076 | 15 |
| *(Same song on each side, issued in a stock sleeve)* | | | |
| I WANT TO HOLD YOUR HAND WMCA Good Guys sleeve | 1964 | Capitol 5112 | 5,000 |
| *(Same number as the more common black/white sleeve)* | | | |
| I'LL GET YOU One-sided record | 1964 | Swan 4152 | 600 |
| *(White promo label)* | | | |
| LADY MADONNA | 1968 | Capitol P-2138 | 300 |
| *(Green promo label, prefix "P" with number)* | | | |
| LET IT BE One-sided record | 1970 | Capitol 2764 | 150 |
| *(Small center hole)* | | | |
| LIKE DREAMERS DO/LOVE OF THE LOVED | 1982 | Backstage 1112 | 25 |
| *(Promotional 45 from "Oui" magazine)* | | | |
| LIKE DREAMERS DO/THREE COOL CATS | 1983 | Backstage 1133 | 25 |
| *(Promotional picture disc)* | | | |
| LOVE ME DO | 1964 | Tollie 9008 | 400 |
| *(White promo label)* | | | |
| LOVE ME DO | 1992 | Capitol 56785 | 40 |
| *(Red vinyl; black vinyl versions $4)* | | | |
| LOVE ME DO Swirl label | 1982 | Capitol PB-5189 | 15 |
| *(Same song on both sides, issued in a stock picture sleeve)* | | | |
| LOVE ME DO/P.S. I LOVE YOU | 1992 | Capitol 7PRO-79551/2 | 50 |
| *(With picture sleeve; offered as a mail-in premium to the first 5,000 buyers of the Love Me Do CD single; most, however, ended up in collector shops)* | | | |
| LOVE OF THE LOVED/MEMPHIS | 1983 | Backstage 1122 | 25 |
| *(Promotional picture disc)* | | | |

| Title | Yr | Label, Number | NM $ |
|---|---|---|---|
| MY BONNIE  The Beatles with Tony Sheridan | 1964 | MGM 13213 | 400 |
| *(Yellow promo label)* | | | |
| MY BONNIE  Tony Sheridan and the Beat Brothers | 1962 | Decca 31382 | 7,500 |
| *(Pink promo label)* | | | |
| OB-LA-DI, OB-LA-DA Mono/stereo | 1976 | Capitol P-4347 | 15 |
| *(White promo label)* | | | |
| PENNY LANE | 1967 | Capitol P-5810 | 750 |
| *(This version does not have the three-second finish; both promos of Penny Lane have green promo labels)* | | | |
| PENNY LANE | 1967 | Capitol P-5810 | 300 |
| *(This version, with an ending trumpet flourish, is about three seconds longer than the stock copy)* | | | |
| PLEASE PLEASE ME | 1964 | Vee Jay 581 | 600 |
| *(White label, blue print; "Promotional Copy" on label)* | | | |
| PLEASE PLEASE ME | 1964 | Vee Jay 581 | 900 |
| *(White label, blue print; no "Promotional Copy" on label)* | | | |
| PLEASE PLEASE ME  "The Beattles" (sic) | 1963 | Vee Jay 498 | 1,500 |
| *(White promo label, thin lettering)* | | | |
| PLEASE PLEASE ME Special promo sleeve | 1964 | Vee Jay 581 | 5,000 |
| *("The Record That Started Beatlemania" promo-only release)* | | | |
| SGT. PEPPER'S LONELY HEARTS CLUB BAND/WITH A LITTLE HELP FROM MY FRIENDS Mono/stereo | 1978 | Capitol P-4612 | 15 |
| *(White promo label)* | | | |
| SHE LOVES YOU/I'LL GET YOU | 1963 | Swan 4152 | 450 |
| *(Thin print, "Don't Drop Out" on label)* | | | |
| SHE LOVES YOU/I'LL GET YOU | 1963 | Swan 4152 | 500 |
| *(Thick print, no "Don't Drop Out" on label)* | | | |
| SHE LOVES YOU/I'LL GET YOU | 1963 | Swan 4152 | 500 |
| *(Flat white label, no "Don't Drop Out" on label)* | | | |
| SIE LIEBT DICH (SHE LOVES YOU)/I'LL GET YOU | 1964 | Swan 4182 | 450 |
| *White label, "Sie Liebt Dich (She Loves You)" on one line* | | | |
| SIE LIEBT DICH (SHE LOVES YOU)/I'LL GET YOU | 1964 | Swan 4182 | 400 |
| *White label, "(She Loves You)" under "Sie Liebt Dich"* | | | |
| SWEET GEORGIA BROWN The Beatles with Tony Sheridan | 1964 | Atco 6302 | 400 |
| *(All-white promo label)* | | | |
| TAXMAN | 1992 | Capitol 17988 | 40 |
| *(Black vinyl; green vinyl versions $4)* | | | |
| THE BEATLES' MOVIE MEDLEY | 1982 | Capitol PB-5100 | 50 |
| *(With "Fab Four on Film" on B-side, not officially released to the public; includes picture sleeve)* | | | |
| THIS BOY George Martin | 1964 | United Artists 745 | 75 |
| *(White promo label)* | | | |
| TWIST AND SHOUT | 1964 | Tollie 9001 | 400 |
| *(White promo label)* | | | |
| TWIST AND SHOUT | 1986 | Capitol P-B-5624 | 10 |
| *(White promo label)* | | | |
| VEE JAY RECORDS, BEATLES CHRISTMAS SLEEVE | 1964 | Vee Jay | 75 |
| *(Used with any VJ Beatles single)* | | | |
| WHY The Beatles with Tony Sheridan | 1964 | MGM 13227 | 400 |
| *(Yellow promo label)* | | | |
| YOU CAN'T DO THAT  Radio KFWBeatles promo | 1964 | Capitol 2637 | 750 |
| *(Record only)* | | | |
| YOU CAN'T DO THAT  KFWB picture sleeve | 1964 | Capitol 2637 | 4,000 |
| *(Picture sleeve has Capitol promo number)* | | | |
| **7-Inch Extended Plays** | | | |
| AIN'T SHE SWEET/CRY FOR A SHADOW//MY BONNIE/THE SAINTS | 1994 | Polydor PRO 1113-7 | 50 |
| *(With picture sleeve; promo issued in conjunction with the "Backbeat" movie)* | | | |
| BEATLES INTRODUCE NEW SONGS | 1964 | Capitol 2720 | 750 |
| *(John introduces songs on one side, Paul on the other)* | | | |
| BEATLES OPEN-END INTERVIEW Compact 33 | 1964 | Capitol 2548 | 350 |
| *(Includes script and EP cover, promo-only release)* | | | |
| BEATLES SECOND ALBUM Jukebox LLP | 1964 | Capitol 2080 | 750 |
| *(Issued with a hard cover)* | | | |
| BEATLES SECOND OPEN-END INTERVIEW COMPACT 33 | 1964 | Capitol 2598 | 300 |
| *(Includes script and EP cover, promo-only release)* | | | |
| BEATLES, BEACH BOYS & KINGSTON TRIO | 1964 | Evatone 8464 | 325 |
| *(Newspaper flexi-disc with three songs)* | | | |
| HELP 33rpm movie spots | 1965 | United Artists | 1,250 |
| *(One-sided record, small center hole)* | | | |
| LET IT BE 33rpm movie spots | 1970 | United Artists | 1,250 |
| *(Small center hole)* | | | |
| MEET THE BEATLES Jukebox LLP | 1964 | Capitol 2047 | 750 |
| *(Issued with a hard cover)* | | | |
| MURRAY THE K & THE BEATLES | 1965 | Fairway 526-1 | 75 |
| *(7" record)* | | | |
| SOMETHING NEW Jukebox LLP | 1964 | Capitol 2108 | 1,250 |
| *(Issued with a hard cover)* | | | |
| SOUVENIR OF THEIR VISIT TO AMERICA | 1964 | Vee Jay 903 | 300 |
| *(White promo label)* | | | |
| SOUVENIR RECORD Promo sampler | 1964 | Capitol 2905 | 275 |
| *(Various artists including the Beatles)* | | | |
| **Albums** | | | |
| AIN'T SHE SWEET | 1964 | Atco 33-169 | 1000 |
| *(White label promo)* | | | |
| AMERICAN TOUR WITH ED RUDY  #3 | 1964 | Radio Pulsebeat News | 40 |
| *(Price includes two inserts)* | | | |
| ARMED FORCES RADIO & TELEVISION SERVICE #113 | 1965 | Department of Defense RL 25-5 | 25 |
| *("She's a Woman" and 13 non-Beatles tracks)* | | | |
| ARMED FORCES RADIO & TELEVISION SERVICE #233 | 1967 | Department of Defense RPL 36-7 | 25 |
| *("Penny Lane" and 11 non-Beatles songs)* | | | |

| Title | Yr | Label, Number | NM $ |
| --- | --- | --- | --- |
| ARMED FORCES RADIO & TELEVISION SERVICE #68 | 1964 | Department of Defense RL 32-4 | 35 |
| ("Please Please Me" and 13 non-Beatles tracks) | | | |
| ARMED FORCES RADIO & TELEVISION SERVICE #69 | 1964 | Department of Defense RL 33-4 | 35 |
| ("From Me to You" and "My Bonnie" and 12 non-Beatles tracks) | | | |
| ARMED FORCES RADIO & TELEVISION SERVICE #90 | 1964 | Department of Defense RL 2-5 | 25 |
| ("Sweet Georgia Brown" and 13 non-Beatles) | | | |
| ARMED FORCES RADIO & TELEVISION SERVICE #92 | 1964 | Department of Defense RL 4-5 | 20 |
| ("Ain't She Sweet" and 13 non-Beatles tracks) | | | |
| ARMED FORCES RADIO & TELEVISION SERVICE #94 | 1964 | Department of Defense RL 6-5 | 30 |
| ("A Hard Day's Night" and "I Should Have Known Better" with 12 other non-Beatle tracks) | | | |
| BEATLEMANIA TOUR COVERAGE | 1964 | I-N-S Radio News DOC-1 | 1,500 |
| (Promo-only open-end interview with script in plain white jacket) | | | |
| BEATLES AGAIN, THE | 1970 | Apple SO-385 | 8,000 |
| (Prototypes with "The Beatles Again" on cover; not released to the general public) | | | |
| BEATLES AT THE HOLLYWOOD BOWL, THE | 1977 | Capitol 11638 | 75 |
| (White cover, title is stamped on) | | | |
| BEATLES CHRISTMAS ALBUM, THE | 1970 | Apple 100 | 100 |
| (From the Beatles Fan Club) | | | |
| BEATLES COLLECTION, THE  Box set of UK LPs | 1980 | Capitol BC-13 | 325 |
| (Price includes promo version of Rarities album) | | | |
| BEATLES WITH TONY SHERIDAN AND GUESTS Mono | 1964 | MGM 4215 | 500 |
| (Yellow promo label) | | | |
| BRITISH ARE COMING, THE | 1984 | Silhouette SM-10013 | 40 |
| White label promo; no numbered sticker | | | |
| GRAMMY TREASURE CHEST | 1975 | Department of the Treasury 75-105 | 20 |
| (33 1/3 rpm U.S. Savings Bonds promo with "Can't Buy Me Love"; red, white and blue label) | | | |
| GRAMMY TREASURE CHEST | 1976 | Department of the Treasury 75-147 | 20 |
| (33 1/3 rpm U.S. Savings Bonds promo with "A Hard Day's Night"; red, white and blue label) | | | |
| GREAT AMERICAN TOUR | 1965 | Lloyds ER MC | 75 |
| (Mostly interviews) | | | |
| GREAT NEW RELEASES FROM THE SOUND CAPITOL OF THE WORLD | 1964 | Capitol 2538 | 50 |
| (Various artists with announcer intros) | | | |
| GREATEST MUSIC EVER SOLD Various artists | 1976 | Capitol 8511 | 40 |
| (Promo-only sampler) | | | |
| A HARD DAY'S NIGHT | 1964 | United Artists 6366 | 900 |
| (White promo label) | | | |
| HEAR THE BEATLES TELL ALL | 1964 | Vee Jay PRO 202 | 10,000 |
| (White label promo with blue print) | | | |
| INTRODUCING THE BEATLES  Mono | 1964 | Vee Jay 1062 | 400 |
| (Blank back cover) | | | |
| INTRODUCING THE BEATLES Stereo | 1964 | Vee Jay 1062 | 750 |
| (Blank back cover) | | | |
| LIKE DREAMERS DO | 1982 | Backstage BSR-1111 | 50 |
| (Gray vinyl promo in white sleeve) | | | |
| LIKE DREAMERS DO | 1982 | Backstage BSR-1111 | 50 |
| (White vinyl promo in white sleeve) | | | |
| LIVE AT THE STAR CLUB IN HAMBURG, GERMANY, 1962 | 1977 | Lingasong LS-2-7001 | 40 |
| (Promo on black vinyl; "D.J. Copy Not for Sale" on labels) | | | |
| LIVE AT THE STAR CLUB IN HAMBURG, GERMANY, 1962 | 1977 | Lingasong LS-2-7001 | 300 |
| (Promo only on blue vinyl) | | | |
| LIVE AT THE STAR CLUB IN HAMBURG, GERMANY, 1962 | 1977 | Lingasong LS-2-7001 | 200 |
| (Promo only on red vinyl) | | | |
| LIVE FROM THE JUDO ARENA Picture disc | 198? | | 40 |
| (Commonly used as a promo, possibly a bootleg) | | | |
| RARITIES | 1979 | Capitol SN-12009 | 300 |
| (Green label; withdrawn before official release; all known copies have a plain white sleeve) | | | |
| REEL MUSIC | 1982 | Capitol SV-12199 | 20 |
| (Yellow vinyl promo; plain white cover with 12-page booklet) | | | |
| REEL MUSIC | 1982 | Capitol SV-12199 | 40 |
| (Yellow vinyl promo; numbered back cover with 12-page booklet) | | | |
| ROLLING STONE MUSIC REPORT | 1984 | Rolling Stone | 50 |
| (Promo-only release) | | | |
| SILVER BEATLES, THE | 1985 | Orange ORC-12880 | 400 |
| (Test pressing; full cover cover slick folded around a white cover. Both contain all 15 Decca audition tracks) | | | |
| SILVER BEATLES, THE | 1985 | Orange ORC-12880 | 300 |
| (Test pressing; white cover with title sticker) | | | |
| SILVER PLATTER SERVICE (Mar 65) Jack Wagner | 1965 | Capitol PRO 3143 | 400 |
| (Lennon/McCartney interview, promo only, rare) | | | |
| SO MUCH YOUNGER Set of five picture discs | 198? | | 40 |
| (Unusual set, hard to find) | | | |
| SOUND TRACK FIVE #56 | 1976 | Veterans Administration | 15 |
| (33 1/3 RPM " Got to Get You into My Life" and five other songs) | | | |
| SPECIAL OPEN-END INTERVIEW WITH THE BEATLES | 1965 | United Artists | 400 |
| (From the movie Help) | | | |
| TALK DOWNUNDER | 1981 | Raven/PVC 8911 | 80 |
| (Promo only in white cover with title sticker. Label reads "For Radio Play Only") | | | |
| THIS IS WHERE IT STARTED Mono | 1966 | Metro MS 563 | 600 |
| (Uncertain of release, an MGM album) | | | |
| UNITED ARTISTS PRESENTS A HARD DAY'S NIGHT | 1964 | United Artists SP-2359/60 | 2000 |
| (Open-end interview with script) | | | |
| UNITED ARTISTS PRESENTS A HARD DAY'S NIGHT | 1964 | United Artists SP-2362/3 | 1500 |
| (Radio spots for movie) | | | |
| UNITED ARTISTS PRESENTS HELP! | 1965 | United Artists UA-Help-A/B | 1500 |
| (Radio spots for movie) | | | |
| UNITED ARTISTS PRESENTS HELP! | 1965 | United Artists UA-Help-Show | 3000 |
| (One-sided interview with script, blue label) | | | |
| UNITED ARTISTS PRESENTS HELP! | 1965 | United Artists UA-Help-INT | 2000 |
| (Open-end interview with script, red label) | | | |

| Title | Yr | Label, Number | NM $ |
|---|---|---|---|
| YELLOW SUBMARINE, THE (A United Artists Release) | 1969 | Apple Films KAL 004 | 2000 |
| *One-sided LP with radio spots for movie* | | | |
| **Compact Discs** | | | |
| ANTHOLOGY I SAMPLER | 1995 | Apple DPRO-10289 | 75 |
| ANTHOLOGY II SAMPLER | 1996 | Apple DPRO-11??? | 75 |
| ANTHOLOGY III SAMPLER | 1996 | Apple | 75 |
| BABY IT'S YOU | 1995 | Apple DPRO-79553 | 60 |
| *(Promo with insert)* | | | |
| CAPITOL 50TH ANNIVERSARY Various artists | 1992 | Capitol (8) | 150 |
| *(Celebration of music 1942-1992 includes Beatles)* | | | |
| CATALOG, THE Capitol 50th anniversary | 1992 | Capitol DPRO-79387 | 20 |
| *(One cut)* | | | |
| CENTURY 21 GOLD DISC | 1987 | Century 21 | 150 |
| *(Part of a music syndication series for radio, some tracks are in stereo for the first time)* | | | |
| FREE AS A BIRD | 1995 | Apple DPRO-11153 | 20 |
| I WANT TO HOLD YOUR HAND | 1994 | Capitol DPRO-79319 | 50 |
| *(Promo CD with swirl on label and picture sleeve)* | | | |
| REAL LOVE | 1996 | Apple DPRO-11187 | 20 |
| SELECTIONS FROM 62-66 & 67-70 | 1994 | Capitol DPRO-79286 | 40 |
| *(Six-song promo sampler from CD releases)* | | | |
| **RADIO SHOWS** | | | |
| **Albums** | | | |
| ALBUM GREATS From the 48-hour series | 1979 | TM Special Products (6) | 125-250 |
| *(Price for Beatles discs of the 53-LP series)* | | | |
| AMERICAN TOP 40 (July 81) Special Beatles show | 1981 | Watermark (4) | 50-75 |
| *(Music and interviews with Casey Kasem)* | | | |
| BBC ROCK HOUR | 1982 | London Wavelength | 40-75 |
| *(Music and interviews)* | | | |
| BBC ROCK HOUR (Dec 84) | 1984 | London Wavelength (2) | 100-150 |
| *(Music and interviews, mostly Christmas material)* | | | |
| BBC TRANSCRIPTION DISC | 197? | BBC Transcription | 1,000-1,500 |
| *(This is from the very rare BBC series and is one of the most desirable Beatles collectibles.)* | | | |
| BBC TRANSCRIPTION DISC | 1988 | BBC Transcription | 500-750 |
| *(Also very rare, music from Sgt. Pepper)* | | | |
| BEATLE INVASION, THE | 1978 | Creative Radio (3) | 40-75 |
| *(Music and interviews)* | | | |
| BEATLE INVASION, THE | 1984 | Creative Radio (3) | 40-75 |
| *(Music and interviews)* | | | |
| BEATLES 20TH ANNIVERSARY SPECIAL (Aug 84) Box set | 1984 | (6) | 125-250 |
| *(Music and interviews)* | | | |
| BEATLES AT THE BEEB (May 82) Box set, Version A | 1982 | London Wavelength (4) | 500-700 |
| *(Only a few sets known, "Version A" in trail-off area)* | | | |
| BEATLES AT THE BEEB (May 83) Box set, Version B | 1983 | London Wavelength (4) | 200-250 |
| *(Repeat of 1982 show with three songs added; Label has "B" on it and "Version B" in trail-off area)* | | | |
| BEATLES AT THE BEEB (May 85) Rebroadcast of '82 show | 1985 | London Wavelength (4) | 125-200 |
| *(No "Version A" in trail-off area)* | | | |
| BEATLES AT THE BEEB (May 85) Rebroadcast of '83 show | 1985 | London Wavelength (4) | 125-200 |
| *(No "B" on label, no "Version B" in trail-off)* | | | |
| BEATLES FROM LIVERPOOL TO LEGEND | 1977 | RKO Radio (15) | 1,000-1,500 |
| *(Music and interviews, includes many unreleased songs)* | | | |
| BEATLES FROM LIVERPOOL TO LEGEND Repeat of 1977 show | 1980 | RKO Radio (15) | 500-750 |
| *(Music and interviews)* | | | |
| BEATLES SILVER ANNIVERSARY SPECIAL | 1987 | United Stations (16) | 125-250 |
| *(Music and interviews)* | | | |
| BEATLES STORY, THE (June 80) | 1980 | London Wavelength (13) | 400-750 |
| *(This version is for radio stations in the UK and USA only, and not available to the public)* | | | |
| BEATLES STORY, THE (Nov 80) | 1980 | London Wavelength (13) | 250-300 |
| *(13-LP picture disc version available to U.S. collectors through a few dealers; London Wavelength claims only 150 sets were made. They came with a book and 28-page script for $249.99 or wholesale for $150 each for up to ten copies shipped out of the UK.)* | | | |
| BEATLES, BEACH BOYS & HOLLY | 198? | Creative Radio | 25-40 |
| *(Samples of the shows by these three acts that are available from Creative Productions)* | | | |
| BREAKS | 198? | (4) | 50-125 |
| *(A series of short interviews with music to be used when needed by a radio station, the four discs have fifty mini-breaks)* | | | |
| A DAY ON THE ROAD | 198? | NBC Radio | 75-125 |
| *(Music and interviews)* | | | |
| DAYS OF THEIR LIVES, THE 30-record set | 1982 | RKO Radio (30) | 600-1,000 |
| *(Music and interviews)* | | | |
| HERE'S TO VETERANS 15-minute public service show | 197? | V. A. 1476 | 650-1,000 |
| *(Co-hosted by Paul McCartney)* | | | |
| HERE'S TO VETERANS 15-minute public service show | 197? | V. A. 1406 | 750-1,250 |
| *(Different artist on flip side)* | | | |
| HIT HEARD AROUND THE WORLD (June 69) SAME AS ABOVE | 1969 | U. S. Army | 100-200 |
| *(George Martin interview/Get Back the song)* | | | |
| IN SOUND (June 69) Features producer George Martin | 1969 | U. S. Army | 100-200 |
| *(Includes the Beatles' "Get Back")* | | | |
| JIM LADD INNERVIEW Two shows | 1982 | Innerview (2) | 30-60 |
| *(Music and interviews)* | | | |
| LONDON WAVELENGTH PRESENTS BEATLES STORY | 1982 | London Wavelength (6) | 150-225 |
| *(Music and interviews)* | | | |
| LOST LENNON TAPES (Jan 88) | 1988 | Westwood One (5) | 100-175 |
| *(Special edition pilot show)* | | | |
| LOST LENNON TAPES (88-92) | 199? | Westwood One (2) | 15-40 |
| *(Weekly shows on vinyl, price for any one volume)* | | | |
| LOST LENNON TAPES (Jan 88-92) | 1992 | Westwood One (448) | 4,000-5,000 |
| *(Price is for the complete set, including pilot. This series ran for 221 weeks and featured many unreleased tracks of the Beatles, Lennon and Ono. The last show ran Apr 92.)* | | | |

| Title | Yr | Label, Number | NM $ |
|---|---|---|---|
| LOVE SONGS OF THE BEATLES (Feb 90) | 1990 | Unistar (4) | 75-100 |
| *(Mostly music and interviews)* | | | |
| MEET THE BEATLES AGAIN (Feb 84) Box set | 1984 | NBC Source (6) | 250-350 |
| *(Music and interviews, photo cover)* | | | |
| RETRO ROCK (Nov 83) | 1983 | Clayton Webster (2) | 200-250 |
| *(Music and interviews)* | | | |
| ROCK AND ROLL NEVER FORGETS | 1984 | Westwood One (5) | 125-250 |
| *(Music and interviews)* | | | |
| ROLLING STONE MAGAZINE (Nov 81) | 1981 | (2) | 25-40 |
| *(Profile show of the Beatles)* | | | |
| ROLLING STONE MAGAZINE (Sept 82) | 1982 | (3) | 30-45 |
| *(Music and interviews)* | | | |
| ROYALTY OF ROCK | 1982 | RKO Radio (2) | 50-75 |
| *(Music and interviews)* | | | |
| ROYALTY OF ROCK | 1983 | RKO Radio (2) | 50-75 |
| *(Music and interviews)* | | | |
| RUBBER SOUL (Sept 87) Profile of the album | 1987 | Album Network (2) | 75-150 |
| *(Music and interview)* | | | |
| RUBBER SOUL TO SGT. PEPPER (Sept 87) | 1987 | Westwood One (4) | 75-125 |
| *(Music and interviews)* | | | |
| SGT. PEPPER'S LONELY HEARTS CLUB BAND (THE BEATLE YEARS) (Oct 83) | 1984 | Westwood One (9) | 500-700 |
| *(Music and interviews)* | | | |
| SGT. PEPPER'S LONELY HEARTS CLUB BAND (THE BEATLE YEARS) (Oct 85) | 1985 | Westwood One (12) | 500-900 |
| *(Music and interviews)* | | | |
| SILVER ANNIVERSARY | 1983 | (3) | 75-100 |
| *(Music and interviews)* | | | |
| SOUNDS OF SOLID GOLD Various artists | 1984 | Marine Vol. 47, 49 or 50 (7) | 60 |
| *(Ex-Beatles or Beatles solo music and interviews. Sounds of Solid Gold is a 13-LP set; price is for each volume)* | | | |
| TICKET TO RIDE (85-88) | 1980s | DIR (2) | 20-40 |
| *(Weekly shows on vinyl, price for any one volume)* | | | |
| TICKET TO RIDE (Jan 85-Dec 88) | 1988 | DIR (414) | 4,000-5,000 |
| *(Complete set on vinyl and CD)* | | | |
| TWIST AND SHOUT (Nov 86) Red label | 1986 | Westwood One (2) | 40-85 |
| *(Music and interviews)* | | | |
| WESTWOOD ONE PRESENTS (Sept 87) | 1987 | Westwood One (2) | 100-150 |
| *(Music and interviews from Rubber Soul)* | | | |
| **Compact Discs** | | | |
| ABC RADIO SPECIAL—BEATLES '95 | 1995 | ABC Radio (2) | 95-175 |
| *(With Paul McCartney interview about the reunion)* | | | |
| BBC BEATLES TAPES (May 90) | 1990 | Westwood One (6) | 300-400 |
| *(Music and interviews)* | | | |
| BBC BEATLES TAPES (May 90) | 1990 | Westwood One | 100-150 |
| *(Show repeated every year)* | | | |
| BBC BEATLES TAPES (June 90) | 1990 | Westwood One | 150-250 |
| *(This version of the show is a thank you to advertising and promotion people, not intended for airplay. Many copies of this very limited edition were damaged at the factory by glue spillage.)* | | | |
| BBC BEATLES TAPES (June 91) | 1991 | Westwood One (6) | 250-300 |
| *(Second edition)* | | | |
| BBC CLASSIC TRACKS (Dec 90) | 1990 | Westwood One | 50-75 |
| *(Various classic live tracks)* | | | |
| BBC CLASSIC TRACKS (June 91) | 1991 | Westwood One (6) | 250-500 |
| *(Various classic live tracks)* | | | |
| BBC CLASSIC TRACKS (Feb 95) | 1995 | Westwood One | 30-60 |
| *(Various classic live tracks)* | | | |
| BBC TRANSCRIPTION DISC | 1992 | BBC Transcription | 400-900 |
| *(CD version of these shows, very rare)* | | | |
| BEATLE YEARS, THE (Apr 92-current) | 199? | Westwood One | 15-20 |
| *(Weekly series replaced Lost Lennon Tapes, price for any one volume)* | | | |
| BEATLE YEARS, THE (Apr 92-Apr 93) | 1993 | Westwood One (52) | 1,250-1,500 |
| *(First full year of the series)* | | | |
| BEATLE YEARS, THE (Apr 93-Apr 98) | 199? | Westwood One (52) | 1,000-1,200 |
| *(Any subsequent full year of the series)* | | | |
| BEATLES AND McCARTNEY (Feb 93) | 1993 | (2) | 75-100 |
| *(Beatles is music and interviews, McCartney is live concert)* | | | |
| BEATLES ANTHOLOGY 2 | 1996 | Album Network (2) | 165-265 |
| *(Music and interviews)* | | | |
| BEATLES ANTHOLOGY 3 (Dec 96) | 1996 | Album Network (3) | 150-250 |
| *(Music and interviews, Derek Taylor is interviewer)* | | | |
| BEATLES AT THE BEEB (May 93) | 1993 | Westwood One (6) | 150-250 |
| *(Music and interviews)* | | | |
| BEATLES CHRISTMAS (90s) | 199? | Westwood One | 35-60 |
| *(Music and interviews)* | | | |
| BEATLES: SGT. PEPPER, A GENERATION AWAY (June 94) | 1994 | Westwood One | 75-100 |
| *(Music and interviews)* | | | |
| IN THE STUDIO (Nov 93) "White Album" profile | 1993 | Album Network (3) | 75-125 |
| *(Music and interviews)* | | | |
| LONG & WINDING ROAD, THE (MAY 94) | 1994 | Westwood One (12) | 300-400 |
| *(Mostly music and interviews but some live material, each CD is a picture disc)* | | | |
| MAKING OF SGT. PEPPER, THE (Aug 93) | 1993 | Album Network | 25-50 |
| *(Profile of the album)* | | | |
| ORIGINAL MASTERS | 1992 | Westwood One (6) | 99-300 |
| *(Music and interviews)* | | | |
| ORIGINAL MASTERS Red and green CDs | 1990 | Westwood One (6) | 500-1,000 |
| *(Music and interviews)* | | | |
| SGT. PEPPER, 25TH ANNIVERSARY (June 92) | 1992 | Unistar (3) | 100-150 |
| *(Mostly music and interviews)* | | | |

| Title | Yr | Label, Number | NM $ |
|---|---|---|---|
| SIXTIES LEGENDS (Aug 92) | 1992 | Unistar (2) | 25-50 |
| *(Mostly music and interviews)* | | | |
| TICKET TO RIDE (88-89) | 1980s | DIR | 15-35 |
| *(Weekly shows on CD, price for any one volume)* | | | |
| TICKET TO RIDE (May 88-Apr 89) | 1989 | DIR (52) | 1,500-2,000 |
| *(The complete CD set)* | | | |
| WESTWOOD ONE SPECIAL (June 91) | 1991 | Westwood One (6) | 250-500 |
| *(Music and interviews with live tracks)* | | | |
| **Reel-to-Reel Tapes** | | | |
| THE BEATLES (80s) Canadian profile | 198? | CHUM Radio | 1,250 |
| *(Music and interviews on 12 10" reels)* | | | |

**BEAUTIFUL SOUTH, THE**
**12-Inch Singles**

| Title | Yr | Label, Number | NM $ |
|---|---|---|---|
| YOU KEEP IT ALL IN (Single Version) (same on both sides) | 1990 | Elektra ED 5444 | 5 |

**BEAVIS & BUTT-HEAD**
**12-Inch Singles**

| Title | Yr | Label, Number | NM $ |
|---|---|---|---|
| COME TO BUTT-HEAD (9 versions) | 1993 | Geffen 4594 | 15 |

**BECK**
**12-Inch Singles**

| Title | Yr | Label, Number | NM $ |
|---|---|---|---|
| LOSER (same on both sides) | 1993 | DGC 4629 | 10 |
| **RADIO SHOWS** | | | |
| **Compact Discs** | | | |
| LIVE FROM THE PIT (Sept 96) | 1996 | | 60 |
| *(Live concert material)* | | | |

**BECK, JEFF**
*Epic promo 45s $5 each*
**Albums**

| Title | Yr | Label, Number | NM $ |
|---|---|---|---|
| EVERYTHING YOU ALWAYS WANTED TO HEAR BY JEFF BECK BUT WERE AFRAID TO ASK FOR | 1977 | Epic AS 151 | 20 |
| *(Promo-only sampler)* | | | |
| THEN AND NOW | 1981 | Epic A2S 850 | 25 |
| *(Promo-only sampler)* | | | |
| **RADIO SHOWS** | | | |
| **Albums** | | | |
| BBC ROCK HOUR (July 84) Live show | 1984 | London Wavelength | 60-125 |
| *(Music quality on these BBC live shows is excellent)* | | | |
| BBC TRANSCRIPTION DISC (Nov 76) Live show | 1976 | BBC Transcription | 150-350 |
| *(Not as hard to find as the first one)* | | | |
| BBC TRANSCRIPTION DISC Live show | 1971 | BBC Transcription | 200-400 |
| *(The ultimate rare radio series)* | | | |
| HIGH VOLTAGE (June 89) | 1989 | Westwood One (2) | 25-65 |
| *(30-minute live concert segment)* | | | |
| IN CONCERT (Feb 87) BBC material | 1987 | Westwood One (2) | 50-125 |
| *(This show was reissued several times)* | | | |
| INNERVIEW (70s) | 197? | Innerview | 20-30 |
| *(Music and interview, released again as #16,3)* | | | |
| LEGENDS OF ROCK (Aug 87) Profile | 1987 | (2) | 20-30 |
| *(Music and interview)* | | | |
| LEGENDS OF ROCK (July 84) Profile | 1984 | NBC Radio (3) | 40-75 |
| *(Music and interview)* | | | |
| NBC SOURCE Profile | 1985 | NBC Radio (3) | 30-50 |
| *(Music and interviews only, unusual for a Source program)* | | | |
| WORLD OF ROCK (Sept 89) Profile | 1989 | DIR (2) | 20-30 |
| *(Music and interview)* | | | |

**BEE GEES**

*Barry, Robin and Maurice Gibb; listings include Andy Gibb, though he was never a Bee Gee. Atco promo 45s $5 each; RSO promo singles $3 each; Atco promo LPs $12 each for single record sets, $20 for double-record sets*

**45s**

| Title | Yr | Label, Number | NM $ |
|---|---|---|---|
| FINE LINE Barry Gibb | 1984 | MCA S45-1242 | 10 |
| *(Promo-only longer version, 6:31)* | | | |
| MARLEY PURT DRIVE Two songs on flip side | 1969 | Atco EP-4535 | 12 |
| *(Promo-only EP from Atco LP 702)* | | | |
| NEW YORK MINING DISASTER 1941/I CAN'T SEE NOBODY | 1967 | Atco 6487 | 25 |
| *(Artist not listed on label)* | | | |
| UNICEF PSAS Cut 7 features the Bee Gees | 1979 | UNICEF DWP 27A | 25 |
| *(7-inch 33 1/3 with small hole, 20 cuts, 30 and 60-second public service spots)* | | | |
| WHAT'S IT ALL ABOUT (June 76) | 1976 | W.I.A.A. 320 | 25 |
| *(Repeat Barry Gibb interviews)* | | | |
| WHAT'S IT ALL ABOUT (May 78) | 1978 | W.I.A.A. 420 | 25 |
| *(Repeat of earlier Bee Gees/Barry Gibb interviews)* | | | |
| WHAT'S IT ALL ABOUT (Sept 75) Barry Gibb | 1975 | W.I.A.A. 283 | 25 |
| *(Features interview with Barry Gibb)* | | | |
| WOULDN'T I BE SOMEONE White/blue promo labels | 1973 | RSO 404 | 10 |
| *(Rare edited 3:24 Mono/Stereo version)* | | | |
| **Albums** | | | |
| SATURDAY NIGHT FEVER SPECIAL DISCO VERSIONS | 1978 | RSO PRO 033 | 50 |
| *(Promo-only sampler; contains an otherwise unavailable extended version of "Stayin' Alive")* | | | |
| SELECT DISCO CUTS FROM "SPIRITS HAVING FLOWN" | 1979 | RSO PRO ??? | 30 |
| *(Promo-only sampler)* | | | |
| THE WORDS AND MUSIC OF MAURICE, BARRY AND ROBIN GIBB | 1979 | RSO SMP-1 | 50 |
| *(Promo-only publisher's sampler)* | | | |

| Title | Yr | Label, Number | NM $ |
|---|---|---|---|
| UNICHAPPELL PUBLISHER'S SAMPLER | 1980 | RSO PUB-1000 | 50 |

**Compact Discs**

| Title | Yr | Label, Number | NM $ |
|---|---|---|---|
| NEW CLASS DISCO | 1994 | RSO 770 | 20 |

*(Promo-only greatest hits album, nine tracks)*

**RADIO SHOWS**

**Albums**

| Title | Yr | Label, Number | NM $ |
|---|---|---|---|
| BEE GEES SPECIAL (Sept 89) Profile | 1989 | Unistar | 10-20 |

*(Music and interviews)*

| Title | Yr | Label, Number | NM $ |
|---|---|---|---|
| FROM AUSTRALIA WITH LOVE (Aug 82) | 1982 | Mutual Radio (3) | 20-30 |

*(Dick Clark presentation; box set music and interviews also includes other Aussies)*

| Title | Yr | Label, Number | NM $ |
|---|---|---|---|
| THE IN SOUND (Aug 67) Series of daily 5-minute shows | 1967 | U. S. Army | 30-50 |

*(One of the shows features the Bee Gees; this show repeated in Apr 68)*

| Title | Yr | Label, Number | NM $ |
|---|---|---|---|
| THE IN SOUND (Oct 67) Features Bee Gees | 1967 | U. S. Army | 100-200 |

*(This series also includes Jimi Hendrix and Jimmy Page)*

| Title | Yr | Label, Number | NM $ |
|---|---|---|---|
| THE IN SOUND (Feb 68) Features Barry Gibb | 1968 | U. S. Army | 25-50 |

*(Show repeated in May 68)*

| Title | Yr | Label, Number | NM $ |
|---|---|---|---|
| ROBERT W. MORGAN (May 78) Music and interviews | 1978 | Watermark 812-6 | 20-40 |

*(Features Andy Gibb, 4th Gibb brother; repeated in May 81)*

| Title | Yr | Label, Number | NM $ |
|---|---|---|---|
| ROBERT W. MORGAN Music and interviews | 1977 | Watermark | 25-60 |

*(This show is part of Series II; other shows in this series in 1978, 1979)*

| Title | Yr | Label, Number | NM $ |
|---|---|---|---|
| NIGHTBIRD (Feb 77) | 1977 | U. S. Army Reserve #301 (2) | 25-40 |

*(Music and interviews, one of four shows on two discs)*

| Title | Yr | Label, Number | NM $ |
|---|---|---|---|
| ROCK AROUND THE WORLD (Jan 77) Music and interviews | 1977 | | 75-100 |

*(Very hard to find series)*

| Title | Yr | Label, Number | NM $ |
|---|---|---|---|
| SOLID GOLD SCRAPBOOK (Sept 86) Profile | 1986 | United Stations | 10-15 |

*(One 60-minute show/disc from a five-disc box set)*

**BEEFEATERS, THE**
*See The Byrds.*

**BELAFONTE, HARRY**
*RCA "Record Prevue" 45s $10-15*

**45s**

| Title | Yr | Label, Number | NM $ |
|---|---|---|---|
| BACK OF THE BUS | 196? | RCA Victor SP45-138 | 15 |

*(With picture sleeve)*

| Title | Yr | Label, Number | NM $ |
|---|---|---|---|
| BY THE TIME I GET TO PHOENIX | 1968 | RCA Victor SP45-181 | 10 |
| QUIET ROOM | 1966 | RCA Victor SP45-155 | 15 |

*(With picture sleeve)*

**7-Inch Extended Plays**

| Title | Yr | Label, Number | NM $ |
|---|---|---|---|
| ALL MY TRIALS | 196? | RCA Victor SP45-54 | 15 |
| BEST OF BELAFONTE | 196? | RCA Victor DJ 84 | 15 |

*(Yellow label)*

| Title | Yr | Label, Number | NM $ |
|---|---|---|---|
| MAMA LOOK AT BUBU | 196? | RCA Victor DJ 77 | 15 |

*(Two songs on each side)*

**BELEW, ADRIAN**
**12-Inch Singles**

| Title | Yr | Label, Number | NM $ |
|---|---|---|---|
| I AM WHAT I AM/MEN IN HELICOPTERS/YOUNG LIONS | 1990 | Atlantic 3324 | 6 |

**BELL, FREDDIE, AND THE BELLBOYS**
*Mercury promo 45s $12*

| Title | Yr | Label, Number | NM $ |
|---|---|---|---|
| ROCK & ROLL White promo label | 1959 | Mercury 20289 | 40 |

**BELLAMY BROTHERS**
*Warner and MCA promo 45s $2; MCA colored vinyl promo 45s $6 each*

**45s**

| Title | Yr | Label, Number | NM $ |
|---|---|---|---|
| OPEN-END INTERVIEW Small center hole | 197? | Warner/Curb 002 | 12 |

*("You Ain't Just Whistlin' Dixie" is flip side)*

**RADIO SHOWS**

**Albums**

| Title | Yr | Label, Number | NM $ |
|---|---|---|---|
| AMERICAN EAGLE (Feb 87) | 1987 | Westwood One | 10-15 |

*(Live concert)*

| Title | Yr | Label, Number | NM $ |
|---|---|---|---|
| SILVER EAGLE (Apr 83) | 1983 | DIR (3) | 20-25 |

*(Entire concert)*

| Title | Yr | Label, Number | NM $ |
|---|---|---|---|
| WESTWOOD ONE PRESENTS (Feb 87) | 1987 | Westwood One | 10-15 |

*(Live concert)*

**BELLY**
**RADIO SHOWS**
**Compact Discs**

| Title | Yr | Label, Number | NM $ |
|---|---|---|---|
| IN CONCERT-NU ROCK (Jan 94) Live concert | 1994 | Westwood One | 15-25 |

**BENATAR, PAT**
*Chrysalis promo 45s $2 each; Chrysalis promo LPs $4 each*

**45s**

| Title | Yr | Label, Number | NM $ |
|---|---|---|---|
| WE BELONG Issued in special gatefold cover | 1984 | Chrysalis 42826 | 15 |

*(Cover is promo only with a typed message insert for DJ)*

| Title | Yr | Label, Number | NM $ |
|---|---|---|---|
| WHAT'S IT ALL ABOUT (July 81) Public service show | 1981 | W. I. A. A. 584 | 25 |

*(Paul Simon on the other side)*

| Title | Yr | Label, Number | NM $ |
|---|---|---|---|
| WHAT'S IT ALL ABOUT (Oct 80) Public service show | 1980 | W. I. A. A. 544 | 20 |

*(Music and interviews)*

**RADIO SHOWS**
**Albums**

| Title | Yr | Label, Number | NM $ |
|---|---|---|---|
| A NIGHT ON THE ROAD (June 81) Profile | 1981 | ABC Radio (3) | 25-60 |

*(Music and interview, box set, scripts, booklet; with the Atlanta Rhythm Section)*

| Title | Yr | Label, Number | NM $ |
|-------|----|--------------|----|
| KING BISCUIT FLOWER HOUR (June 80) Live show | 1980 | DIR/ABC (2) | 40-60 |
| *(With the Cars)* | | | |
| KING BISCUIT FLOWER HOUR (Mar 80) Live show | 1980 | DIR/ABC (2) | 50-75 |
| *(With the Rockets)* | | | |
| LEGENDS OF ROCK (Oct 89) Music and interview | 1989 | (2) | 10-20 |
| *(Repeated several times)* | | | |
| NBC SOURCE (June 82) Live show | 1982 | NBC Radio (3) | 20-35 |
| *(Profile and live music)* | | | |
| NBC SOURCE (May 83) Live show | 1983 | NBC Radio (2) | 15-30 |
| *(With Robert Hazard)* | | | |
| OFF THE RECORD Music and interviews | 1988 | Westwood One (2) | 10-20 |
| *(Repeated many times)* | | | |
| RETRO ROCK (Apr 83) Live show | 1983 | Clayton Webster (2) | 25-40 |
| *(Parts 1 and 2)* | | | |
| SUPERSTAR CONCERT (Mar 84) Live | 1984 | Westwood One (3) | 25-40 |
| *(Repeated several times)* | | | |
| SUPERSTARS LIVE (Mar 84) Live material | 1984 | DIR (3) | 40-75 |
| *(Live concert)* | | | |
| TAB'S SASSY STARS Yellow labels | 1986 | DIR (2) | 25-40 |
| *(Music and interview)* | | | |
| **Compact Discs** | | | |
| ELECTRIC LADYLAND (June 93) | 1993 | Album Network | 200-250 |
| *(Live concert)* | | | |
| IN THE STUDIO (90s) Album profiles | 199? | Album Network | 10-15 |
| *(Music and interview)* | | | |
| KING BISCUIT FLOWER HOUR (June 91) Live show | 1991 | DIR | 25-50 |
| *(Other shows in series)* | | | |
| UP CLOSE  Designer CDs | 1993 | Media America (2) | 30-50 |
| *(Mainly music and interviews)* | | | |

### BENEKE, TEX/RAY EBERLE/THE MODERNAIRES
**45s**

| AND THE BELLS RANG/MERRY CHRISTMAS, BABY | 1965 | Columbia JZSP 111917/8 | 8 |
|---|---|---|---|

### BENNETT, BOYD
*King white label promo singles $18 each; Mercury white label promos $15 each*

### BENNETT, TONY
*Columbia promo 45s not listed $5-15 each depending on age*
**45s**

| EDITION OF HITS | 196? | Columbia (no #) | 10 |
|---|---|---|---|
| *(Promo-only picture sleeve)* | | | |
| I LEFT MY HEART IN SAN FRANCISCO | 1962 | Columbia JZSP 57734 | 15 |
| *(Live version on one side, original on other side)* | | | |
| I LEFT MY HEART IN SAN FRANCISCO | 1962 | Columbia JZSP 56813 | 10 |
| *(Original promo for this classic)* | | | |
| IF I RULED THE WORLD | 195? | Columbia 5-1654 | 10 |
| *(With picture sleeve)* | | | |
| LOVE THEME FROM THE SANDPIPER | 1966 | Columbia 43431 | 10 |
| *(Yellow vinyl)* | | | |
| MY FAVORITE THINGS | 1970 | Columbia AE 28 | 10 |
| *(Promo-only for Christmas Seals, white label with picture sleeve)* | | | |
| WHAT MAKES IT HAPPEN | 1966 | Columbia 43954 | 10 |
| *(Brown vinyl)* | | | |
| WHO CAN I TURN TO | 1965 | Columbia 43141 | 10 |
| *(Red vinyl)* | | | |
| **RADIO SHOWS** | | | |
| **45s** | | | |
| IN THE STUDIO | 198? | Creative Radio D1002 | 20-40 |
| *(7-inch 33 1/3 rpm demo for 3-hour show)* | | | |
| **Albums** | | | |
| IN THE STUDIO | 198? | Creative Radio (3) | 25-40 |
| THE FIRST 40 YEARS | 1991 | | 25-40 |
| *(Music and interviews)* | | | |
| **Compact Discs** | | | |
| GREAT SOUNDS | 1991 | (3) | 25-50 |
| *(Music and interview)* | | | |
| TONY BENNETT (July 91) Profile | 1991 | (3) | 25-40 |
| *(Music and interview)* | | | |

### BENTON, BROOK
**45s**

| YOU'RE ALL I WANT FOR CHRISTMAS/THIS TIME OF THE YEAR | 1963 | Mercury 72214 | 10 |
|---|---|---|---|

### BENTON, WALT
**45s**

| STUCK UP | 1958 | 20th Fox 143 | 40 |
|---|---|---|---|
| *(White promo label)* | | | |

### BERLIN
*Geffen and Columbia promo 45s $4 each*
**12-Inch Singles**

| LIKE FLAMES/LIKE FLAMES (7" Version) | 1986 | Geffen PRO-A-2572 | 8 |
|---|---|---|---|
| NOW IT'S MY TURN/NOW IT'S MY TURN (edit remix) | 1984 | Geffen PRO-A-2147 | 6 |
| PINK AND VELVET (same on both sides) | 1986 | Geffen PRO-A-2632 | 8 |
| SEX (I'M A...)/(Instrumental) | 1982 | Geffen PRO-A-2004 | 16 |

| Title | Yr | Label, Number | NM $ |
|-------|-----|---------------|------|
| TOUCH/NOW IT'S MY TURN/IN MY DREAMS/NO MORE WORDS | 1984 | Geffen PRO-A-2121 | 8 |
| YOU DON'T KNOW (Edit)/YOU DON'T KNOW (LP Version) | 1986 | Geffen PRO-A-2686 | 5 |

**RADIO SHOWS**
**Albums**

| | | | |
|-------|-----|---------------|------|
| IN CONCERT (Apr 84) Live concert | 1984 | Westwood One (2) | 25-50 |
| *(In concert with Big Company)* | | | |
| IN CONCERT (Sept 84) Live concert | 1984 | Westwood One (2) | 40-75 |
| *(With Icicle Works)* | | | |
| INNERVIEW Music and interview | 198? | Innerview | 10-20 |
| *(Show was repeated)* | | | |

**BERRY, CHUCK**
*Other Chess promo 45s (later years) $10 each; Atco promo 45s $5 each; Atco promo LPs $15 each*
**45s**

| | | | |
|-------|-----|---------------|------|
| BROWN EYED HANDSOME MAN | 1956 | Chess 1635 | 150 |
| *(Very rare in promo)* | | | |
| MAYBELLENE  White and blue promo label | 1955 | Chess 1604 | 175 |
| *(Chess promo singles up to 1958 are very rare)* | | | |
| MY DING-A-LING | 1972 | Chess 2131 | 10 |
| *(Orange and blue promo label)* | | | |
| NO MONEY DOWN | 1956 | Chess 1615 | 150 |
| *(Very rare in promo)* | | | |
| OH, BABY DOLL | 1957 | Chess 1664 | 150 |
| *(Very rare in promo)* | | | |
| REELIN' AND ROCKIN' | 1972 | Chess 2136 | 10 |
| *(Orange and blue promo label)* | | | |
| ROLL OVER, BEETHOVEN | 1956 | Chess 1626 | 150 |
| *(Very rare in promo)* | | | |
| SCHOOL DAYS | 1957 | Chess 1653 | 150 |
| *(Very rare in promo)* | | | |
| THIRTY DAYS | 1955 | Chess 1610 | 175 |
| *(Label must also read "Promotion, Not for Sale")* | | | |
| YOU CAN'T CATCH ME | 1957 | Chess 1645 | 150 |
| *(If any of the above titles were pressed as promo 78s their value would be at least double the listed value)* | | | |

**RADIO SHOWS**
**Albums**

| | | | |
|-------|-----|---------------|------|
| IN CONCERT (80s) With George Thorogood | 198? | Westwood One (2) | 50-100 |
| *(Live concert)* | | | |
| NBC SPECIAL (Jan 80) | 1980 | NBC Radio (2) | 25-50 |
| *(Music and interview)* | | | |
| RETRO ROCK (June 82) Live show | 1982 | Clayton Webster | 100-175 |
| *(Rare live concert)* | | | |
| ROYALTY OF ROCK WITH LITTLE RICHARD | 1983 | RKO Radio | 25-40 |
| *(Music and interviews)* | | | |
| SOLID GOLD SCRAPBOOK BIRTHDAY SALUTE (Oct 90) | 1990 | Unistar | 10-15 |
| *(Part of a 5-record, weekly set)* | | | |

**BERRY, JOHN**
*Liberty/Capitol Nashville jukebox 45s $4*
**RADIO SHOWS**
**Compact Discs**

| | | | |
|-------|-----|---------------|------|
| LIVE AT CRAZY HORSE (Sept 94) | 1994 | Westwood One | 30-60 |
| *(Live concert)* | | | |

**BERRY, REED**
**45s**

| | | | |
|-------|-----|---------------|------|
| WHAT A DOLLY | 1957 | 20th Century Fox | 40 |
| *(White promo label)* | | | |

**BEST, PETE**
*Drummer for the Beatles before Ringo Starr*
**45s**

| | | | |
|-------|-----|---------------|------|
| BOYS | 1966 | Cameo 391 | 25 |
| *(White promo label)  See Beatles* | | | |
| CASTING MY SPELL Blue vinyl | 1966 | Mr. Maestro 712 | 100 |
| *(Colored vinyl is available only as a promo)* | | | |
| I CAN'T DO WITHOUT YOU Blue vinyl | 1965 | Mr. Maestro 711 | 100 |
| *(Colored vinyl is available only as a promo)* | | | |
| IF YOU CAN'T GET HER | 1964 | Happening 117 | 60 |
| IF YOU CAN'T GET HER | 1964 | Happening 405 | 40 |

**BETTS, DICKIE**
*Member of the Allman Brothers Band*
**RADIO SHOWS**
**Reel-to-Reel Tapes**

| | | | |
|-------|-----|---------------|------|
| KING BISCUIT FLOWER HOUR (70s) | 197? | DIR/ABC | 75-100 |
| *(With Bob Weir)* | | | |

**BIG AUDIO DYNAMITE**
*Columbia promo 45s $4 each; Columbia promo picture sleeves $3 each*
**12-Inch Singles**

| | | | |
|-------|-----|---------------|------|
| BAD ROCK CITY/BAD ROCK CITY (Edit) | 1986 | Columbia CAS 2647 | 6 |
| C'MON EVERY BEATBOX/C'MON EVERY BEATBOX (Edit) | 1986 | Columbia CAS 2520 | 6 |
| CONTACT (3 versions)/WHO BEATS/IN FULL EFFECT | 1989 | Columbia CAS 01899 | 8 |
| E=MC2 (3 mixes) | 1985 | Columbia CAS 2361 | 6 |

| Title | Yr | Label, Number | NM $ |
|---|---|---|---|
| HOLLYWOOD BOULEVARD (Club Mix) (same on both sides) | 1987 | Columbia CAS 2697 | 6 |
| JAMES BROWN (3 mixes)/IF I WERE JOHN CARPENTER | 1989 | Columbia CAS 01739 | 10 |
| LOOKING FOR A SONG (4 versions) | 1994 | Columbia CAS 6553 | 8 |
| MEDICINE SHOW (London Mix)/MEDICINE SHOW (N.Y. Mix) | 1985 | Columbia CAS 2301 | 8 |
| RUSHDANCE/RUSH (instrumental & LP)/CITY LIGHTS | 1991 | Columbia CAS 4044 | 8 |
| THE BOTTOM LINE (Single Version)/THE BOTTOM LINE (LP Version) | 1985 | Columbia CAS 2252 | 8 |
| THE OTHER 99 (Extended) (same on both sides) | 1988 | Columbia 08133 | 6 |
| V-13 (same on both sides) | 1986 | Columbia CAS 2601 | 6 |
| **Compact Discs** | | | |
| LOOKING FOR A SONG | 199? | Columbia 6567 (2) | 15 |
| **RADIO SHOWS** | | | |
| **Compact Discs** | | | |
| ON THE EDGE (Jan 95) Music and interviews | 1995 | Westwood One | 20-30 |
| *(With Pete Droge and Dink)* | | | |

**BIG BOPPER, THE**
*J. P. Richardson. Mercury promo singles $15 each*

| **Albums** | | | |
|---|---|---|---|
| CHANTILLY LACE | 1958 | Mercury 20402 | 225 |
| *(White promo label)* | | | |

**BIG COUNTRY**
*Mercury promo 45s $5 each*

| **12-Inch Singles** | | | |
|---|---|---|---|
| EAST OF EDEN (same on both sides) | 1984 | Mercury PRO 341 | 6 |
| FIELDS OF FIRE/FIELDS OF FIRE (7" Version) | 1984 | Mercury PRO 239 | 6 |
| JUST A SHADOW (Long)/JUST A SHADOW (Short) | 1984 | Mercury PRO 333 | 6 |
| LOOK AWAY  (same on both sides) | 1986 | Mercury PRO 414 | 6 |
| ONE GREAT THING (same on both sides) | 1986 | Mercury PRO 442 | 6 |
| WHERE THE ROSE... (same on both sides) | 1984 | Mercury PRO 324-1 | 8 |
| **RADIO SHOWS** | | | |
| **Albums** | | | |
| BBC TRANSCRIPTION DISC Live show | 1983 | BBC Transcription | 200-300 |
| *(Very rare radio show series)* | | | |
| COLLEGE CONCERT (Dec 83) | 1983 | London Wavelength | 50-100 |
| *(Live concert)* | | | |
| KING BISCUIT FLOWER HOUR (Apr 83) | 1983 | DIR/ABC (2) | 60-80 |
| *(Live concert)* | | | |
| KING BISCUIT FLOWER HOUR (Apr 84) Live concert | 1984 | DIR (2) | 25-50 |
| *(With Berlin)* | | | |
| SOURCE SPECIAL (July 84) | 1984 | NBC Radio (2) | 50-75 |
| *(Live concert)* | | | |
| **Compact Discs** | | | |
| ON THE EDGE (Oct 93) Music and interviews | 1993 | Album Network | 25-35 |
| *(With The Breeders and Pearl Jam)* | | | |

**BIG HEAD TODD AND THE MONSTERS**
**RADIO SHOWS**

| **Compact Discs** | | | |
|---|---|---|---|
| IN CONCERT (Dec 94) Live concert | 1994 | Westwood One | 25-50 |
| *(With Blues Traveler)* | | | |
| IN CONCERT (July 94) Live concert | 1994 | Westwood One | 25-50 |
| *(With Soul Asylum)* | | | |

**BILLION DOLLAR BABIES**

| **45s** | | | |
|---|---|---|---|
| TOO YOUNG (stereo)/TOO YOUNG (mono) | 1977 | Polydor 14406 | 12 |

**BIONDI, DICK**
**RADIO SHOWS**

| **Albums** | | | |
|---|---|---|---|
| SUPER GOLD ROCK 'N' ROLL | 1976 | Joe Weidensall Productions (3) | 10-12 |
| *(Price for each show, of which at least 15 were aired)* | | | |

**BISHOP, STEPHEN**

| **Albums** | | | |
|---|---|---|---|
| BISH IS BACK | 197? | A-H PR-3079 | 12 |

**BIXBY, BILL, AND BRANDON CRUZ**

| **45s** | | | |
|---|---|---|---|
| BEST FRIEND | 1970 | MGM 14198 | 10 |
| *(Theme from "The Courtship of Eddie's Father" performed by the co-stars)* | | | |

**BJORK**
**RADIO SHOWS**

| **Compact Discs** | | | |
|---|---|---|---|
| IN CONCERT-NU ROCK (Jan 94) | 1994 | Westwood One | 40 |
| *(Live concert)* | | | |
| ON THE EDGE (Jan 94) Music and interviews | 1994 | Westwood One | 10-15 |
| *(With Perry Farell)* | | | |
| ON THE EDGE (Sept 93) Music and interviews | 1993 | Westwood One | 10-15 |
| *(With Lisa Germano and Soul Asylum)* | | | |

| Title | Yr | Label, Number | NM $ |
|---|---|---|---|
| **BLACK AND BLUE** | | | |
| **RADIO SHOWS** | | | |
| **Albums** | | | |
| IN CONCERT (Nov 84) Live concert | 1984 | Westwood One (2) | 40-75 |
| *(Also in concert is Motley Crue)* | | | |
| | | | |
| **BLACK CROWES, THE** | | | |
| *Def American promo singles $4 each* | | | |
| **RADIO SHOWS** | | | |
| **Albums** | | | |
| IN CONCERT (90s) | 199? | Westwood One (2) | 30-50 |
| *(Live concert)* | | | |
| OFF THE RECORD (90s) Profile | 199? | Westwood One (2) | 15-25 |
| *(Music and interviews, several repeats)* | | | |
| SUPERSTAR CONCERT (Dec 90) Box set | 1990 | Westwood One (3) | 30-50 |
| *(Live concert, with Robert Cray)* | | | |
| SUPERSTAR CONCERT (May 91) Box set | 1991 | Westwood One (3) | 40-60 |
| *(Live concert, with Winger)* | | | |
| **Compact Discs** | | | |
| ALBUM NETWORK SPECIAL (Jan 94) | 1994 | Album Network (2) | 60-80 |
| *(Live concert)* | | | |
| ELECTRIC LADYLAND (Nov 91) | 1991 | Album Network (2) | 75-100 |
| *(Music and interviews)* | | | |
| IN CONCERT (Mar 95) Live concert | 1995 | Westwood One | 25-50 |
| *(With Sheryl Crow, Meat Puppets and Candlebox)* | | | |
| LIVE AT THE GREEK THEATRE (Nov 91) | 1991 | (2) | 100-150 |
| *(Live concert)* | | | |
| OFF THE RECORD (Mar 95) | 1995 | Westwood One | 15-25 |
| *(Music and interviews)* | | | |
| ON TOUR (90s) Music and interview | 199? | Media America | 25-75 |
| *(Mainly a profile of the group)* | | | |
| SOUTHERN HARMONY (May 92) Picture CDs | 1992 | (2) | 75-100 |
| *(Mostly live material)* | | | |
| **Reel-to-Reel Tapes** | | | |
| ALBUM NETWORK SPECIAL (Feb 93) | 1993 | Album Network (2) | 75-100 |
| *(Live concert)* | | | |
| WORLD PREMIERE | 1994 | World Premiere | 100-150 |
| *(Live concert on two 10" reels)* | | | |
| | | | |
| **BLACK FLAG** | | | |
| **45s** | | | |
| TV PARTY (same on both sides) | 1981 | SST/Unicorn 95006 | 16 |
| *(Promo only)* | | | |
| | | | |
| **BLACK SABBATH** | | | |
| *Warner promo singles $6 each; Warner promo LPs $15 each* | | | |
| **45s** | | | |
| IRON MAN  Palm trees promo label | 1973 | Warner 7802 | 20 |
| *(The rock classic, 45 reissue)* | | | |
| TOMORROW'S DREAM | 1972 | Warner 7625 | 10 |
| *(White promo label)* | | | |
| **Albums** | | | |
| PARANOID  White promo label | 1971 | Warner 1887 | 20 |
| **Compact Discs** | | | |
| BIBLE ACCORDING TO BLACK SABBATH, THE | 199? | Columbia 2SK 6544 (2) | 25 |
| *(Tribute album with original Black Sabbath versions on second CD)* | | | |
| **RADIO SHOWS** | | | |
| **Albums** | | | |
| CAPTURED LIVE (Nov 83) | 1983 | RKO (3) | 50-100 |
| *(Live concert)* | | | |
| HIGH VOLTAGE (May 89) | 1989 | Westwood One (2) | 25-35 |
| *(Included is a 30-minute live concert from Sabbath)* | | | |
| KING BISCUIT FLOWER HOUR | 1983 | DIR/ABC (2) | 75-100 |
| *(Live concert with Motley Crue)* | | | |
| KING BISCUIT FLOWER HOUR (July 82) | 1982 | DIR/ABC (2) | 50-100 |
| *(Live concert, with the Scorpions)* | | | |
| SUPERGROUPS (Oct 83) Live concert | 1983 | Westwood One (3) | 175-250 |
| *(With Rush)* | | | |
| | | | |
| **BLACK, CILLA** | | | |
| **45s** | | | |
| ACROSS THE UNIVERSE (mono/stereo) | 1970 | DJM 70018 | 12 |
| | | | |
| **BLACK, CLINT** | | | |
| **45s** | | | |
| A BETTER MAN (same on both sides) | 1989 | RCA 8781-7-R | 8 |
| *(Possibly promo only; same track was the B-side of the next Clint Black single, "Killin' Time")* | | | |
| | | | |
| **BLACK, FRANK** | | | |
| **RADIO SHOWS** | | | |
| **Compact Discs** | | | |
| ALBUM NETWORK SPECIAL (June 93) | 1993 | Album Network | 25-50 |

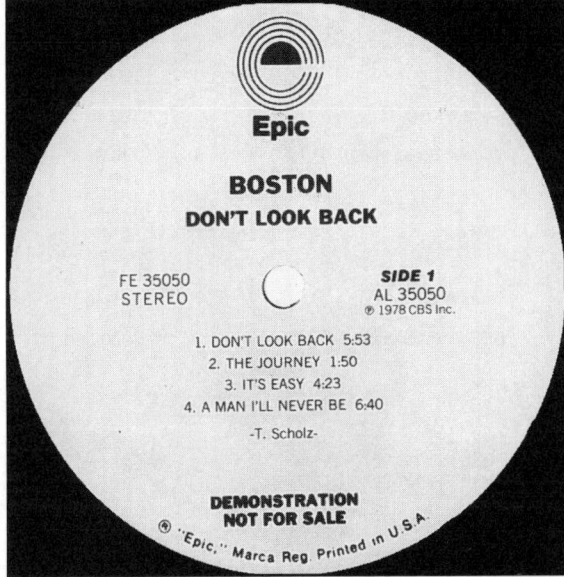

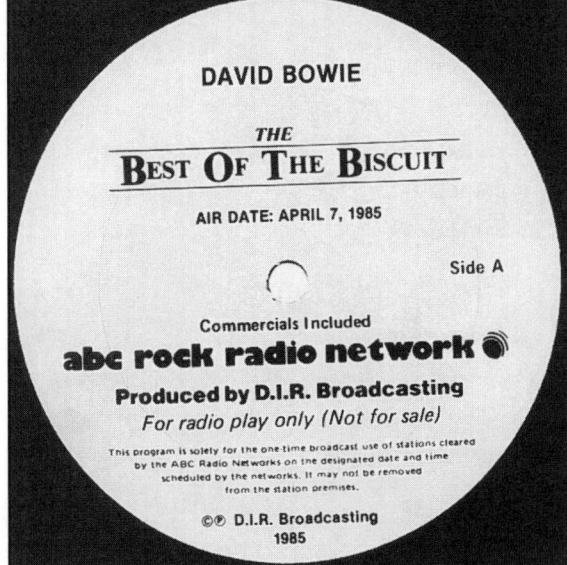

(Top row) All Beatles promos are sought-after, and most are rare. These are two of the rarest. At left is a Decca pink-label promo for the 1962 issue of "My Bonnie," and at right is a white-label promo for the interview album *Hear the Beatles Tell All.* (Middle left) A fairly typical 1970s Epic white promo label, this one from Boston's *Don't Look Back,* the No. 1 followup to their multi-platinum debut. (Middle right) A rarely-seen promo from David Bowie, here's a radio-only extended-play single from 1973 that includes the short version of "Space Oddity." (Bottom left) When the King Biscuit Flower Hour did a rerun, it was called "Best of the Biscuit." Here's one featuring David Bowie. (Bottom right) The King Biscuit Flower Hour was one of the first radio shows to switch to compact discs; it already was sending them out as early as 1987. Here's a David Bowie set on CD from 1989.

| Title | Yr | Label, Number | NM $ |
|-------|----|--------------|------|

**BLACKFOOT**
*Atco promo 45s $4 each*
**RADIO SHOWS**
**Albums**

| Title | Yr | Label, Number | NM $ |
|-------|----|--------------|------|
| IN CONCERT (Dec 84) Live concert | 1984 | Westwood One (2) | 50-100 |
| *(With Golden Earring)* | | | |
| KING BISCUIT FLOWER HOUR (Aug 81) Live concert | 1981 | Westwood One (2) | 40-75 |
| *(With Van Zant)* | | | |
| KING BISCUIT FLOWER HOUR (July 80) Live concert | 1980 | Westwood One (2) | 75-125 |
| *(With Triumph)* | | | |

**BLACKHAWK**
*Arista/Arista Nashville promo CD singles $4 each*
**RADIO SHOWS**
**Compact Discs**

| Title | Yr | Label, Number | NM $ |
|-------|----|--------------|------|
| COUNTRY'S CUTTING EDGE (Nov 93) | 1993 | Westwood One | 10-20 |
| *(Live concert)* | | | |

**BLAINE, HAL**
*Pop/rock era's most recorded and charted drummer*
**7-Inch Extended Plays**

| Title | Yr | Label, Number | NM $ |
|-------|----|--------------|------|
| DRUMS A-GO-GO | 1965 | Dunhill D-2 | 40 |
| *(Rare promo-only release)* | | | |

**BLANC, MEL**
*Capitol yellow and white promo 45s $10 each*
**45s**

| Title | Yr | Label, Number | NM $ |
|-------|----|--------------|------|
| I TAUT I TAW A RECORD DEALER Yellow or white label | 1951 | Capitol PRO-15 | 50 |
| *(Released to record stores for in-store commercial play)* | | | |
| TWEETY'S TWISTMAS TWOUBLE | 1959 | Warner Bros. 5129 | 10 |
| *(White label)* | | | |

**BLANCMANGE**
*Sire promo 45s $3 each*
**RADIO SHOWS**
**Albums**

| Title | Yr | Label, Number | NM $ |
|-------|----|--------------|------|
| BBC ROCK HOUR (Sept 84) Live show | 1984 | London Wavelength | 25-40 |
| *(BBC live concert material)* | | | |
| BBC TRANSCRIPTION DISC  Live show | 1983 | BBC Transcription | 200-350 |
| *(In concert with Hot Chocolate)* | | | |

**BLASTERS, THE**
*Other Warner promo 45s $8 each*
**12-Inch Singles**

| Title | Yr | Label, Number | NM $ |
|-------|----|--------------|------|
| BAREFOOT ROCK/FOOL'S PARADISE/LONG WHITE CADILLAC | 1983 | Slash PRO-A-2017 | 12 |
| COLORED LIGHTS/DARK NIGHT | 1985 | Slash PRO-A-2259 | 8 |

**45s**

| Title | Yr | Label, Number | NM $ |
|-------|----|--------------|------|
| I'M SHAKIN'  Custom label | 1981 | Warner 50047 | 15 |
| *(Original, with picture sleeve, is Slash 109)* | | | |
| RED ROSE Mono/stereo | 1983 | Warner 29566 | 10 |
| *(Little mention of Slash records)* | | | |
| SO LONG BABY GOODBYE Custom label | 1982 | Warner 29975 | 12 |
| *(Mono/stereo promo record)* | | | |

**Albums**

| Title | Yr | Label, Number | NM $ |
|-------|----|--------------|------|
| THE WARNER BROS, MUSIC SHOW | 1985 | Warner Bros. WBMS-130 | 25 |
| *One side: The Blasters; the other side: The Smiths* | | | |

**RADIO SHOWS**
**Albums**

| Title | Yr | Label, Number | NM $ |
|-------|----|--------------|------|
| IN CONCERT (July 85) LIVE | 1985 | Westwood One (2) | 40-75 |
| *(Also in concert is Elliot Faston)* | | | |
| KING BISCUIT FLOWER HOUR (Sept 82) LIVE | 1982 | DIR/ABC (2) | 50-100 |
| *(Also in concert is A Flock Of Seagulls)* | | | |
| SPIN CONCERT  LIVE | 1986 | Spin Magazine | 40-75 |
| *(Live concert)* | | | |

**BLENDERS**
**45s**

| Title | Yr | Label, Number | NM $ |
|-------|----|--------------|------|
| TWO LOVES White promo label | 1958 | Aladdin 3449 | 1,000-1,500 |
| *(Fewer than five copies known, at least one is a promo)* | | | |

**BLENDERS, THE**
*The pop-vocal group*
**45s**

| Title | Yr | Label, Number | NM $ |
|-------|----|--------------|------|
| WAKE UP TO MUSIC | 1958 | RCA Victor 6712 | 50 |
| *(Unusual cut-in, includes an Elvis cut)* | | | |

**7-Inch Extended Plays**

| Title | Yr | Label, Number | NM $ |
|-------|----|--------------|------|
| WAKE UP TO MUSIC Cut-in with Elvis cut | 1958 | RCA Victor DJ 22 | 50-100 |
| *(Rare record)* | | | |

**BLESSING, MICHAEL**
*Better known as Michael Nesmith of the Monkees*
**45s**

| Title | Yr | Label, Number | NM $ |
|-------|----|--------------|------|
| THE NEW RECRUIT | 1965 | Colpix 787 | 50 |
| *(White promo label)* | | | |
| UNTIL IT'S TIME FOR YOU TO GO  White label | 1965 | Colpix 792 | 50 |

| Title | Yr | Label, Number | NM $ |
|---|---|---|---|

**BLIND MELON**
*Capitol promo CD singles $3; Capitol jukebox 45s $4*
**45s**

| | | | |
|---|---|---|---|
| TONES OF HOME (B-side blank) | 1993 | Capitol 7PRO-79??? | 8 |

**RADIO SHOWS**
**Compact Discs**

| | | | |
|---|---|---|---|
| IN CONCERT (Aug 93) Live concert | 1993 | Westwood One (2) | 24-40 |

*(Also in concert the Spin Doctors)*

| | | | |
|---|---|---|---|
| IN CONCERT-NU ROCK (May 93) Live concert | 1993 | Westwood One | 25-40 |

*(This show repeated in Feb 94)*

**BLONDIE**
*Includes Wind in the Willows.  Chrysalis promo 45s $5 each; Chrysalis promo 45s by Debbie Harry $4 each; Geffen promo 45s by Debbie Harry $3 each; Chrysalis LPs with white labels $10-15 each.*
**12-Inch Singles**

| | | | |
|---|---|---|---|
| CALL ME (Remix Extended Version)/NIGHT DRIVE (instrumental) | 1980 | Polydor PRO-124 | 20 |

**45s**

| | | | |
|---|---|---|---|
| IN THE FLESH  Mono/stereo | 1977 | Private Stock 45141 | 18 |

*(Gray colored promo label)*

| | | | |
|---|---|---|---|
| MOMENTS SPENT  Wind in the Willows | 1968 | Capitol P-2274 | 40 |

*(Green Capitol label produced by Artie Kornfeld)*

| | | | |
|---|---|---|---|
| WHAT'S IT ALL ABOUT (Dec 81) Interviews and music | 1981 | W. I. A. A. 603 | 25 |

*(Flip side features Peter, Paul & Mary; both above programs feature interviews with Debbie Harry and Chris Stein)*

| | | | |
|---|---|---|---|
| WHAT'S IT ALL ABOUT (Nov 79) Interviews and music | 1979 | W. I. A. A. 498 | 20 |

*(Flip side features Henry Mancini)*

| | | | |
|---|---|---|---|
| X OFFENDER  Mono/stereo | 1976 | Private Stock 45097 | 20 |

*(Gray colored promo label)*

**Albums**

| | | | |
|---|---|---|---|
| AT HOME WITH DEBBIE HARRY AND CHRIS STEIN | 1981 | Chrysalis CHS 24 PDJ | 50 |

*(Open-end interview with script)*

| | | | |
|---|---|---|---|
| CAPITOL DISC JOCKEY ALBUM (July 68) Various artists | 1968 | Capitol PRO 4583 | 25 |

*(Two songs by Wind in the Willows, including "Moments Spent")*

| | | | |
|---|---|---|---|
| WIND IN THE WILLOWS Pre-Blondie | 1968 | Capitol 2956 | 50 |

*(Blue promo label)*

**RADIO SHOWS**
**Albums**

| | | | |
|---|---|---|---|
| PROFILES IN ROCK (May 80) Profile | 1980 | Watermark | 20-40 |

*(Basically the same show as Robert W. Morgan)*

| | | | |
|---|---|---|---|
| ROBERT KLEIN (Nov 80) Music and interviews | 1980 | | 25-40 |

*(Mostly interview material, with Debbie Harry)*

| | | | |
|---|---|---|---|
| ROBERT W. MORGAN (Apr 80) Profile | 1980 | Watermark | 25-40 |

*(Music and interview)*

| | | | |
|---|---|---|---|
| SUPERGROUPS Live concert | 1980 | DIR (3) | 100-200 |

*(Very rare and high quality show)*

**Compact Discs**

| | | | |
|---|---|---|---|
| ON THE EDGE (Sept 93) Music and interview | 1993 | Westwood One | 25-40 |

*(Also featured are Fluid and Radiohead)*

**BLOOD, SWEAT AND TEARS**
*Columbia white label promo 45s $3 each; ABC label promo 45s $2 each*
**Albums**

| | | | |
|---|---|---|---|
| 1974 CHRISTMAS SEALS  David Clayton-Thomas | 1974 | AS #8086 | 25 |

*(Thomas sings "Magnificent Sanctuary Band")*

| | | | |
|---|---|---|---|
| NUCLEAR BLUES | 1980 | MCA L33-1865 | 15 |

*Promo only on gold vinyl*
**RADIO SHOWS**
**Albums**

| | | | |
|---|---|---|---|
| PIONEERS IN ROCK | 1986 | DIR (2) | 15-25 |

*(With Procol Harum and Chicago)*

| | | | |
|---|---|---|---|
| RETRO ROCK (Dec 81) Live concert | 1981 | (2) | 75-150 |

*(Very rare live concert)*

**BLOODROCK**
*Capitol promo 45s $12 each*
**45s**

| | | | |
|---|---|---|---|
| BLOODROCK INTERVIEW  White promo label | 1972 | Capitol PRO-6581 | 25 |

*(From Sol Smaiizys and Dennis Gray, WXFH Chicago, stock copy of this record, Capitol 3451, has "Help Is On the Way" on flip side)*

| | | | |
|---|---|---|---|
| D.O.A.  Red/yellow promo label | 1970 | Capitol 3099 | 25 |

*(Classic version, "D.O.A." on both sides, rare version)*

| | | | |
|---|---|---|---|
| EROSION  Red/yellow promo label | 1971 | Capitol PRO-6486 | 25 |

*(Promo only, later released as Capitol 3320)*

**BLOSSOMS, THE**
**45s**

| | | | |
|---|---|---|---|
| THINGS ARE CHANGING Public service ads | 1965 | E.E.O.C. | 500 |

*(7" 33rpm with cardboard black/white cover)*

**BLOW MONKEYS**
**12-Inch Singles**

| | | | |
|---|---|---|---|
| DIGGING YOUR SCENE (LP Version) (same on both sides) | 1986 | RCA JR-14326 | 8 |
| WICKED WAYS/WALKING THE BLUE BEAT/ | 1985 | RCA JW-14426 | 10 |
| THE MAN FROM RUSSIA/IT'S NOT UNUSUAL | | | |

| **Title** | **Yr** | **Label, Number** | **NM $** |
|---|---|---|---|
| **BLOW, KURTIS** | | | |
| **45s** | | | |
| CHRISTMAS RAPPIN' PART 1/CHRISTMAS RAPPIN' PART 2 | 1979 | Mercury DJ 562 (MDS-4009) | 8 |
| *(45 promo of 12-inch single)* | | | |
| | | | |
| **BLUE** | | | |
| **RADIO SHOWS** | | | |
| **Compact Discs** | | | |
| IN CONCERT (Oct 92) Live concert | 1992 | Westwood One (2) | 15-25 |
| *(Also Roxy Music and Nirvana)* | | | |
| | | | |
| **BLUE CHEER** | | | |
| **45s** | | | |
| SUMMERTIME BLUES | 1968 | Philips DJP-18 | 10 |
| *(Promo number; white label)* | | | |
| | | | |
| **BLUE MINK** | | | |
| **45s** | | | |
| OUR WORLD | 1969 | Philips DJP-70 | 10 |
| *(Promo number; white label)* | | | |
| | | | |
| **BLUE OYSTER CULT** | | | |
| *Columbia singles $4 each; Columbia promo LPs $10 each* | | | |
| **RADIO SHOWS** | | | |
| **Albums** | | | |
| A NIGHT ON THE ROAD (July 81) | 1981 | ABC Radio (3) | 40-75 |
| *(Box set with scripts, instructions, etc.)* | | | |
| BBC ROCK HOUR (Sept 81) Live concert | 1981 | London Wavelength | 75-150 |
| *(BBC concert material)* | | | |
| CAPTURED LIVE (Apr 84) | 1984 | RKO (2) | 25-50 |
| *(Profile of the group and live music)* | | | |
| FANTASY CONCERT | 1984 | (10) | 75-150 |
| *(Also Dio, INXS, Scandal and others; previously aired live material from other shows)* | | | |
| IN CONCERT (Apr 83) Live concert | 1983 | Westwood One (2) | 25-50 |
| *(With Vandenberg)* | | | |
| IN CONCERT (June 81) Live concert | 1981 | Westwood One (2) | 40-75 |
| *(With Loverboy)* | | | |
| IN CONCERT (May 82) Live concert | 1982 | Westwood One (2) | 50-100 |
| *(Entire live concert is BOC; repeated June 1982)* | | | |
| INNERVIEW  Music and interview | 197? | Innerview Show #18, 27 | 10-15 |
| *(A profile with interviews)* | | | |
| KING BISCUIT FLOWER HOUR (July 86) | 1986 | DIR (2) | 45-75 |
| *(Live concert)* | | | |
| KING BISCUIT FLOWER HOUR (June 84) Live concert | 1984 | DIR/ABC (2) | 45-75 |
| *(With Tony Carey)* | | | |
| KING BISCUIT FLOWER HOUR (Mar 80) LIVE | 1980 | DIR/ABC (2) | 45-75 |
| *(With the Babys)* | | | |
| NBC SOURCE (Feb 82) Live concert | 1982 | NBC Radio (2) | 40-75 |
| *(Different concert than Westwood One or DIR concerts)* | | | |
| | | | |
| **BLUE ZONE U.K.** | | | |
| **45s** | | | |
| JACKIE | 1988 | Arista 9725 | 10 |
| *(Blue vinyl promo)* | | | |
| | | | |
| **BLUES BAND, THE** | | | |
| *Features Paul Jones of Manfred Mann* | | | |
| **RADIO SHOWS** | | | |
| **Albums** | | | |
| BBC TRANSCRIPTION DISC Live concert | 1985 | BBC Transcription | 75-150 |
| | | | |
| **BLUES BROTHERS** | | | |
| *Joliet Jake and Elwood Blues (John Belushi and Dan Aykroyd); Started on Saturday Night Live and developed into movie classic The Blues Brothers; Paul Shaffer was music director on some tracks. Other Atlantic promo 45s $5 each.* | | | |
| **45s** | | | |
| GIMME SOME LOVIN' (same on both sides) | 1980 | Atlantic 3666 | 10 |
| *(Promo only on blue vinyl)* | | | |
| SOUL MAN (same on both sides) | 1985 | Atlantic 89492 | 5 |
| *May be promo only* | | | |
| **Albums** | | | |
| NEIGHBORS  Interviews with Belushi and Aykroyd | 1981 | | 25 |
| *(Promo-only release, Saturday Night Live related)* | | | |
| **RADIO SHOWS** | | | |
| **Albums** | | | |
| KING BISCUIT FLOWER HOUR (July 80) Live concert | 1980 | DIR/ABC (2) | 100-150 |
| *(Rare radio show)* | | | |
| | | | |
| **BLUES PROJECT, THE** | | | |
| **RADIO SHOWS** | | | |
| **Albums** | | | |
| RETRO ROCK (Aug 82) Live concert | 1982 | Clayton Webster (2) | 85-150 |
| *(Rare concert)* | | | |

| **Title** | **Yr** | **Label, Number** | **NM $** |
|---|---|---|---|

**BLUES TRAVELER**
*A&M promo CD singles not listed $3*
**Compact Discs**

| | | | |
|---|---|---|---|
| 1,000,000 PEOPLE CAN'T BE WRONG | 1995 | A&M 31454 8064 2 (2) | 30 |
| *(Promo-only compilation; one disc contains the album "Four," the other highlights from the first three albums)* | | | |
| RUN-AROUND | 1995 | A&M 31458 8341 2 | 7 |
| *(Their biggest hit to date)* | | | |

**RADIO SHOWS**
**Compact Discs**

| | | | |
|---|---|---|---|
| IN CONCERT (Dec 94) Live concert | 1994 | Westwood One | 30-60 |
| *(With Big Head Todd and the Monsters)* | | | |
| KING BISCUIT FLOWER HOUR (Apr 91) Live concert | 1991 | DIR | 35-70 |
| *(Live concert)* | | | |

**BLUR**
*Promo CD singles $5 each*
**RADIO SHOWS**
**Compact Discs**

| | | | |
|---|---|---|---|
| IN CONCERT-NU ROCK (Sept 94) | 1994 | Westwood One | 15-30 |
| *(Live concert)* | | | |

**BOB & SHERI**
*See BEACH BOYS.*

**BOB B. SOXX AND THE BLUE JEANS**
**Albums**

| | | | |
|---|---|---|---|
| ZIP-A-DEE-DOO-DAH | 1963 | Philles 4002 | 750 |
| *(White promo label)* | | | |

**BODEANS**
*Warner promo vinyl singles $3 each; Slash promo CD singles $6 each*
**12-Inch Singles**

| | | | |
|---|---|---|---|
| DREAMS (same on both sides) | 1987 | Slash PRO-A-2950 | 6 |
| SAY ABOUT LOVE (same on both sides) | 1987 | Reprise PRO-A-2913 | 6 |

**RADIO SHOWS**
**Albums**

| | | | |
|---|---|---|---|
| IN CONCERT (Apr 91) Live concert | 1991 | Westwood One (2) | 40-75 |
| *(Repeated Feb 92)* | | | |
| IN CONCERT (Feb 88) Live concert | 1988 | Westwood One (2) | 25-50 |
| *(Live in concert with Love & Rockets)* | | | |
| IN CONCERT (Feb 88) Live concert | 1988 | Westwood One (2) | 20-35 |
| *(Live in concert with Tragically Hip)* | | | |
| IN CONCERT (Feb 92) Live concert | 1992 | Westwood One (2) | 30-60 |
| *(In concert with RTZ)* | | | |

**BODY COUNT**
**12-Inch Singles**

| | | | |
|---|---|---|---|
| THE WINNER LOSES/FLY BY/ESCAPE FROM THE KILLING FIELDS | 1991 | Sire PRO-A-5680 | 7 |

**BOLTON, MICHAEL**
*Columbia promo singles $2 each*
**RADIO SHOWS**
**Albums**

| | | | |
|---|---|---|---|
| KING BISCUIT FLOWER HOUR (June 83) Live | 1983 | DIR (2) | 25-50 |
| *(Rare live concert, with the Call)* | | | |

**Compact Discs**

| | | | |
|---|---|---|---|
| MICHAEL BOLTON STORY (June 91) Profile | 1991 | Unistar | 10-20 |
| *(Music and interview, repeated Dec 91, June 92)* | | | |
| REACHING OUT (Sept 93) | 1993 | (2) | 25-40 |
| *(Music and interviews)* | | | |

**BON JOVI**
*Mercury promo singles $4-$5 each; Includes Jon Bon Jovi*
**Compact Discs**

| | | | |
|---|---|---|---|
| WANTED DEAD OR ALIVE  with poster and insert | 1987 | Mercury CD7P 01 | 60 |
| *(One of the first promo CD singles)* | | | |

**RADIO SHOWS**
**Albums**

| | | | |
|---|---|---|---|
| BON JOVI (Sept 89) | 1989 | MJI Radio | 30-50 |
| *(Music and interview, rare show)* | | | |
| THE BON JOVI STORY (Sept 89) Green and clear vinyl | 1989 | United Stations (2) | 20-40 |
| *(Music and interview)* | | | |
| METALSHOP (Jan 92) Show #460 | 1992 | MJI Productions | 10-15 |
| *(Interviews with Jon Bon Jovi)* | | | |
| OFF THE RECORD (July 89) Music and interview | 1989 | Westwood One (4) | 10-25 |
| *(Parts 1 and 2)* | | | |
| OFF THE RECORD (July 89) Music and interview | 1989 | Westwood One (2) | 10-15 |
| *(This show repeated several times)* | | | |
| THE REAL DEAL (Jan 88) PROFILE | 1988 | DIR (2) | 20-30 |
| *(Music and interview)* | | | |
| ROCK STARS (Apr 87) PROFILE | 1987 | United Stations (2) | 20-40 |
| *(Some live material)* | | | |
| STORY OF BON JOVI (June 89) Music and interviews | 1989 | Unistar (2) | 15-30 |
| *(This show was repeated)* | | | |

| Title | Yr | Label, Number | NM $ |
|---|---|---|---|
| SUPERSTAR CONCERT BOX SET, Live show | 1987 | Westwood One (3) | 30-60 |
| *(This show repeated several times)* | | | |
| **Compact Discs** | | | |
| I'LL SLEEP WHEN I'M DEAD | 1993 | Media America | 125-175 |
| *(Live concert material, very rare)* | | | |
| MEDIA AMERICA SPECIAL (Mar 93) Music and interview | 1993 | Media America (2) | 30-75 |
| *(Some live material)* | | | |
| OFF THE RECORD (Oct 92) Music and interview | 1992 | Westwood One | 15-20 |
| *(CD version of the show)* | | | |
| UP CLOSE | 1989 | Media America (2) | 40-75 |
| *(Profile with some live music)* | | | |
| UP CLOSE Jon Bon Jovi | 1990 | Media America (2) | 40-75 |
| *(Profile of Bon Jovi the group, some live music)* | | | |

## BOND, EDDIE
*Other Mercury 45s $10-20 each*
**45s**

| | | | |
|---|---|---|---|
| BOPPIN' BONNIE | 1958 | Mercury 70941 | 40 |
| *(White promo label)* | | | |
| ROCKIN' DADDY | 1958 | Mercury 70826 | 40 |
| *(White promo label)* | | | |
| SLIP SLIP SLIPPIN' IN | 1958 | Mercury 70882 | 40 |
| *(White promo label)* | | | |

## BONDS, GARY U.S.
*EMI America promo singles $4 each*
**RADIO SHOWS**
**Albums**

| | | | |
|---|---|---|---|
| BBC ROCK HOUR (Jan 82) Live concert | 1982 | London Wavelength | 40-75 |
| *(Rare concert series)* | | | |
| IN CONCERT  Live concert | 1981 | Westwood One (2) | 50-100 |
| *(With Humble Pie)* | | | |
| KING BISCUIT FLOWER HOUR (June 81) Live concert | 1981 | DIR/ABC (2) | 50-75 |
| *(With Jefferson Starship)* | | | |
| KING BISCUIT FLOWER HOUR (Oct 81) Live concert | 1981 | DIR/ABC (2) | 40-75 |
| *(With Garland Jeffreys)* | | | |

## BONGOS, THE
**12-Inch Singles**

| | | | |
|---|---|---|---|
| BRAND NEW WORLD (TRUE LOVE IS ORDINARY) (Edited) | 1985 | RCA JD-14046 | 8 |
| NUMBERS WITH WINGS (Remixed) (Long)/(Short) | 1983 | RCA JD-13578 | 8 |

## BONHAM
**RADIO SHOWS**
**Albums**

| | | | |
|---|---|---|---|
| IN CONCERT (June 90) Live concert | 1990 | Westwood One (2) | 25-40 |
| *(Live with Robin Trower)* | | | |
| METALSHOP (Aug 92) Show #447 | 1992 | MJI Productions | 10-20 |
| *(Music and interview)* | | | |
| **Reel-to-Reel Tapes** | | | |
| HIGH VOLTAGE (90s) LIVE SEGMENT FEATURES BONHAM | 199? | Westwood One | 15-25 |
| *(Also on the live segment Kik Tracee)* | | | |

## BONHAM, TRACY
**45s**

| | | | |
|---|---|---|---|
| SUNSHINE/50 FT. QUEENIE (A Tribute to PJ Harvey) (Live) | 1995 | Island PR7 7227-7 | 5 |
| *(Marbled light blue vinyl with plastic sleeve)* | | | |

## BONOFF, KARLA
*Columbia promo 45s $4 each*
**Albums**

| | | | |
|---|---|---|---|
| PERSONALLY WITH KARLA BONOFF | 1982 | Columbia AS 1423 | 10 |
| *(Promo only called "Interchords")* | | | |
| **RADIO SHOWS** | | | |
| **Albums** | | | |
| IN CONCERT (Mar 83) Live concert | 1983 | Westwood One (2) | 150-250 |
| *(With Jesse Colin Young)* | | | |

## BONZO DOG BAND, THE
**45s**

| | | | |
|---|---|---|---|
| SLUSH (Mono)/SLUSH (Stereo) | 1972 | United Artists 50943 | 10 |
| *(May be promo only)* | | | |

## BOOMTOWN RATS
*Columbia promo singles $5; Columbia promo LPs $10 With Bob Geldof*
**12-Inch Singles**

| | | | |
|---|---|---|---|
| DRAG ME DOWN (same on both sides) | 1984 | Columbia CAS 2170 | 6 |
| RAT TRAP/JOEY'S ON THE STREET | 1979 | Columbia AS 544 | 15 |
| SKIN ON SKIN/TALKING IN CODE | 1982 | Columbia AS 1565 | 7 |
| UP AL NIGHT/MOOD MAMBO/BANANA REPUBLIC | 1981 | Columbia AS 920 | 7 |
| **RADIO SHOWS** | | | |
| **Albums** | | | |
| BBC COLLEGE CONCERT HOUR (Mar 82) | 1982 | London Wavelength | 40-75 |
| *(Live concert)* | | | |

| Title | Yr | Label, Number | NM $ |
|-------|-----|---------------|------|
| BBC ROCK HOUR (Sept 82) Live concert | 1982 | London Wavelength | 40-75 |
| (With A Flock of Seagulls) | | | |
| BBC TRANSCRIPTION DISC Live concert | 1978 | BBC Transcription | 200-300 |
| (Very rare series) | | | |
| BBC TRANSCRIPTION DISC Live concert | 1985 | BBC Transcription | 175-250 |
| (Also very rare) | | | |
| IN CONCERT (Feb 83) Live concert | 1983 | Westwood One (2) | 50-100 |
| (With A Flock of Seagulls) | | | |
| KING BISCUIT FLOWER HOUR (Apr 80) Live concert | 1980 | DIR/ABC (2) | 75-150 |
| (Also very rare) | | | |

## BOONE, PAT

*Republic white promo label 45s $25 each; Dot white promo labels $7 each; Dot blue promo labels $10 each; Dot black promo labels $5 each; Tetragrammaton white promo labels $4 each; Vista white promo labels $3 each; Capitol promo labels $3 each; Warner promo labels $2 each*

**45s**

| Title | Yr | Label, Number | NM $ |
|-------|-----|---------------|------|
| AMERICAN DENTAL ASSOCIATION  Promo spots | 1973 | ADA DWP 973 | 20 |
| (Pat talks about Dental Sealants! 30-second spot, 7-inch 33 1/3 record) | | | |
| BEACH GIRL White promo label | 1964 | Dot 16658 | 25 |
| (Beach Boys related) | | | |
| COLD COLD HEART | 196? | MB11021 | 25 |
| JUNE IS BUSTIN' OUT ALL OVER  Chevrolet ad | 1958 | Dot | 25 |
| (With narrative by Bob Lund) | | | |
| THE HOSTAGE PRAYER  Promo-only release | 1982 | Lamb & Lion 819 | 10 |
| (Small center hole, white label) | | | |
| WATCHING THE RIVER RUN Promo-only release | 1978 | Warner Bros. PRO-S-720 | 10 |
| (Believe it! This is a disco record!) | | | |
| WHEN I'M FEELING GOOD WITH YOU | 1978 | Warner Bros. PRO-S-743 | 10 |
| (With Debby Boone) | | | |
| WISH YOU WERE HERE, BUDDY White label, red vinyl | 1966 | Dot 16933 | 30 |
| (There is also a black vinyl, white promo label version) | | | |

**RADIO SHOWS**

**16-Inch Transcriptions**

| Title | Yr | Label, Number | NM $ |
|-------|-----|---------------|------|
| MUSIC ON DECK: THE PAT BOONE SHOW (60s) | 196? | U. S. Navy | 15-25 |
| (A weekly series of shows) | | | |
| U. S. ARMY PRESENTS (60s) Host is Pat Boone | 196? | U. S. Army | 10-20 |
| (Shows number 39 and 40 are hosted by Boone) | | | |

**Albums**

| Title | Yr | Label, Number | NM $ |
|-------|-----|---------------|------|
| YOUR NAVY PRESENTS MUSIC ON DECK (Apr 67-Apr 69) | 196? | U. S. Navy | 10-20 |
| (Weekly series of 15-minute shows; price for any one show) | | | |
| YOUR NAVY PRESENTS MUSIC ON DECK (Apr 67-Apr 69) | 1969 | U. S. Navy (52) | 500-750 |
| (A complete collection of all 104 shows) Above "Music on Deck" shows have black labels with yellow print | | | |
| YOUR NAVY PRESENTS MUSIC ON DECK (Apr 69) | 1969 | U. S. Navy | 10-15 |
| (Renumbered new series, white labels with blue print) | | | |

## BOONES, THE

**45s**

| Title | Yr | Label, Number | NM $ |
|-------|-----|---------------|------|
| HASTA MANANA (mono/stereo) | 1977 | Warner Bros. 8385 | 5 |
| (Stock copy not known to exist) | | | |

## BOSTON

*Epic promo singles $4 each; MCA promo singles $3 each; Epic promo LPs $15-20 each*

**45s**

| Title | Yr | Label, Number | NM $ |
|-------|-----|---------------|------|
| WHAT'S IT ALL ABOUT (Feb 77) Public service show | 1977 | W. I. A. A. 355 | 25 |
| (Flip side is Charlie Daniels Band) | | | |
| WHAT'S IT ALL ABOUT (Jan 79) Public service show | 1979 | W. I. A. A. 456 | 25 |
| (Interview with Tom Scholz, flip is Bob Seger) | | | |

**RADIO SHOWS**

**Albums**

| Title | Yr | Label, Number | NM $ |
|-------|-----|---------------|------|
| KING BISCUIT FLOWER HOUR Live concert | 1987 | DIR (2) | 25-40 |
| ("The Best of Boston") | | | |
| THIRD STAGE (May 87) | 1987 | MCA Radio (2) | 25-50 |
| (This is the first program of what developed into the UP CLOSE series on CD from Media America) | | | |

**Compact Discs**

| Title | Yr | Label, Number | NM $ |
|-------|-----|---------------|------|
| IN THE STUDIO  Music and interview | 1994 | Media America | 10-15 |
| (An LP is featured, several shows in the series) | | | |
| KING BISCUIT FLOWER HOUR Live concert | 1988 | DIR | 60-125 |
| (A classic live concert) | | | |
| UP CLOSE Music and interview | 1994 | Media America | 25-50 |
| (This series often includes rare live tracks) | | | |

**Reel-to-Reel Tapes**

| Title | Yr | Label, Number | NM $ |
|-------|-----|---------------|------|
| WALK ON | 1995 | World Premiere | 50-100 |
| (Music and interviews) | | | |

## BOSTON POPS ORCHESTRA (FIEDLER)

**45s**

| Title | Yr | Label, Number | NM $ |
|-------|-----|---------------|------|
| WHITE CHRISTMAS/(B-side unknown) | 1959 | RCA Victor KO7W-1589 | 15 |

## BOURGEOIS TAGG

*Virgin promo 45s $3*

**12-Inch Singles**

| Title | Yr | Label, Number | NM $ |
|-------|-----|---------------|------|
| I DON'T MIND AT ALL (same on both sides) | 1987 | Island 2098 | 5 |

**RADIO SHOWS**

**Compact Discs**

| Title | Yr | Label, Number | NM $ |
|-------|-----|---------------|------|
| IN CONCERT (June 88) Live concert | 1988 | Westwood One (2) | 15-25 |
| (With Henry Lee Summer) | | | |

| Title | Yr | Label, Number | NM $ |
|---|---|---|---|
| KING BISCUIT FLOWER HOUR (Jan 88) | 1988 | DIR | 10-20 |
| *(Live concert)* | | | |

**BOW WOW WOW**
*RCA Victor promo 45s $5 each*
**12-Inch Singles**

| | | | |
|---|---|---|---|
| DO YOU WANNA HOLD ME? (Long)/(Short) | 1983 | RCA JD-13535 | 16 |

**45s**

| | | | |
|---|---|---|---|
| THE MILE HIGH CLUB/C-30. C-60, C-90, GO! | 1981 | Studio 54 | 20 |
| *(Promo for show)* | | | |

**RADIO SHOWS**
**Albums**

| | | | |
|---|---|---|---|
| RCA RADIO SERIES Music and interview | 1981 | RCA Victor 4193 | 20 |
| *(Promotional series released by their record company)* | | | |

**BOWIE, DAVID**
*Includes Tin Machine. RCA promo 45s with long/short versions $12 each; RCA promo 45s before 74-0605 $10 each; RCA promo 45s after 10320 $8 each; EMI promo 45s $3-5 each; RCA 12" promo singles $15 each; EMI 12" promo singles $10 each.*
**12-Inch Singles**

| Title | Yr | Label, Number | NM $ |
|---|---|---|---|
| BEAUTY AND THE BEAST | 1977 | RCA 11204 | 20 |
| *(Issued with a picture cover)* | | | |
| BLACK TIE WHITE NOISE (7 versions) | 1993 | Savage 50045 | 15 |
| BLUE JEAN/DANCING WITH THE BIG BOYS | 1984 | EMI America SPRO-9222 | 15 |
| CAT PEOPLE | 1982 | Backstreet L33-1759 | 15 |
| *(Issued with a picture cover)* | | | |
| CHINA GIRL (LONG)/SHAKE IT (LONG) | 1983 | EMI America SPRO-9952 | 15 |
| DAY IN DAY OUT (same on both sides) | 1987 | EMI America SPRO-9985 | 10 |
| DAY IN DAY OUT (4 versions) | 1987 | EMI America SPRO-9996 | 15 |
| FAME 90 (4 mixes) | 1990 | EMI SPRO-04532 | 15 |
| FASHION (long)/FASHION (short) | 1981 | RCA JD-12140 | 12 |
| HEROES | 1977 | RCA 11151 | 25 |
| *(Not issued with a picture cover)* | | | |
| JUMP THEY SAY (5 versions)/PALLAS ATHENA | 1993 | Savage 50039 | 15 |
| LET'S DANCE (same on both sides) | 1983 | EMI America SPRO-9904 | 12 |
| NEVER LET ME DOWN (same on both sides) | 1987 | EMI America SPRO-79090 | 12 |
| PETER AND THE WOLF (Part 1)/PETER AND THE WOLF (Part 2) | 1978 | RCA JD-11306 | 30 |
| SPACE ODDITY/ASHES TO ASHES (2 versions) | 1980 | RCA DJL1-3795 | 20 |
| *(Without stamps)* | | | |
| SPACE ODDITY/ASHES TO ASHES (2 versions) | 1980 | RCA DJL1-3795 | 30 |
| *(With set of stamps)* | | | |
| STAR/WHAT IN THE WORLD/BREAKING GLASS | 1978 | RCA DJL1-3255 | 25 |
| *(White vinyl promo)* | | | |
| TONIGHT (same on both sides) | 1984 | EMI America SPRO-9295 | 15 |
| UNDERGROUND (Long)/UNDERGROUND (Short) | 1986 | EMI America SPRO 9670 | 12 |
| UP THE HILL BACKWARDS | 1980 | RCA 12249 | 20 |
| *(Issued with a picture cover)* | | | |

**45s**

| Title | Yr | Label, Number | NM $ |
|---|---|---|---|
| ABSOLUTE BEGINNERS | 1985 | EMI 7PRO 9627 | 15 |
| *(Promo-only versions)* | | | |
| ALL THE MADMEN  White promo label | 1970 | Mercury DJ-311 | 100 |
| *(Promo-only release)* | | | |
| ASHES TO ASHES | 1980 | RCA 12078 | 15 |
| *(Price includes promo picture sleeve)* | | | |
| BLUE JEAN | 1984 | EMI 8231 | 12 |
| *(Blue vinyl; some stock copies are blue vinyl also)* | | | |
| CAN'T HELP THINKING ABOUT ME | 1967 | Warner Bros 5815 | 200 |
| *(White promo label, stock copies are much more valuable)* | | | |
| CAT PEOPLE | 1983 | Backstreet S45-1767 | 15 |
| *(3:16 version, issued in white sleeve w/printed insert)* | | | |
| CAT PEOPLE | 1983 | Backstreet 12805 | 50 |
| *(Picture disc; with a "filmex" back)* | | | |
| CAT PEOPLE | 1983 | Backstreet 12805 | 50 |
| *(Picture disc; without the "filmex" back)* | | | |
| CAT PEOPLE | 1983 | Backstreet 52024 | 10 |
| *(4:08 version, issued in picture sleeve)* | | | |
| DANCING IN THE STREETS | 1985 | EMI (no#) | 12 |
| *(Common test pressing, no title or artist listed)* | | | |
| DAY IN DAY OUT | 1987 | EMI 8380 | 20 |
| *(Colored vinyl, part of a box set)* | | | |
| FASHION/IT'S NO GAME/TEENAGE WILDLIFE | 1980 | RCA JE-12087 | 400 |
| JOE THE LION Cream-colored label | 1979 | RCA 11887 | 15 |
| *("John, I'm Only Dancing - 72" is other side)* | | | |
| LOVE YOU TILL TUESDAY | 1968 | Deram 85016 | 50 |
| *(White promo label)* | | | |
| MAN WHO SOLD THE WORLD  By Lulu | 1973 | Chelsea 3001 | 40 |
| *(Bowie does backing vocals, that information is not on label)* | | | |
| MEMORY OF A FREE FESTIVAL  White promo label | 1970 | Mercury 73075 | 50 |
| *(Same song on both sides)* | | | |
| MODERN LOVE | 1983 | EMI 501219 | 12 |
| *(Test pressing, no artist listed, two versions of song including one live)* | | | |
| RUBBER BAND | 1968 | Deram 85009 | 60 |
| *(White promo label)* | | | |
| SAVE THE CHILDREN Public service ads | 1984 | DWP 956 | 25 |
| *(Bowie does 30-second ad, cut #5 on 7-inch 33)* | | | |
| SPACE ODDITY  White promo label | 1969 | Mercury 72949 | 50 |
| *(Same song on both sides)* | | | |

| Title | Yr | Label, Number | NM $ |
|---|---|---|---|
| SPACE ODDITY White promo label | 1969 | Mercury DJ-156 | 50 |
| *(Promo-only version)* | | | |
| THE LAUGHING GNOME | 1973 | London 20079 | 50 |
| *(White promo label)* | | | |
| WHAT'S IT ALL ABOUT (Nov 80) Public service program | 1980 | W. I. A. A. 547 | 40 |
| *(Music and interviews, flip is Frank Zappa)* | | | |
| WHITE LIGHT, WHITE HEAT | 1983 | RCA 13660 | 10 |
| *(Cream-colored label, price includes promo picture sleeve)* | | | |
| **7-Inch Extended Plays** | | | |
| DAVID BOWIE | 1972 | RCA EP-45-103 | 25 |
| *(Promo-only record release with promo-only picture cover, yellow label)* | | | |
| **Albums** | | | |
| 1980 ALL CLEAR | 1980 | RCA Victor DJL1-3545 | 20 |
| BOWIE NOW | 1978 | RCA Victor DJL1-2697 | 75 |
| DAVID BOWIE | 1968 | Deram 18003 | 150 |
| *(White promo label)* | | | |
| DAVID BOWIE INTERVIEW | 198? | RCA Victor 3840 | 40 |
| *(Promo-only release)* | | | |
| DAVID BOWIE, MAN OF WORDS, MAN OF MUSIC | 1969 | Mercury 61246 | 200 |
| *(White promo label)* | | | |
| AN EVENING WITH DAVID BOWIE | 1978 | RCA Victor DJL1-3016 | 50 |
| *(Live concert for "Superstars Radio Network")* | | | |
| LET'S TALK | 1983 | EMI America SPRO 9960/9961 | 25 |
| *(Promo-only interview album)* | | | |
| MAN WHO SOLD THE WORLD | 1970 | Mercury 61325 | 100 |
| *(White promo label)* | | | |
| NEVER LET ME DOWN: THE INTERVIEW | 1987 | EMI America SPRO-79112/3 | 25 |
| RISE AND FALL OF ZIGGY STARDUST AND THE SPIDERS FROM MARS | 1990 | Ryko Analogue LSD-4702 | 100 |
| *(Special promo-only package with both the LP and CD versions)* | | | |
| SCARY MONSTERS INTERVIEW | 1980 | RCA Victor DJL1-3840 | 20 |
| SPECIAL RADIO SERIES, VOLUME 1 | 1980 | RCA Victor DJL1-3829 | 25 |
| STAR | 1981 | RCA Victor 3255 | 40 |
| *(White vinyl 12-incher with picture cover; also considered a 12" single)* | | | |
| ZIG ZAG FESTIVAL Promo only, white label | 1970 | Mercury SRD2-29 (2) | 50 |
| *(With other artists)* | | | |
| ZIGGY STARDUST, THE MOTION PICTURE | 1983 | RCA Victor CPL2-4862 | 50 |
| *(Promo version on clear vinyl)* | | | |
| **Compact Discs** | | | |
| BANG BANG | 1987 | EMI | 40 |
| *(Promo-only release)* | | | |
| NEVER LET ME DOWN | 1988 | EMI 31352 | 50 |
| *(Promo-only release)* | | | |
| **RADIO SHOWS** | | | |
| **Albums** | | | |
| BBC BOWIE SPECIAL (Apr 81) Live concert | 1981 | London Wavelength | 40-75 |
| *(BBC concert material)* | | | |
| GOLDEN YEAR SPECIAL (Feb 84) | 1984 | DIR (3) | 60-80 |
| *(A profile of David Bowie)* | | | |
| IN CONCERT (Sept 89) Live concert | 1989 | Westwood One (2) | 75 |
| *(Concert features Tin Machine)* | | | |
| INSIDE TRACK (80s) | 198? | Inside Track (3) | 30-50 |
| *(Music and interview)* | | | |
| KING BISCUIT FLOWER HOUR (80s) Live concert | 198? | DIR/ABC (2) | 45-75 |
| *(Repeated show)* | | | |
| KING BISCUIT FLOWER HOUR (80s) Live concert | 198? | DIR/ABC (2) | 75-150 |
| *(Repeated show)* | | | |
| KING BISCUIT FLOWER HOUR (Jan 80) Live concert | 1980 | DIR/ABC (2) | 80-150 |
| *("John, I'm Only Dreaming" retrospective)* | | | |
| LEGENDS OF ROCK Parts 1 and 2 | 1987 | NBC Radio (4) | 50-75 |
| *(Two weekly 2LP sets)* | | | |
| OFF THE RECORD Parts 1 and 2 | 1990 | Westwood One (4) | 25-40 |
| *(Vinyl version of two shows)* | | | |
| RCA RADIO SERIES Profile | 1981 | RCA Victor | 25-50 |
| *(Part of a series of artist profiles from RCA)* | | | |
| RETRO ROCK (Oct 83) | 1983 | Clayton Webster (2) | 100-150 |
| *(Show repeated in 1984)* | | | |
| ROCK AROUND THE WORLD (May 77) | 1977 | RATW | 100-200 |
| *(Live concert)* | | | |
| ROYALTY OF ROCK  Music and interview | 1983 | RKO Radio | 25 |
| *(This show has been repeated)* | | | |
| SUPER GROUPS (Nov 83) | 1983 | Westwood One (3) | 100-150 |
| *(Much live material)* | | | |
| SUPERSTAR CONCERT (90s) | 199? | Westwood One (3) | 50-100 |
| *(Repeat shows)* | | | |
| TIMOTHY WHITE SESSIONS (Apr 90) Live | 1990 | Westwood One (2) | 50-75 |
| *(This show was also repeated)* | | | |
| WESTWOOD ONE SPECIAL (Sept 89) Live | 1989 | Westwood One (2) | 75-150 |
| *(Featured is Tin Machine)* | | | |
| **Compact Discs** | | | |
| ALBUM NETWORK (Feb 97) | 1997 | Album Network | 75-100 |
| *(With exclusive acoustic tracks and other live tracks)* | | | |
| BBC CLASSIC TRACKS (May 91) Live material | 1991 | London Wavelength | 50-80 |
| *(Repeated several times)* | | | |
| GLASS SPIDER CONCERT SPECIAL (Oct 87) | 1987 | (4) | 400-750 |
| *(Rare live concert)* | | | |
| IN CONCERT-NU ROCK (Dec 93) Live concert | 1993 | Westwood One (2) | 75-100 |
| *(New concert material)* | | | |

| Title | Yr | Label, Number | NM $ |
|---|---|---|---|
| KING BISCUIT FLOWER HOUR (87-88) Live concert | 1987 | DIR (2) | 45-75 |
| *(Two CD concert)* | | | |
| KING BISCUIT FLOWER HOUR (Dec 94) Live concert | 1994 | DIR (2) | 75-150 |
| *(Repeated show)* | | | |
| MASTERS OF ROCK (July 90) | 1990 | Radio Ventures (2) | 60-100 |
| *(Profile, music and interview)* | | | |
| OFF THE RECORD (Apr 93) Parts 1 and 2 | 1993 | Westwood One (2) | 25-45 |
| *(CD version of two shows)* | | | |
| OFF THE RECORD (Sept 93) | 1993 | Westwood One | 15-25 |
| *(Music and interviews, single show)* | | | |
| ON THE EDGE (Dec 93) Music and interview | 1993 | Westwood One | 20-30 |
| *(Profile on Bowie)* | | | |
| ON THE EDGE (May 93) Music and interview | 1993 | Westwood One | 15-25 |
| *(Also featured: Aimee Mann, Radiohead and the Posies)* | | | |
| ONE ON ONE (May 93) Music and interviews | 1993 | | 40-75 |
| *(Hard show to find)* | | | |
| SUPERSTAR CONCERT (Apr 92) Live concert | 1992 | Westwood One (2) | 60-100 |
| *(Repeat shows)* | | | |
| UP CLOSE | 1995 | Media America (2) | 45-75 |
| *(Music and interviews)* | | | |
| UP CLOSE  Profile with some live tracks | 1993 | Media America (2) | 60-100 |
| *(Repeat shows)* | | | |
| **Reel-to-Reel Tapes** | | | |
| KING BISCUIT FLOWER HOUR (Apr 76) Live concert | 1976 | DIR/ABC | 100-200 |
| *(90-minute concert on two reels)* | | | |
| RARITIES (Nov 81) Various artists, on reel | 1981 | Technisonic Studios | 25-40 |
| *(Show #30 is Bowie singing "Space Oddity" in Italian)* | | | |

## BOX OF FROGS
*Epic white promo label 45s $5 each*
**RADIO SHOWS**
**Albums**

| | | | |
|---|---|---|---|
| BBC ROCK HOUR (Sept 84) | 1984 | London Wavelength | 25-35 |
| *(Live concert)* | | | |

## BOY GEORGE
**12-Inch Singles**

| | | | |
|---|---|---|---|
| DON'T TAKE MY MIND ON A TRIP (4 versions)/GIRLFRIEND | 1989 | Virgin 1292 | 8 |
| EVERYTHING I OWN (3 versions)/USE ME | 1987 | Virgin 1052 | 7 |
| LIVE MY LIFE (4 versions) | 1988 | Virgin 1116 | 7 |
| WHISPER (Edit)/WHISPER (LP version) | 1989 | Virgin 2994 | 6 |
| YOU'VE FOUND ANOTHER GUY (3 versions)/I GO WHERE I GO | 1989 | Virgin 1353 | 6 |

## BOY HOWDY
*Curb promo CD singles $3 each*
**RADIO SHOWS**
**Compact Discs**

| | | | |
|---|---|---|---|
| CRAZY HORSE (Aug 94) Live concert | 1994 | | 25-40 |
| *(Live concert material)* | | | |
| SUMMER CONCERT SERIES (July 94) Live concert | 1994 | Westwood One | 40-80 |
| *(In concert with John Anderson)* | | | |

## BOYZ II MEN
**Albums**

| | | | |
|---|---|---|---|
| II | 1994 | Motown 31453 0323-1 | 25 |
| *(Vinyl is promo only; in Motown company cover)* | | | |

## BRAINS, THE
**12-Inch Singles**

| | | | |
|---|---|---|---|
| DREAM LIFE/EYES OF ICE/ASPHALT WONDERLAND/NO TEARS TONIGHT | 1980 | Mercury MK 166 | 15 |
| MONEY CHANGES EVERYTHING/GOLD DUST KIDS | 1980 | Mercury MK 140 | 15 |

## BRAMLETT, DELANEY
**45s**

| | | | |
|---|---|---|---|
| ARE YOU A BEATLE OR A ROLLING STONE | 1974 | Columbia 45950 | 10 |

## BRANDYWINE CHORALE, THE
**45s**

| | | | |
|---|---|---|---|
| CHRISTMAS IS HERE NOW/THE OLD BELL RINGER | 1964 | Coral 98126 | 10 |

## BRANIGAN, LAURA
*Other Atlantic promo singles $2*
**45s**

| | | | |
|---|---|---|---|
| FOOL'S AFFAIR (same on both sides) | 1980 | Atlantic 3770 | 5 |
| *(May be promo only)* | | | |
| LOOKING OUT FOR NUMBER ONE (same on both sides) | 1981 | Atlantic 3807 | 5 |
| *(May be promo only)* | | | |
| LUCKY ONE, THE | 1984 | Atlantic PR 632 | 10 |
| *(With insert)* | | | |
| TELL HIM (same on both sides) | 1981 | Atlantic 3846 | 5 |
| *(May be promo only)* | | | |

**RADIO SHOWS**
**Albums**

| | | | |
|---|---|---|---|
| STARTRACK PROFILE (Jan 85) | 1985 | Unistar (2) | 50-100 |
| *(Live concert)* | | | |

| Title | Yr | Label, Number | NM $ |
|---|---|---|---|

**BRANNEN, JOHN**
*Mercury promo CD singles $3 each*
**RADIO SHOWS**
**Albums**

| | | | |
|---|---|---|---|
| IN CONCERT (Apr 88) Live concert | 1988 | Westwood One (2) | 25-35 |

*(In concert with the Hooters)*

**BRANT, BOBBY**
**45s**

| | | | |
|---|---|---|---|
| PIANO NELLIE | 1958 | East West 124 | 40 |

*(White promo label)*

**BREAD**
*Featuring David Gates. Elektra promo 45s $4 each.*
**45s**

| | | | |
|---|---|---|---|
| WHAT'S IT ALL ABOUT (May 77) Public service show | 1977 | W. I. A. A. 372 | 15 |

*(With David Gates, flip is Bay City Rollers)*
**Albums**

| | | | |
|---|---|---|---|
| BREAD | 1971 | Elektra BRD-1 | 20 |

*(In-store sampler; very similar to the future LP "The Best of Bread")*
**RADIO SHOWS**
**Albums**

| | | | |
|---|---|---|---|
| ROBERT W. MORGAN  Music and interview | 1976 | Watermark | 25-50 |

*(Repeated in 1977)*

**BREAKS, THE**
**12-Inch Singles**

| | | | |
|---|---|---|---|
| SHE WANTS YOU | 1983 | RCA JD-13583 | 10 |

**BREATHE**
*A&M promo singles $3*
**RADIO SHOWS**
**Albums**

| | | | |
|---|---|---|---|
| BREATHE SPECIAL (Oct 90) PROFILE | 1990 | Unistar (2) | 10-20 |

*(Music and interviews)*

**BREEDERS, THE**
*Elektra promo CD singles $6*
**Compact Discs**

| | | | |
|---|---|---|---|
| SECRET HISTORY OF THE BREEDERS | 1994 | Elektra PRCD 8934-2 | 15 |

*(Music and interview)*
**RADIO SHOWS**
**Compact Discs**

| | | | |
|---|---|---|---|
| IN CONCERT-NU ROCK (Jan 95) | 1995 | Westwood One | 10-15 |

*(Live concert)*

| | | | |
|---|---|---|---|
| ON THE EDGE (Oct 93) Music and interviews | 1993 | | 10-15 |

*(With Pearl Jam and Big Country)*

**BRENDA AND THE TABULATIONS**
**45s**

| | | | |
|---|---|---|---|
| AND MY HEART SANG | 196? | Top & Bottom 403 | 10 |

*(One-sided promo)*

**BRENT, RANDY, AND THE HIGHWAY SERENADERS**
**45s**

| | | | |
|---|---|---|---|
| WHAT I WANT FOR CHRISTMAS, IS CHRISTMAS/CANDLES IN HEAVEN | 19?? | Highway 1007 | 5 |

**BREWER, TERESA**
**45s**

| | | | |
|---|---|---|---|
| TAKE A MESSAGE TO JESUS (same on both sides) | 198? | Teresa Brewer TB-1 | 4 |

**BRITT, ELTON**
*RCA Victor white label promo 45s $10 each; ABC Paramount white label promos $5 each; ABC Paramount white label promo LPs $18 each*
**Albums**

| | | | |
|---|---|---|---|
| THE WANDERING COWBOY | 1959 | ABC-Paramount 293 | 25 |

*(White promo label)*

| | | | |
|---|---|---|---|
| THOSE FABULOUS BEVERLY HILLBILLIES | 1961 | RAR-Arts 1000 | 50 |

*(Gold vinyl; made-up group featuring Britt and Zeke Manners)*

**BRONSKI BEAT**
**12-Inch Singles**

| | | | |
|---|---|---|---|
| RUN FROM LOVE/HARD RAIN | 1985 | MCA 17063 | 12 |

**BROOKS, ALBERT**
**45s**

| | | | |
|---|---|---|---|
| A DADDY'S CHRISTMAS (mono/stereo) | 1974 | Asylum XMAS 1 | 150 |

*(With picture sleeve)*

**BROOKS, GARTH**
*Other Capitol promo 45s $5 each; Liberty/Capitol Nashville promo CD singles $6; Liberty/Capitol Nashville jukebox 45s (black vinyl) $4 each*
**45s**

| | | | |
|---|---|---|---|
| CALLING BATON ROUGE | 1994 | Liberty 18136 | 10 |

*(For jukeboxes only, colored vinyl)*

| Title | Yr | Label, Number | NM $ |
|---|---|---|---|
| IF TOMORROW NEVER COMES | 1989 | Capitol PB-44430 | 10 |
| (White promo label) | | | |
| LEARNING TO LIVE AGAIN | 1992 | Liberty 56973 | 10 |
| (For jukeboxes only, red vinyl) | | | |
| **Compact Discs** | | | |
| CD ZOOMING | 1994 | Liberty DPRO-79070 | 30 |
| (Contains excerpts of every song he had released to that time; was supposed to be a giveaway with "The Hits" CD but it was delayed, so it was only available by mail order) | | | |
| ENTERTAINER OF THE YEAR | 1994 | Liberty (no number) | 40 |
| (Fold-open press kit with attached copies of both The Hits and CD Zooming) | | | |
| GARTH BROOKS COLLECTION | 1994 | Liberty 17959 | 25 |
| (Available only at McDonald's) | | | |
| GOTTA DRIVE  With Steve Wariner | 1993 | Arista 2638 | 20 |
| (Garth and Steve discuss Steve's new LP) | | | |
| INTERVIEW FOR IN PIECES ALBUM | 1993 | Liberty DPRO-79004 | 25 |
| (Promo-only 30-minute interview for album) | | | |
| LIMITED SERIES SAMPLER | 1998 | Capitol Nashville DPRO-????? | 40 |
| (Contains the six new songs on the box set; price on this varies widely, but almost always goes for more than the entire box set does!) | | | |
| **RADIO SHOWS** | | | |
| **Compact Discs** | | | |
| ENTERTAINER OF THE YEAR (May 92) | 1992 | Unistar | 10-20 |
| (Music and interview profile) | | | |
| GARTH BROOKS STORY | 1996 | (3) | 10-25 |
| (With acoustic and live tracks) | | | |
| RECORD COMPANY Music and interview | 1994 | | 10-20 |
| (A profile of the artist) | | | |

## BROTHER CANE
**RADIO SHOWS**
**Compact Discs**

| Title | Yr | Label, Number | NM $ |
|---|---|---|---|
| IN CONCERT (Aug 93) Live concert | 1993 | Westwood One | 30-50 |
| (Live with Dire Straits) | | | |
| IN CONCERT (May 94) Live concert | 1994 | Westwood One | 20-30 |
| (Repeated Nov 93, May 94) | | | |
| IN CONCERT (Feb 95) | 1995 | Westwood One | 25-35 |
| (Live concert) | | | |
| SUPERSTAR CONCERT (Dec 93) | 1993 | Westwood One (2) | 25-35 |
| (Live concert) | | | |

## BROTHER PHELPS
**RADIO SHOWS**
**Compact Discs**

| Title | Yr | Label, Number | NM $ |
|---|---|---|---|
| COUNTRY CUTTING EDGE (Nov 93) | 1993 | | 20-25 |
| (Mostly music and interviews) | | | |

## BROTHERS FOUR, THE
**45s**

| Title | Yr | Label, Number | NM $ |
|---|---|---|---|
| CHRISTMAS IS A 'COMIN' | 1965 | Columbia JZSP 116423 | 10 |
| (Special holiday release to radio) | | | |
| DON'T LET THE RAIN COME DOWN | 1964 | Columbia JZSP 78861 | 10 |
| (Brown vinyl) | | | |

## BROUGHTON, EDGAR
**RADIO SHOWS**
**Albums**

| Title | Yr | Label, Number | NM $ |
|---|---|---|---|
| BBC TRANSCRIPTION DISC  Live concert | 1976 | BBC Transcription | 75-100 |
| (Rare live concert series) | | | |

## BROWN, HYLO
*Capitol promo 45s $8 each*
**Albums**

| Title | Yr | Label, Number | NM $ |
|---|---|---|---|
| HYLO BROWN | 1950 | Capitol 1168 | 45 |
| (Capitol promo label) | | | |

## BROWN, JAMES
*Federal white label promo 45s $35 each; King white and yellow label promo 45s $5-10 each*
**45s**

| Title | Yr | Label, Number | NM $ |
|---|---|---|---|
| WHAT'S IT ALL ABOUT (May 80) Public service show | 1980 | W. I. A. A. 517 | 30 |
| (Flip side features The Who) | | | |
| **7-Inch Extended Plays** | | | |
| GRITS & SOUL Jukebox LLP | 1967 | SMASH 703 | 25 |
| (Issued with a hard cover) | | | |
| JB PLAYS NEW BREED Jukebox LLP | 1967 | SMASH 707 | 25 |
| (Issued with a hard cover) | | | |
| LIVE AT THE APOLLO Jukebox special | 1963 | King 826 | 250 |
| (Blue label, issued with a paper sleeve, for jukeboxes) | | | |
| PLEASE, PLEASE, PLEASE  White promo label | 1959 | King 430 | 200 |
| (Promo not issued with cover) | | | |
| **Albums** | | | |
| LIVE AT THE APOLLO | 1963 | King 826 | 500 |
| (White label promo with timing strip on front cover) | | | |
| PURE DYNAMITE! LIVE AT THE ROYAL | 1964 | King 883 | 800 |
| (White label promo; banded for airplay) | | | |

## BROWN, ROY
*Imperial cream-colored promo 45s $15 each*

| Title | Yr | Label, Number | NM $ |
|---|---|---|---|

**BROWN, RUTH**
*Atlantic white promo label 45s $15-30 each depending on year; Decca pink label promo 45s $12 each*

**BROWN, T. GRAHAM**
*Capitol promo 45s $2 each*
**RADIO SHOWS**
**Albums**

| | | | |
|---|---|---|---|
| AMERICAN EAGLE (Aug 86) Live concert | 1986 | Westwood One | 40-60 |

*(In concert live show)*
**Compact Discs**

| | | | |
|---|---|---|---|
| WESTWOOD ONE PRESENTS | 1993 | Westwood One | 25-40 |

*(Live concert)*

**BROWNE, JACKSON**
*Asylum promo 45s $3 each; Asylum promo 12" singles $12 each; Asylum white label promo LPs $12 each*
**12-Inch Singles**

| | | | |
|---|---|---|---|
| BEFORE THE DELUGE  33 rpm | 1979 | Asylum 11442 | 300 |

*(Must be the 33rpm version)*

| | | | |
|---|---|---|---|
| BEFORE THE DELUGE  45 rpm | 1979 | Asylum 11442 | 75 |

*(Must be the 45rpm version; flip side, actually the "A" side of this 12" single, is Bruce Springsteen's "Devil with a Blue Dress Medley")*

| | | | |
|---|---|---|---|
| IN THE SHAPE OF A HEART | 1986 | Asylum 5138 | 10 |

*(Heart-shaped red vinyl)*

| | | | |
|---|---|---|---|
| STAY; THE LOAD-OUT/STAY White promo label, 45RPM | 1977 | Asylum 11389 | 15 |

*(Classic 8:51 version on the B side)*
**Albums**

| | | | |
|---|---|---|---|
| FOR EVERYMAN | 1973 | Asylum 5067 | 25 |

*(White promo label)*
**Compact Discs**

| | | | |
|---|---|---|---|
| RETROSPECTIVE | 1993 | Elektra PRCD 8851-2 (2) | 75 |

*(Promo-only greatest hits CD packaged with then-current release "I'm Alive")*
**RADIO SHOWS**
**Albums**

| | | | |
|---|---|---|---|
| IN CONCERT (Dec 90) Live concert | 1990 | Westwood One (2) | 25-40 |
| *(Repeated show)* | | | |
| OFF THE RECORD (Oct 89) Music and interview | 1989 | Westwood One (2) | 15-20 |
| *(Repeated several times)* | | | |
| POP CONCERT (Apr 87) Live concert | 1987 | Westwood One (2) | 100-200 |
| *(Rare live concert, rare series)* | | | |
| SOUNDS LIKE THE NAVY | 1975 | U.S. Navy (2) | 20-25 |
| SUPERSTAR CONCERT  Box set, live | 1986 | Westwood One (3) | 30-50 |
| *(Repeated several times)* | | | |
| SUPERSTAR CONCERT (Sept 90) Box set, live | 1990 | Westwood One (3) | 30-40 |

*(In concert with Eddie Money)*
**Cassettes**

| | | | |
|---|---|---|---|
| COLUMBIA RECORDS RADIO HOUR | 1996 | Columbia | 150-250 |

*(With Heather Nova, rare series)*
**Compact Discs**

| | | | |
|---|---|---|---|
| IN THE STUDIO (Jan 93) Music and interview | 1993 | Album Network | 15-20 |
| *(Profile of an album)* | | | |
| UP CLOSE Two-CD set, music and interview | 1994 | Media America | 40-80 |

*(Some live material)*

**BROWNS, THE**
*RCA Victor promo singles $3 each*
**45s**

| | | | |
|---|---|---|---|
| DRAGGIN' MAIN STREET Black promo label | 1957 | Fabor 118 | 40 |
| *(DJ sample, features Jim Edward and Maxine Brown)* | | | |
| HERE TODAY AND GONE TOMORROW Black promo label | 1957 | Fabor 126 | 20 |
| *(DJ sample, features Jim Edward, Maxine and Bonnie Brown)* | | | |
| LOOKING BACK TO SEE Black promo label | 1957 | Fabor 107 | 25 |
| *(DJ sample, features Jim Edward and Maxine Brown)* | | | |
| THE GRASS IS GREENER Black promo label | 1957 | Fabor 129 | 20 |

*(By the Abbott Singers, who are Jim Edward, Maxine and Bonnie Brown with Dido Rowley and Lafawn Paul)*
**Albums**

| | | | |
|---|---|---|---|
| JIM EDWARD, MAXINE & BONNIE BROWN | 1957 | RCA Victor 1438 | 50 |

*(White promo label)*

**BRUBECK, DAVE**
*Columbia white label promo 45s $2 each; Columbia white label promo LPs $10-30 depending on year*

**BRUCE, JACK**
*Also see Cream*
**RADIO SHOWS**
**Albums**

| | | | |
|---|---|---|---|
| BBC TRANSCRIPTION DISC Live concert | 1977 | BBC Transcription | 200-300 |
| *(Rare concert, rare series)* | | | |
| KING BISCUIT FLOWER HOUR | 1985 | DIR | 20-40 |

*(Live concert)*
**Compact Discs**

| | | | |
|---|---|---|---|
| KING BISCUIT FLOWER HOUR (Mar 90) Live concert | 1990 | DIR | 30-50 |

*(With J. Geils Band)*

| Title | Yr | Label, Number | NM $ |
|---|---|---|---|
| **BRUCE, LENNY** | | | |
| **7-Inch Extended Plays** | | | |
| CURRAN THEATRE CONCERT | 1958 | Fantasy 2 | 25 |
| *(Promo-only release)* | | | |
| THE LAW, LANGUAGE AND LENNY BRUCE | 1974 | Warner-Spector PRO 598 | 40 |
| *(Promo-only release; includes sleeve and insert)* | | | |
| **Albums** | | | |
| LENNY BRUCE | 1958 | Fantasy 1 | 75 |
| *(Promo-only release)* | | | |
| | | | |
| **BRYANT, JIMMY** | | | |
| *Capitol white label promo 45s $5 each* | | | |
| **Albums** | | | |
| TWO GUITARS COUNTRY STYLE | 1954 | Capitol 520 | 55 |
| *("For Radio and TV use only")* | | | |
| | | | |
| **BUBBLE PUPPY, THE** | | | |
| *Other promo 45s $10 each* | | | |
| **45s** | | | |
| WHAT DO YOU SEE Green vinyl | 1970 | International Artists 138 | 50 |
| *(Colored vinyl version is a promo only)* | | | |
| **Albums** | | | |
| A GATHERING OF PROMISES | 1969 | International Artists 10 | 85 |
| *(White promo label)* | | | |
| | | | |
| **BUCHANAN AND GOODMAN / DICKIE GOODMAN** | | | |
| *Also includes listings of Dickie Goodman; Buchanan and Cella. Rainy Wednesday white label promo Dickie Goodman 45s $10 each* | | | |
| **45s** | | | |
| ATTACK OF THE Z-MONSTER White label | 1984 | Z100 100 | 25 |
| *(Promo only for use around the New York area)* | | | |
| BACK TO EARTH | 1956 | Luniverse 101X | 200 |
| *(Cut-in, general release as "The Flying Saucer")* | | | |
| ELECTION '80 White promo label | 1980 | Prelude 8018 | 12 |
| *(Goodman also recorded a non-promo "Election '84")* | | | |
| HEY E. T. | 1982 | Montage 1220 | 10 |
| *(Produced by Susan Goodman; actually more scarce on stock copy than promo)* | | | |
| KONG White promo label | 1977 | Shock 6 | 10 |
| *(Promo copies of any Goodman record are hard to find)* | | | |
| LUNA TRIP | 1969 | Cotique 173 | 35 |
| *(Very rare as a promo, same colors as stock copy)* | | | |
| MR. JAWS White promo label | 1975 | Cash 451 | 10 |
| *(Goodman's biggest hit as solo artist)* | | | |
| ON CAMPUS | 1969 | Cotique 158 | 35 |
| *(Very rare as a promo, same colors as stock copy)* | | | |
| PUBLIC OPINION | 1956 | Luniverse 102X | Unknown |
| *(Unknown unless some promo copies were pressed)* | | | |
| RUSSIAN BANDSTAND Spencer and Spencer | 1959 | Argo 5331 | 25 |
| *(White promo label, Goodman & Shorr)* | | | |
| STAR WARTS White promo label | 1977 | Janus 271 | 15 |
| *(Goodman's version of "Star Wars")* | | | |
| STRING ALONG WITH PAL-O-MINE Buchanan and Cella | 1959 | ABC Paramount 10033 | 20 |
| *(Not a cut-in)* | | | |
| THE MODIFY THE Hi-Lads (Ramal & Goodman) | 1969 | Capitol 2470 | 25 |
| *(Not a cut-in)* | | | |
| THE PURPLE PEOPLE EATER White promo label | 1973 | Rainy Wednesday 204 | 12 |
| *(Not a cut-in)* | | | |
| **Albums** | | | |
| THE MANY HEADS OF BUCHANAN & GOODMAN | 196? | Rori 3301 | 75 |
| *(Very rare as a promo)* | | | |
| | | | |
| **BUCHANAN, WES** | | | |
| *Other Prep promo 45s $5 each* | | | |
| **45s** | | | |
| GIVE SOME LOVE MY WAY | 1958 | Prep 114 | 50 |
| *(White promo label)* | | | |
| | | | |
| **BUCKINGHAM, LINDSEY** | | | |
| *Also see Fleetwood Mac. Promo 45s $3 each.* | | | |
| **12-Inch Singles** | | | |
| GO INSANE (same on both sides) | 1984 | Elektra 4991 | 6 |
| **Compact Discs** | | | |
| WORDS & MUSIC | 1992 | Warner PROCD-5482 | 40 |
| *(Promo-only CD release)* | | | |
| **RADIO SHOWS** | | | |
| **Albums** | | | |
| IN CONCERT-NU MUSIC (Aug 92) Live concert | 1992 | Westwood One (2) | 30-75 |
| *(Newly recorded live material)* | | | |
| INNERVIEW (70s) Music and interview | 197? | SHOW #22, NUMBER 6 | 25-30 |
| *(Show was repeated the following year)* | | | |
| OFF THE RECORD (Aug 92) PROFILE | 1992 | Westwood One (2) | 10-15 |
| *(Music and interview)* | | | |
| **Compact Discs** | | | |
| SUPERSTAR CONCERT (Feb 93) Live concert | 1993 | Westwood One (2) | 40-80 |
| *(Rare live concert)* | | | |

| Title | Yr | Label, Number | NM $ |
|---|---|---|---|
| **BUCKINGHAMS, THE** | | | |
| *Columbia white label promo 45s $5 each* | | | |
| **45s** | | | |
| SUSAN  White promo label, 2:17 edited version | 1967 | Columbia 44378 | 18 |
| *(Psychedelic bridge is edited; this version not released to the public until 1997)* | | | |
| THE BUCKINGHAMS  Red vinyl | 1966 | Rowe-AMI | 15 |
| *(Jukebox release/promo, about 30 seconds long)* | | | |
| **Albums** | | | |
| KING OF A DRAG  First pressing, 13 tracks | 1966 | USA 107 | 50 |
| *(Actually a stock copy, this version was sent to many radio stations)* | | | |
| | | | |
| **BUCKLEY, JEFF** | | | |
| **Compact Discs** | | | |
| PEYOTE RADIO THEATRE | 1996 | Columbia 6206 | 20 |
| | | | |
| **BUDGIE** | | | |
| *Promo 45s on various labels $6-8 each* | | | |
| **RADIO SHOWS** | | | |
| **Albums** | | | |
| BBC TRANSCRIPTION DISC  Live concert | 1973 | BBC Transcription | 200-350 |
| *(Also features the JSD Band)* | | | |
| | | | |
| **BUFFETT, JIMMY** | | | |
| *MCA promo colored vinyl 45s $6 each; MCA promo black vinyl 45s $2 each* | | | |
| **45s** | | | |
| CHRISTMAS IN THE CARIBBEAN | 1985 | MCA S45-17084 | 10 |
| *(Promo-only release)* | | | |
| PLEASE BYPASS THE HEART | 1985 | MCA 52752 | 10 |
| *(Yellow vinyl)* | | | |
| **Albums** | | | |
| SPECIAL JIMMY BUFFETT SAMPLER | 1978 | ABC SPDJ-43 | 20 |
| **Albums** | | | |
| IN CONCERT (July 81) Live concert | 1981 | Westwood One (2) | 100-200 |
| *(Live concert)* | | | |
| POP CONCERT (Nov 86) Live concert | 1986 | Westwood One (2) | 175-250 |
| *(Live concert)* | | | |
| ROBERT W. MORGAN Music and interview | 1978 | Watermark | 30-50 |
| *(This show was repeated in 1979 and 1980)* | | | |
| STARFLEET (July 80) Live concert | 1980 | (2) | 200-300 |
| *(Rare live concert series)* | | | |
| **Compact Discs** | | | |
| BAROMETER SOUP | 1995 | Album Network (2) | 100-150 |
| *(Music and interviews with some live tracks)* | | | |
| | | | |
| **BUGGLES, THE** | | | |
| **12-Inch Singles** | | | |
| CLEAN CLEAN/LIVING IN THE PLASTIC AGE | 1980 | Island PRO-A-859 | 8 |
| **45s** | | | |
| VIDEO KILLED THE RADIO STAR | 1979 | Island 49114 | 12 |
| *(Original promo of this important single, the first video ever aired on MTV)* | | | |
| VIDEO KILLED THE RADIO STAR | 1983 | Island 99871 | 10 |
| *(Reissue promo)* | | | |
| | | | |
| **BUILT TO SPILL** | | | |
| **45s** | | | |
| UNTRUSTABLE/PART 2 (ABOUT SOMEONE ELSE) | 1996 | Warner Bros. PRO-S-8546 | 5 |
| *Clear vinyl* | | | |
| | | | |
| **BULLETBOYS** | | | |
| **RADIO SHOWS** | | | |
| **Albums** | | | |
| METALSHOP (80s) Show #374 | 198? | DJI Productions | 10-15 |
| *(Live segment in a music and interview show)* | | | |
| | | | |
| **BURDON, ERIC** | | | |
| *Capitol promo 45s $3-5; See The Animals; See War* | | | |
| **45s** | | | |
| SOLEDAD | 1971 | MGM 14296 | 10 |
| *(With Jimmy Witherspoon)* | | | |
| WHAT'S IT ALL ABOUT Public service program | 1975 | W. I. A. A. 259 | 18 |
| *(Grand Funk on B-side)* | | | |
| | | | |
| **BURNETTE BROTHERS, THE** | | | |
| *Johnny and Dorsey Burnette; See Dorsey Burnette; Johnny Burnette Trio* | | | |
| **45s** | | | |
| MY HONEY Cream-colored promo label | 1957 | Imperial 5509 | 50 |
| | | | |
| **BURNETTE, DORSEY** | | | |
| *Of the Johnny Burnette Trio. Era promo 45s $15 each; Condor promo 45s $12 each; Melodyland promo 45s $4 each.* | | | |
| **45s** | | | |
| BE A NAVY MAN (60s) | 196? | Navy Recruiting | 75 |
| *(Issued with a paper picture sleeve)* | | | |
| **Albums** | | | |
| TALL OAK TREE (mono) | 196? | Era 102 | 75 |

| <u>Title</u> | <u>Yr</u> | <u>Label, Number</u> | <u>NM $</u> |
|---|---|---|---|
| **RADIO SHOWS** | | | |
| **Albums** | | | |
| HERE'S TO VETERANS (70s) 15-minute public service show | 197? | The VA 1360 | 100-200 |
| *(Red label, music and interview)* | | | |
| | | | |
| **BURNETTE, JOHNNY** | | | |
| *Of the Johnny Burnette Trio. Liberty white label promo 45s $20 each; Chancellor white label promo 45s $18 each; Other Liberty white promo LPs $50 each.* | | | |
| **45s** | | | |
| BIGGER MAN | 1964 | Magic Lamp 515 | 100 |
| *(Price is for sleeve and record)* | | | |
| SWEET BABY DOLL | 1958 | Freedom 44017 | 40 |
| *(White promo label)* | | | |
| YOU'RE UNDECIDED | 195? | Von 1006 | 150 |
| *(Von promo label)* | | | |
| **Albums** | | | |
| DREAMIN'  White promo label | 1960 | Liberty 7179 | 100 |
| | | | |
| **BURNETTE, JOHNNY, AND THE ROCK 'N' ROLL TRIO** | | | |
| *Johnny and Dorsey Burnette with Paul Burlison* | | | |
| **45s** | | | |
| DRINKING WINE SPO-DEE-O-DEE | 1957 | Coral 61869 | 200 |
| *(Blue promo label)* | | | |
| EAGER BEAVER BABY | 1957 | Coral 61829 | 200 |
| *(Blue promo label)* | | | |
| HONEY HUSH | 1956 | Coral 61719 | 200 |
| *(Blue promo label)* | | | |
| LONESOME TRAIN | 1956 | Coral 61758 | 200 |
| *(Blue promo label)* | | | |
| MIDNIGHT TRAIN | 1956 | Coral 61675 | 200 |
| *(Blue promo label)* | | | |
| ROCKBILLY BOOGIE | 1957 | Coral 61918 | 200 |
| *(Blue promo label)* | | | |
| TEAR IT UP | 1956 | Coral 61651 | 200 |
| *(Blue promo label; stock copies of these promos are worth about 25-50% more)* | | | |
| **Albums** | | | |
| JOHNNY BURNETTE & THE ROCK 'N ROLL TRIO | 1957 | Coral 57080 | 5,000 |
| *(Blue promo label)* | | | |
| | | | |
| **BURNING ROM** | | | |
| **45s** | | | |
| ONCE OVER/BURNING WITH DESIRE | 1982 | A&M 2443 | 8 |
| | | | |
| **BURRITO BROTHERS** | | | |
| *Formerly the Flying Burrito Brothers* | | | |
| **RADIO SHOWS** | | | |
| **Albums** | | | |
| WESTWOOD ONE PRESENTS (Jan 83) Live concert | 1983 | Westwood One | 100-175 |
| *(Rare live concert)* | | | |
| **Compact Discs** | | | |
| UP CLOSE Music and interviews | 1994 | Media America (2) | 25-40 |
| *(Some live material)* | | | |
| | | | |
| **BUS BOYS** | | | |
| **RADIO SHOWS** | | | |
| **Albums** | | | |
| BBC ROCK HOUR (Apr 81) Live show | 1981 | London Wavelength | 35-75 |
| | | | |
| **BUSH** | | | |
| **RADIO SHOWS** | | | |
| **Compact Discs** | | | |
| LIVE FROM THE PIT | 1995 | Global Satellite | 50-75 |
| ON EDGE (Jan 96) | 1996 | | 30 |
| *(With two acoustic tracks by Radiohead)* | | | |
| | | | |
| **BUSH, KATE** | | | |
| *Other EMI promo 45s $5-7 each; Other EMI promo 12" singles $10 each* | | | |
| **12-Inch Singles** | | | |
| CLOUDBURSTING  (same on both sides) | 1985 | EMI America SPRO 9995 | 12 |
| EXPERIMENT IV (same on both sides) | 1986 | EMI America SPRO 9892 | 25 |
| HOUNDS OF LOVE (3:01)/HOUNDS OF LOVE (3:44) | 1985 | EMI America SPRO 9574/5 | 25 |
| RUNNING UP THAT HILL | 1985 | EMI America | 15 |
| *(Gray label, promo prefix)* | | | |
| SUSPENDED IN GAFFA | 1982 | EMI America | 15 |
| *(Same song on each side)* | | | |
| THEM HEAVY PEOPLE | 1978 | EMI America | 15 |
| *(Same song on each side)* | | | |
| **45s** | | | |
| HOUNDS OF LOVE Long and short versions | 1985 | EMI America 7PRO 9606 | 12 |
| *(Promo-only release, issued with a picture sleeve)* | | | |
| THE MAN WITH THE CHILD IN HIS EYES | 1978 | EMI America P-8006 | 15 |
| *(Green promo label)* | | | |
| WUTHERING HEIGHTS | 1978 | EMI America P-8003 | 10 |
| *(Green promo label)* | | | |

| Title | Yr | Label, Number | NM $ |
|---|---|---|---|
| **Albums** | | | |
| HOUNDS OF LOVE  Bio, photos, tied in ribbon | 1986 | EMI America | 40 |
| *(EMI promo label)* | | | |
| HOUNDS OF LOVE  Gray marble vinyl | 1986 | EMI America | 40 |
| *(EMI promo label)* | | | |
| THE KICK INSIDE | 1984 | EMI America 11761 | 40 |
| *(Interview album)* | | | |
| **Compact Discs** | | | |
| CLOUDBURSTING | 1986 | EMI America DPRO 7 900 2 | 60 |
| *(Promo-only CD single)* | | | |
| LOVE AND ANGER | 1989 | Columbia CSK 1859 | 20 |
| ROCKET MAN | 1992 | Polydor CDP 589 | 6 |
| RUBBERBAND GIRL | 1994 | Columbia CSK 5504 | 8 |

## BUTCHER, JON, AXIS
### RADIO SHOWS

| Title | Yr | Label, Number | NM $ |
|---|---|---|---|
| **Albums** | | | |
| BBC ROCK HOUR (Apr 81) | 1981 | London Wavelength | 40-60 |
| *(Live concert)* | | | |
| IN CONCERT (DEC 85) Live concert | 1985 | Westwood One (2) | 30-60 |
| *(With Scandal)* | | | |
| KING BISCUIT FLOWER HOUR (Aug 87) Live concert | 1987 | DIR (2) | 40-75 |
| *(With Mason Ruffner)* | | | |
| KING BISCUIT FLOWER HOUR (Dec 84) Live concert | 1984 | DIR/ABC (2) | 75-125 |
| *(With Stevie Ray Vaughan)* | | | |

## BUTLER, JERRY
*Vee Jay promo 45s $15-30 each depending on year; Abner promo 45s $15-30 each depending on year; Mercury promo 45s $4 each*

| Title | Yr | Label, Number | NM $ |
|---|---|---|---|
| **45s** | | | |
| AWARE OF LOVE White promo-only release | 1963 | Vee Jay 1971 | 30 |
| *(A compact-33 release)* | | | |
| DON'T LET LOVE HANG YOU UP | 1970 | Mercury DJ-152 | 10 |
| *(Special promo number)* | | | |
| FOR YOUR PRECIOUS LOVE | 1958 | Vee Jay 280 | Unknown |
| *(Only a few copies known of the stock copy; promo copies if they exist, would also be very rare)* | | | |
| GOT TO SEE IF I CAN'T GET MOMMY | 1970 | Mercury DJ-177 | 10 |
| *(Special promo number)* | | | |
| WHAT'S IT ALL ABOUT Public service program | 1978 | W. I. A. A. 1147 | 15 |
| *(Marvin Gaye on B-side)* | | | |
| **7-Inch Extended Plays** | | | |
| FOR YOUR PRECIOUS LOVE 4-song promo EP | 196? | Vee Jay 1567 | 100 |
| *(With the El Dorados, Magnificents and Flamingos.* | | | |
| **Albums** | | | |
| JERRY BUTLER ESQUIRE | 1959 | Abner 2001 | 125 |
| *(White promo label)* | | | |

## BUTTHOLE SURFERS

| Title | Yr | Label, Number | NM $ |
|---|---|---|---|
| **10-Inch Singles** | | | |
| CHEWIN' GEORGE LUCAS' CHOCOLATE/GOOFY'S CONCERN/ BEAT THE PRESS/GHANDI/NEEE NEEE | 1993 | Capitol SPRO 79612/3 | 15 |
| *(Promo-only 10-inch on brown vinyl)* | | | |
| **RADIO SHOWS** | | | |
| **Compact Discs** | | | |
| THE ZONE (Dec 96) | 1996 | | 20-40 |
| *(Live concert material)* | | | |

## BUZZCOCKS, THE

| Title | Yr | Label, Number | NM $ |
|---|---|---|---|
| **Albums** | | | |
| ARE EVERYTHING/STRANGE THING + 4 | 1980 | I.R.S. SP-70955 | 15 |
| *Red vinyl; no cover; some come with numbered sticker* | | | |

## BYRD, TRACY
### RADIO SHOWS

| Title | Yr | Label, Number | NM $ |
|---|---|---|---|
| **Compact Discs** | | | |
| LIVE FROM CRAZY HORSE | 1994 | Westwood One | 30-50 |
| *(Live concert)* | | | |

## BYRDS, THE
*Includes the Beefeaters; See Roger (Jim) McGuinn. Columbia white promo label 45s by the Byrds  $10-25 each depending on how early they were released; Capitol white label promo 45s by McGuinn and Hillman, sometimes featuring Clark, are worth $5 each; Columbia white label promo 45s by Roger McGuinn $5-10 each; Asylum white label promo 45s by the Byrds  $8-10 each; Universal label white promo 45s by Hillman and McGuinn  $3; A&M white promo label 45s by Dillard and Clark  $5 each.*

| Title | Yr | Label, Number | NM $ |
|---|---|---|---|
| **45s** | | | |
| 5D Promo-only picture sleeve | 1966 | Columbia ZLP 116003 | 500 |
| *(Very rare sleeve issued with promo single)* | | | |
| ALL I REALLY WANT TO DO  Red vinyl, black print | 1965 | Columbia 43332 | 75 |
| *(Matrix number is JRZSP 72425)* | | | |
| HE WAS A FRIEND OF MINE  White promo label | 1967 | Columbia JZSP 116476 | 15 |
| *(Promo-only release)* | | | |
| I'LL FEEL A WHOLE LOT BETTER Red vinyl, red print | 1965 | Columbia 43332 | 100 |
| *(Matrix number is JRZSP 72495)* | | | |
| MR. TAMBOURINE MAN | 1965 | Columbia ZSP 72245 | 150 |
| *(Red vinyl; no label number, ZSP is the matrix number)* | | | |
| MR. TAMBOURINE MAN Special promo sleeve | 1965 | Columbia 43271 | 300 |
| *(Promotes their appearance on the Hullabaloo TV show)* | | | |
| PLEASE LET ME LOVE YOU  Beefeaters | 1964 | Elektra 45013 | 200 |
| *(Rare first record, before they were the Byrds)* | | | |

| Title | Yr | Label, Number | NM $ |
|-------|----|--------------| ----|
| TURN TURN TURN Red vinyl, white label | 1965 | Columbia 43424 | 100 |
| *(This promo single has an interview on the flip side)* | | | |
| WHAT'S IT ALL ABOUT Public service program | 1974 | W. I. A. A. 236 | 30 |
| *(w/Roger McGuinn, flip side is the Hollies)* | | | |
| WHAT'S IT ALL ABOUT Public service program | 1980 | W. I. A. A. 533 | 25 |
| *(Repeat show, flip is Cheap Trick)* | | | |
| **7-Inch Extended Plays** | | | |
| THE BYRDS | 197? | Columbia 10287 | 25 |
| *(Scholastic Book release 4-song EP released with a paper sleeve)* | | | |
| THE INTERVIEW EP | 1967 | Columbia 116003 | 75 |
| *(This is the same record as "Fifth Dimension")* | | | |
| **Albums** | | | |
| 5D | 1966 | Columbia 2549 | 40 |
| *(White promo label)* | | | |
| BYRDS GREATEST HITS | 1967 | Columbia 2716 | 40 |
| *(White promo label)* | | | |
| BYRDS LIVE | 1981 | Broadcast | 40 |
| MR. TAMBOURINE MAN | 1965 | Columbia 2372 | 45 |
| *(White promo label)* | | | |
| NOTORIOUS BYRD BROTHERS | 1967 | Columbia 2275 | 40 |
| *(White promo label)* | | | |
| SWEETHEART OF THE RODEO | 1968 | Columbia 9670 | 50 |
| *(White promo label, "Special Mono Radio Station Copy", same number as stock stereo version)* | | | |
| TURN TURN TURN | 1965 | Columbia 2454 | 45 |
| *(White promo label)* | | | |
| YOUNGER THAN YESTERDAY | 1967 | Columbia 2646 | 40 |
| *(White promo label)* | | | |
| **RADIO SHOWS** | | | |
| **Albums** | | | |
| CONTINUOUS HISTORY OF ROCK & ROLL Profile | 1982 | Rolling Stone (2) | 40-60 |
| *(Price is for Byrds disc only)* | | | |
| LEGENDS OF ROCK (Mar 88) | 1988 | NBC Radio (2) | 30-50 |
| *(Music and interview)* | | | |
| ROCK AROUND THE WORLD (Oct 76) Profile | 1976 | | 125-200 |
| *(Music and interview, with some live material)* | | | |
| TICKET TO RIDE (Jan 88) FEATURED ON BEATLES SHOW | 1988 | DIR (2) | 25-40 |
| *(Part of a Beatles radio series)* | | | |
| UNISTAR SPECIAL (Mar 91) Profile | 1991 | Unistar (3) | 25-40 |
| *(Music and interview)* | | | |
| **Compact Discs** | | | |
| IN THE STUDIO Album profiles | 1989 | Album Network | 20-35 |
| *(Music and interview)* | | | |
| KING BISCUIT FLOWER HOUR (Mar 91) Live concert | 1991 | DIR | 50-80 |
| *(Features Roger McGuinn)* | | | |
| UP CLOSE Profile | 1990 | Media America (2) | 50-100 |
| *(Contains some live material, show repeated in 1991)* | | | |
| **Reel-to-Reel Tapes** | | | |
| BBC ROCK HOUR (JULY 80) | 1980 | London Wavelength | 150-250 |
| *(Live concert on 7" reel)* | | | |

## BYRNE, DAVID
*Sire promo 45s $5 each See Talking Heads*

**12-Inch Singles**

| Title | Yr | Label, Number | NM $ |
|-------|----|--------------| ----|
| AVA (3 versions)/NINEVEH/MACHU PICCHU | 1991 | Luaka Bop PRO-A-4989 | 7 |
| MAKE BELIEVE MAMBO (4 versions) | 1989 | Sire PRO-A-3800 | 5 |

**RADIO SHOWS**

**Albums**

| Title | Yr | Label, Number | NM $ |
|-------|----|--------------| ----|
| INSIDE TRACK (Sept 83) Music and interview | 1983 | RKO (3) | 25-40 |
| *(Features Ray Davies and Danny Ferry)* | | | |

## BYRNE, DAVID, AND RYUICHI SAKAMOTO
**Albums**

| Title | Yr | Label, Number | NM $ |
|-------|----|--------------| ----|
| THE MAKING OF THE LAST EMPEROR: AN INTERVIEW WITH... | 1988 | Virgin 2204 | 25 |

## BYRNES, EDD "KOOKIE"
*Warner white label promo 45s $20 each*

**7-Inch Extended Plays**

| Title | Yr | Label, Number | NM $ |
|-------|----|--------------| ----|
| EDD "KOOKIE" BYRNES  Promo spots | 1959 | Warner Bros. PRO 102 | 50 |
| *(Issued for DJs to promote new album and TV show)* | | | |
| EDD "KOOKIE" BYRNES Jukebox LLP | 1959 | Warner Bros. 5309 | 200 |
| *(Issued with a paper cover)* | | | |
| **Albums** | | | |
| STAR OF 77 SUNSET STRIP White promo mono label | 1959 | Warner Bros. 1309 | 100 |
| YOU AIN'T HEARD NOTHIN' YET! | 1959 | Warner Bros. | 50 |
| *(Sampler with two Edd Byrnes tracks and one by Roger Smith)* | | | |

| Title | Yr | Label, Number | NM $ |
|---|---|---|---|

## C

**C&C MUSIC FACTORY**
*Columbia promo singles $3*
**RADIO SHOWS**
**Compact Discs**

| | | | |
|---|---|---|---|
| UNISTAR SPECIAL (Nov 91) Profile of the group | 1991 | Unistar | 10-15 |
| *(Music and interview)* | | | |

**CABARET VOLTAIRE**
**12-Inch Singles**

| | | | |
|---|---|---|---|
| COLOURS (4 mixes) | 1991 | Mute ED 5562 | 7 |

**CABBOT, JOHNNY**
**45s**

| | | | |
|---|---|---|---|
| NIGHT & DAY 7" compact single | 1962 | Columbia 42283 | 40 |
| *(For jukeboxes)* | | | |

**CACTUS WORLD NEWS**
**RADIO SHOWS**
**Albums**

| | | | |
|---|---|---|---|
| SPIN CONCERT  Profile | 1986 | Spin Magazine | 20-40 |
| *(Live concert)* | | | |

**CADILLACS, THE**
*Josie promo singles $20-40 each*

**CAESAR, SHIRLEY**
**45s**

| | | | |
|---|---|---|---|
| WON'T YOU COME A-CHRISTMASING (same on both sides) | 198? | Rejoice 2895 | 3 |

**CAFFERTY, JOHN, AND THE BEAVER BROWN BAND**
*Promo singles $2 each*
**RADIO SHOWS**
**Albums**

| | | | |
|---|---|---|---|
| INNERVIEW  Music and interviews | 198? | Clayton Webster | 10-15 |
| *(This show was repeated)* | | | |

**CALE, JOHN**
**12-Inch Singles**

| | | | |
|---|---|---|---|
| DEAD OR ALIVE/HONI SOIT | 1981 | A&M 17154 | 6 |

**Albums**

| | | | |
|---|---|---|---|
| HEAR FEAR | 1975 | Island IXP-2 | 50 |
| *(Promo-only interview album)* | | | |

**CALIFORNIA MUSIC**
*Bruce Johnson and Terry Melcher; Papa Doo Run Run*
**12-Inch Singles**

| | | | |
|---|---|---|---|
| MUSIC MUSIC MUSIC  California Music | 1976 | Warner Bros. 8253 | 15 |
| *(Promo 12" single)* | | | |
| **45s** | | | |
| BE TRUE TO YOUR SCHOOL  Papa Doo Run Run | 1975 | RCA Victor 10404 | 15 |
| *(Cream-colored promo label)* | | | |
| CARMEN  Bruce and Terry | 1965 | Columbia 43238 | 25 |
| *(White promo label)* | | | |
| COME, LOVE  Bruce and Terry | 1965 | Columbia 43479 | 25 |
| *(White promo label)* | | | |
| CUSTOM MACHINE Bruce and Terry | 1964 | Columbia 42956 | 25 |
| *(White promo label)* | | | |
| DON'T RUN AWAY  Bruce and Terry | 1966 | Columbia 43582 | 25 |
| *(White promo label)* | | | |
| DON'T WORRY BABY  California Music | 1974 | RCA Victor 10120 | 20 |
| *(Cream-colored promo label)* | | | |
| I CAN HEAR MUSIC  California | 1978 | RSO 901 | 10 |
| *(White promo label)* | | | |
| I LOVE YOU SO  California Music | 1976 | Warner Bros. 8307 | 10 |
| *(Green promo label)* | | | |
| JAMAICA FAREWELL  California Music | 1975 | RCA Victor 10572 | 15 |
| *(Cream-colored promo label)* | | | |
| MUSIC MUSIC MUSIC  California Music | 1976 | Warner Bros. 8253 | 10 |
| *(Green promo label)* | | | |
| RAINING IN MY HEART  Bruce and Terry | 1965 | Columbia 43378 | 25 |
| *(White promo label)* | | | |
| SKATE BOARD Sidewalk Surfers | 1965 | Jubilee 5496 | 30 |
| *(White promo label)* | | | |
| SUMMER MEANS FUN  Bruce and Terry | 1964 | Columbia 43055 | 25 |
| *(White promo label)* | | | |
| WHY DO FOOLS FALL IN LOVE  California Music | 1975 | RCA Victor 10363 | 20 |
| *(Cream-colored promo label)* | | | |

| Title | Yr | Label, Number | NM $ |
|---|---|---|---|
| **CALL, THE** | | | |
| *Promo 45 rpm singles $3 each* | | | |
| **12-Inch Singles** | | | |
| HEAVY HAND (same on both sides) | 1984 | Mercury PRO 303 | 8 |
| I DON'T WANNA/I DON'T WANNA (Edit) | 1987 | Elektra 5234 | 7 |
| IN THE RIVER (same on both sides) | 1987 | Elektra 5250 | 6 |
| OKLAHOMA/OKLAHOMA (Live)/I STILL BELIEVE (Live) | 1986 | Elektra 5168 | 7 |
| TIME OF YOUR LIFE/ALL ABOUT YOU | 1983 | Mercury MK 242 | 8 |
| WALK WALK (CD Version)/WALK WALK (LP Version) | 1987 | Elektra ED 5271 | 6 |
| WALLS CAME DOWN/DESTINATION | 1982 | Mercury MK 229 | 6 |
| WAR WEARY WORLD (same on both sides) | 1982 | Mercury MK 198 | 6 |
| **RADIO SHOWS** | | | |
| **Albums** | | | |
| INNERVIEW (70s) | 197? | Innerview | 10 |
| *(Music and interview)* | | | |
| KING BISCUIT FLOWER HOUR (June 83) Live show | 1983 | DIR (2) | 25-50 |
| *(Live concert with Michael Bolton)* | | | |
| KING BISCUIT FLOWER HOUR (Sept 86) Live show | 1986 | DIR (2) | 50-75 |
| *(Live concert with The Cure)* | | | |
| | | | |
| **CAMPBELL, GLEN** | | | |
| *Starday promo 45s $4 each; Capitol promo 45s $3 each; other jukebox LLPs $10 each* | | | |
| **45s** | | | |
| DEATH VALLEY | 1961 | Capehart 5008 | 20 |
| *(White promo label)* | | | |
| GUESS I'M DUMB | 1965 | Capitol 5441 | 75 |
| *(Written by Brian Wilson, backing vocal by the Honeys)* | | | |
| THE MIRACLE OF LOVE White promo label | 1962 | Crest 1096 | 12 |
| *(The three above singles are Capehart productions)* | | | |
| ON A GOOD NIGHT (same on both sides) | 1990 | Capitol 7PRO-79107 | 6 |
| *(Vinyl is promo only)* | | | |
| SOMEBODY'S LEAVIN' (same on both sides) | 1990 | Capitol 7PRO-79279 | 6 |
| *(Vinyl is promo only)* | | | |
| TURN AROUND, LOOK AT ME | 1961 | Crest 1087 | 15 |
| *(White promo label)* | | | |
| WALK RIGHT IN | 1963 | Everest 2500 | 10 |
| *(White promo label)* | | | |
| WALKIN' IN THE SUN (same on both sides) | 1990 | Capitol 7PRO-79966 | 6 |
| *Vinyl is promo only* | | | |
| WHAT'S IT ALL ABOUT (Feb 79) Public service show | 1979 | W. I. A. A. 463 | 15 |
| *(Flip side by the Pointer Sisters)* | | | |
| **7-Inch Extended Plays** | | | |
| GLEN CAMPBELL GOOD TIME HOUR (60s) Chevrolet | 196? | Capitol SP 55 | 30 |
| *(Special products release for Chevrolet)* | | | |
| GREATEST HITS (70s) Jukebox LLP with six songs | 197? | Capitol 752 (LLP 156) | 12 |
| *(Issued with a paper cover)* | | | |
| **Albums** | | | |
| BIG BLUEGRASS SPECIAL | 1962 | Capitol 1810 | 55 |
| *(By the Green River Boys featuring Glen Campbell)* | | | |
| **RADIO SHOWS** | | | |
| **Albums** | | | |
| COUNTRY COOKIN' (June 76) Four 15-minute shows | 1976 | U.S. Army Reserve (2) | 15 |
| *(One of the shows is hosted by Campbell)* | | | |
| SILVER PLATTER SERVICE (Oct 65) W/Jack Wagner | 1965 | Capitol 3171 | 20 |
| *(Live interview and new music by Campbell)* | | | |
| **Cassettes** | | | |
| AUSTIN CITY LIMITS (90s) Live show | 199? | Mainstreet | 20-40 |
| *(This radio show released on cassette)* | | | |
| | | | |
| **CAMPER VAN BEETHOVEN** | | | |
| *Also see Cracker.* | | | |
| **12-Inch Singles** | | | |
| PICTURES OF MATCHSTICK MEN (same on both sides) | 1989 | Virgin PR 2865 | 7 |
| | | | |
| **CANDLEBOX** | | | |
| *Maverick promo CD singles $5 each* | | | |
| **RADIO SHOWS** | | | |
| **Compact Discs** | | | |
| IN CONCERT-NU ROCK (Aug 94) | 1994 | Westwood One | 30-60 |
| *(Live concert)* | | | |
| ON THE EDGE (Apr 94) Music and interview | 1994 | Westwood One | 15-30 |
| *(Show also features Possum Dixon and Live)* | | | |
| | | | |
| **CANNED HEAT** | | | |
| **45s** | | | |
| HARLEY DAVIDSON BLUES (mono/stereo) | 1973 | United Artists XW243 | 6 |
| *(Stock copy apparently does not exist)* | | | |
| | | | |
| **CANNON, FREDDY** | | | |
| *Swan white label promo 45s $15 each; Warner Brothers promo 45s $8 each; Sire (London) brown label 45s $5 each; We Make Rock 'N Roll (Capitol) label promo 45s $4 each; Buddah, Metromedia, MCA and Amherst promo 45s $8 each* | | | |
| **45s** | | | |
| KENNYWOOD PARK  KDKA promo | 1987 | HQ (no #) | 30 |
| *(Issued with picture sleeve, both record and sleeve are promo only)* | | | |

| Title | Yr | Label, Number | NM $ |
|---|---|---|---|
| **CANTOR, EDDIE** | | | |
| **78s** | | | |
| THE OLD PIANO ROLL BLUES | 1952 | RCA DJ 949 | 15 |
| *(Promo-only issue with this number)* | | | |
| | | | |
| **CAP-TANS, THE** | | | |
| **45s** | | | |
| ASKING | 1951 | Coral 65071 | 50 |
| *(Blue promo label)* | | | |
| | | | |
| **CAPALDI, JIM** | | | |
| **45s** | | | |
| I'LL KEEP HOLDING ON (same on both sides) | 1984 | Atlantic 89625 | 4 |
| *May be promo only* | | | |
| TONIGHT YOU'RE MINE (same on both sides) | 1983 | Atlantic 89783 | 4 |
| *May be promo only* | | | |
| | | | |
| **CAPITOLS, THE** | | | |
| **45s** | | | |
| I LET HER GO  Green promo label | 1958 | Carlton 461 | 200 |
| | | | |
| **CAPTAIN AND TENNILLE** | | | |
| *A&M white promo label 45s not listed $3 each; Casablanca label promo 45s $2 each* | | | |
| **45s** | | | |
| COMO YO QUIERO SENTIRTE  White promo label | 1975 | A&M 1774 | 10 |
| *("The Way I Want to Touch You" in Spanish)* | | | |
| POR AMOR VIVREMOS | 1975 | A&M 1715 | 10 |
| *("Love Will Keep Us Together" in Spanish)* | | | |
| WHAT'S IT ALL ABOUT (Dec 76) Public service show | 1976 | W. I. A. A. 346 | 15 |
| *(Flip side is Jim Stafford)* | | | |
| **RADIO SHOWS** | | | |
| NBC SOURCE (Nov 80) In concert | 1980 | NBC Radio (2) | 25-50 |
| *(Rare show)* | | | |
| **Albums** | | | |
| ROBERT W. MORGAN  Profile | 1976 | Watermark | 20-35 |
| *(Music and interview)* | | | |
| | | | |
| **CAPTAIN BEEFHEART AND THE MAGIC BAND** | | | |
| *A&M promo singles $20 each; Buddah promo singles $10 each; Mercury, MCA and Epic promo singles $5 each* | | | |
| **45s** | | | |
| CLICK CLACK | 1971 | Reprise PRO 514 | 50 |
| *(Promo-only release, with promo-only sleeve also)* | | | |
| HERE I AM, I ALWAYS AM | 1964 | A&M | 200 |
| *(Test pressing only, flip side of "Moon Child")* | | | |
| TOO MUCH TIME | 1972 | Reprise PRO 547 | 50 |
| *(Promo-only release, with promo-only sleeve also)* | | | |
| **Albums** | | | |
| CLEAR SPOT | 1972 | Reprise 2115 | 50 |
| *(White promo only)* | | | |
| INTERVIEW | 1970 | Reprise PRO 447 | 45 |
| *(White promo label)* | | | |
| TROUT MASK REPLICA | 1969 | Straight 2 STS-1053 | 200 |
| *(White label promo)* | | | |
| TROUT MASK REPLICA | 1969 | Straight 2MS 2027 | 150 |
| *(White label promo with 2027 labels inside 1053 jacket)* | | | |
| | | | |
| **CARAVAN** | | | |
| **RADIO SHOWS** | | | |
| **Albums** | | | |
| BBC TRANSCRIPTION DISC  Live show | 1973 | BBC Transcription | 100-250 |
| *(With Joe Vinegar)* | | | |
| | | | |
| **CARAWAY, BOB** | | | |
| **45s** | | | |
| BALLIN' KEEN | 1958 | Crest 1065 | 45 |
| *(White promo label)* | | | |
| | | | |
| **CAREY, MARIAH** | | | |
| *Columbia promo CDs $4 each* | | | |
| **Compact Discs** | | | |
| MARIAH CAREY Profile | 1991 | Columbia 3087 | 25 |
| *(Music and interview for DJ use, total time 40:45)* | | | |
| **RADIO SHOWS** | | | |
| **Compact Discs** | | | |
| UNISTAR PRESENTS (July 91) Profile | 1991 | Unistar | 15-25 |
| *(Music and interview, repeated in 1992)* | | | |
| | | | |
| **CARLISLE, BELINDA** | | | |
| **45s** | | | |
| SINCE YOU'VE GONE (same on both sides) | 1987 | I.R.S. S45-17262 | 5 |

| Title | Yr | Label, Number | NM $ |
|-------|-----|---------------|------|

**CARLISLES, THE**
*Mercury promo singles with white labels $15 each; Any other label Bill Carlisle 45 (RCA, Hickory, etc.) $5 each; other Mercury LPs with white labels worth $25 each*
**Albums**

| | | | |
|---|---|---|---|
| ON STAGE WITH THE CARLISLES | 1958 | Mercury 20359 | 40 |
| *(White promo label)* | | | |

**RADIO SHOWS**
**16-Inch Transcriptions**

| | | | |
|---|---|---|---|
| U. S. ARMY BAND (60s) Shows 39 and 40 | 196? | U. S. Army | 30-50 |
| *(Music and interviews)* | | | |

**CARMEN, ERIC**
*Also see Raspberries. Arista promo 45s $2 each.*
**45s**

| | | | |
|---|---|---|---|
| SPARROW   by Cyrus Erie | 1970 | Epic 10451 | 15 |
| *(Carmen wrote song and is member of the pre-Raspberries group)* | | | |

**RADIO SHOWS**
**Albums**

| | | | |
|---|---|---|---|
| ROBERT W. MORGAN Music and interview | 1978 | Watermark | 20-35 |
| *(Profile of the artist)* | | | |

**CARNES, KIM**
*EMI promo singles $2 each; EMI test pressing 45s $5 each*
**45s**

| | | | |
|---|---|---|---|
| BAD SEED (mono/stereo) | 1976 | A&M 1807 | 5 |
| *(No stock copies issued)* | | | |

**RADIO SHOWS**
**Albums**

| | | | |
|---|---|---|---|
| KING BISCUIT FLOWER HOUR (Sept 81) Live concert | 1981 | NBC Radio (2) | 75-125 |
| *(Rare radio show)* | | | |

**CAROL AND CHERYL**
**45s**

| | | | |
|---|---|---|---|
| GO GO G.T.O. | 1965 | Colpix 767 | 250 |
| *(White promo label; stock copy even rarer)* | | | |

**CARPENTER, STEVE**
**45s**

| | | | |
|---|---|---|---|
| YOU'RE PUTTING ME ON | 1962 | Brunswick 55322 | 40 |
| *(Yellow promo label)* | | | |

**CARPENTERS**
*A&M promo 45s worth $4 each unless noted*
**45s**

| | | | |
|---|---|---|---|
| DO YOU HEAR WHAT I HEAR? | 1984 | A&M 2700 | 10 |
| *(Promo-only red label)* | | | |
| YOUR BABY DOESN'T LOVE YOU ANYMORE | 198? | A&M | 15 |
| *(Test pressing)* | | | |

**7-Inch Extended Plays**

| | | | |
|---|---|---|---|
| CARPENTERS  Four remixed hits for DJs only | 1985 | A&M 2735 | 15 |
| *(From the LP Yesterday Once More)* | | | |
| CARPENTERS  Jukebox LLP with four songs | 197? | A&M 3502 (LLP 151) | 12 |
| *(Issued with paper sleeve)* | | | |
| CLOSE TO YOU Jukebox LLP with six songs | 197? | A&M 4271 (LLP 125) | 15 |
| *(Issued with paper sleeve)* | | | |
| NOW & THEN  Jukebox LLP with eight songs | 197? | A&M (LLP 222) | 10 |
| *(Issued with paper sleeve)* | | | |
| THE SINGLES  Jukebox LLP with five songs | 197? | A&M (LLP 238) | 10 |
| *(Issued with paper sleeve)* | | | |

**Albums**

| | | | |
|---|---|---|---|
| OFFERING  White promo label | 1970 | A&M 4205 | 40 |
| *(This LP later changed to "Ticket to Ride")* | | | |

**RADIO SHOWS**
**Albums**

| | | | |
|---|---|---|---|
| SOUNDS LIKE THE NAVY | 1975 | U.S. Navy | 20-30 |

**CARR, VIKKI**
**45s**

| | | | |
|---|---|---|---|
| IT CAME UPON A MIDNIGHT CLEAR | 1974 | Columbia AS 85 | 10 |
| *(Promo-only white label with picture sleeve, special Christmas Seals promo item)* | | | |

**CARRACK, PAUL**
*Any label promo 45s $3 each*
**RADIO SHOWS**
**Compact Discs**

| | | | |
|---|---|---|---|
| KING BISCUIT FLOWER HOUR (Apr 88) Live concert | 1988 | DIR | 30-60 |
| *(Carrack with Mike & the Mechanics)* | | | |
| KING BISCUIT FLOWER HOUR (Dec 89) Live concert | 1989 | DIR | 20-40 |
| *(In concert with Squeeze)* | | | |

**CARROLL, JIM**
*Other Atlantic label promos worth $3 each*
**12-Inch Singles**

| | | | |
|---|---|---|---|
| (NO MORE) LUXURIES/VOICES | 1983 | Atlantic 573 | 12 |
| SWEET JANE (same on both sides) | 1983 | Atlantic 593 | 12 |

| Title | Yr | Label, Number | NM $ |
|---|---|---|---|
| **45s** | | | |
| DAY AND NIGHT (same on both sides) | 1981 | Atco 7323 | 4 |
| *(Stock copy may not exist)* | | | |
| PEOPLE WHO DIED | 1980 | Atco 7314 | 10 |
| *(Blue and white promo labels)* | | | |
| SWEET JANE (same on both sides) | 1984 | Atlantic 89687 | 4 |
| *(Stock copy may not exist)* | | | |
| **RADIO SHOWS** | | | |
| **Albums** | | | |
| KING BISCUIT FLOWER HOUR (Feb 81) Live concert | 1981 | DIR/ABC (2) | 60-100 |
| *(In concert with the Pretenders)* | | | |
| KING BISCUIT FLOWER HOUR (May 81) | 1981 | DIR/ABC (2) | 50-100 |
| *(Live concert)* | | | |

**CARROLL, JOHNNY**
*Phillips Int'l. promo label 45s $25 each; other promo label 45s $10-20 each*

| | | | |
|---|---|---|---|
| **45s** | | | |
| HOT ROCK | 1959 | Decca 30013 | 45 |
| *(Pink promo label)* | | | |
| ROCK 'N ROLL RUBY | 1958 | Decca 29940 | 50 |
| *(Pink promo label)* | | | |
| WILD WILD WOMEN | 1958 | Decca 29941 | 45 |
| *(Pink promo label)* | | | |

**CARS, THE**
*Elektra promo 45s $3 each; Elektra promo 45s by Benjamin Orr $2 each*

| | | | |
|---|---|---|---|
| **12-Inch Singles** | | | |
| COMING UP YOU (same on both sides) | 1987 | Elektra 5264 | 6 |
| HELLO AGAIN (Remix)/HELLO AGAIN (LP)/HELLO AGAIN (Dub) | 1984 | Elektra 5014 | 5 |
| YOU ARE THE GIRL (same on both sides) | 1987 | Elektra ED 5249 | 5 |
| **45s** | | | |
| JUST WHAT I NEEDED  Red vinyl | 1978 | Elektra 45491 | 25 |
| *(Red vinyl promo-only release)* | | | |
| **Albums** | | | |
| HEARTBEAT CITY | 1984 | Elektra 60296 | 12 |
| *(Promo-only audiophile pressing on Quiex II vinyl)* | | | |
| SHAKE IT UP Picture disc promo | 1981 | Elektra 567 | 100 |
| *(Picture disc is a promo-only release)* | | | |
| **RADIO SHOWS** | | | |
| **Albums** | | | |
| BBC ROCK HOUR (Nov 80) Live concert | 1980 | London Wavelength | 40-60 |
| *(BBC live concert material)* | | | |
| IN CONCERT | 1989 | Westwood One (2) | 20-40 |
| *(Repeated several times)* | | | |
| INNERVIEW (70s) Music and interview | 197? | Innerview | 10-15 |
| *(Several reissues of this show)* | | | |
| KING BISCUIT FLOWER HOUR (June 80) Live concert | 1980 | DIR/ABC (2) | 40-60 |
| *(Also features Pat Benatar)* | | | |
| KING BISCUIT FLOWER HOUR (June 81) Live concert | 1981 | DIR/ABC (2) | 20-40 |
| *(Also features April Wine)* | | | |
| KING BISCUIT FLOWER HOUR (Mar 80) Live concert | 1980 | DIR/ABC (2) | 40-75 |
| *(Also features the Rockets)* | | | |
| KING BISCUIT FLOWER HOUR (Mar 81) Live concert | 1981 | DIR/ABC (2) | 25-40 |
| *(Also features Eddie Money)* | | | |
| LEGENDS OF ROCK (May 87) Profile | 1987 | NBC Radio (2) | 20-35 |
| *(Music and interview)* | | | |
| NBC SOURCE (Aug 83) | 1983 | NBC Radio (2) | 25-50 |
| *(Live concert)* | | | |
| SOURCE CHRISTMAS COUNTDOWN (Dec 82) | 1982 | NBC Source (3) | 40-60 |
| *(Live concert)* | | | |
| SOURCE SPECIAL (May 84) | 1984 | NBC Radio (3) | 25-40 |
| *(Live concert)* | | | |
| SUPERGROUPS | 198? | ABC Radio SCG 104 (2) | 20-25 |
| SUPERSTAR CONCERT (Apr 85) Box set | 1985 | Westwood One (3) | 25-45 |
| *(Repeated several times)* | | | |
| UP CLOSE | 1986 | MCA Radio (2) | 25-40 |
| *(Music and interviews)* | | | |
| **Compact Discs** | | | |
| BBC CLASSIC TRACKS (Aug 94) Some live | 1994 | London Wavelength | 10-20 |
| *(Material from the BBC)* | | | |
| IN THE STUDIO (July 92) Profile of an album | 1992 | Album Network | 10-20 |
| *(Music and interviews)* | | | |

**CARSON, CHUCK**
*Gaity label promos worth $10-20 each*

| | | | |
|---|---|---|---|
| **45s** | | | |
| MOONLIGHT ROCK | 1957 | Hep 2142 | 75 |
| *(Hep promo label)* | | | |

**CARTER FAMILY, THE**
*RCA Victor Carter Family promo singles $8 each; Decca Carter Family promo singles $5 each; Any Carter Family member promo single on any label $3 Includes Carlene Carter, Roseanne Carter; also see Johnny Cash*

| | | | |
|---|---|---|---|
| **45s** | | | |
| BLUE DOLL White promo label | 1958 | Cadence 1333 | 10 |
| *(By Anita Carter)* | | | |

| Title | Yr | Label, Number | NM $ |
|---|---|---|---|
| MAMA DON'T CRY AT MY WEDDING  White promo label | 1959 | Jamie 1154 | 10 |
| *(By Anita Carter)* | | | |
| **7-Inch Extended Plays** | | | |
| HE'S A REAL GONE GUY/MAYBE  Anita Carter | 1959 | RCA Victor DJ-60 | 15 |
| *(Four-song promo-only EP, other side by Porter Wagoner)* | | | |
| IF I HAD A NEEDLE & THREAD/BELIEVE IT OR NOT  Anita Carter | 1958 | RCA Victor DJ-34 | 10 |
| *(Four-song promo-only EP, other side by Country Partners)* | | | |
| **Albums** | | | |
| ALL TIME FAVORITES | 195? | Acme LP-1 | 85 |
| *(Promo label)* | | | |
| CARTER FAMILY, THE | 1963 | Decca 4404 | 45 |
| *(Pink promo label)* | | | |
| COLLECTION OF FAVORITES, A | 1963 | Decca 4404 | 40 |
| *(Renamed version of "The Carter Family")* | | | |
| COLLECTION OF FAVORITES, A | 1963 | Decca 4404 | 45 |
| *(Pink promo label)* | | | |
| IN MEMORY OF A. P. CARTER | 195? | Acme LP-2 | 100 |
| *(Promo label)* | | | |
| MORE FAVORITES BY THE CARTER FAMILY | 1965 | Decca 4557 | 45 |
| *(Pink promo label)* | | | |
| MOTHER MAYBELLE CARTER | 195? | Ambassador 98069 | 75 |
| *(Promo label)* | | | |
| **RADIO SHOWS** | | | |
| **16-Inch Transcriptions** | | | |
| COUNTRY STYLE USA (50s)  Public service program | 195? | Country Style 113 | 50-85 |
| *(Features the Carter Family)* | | | |
| **Compact Discs** | | | |
| COUNTRY CUTTING EDGE (Nov 93)  Carlene Carter | 1993 | | 15-25 |
| *(Music and interview)* | | | |
| LIVE FROM CRAZY HORSE  Carlene Carter | 1994 | | 40-75 |
| *(Live concert)* | | | |

## CARTER, MEL
**45s**

| Title | Yr | Label, Number | NM $ |
|---|---|---|---|
| SALES STIMULATOR | 1966 | Rowe 1006 | 20 |
| *(Red vinyl, small center hole)* | | | |

## CARTEY, RIC
**45s**

| Title | Yr | Label, Number | NM $ |
|---|---|---|---|
| OOOH-EEE  Promo label | 1957 | Stars 539 | 75 |
| *(Cartey wrote Young Love)* | | | |
| OOOH-EEE  White promo label | 1957 | RCA Victor | 50 |
| *(Flip side is the original version of "Young Love")* | | | |

## CASABLANCA
**RADIO SHOWS**
**Albums**

| Title | Yr | Label, Number | NM $ |
|---|---|---|---|
| BBC TRANSCRIPTION DISC  Live show | 1974 | BBC Transcription | 75-125 |
| *(With Snafu)* | | | |

## CASEY, AL
*Also see Duane Eddy*
**45s**

| Title | Yr | Label, Number | NM $ |
|---|---|---|---|
| SURFIN' HOOTENANNY  Red vinyl | 1963 | Stacy | 40 |
| **Albums** | | | |
| SURFIN' HOOTENANNY  Red vinyl | 1963 | Stacy | 50 |

## CASH, JOHNNY
Sun label promo 45s under #400 $25 each; Sun label color vinyl promo 45s after #1100, $10 each; Columbia promo 45s $4 each; Columbia "stereo/seven" 33s (7") $10 each (Multi-colored labels); Columbia stereo 33s (7") $8 each (orange labels); Columbia white promo label LPs $5-10 each; Mercury or American promo CD singles $3

**45s**

| Title | Yr | Label, Number | NM $ |
|---|---|---|---|
| RIDE THIS TRAIN  Set of five stereo singles | 196? | Columbia JS7-JS12 | 40 |
| *(Issued with envelope cover for jukeboxes only)* | | | |
| RING OF FIRE (same on both sides) | 1963 | Columbia 42788 | 40 |
| *(Red vinyl promo)* | | | |
| RING OF FIRE  Set of five stereo singles | 1963 | Columbia 8853 | 40 |
| *(Issued with envelope cover for jukeboxes only)* | | | |
| **7-Inch Extended Plays** | | | |
| AT FOLSOM PRISON  Jukebox LLP | 197? | Columbia 9639 | 20 |
| *(Blue label, issued with hard cover)* | | | |
| GREATEST HITS VOL. 1  Jukebox LLP | 197? | Columbia 9478 | 18 |
| *(Blue label, issued with paper sleeve)* | | | |
| HAPPINESS IS YOU  Jukebox LLP | 197? | Columbia 9337 | 18 |
| *(Blue label, issued with paper sleeve)* | | | |
| HELLO, I'M JOHNNY CASH  Jukebox LLP | 197? | Columbia 9943 | 20 |
| *(Red label, issued with hard cover)* | | | |
| I WALK THE LINE  Jukebox LLP | 197? | Columbia 8990 | 18 |
| *(Blue label, issued with paper sleeve)* | | | |
| JOHNNY CASH THE LEGEND (70s)  Jukebox LLP with six songs | 197? | Sun 2-118 | 25 |
| *(Yellow label, issued with a paper sleeve)* | | | |
| THE SURVIVORS  Four-song promo-only EP | 1982 | Columbia AE7 1505 | 20 |
| *(With Jerry Lee Lewis and Carl Perkins, issued with promo picture sleeve and recorded live)* | | | |

| Title | Yr | Label, Number | NM $ |
|-------|-----|--------------|------|
| **Albums** | | | |
| 1970 PEPSI-COLA RADIO Interim version | 1970 | Pepsi-Cola 1718 | 100 |
| *(Several tracks)* | | | |
| 1970 PEPSI-COLA RADIO Radio ads including Cash | 1970 | Pepsi-Cola 1706 | 100 |
| *(Several tracks)* | | | |
| 1971 PEPSI-COLA RADIO Interim version | 1971 | Pepsi-Cola 1723 | 100 |
| *(Several tracks)* | | | |
| 1971 PEPSI-COLA RADIO Radio ads | 1971 | Pepsi-Cola 1722 | 100 |
| *(Several tracks)* | | | |
| GOOD EARTH  Radio spots and songs | 1973 | Farm Sales Team | 75 |
| JOHNNY CASH Mail-order from Doral | 197? | Columbia Doral CSP | 40 |
| THE LURE OF THE GRAND CANYON Red promo label | 1961 | Columbia 1622 | 50 |
| *("Demonstration-Not for Sale" in white letters across label)* | | | |
| **RADIO SHOWS** | | | |
| **16-Inch Transcriptions** | | | |
| TREASURY DEPARTMENT Public service show | 1959 | U. S. Treasury 639 | 60-100 |
| *(Music and interview)* | | | |
| **45s** | | | |
| THE JOHNNY CASH SHOW (60s) Public service series | 196? | Social Security | 15 |
| *(7" 33 1/3 demo disc)* | | | |
| **Albums** | | | |
| BBC TRANSCRIPTION DISC  Live Christmas concert | 1978 | BBC Transcription | 300-400 |
| *(The rarest of all Johnny Cash treasures)* | | | |
| COUNTRY COOKIN' (Feb 77) 15-minute show | 1977 | U. S. Army (2) | 15-20 |
| *(Three other programs with three other artists* | | | |
| THE JOHNNY CASH SHOW (60s) Public service series | 196? | Social Security | 25-50 |
| *(Price is for one show)* | | | |
| THE JOHNNY CASH SHOW (60s) Public service series | 196? | Social Security | 300-400 |
| *(Price is for the complete set of shows)* | | | |
| WORLD OF FOLK MUSIC (60s) Show with Bob Dylan | 196? | Social Security | 25-50 |
| *(Music and interviews)* | | | |
| **Cassettes** | | | |
| AUSTIN CITY LIMITS (90s) Live show | 199? | Mainstreet | 40-75 |
| *(Radio show released on cassette)* | | | |

## CASH, ROSEANNE
*Columbia promo 45s $3 each; Columbia promo CD singles $3 each*

| Title | Yr | Label, Number | NM $ |
|-------|-----|--------------|------|
| **Albums** | | | |
| INTERVIEW WITH MARTHA HUME | 1982 | Columbia AS 1527 | 30 |
| *(Generic cover with sticker)* | | | |
| **RADIO SHOWS** | | | |
| **Albums** | | | |
| WESTWOOD ONE PRESENTS (Sept 89) | 1989 | Westwood One | 60-100 |
| *(Live concert)* | | | |

## CASHMAN, TERRY

| Title | Yr | Label, Number | NM $ |
|-------|-----|--------------|------|
| **45s** | | | |
| FOOTBALL U.S.A. (same on both sides) | 1983 | Lifesong 45121 | 4 |
| *(May be promo only)* | | | |

## CASHMERES, THE
*Other Mercury promo $25 each*

| Title | Yr | Label, Number | NM $ |
|-------|-----|--------------|------|
| **45s** | | | |
| DON'T LET IT HAPPEN | 1955 | Mercury 70617 | 45 |
| *(White promo label)* | | | |
| MY SENTIMENTAL HEART | 1954 | Mercury 70501 | 40 |
| *(White promo label)* | | | |
| THERE'S A RUMOR | 1955 | Mercury 70679 | 40 |
| *(White promo label)* | | | |

## CASTOR, JIMMY, BUNCH

| Title | Yr | Label, Number | NM $ |
|-------|-----|--------------|------|
| **45s** | | | |
| I DON'T WANNA LOSE YOU (mono/stereo) | 1976 | Atlantic 3369 | 5 |
| *(May be promo-only)* | | | |

## CELEBRATION FEATURING MIKE LOVE

| Title | Yr | Label, Number | NM $ |
|-------|-----|--------------|------|
| **45s** | | | |
| ALMOST SUMMER/ALMOST SUMMER (KRTH Version) | 1978 | MCA S45-1986 | 10 |
| *(Special promo for Los Angeles radio station)* | | | |

## CHAD AND JEREMY
*World Artists white label promo 45s $12 each; Columbia promo singles $8-10 each; Rocshire white label promo 45s $4 each; World Artists promo LPs $20 each; Columbia white label promo LPs $15 each*

| Title | Yr | Label, Number | NM $ |
|-------|-----|--------------|------|
| **45s** | | | |
| BEFORE AND AFTER Red vinyl | 1965 | Columbia 43277 | 40 |
| *(White promo label)* | | | |
| CHAD STUART & JEREMY CLYDE INTERVIEW Promo only | 1983 | Rocshire 95050 | 15 |
| *(Interview is 6:33, flip is "Bite the Bullet")* | | | |
| I DON'T WANT TO LOSE YOU BABY | 1965 | Columbia 43339 | 15 |
| *(Special promo-only sleeve)* | | | |
| PAXTON QUIGLEY'S HAD THE COURSE White promo label | 1967 | Columbia | 25 |
| *(Price includes promo-only picture sleeve, Nazi-related)* | | | |

| Title | Yr | Label, Number | NM $ |
|---|---|---|---|

**CHAMPS, THE**
*Challenge white label promo 45s worth $10-15 each*
**7-Inch Extended Plays**

| Title | Yr | Label, Number | NM $ |
|---|---|---|---|
| TEQUILA<br>*(White promo label)* | 1958 | Challenge 7100 | 100 |

**CHANTAYS**
*Dot white label promo 45s $10 each*
**45s**

| Title | Yr | Label, Number | NM $ |
|---|---|---|---|
| PIPELINE Green vinyl<br>*(Second release of the single, promo only in color)* | 1966 | Dot 104 (reissue) | 150 |

**CHAPIN, HARRY**
*Elektra white promo label promo 45s $4 each; Boardwalk and other label promos $3 each; Elektra white label promo LPs $8 each*
**12-Inch Singles**

| Title | Yr | Label, Number | NM $ |
|---|---|---|---|
| BETTER PLACE TO BE<br>*(Promo 12" single)* | 1977 | Elektra 45327 | 10 |

**45s**

| Title | Yr | Label, Number | NM $ |
|---|---|---|---|
| OLD TIME MOVIES  From Esquire Socks<br>*(The Chapin brothers and Will Jordan, price includes special picture sleeve)* | 1966 | Rock-Land 664 | 40 |
| TAXI  Long/short versions<br>*(White promo label)* | 1972 | Elektra 45770 | 10 |
| WHAT'S IT ALL ABOUT (Apr 79) Public service show<br>*(Flip is Little Richard)* | 1979 | W. I. A. A. 471 | 30 |
| WHAT'S IT ALL ABOUT (Oct 76) Public service show<br>*(Titled "Cat's in the Cradle," flip is Phoebe Snow)* | 1976 | W. I. A. A. 338 | 25 |
| WHAT'S IT ALL ABOUT (Sept 81) Public service show<br>*(Flip is the Platters)* | 1981 | W. I. A. A. 592 | 30 |
| WORKIN' ON MY LIFE The Chapin Brothers<br>*(White promo label)* | 1969 | Epic 10761 | 10 |

**Albums**

| Title | Yr | Label, Number | NM $ |
|---|---|---|---|
| ENGLISH SPOT PLATTER (80s) U.S. Department of Health and Human Services<br>*(On the two discs, Harry does four 55-second ads)* | 198? | (2) | 25-50 |

**RADIO SHOWS**
**Albums**

| Title | Yr | Label, Number | NM $ |
|---|---|---|---|
| ALISON STEELE  Harry Chapin<br>*(Music and interviews)* | 1980 | | 25-50 |
| KEEP THE CHANGE  Pubic service program<br>*(Series of daily 5-minute public service programs)* | 1981 | Social Security (8) | 75-200 |
| NIGHTBIRD (May 74) One of four 30-minute shows<br>*(Music and interview)* | 1974 | U.S. Army Reserve | 75-100 |
| ROBERT W. MORGAN  Music and interview<br>*(May have been repeated)* | 1978 | Watermark | 50-80 |
| ROBERT W. MORGAN (June 81) Music and interview<br>*(Different show than above)* | 1981 | Watermark | 50-75 |

**Reel-to-Reel Tapes**

| Title | Yr | Label, Number | NM $ |
|---|---|---|---|
| KING BISCUIT FLOWER HOUR (May 76) Live concert<br>*(With Janis Ian)* | 1976 | DIR/ABC (2) | 200-300 |

**CHAPMAN, TRACY**
**12-Inch Singles**

| Title | Yr | Label, Number | NM $ |
|---|---|---|---|
| ALL THAT YOU HAVE IS YOUR SOUL (LP/edit) | 1989 | Elektra 5424 | 5 |
| BABY CAN I HOLD YOU (same on both sides) | 1988 | Elektra 5340 | 6 |
| BORN TO FIGHT (same on both sides) | 1989 | Elektra 5441 | 6 |
| CROSSROADS (same on both sides) | 1989 | Elektra ED 5403 | 6 |
| TALKIN' ABOUT A REVOLUTION (same on both sides) | 1988 | Elektra 5315 | 6 |
| THIS TIME/THIS TIME (Edit) | 1990 | Elektra 5455 | 6 |

**CHARIOTEERS, THE**
**Albums**

| Title | Yr | Label, Number | NM $ |
|---|---|---|---|
| CHARIOTEERS WITH BILLY WILLIAMS<br>*(White promo label)* | 1957 | Harmony 7089 | 40 |

**CHARLATANS, THE**
**45s**

| Title | Yr | Label, Number | NM $ |
|---|---|---|---|
| DATE: MAY 19, 1969<br>*(One-sided, promo only)* | 1969 | Philips 44824 | 60 |

**Albums**

| Title | Yr | Label, Number | NM $ |
|---|---|---|---|
| THE CHARLATANS<br>*(White promo label)* | 1969 | Philips 600309 | 45 |

**CHARLES, RAY**
*Atlantic white label promo 45s to #1200 $35 each; Atlantic white promo label 45s after #1200 $20 each; Atlantic blue label promo 45s $8 each; other ABC Paramount and ABC Jukebox LLPs $12 each; Atlantic white label EPs (if they exist) $250 each; Atlantic white label promo LPs $40 each; ABC Paramount white label promo LPs $15-25 each; Columbia white label promo LPs $5 each; Atco white label promo 45s by the Ikettes $15 each; ABC Paramount white label promo 45s $10 each; ABC Paramount yellow label stereo 7" 33rpm jukebox singles $25 each; ABC white label promo 45s $8 each; Columbia white label promo 45s $3 each.*
**45s**

| Title | Yr | Label, Number | NM $ |
|---|---|---|---|
| CHRISTMAS TIME (same on both sides)<br>*(May be promo-only)* | 1978 | Atlantic 3549 | 6 |
| COCA-COLA JINGLE A GO-GO<br>*(Two ads, Everly Brothers, and yes, that "uh-huh" guy)* | 1963 | Coca-Cola | 200 |
| MODERN SOUNDS IN COUNTRY AND WESTERN MUSIC<br>*(Five-record set with envelope for jukeboxes only, price for each is $15)* | 1962 | ABC Paramount 410-415 | 75 |

| Title | Yr | Label, Number | NM $ |
|---|---|---|---|
| ONE MINT JULEP | 196? | Impulse A-2 S-3 | 25 |
| *(Jukebox-only stereo single)* | | | |
| SMOKEY BEAR RADIO Public service announcement | 1975 | Ad Council 475 | 30 |
| *(Seven cuts in all, issued in hard cover with picture of Smokey, Ray sings a 60-second spot)* | | | |
| SWEET AND SOUR TEARS | 196? | ABC ABCS-480 (5) | 60 |
| *(Set of five jukebox singles from this LP)* | | | |
| WHAT'S IT ALL ABOUT (July 79) Public service show | 1979 | W. I. A. A. 478 | 18 |
| *(Other side is Kenny Rogers)* | | | |
| WHAT'S IT ALL ABOUT (June 82) Public service show | 1982 | W. I. A. A. 630 | 30 |
| *(Flip side is Little Richard)* | | | |
| **7-Inch Extended Plays** | | | |
| ALL-TIME GREAT PERFORMANCES (70s) Jukebox LLP | 197? | ABC PRO-731 (LLP 201) | 15 |
| *(Black label, issued with paper sleeve)* | | | |
| COUNTRY & WESTERN MEETS RHYTHM & BLUES  Jukebox LLP | 1968 | ABC Paramount 520 | 20 |
| *(Issued with hard cover)* | | | |
| CRYING TIME  Jukebox LLP | 1968 | ABC Paramount 544 | 20 |
| *(Issued with hard cover)* | | | |
| DEDICATED TO YOU  Jukebox LLP | 1968 | ABC Paramount 355 | 30 |
| *(Issued with hard cover)* | | | |
| THE GENIUS HITS THE ROAD  Jukebox LLP | 1968 | ABC Paramount 335 | 35 |
| *(Issued with hard cover)* | | | |
| GREATEST HITS  Jukebox LLP | 1968 | ABC Paramount 415 | 30 |
| *(Issued with hard cover)* | | | |
| HAVE A SMILE WITH ME  Jukebox LLP | 1968 | ABC Paramount 495 | 20 |
| *(Issued with hard cover)* | | | |
| INGREDIENTS IN A RECIPE FOR SOUL  Jukebox LLP with six songs | 1968 | ABC Paramount 465 | 25 |
| *(Yellow label, issued with hard cover blank on back)* | | | |
| LIVE IN CONCERT  Jukebox LLP | 1968 | ABC Paramount 500 | 20 |
| *(Issued with hard cover)* | | | |
| MODERN SOUNDS IN COUNTRY AND WESTERN MUSIC Jukebox LLP | 1968 | ABC Paramount 410 | 30 |
| *(Issued with hard cover)* | | | |
| MODERN SOUNDS IN COUNTRY WESTERN VOL. 2  Jukebox LLP | 1968 | ABC Paramount 435 | 30 |
| *(Yellow label, issued with hard cover)* | | | |
| A PORTRAIT OF RAY  Jukebox LLP with six songs | 1968 | ABC Paramount 625 | 15 |
| *(black label, hard cover)* | | | |
| RAY CHARLES  White promo label | 1960 | ABC Paramount 410 | 100 |
| *(Very rare)* | | | |
| SWEET & SOUR TEARS Jukebox LLP with six songs | 1968 | ABC Paramount 480 | 20 |
| *(Yellow label, issued with hard cover blank on back)* | | | |
| WHAT'D I SAY Jukebox LLP | 1968 | Atlantic 8029 | 35 |
| *(Only Jukebox LLP on Atlantic)* | | | |
| **Albums** | | | |
| FRIENDSHIP RADIO SHOW | 1984 | Columbia AS 1920 | 25 |
| **Compact Discs** | | | |
| BUSTED | 1990 | Epic 2129 | 10 |
| *(Promo cartoon cover)* | | | |
| **RADIO SHOWS** | | | |
| **Cassettes** | | | |
| AUSTIN ENCORE | 1994 | Mainstreet | 40-75 |
| *(Live concert on cassette)* | | | |
| **Compact Discs** | | | |
| THE STORY OF RAY CHARLES (June 92) | 1992 | Unistar (2) | 25-40 |
| *(Music and interviews)* | | | |

## CHARMS, THE
*DeLuxe white label promo 45s $25 each; King white label 45s by Otis Williams $15 each*

| **45s** | | | |
|---|---|---|---|
| FIFTY-FIVE SECONDS | 1954 | DeLuxe 6050 | 40 |
| *(White promo label)* | | | |
| HAPPY ARE WE | 1953 | DeLuxe 6014 | 75 |
| *(White promo label)* | | | |
| HEAVEN ONLY KNOWS | 1953 | DeLuxe 6000 | 85 |
| *(White promo label)* | | | |
| MY BABY | 1955 | DeLuxe 6056 | 40 |
| *(White promo label)* | | | |

## CHATEAUS, THE
**45s**

| | | | |
|---|---|---|---|
| LET ME TELL YOU, BABY | 1956 | Epic 9163 | 40 |
| *(White promo label)* | | | |

## CHEAP TRICK
*Epic promo 45s $4-8 each depending on year; Epic promo picture sleeves $3 each; Asylum promo 45s $3 each; Pasha promo singles $3 each; Warner Bros. promo singles $3 each; Epic promo LPs $6 each; Warner Bros. promo CD singles not listed $3; Warner Bros. promo CD singles $3 each*

| **45s** | | | |
|---|---|---|---|
| I WANT YOU TO WANT ME (Alternate Version)// WAITIN' FOR THE MAN/HEROIN (Live) | 1996 | Epic Legacy ES7 8290 | 10 |
| *(Promo-only with title sleeve, giveaway with some copies of the Sex, America, Cheap Trick CD box set)* | | | |
| WHAT'S IT ALL ABOUT (Dec 81) Public service show | 1981 | W. I. A. A. 605 | 25 |
| *(Flip side features Foreigner)* | | | |
| **7-Inch Extended Plays** | | | |
| FOR NESTLE'S CANDY  Special release | 1981 | Columbia P | 15 |
| *(Four songs for Columbia Special Products)* | | | |
| **Albums** | | | |
| FROM TOKYO TO YOU | 1979 | Epic AS 518 | 30 |
| *(Promo-only sampler from Cheap Trick at Budokan)* | | | |

| Title | Yr | Label, Number | NM $ |
|---|---|---|---|
| **Compact Discs** | | | |
| BUSTED | 1990 | Epic ESK 2129 | 20 |
| *(Promo-only release)* | | | |
| THE FLAME | 1988 | Epic ESK 1050 | 8 |
| *(Promo-only, 45 and LP versions)* | | | |
| SAMPLER  Picture disc | 1988 | Epic ESK 1012 | 50 |
| *(Promo-only release)* | | | |
| **RADIO SHOWS** | | | |
| **Albums** | | | |
| IN CONCERT (Aug 82) | 1982 | Westwood One (2) | 25-50 |
| *(Live concert)* | | | |
| IN CONCERT (July 83) | 1983 | Westwood One (2) | 30-50 |
| *(Live concert)* | | | |
| PIONEERS IN MUSIC (Aug 86) Ohio Rock | 1986 | DIR (2) | 30-60 |
| *(With Chrissie Hynde and Devo)* | | | |
| SUPERGROUPS | 1980 | (3) | 150-250 |
| *(Rare live concert material)* | | | |
| **Compact Discs** | | | |
| IN THE STUDIO Album Profile | 1989 | Album Network | 10-20 |
| *(Music and interviews)* | | | |

## CHECKER, CHUBBY

*Parkway white label LPs are $25-50 depending on year ; Parkway white label promo 45s $10-15 each; Cameo white label promo 45s $5 each; Buddah promo 45s $6 each; Seabright promo 45s $3 each; MCA promo 45s worth $3; 12" singles on any label $10 each*

| Title | Yr | Label, Number | NM $ |
|---|---|---|---|
| **45s** | | | |
| MOVE IT  With insert | 1976 | Amherst 716 | 10 |
| *(Insert advertises Checker's appearance on Donny and Marie)* | | | |
| THE TWIST/TWISTIN' U.S.A. Red vinyl | 1961 | Parkway 811 | 200 |
| *(Issued during the second hit run of the song)* | | | |
| THE TWIST/TWISTIN' U.S.A. White promo label | 1961 | Parkway 811 | 25 |
| *(From the second hit run; not to be confused with the white label with blue print stock copy from the first run with "Toot" on the B-side)* | | | |
| THE TWIST/TWISTIN' U.S.A. Yellow vinyl | 1961 | Parkway 811 | 150 |
| *(Also issued during the second hit run)* | | | |
| YOUR HITS AND MINE  Chubby Checker and Bobby Rydell | 1962 | Cameo 12 | 40 |
| *(Promo release only)* | | | |
| **7-Inch Extended Plays** | | | |
| CHUBBY CHECKER  White promo label | 1961 | Parkway 5001 | 100 |
| *(Issued with a paper sleeve)* | | | |

## CHECKERS, THE

*Other King promo 45s $25 each*

| Title | Yr | Label, Number | NM $ |
|---|---|---|---|
| **45s** | | | |
| HEAVEN ONLY KNOWS | 1958 | King 5156 | 45 |
| *(White promo label)* | | | |
| HOUSE WITH NO WINDOWS | 1954 | King 4710 | 85 |
| *(White promo label)* | | | |
| I PROMISE YOU | 1954 | King 4673 | 150 |
| *(White promo label)* | | | |
| MAMA'S DAUGHTER | 1954 | King 4751 | 75 |
| *(White promo label)* | | | |
| TRYING TO HOLD MY GIRL | 1955 | King 4764 | 85 |
| *(White promo label)* | | | |
| WHITE CLIFFS OF DOVER | 1954 | King 4675 | 150 |
| *(White promo label)* | | | |

## CHEERS, THE

*Other Capitol promo 45s $10 each*

| Title | Yr | Label, Number | NM $ |
|---|---|---|---|
| **45s** | | | |
| BLACK DENIM TROUSERS | 1955 | Capitol 3219 | 20 |
| *(White promo label; stock copies list the title as "Black Denim Trousers and Motorcycle Boots")* | | | |

## CHER

*Other Imperial promo 45s $5 each; Kapp, MCA, Warner Bros., Casablanca promo 45s $4 each; Geffen promo 45s $3 each Includes Bonnie Joe Mason, Cherilyn; also see Sonny & Cher*

| Title | Yr | Label, Number | NM $ |
|---|---|---|---|
| **45s** | | | |
| ALL I REALLY WANT TO DO | 1965 | Imperial 66114 | 12 |
| *(Cream-colored promo label)* | | | |
| DREAM BABY  Cherilyn | 1964 | Imperial 66081 | 40 |
| *(White promo label)* | | | |
| RINGO, I LOVE YOU  Bonnie Jo Mason | 1964 | Annette 1000 | 500 |
| *(Stock copy is worth $1,000)* | | | |
| WHAT'S IT ALL ABOUT (Nov 82) Public service show | 1982 | W. I. A. A. 647 | 18 |
| *(Flip side is Roberta Flack)* | | | |
| **Compact Discs** | | | |
| LOVE HURTS | 1992 | Geffen GEFD-24421 | 20 |
| *(CD with custom box and tarot cards, also released as a stock copy)* | | | |
| **RADIO SHOWS** | | | |
| **Compact Discs** | | | |
| THE CHER STORY | 1989 | Unistar | 15-25 |
| *(Music and interviews, repeated)* | | | |

## CHERRY, NENEH

| Title | Yr | Label, Number | NM $ |
|---|---|---|---|
| **12-Inch Singles** | | | |
| BUDDY X (6 versions) | 1992 | Virgin 12776 | 8 |
| BUFFALO STANCE (4 versions) | 1989 | Virgin 1296 | 12 |
| KISSES ON THE WIND (6 versions)/BUFFALO BLUES | 1989 | Virgin 1378 | 8 |

| Title | Yr | Label, Number | NM $ |
|-------|----|--------------| ----|
| MANCHILD (4 versions)/BUFFALO STANCE (Sukka Mix II) | 1989 | Virgin 1403 | 8 |
| MONEY LOVE (2 mixes)/TWISTED | 1992 | Virgin 12709 | 8 |

**CHESTERFIELDS, THE**
**45s**

| I'M IN HEAVEN | 1954 | Chess 1559 | 125 |

*(Chess promo 45s are rare)*

**CHESTNUTS, THE**
**45s**

| DON'T GO | 1954 | Mercury 70489 | 75 |

*(White promo label)*

**CHEVALIER, MAURICE**
**7-Inch Extended Plays**

| MAURICE CHEVALIER | 1958 | MGM 58-EP-51 | 25 |

*(Kaye Ballard on flip)*

**CHICAGO**
*Columbia promo 45s $3-5 each; Full Moon promo 45s $2 each; Warner Brothers promo singles $2 each*
**45s**

| BABY, WHAT A BIG SURPRISE  Promo picture sleeve | 1977 | Columbia 10620 | 10 |
| *(Price is for the promo-only picture sleeve that was issued to a limited number of radio stations)* | | | |
| BEGINNINGS | 1971 | Columbia AS 179 | 10 |
| *(6:28 version, much longer than other single versions)* | | | |
| QUESTIONS 67 AND 68 | 1971 | Columbia 67E68 | 25 |
| *(In English and Japanese!)* | | | |
| TELL ME  James William Guercio | 1973 | Columbia 45886 | 10 |
| *(7:43 version, from movie Elektra Glide in Blue)* | | | |
| WHAT'S IT ALL ABOUT (June 82) Public service show | 1982 | W. I. A. A. 631 | 20 |
| *(Flip side features the Coasters)* | | | |
| WHAT'S IT ALL ABOUT (Nov 75) Public service show | 1975 | W. I. A. A. 291 | 15 |
| *(Same show as above, flip is Lou Rawls)* | | | |
| WHAT'S IT ALL ABOUT (Sept 73) Public service show | 1973 | W. I. A. A. 191 | 25 |
| *(Interview with Robert Lamm and Jim Pankow, flip is the Edgar Winter Group)* | | | |
| WHAT'S IT ALL ABOUT Public service show | 1980 | W. I. A. A. 3024 | 30 |
| *(Flip side features the Rolling Stones)* | | | |
| WHERE DO YOU THINK YOU'RE GOING?  Robert Lamm | 1972 | Columbia AE7 1054 | 15 |
| *(1:15 version, promo only, public service song)* | | | |

**7-Inch Extended Plays**

| CHICAGO ("CALL ON ME") Red-orange label, Jukebox LLP | 1974 | Columbia 7-32810 | 15 |
| *(Issued with hard cover, back is blank)* | | | |
| CHICAGO ("COLOUR MY WORLD") Red label, Jukebox LLP | 1971 | Columbia 7-KGP 24 | 35 |
| *(Issued with hard cover, back is blank)* | | | |
| CHICAGO ("DARLIN' DEAR") Red-orange label, Jukebox LLP | 197? | Columbia 7-32400 | 20 |
| *(Issued with hard cover, group picture on front, back is blank)* | | | |
| CHICAGO ("MOTHER") Red labe, Jukebox LLP | 197? | Columbia 7-30110 | 25 |
| *(Issued with hard cover, back is blank)* | | | |

**Albums**

| CHICAGO | 1976 | Columbia (no #) | 200 |
| *(Box set of 17 records, promo version)* | | | |
| CHICAGO 17 | 1984 | Warner Bros. 25060 | 20 |
| *(Promo pressing on Quiex II vinyl)* | | | |

**RADIO SHOWS**
**Albums**

| 20TH ANNIVERSARY RADIO SPECIAL (May 87) | 1987 | United Stations (3) | 20-30 |
| *(Box set special with other artists)* | | | |
| IN CONCERT (Dec 82) Live concert | 1982 | Westwood One (2) | 25-50 |
| *(Early shows in this series are hard to find)* | | | |
| INNERVIEW (70s) Music and interviews | 197? | Innerview | 15-30 |
| *(Show repeated)* | | | |
| PIONEERS IN ROCK Music and interviews | 1986 | DIR (2) | 20-35 |
| *(With Blood Sweat & Tears and Procol Harum)* | | | |
| RETRO ROCK (Oct 81) Live concert | 1981 | Clayton Webster (2) | 75-125 |
| *(Hard to find concert)* | | | |
| ROBERT W. MORGAN (Nov 80) Music and interviews | 1980 | Watermark | 20-40 |
| *(Show reissued several times)* | | | |
| STARTRACK PROFILE | 1987 | Westwood One (2) | 15-30 |
| *(Later reissued shows split the original concert)* | | | |
| STARTRACK PROFILE Part 1 and 2 | 1987 | Westwood One (4) | 30-60 |
| *(Some live material)* | | | |
| SUPERGROUPS Live concert | 1979 | DIR (3) | 75-140 |
| *(Rare series to find before 1980)* | | | |
| WESTWOOD ONE PRESENTS Live concert | 1983 | Westwood One | 25-40 |
| *(Hard to find series)* | | | |

**Compact Discs**

| IN THE STUDIO Music and interview | 1989 | Album Network | 10-20 |
| *(Featuring an LP each show)* | | | |
| KING BISCUIT FLOWER HOUR (July 88) Live concert | 1988 | DIR | 25-50 |
| *(Repeated June 92)* | | | |
| KING BISCUIT FLOWER HOUR (Nov 94) | 1994 | DIR | 40-75 |
| *(Live concert)* | | | |

**Reel-to-Reel Tapes**

| KING BISCUIT FLOWER HOUR (July 76) Live concert | 1976 | DIR/ABC | 75-100 |
| *(Rare show on two reels, also features Robin Trower)* | | | |

| Title | Yr | Label, Number | NM $ |
|-------|----|--------------| -----|

**CHILD, JANE**
**45s**

| | | | |
|-------|----|--------------|------|
| WELCOME TO THE REAL WORLD | 1991 | WB PRO-S-4388 | 10 |

**CHILLIWACK**
**12-Inch Singles**

| | | | |
|-------|----|--------------|------|
| WHATCHA GONNA DO (same on both sides) | 1982 | Millennium JD-13116 | 10 |

**CHINA CRISIS**
**12-Inch Singles**

| | | | |
|-------|----|--------------|------|
| ARIZONA SKY/ARIZONA SKY (edit) | 1986 | A&M 17445 | 5 |
| THE HIGHEST HIGH/GIFT OF FREEDOM | 1985 | Warner Bros. PRO-A-2302 | 12 |
| WAKE UP (edit)/WAKE UP (LP version) | 1985 | Warner Bros. PRO-A-2343 | 8 |

**RADIO SHOWS**
**Albums**

| | | | |
|-------|----|--------------|------|
| BBC ROCK HOUR (Apr 84) Live concert | 1984 | London Wavelength | 30-60 |
| *(With Wang Chung)* | | | |
| BBC TRANSCRIPTION DISC | 1984 | BBC Transcription | 200-300 |
| *(Live concert)* | | | |
| IN CONCERT (Sept 85) Live concert | 1985 | Westwood One (2) | 40-75 |
| *(With Midnight Oil)* | | | |

**CHIPMUNKS, THE**
*Mercury promo 45s by Ross Bagdasarian $8 each; other Liberty promos $10 each (by Chipmunks, David Seville, Ross Bagdasarian); United Artists promo 45s $5 each; Liberty promo LPs $25. Also includes Alfi & Harry; Ross Bagdasarian; The Bedbugs; David Seville.*
**12-Inch Singles**

| | | | |
|-------|----|--------------|------|
| CALL ME (Disco Version) (same on both sides) | 1980 | Excelsior XEP-2000 | 10 |

**45s**

| | | | |
|-------|----|--------------|------|
| ARMEN'S THEME  David Seville | 1956 | Liberty 55041 | 25 |
| *(White promo label)* | | | |
| CHRISTMAS BLUES/THE CHPMUNK SONG Chipmunks and Canned Heat | 1968 | Liberty 56079 | 15 |
| *(Liberty promo label)* | | | |
| COME ON-A-MY HOUSE  Ross Bagdasarian | 1953 | Coral 60544 | 20 |
| *(Blue promo label)* | | | |
| GOTTA GET TO YOUR HOUSE  David Seville | 1957 | Liberty 55079 | 25 |
| *(White promo label, stock picture sleeve worth $40)* | | | |
| JUDY  David Seville | 1959 | Liberty 55193 | 15 |
| *(White promo label)* | | | |
| LITTLE BRASS BAND David Seville | 1958 | Liberty 55153 | 18 |
| *(White promo label)* | | | |
| THE BIRD ON MY HEAD David Seville | 1958 | Liberty 55140 | 25 |
| *(White promo label)* | | | |
| THE CHIPMUNK SONG  Chipmunks | 1958 | Liberty 55168 | 30 |
| *(White promo label)* | | | |
| THE TROUBLE WITH HARRY Alfi & Harry | 1955 | Liberty 55008 | 25 |
| *(White promo label)* | | | |
| WITCH DOCTOR  David Seville | 1958 | Liberty 55132 | 30 |
| *(White promo label)* | | | |
| YEAH YEAH   The Bedbugs | 1964 | Liberty 55679 | 18 |
| *(Cream-colored promo label)* | | | |

**78s**

| | | | |
|-------|----|--------------|------|
| COME ON-A-MY HOUSE  Ross Bagdasarian | 1953 | Coral 60544 | 30 |
| *(Blue promo label)* | | | |
| HEY BROTHER POUR THE WINE Ross Bagdasarian | 1955 | Mercury 70254 | 10 |
| *(White promo label)* | | | |

**CHIPPER**
**45s**

| | | | |
|-------|----|--------------|------|
| GROOVY CHRISTMAS/TOY SOLDIER | 197? | Malaco 2002 | 6 |

**CHOCOLATE WATCH BAND, THE**
*Tower white promo label 45s $12 each*

**CHORDETTES, THE**
*Columbia promo 78s $15 each; Columbia promo 45s $12 each; Cadence promo 45s $8 each*

**CHRISTIE, LOU**
*Includes The Classics*
**45s**

| | | | |
|-------|----|--------------|------|
| CLOSE YOUR EYES | 1960 | Starr 508 | 50 |
| *(By the Classics, Lou Christie is a member)* | | | |
| THE GYPSY CRIED | 1962 | C & C 102 | 75 |
| WACO (same on both sides) | 1971 | Buddah 231 | 6 |
| *(Stock copy does not exist)* | | | |

**CHURCH, THE**
*Arista promo 45s $5 each; Arista promo CD singles $3 each*
**12-Inch Singles**

| | | | |
|-------|----|--------------|------|
| COLUMBUS (2 versions)/HAPPY HUNTING GROUND | 1986 | Warner Bros. PRO-A-2484 | 12 |
| CONSTANT IN OPAL/SHADOW CABINET | 1984 | Warner Bros. PRO-A-2197 | 15 |
| DESTINATION/DESTINATION (Edit) | 1988 | Arista 9750 | 10 |
| REPTILE (Remix) (same on both sides) | 1988 | Arista 9718 | 10 |
| TANTALIZED (4:57)/TANTALIZED (3:58) | 1985 | Warner Bros. PRO-A-2428 | 15 |
| TERRA NOVA CAIN/TAKE IT BACK//GRIND (Acoustic Version) | 1990 | Arista ADP 2036 | 15 |

STEREO **IN CONCERT** SIDE TWO

Jimmy Buffet

**WESTWOOD ONE**

9540 WASHINGTON BLVD., CULVER CITY, CA 90230 (213) 204-5000

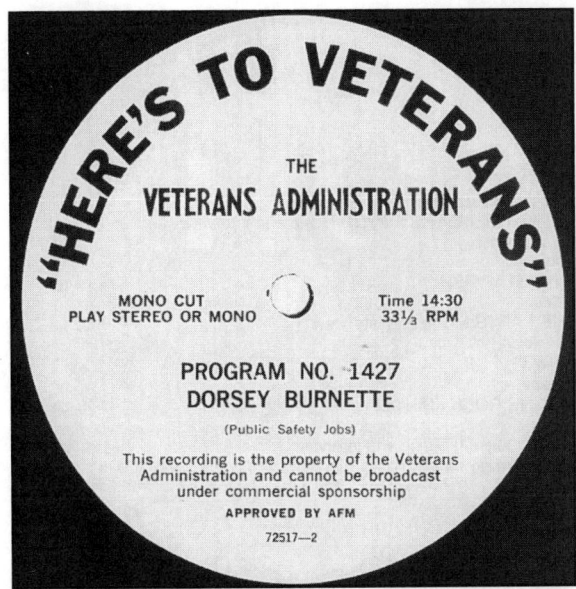

**"HERE'S TO VETERANS"**

THE
**VETERANS ADMINISTRATION**

MONO CUT
PLAY STEREO OR MONO

Time 14:30
33⅓ RPM

**PROGRAM NO. 1427
DORSEY BURNETTE**

(Public Safety Jobs)

This recording is the property of the Veterans
Administration and cannot be broadcast
under commercial sponsorship
**APPROVED BY AFM**
72517—2

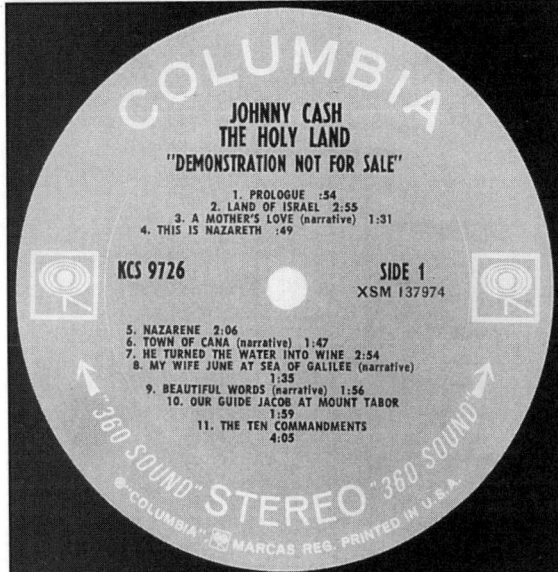

**COLUMBIA**

**JOHNNY CASH
THE HOLY LAND**
"DEMONSTRATION NOT FOR SALE"

1. PROLOGUE :54
2. LAND OF ISRAEL 2:55
3. A MOTHER'S LOVE (narrative) 1:31
4. THIS IS NAZARETH :49

KCS 9726                SIDE 1
                        XSM 137974

5. NAZARENE 2:06
6. TOWN OF CANA (narrative) 1:47
7. HE TURNED THE WATER INTO WINE 2:54
8. MY WIFE JUNE AT SEA OF GALILEE (narrative)
1:35
9. BEAUTIFUL WORDS (narrative) 1:56
10. OUR GUIDE JACOB AT MOUNT TABOR
1:59
11. THE TEN COMMANDMENTS
4:05

©"360 SOUND" STEREO 360 SOUND
©"COLUMBIA" MARCAS REG. PRINTED IN U.S.A.

**MEDIA AMERICA RADIO**
PRESENTS

**UP CLOSE**

DISC 1
8817

**Eric Clapton**

© NEER PERFECT PRODUCTIONS
1988

**NBC Radio
Entertainment**

STEREO
33⅓ RPM                        **4**

**ERIC CLAPTON**
THE BEST OF EVERYTHING

BROADCAST DATE: AUG. 30, 31
SEPT. 1, 2, 1985

Produced by Torus Communications

SD 7001

**CREAM
GOODBYE**

SAMPLE COPY
NOT FOR SALE

**ATCO**        **ONE**        **STEREO**

1. I'M SO GLAD
S. James

2. POLITICIAN
J. Bruce-P. Brown

(ST-C-681513CT)

MFG. BY ATLANTIC RECORDING CORP., 1841 BROADWAY, NEW YORK, N.Y.

(Top left) The Westwood One vinyl series In Concert has a rather attractive label – but the label has Jimmy Buffett's name spelled like an all-you-can-eat affair. (Top right) Dorsey Burnette, who once made a promotional record called "Be a Navy Man," here does a radio show for the Veterans Administration. (Middle left) Most Columbia promos on the "360 Sound" label are white. This Johnny Cash release of *The Holy Land* used the red label but added, in the same typeface, a "demonstration" line. This was atypical for Columbia. (Middle right) Eric Clapton is a frequent radio show subject, as he grabs ratings on classic rock stations. Here's an Up Close CD from 1988. (Bottom left) Another Eric Clapton show, this was meant for broadcast over the Labor Day weekend in 1985. (Bottom right) A "Sample Copy" white label promo of the last official Cream album, *Goodbye.* While this album is stereo, some Atco promo LPs were pressed in mono as late as the early 1970s, years after mono albums were discontinued to the general public.

| Title | Yr | Label, Number | NM $ |
|---|---|---|---|
| **Albums** | | | |
| SUM OF THE PARTS | 1988 | Arista ADP 9713 | 40 |
| *(Interviews and live acoustic tracks)* | | | |
| THREE CHURCH MEMBERS FOUND Music and interview | 198? | Arista | 25-50 |
| *(Issued with a picture cover)* | | | |
| **Compact Discs** | | | |
| LIFE BEFORE STARFISH | 1989 | Arista APCD 9724 | 30 |
| *(Promo-only CD)* | | | |
| SUM OF THE PARTS Music and interview | 1988 | Arista APCD 9713 | 50 |
| *(Promo-only sampler)* | | | |
| **RADIO SHOWS** | | | |
| **Compact Discs** | | | |
| IN CONCERT-NU ROCK (JAN 95) | 1995 | Westwood One | 40-75 |
| *(Live concert)* | | | |
| ON THE EDGE (July 94) Music and interview | 1994 | Westwood One | 20-30 |
| *(With Erasure and Velocity Girl)* | | | |

## CINDERELLA
*Mercury promo 45s $3 each*

| Title | Yr | Label, Number | NM $ |
|---|---|---|---|
| **Compact Discs** | | | |
| HEARTBREAK STATION | 1990 | Mercury CDP 326 | 25 |
| *(Promo CD single in "guitar case" packaging)* | | | |
| **RADIO SHOWS** | | | |
| **Albums** | | | |
| OFF THE RECORD (Feb 91) Music and interview | 1991 | Westwood One (2) | 15-20 |
| *(This show was repeated)* | | | |
| SUPERSTAR CONCERT (Sept 91) | 1991 | Westwood One (3) | 25-40 |
| *(Live concert)* | | | |

## CIRCLE JERKS
**RADIO SHOWS**
**Albums**

| Title | Yr | Label, Number | NM $ |
|---|---|---|---|
| SPIN CONCERT | 1986 | Spin Magazine (2) | 40-60 |
| *(Live concert)* | | | |

## CITY BOY
**45s**

| Title | Yr | Label, Number | NM $ |
|---|---|---|---|
| YOU'RE LEAVING ME (same on both sides) | 1981 | Atlantic 3789 | 4 |
| *(May be promo only)* | | | |

## CLANTON, JIMMY
*Other Ace label promo singles $10-20 each*
**45s**

| Title | Yr | Label, Number | NM $ |
|---|---|---|---|
| OLD ROCK 'N ROLLER (mono/stereo) | 1978 | Starcrest 078 | 5 |
| *(May be promo only)* | | | |
| VENUS IN BLUE JEANS/HIGHWAY BOUND | 1962 | Ace 664 | 25 |
| *(No stock copies exist with this catalog number)* | | | |

## CLAPTON, ERIC
*Polydor promo 45s $8 each; RSO promo 45s $8 each; Duck (Warner Bros.) promo 45s $5 each; Reprise promo 45s $4 each; Duck promo 12" singles $12 each; Warner Bros. promo 12" singles $10 each; other Polydor and RSO promo LPs $10 each; promo CD singles $6-$8*

| Title | Yr | Label, Number | NM $ |
|---|---|---|---|
| **12-Inch Singles** | | | |
| FIGHT (NO MATTER HOW LONG)  The Bunburys | 1988 | Arista ADP-9735 | 25 |
| *(Promo-only 12" single from "One Moment in Time" LP, released for the 1988 Summer Olympics. The Bunburys were Clapton with members of the Bee Gees.)* | | | |
| WHY DOES LOVE GOT TO BE SO SAD  Buckwheat Zydeco | 1988 | Island PR 2425 | 25 |
| *(Promo-only 12" single)* | | | |
| **45s** | | | |
| WHAT'S IT ALL ABOUT (Feb 81) Public service show | 1981 | W. I. A. A. 561 | 30 |
| *(Flip side is Orleans)* | | | |
| WHAT'S IT ALL ABOUT (July 79) Public service show | 1979 | W. I. A. A. 480 | 25 |
| *(Flip side features Suzy Quatro)* | | | |
| **Albums** | | | |
| BACKLESS | 1978 | RSO 1009 | 40 |
| *(White vinyl promo-only release)* | | | |
| CLASSIC CUTS FROM RSO'S COLLECTORS EDITIONS | 1980 | RSO PRO-2-015 | 40 |
| *(White promo labels with special jacket, promo only)* | | | |
| ERIC CLAPTON | 1970 | Atco 33-329 | 100 |
| *(Mono pressing is promo only)* | | | |
| ERIC CLAPTON AT HIS BEST | 1972 | Polydor 3503 | 20 |
| *(White promo label)* | | | |
| SLOWHAND | 1977 | RSO 035 | 25 |
| *(White vinyl promo)* | | | |
| SLOWHAND | 1977 | RSO 3030 | 12 |
| *(White promo label)* | | | |
| TAKING IT HOME Buckwheat Zydeco | 1988 | Island 90968 | 10 |
| *(White promo label)* | | | |
| **Compact Discs** | | | |
| CROSSROADS | 1988 | Polydor (# unknown) | 100 |
| *(Advance copy of box set in 4-CD jewel case)* | | | |
| CROSSROADS SAMPLER | 1989 | Polydor CDP 10 | 30 |
| *(Radio promo from the box set)* | | | |
| ERIC CLAPTON'S GREATEST HITS | 1995 | Warner Bros. (# unknown) | 100 |
| *(Promo-only CD compilation)* | | | |
| RARITIES ON COMPACT DISC VOL. 11 With 19 tracks | 1992 | | 30-60 |
| *(Issued on a regular basis to radio stations)* | | | |

| Title | Yr | Label, Number | NM $ |
|---|---|---|---|
| SELECTIONS FROM CROSSROADS 2 | 1995 | Chronicles PRSAD 00182 | 25 |
| *(Promo-only CD sampler)* | | | |
| **RADIO SHOWS** | | | |
| **Albums** | | | |
| BBC LONDON WAVELENGTH SPECIAL (May 82) | 1982 | London Wavelength (2) | 50-75 |
| *(Mostly music and interview, some live)* | | | |
| BBC ROCK HOUR (May 82) LIVE MATERIAL | 1982 | London Wavelength | 50-80 |
| *(BBC concert material)* | | | |
| BEST OF EVERYTHING (Oct 85) Profile | 1985 | NBC Radio (5) | 100-165 |
| *(Music and interview, issued in a picture box)* | | | |
| CONVERSATION (80s) Music and interview | 198? | London Wavelength (3) | 75-150 |
| *(Issued with a picture cover box)* | | | |
| ERIC CLAPTON IN CONCERT Live material | 1990 | Westwood One (4) | 40-80 |
| *(From several live concerts)* | | | |
| GUITAR  Music and interview | 1981 | | 25-50 |
| *(Hard show to find)* | | | |
| ISLE OF DREAMS  Various artists concert | 1985 | Westwood One (18) | 150-250 |
| *(12-hour "concert" hosted by Clapton, actually a studio-created "event" using prior Westwood One live performances)* | | | |
| ISLE OF DREAMS (86-87) Various artists concert | 1987 | Westwood One (18) | 125-200 |
| *(Repeat of the above)* | | | |
| ISLE OF DREAMS (88-89) Various artists concert | 1989 | Westwood One (9) | 75-125 |
| *(Edited version of the above)* | | | |
| KING BISCUIT FLOWER HOUR (May 85) Live concert | 1985 | DIR (2) | 75-125 |
| *(These shows on two LPs)* | | | |
| LEGENDS OF ROCK (Oct 88) Music and interview | 1988 | NBC Radio (2) | 15-25 |
| *(Profile of Clapton)* | | | |
| NBC SOURCE (Sept 85) Live concert | 1985 | NBC Radio (5) | 100-175 |
| *(Rare concert)* | | | |
| OFF THE RECORD (June 92) | 1992 | Westwood One (2) | 15-20 |
| *(Music and interviews)* | | | |
| OFF THE RECORD (May 90) Two parts | 1990 | Westwood One (4) | 20-30 |
| *(Music and interview)* | | | |
| ROCK AROUND THE WORLD (Nov 76) Music and interview | 1976 | RATW | 75-140 |
| *(Some live tracks)* | | | |
| ROCK STARS (Dec 89) Music and interview | 1989 | (2) | 25-50 |
| *(Some live tracks, repeated in May 90)* | | | |
| SUPERGROUPS (May 85) | 1985 | DIR | 75-125 |
| *(Live concert)* | | | |
| SUPERSTAR CONCERT (Oct 90) Box sets | 1990 | Westwood One (3) | 50-75 |
| *(Reissued several times)* | | | |
| THE BEST OF EVERYTHING (Aug 85) | 1985 | NBC Radio (5) | 100-175 |
| *(Box set with photo cover)* | | | |
| TIMOTHY WHITE SESSIONS (Dec 89) Music and interview | 1989 | (2) | 25-50 |
| *(Show repeated several times, some live tracks)* | | | |
| UP CLOSE Music and interview | 1987 | MCA Radio (2) | 40-75 |
| *(Picture labels, profile of Clapton)* | | | |
| WESTWOOD ONE SPECIAL (May 90) Live material | 1990 | Westwood One (4) | 100-150 |
| *(From several concerts)* | | | |
| **Compact Discs** | | | |
| 24 NIGHTS (Nov 91) Music and interview | 1991 | Album Network (2) | 60-100 |
| *(Live concert)* | | | |
| CREAM OF THE CROP Music and interview | 1993 | Global Satellite (6) | 50-100 |
| *(Some live material)* | | | |
| HISTORY OF ERIC CLAPTON (Sept 92) Profile | 1992 | On The Radio (6) | 125-250 |
| *(Music and interview with many live tracks)* | | | |
| IN THE STUDIO (90s) Album is featured | 199? | Album Network | 15-20 |
| *(Music and interview)* | | | |
| IN THE STUDIO (Nov 92) Special show | 1992 | Album Network (2) | 25-40 |
| *(Music and interview)* | | | |
| KING BISCUIT FLOWER HOUR (90s) Live concert | 199? | DIR | 75-125 |
| *(Later CD shows, mostly repeats of older DIR concerts)* | | | |
| KING BISCUIT FLOWER HOUR (Sept 87) Live concert | 1987 | DIR | 150-250 |
| *(The first radio show released on CD)* | | | |
| MEDIA AMERICA SPECIAL | 1995 | Media America (2) | 125-200 |
| *(Live at the Fillmore, blues-only concert)* | | | |
| OFF THE RECORD (Jan 95) Two parts | 1995 | Westwood One (2) | 30-60 |
| *(Music and interviews)* | | | |
| STILL GOT THE BLUES | 1995 | Westwood One (6) | 75-125 |
| *(Music and interviews)* | | | |
| STORY OF ERIC CLAPTON (May 92) Profile | 1992 | Unistar | 20-35 |
| *(Music and interview)* | | | |
| SUPERSTARS | 1995 | (2) | 50-75 |
| *(With Elton John and Mark Knopfler)* | | | |
| UP CLOSE | 1995 | Media America (3) | 40-75 |
| *(Music and interviews)* | | | |
| UP CLOSE | 1996 | Media America (3) | 40-75 |
| *(Music and interview)* | | | |
| UP CLOSE Music and interview | 1989 | Media America (2) | 20-40 |
| *(Music and interview, repeated in 1994)* | | | |
| UP CLOSE Special show | 1989 | Media America (4) | 40-75 |
| *(Music and interview)* | | | |
| WESTWOOD ONE SPECIAL (Oct 94) | 1994 | Westwood One (2) | 30-60 |
| *(Music and interviews)* | | | |
| **Reel-to-Reel Tapes** | | | |
| FROM THE CRADLE (Oct 94) Music and interview | 1994 | | 50-80 |
| *(Two reels of the world premiere of a new CD release)* | | | |

| Title | Yr | Label, Number | NM $ |
|---|---|---|---|
| KING BISCUIT FLOWER HOUR (Aug 79) Live concert | 1979 | DIR/ABC (2) | 125-225 |
| *(On two reels, with Van Morrison)* | | | |
| KING BISCUIT FLOWER HOUR (Nov 78) Live concert | 1978 | DIR/ABC (2) | 100-200 |
| *(On two reels)* | | | |

## CLARK, DAVE, FIVE
*Epic promo 45s $8-15 each; Epic Memory Lane white label promos $8 each; Epic promo white label LPs $25 each*

**45s**

| | | | |
|---|---|---|---|
| CATCH US IF YOU CAN | 1966 | Auravision/CBS | 25 |
| *(Cardboard record, plays at 33 1/3 rpm; for Fresh Start by Ponds)* | | | |
| DO YOU LOVE ME | 1966 | Columbia Special Products CPS 245 | 25 |
| *("The Lively New Sound" For Nabisco Shreddies Cereal)* | | | |
| MEDLEY: ROCK 'N' ROLL MUSIC, etc.  White promo label | 1969 | Epic 10684 | 12 |
| *(Six songs on "A" side, two on the flip, not an EP)* | | | |
| NINETEEN DAYS (same on both sides) | 1966 | Epic 10076 | 40 |
| *(Promo only on red vinyl)* | | | |
| OVER AND OVER (same on both sides) | 1965 | Epic 9863 | 40 |
| *(Promo only on red vinyl)* | | | |
| PARADISE   White label | 1968 | Epic 10474 | 10 |
| *("34-06" is title of flip side)* | | | |
| THE RED BALLOON  White label, red print | 1968 | Epic 10375 | 15 |
| *(Hard record to find)* | | | |

**Albums**

| | | | |
|---|---|---|---|
| DAVE CLARK INTERVIEW | 1965 | Epic 77238 | 600 |
| *(White promo label)* | | | |
| HAVING A WILD WEEKEND | 1965 | Warner Bros. 3296 | 500 |
| *(Very rare interview LP)* | | | |
| HAVING A WILD WEEKEND | 1965 | Warner Bros. 3248 | 300 |
| *(Radio spots from the record label)* | | | |

**Compact Discs**

| | | | |
|---|---|---|---|
| 55 BY FIVE Picture CD | 1993 | Hollywood 10337 | 25 |
| *(Five track sampler promo-only CD)* | | | |

**RADIO SHOWS**

**Albums**

| | | | |
|---|---|---|---|
| BRITISH INVASION SERIES | 198? | United Stations | 20-30 |
| THE IN SOUND (July 67) Series of 5-minute shows | 1967 | U. S. Army | 15-25 |
| *(One of the shows features the Dave Clark Five)* | | | |
| WORLD OF ROCK (Jan 90) Music and interview | 1990 | (2) | 15-25 |
| *(Dave Clark is a co-host)* | | | |

## CLARK, PETULA
*Coral promo 45s $12 each; MGM promo 45s before 14300 $10 each; Imperial, Warwick, London, Laurie promo 45s $4 each; other Warner Bros. promos $5 each; other label promos $3 each (including MGM after 14300); Warner Bros. jukebox LLPs $12 each; Warner Bros*

**45s**

| | | | |
|---|---|---|---|
| DOWNTOWN | 1964 | Warner Bros. 5494 | 10 |
| *(White promo label)* | | | |

**Albums**

| | | | |
|---|---|---|---|
| PETULA CLARK SWINGS THE JINGLE | 1966 | Coca-Cola 103 | 150 |

## CLASH, THE
*Epic promo 45s $3 each; Epic promo picture sleeves $2 each; other Epic promo LPs $10 each*

**10-Inch Singles**

| | | | |
|---|---|---|---|
| CLAMPDOWN/BRAND NEW CADILLAC/SPANISH BOMBS | 1980 | Epic AS 788 | 25 |
| TRAIN IN VAIN (STAND BY ME) (same on both sides) | 1980 | Epic AS 749 | 25 |

**12-Inch Singles**

| | | | |
|---|---|---|---|
| CLAMPDOWN/LOST IN THE SUPERMARKET/ THE CARD CHEAT/LONDON CALLING | 1979 | Epic AS 723 | 20 |
| FINGERPOPPIN' (AOR Remix) (same on both sides) | 1985 | Epic EAS 2277 | 6 |
| GATES OF THE WEST/GROOVY TIMES/I FOUGHT THE LAW | 1979 | Epic AS 617 | 20 |
| ROCK THE CASBAH/OVERPOWERED BY FUNK/ SHOULD I STAY OR SHOULD I GO/DEATH IS A STAR | 1982 | Epic AS 1464 | 15 |
| THE MAGNIFICENT SEVEN/LIGHTNING STRIKES/ ONE MORE TIME/ONE MORE DUB | 1980 | Epic AS 905 | 15 |
| THIS IS ENGLAND (same on both sides) | 1985 | Epic EAS 2230 | 6 |

**45s**

| | | | |
|---|---|---|---|
| GATES OF THE WEST/GROOVY TIMES | 1979 | Epic AE7 1178 | 8 |
| *(Single included with original pressings of the LP "The Clash")* | | | |

**Albums**

| | | | |
|---|---|---|---|
| COMBAT ROCK | 1982 | Epic AS 99-1595 | 30 |
| *(Camouflage green vinyl promo)* | | | |
| COMBAT ROCK | 1983 | Epic AS 1595 | 30 |
| *(Picture disc, promo-only release)* | | | |
| GIVE 'EM ENOUGH ROPE | 1978 | Epic JE 35543 | 30 |
| *(White label promo; timing strip; back cover has one incorrect song title)* | | | |
| INTERCHORDS | 1981 | Epic AS 952 | 25 |
| *(Music and interview, promo only)* | | | |
| LONDON CALLING | 1980 | Epic E2 36238 | 25 |
| *(White label promo)* | | | |
| SANDINISTA NOW! | 1981 | Epic AS 913 | 20 |
| *(Promo-only sampler)* | | | |
| THE WORLD ACCORDING TO THE CLASH | 1982 | Epic AS 1594 | 40 |
| *(Promo-only sampler)* | | | |

**RADIO SHOWS**

**Albums**

| | | | |
|---|---|---|---|
| INNERVIEW (80s) | 198? | Innerview | 15-25 |
| *(Music and interviews)* | | | |

| Title | Yr | Label, Number | NM $ |
|---|---|---|---|

**CLASSICS IV**
*Other Imperial promo 45s $5 each; MGM and Robox promo 45s $3 each; Imperial promo LPs $8 each With Dennis Yost*
**45s**

| | | | |
|---|---|---|---|
| POLLYANNA The Classics | 1966 | Capitol 5710 | 15 |
| *(Green promo label)* | | | |
| SPECIAL ALBUM SPOT COMMERCIAL | 1969 | Imperial SP-6-A | 18 |
| *(For the song "Everyday with You Girl"; white promo label)* | | | |

**CLAY, CASSIUS**
**45s**

| | | | |
|---|---|---|---|
| I AM THE GREATEST | 1963 | Columbia JZSP 75716 | 40 |
| *(Promo-only single, edited version of the album track)* | | | |
| I AM THE GREATEST Black and white sleeve | 1963 | Columbia JZSP 75716 | 50 |
| *(This rare picture sleeve released with the promo record only)* | | | |
| THE PREDICTION/WILL THE REAL SONNY LISTON PLEASE FALL DOWN | 1964 | Columbia ZSP 75717/77185 | 40 |
| **Albums** | | | |
| I AM THE GREATEST White promo label | 1963 | Columbia 2093 | 75 |
| *(Both the stock copy and promo are very rare)* | | | |

**CLEFS, THE**
**45s**

| | | | |
|---|---|---|---|
| WE THREE | 1956 | Chess 1521 | 150 |
| *(White promo label)* | | | |

**CLEFTONES, THE**
**45s**

| | | | |
|---|---|---|---|
| MY DEAREST DARLING | 1955 | Old Town 1011 | 175 |
| *(White promo label)* | | | |
| THE MASQUERADE IS OVER | 1955 | Old Town | 100 |
| *(White promo label)* | | | |

**CLEMONS, CLARENCE**
*Columbia promo 45s $3 each; Columbia promo picture sleeves $2 each*
**RADIO SHOWS**
**Albums**

| | | | |
|---|---|---|---|
| KING BISCUIT FLOWER HOUR (Aug 84) Live concert | 1984 | DIR (2) | 40-80 |
| *(With Manfred Mann)* | | | |
| KING BISCUIT FLOWER HOUR (Jan 84) Live concert | 1984 | DIR (2) | 30-45 |
| *(With the Animals)* | | | |

**CLICKS, THE**
**45s**

| | | | |
|---|---|---|---|
| COME BACK TO ME | 1955 | Josie 780 | 100 |
| *(White promo label)* | | | |

**CLIFFORD, BUZZ**
*A&M promo 45s $8 each*
**45s**

| | | | |
|---|---|---|---|
| BABY SITTIN' BOOGIE | 1960 | Columbia 41876 | 25 |
| *(White promo label)* | | | |
| FOREVER | 1962 | Columbia 42290 | 15 |
| *(White promo label)* | | | |
| HELLO, MR. MOONLIGHT | 1960 | Columbia 41774 | 15 |
| *(White promo label)* | | | |
| I'LL NEVER FORGET | 1961 | Columbia 42019 | 15 |
| *(White promo label)* | | | |
| MOVING DAY | 1961 | Columbia 42177 | 15 |
| *(White promo label)* | | | |
| THREE LITTLE FISHES | 1961 | Columbia 41797 | 18 |
| *(White promo label)* | | | |
| **Albums** | | | |
| BABY SITTIN' WITH BUZZ | 1961 | Columbia 8416 | 60 |
| *(White promo label)* | | | |

**CLIMAX BLUES BAND**
*Sire promo 45s $3 each; Warner Bros. promo 45s $3 each*
**RADIO SHOWS**
**Albums**

| | | | |
|---|---|---|---|
| BBC ROCK HOUR (Feb 81) Live concert | 1981 | London Wavelength | 75-125 |
| *(Also with Molly Hatchet)* | | | |
| BBC TRANSCRIPTION DISC  Live concert | 1979 | BBC Transcription | 150-300 |
| *(With Molly Hatchet)* | | | |

**CLINE, PATSY**
*Everest white promo label 45s $12 each; Decca green promo label 45s $8 each; Decca pink promo label 45s $6 each; MCA white promo label 45s $2 each; Other Decca pinkpromo label LPs $30-50; Decca white promo label LPs $20*
**45s**

| | | | |
|---|---|---|---|
| I DON'T WANNA | 1957 | Decca 30504 | 25 |
| *(Green promo label)* | | | |
| I DON'T WANNA | 1957 | Everest 20005 | 25 |
| *(White promo label)* | | | |

| Title | Yr | Label, Number | NM $ |
|---|---|---|---|
| **7-Inch Extended Plays** | | | |
| PATSY CLINE  Black label, promo only | 1956 | Patsy Cline (4 Star) EP-25 | 35 |
| *(Four songs including "I Don't Wanna")* | | | |
| PATSY CLINE  Black label, promo only | 1957 | Patsy Cline (4 Star) EP-?? | 25 |
| *(Four songs including "Walking After Midnight")* | | | |
| PATSY CLINE Jukebox LLP | 1963 | Decca 34130 | 25 |
| *(Issued with hard cover and title strips)* | | | |
| PATSY CLINE Jukebox LLP | 1964 | Decca 34131 | 25 |
| *(Issued with hard cover and title strips)* | | | |
| PATSY CLINE Jukebox LLP | 1964 | Decca 34132 | 25 |
| *(Issued with hard cover and title strips)* | | | |
| PATSY CLINE Jukebox LLP | 1964 | Decca 34133 | 25 |
| *(Issued with hard cover and title strips)* | | | |
| **Albums** | | | |
| GOTTA LOT OF RHYTHM IN MY SOUL | 1965 | Metro 540 | 25 |
| *(Yellow promo label)* | | | |
| PATSY CLINE | 1957 | Decca 8611 | 75 |
| *(Pink promo label)* | | | |
| THE PATSY CLINE STORY | 1963 | Decca 176 (2) | 50 |
| *(White promo labels, price includes booklet)* | | | |
| **RADIO SHOWS** | | | |
| **16-Inch Transcriptions** | | | |
| JUBILEE USA (50s) With Patsy Cline | 195? | | 30-50 |
| *(Music and interviews)* | | | |
| NAVY HOEDOWN (50s) With Patsy Cline | 195? | U.S. Navy | 40-60 |
| *(Music and interviews)* | | | |
| **Albums** | | | |
| COUNTRY MUSIC TIME (50s-60s) WITH GUEST PATSY CLINE | 196? | U.S.A.F. | 175-200 |
| *(Live concert, flip is Benny Martin)* | | | |

## CLIQUE, THE
**45s**

| JUDY, JUDY, JUDY (same on both sides) | 1970 | White Whale 367 | 12 |
|---|---|---|---|
| *(May be promo only)* | | | |

## CLOONEY, ROSEMARY
*Columbia and RCA Victor promo singles $3 each*
**45s**

| LOVE, LOOK AWAY  Music in the Air | 1958 | U. S. A. F. 43 | 12 |
|---|---|---|---|
| *(Five-minute public service show)* | | | |
| WHAT IS A BABY  For Gerber Baby Foods | 1958 | Columbia ZTV 27288 | 12 |
| *(Blue label 7-inch 33 1/3 rpm with small hole, flip side has two songs)* | | | |
| **RADIO SHOWS** | | | |
| **16-Inch Transcriptions** | | | |
| MARCH OF DIMES SHOW | 1954 | March of Dimes | 30-50 |
| *(One-time public service show)* | | | |

## CLOVERS, THE
*Atlantic promo 45s $30 each; United Artists promo 45s $25 each; Brunswick promo 45s $15 each; Josie promo 45s $12 each*

## CLUSTERS, THE
**45s**

| FORECAST OF OUR LOVE | 1958 | Epic 9330 | 75 |
|---|---|---|---|
| *(White promo label)* | | | |

## COASTERS, THE
*Atco promo 45s $25 each; Date promo 45s $15 each; King promo 45s $10 each; American International promo 45s $5 each*
**45s**

| WHAT'S IT ALL ABOUT (June 82) Public service show | 1982 | W. I. A. A. 632 | 20 |
|---|---|---|---|
| *(Flip side features Chicago)* | | | |
| **Albums** | | | |
| THE COASTERS | 1958 | Atco 33-101 | 500 |
| *(White promo label)* | | | |
| THE COASTERS GREATEST HITS | 1959 | Atco 33-111 | 250 |
| *(White promo label)* | | | |

## COCHRAN, EDDIE
*Also listings by the Cochran Brothers and the Kelly Four; other Liberty white promo label 45s $30-50 each*
**45s**

| DRIVE IN SHOW | 1957 | Liberty 55087 | 75 |
|---|---|---|---|
| *(White promo label)* | | | |
| OPPORTUNITY | 1959 | Silver 1004 | 40 |
| *(By Jewel and Eddie; white promo label)* | | | |
| PRETTY GIRL | 1958 | Liberty 55138 | 75 |
| *(White promo label)* | | | |
| ROUGH STUFF | 1959 | Capehart 5003 | 50 |
| *(Some promos were issued with a $150 stock picture sleeve)* | | | |
| SKINNY JIM | 1956 | Crest 1026 | 150 |
| *(White promo label)* | | | |
| STROLLIN' GUITAR | 1959 | Silver 1001 | 40 |
| *(By the Kelly Four; white promo label)* | | | |
| TEENAGE HEAVEN | 1959 | Liberty 55177 | 40 |
| *(White promo label)* | | | |
| TWENTY FLIGHT ROCK | 1957 | Liberty 55112 | 75 |
| *(White promo label)* | | | |

| Title | Yr | Label, Number | NM $ |
|---|---|---|---|
| **Albums** | | | |
| EDDIE COCHRAN MEMORIAL ALBUM | 1960 | Liberty 3172 | 150 |
| *(White promo label)* | | | |
| NEVER TO BE FORGOTTEN | 1962 | Liberty 3220 | 125 |
| *(White promo label)* | | | |
| SINGIN' TO MY BABY | 1958 | Liberty 3061 | 300 |
| *(White promo label)* | | | |
| | | | |
| **COCHRAN, JACKIE LEE** | | | |
| **45s** | | | |
| BUY A CAR | 1958 | ABC Paramount 9930 | 75 |
| *(White promo label)* | | | |
| HIP SHAKIN' MAMA | 196? | Sims 107 | 100 |
| *(White promo label)* | | | |
| MAMA, DON'T YOU THINK I KNOW | 195? | Decca 30206 | 75 |
| *(Pink promo label)* | | | |
| | | | |
| **COCHRANE, TOM** | | | |
| *And Red Rider. Capitol promo 45s $3 each; Other Capitol jukebox 45s $4 each; Capitol promo CD singles $3 each.* | | | |
| **45s** | | | |
| LIFE IS A HIGHWAY | 1992 | Capitol 57780 | 6 |
| *(Purple label "For Jukeboxes Only!")* | | | |
| **RADIO SHOWS** | | | |
| **Albums** | | | |
| IN CONCERT (July 92) | 1992 | Westwood One (2) | 25-50 |
| *(Live concert)* | | | |
| IN CONCERT (June 83) Live concert | 1983 | Westwood One (2) | 50-75 |
| *(With Fastway)* | | | |
| IN CONCERT (Oct 86) Live concert | 1986 | Westwood One (2) | 25-50 |
| *(With Bruce Hornsby)* | | | |
| **Compact Discs** | | | |
| KING BISCUIT FLOWER HOUR (Oct 92) Live concert | 1992 | DIR | 20-45 |
| *(With Bryan Adams)* | | | |
| OFF THE RECORD (Apr 92) Profile | 1992 | Westwood One | 10-20 |
| *(Music and interview)* | | | |
| OFF THE RECORD Profile, with Richie Sambora | 1992 | Westwood One | 15-20 |
| *(Music and interview)* | | | |
| | | | |
| **COCKBURN, BRUCE** | | | |
| *A&M promo singles $4; other label promo 45s $3* | | | |
| **Albums** | | | |
| RCA RADIO SERIES  Music and interview | 1981 | RCA Victor | 25 |
| *(Record company promotion)* | | | |
| **Compact Discs** | | | |
| NOTHING BUT A BURNING LIGHT | 198? | Columbia 4222 (2) | 25 |
| *(Promo-only compilation)* | | | |
| **RADIO SHOWS** | | | |
| **Albums** | | | |
| KING BISCUIT FLOWER HOUR (Mar 85) Live concert | 1985 | DIR (2) | 100-150 |
| *(With Scandal)* | | | |
| KING BISCUIT FLOWER HOUR (Nov 84) Live concert | 1984 | DIR (2) | 150-225 |
| *(With Lou Reed)* | | | |
| **Reel-to-Reel Tapes** | | | |
| COLUMBIA RECORDS RADIO HOUR | 1995 | | 100-150 |
| *(With Patty Larkin, Peter Stuart, Jonathan Brooke)* | | | |
| | | | |
| **COCKER, JOE** | | | |
| *A&M promo 45s $4 each; Capitol white label promo 45s not listed $3 each; Capitol 12" promo singles $8 each* | | | |
| **45s** | | | |
| I'LL CRY INSTEAD | 1964 | Philips 40255 | 40 |
| *(White promo label)* | | | |
| WHAT ARE YOU DOING WITH A FOOL LIKE ME (same on both sides) | 1990 | Capitol 7PRO-79025 | 5 |
| *(Vinyl is promo only)* | | | |
| WHEN THE NIGHT COMES (same on both sides) | 1989 | Capitol 7PRO-79711 | 5 |
| *(Vinyl is promo only)* | | | |
| WITH A LITTLE HELP FROM MY FRIENDS White label | 1968 | A&M 991 | 12 |
| *(Special Edit DJ release, time 3:25, very limited)* | | | |
| **Albums** | | | |
| LUXURY YOU CAN AFFORD | 1978 | Asylum 145 | 15 |
| *(Promo-only picture disc)* | | | |
| **RADIO SHOWS** | | | |
| **Albums** | | | |
| KING BISCUIT FLOWER HOUR (Sept 82) Live concert | 1982 | DIR/ABC (2) | 50-80 |
| *(With Marshall Crenshaw)* | | | |
| LEGENDS OF ROCK (Feb 88) Profile | 1988 | NBC Radio (2) | 20-30 |
| *(Music and interview, show repeated Apr 89)* | | | |
| ROCK STARS (Mar 88) BLUE PROMO LABELS | 1988 | Radio Today (2) | 20-30 |
| *(Music and interview, repeated Oct 89)* | | | |
| STORY OF JOE COCKER (JAN 90) Profile | 1990 | Unistar | 15-25 |
| *(Music and interview)* | | | |
| SUPERSTAR CONCERT (June 92) Live concert | 1992 | Westwood One (2) | 30-50 |
| *(Box set)* | | | |
| TOYOTA PRESENTS (70s) Profile | 197? | Toyota (2) | 50-75 |
| *(Music and interview, rare series)* | | | |

| Title | Yr | Label, Number | NM $ |
|---|---|---|---|
| **Compact Discs** | | | |
| BBC CLASSIC TRACKS (July 91) VARIOUS LIVE | 1991 | London Wavelength | 20-40 |
| *(Repeated again Sept 92, July 92)* | | | |
| KING BISCUIT FLOWER HOUR (July 92) Live concert | 1992 | DIR | 25-40 |
| *(Show repeated in Apr 93)* | | | |
| | | | |
| **COCTEAU TWINS** | | | |
| **12-Inch Singles** | | | |
| A KISSED OUT RED FLATBOAT (same on both sides) | 1988 | Capitol SPRO-79512 | 15 |
| HEAVEN OR LAS VEGAS/HEAVEN OR LAS VEGAS (Edit)/DIALS | 1990 | Capitol SPRO-79415/27 | 12 |
| I WEAR YOUR RING (same on both sides) | 1991 | Capitol SPRO-79564 | 15 |
| **Albums** | | | |
| SAMPLER | 1991 | Capitol SPRO 79066/7 | 50 |
| *(Promo-only 10-song collection)* | | | |
| | | | |
| **COE, DAVID ALLAN** | | | |
| *Columbia promo 45s $3 each* | | | |
| **Albums** | | | |
| UNDERGROUND ALBUM | 1978 | DAC Records | 50 |
| *(Promo-only release, rated X)* | | | |
| | | | |
| **COINS, THE** | | | |
| **45s** | | | |
| CHEATIN' BABY | 1954 | Gee 10 | 400 |
| *(White promo label)* | | | |
| LOOK AT ME, GIRL /S. R. BLUES | 1954 | Gee 11 | 300 |
| *(White promo label)* | | | |
| LOOK AT ME, GIRL/TWO LOVES HAVE I | 1954 | Gee 1007 | 150 |
| *(White promo label)* | | | |
| | | | |
| **COLE, LLOYD** | | | |
| **RADIO SHOWS** | | | |
| **Albums** | | | |
| BBC TRANSCRIPTION DISC  Live concert | 1985 | BBC Transcription | 100-175 |
| *(Very rare concert)* | | | |
| BBC TRANSCRIPTION DISC  Live concert | 1986 | BBC Transcription | 75-150 |
| *(Same show as above)* | | | |
| BBC TRANSCRIPTION DISC  Live concert | 1988 | BBC Transcription | 50-100 |
| *(Later versions of this show are easier to find)* | | | |
| | | | |
| **COLE, NAT KING** | | | |
| *Includes King Cole Trio. Capitol promo 45s $3-5 each; Capitol 33-compact jukebox singles $6 each; Capitol jukebox LLPs with hard covers $12 each; Capitol promo LPs $10-15 each.* | | | |
| **45s** | | | |
| COME CLOSER TO ME Blue promo-only label | 1957 | Capitol PRO 679 | 15 |
| *(Promo only, English/Spanish versions)* | | | |
| L-O-V-E Promo-only red label | 1965 | Capitol PRO 2812 | 12 |
| *(Includes introduction to the song, flip has two songs)* | | | |
| LET'S FACE THE MUSIC | 1963 | Capitol 2008 | 50 |
| *(Set of five jukebox-only stereo singles)* | | | |
| LET'S FACE THE MUSIC Set of five stereo 33 1/3 rpm 7-inch singles | 1965 | Capitol SXE-2008 | 40 |
| *(Small center hole, in paper cover, for jukeboxes only)* | | | |
| **7-Inch Extended Plays** | | | |
| L-O-V-E Promo-only red label | 1965 | Capitol PRO 2789 | 15 |
| *(Two versions in six languages, two in English)* | | | |
| TRIPLE HIT PREVIEW | 196? | Capitol PRO 304 | 20 |
| *(Five cuts, two by Nat)* | | | |
| **Albums** | | | |
| MINUTE MASTERS (Jan 66) 20 cuts edited for radio | 1966 | Capitol PRO 2991/2992 | 30 |
| *(White promo-only label)* | | | |
| SILVER PLATTER SERVICE (June 66) with Jack Wagner | 1966 | Capitol PRO 3204 | 15 |
| *(Includes Cole interview and songs from LP)* | | | |
| **Compact Discs** | | | |
| SELECTIONS FROM THE BOX SET | 1993 | Capitol DPRO-79500 | 25 |
| *(Sampler from 4-CD stock set)* | | | |
| | | | |
| **COLE, NATALIE** | | | |
| *Capitol promo 45s $2 each Daughter of Nat King Cole* | | | |
| **RADIO SHOWS** | | | |
| **Albums** | | | |
| BUDWEISER CONCERT SPECIAL (May 86) Live concert | 1986 | (2) | 20-30 |
| *(Rare radio series)* | | | |
| STARDUST MEMORIES (Nov 91) Profile | 1991 | (2) | 15-25 |
| *(Music and interviews)* | | | |
| WESTWOOD ONE SPECIAL (Nov 91) Profile | 1991 | Westwood One (2) | 15-25 |
| *(Music and interview)* | | | |
| **Compact Discs** | | | |
| THE STORY OF NATALIE COLE (Jan 92) Profile | 1992 | Unistar | 10-15 |
| *(Music and interview)* | | | |
| | | | |
| **COLEMAN, CY** | | | |
| **45s** | | | |
| PLAYBOYS THEME Mono/stereo | 1969 | World Pacific 77916 | 10 |
| *(Regular number, but not issued to the public as a 45)* | | | |

| Title | Yr | Label, Number | NM $ |
|-------|-----|---------------|------|

**COLLECTIVE SOUL**
*Atlantic promo CD singles $4 each*
**RADIO SHOWS**
**Compact Discs**

| | | | |
|-------|-----|---------------|------|
| ALBUM NETWORK LIVE | 1994 | Album Network | 30-60 |
| *(Live concert)* | | | |
| IN CONCERT (Feb 95) | 1995 | Westwood One | 40-75 |
| *(Live concert)* | | | |

**COLLINS KIDS, THE**
*Columbia white promo label 45s 21000 series $25-50 each; Columbia white promo label 45s 40800,40900 series $20-40 each; Columbia white promo label 45s 41000,41100 series $30-50 each; Columbia white promo label 45s 41300 and later $10 each including solo*

**COLLINS, JUDY**
*Elektra promo singles $3 each*
**45s**

| | | | |
|-------|-----|---------------|------|
| DRINK A ROUND TO IRELAND Green vinyl | 1982 | Elektra 47437 | 15 |
| *(Only the promo version is green vinyl)* | | | |
| THE HOSTAGE 33 rpm single with small center hole | 1973 | Elektra JC-3 | 12 |
| *(Issued for radio stations with a promo-only picture sleeve)* | | | |
| WHAT'S IT ALL ABOUT (June 79) Public service show | 1979 | W. I. A. A. 475 | 18 |
| *(Flip side is Poco)* | | | |
| WHAT'S IT ALL ABOUT (May 81) Public service show | 1981 | W. I. A. A. 574 | 15 |
| *(Flip side features Stevie Wonder)* | | | |
| WHAT'S IT ALL ABOUT (Oct 82) Public service show | 1982 | W. I. A. A. 642 | 18 |
| *(Flip side is Johnny Ray)* | | | |

**RADIO SHOWS**
**Albums**

| | | | |
|-------|-----|---------------|------|
| POP CONCERT (Sept 88) Live concert | 1988 | Westwood One (2) | 40-100 |
| *(Same concert as above show)* | | | |
| WESTWOOD ONE PRESENTS (Sept 88) Live concert | 1988 | Westwood One (2) | 50-100 |
| *(Judy Collins in concert is hard to find)* | | | |

**Reel-to-Reel Tapes**

| | | | |
|-------|-----|---------------|------|
| ROBERT KLEIN (70s) Profile, music and interview | 197? | | 40-75 |
| *(Also features Debbie Harry of Blondie)* | | | |

**COLLINS, PHIL**
*Atlantic promo 45s $4 each; Atlantic white label promo 45s with no mention of label $6 each; Atlantic promo 12" singles $12 each; Most Atlantic promo CD singles $4 From Genesis; Includes Brand X*
**45s**

| | | | |
|-------|-----|---------------|------|
| I CANNOT BELIEVE IT'S TRUE  Long/short versions | 1982 | Atlantic 89864 | 10 |
| *(Blue promo label, long version is 5:14)* | | | |
| IN THE AIR TONIGHT | 1981 | Atlantic | 20 |
| *(Test pressing)* | | | |
| IN THE AIR TONIGHT  Promo-only number | 1981 | Atlantic PR 655 | 20 |
| *(White promo label)* | | | |
| YOU CAN'T HURRY LOVE | 1982 | Atlantic | 20 |
| *(Test pressing)* | | | |

**Albums**

| | | | |
|-------|-----|---------------|------|
| COLLINS ON COLLINS  Music and interview | 1985 | Atlantic 759 | 18 |
| *(Promo-only candid interview from Atlantic Records)* | | | |
| LIVESTOCK White promo label, by Brand X | 1977 | Passport 9824 | 15 |
| *(Collins is drummer for Brand X; other promo Passport LPs by Brand X have only a promo sticker on stock pressings)* | | | |

**Compact Discs**

| | | | |
|-------|-----|---------------|------|
| GROOVY KIND OF LOVE | 1988 | Atlantic PR 2452-2 | 150 |
| *(Also includes two tracks from Y Kant Tori Read, early Tori Amos)* | | | |
| IN THE AIR TONIGHT | 1990 | Atlantic PRCD 3642-2 | 15 |
| *(Promo only to radio)* | | | |
| THE STORY SO FAR  14 tracks | 1994 | Atlantic 5428 | 18 |
| *(Promo-only CD release)* | | | |
| THE STORY SO FAR  Interview | 1993 | Atlantic 5370 | 25 |
| *(Promo-only 30-minute interview disc)* | | | |

**RADIO SHOWS**
**Albums**

| | | | |
|-------|-----|---------------|------|
| 1986 GRAMMY AWARDS (Feb 86) Various artists | 1986 | MJI Broadcasting (2) | 25-40 |
| *(Hosted by Phil Collins)* | | | |
| BBC ROCK HOUR (Mar 81) Collins/Genesis | 1981 | London Wavelength | 20-40 |
| *(Music and interviews)* | | | |
| CAPTURED LIVE  Live concert | 1983 | RKO (3) | 50-100 |
| *(Also a Genesis version of this show)* | | | |
| COUNTDOWN TO CHRISTMAS (Dec 85) Profile | 1985 | NBC Radio | 12-18 |
| *(Music and interviews of both Collins and Genesis)* | | | |
| HOT ROCKS Profiles both Collins and Genesis | 1986 | United Stations (2) | 20-35 |
| *(Music and interview)* | | | |
| IN CONCERT (Mar 82) | 1982 | Westwood One (2) | 30-50 |
| *(Live concert)* | | | |
| INSIDE TRACKS  Music and interview | 1982 | RKO (3) | 20-40 |
| *(Also a Genesis version of this show)* | | | |
| INSIDE TRACKS (Aug 83) | 1983 | RKO (2) | 20-40 |
| *(With Robert Plant, music and interviews)* | | | |
| KING BISCUIT FLOWER HOUR (Dec 83) Live concert | 1983 | DIR/ABC (2) | 40-60 |
| *(Also includes Chris DeBurgh)* | | | |
| KING BISCUIT FLOWER HOUR (May 86) Live concert | 1986 | DIR (2) | 40-60 |
| *(Phil Collins only)* | | | |

| Title | Yr | Label, Number | NM $ |
|---|---|---|---|
| LEGENDS OF ROCK Profile | 1988 | NBC Radio (2) | 15-25 |
| (Music and interviews) | | | |
| LEGENDS OF ROCK (May 85) Profile | 1985 | NBC Radio (2) | 15-25 |
| (Music and interview) | | | |
| LONDON WAVELENGTH SPECIAL (Dec 82) | 1982 | London Wavelength | 20-30 |
| (Some live material) | | | |
| MASTERS OF ROCK (Feb 89) Collins/Genesis | 1989 | Radio Ventures (2) | 20-30 |
| (Music and interviews) | | | |
| OFF THE RECORD (80s) Profile | 198? | Westwood One (2) | 12-18 |
| (Music and interview) | | | |
| PIONEERS IN MUSIC (May 87) Music and interview | 1987 | DIR (2) | 25-35 |
| (Some live, includes Don Henley and Carl Palmer) | | | |
| THE RECORD COMPANY Profile | 1985 | | 15-25 |
| (Show repeated several times) | | | |
| ROCK SALUTES MOTOWN (June 84) Various artists | 1984 | NBC Radio (5) | 40-60 |
| (Music and interviews, Phil Collins is host) | | | |
| SOLO AND TOGETHER Collins/Genesis | 1987 | Radio International (2) | 20-35 |
| (Music and interviews) | | | |
| STARTRACK PROFILE Both Collins and Genesis | 1988 | Westwood One (2) | 20-35 |
| (Some live mateiral) | | | |
| STARTRACK PROFILE (Sept 85) | 1985 | Westwood One (2) | 20-30 |
| (Some live material) | | | |
| THE STORY OF PHIL COLLINS (July 90) With Genesis | 1990 | Unistar | 12-20 |
| (Music and interview) | | | |
| SUPERSTAR CONCERT (Mar 84) Live concert | 1984 | Westwood One (3) | 40-60 |
| (Box set, repeated several times) | | | |
| SUPERSTARS OF ROCK (May 85) | 1985 | | 15-25 |
| (Music and interview) | | | |
| WORLD OF ROCK (Feb 90) | 1990 | DIR (2) | 15-25 |
| (Music and interviews, Collins is co-host) | | | |
| **Compact Discs** | | | |
| KING BISCUIT FLOWER HOUR (Nov 92) | 1992 | DIR | 40-60 |
| (Show repeated several times) | | | |
| UP CLOSE Profile | 1988 | Media America (2) | 35-50 |
| (Music and interview, some live) | | | |
| WESTWOOD ONE SPECIAL (Sept 94) Collins and Genesis | 1994 | Westwood One (2) | 25-50 |
| (Music and interview) | | | |

## COLLINS, TOMMY

Capitol white and red promo label 45s $6 each; Columbia white promo label 45s $4 each; Tower white promo label 45s $8 each; Music America promo 45s $3 each

**Albums**

| | Yr | Label, Number | NM $ |
|---|---|---|---|
| LIGHT OF THE LORD | 1959 | Capitol 1125 | 75 |
| (Yellow promo label) | | | |
| SONGS I LOVE TO SING | 1961 | Capitol 1436 | 45 |
| (Blue promo label) | | | |
| THE DYNAMIC TOMMY COLLINS | 1966 | Columbia 9310 | 20 |
| (White promo label) | | | |
| THIS IS TOMMY COLLINS | 1959 | Capitol 1196 | 60 |
| (Blue promo label) | | | |
| TOMMY COLLINS ON TOUR | 1968 | Columbia 9578 | 15 |
| (White promo label) | | | |
| WORDS AND MUSIC COUNTRY STYLE | 1957 | Capitol 776 | 100 |
| (Capitol promo label) | | | |

## COLONIALS, THE

**45s**

| | Yr | Label, Number | NM $ |
|---|---|---|---|
| BRING MY BABY BACK | 1954 | Gee 12 | 200 |
| (White promo label) | | | |
| TWO LOVES HAVE I | 1956 | Gee 1007 | 100 |
| (White promo label) | | | |

## COMMODORES

**45s**

| | Yr | Label, Number | NM $ |
|---|---|---|---|
| MACHINE GUN | 1975 | Motown 1307 | 20 |
| (Red vinyl promo) | | | |
| NIGHTSHIFT | 1984 | Motown 1773 | 10 |
| (White label with promotional picture sleeve) | | | |
| SWEET LOVE | 1976 | Motown 1381 | 20 |
| (Yellow vinyl promo) | | | |
| **7-Inch Extended Plays** | | | |
| SAVE THE CHILDREN | 1984 | DWP 956 | 25 |
| (Public service spots) | | | |
| **Reel-to-Reel Tapes** | | | |
| SCHLITZ BEER | 198? | J. Walter Thompson | 25 |
| (Radio spots) | | | |

## COMMUNARDS

MCA promo 45s $3 each

**RADIO SHOWS**

**Albums**

| | Yr | Label, Number | NM $ |
|---|---|---|---|
| BBC TRANSCRIPTION DISC | 1988 | BBC Transcription | 150-250 |
| (Live concert) | | | |

| Title | Yr | Label, Number | NM $ |
|---|---|---|---|

**COMO, PERRY**

*RCA Victor white promo labels 4000-5000 series $20 each; Later RCA Victor white promo label 45s $5-10 each; RCA Victor yellow label promo 45s $3 each*

**45s**

| | | | |
|---|---|---|---|
| THE CHRISTMAS SEAL SONG  "Promotion Disc" | 195? | RCA Victor (no #) | 15 |
| *(Includes an intro to the song by Como)* | | | |
| (Intro) I MAY NEVER PASS THIS WAY AGAIN/ | 1959 | RCA Victor K2NW 6096/7 | 12 |
| (Alternate Intro) I MAY NEVER PASS THIS WAY AGAIN | | | |
| *(Promotional record for Christmas Seals)* | | | |
| I MAY NEVER PASS THIS WAY AGAIN (same on both sides) | 1989 | RCA 9096-7-R | 5 |
| *(Promotional record for Christmas Seals)* | | | |
| ROUTE 66 Promo only, black promo label | 195? | RCA Victor SP-45-72 | 15 |
| *(Flip side is "You Came A Long Way from St. Louis")* | | | |
| RUDOLPH THE RED-NOSED REINDEER/ | 1955 | RCA Victor E3VW 1339/F7OW 9047 | 15 |
| RUDOLPH THE RED-NOSED REINDEER | | | |
| *(B-side by the Three Suns)* | | | |
| SILVER BELLS | 196? | RCA SP-45-189 | 10 |
| *(Promo-only number)* | | | |
| "SPECIAL CHRISTMAS SHOW" | 195? | USAF 85/86 | 15 |
| HOME FOR THE HOLIDAYS/MERRY MERRY CHRISTMAS TO YOU | | | |
| *(B-side by Art Mooney)* | | | |
| THERE'S NO PLACE LIKE HOME FOR THE HOLIDAYS | 196? | RCA Victor SP-45-119 | 12 |
| *(White label, promo-only number, 1954 version)* | | | |
| TOMBOY  Music in the Air series | 1958 | USAF 51 | 12 |
| *(Como song plus opening comment and ad for US Air Force, blue label)* | | | |

**7-Inch Extended Plays**

| | | | |
|---|---|---|---|
| KLEENEX PRESENTS PERRY COMO | 1958 | RCA Victor SPD-28 | 15 |
| *(Six songs, all by Como)* | | | |
| MERRY CHRISTMAS FROM YOUR RCA RECORD DEALER | 195? | RCA Victor SP-45-35 | 12 |
| *(Four songs, one by Como, with paper sleeve)* | | | |
| POP SHOPPER | 195? | RCA Victor SPC-7-13 (3) | 15 |

**COMPUTONES**

**45s**

| | | | |
|---|---|---|---|
| FLIP, FLOP ZU-WAH | 195? | U.G.H.A. 1 | 10 |
| *(Red vinyl)* | | | |

**CONCRETE BLONDE**

*I.R.S. promo 45s $5 each with picture sleeve*

**10-Inch Singles**

| | | | |
|---|---|---|---|
| JONESTOWN/JONESTOWN (Jim Jones Edit)/SIMPLE TWIST OF FATE | 1993 | Capitol SPRO-79245/6 | 20 |

**12-Inch Singles**

| | | | |
|---|---|---|---|
| DANCE ALONG THE EDGE (Edit)/DANCE ALONG THE EDGE (LP) | 1988 | I.R.S. 17310 | 15 |
| STILL IN HOLLYWOOD/I'LL CHEW YOU UP | 1986 | I.R.S. 17231 | 10 |
| TRUE/STILL IN HOLLYWOOD | 1986 | I.R.S. 17268 | 8 |

**Albums**

| | | | |
|---|---|---|---|
| BLOODLETTING | 1990 | I.R.S. 82037 | 25 |
| *(Promo-only, sticker on generic cover, black vinyl. Stock copy has a different number and is on red vinyl.)* | | | |

**RADIO SHOWS**

**Compact Discs**

| | | | |
|---|---|---|---|
| IN CONCERT-NU ROCK (Sept 93) | 1993 | Westwood One | 30-60 |
| *(Live concert)* | | | |
| ON THE EDGE (Nov 93) Music and interview | 1993 | Westwood One | 15-25 |
| *(Also featured is Buffalo Tom)* | | | |

**CONLEE, JOHN**

*MCA and Columbia promo 45s $2 each*

**RADIO SHOWS**

**Albums**

| | | | |
|---|---|---|---|
| SILVER EAGLE (Nov 84) Live concert | 1984 | DIR (3) | 20-30 |
| *(Live concert)* | | | |

**CONLEY, EARL THOMAS**

*Sunbird promo 45s $3; Other RCA Victor promo 45s $2 each; Other RCA Victor colored vinyl promo 45s $5 each*

**45s**

| | | | |
|---|---|---|---|
| ANGEL IN DISGUISE Yellow label, red vinyl | 1984 | RCA Victor 13758 | 12 |
| *(Same on both sides)* | | | |
| HONOR BOUND Blue label, blue vinyl | 1984 | RCA Victor 13960 | 10 |
| *(Remixed 3:14 version)* | | | |
| SMOKEY MOUNTAIN MEMORIES Yellow label, red vinyl | 1982 | RCA Victor 13053 | 12 |
| *(Different flip side)* | | | |
| SOMEWHERE BETWEEN RIGHT AND WRONG Blue vinyl | 1982 | RCA Victor 13320 | 10 |
| *(Same on both sides, except one side is "without horns")* | | | |
| YOUR LOVE'S ON THE LINE Brown label, yellow vinyl | 1983 | RCA Victor 13525 | 10 |
| *(Same on both sides)* | | | |

**RADIO SHOWS**

**Albums**

| | | | |
|---|---|---|---|
| SILVER EAGLE (Oct 84) Live concert | 1984 | (3) | 25-35 |

**CONN, TONY**

**45s**

| | | | |
|---|---|---|---|
| LIKE WOW | 1958 | Decca 30813 | 40 |
| *(Pink promo label)* | | | |
| YOU PRETTY THING | 1958 | Decca 30865 | 40 |
| *(Pink promo label)* | | | |

| Title | Yr | Label, Number | NM $ |
|---|---|---|---|

**CONNIFF, RAY**
*Columbia red vinyl promo 45s $5 each; Other Columbia promo 45s $2 each*
**45s**

| | | | |
|---|---|---|---|
| FROSTY THE SNOWMAN | 1967 | Columbia JZSP 135466 | 10 |
| *(Yellow label promo, no regular number)* | | | |
| PIGGY BANK BOOGIE | 1953 | Brunswick 80244 | 15 |
| *(White promo label)* | | | |
| REAL MEANING OF CHRISTMAS, THE | 1965 | Columbia JZSP 111913 | 10 |
| *(Green vinyl, promo-only white label)* | | | |
| RUDOLPH, THE RED-NOSED REINDEER | 1959 | Columbia | 15 |
| *(Special 10th anniversary promo of the song, white label, no number, flip is same song by Gene Autry)* | | | |

**7-Inch Extended Plays**

| | | | |
|---|---|---|---|
| CHRISTMAS GREETINGS | 1962 | Columbia JZSP 58623 | 15 |
| *(Ray Conniff and the Singers on Band 2, Side 1)* | | | |

**CONTOURS, THE**
*Gordy promo 45s $25 each*
**45s**

| | | | |
|---|---|---|---|
| FUNNY | 1961 | Motown 1012 | 125 |
| *(White promo label)* | | | |
| WHOLE LOTTA WOMAN | 1961 | Motown 1008 | 100 |
| *(White promo label)* | | | |

**Albums**

| | | | |
|---|---|---|---|
| DO YOU LOVE ME | 1962 | Gordy 901 | 200 |
| *(White promo label)* | | | |

**COODER, RY**
**Albums**

| | | | |
|---|---|---|---|
| THE RY COODER RADIO SHOW | 1976 | Reprise PRO 588 | 100 |

**RADIO SHOWS**
**Albums**

| | | | |
|---|---|---|---|
| KING BISCUIT FLOWER HOUR (Apr 81) Live concert | 1981 | DIR/ABC (2) | 75-125 |
| *(With Manfred Mann)* | | | |

**COOKE, SAM**
*Specialty promo 45s $15-20 each; Other Keen promo 45s $10 each; Other RCA Victor promo 45s $5 each; RCA Victor compact-33 singles $10 each (for jukeboxes)*
**45s**

| | | | |
|---|---|---|---|
| A CHANGE IS GONNA COME | 1964 | RCA Victor SP-45-173 | 20 |
| *(Promo-only release, white promo label)* | | | |
| YOU SEND ME | 1957 | Keen 4013 | 25 |
| *(White promo label)* | | | |

**COOLIDGE, RITA**
*A&M promo singles $2 each*
**45s**

| | | | |
|---|---|---|---|
| I WILL NEVER LET YOU GO (same on both sides) | 1983 | A&M 2546 | 4 |
| *(Stock copies do not exist)* | | | |

**RADIO SHOWS**
**Albums**

| | | | |
|---|---|---|---|
| ROBERT W. MORGAN  Profile | 1978 | Watermark | 10-15 |
| *(Music and interview)* | | | |

**COOPER, ALICE**
*Warner Bros. white promo label 45s $8 each; Warner Bros. cream promo label 45s $6 each; Atlantic promo 45s $6 each; MCA white label promo 45s $3 each; Warner Brothers promo LPs $15-20 each*
**12-Inch Singles**

| | | | |
|---|---|---|---|
| CLONES (WE'RE ALL)/MODEL CITIZEN | 1980 | Warner Bros. PRO-A-864 | 15 |
| GIVE IT UP (same on both sides) | 1986 | MCA L33-17205 | 8 |
| HE'S BACK (THE MAN BEHIND THE MASK) (same on both sides) | 1986 | MCA L33-17177 | 8 |
| I GOT A LINE ON YOU (same on both sides) | 1988 | Epic EAS 1347 | 10 |
| I LIKE GIRLS (same on both sides) | 1981 | Warner Bros. PRO-A-1059 | 12 |
| POISON (same on both sides) | 1989 | Epic EAS 1663 | 10 |
| TRASH (same on both sides) | 1989 | Epic EAS 1686 | 10 |

**45s**

| | | | |
|---|---|---|---|
| DON'T BLOW YOUR MIND  The Spiders | 196? | Santa Cruz 003 | 200 |
| *(Stamped and mailed to radio stations)* | | | |
| HELLO HURRAY  Long/short versions | 1973 | Warner Bros. 7673 | 10 |
| *(White promo label)* | | | |
| WHAT'S IT ALL ABOUT (Aug 75) Public service show | 1975 | W. I. A. A. 279 | 25 |
| *("Only Women," flip side is Gladys Knight)* | | | |
| WHAT'S IT ALL ABOUT (Feb 74) Public service show | 1974 | W. I. A. A. 216 | 25 |
| *("Teenage Lament '74," flip is Jim Croce)* | | | |
| WHY DON'T YOU LOVE ME  The Spiders | 196? | Na Scot 112 | 250 |
| *(Stock copies, stamped and mailed to radio stations)* | | | |

**7-Inch Extended Plays**

| | | | |
|---|---|---|---|
| BILLION DOLLAR BABIES  Jukebox LLP | 1973 | Warner Bros. 2685 (LLP 208) | 40 |
| *(Issued with a paper picture sleeve and title strips)* | | | |
| MUSCLE OF LOVE Jukebox LLP | 1973 | Warner Bros. 2748 (LLP 235) | 35 |
| *(Issued with a paper picture sleeve and title strips)* | | | |

**Albums**

| | | | |
|---|---|---|---|
| THE ALICE COOPER RADIO SPECIAL Music and interviews | 1979 | Warner Bros. PRO-A-789 (2) | 40 |
| *(Released by the record label for radio stations)* | | | |
| BATTLE AXE Radio sampler | 1977 | Polydor 30001 | 20 |
| *(By the Billion Dollar Babies, former members of Alice Cooper's band)* | | | |

(Top row) Two different Fantasy promo labels are illustrated by these two Creedence Clearwater Revival albums. (Middle left) An additional reason that radio shows will be collectible in the future: Note that the label of this Crowded House show says "Commercials Included." This was not always the case in the 1970s. (Middle right) It was not uncommon for the King Biscuit Flower Hour to feature two different "lesser" bands at times. Neither the Cure nor the Divinyls were well known in 1986, when this show aired. (Bottom left) An example of a BBC Transcription Disc, this one by Deep Purple. These are highly sought after because they contain re-recorded versions for UK airplay. (Bottom right) An early King Biscuit CD from 1987, this one features Dire Straits, a group that made a much longer version of its *Brothers in Arms* album for CD release in 1985.

| Title | Yr | Label, Number | NM $ |
|---|---|---|---|
| EASY ACTION | 1970 | Warner Bros./Straight 1845 | 100 |
| *(White promo label)* | | | |
| LOVE IT TO DEATH | 1971 | Warner Bros./Straight 1883 | 100 |
| *(White promo label)* | | | |
| PRETTIES FOR YOU | 1969 | Warner Bros./Straight 1051 | 150 |
| *(White promo label)* | | | |
| **Compact Discs** | | | |
| ALICE COOPER PRESENTS STOOPID NEWS | 1991 | Epic ESK 4161 | 20 |
| *(Promo-only music and interviews)* | | | |
| FOUNDATIONS | 1993 | | 18 |
| *(Promo only, music and interviews)* | | | |
| TRASH CAN | 1989 | Epic EK 45137 | 100 |
| *(Promo-only kit includes video, CD, cassette and press kit)* | | | |
| **RADIO SHOWS** | | | |
| **Albums** | | | |
| ALIVE- WHAT'S ALL ABOUT ALICE Profile | 1976 | Entertainment (3) | 100-200 |
| *(Music and interview, rare show and rare material)* | | | |
| DESERT ISLAND DISC (July 91) Profile | 1991 | | 20-35 |
| *(Music and interview)* | | | |
| HIGH VOLTAGE (July 89) Various artists | 1989 | Westwood One (2) | 25-50 |
| *(Alice Cooper featured in live segment)* | | | |
| IN CONCERT (Aug 92) Live concert | 1992 | Westwood One (2) | 50-85 |
| *(Newer material written in the 80s)* | | | |
| INNERVIEW (70s) Profile of Spiders, Alice Cooper | 197? | Innerview | 10-20 |
| *(Music and interview, Series 4, show 13)* | | | |
| METALSHOP (80s) Various artists, Show 387 | 198? | MJI Productions | 15-20 |
| *(Segments of live Alice Cooper tracks)* | | | |
| NIGHTBIRD & COMPANY (Apr 73) 15-minute show | 1973 | U. S. Army (2) | 30-60 |
| *(One of four shows on the two public service* | | | |
| OFF THE RECORD (Dec 89) Music and interview) | 1989 | Westwood One (2) | 15-25 |
| *(This show was repeated)* | | | |
| ROCK CLOCK Live tracks | 1987 | DIR (2) | 25-40 |
| *(With John Waite and The Moody Blues)* | | | |
| SUPERGROUPS Live material | 1980 | DIR (3) | 175-350 |
| *(Rare concert segments from original 70s music)* | | | |
| **Compact Discs** | | | |
| ELECTRIC LADYLAND (Sept 91) Live concert | 1991 | Album Network | 50-100 |
| *(Classic and rare live concert)* | | | |
| KING BISCUIT FLOWER HOUR Live concert | 1988 | DIR | 50-75 |
| *(Alice Cooper only)* | | | |
| **Reel-to-Reel Tapes** | | | |
| WELCOME TO MY NIGHTMARE (July 75) | 1975 | (2) | 100-150 |
| *(Live concert on two 7" reels)* | | | |

## COPAS, COWBOY
*King white promo label 45s $6 each*
**RADIO SHOWS**
**16-Inch Transcriptions**

| | | | |
|---|---|---|---|
| U.S. ARMY BAND (50s) Host is Cowboy Copas | 195? | U. S. Army | 20-35 |
| *(Several shows in this series were hosted by Copas)* | | | |

## COPE, JULIAN
**12-Inch Singles**

| | | | |
|---|---|---|---|
| 5 O'CLOCK WORLD/S.P.Q.R. | 1988 | Island 1288 | 5 |
| CHARLOTTE ANNE/CHARLOTTE ANNE (Edit) | 1988 | Island 2523 | 7 |
| PEGGY SUICIDE SAMPLER | 1991 | Island PR12 6667 | 12 |
| TRAMPOLENE (same on both sides) | 1987 | Island 2000 | 5 |
| WORLD SHUT YOUR MOUTH (same on both sides) | 1987 | Island 988 | 5 |

## COPELAND, STEWART/ADAM ANT
**12-Inch Singles**

| | | | |
|---|---|---|---|
| OUT OF BOUNDS (extended)/OUT OF BOUNDS (LP version) | 1986 | I.R.S. 17166 | 8 |

## COPELAND, STEWART/STANARD RIDGWAY
**12-Inch Singles**

| | | | |
|---|---|---|---|
| DON'T BOX ME IN (same on both sides) | 1983 | A&M 17260 | 10 |

## CORDING, HENRY
**45s**

| | | | |
|---|---|---|---|
| ROCK AND ROLL MOPS | 1958 | Columbia 40762 | 75 |
| *(White promo label)* | | | |

## CORNELIUS, HELEN
**45s**

| | | | |
|---|---|---|---|
| OH HOLY NIGHT/SILENT NIGHT | 1981 | Elektra 47232 | 5 |
| *(B-side by Joe Sun)* | | | |

## CORNELL, DON
**7-Inch Extended Plays**

| | | | |
|---|---|---|---|
| LET'S HAVE AN OLD FASHIONED CHRISTMAS/I'VE GOT THE CHRISTMAS SPIRIT//SING A SONG OF SANTA CLAUS/WINTER'S HERE AGAIN | 195? | Coral 83010 | 15 |
| *(B-side by the Ames Brothers)* | | | |

| Title | Yr | Label, Number | NM $ |
|---|---|---|---|
| **CORNERSHOP** | | | |
| **45s** | | | |
| BRIMFUL OF ASHA/IT'S INDIAN TOBACCO MY FRIEND | 1997 | Luaka Bop/Warner Bros. PRO-S-8869 | 10 |
| *(Red vinyl, promo-only, with picture sleeve and clear vinyl cover)* | | | |
| | | | |
| **CORONETS, THE** | | | |
| **45s** | | | |
| DON'T DEPRIVE ME | 1955 | Sterling 903 | 200 |
| *(Questionable existence as promo)* | | | |
| HUSH | 1955 | Groove 0116 | 150 |
| *(White promo label)* | | | |
| I LOVE YOU MORE | 1955 | Groove 0114 | 125 |
| *(White promo label)* | | | |
| IT WOULD BE HEAVENLY | 1953 | Chess 1553 | 400 |
| *(White promo label, black vinyl; red vinyl stock worth $750)* | | | |
| NADINE | 1953 | Chess 1549 | 200 |
| *(White promo label, black vinyl; red vinyl stock worth $800)* | | | |
| | | | |
| **COSBY, BILL** | | | |
| **45s** | | | |
| CAPTAIN JUNKIE | 1977 | PSA 977 | 15 |
| *(Public service commercial)* | | | |
| **Albums** | | | |
| RADIO SAMPLER ALBUM -- THE BEST OF BILL COSBY | 1969 | Warner Bros. PRO 249 | 20 |
| *(Promo LP with edits of 12 tracks for radio use)* | | | |
| | | | |
| **COSTELLO, ELVIS** | | | |

*Other Columbia and Warner promo 45s $5 each; Columbia promo picture sleeve 45s $3 each; other Columbia and Warner promo 12" singles $10 each; other Warner Bros. promo CD singles $3-5 each*

| Title | Yr | Label, Number | NM $ |
|---|---|---|---|
| **12-Inch Singles** | | | |
| DON'T LET ME BE MISUNDERSTOOD (LIVE) (same on both sides) | 1986 | Columbia CAS 2310 | 15 |
| LOVEABLE (same on both sides) | 1986 | Columbia CAS 2371 | 7 |
| MAN OUT OF TIME/BEYOND BELIEF | 1982 | Columbia AS 1510 | 12 |
| SEVEN DAY WEEKEND (same on both sides) | 1986 | Columbia CAS 2380 | 8 |
| TOKYO STORM WARNING/TOKYO STORM WARNING {PART 1} | 1986 | Columbia CAS 2500 | 6 |
| VERONICA (same on both sides) | 1989 | Warner Bros. PRO-A-3424 | 15 |
| WATCHING THE DETECTIVES | 1978 | Columbia AS 529 | 15 |
| *(White promo label; four-song EP in a 12" single format)* | | | |
| **45s** | | | |
| ALISON/WATCHING THE DETECTIVES | 1977 | Columbia 10705 | 18 |
| *(White promo label)* | | | |
| I CAN'T STAND UP FOR FALLING DOWN | 1980 | Columbia 11251 | 10 |
| *(White promo label; not an EP, but this record has four songs)* | | | |
| MY FUNNY VALENTINE | 1979 | Columbia AE7-1172 | 20 |
| *(Custom label, red vinyl, promo-only release)* | | | |
| NEW AMSTERDAM | 1980 | Columbia 11284 | 10 |
| *(White promo label)* | | | |
| THIS YEAR'S GIRL Stereo/mono | 1978 | Columbia 10762 | 15 |
| *(White promo label)* | | | |
| **7-Inch Extended Plays** | | | |
| LIVE AT HOLLYWOOD HIGH White promo label | 1978 | Columbia AE 1171 | 15 |
| *(Promo-only EP with picture sleeve given away as a bonus with early copies of the Armed Forces LP)* | | | |
| SAVE THE CHILDREN | 1981 | DWP 611 | 25 |
| *(Public service message)* | | | |
| **Albums** | | | |
| ALMOST BLUE | 1981 | Columbia AS-1318 | 40 |
| *(Promo-only radio sampler)* | | | |
| ARMED FORCES | 1979 | Columbia JC 35709 | 15 |
| *(White label promo, includes bonus 7" single)* | | | |
| A CONVERSATION WITH ELVIS COSTELLO | 1982 | Columbia | 50 |
| *(Promo-only release for radio, released at time of Imperial Bedroom LP)* | | | |
| MY AIM IS TRUE | 1978 | Columbia (no #) | 150 |
| *(Promo-only picture disc, highly collectible)* | | | |
| RADIO RADIO Orange vinyl promo | 197? | Columbia AS-443 | 40 |
| *(With tracks by Nick Lowe and Mink DeVille)* | | | |
| SPIKE -- THE ELVIS COSTELLO HOUR | 1989 | Warner Bros. PRO-A-3488 | 30 |
| *(Music and conversation; generic gatefold sleeve with sticker on cover)* | | | |
| TAKING LIBERTIES | 1980 | Columbia AS 847 | 35 |
| *(White promo label, promo-only sampler)* | | | |
| THE TOM SNYDER INTERVIEW | 1981 | Columbia AS-958 | 35 |
| *(Promo-only interview record)* | | | |
| **Compact Discs** | | | |
| 2 1/2 YEARS IN 30 MINUTES | 1993 | Rykodisc VRCD 0271 | 30 |
| *(Promo-only sampler)* | | | |
| BRUTAL YOUTH (WORDS AND MUSIC) | 1994 | Warner Bros. PRO-CD-6955 | 20 |
| *(Music and interviews, promo-only release)* | | | |
| COSTELLO & NIEVE | 1996 | Warner Bros. | 50 |
| *(Promo version of 5-CD single set that was briefly available at retail)* | | | |
| EXCERPTS FROM THE JULIET LETTERS | 1993 | Warner Bros. PRO-CD-6018 | 10 |
| *(Six-track radio sampler)* | | | |
| KOJAK VARIETY | 1995 | Warner Bros. | 300 |
| *(Promo version with two bonus tracks and certificate; only 200 pressed)* | | | |
| LET HIM DANGLE | 1990 | Warner Bros. PRO-CD-3720 | 10 |
| *(Promo-only CD single)* | | | |

| Title | Yr | Label, Number | NM $ |
|-------|-----|---------------|------|
| SPIKE | 1989 | Warner Bros. PRO-CD-3426 | 20 |
| *(Special promo version of hit album)* | | | |
| VERONICA | 1989 | Warner Bros. PRO-CD-3424 | 10 |
| *(Co-written by Paul McCartney)* | | | |
| **RADIO SHOWS** | | | |
| **Albums** | | | |
| BBC CLASSIC TRACKS (Oct 91) | 1991 | | 20-30 |
| *(From several sessions, some live)* | | | |
| BBC TRANSCRIPTION DISC  Live concert | 1984 | BBC Transcription | 350-500 |
| *(One of the most collectible radio shows of* | | | |
| BBC TRANSCRIPTION DISC  Live concert | 1987 | BBC Transcription | 300-450 |
| *(Very rare and desirable)* | | | |
| KING BISCUIT FLOWER HOUR (Dec 84) Live concert | 1984 | DIR (2) | 100-125 |
| *(This concert repeated several times)* | | | |
| KING BISCUIT FLOWER HOUR (July 80) Live concert | 1980 | DIR/ABC (2) | 100-150 |
| *(Early Biscuits are very rare)* | | | |
| KING BISCUIT FLOWER HOUR (Oct 80) Live concert | 1980 | DIR/ABC (2) | 75-125 |
| *(With Devo)* | | | |
| NBC SOURCE (May 84) Live concert | 1984 | NBC Source (2) | 75-125 |
| *(Much of the same material as above)* | | | |
| OFF THE RECORD  Profile | 1986 | Westwood One (2) | 20-40 |
| *(Music and interview)* | | | |
| ROCK AROUND THE WORLD (80s) Profile | 198? | RATW | 40-80 |
| *(Music and interview)* | | | |
| ROCK AROUND THE WORLD (80s) WITH NICK LOWE | 198? | RATW | 40-80 |
| *(Music and interview)* | | | |
| ROCK AROUND THE WORLD (80s) WITH ROBERT GORDON | 198? | RATW | 45-80 |
| *(Music and interview)* | | | |
| ROCK STARS  "Spike" sessions | 1989 | Westwood One | 30-60 |
| *(Live material from several concerts)* | | | |
| ROLLING STONE MAGAZINE RADIO SHOW (Sept 82) | 1982 | Rolling Stone (3) | 75-150 |
| *(Music and interview With Nick Lowe)* | | | |
| SOURCE CONCERT Live concert | 1983 | NBC Source (2) | 75-125 |
| *(Rare concert material)* | | | |
| **Compact Discs** | | | |
| KING BISCUIT FLOWER HOUR (Mar 89) Live concert | 1989 | DIR | 50-80 |
| *(CD versions of above vinyl concerts)* | | | |
| KING BISCUIT FLOWER HOUR (Sept 90) Live concert | 1990 | DIR | 50-75 |
| *(With David Baerwald)* | | | |
| ON THE EDGE (Jan 94) Music and interviews | 1994 | Westwood One | 15-20 |
| *(With the Connells and Verve)* | | | |
| ON THE EDGE (Mar 94) Music and interviews | 1994 | Westwood One | 20-30 |
| *(With Nirvana)* | | | |
| **Reel-to-Reel Tapes** | | | |
| KING BISCUIT FLOWER HOUR (Apr 78) Live concert | 1978 | DIR/ABC (2) | 100-150 |
| *(Live concert on two reels)* | | | |

## COTTON, GENE
*Ariola America promo 45s $4 each*
**45s**

| Title | Yr | Label, Number | NM $ |
|-------|-----|---------------|------|
| CHILD OF PEACE | 1981 | No label, NR 16361 | 8 |
| *(White label promo only, with insert)* | | | |
| WHAT'S IT ALL ABOUT (Dec 78) Public service show | 1978 | W. I. A. A. 454 | 10 |
| *(Flip side features Anne Murray)* | | | |

## COTTON, JOSIE
**12-Inch Singles**

| Title | Yr | Label, Number | NM $ |
|-------|-----|---------------|------|
| JIMMY LOVES MARY-ANNE (same on both sides) | 1984 | Elektra 4958 | 7 |
| **45s** | | | |
| BYE BYE BABY (same on both sides) | 1982 | Elektra 69886 | 3 |
| *(May be promo only)* | | | |

## COUNTING CROWS
*Geffen/Warner promo CD singles $4*
**RADIO SHOWS**
**Compact Discs**

| Title | Yr | Label, Number | NM $ |
|-------|-----|---------------|------|
| IN CONCERT-NU ROCK (Apr 94) Live concert | 1994 | Westwood One (2) | 40-75 |
| *(With Squeeze)* | | | |
| IN CONCERT-NU ROCK (Jan 85) | 1995 | Westwood One | 40-75 |
| *(Live concert)* | | | |
| IN CONCERT-NU ROCK (June 94) Live concert | 1994 | Westwood One (2) | 40-75 |
| *(With Jeff Healy)* | | | |
| ON THE EDGE (Oct 94) Profile of three groups | 1994 | | 20-30 |
| *(Music and interview, also with Dada and Velvet Crush)* | | | |

## COUNTRY JOE (McDONALD) (AND THE FISH)
*Vanguard promo 45s $8 each Popular folk/protest singer/band of the 60s*
**RADIO SHOWS**
**Albums**

| Title | Yr | Label, Number | NM $ |
|-------|-----|---------------|------|
| BBC TRANSCRIPTION DISC Live concert | 1975 | BBC Transcription | 200-350 |
| *(With Barry Melton)* | | | |
| RETRO ROCK (Nov 81) Live concert | 1981 | Clayton Webster | 150-200 |
| *(Very rare concert)* | | | |

| Title | Yr | Label, Number | NM $ |
|---|---|---|---|
| **COVELLE, BUDDY** | | | |
| **45s** | | | |
| BILLY BOY | 1959 | Brunswick 55151 | 50 |
| *(Yellow promo label)* | | | |
| LORRAINE | 1959 | Coral 62181 | 300 |
| *(Blue promo label)* | | | |
| | | | |
| **COWBOY JUNKIES** | | | |
| *RCA promo 45s $4 each; RCA promo CD singles not listed $4 each* | | | |
| **12-Inch Singles** | | | |
| SWEET JANE (same on both sides) | 1988 | RCA 8759 | 12 |
| **Compact Discs** | | | |
| SWEET JANE | 1988 | RCA 8879-2-RDJ | 8 |
| *(First promo issue of this modern-rock hit)* | | | |
| THE COLLECTION | 1994 | RCA RDJ 66349-2 | 50 |
| *(Five CDs with booklets in a CD wallet)* | | | |
| **RADIO SHOWS** | | | |
| **Albums** | | | |
| BBC TRANSCRIPTION DISC Live concert | 1992 | BBC Transcription | 150-300 |
| *(Very rare series)* | | | |
| **Compact Discs** | | | |
| ON THE EDGE (Feb 94) Profile of the group | 1994 | Westwood One | 15-25 |
| *(Music and interview)* | | | |
| | | | |
| **COYNE, KEVIN** | | | |
| **RADIO SHOWS** | | | |
| **Albums** | | | |
| BBC TRANSCRIPTION DISC  Live concert | 1974 | BBC Transcription | 150-300 |
| *(Very rare concert with Robin Trower)* | | | |
| | | | |
| **CRACKER** | | | |
| *Virgin promo CD singles $3-5 each* | | | |
| **Compact Discs** | | | |
| VIRGIN YEARS, THE | 1994 | Virgin DPRO-14129 | 20 |
| *(Promo-only sampler, 8 Cracker tracks, 8 Camper Van Beethoven tracks)* | | | |
| **RADIO SHOWS** | | | |
| **Compact Discs** | | | |
| IN CONCERT-NU ROCK (Sept 94) | 1994 | Westwood One | 20-40 |
| *(Live concert)* | | | |
| | | | |
| **CRADDOCK, BILLY "CRASH"** | | | |
| *Other Columbia promo 45s $12 each; Mercury, King promo 45s $8 each; Cartwheel and ABC promo 45s $3 each* | | | |
| **45s** | | | |
| ALL I WANT IS YOU | 1960 | Columbia 41619 | 15 |
| *(White promo label)* | | | |
| BIRD DOGGIN' | 1958 | Colonial 721 | 25 |
| *(White promo label)* | | | |
| DON'T DESTROY ME | 1959 | Columbia 41470 | 15 |
| *(White promo label)* | | | |
| LULU LEE | 1958 | Date 1007 | 25 |
| *(Green/white promo label)* | | | |
| **7-Inch Extended Plays** | | | |
| RUB IT IN Jukebox LLP | 1974 | ABC PRO-817 | 12 |
| *(Issued with a paper cover)* | | | |
| | | | |
| **CRAMER, FLOYD** | | | |
| **7-Inch Extended Plays** | | | |
| BEHIND CLOSED DOORS/THE MOST BEAUTIFUL GIRL// STAR SPANGLED BANNER/TOP OF THE WORLD | 1974 | RCA Victor DJEO-0272 | 10 |
| | | | |
| **CRAMPS, THE** | | | |
| *Other IRS label promos $10* | | | |
| **12-Inch Singles** | | | |
| BIKINI GIRLS WITH MACHINE GUNS (same on both sides) | 1989 | Enigma EPRO 253 | 10 |
| **45s** | | | |
| GOOGOO MUCK | 1981 | I.R.S. 9021 | 40 |
| *(Promo-only colored vinyl includes picture sleeve)* | | | |
| **Albums** | | | |
| STAY SICK! | 1990 | Enigma 268 | 20 |
| *(Promo-only version)* | | | |
| | | | |
| **CRANBERRIES, THE** | | | |
| *Island promo CD singles $3-5 each* | | | |
| **Compact Discs** | | | |
| TO THE FAITHFUL DEPARTED | 1996 | Island | 40 |
| *(Promo-only package with CD, video, seeds and incense sticks, all in custom box)* | | | |
| **RADIO SHOWS** | | | |
| **Compact Discs** | | | |
| ALBUM NETWORK SPECIAL (Feb 94) | 1994 | Album Network | 50-100 |
| *(Live concert material)* | | | |
| ALBUM NETWORK SPECIAL Picture disc CD | 1993 | Album Network | 40-100 |
| *(Live material from recent concerts)* | | | |

| Title | Yr | Label, Number | NM $ |
|-------|-----|---------------|------|
| IN CONCERT-NU ROCK (May 94) Live concert | 1994 | Westwood One | 50-90 |
| *(New concert material, repeated in Oct)* | | | |
| ON THE EDGE (Sept 93) Music and interview | 1993 | Westwood One | 20-30 |
| *(With Ziggy Marley)* | | | |

**CRASH TEST DUMMIES**
*Arista promo CD singles $3-5 each*
**RADIO SHOWS**
**Compact Discs**

| Title | Yr | Label, Number | NM $ |
|-------|-----|---------------|------|
| ON THE EDGE (Aug 94) Music and interviews | 1994 | Westwood One | 20-30 |
| *(With Sheryl Crow and David Byrne)* | | | |
| ON THE EDGE (Mar 94) Music and interviews | 1994 | Westwood One | 20-35 |
| *(With Lenny Kravitz)* | | | |

**CRAWLER**
**RADIO SHOWS**
**Albums**

| Title | Yr | Label, Number | NM $ |
|-------|-----|---------------|------|
| THE RECORD COMPANY Profile | 1978 | | 15-30 |
| *(Issued with a picture cover)* | | | |

**CRAY, ROBERT**
*Mercury promo 45s $3 each; Mercury promo CDs $3-5 each*
**RADIO SHOWS**
**Albums**

| Title | Yr | Label, Number | NM $ |
|-------|-----|---------------|------|
| BBC TRANSCRIPTION DISC (80s) Live concert | 198? | BBC Transcription | 100-175 |
| *(With Gil Scott Heron)* | | | |
| IN CONCERT (June 87) Live concert | 1987 | Westwood One (2) | 40-60 |
| *(With Europe)* | | | |
| IN CONCERT (Mar 93) Live concert | 1993 | Westwood One (2) | 20-40 |
| *(Robert Cray only)* | | | |
| IN CONCERT (Oct 91) Live concert | 1991 | Westwood One (2) | 20-35 |
| *(With John Hiatt)* | | | |
| KING BISCUIT FLOWER HOUR (June 87) Live concert | 1987 | DIR (2) | 20-40 |
| *(Vinyl version)* | | | |
| OFF THE RECORD (Nov 93) Profile | 1993 | Westwood One (2) | 10-15 |
| *(Music and interview)* | | | |

**Compact Discs**

| Title | Yr | Label, Number | NM $ |
|-------|-----|---------------|------|
| KING BISCUIT FLOWER HOUR | 1987 | DIR | 20-40 |
| *(CD version of the same show, repeated several times)* | | | |
| KING BISCUIT FLOWER HOUR (Oct 95) | 1995 | DIR | 25-40 |
| *(Live concert)* | | | |

**CREAM**
*Includes listings by Derek and the Dominos and Blind Faith; Also see Eric Clapton. Blind Faith Atco white promo 45s $10 each; Derek & the Dominos blue label promo RSO 45s $10 each; Other Atco white promo label 45s $12 each.*
**45s**

| Title | Yr | Label, Number | NM $ |
|-------|-----|---------------|------|
| ANYONE FOR TENNIS | 1967 | Atco 6575 | 15 |
| *(White promo label)* | | | |
| BADGE | 1969 | Atco 6668 | 12 |
| *(White promo label)* | | | |
| LAYLA  Derek & the Dominos | 1971 | Atco 6809 | 18 |
| *(White promo label)* | | | |
| SUNSHINE OF YOUR LOVE | 1967 | Atco 6544 | 20 |
| *(White promo label, reads Plug Side)* | | | |
| WHITE ROOM | 1968 | Atco 6617 | 18 |
| *(White promo label)* | | | |

**7-Inch Extended Plays**

| Title | Yr | Label, Number | NM $ |
|-------|-----|---------------|------|
| WHEELS OF FIRE  White promo label, red print | 1968 | Atco 4525 | 100 |
| *(Promo-only release with picture sleeve)* | | | |

**Albums**

| Title | Yr | Label, Number | NM $ |
|-------|-----|---------------|------|
| BLIND FAITH by Blind Faith | 1969 | Atco 304 | 75 |
| *(White promo label, cover is variation A)* | | | |
| CLASSIC CUTS | 1978 | RSO 015 | 40 |
| *(Promo-only compilation)* | | | |
| DISRAELI GEARS | 1967 | Atco 232 | 85 |
| *(White label promo version of stock LP)* | | | |
| FRESH CREAM | 1967 | Atco 206 | 75 |
| *(White label promo version of stock LP)* | | | |
| GOODBYE | 1969 | Atco 7001 | 30 |
| *(White label promo version of stock LP)* | | | |
| GOODBYE  Promo-only sampler | 1969 | Atco 141 | 50 |
| *(Other side is "Rock 'n Roll" by Vanilla Fudge)* | | | |
| LAYLA Derek & the Dominos | 1970 | Atco 704 (2) | 100 |
| *(White label promo version of stock LP)* | | | |
| LIVE CREAM | 1970 | Atco 328 | 50 |
| *(White label promo version of stock LP)* | | | |
| LIVE CREAM VOLUME II | 1972 | Atco 7005 | 25 |
| *(White label promo version of stock LP)* | | | |
| WHEELS OF FIRE | 1968 | Atco 700 (2) | 100 |
| *(White label promo version of stock LP)* | | | |
| WHEELS OF FIRE | 1968 | Atco 119/120 | 75 |
| *(Promo-only sampler)* | | | |

| Title | Yr | Label, Number | NM $ |
|-------|-----|---------------|------|

**RADIO SHOWS**
**Albums**

| | | | |
|-------|-----|---------------|------|
| LEGENDS OF ROCK (Aug 87) Profile of Clapton and Cream | 1987 | NBC Radio | 20-40 |
| *(Music and interview, some live material)* | | | |
| OFF THE RECORD (June 92) Includes Cream | 1992 | Westwood One (2) | 15-20 |
| *(Show repeated several times)* | | | |
| OFF THE RECORD (May 90) Special show, Clapton and Cream | 1990 | Westwood One (4) | 20-30 |
| *(Music and interview)* | | | |

**Compact Discs**

| | | | |
|-------|-----|---------------|------|
| BBC CLASSIC TRACKS (90s) LIVE MATERIAL | 199? | Westwood One | 20-40 |
| *(Issued several times)* | | | |
| CREAM OF THE CROP  Profile, music and interviews | 1993 | (6) | 50-100 |
| *(Some Cream music, some live performances)* | | | |
| HISTORY OF ERIC CLAPTON (Sept 92) Profile | 1992 | (6) | 125-250 |
| *(Includes Cream material, some live material)* | | | |
| IN THE STUDIO (80s) Profile of an LP | 198? | Album Network | 15-20 |
| *(Music and interview)* | | | |
| IN THE STUDIO (Nov 92) | 1992 | Album Network | 25-40 |
| *(Music and interview)* | | | |

**CREATORS, THE**
**45s**

| | | | |
|-------|-----|---------------|------|
| I'LL STAY HOME | 1962 | Philips 40060 | 75 |
| *(White promo label)* | | | |

**CREEDENCE CLEARWATER REVIVAL**

Includes listings by the Golliwogs, John Fogerty, Tom Fogerty, Blue Ridge Rangers. Other Fantasy promo label 45s $10 each; Other Fantasy red/green promo label 45s for Blue Ridge Rangers $10 each; Fantasy brown promo label 45s for Blue Ridge Rangers $8 each; John Fogerty Asylum promo 45s $5 each; John Fogerty Warner Bros. promo 45s $4 each; John Fogerty Warner Bros. promo 12" singles $12 each; Tom Fogerty Fantasy brown label promo 45s after 715 $4 each; Tom Fogerty Fantasy "lightning" promo labels $3 each; Blue Ridge Rangers promo LPs $20 each. More at John Fogerty.

**12-Inch Singles**

| | | | |
|-------|-----|---------------|------|
| I HEARD IT THROUGH THE GRAPEVINE (11:05) (same on both sides) | 1976 | Fantasy 759-D-LP | 20 |
| MEDLEY Eight-song medley (7:08) | 1985 | Fantasy 238 | 15 |
| *(Blue Fantasy promo label)* | | | |
| VANZ KANT DANZ  John Fogerty | 1985 | Warner Bros. PRO-A-2362 | 25 |
| *(Promo-only 12" single, 5:30/4:04 versions)* | | | |

**45s**

| | | | |
|-------|-----|---------------|------|
| 45 REVOLUTIONS PER MINUTE | 1969 | Fantasy 2832/3 | 40 |
| *(Price includes promo-only picture sleeve)* | | | |
| BAD MOON RISING/LODI | 1969 | Fantasy 622 | 15 |
| *(Red/green label, "Promotion Copy")* | | | |
| BROWN EYED GIRL  The Golliwogs | 1965 | Scorpio 404 | 50 |
| *(Promo label)* | | | |
| COMIN' DOWN THE ROAD  John Fogerty | 1973 | Fantasy 717 | 15 |
| *(Brown stereo/mono promo label)* | | | |
| DON'T TELL ME NO LIES  The Golliwogs | 1964 | Fantasy 590 | 75 |
| *(First record, promo copy is red label,* | | | |
| FACES, PLACES, PEOPLE  Tom Fogerty | 1972 | Fantasy 691 | 12 |
| *(Fantasy brown promo label)* | | | |
| FIGHT FIRE  The Golliwogs | 1966 | Scorpio 405 | 50 |
| *(Promo label)* | | | |
| GOODBYE MEDIA MAN  Tom Fogerty | 1971 | Fantasy 661 | 20 |
| *(Red/green promo label, issued with a picture sleeve)* | | | |
| GREEN RIVER/COMMOTION | 1969 | Fantasy 625 | 15 |
| *(Red/green label, "Promotion Copy")* | | | |
| HAVE YOU EVER SEEN THE RAIN/HEY TONIGHT | 1971 | Fantasy 655 | 15 |
| *(Red/green label, "Promotion Copy")* | | | |
| I HEARD IT THROUGH THE GRAPEVINE | 1976 | RCA Hollywood | 25 |
| *(Test pressing with insert, no print on label)* | | | |
| I PUT A SPELL ON YOU | 1968 | Fantasy 617 | 25 |
| *("Promotional Copy" in black letters on red/green label)* | | | |
| JAMBALAYA (ON THE BAYOU) The Blue Ridge Rangers | 1972 | Fantasy 689 | 12 |
| *(Red/green label, "Promotion Copy")* | | | |
| JOYFUL RESURRECTION  Tom Fogerty | 1973 | Fantasy 702 | 10 |
| *(Fantasy brown promo label)* | | | |
| LADY OF FATIMA Tom Fogerty | 1972 | Fantasy 680 | 15 |
| *(Fantasy red/green promo label)* | | | |
| LOOKIN' OUT MY BACK DOOR/LONG AS I CAN SEE THE LIGHT | 1970 | Fantasy 645 | 15 |
| *(Red/green label, "Promotion Copy")* | | | |
| MEDLEY Two four-song medleys, one on each side | 1985 | Fantasy 957 | 10 |
| *(Blue Fantasy promo label)* | | | |
| MEDLEY U.S.A. | 1981 | Fantasy 917 | 10 |
| *(Fantasy "lightning" promo label)* | | | |
| PORTERVILLE  Creedence Clearwater Revival | 1967 | Scorpio 412 | Unknown |
| *(It's believed that only stock copies were released unde the CCR name)* | | | |
| PORTERVILLE  The Golliwogs | 1967 | Scorpio 412 | 75 |
| *(Promo release only, stock copies unknown)* | | | |
| PROUD MARY/BORN ON THE BAYOU | 1969 | Fantasy 619 | 15 |
| *(Red/green label, "Promotion Copy")* | | | |
| REGGIE  Tom Fogerty | 1973 | Fantasy 715 | 10 |
| *(Fantasy brown promo label)* | | | |
| SOMEDAY NEVER COMES | 1972 | Fantasy 676 | 15 |
| *(Red/green label, "Promotion Copy")* | | | |
| SUSIE Q | 1968 | Fantasy 616 | 25 |
| *("Promotional Copy" in black letters on red/green label)* | | | |

| Title | Yr | Label, Number | NM $ |
|-------|-----|---------------|------|
| TRAVELIN' BAND/WHO'LL STOP THE RAIN | 1970 | Fantasy 637 | 15 |
| *(Red/green label, "Promotion Copy")* | | | |
| VANZ KANT DANZ  John Fogerty | 1985 | Warner Bros. PRO-S-2363 | 18 |
| *(Promo-only 7" single, 4:04 version)* | | | |
| WALKING ON THE WATER  The Golliwogs | 1966 | Scorpio 408 | 50 |
| *(Promo label)* | | | |
| YOU CAME WALKING  The Golliwogs | 1965 | Fantasy 597 | 60 |
| *("Promotional Copy")* | | | |
| YOU GOT NOTHIN' ON ME  The Golliwogs | 1965 | Fantasy 599 | 60 |
| *(Red promo label)* | | | |
| **Albums** | | | |
| BAYOU COUNTRY | 1969 | Fantasy F-8387 | 80 |
| *(White label promo)* | | | |
| COSMO'S FACTORY | 1970 | Fantasy F-8402 | 80 |
| *(White label promo)* | | | |
| CREEDENCE CLEARWATER REVIVAL | 1968 | Fantasy F-8382 | 80 |
| *(White label promo)* | | | |
| GREEN RIVER | 1969 | Fantasy F-8393 | 80 |
| *(White label promo)* | | | |
| MARDI GRAS | 1972 | Fantasy 9404 | 25 |
| *(Brown promo label, reads "Promotional Copy" and "Not for Sale" at top of label in black letters)* | | | |
| PENDULUM White promo label | 1971 | Fantasy 8410 | 50 |
| *(White promo label CCR Fantasy discs are rare)* | | | |
| WILLY AND THE POOR BOYS | 1969 | Fantasy F-8397 | 80 |
| *(White label promo)* | | | |
| **RADIO SHOWS** | | | |
| **Albums** | | | |
| BIRTHDAY TRIBUTE (Nov 90) Tom Fogerty | 1990 | Unistar | 10-15 |
| *(Part of the 5-disc box set "Solid Gold Scrapbook")* | | | |
| DICK CLARK ROCK ROLL & REMEMBER (80s) Various artists | 198? | United Stations (4) | 15-20 |
| *(Interviews with members of CCR)* | | | |
| LEGENDS OF ROCK (Apr 88) Profile of CCR | 1988 | NBC Radio (2) | 20-40 |
| *(Music and interview)* | | | |
| OFF THE RECORD (May 85)  John Fogerty | 1985 | Westwood One (2) | 20-40 |
| *(Music and interview)* | | | |
| **Compact Discs** | | | |
| CREEDENCE CLEARWATER REVIVAL SPECIAL (Oct 92) | 1992 | Unistar (3) | 25-50 |
| *(Music and interview)* | | | |
| OFF THE RECORD (Aug 94) | 1994 | Westwood One | 25-40 |
| *(Music and interviews)* | | | |
| OFF THE RECORD (Mar 93) | 1993 | Westwood One | 20-40 |
| *(Music and interview, show repeated)* | | | |
| STORY OF CREEDENCE CLEARWATER REVIVAL (Aug 92) | 1992 | Unistar (2) | 20-40 |
| *(Music and interview)* | | | |

## CRENSHAW, MARSHALL
*Warner promo 45s $3 each*

**12-Inch Singles**

| Title | Yr | Label, Number | NM $ |
|-------|-----|---------------|------|
| BLUES IS KING (same on both sides) | 1985 | Warner Bros. PRO-A-2410 | 8 |
| CYNICAL GIRL/RAVE ON/SOMEBODY LIKE YOU | 1982 | Warner Bros. PRO-A-2003 | 15 |
| LITTLE WILD ONE (No. 5) (same on both sides) | 1985 | Warner Bros. PRO-A-2366 | 8 |
| MARY JEAN (same on both sides) | 1987 | Warner Bros. PRO-A-2793 | 5 |
| THIS IS EASY (same on both sides) | 1987 | Warner Bros. PRO-A-2752 | 5 |
| WHENEVER YOU'RE ON MY MIND (same on both sides) | 1983 | Warner Bros. PRO-A-2036 | 8 |
| **Compact Discs** | | | |
| COLLECTION, A | 1991 | Paradox 1343 | 20 |
| *(Promo-only sampler)* | | | |
| **RADIO SHOWS** | | | |
| **Albums** | | | |
| BBC COLLEGE CONCERT (Jan 83) | 1983 | London Wavelength | 40-80 |
| *(Live concert, rare series)* | | | |
| KING BISCUIT FLOWER HOUR | 1983 | DIR (2) | 25-50 |
| *(Live concert)* | | | |
| KING BISCUIT FLOWER HOUR (Mar 86) Live concert | 1986 | DIR (2) | 40-60 |
| *(With the Cruzados)* | | | |
| NBC SOURCE (July 83) Live concert | 1983 | NBC Radio (2) | 40-85 |
| *(With Modern English)* | | | |
| **Compact Discs** | | | |
| KING BISCUIT FLOWER HOUR (July 92) Live concert | 1992 | DIR | 25-40 |
| *(With Joe Cocker)* | | | |

## CRESTS, THE
*Coed white promo label 45s $15-20 each*

## CREW CUTS, THE
*Other Mercury white promo label 45s $15 each; RCA Victor promo 45s $5 each; Mercury promo LPs $15 each*

**45s**

| Title | Yr | Label, Number | NM $ |
|-------|-----|---------------|------|
| EARTH ANGEL | 1955 | Mercury 70529 | 25 |
| *(White promo label)* | | | |
| SH-BOOM | 1954 | Mercury 70404 | 25 |
| *(White promo label)* | | | |
| **78s** | | | |
| EARTH ANGEL | 1955 | Mercury 70529 | 40 |
| *(White promo label)* | | | |
| SH-BOOM | 1954 | Mercury 70404 | 30 |
| *(White promo label)* | | | |

| Title | Yr | Label, Number | NM $ |
|---|---|---|---|
| **Albums** | | | |
| THE CREW CUTS SING OUT | 1960 | RCA Victor PR-102 | 30 |
| *(Special products release)* | | | |
| | | | |
| **CRICKETS, THE** | | | |
| *Also see Buddy Holly* | | | |
| **Albums** | | | |
| IN STYLE WITH THE CRICKETS Blue promo label | 1960 | Coral 57320 | 75 |
| *(Does not feature Buddy Holly)* | | | |
| | | | |
| **CROCE, JIM** | | | |
| *ABC white label promo 45s $5 each; ABC white label promo LPs $10 each; Other Lifesong white promo label LPs $8 each* | | | |
| **45s** | | | |
| IT DOESN'T HAVE TO BE THAT WAY (mono/stereo) | 1976 | Lifesong 45018 | 5 |
| *(Promo-only release; Lifesong sleeve has custom sticker, which adds $4 to above)* | | | |
| WHAT'S IT ALL ABOUT (Feb 74) Public service show | 1974 | W. I. A. A. 216 | 25 |
| *(Flip side is Alice Cooper)* | | | |
| WHAT'S IT ALL ABOUT (Nov 73) Public service show | 1973 | W. I. A. A. 201 | 15 |
| *(Flip side is Gary Wright/Spooky Tooth)* | | | |
| WHAT'S IT ALL ABOUT (Nov 74) Public service show | 1974 | W. I. A. A. 243 | 12 |
| *(Flip side is Paul Williams)* | | | |
| **7-Inch Extended Plays** | | | |
| LIFE AND TIMES Jukebox LLP with six songs | 1973 | ABC 769 (LLP 232) | 18 |
| *(Issued with a paper picture cover)* | | | |
| **Albums** | | | |
| GREATEST CHARACTER SONGS | 1978 | Lifesong 35571 | 12 |
| *(White promo label)* | | | |
| **RADIO SHOWS** | | | |
| **Albums** | | | |
| BURNS (PRESENTS JIM CROCE) Music and interview | 1975 | Burns Productions (2) | 50-100 |
| *(A profile and a very rare show)* | | | |
| | | | |
| **CROOM BROTHERS, THE** | | | |
| **45s** | | | |
| ROCK AND ROLL BOOGIE | 1958 | Vee Jay 283 | 40 |
| *(White promo label)* | | | |
| | | | |
| **CROSBY, BING** | | | |
| **45s** | | | |
| AROUND THE WORLD | 1958 | Decca 38031 | 20 |
| *(Green label promo, with promo picture sleeve)* | | | |
| DEAR HEARTS AND GENTLE PEOPLE | 195? | USAF 9 | 20 |
| *(Part of "Music in the Air" series)* | | | |
| HOW LOVELY IS CHRISTMAS/NEVER BE AFRAID | 195? | Bing Crosby (no #) | 20 |
| *(Crowley's Milk promotional item)* | | | |
| I HEARD THE BELLS ON CHRISTMAS DAY/CHRISTMAS IS A-COMIN' | 1956 | Decca 30126 | 12 |
| *(Pink label, black type)* | | | |
| I WISH YOU A MERRY CHRISTMAS/WINTER WONDERLAND// THE LITTLEST ANGEL | 1962 | Warner Bros. PRO 146 | 20 |
| RUDOLPH THE RED-NOSED REINDEER/ I HEARD THE BELLS ON CHRISTMAS DAY | 1956 | Decca 27159/30126 | 20 |
| *(Green label promo with two different numbers on the record!)* | | | |
| **7-Inch Extended Plays** | | | |
| JAN-FEB 1961 SAMPLER | 1961 | Warner Bros. PRO 126 | 15 |
| *(Small center hole, 33 1/3 rpm, 7 cuts)* | | | |
| | | | |
| **CROSBY, DAVID** | | | |
| *A&M promo CD singles $3 each Of Crosby, Stills, Nash & Young; earlier with the Byrds* | | | |
| **RADIO SHOWS** | | | |
| **Albums** | | | |
| LEGENDS OF ROCK (Feb 89) CSNY, mostly Crosby | 1989 | NBC Radio (2) | 20-35 |
| *(Music and interviews)* | | | |
| OFF THE RECORD (July 89) Profile of CSNY | 1989 | Westwood One | 10-20 |
| *(Music and interviews)* | | | |
| WORLD OF ROCK (Mar 89) CSNY, Crosby is co-host | 1989 | DIR (2) | 15-25 |
| *(Music and interviews)* | | | |
| **Compact Discs** | | | |
| KING BISCUIT FLOWER HOUR (May 89) Live concert | 1989 | DIR | 20-40 |
| *(This concert was repeated several times)* | | | |
| **Reel-to-Reel Tapes** | | | |
| LIVE FROM THE WHISKEY David Crosby | 1994 | Entertainment Radio | 50-80 |
| *(Live concert, rare series)* | | | |
| | | | |
| **CROSBY, STILLS, NASH & YOUNG** | | | |
| *Includes listings for Stephen Stills and Graham Nash; separate listings for David Crosby and Neil Young. Atco white promo label 45s for Buffalo Springfield $15 each; Atlantic CSNY promo 45s $5-10 each; Atlantic CSN promo 45s $5 each; Atlantic Stephen Stills promo 45s $4 each; Atlantic Stills-Manassas promo singles $5 each; Columbia white promo label 45s by Stephen Stills $3 each; Atco white promo label LPs for Buffalo Springfield $25 each; Columbia white promo label LPs for Stephen Stills $8 each.* | | | |
| **45s** | | | |
| SOUTHERN CROSS | 1982 | Atlantic 89969 | 10 |
| *(Test pressing, long and short versions)* | | | |
| WOODSTOCK | 1970 | Atlantic 2652 | 10 |
| *(White promo label)* | | | |

| Title | Yr | Label, Number | NM $ |
|---|---|---|---|
| **Albums** | | | |
| 4 WAY STREET | 1971 | Atlantic SD 2-902 | 50 |
| *(White label stereo promo)* | | | |
| CELEBRATION/CSNY MONTH | 197? | Atlantic PR 165 | 100 |
| *(Promo-only radio sampler, mono)* | | | |
| CELEBRATION/CSNY MONTH | 1974 | Atlantic PR 165 | 50 |
| *(Promo-only radio sampler, stereo)* | | | |
| DEJA VU | 1970 | Atlantic SD 7200 | 60 |
| *(White label stereo promo)* | | | |
| IN SYNCH | 1989 | Atlantic PR-2575 | 20 |
| *(Promo-only interview album)* | | | |
| A RAP WITH CROSBY, STILLS, NASH & YOUNG | 1985 | Atlantic 18102 | 40 |
| *(Promo only, music and interview)* | | | |
| **Compact Discs** | | | |
| AMERICAN DREAM | 1988 | Atlantic PR 2552 | 50 |
| *(Promo-only picture disc in Digipak)* | | | |
| BOX SET SAMPLER | 1994 | Atlantic 4283 | 25 |
| *(Promo-only release, 14 songs)* | | | |
| WOODSTOCK | 1992 | Atlantic 2860 | 10 |
| *(The CD single, promo only)* | | | |
| **RADIO SHOWS** | | | |
| **Albums** | | | |
| AT&T SHOWCASE OF ROCK | 1990 | Unistar (3) | 20-40 |
| CLASSIC ROCK  With Neil Young | 1990 | Classic Rock (3) | 20-40 |
| *(Music and interview, some live material)* | | | |
| INNERVIEW (70s) Profile of CSNY | 197? | Innerview | 15-20 |
| *(Music and interviews)* | | | |
| KING BISCUIT FLOWER HOUR (Feb 87) | 1987 | DIR (4) | 50-100 |
| *("Anti-Crack" concert, two shows, CSNY with others)* | | | |
| KING BISCUIT FLOWER HOUR (Nov 79) | 1979 | DIR (3) | 50-100 |
| *(M.U.S.E. concert, CSN with others)* | | | |
| KING BISCUIT FLOWER HOUR (Sept 80) | 1980 | DIR (2) | 35-75 |
| *(Edited version of the original M.U.S.E. concert)* | | | |
| LEGENDS OF ROCK (Aug 87) Two-part profile of CSNY | 1987 | NBC Radio (4) | 25-40 |
| *(Music and interviews)* | | | |
| LEGENDS OF ROCK (May 88) Profile OF CSNY | 1988 | NBC Radio (2) | 15-25 |
| *(Music and interviews)* | | | |
| OFF THE RECORD (90s) CSNY Profile | 1990 | Westwood One (2) | 15-25 |
| *(Music and interviews)* | | | |
| SUPERSTAR CONCERT (80s) Box set, CSNY | 198? | Westwood One (3) | 45-75 |
| *(Live concert, several repeats)* | | | |
| SUPERSTAR CONCERT Box set, with Neil Young | 1987 | Westwood One (3) | 50-100 |
| *(Live concert by Neil Young, several repeats)* | | | |
| WORLD OF ROCK (Mar 89) CSNY, Crosby is co-host | 1989 | DIR (2) | 15-25 |
| *(Various artists, music and interviews)* | | | |
| **Compact Discs** | | | |
| BBC CLASSIC TRACKS (Sept 94) Live BBC material | 1994 | London Wavelength | 20-35 |
| *(Various live tracks)* | | | |
| CSN 25TH ANNIVERSARY SPECIAL (June 94) Profile | 1994 | Album Network | 50-90 |
| *(Music and interviews)* | | | |
| IN THE STUDIO (80s) With CSN/CSNY | 198? | Album Network | 20-30 |
| *(Music and interviews)* | | | |
| IN THE STUDIO (80s) With Neil Young | 198? | Album Network | 30-45 |
| *(Music and interviews)* | | | |
| KING BISCUIT FLOWER HOUR (80s) Live concert | 198? | DIR | 50-80 |
| *(Crosby, Stills, Nash & Young in concert)* | | | |
| KING BISCUIT FLOWER HOUR (Nov 87) Live concert | 1987 | DIR | 20-30 |
| *(With Allman Brothers)* | | | |
| SUPERSTAR CONCERT (Oct 92) Live concert | 1992 | Westwood One (2) | 40-75 |
| *(Crosby Stills & Nash)* | | | |
| UP CLOSE  Edited version of 4-CD set | 1988 | Media America | 35-60 |
| *(Music and interview)* | | | |
| UP CLOSE  Two-part profile of CSNY | 1988 | Media America (2) | 40-80 |
| *(Music and interview)* | | | |

## CROSS, CHRISTOPHER
*Warner Bros. promo 45s $3 each*
**RADIO SHOWS**
**Albums**

| | | | |
|---|---|---|---|
| IN CONCERT (Aug 84) Live concert | 1984 | Westwood One (2) | 75-150 |
| *(Very rare concert)* | | | |
| LIVE  Live concert | 1981 | DIR (3) | 100-175 |
| *(With Leo Sayer)* | | | |
| ROBERT W. MORGAN (Jan 81) Profile | 1981 | Watermark | 10-20 |
| *(Music and interview)* | | | |
| STARTRACK PROFILE (JAN 85) | 1985 | Westwood One (2) | 25-50 |
| *(Music and interview)* | | | |

## CROSSFIRES, THE
*Became The Turtles*
**45s**

| | | | |
|---|---|---|---|
| FIBERGLASS JUNGLE | 1963 | Capco 104 | 40 |
| *(Capco promo label)* | | | |

| Title | Yr | Label, Number | NM $ |
|---|---|---|---|
| **CROW, SHERYL** | | | |
| *A&M promo CD singles $3-5 each* | | | |
| **RADIO SHOWS** | | | |
| **Compact Discs** | | | |
| IN CONCERT (Dec 94) | 1994 | Westwood One | 50-100 |
| *(Live concert)* | | | |
| IN CONCERT (Mar 95) Live concert | 1995 | Westwood One | 25-50 |
| *(With Black Crowes, Meat Puppets and Candlebox)* | | | |
| IN CONCERT-NU ROCK (Dec 94) | 1994 | Westwood One | 50-100 |
| *(Live concert)* | | | |
| | | | |
| **CROWDED HOUSE** | | | |
| *Capitol promo 45s $3 each; Capitol promo CD singles $3-5 each* | | | |
| **12-Inch Singles** | | | |
| CHOCOLATE CAKE (same on both sides) | 1991 | Capitol SPRO-79774 | 10 |
| NOW WE'RE GETTING SOMEWHERE (same on both sides) | 1987 | Capitol SPRO-79169 | 10 |
| WORLD WHERE YOU LIVE/MEAN TO ME/SOMETHING SO STRONG | 1986 | Capitol SPRO-9693/4 | 15 |
| **45s** | | | |
| I FEEL POSSESSED (same on both sides) | 1989 | Capitol 7PRO-79653 | 6 |
| *(Vinyl version appears to be promo-only)* | | | |
| **Compact Discs** | | | |
| KRBE COLLECTORS DISC 12 tracks | 1993 | Capitol | 25 |
| *(Promo-only release, only 1,000 pressed)* | | | |
| LIVE AT THE TOWN & COUNTRY | 1994 | Capitol (2) | 35 |
| *(Promo-only release with 18 tracks)* | | | |
| **RADIO SHOWS** | | | |
| **Albums** | | | |
| KING BISCUIT FLOWER HOUR (May 87) | 1987 | DIR (2) | 50-150 |
| *(Live concert)* | | | |
| **Compact Discs** | | | |
| ON THE EDGE (Feb 94) Music and interviews | 1994 | Westwood One | 20-30 |
| *(Includes Tim Finn and Belly)* | | | |
| | | | |
| **CROWELL, RODNEY** | | | |
| *Warner and Columbia promo 45s $2 each* | | | |
| **RADIO SHOWS** | | | |
| **Albums** | | | |
| LIVE AT GILLEY'S (Dec 89) | 1989 | Westwood One | 15-25 |
| *(Live concert)* | | | |
| WESTWOOD ONE PRESENTS (Dec 89) | 1989 | Westwood One | 25-50 |
| *(Live concert)* | | | |
| **Compact Discs** | | | |
| LIVE AT CRAZY HORSE (July 94) | 1994 | Westwood One | 25-50 |
| *(Live concert)* | | | |
| | | | |
| **CROWNS, THE** | | | |
| **45s** | | | |
| LOVE ME ALWAYS | 1955 | RPM 429 | 75 |
| *(White promo label)* | | | |
| PLEASE DON'T LEAVE ME | 1955 | RPM 438 | 75 |
| *(White promo label)* | | | |
| PLEASE SAY YOU LOVE ME | 1955 | RPM 420 | 75 |
| *(White promo label)* | | | |
| SET MY HEART FREE | 1954 | Modern 944 | 125 |
| *(White promo label)* | | | |
| TRULY | 1955 | RPM 424 | 75 |
| *(White promo label)* | | | |
| | | | |
| **CRUSADERS, THE** | | | |
| **RADIO SHOWS** | | | |
| **Albums** | | | |
| BBC ROCK HOUR (Dec 80) | 1980 | London Wavelength | 40-75 |
| *(Live concert)* | | | |
| | | | |
| **CRUZADOS, THE** | | | |
| **RADIO SHOWS** | | | |
| **Albums** | | | |
| KING BISCUIT FLOWER HOUR (Mar 86) Live concert | 1986 | DIR (2) | 40-60 |
| *(With Marshall Crenshaw)* | | | |
| **Compact Discs** | | | |
| KING BISCUIT FLOWER HOUR (Nov 87) Live concert | 1987 | DIR | 20-30 |
| *(Cruzados only, in concert)* | | | |
| | | | |
| **CRY OF LOVE** | | | |
| **RADIO SHOWS** | | | |
| **Compact Discs** | | | |
| IN CONCERT (JAN 94) | 1994 | Westwood One | 30-50 |
| *(Live concert)* | | | |
| | | | |
| **CRYSTALS, THE** | | | |
| *Other Philles label promo 45s $15-20 each* | | | |
| **45s** | | | |
| (LET'S DANCE) THE SCREW -- PART 1 | 1963 | Philles 111 | 4,000 |
| *(White label)* | | | |

| Title | Yr | Label, Number | NM $ |
|---|---|---|---|
| (LET'S DANCE) THE SCREW -- PART 1 | 1963 | Philles 111 | 6,000 |
| (Light blue label. Matrix numbers are stamped in dead wax. Counterfeits have numbers hand-etched.) | | | |
| HE HIT ME (AND IT FELT LIKE A KISS) | 1962 | Philles 105 | 40 |
| (White promo label) | | | |
| **Albums** | | | |
| CRYSTALS | 1963 | Philles 4003 | 750 |
| (White promo label) | | | |
| CRYSTALS TWIST UPTOWN | 1962 | Philles 4000 | 1,000 |
| (White promo label Philles LPs are very rare) | | | |
| HE'S A REBEL | 1963 | Philles 4001 | 1,000 |
| (White promo label) | | | |

## CULT, THE

Sire promo 45s $5 each

**12-Inch Singles**

| Title | Yr | Label, Number | NM $ |
|---|---|---|---|
| FIRE WOMAN (same on both sides) | 1989 | Sire PRO-A-3435 | 8 |
| LI'L DEVIL (same on both sides) | 1987 | Sire PRO-A-2726 | 6 |
| LOVE REMOVAL MACHINE (7" Edit) (same on both sides) | 1987 | Sire PRO-A-2691 | 7 |
| RAIN (same on both sides) | 1985 | Sire PRO-A-2427 | 15 |
| SHE SELLS SANCTUARY (same on both sides) | 1985 | Sire PRO-A-2394 | 12 |
| THE WITCH/THE WITCH (Edit) | 1992 | Reprise PRO-A-5599 | 8 |
| (Regular black vinyl promo) | | | |
| THE WITCH/THE WITCH (Edit) | 1992 | Reprise PRO-A-5599 | 20 |
| (Purple vinyl promo) | | | |
| WILDFLOWER/WILDFLOWER (Remix) | 1987 | Sire PRO-A-2775 | 12 |
| **Albums** | | | |
| ELECTRIC INTERVIEW | 1987 | Warner Bros. WBMS-147 | 40 |
| **Compact Discs** | | | |
| DREAM TIME | 1989 | Sire | 60 |
| (Radio sampler) | | | |

**RADIO SHOWS**

**Albums**

| Title | Yr | Label, Number | NM $ |
|---|---|---|---|
| BBC TRANSCRIPTION DISC  Live concert | 1986 | BBC Transcription | 200-325 |
| (Very rare series) | | | |
| KING BISCUIT FLOWER HOUR (Sept 86) Live concert | 1986 | DIR (2) | 50-75 |
| (With The Call) | | | |
| **Compact Discs** | | | |
| BBC TRANSCRIPTION DISC  Live concert | 1992 | BBC Transcription | 250-400 |
| (This later show is even more rare!) | | | |
| IN CONCERT (Sept 92) Live concert | 1992 | Westwood One (2) | 40-60 |
| (With King's X) | | | |

## CULTURE CLUB

Featuring Boy George. Other Epic promo 45s $4 each; Epic promo picture sleeves $2 each; Virgin promo 45s by Boy George $3; Virgin promo CD singles by Boy George $3-5.

**12-Inch Singles**

| Title | Yr | Label, Number | NM $ |
|---|---|---|---|
| CHURCH OF THE POISON MIND | 1983 | Epic AS 1752 | 18 |
| (Pre-issue release to radio stations) | | | |
| MOVE AWAY (same on both sides) | 1986 | Virgin/Epic EAS 2296 | 7 |
| TIME/ROMANCE BEYOND THE ALPHABET | 1983 | Epic AS 1642 | 10 |
| **45s** | | | |
| DO YOU REALLY WANT TO HURT ME | 1982 | Epic AE7 1591 | 18 |
| (Promo-only pressing with 2:51 no intro and 3:10 special edit versions) | | | |

**RADIO SHOWS**

**Albums**

| Title | Yr | Label, Number | NM $ |
|---|---|---|---|
| BBC COLLEGE CONCERT (Apr 83) Live concert | 1983 | London Wavelength | 40-75 |
| (With Dexy's Midnight Runners) | | | |
| BBC ROCK HOUR (Nov 84) Live concert | 1984 | London Wavelength | 20-40 |
| (BBC concert material) | | | |
| BBC TRANSCRIPTION DISC  Live concert | 1983 | BBC Transcription | 200-300 |
| (Very rare!) | | | |
| HOT ROCKS (July 86) Profile of Culture Club | 1986 | United Stations (2) | 20-40 |
| (Music and interview) | | | |
| MUSIC OF THE 80S (June 84) Profile of Boy George | 1984 | DIR (2) | 25-50 |
| (Mostly music and interviews) | | | |
| NBC SOURCE (Mar 84) Live concert | 1984 | NBC Radio (2) | 50-75 |
| (Rare live material) | | | |

## CUPP, PAT

**45s**

| Title | Yr | Label, Number | NM $ |
|---|---|---|---|
| LONG GONE DADDY | 1958 | RPM 473 | 45 |
| (White promo label) | | | |

## CURB, MIKE, AND THE WATERFALL

**45s**

| Title | Yr | Label, Number | NM $ |
|---|---|---|---|
| BANDSTAND THEME | 1969 | Forward F-124 | 20 |
| (Promo with promo-only title sleeve; the all-but-forgotten second American Bandstand theme, used from 1969 until Barry Manilow revived the original theme) | | | |

## CURE, THE

Other Sire promo 45s $5 each; Elektra promo 45s $4 each; Sire and Elektra 12" singles $12 each; Elektra promo CD singles $7-10 each

**12-Inch Singles**

| Title | Yr | Label, Number | NM $ |
|---|---|---|---|
| BOYS DON'T CRY (2:36)/BOYS DON'T CRY (5:29) | 1986 | Elektra ED 5175 | 15 |
| CLOSE TO ME (closer mix)/JUST LIKE HEAVEN (dizzy mix)/PRIMARY (red mix) | 1990 | Elektra ED 5513 | 15 |
| CLOSE TO ME (Extended)/CLOSE TO ME (Edit Remix) | 1985 | Elektra ED 5118 | 15 |
| FASCINATION STREET (Extended)/FASCINATION STREET (Remix) | 1989 | Elektra ED 5374 | 7 |

| Title | Yr | Label, Number | NM $ |
|---|---|---|---|
| HOT HOT HOT (3 versions) | 1987 | Elektra ED 5273 | 8 |
| JUST LIKE HEAVEN (Remix)/JUST LIKE HEAVEN (LP Version) | 1987 | Elektra ED 5252 | 18 |
| LET'S GO TO BED (same on both sides) | 1986 | Elektra ED 5146 | 12 |
| LOVE SONG  (same on both sides) | 1989 | Elektra ED 5390 | 8 |
| LOVE SONG (Remix)/LOVE SONG (Extended Remix) | 1989 | Elektra ED 5398 | 12 |
| LULLABY (3 versions) | 1989 | Elektra ED 5418 | 12 |
| NEVER ENOUGH (2 versions)/HAROLD AND JOE/LET'S GO TO BED (Milk Mix) | 1990 | Elektra ED 5489 | 15 |
| PICTURES OF YOU (4:44)/PICTURES OF YOU (8:05) | 1990 | Elektra ED 5452 | 12 |
| **45s** | | | |
| LET'S GO TO BED | 1982 | Sire PRO-S-2022 | 18 |
| *(Also released as Elektra 69537, shorter version)* | | | |
| **Albums** | | | |
| KISS ME, KISS ME, KISS ME | 1987 | Elektra 60737 | 30 |
| *(Promo-only audiophile pressing)* | | | |
| **Compact Discs** | | | |
| KISS ME, KISS ME, KISS ME  Seven-track sampler | 1989 | Elektra | 40 |
| **RADIO SHOWS** | | | |
| **Albums** | | | |
| BBC TRANSCRIPTION DISC Live concert | 1985 | BBC Transcription | 300-450 |
| *(Very rare concert)* | | | |
| BBC TRANSCRIPTION DISC Live concert | 1986 | BBC Transcription | 300-425 |
| *(Very rare)* | | | |
| KING BISCUIT FLOWER HOUR (Feb 86) Live concert | 1986 | DIR (2) | 50-100 |
| *(With the Divinyls)* | | | |
| KING BISCUIT FLOWER HOUR (July 87) Live concert | 1987 | DIR (2) | 40-75 |
| *(With the Outfield)* | | | |
| **Compact Discs** | | | |
| IN CONCERT-NU ROCK (May 96) | 1996 | Westwood One (2) | 50-75 |
| *(Live concert from Glastonbury Festival)* | | | |
| IN CONCERT-NU ROCK (Nov 94) | 1994 | Westwood One | 50-100 |
| *(Live concert)* | | | |
| WESTWOOD ONE SPECIAL (Sept 93) Live concert | 1993 | Westwood One (2) | 75-125 |
| *(Live, mostly unreleased material)* | | | |

**CURTIS, EDDIE**

| | | | |
|---|---|---|---|
| **45s** | | | |
| SHAKE, PRETTY BABY, SHAKE | 1958 | Gee 9 | 125 |
| *(White promo label)* | | | |

**CURTIS, MAC**

| | | | |
|---|---|---|---|
| **45s** | | | |
| GRANDADDY'S ROCKIN' | 195? | King 4949 | 75 |
| *(White promo label)* | | | |
| IF I HAD A WOMAN | 195? | King 4927 | 75 |
| *(White promo label)* | | | |
| THAT AIN'T NOTHIN' BUT RIGHT | 195? | King 4995 | 50 |
| *(White promo label)* | | | |
| YOU AIN'T TREATIN' ME RIGHT | 195? | King 4965 | 60 |
| *(White promo label)* | | | |

**CUTTING CREW**
*Virgin promo 45s $3 each*

| | | | |
|---|---|---|---|
| **12-Inch Singles** | | | |
| (BETWEEN A) ROCK AND A HARD PLACE (LP/Edit) | 1989 | Virgin 2686 | 8 |
| **RADIO SHOWS** | | | |
| **Compact Discs** | | | |
| KING BISCUIT FLOWER HOUR (Aug 87) Live concert | 1987 | DIR | 40-75 |
| *(Rare early CD version)* | | | |
| KING BISCUIT FLOWER HOUR (JAN 88) | 1988 | DIR | 25-50 |
| *(Live concert)* | | | |

**CYRKLE, THE**
*Columbia white promo label 45s $12 each*

| | | | |
|---|---|---|---|
| **45s** | | | |
| CAMARO Issued for Chevrolet | 1967 | Columbia CSM 466 | 40 |
| *(Price includes picture sleeve, flip is by Paul Revere and the Raiders)* | | | |
| RED RUBBER BALL | 1966 | Columbia 43589 | 40 |
| *(Promo-only white label, red vinyl)* | | | |
| TURN-DOWN DAY | 1966 | Columbia 43729 | 40 |
| *(Promo-only white label, red vinyl)* | | | |
| **Albums** | | | |
| RED RUBBER BALL | 1966 | Columbia 2544 | 25 |
| *(White label promo)* | | | |

**CYRUS, BILLY RAY**
*Mercury promo CD singles $3-5 each*

| | | | |
|---|---|---|---|
| **RADIO SHOWS** | | | |
| **Compact Discs** | | | |
| COUNTRY MUSIC TIME | 1994 | U.S. Air Force | 15 |

| Title | Yr | Label, Number | NM $ |
|---|---|---|---|

# D

**D'ARBY, TERENCE TRENT**
*Columbia promo 45s $3 each; Columbia 12" singles not listed $8 each; Columbia promo CD singles $3 each*
**12-Inch Singles**

| | | | |
|---|---|---|---|
| IF YOU LET ME STAY (4 mixes) | 1987 | Columbia CAS 2855 | 8 |
| SIGN YOUR NAME (12" Remix)/ (LP) | 1988 | Columbia CAS 01141 | 12 |
| SIGN YOUR NAME (Lee Perry Remix) | 1987 | Columbia CAS 01181 | 12 |
| *(Advance pressing, no label name on label)* | | | |
| UNDER MY THUMB (Live) (same on both sides) | 198? | Columbia CAS 01070 | 12 |
| *(May only exist as a test pressing)* | | | |
| WISHING WELL (LP Version)/(Cool in the Shade Mix) | 1987 | Columbia CAS 02888 | 8 |

**RADIO SHOWS**
**Albums**

| | | | |
|---|---|---|---|
| BBC TRANSCRIPTION DISC  Live concert | 1988 | BBC Transcription | 300-500 |
| *(Very rare series)* | | | |

**D.J. AND THE CATS**
**45s**

| | | | |
|---|---|---|---|
| SITTING IN SCHOOL | 1959 | Hep 2100 | 50 |
| *(Black promo label)* | | | |

**D.N.A. FEATURING SUZANNE VEGA**
**12-Inch Singles**

| | | | |
|---|---|---|---|
| RUSTED PIPE (5 versions) | 1991 | A&M 75021 7305 1 | 8 |

**DADA**
**RADIO SHOWS**
**Compact Discs**

| | | | |
|---|---|---|---|
| IN CONCERT (June 93) | 1993 | Westwood One | 20-40 |
| *(Live concert)* | | | |
| KING BISCUIT FLOWER HOUR (Feb 93) Live concert | 1993 | DIR | 40-75 |
| *(With Triumph)* | | | |
| ON THE EDGE (Oct 94) Music and interview | 1994 | Westwood One | 20-30 |
| *(With Counting Crows and Velvet Crush)* | | | |

**DALE, DICK**
*Other Capitol promo 45s $20 each; Capitol promo LPs $25 each Member of the Exiles*
**45s**

| | | | |
|---|---|---|---|
| ENLISTMENT TWIST | 1962 | U. S. Army 1301 | 75 |
| *(Public service record, blue vinyl, price includes promo picture sleeve)* | | | |
| JESSIE PEARL | 1960 | Deltone 5014 | 100 |
| *(White label promo)* | | | |
| OOH WHEE, WHEE | 1959 | Deltone 5012 | 50 |
| *(White promo label)* | | | |
| PEPPERMINT MAN Compact single | 196? | Capitol PRO-2320 | 200 |
| *(Orange promo label, promo-only picture sleeve)* | | | |
| STOP TEASIN' | 1959 | Deltone 5013 | 50 |
| *(White promo label)* | | | |
| THUNDER WAVE | 1964 | Capitol PRO-2647 | 35 |
| *(Given away with the "Surf Age" LP)* | | | |

**DALTON, LACY J.**
*Columbia promo 45s $3 each; Universal promo 45s $3 each*
**RADIO SHOWS**
**Albums**

| | | | |
|---|---|---|---|
| LIVE AT GILLEY'S (June 88) | 1988 | Westwood One | 10-20 |
| *(Live concert)* | | | |

**DALTREY, ROGER**
*Other MCA promo 45s $5 each; other Polydor promo 45s $4 each Lead singer of the Who*
**12-Inch Singles**

| | | | |
|---|---|---|---|
| ONE OF THE BOYS | 1977 | MCA 1962 | 15 |
| *(Promo-only 12" single with Steve Gibbons on the flip, issued with a title cover)* | | | |

**45s**

| | | | |
|---|---|---|---|
| GIVING IT ALL AWAY | 1972 | Track (MCA) 40053 | 10 |
| *(White promo label)* | | | |
| THINKING (mono/stereo) | 1973 | Track 40084 | 6 |
| *(May be promo only)* | | | |
| WAITING FOR A FRIEND (same on both sides) | 1981 | Polydor 2153 | 6 |
| *(One label has name misspelled as "Rodger Daltrey")* | | | |
| WHAT'S IT ALL ABOUT (Aug 75) Public service show | 1975 | W. I. A. A. 281 | 25 |
| *(Interviews from "Tommy")* | | | |
| WHAT'S IT ALL ABOUT (July 75) Public service show | 1975 | W. I. A. A. 274 | 25 |
| *(Daltrey and Townshend)* | | | |

**RADIO SHOWS**
**Albums**

| | | | |
|---|---|---|---|
| KING BISCUIT FLOWER HOUR | 1986 | DIR (4) | 50-100 |
| *(Two shows)* | | | |
| KING BISCUIT FLOWER HOUR | 1986 | DIR (2) | 30-60 |
| *(Live concert, repeated)* | | | |
| OFF THE RECORD | 1984 | Westwood One (2) | 20-35 |
| *(Music and interviews)* | | | |
| OFF THE RECORD (Aug 92) Profile with The Who | 1992 | Westwood One (2) | 15-25 |
| *(Music and interview)* | | | |

| Title | Yr | Label, Number | NM $ |
|-------|-----|---------------|------|

**Compact Discs**
KING BISCUIT FLOWER HOUR  Townshend and Daltrey — 1988 — DIR — 40-75
*(Live concert)*
KING BISCUIT FLOWER HOUR (Oct 89) — 1989 — DIR — 30-60
*(Live concert)*
THE STORY OF ROGER DALTREY (Aug 92) Profile with The Who — 1992 — Unistar (3) — 25-75
*(Both solo and with the Who, music and interview)*

## DAMBUILDERS
**RADIO SHOWS**
**Compact Discs**
ON THE EDGE (Aug 94) Music and interview — 1994 — Westwood One — 15-30
*(With Blur and Candlebox)*

## DAMN YANKEES
*Warner Bros. promo 45s $3 each; Warner Bros. 12" singles $10 each; Warner Bros. promo CD singles $3 each*
**RADIO SHOWS**
**Compact Discs**
OFF THE RECORD — 1992 — Westwood One — 15-25
*(Music and interview)*

## DAMNED, THE
**12-Inch Singles**
IN DULCE DECORUM (same on both sides) — 1986 — MCA 17235 — 8

## DANA, VIC
**45s**
SALES STIMULATOR — 1966 — Rowe 1006 — 15
*(Red vinyl, for jukeboxes)*

## DANIELS, CHARLIE, BAND
*Kama Sutra colored promo label 45s $5 each; Epic promo singles $3 each; Epic 12" singles $8 each; Epic white promo label LPs $8 each*
**45s**
THE MIDDLE OF A HEARTACHE — 1976 — Paula 418 — 10
*(White promo label)*
WHAT'S IT ALL ABOUT (Feb 77) Public service show — 1977 — W. I. A. A. 356 — 25
*(Flip side is Boston)*
WHAT'S IT ALL ABOUT (Sept 80) Public service show — 1978 — W. I. A. A. 540 — 18
*(Flip side is Willie Nelson)*
**Albums**
THE CHARLIE DANIELS STORY Music and interviews — 1989 — Epic EAS 1780 — 15
*(Released as a radio show through Epic Records)*
**RADIO SHOWS**
**Albums**
INNERVIEW (70s) Profile of "Uneasy Rider" — 197? — Innerview — 10-15
*(Music and interview)*
LIVE AT GILLEY'S (Feb 87) Live concert — 1987 — Westwood One — 25-75
*(Rare live material)*
PIONEERS IN MUSIC (June 86) Various artists — 1986 — DIR (2) — 20-30
*(Includes Lynyrd Skynyrd, Molly Hatchet and .38 Special)*
PROFILES IN ROCK (July 80) Profile of the band — 1980 — Watermark — 10-15
*(Music and interviews)*
ROBERT W. MORGAN (Dec 80) Profile of the band — 1980 — Watermark — 10-15
*(Music and interviews)*
SKOAL PRESENTS CHARLIE DANIELS AT THANKSGIVING — 1982 — United Stations (3) — 20-30
*(Box set music and interviews)*
SOURCE SPECIAL (Aug 81) — 1981 — NBC Radio (2) — 40-75
*(Live concert)*
TRIPLE (EASTER SPECIAL) — 1982 — Mutual Radio (3) — 20-30
*(Music and interviews with Charlie Daniels Band, Larry Gatlin, Barbara Mandrell)*
WINDOWS WORLD TOUR  Profile of the band — 1982 — Good Vibrations — 10-15
*(Music and interviews)*
**Cassettes**
AUSTIN ENCORE Live concert — 199? — Mainstreet Productions — 20-30
*(Concert issued on cassette to radio stations)*

## DANNY AND THE JUNIORS
*Other ABC Paramount promo 45s $15 each; Other Swan promo 45s $12 each; Mercury promo 45s $15 each; Luv (Bell) promo 45s $8 each*
**45s**
AT THE HOP — 1957 — ABC Paramount 9871 — 25
*(White promo label)*
BACK TO THE HOP — 1962 — Swan 4082 — 20
*(White promo label, stock picture sleeve worth $100)*
CANDY CANE, SUGAR PLUM — 1960 — Swan 4064 — 20
*(White promo label, stock picture sleeve worth $200)*
**78s**
AT THE HOP — 1957 — ABC Paramount 9871 — 100
*(White promo label)*

## DANTE AND THE EVERGREENS
*Madison promo 45s $15 each*

## DANTE, RON
**45s**
THAT'S WHAT LIFE IS ALL ABOUT (mono/stereo) — 1971 — Scepter 12333 — 6
*(Stock copy may not exist)*

| Title | Yr | Label, Number | NM $ |
|-------|-----|---------------|------|

**DANZIG**
**12-Inch Singles**
| HER BLACK WINGS (same on both sides) | 1990 | Def American PRO-A-4121 | 8 |

**DAPPERS, THE**
**45s**
| UNWANTED LOVE | 1956 | Groove 0156 | 150 |
*(White promo label)*

**DARIN, BOBBY**
*Other Decca pink label promo 45s $20 each; Atco all-white promo label 45s $18 each; Atlantic black/white promo label 45s $5 each; Atlantic red/white promo label 45s $4 each; Atlantic blue promo label 45s $3 each*
**45s**
| DEALER IN DREAMS | 1959 | Decca 30225 | 25 |
*(Pink promo label)*
| EARLY IN THE MORNING  The Rinky-Dinks | 1959 | Brunswick 55073 | 75 |
*(Yellow promo label)*
| MELODIE | 1970 | Motown 1183 | 12 |
*(White promo label)*
| SAIL AWAY | 1972 | Motown 1203 | 15 |
*(White promo label)*
| THE GREATEST BUILDER | 1958 | Decca 30031 | 25 |
*(Pink promo label)*
**7-Inch Extended Plays**
| BOBBY DARIN  Four songs, white label | 1974 | Motown PR-4 | 40 |
*(33 rpm, small center hole, issued in paper sleeve)*
| BOBBY DARIN PRESENTS - 18 YELLOW ROSES  Six songs | 1965 | Capitol 2262 | 25 |
*(Artistic Records, issued with a paper picture sleeve; 33 rpm, white label)*
| SCRIPTO PRESENTS BOBBY DARIN  Four songs, 45 rpm | 196? | Capitol 2849 | 15 |
*(Issued with paper color picture sleeve, dark blue label)*
| THIS IS DARIN  All-white promo label | 1958 | Atco 4508 | 50 |
*(Rare, issued without hard cover; if other EP titles were released as promos, their values would be the same)*
**Albums**
| FOR TEENAGERS ONLY  Promo only, white label | 1960 | Atco SP 1001 | 50 |
*(Issued with a paper sleeve)*
| SILVER PLATTER SERVICE (60s)  With Jack Wagner | 196? | Capitol | 25 |
*(There were several shows in this series that included the spotlight on a new Darin LP with interviews)*
**RADIO SHOWS**
**16-Inch Transcriptions**
| NATIONAL GUARD SHOW | 1959 | National Guard | 60 |
*(Darin is guest host, music and interviews)*
**Albums**
| 1963 HEART FUND (Feb 63) | 1963 | Heart Fund | 50 |
*(Five-minute show with Jimmy Durante)*
| FOR CHRISTMAS SEALS  With Chet Atkins | 1964 | Christmas Seals | 75 |
*(15-minute public service show with hard cover)*
| SOLID GOLD SCRAPBOOK (May 89)  Birthday salute | 1989 | United Stations | 10 |
*(From the 5-LP weekly box set)*

**DARREN, JAMES**
**45s**
| ONLY A DREAM AWAY (mono/stereo) | 1977 | Private Stock 45,152 | 5 |
*(Stock copies may not exist)*

**DAS DAMEN**
**45s**
| NOON DAYLIGHT/DAMEN DANCE | 1989 | Twin/Tone TTR 89139 | 8 |
| REVERSE INTO TOMORROW/BUG | 1988 | SST PSST 190 | 15 |
*(No picture sleeve, but with tour dates insert. Deduct 1/3 if insert is missing.)*

**DAVE DEE, DOZY, BEAKY, MICK & TICH**
*Fontana promo 45s $8 each; Atlantic promo 45s $3 each*
**45s**
| I'LL LOVE YOU | 196? | Coca-Cola GMBH 105 112 | 100 |
*(Coca-Cola songs released in Germany, used in USA, price includes picture sleeve)*
| STAYING WITH IT (same on both sides) | 1983 | Atlantic 89757 | 5 |
*(May be promo only)*

**DAVID AND DAVID**
*A&M promo 45s $3 each; A&M promo 12" singles $8 each*
**Albums**
| A&M INTRODUCES DAVID & DAVID  White promo label | 1986 | A&M | 20 |
*(Promo-only record and picture cover)*

**DAVIES, DAVE**
**45s**
| LOVE GETS YOU (same on both sides) | 1983 | Warner Bros. 29509 | 10 |
*(Stock copies are much rarer than promos)*
| MEAN DISPOSITION (same on both sides) | 1983 | Warner Bros. 29425 | 10 |
*(Stock copies not known to exist)*

**DAVIS, BO**
**45s**
| LET'S COAST AWHILE | 1956 | Crest 1027 | 50 |
*(White promo label)*

| Title | Yr | Label, Number | NM $ |
|---|---|---|---|
| **DAVIS, DANNY, AND THE NASHVILLE BRASS** | | | |
| **45s** | | | |
| SILENT NIGHT/JINGLING BRASS | 1970 | RCA Victor 47-9936 | 6 |
| *(Promos available on either yellow or green labels)* | | | |
| **DAVIS, MAC** | | | |
| **45s** | | | |
| SEXY YOUNG GIRL | 1985 | MCA 52765 | 10 |
| *(Promo only on blue vinyl)* | | | |
| **DAVIS, MARTHA** | | | |
| **12-Inch Singles** | | | |
| JUST LIKE YOU (same on both sides) | 1987 | Capitol SPRO 79188 | 6 |
| **Albums** | | | |
| POLICY (RADIO CUE CARD) | 1987 | Capitol CLT-79197/8 | 25 |
| **DAVIS, SAMMY, JR.** | | | |
| **45s** | | | |
| HERE'S A KISS FOR CHRISTMAS (The Christmas Seal Song)/ | 1963 | Reprise (no #) | 15 |
| WHAT KIND OF FOOL AM I | | | |
| **7-Inch Extended Plays** | | | |
| MEL TORME'S CALIFORNIA SUITE | 196? | Reprise PRO-175 | 15 |
| *(Four songs)* | | | |
| **DAWN** | | | |
| **7-Inch Extended Plays** | | | |
| YOU CAN BE MORE THAN YOU ARE | 1975 | Ad Council 975 | 15 |
| *(Public service announcement for U.S. Office of Education)* | | | |
| **DAWSON, WILLIAM, CHORALE** | | | |
| **7-Inch Extended Plays** | | | |
| HERE WE COME A'WASSAILING/IN A CAVE// | 19?? | Sesac 84 | 5 |
| SILENT NIGHT/MERRY ARE THE BELLS | | | |
| **DAY, DENNIS** | | | |
| **78s** | | | |
| SPECIAL INTERVIEW with Mitzi Gaynor | 195? | RCA | 20 |
| *(Promo only)* | | | |
| **DAY, DORIS** | | | |
| **45s** | | | |
| LET NO WALLS DIVIDE/GOD REST YE MERRY, GENTLEMEN | 1961 | Columbia JZSP 55070/1 | 12 |
| *(B-side by Andre Previn)* | | | |
| SILVER BELLS/WINTER WONDERLAND | 1963 | Columbia JZSP 79171/2 | 10 |
| *("Special Album Excerpt" promo)* | | | |
| **DAY, TERRY** | | | |
| *Of Bruce (Johnston) and Terry; better known as Terry Melcher* | | | |
| **45s** | | | |
| BE A SOLDIER | 1963 | Columbia 4-42678 | 25 |
| *(White promo label, stock picture sleeve worth $50)* | | | |
| BE A SOLDIER | 1963 | Columbia 3-42678 | 30 |
| *(Compact 33 for jukeboxes, stock picture sleeve $50)* | | | |
| **DE LA SOUL** | | | |
| **Albums** | | | |
| DE LA SOUL IS DEAD | 1991 | Tommy Boy 1041 | 25 |
| *(Promo-only two-record set)* | | | |
| **DEACON BLUE** | | | |
| **RADIO SHOWS** | | | |
| **Albums** | | | |
| IN CONCERT (July 88) Live concert | 1988 | Westwood One (2) | 20-35 |
| *(With Honeymoon Suite)* | | | |
| **DEAD CAN DANCE** | | | |
| *4AD promo CD singles $6* | | | |
| **RADIO SHOWS** | | | |
| **Compact Discs** | | | |
| ON THE EDGE (Jan 94) Music and interviews | 1994 | Westwood One | 20-30 |
| *(With Blur)* | | | |
| **DEAD MILKMEN, THE** | | | |
| **12-Inch Singles** | | | |
| BIG TIME OPERATOR (same on both sides) | 1987 | Enigma 039 | 8 |
| SMOKIN' BANANA PEELS (Edit) (same on both sides) | 1989 | Enigma EPRO 188 | 8 |
| SMOKIN' BANANA PEELS (LP version + 3 remixes) | 1989 | Enigma EPRO 189 | 10 |
| **DEAN, JIMMY** | | | |
| *Mercury promo 45s $4 each; Columbia red vinyl promo 45s $6 each; Other Columbia promo 45s $3 each; Columbia compact-33s for jukeboxes $5 each; Columbia jukebox LLPs $8 each* | | | |
| **45s** | | | |
| BLUE CHRISTMAS | 1965 | Columbia JZSP 111915 | 20 |
| *(Green vinyl, white label promo-only; number is matrix number)* | | | |

| Title | Yr | Label, Number | NM $ |
|---|---|---|---|
| SILVER BELLS | 1965 | Columbia JZSP 111952 | 12 |
| *(White label, promo only, same song on both sides, number is matrix number)* | | | |
| **RADIO SHOWS** | | | |
| **16-Inch Transcriptions** | | | |
| NAVY HOEDOWN (60s) Music and interview | 196? | U. S. Navy | 20-30 |
| *(Jimmy Dean is the host, several shows)* | | | |

### DeBURGH, CHRIS
*A&M promo 45s $3 each; A&M promo LPs $5 each; A&M promo CD singles $3 each*

| Title | Yr | Label, Number | NM $ |
|---|---|---|---|
| **45s** | | | |
| A SPACEMAN CAME TRAVELLING (mono/stereo) | 1977 | A&M 1998 | 6 |
| *(Stock copies do not exist)* | | | |
| **RADIO SHOWS** | | | |
| **Albums** | | | |
| KING BISCUIT FLOWER HOUR (Aug 84) | 1984 | DIR (2) | 30-50 |
| *(Live concert)* | | | |
| KING BISCUIT FLOWER HOUR (Dec 83) Live concert | 1983 | DIR (2) | 40-60 |
| *(With Phil Collins)* | | | |
| NBC SOURCE (June 83) | 1983 | NBC Radio (2) | 30-50 |
| *(Live concert)* | | | |

### DEE, JIMMY

| Title | Yr | Label, Number | NM $ |
|---|---|---|---|
| **45s** | | | |
| RICK TICK TOCK | 1959 | TNT 161 | 60 |
| *(White promo label)* | | | |
| YOU'RE LATE MISS KATE | 1959 | TNT 152 | 40 |
| *(White promo label)* | | | |

### DEE, JOEY

| Title | Yr | Label, Number | NM $ |
|---|---|---|---|
| **45s** | | | |
| LEARN TO DANCE THE AUTHENTIC PEPPERMINT TWIST | 1962 | Vaseline Hair Tonic | 30 |
| *(Special promo item, includes picture sleeve)* | | | |
| YA YA TWIST/RUNAROUND SUE | 1962 | Monument (# unknown) | 25 |
| *(B-side by Dion)* | | | |

### DEEE-LITE

| Title | Yr | Label, Number | NM $ |
|---|---|---|---|
| **12-Inch Singles** | | | |
| CALL ME (8 versions) | 1994 | Elektra ED 5713 | 20 |
| ESP (3 versions) | 1990 | Elektra ED 5531 | 10 |
| GROOVE IS IN THE HEART (3 mixes)/WHAT IS LOVE? (3 mixes) | 1990 | Elektra ED 5471 | 10 |
| POWER OF LOVE (2 versions)/ | 1990 | Elektra ED 5507 | 10 |
| BUILD THE BRIDGE/HOW DO YOU SAY...LOVE | | | |
| RUNAWAY (7 versions) | 1990 | Elektra ED 5600 | 12 |

### DEEP PURPLE
*Other Warner promo 45s $5 each; Warner promo LPs $10 each Includes listings of Roger Glover; Also see Rainbow*

| Title | Yr | Label, Number | NM $ |
|---|---|---|---|
| **45s** | | | |
| HUSH White promo label | 1968 | Tetragrammaton 1503 | 15 |
| *(Issued with a picture sleeve, not included in value)* | | | |
| THE BIRD HAS FLOWN | 1971 | Tetragrammaton 1519 | 12 |
| *(White promo label)* | | | |
| WOMAN FROM TOKYO White promo label | 1973 | Warner Bros. 7672 | 18 |
| *(5:50/2:56 long/short versions of this classic)* | | | |
| **7-Inch Extended Plays** | | | |
| BURN  Three songs | 1974 | Warner Bros. 2766 (LLP 250) | 25 |
| *(6:00 "Burn" and two other songs; issued with a paper picture sleeve)* | | | |
| MADE IN JAPAN | 1973 | Warner Bros. 2701 (LLP 214) | 30 |
| *(7:27 "Smoke on the Water", 6:45 "Highway Star"; ilssued with a paper picture sleeve)* | | | |
| **RADIO SHOWS** | | | |
| **Albums** | | | |
| BBC ROCK HOUR (June 84) Live concert | 1984 | London Wavelength | 60-100 |
| *(BBC concert material)* | | | |
| BBC TRANSCRIPTION DISC Live concert | 1971 | BBC Transcription | 300-500 |
| *(Very rare series)* | | | |
| BBC TRANSCRIPTION DISC Live concert | 1973 | BBC Transcription | 300-450 |
| *(Almost as rare as the first presentation)* | | | |
| BBC TRANSCRIPTION DISC Live concert | 1980 | BBC Transcription | 175-300 |
| *(With the Jays)* | | | |
| BBC TRANSCRIPTION DISC Live concert | 1981 | BBC Transcription | 200-350 |
| *(Also very hard to find)* | | | |
| CAPTURED LIVE Live concert | 1984 | Captured Live (4) | 60-100 |
| *(Rare live concert)* | | | |
| GUEST DJ Guest host with profile of group | 1983 | MJI Broadcasting (3) | 30-50 |
| *(Also features Paul Stanley of Kiss)* | | | |
| IN CONCERT BBC Classic Concerts | 1988 | Westwood One (2) | 50-85 |
| *(This concert was released several times)* | | | |
| INNERVIEW (70s) With Roger Glover | 197? | Innerview | 20-25 |
| *(Music and interviews)* | | | |
| KING BISCUIT FLOWER HOUR | 1983 | DIR (2) | 75-125 |
| *(Repeated in Jan 87)* | | | |
| OFF THE RECORD (80s) Profile | 198? | Westwood One (2) | 15-25 |
| *(Music and interview)* | | | |
| POP SPECTACULAR (Oct 76) Live concert | 1976 | BBC Transcription | 100-175 |
| *(Live BBC material)* | | | |
| RETRO ROCK (Aug 82) | 1982 | Clayton Webster | 30-50 |
| *(Music and interview)* | | | |

| Title | Yr | Label, Number | NM $ |
|---|---|---|---|
| SUPERSTAR CONCERT (80s) Box set | 198? | Westwood One (3) | 50-85 |
| *(Live concert)* | | | |
| **Compact Discs** | | | |
| BBC CLASSIC TRACKS (Feb 91) Live cuts | 1991 | London Wavelength | 30-40 |
| *(Mainly BBC concert material, several shows)* | | | |
| IN THE STUDIO Profile of an album | 1988 | Album Network | 20-30 |
| *(Music and interview)* | | | |
| SUPERSTAR CONCERT (90s) | 199? | Westwood One (2) | 40-75 |
| *(Live concert)* | | | |
| UP CLOSE Profile of the group | 1991 | Media America (2) | 30-60 |
| *(Music and interview, some live material)* | | | |
| **Reel-to-Reel Tapes** | | | |
| KING BISCUIT FLOWER HOUR (Mar 76) Deep Purple | 1976 | DIR/ABC (2) | 100-175 |
| *(Live concert with Styx)* | | | |
| LIVE ONE (90s) | 199? | | 25-40 |
| *(Music and interviews on 7" reel)* | | | |

## DEEP, THE
**Albums**

| | | | |
|---|---|---|---|
| PSYCHEDELIC MOODS | 1966 | Parkway 7051 | 100 |
| *(Stock copy worth double)* | | | |

## DEF LEPPARD
*Other Mercury promo 45s $4 each; Mercury 12" promo singles $10 each; other Mercury promo CD singles $3-5 each*

**45s**

| | | | |
|---|---|---|---|
| LET IT GO (same on both sides) | 1981 | Mercury 76120 | 10 |
| *(May be promo only)* | | | |
| **Compact Discs** | | | |
| DEF LEPPARD | 1989 | Mercury (5) | 60 |
| *(Promo-only box set)* | | | |
| LET'S GET ROCKED | 1992 | Mercury CDP 641 | 6 |
| *(Promo CD single)* | | | |
| MISS YOU IN A HEARTBEAT | 1994 | Mercury CDP 1090 | 8 |
| *(Promo CD single)* | | | |
| TWO STEPS BEHIND | 1993 | Columbia CSK 5235 | 6 |
| *(Promo CD single, from soundtrack of Last Action Hero)* | | | |
| WOMEN | 1987 | Mercury CDP 02 | 100 |
| *(One of the very first promo CD singles)* | | | |
| **RADIO SHOWS** | | | |
| **Albums** | | | |
| BBC TRANSCRIPTION DISC | 1980 | BBC Transcription | 200-300 |
| *(With the Jaggs, rare early radio show)* | | | |
| IN CONCERT (Mar 86) | 1986 | Westwood One (2) | 75-100 |
| *(Live concert)* | | | |
| IN CONCERT (Mar 88) Live concert | 1988 | Westwood One (2) | 75-100 |
| *(With Thin Lizzy)* | | | |
| INNERVIEW  Music and interview | 1983 | Innerview | 150-200 |
| *(Rare radio show)* | | | |
| METALSHOP (80s) Various artists | 198? | DJM Productions | 15-20 |
| *(Includes segment of live Def Leppard music)* | | | |
| OFF THE RECORD (80s) Profile | 198? | Westwood One (2) | 15-25 |
| *(Music and interviews)* | | | |
| SOURCE SPECIAL (Apr 84) Live concert | 1984 | NBC Source (3) | 80-150 |
| *(This show is hard to find)* | | | |
| THE STORY OF DEF LEPPARD (Nov 88) Profile | 1988 | Unistar (2) | 15-25 |
| *(Music and interviews)* | | | |
| UP CLOSE | 1988 | MCA (2) | 20-30 |
| *(Music and interviews)* | | | |
| **Compact Discs** | | | |
| BBC CLASSIC TRACKS (Sept 90) Live cuts | 1990 | London Wavelength | 15-25 |
| *(Reissued several times)* | | | |
| IN THE STUDIO Profile of an album | 1988 | Album Network | 15-25 |
| *(Music and interviews)* | | | |
| UP CLOSE Profile | 1989 | Media America (2) | 30-50 |
| *(Music and interviews)* | | | |
| **Reel-to-Reel Tapes** | | | |
| SLANG WORLD PREMIERE | 1996 | Album Network | 50-75 |
| *(Preview of new album, with live tracks)* | | | |

## DEL AMITRI
**12-Inch Singles**

| | | | |
|---|---|---|---|
| KISS THIS THING GOODBYE/THE RETURN OF MAGGIE BROWN/ | 1989 | A&M SP-17995 | 12 |
| SLOWLY, IT'S COMING BACK | | | |
| STONE COLD SOBER/ANOTHER LETTER HOME/ | 1990 | A&M 75021 8076 1 | 12 |
| APRIL THE FIRST/MORE THAN YOU'D EVER KNOW | | | |

## DEL FUEGOS, THE
**12-Inch Singles**

| | | | |
|---|---|---|---|
| DON'T RUN WILD (same on both sides) | 1985 | Slash PRO-A-2372 | 6 |
| I STILL WANT YOU/I STILL WANT YOU (Horny Mix) | 1985 | Slash PRO-A-2414 | 6 |
| IT'S ALRIGHT (same on both sides) | 1985 | Slash PRO-A-2486 | 6 |
| LONG SLIDE (same on both sides) | 1987 | Slash PRO-A-2681 | 6 |
| NAME NAMES (same on both sides) | 1987 | Slash PRO-A-2720 | 6 |
| WEAR IT LIKE A CAPE (same on both sides) | 1987 | Slash PRO-A-2769 | 6 |
| **45s** | | | |
| I STILL WANT YOU (LP Version)/ (Horny Mix) | 1986 | Slash 28822 | 4 |

| Title | Yr | Label, Number | NM $ |
|-------|-----|--------------|------|
| **RADIO SHOWS** | | | |
| **Albums** | | | |
| KING BISCUIT FLOWER HOUR (Sept 86) Live concert | 1986 | DIR (2) | 20-35 |
| *(With the Fabulous Thunderbirds)* | | | |
| SPIN CONCERT (Feb 86) | 1986 | Spin Magazine | 25-50 |
| *(Live concert)* | | | |
| | | | |
| **DEL LORDS, THE** | | | |
| **12-Inch Singles** | | | |
| A LOVER'S PRAYER (same on both sides) | 1988 | Enigma 097 | 6 |
| **45s** | | | |
| JUDAS KISS (Radio Edit)/(Vocal Edit) | 1988 | Enigma EPRO 090 | 6 |
| | | | |
| **DEL VIKINGS, THE** | | | |
| *Dot promo 45s $20 each; Mercury white promo label 45s $18 each; Scepter promo 45s $8 each; Mercury white promo label EPs $100 each* | | | |
| **7-Inch Extended Plays** | | | |
| BIG BEAT, THE | 195? | Mercury MEP-39 | 100 |
| *(Promo with three other artists)* | | | |
| **Albums** | | | |
| SWINGING, SINGING DEL VIKINGS RECORDING SESSION | 1958 | Mercury 20353 | 500 |
| *(White promo label)* | | | |
| THEY SING-THEY SWING | 1957 | Mercury 20314 | 500 |
| *(White promo label)* | | | |
| | | | |
| **DELLS, THE** | | | |
| *Vee Jay promo 45s $20 each; Cadet promo 45s $8 each* | | | |
| **Albums** | | | |
| THE DELLS SAMPLER | 1973 | Cadet CADJ-3 | 25 |
| *(Promo-only sampler)* | | | |
| | | | |
| **DEMENSIONS, THE** | | | |
| *Coral blue promo label 45s $25 each* | | | |
| **Albums** | | | |
| MY FOOLISH HEART | 1963 | Coral 57430 | 150 |
| *(Blue promo label)* | | | |
| | | | |
| **DENNY, MARTIN** | | | |
| **45s** | | | |
| OPEN END INTERVIEW | 196? | Liberty MD-514 | 20 |
| *(5:55 interview, both sides same)* | | | |
| QUIET VILLAGE | 1959 | Liberty 55162 | 15 |
| *(His biggest hit, white label promo)* | | | |
| | | | |
| **DENVER, JOHN** | | | |
| *Other RCA Victor promo 45s $3 each; RCA Victor jukebox LLPs $6 each* | | | |
| **12-Inch Singles** | | | |
| BET ON THE BLUES (same on both sides) | 1977 | RCA Victor JD-11189 | 12 |
| **45s** | | | |
| A BABY JUST LIKE YOU | 1979 | RCA Victor 11767 | 10 |
| *(Red vinyl, green promo label)* | | | |
| FLYING FOR ME (same on both sides) | 1986 | RCA PB-14366 | 4 |
| *(No stock copies were issued)* | | | |
| PERHAPS LOVE With Placido Domingo | 198? | Cherry Lane Music 110 | 20 |
| *(Promo-only record and sleeve)* | | | |
| **7-Inch Extended Plays** | | | |
| WOODSY OWL THEATRE | 1975 | US Forest Service 75-05 | 20 |
| *(14 cuts including John Denver)* | | | |
| **Albums** | | | |
| JOHN DENVER HOLIDAY RADIO SHOW, THE | 1984 | RCA Victor DJL1-5398 | 20 |
| JOHN DENVER RADIO SHOW, THE | 1973 | RCA Victor DJL1-0075 | 30 |
| SECOND JOHN DENVER RADIO SHOW, THE | 1974 | RCA Victor DJL1-0683 | 30 |
| **RADIO SHOWS** | | | |
| **Albums** | | | |
| SALUTE TO AMERICA (July 90) With George Bush | 1990 | Dept. of the Interior | 10-20 |
| *(Unusual live performances)* | | | |
| | | | |
| **DEPECHE MODE** | | | |
| *Sire promo 45s $5 each; Sire promo 12" singles $12-15 each; other Sire promo CD singles $8-12 each* | | | |
| **12-Inch Singles** | | | |
| BEHIND THE WHEEL (4 versions) | 1987 | Sire PRO-A-2952 | 20 |
| BLASPHEMOUS RUMOURS/SOMETHING TO DO/REMOTIVATE ME (Edit) | 1985 | Sire PRO-A-2271 | 50 |
| I FEEL YOU (5 versions) | 1993 | Sire PRO-A-6022 | 15 |
| LEAVE IN SILENCE/PHOTOGRAPH/MY SECRET GARDEN (2 versions) | 1982 | Sire PRO-A-1084 | 30 |
| MASTER AND SERVANT (LP version)/ (Black and Blue version) | 1984 | Sire PRO-A-2221 | 30 |
| QUESTION OF LUST (Remix Edit)/(LP Version) | 1986 | Sire PRO-A-2504 | 30 |
| WORLD IN MY EYES (Single Edit)/ (Oil Tank Mix) | 1990 | Sire PRO-A-4507 | 15 |
| **Albums** | | | |
| SELECTIONS FROM THE COMMERCIALLY AVAILABLE BOX SET THREE | 1991 | Sire PRO-A-5242 | 40 |
| SELECTIONS FROM THE COMMERCIALLY AVAILABLE BOX SETS ONE AND TWO | 1991 | Sire PRO-A-5192 | 25 |
| *(Promo-only sampler)* | | | |
| **Compact Discs** | | | |
| BEHIND THE WHEEL | 1988 | Sire PRO-CD-2953 | 20 |
| *(Promo CD single)* | | | |
| CONDEMNATION | 1993 | Sire PRO-CD-???? | 15 |
| *(Promo CD single)* | | | |

| Title | Yr | Label, Number | NM $ |
|---|---|---|---|
| ENJOY THE SILENCE | 1990 | Sire PRO-CD-3976 | 15 |
| *(Promo CD single)* | | | |
| EVERYTHING COUNTS | 1989 | Sire PRO-CD-3485 | 15 |
| *(Promo CD single)* | | | |
| HALO | 1990 | Sire PRO-CD-4362 | 18 |
| *(Promo CD single)* | | | |
| I FEEL YOU | 1993 | Sire PRO-CD-6011 | 15 |
| *(Promo CD single)* | | | |
| NEVER LET ME DOWN AGAIN | 1987 | Sire PRO-CD-2973 | 20 |
| *(Early promo CD single)* | | | |
| ONE CARESS | 1993 | Sire PRO-CD-6626 | 15 |
| *(Promo CD single)* | | | |
| POLICY OF TRUTH | 1990 | Sire PRO-CD-4027 | 15 |
| *(Promo CD single)* | | | |
| STRANGELOVE | 1989 | Sire PRO-CD-3213 | 25 |
| *(Promo CD single)* | | | |
| WALKING IN MY SHOES | 1993 | Sire PRO-CD-6178 | 15 |
| *(Promo CD single)* | | | |
| WORLD IN MY EYES | 1990 | Sire PRO-CD-4441 | 18 |
| *(Promo CD single, first issue)* | | | |
| WORLD IN MY EYES | 1990 | Sire PRO-CD-4531 | 15 |
| *(Promo CD single, second issue)* | | | |
| **RADIO SHOWS** | | | |
| **Albums** | | | |
| BBC TRANSCRIPTION DISC Live concert | 1985 | BBC Transcription | 300-450 |
| *(One of the most collectible concerts on disc)* | | | |
| IN CONCERT (July 85) Live concert | 1985 | Westwood One (2) | 200-300 |
| *(With Katrina & the Waves)* | | | |
| **Compact Discs** | | | |
| ON THE EDGE (Nov 93) Music and interview | 1993 | Westwood One | 20-35 |
| *(With the Gin Blossoms)* | | | |
| WESTWOOD ONE SPECIAL (Aug 93) | 1993 | Westwood One (2) | 75-125 |
| *(Music and interview, some live)* | | | |

**DERBYS, THE**
*Other Mercury white promo label 45s $25 each*

| | | | |
|---|---|---|---|
| **45s** | | | |
| NIGHT AFTER NIGHT | 1960 | Mercury 71437 | 40 |
| *(White promo label)* | | | |

**DEREK AND THE DOMINOS**
*See Eric Clapton*

**DESERT ROSE BAND**
*MCA promo 45s $2 each; MCA promo color vinyl 45s $6 each; MCA Curb promo CD singles $3 each. Also see The Byrds*

| | | | |
|---|---|---|---|
| **45s** | | | |
| ASHES OF LOVE | 1986 | MCA 53048 | 10 |
| *(Blue vinyl promo only)* | | | |
| **RADIO SHOWS** | | | |
| **Albums** | | | |
| WESTWOOD ONE PRESENTS (Feb 90) | 1990 | Westwood One | 50-125 |
| *(Live concert)* | | | |

**DeSHANNON, JACKIE**
*Other Liberty promo 45s $8 each; Imperial promo 45s $5 each; Columbia and Atlantic promo 45s $3 each*

| | | | |
|---|---|---|---|
| **45s** | | | |
| LITTLE YELLOW ROSES | 1963 | Liberty 55602 | 100 |
| *(Yellow vinyl promo)* | | | |

**DeVILLE, WILLY**

| | | | |
|---|---|---|---|
| **12-Inch Singles** | | | |
| ANGEL EYES (same on both sides) | 1987 | A&M 17538 | 6 |

**DEVO**
*Warner promo 45s $6 each; MCA/Backstreet promo 45s $5 each; Asylum white promo label 45s $5 each*

| | | | |
|---|---|---|---|
| **12-Inch Singles** | | | |
| ARE YOU EXPERIENCED?/PLEASE PLEASE | 1984 | Warner Bros. PRO-A-2217 | 10 |
| BABY DOLL (5 versions) | 1988 | Enigma EPRO 148 | 8 |
| GATES OF STEEL/MR'S B'S BALLROOM/WHIP IT | 1980 | Warner Bros. PRO-A-881 | 8 |
| JERKIN' BACK 'N' FORTH//GOING UNDER/THROUGH BEING COOL | 1981 | Warner Bros. PRO-A-993 | 8 |
| POST POST-MODERN MAN (7 versions) | 1990 | Enigma EPRO 298 | 12 |
| SELECTIONS FROM "OH NO! IT'S DEVO" | 1983 | Warner Bros. PRO-A-199 | 15 |
| THAT'S GOOD/SPEED RACER | 1983 | Warner Bros. PRO-1-2006 | 25 |
| *(Promo-only picture disc)* | | | |
| THEME FROM DOCTOR DETROIT (2 versions)/LUV LUV | 1983 | Backstreet L33-1113 | 8 |
| THEME FROM DOCTOR DETROIT (same on both sides) | 1983 | Backstreet L33-1106 | 8 |
| WORKING IN A COAL MINE (same on both sides) | 1981 | Full Moon/Asylum 11523 | 8 |
| **45s** | | | |
| WHAT'S IT ALL ABOUT (Dec 79) Public service show | 1979 | W. I. A. A. 503 | 30 |
| *(With Jerry Casale, flip side is Dire Straits)* | | | |
| WORKING IN A COAL MINE | 1981 | Warner Bros. EP-3595 | 10 |
| *(Same song on each side; issued as a bonus 45 with original copies of the LP "New Traditionalists")* | | | |
| **7-Inch Extended Plays** | | | |
| DUTY NOW FOR THE FUTURE Three-song EP | 1979 | Warner Bros. PRO-S-813 | 20 |
| *(33 rpm promo-only release)* | | | |

| Title | Yr | Label, Number | NM $ |
|---|---|---|---|
| **Albums** | | | |
| SMOOTH NOODLE MAPS | 1990 | Enigma EPRO 326 | 20 |
| *(Promo only, no picture cover)* | | | |
| **RADIO SHOWS** | | | |
| **Albums** | | | |
| KING BISCUIT FLOWER HOUR (Oct 80) Live concert | 1980 | DIR/ABC (2) | 75-125 |
| *(With Elvis Costello)* | | | |
| PIONEERS IN MUSIC (Aug 86) Ohio rock | 1986 | DIR (2) | 30-60 |
| *(With Cheap Trick and Chrissie Hynde)* | | | |
| **Compact Discs** | | | |
| ON TOUR | 1996 | | 20-40 |
| *(Live material, with Satchel and Super 8)* | | | |

**DEXY'S MIDNIGHT RUNNERS**
*Mercury promo 45s $3 each*

| **12-Inch Singles** | | | |
|---|---|---|---|
| THE CELTIC SOUL BROTHERS (same on both sides) | 1982 | Mercury MK 237 | 6 |
| THE CELTIC SOUL BROTHERS/LET'S MAKE THIS PRECIOUS/ALL IN ALL | 1982 | Mercury MK 247 | 8 |
| THIS IS WHAT SHE'S LIKE/ONE OF THOSE THINGS | 1985 | Mercury PRO 387 | 8 |
| **RADIO SHOWS** | | | |
| **Albums** | | | |
| BBC COLLEGE CONCERT (Apr 83) Live concert | 1983 | London Wavelength | 40-75 |
| *(With Culture Club)* | | | |
| NBC SOURCE (Apr 83) | 1983 | NBC Radio | 40-75 |
| *(Live concert)* | | | |
| SUPERGROUPS (May 83) | 1983 | DIR (3) | 75-125 |
| *(With John Cougar Mellencamp)* | | | |

**DFX**

| **RADIO SHOWS** | | | |
|---|---|---|---|
| **Albums** | | | |
| BBC ROCK HOUR (Oct 83) Live concert | 1983 | London Wavelength | 40-75 |

**DIAMOND RIO**
*Arista promo 45s $2 each*

| **RADIO SHOWS** | | | |
|---|---|---|---|
| **Compact Discs** | | | |
| COUNTRY CUTTING EDGE (July 94) | 1994 | Westwood One | 10-20 |
| *(Music and interview)* | | | |

**DIAMOND, NEIL**
*Bang white promo label 45s $10 each; Uni promo 45s $8 each; Capitol white promo label 45s $6 each; other Columbia white promo label 45s $5 each; Columbia promo picture sleeve $3 each; Bang white promo label LPs $18 each. Includes listings by Neil & Jack.*

| **45s** | | | |
|---|---|---|---|
| CLOWN TOWN | 1963 | Columbia 42809 | 600 |
| *(White promo label, flip side is "At Night"; again, promo is less valuable than stock copy)* | | | |
| HEARTLIGHT | 1982 | (Columbia) | 15 |
| *(Test pressing, blank label)* | | | |
| I'M AFRAID  Neil & Jack | 1962 | Duel 517 | 250 |
| *(White promo label is easier to find than stock copy)* | | | |
| SEPTEMBER MORN | 1979 | Columbia AE7 1193 | 12 |
| *(Promo-only number)* | | | |
| SONG SUNG BLUE | 1977 | Columbia AE7 1115 | 15 |
| *(Stereo/mono, white promo label, live version from "Love at the Greek" not released commercially as a single)* | | | |
| TWO-BIT MANCHILD | 1968 | Uni 55075 | 100 |
| *(Red vinyl promo)* | | | |
| WHAT'S IT ALL ABOUT (June 81) Public service show | 1981 | W. I. A. A. 582 | 25 |
| *(Flip side is John Phillips)* | | | |
| YOU ARE MY LOVE AT LAST Neil and Jack | 1962 | Duel 508 | 400 |
| *(White promo label is easier to find than stock copy)* | | | |
| **7-Inch Extended Plays** | | | |
| GOLD Five songs, live | 1970 | Uni 34818 (LLP 127) | 30 |
| *(Issued with a picture paper sleeve)* | | | |
| HIS 12 GREATEST HITS Five songs | 1973 | MCA 34989 | 20 |
| *(Issued with a picture paper sleeve)* | | | |
| STONES Five songs | 1971 | Uni 34871 (LLP 172) | 25 |
| *(Issued with a picture paper sleeve)* | | | |
| **8-Track Tapes** | | | |
| GOLDEN HITS FROM THE GUYS AT BANG (70s) Mono | 197? | Bang | 75 |
| *(Promo-only 8-track with Diamond tracks)* | | | |
| **Albums** | | | |
| NEIL DIAMOND DJ SAMPLER | 1970 | Uni ND-11 | 200 |
| *(Promo-only release)* | | | |
| OPEN-END INTERVIEW | 1972 | Uni 1913 | 300 |
| *(Promo-only release)* | | | |
| **RADIO SHOWS** | | | |
| **Albums** | | | |
| NEIL DIAMOND (May 82) | 1982 | ABC Spotlight (3) | 50-75 |
| *(Profile, music and interview; price includes manual)* | | | |
| ROYALTY OF ROCK  Music and interview | 1983 | | 20-40 |
| *(With Kenny Rogers)* | | | |
| THE IN SOUND (June 67) Various artists | 1967 | U. S. Army | 25-35 |
| *(One of the five shows features Diamond, repeated in Nov 67 and Feb 68)* | | | |

| Title | Yr | Label, Number | NM $ |
|---|---|---|---|

**DIAMONDS, THE**
*Mercury promo singles $15 each; Mercury white promo label EPs $50 each*
**7-Inch Extended Plays**

| | | | |
|---|---|---|---|
| CHOICE SELECTIONS FROM... | 1957 | Mercury MEP-72 | 40 |

*(White promo label, one Diamonds track, with paper cover)*
**Albums**

| | | | |
|---|---|---|---|
| COLLECTION OF GOLDEN HITS | 1956 | Mercury 20213 | 75 |
| *(White promo label)* | | | |
| THE DIAMONDS | 1958 | Mercury 20309 | 75 |
| *(White promo label)* | | | |
| THE DIAMONDS MEET PETE RUGOLO | 1958 | Mercury 20368 | 75 |
| *(White promo label)* | | | |
| THE DIAMONDS OUT WEST | 1960 | Mercury 18940 | 75 |
| *(White promo label)* | | | |

**DIBANGO, MANU**
**12-Inch Singles**

| | | | |
|---|---|---|---|
| BIG BLOW/ALOKO PARTY | 1976 | Island 8680 | 8 |

**DICKENS, LITTLE JIMMY**
*Columbia promo 45s $5-10 each; other Columbia promo LPs $25 each*
**Albums**

| | | | |
|---|---|---|---|
| RAISIN' THE DICKENS | 1957 | Columbia 1047 | 50 |
| *(White promo label)* | | | |

**DICKIES, THE**
**45s**

| | | | |
|---|---|---|---|
| SILENT NIGHT/SOUNDS OF SILENCE | 1978 | A&M 2092 | 8 |
| *(All copies on white vinyl)* | | | |

**DICKSON, BRUCE**
**RADIO SHOWS**
**Albums**

| | | | |
|---|---|---|---|
| IN CONCERT (Oct 90) Live concert | 1990 | Westwood One | 40-75 |
| *(With Judas Priest)* | | | |

**DIDDLEY, BO**
*Checker promo 45s $10 each*
**RADIO SHOWS**
**Compact Discs**

| | | | |
|---|---|---|---|
| SUPERSTARS | 1995 | (2) | 40-60 |
| *(With Ron Wood, live concert)* | | | |

**DIFFIE, JOE**
*Epic promo CD singles $2-4 each*
**RADIO SHOWS**
**Compact Discs**

| | | | |
|---|---|---|---|
| COUNTRY CUTTING EDGE (July 94) | 1994 | Westwood One | 15-20 |
| *(Music and interviews)* | | | |
| LIVE AT THE CRAZY HORSE (Nov 94) | 1994 | Westwood One | 25-40 |
| *(Live concert)* | | | |

**DIFFORD AND TILBROOK**
**12-Inch Singles**

| | | | |
|---|---|---|---|
| PICKING UP THE PIECES (same on both sides) | 1984 | A&M 17283 | 6 |

**DIGABLE PLANETS**
**12-Inch Singles**

| | | | |
|---|---|---|---|
| 9TH WONDER (SLICKER THIS YEAR) (4 versions) | 1994 | Pendulum 19945 | 8 |
| NICKEL BAGS (4 versions)/APPOINTMENT AT THE FAT CLINIC (2 versions) | 1993 | Pendulum 5657 | 8 |

**DINNING, MARK**
*Other MGM promo 45s $8 each*
**45s**

| | | | |
|---|---|---|---|
| TEEN ANGEL | 1959 | MGM 12845 | 15 |
| *(Yellow promo label)* | | | |

**DINOSAUR JR.**
*Sire promo CD singles $3-5 each*
**Compact Discs**

| | | | |
|---|---|---|---|
| OUT THERE | 1993 | Sire PRO-CD-6143 | 15 |
| *(Radio-only sampler)* | | | |

**RADIO SHOWS**
**Compact Discs**

| | | | |
|---|---|---|---|
| IN CONCERT (June 94) Live concert | 1994 | Westwood One | 20-30 |
| *(With James)* | | | |

**DIO**
*Warner Bros. promo 45s $4 each; Warner Bros. promo CD singles $4 each Ronnie James Dio; Also see Black Sabbath*
**Compact Discs**

| | | | |
|---|---|---|---|
| LOCK UP THE WOLVES | 1990 | Warner Bros. 26212-2-DJ | 30 |
| *(Promo-only version, picture CD in leather digipak)* | | | |

**RADIO SHOWS**
**Albums**

| | | | |
|---|---|---|---|
| BBC LONDON WAVELENGTH SPECIAL (Sept 84) Live | 1984 | London Wavelength | 20-35 |
| *(Show repeated)* | | | |

| **Title** | **Yr** | **Label, Number** | **NM $** |
|---|---|---|---|
| CAPTURED LIVE (Feb 84) | 1984 | RKO (2) | 30-50 |
| *(Live concert)* | | | |
| CAPTURED LIVE (Feb 84) PARTS 1 AND 2 | 1984 | RKO (4) | 50-100 |
| *(Concert features Dio)* | | | |
| FROM BLACK SABBATH TO DIO LIVE TRACKS | 1985 | DIR (2) | 30-60 |
| *(Black Sabbath and Ronnie James Dio)* | | | |
| IN CONCERT (Mar 84) Live concert | 1984 | Westwood One (2) | 30-50 |
| *(Features Dio and Fiona)* | | | |
| INNERVIEW (70s) Music and interview | 197? | Innerview | 10-20 |
| *(Features Ronnie James Dio)* | | | |
| KING BISCUIT FLOWER HOUR (Feb 85) Live concert | 1985 | DIR (2) | 40-60 |
| *(With Twisted Sister)* | | | |
| KING BISCUIT FLOWER HOUR (July 82) Live concert | 1982 | DIR (2) | 30-50 |
| *(Concert features "Dio")* | | | |
| KING BISCUIT FLOWER HOUR (Oct 84) Live concert | 1984 | DIR (2) | 25-50 |
| *(With Fastway)* | | | |
| METALSHOP (July 92) Various artists | 1992 | MJI Productions | 10-15 |
| *(Features live cuts by Dio/Black Sabbath)* | | | |
| RETRO ROCK (Dec 83) | 1983 | Clayton Webster (2) | 20-35 |
| *(Music and interview)* | | | |

## DION (AND THE BELMONTS)

Includes listings for Dion; The Belmonts. Laurie promo 45s by Dion & the Belmonts $30 each; Laurie promo 45s by Dion $15 each; Sabrina white promo label 45s by the Belmonts $25 each; Sabina (note different spelling) white promo label 45s by the Belmonts $20 each; Columbia white promo label 45s by Dion $12 each; Columbia white promo label 45s by Dion & the Wanderers $20 each; Columbia white promo label 45s by the Duprees $15 each; Dot white promo label 45s by the Belmonts $12 each; MiaSound promo 45s by Freddy Cannon & The Belmonts $5 each; Warner-Spector promo 45s by Dion $5 each; 3 Seas promo 45s by Dion & the Belmonts $4 each; Day Spring promo 45s by Dion $3 each; Laurie promo LPs by Dion & the Belmonts $150-300 each; Columbia white promo label LPs by Dion $40-50 each.

**45s**

| | | | |
|---|---|---|---|
| BE CAREFUL OF STONES THAT YOU THROW (same on both sides) | 1963 | Columbia 42810 | 100 |
| *(White promo label, blue vinyl)* | | | |
| DONNA THE PRIMA DONNA (same on both sides) | 1963 | Columbia 42852 | 80 |
| *(Promo only on red vinyl)* | | | |
| RUNAROUND SUE/YA YA TWIST | 1962 | Monument (# unknown) | 25 |
| *(B-side by Joey Dee and the Starliters)* | | | |
| SEAGULL/SOFT PARADE | 1972 | Warner Bros. PRO-537 | 15 |
| WANDERER, THE (same on both sides) | 1979 | Warner Bros. PRO-814 | 15 |
| WHAT'S IT ALL ABOUT (Dec 76) Public service show | 1976 | W. I. A. A. 347 | 25 |
| *(Flip side features Olivia Newton-John)* | | | |
| WHEN YOU WISH UPON A STAR | 196? | Laurie LLP 2006 | 500 |
| *(Set of five jukebox 7-inch 33 1/3 records)* | | | |

**RADIO SHOWS**
**Albums**

| | | | |
|---|---|---|---|
| WORLD OF ROCK (May 89) | 1989 | DIR (2) | 20-40 |
| *(Dion is a guest DJ in the series)* | | | |

## DION, CELINE

Epic and 550 Music promo CD singles $4-6

**12-Inch Singles**

| | | | |
|---|---|---|---|
| MY HEART WILL GO ON | 1998 | 550 Music B2S 41125 (2) | 40 |
| *(Eight mixes of the Titanic anthem, white generic sleeve, promo only)* | | | |

## DIRE STRAITS

Warner Bros. promo 45s $4 each; Warner Bros. promo 12" singles $12 each Includes listings of Mark Knopfler

**45s**

| | | | |
|---|---|---|---|
| POOR BOY BLUES  With Chet Atkins | 1990 | Columbia 73556 | 10 |
| *(Red/orange promo label, classic instrumental)* | | | |
| WHAT'S IT ALL ABOUT (Dec 79) Public service show | 1979 | W. I. A. A. 503 | 30 |
| *(Flip side features Devo)* | | | |

**Albums**

| | | | |
|---|---|---|---|
| DIRE STRAITS LIVE | 1980 | Warner Bros. WBMS-109 | 50 |
| *("The Warner Bros. Music Show" promo)* | | | |
| LOVE OVER GOLD | 1982 | Warner Bros. 23728 | 50 |
| *(Promo on Quiex II vinyl; the times of the songs also are listed differently than on stock copies)* | | | |

**RADIO SHOWS**

| | | | |
|---|---|---|---|
| ALBUM NETWORK SPECIAL (June 96) Mark Knopfler | 1996 | Album Network (2) | 100-125 |
| *(Live concert)* | | | |

**Albums**

| | | | |
|---|---|---|---|
| BBC LONDON WAVELENGTH SPECIAL (Mar 84) | 1984 | London Wavelength | 30-50 |
| *(Alchemy special)* | | | |
| BBC LONDON WAVELENGTH SPECIAL (Nov 82) | 1982 | London Wavelength | 30-50 |
| *(Love Over Gold special)* | | | |
| BBC ROCK HOUR (80s) Live concert | 198? | London Wavelength | 75-125 |
| *(Repeated)* | | | |
| BBC TRANSCRIPTION DISC  Live concert | 1978 | BBC Transcription | 200-300 |
| *(With the Motors)* | | | |
| IN CONCERT (May 91) Live concert | 1991 | Westwood One (2) | 30-60 |
| *(With the Kinks)* | | | |
| IN THE STUDIO (80s) Profile of the group | 198? | Westwood One (2) | 15-25 |
| *(Music and interviews)* | | | |
| INNERVIEW (70s) Music and interview | 197? | Innerview | 20-30 |
| *(Repeated several times)* | | | |
| KING BISCUIT FLOWER HOUR (Feb 81) Live concert | 1981 | DIR/ABC (2) | 50-100 |
| *(With Thin Lizzy)* | | | |
| KING BISCUIT FLOWER HOUR (July 81) Live concert | 1981 | DIR/ABC (2) | 40-75 |
| *(With Loverboy)* | | | |
| KING BISCUIT FLOWER HOUR (Nov 85) Live concert | 1985 | DIR (4) | 75-150 |
| *(Two weekly shows, parts 1 and 2)* | | | |

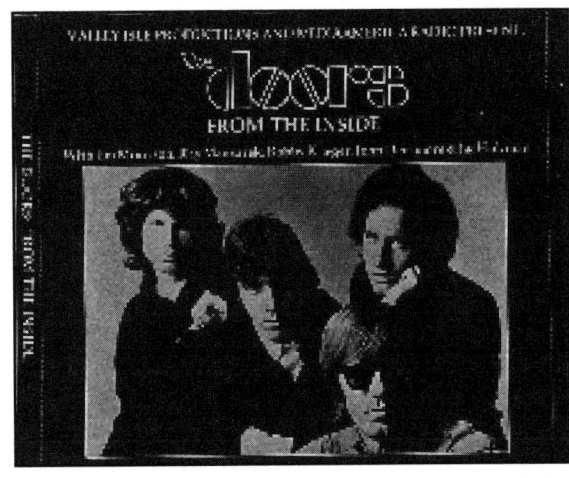

(Top left) A white-label promo of the Doors' only No. 1 album, *Waiting for the Sun.* Promo-label versions of albums that have common stock copies are increasing in value. (Top right) The CD cover for a rare radio show that has both vintage and current interview segments from all four Doors plus Elektra label head Jac Holzman. (Middle left) Promos formerly owned by radio stations are often found marked with notes for the disc jockeys. On this copy of Bob Dylan's *Desire,* "Hurricane" is crossed out with instructions to "use the 45," no doubt because of the language on the LP version. (Middle right) Dylan was on Asylum Records for only about a year. Here is the scarce white-label promo for *Planet Waves,* a No. 1 album. (Bottom left) Dylan radio shows are hard to come by. This 1984 program is among the rarest. (Bottom right) Radio shows are usually associated with classic rock artists, but the 1982 Star Session series featured pop artists, including Sheena Easton.

| Title | Yr | Label, Number | NM $ |
|---|---|---|---|
| KING BISCUIT FLOWER HOUR Live concert | 1984 | DIR/ABC (2) | 40-80 |
| *(Repeated several times)* | | | |
| LEGENDS OF ROCK Profile | 1988 | NBC Radio (2) | 15-25 |
| *(Music and interviews)* | | | |
| LEGENDS OF ROCK Profile, Parts 1 and 2 | 1988 | NBC Radio (4) | 30-60 |
| *(Music and interviews)* | | | |
| NBC PROFILE (July 86) Profile of group | 1986 | NBC Radio (2) | 20-30 |
| *(Music and interview)* | | | |
| SUPERSTAR CONCERT (June 89) Live concert | 1989 | Westwood One (3) | 40-75 |
| *(With Simple Minds)* | | | |
| SUPERSTAR CONCERT Box set | 1986 | Westwood One (3) | 45-75 |
| *(Live concert)* | | | |
| **Compact Discs** | | | |
| BBC CLASSIC TRACKS (June 92) Live cuts | 1992 | Westwood One | 20-30 |
| *(Repeated in Apr 91)* | | | |
| IN CONCERT (Aug 92) Live concert | 1992 | Westwood One | 30-50 |
| *(With Police)* | | | |
| IN CONCERT (Aug 93) Live concert | 1993 | Westwood One | 30-50 |
| *(With Brother Cane)* | | | |
| IN CONCERT (Nov 93) Live concert | 1993 | Westwood One | 30-50 |
| *(From Westwood One concerts)* | | | |
| KING BISCUIT FLOWER HOUR (Sept 87) Live concert | 1987 | DIR (2) | 35-60 |
| *(Repeated several times)* | | | |
| LIVE FROM CENTRAL PARK (90s) | 199? | TBS Syndication | 75-100 |
| *(Rare live concert recorded for Canadian radio, also aired in U.S.)* | | | |
| TIMOTHY WHITE SESSIONS (Mar 92) Music and interview | 1992 | Westwood One (2) | 30-50 |
| *(Some live tracks)* | | | |
| UP CLOSE Profile with some live | 1992 | Media America (2) | 20-40 |
| *(Music and interview)* | | | |

## DIRT BAND
*See Nitty Gritty Dirt Band*

## DIVINYLS
*Chrysalis promo 45s $4 each; Virgin promo CD singles $3 each*

| **12-Inch Singles** | | | |
|---|---|---|---|
| BACK TO THE WALL (same on both sides) | 1988 | Chrysalis VAS 1016 | 5 |
| HEY LITTLE BOY/HEY LITTLE BOY (Extended Remix) | 1988 | Chrysalis VAS 1131 | 6 |
| IN MY LIFE (same on both sides) | 1985 | Chrysalis 2247 | 6 |
| PLEASURE AND PAIN (Live)/IN MY LIFE (Live)/SLEEPING BEAUTY (Live) | 1986 | Chrysalis 2283 | 20 |
| PLEASURE AND PAIN (same on both sides) | 1985 | Chrysalis 2156 | 8 |
| SLEEPING BEAUTY (same on both sides) | 1985 | Chrysalis 2258 | 6 |

**RADIO SHOWS**
**Albums**

| KING BISCUIT FLOWER HOUR (Feb 86) Live concert | 1986 | DIR/ABC (2) | 50-100 |
|---|---|---|---|
| *(In concert with the Cure)* | | | |

## DOBKINS, CARL, JR.
*Decca promo 45s $5 each*
**Albums**

| CARL DOBKINS JR. | 1959 | Decca 8938 | 45 |
|---|---|---|---|
| *(Pink promo label)* | | | |

## DR. DEMENTO
**45s**

| WHAT'S IT ALL ABOUT (Aug 74 and Mar 77) Public service show | 197? | W. I. A. A. 363 | 25 |
|---|---|---|---|
| *(Flip side features Steve Marriott)* | | | |

**RADIO SHOWS**
**Albums**

| THE DR. DEMENTO SHOW (73-92) Various artists | | Westwood One (2) | 10-20 |
|---|---|---|---|
| *(Weekly novelty music show, one of the most popular syndicated radio shows ever!)* | | | |

**Compact Discs**

| THE DR. DEMENTO SHOW (92-present) Various artists | 199? | On The Radio | 15-20 |
|---|---|---|---|
| *(Music and interviews, some original and exclusive music)* | | | |

## DOCTOR FEELGOOD
**RADIO SHOWS**
**Albums**

| BBC TRANSCRIPTION DISC Live concert | 1975 | BBC Transcription | 100-200 |
|---|---|---|---|
| *(Rare concert also features Andrews and Cooper)* | | | |

## DR. HOOK
*Capitol and Casablanca promo 45s $3 each*
**45s**

| WHAT'S IT ALL ABOUT (Nov 78) Public service show | 1978 | W. I. A. A. 450 | 25 |
|---|---|---|---|
| *(Flip side features The Beach Boys)* | | | |

## DODD, JIMMIE
**45s**

| MICKEY MOUSE MAMBO | 1956 | ABC-Paramount 9680 | 50 |
|---|---|---|---|
| *(Standard black label, "Promotion Copy" at lower left)* | | | |

## DODGERS, THE
**45s**

| CAT HOP | 1955 | Aladdin 3259 | 100 |
|---|---|---|---|
| *(White promo label)* | | | |

| Title | Yr | Label, Number | NM $ |
|---|---|---|---|
| LET'S MAKE A WHOLE LOT OF LOVE | 1954 | Aladdin 3259 | 75 |
| *(White promo label)* | | | |

**DOG'S EYE VIEW**
**RADIO SHOWS**
**Compact Discs**

| | | | |
|---|---|---|---|
| ALBUM NETWORK SPECIAL (June 96) | 1996 | Album Network | 20-40 |
| *(Live material)* | | | |

**DOKKEN**
*Elektra promo 45s $3 each; Elektra promo CD singles $2-4 each*
**RADIO SHOWS**
**Albums**

| | | | |
|---|---|---|---|
| IN CONCERT (Mar 85) Live concert | 1985 | Westwood One (2) | 75-125 |
| *(With Whitesnake)* | | | |
| INNERVIEW (80s) Music and interview | 198? | Innerview | 10-15 |
| *(Show was repeated)* | | | |

**DOLBY, THOMAS**
*Capitol promo 45s $4 each*
**12-Inch Singles**

| | | | |
|---|---|---|---|
| AIRWAVES (same on both sides) | 1983 | Capitol SPRO 9980 | 6 |
| GET OUT OF MY MIX (2 mixes) | 1983 | Capitol SPRO 9975 | 8 |
| HUNGER CITY (same on both sides) | 1986 | MCA 17165 | 5 |
| *(As "Dolby's Cube")* | | | |
| HYPERACTIVE! (5:00)/HYPERACTIVE (4:12) | 1984 | Capitol SPRO 9067/8 | 10 |

**RADIO SHOWS**
**Albums**

| | | | |
|---|---|---|---|
| BBC COLLEGE CONCERT (Apr 83) Live concert | 1983 | London Wavelength | 30-60 |
| *(Show was repeated)* | | | |
| BBC ROCK HOUR (Apr 84) | 1984 | London Wavelength | 25-50 |
| *(Music and interview)* | | | |
| ON THE EDGE (Jan 92) Music and interview | 1992 | 10-20 | |
| *(With Mudhoney and the Rembrandts)* | | | |

**DOLCE, JOE**
**45s**

| | | | |
|---|---|---|---|
| THE 12 DAYS OF CHRISTMAS/JINGLE BELL ROCK | 1981 | Montage 1208 | 4 |

**DOMINGO, PLACIDO**
**45s**

| | | | |
|---|---|---|---|
| IT'S CHRISTMAS TIME THIS YEAR (same on both sides) | 1981 | CBS AE7 1789 | 5 |

**DOMINO, FATS**
*Other Imperial cream-colored promo 45s $25 each; Imperial white promo label 45s $15 each; ABC Paramount white promo label 45s $15 each; Mercury pink promo label 45s $12 each; Warner Bros. gray promo label 45s $6 each; Reprise white promo label 45s $10 each; Toot Toot white promo label 45s $5 each; Other Imperial white promo label LPs $50-100 each; ABC Paramount white promo label LPs $50 each; Mercury promo LPs $25 each (unless Mercury 21065 exists as a promo, its value would be around $250 and it would be promo only); United Artists 2LP promo sets $20 each; Other United Artists promo LPs $10 each*

**45s**

| | | | |
|---|---|---|---|
| FATS ON FIRE Set of five stereo singles | 1967 | ABC Paramount 479-1/6 | 200 |
| *(Price is for the complete set of five records)* | | | |
| GOING TO THE RIVER  Red vinyl promo version | 1953 | Imperial 5231 | 300 |
| *(Cream-colored promo label)* | | | |
| HERE COMES FATS DOMINO Set of five stereo singles | 1967 | ABC Paramount 455-1/6 | 200 |
| *(Price is for the complete set of five records)* | | | |
| HOW LONG  Red vinyl promo version | 1952 | Imperial 5209 | 300 |
| *(Cream-colored promo label)* | | | |
| I KNOW  Red vinyl promo version | 1955 | Imperial 5323 | 500 |
| *(Cream-colored promo label)* | | | |
| NOBODY LOVES ME  Red vinyl promo version | 1953 | Imperial 5220 | 300 |
| *(Cream-colored promo label)* | | | |

**7-Inch Extended Plays**

| | | | |
|---|---|---|---|
| COOKIN' WITH FATS  PART 1 | 1957 | Imperial 151 | 175 |
| *(Cream-colored label, issued with hard cover)* | | | |
| COOKIN' WITH FATS  PART 2 | 1957 | Imperial 152 | 175 |
| *(Cream-colored label, issued with hard cover)* | | | |
| FATS '65  Jukebox LLP | 1967 | Mercury LLP | 35 |
| *(Issued with a hard cover)* | | | |
| FATS DOMINO  Cream-colored promo label | 1953 | Imperial 127 | 250 |
| *(Issued with a hard cover)* | | | |
| FATS DOMINO  Cream-colored promo label | 1954 | Imperial 138 | 250 |
| *(Issued with a hard cover)* | | | |
| FATS DOMINO  Cream-colored promo label | 1954 | Imperial 140 | 225 |
| *(Issued with a hard cover)* | | | |
| FATS DOMINO LIVE!  Jukebox LLP | 1967 | ABC Paramount 659 | 20 |
| *(Issued with a hard cover)* | | | |
| FATS DOMINO SWINGS  Jukebox LLP | 1967 | Imperial 2091 | 50 |
| *(Issued with a hard cover)* | | | |
| FATS ON FIRE  Jukebox LLP | 1967 | ABC Paramount 479 | 20 |
| *(Issued with a hard cover)* | | | |
| GETAWAY WITH FATS DOMINO Jukebox LLP | 1967 | ABC Paramount 510 | 20 |
| *(Issued with a hard cover)* | | | |
| HERE COMES FATS | 1956 | Imperial 147 | 250 |
| *(Cream-colored label, issued with hard cover)* | | | |
| HERE COMES FATS DOMINO  Jukebox LLP | 1967 | ABC Paramount 455 | 25 |
| *(Issued with a hard cover)* | | | |

| Title | Yr | Label, Number | NM $ |
|-------|-----|---------------|------|
| HERE STANDS FATS DOMINO  PART 1 | 1956 | Imperial 148 | 175 |
| (Cream-colored label, issued with hard cover) | | | |
| HERE STANDS FATS DOMINO  PART 2 | 1956 | Imperial 149 | 175 |
| (Cream-colored label, issued with hard cover) | | | |
| HERE STANDS FATS DOMINO  PART 3 | 1956 | Imperial 150 | 175 |
| (Cream-colored label, issued with hard cover) | | | |
| ROCK AND ROLLIN' PART 1 | 1954 | Imperial 141 | 200 |
| (Cream-colored label, issued with hard cover) | | | |
| ROCK AND ROLLIN' PART 2 | 1954 | Imperial 142 | 200 |
| (Cream-colored label, issued with hard cover) | | | |
| ROCK AND ROLLIN' PART 3 | 1954 | Imperial 143 | 200 |
| (Cream-colored label, issued with hard cover) | | | |
| THIS IS FATS DOMINO PART 1 | 1955 | Imperial 144 | 200 |
| (Cream-colored label, issued with hard cover) | | | |
| THIS IS FATS DOMINO PART 2 | 1955 | Imperial 145 | 200 |
| (Cream-colored label, issued with hard cover) | | | |
| THIS IS FATS DOMINO PART 3 | 1955 | Imperial 146 | 200 |
| (Cream-colored label, issued with hard cover) | | | |
| **Albums** | | | |
| COOKIN' WITH FATS | 1974 | United Artists UA-LA122-F2 | 15 |
| (White promo label) | | | |
| COOKIN' WITH FATS (SUPERPAK) | 1974 | United Artists UA-LA122-F2 | 300 |
| (Promo with one black vinyl record and one colored vinyl record) | | | |
| FATS  White promo label | 1971 | Reprise 6439 | 250 |
| (Promo-only release) | | | |
| FATS DOMINO ROCK & ROLLIN' | 1956 | Imperial 9009 | 250 |
| (White promo label) | | | |
| FATS DOMINO SWINGS | 1959 | Imperial 9062 | 200 |
| (White promo label) | | | |
| FATS IS BACK | 1968 | Reprise 6304 | 100 |
| (White promo label) | | | |
| HERE STANDS FATS DOMINO | 1957 | Imperial 9038 | 200 |
| (White promo label) | | | |
| MILLION RECORD HITS | 1959 | Imperial 9103 | 150 |
| (White promo label) | | | |
| ROCK & ROLLIN' | 1956 | Imperial 9000 | 300 |
| (White promo label; early Imperial promo LPs are very rare) | | | |
| ROCK & ROLLIN' WITH FATS DOMINO | 1956 | Imperial 9004 | 300 |
| (White promo label) | | | |
| THE FABULOUS MR. D. | 1958 | Imperial 9055 | 200 |
| (White promo label) | | | |
| THE FATS DOMINO SOUND | 1973 | United Artists UAMG-104 | 50 |
| (Edited versions of 30 songs, promo-only release) | | | |
| THIS IS FATS DOMINO | 1956 | Imperial 9028 | 200 |
| (White promo label) | | | |
| **Compact Discs** | | | |
| THEY CALL ME THE FAT MAN | 1993 | EMI DPRO-4843 | 15 |
| (Promo-only 12-track sampler) | | | |
| **RADIO SHOWS** | | | |
| **Cassettes** | | | |
| AUSTIN ENCORE | 1993 | Mainstreet Productions | 40-75 |
| (Live concert) | | | |

## DOMINOES, THE

Other King promo 45s $15 each; Decca promo 45s $12 each; Liberty promo 45s $12 each; Columbia promo 45s by Gene Mumford $8-12 each; Liberty promo LPs $20 each Billy Ward (and the Dominoes).

**45s**

| Title | Yr | Label, Number | NM $ |
|-------|-----|---------------|------|
| CHRISTMAS IN HEAVEN | 1953 | King 1281 | 40 |
| (White promo label) | | | |
| PLEASE GIVE ME ONE MORE CHANCE  Gene Mumford | 1958 | Columbia 41233 | 15 |
| (White promo label, includes photo insert) | | | |
| **Albums** | | | |
| BILLY WARD AND THE DOMINOES | 1958 | Decca 8621 | 250 |
| (Pink promo label) | | | |

## DONEGAN, LONNIE

Mercury and London promo 45s $8 each; Atlantic promo 45s $5 each; Hickory promo 45s $4 each; Atlantic and ABC Paramount promo LPs $25 each

**Albums**

| Title | Yr | Label, Number | NM $ |
|-------|-----|---------------|------|
| AN ENGLISHMAN SINGS FOLK SONGS | 1957 | Mercury 20229 | 100 |
| (White promo label) | | | |

## DONNER, RAL

Other Reprise, Fontana promo 45s $25 each

**45s**

| Title | Yr | Label, Number | NM $ |
|-------|-----|---------------|------|
| GOOD LOVIN'/THE OTHER SIDE OF ME | 1964 | Smash 34774/5 | 40 |
| (A Fontana promo using Smash labels in error and omitting the Fontana number?) | | | |
| I GOT BURNED | 1963 | Reprise 20,141 | 20 |
| (White promo label, stock picture sleeve worth $200) | | | |
| LOVE ISN'T LIKE THAT | 1966 | Red Bird 057 | 50 |
| (Yellow promo label) | | | |

## DONOVAN

Hickory white promo label 45s $5-10 each; Epic white promo label 45s $5 each; Other Epic colored vinyl promo 45s $35 each; Epic orange promo label 45s $4 each; Hickory white promo label LPs $18 each; Epic white promo label LPs $12 each

**45s**

| Title | Yr | Label, Number | NM $ |
|-------|-----|---------------|------|
| SUNSHINE SUPERMAN | 1966 | Epic 10045 | 50 |
| (White label, promo only on red vinyl) | | | |

| Title | Yr | Label, Number | NM $ |
|---|---|---|---|
| WHAT'S IT ALL ABOUT (Nov 76) Public service show | 1976 | W. I. A. A. 343 | 20 |
| (Flip side is Barry White) | | | |
| **RADIO SHOWS** | | | |
| **Albums** | | | |
| BBC TRANSCRIPTION DISC Live concert | 1981 | BBC Transcription | 250-400 |
| (Very rare show and series) | | | |
| INNERVIEW (70s) Profile | 197? | Innerview | 20-30 |
| (Music and interview) | | | |
| ROCK AROUND THE WORLD (May 76) | 1976 | RATW | 100-175 |
| (Some live material) | | | |

## DOOBIE BROTHERS, THE
Other Warner white promo label 45s $4 each

**45s**

| Title | Yr | Label, Number | NM $ |
|---|---|---|---|
| I CHEAT THE HANGMAN | 1975 | Warner Bros. 8161 | 10 |
| (Green promo label, versions are 6:34 and 4:20) | | | |
| NEED A LITTLE TASTE OF LOVE (same on both sides) | 1989 | Capitol 7PRO-79723 | 6 |
| (Vinyl is promo only) | | | |
| **7-Inch Extended Plays** | | | |
| THE CAPTAIN AND ME  Five-song jukebox LLP | 1973 | Warner Bros. 2694 (LLP 221) | 20 |
| (Issued in a paper picture sleeve) | | | |
| WHAT WERE ONCE VICES ARE NOW HABITS  Five songs | 1974 | Warner Bros. 2750 (LLP 247) | 20 |
| (Issued in a paper picture sleeve) | | | |
| **RADIO SHOWS** | | | |
| **Albums** | | | |
| HOT ROCKS (June 86) Michael McDonald | 1986 | United Stations (2) | 25-40 |
| (Music and interviews) | | | |
| INNERVIEW (70s) Profile of group | 197? | Innerview | 10-15 |
| (Music and interviews) | | | |
| KING BISCUIT FLOWER HOUR (July 87) Live concert | 1987 | DIR (2) | 30-50 |
| (Correct labeling of above show) | | | |
| KING BISCUIT FLOWER HOUR (July 87) Live concert | 1987 | DIR (2) | 40-50 |
| (Shipped with the wrong labels but there was an insert to explain the error) | | | |
| KING BISCUIT FLOWER HOUR (Oct 86) Live concert | 1986 | DIR (2) | 30-50 |
| (Repeated several times) | | | |
| LEGENDS OF ROCK (Nov 87) Profile OF GROUP | 1987 | NBC Radio (2) | 15-30 |
| (Music and interviews) | | | |
| OFF THE RECORD (90s) | 199? | Westwood One (2) | 15-20 |
| (Music and interview) | | | |
| ROBERT W. MORGAN (Feb 81) | 1981 | Watermark | 15-25 |
| (Music and interviews) | | | |
| STAR SESSIONS (July 82) Live concert | 1982 | DIR (3) | 75-125 |
| (A hard series to find) | | | |
| STARTRACK PROFILE  Michael McDonald | 1986 | Westwood One (2) | 25-40 |
| (Music and interviews) | | | |
| SUPERSTAR CONCERT (80s) BOX SET Live concert | 198? | Westwood One (3) | 25-50 |
| (Show repeated several times) | | | |
| TIMOTHY WHITE SESSIONS (July 89) | 1989 | Westwood One (2) | 20-35 |
| (Some live material) | | | |
| **Compact Discs** | | | |
| BBC CLASSIC TRACKS (May 94) Live cuts | 1994 | Westwood One | 20-40 |
| (Many of the tracks are live) | | | |
| IN THE STUDIO (June 92) Profile OF AN ALBUM | 1992 | Album Network | 15-25 |
| (Several Doobie shows in this series) | | | |
| KING BISCUIT FLOWER HOUR (Aug 88) Live concert | 1988 | DIR | 30-50 |
| (CD version of the above shows) | | | |
| ROCK STARS (June 89) Profile | 1989 | Radio Today (2) | 20-30 |
| (Music and interviews, some live) | | | |
| SUPERSTAR CONCERT Live concert | 1992 | Westwood One (2) | 25-50 |
| (CD version of the above show) | | | |
| SUPERSTAR CONCERT (Sept 94) Live concert | 1994 | Westwood One (2) | 40-75 |
| (Special reunion concert) | | | |
| UP CLOSE Profile, Music and interviews | 1989 | Media America (2) | 25-40 |
| (Some live material) | | | |

## DOORS, THE
Other Elektra white promo label 45s $10 each (except Elektra 69770, which is $5); Elektra white promo label 12" singles $15 each; other Elektra promo label LPs $40-50 each.  Originally Rick & the Ravens.

**12-Inch Singles**

| Title | Yr | Label, Number | NM $ |
|---|---|---|---|
| LIGHT MY FIRE (edit)/LIGHT MY FIRE (live edit) | 1987 | Elektra ED 5245 | 15 |
| LOVE ME TWO TIMES | 1983 | Elektra 4955 | 75 |
| (Price includes rare picture cover) | | | |
| **45s** | | | |
| BREAK ON THROUGH  White/black promo label | 1966 | Elektra 45611 | 50 |
| (First single as the Doors) | | | |
| HELLO, I LOVE YOU | 1968 | Elektra 45635 | 25 |
| (White/black promo label) | | | |
| HENRIETTA  Rick and the Ravens | 1965 | Aura 4506 | 50 |
| (Rick & the Ravens features Ray Manzarek) | | | |
| LIGHT MY FIRE White/black promo label | 1967 | Elektra 45615 | 50 |
| (Hard to find a mint copy of this promo classic! 2:52 version) | | | |
| PEOPLE ARE STRANGE | 1967 | Elektra 45621 | 35 |
| (White/black promo label) | | | |
| SOUL TRAIN Ray Daniels | 1965 | Aura 4511 | 50 |
| (Same song, different artist listed on label) | | | |
| SOUL TRAIN Rick and the Ravens | 1965 | Aura 4511 | 50 |
| (These promo versions are about as rare as the  stock copies) | | | |

| Title | Yr | Label, Number | NM $ |
|---|---|---|---|
| TOUCH ME | 1969 | Elektra 45646 | 20 |
| *(White/black promo label)* | | | |
| UNKNOWN SOLDIER, THE | 1968 | Elektra 45628 | 25 |
| *(White/black promo label)* | | | |
| WHAT'S IT ALL ABOUT  Public service show | 1973 | W. I. A. A. 122 | 30 |
| *(Music and interviews)* | | | |
| WISHFUL SINFUL | 1969 | Elektra 45656 | 15 |
| *(White/black promo label)* | | | |
| **Albums** | | | |
| 13 | 1970 | Elektra EKS-74079 | 40 |
| *(White label promo)* | | | |
| ABSOLUTELY LIVE | 1970 | Elektra 9002 (2) | 60 |
| *(White promo labels)* | | | |
| DOORS, THE | 1967 | Elektra 4007 | 100 |
| *(White promo label)* | | | |
| L.A. WOMAN | 1971 | Elektra EKS-75011 | 100 |
| *(White promo label)* | | | |
| MORRISON HOTEL/HARD ROCK CAFÉ | 1970 | Elektra EKS-75007 | 100 |
| *(White promo label)* | | | |
| SOFT PARADE, THE | 1969 | Elektra 75005 | 60 |
| *(White promo label)* | | | |
| STRANGE DAYS | 1967 | Elektra 4014 | 75 |
| *(White promo label)* | | | |
| WAITING FOR THE SUN | 1968 | Elektra EKS-74024 | 150 |
| *(White promo label)* | | | |
| **Compact Discs** | | | |
| BREAK ON THROUGH | 1991 | Elektra PRCD-8314-2 | 6 |
| *(Promo CD single from the soundtrack of The Doors, original version)* | | | |
| ROADHOUSE BLUES | 1991 | Elektra PRCD 8361-2 | 10 |
| *(Promo-only CD single release)* | | | |
| **RADIO SHOWS** | | | |
| **Albums** | | | |
| 20TH ANNIVERSARY SALUTE  Profile | 1987 | Radio International (2) | 75-100 |
| *(Music and interviews)* | | | |
| DOORS INTERVIEW | 1979 | Innerview (4) | 100-125 |
| *(Very limited syndication, music and interviews)* | | | |
| DOORS SPECIAL, THE  Black labels, white print | 1987 | Westwood One (2) | 60-125 |
| *(Music and interviews)* | | | |
| IN CONCERT (Dec 91) Live concert | 1991 | Westwood One (2) | 50-100 |
| *(Recorded live in Seattle in the early 70s)* | | | |
| IN SOUND, THE  Various artists | 1967 | U. S. Army | 25-50 |
| *(Several shows, July, Aug, Oct 67; the Doors are the feature of a daily 5-minute program; music and interviews)* | | | |
| INNERVIEW (70s) Profile | 197? | Innerview | 20-40 |
| *(Music and interviews)* | | | |
| JIM LADD INNERVIEW | 1983 | Innerview (4) | 100-125 |
| *(From the "Innerview" series)* | | | |
| NIGHTBIRD & COMPANY (Aug 75) Various artists | 1975 | Army Reserve #223 (2) | 40-60 |
| *(Ray Manzarek is the host of the Doors 15-minute show)* | | | |
| OFF THE RECORD (Dec 91) Profile of the Doors | 1991 | Westwood One (2) | 20-40 |
| *(Music and interview)* | | | |
| ROCK & ROLL NEVER FORGETS (80s) Profile | 198? | Westwood One (5) | 100-150 |
| *(Music and interviews)* | | | |
| ROCK SCOPE  Profile | 1986 | Rock Scope (2) | 50-100 |
| *(Very rare show in a rare series)* | | | |
| SOURCE SPECIAL  Profile | 1981 | NBC Radio (3) | 75-100 |
| *(Music and interviews)* | | | |
| **Compact Discs** | | | |
| DOORS STORY, THE | 1990 | Unistar (3) | 45-80 |
| *(Music and interviews)* | | | |
| FROM THE INSIDE with Jac Holzman | 1988 | Media America (6) | 175-250 |
| *(Mostly music and interviews, some live)* | | | |
| IN THE STUDIO Profile of an album | 1988 | Album Network | 25-40 |
| *(Several Doors shows in this series)* | | | |
| KING BISCUIT FLOWER HOUR  Live concert | 1989 | DIR | 125-200 |
| *(Many copies pressed, but very much in demand)* | | | |
| MEDIA AMERICA SPECIAL | 1996 | Media America (3) | 50-75 |
| *(Retrospective)* | | | |
| ROCK! AT THE CORE with Jimi Hendrix, others | 1989 | (3) | 50-75 |
| *(Music and interview)* | | | |
| SETTING THE RECORD STRAIGHT (Oct 91) "Wrap Up" | 1991 | (4) | 50-100 |
| *(Edited to four CDs version of above show)* | | | |
| SETTING THE RECORD STRAIGHT (Oct 91) Profile | 1991 | (10) | 200-300 |
| *(Music and interviews with many live cuts)* | | | |
| SUPERSTAR CONCERT Live concert | 1990 | Westwood One (2) | 50-80 |
| *(The Vancouver concert in 1970)* | | | |
| TRIBUTE TO JIM MORRISON (June 91) Profile | 1991 | Unistar (3) | 50-100 |
| *(Music and interviews)* | | | |
| UP CLOSE Profile | 1989 | Media America (2) | 50-75 |
| *(Music and interviews, some live material)* | | | |
| UP CLOSE Profile (New show) | 1994 | Media America (2) | 60-100 |
| *(More live material than previous show)* | | | |

**DOUG AND THE SLUGS**
**12-Inch Singles**

| | | | |
|---|---|---|---|
| TOO BAD (same on both sides) | 1981 | RCA JD-12183 | 10 |

| Title | Yr | Label, Number | NM $ |
|-------|----|--------------|----|

**DOUGLAS, CAROL**
**12-Inch Singles**

| Title | Yr | Label, Number | NM $ |
|-------|----|--------------|----|
| NIGHT FEVER (6:20) (same on both sides) | 1978 | Midsong Int'l. L33-1975 | 10 |

**DOUGLAS, MIKE**
**45s**

| Title | Yr | Label, Number | NM $ |
|-------|----|--------------|----|
| SILVER BELLS (mono/stereo) | 1967 | Epic JZSP 135100/1 | 10 |

**DOWELL, JOE**
*Smash promo 45s $12 each*
**45s**

| Title | Yr | Label, Number | NM $ |
|-------|----|--------------|----|
| HOMEWARD ON THE WIND (mono/stereo) | 1973 | Journey 1238 | 6 |
| *(Stock copy not known to exist)* | | | |

**DOWLING, CHET & BILL MINKIN**
**45s**

| Title | Yr | Label, Number | NM $ |
|-------|----|--------------|----|
| CHRISTMAS EVE WITH THE SENATOR//THE OPENING AND THE GIFT LIST/ THE CHRISTMAS HAIRCUT/WHAT TO GET THE KIDS/THE CHRISTMAS CARDS | 1967 | Columbia ZLP 135464/5 | 12 |
| *(Small hole, 33 1/3 rpm; promo for "Senator Bobby's Christmas Party")* | | | |

**DRAMARAMA**
**RADIO SHOWS**
**Compact Discs**

| Title | Yr | Label, Number | NM $ |
|-------|----|--------------|----|
| IN CONCERT (Jan 93) Live concert | 1993 | Westwood One | 75-125 |
| *(With the Ramones)* | | | |
| IN CONCERT (May 92) Live concert | 1992 | Westwood One | 20-40 |
| *(With Drivin' & Cryin')* | | | |

**DRAPER, RUSTY**
**7-Inch Extended Plays**

| Title | Yr | Label, Number | NM $ |
|-------|----|--------------|----|
| 60 SECOND SPECIAL | 195? | Mercury MEP-33 | 20 |
| *(4 songs including "Buzz, Buzz, Buzz," with hard cover sleeve)* | | | |

**DREAM ACADEMY, THE**
*Warner promo 45s $3 each*
**12-Inch Singles**

| Title | Yr | Label, Number | NM $ |
|-------|----|--------------|----|
| EDGE OF FOREVER, THE (same on both sides) | 1986 | Warner Bros. PRO-A-2439 | 8 |
| LIFE IN A NORTHERN TOWN (same on both sides) | 1985 | Warner Bros. PRO-A-2393 | 10 |
| THIS WORLD (same on both sides) | 1985 | Warner Bros. PRO-A-2361 | 8 |

**Albums**

| Title | Yr | Label, Number | NM $ |
|-------|----|--------------|----|
| DREAM ACADEMY | 1985 | Warner Bros. PRO-A-???? | 10 |
| *(Promo-only release)* | | | |

**DREAMERS, THE**
**45s**

| Title | Yr | Label, Number | NM $ |
|-------|----|--------------|----|
| WALKIN' MY BLUES AWAY | 1953 | Mercury 70019 | 75 |
| *(White promo label)* | | | |

**78s**

| Title | Yr | Label, Number | NM $ |
|-------|----|--------------|----|
| I'M GONNA HATE MYSELF IN THE MORNING | 1952 | Mercury 5843 | 100 |
| *(White promo label)* | | | |

**DREW, DAVID**
**45s**

| Title | Yr | Label, Number | NM $ |
|-------|----|--------------|----|
| GREEN EYED LADY | 1988 | MCA 53384 | 10 |
| *(With promo sleeve)* | | | |

**DREW, PATTI**
**Albums**

| Title | Yr | Label, Number | NM $ |
|-------|----|--------------|----|
| WILD IS LOVE | 1979 | Capitol 408 | 25 |
| *(Promo-only picture disc)* | | | |

**DRIFTERS, THE**
*Includes Clyde McPhatter, Ben E. King. Other Atlantic promo 45s $15-20 each; Bell promo 45s $4 each; Atco promo 45s by Ben E. King $5 each; Atlantic promo 45s by Ben E. King $3 each; Atlantic 12" promo singles by Ben E. King $5 each; Atlantic promo 45s by Clyde McPhatter $15-20 each; MGM, Mercury, Amy and Decca promo 45s by Clyde McPhatter $5 each*
**45s**

| Title | Yr | Label, Number | NM $ |
|-------|----|--------------|----|
| CHERRY CHOCOLATE TWIST | 1962 | Quality Checked ZTSC 82592 | 25 |
| *(Number is matrix number, special promo recording)* | | | |
| MONEY HONEY | 1955 | Atlantic 1006 | 60 |
| *(White promo label)* | | | |
| WHITE CHRISTMAS/THE BELLS OF ST. MARY'S | 1956 | Atlantic 1048 | 25 |
| *(White promo label)* | | | |
| WHITE CHRISTMAS Reissue promo | 196? | Atlantic 1048 | 10 |
| *(White/red promo label)* | | | |

**7-Inch Extended Plays**

| Title | Yr | Label, Number | NM $ |
|-------|----|--------------|----|
| I'LL TAKE YOU WHERE THE MUSIC'S PLAYING  Jukebox LLP | 196? | Atlantic 8113 | 50 |
| *(Issued with a hard cover)* | | | |
| SWING THE JINGLE Coca-Cola jingles | 1965 | Coca-Cola | 200 |
| *(Issued to radio stations)* | | | |

**RADIO SHOWS**
**Albums**

| Title | Yr | Label, Number | NM $ |
|-------|----|--------------|----|
| BBC TRANSCRIPTION DISC Ben E. King | 1987 | BBC Transcription | 200-300 |
| *(Live concert, with Los Lobos)* | | | |
| SOLID GOLD SCRAPBOOK (Sept 88) Ben E. King | 1988 | United Stations | 10 |
| *(From the 5-LP weekly set)* | | | |

| Title | Yr | Label, Number | NM $ |
|---|---|---|---|

**DRIVIN' & CRYIN'**
**RADIO SHOWS**
**Compact Discs**

| | | | |
|---|---|---|---|
| IN CONCERT (Mar 93) | 1993 | Westwood One | 20-30 |
| *(Live concert)* | | | |
| IN CONCERT (May 92) Live concert | 1992 | Westwood One | 20-30 |
| *(With Dramarama)* | | | |

**DU DROPPERS, THE**
**45s**

| | | | |
|---|---|---|---|
| DON'T ASK TO BE LONELY | 1957 | Groove 0021 | 50 |
| *(White promo label)* | | | |
| JUST WHISPER | 1955 | Groove 0013 | 50 |
| *(White promo label)* | | | |

**DUDADS, THE**
**45s**

| | | | |
|---|---|---|---|
| I HEARD YOU CALLED ME DEAR | 1955 | DeLuxe 6083 | 50 |
| *(White promo label)* | | | |

**DUDLEY, DAVE**
**45s**

| | | | |
|---|---|---|---|
| THE EAGLE (same on both sides) | 1981 | Sun 1166 | 4 |
| *(Unknown on stock copy)* | | | |

**DUKE, GEORGE**
**12-Inch Singles**

| | | | |
|---|---|---|---|
| 6 O'CLOCK (4 versions) | 1993 | Warner Bros. PRO-A-6463 | 8 |
| BROKEN GLASS (4 versions) | 1986 | Elektra ED 5162 | 8 |
| STRAIGHT FROM THE HEART/PLUCK | 1979 | Epic AE 595 | 10 |
| *(Red vinyl)* | | | |

**DUKES OF STRATOSPHEAR, THE**
*Also see XTC*
**12-Inch Singles**

| | | | |
|---|---|---|---|
| VANISHING GIRL (same on both sides) | 1987 | Geffen PRO-A-2840 | 6 |

**DUKES, THE**
**45s**

| | | | |
|---|---|---|---|
| TEARDROP EYES | 1956 | Imperial 5401 | 40 |
| *(Cream-colored promo label)* | | | |
| WINI BROWN | 1956 | Imperial 5415 | 40 |
| *(Cream-colored promo label)* | | | |

**DUNN, HOLLY**
**RADIO SHOWS**
**Compact Discs**

| | | | |
|---|---|---|---|
| COUNTRY MUSIC TIME | 1994 | | 15-25 |
| *(Music and interview)* | | | |

**DUPREES, THE**
*Coed white promo label 45s $12 each*

**DURAN DURAN**
*Includes Arcadia; Includes Andy Taylor.  Harvest yellow/green promo label 45s $12 each; Capitol white promo label 45s $8 each; Atlantic blue label promo 45s by Arcadia $6 each; Capitol promo label 45s by Arcadia $5 each; Capitol white label promo 45s by John Taylor $4 each; other Capitol 12" singles of group or solo artists, $12 each*
**12-Inch Singles**

| | | | |
|---|---|---|---|
| CARELESS MEMORIES//IS THERE ANYONE OUT THERE/GIRLS ON FILM | 1981 | Harvest SPRO-9662 | 30 |
| DO YOU BELIEVE IN SHAME (same on both sides) | 1989 | Capitol SPRO-79529 | 8 |
| GIRLS ON FILM (Club Version)/GIRLS ON FILM (Radio Version) | 1981 | Harvest SPRO-9680 | 20 |
| HUNGRY LIKE THE WOLF/LONELY IN YOUR NIGHTMARE/RIO | 1982 | Harvest SPRO-9786/7 | 20 |
| NEW MOON ON MONDAY (same on both sides) | 1983 | Capitol SPRO-9060 | 12 |
| PLANET EARTH (Club Version)/PLANET EARTH (Radio Version) | 1981 | Harvest SPRO-9636 | 30 |
| PRESIDENTIAL SUITE (3 remixes of Meet El Presidente)/ | 1987 | Capitol SPRO-79008/9 | 15 |
| SKIN TRADE (2 remixes) | | | |
| REFLEX, THE (LP)/(Single)/(Live)/NEW RELIGION (Live) | 1984 | Capitol SPRO-9093/4 | 15 |
| SAVE A PRAYER (4 versions) | 1984 | Capitol SPRO-9315 | 15 |
| TOO MUCH INFORMATION (4 mixes) | 1993 | Capitol SPRO-79269/70 | 15 |
| WHITE LINES (8 mixes) | 1994 | Capitol SPRO-79544 | 12 |

**45s**

| | | | |
|---|---|---|---|
| ELECTION DAY Arcadia | 1985 | Capitol PB-5501 | 10 |
| *(With custom label, same on both sides)* | | | |
| MEET EL PRESIDENTE | 1987 | Capitol PB-44001 | 10 |
| *(Black vinyl, this promo was issued in a poster fold-out sleeve)* | | | |
| MEET EL PRESIDENTE | 1987 | Capitol PB-44001 | 18 |
| *(White vinyl, issued in clear plastic sleeve, only the promo is white vinyl)* | | | |
| NOTORIOUS | 1986 | Capitol PB-5648 | 20 |
| *(Clear vinyl, issued in clear plastic sleeve, only the promo is clear vinyl)* | | | |
| SAVE A PRAYER White label promo-only release | 1984 | Capitol 7PRO 9330 | 15 |
| *(From the LP "Arena," the stock copy of this song was taken from the LP "Rio")* | | | |
| SKIN TRADE (same on both sides) | 1987 | Capitol 5670 | 20 |
| *(Red vinyl in heavy clear plastic sleeve)* | | | |

**Albums**

| | | | |
|---|---|---|---|
| DURAN GOES DUTCH | 1987 | Capitol 79097/79098 | 40 |
| *(Promo only, five live cuts recorded in Rotterdam)* | | | |

| Title | Yr | Label, Number | NM $ |
|-------|-----|---------------|------|
| **Compact Discs** | | | |
| ALL SHE WANTS IS | 1988 | Capitol DPRO-79456 | 8 |
| *(Promo-only CD single)* | | | |
| COME UNDONE | 1993 | Capitol DPRO-79660 | 8 |
| *(Promo CD single)* | | | |
| COME UNDONE | 1993 | Capitol DPRO-79711 | 8 |
| *(Promo CD single, different mix)* | | | |
| DECADE SAMPLER | 1990 | Capitol DPRO-79607 | 30 |
| *(Promo-only release)* | | | |
| DECADE/ORDINARY WORLD | 1993 | Capitol DPRO-79235 | 25 |
| *(Promo-only release)* | | | |
| I DON'T WANT YOUR LOVE | 1988 | Capitol DPRO-79246 | 8 |
| *(Promo-only CD single)* | | | |
| LIBERTY | 1990 | Capitol 94241 | 25 |
| *(Promo package with CD and cassette)* | | | |
| ORDINARY WORLD | 1993 | Capitol DPRO-79588 | 8 |
| *(Promo CD single)* | | | |
| PERFECT DAY | 1995 | Capitol DPRO-79599 | 8 |
| *(Promo CD single)* | | | |
| SERIOUS | 1990 | Capitol DPRO-79299 | 8 |
| *(Promo CD single)* | | | |
| TOO MUCH INFORMATION | 1993 | Capitol DPRO-79767 | 10 |
| *(First version of promo CD single)* | | | |
| TOO MUCH INFORMATION | 1993 | Capitol DPRO-79816 | 8 |
| *(Reservice of promo CD single)* | | | |
| TOUR SAMPLER  16 tracks | 1993 | Capitol DPRO-79786 | 30 |
| *(Promo-only release)* | | | |
| VIOLENCE OF SUMMER | 1990 | Capitol DPRO-79235 | 8 |
| *(Promo CD single)* | | | |
| VIOLENCE OF SUMMER | 1990 | Capitol DPRO-79288 | 8 |
| *(Promo CD single, different mix)* | | | |
| WHITE LINES | 1994 | Capitol DPRO-????? | 8 |
| *(Promo-only CD single)* | | | |
| **RADIO SHOWS** | | | |
| **Albums** | | | |
| BBC COLLEGE CONCERT HOUR (Sept 82) Live concert | 1982 | London Wavelength | 100-200 |
| *(Very rare live show)* | | | |
| BBC ROCK HOUR (Jan 83) Live concert | 1983 | London Wavelength | 100-200 |
| *(This show repeated in Jan 84)* | | | |
| BBC TRANSCRIPTION DISC Live concert | 1983 | BBC Transcription | 300-500 |
| *(Second show in the series is rarer)* | | | |
| BBC TRANSCRIPTION DISC Live concert | 1982 | BBC Transcription | 200-400 |
| *(Very rare series)* | | | |
| OFF THE RECORD (June 85) Profile of group | 1985 | Westwood One (2) | 20-30 |
| *(Music and interviews)* | | | |
| POP CONCERT (Dec 87) Live concert | 1987 | Westwood One (2) | 75-100 |
| *(Hard to find series)* | | | |
| RETRO ROCK (Apr 84) Live concert | 1984 | Clayton Webster (2) | 100-200 |
| *(Rare concert)* | | | |
| SOURCE CHRISTMAS COUNTDOWN (Dec 83) Live concert | 1983 | NBC Radio (2) | 125-200 |
| *(More limited than above show)* | | | |
| SOURCE SPECIAL (Sept 83) Live show and profile | 1983 | NBC Radio (2) | 100-175 |
| *(Hard to find)* | | | |
| SPOTLIGHT SPECIAL (Aug 84) | 1984 | ABC Radio (2) | 40-75 |
| *(Music and interviews)* | | | |
| SUPERSTAR CONCERT (June 84) Box set | 1984 | Westwood One (3) | 75-100 |
| *(Show repeated)* | | | |
| **Compact Discs** | | | |
| IN CONCERT-NU ROCK (Jan 94) Live concert | 1994 | Westwood One | 100-125 |
| *(New live concert)* | | | |
| ON THE EDGE (Oct 93) Music and interviews | 1993 | | 20-35 |
| *(With School of Fish)* | | | |
| **Reel-to-Reel Tapes** | | | |
| ON TOUR (80s) | 198? | | 75-125 |
| *(Live concert on three 7" reels)* | | | |

**DURY, IAN, AND THE BLOCKHEADS**
*Stiff/Epic promo 45s $6 each*

| | | | |
|-------|-----|---------------|------|
| **12-Inch Singles** | | | |
| HIT ME WITH YOUR RHYTHM STICK/CLEVER BASTARDS | 1978 | Stiff/Epic AE 819 | 12 |
| WAKE UP AND MAKE LOVE TO ME/BILLERICAY DICKIE | 1978 | Stiff SP 19 | 12 |
| **45s** | | | |
| REASONS FOR PROMOTION PT. 3 | 1979 | Stiff/Epic AE7 1190 | 10 |
| *(With Tom Couch and Eddie Gorodetsky)* | | | |
| **RADIO SHOWS** | | | |
| **Albums** | | | |
| BBC ROCK HOUR (Apr 81) Show #215 | 1981 | London Wavelength | 50-80 |
| *(This show was repeated)* | | | |
| BBC TRANSCRIPTION DISC | 1985 | BBC Transcription | 150-250 |
| *(Live concert)* | | | |

**DUVALL, HELEN**
*Other Challenge promo 45s $25 each*

| | | | |
|-------|-----|---------------|------|
| **45s** | | | |
| COMIN' OR GOIN' | 1958 | Challenge 1012 | 45 |
| *(White promo label)* | | | |

| **Title** | **Yr** | **Label, Number** | **NM $** |
|---|---|---|---|

**DYKE, MIKE**
**45s**

| | | | |
|---|---|---|---|
| A CHRISTMAS CARD (same on both sides) | 1986 | Southern Tracks 1073 | 4 |

**DYLAN, BOB**
**45s**

| | | | |
|---|---|---|---|
| BLOWIN' IN THE WIND/DON'T THINK TWICE, IT'S ALL RIGHT | 1963 | Columbia 42856 | 400 |
| *(Regular promo)* | | | |
| BLOWIN' IN THE WIND/DON'T THINK TWICE, IT'S ALL RIGHT | 1963 | Columbia JZSP 75606/7 | 300 |
| *("Special Album Excerpt" promo)* | | | |
| HURRICANE (mono/stereo) | 1975 | Columbia 10245 | 20 |
| *(Plays at 33 1/3 rpm; does not have "Special Rush Reservice" on label)* | | | |
| HURRICANE (mono/stereo) | 1975 | Columbia 10245 | 15 |
| *(Plays at 33 1/3 rpm; has "Special Rush Reservice" on label)* | | | |
| I WANT YOU | 1966 | Columbia 43683 | 50 |
| *(Red vinyl, white promo label)* | | | |
| I WANT YOU   Red label, black vinyl | 1966 | Masterworks 437 | 65 |
| *(Set of five singles with one Dylan, price is for all five)* | | | |
| JUST LIKE A WOMAN | 1966 | Columbia 43792 | 50 |
| *(Red vinyl, white label)* | | | |
| LIKE A ROLLING STONE | 1965 | Columbia 110939 | 65 |
| *(Red vinyl, white promo label)* | | | |
| LIKE A ROLLING STONE | 1965 | Columbia 110939 | 100 |
| *(Numbers on above two singles are matrix numbers; blue vinyl, white promo label)* | | | |
| LIKE A ROLLING STONE   6:00 version/one side | 1965 | Columbia 43346 | 45 |
| *(White promo label)* | | | |
| LIKE A ROLLING STONE   Edited version | 1965 | Columbia 43346 | 40 |
| *(Part 1 and part 2, each just over 3:00, promo-only versions, above two singles are black vinyl)* | | | |
| MIXED UP CONFUSION | 1963 | Columbia 42656 | 200 |
| *(White promo label)* | | | |
| ONE OF US MUST KNOW (SOONER OR LATER) (same on both sides) | 1966 | Columbia (no #) | 100 |
| POSITIVELY 4TH STREET | 1965 | Columbia 43389 | 150 |
| *(Red vinyl, white promo label)* | | | |
| POSITIVELY 4TH STREET/FROM A BUICK 6 | 1965 | Columbia 43389 | 120 |
| *(A-side contains alternate version of "Can You Please Crawl Out Your Window." Evidently must be heard to identify.)* | | | |
| RAINY DAY WOMEN #12 AND #35 | 1966 | Columbia 43592 | 150 |
| *(Red vinyl, white promo label)* | | | |
| SUBTERRANEAN HOMESICK BLUES   The Hitpack | 1965 | Columbia 43242 | 275 |
| *(Price is for three records plus picture sleeves, including "Subterranean," records are red vinyl with white promo labels)* | | | |
| SUBTERRANEAN HOMESICK BLUES (same on both sides) | 1965 | Columbia 43242 | 200 |
| *(Promo only on red vinyl, came separately from The Hiitpack also)* | | | |
| SUBTERRANEAN HOMESICK BLUES Promo picture sleeve | 1965 | Columbia 43242 | 1,500 |
| *(This promo-only sleeve is different than the sleeve from the Hitpack)* | | | |
| SUBTERRANEAN HOMESICK BLUES Regular promo | 1965 | Columbia 43242 | 45 |
| *(Black vinyl and white promo label, without picture sleeve)* | | | |
| WHAT'S IT ALL ABOUT (Oct 82) Public service show | 1982 | W. I. A. A. 645 | 40 |
| *(Flip side features the Rolling Stones)* | | | |

**7-Inch Extended Plays**

| | | | |
|---|---|---|---|
| BRINGING IT ALL BACK HOME Jukebox LLP | 1965 | Columbia 9128 | 150 |
| *(Price includes title strips and inserts)* | | | |
| DISCOTHEQUE DANCE MUSIC   Jukebox 10-EP set | 1965 | Columbia 105001 | 100 |
| *(Two of the 10 discs each have one Dylan song, "Outlaw Blues" and "On the Road")* | | | |
| I AIN'T GOT NO HOME   Picture sleeve | 1971 | Columbia AS 31 | 25 |
| *(Generic Playback sleeve with titles printed on, very scarce, tan color)* | | | |
| I AIN'T GOT NO HOME   Various artists Playback EP | 1971 | Columbia AS 31 | 75 |
| *(One Dylan song on the EP, promo-only release)* | | | |
| STEP LIVELY   Various artists | 1965 | Columbia 319 | 75 |
| *(Special-products release for Keds sneakers, one Dylan track)* | | | |

**Albums**

| | | | |
|---|---|---|---|
| ANOTHER SIDE OF BOB DYLAN | 1964 | Columbia 2193 | 500 |
| *(White promo label)* | | | |
| BASEMENT TAPES, THE | 1975 | Columbia 33682 (2) | 50 |
| *(White promo labels)* | | | |
| BEFORE THE FLOOD | 1974 | Asylum AB-201 | 50 |
| *(White label promo)* | | | |
| BLONDE ON BLONDE | 1966 | Columbia C2L-41 (2) | 750 |
| *(White promo labels)* | | | |
| BLOOD ON THE TRACKS | 1975 | Columbia 33235 | 50 |
| *(White promo label)* | | | |
| BLOOD ON THE TRACKS | 1975 | Columbia 33235 | 7,500 |
| *(Test pressing with alternate versions of most songs, record must be played to identify)* | | | |
| BOB DYLAN | 1967 | Warner/7 Arts 221567 | 1500 |
| *(Publisher's demo with 12 Dylan performances of then-unreleased songs from the "Basement Tapes" era)* | | | |
| BOB DYLAN   White label promo | 1962 | Columbia 1779 | 500 |
| *(First pressings have six Columbia "eyes" on the sides of the label)* | | | |
| BOB DYLAN AT BUDOKAN | 1979 | Columbia 36067 (2) | 40 |
| *(White promo labels)* | | | |
| BOB DYLAN VS A.J. WEBERMAN | 1977 | Folkways 5322 | 150 |
| *(Advance promo, stock copy worth $300; a poor sound quality phone conversation)* | | | |
| BOB DYLAN'S GREATEST HITS | 1967 | Columbia 2663/9463 | 100 |
| *(White promo label)* | | | |
| BRINGIN' IT ALL BACK HOME | 1965 | Columbia 2328 | 500 |
| *(White promo label)* | | | |
| CBS/WNEW INTERVIEW, THE | 1981 | Columbia AS-1259 | 25 |
| *(Promo-only release)* | | | |
| COLUMBIA APRIL DEMONSTRATION RECORD Various artists | 1962 | Columbia XSM 55655 | 2,000 |
| *(Sampler LP for salesmen, no cover; 3 edited tracks from Dylan's first album, which the label calls "Freewheeling.". The title was changed to "Bob Dylan" before release, "Freewheeling" was used as part of the title of his 2nd album)* | | | |

| **Title** | **Yr** | **Label, Number** | **NM $** |
|---|---|---|---|
| DESIRE | 1976 | Columbia 33893 | 40 |
| *(White promo label)* | | | |
| ELECTRIC LUNCH | 1982 | Columbia AS 1471 | 25 |
| *(Promo-only sampler)* | | | |
| FREEWHEELIN' BOB DYLAN  White promo label | 1963 | Columbia 1986 | 25,000 |
| *(First pressings include alternate cuts not listed on cover/label, "Let Me Die In My Footsteps," "Talkin' John Birch Blues," "Rocks and Gravel" and "Gamblin' Willie's Dead Man's Hand." Matrix numbers in dead wax end in "-1" plus a letter)* | | | |
| FREEWHEELIN' BOB DYLAN  White promo label | 1963 | Columbia 1986 | 2,500 |
| *(Promo timing strip on cover lists original tracks but record plays replacement tracks)* | | | |
| FREEWHEELIN' BOB DYLAN  White promo label | 1963 | Columbia 1986 | 750 |
| *(Promo label lists original tracks but plays the replacements)* | | | |
| FREEWHEELIN' BOB DYLAN  White promo label | 1963 | Columbia 1986 | 500 |
| *(Four alternate tracks have been replaced on the label and cover)* | | | |
| HARD RAIN | 1976 | Columbia 34349 | 40 |
| *(White promo label)* | | | |
| HIGHWAY 61 REVISITED | 1965 | Columbia 2389 | 400 |
| *(White promo label, alternate "From A Buick 6." Matrix number in dead wax on that side ends in "-1" plus a letter.)* | | | |
| HIGHWAY 61 REVISITED | 1965 | Columbia 2389 | 300 |
| *(White promo label, does not include alternate version of "From A Buick 6")* | | | |
| INFIDELS | 1983 | Columbia AS 1770 | 20 |
| *Promo-only sampler* | | | |
| JOHN WESLEY HARDING | 1968 | Columbia 2804 | 150 |
| *(White promo label)* | | | |
| PLANET WAVES | 1974 | Asylum 7E-1003 | 50 |
| *(White label promo)* | | | |
| RENALDO AND CLARA | 1976 | Columbia AS 422 | 50 |
| *(Promo-only sampler from the movie. Authentic copies have a sticker on a white cover; counterfeits have the title printed on the cover)* | | | |
| SAVED | 1980 | Columbia AS 798 | 30 |
| *(White promo label, promo-only sampler)* | | | |
| SLOW TRAIN COMING | 1979 | Columbia 36120 | 25 |
| *(White promo label)* | | | |
| STREET LEGAL | 1978 | Columbia 35453 | 30 |
| *(White promo label)* | | | |
| TIME PASSES SLOWLY | 1985 | Columbia CAS-2222 | 25 |
| *(Sampler from the 5-LP Biograph box set)* | | | |
| TIMES THEY ARE A-CHANGIN', THE | 1964 | Columbia 2105 | 500 |
| *(White promo label)* | | | |
| **Compact Discs** | | | |
| BOOTLEG SAMPLER, THE | 1991 | Columbia CSK 3081 | 30 |
| *(Promo-only sampler from The Bootleg Series box set)* | | | |
| DYLAN AND THE DEAD | 1989 | Columbia | 50 |
| *(Promo-only sampler from live LP of the same name)* | | | |
| FOREVER YOUNG | 1988 | Columbia | 50 |
| *(Promo-only sampler, 18 tracks, with picture cover)* | | | |
| KNOCKIN' ON HEAVEN'S DOOR | 1995 | Columbia CSK 7045 | 15 |
| *(Promo-only CD single from Unplugged set)* | | | |
| MOST OF THE TIME | 1993 | Columbia CSK 7332 | 30 |
| *(Promo-only CD single)* | | | |
| MY BACK PAGES | 1993 | Columbia CSK 5323 | 10 |
| *(Promo-only CD single, with many guest stars, from 30th Anniversary concert)* | | | |
| **RADIO SHOWS** | | | |
| **Albums** | | | |
| ALBUM GREATS  From the 53-LP set | 1979 | TM Special Products | 40-60 |
| *(Price is for the Dylan disc only)* | | | |
| DYLAN ON DYLAN (Nov 84) Profile | 1984 | Westwood One (5) | 350-600 |
| *(Very rare music and interviews)* | | | |
| DYLAN ON DYLAN (Oct 85) Repeat, edited version | 1985 | Westwood One (3) | 300-500 |
| *(Very rare music and interviews)* | | | |
| ROCK & RELIGION  Part 10 of a set, Show #131 | 1979 | Rock & Religion | 75-125 |
| *(Brown cover and brown label, very limited public service program)* | | | |
| ROCK AROUND THE WORLD | 1976 | RATW Show #91 | 75-100 |
| *(Music and interviews)* | | | |
| ROYALTY OF ROCK Music and interview | 1983 | | 40-75 |
| *(Grateful Dead is featured on the flip side)* | | | |
| SUPERSTAR CONCERT (Aug 86) Box set | 1986 | Westwood One (3) | 75-150 |
| *(Live concert with Tom Petty)* | | | |
| SUPERSTAR CONCERT (Dec 87) Box set, repeat | 1987 | Westwood One (3) | 75-125 |
| *(Another repeat with Tom Petty)* | | | |
| SUPERSTAR CONCERT (Feb 87) Box set, repeat | 1987 | Westwood One (3) | 75-140 |
| *(Repeat show with Tom Petty)* | | | |
| WORLD OF FOLK MUSIC  Host is Johnny Cash | 1967 | Social Security | 150-200 |
| *(Dylan is the guest and sings two songs)* | | | |
| **Compact Discs** | | | |
| BEATLE YEARS, THE (Mar 95) Bob Dylan | 1995 | Westwood One | 20-35 |
| *(Music and interviews, Bob Dylan is subject of this one show in the series)* | | | |
| BOOTLEG TAPES (May 91) | 1991 | Westwood One (3) | 300-500 |
| *(Mostly unreleased and live material)* | | | |
| THE STORY OF BOB DYLAN (July 92) Profile | 1992 | Unistar (2) | 30-60 |
| *(Music and interview)* | | | |
| UP CLOSE Profile of Dylan | 1989 | Media America (2) | 100-200 |
| *(Music and interviews)* | | | |
| **Reel-to-Reel Tapes** | | | |
| MEDIA AMERICA (90s) Bob Dylan | 199? | Media America | 300-400 |
| *(Live concert on two 10" reels)* | | | |
| THE 30th ANNIVERSARY FROM MADISON SQUARE GARDEN | 1992 | Media America | 200-375 |
| *(Live material on two 10" reels)* | | | |

| **Title** | **Yr** | **Label, Number** | **NM $** |
|---|---|---|---|

## E

### EAGLES

*Including Don Henley; Including Glenn Frey; Including Don Felder. Asylum white promo label 45s $6 each; Asylum promo 45s by Don Henley $4 each; Geffen promo 45s by Don Henley $3 each; MCA promo 45s by Glenn Frey $3 each; Any Don Felder promo 45 $3 each.*

**12-Inch Singles**

| Title | Yr | Label, Number | NM $ |
|---|---|---|---|
| PLEASE COME HOME FOR CHRISTMAS/FUNKY NEW YEAR | 1978 | Asylum 11402 | 20 |

*(Each side has the same two tracks, one side mono, the other stereo)*

**45s**

| Title | Yr | Label, Number | NM $ |
|---|---|---|---|
| HEARTACHE TONIGHT  Small center hole | 1979 | Asylum 12394 | 15 |

*(Rare, label does not identify as a promo)*

| | | | |
|---|---|---|---|
| LYIN' EYES | 1975 | Asylum 45279 | 10 |

*(Promo only, 3:58 and 6:20 versions)*

| | | | |
|---|---|---|---|
| WHAT'S IT ALL ABOUT (Mar 75) Public service show | 1975 | W. I. A. A. 256 | 25 |

*(Label misprint reads "Rick" Frey and Don Henley)*

| | | | |
|---|---|---|---|
| WHAT'S IT ALL ABOUT (Mar 77) Public service show | 1977 | W. I. A. A. 362 | 25 |

*(Flip side is Kris Kristofferson)*

**Compact Discs**

| Title | Yr | Label, Number | NM $ |
|---|---|---|---|
| GET OVER IT | 1995 | Geffen PRCD 4679-2 | 8 |

*(Promo CD single)*

| | | | |
|---|---|---|---|
| LEARN TO BE STILL | 1996 | Geffen PRCD 4713-2 | 8 |

*(Promo-only CD single, no stock copy in any format)*

| | | | |
|---|---|---|---|
| LOVE WILL KEEP US ALIVE | 1995 | Geffen PRCD 46??-2 | 8 |

*(Promo-only CD single, no stock copy in any format)*

| | | | |
|---|---|---|---|
| TOUR COLLECTION 10 tracks | 1994 | Elektra PRCD 8983 | 30 |

*(Promo-only release, exists with both cardboard sleeve and jewel box with insert, no difference in value)*

**RADIO SHOWS**

**Albums**

| Title | Yr | Label, Number | NM $ |
|---|---|---|---|
| BBC ROCK HOUR (Nov 83) Don Felder | 1983 | London Wavelength | 30-50 |

*(Music and interview profile of Felder, Thanksgiving show)*

| | | | |
|---|---|---|---|
| INNERVIEW (70s) Profile of Don Felder | 197? | Innerview | 10-15 |

*(Music and interviews)*

| | | | |
|---|---|---|---|
| KING BISCUIT FLOWER HOUR  A Conversation With... | 198? | DIR (5) | 125-200 |

*(Rare profile of the group)*

| | | | |
|---|---|---|---|
| OFF THE RECORD (90s) Profile of Don Henley | 199? | Westwood One (2) | 15-25 |

*(Repeated, music and interviews)*

| | | | |
|---|---|---|---|
| OFF THE RECORD (90s) Profile of Glenn Frey | 199? | Westwood One (2) | 10-20 |

*(Repeated, music and interviews)*

| | | | |
|---|---|---|---|
| SUPERSTAR CONCERT (80s) Live concert | 198? | Westwood One (3) | 25-40 |

*(Price is for a show featuring any Eagles solo artist)*

| | | | |
|---|---|---|---|
| THE EAGLES SPOTLIGHT SPECIAL Box set | 1980 | ABC Radio (2) | 50-100 |

*(Profile of the group, music and interviews)*

**Compact Discs**

| Title | Yr | Label, Number | NM $ |
|---|---|---|---|
| COMMON THREAD SPECIAL (Oct 93) Various artists | 1993 | (3) | 40-60 |

*(Music and interviews, Eagles songs)*

| | | | |
|---|---|---|---|
| IN THE STUDIO (Oct 92) Profile | 1992 | Media America | 15-25 |

*(Other LPs profiled in this series)*

| | | | |
|---|---|---|---|
| OFF THE RECORD (Aug 94) Profile of reunion | 1994 | Westwood One | 15-30 |

*(Music and interviews)*

| | | | |
|---|---|---|---|
| OFF THE RECORD (Aug 94) Profile of reunion | 1994 | Westwood One (2) | 25-50 |

*(Parts 1 and 2, music and interviews)*

| | | | |
|---|---|---|---|
| OFF THE RECORD (Dec 94) New careers | 1994 | Westwood One | 20-30 |

*(Music and interviews)*

| | | | |
|---|---|---|---|
| ON THE BORDER Profile of the Eagles | 1990 | (3) | 75-100 |

*(Music and interviews)*

| | | | |
|---|---|---|---|
| PINK CHAMPAGNE ON ICE (Nov 90) PROFILE | 1990 | (3) | 75-100 |

*(Music and interviews)*

### EARLE, STEVE

**12-Inch Singles**

| Title | Yr | Label, Number | NM $ |
|---|---|---|---|
| I AIN'T EVER SATISFIED (same on both sides) | 1987 | MCA 17327 | 6 |
| SOMEDAY/FEARLESS HEART/GOOD OL' BOY | 1986 | MCA 17129 | 6 |

### EARLS, THE

**45s**

| Title | Yr | Label, Number | NM $ |
|---|---|---|---|
| REMEMBER ME BABY/AMOR | 1965 | Old Town 1181 | 50 |

*(Assigned 1181 in error, as another record had been released with the number)*

### EARTH, WIND AND FIRE

*Columbia promo 45s $3 each; Columbia promo picture sleeves $2 each; Columbia promo CD singles $3 each*

**12-Inch Singles**

| Title | Yr | Label, Number | NM $ |
|---|---|---|---|
| AND LOVE GOES ON (Single Version) (LP Version) | 1980 | ARC AS 924 | 10 |
| LET ME TALK (Remix)/(Instrumental) | 1980 | ARC AS 853 | 10 |
| MOONWALK/WE'RE LIVING IN OUR OWN TIME | 1983 | Columbia AS 1842 | 8 |
| SIDE BY SIDE/SOMETHING SPECIAL | 1983 | Columbia AS 1648 | 8 |

**45s**

| Title | Yr | Label, Number | NM $ |
|---|---|---|---|
| LET'S GROOVE | 1981 | (Columbia) | 10 |

*(White label test pressing)*

**Albums**

| Title | Yr | Label, Number | NM $ |
|---|---|---|---|
| BEST OF EARTH WIND & FIRE | 1979 | Columbia 035647 | 25 |

*(Promo-only picture disc)*

| Title | Yr | Label, Number | NM $ |
|-------|-----|---------------|------|

**Compact Discs**
GREATEST HITS LIVE SPECIAL RADIO SAMPLER — 1996 — Pyramid PRCD 7212 — 15
*(Promo-only collection)*
**RADIO SHOWS**
**Albums**
ROBERT W. MORGAN (June 81) — 1981 — Watermark — 15-25
*(Music and interviews)*
ROBERT W. MORGAN (Mar 79) — 1979 — Watermark — 20-25
*(Music and interviews)*

**EASTON, ELLIOT**
*Also see The Cars.*
**12-Inch Singles**
SHAYLA (same on both sides) — 1985 — Elektra 5050 — 5
(WEARING DOWN) LIKE A WHEEL (same on both sides) — 1985 — Elektra ED 5033 — 5

**EASTON, SHEENA**
*EMI promo 45s $3 each*
**45s**
ETERNITY — 198? — EMI 7PRO 79035 — 10
*(Promo only, 4:14 and 3:50 versions)*
**RADIO SHOWS**
**Albums**
ROBERT W. MORGAN (Nov 81) — 1981 — Watermark — 10-20
*(Music and interviews)*
STAR SESSIONS (Oct 82) Live concert — 1982 — Westwood One (3) — 100-200
*(Very rare live concert)*
THE STORY OF SHEENA EASTON (Aug 89) Profile — 1989 — Unistar (2) — 15-25
*(Music and interviews)*

**EBONYS, THE**
**45s**
(CHRISTMAS AIN'T CHRISTMAS, NEW YEAR'S AIN'T NEW YEAR'S) WITHOUT THE ONE YOU LOVE (mono/stereo) — 1971 — Philadelphia Int'l. 3513 — 8

**EBSEN, BUDDY**
**45s**
BALLAD OF JED CLAMPETT/MAIL ORDER BRIDE — 1963 — MGM 13210 — 20
*(One of the stars of The Beverly Hillbillies sings its theme! Includes picture sleeve.)*

**ECHO AND THE BUNNYMEN**
*Sire promo 45s $5 each*
**12-Inch Singles**
BEDBUGS AND BALLYHOO (2 versions) — 1987 — Sire PRO-A-2977 — 6
BRING ON THE DANCING HORSES/BRING ON THE DANCING HORSES (7") — 1985 — Sire PRO-A-2398 — 10
NEW DIRECTION (same on both sides) — 1987 — Sire PRO-A-2774 — 6
SEVEN SEAS/SILVER — 1984 — Sire PRO-A-2164 — 12
**RADIO SHOWS**
**Albums**
BBC TRANSCRIPTION DISC  Live concert — 1988 — BBC Transcription — 200-300
*(Very rare series)*
**Compact Discs**
IN CONCERT-NU ROCK (Sept 93) — 1993 — Westwood One — 40-60
*(Live concert)*

**EDDIE AND THE EMPIRES**
**45s**
TEARS IN MY EYES — 1959 — Colpix 112 — 75
*(White promo label)*

**EDDY, DUANE**
*Includes Jimmy (Delbridge) and Duane; Al Casey; Mirriam Johnson.  .Elektra white promo label 45s $3 each; Capitol white promo label 45s $5 each; Stacy white promo label 45s by Al Casey (Combo) $10 each Other Jamie yellow promo label 45s $15 each (Jamie promo singles are rare); Gregmark promo 45s $12 each; Reprise white promo label 45s $10 each; Colpix white promo label 45s $10 each; Congress white promo label 45s $8 each.*
**45s**
DUANE EDDY Set of five stereo jukebox singles — 1960 — Jamie JLP 71-76 — 200
*(Price is for complete set)*
RAMROD — 1957 — Ford 500 — 125
*(Yellow promo label)*
SODA FOUNTAIN GIRL — 195? — Eb. X. Preston 212 — 125
*(By Jimmy and Duane)*
SURFIN' HOOTENANNY  Al Casey — 1960 — Stacy 962 — 25
*(Red vinyl, white promo label)*
THE LONELY ONE Yellow promo label — 1958 — Jamie DE-8 — 30
*(Special DJ release)*
YOUNG AND INNOCENT  Miriam Johnson — 1960 — Jamie 1181 — 12
*(She became Mrs. Duane Eddy, Eddy plays guitar)*

**EDMUNDS, DAVE**
*Member of Rockpile; also see Rockpile. Columbia white promo label 45s $3 each; Columbia white promo label LPs $8 each; Capitol promo CD singles $3 each*
**12-Inch Singles**
DO YOU WANT TO DANCE (same on both sides) — 1985 — Columbia CAS 2077 — 6

| Title | Yr | Label, Number | NM $ |
|---|---|---|---|
| SLIPPING AWAY (same on both sides) | 1982 | Columbia AS 1660 | 8 |
| SOMETHING ABOUT YOU (same on both sides) | 1984 | Columbia AS 1911 | 6 |
| THE WANDERER/DAVE EDMUNDS MEGA-MIX | 1986 | Columbia CAS 02598 | 6 |
| **45s** | | | |
| CLOSER TO THE FLAME (same on both sides) | 1990 | Capitol 7PRO-79973 | 10 |
| **7-Inch Extended Plays** | | | |
| NICK LOWE AND DAVE EDMUNDS SING THE EVERLY BROTHERS | 1980 | Columbia AE7 1219 | 15 |
| *(Bonus record included with first pressings of "Seconds of Pleasure" by Rockpile; includes picture sleeve)* | | | |
| **Albums** | | | |
| COLLEGE NETWORK INTERVIEW | 1978 | Atlantic PR-320 | 50 |
| *(Promo-only interview)* | | | |
| **RADIO SHOWS** | | | |
| **Albums** | | | |
| BBC ROCK HOUR (Aug 83) Live concert | 1983 | London Wavelength | 75-125 |
| *(Rare live concert)* | | | |
| KING BISCUIT FLOWER HOUR (June 82) Live concert | 1982 | DIR/ABC (2) | 60-100 |
| *(With Dwight Twilley)* | | | |
| KING BISCUIT FLOWER HOUR (June 83) Live concert | 1983 | DIR/ABC (2) | 40-75 |
| *(With Robert Hazard)* | | | |
| KING BISCUIT FLOWER HOUR (Mar 87) Live concert | 1987 | DIR (2) | 40-75 |
| *(With Jason & the Scorchers)* | | | |
| **Compact Discs** | | | |
| IN CONCERT (Dec 94) | 1994 | Westwood One | 40-75 |
| *(Live concert)* | | | |
| IN THE STUDIO (90s) Profile of an album | 199? | Media America | 15-20 |
| *(Other LPs profiled in series)* | | | |
| KING BISCUIT FLOWER HOUR  Live concert | 1989 | DIR | 40-75 |
| *(Repeated)* | | | |
| KING BISCUIT FLOWER HOUR (May 90) Live concert | 1990 | DIR (2) | 75-125 |
| *(Special two part concert)* | | | |

## EITZEL, MARK
**45s**

| Title | Yr | Label, Number | NM $ |
|---|---|---|---|
| FREE OF HARM/HELIUM//MISSION ROCK RESORT/FRESH SCREWDRIVER | 1997 | Warner Bros. PRO-S-9058 | 5 |
| *("Soil X Samples" 25; small hole)* | | | |

## EL DORADOS, THE
*Other Vee Jay white promo label 45s $25-40 each*
**45s**

| Title | Yr | Label, Number | NM $ |
|---|---|---|---|
| LIGHTS ARE LOW | 1958 | Vee Jay 302 | 50 |
| *(White promo label)* | | | |
| 3 REASONS WHY | 1958 | Vee Jay 263 | 75 |
| *(White promo label)* | | | |

## ELECTRIC BOYS
**RADIO SHOWS**
**Compact Discs**

| Title | Yr | Label, Number | NM $ |
|---|---|---|---|
| IN CONCERT (Nov 92) Live concert | 1992 | Westwood One (2) | 25-50 |
| *(With Mr. Big and Hardline)* | | | |

## ELECTRIC LIGHT ORCHESTRA
*Other United Artists (Jet) promo 45s $4 each; MCA white promo label 45s $4 each; Other Columbia (Jet) promo 45s by Jeff Lynne $4 each; Virgin white promo label 45s by Jeff Lynne $3 each ELO; Includes Jeff Lynne*
**45s**

| Title | Yr | Label, Number | NM $ |
|---|---|---|---|
| DOIN' THAT CRAZY THING  Jeff Lynne | 198? | Jet AE7 1220 | 12 |
| *(7" single, white label, small center hole)* | | | |
| I'M ALIVE Dark blue promo label | 1980 | MCA 41246 | 10 |
| *(Issued with a "Xanadu" picture sleeve)* | | | |
| TELEPHONE LINE Yellow promo label, green vinyl | 1977 | United Artists 1000 | 18 |
| *(The stock copy of this record is also green vinyl)* | | | |
| WHAT'S IT ALL ABOUT (Aug 77) Public service show | 1977 | W. I. A. A. 384 | 30 |
| *(Flip side is the Who)* | | | |
| WHAT'S IT ALL ABOUT (June 76) Public service show | 1976 | W. I. A. A. 321 | 25 |
| *(Flip side is Three Dog Night)* | | | |
| WHAT'S IT ALL ABOUT (Nov 81) Public service show | 1981 | W. I. A. A. 602 | 20 |
| *(Flip side is Doc Severinsen)* | | | |
| WHAT'S IT ALL ABOUT (Oct 78) Public service show | 1978 | W. I. A. A. 442 | 30 |
| *(Flip side is the Coasters)* | | | |
| **Albums** | | | |
| FACE THE MUSIC | 1975 | United Artists 546 | 25 |
| *(Banded for radio play)* | | | |
| NEW WORLD RECORD, A | 1977 | Jet/United Artists 679 | 20 |
| *(Green vinyl, promo only)* | | | |
| OLE ELO | 1976 | United Artists SP-123 | 50 |
| *(Gold vinyl promo with generic cover)* | | | |
| OLE ELO | 1976 | United Artists SP-123 | 80 |
| *(Red, blue or white vinyl promos with generic cover)* | | | |
| OLE ELO | 1976 | United Artists SP-123 | 100 |
| *(Gold vinyl, cover similar to the released version except for the single line "Ole Elo" – no "Electric Light Orchestra" underneath – at the top of the front cover)* | | | |
| OUT OF THE BLUE | 1977 | Jet/United Artists 823 (2) | 30 |
| *(Blue vinyl discs)* | | | |
| XANADU 10" promo-only picture disc | 1980 | MCA 2315 | 250 |

| Title | Yr | Label, Number | NM $ |
|-------|-----|---------------|------|
| **RADIO SHOWS** | | | |
| **Albums** | | | |
| ABC SPOTLIGHT SPECIAL | 1980 | ABC Radio (2) | 50-100 |
| *(Live concert)* | | | |
| ALISON STEELE Profile | 1980 | | 40-60 |
| *(Music and interviews)* | | | |
| BBC ROCK HOUR (Sept 81) Live concert | 1981 | London Wavelength | 60-100 |
| *(Rare early material)* | | | |
| BBC TRANSCRIPTION DISC Live concert | 1973 | BBC Transcription | 200-400 |
| *(With Wolf)* | | | |
| BBC TRANSCRIPTION DISC Live concert | 1974 | BBC Transcription | 400-600 |
| *(With Ralph McTell)* | | | |
| IN CONCERT (Sept 90) Live concert | 1990 | Westwood One (2) | 50-80 |
| *(Newer live concert material)* | | | |
| LEGENDS OF ROCK (June 88) Profile | 1988 | NBC Radio (2) | 20-35 |
| *(Music and interviews)* | | | |
| RETRO ROCK (Sept 81) Profile of group | 1981 | Clayton Webster (2) | 60-100 |
| *(Some live material)* | | | |
| ROBERT W. MORGAN Profile of group | 1977 | Watermark | 10-15 |
| *(Music and interview)* | | | |
| ROCK AROUND THE WORLD (Apr 77) Live material | 1977 | RATW (2) | 100-200 |
| *(Rare early live material)* | | | |
| **Compact Discs** | | | |
| BBC CLASSIC TRACKS (July 91) | 1991 | | 30-45 |
| *(Various early BBC classic tracks)* | | | |
| IN CONCERT (May 92) Live material | 1992 | Westwood One | 40-75 |
| *(Same show, in CD format)* | | | |
| | | | |
| **ELECTRIC PRUNES, THE** | | | |
| *Other Reprise promo 45s $12 each; Reprise promo LPs $30 each* | | | |
| **45s** | | | |
| HELP US | 1968 | Reprise PRO-305 | 40 |
| *(White label promo-only release)* | | | |
| SANCTUS | 1968 | Reprise PRO-277 | 50 |
| *(White label promo-only release)* | | | |
| | | | |
| **ELEGANTS, THE** | | | |
| **45s** | | | |
| LITTLE STAR | 1958 | Apt 25005 | 40 |
| *(White label promo of their only big hit)* | | | |
| | | | |
| **ELFMAN, DANNY** | | | |
| **12-Inch Singles** | | | |
| GRATITUDE (3 versions) | 1984 | MCA L33-1249 | 12 |
| GRATITUDE (REMIX) (same on both sides) | 1985 | MCA L33-1260 | 10 |
| | | | |
| **ELGART, LES** | | | |
| **7-Inch Extended Plays** | | | |
| MINUTE MAN, THE | 1958 | RCA Victor SP-45-59 | 15 |
| *(Four songs with promo-only sleeve)* | | | |
| **Albums** | | | |
| BANDSTAND BOOGIE | 195? | Columbia | 40 |
| *(Title of LP unknown, white label promo, contains the original Bandstand theme)* | | | |
| | | | |
| **ELGINS, THE** | | | |
| **45s** | | | |
| MADEMOISELLE | 1955 | MGM 12670 | 60 |
| *(Yellow promo label)* | | | |
| | | | |
| **ELLIOTT, BILL, AND THE ELASTIC OZ BAND** | | | |
| **45s** | | | |
| GOD SAVE US/DO THE OZ | 1971 | Apple P-1835 | 25 |
| *Has black star on A-side and unsliced apple on both sides* | | | |
| | | | |
| **ELY, JOE** | | | |
| **12-Inch Singles** | | | |
| LORD OF THE HIGHWAY (same on both sides) | 1987 | Hightone 1001 | 6 |
| MY BABY THINKS SHE'S FRENCH (same on both sides) | 1987 | Hightone 1002 | 5 |
| WHAT'S SHAKIN' TONIGHT (same on both sides) | 1984 | South Coast L33 1168 | 6 |
| **RADIO SHOWS** | | | |
| **Cassettes** | | | |
| AUSTIN ENCORE (90s) Live Concert | 199? | Mainstreet Productions | 40-75 |
| *(Issued on cassette tape)* | | | |
| | | | |
| **EMERSON, LAKE AND PALMER** | | | |
| *Other Atlantic promo singles by ELP or Greg Lake $6 each; Chrysalis white promo label 45s by Greg Lake $3 each; Mercury white promo label 45s by Keith Emerson (Nice) $10 each; Mercury white promo label 2LPs by Keith Emerson $18 each Includes Greg Lake; I* | | | |
| **45s** | | | |
| BRAIN SALAD SURGERY White promo label | 1974 | Manticore 2003 | 10 |
| EXCERPTS FROM MAR Y SOL White promo label | 1972 | Atlantic PR 176 | 40 |
| *(Live versions of "Take A Pebble/Lucky Man" with two other artists on the flip side; this record has a small center hole and a picture sleeve)* | | | |
| FROM THE BEGINNING Long/short versions | 1972 | Cotillion 44158 | 10 |

| Title | Yr | Label, Number | NM $ |
|---|---|---|---|
| LUCKY MAN Long/short versions | 1971 | Cotillion 44106 | 15 |
| *(Rarest version of this classic; there is also a stereo/mono 3:33 promo version of "Lucky Man" of lesser value)* | | | |
| **Albums** | | | |
| ON TOUR WITH EMERSON, LAKE AND PALMER | 1977 | Atlantic PR 281 | 40 |
| WORKS VOLUME 1 | 1977 | Atlantic PR 277 | 15 |
| *(Promo-only sampler)* | | | |
| **Compact Discs** | | | |
| SELECTIONS FROM RETURN OF THE MANTICORE | 1993 | Victory SACD 757 | 20 |
| *(Promo-only sampler from box set)* | | | |
| **RADIO SHOWS** | | | |
| **Albums** | | | |
| IN CONCERT (Nov 86) Live concert | 1986 | Westwood One (2) | 100-150 |
| *(Rare live concert)* | | | |
| KING BISCUIT FLOWER HOUR (Dec 81) Live concert | 1981 | DIR/ABC (2) | 150-350 |
| *(Classic concert)* | | | |
| LEGENDS OF ROCK (June 88) Profile | 1988 | NBC Radio (2) | 25-40 |
| *(Music and interviews)* | | | |
| OFF THE RECORD (Sept 86) Profile of the group | 1986 | Westwood One (2) | 20-30 |
| *(Music and interview)* | | | |
| PIONEERS IN ROCK (Feb 86) Profile of the group | 1986 | DIR (2) | 50-80 |
| *(Music and interviews, some live material)* | | | |
| RETRO ROCK (Sept 81) Live concert | 1981 | Clayton Webster | 75-100 |
| *(Rare early live concert)* | | | |
| SUPERGROUPS (July 82) Live concert | 1982 | DIR (3) | 75-100 |
| *(With Sammy Hagar)* | | | |
| **Compact Discs** | | | |
| KING BISCUIT FLOWER HOUR (Mar 88) Live concert | 1988 | DIR | 50-75 |
| *(Repeated several times)* | | | |
| ON TOUR IN AMERICA (July 92) Live concert | 1992 | Album Network | 100-150 |
| *(Very scarce live concert)* | | | |
| **Reel-to-Reel Tapes** | | | |
| KING BISCUIT FLOWER HOUR (May 78) Live concert | 1978 | DIR/ABC (2) | 100-150 |
| *(On two reels)* | | | |
| | | | |
| **EMF** | | | |
| **12-Inch Singles** | | | |
| IT'S YOU (5 versions) | 1992 | EMI SPRO 04669 | 10 |
| LIES (3 mixes) | 1990 | EMI SPRO 04774/81 | 10 |
| LIES (Head the Ball Mix) | 1991 | EMI SPRO 04810 | 30 |
| *(Promo-only pressing on clear vinyl; 250 made)* | | | |
| **45s** | | | |
| LIES/STRANGE BREW (LIVE) | 1991 | (EMI) 7PRO 4786 | 12 |
| *(Maroon label, small hole, no label name on label)* | | | |
| | | | |
| **EMMITT, RICK** | | | |
| **RADIO SHOWS** | | | |
| **Albums** | | | |
| IN CONCERT (Apr 91) | 1991 | Westwood One (2) | 25-50 |
| *(Live concert)* | | | |
| IN CONCERT (Feb 92) Live concert | 1992 | Westwood One (2) | 25-50 |
| *(With Lita Ford)* | | | |
| | | | |
| **ENGLISH BEAT, THE** | | | |
| *Sire promo 45s $5 each* | | | |
| **12-Inch Singles** | | | |
| TEARS OF A CLOWN/HANDS OFF...SHE'S MINE/TWIST AND CRAWL | 1980 | Sire PRO-A-874 | 15 |
| TOO NICE TO TALK TO/MIRROR IN THE BATHROOM/WALK AWAY | 1981 | Sire PRO-A-988 | 12 |
| **RADIO SHOWS** | | | |
| **Albums** | | | |
| BBC COLLEGE CONCERT (Jan 83) | 1983 | London Wavelength | 25-50 |
| *(Live concert)* | | | |
| NBC SOURCE (Dec 82) Music and interviews | 1982 | NBC Radio (2) | 50-75 |
| *(Christmas countdown with the Go-Gos)* | | | |
| NBC SOURCE (May 83) Music and interviews | 1983 | NBC Radio (2) | 20-35 |
| *(With Music Youth)* | | | |
| | | | |
| **ENGLISH ROCK ENSEMBLE, THE** | | | |
| **RADIO SHOWS** | | | |
| **Albums** | | | |
| BBC TRANSCRIPTION DISC Live concert | 1976 | BBC Transcription | 750-1,250 |
| *(With Rick Wakeman)* | | | |
| | | | |
| **ENIGMA** | | | |
| **12-Inch Singles** | | | |
| AGE OF LONELINESS (3 mixes) | 1994 | Charisma 14174 | 8 |
| MEA CULPA PT. 2 (4 versions) | 1990 | Charisma 1647 | 8 |
| SADENESS (4 versions) | 1990 | Charisma 1591 | 8 |
| | | | |
| **ENO, BRIAN** | | | |
| **45s** | | | |
| THE LION SLEEPS TONIGHT (mono/stereo) | 1975 | Island 036 | 15 |

| Title | Yr | Label, Number | NM $ |
|---|---|---|---|

**Albums**
MUSIC FOR AIRPLAY — 1981 — Jem ENO DJ — 50
*(Promo-only 10-track sampler)*
**Compact Discs**
WORDS AND MUSIC — 1991 — Opal PRO-CD-5886 — 40
*(Promo-only release)*

## ENO, BRIAN, AND DAVID BYRNE
**12-Inch Singles**
THE JEZEBEL SPIRIT/AMERICA IS WAITING/HELP ME SOMEBODY — 1981 — Sire PRO-A-953 — 6

## ENTWISTLE, JOHN
**Albums**
WHO'S OX — 1975 — Track L33-1926 — 50
*(Promo-only sampler)*

## ENUFF Z'NUFF
**RADIO SHOWS**
**Albums**
IN CONCERT (July 90) Live concert — 1990 — Westwood One (2) — 20-35
*(With Little Caeser)*

## ENYA
*Warner Bros./Reprise promo CD singles $3-5 each*
**Compact Discs**
EXILE — 1988 — Geffen PRO-CD-4240 — 7
*(Promo-only CD single)*
ORINOCO FLOW (SAIL AWAY) — 1988 — Geffen PRO-CD-3389 — 8
*(Her most famous song, promo-only CD single)*

## ERASURE
*Sire promo 45s $4 each; Other Sire or Mute promo CD singles $4-6 each*
**12-Inch Singles**

| Title | Yr | Label, Number | NM $ |
|---|---|---|---|
| BLUE SAVANNAH (3 versions) | 1989 | Sire PRO-A-3601 | 18 |
| CHAINS OF LOVE (6 mixes) | 1988 | Sire PRO-A-3186 | 15 |
| CHAINS OF LOVE (7" Remix)/CHAINS OF LOVE (Long Remix) | 1988 | Sire PRO-A-3151 | 15 |
| I LOVE SATURDAY (4 remixes) | 1994 | Mute/Elektra 5716 | 15 |
| LITTLE RESPECT, A (6 versions) | 1988 | Sire PRO-A-3365 | 15 |
| STOP (12" Version)/STOP (7" Version) | 1988 | Sire PRO-A-3471 | 15 |

**45s**
SHE WON'T BE HOME (LONELY CHRISTMAS)/ — 1988 — Sire PRO-S-3409 — 12
GOD REST YE MERRY GENTLEMEN
*(Released with promo insert – add 50%; no picture sleeve)*
**Albums**
ABBA-ESQUE (REMIXES) — 1992 — Mute/Elektra 5621 — 25
*(Promo-only vinyl; remixes of 4-song EP; no special jacket)*
**Compact Discs**
CHAINS OF LOVE — 1987 — Sire PRO-CD-3140 — 20
*(Very early promo CD single)*
LITTLE RESPECT, A — 1988 — Sire PRO-CD-3252 — 10
*(Promo-only CD single)*
**RADIO SHOWS**
**Albums**
BBC TRANSCRIPTION DISC Live concert — 1987 — BBC Transcription — 350-500
*(Very rare concert in a rare series)*
**Compact Discs**
IN CONCERT-NU ROCK (July 93) Live concert — 1993 — Westwood One (2) — 25-50
*(Newly recorded live concert)*
ON THE EDGE (July 94) Music and interviews — 1994 — Westwood One — 20-30
*(With Church and Velocity Girl)*

## ESCAPE CLUB, THE
*Atlantic promo 45s $3 each; Atlantic promo CD singles $2-4 each*
**RADIO SHOWS**
**Compact Discs**
KING BISCUIT FLOWER HOUR (Mar 89) Live concert — 1989 — DIR — 15-25
*(With Hothouse Flowers)*

## ESQUERITA
*Capitol promo 45s $40-75 each*
**Albums**
ESQUERITA — 1959 — Capitol 1186 — 300
*(Very rare as a promo or stock copy)*

## ESTEFAN, GLORIA
*Epic white promo label 45s $2-3 each; Epic promo 12" singles $8 each; Epic promo CD singles $3-6 each; Includes Miami Sound Machine.*
**Compact Discs**
CUTS BOTH WAYS AUDIO CUE CARD — 1989 — Epic ESK 1707 — 30
*(Promo-only interview disc)*
HITS  15 tracks — 1994 — Epic — 25
*(Promo-only greatest hits collection)*

| Title | Yr | Label, Number | NM $ |
|---|---|---|---|
| **RADIO SHOWS** | | | |
| **Albums** | | | |
| THE STORY OF GLORIA ESTEFAN (Aug 89) Profile of Miami Sound Machine | 1989 | Unistar (2) | 35-50 |
| *(Music and interviews)* | | | |
| **Compact Discs** | | | |
| THE STORY OF GLORIA ESTEFAN (Jan 92) Profile of Miami Sound Machine | 1992 | Unistar | 25-50 |
| *(Music and interview, the CD format of same show)* | | | |

## ETHERIDGE, MELISSA
*Island promo 45s $3 each; Island 12" singles $8-12 each; Island promo CD singles not listed $6-8 each.*

| Title | Yr | Label, Number | NM $ |
|---|---|---|---|
| **Compact Discs** | | | |
| BLOCKBUSTER SAMPLER | 1994 | Island | 50 |
| *(Promo-only sampler CD)* | | | |
| HAPPY XMAS (WAR IS OVER) | 1995 | Island | 25 |
| *(Promo-only issue of her live version of the John Lennon classic)* | | | |
| LIVE | 1988 | Island PR 2555 | 20 |
| *(Promo-only release)* | | | |
| LIVE AT THE RECORD PLANT | 1992 | Island | 25 |
| *(Promo-only release)* | | | |
| LIVE AT THE RECORD PLANT (Mar 92) | 1992 | Island | 50-100 |
| *(Live concert)* | | | |
| **RADIO SHOWS** | | | |
| **Albums** | | | |
| IN CONCERT (Sept 88) Live concert | 1988 | Westwood One (2) | 50-100 |
| *(With John Hiatt, rare early concert)* | | | |
| **Compact Discs** | | | |
| IN CONCERT (Sept 93) Live concert | 1993 | Westwood One (2) | 50-100 |
| *(Same as above only solo and some new live tracks added)* | | | |
| LIVE AT THE RECORD PLANT (90s) | 199? | Album Network | 50-75 |
| *(Rare live concert)* | | | |
| OFF THE RECORD (Sept 94) Profile | 1994 | Westwood One | 20-35 |
| *(Music and interviews)* | | | |
| ROCK AND THE ENVIRONMENT Various artists | 1993 | | 50-75 |
| *(Melissa is the host of this music and interview show)* | | | |
| SUPERSTAR CONCERT (Sept 93) Live concert | 1993 | Westwood One | 40-75 |
| *(Live concert with Melissa Etheridge)* | | | |
| UP CLOSE  Profile | 1993 | Media America | 50-100 |
| *(Some live cuts, show repeated in 1994)* | | | |
| **Reel-to-Reel Tapes** | | | |
| MONTREAL CONCERT (Mar 94) Live concert | 1994 | Album Network | 150-300 |
| *(Very rare, released on two reels)* | | | |

## EUROPE
*Epic white promo label 45s $3 each*

| Title | Yr | Label, Number | NM $ |
|---|---|---|---|
| **RADIO SHOWS** | | | |
| **Albums** | | | |
| IN CONCERT (June 87) Live concert | 1987 | Westwood One (2) | 40-60 |
| *(With Robert Cray)* | | | |
| KING BISCUIT FLOWER HOUR (June 87) Live concert | 1987 | DIR (2) | 40-60 |
| *(This group is very limited in live concerts available)* | | | |

## EURYTHMICS
*Epic promo 45s by the Tourists (Pre-Eurythmics) $8 each; RCA cream-colored promo singles $5 each; Any Annie Lennox promo CD singles $4-6 each Includes listings of Annie Lennox*

| Title | Yr | Label, Number | NM $ |
|---|---|---|---|
| **12-Inch Singles** | | | |
| HERE COMES THE RAIN AGAIN (same on both sides) | 1984 | RCA JD-13711 | 12 |
| *(Promo-only 12-inch single)* | | | |
| LOVE YOU LIKE A BALL AND CHAIN (same on both sides) | 1985 | RCA JD-14143 | 8 |
| *(Promo-only 12-inch single)* | | | |
| MISSIONARY MAN (same on both sides) | 1986 | RCA JD-14389 | 6 |
| *(Promo-only 12-inch single)* | | | |
| SEXCRIME (NINETEEN EIGHTY-FOUR) (same on both sides) | 1984 | RCA JR-13961 | 12 |
| *(Promo-only 12-inch single)* | | | |
| THORN IN MY SIDE (same on both sides) | 1986 | RCA 5771 | 8 |
| WHEN TOMORROW COMES (same on both sides) | 1986 | RCA 5726-1-RDAA | 8 |
| WHO'S THAT GIRL? (LIVE) (same on both sides) | 1984 | RCA JR-13837 | 12 |
| WHO'S THAT GIRL? (Long)/WHO'S THAT GIRL? (Short) | 1984 | RCA JD-13803 | 10 |
| *(Promo-only 12-inch single)* | | | |
| WOULD I LIE TO YOU? (same on both sides) | 1985 | RCA JD-14080 | 8 |
| *(Promo-only 12-inch single)* | | | |
| YOU HAVE PLACED A CHILL IN MY HEART (same on both sides) | 1987 | RCA 6986 | 6 |
| **45s** | | | |
| MISSIONARY MAN | 1986 | RCA | 10 |
| *(White label test pressing)* | | | |
| YOU HAVE PLACED A CHILL IN MY HEART (Chill Mix) | 1988 | RCA 7615-7-RAA | 25 |
| *(Most of the value is for the very rare promo-only picture sleeve)* | | | |
| **Albums** | | | |
| ROUGH AND TOUGH -- LIVE AT THE ROXY | 1986 | RCA Victor DJL1-5707 | 30 |
| *(Promo-only 4-song live album)* | | | |
| **Compact Discs** | | | |
| ACOUSTIC EURYTHMICS | 1989 | Arista ASCD-9915 | 15 |
| *(Promo-only release)* | | | |
| ROUGH & TOUGH AT THE ROXY Promo-only release | 1986 | RCA 5629-2-RDJ | 50 |
| *(Some are live tracks; CD version of vinyl EP)* | | | |

| Title | Yr | Label, Number | NM $ |
|-------|-----|---------------|------|

**RADIO SHOWS**
**Albums**

| | | | |
|-------|-----|---------------|------|
| ANNIE LENNOX (Nov 86) Annie Lennox | 1986 | DIR (3) | 75-100 |
| *(Rare live special concert)* | | | |
| IN CONCERT (June 85) Live concert | 1985 | Westwood One (2) | 75-150 |
| *(With John Parr)* | | | |
| MUSIC OF THE 80S (Aug 84) Music and interviews | 1984 | DIR (2) | 100-150 |
| *(Annie Lennox, Cyndi Lauper and Madonna)* | | | |
| NBC SOURCE (June 84) Profile | 1984 | NBC Radio (2) | 35-60 |
| *(Music and interviews)* | | | |
| PENTHOUSE/OMNI COLLEGE ROCK CONCERT (Oct 83) | 1983 | Penthouse/Omni | 50-100 |
| *(Rare early concert)* | | | |
| SUPERSTARS OF ROCK (80s) Various artists | 198? | (3) | 30-50 |
| *(Included are some tracks by the Eurythmics)* | | | |

**EURYTHMICS AND ARETHA FRANKLIN**
**12-Inch Singles**

| | | | |
|-------|-----|---------------|------|
| SISTERS ARE DOIN' IT FOR THEMSELVES (same on both sides) | 1985 | RCA JR-14206 | 8 |
| *B-side by Eurythmics* | | | |

**EVANS, PAUL**

*Guaranteed, Decca, Atco, RCA and Carlton promo 45s $8 each; Kapp, Columbia and Laurie promo singles $5 each; other Guaranteed promo LPs $50 each; other promo LPs $15-25 each*

**Albums**

| | | | |
|-------|-----|---------------|------|
| FABULOUS TEENS | 1960 | Guaranteed 1000 | 75 |
| *(White promo label)* | | | |

**EVERLY BROTHERS, THE**

*Includes Phil Everly. Curb white promo label 45s by Phil Everly $3 each; Elektra white promo label 45s by Phil Everly $3 each; Other Warner promo LPs $25 each Cadence white promo label 45s 1200,1300 series $25 each; Cadence white promo label 45s after 1400 $18 each; Warner white/red promo label 45s in 5000 series $12 each; Warner white promo label 45s in 7000 series $8 each; RCA cream or yellow promo label 45s $10 each; Mercury black promo 45s $4 each; Pye (USA) white promo label 45s by Phil Everly $4 each.*

**45s**

| | | | |
|-------|-----|---------------|------|
| CATHY'S CLOWN Gold vinyl, gold promo label | 1960 | Warner Bros. 5151 | 100 |
| *(Only the promo is colored vinyl)* | | | |
| EBONY EYES Gold vinyl, gold promo label | 1961 | Warner Bros. 5199 | 100 |
| *(There also are regular black vinyl promo versions of these three singles)* | | | |
| PASS THE CHICKEN AND LISTEN | 1971 | RCA Victor SP45-409 | 30 |
| *(Promo-only interview record)* | | | |
| SO SAD Gold vinyl, gold promo label | 1960 | Warner Bros. 5163 | 100 |
| *(The colored promos are very limited)* | | | |
| THE SUN KEEPS SHINING White promo label | 1956 | Columbia 21496 | 250 |
| *(Stock copy worth over $500)* | | | |

**7-Inch Extended Plays**

| | | | |
|-------|-----|---------------|------|
| COCA-COLA JINGLE A GO-GO VOL.1 | 196? | Coca-Cola | 200 |
| *(With another cut by Ray Charles)* | | | |
| COCA-COLA SPOTS | 1965 | Coca-Cola | 200 |
| *(With artists Jan & Dean, Roy Orbison, Shirelles and the Four Seasons)* | | | |
| THE EVERLY BROTHERS  White/red label | 1960 | Warner Bros. 5501 | 40 |
| *(Four songs, issued with a picture sleeve; also issued as red label stock copy)* | | | |
| EVERLY BROTHERS SHOW Jukebox LLP | 197? | Warner Bros. 1858 | 40 |
| *(Includes title strips and paper sleeve)* | | | |
| EVERLY FAMILY SHOW Promo only | 1961 | Warner Bros. 306 | 50 |
| *(Warner promo label, sampler from the record company)* | | | |
| FOREVERLY YOURS | 1960 | Warner Bros. 1381 | 150 |
| *(Gold vinyl, very limited promo-only release)* | | | |
| THE GOLDEN HITS OF THE EVERLY BROTHERS | 1962 | Warner Bros. 1471 | 40 |
| *(Promo-only release)* | | | |
| THE GOLDEN HITS OF THE EVERLY BROTHERS | 1962 | Warner Bros. 1471 | 40 |
| *(White/red promo label, promotion to jukebox vendors)* | | | |
| SONGS OUR DADDY TAUGHT US | 1958 | Cadence 3016 | 50 |
| *(White label test pressing, typewritten titles on an all-white label)* | | | |

**Albums**

| | | | |
|-------|-----|---------------|------|
| BOTH SIDES OF AN EVENING | 1961 | Warner Bros. 1418 | 75 |
| *(White promo label)* | | | |
| CELEBRITIES | 196? | U.S. Marine Corps | 50 |
| *(20 hits, one by the Everly Brothers)* | | | |
| CHRISTMAS WITH THE EVERLY BROTHERS | 1962 | Warner Bros. 1483 | 75 |
| *(White promo label)* | | | |
| A DATE WITH THE EVERLY BROTHERS | 1960 | Warner Bros. 1395 | 75 |
| *(White promo label)* | | | |
| EVERLY BROTHERS REUNION CONCERT (Oct 83) Promo only | 1983 | Passport 4006DJ | 75 |
| *(Recorded live at Albert Hall in Sept 83, special promo cover)* | | | |
| THE EVERLY BROTHERS SING | 1967 | Warner Bros. 1708 | 50 |
| *(White promo label)* | | | |
| GOLDEN HITS OF THE EVERLY BROTHERS | 1962 | Warner Bros. 1471 | 75 |
| *(White promo label)* | | | |
| GREAT COUNTRY HITS | 1963 | Warner Bros. 1513 | 75 |
| *(White promo label)* | | | |
| THE HIT SOUND OF THE EVERLY BROTHERS | 1967 | Warner Bros. 1676 | 50 |
| *(White promo label)* | | | |
| INSTANT PARTY | 1962 | Warner Bros. 1430 | 75 |
| *(White promo label)* | | | |
| IT'S EVERLY TIME  White promo label | 1960 | Warner Bros. 1381 | 100 |
| *(Promo version of the stock copy)* | | | |
| SOUVENIR SAMPLER 10 songs | 1961 | Warner Bros. PRO 135 | 200 |
| *(White promo label with special cover)* | | | |

| Title | Yr | Label, Number | NM $ |
|---|---|---|---|
| TWO YANKS IN LONDON | 1966 | Warner Bros. 1646 | 65 |
| *(White promo label)* | | | |
| WARNER SAMPLER 10-inch LP | 1961 | Warner Bros. PRO 134 | 600 |
| *(White promo label with special cover)* | | | |
| **Compact Discs** | | | |
| HEARTACHES AND HARMONIES SAMPLER | 1994 | Rhino | 20 |
| *(Promo-only sampler from box set)* | | | |
| **RADIO SHOWS** | | | |
| **Albums** | | | |
| ROYALTY OF ROCK | 1983 | Radio Ventures/RKO | 30-50 |
| *(Music and interviews, also features Buddy Holly)* | | | |

**EVERYTHING BUT THE GIRL**
**12-Inch Singles**

| | | | |
|---|---|---|---|
| DON'T LEAVE ME BEHIND (same on both sides) | 1986 | Sire PRO-A-2605 | 7 |

**EXILE**
*Epic and Warner Bros. promo 45s $2 each; Epic promo CD singles $3 each*
**RADIO SHOWS**
**Albums**

| | | | |
|---|---|---|---|
| LIVE FROM DISNEY WORLD (July 86) | 1986 | NBC Radio | 50-80 |
| *(With The Judds)* | | | |
| WESTWOOD ONE PRESENTS (Aug 86) Live concert | 1986 | Westwood One | 20-40 |
| *(This show repeated several times)* | | | |

**EXPOSE**
*Arista promo 45s $3 each; Arista promo CD singles $3 each*
**Compact Discs**

| | | | |
|---|---|---|---|
| TOP TEN HITS OF EXPOSE, THE | 1992 | Arista ASCD-2483 | 12 |
| *(Promo-only compilation)* | | | |
| **RADIO SHOWS** | | | |
| **Albums** | | | |
| THE STORY OF EXPOSE (Aug 89) Profile | 1989 | Unistar (2) | 15-20 |
| *(Music and interviews)* | | | |

**EXTREME**
*A&M promo CD singles not listed $3 each*
**Compact Discs**

| | | | |
|---|---|---|---|
| HOLE HEARTED | 1991 | A&M 75021 7003 2 | 6 |
| *(Promo-only CD single, cardboard sleeve)* | | | |
| **RADIO SHOWS** | | | |
| **Albums** | | | |
| METALSHOP (Oct 92) Various artists | 1992 | MJI Productions | 15-20 |
| *(Group does live set during segment of show)* | | | |
| OFF THE RECORD (Oct 92) | 1992 | Westwood One (2) | 10-15 |
| *(Music and interviews)* | | | |

# F

**FABARES, SHELLEY**
*Other Colpix promo 45s $10 each*
**45s**

| | | | |
|---|---|---|---|
| JOHNNY ANGEL | 1962 | Colpix 621 | 25 |
| *(White promo label)* | | | |
| JOHNNY LOVES ME | 1962 | Colpix 638 | 15 |
| *(White promo label)* | | | |
| WHAT DID THEY DO BEFORE ROCK & ROLL | 1962 | Colpix 631 | 15 |
| *(With Paul Peterson; white promo label)* | | | |

**FABIAN**
*Chancellor black promo label 45s $20 each; Chancellor white promo label 45s $15 each; Dot white promo label 45s $3 each; Chancellor white promo label LPs $30 each. Also includes listings of the Four Dates.*
**45s**

| | | | |
|---|---|---|---|
| BE MY STEADY DATE | 1957 | Chancellor 1024 | 25 |
| *(Fabian with the Four Dates; white promo label)* | | | |
| HEY ROLY POLY | 1957 | Chancellor 1019 | 30 |
| *(By the Four Dates; white promo label)* | | | |
| **7-Inch Extended Plays** | | | |
| THE FABULOUS FABIAN  White promo label | 1958 | Chancellor 5005 | 50 |
| *(Four songs, issued in a plain sleeve)* | | | |

**FABULOUS POODLES**
**12-Inch Singles**

| | | | |
|---|---|---|---|
| PINK CITY TWIST/BIONIC MAN | 1979 | Epic AS 718 | 10 |

**FABULOUS THUNDERBIRDS**
*CBS Associated white promo label 45s $3 each; CBS Associated promo CD singles $3 each*
**45s**

| | | | |
|---|---|---|---|
| (ROCKIN') WINTER WONDERLAND | 1983 | Epic ES7 2594 | 6 |
| *(Promo-only single)* | | | |

| Title | Yr | Label, Number | NM $ |
|---|---|---|---|
| **RADIO SHOWS** | | | |
| **Albums** | | | |
| IN CONCERT (July 89) Live concert | 1989 | Westwood One (2) | 25-40 |
| *(Repeated several times)* | | | |
| IN CONCERT (Mar 91) Live concert | 1991 | Westwood One (2) | 20-30 |
| *(With the Steve Miller Band)* | | | |
| KING BISCUIT FLOWER HOUR Live concert | 1986 | DIR (2) | 30-45 |
| *(Vinyl version)* | | | |
| SUPERSTAR CONCERT Box set | 1986 | Westwood One (3) | 25-40 |
| *(Live concert, repeated several times)* | | | |
| **Compact Discs** | | | |
| IN CONCERT (Sept 92) Live concert | 1992 | Westwood One | 20-35 |
| *(With the Del Fuegos)* | | | |
| KING BISCUIT FLOWER HOUR Live concert | 1987 | DIR | 25-40 |
| *(CD version)* | | | |

## FACES

*Also see Rod Stewart. Other Warner Bros. promo singles $5 each.*

| Title | Yr | Label, Number | NM $ |
|---|---|---|---|
| **45s** | | | |
| CINDY INCIDENTALLY | 1973 | Warner Bros. 7681 | 18 |
| *(Price includes promo-only picture sleeve)* | | | |
| **Albums** | | | |
| FIRST STEP | 1970 | Warner Bros. PRO | 400 |
| *(Price includes a badge, cutouts, press kit, photos and other stuff in a box)* | | | |
| FIRST STEP | 1970 | Warner Bros. 1851 | 25 |
| *(White promo label)* | | | |
| LONG PLAYER | 1971 | Warner Bros. 1892 | 20 |
| *(White promo label)* | | | |
| NOD IS AS GOOD AS A WINK, A | 1971 | Warner Bros. 2574 | 18 |
| *(White promo label)* | | | |
| OOH LA LA | 1973 | Warner Bros. 2665 | 15 |
| *(White promo label)* | | | |
| **RADIO SHOWS** | | | |
| **Albums** | | | |
| BBC COLLEGE CONCERT With Rod Stewart | 1982 | London Wavelength | 25-50 |
| *(Live concert)* | | | |
| BBC TRANSCRIPTION DISC (Mar 76) Live concert | 1976 | BBC Transcription | 750-1,000 |
| *(With Led Zeppelin)* | | | |
| BBC TRANSCRIPTION DISC Live concert | 1972 | BBC Transcription | 150-250 |
| *(Very rare, with Rory Gallagher)* | | | |
| BBC TRANSCRIPTION DISC Live concert | 1973 | BBC Transcription | 200-350 |
| *(Very rare)* | | | |
| BBC TRANSCRIPTION DISC Live concert | 1976 | BBC Transcription | 200-300 |
| *(Very rare)* | | | |
| IN CONCERT | 1987 | Westwood One (2) | 30-60 |
| *(Live concert)* | | | |
| IN CONCERT (June 91) Live concert | 1991 | Westwood One (2) | 25-50 |
| *(With Rod Stewart)* | | | |
| SUPERSTAR CONCERT (Apr 83) | 1983 | Westwood One (3) | 25-50 |
| *(Live concert)* | | | |
| SUPERSTAR CONCERT (Oct 89) | 1989 | Westwood One (3) | 30-50 |
| *(Live concert)* | | | |
| **Compact Discs** | | | |
| KING BISCUIT FLOWER HOUR (Sept 90) Live concert | 1990 | DIR | 25-40 |
| *(With Little Caeser)* | | | |

## FAGEN, DONALD

*Also see Steely Dan. Warner Bros. promo 45s $4 each; WB/Reprise/Giant promo CD singles $3 each.*

| Title | Yr | Label, Number | NM $ |
|---|---|---|---|
| **RADIO SHOWS** | | | |
| **Albums** | | | |
| BBC ROCK HOUR  Live concert | 1983 | London Wavelength | 30-50 |
| *(Rare early concert material)* | | | |
| **Compact Discs** | | | |
| UP CLOSE Special profile show | 1990 | Media America | 50-80 |
| *(Music and interview, some live)* | | | |

## FAITH NO MORE

*Slash/Reprise promo CD singles $3-5 each.*

| Title | Yr | Label, Number | NM $ |
|---|---|---|---|
| **12-Inch Singles** | | | |
| CHINESE ARITHMETIC (radio) (Kick Scream Mix) | 1987 | Slash PRO-A-2823 | 8 |
| FROM OUT OF NOWHERE (same on both sides) | 1989 | Slash PRO-A-3559 | 6 |
| A SMALL VICTORY (3 versions)/MALPRACTICE | 1992 | Slash PRO-A-5757 | 12 |
| WE CARE A LOT (2 mixes)/ANNIE'S SONG | 1987 | Slash PRO-A-2702 | 12 |
| **Compact Discs** | | | |
| LIVE FROM FIVE FAT B**TARDS | 1990 | Slash PRO-CD-4486 | 25 |
| *(Promo-only release; deduct $5 if rubber fish is missing)* | | | |
| 32 CENTS FOR A POSTAGE STAMP?! | 1995 | Slash PRO-CD-7496 | 20 |
| *(Promo-only collection)* | | | |
| **RADIO SHOWS** | | | |
| **Albums** | | | |
| METALSHOP (80s) Various artists | 198? | MJI Productions | 15-25 |
| *(Segment of show features live tracks by Faith No More)* | | | |
| **Compact Discs** | | | |
| IN CONCERT-NU ROCK (Apr 93) | 1993 | Westwood One | 20-35 |
| *(Live concert)* | | | |

| Title | Yr | Label, Number | NM $ |
|---|---|---|---|
| IN CONCERT-NU ROCK (July 95) | 1995 | Westwood One | 30-50 |
| *(Live concert, with Stone Temple Pilots)* | | | |

**FAITH, PERCY**
**45s**

| Title | Yr | Label, Number | NM $ |
|---|---|---|---|
| AWAY IN A MANGER/WE THREE KINGS OF ORIENT ARE | 1965 | Columbia JZSP 111903/4 | 12 |
| *(Promo only on green vinyl)* | | | |
| CHRISTMAS IS . . ./HAPPY HOLIDAY | 1966 | Columbia JZSP 119961/2 | 10 |
| *(Yellow label)* | | | |
| CHRISTMAS IS . . ./HAPPY HOLIDAY | 1967 | Columbia JZSP 119961/2 | 15 |
| *(White label with picture sleeve, 1967 Christmas Seals record)* | | | |

**FAITHFULL, MARIANNE**
*Other London promo 45s $6 each*
**12-Inch Singles**

| Title | Yr | Label, Number | NM $ |
|---|---|---|---|
| BLUE MILLIONAIRE (Long) (Short) | 1983 | Island DMD 627 | 8 |

**45s**

| Title | Yr | Label, Number | NM $ |
|---|---|---|---|
| SISTER MORPHINE Brown/orange promo label | 1969 | London 1022 | 200 |
| *(With the Rolling Stones)* | | | |

**7-Inch Extended Plays**

| Title | Yr | Label, Number | NM $ |
|---|---|---|---|
| GO AWAY FROM MY WORLD Jukebox LLP | 1965 | London 452 | 50 |
| *(Issued with a hard cover)* | | | |

**Albums**

| Title | Yr | Label, Number | NM $ |
|---|---|---|---|
| A CHILD'S ADVENTURE | 1983 | Island 90066 | 15 |
| *(Promo-only Quiex II audiophile pressing)* | | | |

**FALCO**
**45s**

| Title | Yr | Label, Number | NM $ |
|---|---|---|---|
| VIENNA CALLING | 1986 | A&M | 10 |
| *(White label test pressing)* | | | |

**FALCONS, THE**
*Chess and United Artists promo singles $10 each*
**45s**

| Title | Yr | Label, Number | NM $ |
|---|---|---|---|
| PLAY ME (60s) Jukebox promotional sales stimulator | 196? | Rowe AMI (no number) | 25 |
| *(Red vinyl, promo only, less than 60 seconds long)* | | | |

**FALL, THE**
**12-Inch Singles**

| Title | Yr | Label, Number | NM $ |
|---|---|---|---|
| NEW BIG PRINZ (same on both sides) | 1988 | RCA 8826-1-HDAA | 6 |
| VICTORIA (same on both sides) | 1988 | RCA 7617-1 | 6 |

**FAMILY**
**RADIO SHOWS**
**Albums**

| Title | Yr | Label, Number | NM $ |
|---|---|---|---|
| BBC TRANSCRIPTION DISC  Live concert | 1971 | BBC Transcription | 200-400 |
| *(Rare concert in a rare series)* | | | |
| BBC TRANSCRIPTION DISC  Live concert | 1973 | BBC Transcription | 175-350 |
| *(Repeat show)* | | | |
| BBC TRANSCRIPTION DISC  Live concert | 1979 | BBC Transcription | 100-200 |
| *(Not as rare as earlier shows)* | | | |
| POP SPECTACULAR (Jan 77) | 1977 | London Wavelength | 75-150 |
| *(Rare live concert)* | | | |

**FANNY**
*Casablanca and Reprise promo 45s $4 each*
**RADIO SHOWS**
**Albums**

| Title | Yr | Label, Number | NM $ |
|---|---|---|---|
| NIGHTBIRD & COMPANY (June 73) Various artists | 1973 | U. S. Army Reserve (2) | 20-40 |
| *(Fanny hosts one of the four music and interview shows)* | | | |

**FARM, THE**
**12-Inch Singles**

| Title | Yr | Label, Number | NM $ |
|---|---|---|---|
| ALL TOGETHER NOW (6 versions) | 1991 | Sire PRO-A-4798 | 10 |
| GROOVY TRAIN (5 versions) | 1991 | Sire PRO-A-4935 | 10 |
| LOVE SEE NO COLOUR (4 versions) | 1992 | Sire PRO-A-5898 | 8 |

**RADIO SHOWS**
**Compact Discs**

| Title | Yr | Label, Number | NM $ |
|---|---|---|---|
| ON THE EDGE (Jan 93) Music and interviews | 1993 | Westwood One | 15-25 |
| *(With King Missile and the Poppinjays)* | | | |
| ON THE EDGE (July 94) Music and interviews | 1994 | Westwood One | 20-30 |
| *(With Jah Wobble and Toad the Wet Sprocket)* | | | |

**FASCINATORS, THE**
**45s**

| Title | Yr | Label, Number | NM $ |
|---|---|---|---|
| CHAPEL BELLS | 1958 | Capitol 4053 | 50 |
| *(White promo label)* | | | |
| CHAPEL BELLS | 1958 | Capitol 4053 | 65 |
| *(Yellow promo label)* | | | |
| CHAPEL BELLS | 1960 | Capitol 4544 | 50 |
| *(Capitol promo label)* | | | |
| OH, ROSE MARIE | 1959 | Capitol 4247 | 200 |
| *(Yellow promo label)* | | | |

| Title | Yr | Label, Number | NM $ |
|---|---|---|---|
| WHO DO YOU THINK YOU ARE<br>*(White promo label)* | 1959 | Capitol 4137 | 50 |

**FASTER PUSSYCAT**
*Elektra promo CD singles $3-4 each*
**RADIO SHOWS**
**Albums**

| | | | |
|---|---|---|---|
| HIGH VOLTAGE (Jan 90) Various artists<br>*(Segment of the show is live, featuring Faster Pussycat)* | 1990 | Westwood One (2) | 20-35 |

**FASTWAY**
**RADIO SHOWS**
**Albums**

| | | | |
|---|---|---|---|
| IN CONCERT (June 83) Live concert<br>*(With Red Rider)* | 1983 | Westwood One (2) | 30-50 |
| KING BISCUIT FLOWER HOUR (Oct 84) Live concert<br>*(With Dio)* | 1984 | DIR/ABC (2) | 25-50 |

**FATBACK**
**12-Inch Singles**

| | | | |
|---|---|---|---|
| ON THE FLOOR (same on both sides) | 1982 | Spring PRO 184 | 8 |
| YOU'VE GOT THAT MAGIC (6:43) (3:55) | 1984 | Cotillion PR 763 | 8 |

**FATIMA MANSIONS**
**Reel-to-Reel Tapes**

| | | | |
|---|---|---|---|
| ALBUM NETWORK LIVE (July 92)<br>*(Live concert on reel)* | 1992 | Album Network | 175-250 |

**FEATHERBED**
*Also see Barry Manilow.*
**45s**

| | | | |
|---|---|---|---|
| COULD IT BE MAGIC (mono/stereo)<br>*(Stock copy may not exist)* | 1971 | Bell 45,133 | 60 |

**FEATHERS, CHARLIE**
*Later promo 45s after 1960, $10-20 each*
**45s**

| | | | |
|---|---|---|---|
| BOTTLE TO THE BABY<br>*(White promo label)* | 1957 | King 4997 | 60 |
| EVERYBODY'S LOVIN' MY BABY<br>*(White promo label)* | 1957 | King 4971 | 60 |
| NOBODY'S WOMAN<br>*(White promo label)* | 1957 | King 5022 | 60 |
| TOO MUCH ALIKE<br>*(White promo label)* | 1957 | King 5043 | 60 |

**FEELIES, THE**
**12-Inch Singles**

| | | | |
|---|---|---|---|
| AWAY (Edit)/DANCING BAREFOOT | 1988 | A&M 17627 | 8 |

**Albums**

| | | | |
|---|---|---|---|
| PAINT IT BLACK + 5<br>*(Promo-only 6-song sampler)* | 1990 | A&M 75021 7413 1 | 15 |

**FELICIANO, JOSE**
**45s**

| | | | |
|---|---|---|---|
| BALADA DEL PIANISTA (same on both sides)<br>*(May be promo only)* | 1983 | Motown 1673 | 4 |

**FENDERMEN, THE**
*Soma white promo label 45s $20 each*

**FERGUSON, JAY**
**RADIO SHOWS**
**Reel-to-Reel Tapes**

| | | | |
|---|---|---|---|
| STUDIO JAM (May 79)<br>*(Rare radio show on two 7-inch reels)* | 1979 | | 400-600 |

**FERRANTE AND TEICHER**
**45s**

| | | | |
|---|---|---|---|
| LAST TANGO IN PARIS (mono/stereo) | 1973 | United Artists XW205 | 4 |

**FERRY, BRYAN**
**12-Inch Singles**

| | | | |
|---|---|---|---|
| DON'T STOP THE DANCE (LP) (Edit) | 1985 | Warner Bros. PRO-A-2352 | 8 |
| HELP ME (same on both sides) | 1986 | Warner Bros. PRO-A-2577 | 12 |
| THE RIGHT STUFF (same on both sides) | 1987 | Reprise PRO-A-2852 | 6 |
| SLAVE TO LOVE (Long) (Short) | 1985 | Warner Bros. PRO-A-2304 | 8 |

**FEVER TREE**
**45s**

| | | | |
|---|---|---|---|
| SAN FRANSISCO GIRLS (RETURN OF THE NATIVE) (same on both sides)<br>*(Promo only on blue vinyl)* | 1968 | Uni 55060 | 40 |

| Title | Yr | Label, Number | NM $ |
|---|---|---|---|

**FIFTH DIMENSION, THE**

*Also listings of Marilyn McCoo and Billy Davis Jr. Soul City brown promo label 45s $5 each; Soul City black/brown promo label 45s $6 each; Bell white promo label singles $3 each; Any McCoo and Davis promo 45 $3 each.*

**45s**

| | | | |
|---|---|---|---|
| AQUARIUS/LET THE SUNSHINE IN | 1969 | Soul City 772 | 25 |
| *(Brown/black promo label, mono/stereo versions, promo only on gold vinyl)* | | | |
| FIND YOURSELF A STAR  Various artists | 1973 | U.S. Air Force | 15 |
| *(7-inch 33 1/3 record; of the twelve public service ads, the 5th Dimension does one)* | | | |
| UNITED NEGRO COLLEGE FUND  Six public-service ads | 1981 | UNCF 881 | 18 |
| *(White label, 20-30-60 second spots, features McCoo and Davis)* | | | |
| WHAT'S IT ALL ABOUT  Public service show | 197? | W. I. A. A. 245 | 20 |
| *(Flip side is the Pointer Sisters)* | | | |
| WHAT'S IT ALL ABOUT  Public service show | 1980 | W. I. A. A. 445 | 20 |
| *(Flip side features the Kinks)* | | | |
| WHAT'S IT ALL ABOUT (Oct 73) Public service show | 1973 | W. I. A. A. 197 | 20 |
| *(Flip side features B. B. King)* | | | |

**FIFTH ESTATE, THE**

**45s**

| | | | |
|---|---|---|---|
| PARADE OF THE WOODEN SOLDIERS (mono/stereo) | 1969 | Jubilee 5683 | 10 |
| *(Stock copies may not exist – "I Knew You Before I Met You" was the announced B-side)* | | | |

**FIGURES ON A BEACH**

**12-Inch Singles**

| | | | |
|---|---|---|---|
| NO STARS (same on both sides) | 1987 | Sire PRO-A-2745 | 6 |

**FINE YOUNG CANNIBALS**

*MCA/I.R.S. promo 45s $3 each*

**12-Inch Singles**

| | | | |
|---|---|---|---|
| EVER FALLEN IN LOVE (same on both sides) | 1986 | MCA 17259 | 8 |
| JOHNNY COME HOME (same on both sides) | 1986 | MCA 17075 | 8 |
| SHE DRIVES ME CRAZY (LP version) (7:05 remix) | 1989 | I.R.S. 17763 | 8 |
| SUSPICIOUS MINDS (same on both sides) | 1986 | MCA 17124 | 10 |

**RADIO SHOWS**

**Albums**

| | | | |
|---|---|---|---|
| SPIN CONCERT | 198? | Spin Magazine (2) | 25-40 |
| *(Live concert)* | | | |

**FINN, TIM**

**12-Inch Singles**

| | | | |
|---|---|---|---|
| CRESCENDO (same on both sides) | 1989 | Capitol SPRO-79558 | 5 |

**RADIO SHOWS**

**Compact Discs**

| | | | |
|---|---|---|---|
| ON THE EDGE (Feb 94) Music and interviews | 1994 | Westwood One | 15-25 |
| *(With Crowded House and Belly)* | | | |

**FIREFALL**

*Other Atlantic promo 45s $2 each*

**45s**

| | | | |
|---|---|---|---|
| CHRISTMAS IN LOVE Red promo label | 1982 | Atlantic PR 473 | 10 |
| *(Promo only, released for radio stations)* | | | |
| EVERY LITTLE WORD (same on both sides) | 1984 | Atlantic 89702 | 4 |
| *(May be promo only)* | | | |
| FALLING IN LOVE (same on both sides) | 1983 | Atlantic 89833 | 4 |
| *(May be promo only)* | | | |
| LIVIN' AIN'T LIVIN' | 1976 | Atlantic | 10 |
| *(White label test pressing)* | | | |
| LOVE THAT GOT AWAY | 197? | Atlantic | 10 |
| *(White label test pressing)* | | | |
| ONLY TIME WILL TELL (same on both sides) | 1980 | Atlantic 3763 | 4 |
| *(May be promo only)* | | | |
| STRANGE WAY | 1978 | Atlantic | 10 |
| *(White label test pressing)* | | | |
| WHAT'S IT ALL ABOUT (Sept 79) Public service show | 1979 | W. I. A. A. 490 | 15 |
| *(Flip side is Barry Manilow)* | | | |

**FIREHOSE**

**12-Inch Singles**

| | | | |
|---|---|---|---|
| TIME WITH YOU (same on both sides) | 1989 | SST PRO 235 | 10 |

**45s**

| | | | |
|---|---|---|---|
| BRAVE CAPTAIN/PERFECT PAIRS | 1986 | SST PSST-079 | 10 |
| *(Not issued with picture sleeve)* | | | |

**7-Inch Extended Plays**

| | | | |
|---|---|---|---|
| FLYIN' THE FLANNEL/EPOXY, FOR EXAMPLE/ O'ER THE TOWN OF PEDRO/TOO LONG | 1991 | (no label) fHYPE-1 | 8 |
| *(Not issued with picture sleeve)* | | | |

**FIREHOUSE**

**RADIO SHOWS**

**Compact Discs**

| | | | |
|---|---|---|---|
| IN CONCERT (Sept 93) Live concert | 1993 | Westwood One | 25-50 |
| *(With Great White)* | | | |

| Title | Yr | Label, Number | NM $ |
|-------|-----|---------------|------|
| **FIRESIGN THEATRE** | | | |
| **45s** | | | |
| THE HOLYGRAM'S SONG | 1969 | Columbia AE7 1022 | 12 |
| (Promo-only single) | | | |
| **7-Inch Extended Plays** | | | |
| JUST FOLKS -- A FIRESIGN CHAT | 1977 | Butterfly BFEP1 | 15 |
| (Promo-only release) | | | |
| | | | |
| **FIRM, THE** | | | |
| *Atlantic promo 45s $5 each. Features Jimmy Page and Paul Rodgers.* | | | |
| **RADIO SHOWS** | | | |
| **Albums** | | | |
| INNERVIEW (80s) Live music | 198? | Innerview (2) | 30-50 |
| (Special live show) | | | |
| SUPERSTAR CONCERT  Box set | 1985 | Westwood One (3) | 50-75 |
| (Live concert, repeated several times) | | | |
| | | | |
| **FIRST TEAM, THE** | | | |
| **45s** | | | |
| WHEN THE WRONG THING HAPPENS | 1967 | Columbia CSP 787 | 15 |
| (Lou Adessa and Vince Benay; special Chevrolet promo) | | | |
| | | | |
| **FISHBONE** | | | |
| **12-Inch Singles** | | | |
| ? (MODERN INDUSTRY) (LP version)  (Dance Mix) | 1985 | Columbia CAS 2076 | 10 |
| SUNLESS SATURDAY/FISHY SWA SKA/UNDERSTAND ME | 1991 | Columbia CAS 3082 | 6 |
| SWIM (3 versions) | 1993 | Columbia CAS 5252 | 12 |
| | | | |
| **FISHER, EDDIE** | | | |
| **7-Inch Extended Plays** | | | |
| COKE TIME WITH EDDIE FISHER | 195? | RCA Victor 6144X | 20 |
| (Special edition for Coca-Cola, with sleeve) | | | |
| LULLABY IN BLUE | 1957 | RCA Victor DJ-68 (47-6820) | 20 |
| (B-side has two tracks by the Ames Brothers) | | | |
| SOME DAY SOON | 1957 | RCA Victor DJ-41 (47-6746) | 20 |
| (B-side has two tracks by the Sabres) | | | |
| | | | |
| **FIVE AMERICANS, THE** | | | |
| **45s** | | | |
| 7:30 GUIDED TOUR/SEE SAW BABY | 1967 | Abnak 126 | 25 |
| (Promo only on yellow vinyl) | | | |
| CON MAN/LOVIN' IS LOVIN' | 1968 | Abnak 131 | 25 |
| (Promo only on yellow vinyl) | | | |
| GENERATION GAP/THE SOURCE | 1968 | Abnak 132 | 25 |
| (Promo only on yellow vinyl) | | | |
| I SEE THE LIGHT/THE OUTCAST | 1965 | Abnak 109 | 25 |
| (Promo only on yellow vinyl) | | | |
| IF I COULD/NOW THAT IT'S OVER | 1966 | Abnak 116 | 25 |
| (Promo only on yellow vinyl) | | | |
| THE RAIN MAKER/NO COMMUNICATION | 1968 | Abnak 128 | 25 |
| (Promo only on yellow vinyl) | | | |
| REALITY/SYMPATHY | 1966 | Abnak 114 | 25 |
| (Promo only on yellow vinyl) | | | |
| SAY THAT YOU LOVE ME/WITHOUT YOU | 1965 | Abnak 106 | 25 |
| (Promo only on yellow vinyl) | | | |
| SCROOGE/IGNERT WOMAN | 1969 | Abnak 137 | 25 |
| (Promo only on yellow vinyl) | | | |
| SHE'S TOO GOOD TO ME/MOLLY BLACK | 1969 | Abnak 142 | 25 |
| (Promo only on yellow vinyl) | | | |
| SOUND OF LOVE/SYMPATHY | 1967 | Abnak 120 | 25 |
| (Promo only on yellow vinyl) | | | |
| STOP LIGHT/TELL ANN I LOVE HER | 1967 | Abnak 125 | 25 |
| (Promo only on yellow vinyl) | | | |
| VIRGINIA GIRL/CALL ON ME | 1969 | Abnak 134 | 25 |
| (Promo only on yellow vinyl) | | | |
| WESTERN UNION/NOW THAT IT'S OVER | 1967 | Abnak 118 | 25 |
| (Promo only on yellow vinyl) | | | |
| ZIP CODE/SWEET BIRD OF YOUTH | 1967 | Abnak 123 | 25 |
| (Promo only on yellow vinyl) | | | |
| | | | |
| **FIVE DISCS, THE** | | | |
| **45s** | | | |
| I REMEMBER | 1958 | Vik 1327 | 75 |
| (White promo label) | | | |
| NEVER LET YOU GO/THAT WAS THE TIME | 1962 | Cheer 1000 | 300 |
| (White label, promo only) | | | |
| | | | |
| **FIVE KEYS, THE** | | | |
| *Other Aladdin white promo label 45s $200 each; Capitol white promo label 45s $10-15 each* | | | |
| **45s** | | | |
| DEEP IN MY HEART | 1954 | Aladdin 3245 | 375 |
| (White promo label) | | | |
| I'LL FOLLOW YOU | 195? | Groove 0031 | 4,000 |
| (One of the great rarities of record collecting) | | | |

| Title | Yr | Label, Number | NM $ |
|-------|-----|---------------|------|
| MY LOVE | 1955 | Aladdin 3263 | 350 |
| *(White promo label)* | | | |
| SOMEDAY, SWEETHEART | 1954 | Aladdin 3228 | 400 |
| *(White promo label)* | | | |
| STORY OF LOVE | 1956 | Aladdin 3312 | 325 |
| *(White promo label)* | | | |
| **Albums** | | | |
| THE FANTASTIC FIVE KEYS  Blue promo label | 1962 | Capitol 1769 | 125 |
| *(Label reads "For Radio-TV use")* | | | |
| THE FIVE KEYS | 1960 | King 688 | 250 |
| *(Promo label)* | | | |
| THE FIVE KEYS ON STAGE | 1957 | Capitol 828 | 250 |
| *(Promo copies feature the thumb cover; label reads "For Radio-TV Program Use")* | | | |
| FIVE KEYS RHYTHM & BLUES HITS PAST & PRESENT | 1960 | King 692 | 200 |
| *(Promo label)* | | | |

**FIVE MAN ELECTRICAL BAND**
**45s**

| | | | |
|---|---|---|---|
| HELLO MELINDA GOODBYE/SIGNS | 1970 | MGM 14182 | 10 |
| *(Evidently only exists as a promo)* | | | |

**FIVE PEARLS, THE**
**45s**

| | | | |
|---|---|---|---|
| PLEASE LET ME KNOW | 1954 | Aladdin 3265 | 85 |
| *(White promo label)* | | | |

**FIVE SATINS, THE**

*Other Ember white promo label 45s $25-50 each; Cub (MGM) promo 45s $20 each; United Artists promo 45s $18 each; Chancellor promo 45s $12 each; Warner, Roulette and RCA Victor promo 45s $8; Elektra promo 45s $4 each*

**45s**

| | | | |
|---|---|---|---|
| IN THE STILL OF THE NIGHT | 1957 | Ember 1005 | 200 |
| *(White promo label)* | | | |

**FIVE SHILLINGS, THE**
**45s**

| | | | |
|---|---|---|---|
| LETTER TO AN ANGEL | 1958 | Decca 30722 | 40 |
| *(Pink promo label)* | | | |

**FIVE SUPERIORS, THE**
**45s**

| | | | |
|---|---|---|---|
| THERE'S A FOOL BORN EVERY DAY | 1962 | Garpax 44170 | 75 |
| *(White promo label)* | | | |

**FIVE WINGS, THE**
**45s**

| | | | |
|---|---|---|---|
| JOHNNY HAS GONE | 1955 | King 4778 | 100 |
| *(White promo label)* | | | |
| TEARDROPS ARE FALLING | 1955 | King 4781 | 75 |
| *(White promo label)* | | | |

**FIXX, THE**

*MCA white promo label 45s $4 each; RCA and Impact promo CD singles $2-4 each*

**12-Inch Singles**

| | | | |
|---|---|---|---|
| BUILT FOR THE FUTURE (same on both sides) | 1986 | MCA 17175 | 5 |
| BUILT FOR THE FUTURE (3 versions) | 1986 | MCA 17181 | 6 |
| DEEPER AND DEEPER (2 versions) + 2 | 1984 | MCA L33 1184 | 6 |
| *(The "+2" are by Marilyn Martin and Fire Inc., respectively)* | | | |
| DEEPER AND DEEPER (same on both sides) | 1984 | MCA L33 1186 | 6 |
| LESS CITIES, MORE MOVING PEOPLE (7:09)  (same on both sides) | 1984 | MCA L33 1230 | 6 |
| A LETTER TO BOTH SIDES (same on both sides) | 1985 | MCA 17027 | 5 |
| ONE THING LEADS TO ANOTHER (8:00 and 3:23)/THE SIGN OF FIRE | 1983 | MCA L33 1128 | 12 |
| *(Black vinyl)* | | | |
| ONE THING LEADS TO ANOTHER (8:00 and 3:23)/THE SIGN OF FIRE | 1983 | MCA L33 1128 | 25 |
| *(Blue vinyl)* | | | |
| RED SKIES | 1983 | MCA 1102 | 15 |
| *(Red vinyl, promo-only 12" single)* | | | |
| RED SKIES (Long) (Short) | 1987 | MCA 17304 | 7 |
| SAVED BY ZERO (REMIX)/OUTSIDE | 1983 | MCA L33 1109 | 12 |
| THE SIGN OF FIRE/ONE THING LEADS TO ANOTHER (Live)/ | 1983 | MCA L33 1146 | 10 |
| SAVED BY ZERO (Live) | | | |
| SUNSHINE IN THE SHADE (LIVE) (same on both sides) | 1984 | MCA L33 1252 | 6 |
| **45s** | | | |
| SUNSHINE IN THE SHADE | 1984 | MCA 52498 | 12 |
| *(White and blue promo label, yellow vinyl, stock copies are black vinyl)* | | | |
| **Albums** | | | |
| PHANTOMS | 1984 | MCA 1212 | 15 |
| *(Promo only, Side A is three songs, Side B the group has recorded introductions to each LP track)* | | | |
| PHANTOMS | 1984 | MCA 1213 | 15 |
| *(Promo-only release, promo copy of the LP)* | | | |

| Title | Yr | Label, Number | NM $ |
|-------|-----|---------------|------|

**RADIO SHOWS**
**Albums**

| | | | |
|-------|-----|---------------|------|
| BBC ROCK HOUR (Oct 84) Live concert | 1984 | London Wavelength | 25-50 |
| *(Early concert material)* | | | |
| BBC TRANSCRIPTION DISC  Live concert | 1983 | BBC Transcription | 125-200 |
| *(Very rare concert in a very rare series)* | | | |
| IN CONCERT (Sept 83) Live concert | 1983 | Westwood One (2) | 20-40 |
| *(With the Thompson Twins)* | | | |
| INNERVIEW (80s) Profile | 198? | Innerview | 10-15 |
| *(Music and interviews)* | | | |
| KING BISCUIT FLOWER HOUR (Jan 83) Live concert | 1983 | DIR/ABC (2) | 40-80 |
| *(With The Psychedelic Furs)* | | | |
| KING BISCUIT FLOWER HOUR (June 83) Live concert | 1983 | DIR/ABC (2) | 30-50 |
| *(With Billy Idol)* | | | |
| LONDON WAVELENGTH CONCERT (Dec 82) Live concert | 1982 | London Wavelength | 15-25 |
| *(Early concert material)* | | | |
| OFF THE RECORD (80s) PROFILE | 198? | Westwood One (2) | 15-20 |
| *(Music and interviews, repeated several times)* | | | |
| SUPERSTAR CONCERT (Jan 84) Box set, live concert | 1984 | Westwood One (3) | 25-50 |
| *(With Kansas)* | | | |
| SUPERSTAR CONCERT (May 85) Live concert | 1985 | Westwood One (3) | 20-40 |
| *(With John Waite)* | | | |
| SUPERSTAR CONCERT (May 86) Live concert | 1986 | Westwood One (3) | 30-50 |
| *(With The Motels)* | | | |
| SUPERSTAR CONCERT (May 87) Live concert | 1987 | Westwood One (3) | 30-50 |
| *(With Simple Minds)* | | | |

**Compact Discs**

| | | | |
|-------|-----|---------------|------|
| ELECTRIC LADYLAND (Apr 91) | 1991 | Album Network | 25-50 |
| *(Mostly music and interviews)* | | | |
| IN THE STUDIO (Jan 89) PROFILE OF AN ALBUM | 1989 | Album Network | 10-20 |
| *(Music and interviews)* | | | |

**FLACK, ROBERTA**
*Atlantic promo 45s $3 each; Atlantic promo CD singles $2-4 each*
**45s**

| | | | |
|-------|-----|---------------|------|
| MAKE THE WORLD STAND STILL (same on both sides) With Peabo Bryson | 1980 | Atlantic 3775 | 6 |
| *(May be promo only)* | | | |
| 25TH OF LAST DECEMBER | 1978 | Atlantic Atco PR 322 | 10 |
| *(Special promo-only issue, flip is "This Christmas" by Donny Hathaway)* | | | |
| WHAT'S IT ALL ABOUT (Nov 82) Public service show | 1982 | W. I. A. A. 647 | 18 |
| *(Interview with Roberta Flack)* | | | |

**RADIO SHOWS**
**Compact Discs**

| | | | |
|-------|-----|---------------|------|
| THE STORY OF ROBERTA FLACK (Nov 91) Profile | 1991 | Unistar | 15-25 |
| *(Music and interviews, with Maxi Priest)* | | | |

**FLAIRS, THE**
*With Fatso Theus*
**45s**

| | | | |
|-------|-----|---------------|------|
| BE COOL, MY HEART | 1956 | Aladdin 3324 | 50 |
| *(White promo label)* | | | |

**FLAMING LIPS, THE**
**45s**

| | | | |
|-------|-----|---------------|------|
| BALLROOMS OF MARS/SUDDEN DEATH | 1991 | Warner Bros. PRO-S-5452 | 25 |
| *("Soil X Samples #6" on gray vinyl; B-side by Mr. Bungle)* | | | |

**FLAMINGOS, THE**
*Decca promo 45s $25 each; End promo 45s $20 each; Roulette, Vee Jay, Philips and Polydor promo 45s $8 each*
**45s**

| | | | |
|-------|-----|---------------|------|
| DREAM OF A LIFETIME | 1959 | Checker 915 | 50 |
| *(White promo label)* | | | |
| I ONLY HAVE EYES FOR YOU | 1959 | End (no #) | 50 |
| *("DJ Special" 45, matrix number is G-463)* | | | |

**FLANIGAN, DICK**
**45s**

| | | | |
|-------|-----|---------------|------|
| ROUGH AND TOUGH | 195? | Alpine | 60 |
| *(White promo label)* | | | |

**FLASH AND THE PAN**
**12-Inch Singles**

| | | | |
|-------|-----|---------------|------|
| MEDIA MAN (2 versions)/WELCOME TO THE UNIVERSE/RESTLESS | 1980 | Epic AE 761 | 8 |

**45s**

| | | | |
|-------|-----|---------------|------|
| HEY, ST. PETER (Short) (Long) | 1977 | Midland Int'l. JB-10934 | 8 |

**FLATT AND SCRUGGS**
*Columbia promo 45s $5-10 each; Columbia red or white promo label LPs $15-20 each*
**45s**

| | | | |
|-------|-----|---------------|------|
| BALLAD OF JED CLAMPETT | 1962 | Columbia 4-42606 | 25 |
| *(Promo only on red vinyl, same on both sides)* | | | |
| WHAT'S IT ALL ABOUT (May 76) Public service show | 1976 | W. I. A. A. 318 | 10 |
| *(Flip side features Elvin Bishop)* | | | |

| Title | Yr | Label, Number | NM $ |
|---|---|---|---|

**FLEETWOOD MAC**

*Includes some Stevie Nicks, Lindsey Buckingham, Mick Fleetwood's Zoo, Bob Welch, Christine McVie; also see each of these artists. Other Warner Bros. white promo label 45s $8 each; Warner Bros. brown promo label 45s $7 each; Warner Bros. green promo label 45s $5 each; Warner cream-colored promo labels $4 each; Any Christine McVie promo 45s $5 each; Any Bob Welch promo 45s $3 each; Any Lindsey Buckingham promo 45s $3 each; Any other Stevie Nicks promo 45s $4 each; Any Mick Fleetwood's Zoo promo 45s $3 each; Modern promo 12" singles by Stevie Nicks $15 each; Any other solo 12" promo singles $10 each; Epic white promo LPs $20 each; Sire promo 2LPs $15 each.*

**12-Inch Singles**

| Title | Yr | Label, Number | NM $ |
|---|---|---|---|
| BIG LOVE (Extended Remix)/(Remix Edit) | 1987 | Warner Bros. PRO-A-2723 | 10 |
| BIG LOVE (same on both sides) | 1987 | Warner Bros. PRO-A-2688 | 6 |
| EVERYWHERE (same on both sides) | 1987 | Warner Bros. PRO-A-2884 | 6 |
| FIREFLIES (Remix Long Version)(Remix Edit) | 1981 | Warner Bros. PRO-A-932 | 12 |
| GO YOUR OWN WAY/SILVER SPRINGS | 1977 | Warner Bros. PRO-A-652 | 15 |
| HOLD ME (same on both sides) | 1982 | Warner Bros. PRO-A-1040 | 10 |
| ISN'T IT MIDNIGHT (same on both sides) | 1987 | Warner Bros. PRO-A-27?? | 10 |
| SARA (EDIT) (same on both sides) | 1979 | Warner Bros. PRO-A-845 | 10 |
| TANGO IN THE NIGHT (same on both sides) | 1987 | Warner Bros. PRO-A-2728 | 10 |
| THINK ABOUT ME (Remix)/SAVE ME A PLACE | 1980 | Warner Bros. PRO-A-853 | 20 |
| TUSK/NEVER MAKE ME CRY | 1979 | Warner Bros. PRO-A-831 | 12 |

**45s**

| Title | Yr | Label, Number | NM $ |
|---|---|---|---|
| ALBATROSS  Mono/stereo versions | 1969 | Epic 11029 | 15 |
| *(Orange and white promo labels)* | | | |
| ALBATROSS  White promo label | 1969 | Epic JZSP 139609 | 25 |
| *(Flip side is by "Gun")* | | | |
| COMING YOUR WAY | 1969 | Reprise 0860 | 12 |
| *(Reprise promo label)* | | | |
| FOR YOUR LOVE | 1973 | Reprise 1188 | 10 |
| *(Long/short versions)* | | | |
| HEROES ARE HARD TO FIND Brown promo label | 1974 | Reprise 1317 | 12 |
| *(Stereo/mono versions)* | | | |
| I CAN'T WAIT  Stevie Nicks | 1985 | Modern 99565 | 12 |
| *(Issued with a promo-only black/white picture sleeve)* | | | |
| JEWEL-EYED JUDY/STATION MAN | 1971 | Reprise 0984 | 10 |
| *(Reprise promo label)* | | | |
| MAN OF THE WORLD White promo label | 197? | DJM 1007 | 25 |
| *(Label owned by Dick James)* | | | |
| OH WELL - PART 1 White promo label | 1970 | Reprise 1079 | 15 |
| *(Flip side is "The Green Manalishi")* | | | |
| OH WELL, PART 1/OH WELL, PART 2 | 1970 | Reprise 0883 | 10 |
| RATTLESNAKE SHAKE/COMING YOUR WAY | 1969 | Reprise 0860 | 10 |
| THE GREEN MANALISHI White promo label | 1969 | Reprise 0925 | 12 |
| *(Very limited early Reprise promo single)* | | | |
| WHAT'S IT ALL ABOUT (Sept 76) Public service show | 1976 | W. I. A. A. 335 | 25 |
| *(Flip side is Billy Joel)* | | | |

**7-Inch Extended Plays**

| Title | Yr | Label, Number | NM $ |
|---|---|---|---|
| AMERICAN MUSIC CONFERENCE  Various artists | 1977 | AMC 102 | 20 |
| *(Series of 14 public service ads, two by Stevie Nicks)* | | | |
| UNICEF DAY Various artists | 1983 | UNICEF | 20 |
| *(Series of 24 ads, one by Fleetwood Mac)* | | | |

**Albums**

| Title | Yr | Label, Number | NM $ |
|---|---|---|---|
| BUCKINGHAM NICKS  White promo label | 1973 | Polydor 5058 | 75 |
| *(Lindsey Buckingham and Stevie Nicks)* | | | |
| THE FLEETWOOD MAC STORY With Lindsey Buckingham | 1985 | Warner Bros. (2) | 50 |
| *(Music and interviews)* | | | |
| MIRAGE | 1982 | Warner Bros. 23607 | 20 |
| *(Promo on Quiex II vinyl)* | | | |
| RUMOURS | 1977 | Warner Bros. PRO-A-652 | 50 |
| *(Special promo with embossed cover)* | | | |
| TUSK REMIX | 1979 | Warner Bros. PRO-A-866 | 20 |
| *(Promo-only EP)* | | | |

**Compact Discs**

| Title | Yr | Label, Number | NM $ |
|---|---|---|---|
| LITTLE LIES | 1987 | Warner Bros. PRO-CD-2818 | 20 |
| *(3-inch promo CD single with longbox; 5-inch CD single has much less value)* | | | |
| SELECTIONS FROM THE BOX SET | 1994 | Warner Bros. PRO-CD-5905 | 30 |
| *(Promo-only 18-track release)* | | | |

**RADIO SHOWS**

**Albums**

| Title | Yr | Label, Number | NM $ |
|---|---|---|---|
| BBC ROCK HOUR  Stevie Nicks | 1981 | London Wavelength | 50-75 |
| *(Music and interview)* | | | |
| BBC ROCK HOUR (Oct 84) Lindsey Buckingham | 1984 | London Wavelength | 25-50 |
| *(Music and interviews)* | | | |
| BBC TRANSCRIPTION DISC  Live concert | 1973 | BBC Transcription | 500-700 |
| *(One of the most collectible radio shows)* | | | |
| BBC TRANSCRIPTION DISC  Live concert | 1976 | BBC Transcription | 500-700 |
| *(Another very rare show)* | | | |
| BBC TRANSCRIPTION DISC  Profile | 1977 | BBC Transcription | 125-200 |
| *(Not a live concert)* | | | |
| CAPTURED LIVE (80s) | 198? | RKO (2) | 100-200 |
| *(Rare live concert)* | | | |
| COUNTDOWN TO CHRISTMAS (Dec 85) | 1985 | NBC Radio | 20-25 |
| *(Music and interviews)* | | | |
| THE FLEETWOOD MAC STORY Profile | 1990 | Unistar (3) | 25-50 |
| *(Music and interviews)* | | | |
| IN CONCERT | 1984 | Westwood One (2) | 50-100 |
| *(Live concert)* | | | |
| IN CONCERT  Stevie Nicks | 1984 | Westwood One (2) | 60-100 |
| *(Live concert)* | | | |

| Title | Yr | Label, Number | NM $ |
|---|---|---|---|
| IN CONCERT (Apr 84) Christine McVie | 1984 | Westwood One (2) | 75-125 |
| *(Live concert)* | | | |
| IN CONCERT (Dec 92) | 1992 | Westwood One (2) | 25-50 |
| *(Live concert)* | | | |
| IN CONCERT (Mar 84) Mick Fleetwood's Zoo | 1984 | Westwood One (2) | 40-60 |
| *(Live concert)* | | | |
| INNERVIEW (70s) Profile of Fleetwood Mac | 197? | Innerview | 40-60 |
| *(Music and interviews)* | | | |
| KING BISCUIT FLOWER HOUR | 1986 | DIR (2) | 50-100 |
| *(Live concert)* | | | |
| LEGENDS OF ROCK | 1987 | NBC Radio (4) | 30-60 |
| *(Music and interview, Parts 1 and 2)* | | | |
| LEGENDS OF ROCK | 1987 | NBC Radio (2) | 15-25 |
| *(Music and interview)* | | | |
| NBC SOURCE | 1982 | NBC Source (3) | 50-75 |
| *(Mostly live tracks)* | | | |
| NBC SOURCE (Apr 83) Stevie Nicks | 1983 | NBC Radio (2) | 150-225 |
| *(Very rare live concert)* | | | |
| NBC SOURCE (Feb 82) Lindsey Buckingham | 1982 | NBC Radio (2) | 40-75 |
| *(Some live material)* | | | |
| OFF THE RECORD | 1982 | Westwood One (4) | 25-50 |
| *(Music and interview, parts 1 and 2)* | | | |
| OFF THE RECORD | 1982 | Westwood One (2) | 15-25 |
| *(Music and interviews)* | | | |
| OFF THE RECORD  Lindsey Buckingham | 1982 | Westwood One (2) | 15-25 |
| *(Music and interviews)* | | | |
| OFF THE RECORD  Stevie Nicks | 1982 | Westwood One (2) | 20-30 |
| *(Music and interviews)* | | | |
| POP CONCERT | 1988 | Westwood One (2) | 75-100 |
| *(Rare live concerts)* | | | |
| ROBERT W. MORGAN (Apr 80) | 1980 | Watermark (2) | 30-50 |
| *(Music and interviews, two shows)* | | | |
| ROBERT W. MORGAN (Mar 82) Lindsey Buckingham | 1982 | Watermark | 20-30 |
| *(Music and interviews)* | | | |
| ROCK STARS  Stevie Nicks | 1989 | Radio Today (2) | 35-50 |
| *(Music and interviews)* | | | |
| ROCK STARS (Sept 87) | 1987 | Radio Today (2) | 25-40 |
| *(Music and interviews)* | | | |
| SOURCE SPECIAL | 1982 | NBC Source (3) | 50-75 |
| *(Mostly live material)* | | | |
| SPOTLIGHT SPECIAL  Box set | 1980 | ABC Radio (2) | 75-150 |
| *(Mostly music and interviews)* | | | |
| STARTRACK PROFILE  Stevie Nicks | 1986 | Westwood One (2) | 40-60 |
| *(Mostly music and interviews)* | | | |
| STEVIE NICKS SPECIAL (Aug 81) Live concert | 1981 | NBC Source (2) | 100-200 |
| *(One of the earliest Stevie Nicks concerts)* | | | |
| SUPERSTAR CONCERT | 1983 | Westwood One (3) | 50-80 |
| *(Live concert)* | | | |
| SUPERSTAR CONCERT  Box set, Stevie Nicks | 1983 | Westwood One (3) | 60-100 |
| *(Live concert)* | | | |
| SUPERSTAR CONCERT  Lindsey Buckingham | 1984 | Westwood One (3) | 50-75 |
| *(Live concert)* | | | |
| TIMOTHY WHITE SESSIONS | 1987 | Westwood One (2) | 35-60 |
| *(Music and interviews)* | | | |
| **Compact Discs** | | | |
| BBC CLASSIC CUTS (Oct 90) | 1990 | Westwood One | 50-100 |
| *(Mostly music and interviews)* | | | |
| BBC CLASSIC TRACKS (Oct 95) | 1995 | Westwood One | 20-40 |
| *(Concert material)* | | | |
| CLASSIC TRACKS (Dec 95) | 1995 | | 25-40 |
| *(Live material)* | | | |
| IN THE STUDIO | 1989 | Album Network | 20-40 |
| *(Profile of an album)* | | | |
| IN THE STUDIO  Stevie Nicks | 1989 | Album Network | 25-50 |
| *(Profile of an album. This radio series often featured solo and group LP profiles and their values vary slightly depending on which LP is featured.)* | | | |
| KING BISCUIT FLOWER HOUR | 1988 | DIR | 40-75 |
| *(Same live concert, in CD format)* | | | |
| MASTERS OF ROCK (July 90) | 1990 | Radio International (2) | 60-100 |
| *(Some live material)* | | | |
| OFF THE RECORD (Aug 92) Stevie Nicks | 1992 | Westwood One | 20-30 |
| *(Music and interviews, CD format. These "Off the Record" specials were repeated many times, by each solo artist, throughout the 80s.)* | | | |
| SHOWCASE OF ROCK (May 92) | 1992 | Unistar (3) | 40-75 |
| *(Music and interviews)* | | | |
| STEVIE NICKS (Aug 93) Live concert | 1993 | Entertainment Radio | 100-175 |
| *(Very rare and recent live concert)* | | | |
| SUPERSTAR CONCERT (Feb 94) | 1994 | Westwood One (2) | 50-80 |
| *(Live concert, CD format)* | | | |
| SUPERSTAR CONCERT (Jan 95) Stevie Nicks | 1995 | Westwood One (2) | 100-150 |
| *(Live concert)* | | | |
| SUPERSTAR CONCERT (Oct 94) Live concert | 1994 | Westwood One (2) | 50-80 |
| *(Features Nicks, Buckingham and Fleetwood Mac)* | | | |
| SUPERSTAR CONCERT Lindsey Buckingham | 1993 | Westwood One (2) | 50-100 |
| *(Live concert, CD format)* | | | |
| UP CLOSE Stevie Nicks | 1989 | Media America (2) | 60-80 |
| *(Music and interview, some live material)* | | | |
| UP CLOSE Stevie Nicks | 1994 | Media America (2) | 50-75 |
| *(Music and interview, some live material)* | | | |

| Title | Yr | Label, Number | NM $ |
|---|---|---|---|
| **FLEETWOOD, MICK** | | | |
| *Also see Fleetwood Mac.* | | | |
| **12-Inch Singles** | | | |
| ANGEL COME HOME (same on both sides) | 1984 | RCA JR-13744 | 6 |
| I WANT YOU BACK (same on both sides) | 1983 | RCA JR-13616 | 6 |
| | | | |
| **FLESH FOR LULU** | | | |
| **12-Inch Singles** | | | |
| I GO CRAZY (same on both sides) | 1987 | MCA 17280 | 6 |
| I GO CRAZY (same on both sides) | 1987 | Capitol SPRO 79347 | 10 |
| **Albums** | | | |
| FINAL VINYL (EVERY LITTLE WORD + 7 LIVE) | 1989 | Capitol SPRO 79992 | 20 |
| *(Red vinyl; sticker on generic cover)* | | | |
| | | | |
| **FLOCK OF SEAGULLS, A** | | | |
| *Jive/Arista promo singles $3 each* | | | |
| **12-Inch Singles** | | | |
| (IT'S NOT ME) TALKING (same on both sides) | 1983 | Jive 9079 | 8 |
| **RADIO SHOWS** | | | |
| **Albums** | | | |
| BBC ROCK HOUR (Sept 82) | 1982 | London Wavelength | 40-75 |
| *(Music and interviews)* | | | |
| IN CONCERT (Feb 83) | 1983 | Westwood One (2) | 50-100 |
| *(Live concert)* | | | |
| INNERVIEW (80s) | 198? | Innerview | 10-20 |
| *(Music and interviews)* | | | |
| KING BISCUIT FLOWER HOUR (Jan 83) Live concert | 1983 | DIR/ABC (2) | 40-75 |
| *(With Men at Work)* | | | |
| KING BISCUIT FLOWER HOUR (Sept 82) Live concert | 1982 | DIR/ABC (2) | 50-100 |
| *(With the Blasters)* | | | |
| | | | |
| **FLYING BURRITO BROTHERS, THE** | | | |
| *More at Burrito Brothers.* | | | |
| **Albums** | | | |
| HOT BURRITO | 1975 | A&M SP-8070 | 40 |
| *(Promo-only issue with poster)* | | | |
| | | | |
| **FOCUS** | | | |
| *Sire promo 45s $4 each* | | | |
| **RADIO SHOWS** | | | |
| **Albums** | | | |
| BBC TRANSCRIPTION DISC Live concert | 1973 | BBC Transcription | 200-400 |
| *(Very rare)* | | | |
| BBC TRANSCRIPTION DISC Live concert | 1976 | BBC Transcription | 250-500 |
| *(Very rare)* | | | |
| | | | |
| **FOGELBERG, DAN** | | | |
| *Epic/Full Moon white promo label 45s $3 each; Epic promo CD singles $3 each* | | | |
| **45s** | | | |
| LANGUAGE OF LOVE, THE | 1983 | Full Moon/Epic | 10 |
| *(White label test pressing)* | | | |
| LEADER OF THE BAND | 1981 | Full Moon/Epic | 10 |
| *(White label test pressing)* | | | |
| **Albums** | | | |
| INTERCHORDS | 1982 | Full Moon/Epic A2S 1335 | 25 |
| *(Promo-only release)* | | | |
| **RADIO SHOWS** | | | |
| **Albums** | | | |
| IN CONCERT (Apr 85) Live concert | 1985 | Westwood One (2) | 100-200 |
| *(Rare live concert)* | | | |
| IN CONCERT (Apr 95) | 1995 | | 100-150 |
| *(Live concert)* | | | |
| SOURCE SPECIAL (80s) Profile | 198? | NBC Radio (3) | 30-50 |
| *(Music and interviews)* | | | |
| | | | |
| **FOGERTY, JOHN** | | | |
| *More at Creedence Clearwater Revival.* | | | |
| **12-Inch Singles** | | | |
| CHANGE IN THE WEATHER (edit) (LP) | 1986 | Warner Bros. PRO-A-2595 | 8 |
| EYE OF THE ZOMBIE (same on both sides) | 1986 | Warner Bros. PRO-A-2514 | 8 |
| I CAN'T HELP MYSELF (same on both sides) | 1985 | Warner Bros. PRO-A-2337 | 8 |
| KNOCKIN' ON YOUR DOOR (same on both sides) | 1986 | Warner Bros. PRO-A-2637 | 8 |
| ROCK AND ROLL GIRLS/CENTERFIELD | 1985 | Warner Bros. PRO-A-2267 | 8 |
| THE OLD MAN DOWN THE ROAD (same on both sides) | 1984 | Warner Bros. PRO-A-2234 | 8 |
| VANZ KANT DANZ (edit) (LP) | 1985 | Warner Bros. PRO-A-2362 | 8 |
| **Albums** | | | |
| CENTERFIELD | 1985 | Warner Bros. 25203-1 | 20 |
| *(Promo versions on Quiex II audiophile vinyl)* | | | |
| | | | |
| **FOGHAT** | | | |
| *Other Bearsville promo singles $3 each* | | | |
| **12-Inch Singles** | | | |
| STONE BLUE | 1978 | Bearsville PRO-A-725 | 25 |
| *(Promo only on blue vinyl)* | | | |

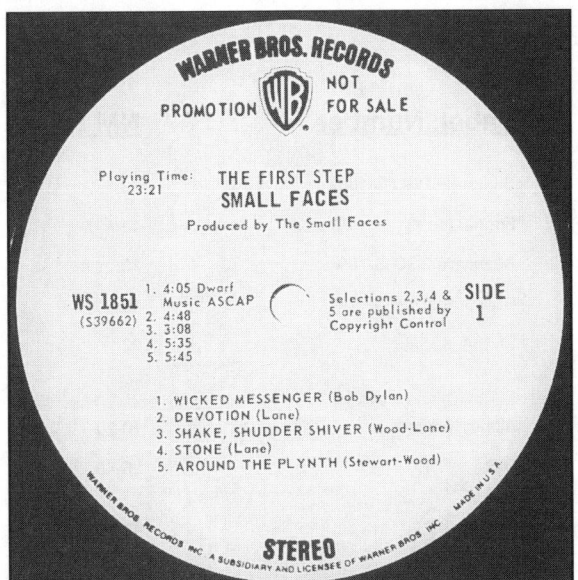

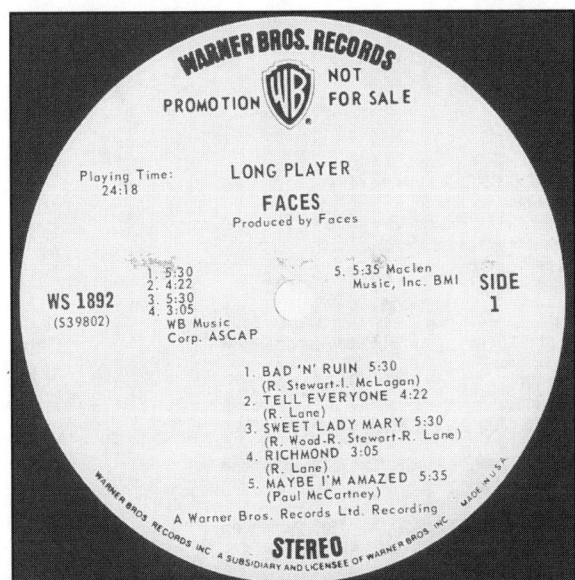

(Top row) The first two albums, on white promo labels, by the Rod Stewart-Ron Wood version of Faces. At left, the promo copies and early stock copies of their Warner Bros. debut still called the group "Small Faces"; this was changed within a year. At right, the second Faces album had the revised band name from the start. (Middle row) The cover and label for a promotional copy of *The Five Keys On Stage!* Note that the cover is the "phallic" version, as a first pressing should be, and that the label not only has a "Sample Album" note, but has a note in the fine print on the label noting this record's promotional nature. (Bottom left) A BBC performance by Fleetwood Mac recorded in 1973, when Bob Welch was still the lead guitarist, even though the show was meant to air in 1976, after Welch was gone! (Bottom right) A King Biscuit Flower Hour appearance by Genesis in 1988, from the tour supporting the *Invisible Touch* album.

| Title | Yr | Label, Number | NM $ |
|---|---|---|---|
| **45s** | | | |
| ALL I WANT FOR CHRISTMAS IS YOU | 1981 | Bearsville PRO-S-1002 | 12 |
| *(Promo-only release)* | | | |
| GOIN' HOME FOR CHRISTMAS | 1986 | Foghat (no #) | 12 |
| *(Promo-only release with picture sleeve)* | | | |
| RUN, RUN, RUDOLPH | 1978 | Bearsville PRO-S-780 | 12 |
| *(Promo-only release)* | | | |
| SLOW RIDE  Long/short versions | 1975 | Bearsville 0306 | 10 |
| *(Brown label promo, long version is 5:55, short 3:45)* | | | |
| WHAT'S IT ALL ABOUT (Aug 76) Public service show | 1976 | W. I. A. A. 328 | 20 |
| *(Flip side is Uriah Heep)* | | | |
| **RADIO SHOWS** | | | |
| **Compact Discs** | | | |
| IN THE STUDIO (July 94) PROFILE OF AN ALBUM | 1994 | Album Network | 10-20 |
| *(Music and interviews)* | | | |
| KING BISCUIT FLOWER HOUR (Oct 88) Live concert | 1988 | DIR | 25-40 |
| *(Rare live concert tracks, with Poco)* | | | |
| **Reel-to-Reel Tapes** | | | |
| KING BISCUIT FLOWER HOUR (Apr 78) Live concert | 1978 | DIR/ABC (2) | 40-75 |
| *(With Winter, Waters and Cotton, on two reels)* | | | |

## FOLEY, RED
*Other Decca promo 45s $5-10 each; Other Decca promo LPs $10-25 each*

| Title | Yr | Label, Number | NM $ |
|---|---|---|---|
| **45s** | | | |
| CRAZY LITTLE GUITAR MAN | 1958 | Decca 30674 | 25 |
| *(Pink promo label)* | | | |
| LET'S ALL SING  Five 7-inch 33rpm singles | 196? | Decca 38119 | 50 |
| *(For the set)* | | | |
| **7-Inch Extended Plays** | | | |
| RED FOLEY'S GOLDEN FAVORITES Jukebox LLP | 196? | Decca 34295 | 15 |
| *(Issued with a hard cover)* | | | |
| THE RED FOLEY SHOW Jukebox LLP | 196? | Decca 74341 | 25 |
| *(Issued with a hard cover, includes Patsy Cline)* | | | |
| **Albums** | | | |
| COMPANY'S COMIN' | 1961 | Decca 4140 | 45 |
| *(Pink promo label)* | | | |
| MY KEEPSAKE ALBUM | 1958 | Decca 8806 | 75 |
| *(Pink promo label)* | | | |
| RED & ERNIE  With Ernest Tubb | 1956 | Decca 8298 | 50 |
| *(Pink promo label)* | | | |
| RED FOLEY DICKIES SOUVENIR ALBUM | 196? | Decca LP | 45 |
| *(Release for the Dickies Company, special products)* | | | |
| SOUVENIR ALBUM | 1956 | Decca 8294 | 75 |
| *(Pink promo label)* | | | |
| **RADIO SHOWS** | | | |
| **16-Inch Transcriptions** | | | |
| JUBILEE USA (50s) | 195? | | 20-35 |
| *(Music and interviews)* | | | |

## FONTANE SISTERS, THE
*RCA Victor promo 78s and 45s $10 each; Dot blue promo and white promo 45s $8 each*

## FOO FIGHTERS

| Title | Yr | Label, Number | NM $ |
|---|---|---|---|
| **12-Inch Singles** | | | |
| EXHAUSTED/WINNEBAGO | 1995 | Capitol/Roswell SPRO 79641/2 | 10 |
| **RADIO SHOWS** | | | |
| **Compact Discs** | | | |
| LIVE FROM THE PIT (Apr 96) | 1996 | | 25-50 |
| *(Live concert)* | | | |

## FOOLS, THE
**RADIO SHOWS**

| Title | Yr | Label, Number | NM $ |
|---|---|---|---|
| **Albums** | | | |
| BBC ROCK HOUR (Oct 80) Live concert | 1980 | London Wavelength | 40-75 |
| *(With Eddie & the Hot Rods)* | | | |

## FORBERT, STEVE

| Title | Yr | Label, Number | NM $ |
|---|---|---|---|
| **45s** | | | |
| OIL SONG, THE | 1979 | Nemperor AE7 1184 | 10 |
| *(Small center hole, plays at 33 1/3 rpm)* | | | |

## FORD, FRANKIE
*Imperial promo 45s $20 each*

## FORD, LITA
*Also see the Runaways. RCA promo 45s $4 each.*
**RADIO SHOWS**

| Title | Yr | Label, Number | NM $ |
|---|---|---|---|
| **Albums** | | | |
| HIGH VOLTAGE (Mar 89) Various artists | 1989 | Westwood One (2) | 40-60 |
| *(Live segment of show features Lita Ford)* | | | |
| IN CONCERT (Apr 85) Live concert | 1985 | Westwood One (2) | 25-40 |
| *(With Survivor)* | | | |
| IN CONCERT (Feb 92) Live concert | 1992 | Westwood One (2) | 20-35 |
| *(With Rick Emmit)* | | | |

| Title | Yr | Label, Number | NM $ |
|---|---|---|---|
| INNERVIEW (80s) PROFILE | 198? | Innerview | 15-20 |
| (Music and interviews) | | | |
| METALSHOP (80s) Various artists | 198? | MJI Productions | 15-25 |
| (Live segment features Lita Ford tracks on show 409) | | | |
| **Compact Discs** | | | |
| IN CONCERT (Oct 94) Live concert | 1994 | Westwood One | 75-150 |
| (With Whitesnake) | | | |

**FORD, TENNESSEE ERNIE**
Capitol promo 45s $4-8 each depending on year; Other Capitol promo LPs $15 each

| | | | |
|---|---|---|---|
| **45s** | | | |
| BALLAD OF DAVY CROCKETT | 1955 | Capitol 3058 | 10 |
| (White promo label) | | | |
| FIRST BORN | 1958 | Capitol 3553 | 10 |
| (Yellow promo label includes Ford's picture on label) | | | |
| SIXTEEN TONS | 1955 | Capitol 3262 | 12 |
| (Promo copy of a classic pop hit) | | | |
| THE REAL STORY OF CHRISTMAS FROM ST. LUKE, CHAPTER 2 | 1972 | Canada Dry 72-6596 | 10 |
| (Special promo for his 1972 Christmas TV special, includes picture sleeve) | | | |
| **7-Inch Extended Plays** | | | |
| NATIONAL WILDLIFE FEDERATION Radio ads | 1964 | ADS Audio 1964 | 18 |
| (PSA spots issued with cover, includes Andy Griffith and Lorne Greene) | | | |
| WHEN PEA-PICKERS GET TOGETHER | 1963 | Green Giant 2566 | 20 |
| (Special promo for the Green Giant Co. and Le Sueur Peas, with picture sleeve) | | | |
| **Albums** | | | |
| OL' ROCKIN' ERN  Yellow promo label | 1957 | Capitol 888 | 50 |
| (Classic rockabilly/country album) | | | |

**FOREIGNER**
Includes listings of Lou Gramm. Other Atlantic promo singles $4 each; Atlantic promo singles by Lou Gramm $3 each.

| | | | |
|---|---|---|---|
| **45s** | | | |
| BLUE MORNING, BLUE DAY  Silver label, blue vinyl | 1978 | Atlantic 3543 | 25 |
| (Only the promo is colored vinyl) | | | |
| WHAT'S IT ALL ABOUT (Aug 80) Public service show | 1980 | W. I. A. A. 536 | 25 |
| (Flip side is Paul Simon) | | | |
| WHAT'S IT ALL ABOUT (Dec 81) Public service show | 1981 | W. I. A. A. 605 | 25 |
| (Flip side is Cheap Trick) | | | |
| **RADIO SHOWS** | | | |
| **Albums** | | | |
| FOREIGNER SPECIAL (Apr 82) | 1982 | ABC Radio (3) | 30-50 |
| (Music and interviews) | | | |
| INNERVIEW (70s) Profile | 197? | Innerview | 10-20 |
| (Music and interviews) | | | |
| KING BISCUIT FLOWER HOUR (Aug 82) Live concert | 1982 | DIR/ABC (2) | 50-75 |
| (With UFO) | | | |
| KING BISCUIT FLOWER HOUR (Mar 80) Live concert | 1980 | DIR/ABC (2) | 50-80 |
| (Repeated several times) | | | |
| LEGENDS OF ROCK (Oct 88) Profile | 1988 | NBC Radio (2) | 25-40 |
| (Music and interviews) | | | |
| NBC SOURCE (June 81) Music and interview | 1981 | NBC Radio (2) | 15-30 |
| (A few live tracks) | | | |
| OFF THE RECORD (80s-90s) | 199? | Westwood One (2) | 10-15 |
| (Music and interviews) | | | |
| PROFILES IN ROCK (June 80) | 1980 | Watermark | 20-25 |
| (Music and interviews) | | | |
| ROCK CLOCK | 1987 | DIR (2) | 20-35 |
| (Music and interviews) | | | |
| SUPERSTAR CONCERT Box set | 1986 | Westwood One (3) | 25-40 |
| (Live concert) | | | |
| SUPERSTAR CONCERT Lou Gramm | 1988 | Westwood One (3) | 20-30 |
| (Live concert) | | | |
| **Compact Discs** | | | |
| IN THE STUDIO  Profile of an album | 1989 | Album Network | 20-30 |
| (Music and interviews) | | | |
| KING BISCUIT FLOWER HOUR (Apr 94) Live concert | 1994 | DIR | 20-35 |
| (With King's X) | | | |
| KING BISCUIT FLOWER HOUR (Sept 91) Live concert | 1991 | DIR | 20-30 |
| (In CD format) | | | |
| LIVE AT ELECTRIC LADYLAND | 1993 | Album Network | 20-40 |
| (Live concert) | | | |
| SUPERSTAR CONCERT (Feb 95) | 1995 | Westwood One (2) | 25-50 |
| (Live concert) | | | |
| SUPERSTAR CONCERT (Oct 92) | 1992 | Westwood One (2) | 25-40 |
| (Live concert) | | | |
| THE STORY OF FOREIGNER (Aug 91) Profile | 1991 | Unistar (3) | 20-40 |
| (Music and interviews) | | | |
| UP CLOSE Profile | 1988 | Media America (2) | 25-40 |
| (Some live tracks) | | | |
| **Reel-to-Reel Tapes** | | | |
| KING BISCUIT FLOWER HOUR (Feb 78) Live concert | 1978 | DIR/ABC | 75-125 |
| (Classic concert with Supertramp) | | | |

| Title | Yr | Label, Number | NM $ |
|---|---|---|---|

**FORESTER SISTERS, THE**
*Warner Bros. promo 45s $2 each*
**RADIO SHOWS**
**Albums**

| Title | Yr | Label, Number | NM $ |
|---|---|---|---|
| AMERICAN EAGLE (July 86) Live concert | 1986 | Westwood One | 10-20 |
| *(Repeated several times)* | | | |
| LIVE FROM DISNEY (Sept 86) Live concert | 1986 | NBC Radio | 10-15 |
| *(Special release live concert)* | | | |
| WESTWOOD ONE PRESENTS (June 90) | 1990 | Westwood One | 10-20 |
| *(Live concert)* | | | |

**FORTUNES, THE**
**Albums**

| Title | Yr | Label, Number | NM $ |
|---|---|---|---|
| IT'S THE REAL THING | 1969 | Coca-Cola (no #) | 60 |

**FOSTER, FRANK, AND THE NIGHTHAWKS**
*Phillips Int'l. white promo label 45s $5 each*
**Albums**

| Title | Yr | Label, Number | NM $ |
|---|---|---|---|
| HEY BOSS MAN! | 1961 | Phillips Int'l. 1975 | 500 |
| *(White promo label)* | | | |

**FOSTER, JERRY**
**45s**

| Title | Yr | Label, Number | NM $ |
|---|---|---|---|
| THE 50'S (same on both sides) | 1982 | Sun 1176 | 4 |
| *(Promo only)* | | | |

**FOSTER, JOHN, AND SONS BLACK DYKE MILLS BAND**
**45s**

| Title | Yr | Label, Number | NM $ |
|---|---|---|---|
| THINGUMYBOB Star on label | 1968 | Apple 1800 | 125 |
| *(Version with the star on the label, sent to radio stations.  Produced by Paul McCartney.)* | | | |

**FOUR BARS, THE**
**45s**

| Title | Yr | Label, Number | NM $ |
|---|---|---|---|
| GRIEF BY DAY, GRIEF BY NIGHT | 1954 | Josie 762 | 150 |
| *(White promo label)* | | | |
| IF I GAVE MY HEART TO YOU | 1954 | Josie 768 | 150 |
| *(White promo label)* | | | |
| WHY DO YOU TREAT ME THIS WAY | 1955 | Josie 783 | 250 |
| *(White promo label)* | | | |

**FOUR CHEERS, THE**
**45s**

| Title | Yr | Label, Number | NM $ |
|---|---|---|---|
| FATAL CHARMS OF LOVE | 1958 | End 1034 | 150 |
| *(White promo label)* | | | |

**FOUR GRADUATES, THE**
*Later became the Happenings*
**45s**

| Title | Yr | Label, Number | NM $ |
|---|---|---|---|
| A LOVELY WAY TO SPEND AN EVENING | 1963 | Rust 5062 | 125 |
| *(White promo label)* | | | |
| CANDY QUEEN | 1963 | Rust 5084 | 175 |
| *(White promo label)* | | | |

**FOUR HORSEMEN, THE**
**45s**

| Title | Yr | Label, Number | NM $ |
|---|---|---|---|
| MY HEARTBEAT | 1958 | United Artists 134 | 75 |
| *(White promo label)* | | | |

**FOUR JACKS, THE**
**45s**

| Title | Yr | Label, Number | NM $ |
|---|---|---|---|
| TIRED OF YOUR SEXY WAYS | 1954 | Aladdin 3274 | 40 |
| *(White promo label)* | | | |

**FOUR KNIGHTS, THE**
*Capitol promo 45s $10-15 each; Capitol promo LPs $50-100 each*
**Albums**

| Title | Yr | Label, Number | NM $ |
|---|---|---|---|
| FOUR KNIGHTS | 1957 | Coral 57221 | 100 |
| *(Blue promo label)* | | | |

**FOUR LADS, THE**
*Okeh promo 45s $15 each; Other Columbia promo 45s $10 each; Columbia stereo single 33s (jukeboxes) $8 each; United Artists promo 45s $4 each; Columbia promo LPs $15 each*
**45s**

| Title | Yr | Label, Number | NM $ |
|---|---|---|---|
| INSIDE THE RECORD SESSION  With Mitch Miller | 1956 | Columbia ZEP 35194 | 15 |
| *(Promo-only interview record)* | | | |
| THE STINGIEST MAN IN TOWN | 1956 | Columbia 40788 | 12 |
| *(Yellow promo label)* | | | |

**4 NON BLONDES**
*Interscope promo CD singles $3-5 each*
**RADIO SHOWS**
**Compact Discs**

| Title | Yr | Label, Number | NM $ |
|---|---|---|---|
| IN CONCERT (Apr 94) Live concert | 1994 | Westwood One | 50-75 |
| *(With the Pretenders)* | | | |

| **Title** | **Yr** | **Label, Number** | **NM $** |
|---|---|---|---|
| SUPERSTAR CONCERT (Apr 94) | 1994 | Westwood One (2) | 30-50 |
| *(Live concert)* | | | |

## FOUR PLAID THROATS
**45s**

| | | | |
|---|---|---|---|
| MY INSPIRATION | 1953 | Mercury 70143 | 175 |
| *(White promo label)* | | | |

## FOUR PREPS, THE
*Other Capitol promo 45s $5-8 each*
**45s**

| | | | |
|---|---|---|---|
| A LETTER TO THE BEATLES | 1964 | Capitol 5143 | 25 |
| *(Green promo label)* | | | |
| BIG MAN | 1958 | Capitol PRO 637 | 30 |
| *(Promo-only pre-release)* | | | |

**7-Inch Extended Plays**

| | | | |
|---|---|---|---|
| DANCING AND DREAMING | 1958 | Capitol PRO 1148 | 25 |
| *(Four song promo-only EP, blue label, no sleeve)* | | | |

## FOUR SEASONS
**45s**

| | | | |
|---|---|---|---|
| BIG GIRLS DON'T CRY/DIRTY DANCING RAP | 1988 | MCA 53440 | 10 |
| *(Re-released thanks to the movie Dirty Dancing)* | | | |
| MOONLIGHT MEMORIES | 1985 | MCA 52724 | 10 |
| *(White label promo)* | | | |
| SHERRY | 196? | Philips 44017 | 15 |
| *(Double Hit Series, unusual white label promo)* | | | |

## FOUR SEASONS, THE
*Includiing the Four Lovers, The Wonder Who, The Topics, Frankie Valli. VJ (Vee Jay) white and blue promo label 45s $18-25 each; VJ (Vee Jay) white promo label 45s $15-20 each; MCA romo 45s $3 each; Philips white/or pink promo label 45s $12 each; Philips double-hit series white promo label 45s $15 each; Motown white promo label 45s $5 each; Philips white promo label 45s by the Wonder Who $10 each; RCA Victor white promo label 45s by the Four Lovers $50 each; Warner Bros. promo 45s $5 each; Philips white promo label 45s by Frankie Valli $6 each; Smash white promo label 45s by Frankie Valli $5 each; Private Stock promo 45s by Frankie Valli $4 each; RSO white promo label 45s by Frankie Valli $3 each; MCA white promo label 45s by Frankie Valli $3 each; Capitol promo 45s by Frankie Valli $4 each; Philips white promo label LPs $25-35 depending on date; any label promo LP by Frankie Valli $10-15 depending on date.*
**45s**

| | | | |
|---|---|---|---|
| BERMUDA | 1961 | Gone 5122 | 60 |
| *(White promo label)* | | | |
| COUSIN BRUCIE GO GO Special release | 1964 | WABC 77 | 45 |
| *(Cousin Brucie is a DJ from WABC Radio)* | | | |
| FORGIVE & FORGET  Frankie Valli | 1954 | Mercury 70381 | 75 |
| *(White promo label)* | | | |
| GIRL IN MY DREAMS The Topics | 196? | Perri 1007 | 40 |
| *(The Four Seasons)* | | | |
| I GO APE  Frankie Tyler (Frankie Valli) | 1958 | Okeh 7103 | 60 |
| *(White promo label)* | | | |
| I'M LONELY  Nickie and the Nitelites | 1959 | Brunswick 55155 | 100 |
| *(Yellow promo label, features Nick Massi)* | | | |
| JOEY REYNOLDS' THEME  Special release | 1965 | WXYZ 121003 | 40 |
| *(Released for WXYZ Radio in Detroit)* | | | |
| JOEY REYNOLDS' THEME  Special release | 1965 | WIBG Radio | 40 |
| *(Released for WIBG Radio in Philadelphia)* | | | |
| LAY ME DOWN (WAKE ME UP) (mono/stereo) | 1970 | Philips 40688 | 15 |
| LITTLE BOY White and blue promo label | 1965 | Vee Jay 713 | 40 |
| *(Label reads "Bunky's pick" with a white star)* | | | |
| MY LIFE FOR YOU The Four Lovers | 1957 | Epic 9255 | 300 |
| *(White promo label)* | | | |
| MY MOTHER'S EYES  "Frankie Valley" | 1953 | Corona 1234 | 175 |
| *(Promo copy)* | | | |
| NEW MEXICAN ROSE/THAT'S THE WAY IT GOES | 1963 | Vee Jay 562 | 30 |
| *(Wrong title on B-side; evidently only exists on promos)* | | | |
| PATCH OF BLUE | 1970 | Philips DJP 59 | 25 |
| *(Red promo label, stereo/mono version)* | | | |
| PEANUTS | 1963 | Vee Jay 901 | 100 |
| *(One-sided promo from E.P.)* | | | |
| PLEASE TAKE A CHANCE  Frankie Valli | 1959 | Decca 30994 | 50 |
| *(Pink promo label)* | | | |
| REAL Frankie Valle and the Romans | 1959 | Cindy 3012 | 65 |
| *(Promo copy)* | | | |
| STAY | 1964 | Vee Jay 582 | 40 |
| *(B-side has a label from The Beatles, VJ #581, on flip)* | | | |
| STAY/PEANUTS | 1964 | Vee Jay 576 | 60 |
| *(White promo label)* | | | |
| WHAT'S IT ALL ABOUT (Dec 80) Public service show | 1980 | W. I. A. A. 553 | 25 |
| *(Featuring Frankie Valli, flip side is Cher)* | | | |
| WHAT'S IT ALL ABOUT (Dec 81) Public service show | 1981 | W. I. A. A. 608 | 25 |
| *(Featuring Frankie Valli, flip side is Grace Slick)* | | | |
| WHERE ARE MY DREAMS? (mono/stereo) | 1971 | Philips 40694 | 15 |
| WILL YOU LOVE ME TOMORROW | 1968 | Philips DJP 19 | 25 |
| *(White promo label, stereo/mono versions)* | | | |

**7-Inch Extended Plays**

| | | | |
|---|---|---|---|
| COCA-COLA JINGLES  Various artists | 1965 | Coca-Cola | 40 |
| *(With Jan & Dean, Roy Orbison and the Shirelles)* | | | |
| COKE JINGLE VOL.1  Various artists | 1963 | Coca-Cola | 200 |
| *(This EP is 7 inches with a small center hole)* | | | |
| GENUINE IMITATION LIFE GAZETTE  Jukebox LLP with five songs | 1968 | Philips 2704 | 40 |
| *(Issued with a hard cover, back side is blank)* | | | |

| Title | Yr | Label, Number | NM $ |
|---|---|---|---|
| HONEY LOVE / PLEASE DON'T LEAVE ME Four Lovers | 1956 | RCA Victor DJ-47 | 125 |
| *(Four Lovers songs on one side, Homer & Jethro other side)* | | | |
| THE FOUR LOVERS  Four Lovers | 1956 | RCA Victor DJ-64 | 100 |
| *(Four Lovers on one side, Teddi King on the other)* | | | |
| **Albums** | | | |
| FOUR SEASONS PRESENT FRANKIE VALLI SOLO | 1965 | Philips 200247 | 40 |
| *(White promo label)* | | | |
| FOUR SEASONS SING BIG HITS BY BACHARACH, DAVID & DYLAN | 1965 | Philips 600193 | 40 |
| *(Group photos on front and back cover)* | | | |
| FOUR SEASONS SING BIG HITS BY BACHARACH, DAVID & DYLAN | 1965 | Philips 600193 | 40 |
| *(White promo label)* | | | |
| FOUR SEASONS SWING THE JINGLE (60s) | 196? | Coca-Cola Products | 400 |
| *(Six cuts for Coca-Cola, issued with a special cover)* | | | |
| JOYRIDE  The Four Lovers | 1956 | RCA Victor 1317 | Unknown |
| *(If a promo version exists, its value would be about $400)* | | | |
| **RADIO SHOWS** | | | |
| SIXTIES LEGENDS (June 92) | 1992 | Unistar (2) | 20-40 |
| *(Music and interviews)* | | | |
| **Albums** | | | |
| SOLID GOLD SCRAPBOOK (May 86) | 1986 | United Stations | 10-15 |
| *(Music and interviews, from the 5-LP weekly box set)* | | | |

**FOUR SPEEDS, THE**

**45s**

| | | | |
|---|---|---|---|
| FOUR ON THE FLOOR | 1963 | Challenge 9202 | 25 |
| *(White promo label)* | | | |
| I NEED YOU BABY | 1954 | DeLuxe 6070 | 40 |
| *(White promo label)* | | | |
| R. P. M. | 1963 | Challenge 9187 | 30 |
| *(White promo label)* | | | |

**FOUR TEENS, THE**

**45s**

| | | | |
|---|---|---|---|
| SPARK PLUG | 1958 | Challenge 59021 | 40 |
| *(White promo label)* | | | |

**FOUR TOPS, THE**

*Motown promo 45s $6-10 each depending on year; Other Columbia promo 45s $12 each; Casablanca promo 45s $3 each; RSO promo 45s $3 each*

**45s**

| | | | |
|---|---|---|---|
| AIN'T THAT LOVE | 1960 | Columbia 41755 | 40 |
| *(White promo label)* | | | |
| COULD IT BE YOU | 1956 | Chess 1623 | 175 |
| *(White promo label)* | | | |
| I CAN'T HELP MYSELF | 1965 | Motown 1076 | 25 |
| *(One-sided record, white promo label)* | | | |
| **7-Inch Extended Plays** | | | |
| FOUR TOPS ON TOP  Jukebox LLP | 1966 | Motown 60647 | 25 |
| *(Issued with a hard cover)* | | | |
| MAIN STREET PEOPLE  Quadraphonic LLP | 1974 | ABC 40012 (LLP 259) | 30 |
| *(Issued with a paper cover)* | | | |
| **RADIO SHOWS** | | | |
| **Albums** | | | |
| SUPER JAM (Sept 91) Live concert | 1991 | (3) | 100-200 |
| *(Very rare live concert, with the Temptations)* | | | |
| **Compact Discs** | | | |
| SIXTIES LEGENDS (Aug 92) Music and interview | 1992 | Unistar (2) | 20-35 |

**FOUR TUNES, THE**

*RCA Victor white promo label 78s and 45s $15 each; Jubilee white promo label 45s $12 each*

**FOUR-EVERS, THE**

**45s**

| | | | |
|---|---|---|---|
| YOU BELONG TO ME | 1962 | Columbia 42303 | 75 |
| *(White promo label)* | | | |

**FOX, NORMAN**

**45s**

| | | | |
|---|---|---|---|
| PIZZA PIE | 1959 | Capitol 4128 | 200 |
| *(Yellow promo label)* | | | |

**FRAMPTON, PETER**

*Includes the Herd; Frampton's Camel. Other A&M white promo label 45s $5 each; A&M red promo label 45s $3 each; Fontana white promo label 45s by the Herd $10 each; A&M promo 45s by Frampton's Camel $8 each; Immediate white promo label 45s by Humble Pie $12 each; A&M promo 45s by Humble Pie $5 each; Atco promo 45s by Humble Pie $4 each; A&M 12" promo singles $8 each; Any promo LP related to Frampton $10-20 each.*

**45s**

| | | | |
|---|---|---|---|
| SHOW ME THE WAY | 1975 | A&M 1693 | 12 |
| *(Test pressing, 3:18)* | | | |
| SHOW ME THE WAY | 1976 | A&M 1795 | 10 |
| *(Test pressing, 3:25)* | | | |
| SHOW ME THE WAY | 1976 | Columbia | 10 |
| *(Test pressing, 3:12)* | | | |
| **Albums** | | | |
| A&M RADIO SPECIAL Promo only | 1979 | A&M | 12 |
| *(Music and interviews)* | | | |

| Title | Yr | Label, Number | NM $ |
|---|---|---|---|
| FRAMPTON IS ALIVE | 1986 | Atlantic PR 848 | 18 |
| *(Promo-only sampler)* | | | |
| I'M IN YOU Picture disc | 1977 | A&M SP-5146 | 50 |
| *(Promo-only picture disc)* | | | |
| PERFECT FIT | 1989 | Atlantic 3093 | 12 |
| *(Question and answer album released by record company)* | | | |
| **RADIO SHOWS** | | | |
| **Albums** | | | |
| BBC ROCK HOUR (June 81) Humble Pie | 1981 | London Wavelength | 50-100 |
| *(Rare live concert)* | | | |
| KING BISCUIT FLOWER HOUR (July 86) | 1986 | DIR (2) | 40-75 |
| *(Repeat show)* | | | |
| WORLD OF ROCK (Nov 89) Various artists | 1989 | DIR (2) | 10-20 |
| *(Music and interview, Frampton is co-host)* | | | |
| **Compact Discs** | | | |
| DESERT ISLAND DISCS (Jan 91) Profile | 1991 | | 10-20 |
| *(Music and interviews)* | | | |
| IN CONCERT (Oct 92) Live concert | 1992 | Westwood One (2) | 25-40 |
| *(Repeat show)* | | | |
| IN THE STUDIO (Nov 92) Profile of an album | 1992 | Album Network | 10-15 |
| *(Several other LPs profiled in this series)* | | | |
| KING BISCUIT FLOWER HOUR (Sept 88) Live concert | 1988 | DIR | 35-60 |
| *(Concerts of Frampton's Camel and Humble Pie)* | | | |
| SUPERSTAR CONCERT (Aug 93) Live concert | 1993 | Westwood One (2) | 25-40 |
| *(Repeated show)* | | | |
| UP CLOSE Profile | 1994 | Media America (2) | 25-40 |
| *(Music and interview, some live tracks)* | | | |
| **Reel-to-Reel Tapes** | | | |
| A CONVERSATION WITH PETER FRAMPTON (Oct 77) | 1977 | DIR (4) | 50-100 |
| *(Two-hour interview from WNEW, New York on four reels. This rare interview concerns the LP "Frampton Comes Alive")* | | | |

## FRANCHI, SERGIO
**12-Inch Singles**

| Title | Yr | Label, Number | NM $ |
|---|---|---|---|
| LAUGH YOU SILLY CLOWN/MORE (THEME FROM MONDO CANE) | 1979 | LAX L33-1836 | 10 |

## FRANCIS, CONNIE

Other MGM yellow promo label 45s $10-15 each; MGM white promo label 45s $5-10 each; Polydor promo 45s $3 each; GSP promo 45s $3 each; MGM promo LPs $20-30 each depending on year.

**45s**

| Title | Yr | Label, Number | NM $ |
|---|---|---|---|
| ARE YOU SATISFIED | 1955 | MGM 12122 | 50 |
| *(Yellow promo label)* | | | |
| EVERYONE NEEDS SOMEONE | 1956 | MGM 12335 | 30 |
| *(Yellow promo label)* | | | |
| FORGETTING | 1956 | MGM 12251 | 40 |
| *(Yellow promo label)* | | | |
| FREDDY Yellow promo label | 1955 | MGM 12015 | 60 |
| *(Her first single)* | | | |
| GOODY GOODBYE | 1955 | MGM 12056 | 50 |
| *(Yellow promo label)* | | | |
| LITTLE BLUE WREN | 1956 | MGM 12375 | 30 |
| *(Yellow promo label)* | | | |
| MY FIRST REAL LOVE | 1956 | MGM 12191 | 40 |
| *(Yellow promo label)* | | | |
| MY HAPPINESS | 1958 | MGM 12738 | 25 |
| *(Yellow promo label)* | | | |
| NO OTHER ONE | 1957 | MGM 12440 | 30 |
| *(Yellow promo label)* | | | |
| A NURSE IN THE U.S. ARMY (same on both sides) | 1966 | MGM 13550 | 30 |
| *(Promotional item for the U.S. Army)* | | | |
| SET OF FIVE JUKEBOX SINGLES | 1960 | MGM STH 411-419 | 50 |
| *(7" stereo singles with small center hole, SB-6 to SB-10; price is each record, $250 for the set)* | | | |
| SET OF FIVE JUKEBOX SINGLES | 1963 | MGM STH 401-410 | 50 |
| *(7" stereo singles with small center hole, SB-46 to SB-50; price is each record, $250 for the set)* | | | |
| STUPID CUPID | 1957 | MGM 12683 | 25 |
| *(Yellow promo label)* | | | |

**7-Inch Extended Plays**

| Title | Yr | Label, Number | NM $ |
|---|---|---|---|
| COUNTRY MUSIC CONNIE STYLE Jukebox LLP | 1967 | MGM 4079 | 25 |
| *(With the Jordanaires, issued with a hard cover)* | | | |
| GREATEST AMERICAN WALTZES Jukebox LLP | 1967 | MGM 4145 | 20 |
| *(Issued with a hard cover)* | | | |
| JEALOUS HEART Jukebox LLP | 1967 | MGM 4355 | 18 |
| *(Issued with a hard cover)* | | | |

**RADIO SHOWS**
**16-Inch Transcriptions**

| Title | Yr | Label, Number | NM $ |
|---|---|---|---|
| BOB CROSBY SHOW Connie Francis is guest | 1960 | U.S. Armed Forces | 50 |
| *(Music and interviews)* | | | |
| CIVIL DEFENSE SHOW Connie Francis is guest | 1959 | Civil Defense | 50 |
| *(Music and interviews)* | | | |
| NATIONAL GUARD SHOW Connie Francis is guest | 1959 | National Guard | 50-100 |
| *(Music and interviews)* | | | |
| **Albums** | | | |
| VOICES OF VISTA (60s) Shows 65 and 86 | 196? | Voices of VISTA | 50 |
| *(Connie Francis is host, music and interviews)* | | | |

| Title | Yr | Label, Number | NM $ |
|---|---|---|---|

**FRANKE AND THE KNOCKOUTS**
*Millennium/RCA promo 45s $3 each*
**RADIO SHOWS**
**Albums**

| | | | |
|---|---|---|---|
| NBC SOURCE (May 82) | 1982 | NBC Radio (2) | 50-100 |
| *(Live concert)* | | | |

**FRANKIE GOES TO HOLLYWOOD**
*Includes Holly Johnson. Other Island promo 45s $5 each; Other Island promo 12" singles $15 each; MCA/Uni promo 45s by Holly Johnson $4 each; MCA/Uni promo 12" singles by Holly Johnson $10 each.*
**12-Inch Singles**

| | | | |
|---|---|---|---|
| RAGE HARD | 1986 | Island PR 945 | 15 |
| *(Promo-only version 4:10)* | | | |
| RELAX | 1984 | Island PR 696 | 25 |
| *(Same version as 7" single PR 695)* | | | |
| RELAX  Clear vinyl test pressing | 1986 | Island PR-706 | 75 |
| *(Price includes letter from Island Records; a promotional package from Island made to look like a test pressing)* | | | |
| RELAX Yellow promo label | 1983 | Island DMD-691 | 30 |
| *(Promo-only 7:20 version)* | | | |
| TWO TRIBES | 1984 | Island PR 657 | 20 |
| *(Same version as the 7" single)* | | | |
| WARRIORS OF THE WASTELAND (2 mixes) | 1986 | Island PR 999 | 8 |
| WELCOME TO THE PLEASUREDOME | 1985 | Island DMD-830 | 18 |
| *(Promo-only 12" single)* | | | |

**45s**

| | | | |
|---|---|---|---|
| RAGE HARD White promo label | 1986 | Island PR 976 | 10 |
| *(Promo-only version 4:03)* | | | |
| RELAX  White promo label | 1982 | Island PR 600 | 15 |
| *(Newer style Island label, promo-only version 3:56)* | | | |
| RELAX Blue promo label | 1982 | Island 99805 | 15 |
| *(Old style Island label, 3:02 version)* | | | |
| RELAX White promo label | 1984 | Island PR 695 | 12 |
| *(Promo-only version 3:55)* | | | |
| RELAX White promo label | 1985 | Island 99653 | 10 |
| *(4:30 "Relax International Live" version)* | | | |
| TWO TRIBES White promo label | 1984 | Island 99695 | 10 |
| *(Same song on both sides)* | | | |

**Albums**

| | | | |
|---|---|---|---|
| LIVERPOOL White promo label | 1986 | Island 90546 | 25 |
| *(Released with a letter and cue-sheet)* | | | |
| ROCK OVER LONDON (80s) Various artists | 198? | Radio International | 10-20 |
| *(Often this show features music and interviews with FGTH)* | | | |

**RADIO SHOWS**
**Albums**

| | | | |
|---|---|---|---|
| INNERVIEW (80s) Profile | 198? | Innerview | 10-20 |
| *(Music and interviews)* | | | |

**FRANKLIN, ARETHA**
*Columbia white promo label 45s $10 each; Atlantic white promo label 45s $8-12 each depending on year; Arista promo singles $3 each*
**12-Inch Singles**

| | | | |
|---|---|---|---|
| GIMME YOUR LOVE (Single Edit) (Extended Remix)/INTERVIEW | 1989 | Arista ADP 9906 | 10 |
| *(With James Brown)* | | | |
| IT WASN'T, IT ISN'T, IT AIN'T NEVER GONNA BE (6:12) (6:20)/(7:35) (5:36) | 1989 | Arista ADP 9877 | 10 |
| *(With Whitney Houston)* | | | |
| JUMP TO IT (6:40) (3:58)/JUST MY DAYDREAM | 1982 | Arista SP-138 | 8 |
| OH HAPPY DAY/THE LORD'S PRAYER//(B-side unknown) | 1988 | Arista ADP 9682 | 12 |
| WHAT A FOOL BELIEVES (Long) (Short) | 1980 | Arista SP-103 | 8 |

**45s**

| | | | |
|---|---|---|---|
| FREEWAY OF LOVE Black promo label, pink vinyl | 1985 | Arista 9354 | 25 |
| *(Only the promo is pink vinyl)* | | | |
| JUMPIN' JACK FLASH  Black label, clear vinyl | 1986 | Arista 9528 | 15 |
| *(With Keith Richards. Early stock copies are also clear vinyl.)* | | | |
| TAKE A LOOK Yellow promo label | 1968 | Columbia JZSP 119505 | 18 |
| *(Promo-only release)* | | | |

**7-Inch Extended Plays**

| | | | |
|---|---|---|---|
| ARETHA FRANKLIN  Four-song promo-only EP | 1968 | Atlantic 33094 | 15 |
| *(7" record, 33rpm, small center hole, issued with picture cover with letter from producer Jerry Wexler)* | | | |
| FOREST FIRES Eight public service ads, one by Aretha | 1980 | Ad Council 879 | 25 |
| *(Issued with a hard cover)* | | | |

**Compact Discs**

| | | | |
|---|---|---|---|
| QUEEN OF SOUL SAMPLER | 1992 | Rhino 90128 | 20 |
| *(Promo-only compilation from box set)* | | | |

**RADIO SHOWS**
**Albums**

| | | | |
|---|---|---|---|
| MILLER CONCERT (May 87) Live concert | 1987 | Miller Beer (2) | 75-125 |
| *(Very rare concert series)* | | | |

**FREBERG, STAN**
*Other Capitol promo 78s $40 each; Other Capitol promo 45s $20-40 each depending on year Recordings also featured Jessie White, Daws Butler and Billy May*
**45s**

| | | | |
|---|---|---|---|
| ABE SNAKE FOR PRESIDENT | 1952 | Capitol 2125 | 50 |
| *(Stock copies of the 45s have about the same value)* | | | |
| BANANA BOAT SONG | 1957 | Capitol 3687 | 20 |
| *(Doesn't have Stan's photo on the label)* | | | |
| BANANA BOAT SONG | 1957 | Capitol 3687 | 35 |
| *(This version has Stan's photo on the label)* | | | |

| Title | Yr | Label, Number | NM $ |
|---|---|---|---|
| A DEAR JOHN AND MARSHA LETTER | 1953 | Capitol 2677 | 25 |
| *(Capitol promo label)* | | | |
| THE GREAT PRETENDER | 1956 | Capitol 3396 | 30 |
| *(White promo label)* | | | |
| GREEN CHRISTMAS | 1959 | Capitol 4097 | 30 |
| *(Has the entire 6:50 version on one side)* | | | |
| GREEN CHRISTMAS  White promo label | 1972 | Capitol 3503 | 25 |
| *(Part 1-3:33 and part 2-3:17)* | | | |
| HEARTBREAK HOTEL | 1956 | Capitol 3480 | 30 |
| *(White promo label)* | | | |
| NUTTIN' FOR CHRISTMAS | 1955 | Capitol 3280 | 25 |
| *(White promo label)* | | | |
| THE OLD PAYOLA ROLL BLUES | 1959 | Capitol 4329 | 35 |
| *(Red promo label, parts 1 and 2)* | | | |
| PERSON TO PEARSON | 1954 | Capitol 2838 | 25 |
| *(With Daws Butler)* | | | |
| SH-BOOM | 1954 | Capitol 2929 | 25 |
| *(White promo label)* | | | |
| ST. GEORGE AND THE DRAGONET | 1953 | Capitol 2596 | 30 |
| *(Usual 45rpm promo label)* | | | |
| TRY | 1951 | Capitol 2029 | 50 |
| *(Some copies were issued with a small center hole insert)* | | | |
| THE WORLD IS WAITING FOR THE SUNRISE | 1952 | Capitol 2279 | 40 |
| *(Some copies have a small center hole insert)* | | | |
| 3 AUDIO ESSAYS  Dialogue | 1962 | Southern Baptist | 100 |
| *(White label, 45rpm, small center hole, issued with hard cover)* | | | |
| WUN'ERFUL, WUN'ERFUL! | 1957 | Capitol 3815 | 25 |
| *("Side uh-one" and "Side uh-two")* | | | |
| WUN'ERFUL, WUN'ERFUL! | 1957 | Capitol PRO 415 | 75 |
| *(Promo only, 7:10 on one side, blank on back)* | | | |
| YA GOT TROUBLE | 1958 | Capitol 3892 | 20 |
| *(White promo label)* | | | |
| THE YELLOW ROSE OF TEXAS | 1955 | Capitol 3249 | 25 |
| *(White promo label)* | | | |
| YULENET | 1954 | Capitol 2986 | 35 |
| *(White promo label)* | | | |
| **7-Inch Extended Plays** | | | |
| BUBBLE-UP  Radio spots | 1965 | Coca-Cola 2227 | 75 |
| *(The same EP and cover as above "Coke" listing)* | | | |
| COKE  Radio spots | 1967 | Coca-Cola 2227 | 75 |
| *(Issued with a cover)* | | | |
| PITTSBURGH PAINT | 1967 | Freberg Ltd. | 75 |
| *(Seven cuts, color cover, includes "Painting on Radio")* | | | |
| SWIMSUITSMANSHIP | 1964 | Capitol 2080 | 100 |
| *(Includes Capitol picture cover)* | | | |
| TOM SWEET AND HIS ELECTRIC MILKY WAY MACHINE | 1959 | Mars U-23300 | 100 |
| *(Seven commercials for Mars Candies on a 7" disc)* | | | |
| **78s** | | | |
| ABE SNAKE FOR PRESIDENT  White promo label | 1952 | Capitol 2125 | 75 |
| *(Rare 78rpm promo)* | | | |
| DINKY PINKY  White promo label | 1950 | Capitol 32113 | 100 |
| *(Side 1 and side 2, from the children's 78rpm set, see Capitol CAS-3162)* | | | |
| ST. GEORGE AND THE DRAGONET  Yellow promo label | 1953 | Capitol 2596 | 75 |
| *(Rare promo 78rpm)* | | | |
| TRY  White promo label | 1951 | Capitol 2029 | 75 |
| *(Rare 78rpm promo)* | | | |
| **Albums** | | | |
| A CHILD'S GARDEN OF FREBERG | 1957 | Capitol 777 | 75 |
| *(Label reads "For Radio-TV Use Only")* | | | |
| A CHILD'S GARDEN OF FREBERG | 1957 | Capitol 777 | 75 |
| *(Yellow promo label)* | | | |
| GO TO CHURCH ON SUNDAY | 1968 | Minnesota Churches | 125 |
| *(60-second public service announcements on behalf of churches in Minnesota)* | | | |
| MORE HERE THAN MEETS THE EAR | 1956 | RAB | 100 |
| *(Six vignettes commissioned by the Radio Advertising Bureau)* | | | |
| SILVER PLATTER SHOW  (Oct 66)  With Jack Wagner | 1966 | Capitol 3219 | 100 |
| *(Includes a 6:51 interview and cuts from "Freberg Underground Show #1")* | | | |
| THE BEST OF THE STAN FREBERG SHOWS | 1958 | Capitol 1035 (2) | 100 |
| *(Label reads "For Radio-TV use only")* | | | |
| THE BEST OF THE STAN FREBERG SHOWS | 1958 | Capitol 1035 (2) | 100 |
| *(Yellow promo labels)* | | | |
| UNCLE STAN WANTS YOU | 1961 | Capitol 80700 | 125 |
| *(Promo-only LP)* | | | |
| WHO LISTENS TO RADIO  Issued with hard cover | 1968 | NAB | 75 |
| *(Issued to radio stations by the National Association of Broadcasters)* | | | |
| **Reel-to-Reel Tapes** | | | |
| LET'S GO TO CHURCH | 1967 | Minnesota Churches | 100 |
| *(Public service commercials for church in general)* | | | |
| NAB RADIO | 1986 | | 15 |
| *(Three radio spots on 5-inch reel)* | | | |

## FREDDIE AND THE DREAMERS

*Capitol and Tower promo 45s $15 each; Mercury promo 45s $12 each; Mercury promo LPs $15 each*

**45s**

| Title | Yr | Label, Number | NM $ |
|---|---|---|---|
| YOU WERE MADE FOR ME | 1965 | Tower 127 | 25 |
| *(White promo label, flip side by the Beat Merchants)* | | | |

| Title | Yr | Label, Number | NM $ |
|---|---|---|---|

**FREE**
*A&M promo 45s $3 each*
**RADIO SHOWS**
**Compact Discs**

| | | | |
|---|---|---|---|
| BBC CLASSIC TRACKS (May 93) | 1993 | Westwood One | 15-30 |
| *(Live tracks from the BBC)* | | | |
| SUPERSTAR CONCERT (Mar 93) Live concert | 1993 | Westwood One (2) | 30-50 |
| *(With Bad Company and The Firm)* | | | |

**FREE DESIGN, THE**
**45s**

| | | | |
|---|---|---|---|
| CLOSE YOUR MOUTH (IT'S CHRISTMAS)/CHRISTMAS IS THE DAY | 1968 | Project 3 1347 | 10 |
| *(Stock copy may not exist)* | | | |

**FREED, ALAN**
**Albums**

| | | | |
|---|---|---|---|
| THE ALAN FREED ROCK & ROLL SHOW | 1957 | Brunswick 54043 | 100 |
| *(Blue promo label)* | | | |

**FRENTE**
**RADIO SHOWS**
**Compact Discs**

| | | | |
|---|---|---|---|
| IN CONCERT-NU ROCK (Oct 94) Live concert | 1994 | Westwood One | 50-100 |
| *(With REM)* | | | |
| ON THE EDGE (May 94) Music and interviews | 1994 | Westwood One | 15-30 |
| *(With New Order)* | | | |

**FREY, GLENN**
**45s**

| | | | |
|---|---|---|---|
| ALLNIGHTER, THE | 1984 | MCA S45-1231 | 10 |
| *(Promo-only single)* | | | |

**FRIZZELL, LEFTY**
*Columbia promo 45s $5-10 each; Columbia promo LPs $10-15 each*

**FRYE, DAVID**
**45s**

| | | | |
|---|---|---|---|
| NIXON MEETS THE GODFATHER (mono/stereo) | 1973 | Buddah 378 | 10 |
| *(May be promo only)* | | | |

**FULLER, BOBBY**
*Capitol promo 45s $12 each*
**45s**

| | | | |
|---|---|---|---|
| NAME LIKE WATERMELON, A | 1970 | Capitol PRO-6123/4 | 20 |
| *(Promo-only single, stock copy on 3028)* | | | |

# G

**G. LOVE AND SPECIAL SAUCE**
**Albums**

| | | | |
|---|---|---|---|
| COAST TO COAST MOTEL | 1994 | Okeh/Epic 7445 | 30 |
| *(Vinyl is promo only)* | | | |

**GABRIEL, PETER**
*Early lead singer with Genesis. Other Mercury promo 45s $8 each; Atco promo 45s $8 each; Atlantic promo 45s $5 each; Geffen promo 45s $3 each; other Geffen promo CD singles $3-5 each.*
**12-Inch Singles**

| | | | |
|---|---|---|---|
| BIG TIME (same on both sides) | 1986 | Geffen PRO-A-2625 | 10 |
| DO IT YOURSELF (D.I.Y.) (same on both sides) | 1978 | Atlantic PR 310 | 22 |
| DON'T GIVE UP (Edit) (LP Version) | 1986 | Geffen PRO-A-2689 | 10 |
| I DON'T REMEMBER/AND THROUGH THE WIRE | 1980 | Mercury MK 157 | 30 |
| I GO SWIMMING (Live)/NO SELF CONTROL (Live)/ | 1984 | Geffen PRO-A-2044 | 12 |
| D.I.Y. (Live)/I DON'T REMEMBER | | | |
| SHOCK THE MONKEY/I HAVE THE TOUCH/KISS OF LIFE | 1982 | Geffen PRO-A-1062 | 10 |
| SLEDGEHAMMER (Edit) (LP Version) | 1986 | Geffen PRO-A-2462 | 12 |
| STEAM (4 versions) | 1992 | Geffen 4488 | 15 |
| WALK THROUGH THE FIRE (Remix) (same on both sides) | 1984 | Atlantic 609 | 12 |

**45s**

| | | | |
|---|---|---|---|
| I DON'T REMEMBER Blue promo label | 1980 | Mercury 76086 | 10 |
| *(Unusual limited blue promo label)* | | | |

**Albums**

| | | | |
|---|---|---|---|
| PETER GABRIEL (SECURITY) | 1982 | Geffen GHS 2011 | 15 |
| *(Promo-only Quiex II audiophile pressing)* | | | |

**Compact Discs**

| | | | |
|---|---|---|---|
| BEFORE US: A BRIEF HISTORY | 1992 | Geffen PRCD-4412 | 20 |
| *(Promo-only compilation of solo material)* | | | |
| DON'T GIVE UP | 1987 | Geffen PRO-CD-2680 | 30 |
| *(With Kate Bush, a very early promo CD single)* | | | |
| IN YOUR EYES | 1989 | WTG PSK 1622 | 20 |
| *(Promo CD release from "Say Anything" soundtrack)* | | | |

| Title | Yr | Label, Number | NM $ |
|---|---|---|---|
| **RADIO SHOWS** | | | |
| **Albums** | | | |
| LEGENDS OF ROCK (July 87) Profile | 1987 | NBC Radio (2) | 20-30 |
| *(Music and interviews)* | | | |
| NBC SOURCE (Nov 86) | 1986 | NBC Radio (2) | 20-30 |
| *(Music and interviews)* | | | |
| OFF THE RECORD (90s) Profile | 199? | Westwood One (2) | 15-25 |
| *(Music and interview, repeated several times)* | | | |
| PROFILE (Nov 86) | 1986 | NBC Radio (2) | 20-35 |
| *(Music and interviews)* | | | |
| TIMOTHY WHITE SESSIONS (June 89) Profile | 1989 | (2) | 20-35 |
| *(Music and interviews)* | | | |
| **Compact Discs** | | | |
| AN INTIMATE CONVERSATION ABOUT US (Aug 93) | 1993 | | 250-500 |
| *(Very rare one-time interview show)* | | | |
| KING BISCUIT FLOWER HOUR (Oct 89) Live concert | 1989 | DIR | 40-60 |
| *(Repeated several times)* | | | |
| UP CLOSE  Profile | 1991 | Media America (2) | 30-50 |
| *(Music and interview, some live tracks)* | | | |
| UP CLOSE (June 91) Tribute to Robert Johnson | 1991 | Media America | 15-25 |
| *(Most shows in this series are double CD sets)* | | | |
| **Reel-to-Reel Tapes** | | | |
| SECRET WORLD LIVE (Sept 94) Pre-release to CD | 1994 | | 25-40 |
| *(Music and interviews about new CD release, on two reels)* | | | |
| | | | |
| **GALLAGHER, RORY** | | | |
| **RADIO SHOWS** | | | |
| **Albums** | | | |
| BBC TRANSCRIPTION DISC Live concert | 1973 | BBC Transcription | 175-250 |
| *(Very rare radio series)* | | | |
| BBC TRANSCRIPTION DISC Live concert | 1979 | BBC Transcription | 125-200 |
| | | | |
| **GALLION, BOB** | | | |
| **45s** | | | |
| MY SQUARE DANCIN' MAMA | 1957 | MGM 12195 | 55 |
| *(Yellow promo label)* | | | |
| | | | |
| **GANG OF FOUR** | | | |
| **12-Inch Singles** | | | |
| CADILLAC (2 versions)/FAVOURITES | 1991 | Polydor 922 | 8 |
| DON'T FIX WHAT AIN'T BROKE (same on both sides) | 1991 | Polydor 925 | 8 |
| I LOVE A MAN IN A UNIFORM (2 versions)/CALL ME UP | 1982 | Warner Bros. PRO-A-1050 | 7 |
| IS IT LOVE (Long Mix)/IS IT LOVE (Short)/MAN WITH A GOOD CAR | 1983 | Warner Bros. PRO-A-2081 | 7 |
| | | | |
| **GAP BAND, THE** | | | |
| **12-Inch Singles** | | | |
| I'M READY (same on both sides) | 1983 | Total Experience 707 | 7 |
| STEPPIN' (OUT) (same on both sides) | 1979 | Mercury MK 124 | 8 |
| YEARNING FOR YOUR LOVE/HUMPIN' | 1980 | Mercury MK 175 | 8 |
| **45s** | | | |
| WE CAN MAKE IT ALRIGHT (same on both sides) | 1990 | Capitol 7PRO-79045 | 6 |
| *Vinyl is promo only* | | | |
| | | | |
| **GARBAGE** | | | |
| **Compact Discs** | | | |
| ONLY HAPPY WHEN IT RAINS | 1996 | Almo Sounds | 6 |
| *(Promo-only CD single, released as stock copy with different number)* | | | |
| STUPID GIRL | 1996 | Almo Sounds | 6 |
| *(Promo-only CD single)* | | | |
| **RADIO SHOWS** | | | |
| **Compact Discs** | | | |
| IN CONCERT-NU ROCK | 1996 | | 40-70 |
| *(Live material)* | | | |
| | | | |
| **GARFUNKEL, ART** | | | |
| *More at Simon and Garfunkel.* | | | |
| **Albums** | | | |
| WATERMARK | 1978 | Columbia JC 34975 | 60 |
| *(Test pressing or white label promo with "Fingerpaint" on side 2)* | | | |
| | | | |
| **GARLAND, JUDY** | | | |
| **Albums** | | | |
| IN CONCERT, SAN FRANSICO | 197? | Mark 56 | 50 |
| *(Promo picture disc)* | | | |
| SILVER PLATTER SERVICE (60s) With Jack Wagner | 196? | Capitol PRO-3164 | 50 |
| *(Includes Judy Garland phone interview)* | | | |
| **RADIO SHOWS** | | | |
| **Albums** | | | |
| GUARD SESSIONS | 1967 | National Guard 301-4 | 50-75 |
| *(Four public service shows issued with hard cover)* | | | |

| Title | Yr | Label, Number | NM $ |
|-------|----|--------------| -----|

**GATES, DAVID**
*Lead singer of Bread. Elektra promo 45s $3 each.*
**45s**

| Title | Yr | Label, Number | NM $ |
|-------|----|--------------| -----|
| COME HOME FOR CHRISTMAS | 1981 | Arista AS 0653 | 10 |
| *(Promo-only 45; a B-side was assigned but never issued)* | | | |
| LOVIN' AT NIGHT | 1961 | Robbins 1008 | 75 |
| *(White promo label)* | | | |
| SWINGIN' BABY DOLL | 1959 | East West 123 | 125 |
| *(White promo label)* | | | |

**GATLIN, LARRY, AND THE GATLIN BROTHERS BAND**
*Monument promo 45s $3 each; Columbia promo 45s $2 each.*
**45s**

| Title | Yr | Label, Number | NM $ |
|-------|----|--------------| -----|
| BOOGIE AND BEETHOVEN (same on both sides) | 1990 | Capitol 7PRO-79053 | 5 |
| *(Vinyl is promo only)* | | | |
| COUNTRY GIRL HEART (same on both sides) | 1991 | Capitol 7PRO-79378 | 5 |
| *(Vinyl is promo only)* | | | |

**45s**

| Title | Yr | Label, Number | NM $ |
|-------|----|--------------| -----|
| WHAT'S IT ALL ABOUT (Jan 81) Public service show | 1981 | W. I. A. A. 557/613 | 30 |
| *(Flip side features Robert Plant)* | | | |

**RADIO SHOWS**
**Albums**

| Title | Yr | Label, Number | NM $ |
|-------|----|--------------| -----|
| AMERICAN EAGLE (July 86) Live concert | 1986 | Westwood One | 15-25 |
| *(With the Gatlin Brothers)* | | | |
| SILVER EAGLE (Apr 82) Live concert | 1982 | Westwood One (3) | 30-50 |
| *(Larry Gatlin and the Gatlin Brothers)* | | | |
| WESTWOOD ONE PRESENTS (Aug 89) | 1989 | Westwood One | 15-25 |
| *(Live concert)* | | | |

**GAYE, MARVIN**
*Other Tamla promo singles $5-15 each depending on year; Motown promo singles $5 each; Columbia promo singles $3 each*
**12-Inch Singles**

| Title | Yr | Label, Number | NM $ |
|-------|----|--------------| -----|
| MASOCHISTIC BEAUTY/(Instrumental) | 1985 | Columbia CAS 2124 | 6 |

**45s**

| Title | Yr | Label, Number | NM $ |
|-------|----|--------------| -----|
| I WANT YOU White promo label, yellow vinyl | 1976 | Tamla 54264 | 15 |
| *(Only the promo is yellow vinyl)* | | | |
| MASQUERADE (IS OVER)/WITCHCRAFT | 1962 | Tamla (no #) | 600 |
| *(As "Marvin Gay"; label states "Single Not Available extracted from Album (TM-221)")* | | | |
| TEEN BEAT SONG/LORAINE ALTERMAN INTERVIEWS MARVIN GAYE | 1966 | Detroit Free Press (no #) | 150 |
| THIS IS THE LIFE/MY WAY | 1965 | Tamla S4KM 0741/2 | 50 |
| WHAT'S IT ALL ABOUT (July 80) Public service show | 1980 | W. I. A. A. 530 | 18 |
| *(Flip side features Meat Loaf)* | | | |
| WORLD IS RATED X  Promo record, promo sleeve | 1986 | Tamla 1836 | 10 |
| *(The picture sleeve is a promo)* | | | |
| YOU'RE THE MAN  White promo label, red vinyl | 1972 | Tamla 54221 | 25 |
| *(Only the promo is red vinyl)* | | | |

**7-Inch Extended Plays**

| Title | Yr | Label, Number | NM $ |
|-------|----|--------------| -----|
| MARVIN GAYE GREATEST HITS  Jukebox LLP | 1967 | Tamla 5708 | 50 |
| *(Issued with a hard cover)* | | | |

**Albums**

| Title | Yr | Label, Number | NM $ |
|-------|----|--------------| -----|
| THE MASTER 1961-1984 | 1995 | Motown 37463 1296-1 | 20 |
| *(Vinyl is promo only; 8-song sampler from box set)* | | | |

**Compact Discs**

| Title | Yr | Label, Number | NM $ |
|-------|----|--------------| -----|
| THE MASTER 1961-1984 SAMPLER | 1995 | Motown | 15 |
| *(Single-CD promo compilation from box set)* | | | |

**RADIO SHOWS**

| Title | Yr | Label, Number | NM $ |
|-------|----|--------------| -----|
| SIXTIES LEGENDS (July 92) Profile | 1992 | Unistar (2) | 20-35 |
| *(Music and interviews)* | | | |

**Albums**

| Title | Yr | Label, Number | NM $ |
|-------|----|--------------| -----|
| THE IN SOUND (Jan 68) Various artists | 1968 | U.S. Army | 10-20 |
| *(Includes interview with Marvin Gaye)* | | | |
| WESTWOOD ONE PRESENTS  Tribute to Marvin Gaye | 1984 | Westwood One | 75-125 |
| *(Music and interviews)* | | | |

**GAYLE, CRYSTAL**
**Albums**

| Title | Yr | Label, Number | NM $ |
|-------|----|--------------| -----|
| SOMEBODY LOVES YOU | 1978 | United Artists 856 | 50 |
| *(Hard to find promo-only picture disc)* | | | |

**RADIO SHOWS**
**Albums**

| Title | Yr | Label, Number | NM $ |
|-------|----|--------------| -----|
| WHILE I DREAM | 1976 | Burns Media Consultants | 30-50 |
| *(Obscure radio show on the LP of the same name)* | | | |

**GAYNOR, GLORIA**
**12-Inch Singles**

| Title | Yr | Label, Number | NM $ |
|-------|----|--------------| -----|
| ANYBODY WANNA PARTY (same on both sides) | 1978 | Polydor PD-D-507 | 8 |
| LET ME KNOW (I HAVE A RIGHT) (2 versions) | 1979 | Polydor PRO 111 | 8 |
| LET'S MEND WHAT'S BEEN BROKEN (same on both sides) | 1981 | Polydor PD-D-517 | 8 |
| LOVE IS A HEARTBEAT AWAY (2 versions) | 1979 | MCA L33-1847 | 10 |
| MOST OF ALL/AS TIME GOES BY | 1977 | Polydor PRO 107 | 10 |
| SUBSTITUTE (same on both sides) | 1978 | Polydor PD-D-504 | 8 |

**45s**

| Title | Yr | Label, Number | NM $ |
|-------|----|--------------| -----|
| AMERICA (same on both sides) | 1983 | Atlantic 89824 | 4 |
| *(May be promo only)* | | | |

| Title | Yr | Label, Number | NM $ |
|---|---|---|---|

**GEILS, J., BAND**
**45s**

| | | | |
|---|---|---|---|
| COME BACK (Long) (Edit) | 1980 | EMI America 8032 | 5 |

**GELDOF, BOB**
*Atlantic promo 45s $3 each Of the Boomtown Rats; Creator of Band Aid*
**12-Inch Singles**

| | | | |
|---|---|---|---|
| HEARTLESS HEART/PULLED APART BY HORSES | 1986 | Atlantic 2026 | 8 |

**Albums**

| | | | |
|---|---|---|---|
| QUESTIONS AND ANSWERS | 1987 | Atlantic 1010 | 15 |

*(Promo-only interview LP)*
**RADIO SHOWS**
**Compact Discs**

| | | | |
|---|---|---|---|
| ON THE EDGE (June 93) Profile of three acts | 1993 | Westwood One | 20-30 |

*(Music and interviews, with World Party and Judybats)*

**GENE LOVES JEZEBEL**
**12-Inch Singles**

| | | | |
|---|---|---|---|
| SUSPICION (same on both sides) | 1987 | Geffen PRO-A-2800 | 10 |
| TANGLED UP IN YOU (2 mixes)/JEALOUS (2 mixes) | 1990 | Geffen 4157 | 10 |
| TWENTY KILLER HURTS (3 versions) | 1987 | Geffen PRO-A-2998 | 8 |

**Albums**

| | | | |
|---|---|---|---|
| GEFFEN MUSIC SHOW Music and interviews | 1986 | Geffen | 10 |

*(Promotional show from the record label)*
**RADIO SHOWS**
**Compact Discs**

| | | | |
|---|---|---|---|
| IN CONCERT-NU ROCK (Mar 93) | 1993 | Westwood One | 40-60 |

*(Live concert)*

| | | | |
|---|---|---|---|
| ON THE EDGE (Feb 93) Profile of three acts | 1993 | Westwood One | 20-30 |

*(Music and interviews, with Blind Melon and Stereo MCs)*

**GENERAL PUBLIC**
**12-Inch Singles**

| | | | |
|---|---|---|---|
| COME AGAIN (same on both sides) | 1986 | I.R.S. 17271 | 6 |
| TOO MUCH OR NOTHING (Long) (Short) | 1986 | I.R.S. 17192 | 5 |

**GENESIS**
*Includes listings of Mike & the Mechanics. Also see Tony Banks; Phil Collins; Peter Gabriel. Other Atco promo 45s $8 each; Other Atlantic promo 45s $5 each; Atlantic promo 45s by Mike & the Mechanics $3 each; Buddah promo 2LPs $12 each; Atlantic promo CD singles $3-5 each.*
**12-Inch Singles**

| | | | |
|---|---|---|---|
| ABACAB (same on both sides) | 1981 | Atlantic PR 416 | 10 |
| GO WEST YOUNG MAN (same on both sides) | 1978 | Atlantic PR 311 | 20 |
| ILLEGAL ALIEN//HOME BY THE SEA/SECOND HOME BY THE SEA | 1983 | Atlantic PR 581 | 8 |
| INVISIBLE TOUCH (same on both sides) | 1986 | Atlantic PR 897 | 6 |
| INVISIBLE TOUCH (Special Remix) (same on both sides) | 1986 | Atlantic PR 924 | 12 |
| MAMA (same on both sides) | 1983 | Atlantic PR 535 | 8 |
| MAN ON THE CORNER (same on both sides) | 1981 | Atlantic PR 425 | 8 |
| NO REPLY AT ALL (4:37) (4:00) | 1981 | Atlantic PR 404 | 10 |
| TONIGHT, TONIGHT, TONIGHT | 1986 | Atlantic PR-965 | 12 |

*(Short and long versions)*

| | | | |
|---|---|---|---|
| TURN IT ON AGAIN | 1982 | Atlantic | 15 |

*(Live and studio versions)*
**45s**

| | | | |
|---|---|---|---|
| PAPERLATE  White promo label | 1982 | Atlantic PR 453 | 12 |

*(Promo-only version 3:15)*

| | | | |
|---|---|---|---|
| SILENT SUN/THAT'S ME | 1968 | Parrot 3018 | 100 |

*(May be promo only)*

| | | | |
|---|---|---|---|
| THAT'S ALL | 1984 | Atlantic | 15 |

*(White label test pressing)*

| | | | |
|---|---|---|---|
| THE LAMB LIES DOWN ON BROADWAY  White/blue labels | 1974 | Atco 7013 | 12 |

*(Stereo/mono versions)*

| | | | |
|---|---|---|---|
| YOUR OWN SPECIAL WAY White/blue labels | 1976 | Atlantic 7076 | 10 |

*(Stereo/mono versions)*
**7-Inch Extended Plays**

| | | | |
|---|---|---|---|
| NURSERY CRYME | 197? | Buddah | 20 |

*(Promo-only EP)*

| | | | |
|---|---|---|---|
| PROFILES IN GOLD ALBUM 2  Four artists | 197? | Warner Bros. 7502 | 10 |

*(With paper cover, one Genesis song, for Coca-Cola and Burger King)*
**Compact Discs**

| | | | |
|---|---|---|---|
| TWO SONGS FROM THE LONGS | 1993 | Atlantic PRCD 4997 | 20 |

*(Promo-only CD from the record label)*
**RADIO SHOWS**
**Albums**

| | | | |
|---|---|---|---|
| 1986 GRAMMY AWARDS (Feb 86) Hosted by Collins | 1986 | MJI Broadcasting (2) | 25-40 |

*(Various artists, music and interviews)*

| | | | |
|---|---|---|---|
| 3 INTO 1 LONDONWAVE CONCERT (Apr 84) | 1984 | London Wavelength (3) | 40-75 |

*(Rare early live concert)*

| | | | |
|---|---|---|---|
| BBC ROCK HOUR | 1981 | London Wavelength | 20-40 |

*(Mostly music and interviews)*

| | | | |
|---|---|---|---|
| BBC ROCK HOUR (Mar 81) Collins/Genesis | 1981 | London Wavelength | 20-40 |

*(Mostly music and interviews)*

| | | | |
|---|---|---|---|
| BBC TRANSCRIPTION DISC  Live concert | 1978 | BBC Transcription | 250-425 |

*(Rarest of the live Genesis concerts)*

| Title | Yr | Label, Number | NM $ |
|---|---|---|---|
| BBC TRANSCRIPTION DISC  Music and interviews | 1986 | BBC Transcription | 100-200 |
| *(A very rare radio series)* | | | |
| CAPTURED LIVE  Phil Collins | 1983 | RKO (3) | 50-100 |
| *(Live concert)* | | | |
| CAPTURED LIVE (July 84) | 1984 | RKO (3) | 50-100 |
| *(Live concert)* | | | |
| COUNTDOWN TO CHRISTMAS (Dec 85) Phil Collins/Genesis | 1985 | NBC Radio | 15-25 |
| *(Music and interviews)* | | | |
| HOT ROCKS Genesis/Collins | 1986 | United Stations (2) | 25-40 |
| *(Mostly music and interviews)* | | | |
| INSIDE TRACKS (Feb 83) | 1983 | RKO (3) | 20-40 |
| *(Music and interviews)* | | | |
| INSIDE TRACKS Phil Collins | 1982 | RKO (3) | 20-40 |
| *(Phil Collins and Steve Winwood)* | | | |
| KING BISCUIT FLOWER HOUR Mike & the Mechanics | 1986 | DIR (2) | 20-40 |
| *(Live concert, repeated several times)* | | | |
| KING BISCUIT FLOWER HOUR (June 87) | 1987 | DIR (4) | 75-150 |
| *(Live super special concert, edited version)* | | | |
| KING BISCUIT FLOWER HOUR (May 86) Phil Collins | 1986 | DIR (2) | 40-60 |
| *(Live concert, repeated several times)* | | | |
| KING BISCUIT FLOWER HOUR (Nov/Dec 86) | 1986 | DIR (8) | 175-300 |
| *(Live super special concert)* | | | |
| LEGENDS OF ROCK | 1988 | NBC Radio (2) | 15-25 |
| *(Music and interviews)* | | | |
| LEGENDS OF ROCK  Peter Gabriel | 1988 | NBC Radio (2) | 20-30 |
| *(Music and interviews)* | | | |
| LEGENDS OF ROCK  Phil Collins | 1988 | NBC Radio (2) | 15-25 |
| *(Music and interviews)* | | | |
| LEGENDS OF ROCK (Jan 87) | 1987 | NBC Radio (4) | 25-40 |
| *(Music and interviews, parts 1 and 2)* | | | |
| LONDON PROFILE (80s) | 198? | Westwood One | 15-25 |
| *(Music and interviews)* | | | |
| LONDON WAVELENGTH Box set | 1983 | London Wavelength (3) | 75-125 |
| *(Mostly live material)* | | | |
| LONDON WAVELENGTH SPECIAL (Dec 82) | 1982 | London Wavelength (2) | 25-50 |
| *(Live concert)* | | | |
| MASTERS OF ROCK  Group and solos | 1989 | Radio Ventures (2) | 20-30 |
| *(Music and interviews)* | | | |
| MELLO YELLOW | 1983 | ABC Radio (3) | 75-125 |
| *(Rare early live concert)* | | | |
| NBC SOURCE (80s) | 198? | NBC Radio (2) | 100-175 |
| *(Rare early live concert)* | | | |
| NBC SOURCE (Nov 80) | 1980 | NBC Radio (2) | 20-40 |
| *(Music and interviews)* | | | |
| OFF THE RECORD (80s) | 198? | Westwood One (2) | 12-18 |
| *(Music and interviews, repeated)* | | | |
| OFF THE RECORD (80s) Mike & the Mechanics | 198? | Westwood One (2) | 10-15 |
| *(Music and interviews, repeated)* | | | |
| OFF THE RECORD (80s) Phil Collins | 198? | Westwood One (2) | 12-18 |
| *(Music and interviews, repeated)* | | | |
| PROFILE (Nov 86) Peter Gabriel | 1986 | NBC Radio (2) | 20-35 |
| *(Music and interviews)* | | | |
| ROCK AROUND THE WORLD | 1976 | RATW | 40-60 |
| *(Music and interviews)* | | | |
| ROCK CONNECTIONS (Apr 87) | 1987 | CBS RadioRadio | 10-20 |
| *(Music and interviews)* | | | |
| ROCK SALUTES MOTOWN (June 84) Box set | 1984 | NBC Radio (5) | 40-60 |
| *(Various artists, Collins is host, music and interviews)* | | | |
| SOLO & TOGETHER Collins/Genesis | 1987 | Radio International (2) | 20-35 |
| *(Music and interviews)* | | | |
| STARTRACK PROFILE  Genesis/Collins | 1988 | Westwood One (2) | 20-30 |
| *(Music and interviews)* | | | |
| SUPERSTAR CONCERT  Box set | 1983 | Westwood One (3) | 40-60 |
| *(Live concert, repeated several times)* | | | |
| SUPERSTAR CONCERT  For the Prince's Trust | 1985 | Westwood One (3) | 50-75 |
| *(Various artists live concert, lots of Genesis)* | | | |
| SUPERSTAR CONCERT  Phil Collins | 1984 | Westwood One (3) | 40-60 |
| *(Live concert, repeated several times)* | | | |
| WORLD OF ROCK Phil Collins | 1990 | DIR (2) | 10-25 |
| *(Music and interviews, Phil is co-host)* | | | |
| WORLD OF ROCK (Apr 89) Mike Rutherford | 1989 | DIR (2) | 10-20 |
| *(Music and interviews, Mike is co-host)* | | | |
| **Compact Discs** | | | |
| BBC CLASSIC TRACKS (July 91) | 1991 | Westwood One | 20-35 |
| *(Classic live tracks from the BBC)* | | | |
| KING BISCUIT FLOWER HOUR | 1987 | DIR | 40-60 |
| *(Live concert, repeated)* | | | |
| KING BISCUIT FLOWER HOUR (Aug 88) | 1988 | DIR | 75-125 |
| *(With King Crimson)* | | | |
| KING BISCUIT FLOWER HOUR (Oct 89) Peter Gabriel | 1989 | DIR | 40-60 |
| *(Live concert, repeated several times)* | | | |
| KING BISCUIT FLOWER HOUR Mike & the Mechanics | 1989 | DIR | 20-40 |
| *(Live concert, repeated)* | | | |
| RADIO TODAY  Mike Rutherford/Mechanics | 1989 | Radio International (2) | 20-30 |
| *(Music and interviews)* | | | |
| ROCK STARS Mike & the Mechanics | 1989 | Radio International (2) | 30-40 |
| *(Material from live concerts)* | | | |

| Title | Yr | Label, Number | NM $ |
|---|---|---|---|
| UP CLOSE | 1988 | Media America (2) | 35-50 |
| *(Mostly music and interviews, some live material)* | | | |
| UP CLOSE Phil Collins | 1988 | Media America (2) | 35-50 |
| *(Mostly music and interviews, some live material)* | | | |

**GENO, SONNY**
**45s**

| Title | Yr | Label, Number | NM $ |
|---|---|---|---|
| DON'T LEAVE ME, BABY | 1955 | Apollo 470 | 75 |
| *(White promo label)* | | | |
| SOMETHING TO REMEMBER YOU BY | 1954 | Apollo 464 | 75 |
| *(White promo label)* | | | |

**GENTLE GIANT**
**45s**

| Title | Yr | Label, Number | NM $ |
|---|---|---|---|
| WORDS FROM THE WISE | 197? | Capitol PRO-8951 | 20 |
| *(Promo only on orange vinyl)* | | | |

**GENTRYS, THE**
**45s**

| Title | Yr | Label, Number | NM $ |
|---|---|---|---|
| CINNAMON GIRL/I JUST GOT THE NEWS | 1970 | Sun 1114 | 10 |
| *(Promo only on blue vinyl)* | | | |

**GEORGIA SATELLITES**
*Elektra promo 45s $3 each; Elektra promo CD singles $3 each*
**RADIO SHOWS**
**Albums**

| Title | Yr | Label, Number | NM $ |
|---|---|---|---|
| IN CONCERT (Feb 87) Live concert | 1987 | Westwood One (2) | 35-50 |
| *(With Robert Cray)* | | | |
| KING BISCUIT FLOWER HOUR (Apr 87) Live concert | 1987 | DIR (2) | 50-80 |
| *(This show was repeated)* | | | |
| SUPERSTAR CONCERT (Aug 88) Live concert | 1988 | Westwood One (3) | 40-75 |
| *(With Henry Lee Summer)* | | | |

**GETSET V.O.P.**
**12-Inch Singles**

| Title | Yr | Label, Number | NM $ |
|---|---|---|---|
| TIMBERLANDS FOR XMAS (House of the Seven Do's)/ | 1993 | Polydor PRO 1085-1 | 8 |
| TIMBERLANDS FOR CHRISTMAS (Alternate Mix)//TIMBERLAND | | | |

**GIBB, ROBIN**
*More at Bee Gees.*
**12-Inch Singles**

| Title | Yr | Label, Number | NM $ |
|---|---|---|---|
| SECRET AGENT/ROBOT | 1984 | Mirage PR 775 | 10 |

**45s**

| Title | Yr | Label, Number | NM $ |
|---|---|---|---|
| IN YOUR DIARY (same on both sides) | 1984 | Mirage 99688 | 4 |
| *(Stock copy unknown)* | | | |

**GIBSON, STEVE, AND HIS RED CAPS**
*Including Damita Jo. Other Mercury promo 45s $18 each; Other RCA Victor promo 45s $15 each; Other ABC Paramount promo 45s $12 each; Hunt promo 45s $12 each; RCA Victor promo 45s by Damita Jo $8 each; Mercury promo 45s by Damita Jo $5 each; ABC Paramount promo LPs by Damita Jo and Red Caps $30 each.*
**45s**

| Title | Yr | Label, Number | NM $ |
|---|---|---|---|
| HOW I CRY | 1958 | RCA Victor 6345 | 18 |
| *(White promo label)* | | | |
| IF YOU GO AWAY Damita Jo | 1966 | Epic 10061 | 18 |
| *(Yellow vinyl, white promo label)* | | | |
| SILHOUETTES | 1958 | ABC-Paramount 9856 | 15 |
| *(White promo label)* | | | |

**78s**

| Title | Yr | Label, Number | NM $ |
|---|---|---|---|
| HOW I CRY | 1957 | RCA Victor 6345 | 25 |
| *(White promo label)* | | | |
| I'LL NEVER LOVE ANYONE ELSE | 1955 | Mercury 8380 | 40 |
| *(White promo label)* | | | |
| SHAME | 1951 | RCA Victor 4294 | 50 |
| *(White promo label)* | | | |
| THE THING | 1950 | RCA Victor 3986 | 50 |
| *(White promo label)* | | | |
| THREE DOLLARS AND NINETY-EIGHT CENTS | 1951 | RCA Victor 4076 | 50 |
| *(White promo label)* | | | |
| WEDDING BELLS | 1954 | Mercury 8069 | 50 |
| *(White promo label)* | | | |

**GILBERTO, ASTRUD**
**45s**

| Title | Yr | Label, Number | NM $ |
|---|---|---|---|
| ARUANDA/DINDI | 1967 | Verve 10532 | 8 |
| LOOK TO THE RAINBOW/LUGAR BONITA | 1967 | Verve 10534 | 8 |
| MANHA DE CARNIVAL/BERIMBAU | 1967 | Verve 10533 | 8 |
| ONCE UPON A SUMMERTIME/ONCE I LOVED | 1967 | Verve 10531 | 8 |
| SO NICE/WISH ME A RAINBOW | 1967 | Verve 10535 | 8 |

*(The above five 45s are yellow label promos, part of a "Celebrity Series" box set for jukebox operators. Add another $10 for the box, title strips and artist bio.)*

| Title | Yr | Label, Number | NM $ |
|---|---|---|---|

**GILL, VINCE**
*RCA Victor promo 45s $3 each; MCA promo 45s $3 each; MCA promo CDs $3 each*
**RADIO SHOWS**
**Compact Discs**

| | | | |
|---|---|---|---|
| COUNTRY CONCERT (July 94) | 1994 | Westwood One (2) | 35-50 |
| *(Live concert)* | | | |

**GILLAN**
**RADIO SHOWS**
**Albums**

| | | | |
|---|---|---|---|
| BBC TRANSCRIPTION DISC Live concert | 1981 | BBC Transcription | 175-350 |
| *(With Siouxsie and the Banshees)* | | | |

**GILLEY, MICKEY**
*TCF/Fox promo 45s $6 each; Paula white promo label 45s $5 each; Playboy promo 45s $4 each; Other Epic promo 45s $3 each; Airborne (Capitol) promo 45s $3 each*
**45s**

| | | | |
|---|---|---|---|
| CALL ME SHORTY | 1958 | DOT 15706 | 75 |
| *(Black promo label)* | | | |
| I'M SPENDING CHRISTMAS WITH YOU | 1981 | Epic AE7 1774 | 10 |
| *(Promo-only holiday single for radio)* | | | |
| MICKEY GILLEY CHRISTMAS MEDLEY Promo only | 1981 | Epic AE7 1356 | 10 |
| *(Two medleys, 2:51 and 3:34)* | | | |

**RADIO SHOWS**
**Albums**

| | | | |
|---|---|---|---|
| LIVE AT GILLEY'S (Feb 84) Live concert | 1984 | Westwood One | 10-20 |
| *(Show was repeated)* | | | |
| WESTWOOD ONE PRESENTS (Nov 89) Live concert | 1989 | Westwood One | 10-20 |

**GILMOUR, DAVID**
*Member of Pink Floyd.*
**RADIO SHOWS**
**Albums**

| | | | |
|---|---|---|---|
| IN CONCERT (Mar 85) Live concert | 1985 | Westwood One (2) | 150-225 |
| *(Rare live concert)* | | | |
| INNERVIEW (70s) Profile | 197? | Innerview | 10-20 |
| *(Music and interviews)* | | | |
| SUPER CONCERT (Nov 86) Live concert | 1986 | DIR (3) | 40-75 |

**GIN BLOSSOMS**
*A&M promo CD singles $3 each*
**RADIO SHOWS**
**Compact Discs**

| | | | |
|---|---|---|---|
| ALBUM NETWORK SPECIAL (Apr 96) | 1996 | Album Network (2) | 50-75 |
| *(Live concert material)* | | | |
| IN CONCERT (Mar 95) | 1995 | Westwood One | 25-50 |
| *(Live concert)* | | | |
| IN CONCERT (Oct 93) Live concert | 1993 | Westwood One | 25-50 |
| *(This show also repeated)* | | | |
| IN CONCERT-NU ROCK (Jan 95) | 1995 | Westwood One | 25-50 |
| *(Live concert)* | | | |
| IN CONCERT-NU ROCK (Nov 93) Live concert | 1993 | Westwood One | 25-50 |
| *(New concert material)* | | | |
| ON THE EDGE (May 94) Music and interviews | 1994 | Westwood One | 15-25 |
| *(With the Pretenders)* | | | |
| ON THE EDGE (Nov 93) Music and interviews | 1993 | Westwood One | 25-35 |
| *(With Depeche Mode)* | | | |
| ON THE EDGE (Oct 94) Music and interviews | 1994 | Westwood One | 15-25 |
| *(With Oasis)* | | | |
| ON TOUR (June 96) | 1996 | | 25-40 |
| *(Live material, with Filter and Seven Mary Three)* | | | |
| SUPERSTAR CONCERT Live concert | 1993 | Westwood One (2) | 25-50 |
| *(Live concert, show repeated)* | | | |

**GINGER AND THE SNAPS**
*The Honeys*
**45s**

| | | | |
|---|---|---|---|
| SEVEN DAYS IN SEPTEMBER | 1965 | MGM 13413 | 75 |
| *(Yellow promo label)* | | | |

**GIORDANO, LOU**
**45s**

| | | | |
|---|---|---|---|
| STAY CLOSE TO ME  Yellow promo label | 1959 | Brunswick 55115 | 500 |
| *(With Buddy Holly and Phil Everly)* | | | |

**GIUFFRIA**
*MCA promo 45s $3 each*
**RADIO SHOWS**
**Albums**

| | | | |
|---|---|---|---|
| KING BISCUIT FLOWER HOUR (Mar 85) Live concert | 1985 | DIR (2) | 50-80 |
| *(With Accept)* | | | |

(Top left) The Source, which was NBC Radio's "young adult" service, had a "Christmas Countdown" concert series. This one features the appropriate double bill of The English Beat and the Go-Go's. (Top right) For Grateful Dead fans who are not tape traders, finding a promo copy of a concert album is a goal. Even the white-label promo of *Europe '72* had the skull on the label. (Middle left) While many amateur tapes of Grateful Dead concerts are well recorded, those taped for use as radio shows *definitely* were well recorded. Here's a King Biscuit Flower Hour appearance, part 1 of 2 shows. (Middle right) A concert from Heart's comeback period aired on the King Biscuit Flower Hour on Dec. 8, 1985. (Bottom row) The jacket and label for a special on the revived Heart, which aired around Valentine's Day of 1986.

| Title | Yr | Label, Number | NM $ |
|---|---|---|---|

**GLAD SINGERS, THE**
**45s**

| DECK THE HALLS/HAPPY NEW YEAR | 1965 | Columbia JZSP 111919/20 | 12 |

*(Promo only on green vinyl)*

**GLASER, TOMPALL**
**Albums**

| THIS LAND FOLK SONGS  Pink promo label | 1960 | Decca 4041 | 40 |

**GLEASON, JACKIE**

*Also includes other members of the Honeymooners cast. Decca promo 78s and 45s $15 each (Decca 274 has a stock picture sleeve for $30); Capitol promo 78s and 45s (Orchestral) $2 each; Capitol promo 78s and 45s (Novelty) $8 each (Including Frank Fontaine 45s); ABC Paramount promo 45s by Frank Fontaine $5 each; Columbia promo 78s and 45s by Art Carney (Ed Norton) $10-15 each; RCA Victor promo 78s and 45s by Audrey Meadows (Alice) $8 each; Capitol jukebox LLPs $5 each.*

**45s**

| SEASON'S GREETINGS FROM BULOVA | 1955 | Bulova (Capitol) | 75 |

*(Beautiful promo-only 45 in a hard picture cover from Bulova and Jackie himself, very rare)*

**7-Inch Extended Plays**

| A PERSONAL MESSAGE TO DISC JOCKEYS | 1958 | Capitol PRO-762 | 50 |

*(Five cuts, promo-only release)*

| SONGS I SING ON THE JACKIE GLEASON SHOW | 1966 | ABC-Paramount 442 | 25 |

*(Frank Fontaine, jukebox LLP with a hard cover)*

**RADIO SHOWS**
**45s**

| LIMEHOUSE BLUES | 195? | U.S. Air Force 138 | 20 |

*(Part of Music in the Air series)*

**Albums**

| HERE'S TO VETERANS (60s) | 196? | Veterans Administration (Public service) | 100-200 |

*(Music and interviews)*

**GLENN, GLEN**
**45s**

| EVERYBODY'S MOVIN' | 195? | Era 1061 | 40 |

**GLITTER, GARY**

*Other Bell promo 45s $6 each*

**45s**

| I LOVE YOU LOVE ME LOVE | 1973 | Bell 45,438 | 12 |

*(White promo label, UK mega-hit)*

| I'M THE LEADER OF THE GANG | 1973 | Bell 45,398 | 12 |

*(White promo label, UK mega-hit)*

**Compact Discs**

| ROCK AND ROLL PART 2 (THE HEY SONG) | 1994 | Tommy Boy | 8 |

*(Promo CD single, reissued in conjunction with its appearance on ESPN Jock Jams)*

**GO WEST**

*Chrysalis promo 45s $3 each; Chrysalis promo CD singles $3 each; EMI promo CD singles $3 each*

**12-Inch Singles**

| DON'T LOOK DOWN (3 versions) | 1987 | Chrysalis VAS 2760 | 7 |

**RADIO SHOWS**
**Albums**

| BBC TRANSCRIPTION DISC Live concert | 1985 | BBC Transcription | 100-200 |

*(With Katrina & the Waves)*

| IN CONCERT (Oct 85) Live concert | 1985 | Westwood One (2) | 50-100 |

*(With Marillion)*

**GO-GO'S**

*Includes Belinda Carlisle; Includes Jane Wiedlin. IRS promo 45s $6 each; IRS promo 45s by Belinda Carlisle $3 each; MCA promo 45s by Belinda Carlisle $3 each; IRS promo 45s by Jane Wiedlin $3 each; EMI Manhattan promo 45s by Jane Wiedlin $3 each; IRS promo 12" singles $10 each; Promo 12" singles by members solo $6 each*

**12-Inch Singles**

| COOL JERK (6 versions) | 1990 | I.R.S. 75021 7480 1 | 8 |
| HEAD OVER HEELS (same on both sides) | 1984 | I.R.S. 70973 | 8 |
| OUR LIPS ARE SEALED/TONIGHT/WE GOT THE BEAT | 1981 | I.R.S. 70956 | 8 |
| VACATION/BEATNIK BEACH | 1982 | I.R.S. 70961 | 8 |
| WE GOT THE BEAT/HOW MUCH MORE | 1982 | I.R.S. 70959 | 8 |

**45s**

| WE GOT THE BEAT | 1982 | A&M | 10 |

*(White label test pressing)*

| WHAT'S IT ALL ABOUT (Mar 82) Public service show | 1982 | W. I. A. A. 615 | 25 |

*(Flip side is Quarterflash)*

**RADIO SHOWS**
**Albums**

| IN CONCERT (Dec 81) Live concert | 1981 | Westwood One (2) | 150-250 |

*(With the Blasters)*

| IN CONCERT (July 82) Live concert | 1982 | Westwood One (2) | 200-300 |

*(Very rare concert)*

| INNERVIEW (80s) Profile | 198? | Innerview | 15-25 |

*(Music and interviews)*

| NBC SOURCE (Dec 82) Christmas countdown | 1982 | NBC Radio (2) | 50-75 |

*(With English Beat)*

| Title | Yr | Label, Number | NM $ |
|---|---|---|---|
| **GODLEY AND CREME** | | | |
| **45s** | | | |
| WEDDING BELLS (same on both sides) | 1982 | Mirage 4036 | 4 |
| *(May be promo only)* | | | |
| | | | |
| **GOFFIN, LOUISE** | | | |
| **Albums** | | | |
| WORDS AND MUSIC | 1986 | Warner Bros. WBMS-152 | 20 |
| *(Part of the Warner Bros. Music Show series)* | | | |
| | | | |
| **GOLDBERG-MILLER BLUES BAND** | | | |
| **45s** | | | |
| MORE SOUL THAN SOULFUL/MOTHER SONG | 1965 | Epic 9865 | 25 |
| *(Promo only on blue vinyl)* | | | |
| | | | |
| **GOLDEN EARRING** | | | |
| *Track promo 45s $5 each; Other label promo 45s $3 each* | | | |
| **RADIO SHOWS** | | | |
| **Albums** | | | |
| IN CONCERT (Dec 84) Live concert | 1984 | Westwood One (2) | 50-100 |
| *(With Blackfoot)* | | | |
| NBC SOURCE (Apr 83) | 1983 | NBC Radio (2) | 75-125 |
| *(Live concert)* | | | |
| NBC SOURCE (Nov 83) | 1983 | NBC Radio (2) | 30-50 |
| *(With Zebra)* | | | |
| SOURCE CONCERT (May 84) | 1984 | NBC Radio (3) | 30-50 |
| *(Music and interviews)* | | | |
| | | | |
| **GOLDEN WEST COLLEGE COMMERCIAL MUSIC PROGRAM, THE** | | | |
| **7-Inch Extended Plays** | | | |
| CHRISTMAS WITH YOU/THE JOY OF CHRISTMAS// CHRISTMAS/TIME FOR THE HOLLY | 1979 | (no label) GWC-79-102 | 6 |
| | | | |
| **GOLDSBORO, BOBBY** | | | |
| **Albums** | | | |
| BOBBY GOLDSBORO FAMILY ALBUM, THE | 1971 | United Artists SP-58 | 50 |
| *(Promo-only compilation)* | | | |
| DORAL PRESENTS BOBBY GOLDSBORO | 197? | Doral 2604 | 25 |
| *(Available by mail-order through Doral cigarettes)* | | | |
| | | | |
| **GOLLIWOGS, THE** | | | |
| *See Creedence Clearwater Revival.* | | | |
| | | | |
| **GONZALES, BABS** | | | |
| **45s** | | | |
| BE-BOP SANTA CLAUS/WATCH THEM RESOLUTIONS | 1955 | King 4836 | 15 |
| | | | |
| **GOO GOO DOLLS** | | | |
| **RADIO SHOWS** | | | |
| **Compact Discs** | | | |
| LIVE FROM THE PIT (June 96) | 1996 | (2) | 20-40 |
| *(Live material, with Toadies)* | | | |
| ON TOUR (June 96) | 1996 | | 20-40 |
| *(Live material, with Morphine and Dog's Eye View)* | | | |
| | | | |
| **GOOD RATS, THE** | | | |
| **Albums** | | | |
| RATS THE WAY YOU LIKE IT (Live) | 1978 | Passport SP-20 | 60 |
| *(Promo-only release)* | | | |
| | | | |
| **GOODMAN, BENNY** | | | |
| **Albums** | | | |
| BENNY RIDES AGAIN | 1960 | Chess LP-1440 | 100 |
| *(Multi-color swirl vinyl)* | | | |
| | | | |
| **GOODMAN, DICKIE** | | | |
| *See Buchanan and Goodman.* | | | |
| | | | |
| **GORDON, ROBERT** | | | |
| *Other RCA promo 45s $5 each; Private Stock promo 45s $4 each* | | | |
| **45s** | | | |
| BLUE CHRISTMAS (mono/stereo) | 1978 | RCA JH-11452 | 6 |
| IT'S ONLY MAKE BELIEVE  Cream-colored promo label | 1979 | RCA Victor JB-11471 | 25 |
| *(White vinyl and promo-only picture sleeve; stock copy has white vinyl but has "PB" prefix)* | | | |
| **Albums** | | | |
| ESSENTIAL ROBERT GORDON | 1979 | RCA Victor DJL1-3411 | 30 |
| *(Promo-only live album with tracks from Tuff Darts)* | | | |
| ROCK BILLY BOOGIE | 1979 | RCA Victor 3294 | 25 |
| *(White vinyl promo release)* | | | |

| Title | Yr | Label, Number | NM $ |
|---|---|---|---|

**GORE, LESLEY**
*Mercury promo 45s $10 each; A&M promo 45s $3 each; Manhattan promo 45s duet $3 each; Mercury promo LPs $10 each*
**45s**

| | | | |
|---|---|---|---|
| WEDDING BELL BLUES | 1969 | Mercury DJ-142 | 15 |
| *(Promo 45 with special DJ number)* | | | |

**GORME, EYDIE**
*ABC-Paramount promo 45s $6 each; Manhattan (Capitol) promo 45s duets $4 each; ABC-Paramount promo LPs $10 each*
**45s**

| | | | |
|---|---|---|---|
| ALEGRE NAVIDAD/BLANCA NAVIDAD | 1966 | Columbia JZSP 116419/20 | 10 |
| *(With Trio Los Panchos)* | | | |
| CINNAMON SKIN  With Trio Los Panchos | 1965 | Columbia JZSP 78862 | 10 |
| *(Yellow vinyl, white promo label, promo-only release)* | | | |
| I WANT TO STAY HERE With Steve Lawrence | 1963 | Columbia 42815 | 10 |
| *(Red vinyl, white promo label)* | | | |
| I WANT YOU TO MEET MY BABY | 1964 | Columbia 43082 | 10 |
| *(Red vinyl, white promo label)* | | | |

**7-Inch Extended Plays**

| | | | |
|---|---|---|---|
| TONIGHT I'LL SAY A PRAYER (60s) Jukebox LLP | 196? | RCA Victor 334 (LLP 138) | 10 |
| *(Issued with a paper cover)* | | | |

**GOULET, ROBERT**
*Other Columbia promo 45s $2 each*
**45s**

| | | | |
|---|---|---|---|
| AUTUMN LEAVES | 1964 | Columbia JZSP 78866 | 10 |
| *(Purple vinyl, white label, promo-only release)* | | | |
| DECEMBER TIME/SILVER BELLS | 1963 | Columbia JZSP 76415/6 | 10 |
| THE VERY THOUGHT OF YOU | 1964 | Columbia JZSP 78864 | 10 |
| *(Gold vinyl, white label, promo-only release)* | | | |
| THIS CHRISTMAS I SPEND WITH YOU/WHITE CHRISTMAS | 1965 | Columbia JZSP 111805/6 | 10 |
| *(Promotional record for Christmas Seals)* | | | |
| WHAT KIND OF FOOL AM I | 1963 | Columbia JZSP 58174 | 10 |
| *(Yellow vinyl, promo-only silver label)* | | | |

**GOWANS, SONNY**
**45s**

| | | | |
|---|---|---|---|
| ROCKIN' BY MYSELF | 195? | United Artists 114 | 50 |
| *(White promo label)* | | | |

**GRABEAU, BOBBY**
**45s**

| | | | |
|---|---|---|---|
| SOUVENIRS OF CHRISTMAS/ONCE A FOOL | 19?? | Class 805 | 5 |
| *(B-side by Ann Young)* | | | |

**GRAHAM CENTRAL STATION**
*More at Larry Graham.*
**12-Inch Singles**

| | | | |
|---|---|---|---|
| ENTROW (2 versions) | 1976 | Warner Bros. PRO-A-639 | 15 |
| NOW DO U WANTA DANCE (same on both sides) | 1977 | Warner Bros. PRO-A-673 | 15 |

**GRAHAM, BILL**
*Bill Graham is famous as a producer/promoter.*
**RADIO SHOWS**
**Compact Discs**

| | | | |
|---|---|---|---|
| BILL GRAHAM PRESENTS (Oct 92) Various artists | 1992 | (3) | 50-100 |
| *(Rare live material from Dylan, Gabriel, Santana, Stones and others)* | | | |

**GRAHAM, LARRY**
*More at Graham Central Station.*
**12-Inch Singles**

| | | | |
|---|---|---|---|
| DON'T STOP WHEN YOU'RE HOT (edit)/(LP version) | 1982 | Warner Bros. PRO-A-1027 | 8 |
| I'M SICK AND TIRED (same on both sides) | 1983 | Warner Bros. PRO-A-2065 | 8 |
| SOONER OR LATER/(Instrumental) | 1982 | Warner Bros. PRO-A-1046 | 8 |

**GRAHAM, SCOTTY**
**78s**

| | | | |
|---|---|---|---|
| EASY TO SAY With the Ravens | 1950 | National 9141 | 200 |
| *(White label promo)* | | | |

**GRAMM, LOU**
*More at Foreigner.*
**Albums**

| | | | |
|---|---|---|---|
| Q&A | 1987 | Atlantic 1020 | 15 |
| *(Promo-only interview album)* | | | |

**GRAND FUNK RAILROAD**
*Includes Mark Farner, Terry Knight and the Pack.  Capitol promo label 45s $5 each; Other MCA promo 45s $4 each; Full Moon promo 45s $3 each; Lucky Eleven promo 45s by Terry Knight (& the Pack) $10 each; Cameo white promo label 45s by Terry Knight $8 each; Capitol promo 45s by Terry Knight $6 each; Lucky Eleven promo 45s by Mark Farner $10 each.*
**45s**

| | | | |
|---|---|---|---|
| JUST COULDN'T WAIT  Blue promo label | 1976 | MCA 40641 | 12 |
| *(Produced by Frank Zappa)* | | | |
| SOME KIND OF WONDERFUL | 1974 | Capitol | 15 |
| *(White label test pressing)* | | | |

| Title | Yr | Label, Number | NM $ |
|---|---|---|---|
| WE'RE AN AMERICAN BAND  Gold vinyl promo | 1973 | Capitol P-3660 | 20 |
| *(Some of the stock copies are also gold vinyl)* | | | |
| WHAT'S IT ALL ABOUT (Mar 76)  Public service show | 1976 | W. I. A. A. 309 | 18 |
| *(Flip side is Jose Feliciano)* | | | |
| **7-Inch Extended Plays** | | | |
| GRAND FUNK RAILROAD  Six-song EP | 1972 | Capitol SPRO-6502 | 15 |
| *(Promo-only release includes 5:30 version of "Closer to Home")* | | | |
| **RADIO SHOWS** | | | |
| **Compact Discs** | | | |
| IN THE STUDIO | 1989 | Album Network | 15-25 |
| *(Profile of an album, music and interviews)* | | | |

## GRANDMASTER FLASH

| Title | Yr | Label, Number | NM $ |
|---|---|---|---|
| **12-Inch Singles** | | | |
| ALL WRAPPED UP (3 versions) | 1987 | Elektra 5233 | 5 |
| ALTERNATIVE GROOVE (3 versions) | 1985 | Elektra 5079 | 7 |
| BEHIND CLOSED DOORS (2 versions) | 1986 | Elektra 5154 | 5 |
| FLY GIRL (6 versions) | 1988 | Elektra ED 5301 | 6 |
| GOLD (6 versions) | 1988 | Elektra 5279 | 6 |
| MAGIC CARPET RIDE (3 versions) | 1988 | Elektra 5319 | 6 |
| STYLE (PETER GUNN THEME) (3 versions) | 1986 | Elektra 5134 | 7 |

## GRANT, AMY

*A&M promo CD singles $4-6 each*

| Title | Yr | Label, Number | NM $ |
|---|---|---|---|
| **Albums** | | | |
| CHRISTMAS ALBUM, A | 1985 | Myrrh | 40 |
| *(Promo-only picture disc)* | | | |
| **Compact Discs** | | | |
| HOUSE OF LOVE | 1994 | A&M | 30 |
| *(Promo-only, music and interviews, not to be confused with all-music stock copy)* | | | |
| LEAD ME ON | 1988 | Myrrh | 150 |
| *(Promo-only gold picture disc, autographed and hand-numbered)* | | | |

## GRASS ROOTS, THE

*Including Rob Grill. Dunhill white promo label 45s $5 each; Haven (Capitol) promo 45s $3 each; Mercury promo 45s by Rob Grill $3 each; MCA promo 45s by Grass Roots and/or Rob Grill $3*

| Title | Yr | Label, Number | NM $ |
|---|---|---|---|
| **45s** | | | |
| HERE COMES THAT FEELING AGAIN | 1982 | MCA 52058 | 10 |
| *(Promo-only white label, same on both sides)* | | | |
| **7-Inch Extended Plays** | | | |
| THEIR 16 GREATEST HITS  Six-song jukebox LLP | 1974 | ABC Command 40013 | 25 |
| *(Quadraphonic; issued with paper picture sleeve)* | | | |
| THEIR 16 GREATEST HITS  Six-song jukebox LLP | 1974 | ABC Dunhill 50107 | 20 |
| *(Issued with a paper picture sleeve)* | | | |

## GRATEFUL DEAD, THE

*Includes Jerry Garcia and Mickey Hart. Other Warner Bros. promo 45s $12 each; Other Grateful Dead white promo label 45s $15 each; Other Arista promo 45s $10 each; Other Arista promo 12" singles $20 each; Warner Bros. white promo label 45s by Jerry Garcia $6 each; Douglas (CBSs) white promo label 45s by Jerry Garcia $6 each; Warner white promo label 45s by Mickey Hart $6 each; Other Warner white promo label LPs $30-40 each; Other Arista promo CD singles $6-8 each.*

| Title | Yr | Label, Number | NM $ |
|---|---|---|---|
| **12-Inch Singles** | | | |
| THROWING STONES (ASHES ASHES) (LP version)/(Edit Remix) | 1987 | Arista ADP 9757 | 12 |
| TOUCH OF GREY | 1987 | Arista 9606 | 12 |
| *(Promo 12" single)* | | | |
| **45s** | | | |
| DARK STAR  White promo label | 1968 | Warner Bros. 7186 | 20 |
| *(Stock picture sleeve worth $300)* | | | |
| DON'T EASE ME IN | 1966 | Scorpio 201 | 100 |
| *(Very rare promo record)* | | | |
| FRANKLIN'S TOWER | 1975 | Grateful Dead 762 | 10 |
| *(Stock copies worth much more)* | | | |
| LET IT ROCK  Jerry Garcia | 1974 | Round 4504 | 12 |
| *(White promo label)* | | | |
| MR. CHARLIE | 1972 | Warner Bros. 7667 | 10 |
| *(Burbank-label promo copy)* | | | |
| MUSIC NEVER STOPPED, THE | 1975 | Grateful Dead 718 | 10 |
| *(White label)* | | | |
| SOUTH SIDE STRUT  Jerry Garcia with Howard Wales | 1971 | Douglas 6501 | 15 |
| TOUCH OF GREY  Black label, gray vinyl | 1987 | Arista 9606 | 15 |
| *(Many stock copies were also available in gray vinyl)* | | | |
| U.S. BLUES | 1973 | Grateful Dead 45-03 | 20 |
| *(With promo picture sleeve)* | | | |
| **7-Inch Extended Plays** | | | |
| AMERICAN BEAUTY  Jukebox LLP | 1970 | Warner Bros. 1893 (LLP 226) | 50 |
| *(Five songs, issued with a paper picture sleeve)* | | | |
| AMERICAN BEAUTY RADIO SPOTS | 1970 | Warner Bros. PRO-438 | 75 |
| *(Promo-only release)* | | | |
| EUROPE '72  Promo EP | 1972 | Warner Bros. PRO-544 | 50 |
| *(White promo label)* | | | |
| PLAYBACK  One track by Jerry Garcia | 1969 | Playback | 15 |
| *(Issued with newsletter insert)* | | | |
| PREVENT FOREST FIRES  Public service spots, one by Grateful Dead | 1984 | Ad Council 184 | 50 |
| *(Very rare public service ads)* | | | |
| PREVENT FOREST FIRES  Public service spots, one by Mickey Hart | 1989 | Ad Council 188 | 40 |
| *(Issued with a paper picture sleeve)* | | | |
| SAMPLER FOR DEADHEADS  Promo EP | 1976 | Round 02/03 (2) | 50 |
| *(White promo labels)* | | | |

| Title | Yr | Label, Number | NM $ |
|---|---|---|---|
| SHAKEDOWN STREET RADIO SPOTS | 1977 | Arista | 40 |
| *(Promo-only release)* | | | |
| WORKINGMAN'S DEAD RADIO SPOTS | 1970 | Warner Bros. PRO-414 | 75 |
| *(Promo-only release)* | | | |
| **Albums** | | | |
| EUROPE '72 | 1972 | Warner Bros. 2668 (3) | 75 |
| *(Three-record set, white promo labels)* | | | |
| FOR DEAD HEADS | 1975 | United Artists SP-114 | 40 |
| *(Promo-only release)* | | | |
| GRATEFUL DEAD SAMPLER | 1977 | Arista SP-35 | 40 |
| *(Promo-only release)* | | | |
| GRATEFUL DEAD TALK TO THEMSELVES | 1987 | Arista 9630 | 30 |
| *(Promo-only interview record)* | | | |
| TERRAPIN STATION | 1977 | Arista 7001 | 35 |
| *(Special promo banded version for radio)* | | | |
| Wake of the Flood | 1973 | Grateful Dead GD-01 | 400 |
| *(Green vinyl meant for fan-club members; ironically, most copies were damaged in a flood before distribution)* | | | |
| **Compact Discs** | | | |
| ANTE UP (THE BUILT TO LAST INTERVIEW) | 1989 | Arista ASCD-9921 | 40 |
| *(Music and interviews)* | | | |
| DEADICATED | 198? | Arista | 40 |
| *(Promotional CD released by their record company)* | | | |
| DYLAN AND THE DEAD | 1989 | Columbia | 40 |
| *(Promotional sampler)* | | | |
| TOUCH OF GREY | 1987 | Arista ASCD-9606 | 10 |
| *(Promo-only CD single)* | | | |
| **RADIO SHOWS** | | | |
| **Albums** | | | |
| GRATEFUL DEAD HOUR (88-89) Whole series | 1989 | MJI (52) | 5,000-8,500 |
| *(Entire first year of the show on LP. The show continues to air to this day, but is transmitted via satellite uplink to each station.)* | | | |
| GRATEFUL DEAD HOUR (Sept 88) Debut show | 1988 | MJI | 150-200 |
| *(Aired on September 5, 1988)* | | | |
| GRATEFUL DEAD HOUR (Sept 88-Aug 89) | 198? | MJI | 50-100 |
| *(Weekly show, music and interviews, many live tracks, price is per show from 2-52)* | | | |
| INNERVIEW  Live show | 1980 | Innerview (2) | 80-125 |
| *(Live concert presentation)* | | | |
| INNERVIEW  Music and interviews | 1980 | Innerview (2) | 25-50 |
| *(Two shows, part 1 and part 2)* | | | |
| JERRY GARCIA RADIO SPECIAL | 1991 | | 20-40 |
| *(Music and interviews)* | | | |
| KING BISCUIT FLOWER HOUR | 1982 | DIR/ABC (2) | 100-200 |
| *(Live concert)* | | | |
| KING BISCUIT FLOWER HOUR  Bobby and the Midnights | 1982 | DIR/ABC (2) | 75-100 |
| *(Live concert)* | | | |
| KING BISCUIT FLOWER HOUR (June 80) | 1980 | DIR/ABC (3) | 150-300 |
| *(Rare live concert)* | | | |
| LEGENDS OF ROCK  Profile | 1987 | NBC Radio (2) | 25-40 |
| *(Music and interviews)* | | | |
| OFF THE RECORD (80s) Music and interviews | 198? | Westwood One (2) | 20-35 |
| *(Show repeated several times)* | | | |
| OFF THE RECORD (Sept 80) With Jerry Garcia | 1980 | Westwood One (2) | 20-35 |
| *(Music and interviews)* | | | |
| ROAD AHEAD, THE  With one live cut | 1980 | DIR | 35-50 |
| *(King Biscuit Flower Hour - Honda Highlights sampler promo LP with special cover)* | | | |
| SOURCE SPECIAL (Dec 81) | 1981 | NBC Source (3) | 40-75 |
| *(Music and interviews and some live)* | | | |
| WHAT KEEPS THE DEAD ALIVE (Mar 85) | 1985 | Westwood One (2) | 40-75 |
| *(Music and interviews)* | | | |
| **Compact Discs** | | | |
| 27 YEARS PLAYING IN THE SAME BAND (June 92) Live material | 1992 | (4) | 75-150 |
| *(Concert profile of the Grateful Dead)* | | | |
| ALL AMERICAN JAM | 1996 | (3) | 50-75 |
| *(With Journey, Boston, Allman Brothers, Aerosmith, Doobie Brothers)* | | | |
| AMERICAN BEAUTY (June 92) Profile | 1992 | Media America (4) | 40-75 |
| *(Music and interviews)* | | | |
| HUNDRED YEAR HALL (Sept 95) | 1995 | Album Network (2) | 50-75 |
| *(World premiere of the album of the same name, music and interviews)* | | | |
| IN THE STUDIO | 1996 | Album Network | 35-50 |
| *(Music and interviews, subject is "The Arista Years")* | | | |
| KING BISCUIT FLOWER HOUR (90s) Live concert | 199? | DIR | 40-60 |
| *(Edited repeats of above show)* | | | |
| KING BISCUIT FLOWER HOUR (Feb 88) Part 1 and 2 | 1988 | DIR (2) | 200-300 |
| *(Special live concert of new material)* | | | |
| ROCK STARS (Nov 89) Music and interviews | 1989 | Radio Today (2) | 50-100 |
| *(Some live tracks)* | | | |
| TIMOTHY WHITE SESSIONS (Nov 96) | 1996 | (2) | 75-100 |
| *(Music and interviews, plus performances by Bob Weir and Rob Wasserman)* | | | |
| UP CLOSE Parts 1 and 2 | 1989 | Media America (4) | 125-200 |
| *(Mostly music and interviews, some live tracks, repeated in 1992)* | | | |
| **Reel-to-Reel Tapes** | | | |
| KING BISCUIT FLOWER HOUR (July 78) Live concert | 1978 | DIR/ABC (2) | 100-200 |
| *(Repeat of the Englishtown material)* | | | |
| KING BISCUIT FLOWER HOUR (July 79) Live concert | 1979 | DIR/ABC (2) | 100-200 |
| *(Repeat show from earlier)* | | | |
| KING BISCUIT FLOWER HOUR (Nov 77) Live concert | 1977 | DIR/ABC (2) | 150-225 |
| *(Concert at Englishtown, on two reels)* | | | |

| Title | Yr | Label, Number | NM $ |
|---|---|---|---|
| **GREAT BUILDINGS** | | | |
| **12-Inch Singles** | | | |
| COMBAT ZONE + 2 | 1981 | Columbia AS 927 | 6 |
| | | | |
| **GREAT WHITE** | | | |
| *Capitol promo 45s $3 each; Capitol promo CDs $3-5 each.* | | | |
| **Compact Discs** | | | |
| BACK TRACKS 1986-1991 | 1992 | Capitol DPRO-79286 | 30 |
| *(Promo-only compilation)* | | | |
| HOOKED | 1991 | Capitol 95330 | 30 |
| *(CD and cassette in custom box with fishnet wrapping)* | | | |
| LIVE AT THE RITZ | 1988 | Capitol DPRO-79305 | 30 |
| *(Promo-only live concert)* | | | |
| **RADIO SHOWS** | | | |
| **Albums** | | | |
| IN CONCERT Live concert | 1989 | Westwood One (2) | 25-50 |
| *(Repeated several times)* | | | |
| OFF THE RECORD (Nov 91) Profile | 1991 | Westwood One (2) | 10-15 |
| *(Music and interviews)* | | | |
| **Compact Discs** | | | |
| LIVE AT ELECTRIC LADYLAND (May 91) | 1991 | Album Network | 25-50 |
| *(Live concert)* | | | |
| | | | |
| **GREEN DAY** | | | |
| *Other Reprise promo CD singles $4-6 each* | | | |
| **Albums** | | | |
| DOOKIE | 1994 | Reprise 45529 | 35 |
| *(Promo version on clear green vinyl in plain white cover)* | | | |
| DOOKIE | 1994 | Reprise 45529 | 30 |
| *(Promo version on milky pale-green vinyl)* | | | |
| **Compact Discs** | | | |
| BASKET CASE | 1994 | Reprise | 8 |
| *(Promo-only CD single)* | | | |
| GEEK STINK BREATH | 1995 | Reprise PRO-CD-7866 | 8 |
| *(Promo-only CD single)* | | | |
| J.A.R. | 1995 | Reprise PRO-CD-7843 | 8 |
| *(Promo-only CD single)* | | | |
| LONGVIEW | 1994 | Reprise | 8 |
| *(Promo-only CD single)* | | | |
| WHEN I COME AROUND | 1994 | Reprise | 8 |
| *(Promo-only CD single)* | | | |
| **RADIO SHOWS** | | | |
| **Compact Discs** | | | |
| IN CONCERT (Nov 94) Live concert | 1994 | Westwood One | 30-60 |
| *(With the Pretenders)* | | | |
| IN CONCERT-NU ROCK (Nov 94) | 1994 | Westwood One | 30-60 |
| *(Live concert)* | | | |
| | | | |
| **GREEN ON RED** | | | |
| **Albums** | | | |
| BBC TRANSCRIPTION DISC | 1985 | BBC Transcription | 100-175 |
| *(Live concert)* | | | |
| | | | |
| **GREEN, AL** | | | |
| **7-Inch Extended Plays** | | | |
| I'M STILL IN LOVE WITH YOU | 1972 | Hi SB 685 | 15 |
| *(Jukebox LLP, issued with hard cover)* | | | |
| | | | |
| **GREENE, LORNE** | | | |
| *Other RCA Victor promo 45s $3 each* | | | |
| **45s** | | | |
| RINGO | 1964 | RCA Victor 47-8444 | 12 |
| *(White promo label)* | | | |
| **7-Inch Extended Plays** | | | |
| WELCOME TO THE PONDEROSA  Jukebox LLP | 1964 | RCA Victor 2843 | 25 |
| *(Issued with a hard cover)* | | | |
| **Albums** | | | |
| PALAVER WITH THE MAN | 1965 | RCA Victor SP-33-327 | 50 |
| *(Promo-only interview record with script)* | | | |
| | | | |
| **GREENWOOD, LEE** | | | |
| **45s** | | | |
| CHRISTMAS TO CHRISTMAS (LOVING YOU) | 1985 | MCA 52733 | 10 |
| CHRISTMAS TO CHRISTMAS (LOVING YOU) | 1987 | MCA S45-17739 | 10 |
| | | | |
| **GRIFFIN, BUCK** | | | |
| **45s** | | | |
| BOW MY BACK | 1958 | MGM 12439 | 50 |
| *(Yellow promo label)* | | | |
| JESSIE LEE | 1958 | MGM 12597 | 50 |
| *(Yellow promo label)* | | | |
| STUTTERIN' PAPA | 1957 | MGM 12284 | 50 |
| *(Yellow promo label)* | | | |

| Title | Yr | Label, Number | NM $ |
|-------|-----|--------------|------|

**GRIFFINS, THE**
**45s**

| BAD LITTLE GIRL | 1955 | Mercury 70650 | 85 |
| *(White promo label)* | | | |
| FOREVER MORE | 1956 | Wing 90067 | 55 |
| *(White promo label)* | | | |
| I SWEAR BY ALL THE STARS ABOVE | 1955 | Mercury 70558 | 75 |
| *(White promo label)* | | | |
| MY BABY'S GONE | 1956 | Mercury 70913 | 65 |
| *(White promo label)* | | | |

**GROUNDHOGS, THE**
**RADIO SHOWS**
**Albums**

| BBC TRANSCRIPTION DISC | 1972 | BBC Transcription | 200-350 |
| *(Live concert)* | | | |

**GTR**
*Arista promo 45s $4 each Some of the members from the group Yes*
**RADIO SHOWS**

| KING BISCUIT FLOWER HOUR (Aug 86) | 1986 | DIR (3) | 50-150 |
| *(Live concert)* | | | |
| KING BISCUIT FLOWER HOUR (Nov 86) Live concert | 1986 | DIR (2) | 40-100 |
| *(Live concert)* | | | |

**GUADALCANAL DIARY**
**12-Inch Singles**

| ALWAYS SATURDAY (Edit) (LP Version) | 1989 | Elektra ED 5359 | 5 |
| GET OVER IT (same on both sides) | 1987 | Elektra ED 5291 | 5 |
| LIPS OF STEEL (same on both sides) | 1987 | Elektra ED 5272 | 5 |
| LITANY (same on both sides) | 1987 | Elektra ED 5256 | 5 |
| LONELY STREET (same on both sides) | 1986 | Elektra ED 5155 | 5 |
| PRETTY IS AS PRETTY DOES (same on both sides) | 1989 | Elektra ED 5379 | 5 |
| SPIRIT TRAIN (same on both sides) | 1986 | Elektra ED 5172 | 5 |
| TRAIL OF TEARS (same on both sides) | 1985 | Elektra ED 5071 | 6 |
| **Albums** | | | |
| FLIP-FLOP | 1989 | Elektra 60848 | 10 |
| *(Promo-only white label audiophile vinyl)* | | | |

**GUESS WHO, THE**
*Includes listings of Burton Cummings and Chad Allen. In Canada, pre-Guess Who was the Expressions, and Chad Allen's backup group was the Reflections. Scepter white promo label 45s $8 each; Other RCA promo 45s $4 each; Portrait promo 45s by Burton Cummings $4 each; Alfa promo 45s by Burton Cummings $3 each.*
**45s**

| ALBERT FLASHER  Yellow promo label | 1971 | RCA Victor SPS-45-259 | 12 |
| *(Promo only at the time of its release)* | | | |
| FRIENDS OF MINE  Yellow promo label | 1970 | RCA Victor SPS-45-223 | 25 |
| *(Part 1 and part 2, total time 10:12)* | | | |
| GUNS GUNS GUNS  Yellow promo label | 1972 | RCA Victor SP-45-320 | 20 |
| *(Promo-only stereo/mono versions)* | | | |
| HIS GIRL | 1967 | Amy 976 | 25 |
| *(Blue promo label, promo only)* | | | |
| SHE'S ALL MINE | 1967 | Amy 967 | 25 |
| *(Blue promo label, promo only)* | | | |
| THIS TIME LONG AGO | 1969 | Fontana 1597 | 18 |
| *(White promo label)* | | | |
| TRIBUTE TO BUDDY HOLLY  Chad Allen | 1962 | Canadian American 802 | 30 |
| *(White promo label, Chad Allen & the Reflections)* | | | |
| WHAT'S IT ALL ABOUT (Sept 77) Public service show | 1977 | W. I. A. A. 387 | 18 |
| *(With Burton Cummings, flip side is Al Stewart)* | | | |
| WHO INVENTED THE TWIST  Chad Allen | 1963 | Radiant 1508 | 15 |
| *(Orange promo label)* | | | |
| **Albums** | | | |
| TRACK AND DIALOGUE | 1979 | Hilltak 331 | 25 |
| *(Promo-only interview record)* | | | |
| **RADIO SHOWS** | | | |
| **Albums** | | | |
| INNERVIEW (80s) Burton Cummings | 198? | Innerview | 10-20 |
| *(Music and interviews)* | | | |
| **Compact Discs** | | | |
| IN THE STUDIO (90s) Profile | 199? | Album Network | 10-20 |
| *(Music and interviews)* | | | |

**GUITAR, BILLY**
**45s**

| HERE COMES THE NIGHT | 1958 | Decca 30634 | 60 |
| *(Decca promo label)* | | | |

**GUNS N' ROSES**
*Including Slash. Other Geffen promo 45s $8 each; other Geffen promo CD singles $6-8 each.*
**45s**

| WELCOME TO THE JUNGLE | 1987 | Geffen 27759 | 10 |
| *(Black promo label)* | | | |

| Title | Yr | Label, Number | NM $ |
|---|---|---|---|
| **Compact Discs** | | | |
| 14 YEARS | 1992 | Geffen PRO-4418 | 10 |
| *(Promo CD single)* | | | |
| AEROSMITH/GUNS N' ROSES | 1988 | Geffen PRO-CD-3132 | 15 |
| *(Promo-only sampler, three tracks by Aerosmith, two by G N' R)* | | | |
| AIN'T IT FUN | 1993 | Geffen PRO-4579 | 8 |
| *(Promo-only CD single)* | | | |
| DEAD HORSE | 1993 | Geffen PRO-4511 | 8 |
| *(Promo-only CD single)* | | | |
| DON'T CRY | 1991 | Geffen PRO-4232 | 15 |
| *(Promo CD single)* | | | |
| ESTRANGED  3 edit versions | 1993 | Geffen | 50 |
| *(White CD in cardboard sleeve)* | | | |
| GARDEN OF EDEN | 1991 | Geffen PRO-4366 | 25 |
| *(Promo-only CD single)* | | | |
| GUNS N' RADIO  12 tracks | 1992 | Geffen PRO-4340 | 50 |
| *(Promo-only sampler)* | | | |
| KNOCKIN' ON HEAVEN'S DOOR | 1990 | Geffen PRO-4140 | 20 |
| *(Promo-only CD single)* | | | |
| LIVE AND LET DIE | 1991 | Geffen PRO-4352 | 8 |
| *(Promo-only CD single)* | | | |
| NIGHTRAIN | 1988 | Geffen PRO-CD-3625 | 8 |
| *(Promo-only CD single)* | | | |
| NOVEMBER RAIN | 1992 | Geffen PRO-4387 | 20 |
| *(Promo-only CD single, full-length version)* | | | |
| NOVEMBER RAIN  Six versions | 1992 | Hitmakers | 50 |
| *(Promo-only release, around 300 made)* | | | |
| ON TOUR NOW  11 tracks | 1992 | Geffen PRO-4441 | 30 |
| *(Promo-only sampler)* | | | |
| PATIENCE | 1989 | Geffen PRO-CD-3437 | 8 |
| *(Promo-only CD single)* | | | |
| PRETTY TIED UP | 1992 | Geffen PRO-4386 | 20 |
| *(Promo-only release)* | | | |
| SELECTIONS FROM USE YOUR ILLUSION I & II | 1991 | Geffen PRO-4328 | 20 |
| *(Promo-only sampler)* | | | |
| SWEET CHILD O' MINE  One version | 1988 | Geffen PRO-CD-3147 | 12 |
| *(Promo CD single)* | | | |
| SWEET CHILD O' MINE  Three versions | 1988 | Geffen PRO-CD-3077 | 35 |
| *(Promo-only release)* | | | |
| SYMPATHY FOR THE DEVIL | 1994 | Geffen | 30 |
| *(Promo-only CD single)* | | | |
| USE YOUR ILLUSION I & II | 1991 | Geffen PRO-4244 (2) | 300 |
| *(Special promo release with numbered metal plaque in a hardbound cloth cover)* | | | |
| WELCOME TO THE JUNGLE | 1987 | Geffen PRO-CD-2668 | 15 |
| *(Promo-only CD single, one of the first)* | | | |
| YESTERDAYS | 1992 | Geffen PRO-4470 | 10 |
| *(Promo-only CD single)* | | | |
| YOU COULD BE MINE | 1991 | Geffen PRO-4235 | 10 |
| *(Promo-only CD single)* | | | |
| **RADIO SHOWS** | | | |
| **Albums** | | | |
| HIGH VOLTAGE  Various artists | 1989 | Westwood One (2) | 30-40 |
| *(Live segment of the show features G N' R)* | | | |
| IN CONCERT (Apr 88)  Live concert | 1988 | Westwood One (2) | 75-150 |
| *(Rare concert with White Lion)* | | | |
| IN CONCERT  Live concert | 1990 | Westwood One (2) | 75-125 |
| *(Rare concert with Motley Crue)* | | | |
| METALSHOP (June 92)  Various artists | 1992 | MJI Productions (2) | 15-35 |
| *(One segment of the show features live Slash tracks)* | | | |
| METALSHOP (Sept 88)  Various artists | 1988 | MJI Productions (2) | 20-40 |
| *(One segment of the show features live G N' R tracks)* | | | |
| OFF THE RECORD (90s)  Profile | 199? | Westwood One (2) | 20-30 |
| *(Music and interviews)* | | | |
| SUPERSTAR CONCERT (June 91)  Live concert | 1991 | Westwood One (3) | 75-100 |
| *(This show was repeated)* | | | |
| **Compact Discs** | | | |
| IN CONCERT (May 94)  Live concert | 1994 | Westwood One (2) | 30-50 |
| *(Live concert with Cracker and Candlebox)* | | | |
| KING BISCUIT FLOWER HOUR (June 91)  Live concert | 1991 | DIR | 50-100 |
| *(New material in live concert)* | | | |
| OFF THE RECORD (Apr 94)  Profile | 1994 | Westwood One (2) | 25-40 |
| *(Double show, parts 1 and 2, music and interviews)* | | | |
| SLASH AND THE HARD EDGE OF ROCK | 1991 | Media America (3) | 100-175 |
| *(Music and interview plus live tracks)* | | | |
| SUPERSTAR CONCERT (Sept 92)  Live concert | 1992 | Westwood One (4) | 100-175 |
| *(Extended concert, parts 1 and 2)* | | | |

## GUTHRIE, ARLO

| Title | Yr | Label, Number | NM $ |
|---|---|---|---|
| **45s** | | | |
| MOTORCYCLE SONG/THE PAUSE OF MR. CLAUS | 1970 | Reprise PRO 304 | 20 |
| *(Double-sided promo-only release)* | | | |
| **7-Inch Extended Plays** | | | |
| OUTLASTING THE BLUES | 1979 | Warner Bros. PRO-S-813 | 10 |
| *(Four tracks, two with his backing group Shenandoah)* | | | |

| Title | Yr | Label, Number | NM $ |
|-------|----|----|------|

## H

**HACKERT, VALINE**
*Buddy Covelle*
**45s**

| Title | Yr | Label, Number | NM $ |
|-------|----|----|------|
| BILLY BOY | 1959 | Brunswick 55151 | 100 |
| *(Yellow promo label)* | | | |

**HACKETT, STEVE**
*See Yes*
**RADIO SHOWS**
**Albums**

| Title | Yr | Label, Number | NM $ |
|-------|----|----|------|
| BBC ROCK HOUR (Dec 81) Live concert | 1981 | London Wavelength | 40-75 |
| *(With Billy Squier)* | | | |
| BBC TRANSCRIPTION DISC  Live concert | 1979 | BBC Transcription | 200-375 |
| *(Very rare live concert)* | | | |

**HADAWAY, HENRY, ORCHESTRA AND CHORUS**
**45s**

| Title | Yr | Label, Number | NM $ |
|-------|----|----|------|
| TURNED ON WINTER MEDLEY (same on both sides) | 1982 | RCA JH-13378 | 4 |

**HAGAN, SAMMY, AND THE VISCOUNTS**
*Other Capitol promo 45s $10-15 each*
**7-Inch Extended Plays**

| Title | Yr | Label, Number | NM $ |
|-------|----|----|------|
| SNUGGLE BUNNY | 1959 | Capitol PRO 528 | 50 |
| *(Promo-only 4-track EP)* | | | |

**HAGAR, SAMMY**
*Other Geffen promo 45s $3 each; Became a member of Van Halen.*
**45s**

| Title | Yr | Label, Number | NM $ |
|-------|----|----|------|
| I CAN'T DRIVE 55 | 1984 | Geffen 29173 | 12 |
| *(Same on both sides, with picture sleeve and "traffic ticket" insert, not included with stock copies)* | | | |
| TWO SIDES OF LOVE | 1984 | Geffen 29246 | 10 |
| *(Same on both sides, red vinyl, with picture sleeve; stock copy also red vinyl)* | | | |
| **Compact Discs** | | | |
| SAMMY HAGAR RETURNS HOME | 1987 | Geffen PRO-CD-2832 | 18 |
| *(Promo-only, music and interview)* | | | |
| **RADIO SHOWS** | | | |
| **Albums** | | | |
| BBC LONDON WAVELENGTH CONCERT (Mar 82) | 1982 | London Wavelength | 15-25 |
| *(Live concert)* | | | |
| BBC ROCK HOUR (Mar 82) Live concert | 1982 | London Wavelength | 20-40 |
| *(Live concert)* | | | |
| IN CONCERT (Aug 82) Live concert | 1982 | Westwood One (2) | 25-40 |
| *(Vinyl version)* | | | |
| INNERVIEW (80s) Profile | 198? | Innerview | 10-15 |
| *(Music and interviews)* | | | |
| SOURCE CONCERT (Sept 84) | 1984 | NBC Radio (2) | 25-40 |
| *(Live concert)* | | | |
| SUPERGROUPS (July 82) Live concert | 1982 | DIR (3) | 75-100 |
| *(With Emerson, Lake & Palmer)* | | | |
| SUPERSTAR CONCERT (Aug 84) Box set | 1984 | Westwood One (3) | 25-40 |
| *(Live concert)* | | | |
| **Compact Discs** | | | |
| IN CONCERT (June 94) Live concert | 1994 | Westwood One | 25-40 |
| *(CD version)* | | | |
| IN THE STUDIO (90s) Profile of an album | 199? | Album Network | 10-15 |
| *(Music and interviews)* | | | |

**HAGEN, NINA**
**12-Inch Singles**

| Title | Yr | Label, Number | NM $ |
|-------|----|----|------|
| SMACK JACK/COSMA SHIVA/BORN IN XLXAX | 1982 | Columbia AS 1506 | 10 |

**HAGGARD, MERLE**
*Capitol promo 45s $3 each*
**45s**

| Title | Yr | Label, Number | NM $ |
|-------|----|----|------|
| JUST BETWEEN THE TWO OF US With Bonnie Owens | 1965 | Tally 181 | 15 |
| *(Yellow promo label)* | | | |
| SAM HILL | 1964 | Tally 178 | 15 |
| *(Yellow promo label)* | | | |
| SANTA CLAUS AND POPCORN | 1982 | Epic AE7 1777 | 10 |
| *(Promo-only 45 rpm release)* | | | |
| SING A SAD SONG | 1964 | Tally 155 | 18 |
| *(Yellow promo label)* | | | |
| STRANGERS | 1964 | Tally 179 | 15 |
| *(Yellow promo label)* | | | |
| **7-Inch Extended Plays** | | | |
| OKIE FROM MUSKOGEE  Jukebox LLP | 1970 | Capitol 384 | 12 |
| *(Issued with a soft cardboard cover)* | | | |
| **Albums** | | | |
| LAND OF MANY CHURCHES | 1971 | Capitol 803 (2) | 55 |
| *(Each side recorded live from a different Nashville area church)* | | | |
| TRULY THE BEST OF MERLE HAGGARD | 1971 | Capitol 823 | 40 |

| Title | Yr | Label, Number | NM $ |
|-------|----|--------------|------|

**RADIO SHOWS**
**Albums**

| Title | Yr | Label, Number | NM $ |
|-------|----|--------------|------|
| HERE'S TO VETERANS (60s) Public service show | 196? | Veterans Administration | 40-60 |
| *(Music and interviews)* | | | |
| LIVE AT GILLEY'S (May 87) | 1987 | Westwood One | 20-30 |
| *(Live concert)* | | | |
| ON A COUNTRY ROAD (Jan 83) Various artists box set | 1983 | Mutual Radio (3) | 20-30 |
| *(The live segment features Haggard in concert)* | | | |
| SILVER EAGLE II  Live concert | 1981 | DIR (2) | 75-100 |
| *(Canadian version, quite rare, pressed for use in Canada and the USA)* | | | |
| THE SILVER EAGLE | 1981 | DIR (3) | 40-60 |
| *(Live concert)* | | | |
| WILLIE & MERLE (June 82) Box set, music and interviews | 1982 | Mutual Radio (3) | 30-50 |
| *(Willie Nelson and Merle Haggard)* | | | |

**HAIRCUT ONE HUNDRED**
**12-Inch Singles**

| Title | Yr | Label, Number | NM $ |
|-------|----|--------------|------|
| FANTASTIC DAY (Extended)/SKI CLUB/ | 1982 | Arista SP-139 | 8 |
| LOVE'S GOT ME (Extended)/CALLING CAPTAIN AUTUMN (Extended) | | | |

**45s**

| Title | Yr | Label, Number | NM $ |
|-------|----|--------------|------|
| FAVOURITE SHIRTS (BOY MEETS GIRL) (same on both sides) | 1982 | Arista 0708 | 4 |
| *(Stock copy may not exist)* | | | |

**HALE AND THE HUSHABYES**
**45s**

| Title | Yr | Label, Number | NM $ |
|-------|----|--------------|------|
| YES SIR, THAT'S MY BABY | 1964 | Apogee | 150 |
| *(White promo label)* | | | |
| YES SIR, THAT'S MY BABY | 1964 | Reprise 0299 | 100 |
| *(Includes Brian Wilson, Sonny & Cher, Blossoms, Jack Nitzsche, Jackie DeShannon, Darlene Love and others)* | | | |

**HALE, CORKY**
**45s**

| Title | Yr | Label, Number | NM $ |
|-------|----|--------------|------|
| CHRISTMAS DAY/TWINKY (THE STAR THAT COULDN'T SHINE) | 1968 | Columbia 44713 | 10 |
| *(Stock copy may not exist)* | | | |

**HALEY, BILL, AND HIS COMETS**

*Other Decca promo singles $10-20 each depending on year; Other Warner promo 45s $10 each; United Artists white promo label 45s $8 each; any Decca promo EPs, if they exist, around $100 each;  Other promo Decca LPs $20-50 each depending on year; Other Warner promo LPs $15-20 each; Vocalion, Kama Sutra, Janus, Valiant, Crescendo promo LPs $15-25 each*

**45s**

| Title | Yr | Label, Number | NM $ |
|-------|----|--------------|------|
| CANDY KISSES  Promo label, yellow vinyl | 1960 | Warner Bros. 5145 | 50 |
| ROCK AROUND THE CLOCK  Pink promo label | 1954 | Decca 29124 | 100 |
| *(This version must have black lines on both sides of Decca)* | | | |
| SHAKE, RATTLE AND ROLL  Pink promo label | 1954 | Decca 29204 | 50 |
| *(This version does not have a star under the Decca on label)* | | | |

**7-Inch Extended Plays**

| Title | Yr | Label, Number | NM $ |
|-------|----|--------------|------|
| HI-FI DEMONSTRATION RECORD  Various artists | 1958 | Decca 38088 | 25 |
| *(Four Decca artists, one track is Bill Haley. Issued with a paper picture sleeve.)* | | | |

**78s**

| Title | Yr | Label, Number | NM $ |
|-------|----|--------------|------|
| ROCK AROUND THE CLOCK  Pink promo label | 1954 | Decca 29124 | 250 |
| *(The classic of promo collectible singles)* | | | |

**Albums**

| Title | Yr | Label, Number | NM $ |
|-------|----|--------------|------|
| BILL HALEY'S CHICKS | 1959 | Decca 8821 | 75 |
| *(Pink promo label)* | | | |
| COMETS | 1960 | Warner Bros. 1378 | 65 |
| *(White promo label)* | | | |
| MUSIC FOR THE BOYFRIEND | 1956 | Decca 8315 | 175 |
| *(Pink promo label)* | | | |
| ROCK 'N' ROLL | 1973 | Crescendo 2077 | 20 |
| *(White promo label)* | | | |
| ROCK 'N' ROLL REVIVAL | 196? | Valiant 1831 | 30 |
| *(White promo label)* | | | |
| ROCK AND ROLL STAGE SHOW | 1956 | Decca 8345 | 200 |
| *(Pink promo label)* | | | |
| ROCK AROUND THE CLOCK  Pink promo label | 1956 | Decca 8225 | 250 |
| *(The first Decca rock-related 12" LP)* | | | |
| ROCK AROUND THE COUNTRY | 1976 | Crescendo 2097 | 18 |
| *(White promo label)* | | | |
| ROCKIN' AROUND THE WORLD | 1957 | Decca 8692 | 125 |
| *(Pink promo label)* | | | |
| ROCKIN' THE JOINT | 1958 | Decca 8775 | 100 |
| *(Pink promo label)* | | | |
| ROCKIN' THE OLDIES | 1957 | Decca 8569 | 150 |
| *(Pink promo album)* | | | |
| STRICTLY INSTRUMENTAL | 1959 | Decca 8964 | 65 |
| *(Pink promo label)* | | | |

**HALL, DARYL, AND JOHN OATES**

*Other Atlantic promo 45s $5 each; Other RCA promo 45s $3-5 each; Arista promo 45s $3 each; Other RCA and Arista promo 12" singles $8 each; RCA Victor promo 45s by Daryl Hall $3 each; RCA Victor promo 12" singles by Daryl Hall $6 each;  Arista promo CD singles $2-4 each*

**12-Inch Singles**

| Title | Yr | Label, Number | NM $ |
|-------|----|--------------|------|
| ADULT EDUCATION (Special Extended Mix Long)/ | 1984 | RCA JD-13736 | 10 |
| (Special Extended Mix Short) | | | |
| AUGUST DAY/I DON'T WANNA LOSE YOU | 1977 | RCA JD-11431 | 12 |
| DO WHAT YOU WANT, BE WHAT YOU ARE (LP) (Short Version) | 1976 | RCA JD-11302 | 15 |
| DREAMTIME (same on both sides)  Daryl Hall | 1986 | RCA PD-14386 | 6 |

| Title | Yr | Label, Number | NM $ |
|---|---|---|---|
| JINGLE BELL ROCK  Picture disc | 1983 | RCA JM-13705 | 25 |
| (One side John, other side Daryl, promo-only picture disc) | | | |
| JINGLE BELL ROCK (same on both sides) | 1984 | RCA JD-13983 | 12 |
| MANEATER (Special Extended Club Mix)/I CAN'T GO FOR THAT (Club Mix) | 1982 | RCA JD-13403 | 12 |
| METHOD OF MODERN LOVE/BANK ON YOUR LOVE | 1984 | RCA JD-13972 | 10 |
| NITE AT THE APOLLO LIVE! , A: | 1985 | RCA JR-14180 | 8 |
| THE WAY YOU DO THE THINGS YOU DO/MY GIRL (same on both sides) | | | |
| POSSESSION OBSESSION (Special New Mix) (same on both sides) | 1985 | RCA JR-14100 | 8 |
| SAY IT ISN'T SO/WAIT FOR ME (Live) | 1983 | RCA JD-13659 | 12 |
| SOME THINGS ARE BETTER LEFT UNSAID (Special New Mix) | 1985 | RCA JD-14038 | 8 |
| (same on both sides) | | | |

**45s**

| | | | |
|---|---|---|---|
| DEEP RIVER BLUES White promo label | 1976 | Chelsea 3065 | 10 |
| (Actually the stock copy is harder to find) | | | |
| I CAN'T GO FOR THAT (NO CAN DO) (Club Mix) | 1981 | RCA JB-12361 | 10 |
| (Promo only) | | | |
| IT'S A LAUGH | 1978 | RCA | 10 |
| (White label test pressing) | | | |
| JINGLE BELL ROCK  Black label, green vinyl | 1984 | RCA 14259 | 20 |
| (One side by Daryl, other side by John, not released to the general public in any form) | | | |
| JINGLE BELL ROCK  Black label, red vinyl | 1984 | RCA 14259 | 20 |
| (Same single as above, different color; both versions of "Jingle Bell Rock" promo were issued with a picture sleeve, which is included in the price listed.) | | | |
| SAY IT ISN'T SO | 1983 | RCA 13654 | 10 |
| (Promo-only Adult Contemporary mix) | | | |
| SHE'S GONE (Long version)/(45 version) | 1976 | Atlantic 3332 | 6 |
| WHAT'S IT ALL ABOUT (Feb 77) Public service show | 1977 | W.I.A.A. 359 | 20 |
| (Flip is Tommy Roe) | | | |
| WHAT'S IT ALL ABOUT (Apr 82) Public service show | 1982 | W. I. A. A. 621 | 25 |
| (Flip side features the Police) | | | |

**7-Inch Extended Plays**

| | | | |
|---|---|---|---|
| SOMETHING FOR NOTHING  Various artists | 1973 | Atlantic PR-195 | 12 |
| (Four songs, four artists, one by Hall & Oates, issued w/paper sleeve) | | | |
| SHE'S GONE | 1973 | Atlantic PR-265 | 15 |
| (Four songs, all by Hall & Oates) | | | |

**Albums**

| | | | |
|---|---|---|---|
| RCA SPECIAL RADIO SERIES | 1981 | RCA Victor 4179 | 25 |
| (Music and interviews) | | | |

**RADIO SHOWS**

**Albums**

| | | | |
|---|---|---|---|
| ABC SPOTLIGHT SPECIAL | 1982 | ABC Radio | 20-35 |
| (Music and interviews) | | | |
| DICK CLARK PRESENTS (Apr 84)  Box set | 1984 | Mutual Radio (3) | 20-30 |
| (Music and interviews, with Air Supply) | | | |
| DYNAMIC DUOS (May 82)  Box set | 1982 | Mutual Radio (3) | 20-35 |
| (Music and interviews, also Seals & Crofts, England Dan and John Ford Coley) | | | |
| KING BISCUIT FLOWER HOUR (Sept 80)  Live concert | 1980 | DIR/ABC (2) | 50-75 |
| (This show repeated several times) | | | |
| NBC RADIO (Dec 85)  Profile | 1985 | NBC Radio | 20-35 |
| (Music and interviews) | | | |
| NBC SOURCE (Feb 81)  Live concert | 1981 | NBC Radio (2) | 75-150 |
| (This show was repeated six months later) | | | |
| RETRO ROCK (Nov 81) | 1981 | Clayton Webster | 50-100 |
| (Rare live concert) | | | |
| ROBERT W. MORGAN (Mar 81) | 1981 | Watermark | 10-20 |
| (Music and interviews, repeated in Aug) | | | |
| ROCK ON THE ROAD | 1984 | ABC Radio (2) | 75-150 |
| (Includes five live tracks) | | | |
| SUPERGROUPS (80s)  Live concert | 198? | DIR (3) | 75-150 |
| (Rare live concert) | | | |
| TBS SYNDICATION  Live from Central Park | 198? | TBS Broadcasting | 50-100 |
| (Live concert with Dire Straits) | | | |

**Reel-to-Reel Tapes**

| | | | |
|---|---|---|---|
| KING BISCUIT FLOWER HOUR (Dec 78)  "The British Biscuit" | 1978 | DIR/ABC (2) | 75-150 |
| (Live concert on two reels) | | | |

**HALL, ROY**

**45s**

| | | | |
|---|---|---|---|
| DIGGIN' THE BOOGIE | 195? | Decca 30060 | 40 |
| (Pink promo label) | | | |

**HALL, SANDI**

**45s**

| | | | |
|---|---|---|---|
| A CHRISTMAS-Y DAY (same on both sides) | 1982 | K-Tel KS-077 | 4 |

**HALL, TOM T.**

*Mercury and RCA Victor promo 45s $3 each*

**7-Inch Extended Plays**

| | | | |
|---|---|---|---|
| NATIONAL GUARD  Six PSA ads | 1982 | EGR 1282 | 12 |
| (Tom T. Hall has two ads, 60-second and 30-second) | | | |
| THE STORY TELLER  33 1/3 rpm, 6 songs | 1972 | Mercury PL-24 | 12 |
| (White promo label, large center hole) | | | |

**RADIO SHOWS**

**Albums**

| | | | |
|---|---|---|---|
| COUNTRY COOKIN' (Sept 75)  Various artists | 1975 | Army Reserve (2) | 15-25 |
| (Four shows including Wanda Jackson and Tom T. Hall) | | | |

| Title | Yr | Label, Number | NM $ |
|---|---|---|---|
| COUNTRY MUSIC TIME (80s) | 198? | U.S. Air Force | 10-15 |
| *(Music and interviews)* | | | |
| COUNTRY SESSIONS (80s) | 198? | NBC Radio | 10-20 |
| *(Music and interviews)* | | | |

### HALOS, THE
**45s**

| | | | |
|---|---|---|---|
| COME SOFTLY TO ME | 1966 | Congress 262 | 12 |
| *(May be promo-only)* | | | |

### HAMILL, CLAIRE
**RADIO SHOWS**
**Albums**

| | | | |
|---|---|---|---|
| BBC TRANSCRIPTION DISC  Live concert | 1973 | BBC Transcription | 100-200 |
| *(With John Prine)* | | | |

### HAMILTON, GEORGE, IV
**45s**

| | | | |
|---|---|---|---|
| ONLY THE BEST (mono/stereo) | 1978 | ABC 12342 | 5 |
| *(May be promo only)* | | | |

**7-Inch Extended Plays**

| | | | |
|---|---|---|---|
| ON CAMPUS | 1958 | ABC-Paramount 220 | 50 |
| *(Promo label with picture sleeve)* | | | |

### HAMILTON, ROY
*Other Epic promo 45s $5 each; Epic Memory Lane promo 45s $3 each; RCA Victor promo 45s $3 each*
**45s**

| | | | |
|---|---|---|---|
| SOFT 'N' WARM  Compact 33 stereo singles | 1961 | Epic SE-6 | 60 |
| *(Five 7-inch singles with small center hole; $12 each; for jukebox use)* | | | |

### HAMLISCH, MARVIN
**45s**

| | | | |
|---|---|---|---|
| THEME FROM "ORDINARY PEOPLE" (same on both sides) | 1980 | Planet 45922 | 4 |

### HAMMER, MC
**45s**

| | | | |
|---|---|---|---|
| (HAMMER HAMMER) THEY PUT ME IN THE MIX (same on both sides) | 1989 | Capitol 7PRO-79667 | 6 |
| DANCIN' MACHINE (same on both sides) | 1990 | Capitol 7PRO-79893 | 6 |
| HAVE YOU SEEN HER (same on both sides) | 1990 | Capitol 7PRO-79150 | 10 |
| PRAY (Radio Edit)/ (LP Version) | 1990 | Capitol 7PRO-79284/95 | 10 |
| U CAN'T TOUCH THIS (same on both sides) | 1990 | Capitol 7PRO-79072 | 20 |

### HAMPTON, PAUL
*Other Columbia and Dot promo 45s $4 each*
**45s**

| | | | |
|---|---|---|---|
| ROCKIN' DOLL | 1959 | Columbia 41089 | 25 |
| *(White promo label)* | | | |
| SLAM BAM THANK YA MA'AM | 1959 | Columbia 41145 | 25 |
| *(White promo label)* | | | |

### HANCOCK, HERBIE
**12-Inch Singles**

| | | | |
|---|---|---|---|
| EVERYBODY'S BROKE (3:53)/(7:05) | 1981 | Columbia AS 1251 | 8 |
| GETTIN' TO THE GOOD PART/THE FUN TRACKS | 1982 | Columbia AS 1504 | 8 |
| GO FOR IT (6:58)/(7:32) | 1980 | Columbia AS 751 | 8 |
| LITE ME UP (long)/(short) | 1982 | Columbia AS 1413 | 8 |
| MAGIC NUMBER (Remix)/(Edit) | 1981 | Columbia AS 1333 | 8 |
| MAGIC NUMBER/EVERYBODY'S BROKE | 1981 | Columbia AS 1262 | 8 |
| SATURDAY NIGHT/MAKING LOVE | 1980 | Columbia AS 814 | 8 |

### HANEY, RAY
**45s**

| | | | |
|---|---|---|---|
| THE PICTURE ON THE CHRISTMAS CARD/STORY OF A CHRISTMAS TREE | 1955 | MGM 12106 | 12 |

### HAPPENINGS, THE
**45s**

| | | | |
|---|---|---|---|
| HAVE YOURSELF A MERRY LITTLE CHRISTMAS (same on both sides) | 1966 | B.T. Puppy 181 | 30 |
| *(Stock copies do not exist)* | | | |
| MAKE YOUR OWN KIND OF MUSIC (mono/stereo) | 1971 | Jubilee 5721 | 6 |
| *(Stock copies may not exist)* | | | |

### HAPPY MONDAYS
**12-Inch Singles**

| | | | |
|---|---|---|---|
| STEP ON (4 versions) | 1990 | Elektra ED 5469 | 8 |
| SUNSHINE AND LOVE (3 mixes) | 1992 | Elektra ED 5637 | 8 |

### HARLAND, BILLY
**45s**

| | | | |
|---|---|---|---|
| SCHOOL HOUSE ROCK | 1958 | Brunswick 55066 | 125 |
| *(Yellow promo label)* | | | |

| Title | Yr | Label, Number | NM $ |
|---|---|---|---|
| **HARPER, ROY** | | | |
| **Albums** | | | |
| INTRODUCTION TO ROY HARPER | 1976 | Chrysalis PRO-620 | 30 |
| **RADIO SHOWS** | | | |
| **Albums** | | | |
| BBC TRANSCRIPTION DISC | 1974 | BBC Transcription | 75-150 |
| *(Live concert)* | | | |
| | | | |
| **HARRIS, EMMYLOU** | | | |
| *Jubilee white promo label 45s $10 each; Reprise promo 45s $5 each; Warner Bros. promo 45s $4 each; Warner Bros. promo CD singles $3 each; Asylum promo CD singles $3 each* | | | |
| **45s** | | | |
| LIGHT OF THE STABLE/IT CAME UPON A MIDNIGHT CLEAR | 1987 | Warner Bros. PRO-S-2872 | 10 |
| *(B-side by Highway 101)* | | | |
| **Albums** | | | |
| GLIDING BIRD  First pressing, color cover, promo | 1969 | Jubilee 8031 | 50 |
| *(Rare first album)* | | | |
| WARNERS PROMOTIONAL ALBUM | 1987 | Warner Bros. | 15 |
| *(Issued with a special picture cover)* | | | |
| **RADIO SHOWS** | | | |
| **Albums** | | | |
| AMERICAN EAGLE (Jan 87) Live concert | 1987 | Westwood One | 75-125 |
| *(With Don Williams)* | | | |
| LIVE AT GILLEY'S (Apr 83) Live concert | 1983 | Westwood One | 100-175 |
| *(Short but rare live concert)* | | | |
| **Reel-to-Reel Tapes** | | | |
| KING BISCUIT FLOWER HOUR (Sept 76) "The British Biscuit" | 1976 | DIR/ABC (2) | 100-150 |
| *(Live concert with Thin Lizzy)* | | | |
| | | | |
| **HARRIS, MAJOR** | | | |
| **45s** | | | |
| LOVING YOU IS MELLOW (mono/stereo) | 1975 | Atlantic 3299 | 5 |
| *(May be promo-only)* | | | |
| | | | |
| **HARRIS, RICHARD** | | | |
| *Other ABC/Dunhill promo 45s $3 each; Other Atlantic promo 33s and 45s $2 each* | | | |
| **45s** | | | |
| MAC ARTHUR PARK  Stereo single | 1968 | Dunhill D-32 | 18 |
| *(7:20 version, small center hole, promo only)* | | | |
| THE PROPHET | 1974 | (Atlantic) 3238 | 10 |
| *(White promo label)* | | | |
| **7-Inch Extended Plays** | | | |
| THE PROPHET With Kahlil Gibran | 1974 | Atlantic PR-221 | 10 |
| *(Promo-only record and sleeve)* | | | |
| A TRAMP SHINING  Jukebox LLP | 1968 | Dunhill 50032 | 15 |
| *(With "MacArthur Park," issued with hard cover)* | | | |
| THE YARD WENT ON FOREVER  Jukebox LLP | 1969 | ABC Dunhill 50042 | 12 |
| *(Issued with a hard cover)* | | | |
| | | | |
| **HARRIS, WYNONIE** | | | |
| *Other promo King 45s $20-30 each* | | | |
| **45s** | | | |
| DON'T TAKE MY WHISKEY AWAY FROM ME | 1954 | King 4724 | 40 |
| *(White promo label)* | | | |
| SHAKE THAT THING | 1954 | King 4716 | 40 |
| *(White promo label)* | | | |
| | | | |
| **HARRISON, GEORGE** | | | |
| *Member of the Beatles; Member of the Traveling Wilburys* | | | |
| **12-Inch Singles** | | | |
| ALL THOSE YEARS AGO | 1981 | Dark Horse PRO-A-949 | 25 |
| *(Released as a promo only. The song "All Those Years Ago" also features Paul McCartney and Ringo Starr.)* | | | |
| DEVIL'S RADIO | 1987 | Dark Horse PRO-A-2889 | 30 |
| *(Released as a promo only, with a picture cover)* | | | |
| GOT MY MIND SET ON YOU | 1987 | Dark Horse PRO-A-2845 | 25 |
| *(Released as a promo only)* | | | |
| I DON'T WANT TO DO IT  Red label | 1985 | Columbia 2034 | 20 |
| *(George is one of three artists on the record)* | | | |
| I DON'T WANT TO DO IT  Red label | 1985 | Columbia 2085 | 20 |
| *(Only the Harrison song is on this record, both sides)* | | | |
| WAKE UP MY LOVE | 1982 | Dark Horse PRO-A-1075 | 25 |
| *(Same song on both sides)* | | | |
| WHEN WE WAS FAB | 1987 | Dark Horse PRO-A-2885 | 25 |
| *(Released as a promo only)* | | | |
| **45s** | | | |
| ALL THOSE YEARS AGO  Mono/stereo versions | 1981 | Dark Horse 49725 | 15 |
| *(Same song on both sides)* | | | |
| BANGLA DESH  Star on Apple label | 1971 | Apple 1836 | 12 |
| *(Not a legal promo, this version was sent to radio stations.)* | | | |
| BLACK IS BLACK  Lord Sitar | 1968 | Capitol 5972 | 100 |
| *(No, this isn't George; but we can dream…Green label promo; the stock copy of this record, much easier to find, is worth around $20.)* | | | |
| BLOW AWAY Mono/stereo versions | 1979 | Dark Horse 8763 | 15 |
| *(Same song on both sides)* | | | |
| CHEER DOWN | 1989 | Warner Bros. 22807 | 200 |
| *(Very rare, label must read "Promotion Not for Sale")* | | | |

| Title | Yr | Label, Number | NM $ |
|---|---|---|---|
| CRACKERBOX PALACE  Mono/stereo versions | 1977 | Dark Horse 8313 | 15 |
| *(Same song on both sides)* | | | |
| DARK HORSE  Mono/stereo versions | 1974 | Apple P-1877 | 40 |
| *(White promo label, this is the 3:52 version on both sides)* | | | |
| DARK HORSE  Mono/stereo versions | 1974 | Apple P-1877 | 60 |
| *(White promo label, this is the 2:48 version on both sides)* | | | |
| DING DONG, DING DONG (remixed mono/edited stereo) | 1974 | Apple P-1879 | 40 |
| GIVE ME LOVE  Mono/stereo versions | 1973 | Apple PRO 6676 | 50 |
| *(Green Apple label, same song on both sides)* | | | |
| GOT MY MIND SET ON YOU | 1987 | Dark Horse 28178 | 15 |
| *(Most copies can be found with a picture sleeve, worth about $3)* | | | |
| I DON'T WANT TO DO IT  White promo label | 1985 | Columbia 04887 | 15 |
| *(George's only 45rpm on Columbia)* | | | |
| I REALLY LOVE YOU | 1982 | Dark Horse 29744 | 15 |
| *(Same songs on both sides)* | | | |
| LOVE COMES TO EVERYONE  Mono/stereo versions | 1979 | Dark Horse 8844 | 15 |
| *(Same song on both sides. The picture sleeve for this song is very rare, worth $750 or more; it is a stock sleeve, but is most likely to be found on a promo record in a radio station.)* | | | |
| MY SWEET LORD Star on Apple label | 1970 | Apple 2995 | 15 |
| *(Not a legal promo, this version was shipped to radio stations.)* | | | |
| TEARDROPS  Mono/stereo versions | 1981 | Dark Horse 49785 | 15 |
| *(Same song on both sides)* | | | |
| THIS GUITAR Mono/stereo versions | 1975 | Apple P-1885 | 50 |
| *(Same song on both sides, Apple green label, also this is the last record, Apple 1885, in the original Apple label series)* | | | |
| THIS IS LOVE | 1988 | Dark Horse 27913 | 15 |
| *(Often found with a picture sleeve worth $4)* | | | |
| THIS SONG  Mono/stereo versions | 1976 | Dark Horse 8294 | 25 |
| *(Same song on both sides)* | | | |
| THIS SONG  Promo-only picture sleeve | 1976 | Dark Horse 8294 | 40 |
| *(This picture sleeve is in the form of a letter to the DJ and is different from the picture sleeve found on the stock copy.)* | | | |
| WAKE UP MY LOVE | 1982 | Dark Horse 29864 | 15 |
| *(Same song on both sides)* | | | |
| WHAT IS LIFE Star on Apple label | 1971 | Apple 1828 | 12 |
| *(Not a legal promo, this version was shipped to radio stations.)* | | | |
| WHEN WE WAS FAB | 1987 | Dark Horse 28131 | 15 |
| *(Same song on both sides)* | | | |
| YOU  Mono/stereo versions | 1975 | Apple P-1884 | 40 |
| *(Brown and blue promo label)* | | | |
| **7-Inch Extended Plays** | | | |
| THE CONCERT FOR BANGLA DESH  White label | 1971 | Apple/20th Century Fox 791 | 1,000 |
| *(7", one-sided with four movie promo cuts, 30- and 60-second)* | | | |
| **Albums** | | | |
| DARK HORSE RADIO SPECIAL | 1974 | Dark Horse (no #) | 400 |
| *(Promo-only; George Harrison introduces his new record label and artists)* | | | |
| GONE TROPPO | 1982 | Dark Horse 23724 | 25 |
| *(Promo on Quiex II vinyl)* | | | |
| MONSTERS  Various artists sampler | 197? | Warner Bros. PRO-796 (2) | 15 |
| *(Includes a track by Harrison)* | | | |
| PERSONAL MUSIC DIALOGUE AT 33 & 1/3 | 1976 | Dark Horse PRO-649 | 50 |
| *(Promo-only release from label)* | | | |
| **Compact Discs** | | | |
| CHEER DOWN | 1989 | Warner Bros. PRO-CD-3647 | 20 |
| *(Promo-only CD single)* | | | |
| CLOUD 9 | 1988 | Dark Horse PRO-CD-2924 | 30 |
| *(Promo-only CD single)* | | | |
| CLOUD NINE | 1987 | Dark Horse 25643 | 35 |
| *(Picture disc version of the stock album)* | | | |
| GOT MY MIND SET ON YOU | 1987 | Dark Horse PRO-CD-2846 | 30 |
| *(Promo-only CD single)* | | | |
| LIVE IN JAPAN SAMPLER | 1992 | Dark Horse PRO-CD-5555 | 40 |
| *(Five-track sampler from 2-CD set)* | | | |
| POOR LITTLE GIRL | 1989 | Dark Horse PRO-CD-3775 | 15 |
| *(Promo-only CD single, 4:32 and 3:25 versions)* | | | |
| THIS IS LOVE | 1988 | Dark Horse PRO-CDS-3068 | 60 |
| *(3-inch promo-only CD single)* | | | |
| THIS IS LOVE | 1988 | Dark Horse PRO-CD-3068 | 15 |
| *(Promo-only 5-inch CD single, not to be confused with smaller 3-inch promo)* | | | |
| **RADIO SHOWS** | | | |
| **Albums** | | | |
| HOT ROCKS (Dec 87) | 1987 | United Stations (2) | 35-50 |
| *(Music and interviews)* | | | |
| INNERVIEW Profile of Harrison/Beatles | 1978 | Innerview | 30-60 |
| *(Rare show, music and interviews)* | | | |
| LEGENDS OF ROCK (Dec 87) Music and interviews | 1987 | NBC Radio (2) | 40-55 |
| *(This show was repeated in 1988)* | | | |
| LEGENDS OF ROCK (June 87) Profile | 1987 | NBC Radio (2) | 35-50 |
| *(Music and interview)* | | | |
| OFF THE RECORD (Mar 88) Music and interview | 1988 | Westwood One (2) | 35-50 |
| *(This show was repeated)* | | | |
| ROCK STARS (Dec 87) Music and interviews | 1987 | Radio Today (2) | 35-50 |
| *(Blue labels)* | | | |
| ROCK, ROLL & REMEMBER  Dick Clark is host | 1989 | United Stations (4) | 20-35 |
| *(Harrison special w/interviews and music)* | | | |
| STARTRACK PROFILE (Feb 88) Profile | 1988 | Westwood One (2) | 40-75 |
| *(Includes Beatles material)* | | | |
| STARTRACK PROFILE (Oct 88) Profile | 1988 | Westwood One (2) | 35-60 |
| *(Same show as above)* | | | |

| Title | Yr | Label, Number | NM $ |
|---|---|---|---|
| **Compact Discs** | | | |
| IN THE STUDIO Music and interview | 1994 | (2) | 100-150 |
| *(Interview on the making of "Live in Japan")* | | | |
| IN THE STUDIO (Aug 92) Profile of an album | 1992 | Album Network (2) | 40-100 |
| *(Special 2CD "Live In Japan" special)* | | | |
| IN THE STUDIO (Jan 90) Profile of an album | 1990 | Album Network | 30-60 |
| *(Music and interview, LP is "Dark Horse")* | | | |
| MASTERS OF ROCK (July 89) Music and interview | 1989 | Radio Ventures | 50-100 |
| *(Rare show)* | | | |
| TICKET TO RIDE | 1988 | DIR | 20-40 |
| *(This show, part of a series, highlights Harrison)* | | | |
| UP CLOSE (Aug 92) Profile, Parts 1 and 2 | 1992 | Media America (4) | 100-175 |
| *(Mostly music and interviews)* | | | |
| | | | |
| **HARRISON, JERRY** | | | |
| *More at Talking Heads.* | | | |
| **12-Inch Singles** | | | |
| MAN WITH A GUN (2 versions) | 1988 | Sire PRO-A-3165 | 6 |
| | | | |
| **HARRY, DEBBIE** | | | |
| *More at Blondie.* | | | |
| **12-Inch Singles** | | | |
| FRENCH KISSIN' (Remix)/FRENCH KISSIN' (LP Version) | 1986 | Geffen PRO-A-2594 | 7 |
| | | | |
| **HART, COREY** | | | |
| *EMI promo 45s $3 each* | | | |
| **RADIO SHOWS** | | | |
| **Albums** | | | |
| INNERVIEW (80s) Profile | 198? | Innerview | 10-20 |
| *(Music and interviews)* | | | |
| | | | |
| **HATHAWAY, DONNY** | | | |
| **45s** | | | |
| THIS CHRISTMAS | 1978 | Atlantic Atco PR 322 | 10 |
| *(Special promo-only release, flip is by Roberta Flack)* | | | |
| | | | |
| **HAWKINS, DALE** | | | |
| *Checker promo 45s $15 each* | | | |
| | | | |
| **HAWKINS, HAWKSHAW** | | | |
| **RADIO SHOWS** | | | |
| **16-Inch Transcriptions** | | | |
| LEATHERNECK JAMBOREE (50s) Hawkins was a guest | 195? | Armed Forces | 25-40 |
| *(Music and interviews)* | | | |
| U. S. ARMY BAND (50s) Hawkins was the host | 195? | U.S. Army | 25-40 |
| *(Music and interviews)* | | | |
| | | | |
| **HAWKINS, RONNIE** | | | |
| *Also see John Lennon; Roulette promo 45s $10-20 each; Monument promo 45s $3 each* | | | |
| **45s** | | | |
| FORTY DAYS | 1959 | Roulette 4154 | 35 |
| *(Roulette promo label)* | | | |
| LONELY HOURS | 1960 | Roulette 4228 | 25 |
| *(Roulette promo label)* | | | |
| **Albums** | | | |
| RONNIE HAWKINS | 1959 | Roulette 25078 | 40 |
| *(Roulette promo label, mono)* | | | |
| | | | |
| **HAWKINS, SCREAMIN' JAY** | | | |
| *Epic promo 45s $5 each* | | | |
| **Albums** | | | |
| AT HOME WITH SCREAMIN' JAY | 1956 | Epic 3448 | 225 |
| *(White promo label)* | | | |
| I PUT A SPELL ON YOU | 1957 | Epic 3457 | 100 |
| *(White promo label)* | | | |
| | | | |
| **HAWKINS, SOPHIE B.** | | | |
| **12-Inch Singles** | | | |
| RIGHT BESIDE YOU (4 versions) | 1994 | Columbia CAS 6237 | 10 |
| | | | |
| **HAWKS, MICKEY** | | | |
| **45s** | | | |
| HIDI HIDI HIDI | 195? | Profile 4007 | 40 |
| *(White promo label)* | | | |
| SCREAMIN' MIMI JEANIE | 195? | Profile 4010 | 50 |
| *(White promo label)* | | | |
| | | | |
| **HAWKS, THE** | | | |
| **45s** | | | |
| ALL WOMEN ARE THE SAME | 1954 | Imperial 5317 | 50 |
| *(Cream-colored promo label)* | | | |
| IT AIN'T THAT WAY | 1954 | Imperial 5292 | 75 |
| *(Cream-colored promo label)* | | | |
| IT'S TOO LATE NOW | 1955 | Imperial 5332 | 50 |
| *(Cream-colored promo label)* | | | |

| Title | Yr | Label, Number | NM $ |
|---|---|---|---|
| JOE, THE GRINDER | 1954 | Imperial 5266 | 100 |
| *(Cream-colored promo label)* | | | |
| NOBODY BUT YOU | 1954 | Imperial 5306 | 50 |
| *(Cream-colored promo label)* | | | |
| SHE'S ALL RIGHT | 1954 | Imperial 5281 | 100 |
| *(Cream-colored promo label)* | | | |
| WHY OH WHY | 1955 | Post 2004 | 50 |
| *(White promo label)* | | | |

**HAWKWIND**
**RADIO SHOWS**
**Albums**

| BBC TRANSCRIPTION DISC Live concert | 1972 | BBC Transcription | 400-600 |
|---|---|---|---|
| *(Very rare show)* | | | |

**HAYES, BILL**
*Other ABC-Paramount promo 45s $5 each*
**45s**

| BOP BOY | 1958 | ABC-Paramount | 40 |
|---|---|---|---|
| *(White promo label)* | | | |

**HAYES, ISAAC**
**Albums**

| FUNKY JUNKY | 1995 | Pointblank SPRO-12787 | 15 |
|---|---|---|---|
| *(Vinyl is promo only)* | | | |

**HAZARD, ROBERT**
*RCA Victor promo 45s $4 each*
**RADIO SHOWS**
**Albums**

| KING BISCUIT FLOWER HOUR (June 83) Live concert | 1983 | DIR/ABC (2) | 40-75 |
|---|---|---|---|
| *(With Dave Edmunds)* | | | |
| NBC SOURCE (May 83) | 1983 | NBC Radio (2) | 15-30 |
| *(Music and interviews)* | | | |

**HEAD, HANDS & FEET**
**RADIO SHOWS**
**Albums**

| BBC TRANSCRIPTION DISC | 1972 | BBC Transcription | 125-200 |
|---|---|---|---|
| *(Live concert)* | | | |

**HEAD, ROY**
*Scepter and Mercury promo 45s $8 each*
**45s**

| KISS YOU AND MAKE IT BETTER (mono/stereo) | 1979 | ABC 12462 | 4 |
|---|---|---|---|
| *(May be promo only)* | | | |

**HEADCRASH**
**45s**

| SAFEHOUSE/STAINS | 1996 | Discovery PRO 74539-7 | 5 |
|---|---|---|---|
| *(With insert in generic, promo-stamped sleeve)* | | | |

**HEADROOM, MAX**
**45s**

| MERRY CHRISTMAS SANTA CLAUS (YOU'RE A LOVELY GUY) | 1985 | Chrysalis 44000 | 4 |
|---|---|---|---|
| *(Promo version, same on both sides)* | | | |

**HEALEY, JEFF, BAND**
*Arista promo 45s $3 each; Arista promo CD singles $2-3 each*
**RADIO SHOWS**
**Compact Discs**

| IN CONCERT (Apr 94) Live concert | 1994 | Westwood One | 20-30 |
|---|---|---|---|
| *(Live with Chris Whitten)* | | | |
| IN CONCERT (Feb 91) Live concert | 1991 | Westwood One (2) | 25-50 |
| *(Jeff Healey Band only)* | | | |
| IN CONCERT (June 92) Live concert | 1992 | Westwood One (2) | 40-75 |
| *(Live with Counting Crows)* | | | |
| OFF THE RECORD (Feb 92) Profile | 1992 | Westwood One (2) | 10-15 |
| *(Music and interviews)* | | | |
| UP CLOSE  Profile | 1993 | Media America (2) | 20-35 |
| *(Some live material)* | | | |

**HEART**
*Other Mushroom promo 45s $6 each; Portrait (CBS) promo 45s $5 each; Capitol white promo label 45s $4 each; Other Capitol promo CD singles $3-5 each; any promo 45s by Ann Wilson or Nancy Wilson $3 each; Other 12" singles by Heart, group or solo, $8 each*
**12-Inch Singles**

| DREAMBOAT ANNIE | 1976 | Mushroom 7023 | 12 |
|---|---|---|---|
| *(The only Mushroom 12" single, long and short versions)* | | | |

**45s**

| MAGIC MAN  Mono AM Play/Stereo FM Play | 1975 | Mushroom 7011 | 10 |
|---|---|---|---|
| *(Long 5:35 and short 2:45 versions)* | | | |
| WHAT'S IT ALL ABOUT (Aug 80) Public service show | 1980 | W. I. A. A. 537 | 25 |
| *(Flip side features Grace Slick)* | | | |

| Title | Yr | Label, Number | NM $ |
|---|---|---|---|
| **Albums** | | | |
| HEART | 1980 | Epic AS 884 | 20 |
| *(Promo-only sampler from "Greatest Hits/Live")* | | | |
| MAGAZINE | 1978 | Mushroom 5008 | 40 |
| *(Promo-only picture disc, not to be confused with stock picture disc, which is individually numbered)* | | | |
| **Compact Discs** | | | |
| BRIGADE | 1990 | Capitol DPRO-79667 | 20 |
| *(Promo-only packaging in black box)* | | | |
| HERE IS CHRISTMAS | 1989 | Capitol DPRO-79??? | 12 |
| *(Promo-only CD single, by "Ann and Nancy Wilson")* | | | |
| **RADIO SHOWS** | | | |
| **Albums** | | | |
| BBC ROCK HOUR (July 82) Live concert | 1982 | London Wavelength | 40-75 |
| *(This show was repeated)* | | | |
| CAPTURED LIVE (May 84) Live concert | 1984 | RKO (2) | 40-75 |
| *(With Kansas, same shows)* | | | |
| CAPTURED LIVE (May 84) Parts 1 and 2, live concert | 1984 | RKO (4) | 75-150 |
| *(With Kansas)* | | | |
| HOT ROCKS (May 86) Music and interviews | 1986 | United Stations (2) | 20-35 |
| *(Show was repeated)* | | | |
| INNERVIEW (70s) Profile | 197? | Innerview | 15-25 |
| *(Music and interviews)* | | | |
| KING BISCUIT FLOWER HOUR Live concert | 1985 | DIR/ABC (2) | 25-50 |
| *(Vinyl version)* | | | |
| NBC SOURCE (Feb 84) Live concert | 1984 | NBC Radio (2) | 75-150 |
| *(Rare early live concert)* | | | |
| OFF THE RECORD (Feb 92) Music and interviews | 1992 | Westwood One (2) | 15-25 |
| *(This show repeated several times)* | | | |
| PIONEERS IN MUSIC (Apr 87) | 1987 | DIR (2) | 20-40 |
| *(Music and interviews, with the Pretenders)* | | | |
| PROFILES IN ROCK (July 80) | 1980 | Watermark | 15-25 |
| *(Music and interviews)* | | | |
| RETRO ROCK (Feb 82) Music and interviews | 1982 | Clayton Webster (2) | 40-75 |
| *(With some live tracks)* | | | |
| RETRO ROCK (Sept 84) Music and interviews | 1984 | Clayton Webster (2) | 30-60 |
| *(Not the same show as above, less live)* | | | |
| ROBERT W. MORGAN (Nov 79) | 1979 | Watermark | 15-25 |
| *(Music and interviews)* | | | |
| ROCK AND THE ENVIRONMENT (Apr 92) Ann and Nancy Wilson | 1992 | (2) | 15-25 |
| *(Music and interviews)* | | | |
| SUPERSTAR CONCERT  Box set | 1987 | Westwood One (3) | 45-80 |
| *(Live concert, repeated several times)* | | | |
| WESTWOOD ONE SNEAK PREVUE (Aug 83) | 1983 | Westwood One | 20-35 |
| *(Music and interviews)* | | | |
| WHAT ABOUT LOVE (Feb 87) (An Audio Valentine) | 1987 | Radio International | 20-35 |
| *(Rare one time special, with red/white photo cover)* | | | |
| **Compact Discs** | | | |
| KING BISCUIT FLOWER HOUR Live concert | 1989 | DIR | 25-50 |
| *(This CD version corrected for broadcast)* | | | |
| KING BISCUIT FLOWER HOUR (Oct 87) | 1987 | DIR | 150-250 |
| *(Very rare show, called back by DIR)* | | | |
| SUPERSTARS (Jan 95) | 1995 | (2) | 75-100 |
| *(Live concert material)* | | | |
| UP CLOSE  Profile | 1990 | Album Network (2) | 25-40 |
| *(Music and interviews, some live tracks)* | | | |
| UP CLOSE  Profile | 1994 | Album Network (2) | 20-35 |
| *(Music and interviews)* | | | |

## HEARTBEATS, THE

*Other Hull promo 45s $50-75 each; Gee promo 45s $40 each; Roulette promo 45s $25 each*

| Title | Yr | Label, Number | NM $ |
|---|---|---|---|
| **45s** | | | |
| CRAZY FOR YOU | 1955 | Hull 711 | 750 |
| *(Ropes promo label)* | | | |
| PEOPLE ARE TALKING | 1956 | Hull 716 | 175 |
| *(White promo label)* | | | |
| A THOUSAND MILES AWAY | 1956 | Hull 720 | 150 |
| *(White promo label; the answer song is "Daddy's Home" Shep & Limelites, Hull 740)* | | | |

## HEARTBREAKERS, THE

*Frank Zappa involvement on the Donna record*

| Title | Yr | Label, Number | NM $ |
|---|---|---|---|
| **45s** | | | |
| EVERY TIME I SEE YOU | 1964 | Donna 1381 | 60 |
| *(White promo label)* | | | |
| HEARTBREAKER | 1951 | RCA Victor 4327 | 400 |
| *(White promo label)* | | | |
| I'M ONLY FOOLING MY HEART | 1951 | RCA Victor 4508 | 400 |
| *(White promo label)* | | | |
| MY LOVE | 195? | Vik 0299 | 200 |
| *(White promo label)* | | | |
| ONE, TWO, I LOVE YOU | 195? | Vik 0261 | 100 |
| *(White promo label)* | | | |
| THERE IS TIME | 1952 | RCA Victor 4849 | 250 |
| *(White promo label)* | | | |
| WHY DON'T I | 1952 | RCA Victor 4662 | 300 |
| *(White promo label)* | | | |

| Title | Yr | Label, Number | NM $ |
|-------|----|--------------|----|
| **78s** | | | |
| HEARTBREAKER | 1951 | RCA Victor 4327 | 200 |
| *(White promo label)* | | | |
| I'M ONLY FOOLING MY HEART | 1951 | RCA Victor 4508 | 200 |
| *(White promo label)* | | | |
| THERE IS TIME | 1952 | RCA Victor 4849 | 150 |
| *(White promo label)* | | | |
| WHY DON'T I | 1952 | RCA Victor 4662 | 200 |
| *(White promo label)* | | | |
| | | | |
| **HEAVEN** | | | |
| **RADIO SHOWS** | | | |
| **Albums** | | | |
| BBC ROCK HOUR (Jan 84) | 1984 | London Wavelength | 40-75 |
| *(Live concert)* | | | |
| | | | |
| **HEAVEN 17** | | | |
| **12-Inch Singles** | | | |
| (BIG) TROUBLE (2 versions) | 1986 | Virgin 1049 | 6 |
| PENTHOUSE AND PAVEMENT (4 versions) | 1993 | Virgin 12667 | 8 |
| | | | |
| **HENDRIX, JIMI** | | | |
| *Other Reprise promo 45s $10 each; Other Reprise promo LPs $20 each; United Artists promo LP $25* | | | |
| **12-Inch Singles** | | | |
| AND A HAPPY NEW YEAR Promo-only release | 1979 | Reprise PRO-840 | 100 |
| *(Price includes a picture sleeve cover)* | | | |
| **45s** | | | |
| ALL ALONG THE WATCHTOWER | 1968 | Reprise 0767 | 25 |
| *(White promo label)* | | | |
| AND A HAPPY NEW YEAR Promo-only release | 1974 | Reprise PRO-595 | 300 |
| *(Price includes the picture sleeve that was issued with the record)* | | | |
| CAN YOU PLEASE CRAWL OUT YOUR WINDOW?/ | | | |
| BURNING OF THE MIDNIGHT LAMP | 1998 | MCA 55454 | 10 |
| *(Promo only on orange vinyl with cardboard picture sleeve; given out at Best Buy with purchase of 'BBC Sessions" CD)* | | | |
| CROSSTOWN TRAFFIC | 1968 | Reprise 0792 | 20 |
| *(White promo label)* | | | |
| DOLLY DAGGER | 1971 | Reprise 1044 | 20 |
| *(White promo label)* | | | |
| FIRE  Brown promo label | 1983 | Reprise 29845 | 12 |
| *(Stereo/mono versions)* | | | |
| FOXY LADY | 1967 | Reprise 0641 | 25 |
| *(White promo label)* | | | |
| FREEDOM  White promo label | 1971 | Reprise 1000 | 25 |
| *(Same track on both sides)* | | | |
| GLORIA  One-sided, issued with LP | 1985 | Reprise 2293 | 12 |
| *(Price includes paper picture cover)* | | | |
| HEY JOE  White promo label | 1967 | Reprise 0572 | 50 |
| *(His first record for Reprise)* | | | |
| IF 6 WAS 9 | 1969 | Reprise 0853 | 25 |
| *(White promo label)* | | | |
| JOHNNY B. GOODE | 1972 | Reprise 1082 | 18 |
| *(White promo label)* | | | |
| PURPLE HAZE | 1967 | Reprise 0597 | 25 |
| *(White promo label)* | | | |
| STEPPING STONE | 1970 | Reprise 0905 | 75 |
| *(The stock copy is even rarer, worth $100)* | | | |
| THE WIND CRIES MARY | 1972 | Reprise 1118 | 25 |
| *(White promo label)* | | | |
| UP FROM THE SKIES | 1968 | Reprise 0665 | 25 |
| *(White promo label)* | | | |
| **Albums** | | | |
| ARE YOU EXPERIENCED White promo label | 1967 | Reprise R-6261 | 250 |
| *(Stock copy mono copies of this LP are very rare)* | | | |
| AXIS: BOLD AS LOVE  White promo label | 1967 | Reprise R-6281 | 300 |
| *(Stock copy mono copies of this LP are very rare)* | | | |
| CRASH LANDING | 1975 | Reprise 2204 | 100 |
| *(White promo label)* | | | |
| CRAWDADDY INTERVIEW | 1975 | CRAWDADDY | 150-200 |
| *(Promo-only release issued by Crawdaddy magazine)* | | | |
| ELECTRIC LADYLAND  White promo label | 1968 | Reprise RS-6307 (2) | 150 |
| *(This version in stereo)* | | | |
| ELECTRIC LADYLAND  White promo label | 1968 | Reprise R-6307 (2) | 800 |
| *(This version is in mono)* | | | |
| HISTORIC PERFORMANCES AT THE MONTEREY | 1970 | Reprise 2029 | 125 |
| INTERNATIONAL POP FESTIVAL | | | |
| *(White promo label)* | | | |
| IN THE WEST | 1972 | Reprise 2049 | 100 |
| *(White promo label)* | | | |
| MIDNIGHT LIGHTNING | 1975 | Reprise 2229 | 100 |
| *(White promo label)* | | | |
| RAINBOW BRIDGE | 1971 | Reprise 2040 | 100 |
| *(White promo label)* | | | |
| SMASH HITS | 1969 | Reprise 2025 | 125 |
| *(White promo label)* | | | |
| SOUNDTRACK RECORDINGS FROM THE FILM JIMI HENDRIX | 1973 | Reprise 2-6481 (2) | 175 |
| *(White promo label)* | | | |

| Title | Yr | Label, Number | NM $ |
|---|---|---|---|
| THE CRY OF LOVE | 1970 | Reprise 2034 | 100 |
| (White promo label) | | | |
| WAR HEROES | 1972 | Reprise 2103 | 100 |
| (White promo label) | | | |
| **Compact Discs** | | | |
| BAND OF GYPSYS | 1995 | Capitol DPRO-79534 | 20 |
| (Sampler from reissue of the 1970 LP) | | | |
| BETWEEN THE LINES | 1990 | Reprise PRO-CD-4541 | 15 |
| (Promo-only sampler) | | | |
| RADIO RADIO | 1989 | Rykodisc PRO 0078 | 40 |
| (Promo-only sampler from Radio One LP) | | | |
| RARITIES ON COMPACT DISC VOLUME 1 | 1991 | On the Radio | 70 |
| (First of a series of sought-after CDs for radio use) | | | |
| RARITIES ON COMPACT DISC VOLUME 1 | 1994 | On the Radio | 30 |
| (Reissue of 1991 disc, has 1994 date clearly indicated) | | | |
| STEPPING STONE | 1995 | MCA 3357 | 15 |
| (Promo CD single) | | | |
| **RADIO SHOWS** | | | |
| **Albums** | | | |
| BBC ROCK HOUR (Nov 81) Music and interviews | 1981 | London Wavelength | 75-125 |
| (Some live tracks) | | | |
| BBC ROCK HOUR (Oct 84) Music and interviews | 1984 | London Wavelength | 80-150 |
| (Some live tracks) | | | |
| THE IN SOUND (Oct 67) 5-minute public service show | 1967 | U.S. Army | 150-250 |
| (Jimi Hendrix is one of the features, Jimmy Page is another, music and interviews, very rare record) | | | |
| JIMI HENDRIX  Profile | 1981 | London Wavelength (5) | 175-250 |
| (Mostly music and interviews) | | | |
| JIMI HENDRIX SPECIAL (Sept 88) | 1988 | Westwood One (4) | 125-250 |
| (Show includes many rare unreleased concert performances) | | | |
| JIMI HENDRIX STORY | 1990 | United Stations (3) | 75-125 |
| (Music and interviews) | | | |
| LIVE & UNRELEASED (Sept 88) Very rare | 1988 | (8) | 150-225 |
| (Eight-record radio show of rare live material) | | | |
| NBC SOURCE (Nov 82) The Tribute Special | 1982 | NBC Radio (5) | 85-150 |
| (Three-hour show, music and interviews) | | | |
| ROCK AND ROLL NEVER FORGETS Profile | 1984 | Westwood One (5) | 125-250 |
| (Mostly music and interviews) | | | |
| ROLLING STONE CONTINUOUS HISTORY OF ROCK | 1982 | Rolling Stone (2) | 30-50 |
| (2-LP segment on Hendrix from a series in rock history) | | | |
| ROYALTY OF ROCK Profile | 1982 | RKO | 30-60 |
| (Music and interviews) | | | |
| **Compact Discs** | | | |
| ALBUM NETWORK SPECIAL (Nov 93) Based on tribute LP | 1993 | Album Network (2) | 40-75 |
| (Music and interviews) | | | |
| BBC CLASSIC TRACKS (Feb 93) Live tracks | 1993 | Westwood One | 25-50 |
| (From various live performances) | | | |
| HENDRIX AT THE BEEB (Nov 92) Live material | 1992 | London Wavelength (3) | 100-150 |
| (Many BBC unreleased live tracks, most of which have been released legitimately now) | | | |
| IN FROM THE STORM | 1995 | Media America (3) | 80-120 |
| (Music and interviews, some live tracks) | | | |
| INSIDE THE EXPERIENCE (Aug 90) Music and interviews | 1990 | Media America (3) | 75-125 |
| (Released in a picture box) | | | |
| LABOR DAY SPECIAL (Sept 90) | 1990 | Media America (3) | 75-125 |
| (Music and interviews) | | | |
| OFF THE RECORD | 1996 | (2) | 100-125 |
| (Music and interviews, rare tracks) | | | |
| OFF THE RECORD (Nov 95) | 1995 | (2) | 50-75 |
| (Music and interviews, one live track) | | | |
| ROCK AT THE CORE  With others | 1989 | (3) | 40-75 |
| (Music and interviews) | | | |
| SET, RECORD, START (90s) | 199? | (3) | 100-150 |
| (Some live tracks and some music and interview) | | | |
| SETTING THE RECORD STRAIGHT (Sept 92) Live material | 1992 | Westwood One (3) | 100-150 |
| (Much unreleased material, produced by Eddie Kramer, who was Jimi's original engineer) | | | |
| THE OTHER SIDE OF LOVE ROCK | 1988 | Media America (3) | 75-125 |
| (Mostly music and interviews) | | | |
| UP CLOSE  Profile | 1990 | Media America (2) | 75-125 |
| (Music and interview with some live tracks) | | | |

## HENLEY, DON
*More at the Eagles*
**45s**

| Title | Yr | Label, Number | NM $ |
|---|---|---|---|
| BOYS OF SUMMER, THE | 1984 | Geffen 29141 | 10 |
| (With promo-only insert) | | | |

## HERMAN'S HERMITS
*Featuring Peter Noone; MGM promo 45s $6 each; Private Stock promo 45s $3 each; Buddah promo 45s $3 each; Casablanca promo 45s by Peter Noone $4 each; Johnson (CBS) promo 45s by Peter Noone $2 each*
**45s**

| Title | Yr | Label, Number | NM $ |
|---|---|---|---|
| OH YOU PRETTY THINGS  With David Bowie | 1971 | Bell 45,131 | 25 |
| (White promo label, stock copy is very rare, worth over $50) | | | |

## HERROLD, DENNIS
**45s**

| Title | Yr | Label, Number | NM $ |
|---|---|---|---|
| HIP HIP BABY | 1955 | Imperial 5482 | 50 |
| (Cream-colored promo label) | | | |

(Top left) Jimi Hendrix promos are highly sought-after. Here is a label from the soundtrack of the movie *Jimi Hendrix*, which has not been released on CD. (Top right) The Spin Radio Concert was an alternative to the King Biscuit Flower Hour with more "modern" acts. Here's a rare performance by Husker Du when the band was still on SST Records, before its ill-fated major-label plunge. (Middle left) Another in the seemingly infinite number of radio-show concert series was A Night On The Road. This episode from 1981 featured Jethro Tull. (Middle right) Elton John's 1974 recording for the BBC was issued on this transcription disc from 1978. (Bottom row) Elton John was another act that garnered good ratings for local stations. Here are a Star Session from 1982 and a King Biscuit Flower Hour from 1987, one of the last vinyl editions of the KBFH.

| Title | Yr | Label, Number | NM $ |
|-------|-----|---------------|------|

**HERSH, KRISTIN**
**45s**
COUNTING BACKWARDS (LIVE)/COUNTING SHEEP (LIVE)   1991   Warner Bros. PRO-S-4663   10
*("Soil Samples" series; B-side by the Judybats; green vinyl)*

**HESS, BENNIE**
**45s**
ELVIS PRESLEY BOOGIE   1961   Spade 2202   45
*(Promo label)*
TENNESSEE MAMA BLUES   1961   Tap 1016   40
*(Promo label)*
THE LIFE OF JIMMIE RODGERS   196?   Showland 241973   75
*(Issued in a picture sleeve that is also quite rare and is included in the price)*
WALKING THAT LAST MILE   1961   Major 1006   65
*(Promo label)*
WILD HOG HOP   1959   Major 1001   150
*(Promo label)*
WILD HOG HOP   1961   Spade 1975   40
*(Promo label)*

**HI-LITES, THE**
**45s**
I FOUND LOVE   1954   Okeh 7046   100
*(White promo label)*

**HIATT, JOHN**
*EMI promo singles $3 each; A&M promo CD singles $3-5 each; Capitol promo CD singles $2-3 each*
**Compact Discs**
PERFECTLY GOOD GUITAR   1993   A&M 31454 0135-2   50
*(Promo-only release with black guitar box)*
WALK ON SAMPLER   1995   Capitol DPRO-10280   30
*(Promo-only release)*
**RADIO SHOWS**
**Albums**
IN CONCERT (90s) Live concert   199?   Westwood One (2)   20-35
*(With Robert Cray)*
IN CONCERT (Nov 90) Live concert   1990   Westwood One (2)   25-40
*(With Michael Penn)*
KING BISCUIT FLOWER HOUR (Mar 85) Live concert   1985   DIR (2)   30-50
*(With Missing Persons)*
RETRO ROCK (Jan 84) Live concert   1984   Clayton Webster   40-100
*(With Marshall Crenshaw)*
**Compact Discs**
IN CONCERT (Jan 94) Live concert   1994   Westwood One   25-50
*(Solo concert)*
KING BISCUIT FLOWER HOUR (Oct 87) Live concert   1987   DIR   20-35
*(Solo live concert)*

**HICKEY, ERSEL**
*Epic white promo label 45s $10 each*
**7-Inch Extended Plays**
IN LOVE'S HAND   1958   Epic 7206   125
*(White promo label)*

**HICKS, JOHNNY**
*Other Columbia promo 45s $25 each*
**45s**
PICK UP BLUES   1955   Columbia 21064   75
*(White promo label)*

**HIGH LETTERS, THE**
**45s**
HELLO, DEAR   1956   Vee Jay 184   125
*(White promo label)*

**HIGHWAY 101**
*Includes listings by Paulette Carlson; Other Warner Bros. promo 45s $2 each; Warner Bros. promo CD singles $2 each*
**45s**
IT CAME UPON A MIDNIGHT CLEAR/LIGHT OF THE STABLE   1987   Warner Bros. PRO-S-2872   10
*(B-side by Emmylou Harris)*
**RADIO SHOWS**
**Albums**
WESTWOOD ONE PRESENTS (May 89) Live concert   1989   Westwood One   30-60

**HIGHWAYMEN, THE**
**45s**
ROLL ON COLUMBIA   196?   United Artists 679   12
*(Stereo, small hole, 33 1/3 rpm)*

**HILL, FAITH**
*Other Warner Bros. promo CD singles $3-5 each*
**Compact Discs**
WILD ONE   1993   Warner Bros. PRO-CD-6445   8
*(Promo CD single, her first hit)*

| Title | Yr | Label, Number | NM $ |
|---|---|---|---|

**RADIO SHOWS**
**Compact Discs**

| | | | |
|---|---|---|---|
| COUNTRY CUTTING EDGE (Nov 93) | 1993 | Westwood One | 10-20 |

*(Music and interviews)*

**HILL, JAYCEE**
*Other Epic promo 45s $10-20 each*
**45s**

| | | | |
|---|---|---|---|
| ROMP STOMPIN' BOOGIE | 1954 | Epic 9185 | 40 |

*(White promo label)*

**HITCHCOCK, ROBYN, AND THE EGYPTIANS**
**12-Inch Singles**

| | | | |
|---|---|---|---|
| BALLOON MAN (same on both sides) | 1988 | A&M SP-17537 | 10 |
| BALLOON MAN/A GLOBE OF FROGS (ELECTRIC)/THE GHOST SHIP | 1988 | A&M SP-17530 | 15 |
| *(Green vinyl)* | | | |
| DARK GREEN ENERGY + 2 | 1991 | A&M 75021 7277 1 | 10 |
| FLESH NUMBER ONE/LEGALIZED MURDER | 1988 | A&M SP-17549 | 15 |
| *(Blue vinyl)* | | | |
| INTERVIEW WITH DEIDRE O'DONOGHUE | 1989 | A&M SP-17765 | 12 |
| MADONNA OF THE WASPS/ONE LONG PAIR OF EYES (Acoustic)/ | 1989 | A&M SP-17697 | 12 |
| MORE THAN THIS | | | |
| *(Purple vinyl)* | | | |
| OCEANSIDE + 2 | 1991 | A&M 75021 7300 1 | 10 |
| ONE LONG PAIR OF EYES (Edit)/THE GHOST IN YOU (Live)/ | 1989 | A&M 17729 | 18 |
| FREEZE (Sunset Mix) | | | |
| *(Red vinyl)* | | | |
| SO YOU THINK YOU'RE IN LOVE/WATCH YOUR INTELLIGENCE | 1991 | A&M 75021 7271 1 | 10 |

**45s**

| | | | |
|---|---|---|---|
| HEAVEN/LISTENING TO THE HIGSONS | 1985 | Relativity 8076 | 10 |

**HODGSON, ROGER**
*More at Supertramp; A&M promo 45s $3 each*
**Albums**

| | | | |
|---|---|---|---|
| INNERVIEW  Profile | 1985 | Innerview | 10-20 |

*(Show repeated several times)*

**HOGS, THE**
**45s**

| | | | |
|---|---|---|---|
| BLUES THEME  Promo label | 1966 | Hanna-Barbera  511 | 50 |

*(Produced by Frank Zappa)*

**HOLE**
*Geffen promo CD singles $5-8 each*
**RADIO SHOWS**
**Compact Discs**

| | | | |
|---|---|---|---|
| IN CONCERT - NU ROCK (Aug 95) | 1995 | Westwood One | 40-60 |

*(Live concert material)*

**HOLIDAYS, THE**
**45s**

| | | | |
|---|---|---|---|
| SEND BACK MY LOVE/DEACON BROWN | 1962 | Galaxy 714 | 30 |

*(Promo on colored vinyl)*

**HOLLIES, THE**
*Includes listings by Allan Clarke, Terry Sylvester .Imperial cream-colored promo 45s $12 each; Epic white promo label 45s $5-10 each depending on year; Epic white promo label Memory Lane 45s $10 each; Atlantic promo 45s $4 each; Epic promo 45s by Terry Sylvester $5 each; Atlantic promo 45s by Allan Clarke $3 each; Imperial white promo label LPs $40 each; Epic white label promo LPs $15-20 each*
**12-Inch Singles**

| | | | |
|---|---|---|---|
| DRAGGIN' MY HEELS | 1977 | Epic ASD-387 | 12 |
| *(Promo-only 12" single)* | | | |
| STOP IN THE NAME OF LOVE (same on both sides) | 1983 | Atlantic PR 502 | 6 |

**45s**

| | | | |
|---|---|---|---|
| AFTER THE FOX  With Peter Sellers | 1967 | United Artists 50079 | 15 |
| *(White promo label)* | | | |
| STAY | 1963 | Liberty 55674 | 25 |
| *(Cream-colored promo label, first record)* | | | |

**Albums**

| | | | |
|---|---|---|---|
| EVERYTHING YOU ALWAYS WANTED TO HEAR | 1976 | Epic AS-138 | 20 |

*(Promo-only greatest hits LP of Epic material)*
**RADIO SHOWS**
**Albums**

| | | | |
|---|---|---|---|
| BBC TRANSCRIPTION DISC Live concert | 1974 | BBC Transcription (2) | 400-650 |
| *(Special rare double show)* | | | |
| BBC TRANSCRIPTION DISC Profile | 1974 | BBC Transcription (3) | 500-800 |

*(Very special music and interview show, and one of the rarest radio shows because to put together all three discs in the show is almost impossible)*

| | | | |
|---|---|---|---|
| NBC SOURCE (Oct 83) Live concert | 1983 | NBC Radio (2) | 200-400 |

*(Very rare live concert)*

**HOLLOWAY, BRENDA**
**45s**

| | | | |
|---|---|---|---|
| PLAY IT COOL, STAY IN SCHOOL | 1966 | Tamla 206312 | 600 |

*(Promo for Women's Ad Club of Detroit)*

| Title | Yr | Label, Number | NM $ |
|-------|-----|---------------|------|

## HOLLY, BUDDY / THE CRICKETS

*Includes listings of the Crickets, Camps, Ivan, Nikki Sullivan, Sonny Curtis, Jerry Allison, Jerry Naylor, the Norman Petty Trio, the Bowman Brothers and the Picks, which include Buddy Holly. Also includes other records to which Buddy Holly contributed guitar and/or backing vocals. Also see Waylon Jennings; Bobby Vee; Norman Petty Trio.Any promo 45s by Tommy Allsup $3 each; Metromedia or Reprise promo LPs by Tommy Allsup $5-10 each; Dot promo 45s by Sonny Curtis $50 each; Dimension promo 45s by Sonny Curtis $20 each; Viva promo 45s by Sonny Curtis $12-15 each; Ovation promo 45s by Sonny Curtis $6 each; Mercury and A&M promo 45s by Sonny Curtis $5 each; Capitol promo singles by Sonny Curtis $4 each; Other Elektra promo 45s by Sonny Curtis $3 each; Elektra promo LPs by Curtis $10 each; Skyla promo 45s by Jerry Naylor $12 each; Tower, Columbia and MCA promo singles by Jerry Naylor $3 each.*

**45s**

| Title | Yr | Label, Number | NM $ |
|-------|-----|---------------|------|
| ALL OVER YOU  The Crickets | 1964 | Liberty 55696 | 20 |
| *(Cream-colored promo label)* | | | |
| APRIL AVENUE  The Crickets | 1963 | Liberty 55603 | 20 |
| *(Cream-colored promo label)* | | | |
| BLUE DAYS-BLACK NIGHTS | 1956 | Decca 29854 | 300 |
| *(Blue promo label)* | | | |
| BROWN-EYED HANDSOME MAN | 1963 | Coral 62369 | 125 |
| *(Blue promo label)* | | | |
| CHRISTMAS COUNTRY MESSAGES  Various artists | 1981 | Elektra 47254 | 12 |
| *(Promo-only release, nine messages including one by Sonny Curtis)* | | | |
| DARDANELLA  The Raiders (Tommy Allsup) | 1961 | Liberty 55393 | 30 |
| *(Cream-colored promo label)* | | | |
| DON'T EVER CHANGE  The Crickets | 1962 | Liberty 55441 | 30 |
| *(Cream-colored promo label)* | | | |
| EARLY IN THE MORNING | 1958 | Coral 62006 | 200 |
| *(Blue promo label)* | | | |
| EARLY IN THE MORNING | 1962 | Coral 62006 | 75 |
| *(Yellow promo label)* | | | |
| FRANKIE FRANKENSTEIN  Ivan | 1958 | Coral 62081 | 200 |
| *(Blue promo label, written by Jack Huddle and Norman Petty)* | | | |
| FRANKIE FRANKENSTEIN  Ivan | 1967 | Coral 65607 | 100 |
| *(Silver Star series, promo label)* | | | |
| FROM ME TO YOU  The Crickets | 1964 | Liberty 55668 | 50 |
| *(Cream-colored promo label, flip side is "Please Please Me")* | | | |
| GIRL ON MY MIND | 1958 | Decca 30650 | 200 |
| *(Blue label)* | | | |
| HEARTBEAT | 1958 | Coral 62051 | 200 |
| *(Blue promo label)* | | | |
| HEARTBEAT | 1962 | Coral 62051 | 75 |
| *(Yellow promo label)* | | | |
| HEY, PUNKIN'  Bowman Brothers | 1958 | Columbia 41176 | 40 |
| *(White promo label)* | | | |
| I CRY ALL THE TIME  The Hollyhawks (Niki Sullivan) | 1963 | Jubilee 5441 | 25 |
| *(White promo label)* | | | |
| I PLEDGE MY LOVE TO YOU  Sonny Curtis | 1964 | Liberty 55710 | 15 |
| *(Cream-colored promo label)* | | | |
| I THINK I'VE CAUGHT THE BLUES The Crickets | 1965 | Liberty 55742 | 15 |
| *(Cream-colored promo label)* | | | |
| IT DOESN'T MATTER ANYMORE | 1959 | Coral 62074 | 200 |
| *(Blue promo label)* | | | |
| IT DOESN'T MATTER ANYMORE | 1962 | Coral 62074 | 75 |
| *(Yellow promo label)* | | | |
| IT DOESN'T MATTER ANYMORE  Buddy Holly/The Crickets | 1978 | MCA 40905 | 10 |
| *(White promo label, issued with a picture sleeve included in the price)* | | | |
| IT'S SO EASY  The Crickets | 1958 | Brunswick 55094 | 150 |
| *(Yellow promo label)* | | | |
| JOLE BLON  Waylon Jennings | 1959 | Brunswick 55130 | 150 |
| *(Yellow promo label, Holly plays guitar; maroon label stock copy twice as valuable)* | | | |
| LINDA LOU  Jim Pewter (with Allison and Curtis) | 1972 | MGM 14446 | 12 |
| *(Yellow promo label)* | | | |
| LISTEN TO ME | 1958 | Coral 61947 | 200 |
| *(Blue promo label)* | | | |
| LISTEN TO ME | 1962 | Coral 61947 | 75 |
| *(Yellow promo label)* | | | |
| LITTLE HOLLYWOOD GIRL  The Crickets | 1962 | Liberty 55495 | 25 |
| *(Cream-colored promo label)* | | | |
| LOVE IS STRANGE | 1969 | Coral 62558 | 75 |
| *(Blue promo label; a promo-only DJ insert sheet was issued with the promo single, it's worth an additional $50; some promo copies were sent in a stock picture sleeve worth an additional $25-30)* | | | |
| LOVE ME | 1958 | Decca 30543 | 300 |
| *(Green promo label, rarer of two versions)* | | | |
| LOVE ME | 1958 | Decca 30543 | 200 |
| *(Blue label)* | | | |
| LOVE'S MADE A FOOL OF YOU  The Crickets | 1959 | Brunswick 55124 | 150 |
| *(Yellow promo label, Buddy Holly is not on this record)* | | | |
| MAYBE BABY | 1964 | Coral 62407 | 80 |
| *(Blue promo label)* | | | |
| MAYBE BABY  The Crickets | 1958 | Brunswick 50053 | 150 |
| *(Yellow promo label)* | | | |
| MODERN DON JUAN | 1956 | Decca 30166 | 300 |
| *(Blue promo label)* | | | |
| MOONDREAMS  Norman Petty Trio | 1957 | Columbia 41039 | 50 |
| *(White promo label, Holly on guitar)* | | | |
| MOONDREAMS  The Picks | 1957 | Columbia 41096 | 75 |
| *(White promo label)* | | | |
| MORE THAN I CAN SAY  The Crickets | 1960 | Coral 62198 | 40 |
| *(Blue promo label)* | | | |
| MY LITTLE GIRL  The Crickets | 1963 | Liberty 55540 | 20 |
| *(Cream-colored promo label)* | | | |

| Title | Yr | Label, Number | NM $ |
|-------|-----|---------------|------|
| NOW HEAR THIS  The Crickets | 1965 | Liberty 55767 | 15 |
| *(Cream-colored promo label)* | | | |
| OH BOY  The Crickets | 1957 | Brunswick 50035 | 150 |
| *(Yellow promo label)* | | | |
| ONE FADED ROSE  Charlie Phillips | 1962 | Coral 61908 | 50 |
| *(Blue promo label, Holly plays guitar)* | | | |
| PATTY BABY  Rick Tucker and the Picks | 1957 | Columbia 41041 | 75 |
| *(White promo label)* | | | |
| PEGGY SUE | 1957 | Coral 61885 | 200 |
| *(Blue promo label)* | | | |
| PEGGY SUE | 1962 | Coral 61885 | 75 |
| *(Yellow promo label)* | | | |
| PEGGY SUE GOT MARRIED | 1959 | Coral 62134 | 200 |
| *(Blue promo label, look carefully at the artist; there is a version of the same song by the Crickets on Coral)* | | | |
| PEGGY SUE GOT MARRIED | 1962 | Coral 62134 | 75 |
| *(Yellow promo label)* | | | |
| PEGGY SUE GOT MARRIED  The Crickets | 1960 | Coral 62238 | 40 |
| *(Blue promo label; don't confuse this Crickets version with the Buddy Holly version worth much more)* | | | |
| PUNISH HER  Bobby Vee and the Crickets | 1962 | Liberty 55479 | 25 |
| *(Cream-colored promo label)* | | | |
| RAVE ON | 1958 | Coral 61985 | 200 |
| *(Blue promo label)* | | | |
| RAVE ON | 1962 | Coral 61985 | 75 |
| *(Yellow promo label)* | | | |
| RAVE ON | 1968 | Coral 62554 | 40 |
| *(Blue promo label)* | | | |
| REAL WILD CHILD Ivan | 1958 | Coral 62017 | 100 |
| *(Blue promo label, Buddy Holly on guitar)* | | | |
| RED HEADED STRANGER  Sonny Curtis | 1959 | Coral 62207 | 40 |
| *(Blue promo label)* | | | |
| REMINISCING | 1962 | Coral 62329 | 175 |
| *(Blue promo label)* | | | |
| ROCK AROUND WITH OLLIE VEE | 1963 | Coral 62390 | 100 |
| *(Blue promo label)* | | | |
| SLIPPIN' AND SLIDIN' | 1965 | Coral 62448 | 60 |
| *(Blue promo label)* | | | |
| STARLIGHT  Jack Huddle | 1958 | Kapp 207 | 200 |
| *(White and red promo label, Holly plays guitar)* | | | |
| STAY CLOSE TO ME  Lou Giordano | 1959 | Brunswick 55115 | 500 |
| *(Yellow promo label, also features Phil Everly. Maroon label stock copy twice as valuable)* | | | |
| T-SHIRT  The Crickets | 1988 | Epic 08028 | 10 |
| *(Price includes promo-only picture sleeve; produced by Paul McCartney)* | | | |
| THAT'LL BE THE DAY | 1958 | Decca 30434 | 200 |
| *(Blue promo label)* | | | |
| THAT'LL BE THE DAY | 1971 | Coral 65618 | 50 |
| *(Blue Silver Star series promo label)* | | | |
| THAT'LL BE THE DAY  The Crickets | 1957 | Brunswick 55009 | 150 |
| *(Yellow promo label)* | | | |
| THE BALLAD OF BATMAN The Campers | 1966 | Parkway 974 | 40 |
| *(White promo new style label)* | | | |
| THE BALLAD OF BATMAN The Camps | 1966 | Parkway 974 | 50 |
| *(White promo old style label, which may include a stock picture sleeve worth another $50)* | | | |
| THE REAL BUDDY HOLLY STORY  Sonny Curtis | 1980 | Elektra 46616 | 10 |
| *(White promo label)* | | | |
| THINK IT OVER  The Crickets | 1958 | Brunswick 55072 | 150 |
| *(Yellow promo label)* | | | |
| THREE STEPS TO HEAVEN  Niki Sullivan | 1958 | Dot 15751 | 100 |
| *(Rare Dot promo label)* | | | |
| TRUE LOVE WAYS | 1959 | Coral 62210 | 200 |
| *(Blue promo label)* | | | |
| TRUE LOVE WAYS | 1962 | Coral 62210 | 75 |
| *(Yellow promo label)* | | | |
| TRUE LOVE WAYS | 1963 | Coral 62352 | 150 |
| *(Blue promo label)* | | | |
| TRUE LOVE WAYS  The Crickets | 1972 | Barnaby 2061 | 12 |
| *(Mono/stereo versions, white promo label)* | | | |
| WHAT'S IT ALL ABOUT (July 81) Public service show | 1981 | W. I. A. A. 585 | 40 |
| *(Music and interviews)* | | | |
| WHEN YOU ASK ABOUT LOVE The Crickets | 1959 | Brunswick 55153 | 150 |
| *(Yellow promo label, Buddy Holly is not on this record)* | | | |
| WHOLE LOTTA LOVIN'  Jim Robinson | 1958 | Epic 9234 | 50 |
| *(White promo label, Holly plays guitar)* | | | |
| WORDS OF LOVE | 1957 | Coral 61852 | 300 |
| *(Blue promo label)* | | | |
| WORDS OF LOVE | 1962 | Coral 61852 | 100 |
| *(Yellow promo label)* | | | |
| **Albums** | | | |
| BEATLE HITS  Sonny Curtis | 1965 | Imperial 9276 | 40 |
| *(White promo label)* | | | |
| BOBBY VEE MEETS THE CRICKETS  Bobby Vee and the Crickets | 1961 | Liberty 3228 | 75 |
| *(White promo label)* | | | |
| BUDDY HOLLY | 1958 | Coral 57210 | 750 |
| *(Blue promo label)* | | | |
| BUDDY HOLLY & THE CRICKETS | 1962 | Coral 57405 | 600 |
| *(Blue promo label)* | | | |
| BUDDY HOLLY STORY | 1959 | Coral 57279 | 600 |
| *(Blue promo label)* | | | |

| Title | Yr | Label, Number | NM $ |
|---|---|---|---|
| BUDDY HOLLY STORY VOL. 2 | 1960 | Coral 57326 | 600 |
| *(Blue promo label)* | | | |
| BUDDY HOLLY'S GREATEST HITS | 1967 | Coral 57492 | 250 |
| *(Yellow promo label)* | | | |
| CALIFORNIA SUN  The Crickets | 1964 | Liberty 7351 | 50 |
| *(White promo label)* | | | |
| THE CHIRPING CRICKETS  The Crickets | 1957 | Brunswick 54038 | 1,000 |
| *(Yellow promo label)* | | | |
| GIANT | 1969 | Coral 57504 | 175 |
| *(Yellow promo label)* | | | |
| HOLLY IN THE HILLS | 1965 | Coral 57463 | 300 |
| *(Yellow promo label)* | | | |
| IN STYLE WITH THE CRICKETS  The Crickets | 1959 | Coral 57320 | 200 |
| *(Blue promo label)* | | | |
| MOONBEAMS  Norman Petty Trio | 1958 | Columbia 1092 | 300 |
| *(On one cut, "Moondreams," Buddy Holly plays guitar; there is also an EP from this album but it does not include the track "Moondreams.")* | | | |
| REMINISCING | 1963 | Coral 57426 | 400 |
| *(Blue promo label)* | | | |
| ROCKIN' 50'S ROCK N' ROLL  The Crickets | 1970 | Barnaby 30268 | 25 |
| *(White promo label)* | | | |
| SHOWCASE | 1964 | Coral 57450 | 300 |
| *(Yellow promo label)* | | | |
| SOMETHING OLD, SOMETHING NEW  The Crickets | 1963 | Liberty 3272 | 100 |
| *(White promo label)* | | | |
| THAT'LL BE THE DAY | 1958 | Decca 8707 | 1,250 |
| *(Pink promo label)* | | | |
| **RADIO SHOWS** | | | |
| **Albums** | | | |
| AMERICAN EAGLE  Various artists | 1987 | DIR (3) | 75 |
| *(Jerry Lee Lewis, Carl Perkins and Buddy Holly)* | | | |
| BUDDY HOLLY | 1987 | Creative Radio (2) | 75 |
| *(Another edited version of above show, for broadcast anytime during 1987)* | | | |
| BUDDY HOLLY SPECIAL WITH HOST JIM PEWTER | 198? | Creative Radio (4) | 100 |
| *(Four-hour radio show, add $20 if the demo disc is included)* | | | |
| EARTH NEWS (Jan 78) | 1978 | Earth News | 40 |
| *(This entire week of daily features are devoted to Buddy Holly)* | | | |
| ROYALTY OF ROCK  Profile | 1982 | RKO | 30-50 |
| *(Music and interviews, also features the Everly Brothers)* | | | |
| A TRIBUTE TO BUDDY HOLLY WITH HOST JERRY NAYLOR | 1985 | Creative Radio (2) | 75 |
| *(Edited version of 4-hour show, for broadcast anytime in 1985)* | | | |

## HOLMES, RUPERT

*Includes the Buoys and Street People; Epic, Infinity and MCA promo 45s $3 each; Other Scepter & Polydor promo 45s by the Buoys $5 each; Musicor promo 45s by Street People $4 each*

**45s**

| Title | Yr | Label, Number | NM $ |
|---|---|---|---|
| GIVE UP YOUR GUNS  The Buoys | 1971 | Scepter 12318 | 10 |
| *(4:14 and 3:00 versions, the latter only exists on promo)* | | | |
| TIMOTHY  The Buoys | 1971 | Scepter 12275 | 12 |
| *(With edited, bleeped version of song)* | | | |
| TIMOTHY  The Buoys | 1971 | Scepter 12275 B | 12 |
| *(With revised lyric for radio play)* | | | |
| WHAT'S IT ALL ABOUT (Apr 80) Public service show | 1980 | W. I. A. A. 520 | 25 |
| *(Flip side features The Police)* | | | |
| WHAT'S IT ALL ABOUT (Feb 82) Public service show | 1982 | W. I. A. A. 611 | 15 |
| *(Flip side features Gladys Knight & the Pips)* | | | |

## HOLT, DAN

*With Bob Eveslage; Other promo Clowd 45s $3 each*

**45s**

| Title | Yr | Label, Number | NM $ |
|---|---|---|---|
| YOU DON'T KNOW WHAT YOU'VE GOT UNTIL YOU LOSE IT | 1988 | Clowd 8804 | 75 |
| *(Red promo label, only six promo copies pressed)* | | | |

## HOMER AND JETHRO

*Other RCA Victor promo 78s and 45s $10-15 each*

**45s**

| Title | Yr | Label, Number | NM $ |
|---|---|---|---|
| I WANT TO HOLD YOUR HAND | 1964 | RCA Victor 8345 | 15 |
| *(White promo label)* | | | |

**7-Inch Extended Plays**

| Title | Yr | Label, Number | NM $ |
|---|---|---|---|
| HOUND DOG/SCREEN DOOR | 1957 | RCA Victor DJ-20 (6706) | 25 |
| *(Two songs on other side by Terry Fell)* | | | |

## HONDELLS, THE

*Mercury promo 45s $15-25 each*

## HONEYMOON SUITE

*Warner Bros. promo 45s $3 each*

**12-Inch Singles**

| Title | Yr | Label, Number | NM $ |
|---|---|---|---|
| ALL ALONG YOU KNEW (LP version) (Single Version) | 1985 | Warner Bros. PRO-A-2539 | 6 |
| BURNING IN LOVE (same on both sides) | 1984 | Warner Bros. PRO-A-2202 | 8 |
| FEEL IT AGAIN (same on both sides) | 1985 | Warner Bros. PRO-A-2437 | 6 |
| NEW GIRL NOW/WAVE BABIES | 1984 | Warner Bros. PRO-A-2165 | 8 |
| WHAT DOES IT TAKE (same on both sides) | 1985 | Warner Bros. PRO-A-2515 | 6 |

**RADIO SHOWS**

**Albums**

| Title | Yr | Label, Number | NM $ |
|---|---|---|---|
| IN CONCERT (July 88) Live concert | 1988 | Westwood One (2) | 20-35 |
| *(With Deacon Blue)* | | | |
| KING BISCUIT FLOWER HOUR (Sept 84) Live concert | 1984 | DIR/ABC (2) | 20-40 |
| *(With Saga)* | | | |

| Title | Yr | Label, Number | NM $ |
|---|---|---|---|

**HONEYS, THE**
*Beach Boys related; Includes the Blossoms, Ginger & The Snaps;  Also see the Beach Boys, Ginger & the Snaps, the Honey Bees, Rachel & the Revolvers; the early Capitol releases were not available as promos (radio stations got stock copies)*
**45s**

| Title | Yr | Label, Number | NM $ |
|---|---|---|---|
| HE'S A DOLL | 1964 | Warner Bros. 5430 | 75 |
| *(White promo label, stock copies worth at least twice as much)* | | | |
| SEVEN DAYS IN SEPTEMBER  Ginger and the Snaps | 1965 | MGM 13413 | 75 |
| *(Yellow promo label)* | | | |
| THINGS ARE CHANGING With the Blossoms | 1965 | E.E.O.C. | 500 |
| *(7" 33rpm radio ads with cover, the Blossoms include members of the Honeys)* | | | |
| TONIGHT YOU BELONG TO ME | 1969 | Capitol 2554 | 45 |
| *(Promo copy)* | | | |

**HOODOO GURUS**
**12-Inch Singles**

| Title | Yr | Label, Number | NM $ |
|---|---|---|---|
| BITTERSWEET (same on both sides) | 1985 | Big Time 1001 | 6 |
| DEATH DEFYING (REMIX) (same on both sides) | 1985 | Elektra 5151 | 6 |
| GOOD TIME (same on both sides) | 1987 | Elektra 5215 | 6 |
| I WANT YOU BACK (EDIT) (same on both sides) | 1984 | A&M 17286 | 6 |
| OUT THAT DOOR (same on both sides) | 1987 | Elektra 5235 | 5 |
| POISON PEN (same on both sides) | 1985 | Big Time 1002 | 5 |
| WHAT'S MY SCENE (same on both sides) | 1987 | Elektra 5255 | 5 |

**HOOKER, JOHN LEE**
**RADIO SHOWS**
**Compact Discs**

| Title | Yr | Label, Number | NM $ |
|---|---|---|---|
| LIVE FROM THE HOUSE OF BLUES (Sept 95) | 1995 | (2) | 60-100 |
| *(As "John Lee Hooker and Friends," live concert material)* | | | |

**HOOKFOOT**
**RADIO SHOWS**
**Albums**

| Title | Yr | Label, Number | NM $ |
|---|---|---|---|
| BBC TRANSCRIPTION DISC  Live concert | 1974 | BBC Transcription | 75-150 |
| *(With Tempest)* | | | |

**HOOTERS**
*Columbia white promo label 45s $4 each; Columbia promo CD singles $3 each; MCA promo CD singles $2 each*
**12-Inch Singles**

| Title | Yr | Label, Number | NM $ |
|---|---|---|---|
| ALL YOU ZOMBIES (long & short) | 1985 | Columbia AS 2043 | 15 |
| DAY BY DAY (same on both sides) | 1985 | Columbia CAS 2232 | 6 |
| JOHNNY B (same on both sides) | 1987 | Columbia CAS 2734 | 6 |
| **Compact Discs** | | | |
| ZIG ZAG | 1989 | Columbia CSK 1832 | 20 |
| *(Promo-only full-length picture disc CD)* | | | |
| **RADIO SHOWS** | | | |
| **Albums** | | | |
| IN CONCERT (Feb 85) Live concert | 1985 | Westwood One (2) | 20-35 |
| *(Hooters live solo concert, repeated)* | | | |
| OFF THE RECORD (Feb 90) Profile | 1990 | Westwood One (2) | 10-15 |
| *(Music and interviews)* | | | |
| SUPERSTAR CONCERT (Oct 85) Live concert | 1985 | Westwood One (3) | 25-50 |
| *(With Tears for Fears)* | | | |
| **Compact Discs** | | | |
| KING BISCUIT FLOWER HOUR  Live concert | 1988 | DIR | 25-40 |
| *(Hooters live solo concert)* | | | |

**HOOTIE AND THE BLOWFISH**
**Compact Discs**

| Title | Yr | Label, Number | NM $ |
|---|---|---|---|
| HOLD MY HAND | 1994 | Atlantic | 8 |
| *(Promo CD single, stock copies worth $4)* | | | |
| I GO BLIND | 1996 | Atlantic | 8 |
| *(Promo-only CD single, no stock copies issued)* | | | |
| LET HER CRY | 1995 | Atlantic | 8 |
| *(Promo CD single, stock copies worth $4)* | | | |
| OLD MAN & ME (WHEN I GET TO HEAVEN) | 1996 | Atlantic PRCD 6694 | 8 |
| *(Promo CD single, stock copies worth $4)* | | | |
| ONLY WANNA BE WITH YOU | 1995 | Atlantic | 8 |
| *(Promo CD single, stock copies worth $4)* | | | |
| TIME | 1995 | Atlantic | 8 |
| *(Promo CD single, stock copies worth $4)* | | | |
| TUCKER'S TOWN | 1996 | Atlantic | 8 |
| *(Promo CD single, stock copies worth $4)* | | | |
| **RADIO SHOWS** | | | |
| **Compact Discs** | | | |
| IN CONCERT (Jan 95) | 1995 | Westwood One | 30-60 |
| *(Live concert)* | | | |

**HOPE, BOB**
*RCA Victor promo 45s $8 each*
**RADIO SHOWS**
**Albums**

| Title | Yr | Label, Number | NM $ |
|---|---|---|---|
| NBC CHRISTMAS (Dec 82) | 1982 | NBC Radio (2) | 15-25 |
| *(Music and interviews)* | | | |

| Title | Yr | Label, Number | NM $ |
|---|---|---|---|
| **HOPKINS, LIGHTNIN'** | | | |
| **Albums** | | | |
| ON STAGE | 1962 | Imperial 9180 | 125 |
| *(White promo label)* | | | |
| | | | |
| **HORNE, LENA** | | | |
| **45s** | | | |
| LET IT SNOW! LET IT SNOW! LET IT SNOW! (same on both sides) | 1966 | United Artists 1661 | 8 |
| *(Silver Spotlight Series promo)* | | | |
| | | | |
| **HORNSBY, BRUCE, AND THE RANGE** | | | |
| *RCA Victor promo 45s $3 each; RCA promo CD singles $3 each* | | | |
| **Compact Discs** | | | |
| FOR IN-STORE PLAY | 1990 | RCA 2456-2-RDJ | 15 |
| *(Promo only for record stores, 13 tracks)* | | | |
| HARBOR LIGHTS | 1993 | RCA RJC-66230-2 | 20 |
| *(Promo-only picture disc in custom packaging)* | | | |
| LIVE-THE WAY IT IS TOUR | 1987 | RCA 6275-2-RDJ | 40 |
| *(Live concert promo-only CD release)* | | | |
| SONY DIGITAL MASTERS SERIES | 1991 | RCA RDJ-61000 | 80 |
| *(Promo-only release)* | | | |
| **RADIO SHOWS** | | | |
| **Albums** | | | |
| IN CONCERT | 1987 | Westwood One (2) | 30-50 |
| *(Live concert)* | | | |
| IN CONCERT (Oct 86) Live concert | 1986 | Westwood One (2) | 25-50 |
| *(With Red Riders)* | | | |
| KING BISCUIT FLOWER HOUR (Apr 87) Live concert | 1987 | DIR (2) | 25-40 |
| *(With Red Rider)* | | | |
| OFF THE RECORD (May 88) Music and interviews | 1988 | Westwood One (2) | 15-25 |
| *(Repeated several times)* | | | |
| POP CONCERT | 1986 | Westwood One (2) | 20-35 |
| *(Live concert)* | | | |
| SUPERSTAR CONCERT (Aug 88) Box set | 1988 | Westwood One (3) | 20-40 |
| *(Live concert, several repeats)* | | | |
| **Compact Discs** | | | |
| KING BISCUIT FLOWER HOUR (Dec 87) Live concert | 1987 | DIR | 25-40 |
| *(Hard to find this date)* | | | |
| KING BISCUIT FLOWER HOUR (Jan 93) Live concert | 1993 | DIR | 15-25 |
| *(Same show, easier to find)* | | | |
| MASTERS OF ROCK (July 90) Profile | 1990 | Radio Ventures (2) | 20-30 |
| *(Music and interviews)* | | | |
| OFF THE RECORD (May 93) Music and interviews | 1993 | Westwood One | 15-25 |
| *(Repeated several times)* | | | |
| UP CLOSE  Profile | 1993 | Media America (2) | 20-40 |
| *(Music and interviews, some live tracks)* | | | |
| | | | |
| **HORSLIPS** | | | |
| **45s** | | | |
| SHAKIN' ALL OVER (mono/stereo) | 1979 | Mercury 76072 | 6 |
| *May be promo only* | | | |
| | | | |
| **HORTON, JOHNNY** | | | |
| *Dot blue promo label 45s $15 each; Other Columbia white promo label 45s $10 each; Columbia 33rpm stereo singles (jukebox) $25 each; Columbia white promo label LPs $25-40 each depending on year* | | | |
| **45s** | | | |
| THE BATTLE OF NEW ORLEANS | 1959 | Columbia 41339 | 20 |
| *(Stock picture sleeve worth $20)* | | | |
| HONKY TONK HARDWOOD FLOOR | 1959 | Columbia 41110 | 40 |
| *(White promo label)* | | | |
| HONKY TONK MAN | 1956 | Columbia 21504 | 25 |
| *(White promo label)* | | | |
| I'LL DO EVERY TIME | 1958 | Columbia 40986 | 15 |
| *(White promo label)* | | | |
| I'M A ONE WOMAN MAN | 1957 | Columbia 21538 | 20 |
| *(White promo label)* | | | |
| I'M COMING HOME | 1958 | Columbia 40813 | 20 |
| *(White promo label)* | | | |
| THE LOVE OF A GIRL | 1953 | Mercury 70227 | 25 |
| *(White promo label)* | | | |
| LOVER'S ROCK | 1958 | Columbia 41043 | 25 |
| *(White promo label)* | | | |
| RIDIN' THE SUNSHINE SPECIAL | 1956 | Mercury 70636 | 30 |
| *(White promo label)* | | | |
| TENNESSEE JIVE  White promo label | 1953 | Mercury 70100 | 25 |
| *(First record)* | | | |
| THERE'LL NEVER BE ANOTHER MARY | 1955 | Mercury 70462 | 25 |
| *(White promo label)* | | | |
| THE WOMAN I NEED | 1958 | Columbia 40919 | 15 |
| *(White promo label)* | | | |
| **7-Inch Extended Plays** | | | |
| FREE `N' EASY SONGS  With the Four B's | 1959 | SESAC AD-26 | 75 |
| *(Promo-only release to radio stations)* | | | |
| **78s** | | | |
| HONKY TONK MAN | 1956 | Columbia 21504 | 40 |
| *(White promo label)* | | | |

| Title | Yr | Label, Number | NM $ |
|-------|-----|---------------|------|
| I'M A ONE WOMAN MAN | 1957 | Columbia 21538 | 40 |
| *(White promo label)* | | | |
| I'M COMING HOME | 1958 | Columbia 40813 | 50 |
| *(Rare 78rpm white promo label)* | | | |
| THE LOVE OF A GIRL | 1953 | Mercury 70227 | 50 |
| *(White promo label)* | | | |
| RIDIN' THE SUNSHINE SPECIAL | 1956 | Mercury 70636 | 35 |
| *(White promo label)* | | | |
| TENNESSEE JIVE  White promo label | 1953 | Mercury 70100 | 50 |
| *(Mercury promo 78s are rare)* | | | |
| THERE'LL NEVER BE ANOTHER MARY | 1955 | Mercury 70462 | 40 |
| *(White promo label)* | | | |
| **Albums** | | | |
| FREE `N' EASY SONGS  With the Four B's | 1959 | SESAC 1201 | 125 |
| *(Promo-only release to radio stations)* | | | |
| THE FANTASTIC JOHNNY HORTON | 1959 | Mercury 20478 | 100 |
| *(White promo label)* | | | |

## HOT CHOCOLATE

Other RAK (USA) promo 45s $6 each; Other Bell promo 45s $5 each; Other Big Tree promo singles $3 each; Infinity promo 45s $3 each; On Apple as Hot Chocolate Band, no promos known

**45s**

| | | | |
|-------|-----|---------------|------|
| BROTHER LOUIE  White promo label, original version | 1973 | Rak (CBS) 4515 | 12 |
| *(This is the original, 4:23 version)* | | | |
| BROTHER LOUIE Blue promo label, 4:56 version | 1974 | Big Tree 16101 | 10 |
| *(Label says original, this is the "B" side)* | | | |
| EMMA  White promo label | 1974 | Bell 45,466 | 10 |
| *(Stereo/mono versions of this rock classic, was a hit on Big Tree)* | | | |
| IT STARTED WITH A KISS White promo label | 1982 | Capitol SPRO-8157 | 10 |
| *(Promo-only release)* | | | |

**RADIO SHOWS**
**Albums**

| | | | |
|-------|-----|---------------|------|
| BBC TRANSCRIPTION DISC Live concert | 1980 | BBC Transcription | 200-325 |
| *(Rare live concert in a rare series)* | | | |
| BBC TRANSCRIPTION DISC Live concert | 1983 | BBC Transcription | 200-325 |
| *(Rare live concert with Blanchmange)* | | | |

## HOTHOUSE FLOWERS

**12-Inch Singles**

| | | | |
|-------|-----|---------------|------|
| DON'T GO (same on both sides) | 1988 | London 604 | 6 |
| FEET ON THE GROUND (LP and Live)/ | | | |
| CARRICKFERGUS/BETTER AND BETTER | 1988 | London PRO 715 | 10 |
| **Albums** | | | |
| CONVERSATION AND MUSIC WITH HOTHOUSE FLOWERS | 1988 | London 085 | 15 |
| LIVE | 1990 | London 884-1 | 25 |
| *(Six-song promo-only live EP)* | | | |
| **Cassettes** | | | |
| HOME | 1992 | London | 40 |
| *(Promo pack with viedo, cassette, and newspaper, released only to radio stations)* | | | |

**RADIO SHOWS**
**Compact Discs**

| | | | |
|-------|-----|---------------|------|
| KING BISCUIT FLOWER HOUR (Apr 89) Live concert | 1989 | DIR | 15-25 |
| *(With Escape Club)* | | | |

## HOUSE OF PAIN

**12-Inch Singles**

| | | | |
|-------|-----|---------------|------|
| WHO'S THE MAN? (same on both sides) | 1993 | Uptown 2606 | 7 |

## HOUSE OF SCHOCK

**12-Inch Singles**

| | | | |
|-------|-----|---------------|------|
| MIDDLE OF NOWHERE (same on both sides) | 1988 | Capitol SPRO-79277 | 5 |

## HOUSEMARTINS, THE

**12-Inch Singles**

| | | | |
|-------|-----|---------------|------|
| HAPPY HOUR (same on both sides) | 1986 | Elektra 5174 | 7 |
| **Albums** | | | |
| THE PEOPLE WHO GRINNED THEMSELVES TO DEATH | 1987 | Elektra 60761 | 12 |
| *(Promo-only audiophile pressing)* | | | |

## HOUSTON, DAVID

Other RCA Victor promo 45s $8 each; Epic promo 45s $2 each

**45s**

| | | | |
|-------|-----|---------------|------|
| ALL I DO IS DREAM OF YOU | 1958 | NRC 005 | 25 |
| *(White promo label)* | | | |
| SUGAR SWEET | 1956 | RCA Victor 6611 | 18 |
| *(White promo label)* | | | |
| **7-Inch Extended Plays** | | | |
| ALMOST PERSUADED  Jukebox LLP | 1975 | Epic 26342 | 10 |
| *(Issued with paper cover)* | | | |
| BLUE PRELUDE/I'LL ALWAYS HAVE IT ON MY MIND | 1957 | RCA Victor DJ-15 | 15 |
| *(Promo EP, flip side features Porter Wagoner)* | | | |
| I AIN'T GOIN' THERE NO MORE/SOMEONE ELSE'S ARMS | 1957 | RCA Victor DJ-79 | 15 |
| *(Promo EP, flip side is Bobby John)* | | | |
| YOU MEAN THE WORLD TO ME  Jukebox LLP | 1975 | Epic 26338 | 10 |
| *(Issued with paper cover)* | | | |

| Title | Yr | Label, Number | NM $ |
|---|---|---|---|
| **HOUSTON, THELMA** | | | |
| **12-Inch Singles** | | | |
| HIGH (4 versions) | 1990 | Reprise PRO-A-4475 | 8 |
| I'D RATHER SPEND THE BAD TIMES WITH YOU (3 versions) | 1984 | MCA L33-1253 | 8 |
| OUT OF MY HANDS (REMIX) (same on both sides) | 1990 | Reprise PRO-A-4487 | 8 |
| WORKING GIRL (3:45)/(5:00) | 1983 | MCA L33-1795 | 8 |
| **45s** | | | |
| DON'T LEAVE ME THIS WAY (Long Version)/(Short Version) | 1977 | Tamla 54278 | 6 |
| EVERYBODY GETS TO GO TO THE MOON (same on both sides) | 1969 | ABC Dunhill 11 | 15 |
| *(Special Apollo 11 promotional item)* | | | |
| | | | |
| **HOUSTON, WHITNEY** | | | |
| *Arista promo 45s $4 each; Arista promo CD singles $3-5 each* | | | |
| **RADIO SHOWS** | | | |
| **Compact Discs** | | | |
| ALL MY LOVE (Aug 93) Music and interviews | 1993 | | 75-125 |
| *(Rare radio show)* | | | |
| WESTWOOD ONE SPECIAL (90s) | 199? | Westwood One (2) | 40-75 |
| *(Music and interviews)* | | | |
| | | | |
| **HOWARD, GREGORY** | | | |
| **45s** | | | |
| WHEN IN LOVE | 1963 | Kapp 536 | 75 |
| *(Vocals by the Cadillacs)* | | | |
| | | | |
| **HOWELL, LOYD** | | | |
| **45s** | | | |
| LITTLE FROGGY WENT A COURTIN' | 1961 | Nashville 5028 | 100 |
| *(White promo label)* | | | |
| | | | |
| **HUDDLE, JACK** | | | |
| **45s** | | | |
| STARLIGHT | 1959 | Kapp 207 | 100 |
| *(Buddy Holly on guitar)* | | | |
| | | | |
| **HUDGINS, JOE** | | | |
| **45s** | | | |
| WHERE'D YOU STAY LAST NIGHT | 195? | Robbins 1005 | 45 |
| *(Promo label)* | | | |
| | | | |
| **HUGO AND LUIGI** | | | |
| **45s** | | | |
| RCA VICTOR SPECIAL DJ SPOTS | 1959 | RCA Victor SP-45-101 | 10 |
| | | | |
| **HUM** | | | |
| **45s** | | | |
| COMIN' HOME/PUPPETS | 1997 | RCA RDAB 65343-7 | 8 |
| *(Promo-only single with picture sleeve)* | | | |
| | | | |
| **HUMAN LEAGUE** | | | |
| **12-Inch Singles** | | | |
| (KEEP FEELING) FASCINATION (4:56)/ (6:12) | 1983 | A&M 17227 | 8 |
| THE LEBANON (LP Version) (Single Version) | 1984 | A&M 17276 | 8 |
| TELL ME WHEN (4 versions) | 1995 | EastWest 5731 | 8 |
| **45s** | | | |
| LEBANON, THE | 198? | A&M | 10 |
| *(White label test pressing)* | | | |
| LIFE ON YOUR OWN (same on both sides) | 1984 | A&M 2661 | 5 |
| *(No stock copies issued)* | | | |
| LOUISE | 198? | ElectroSound | 10 |
| *(White label test pressing)* | | | |
| | | | |
| **HUMANS, THE** | | | |
| *A&M promo 45s $5 each* | | | |
| **12-Inch Singles** | | | |
| DON'T BE AFRAID OF THE DARK/GET YOU TONIGHT/LIGHTNING | 1981 | I.R.S. 70957 | 5 |
| **7-Inch Extended Plays** | | | |
| HUMANS  One-sided record | 1979 | A&M 17900 | 40 |
| *(Five-song promo-only release)* | | | |
| | | | |
| **HUMBLE PIE** | | | |
| *Also see Peter Frampton; A&M white promo label 45s $6 each* | | | |
| **45s** | | | |
| I DON'T NEED NO DOCTOR | 1971 | A&M 1282 | 10 |
| *(White label promo)* | | | |
| NATURAL BORN WOMAN | 1969 | Immediate 001 | 25 |
| *(White promo label)* | | | |
| THIRTY DAYS IN THE HOLE | 1972 | A&M 1366 | 10 |
| *(White label promo)* | | | |
| **RADIO SHOWS** | | | |
| **Albums** | | | |
| BBC ROCK HOUR (June 81) | 1981 | London Wavelength | 50-100 |
| *(Live concert)* | | | |

| Title | Yr | Label, Number | NM $ |
|-------|-----|---------------|------|
| IN CONCERT  Live concert | 1981 | Westwood One (2) | 50-100 |
| *(With Gary U.S. Bonds)* | | | |
| KING BISCUIT FLOWER HOUR (Apr 81) Live concert | 1981 | DIR/ABC (2) | 50-100 |
| *(With Loverboy)* | | | |
| **Compact Discs** | | | |
| KING BISCUIT FLOWER HOUR (Sept 88) Live concert | 1988 | DIR | 40-75 |
| *(With Frampton's Camel and Humble Pie)* | | | |

### HUMPERDINCK, ENGELBERT
*Parrot/London promo 45s $2 each*

**45s**

| | | | |
|-------|-----|---------------|------|
| CHRISTMAS SONG | 1978 | Epic AE7 1170 | 10 |
| *(1978 "Christmas Seals" song, with promo-only picture sleeve)* | | | |
| THE LORD'S PRAYER  Promo-only release | 1980 | Epic AE7 1205 | 10 |
| *(White promo label)* | | | |

**7-Inch Extended Plays**

| | | | |
|-------|-----|---------------|------|
| LIVE AT THE RIVIERA  Jukebox LLP | 1972 | Parrot SBG 82 | 10 |
| *(Issued with a hard cover)* | | | |
| WE MADE IT HAPPEN Jukebox LLP | 1972 | Parrot SBG 80 | 10 |
| *(Issued with a hard cover)* | | | |

**Albums**

| | | | |
|-------|-----|---------------|------|
| LAST OF THE ROMANTICS | 1978 | Epic 35020 | 40 |
| *(Promo-only picture disc)* | | | |

### HUNT, SLIM
**45s**

| | | | |
|-------|-----|---------------|------|
| WELCOME HOME, BABY | 1955 | Excello 2055 | 50 |
| *(White promo label)* | | | |

### HUNTER, IAN
*Lead singer of Mott The Hoople*
**RADIO SHOWS**
**Albums**

| | | | |
|-------|-----|---------------|------|
| BBC TRANSCRIPTION DISC | 1980 | BBC Transcription | 300-400 |
| *(Live concert)* | | | |
| IN CONCERT (Mar 82) Live concert | 1982 | Westwood One (2) | 40-75 |
| *(With Quarterflash)* | | | |
| KING BISCUIT FLOWER HOUR (May 82) Live concert | 1982 | DIR/ABC (2) | 40-75 |
| *(With Prism)* | | | |
| **Compact Discs** | | | |
| KING BISCUIT FLOWER HOUR (Dec 89) Live concert | 1989 | DIR | 40-75 |
| *(With Mott The Hoople)* | | | |
| **Reel-to-Reel Tapes** | | | |
| STUDIO JAM (June 79) | 1979 | (2) | 200-400 |
| *(Live material on two reels)* | | | |

### HUNTER, IVORY JOE
*MGM promo singles $15 each; Dot promo 45s $12 each*
**Albums**

| | | | |
|-------|-----|---------------|------|
| I GET THAT LONESOME FEELING | 1957 | MGM 3488 | 300 |
| *(Yellow promo label)* | | | |

### HUNTERS & COLLECTORS
**12-Inch Singles**

| | | | |
|-------|-----|---------------|------|
| BACK ON THE BREADLINE (same on both sides) | 1988 | I.R.S. 17634 | 5 |
| FARAWAY MAN (LIVE)/SAY GOODBYE (LIVE)/ | 1988 | I.R.S. 17705 | 10 |
| BACK ON THE BREADLINE (LIVE)/PARTING GLASS (LIVE) | | | |
| THROW YOUR ARMS/SAY GOODBYE/ANYBODY | 1986 | I.R.S. 17224 | 6 |

### HURRICANES, THE
**45s**

| | | | |
|-------|-----|---------------|------|
| DEAR MOTHER | 1956 | King 4947 | 75 |
| *(White promo label)* | | | |
| FALLEN ANGEL | 1957 | King 5018 | 75 |
| *(White promo label)* | | | |
| MAYBE IT'S FOR THE BEST | 1956 | King 4867 | 100 |
| *(White promo label)* | | | |
| POOR LITTLE DANCING GIRL | 1955 | King 4817 | 125 |
| *(White promo label)* | | | |
| RAINING IN MY HEART | 1956 | King 4898 | 75 |
| *(White promo label)* | | | |

### HUSKER DU
*Warner Bros. promo 45s $5 each*
**12-Inch Singles**

| | | | |
|-------|-----|---------------|------|
| COULD YOU BE THE ONE (same on both sides) | 1987 | Warner Bros. PRO-A-2654 | 7 |
| SORRY SOMEHOW (same on both sides) | 1986 | Warner Bros. PRO-A-2524 | 8 |
| **45s** | | | |
| CELEBRATED SUMMER/NEW DAY RISING | 1984 | SST PSST 031 | 15 |
| **Albums** | | | |
| EIGHT MILES HIGH/6 FROM ZEN ARCADE | 1984 | SST PSST E27 | 30 |
| *(Promo sampler, etched design on side 1, sticker cover)* | | | |
| WAREHOUSE INTERVIEW | 1987 | Warner Bros. WBMS-145 (2) | 25 |
| *(Promo only, music and interviews)* | | | |

| Title | Yr | Label, Number | NM $ |
|---|---|---|---|
| WAREHOUSE: SONGS AND STORIES | 1987 | Warner Bros. PRO-A-2719 | 8 |
| *(Promo-only four-song sampler)* | | | |
| **Compact Discs** | | | |
| DO YOU REMEMBER? | 1992 | Warner Bros. PRO-CD-6853 | 25 |
| *(Promo-only greatest hits set)* | | | |
| **RADIO SHOWS** | | | |
| **Albums** | | | |
| SPIN CONCERT (June 86) College series | 1986 | BBC Radio (2) | 150-250 |
| *(Very rare radio show)* | | | |

**HUSKY, FERLIN**

*Includes listings of Terry Preston and Simon Crum; King white promo label 45s $6 each; Other Capitol promo 45s $3 each; ABC promo 45s $2 each; Other Terry Preston Capitol promo 45s $10 each; Other Capitol promo 45s by Simon Crum $3 each; ABC promo 45s by Simon Crum $2 each; Other Capitol promo LPs $15 each*

| Title | Yr | Label, Number | NM $ |
|---|---|---|---|
| **45s** | | | |
| BOP CAT BOP  Simon Crum | 1957 | Capitol 3460 | 30 |
| *(Rockabilly)* | | | |
| COUNTRY MUSIC IS HERE TO STAY  Simon Crum | 1959 | Capitol 4073 | 15 |
| *(Impersonations)* | | | |
| CUZZ YORE SO SWEET  Simon Crum | 1955 | Capitol 3063 | 25 |
| *(In 1955 Ferlin Husky sold more records as Simon Crum)* | | | |
| GONE | 1957 | Capitol 3628 | 15 |
| *("Smash Hit Record" on yellow promo label)* | | | |
| GONE  Terry Preston | 1953 | Capitol 2298 | 50 |
| *(The original version, later a hit as Ferlin Husky)* | | | |
| HANK'S SONG | 1953 | Capitol 2397 | 40 |
| *(Tribute to Hank Williams written by Tommy Collins)* | | | |
| A HILLBILLY'S DECK OF CARDS  Simon Crum | 1956 | Capitol 3270 | 10 |
| *(Some of these Capitol promos were yellow colored)* | | | |
| I WANT YOU SO  Terry Preston | 1952 | Capitol 1947 | 25 |
| *(White promo label)* | | | |
| LAUGH LAUGH LAUGH Cousin Herb Henson | 1954 | Capitol 2824 | 18 |
| *(Features the famous laugh of Ferlin Husky)* | | | |
| MORGAN POISONED THE WATERHOLE Simon Crum | 1960 | Capitol 4252 | 10 |
| *(Blue promo label)* | | | |
| MY FOOLISH HEART  Terry Preston | 1953 | Capitol 2391 | 18 |
| *(White promo label)* | | | |
| WANG DANG DO | 1958 | Capitol 3862 | 15 |
| *(White promo label)* | | | |
| **78s** | | | |
| ROAD TO HEAVEN  Terry Preston | 1951 | 4-Star 1516 | 25 |
| *(Ferlin Husky was recording early tracks for the King label)* | | | |
| **Albums** | | | |
| BORN TO LOSE | 1959 | Capitol 1204 | 25 |
| *(Colored promo label)* | | | |
| BOULEVARD OF BROKEN DREAMS | 1957 | Capitol 880 | 30 |
| *(Colored promo label)* | | | |
| SITTIN' ON A RAINBOW | 1959 | Capitol 976 | 25 |
| *(Colored promo label)* | | | |
| SONGS OF THE HOME AND HEART | 1956 | Capitol 718 | 40 |
| *(Colored promo label)* | | | |
| THE UNPREDICTABLE SIMON CRUM  Simon Crum | 1963 | Capitol 1880 | 100 |
| *(Promo label)* | | | |
| **RADIO SHOWS** | | | |
| **16-Inch Transcriptions** | | | |
| COUNTRY MUSIC TIME (60s) Various artists | 196? | U.S. Army | 20-30 |
| *(Music and interviews)* | | | |
| COUNTRY STYLE U. S. A.  Various artists | 1956 | PSA Radio | 15-25 |
| *(Music and interviews)* | | | |
| U. S. ARMY BAND (60s) Various artists | 196? | U.S. Army | 15-25 |
| *(Music and interviews, Husky is the host)* | | | |

**HYLAND, BRIAN**

*Other Kapp white/red promo label 45s $25 each; Other ABC Paramount white promo label 45s $10 each; Philips white promo label 45s $6 each; Uni label promo 45s $5 each*

| Title | Yr | Label, Number | NM $ |
|---|---|---|---|
| **45s** | | | |
| IF MARY'S THERE White promo label, red vinyl | 1963 | ABC-Paramount 10400 | 30 |
| *(Only the promo is red vinyl, same song on both sides)* | | | |
| ITSY BITSY TEENIE WEENIE YELLOW POLKADOT BIKINI | 1960 | Kapp 342 | 30 |
| *(White/red promo label)* | | | |
| LOP-SIDED OVER-LOADED | 1960 | Kapp 363 | 20 |
| *(White/red promo label)* | | | |

| **Title** | **Yr** | **Label, Number** | **NM $** |
|---|---|---|---|

# I

**IAN AND THE ZODIACS**
**7-Inch Extended Plays**

| | | | |
|---|---|---|---|
| IAN & THE ZODIACS  Jukebox LLP | 1965 | Philips 807 | 50 |

*(Issued with a hard cover)*

**IAN, JANIS**
*Columbia white promo label 45s $3 each; Polydor white promo label 45s $2 each*
**45s**

| | | | |
|---|---|---|---|
| SOCIETY'S CHILD  Brown promo label | 1966 | Verve Folkways 5027 | 12 |

*(Folkways version, not Forecast)*

| | | | |
|---|---|---|---|
| WHAT'S IT ALL ABOUT (Aug 75) Public service show | 1975 | W. I. A. A. 278 | 18 |

*(Flip side is Jim Stafford)*

| | | | |
|---|---|---|---|
| WHAT'S IT ALL ABOUT  Public service show | 1980 | W. I. A. A. 218 | 30 |

*(Flip side features the Rolling Stones)*
**Albums**

| | | | |
|---|---|---|---|
| INNERVIEW (70s) Profile | 197? | Innerview | 10-20 |

*(Music and interviews)*
**RADIO SHOWS**
**Reel-to-Reel Tapes**

| | | | |
|---|---|---|---|
| KING BISCUIT FLOWER HOUR (70s) Live concert | 197? | DIR/ABC (2) | 100-150 |

*(On two reels, live with 10CC)*

| | | | |
|---|---|---|---|
| KING BISCUIT FLOWER HOUR (May 76) Live concert | 1976 | DIR/ABC (2) | 200-300 |

*(On two reels, live with Harry Chapin)*

**ICE-T**
**12-Inch Singles**

| | | | |
|---|---|---|---|
| MIND OVER MATTER (4 versions) | 1991 | Sire PRO-A-5367 | 8 |
| NEW JACK HUSTLER (3 versions) | 1991 | Giant PRO-A-4643 | 8 |
| RICOCHET (3 versions)/MIND OVER MATTER (4 versions) | 1991 | Sire PRO-A-5143 | 8 |

**Albums**

| | | | |
|---|---|---|---|
| O.G. ORIGINAL GANGSTER | 1991 | Sire PRO-A-4959 | 40 |

*(Promo-only radio-ready version of album otherwise unavailable on U.S. vinyl)*

**ICEHOUSE**
*Chrysalis promo 45s $4 each*
**12-Inch Singles**

| | | | |
|---|---|---|---|
| CROSS THE BORDER/IVA DAVIES INTERVIEW | 1986 | Chrysalis VAS 2389 | 20 |

*(Released with cue sheets)*

| | | | |
|---|---|---|---|
| ELECTRIC BLUE (3 versions) | 1988 | Chrysalis VAS 2899 | 15 |

*Blue vinyl promo*

| | | | |
|---|---|---|---|
| NO PROMISES (3 versions) | 1986 | Chrysalis VAS 2362 | 10 |
| NO PROMISES (same on both sides) | 1986 | Chrysalis VAS 2305 | 7 |
| PARADISE (2 versions)/NO PROMISES (Live)/CROSS THE BORDER (Live) | 1986 | Chrysalis VAS 2519 | 6 |
| TAKING THE TOWN (same on both sides) | 1984 | Chrysalis AS 1859 | 8 |

**RADIO SHOWS**

| | | | |
|---|---|---|---|
| KING BISCUIT FLOWER HOUR (Oct 81) Live concert | 1981 | DIR/ABC (2) | 50-80 |

*(With the Michael Stanley Band)*
**Albums**

| | | | |
|---|---|---|---|
| BBC ROCK HOUR (Oct 81) | 1981 | London Wavelength | 45-80 |

*(Live concert)*

**ICICLE WORKS**
**12-Inch Singles**

| | | | |
|---|---|---|---|
| IN THE CAULDRON OF LOVE (same on both sides) | 1984 | Arista 9217 | 8 |
| UNDERSTANDING JANE (same on both sides) | 1987 | RCA 6444 | 8 |

**RADIO SHOWS**
**Albums**

| | | | |
|---|---|---|---|
| IN CONCERT (Sept 84) Live concert | 1984 | Westwood One (2) | 40-75 |

*(With Berlin)*

**IDOL, BILLY**
*Chrysalis promo 45s $4 each; Chrysalis promo CD singles $2-4 each.*
**12-Inch Singles**

| | | | |
|---|---|---|---|
| BLUE HIGHWAY (same on both sides) | 1983 | Chrysalis AS 1831 | 6 |
| EYES WITHOUT A FACE (LP version)/(single) | 1984 | Chrysalis AS 1856 | 8 |
| FLESH FOR FANTASY (2 versions) | 1984 | Chrysalis AS 1894 | 10 |
| FLESH FOR FANTASY (2 versions) | 1984 | Chrysalis AS 1901 | 6 |
| HEROIN (9 versions) | 1994 | Chrysalis 24826 | 15 |

*(White vinyl promo-only release)*

| | | | |
|---|---|---|---|
| REBEL YELL (same on both sides) | 1983 | Chrysalis AS 1761 | 7 |
| SWEET SIXTEEN (same on both sides) | 1987 | Chrysalis VAS 2672 | 8 |
| TO BE A LOVER (same on both sides) | 1986 | Chrysalis VAS 2449 | 8 |

**Albums**

| | | | |
|---|---|---|---|
| INTERVIEW | 1983 | Chrysalis VAS 2610 | 15 |

**RADIO SHOWS**
**Albums**

| | | | |
|---|---|---|---|
| IN CONCERT (Nov 82) Live concert | 1982 | Westwood One (2) | 25-40 |

*(With George Thorogood)*

| Title | Yr | Label, Number | NM $ |
|---|---|---|---|
| IN CONCERT (Nov 83) Live concert | 1983 | Westwood One (2) | 25-40 |
| *(With INXS)* | | | |
| KING BISCUIT FLOWER HOUR (June 83) Live concert | 1983 | DIR/ABC (2) | 30-50 |
| *(With The Fixx)* | | | |
| KING BISCUIT FLOWER HOUR (Oct 84) Live concert | 1984 | DIR (2) | 25-40 |
| *(Billy Idol solo)* | | | |
| SUPERGROUPS (June 84) Live concert | 1984 | DIR (2) | 40-75 |
| *(Rare concert)* | | | |
| SUPERSTAR CONCERT Box set | 1988 | Westwood One (3) | 15-30 |
| *(Live concert)* | | | |
| **Compact Discs** | | | |
| IN CONCERT (Dec 93) Live concert | 1993 | Westwood One | 25-40 |
| *(Repeated several times)* | | | |
| KING BISCUIT FLOWER HOUR (Apr 90) Live concert | 1990 | DIR | 20-30 |
| *(Repeated)* | | | |
| KING BISCUIT FLOWER HOUR (Nov 87) Live concert | 1987 | DIR | 30-50 |
| *(Early KBFH CDs are rare)* | | | |
| OFF THE RECORD (June 93) Profile | 1993 | Westwood One | 10-15 |
| *(Music and interviews)* | | | |
| ON THE EDGE (June 93) Profile | 1993 | Westwood One | 10-15 |
| *(Music and interviews)* | | | |
| THE STORY OF BILLY IDOL (June 90) Profile | 1990 | Unistar (2) | 20-35 |
| *(Music and interviews)* | | | |

**IGGY POP /THE STOOGES**
*A&M promo 45s $4 each; Other Virgin promo CD singles $3 each*

| **12-Inch Singles** | | | |
|---|---|---|---|
| COLD METAL (2 mixes)/TOUGH BABY (2 mixes) | 1988 | A&M 17608 | 8 |
| CRY FOR LOVE (same on both sides) | 1986 | A&M 17426 | 6 |
| ISOLATION (same on both sides) | 1986 | A&M 17444 | 8 |
| KNOCKING 'EM DOWN/AMBITION/LOCO MOSQUITO | 1980 | Arista SP-81 | 20 |
| REAL WILD CHILD (2 mixes) | 1986 | A&M 17446 | 8 |
| **45s** | | | |
| DOWN ON THE STREET  The Stooges | 1970 | Elektra 45695 | 15 |
| *(White promo label)* | | | |
| I WANNA BE YOUR DOG  The Stooges | 1969 | Elektra 45664 | 18 |
| *(White promo label)* | | | |
| SEARCH AND DESTROY  The Stooges | 1971 | Columbia 45877 | 25 |
| *(White promo label)* | | | |
| **Albums** | | | |
| FUN HOUSE  The Stooges | 1970 | Elektra 74101 | 60 |
| *(White promo label)* | | | |
| LIVE AT THE CHANNEL 7/19/88 | 1988 | A&M SP-17641 | 40 |
| *(Numbered, rubber-stamped promo-only edition)* | | | |
| RAW POWER  The Stooges | 1973 | Columbia 32111 | 50 |
| *(Promo or stock copy)* | | | |
| THE STOOGES  The Stooges | 1969 | Elektra 74051 | 75 |
| *(White promo label)* | | | |
| **Compact Discs** | | | |
| BUTT TOWN | 1990 | Virgin PRCD BUTT | 20 |
| *(Rare promo CD single)* | | | |
| COLD METAL | 1988 | A&M CD-17573 | 8 |
| *(Promo-only CD single)* | | | |
| HIGH ON YOU | 1988 | A&M CD-17632 | 8 |
| *(Promo-only CD single)* | | | |
| LIVE AT THE CHANNEL 7/19/88 | 1988 | A&M CD-17641 | 30 |
| *(Promo-only release, 12 tracks)* | | | |
| **RADIO SHOWS** | | | |
| KING BISCUIT FLOWER HOUR (Jan 87) Live concert | 1987 | DIR | 75-125 |
| *(With Lou Reed)* | | | |
| **Albums** | | | |
| ROCK AROUND THE WORLD (May 77) Live concert | 1977 | RATW | 100-200 |
| *(With David Bowie)* | | | |
| **Compact Discs** | | | |
| KING BISCUIT FLOWER HOUR (Feb 89) | 1989 | DIR | 25-40 |
| *(Live concert)* | | | |
| KING BISCUIT FLOWER HOUR (Sept 88) | 1988 | DIR | 50-75 |
| *(Live concert)* | | | |

**IMPALAS, THE**
*Other Cub promo 45s $25 each*

| **45s** | | | |
|---|---|---|---|
| SORRY (I RAN ALL THE WAY HOME) | 1959 | Cub 9022 | 30 |
| *(Cub promo label)* | | | |

**IMPRESSIONS, THE**
*Featuring Jerry Butler; Curtis Mayfield*

| **45s** | | | |
|---|---|---|---|
| FOR YOUR PRECIOUS LOVE | 1958 | Vee Jay 280 | Unknown |
| *(Only a few copies known of the stock copy; promo copies if they exist, would also be very rare)* | | | |
| MERRY CHRISTMAS HAPPY NEW YEAR | 197? | Curtom SP-3 | 15 |
| *(Promo only, B-side is blank)* | | | |
| WHAT'S IT ALL ABOUT  (Jan 76) Public service show | 1976 | W.I.A.A. 298 | 15 |
| *(Flip side is Billy Swan)* | | | |

| Title | Yr | Label, Number | NM $ |
|---|---|---|---|
| **7-Inch Extended Plays** | | | |
| ONE BY ONE | 196? | ABC 523 | 20 |
| *(Jukebox LLP, with cover)* | | | |
| TEEN DELIGHTS | 1958 | Vee Jay 1091 | 100 |
| *(No cover, promo only, also includes El Dorados, Magnificents and Flamingos)* | | | |
| | | | |
| **IMUS, DON** | | | |
| *Also known as "Imus in the Morning"; Other RCA promo 45s $8 each* | | | |
| **45s** | | | |
| 1200 HAMBURGERS TO GO  Yellow promo label | 1972 | RCA Victor 1031 | 15 |
| *(Flip side is The Reverend Billy Sol Hargis)* | | | |
| HOLYLAND RECORD PACKAGE  Yellow promo label | 1972 | RCA Victor SPS-45-372 | 12 |
| *(By Imus' fictional televangelist, Billy Sol Hargis)* | | | |
| PLAY THAT COUNTRY JUKEBOX  Cream promo label | 1975 | RCA Victor 10170 | 12 |
| *(Country version of Life Is A Rock)* | | | |
| SON OF CHECKERS  White promo label | 1973 | RCA Victor SPS-45-512 | 30 |
| *(Cut-in, long/short versions, 5:24 and 4:07)* | | | |
| SON OF CHECKERS  Yellow promo label | 1973 | RCA Victor 0982 | 20 |
| *(Cut-in, 4:07 version)* | | | |
| THE PRESIDENTIAL DEBATE  Mono/stereo versions | 1976 | Epic 50305 | 20 |
| *(Cut-in, 2:36 versions)* | | | |
| | | | |
| **IN CROWD, THE** | | | |
| *Other Abnak promo 45s $3 each* | | | |
| **45s** | | | |
| BIG CITIES | 1967 | Abnak 121 | 12 |
| *(Yellow vinyl, yellow promo label)* | | | |
| HANGIN' FROM YOUR LOVIN' TREE | 1968 | Abnak 129 | 12 |
| *(Yellow vinyl, yellow promo label)* | | | |
| | | | |
| **INDIGO GIRLS** | | | |
| *Epic promo 45s $5 each; Epic promo CD singles $4-6 each* | | | |
| **Albums** | | | |
| SHADES OF INDIGO: AN INTERVIEW BY SHAWN COLVIN | 1990 | Epic EAS 2201 | 40 |
| **Compact Discs** | | | |
| 1,200 CURFEWS | 1995 | Epic E2K 67229 | 80 |
| *(2-CD promo in book with wood panels)* | | | |
| ACOUSTIC EVENING WITH THE INDIGO GIRLS & | 1992 | Epic ESK 4632 | 80 |
| THE ALLMAN BROTHERS BAND | | | |
| *(Seven tracks by each band, promo only)* | | | |
| BREAKING CURFEW | 1995 | Epic ESK 7382 | 30 |
| *(Promo-only sampler from double live CD)* | | | |
| INDIGO GIRLS | 1989 | Epic ESK 1486 | 20 |
| *(Promo-only sampler from major-label debut)* | | | |
| SHADES OF INDIGO | 1990 | Epic ESK 2201 | 20 |
| *(Promo-only interview disc)* | | | |
| THREE HITS | 1993 | Epic ESK 4864 | 20 |
| *(Promo-only sampler)* | | | |
| **RADIO SHOWS** | | | |
| **Compact Discs** | | | |
| ON THE EDGE (Aug 94) Music and interviews | 1994 | Westwood One | 35-50 |
| *(With L7 and Love Spit Love)* | | | |
| | | | |
| **INK SPOTS, THE** | | | |
| *Other white promo label King 45s $25 each; Decca pink promo label 45s $5 each; Decca promo LPs $15-20 each; "X" (RCA Victor) promo 45s by Bill Kenny $10 each; Decca promo 45s by Bill Kenny $6 each* | | | |
| **45s** | | | |
| HERE IN MY LONELY ROOM | 1953 | King 4670 | 75 |
| *(White promo label)* | | | |
| MELODY OF LOVE | 1954 | King 1336 | 40 |
| *(White promo label)* | | | |
| MELODY OF LOVE | 1955 | King 1429 | 40 |
| *(White promo label)* | | | |
| SOMEONE'S ROCKING MY DREAMBOAT | 195? | King 1415 | 40 |
| *(White label promo with biography of group on label)* | | | |
| WHEN YOU COME TO THE END OF THE DAY | 1954 | King 1425 | 40 |
| *(White promo label)* | | | |
| **7-Inch Extended Plays** | | | |
| BEST OF THE INK SPOTS  Jukebox LLP | 1972 | Decca 7182 (LLP 148) | 10 |
| *(Issued in a paper sleeve)* | | | |
| | | | |
| **INMAN, AUTRY** | | | |
| *Decca promo 45s $5 each; Jubilee promo 45s $4 each; United Artists promo 45s $4 each; Sims promo 45s $3 each; RCA Victor promo 45s $4 each; Epic promo 45s $2 each* | | | |
| **45s** | | | |
| BE BOP BABY | 1955 | Decca 29936 | 30 |
| *(Pink promo label)* | | | |
| NITECLUBBIN'  White promo label | 1967 | Risque 103 | 15 |
| *(Party record)* | | | |
| THAT'S ALL RIGHT | 1953 | Decca 28629 | 18 |
| *(Pink promo label)* | | | |
| | | | |
| **INMATES, THE** | | | |
| **12-Inch Singles** | | | |
| THE WALK/DIRTY WATER | 1979 | Polydor 123 | 10 |

| Title | Yr | Label, Number | NM $ |
|---|---|---|---|
| **INNOCENTS, THE** | | | |
| *More at Kathy Young* | | | |
| **Albums** | | | |
| INNOCENTLY YOURS | 1961 | Indigo 503 | 500 |
| *(Special promo advance copy in white cover with raised blue letters)* | | | |
| | | | |
| **INSPIRATIONS, THE** | | | |
| **45s** | | | |
| RAINDROPS | 1955 | Apollo 494 | 75 |
| *(White promo label)* | | | |
| | | | |
| **INSPIRATORS, THE** | | | |
| **45s** | | | |
| STARLIGHT TONIGHT | 1958 | Old Town 1053 | 50 |
| *(White promo label)* | | | |
| | | | |
| **INTERNATIONAL STRING BAND** | | | |
| **RADIO SHOWS** | | | |
| **Albums** | | | |
| BBC TRANSCRIPTION DISC  Live concert | 1973 | BBC Transcription | 200-300 |
| *(Very rare radio series)* | | | |
| BBC TRANSCRIPTION DISC  Live concert | 1974 | BBC Transcription | 150-250 |
| *(Very rare concert)* | | | |
| | | | |
| **INTERNATIONAL SUBMARINE BAND, THE** | | | |
| **45s** | | | |
| RUSSIANS ARE COMING | 196? | Ascot 2218 | 18 |
| *(White promo label)* | | | |
| SUM UP BROKE | 1967 | Columbia 43953 | 15 |
| *(White promo label)* | | | |
| | | | |
| **INXS** | | | |
| *Atco promo 45s $4 each; Atlantic promo 45s $3 each; Other Atlantic promo CD singles $4-6 each* | | | |
| **12-Inch Singles** | | | |
| BITTER TEARS (Lorimer Remix)/(Instrumental) | 1990 | Atlantic 1616 | 8 |
| BURN FOR YOU (3 versions) | 1984 | Atco PR 639 | 12 |
| DEVIL INSIDE (LP version)/(edit) | 1987 | Atlantic PR 2191 | 8 |
| DEVIL INSIDE (Remix)/(Edit)/ON THE ROCKS | 1987 | Atlantic 1137 | 6 |
| DON'T CHANGE (same on both sides) | 1982 | Atco PR 499 | 12 |
| GOOD TIMES (same on both sides)  With Jimmy Barnes | 1986 | Atlantic PR 2050 | 8 |
| I SEND A MESSAGE (Remix)/(LP Version) | 1984 | Atco PR 618 | 12 |
| KISS THE DIRT (same on both sides) | 1985 | Atlantic 885 | 12 |
| LISTEN LIKE THIEVES (3 versions) | 1985 | Atlantic 936 | 8 |
| LISTEN LIKE THIEVES (same on both sides) | 1985 | Atlantic PR 865 | 8 |
| NEED YOU TONIGHT (same on both sides) | 1987 | Atlantic PR 2116 | 8 |
| NEW SENSATION (3 versions) | 1988 | Atlantic 1172 | 8 |
| THE ONE THING (Extended)/(Edit) | 1983 | Atco PR 481 | 8 |
| ORIGINAL SIN (3 versions) | 1984 | Atco PR 586 | 20 |
| PLEASE (YOU GOT THAT...) (3 dub versions)/FREEDOM DEEP (12" Version) | 1993 | Atlantic 2078 | 15 |
| SUICIDE BLONDE (4 mixes) | 1990 | Atlantic 1550 | 8 |
| TASTE IT (3 versions) | 1992 | Atlantic 1933 | 15 |
| THIS TIME (same on both sides) | 1985 | Atlantic 788 | 7 |
| TO LOOK AT YOU (long & short) | 1983 | Atco PR 527 | 15 |
| WHAT YOU NEED (same on both sides) | 1985 | Atlantic PR 824 | 8 |
| WHAT YOU NEED (LP)/(Extended) | 1985 | Atlantic 910 | 12 |
| **Albums** | | | |
| THE NEW SENSATION Music and interviews | 1988 | Atlantic (2) | 20 |
| *(Promo-only release)* | | | |
| **Compact Discs** | | | |
| NEVER TEAR US APART | 1988 | Atlantic PR 2399 | 10 |
| *(Promo-only CD single, stock copies on 45 and cassette)* | | | |
| NEW MUSIC FROM INXS (COMPILATION) | 1990 | Atlantic PRCD-3416 | 30 |
| *(Promo-only collection)* | | | |
| PROFILED Music and interviews | 1992 | Atlantic PRCD-3675 | 20 |
| *(Promo-only release)* | | | |
| **RADIO SHOWS** | | | |
| **Albums** | | | |
| IN CONCERT  Live concert | 1986 | Westwood One (2) | 30-50 |
| *(Inxs only)* | | | |
| IN CONCERT (Nov 83) Live concert | 1983 | Westwood One (2) | 25-40 |
| *(With Billy Idol)* | | | |
| INNERVIEW (80s) Profile | 198? | Innerview | 10-20 |
| *(Music and interviews)* | | | |
| OFF THE RECORD (Jan 88) Profile | 1988 | Westwood One (2) | 10-15 |
| *(Music and interviews)* | | | |
| SUPERSTAR CONCERT Live concert | 1988 | Westwood One (3) | 25-50 |
| *(Box set, repeated)* | | | |
| **Compact Discs** | | | |
| IN CONCERT-NU ROCK (Nov 93) Live concert | 1993 | Westwood One | 40-75 |
| *(New live concert)* | | | |
| MASTERS OF ROCK (Oct 90) Profile | 1990 | Radio Ventures (2) | 20-40 |
| *(Music and interviews)* | | | |

| Title | Yr | Label, Number | NM $ |
|---|---|---|---|
| OFF THE RECORD (Sept 92) Profile | 1992 | Westwood One | 15-20 |
| *(Music and interviews)* | | | |
| ON THE EDGE (Jan 93) Profile | 1993 | Westwood One | 10-20 |
| *(Music and interviews)* | | | |
| SUPERSTAR CONCERT (Nov 93) Live concert | 1993 | Westwood One | 25-50 |
| *(CD version, repeated)* | | | |
| UP CLOSE  Profile | 1988 | Media America (2) | 25-50 |
| *(Music and interviews, some live tracks)* | | | |
| UP CLOSE  Profile | 1993 | Media America (2) | 30-50 |
| *(Music and interviews, some live tracks)* | | | |

## IRON MAIDEN
### Compact Discs

| Title | Yr | Label, Number | NM $ |
|---|---|---|---|
| BE QUICK OR BE DEAD | 1992 | Epic ESK 4551 | 20 |
| *(Promo-only CD single)* | | | |
| BRING YOUR DAUGHTER TO THE SLAUGHTER | 1991 | Epic ESK 4007 | 20 |
| *(Promo-only CD single, picture disc)* | | | |
| FROM HERE TO ETERNITY | 1992 | Epic ESK 4758 | 10 |
| *(Promo-only CD single)* | | | |
| FUGITIVE, THE | 1992 | Epic ESK 4648 | 20 |
| *(Promo-only interview disc)* | | | |
| HOLY SMOKE | 1990 | Epic ESK 2194 | 8 |
| *(Promo-only CD single)* | | | |
| LORD OF THE FLIES | 1996 | CMC International 82660 | 15 |
| *(Promo-only CD single)* | | | |
| NO PRAYER FOR THE DYING | 1990 | Epic ESK 73695 | 25 |
| *(Promo-only CD single, was released as a stock copy cassette)* | | | |
| TAILGUNNER | 1990 | Epic ESK 2233 | 30 |
| *(Promo-only CD single, picture disc)* | | | |
| VIRUS | 1996 | Castle Communications PROC 6-2 | 20 |
| *(Promo-only sampler)* | | | |
| WASTING LOVE | 1992 | Epic ESK 4640 | 10 |
| *(Promo-only CD single)* | | | |

### RADIO SHOWS
### Albums

| Title | Yr | Label, Number | NM $ |
|---|---|---|---|
| INNERVIEW (80s) Profile | 198? | Innerview | 10-20 |
| *(Music and interviews)* | | | |
| NBC SOURCE (Sept 82) | 1982 | NBC Radio (2) | 200-400 |
| *(Live concert material, one of their only radio shows)* | | | |

## ISAAK, CHRIS
*Reprise promo 45s $4 each; Reprise promo CD singles $3 each*
### 12-Inch Singles

| Title | Yr | Label, Number | NM $ |
|---|---|---|---|
| DANCIN'/GONE RIDIN' | 1985 | Warner Bros. PRO-A-2265 | 8 |
| GONE RIDIN' (same on both sides) | 1985 | Warner Bros. PRO-A-2359 | 8 |
| HEART FULL OF SOUL (same on both sides) | 1987 | Warner Bros. PRO-A-2736 | 8 |
| LIVIN' FOR YOUR LOVER (same on both sides) | 1985 | Warner Bros. PRO-A-2332 | 8 |
| YOU OWE ME SOME KIND OF LOVE (same on both sides) | 1987 | Warner Bros. PRO-A-2682 | 8 |

### RADIO SHOWS
### Albums

| Title | Yr | Label, Number | NM $ |
|---|---|---|---|
| IN CONCERT (July 91) Live concert | 1991 | Westwood One (2) | 30-60 |
| *(Rare live concert)* | | | |

### Compact Discs

| Title | Yr | Label, Number | NM $ |
|---|---|---|---|
| ON THE EDGE (Sept 93) Music and interviews | 1993 | | 20-30 |
| *(With Urge Overkill and the Posies)* | | | |

## ISLEY BROTHERS, THE
*RCA Victor promo 45s $12 each; Atlantic, Wand and United Artists promo 45s $8 each; Tamla promo 45s $6 each; T-Neck promo 45s $5 each.*
### 12-Inch Singles

| Title | Yr | Label, Number | NM $ |
|---|---|---|---|
| COLDER ARE MY NIGHTS (Edit Version) (LP Version) | 1985 | Warner Bros. PRO-A-2378 | 8 |
| HURRY UP AND WAIT (3:54) (4:09) | 1981 | T-Neck AS 947 | 8 |
| SENSITIVE LOVER (4 versions) | 1992 | Warner Bros. PRO-A-5417 | 8 |
| SPEND THE NIGHT (Edit)/COLDER ARE MY NIGHTS (Edit)/ | 1989 | Warner Bros. PRO-A-4511 | 8 |
| SMOOTH SAILIN' TONIGHT (Edit) | | | |

### 45s

| Title | Yr | Label, Number | NM $ |
|---|---|---|---|
| EVERYBODY'S GONNA ROCK AND ROLL | 1958 | Gone 5022 | 100 |
| *(White promo label)* | | | |
| THE DRAG | 1959 | Gone 5048 | 25 |
| *(White promo label)* | | | |

### Albums

| Title | Yr | Label, Number | NM $ |
|---|---|---|---|
| EVERYTHING YOU ALWAYS WANTED TO HEAR BY THE ISLEY BROTHERS BUT WERE AFRAID TO ASK FOR | 1976 | T-Neck ASZ 137 | 20 |
| *(Promo-only compilation)* | | | |
| MISSION TO PLEASE | 1996 | Island 7243 | 20 |
| *(Promo-only vinyl in generic cover)* | | | |

## IT'S A BEAUTIFUL DAY
*Includes listings of David LaFlamme; Other Columbia promo 45s $5 each; Other Columbia white promo label LPs $20 each*
### 45s

| Title | Yr | Label, Number | NM $ |
|---|---|---|---|
| WHITE BIRD | 1969 | Columbia 44928 | 18 |
| *(Mono/stereo versions of the classic)* | | | |
| WHITE BIRD | 1972 | Columbia 45788 | 15 |
| *(Mono/stereo Special Rush Reservice copy)* | | | |

| Title | Yr | Label, Number | NM $ |
|---|---|---|---|
| WHITE BIRD  David LaFlamme | 1976 | Amherst 717 | 10 |
| *(Mono/stereo solo version, issued with a picture sleeve)* | | | |
| **Albums** | | | |
| A THOUSAND AND ONE NIGHTS | 1973 | Columbia KC 32660 | 50 |
| *(May have been canceled before commercial release)* | | | |

**IVAN**
*Jerry Allison with Buddy Holly*
**45s**

| | | | |
|---|---|---|---|
| FRANKIE FRANKENSTEIN | 1958 | Coral 62081 | 200 |
| *(Blue promo label)* | | | |
| REAL WILD CHILD | 1958 | Coral 62017 | 100 |
| *(Blue promo label)* | | | |
| REAL WILD CHILD | 196? | Coral 65607 | 100 |
| *(Blue promo label, silver star series)* | | | |

**IVES, BURL**
*Decca promo 45s $2 each; Decca jukebox LLPs $4 each*
**45s**

| | | | |
|---|---|---|---|
| THE CHRISTMAS LEGEND OF MONKEY JOE/ IT'S GONNA BE A MIXED UP XMAS | 1978 | Monkey Joe MJ-1 | 10 |
| A HOLLY JOLLY CHRISTMAS | 1980 | MCA 31695 | 10 |
| *(Sample copy, unusual reissue with original Decca number on blue rainbow MCA label)* | | | |
| **7-Inch Extended Plays** | | | |
| SUMMER MAGIC | 1963 | Buena Vista AL-701 | 25 |
| *(Promo EP for Alcoa, 7 tracks, picture sleeve, also features Hayley Mills)* | | | |

# J

**J. GEILS BAND**
*Featuring Peter Wolf; more at "Geils" ; Other Atlantic promo 45s $4 each (Atlantic 3411 lists artist as "Geils"); Other EMI green promo label 45s $3 each; Other EMI gray promo label 45s $2 each; EMI promo 45s by Peter Wolf $3 each; EMI promo 12" singles by Peter Wolf $8 each*
**45s**

| | | | |
|---|---|---|---|
| CENTERFOLD | 1981 | EMI | 10 |
| *(Test pressing of their biggest hit)* | | | |
| FLAMETHROWER  Long/short versions | 1981 | EMI SPRO 9743 | 10 |
| *(Promo-only versions)* | | | |
| FREEZE-FRAME  Long/short versions | 1981 | EMI SPRO 9741 | 10 |
| *(Promo-only versions)* | | | |
| HARD DRIVIN' MAN | 1972 | Atlantic 2929 | 10 |
| *(Red and white promo labels)* | | | |
| I DO | 1982 | EMI | 10 |
| *(Test pressing, with stamped title on white sleeve)* | | | |
| **7-Inch Extended Plays** | | | |
| BLOODSHOT  Jukebox LLP | 1973 | Atlantic 7260 (LLP 219) | 15 |
| *(Issued in a paper sleeve)* | | | |
| **Albums** | | | |
| BLOODSHOT | 1973 | Atlantic 7260 | 20 |
| *(Red vinyl promo; some stock copies also exist on red vinyl)* | | | |
| SANCTUARY | 1979 | EMI 17006 | 20 |
| *(Picture disc; promo only)* | | | |
| **RADIO SHOWS** | | | |
| **Albums** | | | |
| BBC LONDON WAVELENGTH (Dec 81) Live concert | 1981 | London Wavelength | 20-40 |
| *(J. Geils Band only)* | | | |
| WORLD OF ROCK (Apr 90) Various artists | 1990 | DIR (2) | 10-20 |
| *(Peter Wolf is co-host of the show)* | | | |
| **Compact Discs** | | | |
| IN THE STUDIO (Sept 90) Profile of an album | 1990 | Album Network | 10-20 |
| *(Music and interviews)* | | | |
| KING BISCUIT FLOWER HOUR (Jan 94) Live concert | 1994 | DIR | 40-75 |
| *(With Jack Bruce)* | | | |
| KING BISCUIT FLOWER HOUR (May 88) Live concert | 1988 | DIR | 60-100 |
| *(With Slade)* | | | |

**JACK AND JIM**
**45s**

| | | | |
|---|---|---|---|
| TARZAN & JANE | 1959 | Brunswick 55141 | 40 |
| *(Yellow promo label)* | | | |

**JACKS, THE**
*Other RPM promo 45s $25 each*
**45s**

| | | | |
|---|---|---|---|
| I'M CONFESSIN' | 1955 | RPM 433 | 60 |
| *(White promo label)* | | | |
| WHY DON'T YOU WRITE ME | 1955 | RPM 428 | 80 |
| *(White promo label)* | | | |

| Title | Yr | Label, Number | NM $ |
|---|---|---|---|

**JACKSON, ALAN**
*Arista promo 45s $3 each; Arista promo CD singles $3 each*
**Compact Discs**

| | | | |
|---|---|---|---|
| GREATEST HITS COLLECTION | 1995 | Arista 07822-18801-2 | 20 |
| *(Promo CD in special 6x12 packaging not available commercially)* | | | |
| MUSIC ROW THEATER | 199? | Arista ASCD-2479 | 20 |
| *(Promo-only record company radio show)* | | | |

**RADIO SHOWS**
**Compact Discs**

| | | | |
|---|---|---|---|
| ALAN JACKSON STORY (July 93) | 1993 | Unistar | 20-35 |
| *(Profile of the artist)* | | | |
| COUNTRY CONCERT (Aug 96) | 1996 | Westwood One (2) | 30-50 |
| *(Live concert material)* | | | |
| WHO I AM | 1994 | Westwood One | 20-40 |
| *(Special preview of his then-new album)* | | | |

**JACKSON, JANET**
*Other A&M promo 45s $5 each; A&M promo 12" singles $8 each*
**45s**

| | | | |
|---|---|---|---|
| YOUNG LOVE   White promo label | 1982 | A&M 2440 | 12 |
| *(First record, released with a rare picture sleeve)* | | | |

**Compact Discs**

| | | | |
|---|---|---|---|
| AGAIN | 1993 | Virgin DPRO-12801 | 10 |
| *(Promo CD single, not to be confused with less valuable stock copy)* | | | |
| ALRIGHT | 1990 | A&M CD-17981 | 10 |
| *(Promo-only CD single, different mixes)* | | | |
| ALRIGHT | 1990 | A&M CD-17978 | 10 |
| *(Promo-only CD single)* | | | |
| ANY TIME, ANY PLACE | 1994 | Virgin DPRO-14151 | 8 |
| *(Promo CD single, not to be confused with less valuable stock copy)* | | | |
| BECAUSE OF LOVE | 1994 | Virgin DPRO-14111 | 8 |
| *(Promo CD single, not to be confused with less valuable stock copy)* | | | |
| BLACK CAT | 1990 | A&M 75021 7972 2 | 15 |
| *(Promo CD single, not to be confused with less valuable stock copy)* | | | |
| COME BACK TO ME | 1990 | A&M 75021 7939 2 | 10 |
| *(Promo-only CD single)* | | | |
| ESCAPADE | 1989 | A&M CD-18002 | 10 |
| *(Promo-only CD single)* | | | |
| GO DEEP | 1998 | Virgin DPRO-????? | 8 |
| *(Promo-only CD single)* | | | |
| GOT 'TIL IT'S GONE | 1997 | Virgin DPRO-????? | 8 |
| *(Promo-only CD single, released commercially as B-side of "Together Again")* | | | |
| IF | 1993 | Virgin DPRO-12808 | 10 |
| *(Promo CD single, not to be confused with less valuable stock copy)* | | | |
| JANET JACKSON'S RHYTHM NATION 1814 | 1989 | A&M CD 3920 | 20 |
| *(Promo-only box with CD, cassette and pin)* | | | |
| LOVE WILL NEVER DO (WITHOUT YOU) | 1990 | A&M 75021 7444 2 | 10 |
| *(Promo-only CD single)* | | | |
| MISS YOU MUCH | 1989 | A&M CD-17885 | 10 |
| *(Promo-only CD single)* | | | |
| MISS YOU MUCH | 1989 | A&M CD-17917 | 10 |
| *(Promo-only CD single, different mixes)* | | | |
| REMIXES, THE | 1989 | A&M CD-17966 | 20 |
| *(Promo-only collection of Rhythm Nation remixes)* | | | |
| RHYTHM NATION | 1989 | A&M CD-17915 | 10 |
| *(Promo-only CD single)* | | | |
| RHYTHM NATION | 1989 | A&M CD-17928 | 10 |
| *(Promo-only CD single, different mixes)* | | | |
| STATE OF THE WORLD | 1990 | A&M 75021 7514 2 | 12 |
| *(Promo-only CD single; only stock single release was as a Collectables 45)* | | | |
| THAT'S THE WAY LOVE GOES | 1993 | Virgin DPRO-12773 | 10 |
| *(Promo-only CD single)* | | | |
| THAT'S THE WAY LOVE GOES | 1993 | Virgin DPRO-12795 | 10 |
| *(Promo-only CD single, different mixes)* | | | |
| TOGETHER AGAIN | 1997 | Virgin DPRO-????? | 8 |
| *(Promo CD single, not to be confused with less valuable stock copy)* | | | |
| YOU WANT THIS | 1994 | Virgin DPRO-14??? | 10 |
| *(Promo CD single, not to be confused with less valuable stock copy)* | | | |

**RADIO SHOWS**
**Albums**

| | | | |
|---|---|---|---|
| THE STORY OF JANET JACKSON Profile | 1990 | Unistar (2) | 20-40 |
| *(Music and interviews)* | | | |

**JACKSON, JERMAINE**
*Any other promo 45s $3 each; Any promo 12" single $7 each; Any promo LP $5 each*
**12-Inch Singles**

| | | | |
|---|---|---|---|
| DON'T TAKE IT PERSONAL (same on both sides) | 1989 | Arista ADP 9876 | 8 |
| DYNAMITE/(Instrumental)/TELL ME I'M NOT DREAMING (Instrumental) | 1984 | Arista AD1 9222 | 6 |
| TELL ME I'M NOT DREAMIN' (TOO GOOD TO BE TRUE)/ | 1984 | Arista ADP 9189 | 10 |
| DO WHAT YOU DO/ESCAPE FROM THE PLANET | | | |
| VERY SPECIAL PART/(Instrumental) | 1982 | Motown PR 108 | 10 |

**45s**

| | | | |
|---|---|---|---|
| DYNAMITE   Red vinyl | 1984 | Arista 9190 | 25 |
| *(Only the promo version is red vinyl)* | | | |

| Title | Yr | Label, Number | NM $ |
|---|---|---|---|
| **RADIO SHOWS** | | | |
| **Albums** | | | |
| MILLER SOUND EXPRESS (Jan 87) Live concert | 1987 | Miller (2) | 60-125 |
| *(Rare live concert, rare radio series)* | | | |
| STARTRACK PROFILE | 1986 | NBC Radio (2) | 20-40 |
| *(Mostly music and interviews)* | | | |
| | | | |
| **JACKSON, JOE** | | | |
| *A&M promo 45s $3 each; A&M promo CD singles $2-4 each* | | | |
| **12-Inch Singles** | | | |
| HOME TOWN (same on both sides) | 1986 | A&M 17395 | 6 |
| RIGHT AND WRONG (4:35)/(4:11) | 1986 | A&M 17374 | 6 |
| STEPPIN' OUT (LP version)/(edit) | 1982 | A&M 17201 | 8 |
| WILD WEST/RIGHT AND WRONG/HOME TOWN/TONIGHT | 1986 | A&M 17375 | 6 |
| **Albums** | | | |
| JOE JACKSON  Promo-only release | 1986 | A&M | 20 |
| *(Music and interviews)* | | | |
| **RADIO SHOWS** | | | |
| **Albums** | | | |
| BBC LONDON WAVELENGTH (May 84) | 1984 | London Wavelength | 15-25 |
| *(Music and interviews)* | | | |
| BBC ROCK HOUR (Jan 81) | 1981 | London Wavelength | 40-75 |
| *(Live concert)* | | | |
| IN CONCERT | 1983 | Westwood One (2) | 40-75 |
| *(Live concert)* | | | |
| KING BISCUIT FLOWER HOUR (May 80) Live concert | 1980 | DIR/ABC (2) | 75-125 |
| *(Joe Jackson solo concert)* | | | |
| NBC SOURCE (Apr 86) | 1986 | NBC Radio (2) | 20-40 |
| *(This version is music and interviews)* | | | |
| NBC SOURCE (May 80) Live concert | 1980 | NBC Radio (2) | 75-125 |
| *(This version is live)* | | | |
| **Compact Discs** | | | |
| IN CONCERT-NU ROCK (Sept 93) | 1993 | Westwood One | 30-50 |
| *(Live concert)* | | | |
| | | | |
| **JACKSON, LA TOYA** | | | |
| *Any other promo 45s $3 each; Any promo 12" single $7 each; Any promo LP $5 each* | | | |
| **45s** | | | |
| I DON'T WANT YOU TO GO | 1981 | Polydor 2188DJ | 10 |
| *(Red promo label)* | | | |
| **Albums** | | | |
| MY SPECIAL LOVE | 1981 | Polydor 6328 | 12 |
| *(White promo label)* | | | |
| | | | |
| **JACKSON, MAHALIA** | | | |
| **45s** | | | |
| HAPPY BIRTHDAY TO YOU, OUR LORD/SILVER BELLS | 1968 | Columbia JZSP 137705/6 | 5 |
| SILENT NIGHT/THE LORD'S PRAYER | 197? | Nashboro 750 | 4 |
| *(Reissue of Kenwood 750, possibly promo only)* | | | |
| | | | |
| **JACKSON, MICHAEL** | | | |
| *Other Motown promo singles $8 each; Other Epic promo 45s $4 each; Epic promo picture sleeve 45s $4 each; Other promo 12" singles $10-12 each; Epic or Motown promo LPs $10 each* | | | |
| **12-Inch Singles** | | | |
| FAREWELL MY SUMMER LOVE | 1984 | Motown PR 153B | 10 |
| *(The 4:21 version on a promo 12-inch single)* | | | |
| IN THE CLOSET (11 versions) | 1991 | Epic ES 4533 | 30 |
| JAM (13 versions) | 1991 | Epic ES 4580 | 30 |
| THRILLER | 1983 | Epic AS 1805 | 18 |
| *(The 5:56 version on a promo label)* | | | |
| **45s** | | | |
| BEN  White promo label | 1972 | Motown | 125 |
| *(Promo issued without number, had authentic rat sounds under the music, which was removed for later promo and all stock copies)* | | | |
| BODY LANGUAGE | 1976 | Motown 1375 | 500 |
| *(Unreleased, only exists on acetate)* | | | |
| THE BOOGIE MAN | 1974 | Motown 1230 | 500 |
| *(Unreleased, only exists on acetate)* | | | |
| DOGGIN' AROUND | 1975 | Motown 1270 | 500 |
| *(Unreleased, only exists on acetate)* | | | |
| EASE ON DOWN THE ROAD  With Diana Ross | 1978 | MCA 40947 | 10 |
| *(White promo label, from the soundtrack of The Wiz)* | | | |
| THE GIRL IS MINE  With Paul McCartney | 1982 | Epic 03288 | 10 |
| *(Promo-only edited version, 3:32)* | | | |
| SOMEONE IN THE DARK  White promo label | 1982 | MCA 1786 | 150 |
| *(Fewer than five copies known, from the MCA set, 4:58 and 3:04 versions)* | | | |
| THRILLER | 1983 | Epic AE7 1829 | 15 |
| *(Promo-only long/short versions, 5:11 each/with and without rap)* | | | |
| **7-Inch Extended Plays** | | | |
| BEN RADIO SPOT ANNOUNCEMENTS | 1972 | Cinerama Releasing | 300 |
| *(Yellow label, regular 45rpm center hole, one-sided, very rare)* | | | |
| DRUNK DRIVING CAMPAIGN  PSA ads | 1984 | Nat'l. Highway Traffic Safety Comm. 684 | 100 |
| *(7" 33rpm with three cuts for traffic safety to music of "Beat It")* | | | |

| Title | Yr | Label, Number | NM $ |
|---|---|---|---|
| **Albums** | | | |
| BEN | 1972 | Motown | 40 |
| *(White promo label)* | | | |
| FAREWELL MY SUMMER LOVE | 1984 | Motown 6101 | 12 |
| *(White promo label)* | | | |
| ONE DAY AT A TIME | 1981 | Motown 956 | 12 |
| *(White promo label)* | | | |
| **Compact Discs** | | | |
| BAD | 1987 | Epic ESK 2808 | 12 |
| *(Promo-only CD single)* | | | |
| BAD MIXES, THE | 1988 | Epic/Monster Music ESK 1215MC | 400 |
| *(Promo-only CD, limited to 6,000 numbered copies)* | | | |
| DIRTY DIANA | 1988 | Epic ESK 1110 | 20 |
| *(Promo-only CD single)* | | | |
| GONE TOO SOON | 1993 | Epic ESK 5562 | 15 |
| *(Promo-only CD single)* | | | |
| IN THE CLOSET | 1992 | Epic ESK 4537 | 15 |
| *(Promo-only CD single, not to be confused with two stock versions)* | | | |
| MAN IN THE MIRROR | 1988 | Epic ESK 1006 | 15 |
| *(Promo-only CD single)* | | | |
| REMEMBER THE TIME | 1992 | Epic ESK 4457 | 12 |
| *(Promo-only CD single, different mix)* | | | |
| REMEMBER THE TIME | 1992 | Epic ESK 4456 | 12 |
| *(Promo-only CD single)* | | | |
| SMOOTH CRIMINAL | 1988 | Epic ESK 1274 | 12 |
| *(Promo-only CD single)* | | | |
| THEY DON'T CARE ABOUT US | 1996 | Epic ESK 7723 | 12 |
| *(CD single, promo-only number)* | | | |
| THIS TIME AROUND | 1996 | Epic ESK 7251 | 12 |
| *(Promo-only CD single)* | | | |
| WAY YOU MAKE ME FEEL, THE | 1987 | Epic ESK 2862 | 10 |
| *(Promo-only CD single)* | | | |
| **RADIO SHOWS** | | | |
| **Albums** | | | |
| BIRTHDAY SALUTE (Aug 90) FROM SOLID GOLD SCRAPBOOK | 1990 | Unistar | 10-15 |
| *(Music and interviews)* | | | |
| HOT ROCKS (Apr 88) | 1988 | United Stations | 20-40 |
| *(Music and interviews)* | | | |
| PROFILE OF MICHAEL JACKSON (Aug 86) | 1986 | Unistar | 10-15 |
| *(Music and interviews from Solid Gold Scrapbook)* | | | |
| SPOTLIGHT SPECIAL  Profile of Michael Jackson | 1983 | ABC Radio (2) | 20-40 |
| *(Music and interviews)* | | | |
| **Compact Discs** | | | |
| THE STORY OF MICHAEL JACKSON (Jan 92) Profile | 1992 | Unistar | 20-40 |
| *(Music and interviews, several repeats)* | | | |
| THE STORY OF MICHAEL JACKSON (Jan 92) Profile | 1992 | Unistar (2) | 25-50 |
| *(Music and interviews, extended version)* | | | |
| THE STORY OF MICHAEL JACKSON (May 91) Profile | 1991 | Unistar (3) | 30-60 |
| *(Music and interviews special)* | | | |
| **Reel-to-Reel Tapes** | | | |
| THRILLER | 1983 | | 100-150 |
| *(Music and interviews on two 7" reels)* | | | |

**JACKSON, MILLIE**

**12-Inch Singles**

| | | | |
|---|---|---|---|
| ALL THE WAY LOVER/YOU CREATED A MONSTER | 1977 | Spring 028 | 10 |

**JACKSON, REBBIE**

*Any other promo 45s $3 each; Any promo 12" single $7 each; Any promo LP $5 each*

**45s**

| | | | |
|---|---|---|---|
| CENTIPEDE  White promo label | 1984 | Columbia 04547 | 10 |
| *(This single was released with a picture sleeve marked "Demonstration Not for Sale")* | | | |

**JACKSON, WANDA**

*Other Capitol promo 45s $5 each*

**45s**

| | | | |
|---|---|---|---|
| BABY LOVES HIM | 1957 | Capitol 3637 | 50 |
| *(White promo label)* | | | |
| COOL LOVE | 1957 | Capitol 3764 | 30 |
| *(White promo label)* | | | |
| FUJIYAMA MAMA | 1957 | Capitol 3843 | 35 |
| *(White promo label)* | | | |
| HONEY BOP | 1957 | Capitol 3941 | 30 |
| *(White promo label)* | | | |
| HOT DOG! THAT MADE HIM MAD | 1956 | Capitol 3575 | 40 |
| *(White promo label)* | | | |
| I GOTTA KNOW | 1956 | Capitol 3485 | 40 |
| *(White promo label)* | | | |
| IF YOU DON'T SOMEBODY ELSE WILL | 1954 | Decca 29267 | 12 |
| *(Pink promo label)* | | | |
| IT'S THE SAME WORLD | 1955 | Decca 29677 | 15 |
| *(Pink promo label)* | | | |
| LET ME EXPLAIN | 1957 | Capitol 3683 | 30 |
| *(White promo label)* | | | |

| Title | Yr | Label, Number | NM $ |
|---|---|---|---|
| LET'S HAVE A PARTY  Red promo label | 1960 | Capitol 4397 | 30 |
| *(With Gene Vincent and his Blue Caps)* | | | |
| MEAN MEAN MAN | 1958 | Capitol 4026 | 40 |
| *(White promo label)* | | | |
| MEAN MEAN MAN | 1960 | Capitol 4469 | 20 |
| *(Red promo label)* | | | |
| RIOT IN CELL BLOCK NUMBER NINE | 1961 | Capitol 4520 | 20 |
| *(Red promo label)* | | | |
| ROCK YOUR BABY | 1958 | Capitol 4081 | 20 |
| *(White promo label)* | | | |
| TEARS AT THE GRAND OLE OPRY | 1955 | Decca 29514 | 18 |
| *(Pink promo label)* | | | |
| THE RIGHT TO LOVE  Pink promo label | 1954 | Decca 29253 | 15 |
| *(The first Wanda Jackson solo single)* | | | |
| WASTED | 1956 | Decca 29803 | 10 |
| *(Pink promo label)* | | | |
| YOU CAN'T HAVE MY LOVE  Pink promo label | 1954 | Decca 29140 | 18 |
| *(Duet with Billy Gray)* | | | |

**7-Inch Extended Plays**

| Title | Yr | Label, Number | NM $ |
|---|---|---|---|
| WONDERFUL WANDA  Jukebox LLP | 1962 | Capitol 1776 | 35 |
| *(Issued with a hard cover)* | | | |

**Albums**

| Title | Yr | Label, Number | NM $ |
|---|---|---|---|
| LOVIN' COUNTRY  Pink promo label | 1962 | Decca 4224 | 75 |
| *(1962 release of her 1954-55 Decca singles)* | | | |
| ROCKIN' WITH WANDA  Promo label | 1960 | Capitol 1384 | 500 |
| *(Stock copy worth $400, the promo is rarer!)* | | | |
| THERE'S A PARTY GOIN' ON  Promo label | 1961 | Capitol 1511 | 200 |
| *(Stereo stock copy is worth even more!)* | | | |
| WANDA JACKSON  Promo label | 1958 | Capitol 1041 | 250 |
| *(Her first album)* | | | |

**RADIO SHOWS**

**Albums**

| Title | Yr | Label, Number | NM $ |
|---|---|---|---|
| COUNTRY COOKIN' (Sept 75) Various artists | 1975 | U.S. Army Reserve (2) | 25-50 |
| *(One of the four shows features Wanda Jackson, music and interviews)* | | | |

## JACKSONS, THE

Also includes The Jackson 5; Other Motown white promo label 45s $6-12 each depending on year; Other Epic white promo label 45s $5 each; Epic promo picture sleeves $5 each; Other 12" promo singles $10 each; Other Epic white promo label LPs $12 each

**12-Inch Singles**

| Title | Yr | Label, Number | NM $ |
|---|---|---|---|
| HEARTBREAK HOTEL | 1980 | Epic AS 894 | 12 |
| *(The 4:49 version, promo only)* | | | |
| JACKSON FIVE MOTOWN MEDLEY | 1984 | Motown PR 153 B | 10 |
| *(The 6:49 version, promo only)* | | | |

**45s**

| Title | Yr | Label, Number | NM $ |
|---|---|---|---|
| BIG BOY Promo label | 1968 | Steeltown 681 | 150 |
| *(Same value for stock or promo, both rare)* | | | |
| FEELIN' ALRIGHT  White promo label | 1971 | Motown DJ 719 | 25 |
| *(Diana Ross and the Jackson Five, promo-only release)* | | | |
| FOREVER CAME TODAY  White promo label | 1975 | Motown 1356F | 25 |
| *(Promo only on blue vinyl)* | | | |
| GET IT TOGETHER  White promo label | 1973 | Motown 1277F | 25 |
| *(Promo only on red vinyl)* | | | |
| I FOUND THAT GIRL (same on both sides) | 1970 | Motown 1166 | 20 |
| *(Red vinyl)* | | | |
| JACKSON FIVE  Cereal box records, five songs | 1971 | Motown Sound | 25 |
| *(Five different versions, on cardboard)* | | | |
| JACKSON FIVE  Cereal box records, three songs | 1971 | Motown Sound | 25 |
| *(Three different versions, on cardboard)* | | | |
| LET ME CARRY YOUR SCHOOL BOOKS  Orange label | 1969 | Steeltown 688 | 175 |
| *(By The Ripples & Waves plus Michael)* | | | |
| THE LOVE YOU SAVE  White promo label | 1970 | Motown 1166 | 30 |
| *(This version is blank on the flip side)* | | | |
| MAYBE TOMORROW  White label, red print | 1971 | Motown 1186F | 12 |
| *(Rarest of several variations of this promo)* | | | |
| MEDLEY: I WANT YOU BACK/ABC/THE LOVE YOU SAVE | 1981 | Epic AE7 1352 | 15 |
| *(White promo label, promo only)* | | | |
| SANTA CLAUS IS COMIN' TO TOWN  White promo label | 1970 | Motown 1174DJ | 25 |
| *(Same song on both sides)* | | | |
| WE DON'T HAVE TO BE OVER 21  Blue label | 1968 | Steeltown 682 | 150 |
| *(Same value for stock or promo, both rare)* | | | |
| WHAT'S IT ALL ABOUT (July 77) Public service show | 1977 | W.I.A.A. 380 | 25 |
| *(Flip side is Marilyn McCoo and Billy Davis)* | | | |

**7-Inch Extended Plays**

| Title | Yr | Label, Number | NM $ |
|---|---|---|---|
| THIRD ALBUM  Jukebox LLP | 1971 | Motown 60718 (LLP 132) | 50 |
| *(Issued with paper sleeve and title strips)* | | | |

**Albums**

| Title | Yr | Label, Number | NM $ |
|---|---|---|---|
| GOIN' PLACES | 1978 | Epic 34835 | 25 |
| *(Promo-only picture disc)* | | | |
| SOULSATION! | 1995 | Motown 37463 1294-1 | 20 |
| *(Vinyl is promo only; 4-song sampler from box set)* | | | |

**Reel-to-Reel Tapes**

| Title | Yr | Label, Number | NM $ |
|---|---|---|---|
| 1984 JACKSONS RADIO Pepsi commercials | 198? | Pepsi-Cola | 200 |
| *(5" reel-to-reel tape in box with color photo on front; three 60-second ads)* | | | |

| Title | Yr | Label, Number | NM $ |
|---|---|---|---|
| **JADES, THE** | | | |
| **45s** | | | |
| PRIVILEGE (same on both sides) | 1967 | Uni 55032 | 8 |
| | | | |
| **JAGGER, MICK** | | | |
| *More at The Rolling Stones* | | | |
| **12-Inch Singles** | | | |
| BEAST OF BURDEN  Bette Midler | 1983 | Atlantic PR-573 | 10 |
| *(Promo-only 12" single, Jagger sings along)* | | | |
| JUST ANOTHER NIGHT | 1985 | Columbia | 12 |
| *(Promo 12" single with cover)* | | | |
| LUCKY IN LOVE | 1985 | Columbia 2060 | 12 |
| *(Promo 12" single with cover)* | | | |
| RUTHLESS PEOPLE | 1986 | Epic 05931 | 12 |
| *(Promo 12" single)* | | | |
| **45s** | | | |
| BUK-IN-HAM PALACE  With Peter Tosh | 1979 | Rolling Stones 20000 | 10 |
| *(Long and short versions)* | | | |
| JUST ANOTHER NIGHT | 1985 | Columbia 04743 | 10 |
| *(White promo label with promo picture sleeve)* | | | |
| LET'S WORK | 1987 | Columbia 07306 | 15 |
| *(Promo record and picture sleeve)* | | | |
| LUCKY IN LOVE | 1985 | Columbia 04893 | 12 |
| *(White promo label with promo picture sleeve)* | | | |
| RUTHLESS PEOPLE | 1986 | Epic 06211 | 10 |
| *(White promo label)* | | | |
| SAY YOU WILL | 1987 | Columbia 07703 | 20 |
| *(Promo record and picture sleeve)* | | | |
| THROWAWAY | 1987 | Columbia 07653 | 10 |
| *(White promo label)* | | | |
| **Albums** | | | |
| INTERVIEW WITH MICK JAGGER BY TOM DONAHUE | 1971 | ROLLING STONES 164 | 200 |
| *(White promo label)* | | | |
| INTERVIEW WITH MICK JAGGER BY TOM DONAHUE | 1971 | ROLLING STONES 164 | 150 |
| *(Yellow promo label)* | | | |
| PERFORMANCE | 1970 | Warner Bros. 2554 | 40 |
| *(White promo label)* | | | |
| **Compact Discs** | | | |
| DON'T TEAR ME UP | 1993 | Atlantic PRCD 5015 | 8 |
| *(Promo-only CD single)* | | | |
| LET'S WORK | 1987 | Columbia CSK 2271 | 8 |
| *(Promo-only CD single)* | | | |
| OUT OF FOCUS | 1993 | Atlantic PRCD 5152 | 8 |
| *(Promo-only CD single)* | | | |
| SWEET THING | 1993 | Atlantic PRCD 4800 | 8 |
| *(Promo-only CD single)* | | | |
| SWEET THING | 1993 | Atlantic PRCD 4939 | 8 |
| *(Promo-only CD single, different mix)* | | | |
| TOGETHER AND SOLO  Stones, Jagger, Richards | 199? | (3) | 60 |
| *(Promo-only release)* | | | |
| WANDERING SPIRIT, THE | 1993 | Atlantic 5002 | 30 |
| *(Promo-only release)* | | | |
| WIRED ALL NIGHT | 1993 | Atlantic PRCD 5020 | 8 |
| *(Promo-only CD single)* | | | |
| **RADIO SHOWS** | | | |
| **Albums** | | | |
| EARTH NEWS RADIO  Jagger and Keith Richards | 1981 | Earth News | 15-30 |
| *(Daily features)* | | | |
| INSIDE TRACK (June 83) Jagger, David Lee Roth | 1983 | RKO (3) | 50-100 |
| *(Music and interviews)* | | | |
| INSIDE TRACK (Mar 82) Jagger, David Lee Roth | 1982 | RKO (2) | 40-75 |
| *(Music and interviews)* | | | |
| INSIDE TRACK (Mar 82) Jagger, Richards, Bill Wyman | 1982 | RKO (3) | 50-80 |
| *(Music and interviews)* | | | |
| NBC SOURCE | 1983 | NBC Radio | 75-125 |
| *(Special interview show with photo cover)* | | | |
| NBC SOURCE (Jan 83) | 1983 | NBC Radio (3) | 40-75 |
| *(Music and interviews)* | | | |
| RADIO CONTROL (Nov 87) | 1987 | DIR (2) | 200-300 |
| *(Mostly music and interviews, rare show)* | | | |
| **Compact Discs** | | | |
| KING BISCUIT FLOWER HOUR (June 88) | 1988 | DIR | 125-200 |
| *(Live material from "Under Radio Control")* | | | |
| UP CLOSE | 1993 | Media America (2) | 75-125 |
| | | | |
| **JAM, THE** | | | |
| *Featuring Paul Weller; Also see The Style Council; Other Polydor promo 45s $5 each.* | | | |
| **12-Inch Singles** | | | |
| TOWN CALLED MALICE (same on both sides) | 1982 | Polydor 180 | 10 |
| **45s** | | | |
| GOING UNDERGROUND/DREAMS OF CHILDREN | 1980 | Polydor PRO 145 | 8 |
| IN THE CITY  White promo label | 1977 | Polydor 14442 | 25 |
| *(Issued with a picture sleeve, included in the price)* | | | |
| MR. CLEAN  White promo label | 1979 | Polydor 14566 | 10 |
| *(Both sides are the same)* | | | |

| Title | Yr | Label, Number | NM $ |
|---|---|---|---|
| THE BUTTERFLY COLLECTOR  White label, yellow vinyl | 1979 | Polydor 14553 | 12 |
| *(Some stock copies also are yellow vinyl)* | | | |
| TOWN CALLED MALICE  Red promo label | 1982 | Polydor 2206 DJ | 10 |
| *(Scarce promo version of this British classic)* | | | |
| **RADIO SHOWS** | | | |
| **Albums** | | | |
| BBC COLLEGE CONCERT HOUR | 1982 | London Wavelength | 40-75 |
| *(Rare live concert)* | | | |
| BBC ROCK HOUR (June 81) Live concert | 1981 | London Wavelength | 100-200 |
| *(Rare concert)* | | | |
| BBC TRANSCRIPTION DISC Live concert | 1980 | BBC Transcription | 275-450 |
| *(Very rare concert in a rare series)* | | | |
| KING BISCUIT FLOWER HOUR  Live concert | 1985 | DIR/ABC (2) | 40-75 |
| *(Rare live concert)* | | | |

## JAMAL, AHMAD
**45s**

| Title | Yr | Label, Number | NM $ |
|---|---|---|---|
| IT'S THAT TIME OF YEAR AGAIN (same on both sides) | 1985 | Atlantic 89476 | 5 |
| *(With Larry Goshorn; may be promo only)* | | | |

## JAMES
*Other Fontana promo CD singles $2-3 each*

**12-Inch Singles**

| Title | Yr | Label, Number | NM $ |
|---|---|---|---|
| WHAT FOR?/JAMES WHO? (interview) | 1988 | Sire PRO-A-3127 | 10 |
| **Compact Discs** | | | |
| LAID | 1994 | Fontana CDP 1010 | 8 |
| *(Promo-only CD single; their best-known hit in the U.S.)* | | | |
| **RADIO SHOWS** | | | |
| **Compact Discs** | | | |
| IN CONCERT-NU ROCK (June 94) Live concert | 1994 | Westwood One | 30-60 |
| *(With Dinosaur Jr.)* | | | |
| ON THE EDGE (Feb 94) Music and interviews | 1994 | Westwood One | 20-35 |
| *(With Soundgarden)* | | | |

## JAMES GANG, THE
*Featuring Joe Walsh; ABC promo 45s $5 each*

**RADIO SHOWS**
**Compact Discs**

| Title | Yr | Label, Number | NM $ |
|---|---|---|---|
| IN THE STUDIO (Mar 92) Profile of an album | 1992 | Album Network | 15-30 |
| *(Music and interviews)* | | | |

## JAMES, JESSIE
**45s**

| Title | Yr | Label, Number | NM $ |
|---|---|---|---|
| RED HOT ROCKIN' BLUES | 195? | Kent 314 | 75 |
| *(Kent promo label)* | | | |

## JAMES, RICK
**12-Inch Singles**

| Title | Yr | Label, Number | NM $ |
|---|---|---|---|
| GIVE IT TO ME BABY (3 versions) | 1981 | Motown PR-81 | 12 |
| LOVE GUN (10:03) (3:45) | 1979 | Motown PR-60 | 12 |
| SEXUAL LOVE AFFAIR (Club) (Remix Edit) (LP) | 1988 | Reprise PRO-A-3376 | 8 |
| YOU AND I (8:04) (same on both sides) | 1978 | Motown 981 | 10 |

## JAMES, SONNY
*Other Capitol promos $2-5 each depending on year; Capitol compact 33 stereo singles (for jukeboxes) $12 each; Columbia promo 45s $2 each; Dot promo 45s $6 each.*

**45s**

| Title | Yr | Label, Number | NM $ |
|---|---|---|---|
| BIMBO | 1958 | NRC 061 | 12 |
| *(White promo label)* | | | |
| JENNY LOU | 1958 | NRC 050 | 10 |
| *(White promo label)* | | | |
| LOVESICK BLUES | 1957 | Capitol 3734 | 15 |
| *(Photo of Sonny James on yellow label)* | | | |
| SONNY JAMES  "Sales Stimulator," red vinyl | 1966 | Rowe AMI | 30 |
| *(For jukebox owners, about 60 seconds long)* | | | |
| YOUNG LOVE | 1957 | Capitol 3602 | 15 |
| *(Promo label)* | | | |
| YOUNG LOVE | 1959 | Groove G4-1 | 25 |
| *(Newly recorded version produced by Chet Atkins)* | | | |
| **7-Inch Extended Plays** | | | |
| THE SENSATIONAL SONNY JAMES  Jukebox LLP | 1972 | Capitol 804 (LLP 159) | 10 |
| *(Issued with a paper sleeve)* | | | |
| **Albums** | | | |
| IN-PRISON INTERVIEW | 197? | CBS 148780 | 20 |
| *(Promo-only interview album)* | | | |

## JAMES, TOMMY (AND THE SHONDELLS)
*Roulette promo 45s $8-10 each*

**45s**

| Title | Yr | Label, Number | NM $ |
|---|---|---|---|
| HANKY PANKY | 1963 | Snap 102 | 40 |
| *(White promo label)* | | | |
| HANKY PANKY | 1966 | Red Fox 110 | 40 |
| *(White promo label)* | | | |

| Title | Yr | Label, Number | NM $ |
|---|---|---|---|
| **JAMES, VINNIE** | | | |
| **RADIO SHOWS** | | | |
| **Albums** | | | |
| OFF THE RECORD Music and interviews | 1991 | Westwood One (2) | 10-20 |
| *(With Billy Falcon)* | | | |
| | | | |
| **JAN AND DEAN** | | | |
| *Includes listings by Jan & Arnie, Jan, Rally Packs, Laughing Gravy, Legendary Masked Surfers, and Mike Love & Dean Torrence; Other Liberty promo 45s $18 each; Liberty promo LPs $25-40 each depending on year* | | | |
| **45s** | | | |
| BABY TALK  Jan & Arnie | 1959 | Dore 522 | 500 |
| *(Is actually Jan & Dean)* | | | |
| BABY TALK  White promo label | 1959 | Dore 522 | 75 |
| *(Correctly lists Jan & Dean as the artist)* | | | |
| BLUE MOON SHUFFLE  Jan Berry | 1973 | Ode 66034 | 15 |
| *(Same song on both sides)* | | | |
| CINDY | 1960 | Dore 548 | 35 |
| *(White promo label)* | | | |
| CLEMENTINE | 1960 | Dore 539 | 40 |
| *(White promo label)* | | | |
| DA DOO RON RON  Mike Love & Dean Torrence | 1982 | Hitbound 101 | 10 |
| *(White promo label, promo-only release)* | | | |
| DEAD MAN'S CURVE | 1972 | United Artists 092 | 25 |
| *(Yellow promo label, promo-only release on UA)* | | | |
| DON'T YOU JUST KNOW IT  Jan | 1973 | Ode 66034 | 50 |
| *(Rare promo copy features Brian Wilson, flip side is "Blue Moon Shuffle")* | | | |
| FUN CITY | 1975 | Ode 66111 | 15 |
| *(Artist is Jan Berry, not Dean)* | | | |
| GAS MONEY Jan & Arnie | 1958 | Arwin 111 | 75 |
| *(Rare pink promo label)* | | | |
| GAS MONEY  Jan & Arnie | 1960 | Dot 16116 | 75 |
| *(Rare white or blue promo label)* | | | |
| GEE | 1960 | Dore 576 | 25 |
| *(White label, stock picture sleeve worth $200)* | | | |
| GIRL, YOU'RE BLOWING MY MIND | 1968 | Warner Bros. 7240 | 75 |
| *(White promo label, promo-only release)* | | | |
| GONNA HUSTLE YOU  The Legendary Masked Surfers | 1972 | United Artists 50958 | 25 |
| *(Yellow promo label; is actually Dean with Bruce Johnson and Terry Melcher)* | | | |
| HEART AND SOUL | 1961 | Challenge 9111 | 50 |
| *(White promo label)* | | | |
| I KNOW MY MIND | 1968 | Warner Bros. 7219 | 25 |
| *(White promo label)* | | | |
| I LOVE LINDA  Jan & Arnie | 1958 | Arwin 113 | 75 |
| *(White promo label)* | | | |
| JENNIE LEE  Jan & Arnie | 1957 | Arwin 108 | 100 |
| *(Rare pink promo label)* | | | |
| JENNY LEE | 1972 | United Artists 50859 | 20 |
| *(Stock picture sleeve is worth $25)* | | | |
| LITTLE QUEENIE  Jan Berry | 1977 | A&M 1957 | 12 |
| *(Stereo/mono versions)* | | | |
| LOVE AND HATE | 1967 | Warner Bros. 7151 | 25 |
| *(White promo label)* | | | |
| MOTHER EARTH  Jan Berry | 1973 | Ode 66023 | 15 |
| *(Flip is "Blue Moon Shuffle")* | | | |
| MOVE OUT, LITTLE MUSTANG  The Rally Packs | 1964 | Imperial 66036 | 30 |
| *(White promo label, Jan & Dean on backing vocals)* | | | |
| MY FAVORITE DREAM | 1962 | Liberty 55496 | 50 |
| *(Cream-colored promo, hard title to find)* | | | |
| OCEAN PARK ANGEL/WIPE OUT | 1981 | J&D 1271 | 10 |
| *(B-side by the Surfaris)* | | | |
| SHE'S STILL TALKING BABY TALK | 1962 | Liberty 55522 | 40 |
| *(Cream-colored promo, hard title to find)* | | | |
| SIDEWALK SURFIN' | 1976 | United Artists 670 | 15 |
| *(Yellow promo label)* | | | |
| SING SANG A SONG  Jan Berry | 1976 | Ode 66120 | 15 |
| *(Produced by Jim Pewter)* | | | |
| SKATEBOARD SURFIN' U.S.A.  Jan Berry | 1978 | A&M 2020 | 12 |
| *(Stereo/mono versions)* | | | |
| SOMETHING A LITTLE BIT DIFFERENT | 1961 | Challenge 9120 | 40 |
| *(White promo label)* | | | |
| SUMMER MEANS FUN The Legendary Masked Surfers | 1973 | United Artists 270 | 20 |
| *(Yellow promo label)* | | | |
| THERE'S A GIRL White promo label | 1959 | Dore 531 | 50 |
| *(Written and produced by Herb Alpert)* | | | |
| TINSEL TOWN  1 Jan 1 | 1973 | Ode 66050 | 15 |
| *(Flip is "Blow Up Music")* | | | |
| UNIVERSAL COWARD Jan Berry | 1966 | Liberty 55845 | 25 |
| *(Stock copy picture sleeve is worth $100)* | | | |
| VEGETABLES Laughing Gravy | 1967 | White Whale 261 | 100 |
| *(Is actually Dean, blue promo label)* | | | |
| WE GO TOGETHER | 1960 | Dore 555 | 30 |
| *(White label, stock picture sleeve worth $75)* | | | |
| YELLOW BALLOON | 1967 | Columbia 44036 | 40 |
| *(White promo label)* | | | |

| Title | Yr | Label, Number | NM $ |
|-------|-----|---------------|------|
| **7-Inch Extended Plays** | | | |
| COCA-COLA  Radio ads | 1965 | Coca-Cola | 200 |
| *(Cuts by Jan & Dean, Shirelles, Roy Orbison and Four Seasons)* | | | |
| **Albums** | | | |
| JAN & DEAN SWING THE JINGLE  Five radio ads | 1965 | Coca-Cola | 500 |
| *(Issued by Coca-Cola with a picture cover)* | | | |
| SAVE FOR A RAINY DAY  White promo label | 1967 | Columbia 9461 | 750 |
| *(Only known to exist as test pressings)* | | | |
| **RADIO SHOWS** | | | |
| **Albums** | | | |
| THE BEACH YEARS | 1976 | Rock Shoppe (6) | 50-125 |
| *(With Jan & Dean, Dick Dale, Surfaris and others)* | | | |
| 4TH OF JULY SUMMER BEACH PARTY (June 84) | 1984 | United Stations (3) | 25-50 |
| *(Box set includes music of the Beach Boys, Jan & Dean, Motels and others)* | | | |
| **JANE'S ADDICTION** | | | |
| *Other Warner Bros. promo CD singles $6-8 each* | | | |
| **Albums** | | | |
| WORDS AND MUSIC | 1988 | Warner Bros. PRO-A-3369 | 40 |
| *(Promo-only interview album)* | | | |
| **Compact Discs** | | | |
| BEEN CAUGHT STEALING | 1989 | Warner Bros. PRO-CD-4039 | 20 |
| *(Promo CD single in cloth package with miniature handcuffs attached)* | | | |
| **RADIO SHOWS** | | | |
| **Compact Discs** | | | |
| ON THE EDGE (Sept 93) Music and interviews | 1993 | | 20-35 |
| *(Featuring Perry Farrell, with the Verve and Smashing Pumpkins)* | | | |
| **JANO, JOHNNY** | | | |
| **45s** | | | |
| HAVING A WHOLE LOT OF FUN | 1958 | Excello 2099 | 45 |
| *(White promo label)* | | | |
| **JAPAN** | | | |
| **12-Inch Singles** | | | |
| LIFE IN JAPAN (Long)/(Short) | 1979 | Ariola America PRO 7756 | 10 |
| SOMETIMES I FEEL SO LOW (same on both sides) | 1978 | Ariola America PRO 7727 | 20 |
| **JARREAU, AL** | | | |
| **45s** | | | |
| CHRISTMAS SONG, THE | 1982 | Warner Bros. PRA | 12 |
| *(Green label, promo only, 4:13 version with Al Jarreau greeting, includes picture sleeve)* | | | |
| **JARRETT, KEITH** | | | |
| **12-Inch Singles** | | | |
| COUNTRY/MY SONG | 1978 | ECM PRO-A-768 | 10 |
| FLYING PART 1 AND 2/PRISM | 1984 | ECM PRO-A-2186 | 6 |
| GOD BLESS THE CHILD (Edit)/THE MASQUERADE IS OVER | 1983 | ECM PRO-A-2072 | 6 |
| MON COEUR EST ROUGE (2 versions)/HEARTLAND | 1982 | ECM PRO-A-1088 | 8 |
| **JARVIS, FELTON** | | | |
| **45s** | | | |
| SWINGIN' CAT | 195? | Thunder 1023 | 40 |
| *(Gray promo label)* | | | |
| **JASON AND THE SCORCHERS** | | | |
| *EMI promo 45s $3 each; A&M promo CD singles $2 each* | | | |
| **RADIO SHOWS** | | | |
| **Albums** | | | |
| IN CONCERT (May 85) Live concert | 1985 | Westwood One (2) | 20-35 |
| *(With Howard Jones)* | | | |
| KING BISCUIT FLOWER HOUR (Apr 84) Live concert | 1984 | DIR/ABC (2) | 75-125 |
| *(With Al Yankovic)* | | | |
| KING BISCUIT FLOWER HOUR (Mar 87) Live concert | 1987 | DIR (2) | 40-75 |
| *(With Dave Edmunds)* | | | |
| **JAYTONES, THE** | | | |
| **45s** | | | |
| THE CLOCK | 1958 | Brunswick 55087 | 50 |
| *(Yellow promo label)* | | | |
| **JEFFERSON AIRPLANE/STARSHIP** | | | |
| *Includes listings of Grace Slick, Mickey Thomas, Paul Kantner, Marty Balin, The Great Society; Other RCA Victor white promo label 45s $12 each; other RCA Victor yellow promo label 45s $10 each; Other RCA Victor and Grunt black label promo 45s $4 each; RCA Victor promo 45s by Paul Kantner, Mickey Thomas or Grace Slick $3 each; MCA promo 45s by Mickey Thomas $3 each; EMI promo 45s by Marty Balin $3 each; Grunt/RCA Victor promo 12" Starship singles $8 each.* | | | |
| **45s** | | | |
| BALLAD OF YOU & ME & POONEIL  Jefferson Airplane | 1967 | RCA Victor 9297 | 15 |
| *(White promo label)* | | | |
| BLUES FROM AN AIRPLANE  Jefferson Airplane | 1966 | RCA Victor 8848 | 20 |
| *(White promo label)* | | | |
| BRINGING ME DOWN  Jefferson Airplane | 1966 | RCA Victor 8967 | 20 |
| *(White promo label)* | | | |

| **Title** | **Yr** | **Label, Number** | **NM $** |
|---|---|---|---|
| A CHILD IS COMING Paul Kantner and Jefferson Starship | 1971 | RCA Victor 0426 | 15 |
| *(Yellow promo label)* | | | |
| CROWN OF CREATION  Jefferson Airplane | 1970 | RCA Victor 9644 | 12 |
| *(Yellow promo label)* | | | |
| IT'S NO SECRET  Jefferson Airplane | 1966 | RCA Victor 8769 | 25 |
| *(White promo label)* | | | |
| LIGHT THE SKY ON FIRE  Jefferson Starship, black promo label | 1978 | Grunt 11426 | 12 |
| *(Included in price is a promo-only picture sleeve)* | | | |
| LONG JOHN SILVER  Jefferson Airplane, black promo label | 1972 | Grunt SP-45-357 | 15 |
| *(This promo-only version was issued with a stock picture sleeve that is not included in the price)* | | | |
| MY BEST FRIEND Jefferson Airplane | 1967 | RCA Victor 9063 | 18 |
| *(White promo label)* | | | |
| RUNAWAY (Long)/(Short)  Jefferson Starship | 1978 | Grunt JB-11274 | 10 |
| *(With promo-only picture sleeve, similar to stock copy but lists only one song)* | | | |
| SALLY GO 'ROUND THE ROSES  The Great Society | 1968 | Columbia 44583 | 25 |
| *(With Grace Slick, white promo label)* | | | |
| SARA  Starship, black label, blue vinyl | 1985 | RCA Victor 14253 | 15 |
| *(Some stock copies also are on blue vinyl.)* | | | |
| SOMEBODY TO LOVE  Jefferson Airplane | 1967 | RCA Victor 9140 | 25 |
| *(White promo label)* | | | |
| SOMEONE TO LOVE  The Great Society | 1966 | North Beach 1001 | 250 |
| *(Designed to be serviced to radio stations. Early version of a song later recorded by Jefferson Airplane as "Somebody to Love.")* | | | |
| VOLUNTEERS  Jefferson Airplane | 1970 | RCA Victor 0245 | 10 |
| *(Yellow promo label)* | | | |
| WHAT'S IT ALL ABOUT (Aug 80) Public service show | 1980 | W.I.A.A. 537 | 25 |
| *(Features Grace Slick, flip side is Heart)* | | | |
| WHITE RABBIT  Jefferson Airplane | 1967 | RCA Victor 9348 | 25 |
| *(White promo label)* | | | |
| WHITE RABBIT  Jefferson Airplane, black promo label, white vinyl | 1977 | Grunt 10988 | 25 |
| *(Only the promo is white vinyl)* | | | |
| **7-Inch Extended Plays** | | | |
| LEVI'S RADIO COMMERCIAL | 196? | Levi Strauss & Co. | 500 |
| *(Very rare record of ads for the jeans)* | | | |
| **Albums** | | | |
| BLOWS AGAINST THE EMPIRE | 1970 | RCA Victor 4448 | 80 |
| *(Special promo release, clear vinyl release for DJs)* | | | |
| **Compact Discs** | | | |
| JEFFERSON AIRPLANE LOVES YOU | 1992 | RCA RDJ-66113-2 | 15 |
| *(Promo CD sampler, regular silver disc)* | | | |
| JEFFERSON AIRPLANE LOVES YOU | 1992 | RCA RDJ-66113-2 | 20 |
| *(Promo CD sampler, colored disc)* | | | |
| **RADIO SHOWS** | | | |
| **Albums** | | | |
| INNERVIEW (70s) Jefferson Airplane | 197? | Innerview | 10-15 |
| *(Music and interviews, several repeats)* | | | |
| KING BISCUIT FLOWER HOUR (June 81) Jefferson Starship | 1981 | DIR/ABC (2) | 50-75 |
| *(Live concert with Gary U. S. Bonds)* | | | |
| LEGENDS OF ROCK Jefferson Airplane | 1987 | NBC Radio (2) | 20-35 |
| *(Music and interviews)* | | | |
| MELLO YELLO CONCERT | 1981 | DIR/ABC (3) | 40-80 |
| *(Rare concert)* | | | |
| OFF THE RECORD (80s) Jefferson Starship | 198? | Westwood One (2) | 15-25 |
| *(Music and interviews)* | | | |
| OFF THE RECORD (Oct 81) Jefferson Starship | 1981 | Westwood One (3) | 20-40 |
| *(Music and interviews)* | | | |
| PROFILES IN ROCK (Mar 80) Jefferson Airplane | 1980 | Watermark | 15-25 |
| *(Music and interviews)* | | | |
| RETRO ROCK  Jefferson Starship | 1982 | Clayton Webster (2) | 30-50 |
| *(Some live material)* | | | |
| SOURCE SPECIAL  Live concert | 1981 | NBC Source (3) | 40-60 |
| *(Rare live concert)* | | | |
| SUPERGROUPS  Jefferson Starship | 1983 | DIR (2) | 50-100 |
| *(Live concert with Missing Persons)* | | | |
| SUPERSTAR CONCERT (Mar 86) Starship | 1986 | Westwood One (2) | 20-35 |
| *(Live concert)* | | | |
| **Compact Discs** | | | |
| IN THE STUDIO (90s) Profile of an album | 199? | Album Network | 10-20 |
| *(Music and interviews)* | | | |
| KING BISCUIT FLOWER HOUR (Oct 89) Starship/Airplane | 1989 | DIR | 40-75 |
| *(Live concert, several repeats)* | | | |
| ROCK STARS (Sept 89) Jefferson Starship | 1989 | Radio International (2) | 20-30 |
| *(Music and interviews)* | | | |
| UP CLOSE  Profile of Starship/Airplane | 1989 | Media America (2) | 25-45 |
| *(Music and interviews)* | | | |

## JEFFREYS, GARLAND

| **12-Inch Singles** | | | |
|---|---|---|---|
| MODERN LOVERS/R.O.C.K./GHOST OF A CHANCE | 1981 | Epic AS 962 | 10 |
| **45s** | | | |
| INTERVIEW WITH GARLAND JEFFREYS | 1981 | Epic AE7 1225 | 8 |
| **7-Inch Extended Plays** | | | |
| GARLAND JEFFREYS | 1981 | Epic AE7 1223 | 10 |
| *(Promo-only sampler)* | | | |
| WAYS OF ESCAPE | 1981 | Epic AE7 1225 | 10 |
| *(Promo-only sampler)* | | | |

| Title | Yr | Label, Number | NM $ |
|---|---|---|---|
| **RADIO SHOWS** | | | |
| **Albums** | | | |
| KING BISCUIT FLOWER HOUR (Oct 81) Live concert | 1981 | DIR/ABC (2) | 40-75 |
| *(With Gary U. S. Bonds)* | | | |
| | | | |
| **JEJEUNE & THE JAYBOPS** | | | |
| **45s** | | | |
| THUNDERIN' GUITAR  Red vinyl | 195? | Zero 3279 | 150 |
| *(100 copies pressed on Minnesota label)* | | | |
| | | | |
| **JELLYFISH** | | | |
| *Other Charisma promo CD singles $3 each* | | | |
| **Compact Discs** | | | |
| BABY'S COMING BACK | 1990 | Charisma PRCD 008 | 8 |
| *(Promo-only CD single, the closest thing this band had to a U.S. hit)* | | | |
| THAT IS WHY | 1990 | Charisma PRCD 019 | 20 |
| *(Promo-only CD single in "Aqua Pak")* | | | |
| **RADIO SHOWS** | | | |
| **Compact Discs** | | | |
| IN CONCERT-NU ROCK (July 93) | 1993 | Westwood One | 40-80 |
| *(Live concert)* | | | |
| ON THE EDGE (Apr 93) Music and interviews | 1993 | Westwood One | 20-30 |
| *(With Living Colour)* | | | |
| | | | |
| **JENNINGS, WAYLON** | | | |
| *Other RCA Victor promo 45s $3 each; Other RCA Victor colored vinyl promo 45s $8 each; Other MCA promo 45s $2 each; Other MCA colored vinyl promo 45s $7 each* | | | |
| **45s** | | | |
| AMANDA  Blue label, blue vinyl | 1979 | RCA 11596 | 20 |
| *(Stereo/mono versions, only the promo is blue vinyl)* | | | |
| AMERICA  Silver label, blue vinyl | 1984 | RCA 13908 | 15 |
| *(Long/short versions 3:43/3:25, only promo is blue vinyl)* | | | |
| THE DOCK OF THE BAY  Green label, red vinyl | 1982 | RCA 13319 | 15 |
| *(Waylon and Willie Nelson)* | | | |
| FALLIN' OUT  White label, yellow vinyl | 1987 | MCA 53088 | 10 |
| *(Only the promo version is yellow vinyl)* | | | |
| FOUR STRONG WINDS  White promo label | 1964 | A&M 739 | 25 |
| *(Produced by Herb Alpert)* | | | |
| I'LL BE ALRIGHT  Orange label, yellow vinyl | 1981 | RCA 12245 | 12 |
| *("Wild Side of Life" on flip side)* | | | |
| JOLE BLON  Yellow promo label | 1959 | Brunswick 55130 | 200 |
| *(Buddy Holly on guitar, Waylon was a member of the touring Crickets)* | | | |
| JUST TO SATISFY YOU  Silver label, blue vinyl | 1982 | RCA 13073 | 15 |
| *(Waylon and Willie Nelson)* | | | |
| LIVING LEGENDS  Red label, green vinyl | 1983 | RCA 13543 | 12 |
| *(Only the promo version is red vinyl)* | | | |
| LUCKENBACH, TEXAS  White label, "RCA" in script print | 1977 | RCA 10924 | 15 |
| *(Very limited and unusual promo from RCA)* | | | |
| MY BABY WALKS ALL OVER ME  Striped promo label | 1966 | Ramco 1989 | 25 |
| *("Never Again" on flip side)* | | | |
| MY WORLD  Striped promo label | 1967 | Ramco 1997 | 25 |
| *(Both sides are the same)* | | | |
| NEVER AGAIN | 1964 | Trend 102 | 35 |
| *(White/yellow promo label)* | | | |
| RAVE ON  White promo label | 1964 | A&M 722 | 25 |
| *(Produced by Herb Alpert)* | | | |
| ROSE IN PARADISE  White label, red vinyl | 1987 | MCA 53009 | 12 |
| *(Only the promo version is red vinyl)* | | | |
| THE STAGE | 1964 | Trend 106 | 25 |
| *(White/yellow promo label)* | | | |
| WALTZ ME TO HEAVEN  Yellow label, yellow vinyl | 1984 | RCA 13984 | 12 |
| *(Same on both sides)* | | | |
| WHAT'S IT ALL ABOUT (Jan/Feb 84) Public service show | 1984 | W.I.A.A. 214 | 25 |
| *(Flip side features Don McLean)* | | | |
| WHAT'S IT ALL ABOUT (Oct 75) Public service show | 1975 | W.I.A.A. 288 | 18 |
| *(Flip side is the Dirt Band)* | | | |
| WHAT'S IT ALL ABOUT (Nov 82) Public service show | 1982 | W.I.A.A. 649 | 15 |
| *(Flip side is Roy Clark)* | | | |
| WILL THE WOLF SURVIVE  White label, yellow vinyl | 1986 | MCA 52830 | 10 |
| *(Only the promo version is yellow vinyl)* | | | |
| WORKING WITHOUT A NET  Red label, red vinyl | 1983 | RCA 13580 | 12 |
| *(Waylon and Jerry Reed)* | | | |
| WORKING WITHOUT A NET  White label, blue vinyl | 1986 | MCA 52776 | 10 |
| *(Only the promo version is blue vinyl)* | | | |
| **Albums** | | | |
| DON'T THINK TWICE  Produced by Herb Alpert | 1969 | A&M 4238 | 40 |
| *(White promo label)* | | | |
| GET INTO WAYLON JENNINGS  White promo label | 1972 | RCA Victor SPS 570 | 50 |
| *(Promo-only sampler sent to radio stations)* | | | |
| WAYLON & WILLIE  Promo label, gold vinyl | 1978 | RCA Victor 2686 | 40 |
| *(Only the promo is gold vinyl)* | | | |
| **RADIO SHOWS** | | | |
| **Albums** | | | |
| AMERICAN EAGLE | 1984 | DIR (3) | 50-75 |
| *(Live concert)* | | | |
| WAYLON & WILLIE | 198? | Mutual Radio (3) | 20-30 |
| *(Music and interviews)* | | | |

(Top left) The Jordanaires, best known as Elvis Presley's backing vocalists, were a gospel group when they weren't singing backup for someone. Here's a "Country Music Time" radio show from the U.S. Air Force Recruiting Service. (Top right) A radio show from about the time of Kansas' live double album of the same name; despite the 1976 copyright date on the label, this show aired in 1978. (Middle row) These two Kinks shows, both from 1987, illustrate the change in distribution of the King Biscuit Flower Hour from records to compact discs. KBFH shows usually were sent to radio stations in generic sleeves, which is why the labels are illustrated. (Bottom left) A white-label promo of *Arthur* by the Kinks lists the playing times of each track left of the center hole. Stock copies omitted this detail. (Bottom right) A Best of the Biscuit program featuring both a post-makeup Kiss and a pre-"Smokin' in the Boys' Room" Motley Crue is highly sought after by fans of both groups.

| **Title** | **Yr** | **Label, Number** | **NM $** |
|---|---|---|---|
| **JERRY AND THE LANDSLIDERS** | | | |
| **45s** | | | |
| GET OFF MY ROOF/WHITE CHRISTMAS | 197? | Holiday 1026 | 12 |
| *(B-side by the Statues)* | | | |
| | | | |
| **JESUS AND MARY CHAIN, THE** | | | |
| *Def American/American promo CD singles $2-4 each* | | | |
| **12-Inch Singles** | | | |
| BLUES FROM A GUN (same on both sides) | 1989 | Warner Bros. PRO-A-3750 | 12 |
| HAPPY WHEN IT RAINS (same on both sides) | 1987 | Warner Bros. PRO-A-2857 | 8 |
| REVERENCE (4 versions) | 1992 | Def American PRO-A-5340 | 15 |
| **Compact Discs** | | | |
| 7 YEARS ON THE LEADING EDGE/10 SMASH HITS | 1992 | Def American PRO-CD-5336 | 25 |
| *(Promo-only 2-CD set; the other CD contains "Reverence")* | | | |
| **RADIO SHOWS** | | | |
| **Albums** | | | |
| SPIN CONCERT  Live concert | 1987 | Spin Magazine (2) | 50-75 |
| *(Rare live concert)* | | | |
| **Compact Discs** | | | |
| IN CONCERT-NU ROCK (Mar 95) | 1995 | Westwood One | 35-65 |
| *(Live concert)* | | | |
| ON THE EDGE (Sept 94) Music and interviews | 1994 | Westwood One | 10-20 |
| *(With Sam Phillips and Killing Joke)* | | | |
| | | | |
| **JESUS JONES** | | | |
| *Other SBK promo CD singles $2-4 each* | | | |
| **Albums** | | | |
| A CONVERSATION WITH JESUS | 1990 | SBK 05348 | 20 |
| *(Generic cover with sticker)* | | | |
| **Compact Discs** | | | |
| A PERVERSE CONVERSATION WITH JESUS JONES | 1993 | SBK DPRO-04704 | 15 |
| *(Promo-only release)* | | | |
| REAL REAL REAL | 1991 | SBK DPRO-05402 | 8 |
| *(Promo CD single of their second-biggest U.S. hit)* | | | |
| REAL REAL REAL | 1991 | SBK DPRO-05405 | 8 |
| *(Promo CD single of their second-biggest U.S. hit, different mixes)* | | | |
| RIGHT HERE, RIGHT NOW | 1991 | SBK DPRO-05376 | 8 |
| *(Promo CD single of their biggest U.S. hit)* | | | |
| RIGHT HERE, RIGHT NOW | 1991 | SBK DPRO-05387 | 8 |
| *(Another promo CD single of their biggest U.S. hit, different mixes)* | | | |
| **RADIO SHOWS** | | | |
| **Albums** | | | |
| BBC TRANSCRIPTION DISC  Live concert | 1991 | BBC Transcription | 300-450 |
| *(Very rare series)* | | | |
| SPIN CONCERT  Live concert | 1986 | Spin Magazine | 100-175 |
| *(Rare concert)* | | | |
| | | | |
| **JETHRO TULL** | | | |
| *Other Reprise promo 45s $8 each; Chrysalis green promo label 45s $6 each; Chrysalis white promo label 45s $4 each; Chrysalis promo 12" singles $12 each; Chrysalis or Reprise promo LPs $20 each* | | | |
| **12-Inch Singles** | | | |
| RING OUT, SOLSTICE BELLS White promo label | 1976 | Chrysalis CHS 3 PDJ | 25 |
| *(12" promo-only EP with three other songs)* | | | |
| **45s** | | | |
| BUNGLE IN THE JUNGLE  Green promo label | 1974 | Chrysalis 2101 | 20 |
| *(Price includes a stock picture sleeve that was issued with some promos)* | | | |
| LIVING IN THE PAST/DRIVING SONG | 1969 | Reprise 0845 | 20 |
| *(May be white label promo only)* | | | |
| LOVE STORY/SONG FOR JEFFREY | 1969 | Reprise 0815 | 15 |
| *(Their first single, may be promo only)* | | | |
| REASONS FOR WAITING  White promo label | 1969 | Reprise 0886 | 15 |
| *(Stock copy for Reprise 0886 has different A side)* | | | |
| TEACHER | 1970 | Reprise 0899 | 10 |
| *(White promo label)* | | | |
| WHAT'S IT ALL ABOUT (Jan 80) Public service show | 1980 | W.I.A.A. 506 | 18 |
| *(Flip side is Robert Palmer)* | | | |
| WHAT'S IT ALL ABOUT (May 81) Public service show | 1981 | W.I.A.A. 578 | 20 |
| *(Flip side by the Police)* | | | |
| **7-Inch Extended Plays** | | | |
| AQUALUNG  Jukebox LLP | 1971 | Chrysalis 1044 (LLP 242) | 40 |
| *(Issued with a paper sleeve)* | | | |
| STAND UP  Radio spots | 1969 | Reprise PRO-353 | 50 |
| *(Released for radio only)* | | | |
| **Albums** | | | |
| THE JETHRO TULL RADIO SHOW | 1975 | Chrysalis PRO 623 | 50 |
| A PASSION PLAY | 1973 | Chrysalis 1040 | 25 |
| *(Banded version for airplay)* | | | |
| THICK AS A BRICK | 1972 | Reprise 2072 | 30 |
| *(Banded version for airplay)* | | | |
| **Compact Discs** | | | |
| ANOTHER CHRISTMAS SONG | 1989 | Chrysalis DPRO 23471 | 20 |
| *(Promo-only 4-track CD)* | | | |

| Title | Yr | Label, Number | NM $ |
|---|---|---|---|
| **RADIO SHOWS** | | | |
| **Albums** | | | |
| ALLISON STEELE (70s) Profile of Ian Anderson | 197? | | 25-40 |
| *(Music and interviews)* | | | |
| BBC LONDON WAVELENGTH (June 82) Profile | 1982 | London Wavelength | 25-40 |
| *(The Broadsword and the Beast Special)* | | | |
| BBC ROCK HOUR | 1982 | London Wavelength (2) | 20-30 |
| *(Music and interviews)* | | | |
| BBC ROCK HOUR (Dec 84) Live concert | 1984 | London Wavelength | 75-125 |
| *(Rare live tracks from the BBC)* | | | |
| BBC TRANSCRIPTION DISC Live concert | 1984 | BBC Transcription | 300-400 |
| *(Very rare live concert)* | | | |
| CAPTURED LIVE (Jan 83) Live concert | 1983 | RKO | 75-150 |
| *(Rare live concert)* | | | |
| IN CONCERT (Sept 91) Live concert | 1991 | Westwood One (2) | 50-80 |
| *(With Procol Harum)* | | | |
| KING BISCUIT FLOWER HOUR (Dec 84) Live concert | 1984 | DIR/ABC (2) | 75-150 |
| *(Rare live concert)* | | | |
| LEGENDS OF ROCK (Nov 87) Profile | 1987 | NBC Radio (2) | 20-30 |
| *(Music and interviews)* | | | |
| LEGENDS OF ROCK (Nov 87) Profile | 1987 | NBC Radio (4) | 30-50 |
| *(Music and interviews)* | | | |
| LONDON WAVELENGTH (Oct 84) HITLINE | 1984 | London Wavelength | 20-30 |
| *(Music and interview)* | | | |
| A NIGHT ON THE ROAD (June 81) Box set | 1981 | ABC Radio (3) | 75-150 |
| *(Mostly music and interviews)* | | | |
| PIONEERS IN ROCK (Jan 86) | 1986 | DIR (2) | 20-40 |
| *(Some live tracks from various concerts)* | | | |
| TOYOTA PRESENTS (70s) Profile of Ian Anderson | 197? | Toyota (2) | 20-30 |
| *(Music and interviews)* | | | |
| WORLD OF ROCK (Dec 89) Various artists | 1989 | DIR (2) | 20-35 |
| *(Ian Anderson is co-host of this show)* | | | |
| **Compact Discs** | | | |
| BBC CLASSIC TRACKS (Aug 93) | 1993 | Westwood One | 20-40 |
| *(Mostly live tracks)* | | | |
| BBC CLASSIC TRACKS (Mar 91) | 1991 | Westwood One | 30-60 |
| *(Mostly rare live tracks)* | | | |
| CLASSIC CD (Nov 90) | 1990 | Westwood One (2) | 50-75 |
| *(Mostly live tracks)* | | | |
| IN CONCERT (Feb 93) Live concert | 1993 | Westwood One (2) | 50-75 |
| *(Live recent material)* | | | |
| IN CONCERT (Feb 94) Live concert | 1994 | Westwood One (2) | 45-60 |
| *(In concert with SLAB)* | | | |
| IN THE STUDIO (Dec 89) Profile of an album | 1989 | Album Network | 20-40 |
| *(Music from, and interviews about, "Benefit")* | | | |
| IN THE STUDIO (Dec 91) Profile of an album | 1991 | Album Network | 20-40 |
| *(Music from, and interviews about, "Thick as a Brick")* | | | |
| IN THE STUDIO (May 91) Profile of an album | 1991 | Album Network | 20-40 |
| *(Music from, and interviews about, "Aqualung")* | | | |
| KING BISCUIT FLOWER HOUR (Jan 88) Live concert | 1988 | DIR | 50-100 |
| *(Rare KBFH silver CD)* | | | |
| KING BISCUIT FLOWER HOUR (May 88) | 1988 | DIR | 40-75 |
| *(Live concert)* | | | |
| KING BISCUIT FLOWER HOUR (Jan 91) Live concert | 1991 | DIR | 20-40 |
| *(With King's X)* | | | |
| KING BISCUIT FLOWER HOUR (Mar 91) Live concert | 1991 | DIR | 40-75 |
| *(With Procol Harum)* | | | |
| KING BISCUIT FLOWER HOUR (Sept 94) | 1994 | DIR | 30-50 |
| *(Live concert)* | | | |
| MASTERS OF ROCK (June 89) | 1989 | Radio Ventures (2) | 20-30 |
| *(Music and interviews)* | | | |
| ROCK STARS (Dec 89) Profile | 1989 | Radio Today (2) | 25-50 |
| *(Music and interviews)* | | | |
| ROCK STARS (Nov 87) Profile | 1987 | Radio Today (2) | 25-50 |
| *(Music and interviews)* | | | |
| THE STORY OF JETHRO TULL (Oct 91) Profile | 1991 | Unistar (3) | 40-75 |
| *(Music and interviews)* | | | |
| UP CLOSE  Profile | 1990 | Media America (2) | 25-50 |
| *(Music and interviews, some live tracks)* | | | |

## JETS, THE

**45s**

| Title | Yr | Label, Number | NM $ |
|---|---|---|---|
| GOT A LITTLE SHADOW | 1954 | Aladdin 3247 | 175 |
| *(White promo label)* | | | |
| HEAVEN ABOVE ME | 1956 | Gee 1020 | 200 |
| *(White promo label)* | | | |

## JETT, JOAN, AND THE BLACKHEARTS

*Member of the Runaways; .Boardwalk promo 45s $4 each; MCA/Blackheart white promo label 45s $3 each; CBS/Blackheart label promo 45s $3 each; Any promo CD single $3-5 each*

**12-Inch Singles**

| Title | Yr | Label, Number | NM $ |
|---|---|---|---|
| CHERRY BOMB | 1985 | MCA L33-1226 | 20 |
| *(Red vinyl, promo-only 12" single)* | | | |
| CRIMSON AND CLOVER (AOR Remix) (same on both sides) | 1982 | Boardwalk 012 | 15 |
| DO YOU WANNA TOUCH ME (OH YEAH)/SUMMERTIME BLUES | 1982 | Boardwalk 019 | 15 |
| DON'T SURRENDER (6:42)/(4:04) | 1991 | Blackheart ZAS 4256 | 12 |
| EVERYDAY PEOPLE (Short)/(Long) | 1983 | MCA L33-1121 | 8 |

| Title | Yr | Label, Number | NM $ |
|-------|-----|---------------|------|
| FAKE FRIENDS (same on both sides) | 1983 | MCA L33-1117 | 10 |
| GOOD MUSIC (3:29)/(5:45) | 1985 | Blackheart ZAS 2517 | 12 |
| I HATE MYSELF FOR LOVING YOU (same on both sides) | 1988 | Blackheart ZAS 1094 | 12 |
| I LOVE YOU LOVE/NEW ORLEANS/LITTLE DRUMMER BOY | 1984 | MCA L33-1247 | 15 |
| LIGHT OF DAY/ROADRUNNER | 1987 | Blackheart BH 007 | 20 |
| LITTLE DRUMMER BOY/VICTIM OF CIRCUMSTANCE | 1981 | Boardwalk 005 | 20 |
| ROADRUNNER/YOU GOT ME FLOATIN'/THIS MEANS WAR | 1986 | Blackheart ZAS 2559 | 20 |

**45s**

| | | | |
|---|---|---|---|
| CONEY ISLAND WHITEFISH  Flexidisc | 1983 | Evatone 83193 (#22) | 10 |
| *(From Trouser Press magazine)* | | | |
| LITTLE DRUMMER BOY | 1981 | Boardwalk NBS-7-006 | 15 |
| *(Same on both sides, promo only)* | | | |

**RADIO SHOWS**

| | | | |
|---|---|---|---|
| INSIDE TRACK (June 83) | 1983 | RKO Radio (2) | 75-125 |
| *(Mick Jagger, David Lee Roth and Joan Jett)* | | | |
| KING BISCUIT FLOWER HOUR (Feb 82) Live concert | 1982 | DIR/ABC (2) | 100-200 |
| *(With The Romantics)* | | | |

## JEWEL

*Atlantic promo CD singles $3-5 each*

**RADIO SHOWS**

**Compact Discs**

| | | | |
|---|---|---|---|
| IN CONCERT - NU ROCK (Nov 96) | 1996 | | 50-80 |
| *(Live concert material)* | | | |

## JIM & ROD

**45s**

| | | | |
|---|---|---|---|
| DIDN'T IT ROCK | 1958 | Challenge 59034 | 50 |
| *(White promo label)* | | | |

## JIVERS, THE

**45s**

| | | | |
|---|---|---|---|
| CHERIE | 1956 | Aladdin 3329 | 100 |
| *(White promo label)* | | | |
| RAY PEARL | 1956 | Aladdin 3347 | 75 |
| *(White promo label)* | | | |

## JO BOXERS

*RCA Victor promo 45s $3 each*

**RADIO SHOWS**

**Albums**

| | | | |
|---|---|---|---|
| BBC TRANSCRIPTION DISC  Live concert | 1983 | BBC Transcription | 100-200 |
| *(Very rare live concert)* | | | |

## JO JO ZEP AND THE FALCONS

**12-Inch Singles**

| | | | |
|---|---|---|---|
| HIT AND RUN/THE SHAPE I'M IN | 1979 | Columbia AS 820 | 12 |
| THE LOSING GAME (3 versions) | 1983 | A&M 17249 | 8 |

## JODIMARS, THE

**45s**

| | | | |
|---|---|---|---|
| CLARABELLA | 1958 | Capitol 3588 | 15 |
| *(White promo label)* | | | |
| CLOUD 99 | 1958 | Capitol 3633 | 15 |
| *(White promo label)* | | | |
| DANCIN' THE BOP | 1957 | Capitol 3360 | 20 |
| *(White promo label)* | | | |
| LET'S ALL ROCK TOGETHER | 1957 | Capitol 3285 | 20 |
| *(White promo label)* | | | |
| ONE GRAIN OF SAND  Marshall and Wes | 1958 | Milestone 107 | 20 |
| *(Audition copy, with the Jodimars)* | | | |
| RATTLE MY BONES | 1957 | Capitol 3436 | 18 |
| *(White promo label)* | | | |
| RATTLE SHAKIN' DADDY | 1958 | Capitol 3512 | 15 |
| *(White promo label)* | | | |

## JOEL, BILLY

*Includes listings for the Hassles; Columbia or Epic white promo label 45s $3 each; Columbia or Epic promo picture sleeves $3 each; Columbia promo 12" singles $8 each; Columbia white promo label LPs $10 each.*

**45s**

| | | | |
|---|---|---|---|
| EVERY STEP I TAKE  The Hassles | 1967 | United Artists 50258 | 18 |
| *(White promo label)* | | | |
| 4 O'CLOCK IN THE MORNING  The Hassles | 1968 | United Artists 50450 | 18 |
| *(White promo label)* | | | |
| NIGHT AFTER DAY  The Hassles | 1968 | United Artists 50513 | 15 |
| *(White promo label)* | | | |
| SHE'S GOT A WAY | 1971 | Family Productions 0900 | 15 |
| *(Dark blue label, stock copy is much scarcer)* | | | |
| TOMORROW IS TODAY | 1971 | Family Productions 0906 | 15 |
| *(Dark blue label, stock copy is much scarcer)* | | | |
| TRAVELING BAND  The Hassles | 1969 | United Artists 50586 | 12 |
| *(White promo label)* | | | |
| WHAT'S IT ALL ABOUT (Oct 81) Public service show | 1981 | W.I.A.A. 600 | 20 |
| *(Flip side is Kenny Loggins)* | | | |

| Title | Yr | Label, Number | NM $ |
|---|---|---|---|
| WHAT'S IT ALL ABOUT (Sept 76) Public service show | 1976 | W.I.A.A. 336 | 25 |
| *(Flip side is Fleetwood Mac)* | | | |
| YOU'VE GOT ME HUMMIN' The Hassles | 1967 | United Artists 50215 | 20 |
| *(White promo label, first record by Joel)* | | | |
| **Albums** | | | |
| BILLY JOEL INTERVIEW | 1982 | Columbia AS-1343 | 20 |
| *(Promo-only release)* | | | |
| INTERCHORDS | 1977 | Columbia | 25 |
| *(Promo only, music and interviews)* | | | |
| SOUVENIR | 1976 | Columbia AS 326 | 20 |
| *(Promo-only LP with one side live, one side a compilation of studio tracks)* | | | |
| **Compact Discs** | | | |
| ALL ABOUT SOUL | 1993 | Columbia CSK 5469 | 8 |
| *(Promo CD single)* | | | |
| ALL SHOOK UP | 1992 | Epic ESK 74422 | 8 |
| *(Promo CD single)* | | | |
| AND SO IT GOES | 1990 | Columbia CSK 73602 | 8 |
| *(Promo CD single)* | | | |
| BACK IN THE U.S.S.R. | 1987 | Columbia CSK 2834 | 8 |
| *(Promo CD single)* | | | |
| DOWNEASTER "ALEXA," THE | 1990 | Columbia CSK 73333 | 8 |
| *(Promo CD single, the first Billy Joel single not to be issued in the U.S. on 45)* | | | |
| HEY GIRL | 1997 | Columbia | 8 |
| *(Promo CD single, not released as a commercial single in U.S.)* | | | |
| I GO TO EXTREMES | 1989 | Columbia CSK 73091 | 8 |
| *(Promo CD single)* | | | |
| LULLABYE | 1993 | Columbia CSK 5631 | 8 |
| *(Promo CD single)* | | | |
| NO MAN'S LAND | 1993 | Columbia CSK 5278 | 8 |
| *(Promo CD single, released commercially as B-side of "River of Dreams")* | | | |
| RIVER OF DREAMS | 1993 | Columbia CSK 5277 | 8 |
| *(Promo CD single)* | | | |
| THAT'S NOT HER STYLE -- THE STORM FRONT TOUR CD | 1990 | Columbia CSK 2127 | 20 |
| *(Promo-only tour CD)* | | | |
| TO MAKE YOU FEEL MY LOVE | 1997 | Columbia | 8 |
| *(Promo CD single)* | | | |
| WE DIDN'T START THE FIRE | 1989 | Columbia CSK 73021 | 12 |
| *(Promo CD single)* | | | |
| **RADIO SHOWS** | | | |
| **Albums** | | | |
| ALLISON STEELE (70s) Profile | 197? | | 20-40 |
| *(Rare music and interview series)* | | | |
| LEGENDS OF ROCK (June 89) Profile | 1989 | NBC Radio (4) | 25-50 |
| *(Part one and two, music and interviews)* | | | |
| LEGENDS OF ROCK (June 89) Profile | 1989 | NBC Radio (2) | 15-25 |
| *(Music and interviews)* | | | |
| NBC SOURCE (Nov 81) | 1981 | NBC Radio (3) | 30-50 |
| *(Music and interviews)* | | | |
| PIONEERS IN MUSIC | 1986 | DIR (2) | 20-40 |
| *(Some live tracks from various concerts)* | | | |
| RETRO ROCK (Jan 83) Live concert | 1983 | Clayton Webster (2) | 100-175 |
| *(Joel live concerts are rare)* | | | |
| ROBERT W. MORGAN | 1981 | Watermark | 25-50 |
| *(Music and interviews, red strip, issued with a title cover)* | | | |
| ROBERT W. MORGAN (Feb 79) | 1979 | Watermark | 20-25 |
| *(Music and interviews)* | | | |
| ROBERT W. MORGAN (Feb 81) | 1981 | Watermark | 15-25 |
| *(Music and interviews, green strip)* | | | |
| ROYALTY OF ROCK  Profile | 1983 | Watermark | 10-15 |
| *(Music and interviews)* | | | |
| STARTRACK PROFILE | 1985 | Westwood One (4) | 25-50 |
| *(Music and interviews)* | | | |
| STORY OF BILLY JOEL (Jan 83) Profile | 1983 | Unistar (2) | 20-40 |
| *(Music and interviews)* | | | |
| STORY OF BILLY JOEL (Mar 86) Profile | 1986 | Unistar (2) | 25-50 |
| *(Music and interviews with some live tracks)* | | | |
| WESTWOOD ONE SPECIAL (Nov 82) | 1982 | Westwood One (2) | 20-35 |
| *(Music and interviews)* | | | |
| **Compact Discs** | | | |
| IN THE STUDIO (Sept 90) Profile of an album | 1990 | Album Network | 15-25 |
| *(Music and interviews)* | | | |
| PIANO MEN (May 94) Profiles | 1994 | Westwood One (3) | 40-75 |
| *(Music and interviews, with Elton John)* | | | |
| UP CLOSE  Profile | 1990 | Media America (2) | 25-40 |
| *(Mostly music and interviews)* | | | |
| UP CLOSE  Profile | 1994 | Media America (2) | 30-60 |
| *(Music and interviews with some live tracks)* | | | |
| | | | |
| **JOHANSEN, DAVID** | | | |
| *Also known as Buster Poindexter; More at New York Dolls; Blue Sky promo 45s $4 each* | | | |
| **12-Inch Singles** | | | |
| HERE COMES THE NIGHT/YOU FOOL YOU/+ 2 | 1981 | Blue Sky AS 972 | 6 |
| SWAHETO WOMAN (Long)/(Short) | 1979 | Blue Sky AS 740 | 15 |
| **Albums** | | | |
| DAVID JOHANSEN GROUP LIVE | 197? | Blue Sky AS 519 | 30 |
| *(Promo-only sampler)* | | | |

| Title | Yr | Label, Number | NM $ |
|-------|-----|---------------|------|
| LIVE AND SAMPLER | 1981 | Blue Sky AS 1281 | 12 |
| *(Promo-only four-song sampler)* | | | |

**RADIO SHOWS**

**Albums**

| | | | |
|-------|-----|---------------|------|
| CONCERT MAGAZINE (July 83) Music and interviews | 1983 | Concert Magazine (2) | 20-40 |

## JOHN, ELTON

*Uni promo 45s $12 each; MCA white promo label 45s $6 each; Geffen white promo label 45s $5 each; Geffen black promo label 45s $4 each; MCA (Rocket) yellow label promo 45 by Elton John and Kiki Dee $5; Geffen black promo label 45 by Elton John and Millie Jackson $3; Columbia promo 45 by Elton John and George Michael $4; Other 12" promo singles $12-15 each*

**12-Inch Singles**

| | | | |
|-------|-----|---------------|------|
| ACT OF WAR (Edit)/(Instrumental) | 1985 | Geffen PRO-A-2324 | 6 |
| *(With Millie Jackson)* | | | |
| BITE YOUR LIP (GET UP AND DANCE) (same on both sides) | 1977 | MCA L33-1172 | 10 |
| CANDLE IN THE WIND (LIVE) (same on both sides) | 1987 | MCA L33-17458 | 6 |
| EMPTY GARDEN (HEY HEY JOHNNY) (Long)/(Short) | 1981 | Geffen PRO-A-1463 | 10 |
| GET UP AND DANCE | 1977 | MCA 1174 | 25 |
| *(Blue vinyl promo-only 12" single)* | | | |
| HEARTACHE ALL OVER THE WORLD (2 edit versions) | 1986 | Geffen PRO-A-2569 | 6 |
| I'M STILL STANDING (same on both sides) | 1983 | Geffen PRO-A-2025 | 8 |
| JOHNNY B. GOODE (same on both sides) | 1979 | MCA L33-1854 | 8 |
| KISS THE BRIDE (LP Version) (Edit) | 1983 | Geffen PRO-A-2066 | 6 |
| NOBODY WINS/NOBODY WINS (French Version) | 1981 | Geffen PRO-A-948 | 12 |
| SAD SONGS (SAY SO MUCH) (same on both sides) | 1984 | Geffen PRO-A-2160 | 6 |
| SASSON PRESENTS ELTON JOHN | 1984 | Geffen PRO-A-2176 | 20 |
| *(One-sided promo with two versions of "Sad Songs (Say So Much)" and an etched facsimile autograph on B-side)* | | | |
| TAKE ME TO THE PILOT (LIVE) (same on both sides) | 1987 | MCA L33-17475 | 6 |
| VICTIM OF LOVE  Four-record box set | 1979 | MCA L33-1848 | 100 |
| *(Promo-only 12" singles in a photo box set and individually numbered)* | | | |
| VICTIM OF LOVE (same on both sides) | 1979 | MCA L33-1850 | 6 |
| WHO WEARS THESE SHOES? (same on both sides) | 1984 | Geffen PRO-A-2188 | 6 |
| WRAP HER UP (same on both sides) | 1985 | Geffen PRO-A-2374 | 6 |

**45s**

| | | | |
|-------|-----|---------------|------|
| BORDER SONG  Red/pink/orange label | 1970 | Congress 6022 | 30 |
| *(Stock copy is much rarer. Uni reissue is much more common.)* | | | |
| EMPTY GARDEN  Gray promo label | 1982 | Geffen 50049 | 12 |
| *(Long/short versions, song is about John Lennon)* | | | |
| FANFARE/CHLOE  Gray promo label | 1981 | Geffen 49788 | 10 |
| *(Long/short versions, including promo-only 6:06 version)* | | | |
| FROM DENVER TO L.A.  White promo label | 1970 | Viking 1010 | 30 |
| *(Same song on both sides, stock copy with instrumental B-side is much rarer)* | | | |
| LADY SAMANTHA  Red/pink/orange label | 1969 | Congress 6017 | 30 |
| *(Flip side is "It's Me that You Need", stock copy is much rarer)* | | | |
| LADY SAMANTHA  White promo label | 1969 | DJM 70008 | 100 |
| *(Flip side is "All Across the Havens", stock copy is much rarer)* | | | |
| LOVE SONG  Yellow promo label | 1976 | MCA 1938 | 25 |
| *(Long/short 5:32/4:40 versions, promo only)* | | | |
| PHILADELPHIA FREEDOM | 1975 | MCA 40364 | 50 |
| *(Picture sleeve from WFIL radio in Philadelphia comprises most of the value)* | | | |
| PINBALL WIZARD  White promo label | 1975 | Polydor PRO-002 | 25 |
| *(Promo-only release, flip side is Tina Turner)* | | | |
| SAD SONGS  Gray promo label | 1984 | Geffen 29292 | 10 |
| *(Special radio mix, unreleased 4:05 version)* | | | |
| SONG FOR GUY/LOVESICK | 1979 | MCA 40993 | 5 |
| *(The only MCA single where the stock copy is harder to find than the promo)* | | | |
| STEP INTO CHRISTMAS  White promo label | 1973 | MCA 65018 | 10 |
| *(Classic Christmas record that is hard to find as a promo)* | | | |
| TINY DANCER/RAZOR FACE | 1971 | Uni 55318 | 10 |
| *(With a severely truncated version of the A-side)* | | | |
| WHAT'S IT ALL ABOUT (Feb 73) Public service show | 1973 | W.I.A.A. 163 | 25 |
| *(Flip side is Don McLean)* | | | |
| WHAT'S IT ALL ABOUT (July 75) Public service show | 1975 | W.I.A.A. 272 | 20 |
| *(Flip side is Bobby Vinton)* | | | |
| WHAT'S IT ALL ABOUT (Mar 79) Public service show | 1979 | W.I.A.A. 467 | 25 |
| *(Flip side is the Spinners)* | | | |
| WHAT'S IT ALL ABOUT (Sept 76) Public service show | 1976 | W.I.A.A. 333 | 18 |
| *(Flip side is Anne Murray)* | | | |

**7-Inch Extended Plays**

| | | | |
|-------|-----|---------------|------|
| DON'T SHOOT ME I'M ONLY THE PIANO PLAYER  Jukebox LLP | 1973 | MCA 349671 (LLP 207) | 30 |
| *(Issued with a paper sleeve)* | | | |
| TUMBLEWEED CONNECTION  Jukebox LLP | 1971 | Uni 1903 (LLP 143) | 35 |
| *(Issued with a paper sleeve)* | | | |

**Albums**

| | | | |
|-------|-----|---------------|------|
| BERNIE TAUPIN AND INTERVIEW | 1987 | RCA 6420 (2) | 25 |
| *(Music and interviews)* | | | |
| BREAKING HEARTS | 1984 | Geffen GHS 24031 | 20 |
| *(Promo pressing on Quiex II vinyl)* | | | |
| CAPTAIN FANTASTIC & THE BROWN DIRT COWBOY | 1975 | MCA 2142 | 50 |
| *(Promo-only picture disc)* | | | |
| CAPTAIN FANTASTIC & THE BROWN DIRT COWBOY | 1975 | MCA 2142 | 300 |
| *(Brown vinyl version, autographed by Elton and Bernie Taupin, promo only)* | | | |
| FRIENDS  Open-end interview | 1971 | Paramount DJ-1 | 100 |
| *(White label promo-only LP)* | | | |
| THE GAMES  Various artists, soundtrack | 1970 | Viking 105 | 100 |
| *(Promo-only release with one Elton John cut)* | | | |
| SINGLE MAN, A  Promo picture disc | 1978 | MCA 1995 | 45 |
| *(Do not confuse with the common stock copy picture disc; msut read "Promotional")* | | | |

| **Title** | **Yr** | **Label, Number** | **NM $** |
|-----------|--------|-------------------|----------|
| **Compact Discs** | | | |
| CAN YOU FEEL THE LOVE TONIGHT | 1994 | Hollywood PRCD 10441 | 20 |
| *(Promo CD single, with "Lion King" cover)* | | | |
| CIRCLE OF LIFE | 1994 | Hollywood PRCD 10480 | 15 |
| *(Promo CD single, with "Lion King" cover)* | | | |
| CLASSIC ELTON JOHN | 1994 | CEMA S2-179?? | 10 |
| *(Special products issue, only available at McDonald's)* | | | |
| CLUB AT THE END OF THE STREET | 1989 | MCA CD-18303 | 10 |
| *(Promo-only CD single)* | | | |
| DON'T GO BREAKIN' MY HEART  With RuPaul | 1994 | MCA 2967 | 8 |
| *(Promo-only CD single)* | | | |
| ELTON JOHN/BERNIE TAUPIN COLLECTION, THE | 1990 | Polygram PIP-CD-002 (2) | 60 |
| *(Promo-only 32-track release)* | | | |
| EXCERPTS FROM "TO BE CONTINUED" | 1990 | MCA 9070 | 30 |
| *(Sampler from out-of-print 4 CD box set)* | | | |
| HEALING HANDS | 1989 | MCA | 8 |
| *(Promo-only CD single)* | | | |
| I DON'T WANNA GO ON WITH YOU LIKE THAT | 1988 | MCA CD-17535 | 20 |
| *(Promo-only CD single)* | | | |
| LAST SONG, THE | 1992 | MCA 2425 | 8 |
| *(Promo-only CD single)* | | | |
| MADMAN ACROSS THE WATER | 1992 | Polydor CDP 819 | 8 |
| *(Promo-only CD single, from "Rare Masters")* | | | |
| ONE, THE | 1992 | MCA 2262 | 8 |
| *(Promo-only CD single)* | | | |
| ONE, THE | 1992 | MCA 2302 | 8 |
| *(Promo-only CD single, different mix)* | | | |
| RUNAWAY TRAIN  With Eric Clapton | 1992 | MCA 2305 | 8 |
| *(Promo-only CD single)* | | | |
| SACRIFICE | 1989 | MCA 18061 | 8 |
| *(Promo-only CD single)* | | | |
| SELECTIONS FROM RARE MASTERS | 1993 | Polydor SACD 535 | 30 |
| *(Promo-only single-CD condensation of double-CD release)* | | | |
| SIMPLE LIFE | 1993 | MCA 2539 | 8 |
| *(Promo-only CD single)* | | | |
| TRUE LOVE  With Kiki Dee | 1994 | MCA 2875 | 8 |
| *(Promo-only CD single)* | | | |
| WORD IN SPANISH, A | 1988 | MCA CD-17640 | 10 |
| *(Promo-only CD single)* | | | |
| YOU GOTTA LOVE SOMEONE | 1990 | MCA 1135 | 8 |
| *(Promo-only CD single)* | | | |
| **RADIO SHOWS** | | | |
| **Albums** | | | |
| ALBUM GREATS | 1979 | TM Special Products | 20-40 |
| *(Only the Elton John discs)* | | | |
| BBC LONDON WAVELENGTH (July 81) | 1981 | London Wavelength | 20-35 |
| *(Music and interview, repeated in 1984)* | | | |
| BBC ROCK HOUR (Dec 80) | 1980 | London Wavelength (2) | 20-30 |
| *(Music and interviews)* | | | |
| BBC ROCK HOUR (Sept 84) | 1984 | London Wavelength (2) | 40-75 |
| *(Live concert)* | | | |
| BBC TRANSCRIPTION DISC  Live concert | 1974 | BBC Transcription (2) | 500-750 |
| *(Part one and part two of a very rare concert)* | | | |
| BBC TRANSCRIPTION DISC  Live concert | 1979 | BBC Transcription (2) | 450-600 |
| *(Repeat of the above)* | | | |
| BBC TRANSCRIPTION DISC  Live concert | 1984 | BBC Transcription (2) | 300-500 |
| *(Another repeat concert)* | | | |
| COUNTDOWN TO CHRISTMAS (Dec 85) | 1985 | NBC Radio | 10-20 |
| *(Music and interviews)* | | | |
| DICK CLARK PRESENTS ELTON JOHN (July 81) Box set | 1981 | Mutual Radio (3) | 50-100 |
| *(Music and interviews)* | | | |
| ELTON JOHN (Aug 90) Solid Gold Scrapbook disc | 1990 | Unistar | 10-15 |
| *(Music and interviews, from a 5-LP box set)* | | | |
| ELTON JOHN SPECIAL (Aug 82) | 1982 | Westwood One (2) | 25-45 |
| *(Music and interviews)* | | | |
| ELTON JOHN STORY (Sept 89) Profile | 1989 | United Stations (2) | 20-30 |
| *(Music and interviews)* | | | |
| HOT ROCKS  Profile | 1988 | United Stations (2) | 20-30 |
| *(Music and interviews)* | | | |
| IN CONCERT  Live concert | 1987 | Westwood One (2) | 40-75 |
| *(BBC concert material)* | | | |
| KING BISCUIT FLOWER HOUR  Live concert | 1985 | DIR/ABC (2) | 30-60 |
| *(Repeated several times)* | | | |
| KING BISCUIT FLOWER HOUR  Parts 1 and 2 | 1987 | DIR (4) | 60-125 |
| *(Live concert)* | | | |
| LEGENDS OF ROCK (Apr 88) Profile | 1988 | NBC Radio (4) | 25-50 |
| *(Music and interviews, parts 1 and 2)* | | | |
| LEGENDS OF ROCK (Apr 88) Profile | 1988 | NBC Radio (2) | 15-25 |
| *(Music and interviews, some live tracks; this show was repeated in 1989)* | | | |
| NBC SOURCE (Dec 82) Live concert | 1982 | NBC Radio (2) | 100-150 |
| *(Rare live concert)* | | | |
| PIONEERS IN MUSIC  Profile of "Piano Men" | 1986 | DIR (2) | 30-50 |
| *(Live tracks from concerts of three piano/singers: Elton John, Joe Jackson and Billy Joel)* | | | |
| POP CONCERT  Live concert | 1986 | Westwood One (2) | 40-60 |
| *(This show was repeated)* | | | |

| **Title** | **Yr** | **Label, Number** | **NM $** |
|---|---|---|---|
| PROFILE OF ELTON JOHN & BERNIE TAUPIN (May 86) | 1986 | United Stations | 10-15 |
| *(Disc from Solid Gold Scrapbook, music and interviews)* | | | |
| SPOTLIGHT SPECIAL (June 83) | 1983 | ABC Radio (2) | 25-50 |
| *(Music and interviews)* | | | |
| STAR SESSION (Sept 82) Green labels | 1982 | ABC Radio (3) | 50-100 |
| *(Rare live concert)* | | | |
| STARTRACK PROFILE | 1986 | Westwood One (2) | 20-40 |
| *(Music and interviews)* | | | |
| STARTRACK PROFILE (Dec 86) | 1986 | Westwood One (2) | 40-60 |
| *(Music, interviews and live tracks)* | | | |
| STARTRACK PROFILE (Dec 86) Three 2-LP sets | 1986 | Westwood One (6) | 125-200 |
| *(Price is for all three sets)* | | | |
| SUPERSTAR CONCERT  Box set, Prince's Trust | 1986 | Westwood One (3) | 40-80 |
| *(Various artists, live concert, repeated)* | | | |
| SUPERSTAR CONCERT  Live concert | 1985 | Westwood One (3) | 30-60 |
| *(Vinyl box set)* | | | |
| WORLD OF ROCK (Mar 90) Various artists | 1990 | DIR (2) | 10-20 |
| *(Music and interviews, Elton John is co-host)* | | | |
| **Compact Discs** | | | |
| AIDS CHARITIES BENEFIT SPECIAL Various artists | 1992 | (2) | 30-50 |
| *(Includes tracks by Elton John)* | | | |
| BBC CLASSIC TRACKS (Jan 91) | 1991 | Westwood One | 20-40 |
| *(Classic live tracks, repeated several times)* | | | |
| I'M STILL STANDING (July 96) | 1996 | Westwood One (3) | 75-100 |
| *(Music and interviews, some live tracks)* | | | |
| IN CONCERT (Nov 91) Live concert | 1991 | Westwood One (2) | 40-75 |
| *(BBC concert material)* | | | |
| IN THE STUDIO Profile of an album (Nov 88) | 1988 | Album Network | 10-15 |
| *(Several shows in this series, music and interviews)* | | | |
| KING BISCUIT FLOWER HOUR  Live concert | 1987 | DIR | 75-125 |
| *(Rare KBFH silver CD)* | | | |
| KING BISCUIT FLOWER HOUR  Parts 1 and 2 | 1988 | DIR (2) | 75-125 |
| *(Live concert on double CD)* | | | |
| KING BISCUIT FLOWER HOUR (Aug 92) Live concert | 1992 | DIR (2) | 30-50 |
| *(Repeated several times)* | | | |
| KING BISCUIT FLOWER HOUR (June 95) | 1995 | DIR | 50-75 |
| *(Live concert)* | | | |
| OFF THE RECORD (Aug 93) Profile | 1993 | Westwood One | 20-40 |
| *(Music and interviews)* | | | |
| OFF THE RECORD (Jan 94) Profile of "Duets" LP | 1994 | Westwood One | 25-50 |
| *(Music and interviews)* | | | |
| PIANO MEN, THE (May 94) Profile of Elton John and Billy Joel | 1994 | Westwood One (3) | 40-75 |
| *(Music and interviews)* | | | |
| STORY OF ELTON JOHN (June 89) Profile | 1989 | Unistar (3) | 25-50 |
| *(Music and interviews)* | | | |
| SUPERSTAR CONCERT (Feb 94) Live concert | 1994 | Westwood One (2) | 40-75 |
| *(New material)* | | | |
| THE STORY OF ELTON JOHN (Aug 92) Profile | 1992 | Unistar | 20-40 |
| *(Music and interviews)* | | | |
| **Reel-to-Reel Tapes** | | | |
| KING BISCUIT FLOWER HOUR (Aug 76) | 1976 | DIR/ABC | 100-200 |
| *(Two-hour live concert on four 7" reels)* | | | |

## JOHNNY AND THE DISTRACTIONS
**RADIO SHOWS**
**Albums**

| KING BISCUIT FLOWER HOUR (July 82) Live concert | 1982 | DIR/ABC (2) | 20-40 |
|---|---|---|---|
| *(With the Outlaws)* | | | |

## JOHNNY AND THE DWELLERS
**45s**

| DEPRESSION/RUDOLF THE RED-NOSED REINDEER | 1994 | EMI SPRO 19949 | 10 |
|---|---|---|---|
| *(B-side by the Ventures; promo only with picture sleeve)* | | | |

## JOHNNY AND THE HURRICANES
*Warwick promo 45s $20 each; Big Top promo 45s $18 each; Mala promo 45s $8 each*

## JOHNSON, CLIFF
**45s**

| GO 'WAY HOUND DOG | 195? | Columbia 40865 | 40 |
|---|---|---|---|
| *(White promo label)* | | | |

## JOHNSON, MARV
**45s**

| COME TO ME | 1959 | Tamla 101 | 175 |
|---|---|---|---|
| *(White promo label)* | | | |

## JOHNSON, MICHAEL
**45s**

| THERE'S A NEW KID IN TOWN (same on both sides) | 1985 | RCA Victor JK-14239 | 3 |
|---|---|---|---|

## JOHNSTON, BRUCE
*Of the Beach Boys, the Surf Stompers and Vettes; Columbia promo 45s and 12" singles $5 each; Columbia promo LPs $18 each*
**45s**

| DO THE SURFER STOMP  Surf Stompers | 1962 | Donna 1354 | 40 |
|---|---|---|---|
| *(White promo label)* | | | |

| Title | Yr | Label, Number | NM $ |
|---|---|---|---|
| LITTLE FORD RAGTOP  The Vettes | 1963 | MGM 13186 | 25 |
| *(Yellow promo label)* | | | |
| SOUPY SHUFFLE STOMP  Bruce Johnston | 1962 | Donna 1364 | 25 |
| *(White promo label)* | | | |
| THE ORIGINAL SURFER STOMP  Surf Stompers | 1961 | Del-Fi 4202 | 75 |
| *(White promo label)* | | | |

## JOHNSTON, TOM
*Of the Doobie Brothers; Warner Bros. promo 45s $3 each*
**RADIO SHOWS**
**Albums**

| | | | |
|---|---|---|---|
| KING BISCUIT FLOWER HOUR (Aug 81) Live concert | 1981 | DIR/ABC (2) | 25-40 |
| *(With Billy Squier)* | | | |

## JOLSON, AL
**RADIO SHOWS**
**Albums**

| | | | |
|---|---|---|---|
| HERE'S TO VETS | 195? | V.A. #1466 | 40 |
| *(Al Jolson is host; music and interviews)* | | | |

## JON AND ROBIN AND THE IN CROWD
**45s**

| | | | |
|---|---|---|---|
| CAN'T MAKE IT WITH YOU/IF I NEED SOMEONE | 1966 | Abnak 113 | 15 |
| *(Promo only on yellow vinyl)* | | | |
| DO IT AGAIN A LITTLE BIT SLOWER/IF I NEED SOMEONE | 1967 | Abnak 119 | 16 |
| *(Promo only on yellow vinyl)* | | | |
| DR. JON (THE MEDICINE MAN)/LOVE ME BABY | 1968 | Abnak 127 | 12 |
| *(Promo only on yellow vinyl)* | | | |
| DRUMS/YOU DON'T CARE | 1967 | Abnak 122 | 15 |
| *(Promo only on yellow vinyl)* | | | |
| GIFT OF LOVE/GIFT OF LOVE (COUNTRY STYLE) | 1969 | Abnak 135 | 12 |
| *(Promo only on yellow vinyl)* | | | |
| GIVE ME YOUR LOVE/LONELY ONE | 1969 | Abnak 138 | 12 |
| *(Promo only on yellow vinyl)* | | | |
| HEY GIRL/IF I NEED SOMEONE | 1966 | Abnak 115 | 15 |
| *(Promo only on yellow vinyl)* | | | |
| I WANT SOME MORE/LOVE ME BABY | 1967 | Abnak 124 | 15 |
| *(Promo only on yellow vinyl)* | | | |
| IF YOU GOT IT, FLAUNT IT/I'LL COME RUNNING TO YOU | 1969 | Abnak 141 | 12 |
| *(Promo only on yellow vinyl)* | | | |
| LONELY ONE/HOW COME | 1965 | Abnak 111 | 15 |
| *(Promo only on yellow vinyl)* | | | |
| SAVE ME, SAVE ME/THURSDAY MORNING | 1968 | Abnak 133 | 12 |
| *(Promo only on yellow vinyl)* | | | |
| THERE'S AN AMERICAN FLAG ON THE MOON | 1969 | Abnak 140 | 12 |
| *(Promo only on yellow vinyl)* | | | |
| YOU GOT STYLE/THURSDAY MORNING | 1968 | Abnak 130 | 12 |
| *(Promo only on yellow vinyl)* | | | |

## JONES, FLOYD
**45s**

| | | | |
|---|---|---|---|
| EARLY MORNING | 195? | Chess 1527 | 45 |
| *(Blue/white promo label)* | | | |
| FLOYD'S BLUES | 1955 | Vee Jay 126 | 100 |
| *(White promo label)* | | | |
| SCHOOLDAYS ON MY MIND | 1955 | Vee Jay 111 | 100 |
| *(White promo label)* | | | |

## JONES, GEORGE
*Recorded as Thumper Jones for Starday and Hank Jones for Tops, but no promos exist on either; Mercury white promo label 45s $10 each including duets; Mercury Celebrity Series white promo label 45s $8 each; United Artists white promo label 45s $6 each; Musicor white promo 45s $5 each including duets; Epic promo 45s $2 each including duets; Other Mercury white promo albums $25-40 each depending on year; United Artists promo LPs $20 each including duets; Musicor white promo label LPs $12 each including duets; Epic promo LPs $5 each including duets*
**45s**

| | | | |
|---|---|---|---|
| TALL TALL TREES  Stereo 7" single | 1960 | Mercury 7048 | 50 |
| *(Small center hole, blue label, jukebox single)* | | | |
| WHITE LIGHTNING  Stereo 7" single | 1960 | Mercury 7045 | 100 |
| *(Small center hole, blue label, jukebox single)* | | | |
| WHO SHOT SAM  Stereo 7" single | 1960 | Mercury 7049 | 75 |
| *(Small center hole, blue label, jukebox single)* | | | |
| WHY BABY WHY  Stereo 7" single | 1960 | Mercury 7046 | 75 |
| *(Small center hole, blue label, jukebox single)* | | | |
| THE WINDOW UP ABOVE   Stereo 7" single | 1960 | Mercury 7047 | 50 |
| *(Small center hole, blue label, jukebox single)* | | | |

**7-Inch Extended Plays**

| | | | |
|---|---|---|---|
| COUNTRY CHURCH TIME  VOL. 1, 2 ,3  White label promos | 1961 | Mercury 4035/6/7 | 50 |
| *(Each record)* | | | |
| EP Various artists | 1958 | Dixie 501 | 200 |
| *(George Jones song, "Why Baby Why," no cover)* | | | |
| EP Various artists | 1958 | Dixie 525 | 150 |
| *(One George Jones song, "Don't Do this to Me," no cover)* | | | |
| EP Various artists | 1958 | Dixie 505 | 150 |
| *(One George Jones song, "Heartbreak Hotel," no cover)* | | | |
| GEORGE JONES  Jukebox LLP | 1965 | Starday 335 | 100 |
| *(Issued with a beautiful color hard cover, very rare)* | | | |
| GEORGE JONES' GREATEST HITS VOL. 1, 2, 3  White label promos | 1961 | Mercury 4048/49/50 | 50 |
| *(Each record)* | | | |

| Title | Yr | Label, Number | NM $ |
|---|---|---|---|
| THUMPER JONES | 1958 | Dixie 502 | 175 |
| *(Songs by "Thumper Jones," no cover)* | | | |
| WHITE LIGHTNING VOL. 1, 2, 3  White label promos | 1959 | Mercury 3399/3400/3401 | 50 |
| *(Each record)* | | | |
| **Albums** | | | |
| COUNTRY CHURCH TIME  Mono | 1959 | Mercury 20462 | 150 |
| *(White promo label)* | | | |
| 14 COUNTRY FAVORITES  Mono | 1957 | Mercury 20306 | 125 |
| *(His first Mercury album, white promo label)* | | | |
| GEORGE JONES SALUTES HANK WILLIAMS  Mono | 1960 | Mercury 20596 | 75 |
| *(White promo label)* | | | |
| GEORGE JONES SINGS WHITE LIGHTNING AND OTHER FAVORITES  Mono | 1959 | Mercury 20477 | 150 |
| *(White promo label)* | | | |
| THE NOVELTY SIDE OF GEORGE JONES  Mono | 1963 | Mercury 60793 | 75 |
| *(White promo label)* | | | |
| **RADIO SHOWS** | | | |
| **Albums** | | | |
| AMERCIAN EAGLE (Jan 87) Live concert | 1987 | DIR (3) | 50-100 |
| *(With Tammy Wynette)* | | | |
| AMERICAN EAGLE Live concert | 1982 | DIR (3) | 50-100 |
| *(Rare live concert, repeated)* | | | |
| COUNTRY SESSIONS  Profile | 1982 | Country Sessions | 20-40 |
| *(Music and interviews)* | | | |
| LIVE AT GILLEY'S  Live concert | 1985 | Westwood One | 25-50 |
| *(Also live, repeated)* | | | |
| THE SILVER EAGLE  Canadian pressing for U.S. use | 1981 | DIR (3) | 40-75 |
| *(Live concert with Ronnie Milsap)* | | | |
| WESTWOOD ONE PRESENTS (June 87) Live concert | 1987 | Westwood One | 25-50 |
| *(Repeated in 1989 and 1990)* | | | |

## JONES, HOWARD
*Elektra promo 45s $2 each; Elektra promo LPs $6 each*

**12-Inch Singles**

| Title | Yr | Label, Number | NM $ |
|---|---|---|---|
| ALL I WANT (2 versions)/YOU KNOW I LOVE YOU... DON'T YOU? (LIVE) | 1986 | Elektra 5207 | 5 |
| LIFE IN ONE DAY/LIFE IN ONE DAY (Remix Part 1 & 2) | 1985 | Elektra 5065 | 6 |
| LIKE TO GET TO KNOW YOU WELL (Short)/(Long) | 1985 | Elektra 5091 | 10 |
| NEW SONG (2 versions)/CONDITIONING/CHANGE THE MAN | 1983 | Elektra 4944 | 10 |
| PEARL IN THE SHELL (Long)/(Short) | 1984 | Elektra 4992 | 8 |
| THE PRISONER (3 versions) | 1989 | Elektra 5385 | 8 |
| THINGS CAN ONLY GET BETTER (LP) (Remix) | 1985 | Elektra 5043 | 8 |
| WHAT IS LOVE (Long)/(Short) | 1983 | Elektra 4965 | 5 |
| YOU KNOW I LOVE YOU...DON'T YOU? (LP)/(Edit) | 1986 | Elektra 5178 | 6 |
| **Albums** | | | |
| CROSS THAT LINE | 1989 | Elektra 60794 | 10 |
| *(Promo-only white label audiophile vinyl)* | | | |
| **RADIO SHOWS** | | | |
| **Albums** | | | |
| BBC LONDON WAVELENGTH (Feb 84) Live concert | 1984 | London Wavelength | 20-40 |
| *(With Paul Young)* | | | |
| BBC LONDON WAVELENGTH (July 84) | 1984 | London Wavelength | 25-50 |
| *(Live solo concert)* | | | |
| BBC ROCK HOUR | 1984 | London Wavelength | 25-50 |
| *(Live concert)* | | | |
| IN CONCERT (May 85) Live concert | 1985 | Westwood One (2) | 20-35 |
| *(With Jason & the Scorchers)* | | | |
| **Compact Discs** | | | |
| THE HOWARD JONES STORY (June 92) Profile | 1992 | Unistar | 10-20 |
| *(Music and interviews)* | | | |

## JONES, MICK
**Albums**

| Title | Yr | Label, Number | NM $ |
|---|---|---|---|
| JONES ALONE | 1989 | Atlantic 2995 | 15 |
| *(Promo-only preview album)* | | | |

## JONES, QUINCY
*Mercury promo 45s $3 each; Mercury promo LPs $8 each*

**7-Inch Extended Plays**

| Title | Yr | Label, Number | NM $ |
|---|---|---|---|
| QUINCY'S GOT A BRAND NEW BAG  Jukebox LLP | 1969 | Mercury 663 | 15 |
| *(Issued with a hard cover)* | | | |
| **Albums** | | | |
| GO WEST, MAN! | 1957 | ABC-Paramount 186 | 25 |
| *(White label promo)* | | | |
| **RADIO SHOWS** | | | |
| **Albums** | | | |
| WESTWOOD ONE CONCERT (Mar 83) | 1983 | Westwood One (2) | 200-400 |
| *(Rare live concert)* | | | |

## JONES, SPIKE /HIS CITY SLICKERS
*Other RCA Victor promo 78s $30 each; Other RCA Victor promo 45s $25 each; Other Liberty promo 45s $10-18 each (depending on novelty or mood music); Liberty promo LPs $25 each; MGM promo LPs $20 each*

**45s**

| Title | Yr | Label, Number | NM $ |
|---|---|---|---|
| DANCE OF THE HOURS | 1970 | RCA Victor 0532 | 18 |
| *(Yellow promo label)* | | | |
| I WANT EDDIE FISHER FOR CHRISTMAS | 1954 | RCA Victor 5920 | 25 |
| *(White promo label)* | | | |

| Title | Yr | Label, Number | NM $ |
|---|---|---|---|
| I WANT THE SOUTH TO WIN THE WAR FOR CHRISTMAS | 1959 | Kapp 314 | 50 |
| *(White and brown label)* | | | |
| I'M IN THE MOOD FOR LOVE | 1960 | Liberty 55718 | 20 |
| *(Cream-colored promo label)* | | | |
| SUNSET STRIP | 1959 | Liberty 55253 | 20 |
| *(White promo label)* | | | |
| **78s** | | | |
| ALL I WANT FOR CHRISTMAS  Promo-only trailers | 1950 | RCA Victor DJ-613 | 200 |
| *(7", seven cuts with RCA designs engraved on flip)* | | | |
| ANDRE KOROSHOVSKY AND HIS FOSTER PARENT SPIKE JONES | 1950 | RCA Victor 1299 | 250 |
| *(12", promo only, 2 cuts, used with "Mommy, Won't You Buy a Baby Brother," theme for Foster Parents Plan for War Children)* | | | |
| **Albums** | | | |
| OMNIBUST | 1959 | Liberty 7140 | 50 |
| *(Red vinyl)* | | | |
| THIS IS STEREO  Sampler LP narrated by Spike Jones | 1958 | Liberty 101 | 75 |
| *(White promo label)* | | | |
| **RADIO SHOWS** | | | |
| **Albums** | | | |
| DOCTOR DEMENTO (Feb 88) Dr. Demento | 1988 | Westwood One (2) | 20-35 |
| *(Spike Jones Special, music and interviews)* | | | |
| **Digital Audio Tapes** | | | |
| PRIME CUTS (Jan 85) Merrill Piepkorn and Fred Heggeness | 1985 | FH Productions | 20-30 |
| *(Spike Jones Special with guests Dale Mattson and Kyle Wilkins; music and interviews)* | | | |

## JONES, TOM

*Parrot promo 45s $4 each; Epic promo 45s $2 each; Mercury promo 45s $2 each*

| Title | Yr | Label, Number | NM $ |
|---|---|---|---|
| **12-Inch Singles** | | | |
| IF I ONLY KNEW (4 versions) | 1994 | Interscope 2172 | 10 |
| SITUATION (5 versions) | 1994 | Interscope 2194 | 10 |
| **45s** | | | |
| CHILLS AND FEVER White promo label | 1966 | Tower 190 | 12 |
| *(Tower promo 45s are rare)* | | | |
| HIT MEDLEY/ROCK AND ROLL MEDLEY Orange label | 1971 | Parrot DPAS 49/50 | 25 |
| *(Promo-only release, issued with a promo picture cover)* | | | |
| I WAS A FOOL White promo label | 1966 | Tower 176 | 15 |
| *(The first two singles have stock picture sleeves that may be found with the promo, value $20 each)* | | | |
| LITTLE LONELY ONE  White promo label | 1965 | Tower 126 | 20 |
| *(Tom's first record)* | | | |
| **7-Inch Extended Plays** | | | |
| LIVE IN LAS VEGAS  Jukebox LLP | 1971 | Parrot 83 | 18 |
| *(Issued with a hard cover)* | | | |
| TOM  Jukebox LLP | 1971 | Parrot 78 | 20 |
| *(Issued with a hard cover)* | | | |
| **Albums** | | | |
| SPECIAL TOM JONES INTERVIEW | 1970 | Parrot XPAS-1 | 100 |
| *(Promo-only open-end interview with gatefold cover and script)* | | | |

## JOPLIN, JANIS

*Includes Big Brother & the Holding Company;  Columbia white promo label 45s by Janis Jopin $12 each; Mainstream white promo label 45s by Big Brother & the Holding Company $15 each; Columbia white promo label 45s by Big Brother & the Holding Company $8 each*

| Title | Yr | Label, Number | NM $ |
|---|---|---|---|
| **45s** | | | |
| KEEP ON Big Brother and the Holding Company | 1970 | Columbia 45284 | 12 |
| *(White promo/blue promo labels)* | | | |
| PIECE OF MY HEART   Big Brother and the Holding Company | 1968 | Columbia 44626 | 15 |
| *(White promo label)* | | | |
| **Albums** | | | |
| A COLLECTION | 1982 | Columbia AS 1377 | 20 |
| **Compact Discs** | | | |
| SIX SIDES OF JANIS | 1993 | Columbia CSK 5223 | 20 |
| *(Promo only sampler CD)* | | | |
| **RADIO SHOWS** | | | |
| **Albums** | | | |
| BBC LONDON WAVELENGTH (Apr 82) Janis Joplin special | 1982 | London Wavelength | 50-75 |
| *(Mostly music and interviews)* | | | |
| RETRO ROCK | 1982 | Clayton Webster | 50-75 |
| *(Mostly music and interviews)* | | | |
| ROYALTY OF ROCK Profile | 1982 | | 25-40 |
| *(Music and interviews)* | | | |

## JORDAN, LOUIS

*Decca pink promo label 45s $10-20 each; Other Mercury white promo label 45s $10 each; TRC (ABC) white promo label 45s $8 each; Other Decca promo LPs $25 each*

| Title | Yr | Label, Number | NM $ |
|---|---|---|---|
| **45s** | | | |
| CHOO CHOO CH' BOOGIE | 1956 | Mercury 71025 | 25 |
| *(White promo label)* | | | |
| FIRE | 1957 | Mercury 71106 | 15 |
| *(White promo label)* | | | |
| ROCK DOC | 1957 | Mercury 71052 | 20 |
| *(White promo label)* | | | |
| SWEET HUNK OF JUNK | 1958 | Mercury 71319 | 15 |
| *(White promo label)* | | | |
| **Albums** | | | |
| LET THE GOOD TIMES ROLL | 1958 | Decca 8551 | 100 |
| *(Pink promo label)* | | | |

| Title | Yr | Label, Number | NM $ |
|---|---|---|---|
| LOUIS JORDAN'S GREATEST HITS | 1968 | Decca 75035 | 40 |
| *(White promo label)* | | | |
| MAN, WE'RE WAILIN' | 1957 | Mercury 20331 | 125 |
| *(White promo label)* | | | |
| SOMEBODY UP THERE DIGS ME | 1957 | Mercury 20242 | 150 |
| *(White promo label)* | | | |

## JORDANAIRES, THE

Legendary backup group, they appear on most of Elvis Presley's 1950s and 1960s hits; Capitol white promo label 45s $5 each; Decca pink promo label 45s $6 each; Capitol promo LPs $15-20 each; Decca promo LPs $50 each; Columbia white promo label LPs $20 each

**45s**

| Title | Yr | Label, Number | NM $ |
|---|---|---|---|
| LITTLE MISS RUBY  White promo label | 1958 | Capitol 3940 | 12 |
| *(From movie "Country Music Holiday")* | | | |
| ROCK 'N ROLL RELIGION  White promo label | 1957 | Capitol 3420 | 10 |
| *(Much of their Capitol material was gospel)* | | | |
| SUGAREE  White promo label, no photo | 1957 | Capitol 3610 | 10 |
| *(As close as they came to solo rockabilly)* | | | |
| SUGAREE  Yellow label promo with group's photo | 1957 | Capitol 3610 | 15 |
| *(Written by Marty Robbins)* | | | |
| WELLA WELLA HONEY  White promo label | 1958 | Capitol 4025 | 10 |

**7-Inch Extended Plays**

| Title | Yr | Label, Number | NM $ |
|---|---|---|---|
| THE JORDANAIRES  Blue label | 1956 | SESAC 46 | 25 |
| *(There were dozens of Seasac EPs that featured the group, all of which are promo only and any of which go for $25 each)* | | | |

**Albums**

| Title | Yr | Label, Number | NM $ |
|---|---|---|---|
| OF RIVERS AND PLAINS  Blue label | 1956 | SESAC 1401 | 100 |
| *(Promo only, for radio stations)* | | | |
| SPOTLIGHT ON THE JORDANAIRES | 1962 | Capitol 1742 | 40 |
| *(Promo blue label)* | | | |

**RADIO SHOWS**

**16-Inch Transcriptions**

| Title | Yr | Label, Number | NM $ |
|---|---|---|---|
| COUNTRY STYLE USA (50s) The Jordanaires are guests | 195? | Public Service | 25-50 |
| *(Music and interviews, several shows)* | | | |
| U. S. ARMY (60s) The Jordanaires are guests | 196? | U.S. Army | 25-50 |
| *(Music and interviews, several shows)* | | | |

**Albums**

| Title | Yr | Label, Number | NM $ |
|---|---|---|---|
| COUNTRY MUSIC TIME | 1965 | U.S. Air Force | 25-50 |
| *(Orange and white label, flip side is the Wilburn Brothers)* | | | |
| COUNTRY MUSIC TIME | 1966 | U.S. Air Force | 25-50 |
| *(Brown and white label, flip side is Mac Wiseman)* | | | |
| COUNTRY MUSIC TIME | 1981 | U.S. Air Force | 15-25 |
| *(Music and interviews)* | | | |

## JOURNEY

Includes listings of Steve Perry; Columbia white promo label 45s $3 each; Geffen promo 45s $3 each; Columbia promo picture sleeves $3 each; Columbia promo LPs and 12" singles $6 each; Columbia promo 45s by Steve Perry $2 each; Columbia promo picture sleeve by Steve Perry $3 each

**12-Inch Singles**

| Title | Yr | Label, Number | NM $ |
|---|---|---|---|
| JUST THE SAME WAY (stereo/mono) | 1979 | Columbia AS 568 | 10 |
| ONLY THE YOUNG (same on both sides) | 1985 | Geffen PRO-A-2240 | 6 |

**45s**

| Title | Yr | Label, Number | NM $ |
|---|---|---|---|
| DON'T FIGHT IT  Steve Perry with Kenny Loggins | 1982 | Allied | 10 |
| *(Test pressing)* | | | |
| KOHOUTEK  Promo-only 6:47 version | 1974 | Columbia AS 128 | 18 |
| *(Seven-inch record, small center hole)* | | | |
| WHAT'S IT ALL ABOUT (Aug 81) Public service show | 1981 | W.I.A.A. 587 | 18 |
| *(Flip side is Gary Paxton)* | | | |
| WHAT'S IT ALL ABOUT (Aug 82) Public service show | 1982 | W.I.A.A. 624 | 18 |
| *(Flip side is the Pointer Sisters)* | | | |

**7-Inch Extended Plays**

| Title | Yr | Label, Number | NM $ |
|---|---|---|---|
| ROCK MINI ALBUM  Four songs, four artists | 1981 | CSP (CBS) 16174 | 10 |
| *(Issued with a paper cover, Journey does "Any Way You Want It")* | | | |

**Albums**

| Title | Yr | Label, Number | NM $ |
|---|---|---|---|
| A CANDID CONVERSATION | 1977 | Columbia AS-1606 | 15 |
| *(Promo-only release)* | | | |
| JOURNEY | 1975 | Columbia AS-914 | 15 |
| *(Promo-only release)* | | | |

**RADIO SHOWS**

**Albums**

| Title | Yr | Label, Number | NM $ |
|---|---|---|---|
| BBC LONDON WAVELENGTH (May 81) | 1981 | London Wavelength | 20-35 |
| *(Music and interviews)* | | | |
| BBC LONDON WAVELENGTH (May 81) Profile | 1981 | London Wavelength (3) | 30-60 |
| *(Music and interviews)* | | | |
| HOT ROCKS (June 86) | 1986 | United Stations (2) | 20-30 |
| *(Music and interviews)* | | | |
| KING BISCUIT FLOWER HOUR Live concert | 1982 | DIR/ABC (2) | 25-40 |
| *(Repeated)* | | | |
| LEGENDS OF ROCK (July 87) Profile of Journey | 1987 | NBC Radio (4) | 20-40 |
| *(Music and interviews, parts 1 and 2)* | | | |
| PIONEERS IN ROCK (Mar 86) | 1986 | DIR (2) | 20-40 |
| *(Various live tracks from concerts)* | | | |
| RETRO ROCK (June 83) | 1983 | Clayton Webster (2) | 20-35 |
| *(Music and interviews)* | | | |
| ROBERT W. MORGAN (Nov 81) JOURNEY | 1981 | Watermark | 15-25 |
| *(Music and interviews)* | | | |
| STARTRACK PROFILE (Oct 83) | 1983 | Westwood One (2) | 20-35 |
| *(Music and interviews)* | | | |

| Title | Yr | Label, Number | NM $ |
|---|---|---|---|
| SUPERSTAR CONCERT (June 86) Box set | 1986 | Westwood One (3) | 25-50 |
| *(Live concert, repeated)* | | | |
| **Compact Discs** | | | |
| IN THE STUDIO (July 91) Profile of an album | 1991 | Album Network | 10-15 |
| *(Music and interviews)* | | | |
| KING BISCUIT FLOWER HOUR (Dec 91) Live concert | 1991 | DIR | 25-40 |
| *(Repeated)* | | | |
| OFF THE RECORD (Aug 94) Steve Perry | 1994 | Westwood One | 10-15 |
| *(Music and interviews)* | | | |
| UP CLOSE  Steve Perry/Journey | 1994 | Media America (2) | 25-40 |
| *(Music and interviews)* | | | |
| UP CLOSE Steve Perry | 1989 | Media America (2) | 20-40 |
| *(Music and interviews)* | | | |

**JOY DIVISION**
**45s**

| Title | Yr | Label, Number | NM $ |
|---|---|---|---|
| LOVE WILL TEAR US APART/THESE DAYS | 1980 | Factory FACUS 23 | 100 |
| *(White label promo)* | | | |

**JUDAS PRIEST**
*Columbia promo 45s $4 each*
**Compact Discs**

| Title | Yr | Label, Number | NM $ |
|---|---|---|---|
| SHARPEST CUTS, THE | 1990 | Columbia CSK 2133 | 30 |
| *(Promo-only sampler; 10 tracks listed on inlay card, and CD plays 10)* | | | |
| SHARPEST CUTS, THE | 1990 | Columbia CSK 2133 | 20 |
| *(Promo-only sampler; 10 tracks listed on inlay card, but CD only plays 9)* | | | |

**RADIO SHOWS**
**Albums**

| Title | Yr | Label, Number | NM $ |
|---|---|---|---|
| BBC LONDON WAVELENGTH (Feb 82) | 1982 | London Wavelength | 35-70 |
| *(Some live material)* | | | |
| BBC ROCK HOUR (May 82) Live concert | 1982 | London Wavelength | 40-75 |
| *(Mostly live concert)* | | | |
| BBC ROCK HOUR (Feb 84) Live concert | 1984 | London Wavelength | 75-125 |
| *(Rare live concert)* | | | |
| IN CONCERT (Dec 83) Live concert | 1983 | Westwood One (2) | 85-150 |
| *(Repeated)* | | | |
| IN CONCERT (Sept 88) Live concert | 1988 | Westwood One (2) | 75-150 |
| *(Repeated)* | | | |
| IN CONCERT (Nov 90) Live concert | 1990 | Westwood One (2) | 40-75 |
| *(With Bruce Dickinson)* | | | |
| INNERVIEW (80s) Profile OF JUDAS PRIEST | 198? | Innerview | 15-25 |
| *(Music and interviews)* | | | |
| KING BISCUIT FLOWER HOUR (Mar 83) Live concert | 1983 | DIR/ABC (2) | 75-150 |
| *(Repeated)* | | | |
| KING BISCUIT FLOWER HOUR (Sept 84) Live concert | 1984 | DIR/ABC (2) | 50-100 |
| *(Repeated)* | | | |
| NIGHT ON THE ROAD, A (June 82) | 1982 | ABC Radio (3) | 40-75 |
| *(Mostly music and interviews)* | | | |
| ON TOUR SPECIAL Profile | 1984 | (3) | 40-75 |
| *(Music and interviews)* | | | |
| SUPERGROUPS | 1982 | ABC Radio (3) | 100-175 |
| *(Rare live concert)* | | | |
| SUPERGROUPS (Aug 83) Various artists | 1983 | ABC Radio (3) | 75-150 |
| *(Concerts that include U2)* | | | |

**Compact Discs**

| Title | Yr | Label, Number | NM $ |
|---|---|---|---|
| KING BISCUIT FLOWER HOUR (May 91) Live concert | 1991 | DIR | 40-75 |
| *(Repeated)* | | | |
| METALSHOP (Sept 92) Various artists | 1992 | MJI Productions | 15-25 |
| *(Features Rob Halford from Judas Priest)* | | | |

**JUDD, WYNONNA**
*Other Curb/MCA/Universal promo CD singles $2-3 each*
**Compact Discs**

| Title | Yr | Label, Number | NM $ |
|---|---|---|---|
| GIRLS WITH GUITARS | 1994 | Curb/MCA 54875 | 15 |
| *(Promo-only CD single in guitar-shaped case)* | | | |
| WYNONNA SAMPLER | 1996 | Curb/MCA 3666 | 15 |
| *(Promo-only sampler)* | | | |

**JUDDS, THE**
*Wynonna and Naomi; Also see Wynonna Judd; Other RCA Victor promo 45s $3 each*
**45s**

| Title | Yr | Label, Number | NM $ |
|---|---|---|---|
| HAD A DREAM  Brown promo label, red vinyl | 1983 | RCA PB-13673 | 20 |
| *(Only the promo version is red vinyl)* | | | |

**RADIO SHOWS**
**Albums**

| Title | Yr | Label, Number | NM $ |
|---|---|---|---|
| FAREWELL TO THE JUDDS (Aug 91) | 1991 | (3) | 50-80 |
| *(Mostly music and interviews, some live tracks)* | | | |
| LIVE FROM DISNEY WORLD (July 86) Live concert | 1986 | NBC Radio | 50-80 |
| *(With Exile)* | | | |
| LIVE IN HOLLAND (80s) Live concert | 198? | Westwood One | 40-75 |
| *(Rare live concert)* | | | |
| THE JUDDS CHRISTMAS PRESENT (Dec 86) | 1986 | Mutual Radio (3) | 25-50 |
| *(Mostly music and interviews, some live)* | | | |
| WESTWOOD ONE PRESENTS (June 90) | 1990 | Westwood One | 40-75 |
| *(Mostly live concert)* | | | |

| Title | Yr | Label, Number | NM $ |
|-------|-----|---------------|------|

# K

**KAJAGOOGOO**
*EMI promo 45s $4 each*
**RADIO SHOWS**
**Albums**

| | | | |
|-------|-----|---------------|------|
| BBC ROCK HOUR (July 83) | 1983 | London Wavelength | 75-150 |

*(Live concert)*

**KAK**
*Epic promo 45s $5 each*
**45s**

| | | | |
|-------|-----|---------------|------|
| EVERYTHING'S CHANGING (Long Version)/(Edited Version) | 1968 | Epic 10383 | 20 |

*(May be promo only)*
**Albums**

| | | | |
|-------|-----|---------------|------|
| KAK | 1969 | Epic BN 26429 | 50 |

*(White promo label)*

**KALEIDOSCOPE**
*Epic promo 45s $8 each*
**Albums**

| | | | |
|-------|-----|---------------|------|
| A BEACON FROM MARS | 1967 | Epic 24333 | 40 |
| *(White promo label)* | | | |
| SIDE TRIPS | 1967 | Epic 24304 | 75 |

*(White promo label)*

**KALIN TWINS, THE**
*Other Decca promo 45s $18 each*
**45s**

| | | | |
|-------|-----|---------------|------|
| WHEN | 1958 | Decca 30642 | 30 |

*(Green promo label)*
**Albums**

| | | | |
|-------|-----|---------------|------|
| THE KALIN TWINS | 1959 | Decca 8812 | 125 |

*(Pink promo label)*

**KALLEN, KITTY**
*Other Decca promo 45s $5 each*
**45s**

| | | | |
|-------|-----|---------------|------|
| PERSONAL INTRODUCTION TO 1954 CHRISTMAS SEALS | 1954 | Columbia 78079 | 25 |
| *(One-sided, red/white promo label)* | | | |
| THE SPIRIT OF CHRISTMAS | 1954 | Decca 29315 | 12 |

*(White/red promo label, 1954 Christmas Seals song, issued with stock picture sleeve not included above)*

**KANE, PAUL**
*More at Paul Simon*
**45s**

| | | | |
|-------|-----|---------------|------|
| HE WAS MY BROTHER | 1964 | Tribute 128 | 50 |

*(White promo label)*

**KANSAS**
*Kirshner and CBS promo 45s $3 each; CBS label promo picture sleeves $3 each*
**12-Inch Singles**

| | | | |
|-------|-----|---------------|------|
| CAN'T CRY ANYMORE (same on both sides) | 1987 | MCA L33-17306 | 6 |
| MAINSTREAM/EVERYBODY'S MY FRIEND | 1983 | CBS Associated 1747 | 6 |
| PLAY THE GAME TONIGHT/CONFESSIONS PRE-RELEASE MONTAGE | 1982 | Kirshner 1451 | 8 |
| RIGHT AWAY/DIAMONDS AND PEARLS | 1982 | Kirshner 1534 | 8 |

**45s**

| | | | |
|-------|-----|---------------|------|
| POWER | 1985 | MCA S45-17290 | 10 |
| *(Promo-only number)* | | | |
| POWER | 1985 | MCA 52958 | 10 |
| *(Test pressing)* | | | |
| WHAT'S IT ALL ABOUT (Oct 80) Public service show | 1980 | W.I.A.A. 545 | 15 |

*(Flip side is William Bell)*
**Albums**

| | | | |
|-------|-----|---------------|------|
| POINT OF KNOW RETURN | 1977 | Kirshner 34929 | 50 |
| *(Promo-only picture disc)* | | | |
| TWO FOR THE SHOW | 1978 | Kirshner AS-555 | 20 |

*(Promo-only sampler)*
**RADIO SHOWS**
**Albums**

| | | | |
|-------|-----|---------------|------|
| BBC ROCK HOUR (May 82) KANSAS | 1982 | London Wavelength | 30-50 |
| *(Music and interviews)* | | | |
| CAPTURED LIVE (May 84) Live concert | 1984 | RKO (4) | 75-150 |
| *(With Heart)* | | | |
| IN CONCERT (Dec 82) Live concert | 1982 | Westwood One (2) | 100-150 |
| *(With Pat Travers)* | | | |
| INNERVIEW (70s) KANSAS PROFILE | 197? | Innerview | 20-30 |
| *(Music and interviews)* | | | |
| KING BISCUIT FLOWER HOUR (Aug 88) Live concert | 1988 | DIR (2) | 50-100 |
| *(With Queen)* | | | |
| KING BISCUIT FLOWER HOUR (Feb 83) | 1983 | DIR (2) | 75-150 |
| *(Live concert)* | | | |
| NBC SOURCE (Dec 80) Live concert | 1980 | NBC Radio (2) | 75-125 |

*(Early rare concert)*

| Title | Yr | Label, Number | NM $ |
|---|---|---|---|
| NBC SOURCE SPECIAL (Apr 81) KANSAS | 1981 | NBC Radio (2) | 20-40 |
| *(Music and interviews)* | | | |
| A NIGHT ON THE ROAD (June 82) | 1982 | ABC Radio (3) | 100-175 |
| *(Music and interviews with some live tracks)* | | | |
| SUPERSTAR CONCERT (Jan 84) Live concert | 1984 | Westwood One (3) | 25-50 |
| *(With the Fixx)* | | | |
| **Compact Discs** | | | |
| IN THE STUDIO (Sept 92) Profile of an album | 1992 | Album Network | 10-20 |
| *(Music and interviews)* | | | |
| KING BISCUIT FLOWER HOUR (Jan 91) Live concert | 1991 | DIR | 20-40 |
| *(With King's X)* | | | |
| KING BISCUIT FLOWER HOUR (Jan 95) | 1995 | DIR | 25-40 |
| *(Live concert)* | | | |
| KING BISCUIT FLOWER HOUR (June 89) | 1989 | DIR | 40-75 |
| *(Live concert)* | | | |
| KING BISCUIT FLOWER HOUR (Mar 93) | 1993 | DIR | 20-40 |
| *(Live concert)* | | | |
| LIVE FROM THE WHISKEY (Aug 93) | 1993 | Entertainment Radio | 40-60 |
| *(Live concert)* | | | |
| SUPERSTARS (Oct 95) | 1995 | (2) | 50-75 |
| *(Live concert material)* | | | |

## KATRINA AND THE WAVES
*Capitol promo singles $3 each*

**12-Inch Singles**

| Title | Yr | Label, Number | NM $ |
|---|---|---|---|
| DO YOU WANT CRYING (Extended Mix)/(Single Version) | 1985 | Capitol SPRO 9359 | 6 |
| IS THAT IT (LP)/(extended) | 1986 | Capitol SPRO 9645 | 6 |
| LOVELY LINDSAY (same on both sides) | 1986 | Capitol SPRO 9716 | 6 |
| QUE TE QUIERO (same on both sides) | 1985 | Capitol SPRO 9514 | 8 |
| RED WINE AND WHISKEY (same on both sides) | 1985 | Capitol SPRO 9413 | 10 |
| *(Red vinyl)* | | | |
| THAT'S THE WAY (same on both sides) | 1989 | SBK 05311 | 7 |
| WALKING ON SUNSHINE (5:37)/(4:00) | 1985 | Capitol SPRO 9372/3 | 10 |

**RADIO SHOWS**

**Albums**

| Title | Yr | Label, Number | NM $ |
|---|---|---|---|
| BBC TRANSCRIPTION DISC  Live concert | 1985 | BBC Transcription | 100-200 |
| *(With Go West)* | | | |
| IN CONCERT (July 85) Live concert | 1985 | Westwood One (2) | 200-300 |
| *(With Depeche Mode)* | | | |
| KING BISCUIT FLOWER HOUR (June 85) Live concert | 1985 | DIR (2) | 50-100 |
| *(With Fiona)* | | | |

## KATZ, MICKEY
*Other Capitol promo 45s $10 each*

**45s**

| Title | Yr | Label, Number | NM $ |
|---|---|---|---|
| HANSEL AND GENSEL | 1958 | Capitol PRO-1241 | 15 |
| *(Red promo label, promo-only release)* | | | |

## KBC BAND
*Arista promo 45s $3 each*

**RADIO SHOWS**

**Albums**

| Title | Yr | Label, Number | NM $ |
|---|---|---|---|
| KING BISCUIT FLOWER HOUR (June 87) | 1987 | DIR (2) | 75-100 |
| *(Live concert)* | | | |

## KC AND THE SUNSHINE BAND
**45s**

| Title | Yr | Label, Number | NM $ |
|---|---|---|---|
| WHAT'S IT ALL ABOUT (70s) Public serivce show | 197? | W.I.A.A. 312 | 20 |
| *(Flip side is Asleep At The Wheel)* | | | |

## KELLUM, MURRY
**45s**

| Title | Yr | Label, Number | NM $ |
|---|---|---|---|
| MEMPHIS SUN (mono/stereo) | 1978 | Plantation 176 | 5 |
| *(Released only as a promo)* | | | |

## KELLY, AL
**45s**

| Title | Yr | Label, Number | NM $ |
|---|---|---|---|
| AN EXCLUSIVE INTERVIEW WITH SANTA CLAUS/ O COME, ALL YE FAITHFUL/LO! HOW A ROSE E'ER BLOOMING/SILENT NIGHT | 1957 | RCA Thesaurus HO7H-0934 | 15 |
| *(B-side by Domenico Savino and His Orchestra)* | | | |

## KENDRICKS, EDDIE
*More at The Temptations*

**12-Inch Singles**

| Title | Yr | Label, Number | NM $ |
|---|---|---|---|
| AIN'T NO SMOKE WITHOUT FIRE (5:58)/WHIP (5:05) | 1978 | Arista SP-15 | 12 |

**45s**

| Title | Yr | Label, Number | NM $ |
|---|---|---|---|
| I DON'T NEED NOBODY ELSE (same on both sides) | 1981 | Atlantic 3874 | 5 |
| *(May be promo only)* | | | |

## KENTON, STAN
**45s**

| Title | Yr | Label, Number | NM $ |
|---|---|---|---|
| THE TWELVE DAYS OF CHRISTMAS/ O TANNENBAUM/WE THREE KINGS OF ORIENT ARE | 197? | Creative World 1001 | 4 |

| Title | Yr | Label, Number | NM $ |
|---|---|---|---|

**KENTUCKY HEADHUNTERS**
*Mercury promo 45s $2 each; Mercury promo CD singles $2-3 each*
**RADIO SHOWS**
**Compact Discs**

| | | | |
|---|---|---|---|
| COUNTRY CONCERTS (July 93) | 1993 | Westwood One | 30-60 |
| *(Live concert)* | | | |
| THE STORY OF THE KENTUCKY HEADHUNTERS | 1992 | Unistar (2) | 15-25 |
| *(Music and interviews)* | | | |

**KERR, ANITA, SINGERS**
**7-Inch Extended Plays**

| | | | |
|---|---|---|---|
| DECK THE HALLS/ALL THROUGH THE NIGHT// | 197? | Sesac AD-56 | 6 |
| RISE UP SHEPHERD AND FOLLER/CHRISTMAS IS THE DAY | | | |
| ON THIS HOLY NIGHT/BRING A TORCH, JEANETTE, ISABELLA// | 197? | Sesac AD-49 | 6 |
| SLEEP, SWEET JESUS, SLEEP/THE 12 DAYS OF CHRISTMAS | | | |

**KERSHAW, DOUG**
*Includes Rusty & Doug; Hickory promo 45s $10 each (Rusty and Doug); RCA Victor promo 45s $4 each; Reprise promo 45s $3 each; Reprise/Warner white promo label LPs $8 each*
**RADIO SHOWS**
**Albums**

| | | | |
|---|---|---|---|
| LIVE AT GILLEY'S (Apr 87) | 1987 | Westwood One | 100-175 |
| *(Live concert)* | | | |

**KERSHAW, SAMMY**
*Mercury promo CD singles $2-3 each*
**RADIO SHOWS**
**Compact Discs**

| | | | |
|---|---|---|---|
| COUNTRY CONCERTS (July 93) | 1993 | Westwood One | 30-60 |
| *(Live concert)* | | | |
| COUNTRY CUTTING EDGE (Jan 94) | 1994 | Westwood One | 10-20 |
| *(Music and interviews)* | | | |

**KEYNOTES, THE**
**45s**

| | | | |
|---|---|---|---|
| IN THE EVENING | 1956 | Apollo 503 | 125 |
| *(White promo label)* | | | |
| ONE LITTLE KISS | 1957 | Apollo 513 | 85 |
| *(White promo label)* | | | |
| REALLY WISH YOU WERE HERE | 1956 | Apollo 493 | 125 |
| *(White promo labels)* | | | |
| A STAR | 1955 | Apollo 484 | 100 |
| *(White promo label)* | | | |
| SUDDENLY | 1953 | Apollo 478 | 125 |
| *(White promo label)* | | | |
| ZUP, ZUP | 1956 | Apollo 498 | 80 |
| *(White promo label)* | | | |

**KEYTONS, THE**
**45s**

| | | | |
|---|---|---|---|
| WONDER OF THE WORLD | 1957 | Old Town 1041 | 40 |
| *(White promo label)* | | | |

**KICK AXE**
**RADIO SHOWS**
**Albums**

| | | | |
|---|---|---|---|
| KING BISCUIT FLOWER HOUR (Oct 84) Live concert | 1984 | DIR (2) | 30-50 |
| *(With Twisted Sister)* | | | |

**KID CREOLE AND THE COCONUTS**
**12-Inch Singles**

| | | | |
|---|---|---|---|
| ANNIE, I'M NOT YOUR DADDY (Long)/(Short) | 1983 | Sire PRO-A-2005 | 6 |
| GOING PLACES/IN THE JUNGLE/TABLE MANNERS | 1981 | Sire PRO-A-969 | 10 |
| I'M A WONDERFUL THING, BABY (LP)/(Edit) | 1982 | Sire PRO-A-1026 | 7 |
| MY MALE CURIOSITY (same on both sides) | 1984 | Atlantic PR 610 | 8 |
| PEOPLE WILL TALK | 1989 | Musician 5369 | 6 |
| STOOL PIGEON (Extended)/ANNIE, I'M NOT YOUR DADDY/I'M CORRUPT | 1982 | Sire PRO-A-1064 | 7 |

**45s**

| | | | |
|---|---|---|---|
| MY MALE CURIOSITY (edit)/(LP) | 1984 | Atlantic 89664 | 4 |
| *(Apparently, no stock copy exists)* | | | |

**KIDDS, THE**
**45s**

| | | | |
|---|---|---|---|
| ARE YOU FORGETTING ME? | 1955 | Imperial 5335 | 250 |
| *(White promo label)* | | | |

**KIHN, GREG**
*Beserkley promo 45s $3 each*
**RADIO SHOWS**
**Albums**

| | | | |
|---|---|---|---|
| BBC ROCK HOUR (Apr 82) | 1982 | London Wavelength | 15-25 |
| *(Music and interviews)* | | | |
| IN CONCERT (Apr 85) | 1985 | Westwood One (2) | 20-30 |
| *(Live concert)* | | | |
| IN CONCERT (June 84) Live concert | 1984 | Westwood One (2) | 20-40 |
| *(With Wang Chung)* | | | |

| Title | Yr | Label, Number | NM $ |
|---|---|---|---|
| IN CONCERT (May 83) Live concert | 1983 | Westwood One (2) | 40-75 |
| *(With Psychedelic Furs)* | | | |
| INNERVIEW (80s) Profile | 198? | Innerview | 10-15 |
| *(Music and interviews)* | | | |
| KING BISCUIT FLOWER HOUR  Live concert | 1983 | DIR/ABC (2) | 20-30 |
| *(Repeated)* | | | |
| KING BISCUIT FLOWER HOUR (June 86) Live concert | 1986 | DIR (2) | 20-35 |
| *(With John Cafferty)* | | | |
| KING BISCUIT FLOWER HOUR (May 81) Live concert | 1981 | DIR/ABC (2) | 10-20 |
| *(With Willie Nile)* | | | |
| KING BISCUIT FLOWER HOUR (Sept 81) Live concert | 1981 | DIR/ABC (2) | 40-75 |
| *(With Rockpile)* | | | |
| NBC SOURCE (Sept 83) | 1983 | NBC Radio (3) | 15-30 |
| *(Music and interviews)* | | | |
| OFF THE RECORD (July 84) Profile | 1984 | Westwood One (2) | 10-15 |
| *(Music and interviews, repeated)* | | | |

## KING
*Epic promo 45s $3 each; Epic promo 12" singles $6 each*
### RADIO SHOWS
**Albums**

| | | | |
|---|---|---|---|
| BBC ROCK HOUR  Live concert | 1985 | London Wavelength | 60-120 |
| *(With Working Week)* | | | |
| BBC TRANSCRIPTION DISC  Live concert | 1985 | BBC Transcription | 75-150 |
| *(Rare solo concert)* | | | |
| BBC TRANSCRIPTION DISC  Live concert | 1985 | BBC Transcription | 60-120 |
| *(With Working Week)* | | | |

## KING CRIMSON
*Atlantic promo 45s $8 each; Warner Bros. promo 45s $6 each; Warner promo-only 12" singles $8 each*
### 12-Inch Singles

| | | | |
|---|---|---|---|
| SLEEPLESS (Long Version)/(Short Version) | 1984 | Warner Bros. PRO-A-2131 | 8 |
| 3 OF A PERFECT PAIR/MAN WITH AN OPEN HEART | 1984 | Warner Bros. PRO-A-2148 | 8 |
| **Albums** | | | |
| THE RETURN OF KING CRIMSON | 1981 | Warner Bros. WBMS-119 | 60 |
| *(Promo-only interview and music show)* | | | |

### RADIO SHOWS
**Albums**

| | | | |
|---|---|---|---|
| BBC CONCERT (Mar 83) | 1983 | London Wavelength | 40-75 |
| *(Mostly music and interviews)* | | | |
| BBC ROCK HOUR (May 84) Live concert | 1984 | London Wavelength | 100-200 |
| *(With Pink Floyd)* | | | |
| BBC TRANSCRIPTION DISC  Live concert | 1974 | BBC Transcription | 400-650 |
| *(Very rare concert)* | | | |
| KING BISCUIT FLOWER HOUR (Aug 84) Live concert | 1984 | DIR/ABC (2) | 150-250 |
| *(Rare early concert)* | | | |
| NIGHTBIRD & COMPANY (July 74) Various artists | 1974 | U.S. Army (2) | 40-75 |
| *(One of the four shows features King Crimson)* | | | |
| **Compact Discs** | | | |
| KING BISCUIT FLOWER HOUR (Aug 88) Live concert | 1988 | DIR | 75-125 |
| *(With Genesis)* | | | |

## KING CURTIS
*Atco promo 45s $15 each; ABC Paramount, RCA Victor and Capitol promo 45s $8 each; Atco jukebox LLPs $12 each*
### 45s

| | | | |
|---|---|---|---|
| COUNTRY SOUL  Set of five Compact 33 singles | 1963 | Capitol 1756 | 40 |
| *(Or $8 each; jukebox releases)* | | | |

## KING FAMILY, THE
### 45s

| | | | |
|---|---|---|---|
| GO TELL IT ON THE MOUNTAIN/HERE THE SLEDGES WITH THE BELLS | 1965 | Warner Bros PRO 216 | 10 |

## KING SISTERS, THE
### 45s

| | | | |
|---|---|---|---|
| HOLIDAY OF LOVE/OVER THE RIVER | 1958 | Capitol 4099 | 12 |

## KING TOPPERS, THE
### 45s

| | | | |
|---|---|---|---|
| YOU WERE WAITING FOR ME | 1957 | Josie 811 | 45 |
| *(White promo label)* | | | |

## KING'S X
*Atlantic and Megaforce promo CD singles $2-3 each*
### Compact Discs

| | | | |
|---|---|---|---|
| BUILDING BLOX | 1994 | Atlantic PRCD-5494 | 18 |
| *(Promo-only sampler)* | | | |

### RADIO SHOWS
**Compact Discs**

| | | | |
|---|---|---|---|
| IN CONCERT (Sept 92) Live concert | 1992 | Westwood One | 30-50 |
| *(With The Cult)* | | | |
| KING BISCUIT FLOWER HOUR (Apr 94) Live concert | 1994 | DIR | 20-35 |
| *(With Foreigner)* | | | |
| KING BISCUIT FLOWER HOUR (Jan 91) Live concert | 1991 | DIR | 20-40 |
| *(With Jethro Tull)* | | | |

| Title | Yr | Label, Number | NM $ |
|---|---|---|---|
| KING BISCUIT FLOWER HOUR (Jan 91) Live concert | 1991 | DIR | 20-40 |
| *(With Kansas)* | | | |
| KING BISCUIT FLOWER HOUR (Jan 91) Live concert | 1991 | DIR | 40-60 |
| *(With Boston)* | | | |

**KING, B.B.**
**12-Inch Singles**

| Title | Yr | Label, Number | NM $ |
|---|---|---|---|
| THE BLUES COME OVER ME (6 versions) | 1991 | MCA 2118 | 6 |
| LAY ANOTHER LOG ON THE FIRE/GO ON | 1989 | MCA L33-17810 | 6 |
| MY LUCILLE (Extended)/INTO THE NIGHT | 1985 | MCA L33-1284 | 8 |

**KING, BEN E.**
*Of the Drifters; Atco promo 45s $10 each; Manhattan promo 45s $3 each*
**45s**

| Title | Yr | Label, Number | NM $ |
|---|---|---|---|
| STAND BY ME MEDLEY (same on both sides) | 1986 | Atlantic 89361 | 18 |
| *(Contains excerpts from all 10 songs on the "Stand By Me" soundtrack album; this is listed here because it uses the same number as the stock release of "Stand By Me." Also includes promo-only picture sleeve.)* | | | |
| WHAT'S IT ALL ABOUT (Oct 73) Public service show | 1973 | W.I.A.A. 197 | 20 |
| *(Flip side features 5th Dimension)* | | | |

**7-Inch Extended Plays**

| Title | Yr | Label, Number | NM $ |
|---|---|---|---|
| BEN E. KING'S GREATEST HITS  Jukebox LLP | 1972 | Atlantic 165 | 35 |
| *(Issued with a hard cover)* | | | |

**Albums**

| Title | Yr | Label, Number | NM $ |
|---|---|---|---|
| AUDIO BIOGRAPHY | 1972 | Mandala MLP-3008 | 30 |
| *(Promo-only interview by Richard Robinson)* | | | |

**RADIO SHOWS**
**Albums**

| Title | Yr | Label, Number | NM $ |
|---|---|---|---|
| BBC TRANSCRIPTION DISC  Live concert | 1987 | BBC Transcription | 200-300 |
| *(With Los Lobos)* | | | |

**KING, CAROLE**
*Other Dimension promo 45s $15 each; Ode promo 45s $3 each; Ode promo 33rpm singles $8 each; Dimension promo 45s by the Cookies $10-15 each; Ode promo 45s by the City $7 each.*
**12-Inch Singles**

| Title | Yr | Label, Number | NM $ |
|---|---|---|---|
| MAIN STREET SATURDAY NIGHT/DISCO TECH | 1978 | Capitol SPRO-8863/4 | 12 |
| ONE TO ONE (same on both sides) | 1982 | Atlantic PR 427 | 8 |

**45s**

| Title | Yr | Label, Number | NM $ |
|---|---|---|---|
| BABY SITTIN' | 1958 | ABC-Paramount 9986 | 100 |
| *(White promo label)* | | | |
| CHICKEN SOUP WITH RICE | 1975 | Ode 66112 SP | 18 |
| *(Special release through Scholastic Book Services, plays at 33 1/3 rpm, with picture sleeve)* | | | |
| CITY STREETS (same on both sides) | 1989 | Capitol 7PRO-79520 | 10 |
| *(Includes promo-only picture sleeve)* | | | |
| GOIN' WILD | 1958 | ABC-Paramount 9921 | 100 |
| *(White promo label)* | | | |
| HE'S A BAD BOY | 1961 | Dimension 1000 | 15 |
| *(Black promo label)* | | | |
| IT MIGHT AS WELL RAIN UNTIL SEPTEMBER | 1962 | Companion 2000 | 150 |
| *(White promo label)* | | | |
| IT MIGHT AS WELL RAIN UNTIL SEPTEMBER | 1962 | Dimension 2000 | 15 |
| *(Blue promo label)* | | | |
| OH, NEIL | 1959 | Alpine 57 | 500 |
| *(Answer song for Oh Carol by Neil Sedaka)* | | | |
| QUEEN OF THE BEACH | 1959 | RCA Victor 7560 | 75 |
| *(White promo label)* | | | |
| SPENDING TIME (same on both sides) | 1984 | Atlantic 89694 | 4 |
| *(May be promo only)* | | | |

**7-Inch Extended Plays**

| Title | Yr | Label, Number | NM $ |
|---|---|---|---|
| CAROLE KING MUSIC  Jukebox LLP | 1973 | Ode 77013 (LLP 180) | 12 |
| *(Issued with a soft cover)* | | | |
| TAPESTRY  Jukebox LLP | 1973 | Ode 77009 | 15 |
| *(Issued with a hard cover)* | | | |

**KING, PEE WEE**
*RCA Victor white promo label 78s $12 each; RCA Victor promo 45s $6-10 each; Top Rank and Jaro promo 45s $5 each; Landa promo 45s $3 each*

**KING, PETE, CHORALE**
**45s**

| Title | Yr | Label, Number | NM $ |
|---|---|---|---|
| WHITE CHRISTMAS (same on both sides) | 196? | Kapp AS-918X | 8 |

**KINGSMEN, THE**
*Wand promo 45s $6 each*

**KINGSTON TRIO, THE**
*Includes listings of Dave Guard, The New Kingston Trio; Other Capitol promo 45s $5-8 each depending on year; Decca pink label promo 45s $8 each; Tetragrammaton promo 45s $6 each; Nautilus promo 45s $5 each; Capitol promo 45s by the New Kingston Trio $2 each; Other Capitol promo LPs $40 each; Capitol DJ sampler promo LPs $12 each*
**45s**

| Title | Yr | Label, Number | NM $ |
|---|---|---|---|
| BEST OF THE KINGSTON TRIO Set of five 7-inch stereo jukebox singles | 1961 | Capitol SM-1705 | 75 |
| *(Small center hole, $15 each)* | | | |
| BIG SHIP GLORY | 1977 | Mountain Creek 301 | 25 |
| COREY, COREY | 1960 | Capitol 2007 | 40 |
| *(Issued with a promo-only picture sleeve, included in the price)* | | | |
| EL MATADOR  Music in the Air | 1960 | U.S. Air Force | 40 |
| *(Public service radio show, flip is by Dinah Shore)* | | | |
| EVERGLADES  Music in the Air | 1960 | U.S. Air Force | 40 |
| *(Public service radio show, flip is by the Four Preps)* | | | |

| Title | Yr | Label, Number | NM $ |
|---|---|---|---|
| HAUL AWAY  For the "New March of Dimes" | 1959 | Capitol 2783 | 40 |
| *(Promo-only record and picture sleeve, included in price)* | | | |
| IT TAKES A WORRIED MAN  Music in the Air | 1960 | U.S. Air Force #29 | 40 |
| *(Public service radio show (5:00), flip is by Sonny James)* | | | |
| LAST MONTH OF THE YEAR Set of five 7-inch stereo jukebox singles | 1960 | Capitol XE-1446 | 100 |
| *(Small center hole, $20 each)* | | | |
| MERRY MINUET | 1959 | Capitol PRO-856 | 40 |
| *(Rare promo single includes "Tick, Tick, Tick")* | | | |
| NEW FRONTIER Set of five 7-inch stereo jukebox singles | 1962 | Capitol SXE-1809 | 75 |
| *(Small center hole, $15 each)* | | | |
| PLANE WRECK AT LOS GATOS  Dave Guard | 1962 | Capitol 4787 | 10 |
| *(With the Whiskeyhill Singers)* | | | |
| STRING ALONG Set of five 7-inch stereo jukebox singles | 1960 | Capitol X-1407 | 75 |
| *(Small center hole, $15 each)* | | | |
| TOM DOOLEY  White promo label | 1958 | Capitol 4049 | 30 |
| *(Promo copy of the classic single)* | | | |

**7-Inch Extended Plays**

| Title | Yr | Label, Number | NM $ |
|---|---|---|---|
| ALL TOGETHER NOW  Various artists, General Electric promo | 1958 | Capitol 2537 | 20 |
| *(Includes one Kingston Trio song)* | | | |
| COOL CARGO  7-Up promo | 1960 | Capitol 2670 | 40 |
| *(Green or blue label, issued with a hard cover)* | | | |
| THE KINGSTON TRIO  Jukebox LLP | 1968 | Capitol 1577 | 25 |
| *(Issued with a hard cover)* | | | |
| KINGSTON TRIO #16  Jukebox LLP | 1968 | Capitol 1871 | 25 |
| *(Issued with a hard cover)* | | | |
| KINGSTON TRIO'S THREE HIT ALBUMS | 1959 | Capitol 1212 | 50 |
| *(Four songs from two albums)* | | | |
| MINUTE MASTERS  Various artists | 1960 | Capitol 1529 | 20 |
| *(Ten cuts, all edited, one Kingston Trio)* | | | |
| NEW FRONTIER  Jukebox LLP | 1968 | Capitol 1809 | 25 |
| *(Issued with a hard cover)* | | | |
| THE NEW FRONTIER | 1962 | Capitol PRO-2330 | 25 |
| *(Flip side is by Frank Sinatra)* | | | |
| SHORT SELECTIONS  Various artists | 1959 | Capitol 1266 | 20 |
| *(Ten cuts, all edited, one Kingston Trio)* | | | |
| TIJUANA JAIL  Red label | 1959 | Capitol 1129 | 100 |
| *(This very rare stereo EP with a hard cover was used as a jukebox LLP)* | | | |
| TIME TO THINK  Songs from the album | 1963 | Capitol PRO-2529 | 25 |
| *(Promo-only release)* | | | |

**Albums**

| Title | Yr | Label, Number | NM $ |
|---|---|---|---|
| BALANCED FOR BROADCAST (Mar 65) Various artists | 1965 | Capitol PRO-2809 | 15 |
| *(Trio does "Reverend Mr. Black")* | | | |
| EXCERPTS (Jan 59) Various artists | 1959 | Capitol PRO-828 (2) | 60 |
| *(Thirty-two cuts, one by Trio, "New York Girls")* | | | |
| EXCERPTS (June 59) Various artists | 1959 | Capitol PRO-1116 | 40 |
| *(Seventeen cuts, two by Trio, "MTA" and "All My Sorrows")* | | | |
| EXCERPTS (Oct 59) Various artists | 1959 | Capitol PRO-1263 | 40 |
| *(Fourteen cuts, two by Trio, "Molly Dee" and "Across the Wide Missouri")* | | | |
| EXCERPTS (Feb 61) Various artists | 1961 | Capitol PRO-1759 | 20 |
| *(Sixteen cuts, Trio does two, "En El Agua" and "Blue Eyed Gal")* | | | |
| EXCERPTS (May 62) Various artists | 1962 | Capitol PRO-2048 | 25 |
| *(Fourteen cuts, including two by Dave Guard and the Whiskeyhill Singers, "The Banks of the Ohio" and "Ride On Railroad Bill")* | | | |
| EXCERPTS  Various artists | 1962 | Capitol PRO-2125 | 20 |
| *(Fourteen cuts, Trio does two, "One More Town" and "Old Joe Clark")* | | | |
| EXCERPTS (Aug 63) Various artists | 1963 | Capitol PRO-2414 | 20 |
| *(Sixteen cuts, Trio does "Desert Pete")* | | | |
| EXCERPTS (Jan 64) Various artists | 1964 | Capitol PRO-2519 | 20 |
| *(Fourteen cuts, one by Trio, "Ally Ally Oxen Free")* | | | |
| EXCERPTS (June 64) Various artists | 1964 | Capitol PRO-2656 | 25 |
| *(Twenty-two edited cuts, one by Trio, "The World I Used to Know")* | | | |
| EXCERPTS (May 64) Various artists | 1964 | Capitol PRO-2615 | 15 |
| *(Sixteen cuts, one by Trio, "Let's Get Together")* | | | |
| FROM THE HUNGRY I  Black promo label | 1959 | Capitol 1107 | 50 |
| *("For Radio-TV Program use" label)* | | | |
| INSTANT HITS (Jan 64) Various artists | 1964 | Capitol PRO-2508 (2) | 35 |
| *(Forty-six edited cuts, one by the Trio)* | | | |
| INSTANT MUSIC (Mar 63) Various artists, white label | 1963 | Capitol PRO-2292 | 35 |
| *(Twenty-two cuts, four edited songs from Trio)* | | | |
| SILVER PLATTER SERVICE (Aug 63) With Jack Wagner | 1963 | Capitol PRO-3064 | 50 |
| *(Includes Kingston Trio interview and "Marcelle Vahine")* | | | |
| SILVER PLATTER SERVICE (Dec 63) With Jack Wagner | 1963 | Capitol PRO-3081 | 15 |
| *(Includes one Trio song, "Chilly Winds")* | | | |
| SILVER PLATTER SERVICE (June 64) With Jack Wagner | 1964 | Capitol PRO-3109 | 15 |
| *(Includes one Trio song, "World I Used to Know")* | | | |
| SILVER PLATTER SERVICE (July 64) With Jack Wagner | 1964 | Capitol PRO-3112 | 15 |
| *(Includes one Trio song, "Walkin' this Road to My Town")* | | | |
| THE KINGSTON TRIO  Yellow promo label | 1958 | Capitol 996 | 100 |
| *(Early Capitol promos are scarce)* | | | |
| WHO'S NEWS  Various artists, paper sleeve | 1960 | Capitol NP-1 | 15 |
| *(Yellow label, eleven tracks, one by the Kingston Trio)* | | | |

**RADIO SHOWS**

**16-Inch Transcriptions**

| Title | Yr | Label, Number | NM $ |
|---|---|---|---|
| CIVIL DEFENSE SHOW | 1959 | Civil Defense | 50-100 |
| *(Music and interviews, Kingston Trio are hosts)* | | | |
| TREASURY DEPARTMENT | 1960 | U.S. Treasury | 50-100 |
| *(Music and interviews, Kingston Trio are hosts)* | | | |

| Title | Yr | Label, Number | NM $ |
|-------|-----|---------------|------|

**KINGTONES, THE**
**45s**

| Title | Yr | Label, Number | NM $ |
|-------|-----|---------------|------|
| IT DOESN'T MATTER ANYMORE | 1969 | Cotillion 44069 | 50 |
| *(White promo label)* | | | |

**KINISON, SAM**
**45s**

| Title | Yr | Label, Number | NM $ |
|-------|-----|---------------|------|
| WILD THING | 1988 | Warner Bros. PRO-S-3396 | 15 |
| *(Promo-only 45)* | | | |

**KINKS, THE**

*Includes listings of Dave Davies; Reprise white promo label 45s before 0540 $18 each; Reprise white or brown promo 45s including and after 0540 $25 each; RCA Victor yellow promo label 45s $12 each; Other Arista promo 45s $5 each; MCA white promo label 45s $4 each; Arista oldies promo 45s $5 each; Warner Bros. promo 45s by Dave Davies $3 each; Other Arista and MCA 12" promo singles $10 each; Other Reprise white promo label LPs $20-30 depending on year*

**12-Inch Singles**

| Title | Yr | Label, Number | NM $ |
|-------|-----|---------------|------|
| ART LOVER (Live)/DESTROYER (Live) | 1988 | MCA L33-17531 | 6 |
| DO IT AGAIN (same on both sides) | 1984 | Arista ADP 9297 | 6 |
| DON'T FORGET TO DANCE (same on both sides) | 1983 | Arista ADP 9095 | 6 |
| FATHER CHRISTMAS | 1978 | Arista SP-34 | 15 |
| *(Promo-only release as a 12-inch)* | | | |
| HOW ARE YOU (same on both sides) | 1987 | MCA L33-17345 | 6 |
| LOST AND FOUND (same on both sides) | 1987 | MCA L33-17260 | 6 |
| THE ROAD (same on both sides) | 1988 | MCA L33-17460 | 8 |
| THE ROAD (EDIT) (same on both sides) | 1988 | MCA L33-17498 | 6 |
| ROCK 'N' ROLL CITIES (same on both sides) | 1987 | MCA L33-17207 | 6 |
| SUMMER'S GONE (same on both sides) | 1983 | Arista ADP 9337 | 6 |
| (WISH I COULD FLY LIKE) SUPERMAN (3:45) (5:58) | 1979 | Arista SP-45 | 15 |

**45s**

| Title | Yr | Label, Number | NM $ |
|-------|-----|---------------|------|
| CATCH ME NOW I'M FALLING | 1979 | Arista 0458 | 10 |
| *(Intro version 4:02 and 3:31 regular version)* | | | |
| LONG TALL SALLY  White promo label | 1964 | Cameo 308 | 300 |
| *(Stock copy very rare, worth $100 more)* | | | |
| LONG TALL SALLY  White promo label | 1965 | Cameo 345 | 100 |
| *(Stock copy very rare, worth $100 more)* | | | |
| SLEEPWALKER | 1977 | Arista SP-5 | 20 |
| *(Yellow vinyl, includes promo-only picture sleeve)* | | | |
| SUPERSONIC ROCKET SHIP | 1972 | RCA Victor SPS-45-380 | 15 |
| *(Released commercially as 74-0807)* | | | |
| WHAT'S IT ALL ABOUT  Public service show | 1980 | W.I.A.A. 445 | 20 |
| *(Flip side is Marilyn McCoo)* | | | |
| WHAT'S IT ALL ABOUT  Public service show | 1981 | W.I.A.A. 493 | 20 |
| *(Flip side is Rex Smith)* | | | |
| WHAT'S IT ALL ABOUT (Feb 81) Public service show | 1981 | W.I.A.A. 560 | 20 |
| *(Interview with Ray Davies, flip side is Glen Campbell)* | | | |
| WHAT'S IT ALL ABOUT (July 77) Public service show | 1977 | W.I.A.A. 377 | 25 |
| *(Interview with Ray Davies, flip side is Charley Pride)* | | | |
| YOU STILL WANT ME | 1965 | Cameo 348 | Unknown |
| *(Release uncertain)* | | | |

**7-Inch Extended Plays**

| Title | Yr | Label, Number | NM $ |
|-------|-----|---------------|------|
| ARTHUR  Radio spots | 1969 | Reprise PRO-352 | 150 |
| *(White promo label)* | | | |
| A FISTFUL OF KINKS | 1980 | Arista SP-85 | 30 |
| *(An EP sampler from Arista)* | | | |
| LOW BUDGET  Radio spots | 1979 | Arista | 50 |
| *(White promo label)* | | | |
| MISFITS  Square-shaped EP | 1978 | Arista SP-22 | 30 |
| *(Issued in an octagonal sleeve)* | | | |
| A ROCK AND ROLL FANTASY | 1978 | Arista 2623 | 40 |
| *(Promo-only white label record sent out to radio stations only)* | | | |

**Albums**

| Title | Yr | Label, Number | NM $ |
|-------|-----|---------------|------|
| GOD SAVE THE KINKS BOX | 1969 | Reprise PRO-328 | 500 |
| *(Mail-order box with decal, postcard, bag of grass, two pins, letter, Kinks consumer guide and "Then Now and In Between" LP, price is for complete package)* | | | |
| GREAT LOST KINKS ALBUM | 1973 | Reprise 2127 | 75 |
| *(Promo-only album, price includes insert)* | | | |
| KINDA KINKS | 1965 | Reprise 6173 | 200 |
| *(White promo label)* | | | |
| KINKS KINKDOM | 1965 | Reprise R-6184 | 200 |
| *(White promo label)* | | | |
| THE KINK KONTROVERSY | 1966 | Reprise R-6197 | 200 |
| *(White promo label)* | | | |
| KINKS SIZE | 1965 | Reprise 6158 | 200 |
| *(White promo label)* | | | |
| A LOOK AT THINK VISUAL | 1986 | MCA 17281 | 40 |
| *(Music and interviews)* | | | |
| LOW BUDGET RADIO INTERVIEW | 1979 | Arista SP-69 | 40 |
| *(Promo label and cover)* | | | |
| MISFITS | 1978 | Arista AL 4167 | 30 |
| *(White label promo)* | | | |
| SLEEPWALKER | 1977 | Arista AL 4106 | 30 |
| *(White label promo)* | | | |
| SOMETHING ELSE BY THE KINKS | 1968 | Reprise R-6272 | 300 |
| *(White label mono promo; no stock copies were issued in mono)* | | | |
| THEN, NOW & IN-BETWEEN | 1969 | Reprise PRO-328 | 50 |
| *(Record only)* | | | |
| YOU REALLY GOT ME | 1965 | Reprise 6143 | 400 |
| *(White promo label)* | | | |

| Title | Yr | Label, Number | NM $ |
|-------|-----|---------------|------|
| **RADIO SHOWS** | | | |
| **Albums** | | | |
| BBC LONDON WAVELENGTH (Nov 81) KINKS | 1981 | London Wavelength | 25-40 |
| *(Music and interviews)* | | | |
| BBC ROCK HOUR | 1981 | London Wavelength | 25-40 |
| *(Music and interviews)* | | | |
| BBC ROCK HOUR (Jan 82) Live concert | 1982 | London Wavelength | 40-75 |
| *(Repeated Dec 84)* | | | |
| BBC TRANSCRIPTION DISC  Live concert | 1978 | BBC Transcription | 300-400 |
| *(Very rare live concert)* | | | |
| CAPTURED LIVE (Oct 83) Live concert | 1983 | RKO Radio (3) | 85-140 |
| *(Rare live concert material)* | | | |
| IN CONCERT  Live concert | 1986 | Westwood One (2) | 40-75 |
| *(Repeated)* | | | |
| IN CONCERT (May 91) Live concert | 1991 | Westwood One (2) | 30-60 |
| *(With Dire Straits)* | | | |
| INSIDE TRACK (Oct 83) KINKS | 1983 | RKO Radio (3) | 25-40 |
| *(With Danny Ferry and David Byrne)* | | | |
| KING BISCUIT FLOWER HOUR  Live concert | 1985 | DIR (2) | 75-125 |
| *(Repeated)* | | | |
| KING BISCUIT FLOWER HOUR  Live concert | 1987 | DIR (4) | 100-175 |
| *(Parts one and two)* | | | |
| OFF THE RECORD (June 85) Profile | 1985 | Westwood One (2) | 15-25 |
| *(Music and interviews, repeated)* | | | |
| RETRO ROCK (Aug 82) Live concert | 1982 | Clayton Webster | 75-125 |
| *(Rare early concert material)* | | | |
| SOURCE CONCERT  Live concert | 1982 | NBC Radio (3) | 40-85 |
| *(Rare early concert)* | | | |
| SUPERGROUPS (Aug 82) Live concert | 1982 | Westwood One (3) | 75-150 |
| *(Rare concert material)* | | | |
| SUPERSTAR CONCERT (July 88) Live concert | 1988 | Westwood One (3) | 25-40 |
| *(Box set, repeated)* | | | |
| WORLD OF ROCK (80s) Various artists | 198? | DIR (2) | 15-25 |
| *(Ray Davies is a co-host)* | | | |
| **Compact Discs** | | | |
| BBC CLASSIC TRACKS (Feb 91) | 1991 | Westwood One | 20-35 |
| *(Live tracks from past BBC concerts)* | | | |
| IN CONCERT (Jan 94) Live concert | 1994 | Westwood One | 30-60 |
| *(CD format, repeated)* | | | |
| IN THE STUDIO (90s) Profile of an album | 199? | Album Network | 15-25 |
| *(Music and interviews)* | | | |
| KING BISCUIT FLOWER HOUR (Dec 92) Live concert | 1992 | DIR | 20-35 |
| *(Repeated and pressed in high numbers)* | | | |
| KING BISCUIT FLOWER HOUR (Oct 92) Live concert | 1992 | DIR | 20-40 |
| *(With Michael Penn)* | | | |
| MASTERS OF ROCK (May 90) | 1990 | Radio Ventures (2) | 20-35 |
| *(Mostly music and interviews)* | | | |
| SUPERSTAR CONCERT (July 93) Live concert | 1993 | Westwood One (2) | 25-40 |
| *(Repeated)* | | | |
| UP CLOSE  Profile | 1990 | Media America (2) | 45-75 |
| *(Mostly music and interviews, some live tracks)* | | | |

## KIRK, T.J.
**45s**

| Title | Yr | Label, Number | NM $ |
|-------|-----|---------------|------|
| SOUL POWER (Part 1)/SOUL POWER (Part 2) | 1995 | Warner Bros. PRO-A-7591 | 3 |

## KIRKLAND, EDDIE
**45s**

| Title | Yr | Label, Number | NM $ |
|-------|-----|---------------|------|
| IT'S TIME | 1952 | RPM 367 | 50 |
| *(White promo label)* | | | |

## KISS

*Including listings of Ace Frehley, Peter Criss, Gene Simmons, Paul Stanley, Vinnie Vincent Explosion; Other Casablanca brown promo label 45s $10 each; Mercury black promo label 45s $8 each; Casablanca promo 45s by Ace Frehley $10-20 each; Atlantic promo 45s by Ace Frehley $3 each; Megaforce promo singles by Ace Frehley $4 each; Casablanca promo 45s by Criss, Simmons and Stanley $4 each; Other promo 45s by Vinnie Vincent Invasion $4 each; Other Mercury promo 12" singles $12 each; Other Casablanca promo LPs $25 each; Casablanca promo LPs by Criss, Simmons, Stanley and Frehley $25 each*

**12-Inch Singles**

| Title | Yr | Label, Number | NM $ |
|-------|-----|---------------|------|
| ALL HELL'S BREAKING LOOSE (same on both sides) | 1983 | Mercury 244-1 | 15 |
| CRAZY NIGHTS (same on both sides) | 1987 | Mercury 531-1 | 12 |
| HEAVEN'S ON FIRE (same on both sides) | 1984 | Mercury 311-1 | 15 |
| I WAS MADE FOR LOVIN' YOU | 1978 | Casablanca 298 | 25 |
| *(One-sided 12" promo single)* | | | |
| LICK IT UP (same on both sides) | 1983 | Mercury 229-1 | 15 |
| REASON TO LIVE (same on both sides) | 1987 | Mercury 559-1 | 12 |
| TEARS ARE FALLING (same on both sides) | 1985 | Mercury 377-1 | 15 |
| THRILLS IN THE NIGHT (same on both sides) | 1984 | Mercury 326-1 | 15 |
| TURN ON THE NIGHT (same on both sides) | 1987 | Mercury 572-1 | 12 |
| **45s** | | | |
| BETH | 1976 | Casablanca BETH 1 DJ | 50 |
| *(Special prerelease, stereo/mono versions)* | | | |
| BETH | 1976 | Casablanca NBX 863 | 40 |
| *(Stereo/mono versions; originally the B-side of "Detroit Rock City")* | | | |
| C'MON AND LOVE ME | 1975 | Casablanca 841 | 18 |
| *(Stereo/mono versions)* | | | |
| DETROIT ROCK CITY | 1987 | Casablanca NB 863 | 50 |
| *(Stereo/mono versions, original A-side of 45 with "Beth" on B-side)* | | | |

| Title | Yr | Label, Number | NM $ |
|---|---|---|---|
| FLAMING YOUTH | 1976 | Casablanca 858 | 20 |
| *(Stereo/mono versions; some copies of this promo were shipped with stock picture sleeves, worth an additional $50 each)* | | | |
| HARD LUCK WOMAN | 1976 | Casablanca 873 | 12 |
| *(Stereo/mono versions)* | | | |
| KISSIN' TIME | 1974 | Casablanca 0011 | 25 |
| *(Dark blue label promo, Warner Bros. distribution)* | | | |
| LET ME GO, ROCK 'N ROLL | 1974 | Casablanca 823 | 18 |
| *(Stereo/mono versions)* | | | |
| NOTHIN' TO LOSE | 1974 | Casablanca 0004 | 25 |
| *(First record)* | | | |
| ROCK AND ROLL ALL NITE | 1975 | Casablanca 829 | 18 |
| *(Stereo/mono versions, studio)* | | | |
| ROCK AND ROLL ALL NITE | 1975 | Casablanca 850 | 15 |
| *(Stereo/mono versions, live)* | | | |
| ROCK AND ROLL ALL NITE | 1992 | Mercury PRO-1086 | 50 |
| *(Promo-only one-sided record)* | | | |
| SHOUT IT OUT LOUD | 1976 | Casablanca 854 | 20 |
| *(Stereo/mono 2:38 versions)* | | | |
| SHOUT IT OUT LOUD | 1976 | Casablanca 854 | 15 |
| *(Stereo/mono 2:50 versions)* | | | |
| SNEAK PEAK  Vinnie Vincent Invasion | 1988 | Chrysalis 43253 | 40 |
| *(Promo-only one-sided record and promo picture sleeve; very limited as a giveaway item at a Kiss Convention)* | | | |
| STRUTTER | 1974 | Casablanca 0015 | 20 |
| *(Dark blue label promo, Warner Bros. distribution)* | | | |
| WHAT'S IT ALL ABOUT (Feb 81) Public service show | 1981 | W.I.A.A. 563 | 35 |
| *(Interviews with Gene Simmons, flip side is Devo!)* | | | |
| **Albums** | | | |
| ALIVE! | 1975 | Casablanca 7020 (2) | 50 |
| *(Promo version, labeled as such)* | | | |
| ALIVE II | 1977 | Casablanca 7076 (2) | 50 |
| *(Promo version, labeled as such)* | | | |
| ASSEMBLED ESPECIALLY FOR RADIO | 1978 | Casablanca | 40 |
| *(Promo-only sampler from the four Kiss solo albums)* | | | |
| CREATURES OF THE NIGHT | 1982 | Casablanca 7261 | 40 |
| *(Promo version, labeled as such)* | | | |
| CRISS, FREHLEY, SIMMONS, STANLEY | 1978 | Casablanca NB 20137 | 40 |
| *(Promo-only sampler from the band's solo albums)* | | | |
| DESTROYER | 1976 | Casablanca 7025 | 40 |
| *(Promo version, labeled as such)* | | | |
| DOUBLE PLATINUM | 1978 | Casablanca 7100 (2) | 50 |
| *(Promo version, labeled as such)* | | | |
| DRESSED TO KILL | 1975 | Casablanca 7016 | 40 |
| *(Promo version, labeled as such)* | | | |
| DYNASTY | 1979 | Casablanca 7152 | 30 |
| *(Promo version, labeled as such)* | | | |
| FIRST KISS, LAST LICKS | 1990 | Mercury 792 | 100 |
| *(Promo-only release)* | | | |
| HOTTER THAN HELL | 1974 | Casablanca 7006 | 40 |
| *(Promo version, labeled as such)* | | | |
| KISS | 1974 | Casablanca 9001 | 200 |
| *(First Kiss LP, rare white promo label)* | | | |
| LOVE GUN | 1977 | Casablanca 7057 | 30 |
| *(Promo version, labeled as such)* | | | |
| ORIGINALS, THE | 1976 | Casablanca 7032 (3) | 200 |
| *(Repackage of first three Kiss LPs, white promo labels)* | | | |
| RETURN TO CASABLANCA | 1978 | Casablanca 20131 | 35 |
| *(Promo-only release)* | | | |
| ROCK AND ROLL OVER | 1976 | Casablanca 7037 | 30 |
| *(Promo version, labeled as such)* | | | |
| ROCK AND ROLL OVER SPECIAL EDITION | 1976 | Casablanca 7037 | 75 |
| *(Promo-only release, white promo label)* | | | |
| SPECIAL ALBUM FOR THEIR SUMMER TOUR | 1978 | Casablanca KISS-76 | 75 |
| *(Promo-only release)* | | | |
| A TASTE OF PLATINUM | 1978 | Casablanca 20128 | 40 |
| *(Promo-only release)* | | | |
| UNMASKED | 1980 | Casablanca 7225 | 30 |
| *(Promo version, labeled as such)* | | | |
| **Compact Discs** | | | |
| ALIVE III, THE TRILOGY | 1993 | Mercury (5) | 90 |
| *(All three live albums in one promo-only collection)* | | | |
| CRAZY CRAZY NIGHTS | 1988 | Mercury CDP 04 | 12 |
| *(Very early promo CD single)* | | | |
| DOMINO | 1992 | Mercury CDP 681 | 12 |
| *(Promo-only CD single)* | | | |
| EVERY TIME I LOOK AT YOU | 1992 | Mercury | 12 |
| *(Promo-only CD single)* | | | |
| FOREVER | 1989 | Mercury CDP 195 | 10 |
| *(Promo-only CD single, one of their biggest hits)* | | | |
| GOD GAVE ROCK AND ROLL TO YOU | 1991 | Interscope PRCD 4076 | 20 |
| *(Promo-only CD single, picture disc)* | | | |
| GOD GAVE ROCK AND ROLL TO YOU | 1991 | Interscope | 10 |
| *(Promo-only CD single, silver disc with insert card)* | | | |
| HIDE YOUR HEART | 1989 | Mercury CDP 140 | 12 |
| *(Promo-only CD single)* | | | |
| I JUST WANNA | 1992 | Mercury CDP 707 | 10 |
| *(Promo-only CD single)* | | | |

| Title | Yr | Label, Number | NM $ |
|---|---|---|---|
| I LOVE IT LOUD | 1992 | Mercury CDP 882 | 10 |
| *(Promo-only CD single)* | | | |
| LET'S PUT THE X IN SEX | 1988 | Mercury CDP 35 | 10 |
| *(Promo-only CD single)* | | | |
| NEW YORK GROOVE | 1996 | Mercury MECP 120 | 30 |
| *(Bonus CD single available only at Blockbuster Music to buyers of the Kiss CD "You Wanted the Best, You Got the Best!")* | | | |
| UNHOLY | 1992 | Mercury CDP 666 | 15 |
| *(Promo-only CD single)* | | | |

**RADIO SHOWS**
**Albums**

| | | | |
|---|---|---|---|
| GUEST DJ  Various artists | 1983 | PFM (3) | 30-50 |
| *(Members of Kiss co-host the show)* | | | |
| IN CONCERT (Jan 85) | 1985 | Westwood One (2) | 175-250 |
| *(With Twisted Sister)* | | | |
| KING BISCUIT FLOWER HOUR (Dec 84) Live concert | 1984 | ABC/DIR (2) | 175-250 |
| *(With Motley Crüe)* | | | |
| KING BISCUIT FLOWER HOUR (Mar 86) Metal Mania | 1986 | DIR (2) | 50-100 |
| *(Various artists including Kiss)* | | | |
| THE KISS STORY (May 90) Kiss Konfidential | 1990 | Unistar (2) | 100-175 |
| *(Rare and very collectible)* | | | |
| METALSHOP (Oct 92) Various artists | 1992 | MJI Broadcasting | 20-35 |
| *(Featured artist segment features Kiss)* | | | |

**Compact Discs**

| | | | |
|---|---|---|---|
| FOR ROCKERS ONLY  With Ace Frehley | 1988 | DSP Productions | 40-75 |
| *(Series of daily tracks, all Kiss related)* | | | |
| RADIO TODAY | 1993 | Radio International | 75-125 |
| *(Music and interviews)* | | | |

**KISSING THE PINK**
**RADIO SHOWS**
**Albums**

| | | | |
|---|---|---|---|
| BBC TRANSCRIPTION DISC  Live concert | 1983 | BBC Transcription | 100-200 |
| *(With JoBoxers)* | | | |

**KIX**
*Atlantic promo 45s $3 each; Atlantic and EastWest promo CD singles $2 each*
**RADIO SHOWS**
**Albums**

| | | | |
|---|---|---|---|
| IN CONCERT (Feb 90) Live concert | 1990 | Westwood One (2) | 20-40 |
| *(With Skid Row)* | | | |
| NBC SOURCE (June 83) | 1983 | NBC Radio (2) | 20-35 |
| *(With Zebra)* | | | |

**KNACK, THE**
*Charisma promo CD singles $2 each*
**12-Inch Singles**

| | | | |
|---|---|---|---|
| ART WAR | 1981 | Capitol SPRO-9712 | 10 |
| *(Promo-only 12" single)* | | | |
| ART WAR/AFRICA/PAY THE DEVIL | 1981 | Capitol SPRO 9713 | 6 |

**45s**

| | | | |
|---|---|---|---|
| BABY TALKS DIRTY  White/pink promo label | 1980 | Capitol P-4822 | 12 |
| *(Mono/stereo version)* | | | |
| BOYS GO CRAZY  White promo label | 1981 | Capitol P-5078 | 10 |
| *(Both sides are the same)* | | | |
| CAN'T PUT A PRICE ON LOVE  White promo label | 1980 | Capitol P-4853 | 10 |
| *(Mono/stereo version)* | | | |
| GOOD GIRLS DON'T   White promo label | 1979 | Capitol P-4771 | 10 |
| *(Mono/stereo version)* | | | |
| MY SHARONA  White promo label (3:58) | 1979 | Capitol P-4731 | 15 |
| *(Mono/stereo original promo version of this classic rock era record)* | | | |
| MY SHARONA  Gray custom label | 1994 | Capitol/RCA 62800 | 15 |
| *(Technically not a promo, but was mostly distributed to the jukebox trade; B-side is "Tempted" by Squeeze; price includes picture sleeve)* | | | |
| PAY THE DEVIL  White promo label | 1981 | Capitol P-5054 | 10 |
| *(Mono/stereo version)* | | | |

**KNICKERBOCKERS, THE**
*Challenge promo 45s $4 each*
**Albums**

| | | | |
|---|---|---|---|
| LIES | 1966 | Challenge 622 | 80 |
| *(White promo label)* | | | |

**KNIGHT, GLADYS, AND THE PIPS**
*Fury white promo label 45s $15-20 each; Soul white promo label 45s $5 each; Buddah promo 45s $4 each; Columbia and MCA white promo label 45s $2 each*
**12-Inch Singles**

| | | | |
|---|---|---|---|
| I WILL FIGHT/GOD IS | 1981 | Columbia AS 1307 | 8 |
| IT'S GONNA TAKE ALL OUR LOVE (same on both sides) | 1988 | MCA L33-17561 | 8 |
| LOVE OVERBOARD (4 versions) | 1987 | MCA L33-17431 | 8 |
| LOVE OVERBOARD (6:10) (5:44) | 1987 | MCA L33-17444 | 8 |
| LOVIN' ON NEXT TO NOTHIN' (4 versions) | 1987 | MCA L33-17429 | 8 |
| MEET ME IN THE MIDDLE (6 versions) | 1991 | MCA 2080 | 8 |
| MEN (5 versions) | 1990 | MCA 1456 | 8 |
| SUPERWOMAN (4 versions) | 1991 | MCA 1694 | 8 |
| TASTE OF BITTER LOVE/BOURGIE, BOURGIE | 1980 | Columbia AS 803 | 10 |
| THIS TIME (4 versions) | 1994 | MCA 3311 | 8 |
| WHERE WOULD I BE (3 versions) | 1991 | MCA 1621 | 8 |

| Title | Yr | Label, Number | NM $ |
|---|---|---|---|
| **45s** | | | |
| EVERY BEAT OF MY HEART  White promo label | 1961 | Vee Jay 386 | 25 |
| *(Also on Huntom-no promo known-and Fury labels)* | | | |
| MARCH OF DIMES  12 public service spots | 198? | B V 8000 | 25 |
| *(Gladys Knight does one 30-second and one 60-second ad)* | | | |
| SILENT NIGHT | 1974 | Buddah 1974 | 15 |
| *(Promo-only 45 and picture sleeve)* | | | |
| WHAT'S IT ALL ABOUT (Aug 75) Public service show | 1975 | W.I.A.A. 280 | 25 |
| *(Flip side is Alice Cooper)* | | | |
| WHAT'S IT ALL ABOUT (Feb 82) Public service show | 1982 | W.I.A.A. 612 | 15 |
| *(Flip side is Rupert Holmes)* | | | |
| WHISTLE, MY LOVE  The Pips | 1958 | Brunswick 55048 | 100 |
| *(Yellow promo label, first record)* | | | |
| **Albums** | | | |
| GREATEST HITS | 1970 | Soul 723 | 15 |
| *(White promo label)* | | | |
| **RADIO SHOWS** | | | |
| **Albums** | | | |
| ROBERT W. MORGAN Profile | 1976 | Watermark | 20-35 |
| *(Music and interviews)* | | | |

## KNOX, BUDDY

*Roulette promo 45s $12 each; Liberty promo 45s $10 each; Reprise promo 45s $8 each; United Artists promo 45s $5 each*

## KOFI

| | | | |
|---|---|---|---|
| **Albums** | | | |
| A VERY REGGAE CHRISTMAS | 1994 | Atlantic DMD 2182 | 15 |
| *(Promo only on green vinyl; generic white cover with custom sticker)* | | | |

## KOOL AND THE GANG

*DeLite promo 45s $3 each*

| | | | |
|---|---|---|---|
| **12-Inch Singles** | | | |
| RAINDROPS (3 versions) | 1989 | Mercury 739-1 | 5 |
| STONE LOVE (2 versions)/DANCE CHAMPION | 1986 | Mercury 478-1 | 6 |
| STRAIGHT AHEAD (same on both sides) | 1983 | DeLite 278-1 | 6 |
| TAKE MY HEART (same on both sides) | 1983 | DeLite 179-1 | 6 |
| TONIGHT (same on both sides) | 1983 | DeLite 261-1 | 6 |
| **45s** | | | |
| WHAT'S IT ALL ABOUT (Feb 76) Public service show | 1976 | W.I.A.A. 303 | 12 |
| *(Flip side features The Lettermen)* | | | |
| WHAT'S IT ALL ABOUT (Mar 75) Public service show | 1975 | W.I.A.A. 256 | 25 |
| *(Flip side features The Eagles)* | | | |
| **Albums** | | | |
| HISTORY OF KOOL AND THE GANG | 1979 | De-Lite MK-48 | 15 |
| **Reel-to-Reel Tapes** | | | |
| COKE  60-second commercial spots | 1984 | Coke AT-684 | 50 |
| *(Seven commercials, one by Kool & the Gang)* | | | |
| **RADIO SHOWS** | | | |
| **Albums** | | | |
| ROBERT W. MORGAN (Apr 81) | 1981 | Watermark | 15-25 |
| *(Music and interviews)* | | | |
| STARTRACK PROFILE (May 85) | 1985 | Westwood One (2) | 20-30 |
| *(Music and interviews)* | | | |

## KOOL GENTS, THE

| | | | |
|---|---|---|---|
| **45s** | | | |
| THIS IS THE NIGHT | 1955 | Vee Jay 173 | 65 |
| *(White promo label)* | | | |
| YOU KNOW | 1956 | Vee Jay 207 | 60 |
| *(White promo label)* | | | |

## KOSTELANETZ, ANDRE

| | | | |
|---|---|---|---|
| **45s** | | | |
| MEDLEY: SANTA CLAUS IS COMING TO TOWN & HAVE YOURSELF A MERRY LITTLE CHRISTMAS/CHRISTMAS CHOPSTICKS | 1963 | Columbia JZSP 76389/90 | 10 |
| O COME ALL YE FAITHFUL/OH TANNENBAUM | 1965 | Columbia JZSP 111905/6 | 12 |
| *(Green vinyl)* | | | |
| O COME ALL YE FAITHFUL/OH TANNENBAUM | 1965 | Columbia JZSP 111905/6 | 8 |
| *(Black vinyl)* | | | |

## KRAFTWERK

*Other Mercury and Warner Bros. promo 45s $4 each*

| | | | |
|---|---|---|---|
| **12-Inch Singles** | | | |
| POCKET CALCULATOR/DENTAKU | 1981 | Warner Bros. PRO-A-951 | 12 |
| ROBOTNIK/THE ROBOTS/ROBOTRONIK | 1991 | Elektra ED 5551 | 12 |
| **45s** | | | |
| AUTOBAHN | 1974 | Mercury DJ-9 | 15 |
| *(Promo-only 5:46/3:27 versions)* | | | |
| POCKET CALCULATOR | 1981 | Warner Bros. 49723 | 18 |
| *(Yellow vinyl, yellow promo label, clear picture sleeve included in price; this also was released as a stock copy)* | | | |

| Title | Yr | Label, Number | NM $ |
|-------|----|----|------|
| **KRAVITZ, LENNY** | | | |
| **Compact Discs** | | | |
| ARE YOU GONNA GO MY WAY | 1993 | Virgin DPRO-12755 | 8 |
| *(Promo-only CD single)* | | | |
| BELIEVE | 1993 | Virgin DPRO-12781 | 8 |
| *(Promo-only CD single)* | | | |
| CAN'T GET YOU OFF MY MIND | 1995 | Virgin DPRO-11071 | 8 |
| *(Promo-only CD single)* | | | |
| CIRCUS | 1995 | Virgin DPRO-11045 | 8 |
| *(Promo-only CD single)* | | | |
| FIELDS OF JOY | 1991 | Virgin PRCD 5981 | 8 |
| *(Promo-only CD single)* | | | |
| HEAVEN HELP | 1993 | Virgin DPRO-14105 | 8 |
| *(Promo-only CD single)* | | | |
| I BUILT THIS GARDEN FOR US | 1990 | Virgin PRCD WEED | 10 |
| *(Promo-only CD single)* | | | |
| IS THERE ANY LOVE IN YOUR HEART | 1993 | Virgin DPRO-12803 | 18 |
| *(Promo-only collection)* | | | |
| IT AIN'T OVER 'TIL IT'S OVER | 1991 | Virgin PRCD 3883 | 8 |
| *(Promo-only CD single)* | | | |
| LET LOVE RULE | 1989 | Virgin PRCD 2864 | 8 |
| *(Promo-only CD single)* | | | |
| MAMA SAID SAMPLER | 1991 | Virgin 3941 | 12 |
| *(Promo-only collection)* | | | |
| MR. CAB DRIVER | 1990 | Virgin PRCD 3272 | 8 |
| *(Promo-only CD single)* | | | |
| SAMPLER WITH SOUL | 1991 | Virgin 3869 | 15 |
| *(Promo-only collection)* | | | |
| SPINNING AROUND OVER YOU | 1993 | Virgin DPRO-14115 | 10 |
| *(Promo-only CD single)* | | | |
| STAND BY MY WOMAN | 1990 | Virgin PRCD 4099 | 8 |
| *(Promo-only CD single)* | | | |
| STOP DRAGGIN' | 1990 | Virgin PRCD 4377 | 8 |
| *(Promo-only CD single)* | | | |
| WHAT COMES AROUND GOES AROUND | 1991 | Virgin PRCD 4274 | 10 |
| *(Promo-only CD single)* | | | |
| **RADIO SHOWS** | | | |
| **Compact Discs** | | | |
| OFF THE RECORD (Sept 95) | 1995 | Westwood One | 15-25 |
| *(Music and interviews)* | | | |
| ON THE EDGE (Sept 93) Music and interviews | 1993 | Westwood One | 15-25 |
| *(With Sting)* | | | |
| **Reel-to-Reel Tapes** | | | |
| WORLD PREMIERE | 1995 | Album Network | 60-80 |
| *(With live tracks)* | | | |
| | | | |
| **KRISTOFFERSON, KRIS** | | | |
| *Monument promo 45s $3 each* | | | |
| **45s** | | | |
| WHAT'S IT ALL ABOUT (Dec 75) Public service show | 1975 | W.I.A.A. 294 | 10 |
| *(Flip side features Anne Murray)* | | | |
| WHAT'S IT ALL ABOUT (Mar 75) Public service show | 1975 | W.I.A.A. 267 | 15 |
| *(Flip side features Loggins and Messina)* | | | |
| WHAT'S IT ALL ABOUT (Mar 77) Public service show | 1977 | W.I.A.A. 362 | 25 |
| *(Flip side features The Eagles)* | | | |
| | | | |
| **KROKUS** | | | |
| *Arista promo 45s $3 each* | | | |
| **RADIO SHOWS** | | | |
| **Albums** | | | |
| BBC LONDON WAVELENGTH (May 81) Live concert | 1981 | London Wavelength | 35-70 |
| *(Rare early concert)* | | | |
| BBC ROCK HOUR (Sept 80) | 1980 | London Wavelength | 25-50 |
| *(Some music and interviews, repeated May 1981)* | | | |
| IN CONCERT (Apr 82) Live concert | 1982 | Westwood One (2) | 40-75 |
| *(With Tommy Tutone)* | | | |
| IN CONCERT (June 83) Live concert | 1983 | Westwood One (2) | 40-75 |
| *(With Quiet Riot)* | | | |
| INNERVIEW (80s) Profile | 198? | Innerview | 10-15 |
| *(Music and interviews)* | | | |
| KING BISCUIT FLOWER HOUR (Aug 82) Live concert | 1982 | DIR/ABC (2) | 100-200 |
| *(With ZZ Top)* | | | |
| KING BISCUIT FLOWER HOUR (Jan 85) | 1985 | DIR (2) | 40-75 |
| *(Live concert)* | | | |

| Title | Yr | Label, Number | NM $ |
|-------|----|--------------|------|

## L

**L.A. GUNS**
*Other Polydor promo CD singles $2-3 each*
**Compact Discs**

| Title | Yr | Label, Number | NM $ |
|-------|----|--------------|------|
| BALLAD OF JAYNE, THE | 1990 | Polydor CDP 210 | 8 |

*(Promo-only CD single, their biggest hit)*
**RADIO SHOWS**
**Albums**

| Title | Yr | Label, Number | NM $ |
|-------|----|--------------|------|
| HIGH VOLTAGE (Feb 90) Various artists | 1990 | Westwood One (2) | 20-35 |

*(Live segment of the show is L. A. Guns)*

| Title | Yr | Label, Number | NM $ |
|-------|----|--------------|------|
| METALSHOP (Aug 91) Various artists | 1991 | MJI Broadcasting (2) | 10-15 |

*(L. A. Guns featured on guest segment)*

| Title | Yr | Label, Number | NM $ |
|-------|----|--------------|------|
| OFF THE RECORD (Aug 91) Profile OF GROUP | 1991 | Westwood One (2) | 10-15 |

*(Music and interviews)*

**L.L. COOL J**
**12-Inch Singles**

| Title | Yr | Label, Number | NM $ |
|-------|----|--------------|------|
| NOW I'M COMIN'/(Instrumental) | 1993 | Def Jam CAS 05010 | 8 |
| PINK COOKIES IN A PLASTIC BAG GETTING CRUSHED BY BUILDINGS | 1992 | Def Jam CAS 05193 | 8 |
| STRICTLY BUSINESS (4 mixes) | 1991 | Uptown 1696 | 8 |
| TO DA BREAK OF DAWN (4 mixes) | 1990 | Motown 18371 | 6 |

**L7**
**45s**

| Title | Yr | Label, Number | NM $ |
|-------|----|--------------|------|
| CAN I RUN/BAGGAGE (Live) | 1995 | Slash PRO-S-7783 | 5 |

**RADIO SHOWS**
**Albums**

| Title | Yr | Label, Number | NM $ |
|-------|----|--------------|------|
| IN CONCERT (Feb 93) Live concert | 1993 | Westwood One (2) | 40-75 |

*(With Psychedelic Furs)*
**Compact Discs**

| Title | Yr | Label, Number | NM $ |
|-------|----|--------------|------|
| ON THE EDGE (Sept 94) Music and interviews | 1994 | Westwood One | 25-35 |

*(With the Indigo Girls and Love Spit Love)*

**LaBEEF, SLEEPY**
*Also known as Tommy LaBeef; Columbia white promo label 45s $4 each; Sun promo yellow vinyl 45s $6 each*
**45s**

| Title | Yr | Label, Number | NM $ |
|-------|----|--------------|------|
| ALL THE TIME | 1958 | Mercury 71179 | 40 |

*(White promo label)*

| Title | Yr | Label, Number | NM $ |
|-------|----|--------------|------|
| GHOST RIDERS IN THE SKY (same on both sides) | 1975 | Sun 1133 | 4 |

*(Promo only)*

| Title | Yr | Label, Number | NM $ |
|-------|----|--------------|------|
| I'M THROUGH  White promo label | 1958 | Mercury 71112 | 40 |

*(Earlier version on Starday worth more, no promo known)*

| Title | Yr | Label, Number | NM $ |
|-------|----|--------------|------|
| RIDE ON, JOSEPHINE | 1959 | Wayside 1937 | 60 |

*(Promo label)*

| Title | Yr | Label, Number | NM $ |
|-------|----|--------------|------|
| RIDE ON, JOSEPHINE | 1959 | Wayside 1651 | 75 |

*(Promo label)*

| Title | Yr | Label, Number | NM $ |
|-------|----|--------------|------|
| TORE UP  Tommy LaBeef | 1959 | Wayside 1654 | 100 |

*(Promo label)*

**LaBELLE, PATTI**
**12-Inch Singles**

| Title | Yr | Label, Number | NM $ |
|-------|----|--------------|------|
| ALL RIGHT NOW (6 versions) | 1992 | MCA 2433 | 8 |
| ALL THIS LOVE (3 versions) | 1994 | MCA 3140 | 8 |
| ALL THIS LOVE (4 versions) | 1994 | MCA 3160 | 8 |
| I CAN'T COMPLAIN/(Instrumental) | 1989 | MCA L33-18108 | 8 |
| JUST THE FACTS (same on both sides) | 1987 | MCA L33-17339 | 8 |
| SOMEBODY LOVES YOU BABY (4 versions) | 1991 | MCA 2074 | 8 |
| 'TWAS LOVE/REASON FOR THE SEASON | 1990 | MCA 1131 | 8 |
| YO MISTER (same on both sides) | 1989 | MCA L33-18014 | 8 |

**LAFETS & KITTY**
**45s**

| Title | Yr | Label, Number | NM $ |
|-------|----|--------------|------|
| CAN CAN ROCK AND ROLL | 1957 | Apollo 520 | 60 |

*(White promo label)*

**LAINE, DENNY**
*Early member of The Moody Blues; also a member of Wings (Paul McCartney and Co.) 1971-79; Capitol promo 45s $6 each*
**Albums**

| Title | Yr | Label, Number | NM $ |
|-------|----|--------------|------|
| HOLLY DAYS | 1976 | Capitol 11588 | 50 |

*(Issued in a plain white cover with 1976 copyright, later stock copies have a 1977 copyright)*

**LAINE, FRANKIE**
*ABC jukebox LLPs $10 each with covers*

**LAMPKIN, TOMMY**
**45s**

| Title | Yr | Label, Number | NM $ |
|-------|----|--------------|------|
| ETERNAL LOVE | 1956 | Imperial 5361 | 75 |

*(Cream-colored promo label)*

| Title | Yr | Label, Number | NM $ |
|---|---|---|---|
| **LANE, ROBIN, AND THE CHARTBUSTERS** | | | |
| **RADIO SHOWS** | | | |
| **Albums** | | | |
| BBC ROCK HOUR (Oct 80) | 1980 | London Wavelength | 40-75 |
| (Live concert) | | | |
| | | | |
| **LANG, K.D.** | | | |
| *Sire promo 45s $4 each; Sire and Warner Bros. promo CD singles $3-5 each* | | | |
| **12-Inch Singles** | | | |
| MISS CHATELAINE (4 remixes) | 1992 | Sire PRO-A-6052 | 15 |
| TURN ME ROUND (same on both sides) | 1987 | Sire PRO-A-2697 | 10 |
| **Albums** | | | |
| MAKING OF SHADOWLAND, THE | 1988 | Sire PRO-A-3120 | 25 |
| (Promo-only LP, music and interview) | | | |
| **RADIO SHOWS** | | | |
| **Albums** | | | |
| LIVE AT GILLEY'S (80s) Live concert | 198? | Westwood One | 75-125 |
| (Rare live concert) | | | |
| WESTWOOD ONE PRESENTS (Mar 90) Live concert | 1990 | Westwood One | 150-225 |
| (Very rare live concert) | | | |
| **Compact Discs** | | | |
| ON THE EDGE (Nov 93) Music and interviews | 1993 | Westwood One | 10-20 |
| (With the Lemonheads and R.E.M.) | | | |
| | | | |
| **LANIN, LESTER** | | | |
| **45s** | | | |
| CHRISTMAS MEDLEY/JINGLE BELLS | 1967 | Epic JZSP 123259/60 | 8 |
| DANCE OF THE SUGAR-PLUM FAIRIES/RING IN THE NEW | 1967 | Epic JZSP 123257/8 | 8 |
| WINTER WONDERLAND/SLEIGH RIDE | 1967 | Epic JZSP 123255/6 | 8 |
| | | | |
| **LARKS, THE** | | | |
| *Other Apollo white promo label 45s $125 each and higher* | | | |
| **45s** | | | |
| HONEY FROM THE BEE | 1955 | Apollo 475 | 100 |
| (White promo label) | | | |
| | | | |
| **LAUPER, CYNDI** | | | |
| *Epic and Portrait promo 45s $3 each; Other Epic promo CD singles $3 each* | | | |
| **12-Inch Singles** | | | |
| CHANGE OF HEART (AOR Mix) (same on both sides) | 1986 | Portrait AS 2560 | 6 |
| THE GOONIES 'R' GOOD ENOUGH (same on both sides) | 1985 | Portrait AS 2084 | 6 |
| TRUE COLORS (same on both sides) | 1986 | Portrait AS 2450 | 6 |
| **Compact Discs** | | | |
| I DROVE ALL NIGHT | 1989 | Epic ESK 1564 | 8 |
| (Promo-only CD single) | | | |
| **RADIO SHOWS** | | | |
| **Albums** | | | |
| MUSIC OF THE 80S (Aug 84) Music and interviews | 1984 | DIR (2) | 100-150 |
| (With Annie Lennox and Madonna) | | | |
| | | | |
| **LAURELS, THE, WITH BOBBY RELF** | | | |
| **45s** | | | |
| TRULY, TRULY | 1955 | "X" 0143 | 250 |
| (White promo label) | | | |
| | | | |
| **LAWRENCE, BILL** | | | |
| **45s** | | | |
| HEY BABY | 1957 | Freedom 44004 | 40 |
| (White promo label) | | | |
| | | | |
| **LAWRENCE, STEVE** | | | |
| *Includes Steve Lawrence and Eydie Gorme; ABC Paramount promo 45s $8 each; Coral promo 45s $6 each; Columbia promo 45s, solo or duet, $4 each; MGM promo 45s by Steve & Eydie $2 each* | | | |
| **45s** | | | |
| BLUESETTE | 1964 | Columbia JZSP 78856 | 10 |
| (Red vinyl, white promo label) | | | |
| I WANT TO STAY HERE  Steve & Eydie | 1966 | Columbia 42815 | 10 |
| (Red vinyl, white promo label) | | | |
| **7-Inch Extended Plays** | | | |
| STEVE LAWRENCE'S GREATEST HITS | 196? | Columbia 8670 | 10 |
| (Jukebox LLP, issued with a hard cover) | | | |
| WE GOT US  Steve & Eydie | 1958 | ABC-Paramount | 15 |
| (Promo-only EP, no cover issued) | | | |
| **Albums** | | | |
| THE SKITCH HENDERSON ORCHESTRA (60s) | 196? | SESAC 1455 | 50 |
| (With Steve Lawrence, promo-only release) | | | |
| | | | |
| **LAWRENCE, TRACY** | | | |
| *Atlantic promo CD singles $2-3 each* | | | |
| **RADIO SHOWS** | | | |
| **Compact Discs** | | | |
| COUNTRY CUTTING EDGE (June 94) Live concert | 1994 | Westwood One | 25-50 |

| **Title** | **Yr** | **Label, Number** | **NM $** |
|---|---|---|---|

**LED ZEPPELIN**
*Includes singles by Led Zeppelin and Listen, and both group and solo LPs; also see Jimmy Page; Robert Plant; The Yardbirds*

**45s**

| Title | Yr | Label, Number | NM $ |
|---|---|---|---|
| BLACK DOG  Regular promo single | 1971 | Atlantic 2849 | 30 |
| *(Same track on both sides)* | | | |
| CANDY STORE ROCK  Mono/stereo versions | 1977 | Swan Song 70110 | 20 |
| *(White label/blue label)* | | | |
| D'YER MAK'ER  Mono long (4:19)/short (3:15) versions | 1973 | Atlantic 2986 | 30 |
| *(Red/white promo labels)* | | | |
| D'YER MAK'ER  Stereo long (4:19) version | 1973 | Atlantic 2986 | 30 |
| *(Same track on both sides, blue labels)* | | | |
| DAZED AND CONFUSED  Promo-only release | 1969 | Atlantic 1019 | 750 |
| *(Price includes promo-only paper sleeve)* | | | |
| FOOL IN THE RAIN  Long/short versions | 1979 | Swan Song 71003 | 20 |
| *(Blue label)* | | | |
| GALLOWS POLE  Mono/stereo versions | 1971 | Atlantic PR-157 | 150 |
| *(Promo-only release)* | | | |
| GOOD TIMES BAD TIMES  Promo label | 1969 | Atlantic 2613 | 50 |
| *(Both sides are the same)* | | | |
| IMMIGRANT SONG  One-sided promo | 1970 | Atlantic 2777 | 150 |
| *(All red label)* | | | |
| IMMIGRANT SONG  Regular promo single | 1970 | Atlantic 2777 | 30 |
| *(Same on both sides, red/white labels)* | | | |
| LIVING LOVING MAID  Original B-side | 1969 | Atlantic 2690 | 150 |
| *(One-sided record, all red label)* | | | |
| OVER THE HILLS AND FAR AWAY  Mono/stereo versions | 1973 | Atlantic 2970 | 30 |
| *(Blue and red/white labels)* | | | |
| ROCK AND ROLL  Mono/stereo versions | 1972 | Atlantic 2865 | 30 |
| *(Blue/red, white/red labels)* | | | |
| STAIRWAY TO HEAVEN  20th anniversary issue | 1992 | Atlantic | 100 |
| *(Promo vinyl and CD, 1,000 copies pressed)* | | | |
| STAIRWAY TO HEAVEN  Mono/stereo, 7:55 version | 1971 | Atlantic PR-175 | 100 |
| *(White promo label on both sides, promo only; a paper picture sleeve was also released with this; together, the two go for $250 or more)* | | | |
| STAIRWAY TO HEAVEN  Stereo, 7:55 version | 1973 | Atlantic PR-269 | 75 |
| *(Also a promo-only release, no picture sleeve, both sides are the same, blue promo labels)* | | | |
| TRAMPLED UNDER FOOT  Mono/stereo versions | 1975 | Swan Song 70102 | 20 |
| *(White label/blue label)* | | | |
| WHAT'S IT ALL ABOUT (Feb 82) Public service show | 1982 | W.I.A.A. 613 | 30 |
| *(Interviews with Robert Plant, flip is Supertramp)* | | | |
| WHAT'S IT ALL ABOUT (Jan 81) Public service show | 1981 | W.I.A.A. 557 | 30 |
| *(Interviews with Robert Plant, flip is Larry Gatlin)* | | | |
| WHOLE LOTTA LOVE  Red/white and white promo labels | 1969 | Atlantic/Atco 2690/6779 | 50 |
| *(Flip side is same song by King Curtis, on Atco)* | | | |
| WHOLE LOTTA LOVE  Red/white labels | 1969 | Atlantic 2690 | 50 |
| *(Both sides "Plug Side," 5:33 mono and 3:12 mono versions)* | | | |
| WHOLE LOTTA LOVE  Regular promo single | 1969 | Atlantic 2690 | 30 |
| *(Red/white labels)* | | | |
| YOU BETTER RUN  by Listen | 1967 | Columbia 43967 | 100 |
| *(White promo label)* | | | |

**7-Inch Extended Plays**

| Title | Yr | Label, Number | NM $ |
|---|---|---|---|
| CONCERTS FOR THE PEOPLE OF KAMPUCHEA  Various artists | 1981 | Atlantic PR-388 | 100 |
| *(Promo only, includes one Robert Plant track)* | | | |
| HOUSES OF THE HOLY  Jukebox LLP | 1973 | Atlantic 7255 (LLP 213) | 150 |
| *(Issued with a paper cover)* | | | |
| LED ZEPPELIN  Jukebox LLP | 1971 | Atlantic 7208 (LLP 171) | 200 |
| *(Issued with a paper sleeve; includes Black Dog, Rock and Roll, Stairway to Heaven)* | | | |
| SAVE THE CHILDREN  Various artists | 1980 | DWP 567 | 100 |
| *(20 cuts, cut 6 is a 30-second spot by Led Zeppelin)* | | | |
| STAIRWAY TO HEAVEN | 197? | Atlantic | 250 |
| *(Considered by many to be an EP, this is the rare promo picture disc version)* | | | |

**Albums**

| Title | Yr | Label, Number | NM $ |
|---|---|---|---|
| HOUSES OF THE HOLY  Mono | 1973 | Atlantic 7255 | 400 |
| *(Very rare mono white promo label version)* | | | |
| HOUSES OF THE HOLY  Stereo | 1973 | Atlantic 7255 | 200 |
| *(Rare white stereo promo label)* | | | |
| LED ZEPPELIN  Mono | 1969 | Atlantic 8216 | 200 |
| *(White promo label, no stock copies are in mono)* | | | |
| LED ZEPPELIN  Record store sampler | 1969 | Atlantic 135 | 200 |
| *(Also known as "Climb Aboard Led Zeppelin," this promo-only sampler has Dusty Springfield on the B-side.)* | | | |
| LED ZEPPELIN  Stereo | 1969 | Atlantic 8216 | 150 |
| *(White promo label)* | | | |
| LED ZEPPELIN II  Mono | 1969 | Atlantic 8236 | 200 |
| *(White promo label, no stock copies are in mono)* | | | |
| LED ZEPPELIN II  Stereo | 1969 | Atlantic 8236 | 150 |
| *(White promo label)* | | | |
| LED ZEPPELIN III  Mono | 1970 | Atlantic 7201 | 200 |
| *(White promo label, no stock copies are in mono)* | | | |
| LED ZEPPELIN III  Stereo | 1970 | Atlantic 7201 | 150 |
| *(White promo label)* | | | |
| LED ZEPPELIN IV | 1971 | Atlantic 7208 | 200 |
| *(White promo label, includes "Stairway to Heaven")* | | | |
| ROBERT PLANT  Promo-only release | 1988 | Atlantic | 20 |
| *(Music and interviews)* | | | |
| ROBERT PLANT  Promo-only release with special cover | 1988 | Atlantic (2) | 25 |
| *(Music and interviews about new album)* | | | |

| Title | Yr | Label, Number | NM $ |
|-------|----|--------------| ----|
| **Compact Discs** | | | |
| BABY COME ON HOME | 1995 | Atlantic PRCD 5255 | 10 |
| *(Promo-only CD single)* | | | |
| OVER THE HILLS AND FAR AWAY | 1990 | Atlantic PRCD 3717 | 10 |
| *(Promo-only CD single)* | | | |
| PROFILED | 1990 | Atlantic PRCD 3629 | 20 |
| *(Music and interviews)* | | | |
| TRAVELING RIVERSIDE BLUES | 1990 | Atlantic PRCD 3627 | 10 |
| *(Promo-only CD single)* | | | |
| **RADIO SHOWS** | | | |
| **Albums** | | | |
| ALBUM GREATS  Various artists | 1979 | TM Special Products (2) | 30-60 |
| *(Price is for just the Led Zeppelin discs)* | | | |
| BBC ROCK HOUR (Oct 80) | 1980 | London Wavelength | 175-250 |
| *(Live concert)* | | | |
| BBC ROCK HOUR (Dec 83) Robert Plant | 1983 | London Wavelength | 25-40 |
| *(Music and interviews)* | | | |
| BBC ROCK HOUR (Nov 84) | 1984 | London Wavelength | 150-225 |
| *(Live concert)* | | | |
| BBC TRANSCRIPTION DISC | 1971 | BBC Transcription | 500-700 |
| *(Very rare live concert)* | | | |
| BBC TRANSCRIPTION DISC | 1976 | BBC Transcription | 500-700 |
| *(Very rare live concert)* | | | |
| CONTINUOUS HISTORY OF ROCK & ROLL (Nov 81) Various artists | 1981 | Rolling Stone (2) | 50-100 |
| *(Price is for just the Led Zeppelin discs)* | | | |
| COUNTDOWN TO CHRISTMAS (Dec 85) | 1985 | NBC Source | 20-35 |
| *(Music and interviews)* | | | |
| HIGH VOLTAGE (June 89) Various artists | 1989 | Westwood One (2) | 40-75 |
| *(Live segment of the show is Led Zeppelin live)* | | | |
| HIGH VOLTAGE Various artists | 1989 | Westwood One (2) | 40-75 |
| *(Live segment of the show is Jimmy Page live)* | | | |
| HIGH VOLTAGE Various artists | 1989 | Westwood One (2) | 35-65 |
| *(Live segment of the show is Robert Plant live)* | | | |
| IN CONCERT | 1986 | Westwood One (2) | 50-100 |
| *(Live concert, repeated several times)* | | | |
| INNERVIEW (July 75) | 1975 | Sound Communications (2) | 300-500 |
| *(Hosted by JJ Jackson, presented by Toyota)* | | | |
| INNERVIEW | 1976 | Sound Communications | 125-200 |
| *(Edited version of above show)* | | | |
| INNERVIEW  Robert Plant | 1978 | Sound Communications | 75-100 |
| *(Music and interviews)* | | | |
| INSIDE TRACKS (Aug 83) Robert Plant and others | 1983 | Inside Tracks | 30-50 |
| *(Also features Phil Collins, music and interviews)* | | | |
| KING BISCUIT FLOWER HOUR  Robert Plant | 1984 | DIR/ABC (2) | 50-100 |
| *(Live concert)* | | | |
| KING BISCUIT FLOWER HOUR (Feb 84) Robert Plant | 1984 | DIR/ABC (2) | 50-100 |
| *(Side 4, usually blank, has live version of "Big Log")* | | | |
| KING BISCUIT FLOWER HOUR -- BIG LOG (Feb 84) Robert Plant | 1984 | DIR/ABC | 10 |
| *(For the "Big Log" record only of the Feb 85 show)* | | | |
| LED ZEPPELIN STORY | 1989 | United Stations (3) | 50-100 |
| *(Music and interviews)* | | | |
| LEGENDS OF ROCK  Jimmy Page | 1989 | NBC Radio (2) | 20-40 |
| *(Music and interviews)* | | | |
| LEGENDS OF ROCK  Robert Plant | 1987 | NBC Radio (2) | 20-40 |
| *(Music and interviews)* | | | |
| LEGENDS OF ROCK  Robert Plant | 1988 | NBC Radio (4) | 25-50 |
| *(Parts one and two, music and interviews)* | | | |
| LEGENDS OF ROCK (Sept 87) | 1987 | NBC Radio (4) | 35-50 |
| *(Parts one and two, music and interviews with some live)* | | | |
| LONDON WAVELENGTH | 1982 | London Wavelength | 150-225 |
| *(Live concert)* | | | |
| MAXELL PRESENTS (Dec 82) | 1982 | Maxell (2) | 1,000-1,500 |
| *(The ultimate live concert radio show, issued with a special hard cover)* | | | |
| METALSHOP (Feb 85) Jimmy Page/The Firm | 1985 | MJI (2) | 20-40 |
| *(Various artists, special segment is Page/Firm)* | | | |
| NIGHTBIRD & COMPANY (May 75) Various artists | 1975 | Army Reserve (2) | 75-125 |
| *(Two of the four shows feature Led Zeppelin)* | | | |
| OFF THE RECORD  Robert Plant | 1983 | Westwood One (2) | 15-25 |
| *(Repeated several times)* | | | |
| OFF THE RECORD  Robert Plant | 1984 | Westwood One (4) | 25-35 |
| *(Parts one and two)* | | | |
| OFF THE RECORD (Apr 85) The Firm | 1985 | Westwood One (2) | 15-25 |
| *(Repeated)* | | | |
| OFF THE RECORD (June 88) Jimmy Page | 1988 | Westwood One (4) | 30-40 |
| *(Parts one and two)* | | | |
| ROBERT PLANT  Robert Plant | 1984 | London Wavelength (2) | 50-100 |
| *(Music and interviews, black labels)* | | | |
| THE ROBERT PLANT STORY | 1990 | Unistar (3) | 30-50 |
| *(Music and interviews)* | | | |
| ROCK AND ROLL NEVER FORGETS | 198? | Westwood One (3) | 50-80 |
| *(Music and interviews)* | | | |
| ROYALTY OF ROCK | 1983 | RKO (2) | 40-75 |
| *(Music and interviews)* | | | |
| SOURCE CHRISTMAS SPECIAL (Dec 83)  Robert Plant | 1983 | NBC Source (6) | 100-150 |
| *(Music and interviews)* | | | |
| SOURCE SPECIAL | 1982 | NBC Source (6) | 150-200 |
| *(Mostly music and interviews)* | | | |

| **Title** | **Yr** | **Label, Number** | **NM $** |
|---|---|---|---|
| SOURCE SPECIAL  Robert Plant | 1982 | NBC Source (6) | 100-150 |
| *(Mostly music and interviews)* | | | |
| SOURCE SPECIAL  Robert Plant | 1983 | NBC Source (2) | 30-50 |
| *(Music and interviews)* | | | |
| A STAIRWAY TO HEAVEN (Nov 88) | 1988 | Westwood One (3) | 40-75 |
| *(Music and interviews)* | | | |
| SUPERSTAR CONCERT  The Firm | 1985 | Westwood One (3) | 40-80 |
| *(Live concert)* | | | |
| SUPERSTAR CONCERT  Robert Plant | 1986 | Westwood One (3) | 40-75 |
| *(Live concert, repeated)* | | | |
| SUPERSTAR CONCERT  Jimmy Page | 1988 | Westwood One (3) | 50-100 |
| *(Live concert, repeated)* | | | |
| SUPERSTAR CONCERT (Aug 88) | 1988 | Westwood One (3) | 40-75 |
| *(With Foreigner and Yes)* | | | |
| SUPERSTAR CONCERT (Feb 91) Robert Plant | 1991 | Westwood One (3) | 40-75 |
| *(With Neil Young and Van Halen)* | | | |
| SUPERSTAR CONCERT (Mar 93) The Firm | 1993 | Westwood One (3) | 30-50 |
| *(With Bad Company and Free)* | | | |
| **Compact Discs** | | | |
| 25TH ANNIVERSARY OF MAKING OF LED ZEPPELIN I (Jan 94) | 1994 | Album Network (2) | 40-80 |
| *(Designer CDs, music and interviews)* | | | |
| BBC CLASSIC TRACKS (90s) | 199? | Westwood One | 20-40 |
| *(Several shows, mostly live tracks)* | | | |
| BRING IT ON HOME (Nov 90) | 1990 | Media America (4) | 125-250 |
| *(Mostly music and interviews)* | | | |
| CLASSIC CUTS (Oct 90) | 1990 | WWI/Source (2) | 100-175 |
| *(Mostly live cuts)* | | | |
| CROSSROADS (July 90) Various artists | 1990 | (3) | 40-75 |
| *(Music and interviews, including Led Zeppelin)* | | | |
| THE FINAL CHAPTER (Sept 91) | 1991 | Westwood One (6) | 150-225 |
| *(Mostly live with some music and interviews)* | | | |
| FOR ROCKERS ONLY | 1988 | DSP Productions | 20-30 |
| *(Series of daily shows, all shows are Led Zeppelin)* | | | |
| IN CONCERT (Aug 92) | 1992 | Westwood One (2) | 60-125 |
| *(Live concert, repeated)* | | | |
| IN CONCERT (May 92) Led Zeppelin/Nirvana | 1992 | Westwood One (2) | 75-125 |
| *(Live concert)* | | | |
| IN THE STUDIO  Robert Plant | 1988 | Album Network | 15-25 |
| *(Profile of an album, music and interviews)* | | | |
| IN THE STUDIO  Robert Plant | 1990 | Album Network | 10-25 |
| *(World premiere of "Manic Nirvana," music and interviews)* | | | |
| IN THE STUDIO (Nov 88) | 1988 | Album Network | 25-40 |
| *(Profile of an album, music and interviews)* | | | |
| IN THE STUDIO  Page & Plant | 1995 | Album Network | 20-40 |
| *(Profile of the making of "No Quarter")* | | | |
| IT'S BEEN A LONG TIME (Sept 90) | 1990 | (6) | 150-275 |
| *(Six-hour documentary including some live tracks)* | | | |
| KING BISCUIT FLOWER HOUR  Robert Plant | 1989 | DIR | 40-80 |
| *(Live concert)* | | | |
| LABOR DAY SPECIAL (Sept 90) | 1990 | Westwood One (6) | 125-250 |
| *(Live tracks; music and interviews)* | | | |
| LED ZEPTEMBER | 1993 | Premier Radio (3) | 75-125 |
| *(Mostly music and interviews)* | | | |
| LEDDED AND UN-LEDDED (May 95) | 1995 | Westwood One (8) | 100-200 |
| *(Career retrospective and live Page/Plant tracks)* | | | |
| OFF THE RECORD (Sept 93) Coverdale/Page | 1993 | Westwood One | 20-30 |
| *(Music and interviews)* | | | |
| ON THE EDGE (Mar 95) Led Zeppelin tribute | 1995 | | 30-60 |
| *(Music and interviews, all cover songs from the CD)* | | | |
| RARITIES VOL. 7 | 1991 | | 30-60 |
| *(Rare tracks now on CD)* | | | |
| SHOWCASE OF ROCK (Feb 92) | 1992 | Unistar (3) | 40-75 |
| *(Music and interviews)* | | | |
| SILVER ANNIVERSARY (July 93) | 1993 | Westwood One (6) | 90-150 |
| *(Music and interviews with many live tracks)* | | | |
| SUPERSTAR CONCERT (Aug 94) | 1994 | Westwood One (2) | 40-75 |
| *(Live concert)* | | | |
| SUPERSTAR CONCERT (July 93) | 1993 | Westwood One (2) | 40-80 |
| *(Live concert)* | | | |
| SUPERSTAR CONCERT (Sept 93) Robert Plant | 1993 | Westwood One (2) | 40-75 |
| *(Live concert, repeated)* | | | |
| SUPERSTARS (July 95) | 1995 | (2) | 50-80 |
| *(Live concert material)* | | | |
| SUPERSTARS (Mar 95) Robert Plant | 1995 | (2) | 40-70 |
| *(Live concert material)* | | | |
| TRIBUTE TO BONHAM (Sept 90) | 1990 | Westwood One (6) | 40-80 |
| *(Music and interviews, with many live tracks)* | | | |
| UP CLOSE  Jimmy Page | 1988 | Media America (2) | 50-100 |
| *(Music and interviews with some live)* | | | |
| UP CLOSE  Robert Plant | 1989 | Media America (4) | 75-150 |
| *(Parts one and two, music and interviews)* | | | |
| UP CLOSE  Robert Plant | 1989 | Media America (2) | 40-80 |
| *(Music and interviews, some live tracks)* | | | |
| UP CLOSE | 1990 | Media America (4) | 75-150 |
| *(Parts one and two, music and interviews)* | | | |
| UP CLOSE  Robert Plant | 1993 | Media America (3) | 50-100 |
| *(Edited version of earlier shows, music and interviews)* | | | |

| Title | Yr | Label, Number | NM $ |
|-------|-----|---------------|------|
| UP CLOSE  Plant & Page | 1994 | Media America (4) | 125-200 |
| *(Parts one and two, mostly music and interviews)* | | | |
| **Reel-to-Reel Tapes** | | | |
| WORLD PREMIERE (Mar 93) Coverdale/Page | 1993 | | 40-80 |
| *(Music and interviews)* | | | |

**LEE, ALVIN**
*Also see Ten Years After*

| Title | Yr | Label, Number | NM $ |
|-------|-----|---------------|------|
| **12-Inch Singles** | | | |
| DETROIT DIESEL (same on both sides) | 1986 | 21 Records PR 918 | 6 |
| SHOT IN THE DARK (same on both sides) | 1986 | 21 Records PR 956 | 6 |
| **45s** | | | |
| CAN'T STOP (same on both sides) | 1982 | Atlantic 4004 | 4 |
| *(May be promo only)* | | | |
| RIDIN' TRUCKIN' (same on both sides) | 1981 | Atlantic 3792 | 4 |
| *(May be promo only)* | | | |
| **RADIO SHOWS** | | | |
| **Albums** | | | |
| BBC ROCK HOUR (Feb 81) Live concert | 1981 | London Wavelength | 40-80 |
| *(Rare early concert)* | | | |
| **Compact Discs** | | | |
| KING BISCUIT FLOWER HOUR (Oct 88) Live concert | 1988 | DIR | 25-50 |
| *(With Elvin Bishop)* | | | |

**LEE, BRENDA**
*Other Decca promo 45s $5-8 each; Other MCA color vinyl promo 45s $8 each; MCA promo 45s $2 each; Other jukebox LLPs $8 each; Other Decca promo LPs $15-20 each*

| Title | Yr | Label, Number | NM $ |
|-------|-----|---------------|------|
| **45s** | | | |
| CHRISTY CHRISTMAS | 1956 | Decca 30107 | 20 |
| *(Pink promo label; same record as 88215 but released for the pop market)* | | | |
| DYNAMITE | 1957 | Decca 30333 | 18 |
| *(Pink promo label)* | | | |
| EMOTIONS  Five 7-inch stereo jukebox 33s | 1967 | Decca 38275 | 40 |
| *(Or $8 each)* | | | |
| A GOOD LOVE DON'T COME THAT EASY | 1981 | KFC 005 | 12 |
| *(White promo label, songwriter contest winner on the "Kentucky Fried Chicken" (MCA) label)* | | | |
| I'M GONNA LASSO SANTA CLAUS | 1956 | Decca 88215 | 40 |
| *(Pink promo label)* | | | |
| JAMBALAYA | 1956 | Decca 30050 | 25 |
| *(Pink promo label)* | | | |
| LET'S JUMP THE BROOMSTICK | 1959 | Decca 30885 | 25 |
| *(Green promo label)* | | | |
| MERRY CHRISTMAS  Five 7-inch stereo jukebox 33s | 1966 | Decca 34267 | 50 |
| *(Or $10 each)* | | | |
| ONE STEP AT A TIME | 1957 | Decca 30198 | 18 |
| *(White promo label)* | | | |
| ONE TEENAGER TO ANOTHER | 1957 | Decca 30411 | 18 |
| *(Pink promo label)* | | | |
| RING-A MY PHONE | 1958 | Decca 30673 | 25 |
| *(Green promo label)* | | | |
| ROCK THE BOP | 1958 | Decca 30535 | 25 |
| *(Green promo label)* | | | |
| ROCKIN' AROUND THE CHRISTMAS TREE | 1958 | Decca 30776 | 20 |
| *(Pink promo label, stock picture sleeve worth $30)* | | | |
| TWO HEARTS | 1986 | MCA 52804 | 10 |
| *(Red vinyl, white promo label)* | | | |
| WHY YOU BEEN GONE SO LONG | 1985 | MCA 52720 | 10 |
| *(Yellow vinyl, white promo label)* | | | |
| **7-Inch Extended Plays** | | | |
| 1976 FAN FAIR SPOTS Various artists | 1976 | Country Music UR699 | 18 |
| *(Series of 16 30-second ads, two by Brenda Lee)* | | | |
| ALL ALONE AM I  Jukebox LLP | 1963 | Decca 34108 | 20 |
| *(Issued with a hard cover)* | | | |
| BRENDA AND PETE  Jukebox LLP | 1968 | Decca 34528 | 12 |
| *(With Pete Fountain, issued with hard cover)* | | | |
| BY REQUEST  Jukebox LLP | 1964 | Decca 34242 | 15 |
| *(Issued with a hard cover)* | | | |
| BY REQUEST  Jukebox LLP | 1964 | Decca 34243 | 15 |
| *(Issued with a hard cover)* | | | |
| LET ME SING  Jukebox LLP | 1963 | Decca 34204 | 18 |
| *(Issued with a hard cover)* | | | |
| MERRY CHRISTMAS  Jukebox LLP | 1964 | Decca 34254 | 20 |
| *(Issued with a hard cover)* | | | |
| SINCERELY  Jukebox LLP | 1962 | Decca 34051 | 25 |
| *(Issued with a hard cover)* | | | |
| THAT'S ALL  Jukebox LLP | 1962 | Decca 34099 | 25 |
| *(Issued with a hard cover)* | | | |
| TOO MANY RIVERS  Jukebox LLP | 1966 | Decca 34341 | 15 |
| *(Issued with a hard cover)* | | | |
| **78s** | | | |
| I'M GONNA LASSO SANTA CLAUS | 1956 | Decca 88215 | 40 |
| *(Pink promo label, stock picture sleeve worth $75)* | | | |
| **Albums** | | | |
| GRANDMA, WHAT GREAT SONGS YOU SANG | 1959 | Decca 8873 | 50 |
| *(Pink promo label)* | | | |

| **Title** | **Yr** | **Label, Number** | **NM $** |
|---|---|---|---|
| **RADIO SHOWS** | | | |
| **16-Inch Transcriptions** | | | |
| COUNTRY STYLE USA | 1960 | PSA | 75 |
| *(Music and interviews)* | | | |
| | | | |
| **LEE, JIMMY** | | | |
| **45s** | | | |
| LOVE ME  With Wayne Walker | 1957 | Chess 4863 | 100 |
| *(White promo label)* | | | |
| | | | |
| **LEE, JOHNNY** | | | |
| **45s** | | | |
| PLEASE COME HOME FOR CHRISTMAS/SILVER BELLS | 1981 | Elektra 47230 | 5 |
| *(B-side by Tompall and the Glaser Brothers)* | | | |
| | | | |
| **LEE, MYRON, AND THE CADDIES** | | | |
| *ABC Paramount promo 45s $15 each* | | | |
| | | | |
| **LEE, PEGGY** | | | |
| *Decca promo 45s $8 each; Other Capitol promo 45s $4 each* | | | |
| **45s** | | | |
| YOU CAME A LONG WAY FROM ST. LOUIS | 1959 | Capitol (no #) | 15 |
| *(With George Shearing, blue promo label, recorded live at the 1959 Miami DJ convention)* | | | |
| **7-Inch Extended Plays** | | | |
| PEGGY LEE'S GREATEST HITS  Jukebox LLP | 1972 | Capitol 1591 (LLP 152) | 10 |
| *(Issued with a paper cover)* | | | |
| THEN WAS THEN | 1964 | Capitol 2388 | 15 |
| *(33-compact, issued with a hard cover)* | | | |
| | | | |
| **LEE, TERRY, AND THE POOR BOYS** | | | |
| *This group, and Bobby Vee's Shadows, replaced Buddy Holly on stage in Moorhead, MN in February 1959* | | | |
| **45s** | | | |
| MY LITTLE SUE | 1958 | Soma 1116 | 300 |
| *(Not a promo, white label used for promo purposes)* | | | |
| | | | |
| **LEFEVRE, RAYMOND** | | | |
| **45s** | | | |
| SILVER BELLS (mono/stereo) | 196? | Kapp AS-949 | 8 |
| | | | |
| **LEGENDARY STARDUST COWBOY, THE** | | | |
| **45s** | | | |
| PARALYZED | 1968 | Mercury 72862 | 40 |
| *(White promo label)* | | | |
| | | | |
| **LEGENDS, THE** | | | |
| **45s** | | | |
| THE LEGEND OF LOVE | 1958 | Hull 727 | 50 |
| *(White promo label)* | | | |
| | | | |
| **LEMONHEADS, THE** | | | |
| *Atlantic promo CD singles $3-5 each* | | | |
| **12-Inch Singles** | | | |
| CONFETTI (Remix)/MY DRUG BUDDY | 1992 | Atlantic SAM 1126 | 8 |
| HALF THE TIME/LEFT FOR DEAD/LI'L SEED | 1990 | Atlantic 3499 | 8 |
| INTO YOUR ARMS/MISS OTIS REGRETS | 1993 | Atlantic SAM 1253 | 8 |
| MRS. ROBINSON/BEING AROUND | 1992 | Atlantic SAM 1164 | 8 |
| **45s** | | | |
| STYLE/ACOUSTIC RICK JAMES STYLE | 1993 | Atlantic PR 5336 | 6 |
| *(White label promo with small hole)* | | | |
| **Albums** | | | |
| COME ON FEEL THE LEMONHEADS | 1993 | Atlantic SAM 1267 | 20 |
| *Promo-only four-song sampler* | | | |
| **RADIO SHOWS** | | | |
| **Compact Discs** | | | |
| IN CONCERT-NU ROCK (Apr 94) | 1994 | Westwood One | 40-75 |
| *(Live concert)* | | | |
| ON THE EDGE (Nov 93) Music and interviews | 1993 | Westwood One | 10-20 |
| *(With R.E.M. and k.d. lang)* | | | |
| | | | |
| **LENNON, FREDDIE** | | | |
| *Father of John Lennon* | | | |
| **45s** | | | |
| THAT'S MY LIFE | 1966 | Jerden 792 | 75 |
| *(White promo label)* | | | |
| | | | |
| **LENNON, JOHN** | | | |
| *Includes Lennon/Yoko Ono and Plastic Ono Band records, but not Yoko Ono solo;  Also see The Beatles, Yoko Ono; Capitol purple jukebox color vinyl 45s $5 each* | | | |
| **12-Inch Singles** | | | |
| HAPPY XMAS | 1982 | Geffen PRO-A-1079 | 30 |
| *(Promo-only 12" single)* | | | |
| HAPPY XMAS | 1986 | Capitol SPRO-9894 | 200 |
| *(Promo-only 12" single, white vinyl, plastic clear sleeve,released to promote Central Virgina Food Bank)* | | | |
| HAPPY XMAS | 1986 | Capitol SPRO-9929 | 50 |
| *(Promo-only 12" single, white vinyl, plastic clear sleeve)* | | | |
| IMAGINE | 1986 | Capitol SPRO-9585 | 40 |
| *(Promo-only 12" single)* | | | |

| Title | Yr | Label, Number | NM $ |
|---|---|---|---|
| NOBODY TOLD ME | 1983 | Polydor PRO-250 | 30 |
| *(Red promo label 12" single, black vinyl)* | | | |
| NOBODY TOLD ME | 1983 | Polydor PRO-250 | 50 |
| *(Red promo label 12" single, purple vinyl)* | | | |
| ROCK AND ROLL PEOPLE | 1986 | Capitol SPRO-9917 | 60 |
| *(Promo-only 12" single)* | | | |
| STAND BY ME | 1988 | Capitol SPRO-79453 | 40 |
| *(Purple label 12" promo single)* | | | |
| STARTING OVER | 1980 | Geffen PRO-A-919 | 60 |
| *(Promo-only 12" single, with 4:17 version otherwise unavailable)* | | | |
| **45s** | | | |
| #9 DREAM | 1974 | Apple P-1878 | 50 |
| *(Mono/stereo versions, same song on flip)* | | | |
| AIN'T THAT A SHAME | 1975 | Apple P-1883 | 200 |
| *(Promo-only mono/stereo versions, same song on flip)* | | | |
| BORROWED TIME | 1984 | Polydor 821 204 | 15 |
| *(Red promo label, long 4:30/short 3:45 versions)* | | | |
| EVERY MAN HAS A WOMAN WHO LOVES HIM | 1984 | Polydor 881 378 | 15 |
| *(Red promo label, both sides the same)* | | | |
| GIVE PEACE A CHANCE | 1994 | Capitol 17783 | 75 |
| *(Purple label, limited pressing for a plaque)* | | | |
| GIVE PEACE A CHANCE  Plastic Ono Band | 1969 | Americom 435 | 1,000 |
| *(Four-inch flexidisc sold in vending machines)* | | | |
| HAPPY XMAS | 1982 | Geffen 29855 | 15 |
| *(Mono/stereo versions)* | | | |
| HAPPY XMAS  John & Yoko/Plastic Ono Band | 1971 | Apple 47663 | 750 |
| *(Very rare promo version, white label)* | | | |
| I'M STEPPING OUT | 1984 | Polydor 821 107 | 15 |
| *(Red promo label, long 4:06/short 3:33 versions)* | | | |
| IMAGINE | 1994 | Capitol 57849 | 60 |
| *(Purple label, limited pressing for a plaque)* | | | |
| INSTANT KARMA  John Ono Lennon | 1970 | Apple 1818 | 200 |
| *(One-sided promo, no mention of promo on the record)* | | | |
| JEALOUS GUY | 1988 | Capitol 44230 | 20 |
| *(White promo label, price includes picture sleeve)* | | | |
| JOHN LENNON ON RONNIE HAWKINS: THE SHORT RAP/THE LONG RAP | 1970 | Cotillion PR-104/5 | 90 |
| *(No promo markings on white label)* | | | |
| JOHN LENNON ON RONNIE HAWKINS: THE SHORT RAP/THE LONG RAP | 1970 | Cotillion PR-104/5 | 80 |
| *(White label with promo markings)* | | | |
| JOHN LENNON ON RONNIE HAWKINS: THE SHORT RAP/THE LONG RAP | 1970 | Atlantic PR-104/5 | 100 |
| JOHN LENNON RADIO PLAY | 1970 | Eva-Tone 7 | 600 |
| *(Flexi-disc, included with a copy of Aspen Magazine)* | | | |
| KYA 1969 PEACE TALK | 1969 | KYA Radio | 200 |
| *(An interview from KYA radio)* | | | |
| MIND GAMES | 1973 | Apple P-1868 | 50 |
| *(Mono/stereo versions)* | | | |
| MOTHER  John Lennon Plastic Ono Band | 1970 | Apple 1827 | 15 |
| *(Not a promo but this version with a star on the label was shipped to radio stations)* | | | |
| NOBODY TOLD ME | 1983 | Polydor 817 254 | 25 |
| *(Red promo label, purple vinyl that has to be checked by holding the record up to a light)* | | | |
| NOBODY TOLD ME | 1983 | Polydor 817 254 | 15 |
| *(Red promo label)* | | | |
| POWER TO THE PEOPLE  John Lennon/Plastic Ono Band | 1971 | Apple 1830 | 15 |
| *(Star on the label, actually not a promo)* | | | |
| ROCK 'N' ROLL RADIO SPOT | 1975 | Quaye/Trident 3419 | 500 |
| *(Very rare, for radio only)* | | | |
| SLIPPIN' AND SLIDIN' | 1975 | Apple P-1883 | 200 |
| *(Promo-only mono/stereo versions, same song on flip)* | | | |
| STAND BY ME | 1975 | Apple P-1881 | 50 |
| *(Mono/stereo versions)* | | | |
| STARTING OVER | 1980 | Geffen 49604 | 15 |
| *(Flip side is same song)* | | | |
| A TRIBUTE TO JOHN LENNON | 1987 | Quaker Granola Dipps | 25 |
| *(Cardboard record)* | | | |
| WATCHING THE WHEELS | 1981 | Geffen 49695 | 15 |
| *(Flip side is Yoko Ono)* | | | |
| WHAT YOU GOT | 1974 | Apple P-1878 | 100 |
| *(Mono/stereo versions, "#9 Dream" is the hit side of Apple 1878)* | | | |
| WHAT'S IT ALL ABOUT (Nov 75) Public service show | 1975 | W.I.A.A. 290 | 35 |
| *(Flip side is Marvin Hamlisch)* | | | |
| WHAT'S IT ALL ABOUT (Feb 81) Public service show | 1981 | W.I.A.A. 565 | 50 |
| *(Extended version, 10:05, both sides John Lennon, rare)* | | | |
| WHAT'S IT ALL ABOUT (July 82) Public service show | 1982 | W.I.A.A. 635 | 40 |
| *(Extended version, 10:05, both sides John Lennon)* | | | |
| WHATEVER GETS YOU THROUGH THE NIGHT John Lennon and the Plastic Ono Nuclear Band | 1974 | Apple P-1874 | 50 |
| *(Mono/stereo versions)* | | | |
| WOMAN | 1981 | Geffen 49644 | 15 |
| *(Flip side is Yoko Ono)* | | | |
| **Albums** | | | |
| DOUBLE FANTASY | 1980 | Nautilus 47 | 500 |
| *(Issued in a plain white jacket)* | | | |
| I APOLOGIZE | 1966 | Sterling 8893 | 50 |
| *(Mail order item from the Chicago Tribune)* | | | |
| THE JOHN LENNON COLLECTION | 1982 | Geffen 2023 | 50 |
| *(The Quiex II vinyl version)* | | | |
| REFLECTIONS AND POETRY | 1984 | Silhouette 10012 (2) | 50 |
| *(Includes poster; labels must identify set as promo)* | | | |

| Title | Yr | Label, Number | NM $ |
|---|---|---|---|
| SILVER PLATTER SERVICE (Mar 65) Jack Wagner | 1965 | Capitol PRO 3143 | 400 |
| *(McCartney/Lennon interview, promo only, rare)* | | | |
| SOME TIME IN NEW YORK CITY | 1972 | Apple 3392 (2) | 1,000 |
| *(White promo labels)* | | | |
| **Compact Discs** | | | |
| JEALOUS GUY | 1988 | Capitol DPRO-79417 | 10 |
| *(Promo CD in hard picture cover)* | | | |
| **RADIO SHOWS** | | | |
| **Albums** | | | |
| ALBUM GREATS | 1979 | TIM Special Products | 20-40 |
| *(The one Lennon disc from the set)* | | | |
| BBC PRESENTS A TRIBUTE (Dec 82) | 1982 | (5) | 150-275 |
| *(Box set, very rare, music and interviews)* | | | |
| BBC TRANSCRIPTION DISC Music and interviews | 1980 | BBC Transcription (5) | 600-800 |
| *(The rarest of Lennon shows)* | | | |
| CELEBRATION  Profile | 1982 | NBC Radio (5) | 75-125 |
| *(Music and interviews)* | | | |
| DRAKE-CHENAULT SAMPLER  Various artists | 1982 | Drake-Chenault (2) | 20-40 |
| *(Side 4 includes Don Imus/WNBC New York, tribute to Lennon)* | | | |
| EVERY MAN HAS A WOMAN (Dec 84) John & Yoko | 1984 | MJI Broadcasting (2) | 30-50 |
| *(Music and interviews)* | | | |
| HISTORY OF ROCK & ROLL (May 84) | 1984 | Drake-Chenault | 20-40 |
| *(Price is for the Lennon disc only)* | | | |
| IN HIS OWN WRITE (July 86) | 1986 | Westwood One (2) | 25-50 |
| *(Music and interviews)* | | | |
| INSIDE TRACK (Dec 82) | 1982 | Inside Track (3) | 25-40 |
| *(Music and interviews)* | | | |
| JOHN LENNON REMEMBERED (Dec 87) | 1987 | (5) | 30-60 |
| *(Music and interviews)* | | | |
| JOHN LENNON STORY | 1981 | London Wavelength (6) | 200-300 |
| *(Mostly music and interviews)* | | | |
| JOHN LENNON STORY  Edited version | 1981 | London Wavelength (5) | 100-200 |
| *(Mostly music and interviews)* | | | |
| LEGENDS OF ROCK (Jan 89) Year-end update | 1989 | NBC Radio (4) | 25-50 |
| *(Music and interviews)* | | | |
| LEGENDS OF ROCK (Oct 88) | 1988 | NBC Radio (2) | 40-60 |
| *(Music and interviews)* | | | |
| LENNON | 1988 | United Stations (3) | 75-100 |
| *(Music and interviews)* | | | |
| LENNON UNISTAR SPECIAL (Dec 89) Profile | 1989 | Unistar (4) | 40-75 |
| *(Music and interviews)* | | | |
| LOST LENNON TAPES Lennon/Ono/Beatles | 199? | Westwood One (2) | 15-40 |
| *(Price is for each weekly 2LP show)* | | | |
| LOST LENNON TAPES (Jan 88) Lennon/Ono/Beatles | 1988 | Westwood One (5) | 100-175 |
| *(Special edition pilot show)* | | | |
| LOST LENNON TAPES (Jan 88-92) Lennon/Ono/Beatles | 1992 | Westwood One (448) | 4,000-5,000 |
| *(Price is for the complete set, including pilot. This series ran for 221 weeks and featured many unreleased tracks of the Beatles, Lennon and Ono.)* | | | |
| NATIONAL MUSIC SURVEY (Dec 81) Various artists | 1981 | Mutual Radio (3) | 25-40 |
| *(Includes interviews with Lennon)* | | | |
| NBC SOURCE  Profile | 1981 | NBC Radio (5) | 75-125 |
| *(Music and interviews)* | | | |
| A PRESENT FOR YOKO  John & Yoko | 1984 | Westwood One | 40-75 |
| *(Music and interviews)* | | | |
| RETRO ROCK JOHN LENNON | 1983 | Clayton Webster (2) | 50-100 |
| *(Music and interviews)* | | | |
| ROBERT KLEIN SPECIAL (Jan 87) Lennon and others | 1987 | (4) | 40-75 |
| *(Music and interviews, with May Pang and Martha Quinn)* | | | |
| ROCK AND ROLL NEVER FORGETS  Profile | 1983 | Westwood One (5) | 100-175 |
| *(Music and interviews)* | | | |
| ROCK AND ROLL NEVER FORGETS  Profile | 1983 | Westwood One (6) | 125-200 |
| *(Music and interviews)* | | | |
| ROCK, ROLL AND REMEMBER Various artists | 1988 | United Stations (4) | 20-40 |
| *(Shows that features Lennon interviews)* | | | |
| ROYALTY OF ROCK | 1982 | Watermark | 20-35 |
| *(Music and interviews)* | | | |
| SOLID GOLD SCRAPBOOK (Oct 86) Profile | 1986 | United Stations | 15-25 |
| *(One of the five discs in the box set)* | | | |
| THEY SAY IT'S YOUR BIRTHDAY (Oct 90) | 1990 | Westwood One (2) | 25-35 |
| *(Music and interviews)* | | | |
| TICKET TO RIDE Beatles/Lennon | 198? | DIR (2) | 20-40 |
| *(Weekly shows on vinyl, price for any one volume)* | | | |
| TICKET TO RIDE (Jan 85-Apr 89) Beatles/Lennon | 1989 | DIR (414) | 4,000-5,000 |
| *(Complete set of shows, vinyl and CD. This series ran for 209 weeks and featured a Beatles-related theme weekly with a guest artist.)* | | | |
| **Compact Discs** | | | |
| THE BEATLE YEARS (Apr 92-Apr 93) Beatles/Lennon | 1993 | Westwood One (52) | 1,250-1,500 |
| *(First full year of the series)* | | | |
| THE BEATLE YEARS (Apr 92-present) Beatles/Lennon | 199? | Westwood One | 15-20 |
| *(Weekly series replaced Lost Lennon Tapes, price for any one volume)* | | | |
| THE BEATLE YEARS (Apr 93-Apr 98) Beatles/Lennon | 199? | Westwood One (52) | 1,000-1,200 |
| *(Any subsequent full year of the series)* | | | |
| HIS LAST INTERVIEWS (Dec 91) | 1991 | (4) | 40-75 |
| *(Music and interviews)* | | | |
| KING BISCUIT FLOWER HOUR  Live concert | 1990 | DIR | 40-75 |
| *(With Warren Zevon)* | | | |
| KING BISCUIT FLOWER HOUR (Oct 90) Live concert | 1990 | DIR | 50-100 |
| *(With Todd Rundgren)* | | | |
| MASTERS OF ROCK (Oct 89) | 1989 | Radio Ventures | 75-100 |
| *(Music and interviews, repeated month later)* | | | |

| Title | Yr | Label, Number | NM $ |
|---|---|---|---|
| REMEMBER LENNON (Dec 90) JOHN LENNON | 1990 | ABC Radio (4) | 125-250 |
| *(Music and interviews, rare show)* | | | |
| TICKET TO RIDE Beatles/Lennon | 198? | DIR | 15-35 |
| *(Weekly shows on CD, price for any one volume)* | | | |
| TICKET TO RIDE (May 88-Apr 89) Beatles/Lennon | 1989 | DIR (52) | 1,500-2,000 |
| *(Complete set of CD shows)* | | | |
| **Reel-to-Reel Tapes** | | | |
| MAN, MEMORY OF JOHN LENNON (Jan 81) | 1981 | RKO Radio (3) | 50-100 |
| *(Music and interview, not available on disc)* | | | |

## LENNON, JULIAN
*Atlantic blue label promo 45s $3 each; Atlantic 12" promo singles $12 each; Atlantic promo CD singles $4-6 each*

**45s**

| | | | |
|---|---|---|---|
| TIME WILL TEACH US ALL | 1986 | Capitol P-B-5618 | 10 |
| *(With Stevie Wonder, produced by Dave Clark)* | | | |

**RADIO SHOWS**

**Albums**

| | | | |
|---|---|---|---|
| HOT ROCKS (June 86) | 1986 | United Stations (2) | 20-35 |
| *(Music and interviews)* | | | |
| INNERVIEW | 1985 | Innerview | 15-25 |
| *(Music and interviews)* | | | |
| JULIAN LENNON SPECIAL (May 85) | 1985 | Radio International (2) | 40-75 |
| *(Julian is host, nice photo cover)* | | | |
| POP CONCERT (May 87) Live concert | 1987 | Westwood One (2) | 100-175 |
| *(Julian's only live concert)* | | | |
| ROCK CONNECTION | 1986 | CBS RadioRadio | 25-40 |
| *(Music and interviews, host is Mike Harrison)* | | | |

## LENNOX, ANNIE
*Of the Eurythmics; Arista promo CD singles $3-5 each*

**Compact Discs**

| | | | |
|---|---|---|---|
| IN-STORE SAMPLER | 1995 | Arista ASCD 2873 | 15 |
| *(Promo-only collection)* | | | |
| IN-STORE SAMPLER | 1995 | Arista ASCD 2873 (2) | 40 |
| *(Expanded version of one-CD set, with an Album Network various-artists CD included)* | | | |

**RADIO SHOWS**

**Compact Discs**

| | | | |
|---|---|---|---|
| ON THE EDGE (Jan 93) Music and interviews | 1993 | | 15-25 |
| *(With John Wesley Harding and Nine Inch Nails)* | | | |

## LENYA, LOTTE, AND JACK GILFORD
**45s**

| | | | |
|---|---|---|---|
| IT COULDN'T PLEASE ME MORE | 1966 | Columbia JZSP 117536 | 10 |
| *(Yellow vinyl, promo only)* | | | |

## LeROUX
**7-Inch Extended Plays**

| | | | |
|---|---|---|---|
| SEASONS GREETINGS/YOU KNOW HOW THOSE BOYS ARE// ADDICTED/LAST SAFE PLACE ON EARTH | 1981 | RCA Victor JF-13012 | 6 |
| *(Promo only on green vinyl)* | | | |

## LET'S ACTIVE
**12-Inch Singles**

| | | | |
|---|---|---|---|
| BLUE LINE (same on both sides) | 1984 | I.R.S. 70981 | 6 |
| EVERY DOG HAS ITS DAY (same on both sides) | 1988 | I.R.S. 17627 | 5 |
| IN LITTLE WAYS/TALKING TO MYSELF/LAST CHANCE TOWN | 1986 | I.R.S. 17133 | 5 |
| WATER'S PART/BLUE LINE | 1984 | I.R.S. 70983 | 8 |

## LETTERMEN, THE
*Capitol promo 45s $2 each*

**45s**

| | | | |
|---|---|---|---|
| LOVE | 1971 | Capitol PRO-6315 | 10 |
| *(Promo-only mix, cover of a John Lennon song)* | | | |
| WHAT'S IT ALL ABOUT (Feb 76) Public service show | 1976 | W.I.A.A. 303 | 12 |
| *(Flip side features Kool & The Gang)* | | | |

**7-Inch Extended Plays**

| | | | |
|---|---|---|---|
| COLLEGE STANDARDS  Jukebox LLP | 196? | Capitol 1829 | 12 |
| *(Issued with a hard cover)* | | | |

## LEVEL 42
**12-Inch Singles**

| | | | |
|---|---|---|---|
| LESSONS IN LOVE (same on both sides) | 1987 | Polydor 492 | 12 |
| RUNNING IN THE FAMILY (same on both sides) | 1987 | Polydor PRO 522-1 | 12 |

## LEWIS, BARBARA
*Atlantic promo 45s $3 each; Other Atlantic promo LPs $12 each*

**Albums**

| | | | |
|---|---|---|---|
| THE BEST OF BARBARA LEWIS | 1971 | Atlantic 8286 | 15 |
| *(White promo label)* | | | |

## LEWIS, BOBBY
*Roulette promo 45s $15 each; Beltone promo 45s $12 each; United Artists promo 45s (different singer with same name) $4 each*

| Title | Yr | Label, Number | NM $ |
|---|---|---|---|

### LEWIS, GARY, AND THE PLAYBOYS
*Liberty promo 45s $4 each*
**45s**

| | | | |
|---|---|---|---|
| DOIN' THE FLAKE | 1965 | Liberty 65-227-1 | 25 |
| *(Three songs for Kellogg's Corn Flakes, includes promo picture sleeve)* | | | |
| WAY WAY OUT | 1967 | Liberty (no #) | 500 |
| *(Unreleased theme song to a movie; only two known copies)* | | | |

### LEWIS, HUEY, AND THE NEWS
*Other Chrysalis promo 45s $3 each; Chrysalis 12" promo singles $6 each; Chrysalis, EMI and Elektra promo CD singles $3 each*
**45s**

| | | | |
|---|---|---|---|
| DO YOU BELIEVE IN LOVE  White label, red vinyl | 1982 | Chrysalis 2589 | 12 |
| *(Only the promo version is red vinyl, issued with special heart hard cover)* | | | |

**Compact Discs**

| | | | |
|---|---|---|---|
| FOUR CHORDS AND SEVERAL YEARS AGO | 1994 | Elektra PR 8975 | 15 |
| *(Special promo package, with CD and 45 rpm record in 78-rpm-style "album")* | | | |
| HARD AT PLAY | 1991 | EMI 93355 | 15 |
| *(Regular stock copy packaged in promo-only press kit)* | | | |

**RADIO SHOWS**
**Albums**

| | | | |
|---|---|---|---|
| HUEY LEWIS CONCERT (Mar 84)  Live concert | 1984 | NBC Source (2) | 20-40 |
| *(Rare live concert)* | | | |
| IN CONCERT-NU ROCK (July 91) | 1991 | Westwood One (2) | 15-20 |
| *(Live concert)* | | | |
| INNERVIEW (80s)  Profile | 198? | Innerview | 10-15 |
| *(Music and interviews)* | | | |
| KING BISCUIT FLOWER HOUR  Live concert | 1982 | DIR/ABC (2) | 20-40 |
| *(Repeated several times)* | | | |
| OFF THE RECORD (June 91)  Profile | 1991 | Westwood One (2) | 10-15 |
| *(Music and interviews, repeated)* | | | |
| STARTRACK PROFILE (Feb 87)  Live concert | 1987 | Westwood One (2) | 15-25 |
| *(Repeated)* | | | |
| SUPERSTAR CONCERT  Live concert | 1984 | Westwood One (3) | 15-30 |
| *(Repeated several times)* | | | |

**Compact Discs**

| | | | |
|---|---|---|---|
| IN THE STUDIO (Sept 93)  Profile of an album | 1993 | Album Network | 10-15 |
| *(Music and interviews)* | | | |
| KING BISCUIT FLOWER HOUR (May 92)  Live concert | 1992 | DIR | 15-30 |
| *(Repeated several times)* | | | |
| STORY OF HUEY LEWIS (June 91)  Profile | 1991 | Unistar | 10-15 |
| *(Music and interviews)* | | | |

### LEWIS, JERRY LEE
*Smash white promo label 45s $4 each; Mercury white promo label 45s $3 each; Sun (SSS) white promo label 45s $2 each; Other Sun promo yellow vinyl 45s $6 each; Elektra white promo label 45s $2 each; America/Smash promo 45s $3 each; Any promo CD single $3*
**45s**

| | | | |
|---|---|---|---|
| COLD, COLD HEART | 197? | Sun 1141 | 12 |
| *(Yellow vinyl, white promo label)* | | | |
| I CAN'T SEEM TO SAY GOODBYE  Yellow vinyl | 1968 | Sun 1115 | 10 |
| *(White promo label)* | | | |
| LONELY WEEKENDS | 196? | Mercury DJ-345 | 12 |
| *(White promo label, special DJ number)* | | | |
| SAVE THE LAST DANCE FOR ME  Yellow vinyl | 1978 | Sun 1139 | 12 |
| *(Yellow promo label)* | | | |
| WAITING FOR A TRAIN  Yellow vinyl | 1968 | Sun 1119 | 10 |
| *(Yellow promo label)* | | | |
| WHAT'S MADE MILWAUKEE FAMOUS  White promo label | 1968 | Mercury DJ-16 | 10 |
| YOUR LOVING WAYS  Yellow vinyl | 1968 | Sun 1128 | 10 |
| *(Yellow promo label)* | | | |

**7-Inch Extended Plays**

| | | | |
|---|---|---|---|
| A TASTE OF COUNTRY  Jukebox LLP | 1969 | Sun 114 | 25 |
| *(Issued with a paper cover)* | | | |
| GOLDEN CREAM OF THE COUNTRY  Jukebox LLP | 1969 | Sun 108 (LLP 155) | 25 |
| *(Issued with a paper cover)* | | | |
| JERRY LEE LEWIS  Promo-only release | 1969 | Smash SEP-2 | 40 |
| *(White promo label)* | | | |
| OPEN-END INTERVIEW  Promo-only release | 1969 | Smash DJS-28 | 35 |
| *(White promo label)* | | | |
| THE SURVIVORS  Lewis, Johnny Cash, Carl Perkins | 1982 | Columbia AE7 1505 | 25 |
| *(Promo-only EP with four songs, recorded live in Germany; there is also a promo-only paper sleeve)* | | | |

**Albums**

| | | | |
|---|---|---|---|
| THE GREATEST LIVE SHOW ON EARTH | 1964 | Mercury 27056 | 40 |
| *(White promo label)* | | | |
| JERRY LEE LEWIS-SOUL MY WAY | 1967 | Mercury 27097 | 45 |
| *(White promo label)* | | | |
| JERRY LEE'S GREATEST | 1961 | Sun SLP-1265 | 800 |
| *(White label promo from the original Sun label)* | | | |
| SOUTHERN ROOTS-A RADIO SPECIAL | 1973 | Mercury MK-3 (690) | 50 |
| *(For radio only, white promo label)* | | | |

**RADIO SHOWS**
**Albums**

| | | | |
|---|---|---|---|
| AMERICAN EAGLE  Live concert | 1982 | DIR (3) | 40-75 |
| *(Repeated)* | | | |
| AMERICAN EAGLE  Live concert | 1987 | DIR (3) | 50-80 |
| *(Includes Carl Perkins and the Crickets)* | | | |
| LIVE AT GILLEY'S  Live concert | 1983 | Westwood One | 25-50 |
| *(Repeated)* | | | |

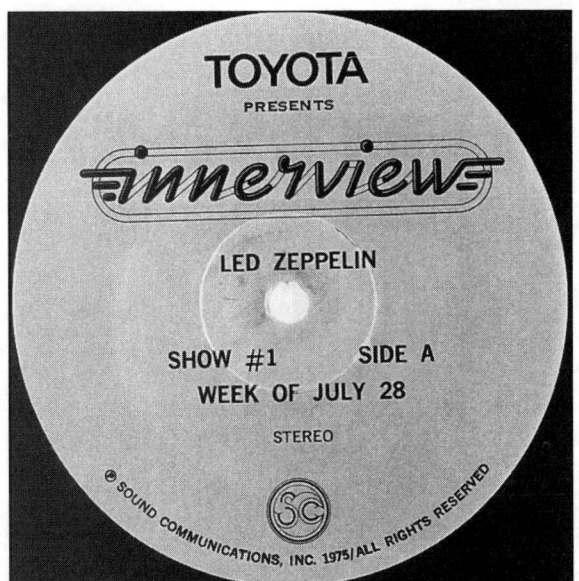

(Top left) There weren't many radio shows that featured Led Zeppelin in the years they were still an official band. Here's an Innerview show from 1975; note the sponsorship right on the label. (Top right) The Little River Band makes an unusual radio show appearance thanks to the Star Session series of the early 1980s. (Middle left) The short-lived Retro Rock radio show, from the little-known Clayton Webster Corporation, had chintzy labels even by radio show standards: It used the same label for every show and simply affixed labels to the label to tell the programmer which show it was. (Middle right) The original Lynyrd Skynyrd made appearances on the King Biscuit Flower Hour, so it was natural that when the group reformed in the mid-1980s, it would again be on the KBFH. (Bottom left) A short-lived radio show from the syndicators of the King Biscuit Flower Hour had the interesting combination of Madonna and Sade on the same show. (Bottom right) An older edition of the King Biscuit Flower Hour, complete with the elaborate graphics, features Manfred Mann and Ry Cooder.

| Title | Yr | Label, Number | NM $ |
|---|---|---|---|

**LIGHTFOOT, GORDON**
*United Artists promo 45s $5 each; Reprise promo 45s $3 each*
**7-Inch Extended Plays**

| Title | Yr | Label, Number | NM $ |
|---|---|---|---|
| SUNDOWN  Jukebox LLP | 1974 | Reprise 2177 (LLP 251) | 15 |

*(Issued with a paper cover)*
**RADIO SHOWS**
**Albums**

| Title | Yr | Label, Number | NM $ |
|---|---|---|---|
| STARTRACK PROFILE (Sept 86) | 1986 | Westwood One (2) | 50-100 |

*(Music and interviews)*

**LIGHTHOUSE**
*Evolution promo 45s $5 each*
**RADIO SHOWS**
**Albums**

| Title | Yr | Label, Number | NM $ |
|---|---|---|---|
| NIGHTBIRD & COMPANY (July 73) Various artists | 1973 | U.S. Army (2) | 20-35 |

*(One of the four shows features Lighthouse)*

**LILE, FORD**
**45s**

| Title | Yr | Label, Number | NM $ |
|---|---|---|---|
| WHO SAID IT'S CHRISTMAS IN SAN FRANCISCO | 19?? | Pennant 106 | 6 |

**LIME SPIDERS**
**7-Inch Extended Plays**

| Title | Yr | Label, Number | NM $ |
|---|---|---|---|
| SPACE CADET/JUST ONE SOLUTION/ACTION WOMEN/STONE FREE | 1987 | Virgin 99393 | 25 |

*(Promo-only live versions; green vinyl, includes picture sleeve)*

**LIMELITERS, THE**
*Other RCA Victor promo 45s by the Limeliters, Glenn Yarbrough or Alex Hassilev $3 each; Columbia promo 45s by Ernie Sheldon $3 each; Warner Bros.promo 45s $5  each; Any other label promo by the group or solo $2 each*
**45s**

| Title | Yr | Label, Number | NM $ |
|---|---|---|---|
| FOLK MATINEE Jukebox singles | 1962 | RCA Victor 2547 | 20 |
| *(Five stereo singles, small center hole, $4 each)* | | | |
| THE HAMMER SONG  White promo label | 1958 | Elektra 8 A | 10 |
| *(First single as a folk group)* | | | |
| THE SLIGHTLY FABULOUS LIMELITERS  Jukebox singles | 1961 | RCA Victor 2393 | 20 |

*(Five stereo singles worth $4 each)*
**7-Inch Extended Plays**

| Title | Yr | Label, Number | NM $ |
|---|---|---|---|
| SING OUT  Promo-only four-song EP | 1962 | RCA Victor SP-45-116 | 10 |

*(Includes a promo-only paper sleeve)*

**LINDISFARNE**
*Elektra or Atco promo singles $3 each*
**RADIO SHOWS**
**Albums**

| Title | Yr | Label, Number | NM $ |
|---|---|---|---|
| BBC TRANSCRIPTION DISC | 1974 | BBC Transcription | 125-250 |

*(Rare live concert)*

**LISTEN**
*Features Robert Plant*
**45s**

| Title | Yr | Label, Number | NM $ |
|---|---|---|---|
| YOU BETTER RUN | 1967 | Columbia 43967 | 100 |

*(White promo label)*

**LITTLE ANTHONY AND THE IMPERIALS**
*DCP promo 45s $8 each; United Artists promo 45s $6 each; Avco promo 45s $5 each*
**45s**

| Title | Yr | Label, Number | NM $ |
|---|---|---|---|
| TEARS ON MY PILLOW | 1957 | End 1027 | 25 |

*(White promo label)*

**LITTLE BOOKER**
**45s**

| Title | Yr | Label, Number | NM $ |
|---|---|---|---|
| THINKIN' 'BOUT MY BABY | 1954 | Imperial 5293 | 50 |

*(Cream-colored promo label)*

**LITTLE CAESAR**
*DGC promo CD singles $2-4 each*
**RADIO SHOWS**
**Albums**

| Title | Yr | Label, Number | NM $ |
|---|---|---|---|
| HIGH VOLTAGE (Nov 90) Various artists | 1990 | Westwood One (2) | 15-25 |
| *(Live segment features Little Caesar)* | | | |
| IN CONCERT (July 90) Live concert | 1990 | Westwood One (2) | 10-20 |

*(With ENUFF Z'NUFF)*
**Compact Discs**

| Title | Yr | Label, Number | NM $ |
|---|---|---|---|
| KING BISCUIT FLOWER HOUR (Sept 90) Live concert | 1990 | DIR | 20-30 |

*(With George Thorogood)*

**LITTLE FEAT**
*Warner Bros. promo 45s $3 each; Warner Bros. and Morgan Creek promo CD singles $3 each*
**Albums**

| Title | Yr | Label, Number | NM $ |
|---|---|---|---|
| HOY-HOY! | 1981 | Warner Bros. PRO-A-984 | 20 |

*(Single-album sampler of 2-LP set)*
**RADIO SHOWS**
**Albums**

| Title | Yr | Label, Number | NM $ |
|---|---|---|---|
| IN CONCERT  Live concert | 1988 | Westwood One (2) | 30-50 |

*(Repeated)*

| Title | Yr | Label, Number | NM $ |
|---|---|---|---|
| LEGENDS OF ROCK (June 89) Profile | 1989 | NBC Radio (2) | 15-25 |
| *(Music and interviews)* | | | |
| OFF THE RECORD (Sept 89) Profile | 1989 | Westwood One (2) | 10-20 |
| *(Music and interviews, repeated)* | | | |
| RETRO ROCK (Dec 81) Profile | 1981 | Clayton Webster (2) | 25-50 |
| *(Music and interviews)* | | | |
| ROCK STARS (Dec 88) Profile | 1988 | United Stations (2) | 15-25 |
| *(Music and interviews)* | | | |
| SUPERSTAR CONCERT (90s) Live concert | 199? | Westwood One (3) | 25-50 |
| *(Repeated)* | | | |
| WORLD OF ROCK (June 89) Various artists | 1989 | DIR (2) | 20-30 |
| *(Little Feat is co-host for this show)* | | | |
| **Compact Discs** | | | |
| BBC CLASSIC TRACKS (Aug 94) | 1994 | Westwood One | 25-50 |
| *(Various classic live tracks)* | | | |
| ELECTRIC LADYLAND (Oct 90) | 1990 | Westwood One | 35-50 |
| *(Music and interviews)* | | | |
| IN CONCERT (Oct 93) Live concert | 1993 | Westwood One | 25-50 |
| *(Repeated)* | | | |
| IN THE STUDIO (90s) Profile of an album | 199? | Album Network | 10-15 |
| *(Music and interviews)* | | | |
| KING BISCUIT FLOWER HOUR (July 92) Live concert | 1992 | DIR | 25-40 |
| *(With Blues Traveler)* | | | |
| KING BISCUIT FLOWER HOUR (Oct 94) | 1994 | DIR | 25-50 |
| *(Live concert)* | | | |
| UP CLOSE | 1991 | Media America (2) | 30-50 |
| *(With Little Feat and Lynyrd Skynyrd)* | | | |
| UP CLOSE  Profile | 1989 | Media America (2) | 20-30 |
| *(Music and interviews, repeated)* | | | |

## LITTLE RICHARD

*Of the Deuces of Rhythm; Reprise promo 45s $8 each; WTG (CBS) promo 45s w/Philip Bailey $3; Okeh promo LP $30 each; Epic promo LP $25; Reprise promo LP $20 each; Polydor and Grudge promo CD singles $3 each*

| Title | Yr | Label, Number | NM $ |
|---|---|---|---|
| **12-Inch Singles** | | | |
| GREAT GOSH A' MIGHTY! (same on both sides) | 1986 | MCA L33-17101 | 8 |
| **45s** | | | |
| AIN'T NOTHIN' HAPPENIN' | 1952 | RCA Victor 4772 | 300 |
| *(White promo label)* | | | |
| ALWAYS The Deuces of Rhythm | 1954 | Peacock 1628 | 50 |
| *(Multi-colored promo label)* | | | |
| BAMA LAMA BAMA LOO | 1964 | Specialty 692 | 25 |
| *(White promo label)* | | | |
| THE COMMANDMENTS OF LOVE | 1967 | Okeh 7262 | 20 |
| *(White promo label)* | | | |
| A FOOL AT THE WHEEL  The Deuces of Rhythm | 1953 | Peacock 1616 | 200 |
| *(Multi-colored promo label)* | | | |
| GET RICH QUICK | 1952 | RCA Victor 4582 | 300 |
| *(White promo label)* | | | |
| HE GOT WHAT HE WANTED | 1962 | Mercury 71963 | 12 |
| *(White promo label)* | | | |
| JOY, JOY, JOY | 1962 | Mercury 71884 | 15 |
| *(White promo label)* | | | |
| KEEP A-KNOCKIN' | 1964 | Specialty 697 | 25 |
| *(White promo label)* | | | |
| THE MOST I CAN OFFER | 1964 | Specialty 686 | 30 |
| *(White promo label)* | | | |
| PLEASE HAVE MERCY ON ME | 1952 | RCA Victor 5025 | 300 |
| *(White promo label)* | | | |
| POOR DOG | 1967 | Okeh 7251 | 15 |
| *(White promo label)* | | | |
| ROCKIN' WITH THE KING  Canned Heat | 1971 | United Artists 50892 | 10 |
| *(White promo label, Little Richard on backing vocals)* | | | |
| TAXI BLUES | 1951 | RCA Victor 4392 | 300 |
| *(White promo label)* | | | |
| WHAT'S IT ALL ABOUT (May 79) Public service show | 1979 | W.I.A.A. 472 | 30 |
| *(Flip side is Harry Chapin)* | | | |
| **78s** | | | |
| AIN'T NOTHIN' HAPPENIN' | 1952 | RCA Victor 4772 | 400 |
| *(White promo label)* | | | |
| GET RICH QUICK | 1952 | RCA Victor 4582 | 400 |
| *(White promo label)* | | | |
| PLEASE HAVE MERCY ON ME | 1952 | RCA Victor 5025 | 400 |
| *(White promo label)* | | | |
| TAXI BLUES | 1951 | RCA Victor 4392 | 500 |
| *(White promo label)* | | | |
| **Albums** | | | |
| COMIN' HOME | 1963 | Coral 57446 | 40 |
| *(Blue promo label)* | | | |
| IT'S REAL | 1961 | Mercury 20656 | 40 |
| *(White promo label)* | | | |
| **RADIO SHOWS** | | | |
| **Albums** | | | |
| ROYALTY OF ROCK | 1983 | Watermark | 20-40 |
| *(With Chuck Berry, music and interviews)* | | | |
| SOUNDS LIKE THE NAVY | 1975 | U.S. Navy (2) | 20-40 |
| *(Public service radio show)* | | | |

| Title | Yr | Label, Number | NM $ |
|---|---|---|---|
| **LITTLE RIVER BAND** | | | |
| *Harvest promo 45s $4 each; Other Capitol promo 45s $3 each; MCA promo 45s $2 each* | | | |
| **45s** | | | |
| WE TWO  White promo label | 1983 | Capitol SPRO-9936 | 10 |
| *(3:58 promo edited version)* | | | |
| **RADIO SHOWS** | | | |
| **Albums** | | | |
| BBC ROCK HOUR (Feb 82) | 1982 | London Wavelength | 40-75 |
| *(Live concert)* | | | |
| BBC TRANSCRIPTION DISC  Live concert | 1982 | BBC Transcription | 200-325 |
| *(Very rare concert)* | | | |
| IN CONCERT (May 85) Live concert | 1985 | Westwood One (2) | 40-75 |
| *(With Graham Parker)* | | | |
| KING BISCUIT FLOWER HOUR (Nov 81) Live concert | 1981 | DIR (2) | 60-100 |
| *(With Mink DeVille)* | | | |
| ON STAGE | 198? | (3) | 100-175 |
| *(Rare live concert)* | | | |
| ROBERT W. MORGAN  Profile | 1979 | Watermark | 15-25 |
| *(Music and interviews)* | | | |
| ROCK AROUND THE WORLD (Dec 76) Live concert | 1976 | RATW | 50-100 |
| *(With Dwight Twilly)* | | | |
| ROYALTY OF ROCK | 1983 | Watermark | 15-30 |
| *(Music and interviews)* | | | |
| STAR SESSION | 1983 | DIR (3) | 50-100 |
| *(Profile with live tracks)* | | | |
| | | | |
| **LITTLE TEXAS** | | | |
| *Warner Bros. promo CD singles $2-4 each* | | | |
| **RADIO SHOWS** | | | |
| **Compact Discs** | | | |
| COUNTRY CONCERT (June 93) | 1993 | Westwood One | 20-40 |
| *(Music and interviews, some live)* | | | |
| | | | |
| **LITTLE VILLAGE** | | | |
| **RADIO SHOWS** | | | |
| **Albums** | | | |
| OFF THE RECORD (May 92) Profile | 1992 | Westwood One (2) | 10-15 |
| *(Music and interviews)* | | | |
| **Compact Discs** | | | |
| IN CONCERT (June 92) | 1992 | Westwood One (2) | 20-30 |
| *(Live concert)* | | | |
| | | | |
| **LIVE** | | | |
| *Other Radioactive promo CD singles $2 each* | | | |
| **Compact Discs** | | | |
| I ALONE | 1994 | Radioactive | 10 |
| *(Promo-only CD single, also contains acoustic version unavailable elsewhere)* | | | |
| WHITE, DISCUSSION | 1995 | Radioactive 3083 | 10 |
| *(Promo-only CD single)* | | | |
| **RADIO SHOWS** | | | |
| **Compact Discs** | | | |
| ALBUM NETWORK (Dec 94) | 1994 | Album Network | 40-75 |
| *(Live concert)* | | | |
| IN CONCERT (Sept 94) | 1994 | Westwood One | 25-50 |
| *(Live concert)* | | | |
| IN CONCERT-NU ROCK (Aug 94) | 1994 | Westwood One | 25-50 |
| *(Live concert)* | | | |
| SUPERSTAR CONCERT (Sept 94) | 1994 | Westwood One (2) | 25-50 |
| *(Live concert)* | | | |
| | | | |
| **LIVING COLOUR** | | | |
| *Epic promo CD singles $3-5 each* | | | |
| **12-Inch Singles** | | | |
| AUSLANDER (4 versions) | 1993 | Epic EAS 5140 | 10 |
| CULT OF PERSONALITY + 4 live songs | 1988 | Epic EAS 01265 | 10 |
| LEAVE IT ALONE | 1990 | (No label) 4952 | 15 |
| *(Red vinyl, white label, song title/group only)* | | | |
| MIDDLEMAN (same on both sides) | 1988 | Epic EAS 01074 | 7 |
| SUNSHINE OF YOUR LOVE (2 versions) | 1994 | Epic EAS 6296 | 7 |
| TYPE/FINAL SOLUTION/SAILIN' ON (Live) | 1990 | Epic EAS 2147 | 18 |
| *(Promo-only on yellow vinyl with picture cover)* | | | |
| **RADIO SHOWS** | | | |
| **Albums** | | | |
| IN CONCERT Live concert | 1990 | Westwood One (2) | 20-35 |
| *(Living Colour solo concert)* | | | |
| IN CONCERT (Aug 89) Live concert | 1989 | Westwood One (2) | 25-40 |
| *(With Love & Rockets)* | | | |
| OFF THE RECORD Profile | 1990 | Westwood One (2) | 10-15 |
| *(Music and interviews)* | | | |
| **Compact Discs** | | | |
| LIVE AT ELECTRIC LADYLAND (Dec 90) Live concert | 1990 | Westwood One | 75-125 |
| *(Hard to find series)* | | | |
| OFF THE RECORD (May 93) Profile | 1993 | Westwood One | 20-30 |
| *(With Soul Asylum)* | | | |

| Title | Yr | Label, Number | NM $ |
|---|---|---|---|
| ON THE EDGE (Apr 93) Music and interviews | 1993 | Westwood One | 20-30 |
| *(With Jellyfish)* | | | |
| UP CLOSE Profile | 1993 | Media America (2) | 15-25 |
| *(Music and interviews)* | | | |

**LIVING VOICES**
**45s**

| | | | |
|---|---|---|---|
| CHRISTMAS IS CHRISTMAS (ALL OVER THE WORLD)/LONG LONG KISS | 197? | RCA JPC6-5314/5292 | 8 |
| *A-side with the Living Strings; white label promo with no RCA logo* | | | |
| FLYING HOME FOR CHRISTMAS (mono/stereo) | 1977 | RCA JH-11155 | 5 |

**LLOYD, DAVID, AND HIS LONDON ORCHESTRA**
**7-Inch Extended Plays**

| | | | |
|---|---|---|---|
| LIVE AND LET DIE | 1973 | SESAC AD-95 | 12 |
| *(With paper cover)* | | | |

**LLOYD, JAY B.**
*Bill Black; Also recorded as Bill Black's Combo*
**45s**

| | | | |
|---|---|---|---|
| I'M SO LONELY | 1958 | Hi 2028 | 50 |
| *(Hi promo label)* | | | |
| YOU'RE JUST MY KIND | 1958 | ABC-Paramount 9922 | 50 |
| *(White promo label)* | | | |

**LOBO**
**45s**

| | | | |
|---|---|---|---|
| AM I GOING CRAZY (OR JUST OUT OF HER MIND) (same on both sides) | 1985 | Evergreen 1028 | 5 |
| *(Promo copies have incorrect title; correct title ends in "..Out of My Mind")* | | | |
| CARIBBEAN CARNIVAL (same on both sides) | 1981 | Atlantic 3851 | 5 |
| *(May be promo only)* | | | |

**LOCAL H**
**45s**

| | | | |
|---|---|---|---|
| DISGRUNTLED CHRISTMAS/WHITE CHRISTMAS | 1994 | Island PR7 6902-7 | 8 |
| *(B-side by Sybil Vane; green vinyl)* | | | |

**LOFGREN, NILS**
*A&M promo 45s $5 each*
**12-Inch Singles**

| | | | |
|---|---|---|---|
| ACROSS THE TRACKS/DADDY DREAM | 1983 | Backstreet L33-1127 | 8 |
| DELIVERY NIGHT (same on both sides) | 1985 | Columbia CAS 2173 | 6 |
| SECRETS IN THE STREET (same on both sides) | 1985 | Columbia CAS 2100 | 6 |

**Albums**

| | | | |
|---|---|---|---|
| AUTHORIZED BOOTLEG | 1976 | A&M SP-8362 | 25 |
| *(Ironically, this promo-only live album has been bootlegged!)* | | | |

**RADIO SHOWS**
**Albums**

| | | | |
|---|---|---|---|
| BBC LONDON WAVELENGTH (Nov 81) | 1981 | London Wavelength | 20-40 |
| *(Mostly music and interviews)* | | | |
| IN CONCERT (July 91) Live concert | 1991 | Westwood One (2) | 30-50 |
| *(With Midnight Oil)* | | | |
| KING BISCUIT FLOWER HOUR (Dec 81) Live concert | 1981 | DIR (2) | 40-75 |
| *(With the Henry Paul Band)* | | | |
| OFF THE RECORD Music and interviews | 1991 | Westwood One (2) | 10-20 |
| *(Repeated)* | | | |

**LOGGINS AND MESSINA**
*Includes Kenny Loggins listings; Other Columbia promo 45s $4 each; Columbia promo 45s by Kenny Loggins $3 each; Columbia promo picture sleeves by Kenny Loggins $2 each*
**45s**

| | | | |
|---|---|---|---|
| ANGRY EYES | 1976 | Columbia 10444 | 12 |
| *(Price includes promo-only large center hole picture sleeve)* | | | |
| JUST BEFORE THE NEWS | 1972 | Columbia AE7 1060 | 15 |
| *(Promo-only record and picture sleeve, 1:06 long)* | | | |
| WHAT'S IT ALL ABOUT (Mar 75) Public service show | 1975 | W.I.A.A. 267 | 15 |
| *(Loggins & Messina, flip side is Kris Kristofferson)* | | | |
| WHAT'S IT ALL ABOUT (Apr 79) Public service show | 1979 | W.I.A.A. 470 | 12 |
| *(Kenny Loggins, flip side is Ellen McIlwaine)* | | | |
| WHAT'S IT ALL ABOUT (Oct 81) Public service show | 1981 | W.I.A.A. 600 | 20 |
| *(Flip side features Billy Joel)* | | | |

**7-Inch Extended Plays**

| | | | |
|---|---|---|---|
| LISTEN TO A COUNTRY SONG | 197? | Columbia AS7 1033 | 10 |
| *(Part of Playback series, with cardboard inner sleeve)* | | | |
| PLAYBACK | 1972 | Columbia Playback AS 36 | 15 |
| *(Two songs, "Long Tail Cat" and "Listen to a Country Song," issued with a paper picture sleeve with artist information)* | | | |

**Albums**

| | | | |
|---|---|---|---|
| KENNY LOGGINS | 1981 | Columbia AS-946 | 15 |
| *(Promo-only sampler)* | | | |

**RADIO SHOWS**
**Albums**

| | | | |
|---|---|---|---|
| INNERVIEW (80s) | 198? | Innerview | 10-20 |
| *(Music and interviews)* | | | |
| ROBERT W. MORGAN  Dave Loggins | 1979 | Watermark | 15-25 |
| *(Demo show, red artist strip, with hard title cover)* | | | |

| Title | Yr | Label, Number | NM $ |
|---|---|---|---|
| ROBERT W. MORGAN  Jim Messina | 1981 | Watermark | 10-20 |
| *(Music and interviews)* | | | |
| SPOTLIGHT SPECIAL | 1982 | ABC Radio (2) | 25-40 |
| *(Music and interviews)* | | | |
| STARTRACK PROFILE (Apr 85) Kenny Loggins | 1985 | (4) | 25-50 |
| *(Two shows, music and interviews)* | | | |

## LOMAX, JACKIE
**45s**

| | | | |
|---|---|---|---|
| SOUR MILK SEA/(I) FALL INSIDE YOUR EYES | 1971 | Apple PRO-6240/1 | 30 |
| **Albums** | | | |
| AN INTERVIEW WITH JACKIE LOMAX | 1972 | Warner Bros. PRO 520 | 40 |

## LONDON, JULIE
*Other Liberty white promo 45s $8 each; Liberty white promo label LPs $18 each*
**45s**

| | | | |
|---|---|---|---|
| CRY ME A RIVER | 1959 | Liberty 55227 | 10 |
| *(White promo label)* | | | |
| JULIE AT HOME  Five stereo 33 1/3 rpm singles | 1963 | Liberty SE-11 | 50 |
| *(Seven-inch records with small center hole, $10 each)* | | | |
| **7-Inch Extended Plays** | | | |
| JULIE LONDON Jukebox LLP | 1964 | Liberty 7342 | 10 |
| *(Issued with a hard cover)* | | | |

## LONE JUSTICE
**12-Inch Singles**

| | | | |
|---|---|---|---|
| I FOUND LOVE (same on both sides) | 1986 | Geffen PRO-A-2645 | 6 |
| SHELTER (same on both sides) | 1986 | Geffen PRO-A-2596 | 6 |
| SWEET SWEET BABY (LP) (Remix) | 1985 | Geffen PRO-A-2329 | 6 |
| WAYS TO BE WICKED (same on both sides) | 1985 | Geffen PRO-A-2275 | 5 |

## LOPEZ, TRINI
*Other King promo 45s $8 each; Reprise promo 45s $4 each; Reprise promo LPs $8 each; Warner Fresca EP $5 each; Reprise promo 33s $8 each; Reprise promo jukebox LLPs $8-15 each*
**45s**

| | | | |
|---|---|---|---|
| EL NINO DEL TAMBOR/NOCHO DE PAZ (LET THERE BE PEACE) | 1968 | Reprise 0801 | 8 |
| *(Stock copy may not exist)* | | | |
| I'M GRATEFUL | 1959 | King 5234 | 12 |
| *(White promo label)* | | | |
| NOLA | 1959 | King 5173 | 18 |
| *(White promo label)* | | | |
| SINCE I DON'T HAVE YOU | 1959 | King 5187 | 12 |
| *(White promo label)* | | | |
| **7-Inch Extended Plays** | | | |
| DEPARTMENT OF COMMERCE  Radio ads | 1971 | AAVP 71664 | 10 |
| *(All eight PSA spots by Trini Lopez)* | | | |

## LORDS OF THE NEW CHURCH
*I.R.S. promo 45s $4 each; Any other I.R.S. promo 12" singles $8 each*
**12-Inch Singles**

| | | | |
|---|---|---|---|
| HOLY WAR/OPEN YOUR EYES | 1982 | I.R.S. 70962 | 8 |
| THE METHOD TO MY MADNESS (same on both sides) | 1985 | I.R.S. 70985 | 18 |
| **RADIO SHOWS** | | | |
| **Albums** | | | |
| BBC COLLEGE CONCERT HOUR (Oct 82) | 1982 | London Wavelength | 100-200 |
| *(Live concert)* | | | |

## LOS BRAVOS
*Press (London) promo 45s $8-10 each*
**7-Inch Extended Plays**

| | | | |
|---|---|---|---|
| SWING THE JINGLE Various artists | 196? | Coca-Cola | 100 |
| *(45rpm jingles for Coca-Cola, picture sleeve)* | | | |

## LOS LOBOS
*Warner Bros/Slash promo 45s $3 each; Warner Bros./Slash promo CD singles $2-3 each*
**12-Inch Singles**

| | | | |
|---|---|---|---|
| DON'T WORRY BABY/WILL THE WOLF SURVIVE? | 1984 | Slash PRO-A-2226 | 7 |
| IS THAT ALL THERE IS (same on both sides) | 1987 | Slash PRO-A-2685 | 7 |
| LA BAMBA/LA BAMBA (Fade) | 1987 | Slash PRO-A-2737 | 8 |
| SET ME FREE (ROSA LEE) (same on both sides) | 1987 | Slash PRO-A-2690 | 5 |
| SHAKIN' SHAKIN' SHAKES (same on both sides) | 1986 | Slash PRO-A-2640 | 8 |
| WILL THE WOLF SURVIVE? (Remix Edit)/(LP Version) | 1984 | Slash PRO-A-2252 | 7 |
| **Compact Discs** | | | |
| WORLD PACK: AN AOR SAMPLER | 1994 | Slash PRO-CD-6578 | 12 |
| *(Promo-only collection for FM radio)* | | | |
| **RADIO SHOWS** | | | |
| **Albums** | | | |
| BBC TRANSCRIPTION DISC Live concert | 1987 | BBC Transcription | 200-300 |
| *(Very rare concert, with Ben E. King)* | | | |
| IN CONCERT (Dec 87) Live concert | 1987 | Westwood One (2) | 20-30 |
| *(Solo live concert)* | | | |
| IN CONCERT (Feb 85) Live concert | 1985 | Westwood One (2) | 25-50 |
| *(With the Romantics)* | | | |

| Title | Yr | Label, Number | NM $ |
|---|---|---|---|
| IN CONCERT (June 85) Live concert | 1985 | Westwood One (2) | 25-50 |
| *(With the Payolas)* | | | |
| KING BISCUIT FLOWER HOUR Live concert | 1985 | DIR (2) | 25-35 |
| *(With Dwight Twilley)* | | | |
| KING BISCUIT FLOWER HOUR (Jan 85) Live concert | 1985 | DIR (2) | 20-30 |
| *(With Romeo Void)* | | | |

## LOUDERMILK, JOHN D.
*Includes Johnny Dee and Ebe Sneezer & the Epidemics; Other Columbia promo 45s $8 each; RCA Victor promo 45s $5 each; Music is Medicine (CBS) promo 45s $2 each*
### 45s

| | | | |
|---|---|---|---|
| 1,000 CONCRETE BLOCKS  Johnny Dee | 1959 | Colonial 435 | 30 |
| *(White promo label)* | | | |
| ASIATIC FLU   Ebe Sneezer and His Epidemics | 1959 | Colonial 436 | 40 |
| *(White promo label)* | | | |
| SITTIN' IN THE BALCONY  Johnny Dee | 1958 | Colonial 430 | 40 |
| *(White promo label, this is the original B-side)* | | | |
| TEENAGE QUEEN  Johnny Dee | 1959 | Colonial 433 | 35 |
| *(White promo label)* | | | |
| TOBACCO ROAD | 1960 | Columbia 41562 | 12 |
| *(White promo label)* | | | |

## LOUDNESS
### RADIO SHOWS
### Albums

| | | | |
|---|---|---|---|
| IN CONCERT (Sept 85) Live concert | 1985 | Westwood One (2) | 40-75 |
| *(With Mama's Boys and Y & T)* | | | |

## LOUVIN BROTHERS, THE
*Capitol white promo label 45s $5 each*
### Albums

| | | | |
|---|---|---|---|
| COUNTRY LOVE BALLADS | 1959 | Capitol 1106 | 50 |
| *(Blue promo label)* | | | |
| ENCORE | 1961 | Capitol 1547 | 40 |
| *(Blue promo label)* | | | |
| THE LOUVIN BROTHERS | 1957 | MGM 3426 | 125 |
| *(Yellow promo label)* | | | |
| NEARER MY GOD TO THEE | 1957 | Capitol 825 | 40 |
| *(Yellow promo label)* | | | |
| SATAN IS REAL | 1960 | Capitol 1277 | 50 |
| *(Blue promo label)* | | | |
| TRAGIC SONGS OF LIFE | 1956 | Capitol 769 | 40 |
| *(Yellow promo label)* | | | |
| A TRIBUTE TO THE DELMORE BROTHERS | 1960 | Capitol 1449 | 75 |
| *(Blue promo label)* | | | |

### RADIO SHOWS
### Albums

| | | | |
|---|---|---|---|
| LOUVIN BROTHERS AND ERNEST TUBB (60s) | 196? | U.S. Air Force | 20-40 |
| *(Music and interviews)* | | | |

## LOVE
### Albums

| | | | |
|---|---|---|---|
| FOREVER CHANGES | 1967 | Elektra EKL-4013 | 150 |
| *(White label promo, mono)* | | | |
| FOUR SAIL | 1969 | Elektra EKS-74049 | 80 |
| *(White label promo)* | | | |
| LOVE | 1966 | Elektra EKL-4001 | 300 |
| *(White label promo, mono)* | | | |

## LOVE AND ROCKETS
*Beggars Banquet/RCA promo CD singles $3-5 each*
### 12-Inch Singles

| | | | |
|---|---|---|---|
| BALL OF CONFUSION (same on both sides) | 1986 | Big Time 6035 | 8 |
| DOG END OF THE DAY GONE BY (2 versions)/INTERVIEW | 1988 | RCA 8758 | 15 |
| KUNDALINI EXPRESS (same on both sides) | 1986 | Big Time 6018 | 8 |
| MIRROR PEOPLE (same on both sides) | 1987 | Big Time 6067 | 10 |
| NO NEW TALE TO TELL (same on both sides) | 1987 | Big Time 6063 | 10 |
| WAITING FOR THE FLOOD (same on both sides) | 1987 | Big Time 6071 | 10 |

### RADIO SHOWS
### Albums

| | | | |
|---|---|---|---|
| IN CONCERT (Aug 88) Live concert | 1988 | Westwood One (2) | 25-40 |
| *(With Living Colour)* | | | |
| IN CONCERT (Feb 88) Live concert | 1988 | Westwood One (2) | 30-60 |
| *(With the BoDeans)* | | | |

## LOVE SPIT LOVE
### RADIO SHOWS
### Compact Discs

| | | | |
|---|---|---|---|
| IN CONCERT-NU ROCK (Dec 94) | 1994 | Westwood One | 30-60 |
| *(Live concert)* | | | |

## LOVE, DARLENE
*Other Philles promo 45s $25 each; Warner/Spector promo 45s $10 each; Reprise promo 45s $8 each*
### 45s

| | | | |
|---|---|---|---|
| HE'S A QUIET GUY | 1964 | Philles 123 | 150 |
| *(Philles white promo label)* | | | |

| Title | Yr | Label, Number | NM $ |
|-------|-----|---------------|------|
| **Compact Discs** | | | |
| ALL ALONE ON CHRISTMAS | 1992 | Fox 10003 | 8 |
| *(Promo-only CD single)* | | | |
| | | | |
| **LOVELESS, PATTY** | | | |
| *MCA promo 45s $3 each; MCA promo CD singles $2 each; Epic promo CD singles $3 each.* | | | |
| **RADIO SHOWS** | | | |
| **Albums** | | | |
| LIVE AT GILLEY'S (Aug 88) Live concert | 1988 | Westwood One | 25-50 |
| *(Rare earlier concert)* | | | |
| **Compact Discs** | | | |
| COUNTRY CONCERT | 1993 | Westwood One | 40-60 |
| *(Live concert)* | | | |
| LIVE AT CRAZY HORSE | 1993 | Album Network | 40-75 |
| *(Live concert)* | | | |
| | | | |
| **LOVERBOY** | | | |
| *Other Columbia promo 45s and promo sleeves $2 each* | | | |
| **45s** | | | |
| TURN ME LOOSE (Long)/(Short) | 1981 | Columbia 11421 | 8 |
| **RADIO SHOWS** | | | |
| **Albums** | | | |
| IN CONCERT (Feb 82) Live concert | 1982 | Westwood One (2) | 20-30 |
| *(With the Rockets)* | | | |
| IN CONCERT (June 81) Live concert | 1981 | Westwood One (2) | 40-80 |
| *(With Blue Oyster Cult)* | | | |
| KING BISCUIT FLOWER HOUR (Apr 81) Live concert | 1981 | DIR/ABC (2) | 50-100 |
| *(With Humble Pie)* | | | |
| KING BISCUIT FLOWER HOUR (July 81) Live concert | 1981 | DIR/ABC (2) | 50-75 |
| *(With Dire Straits)* | | | |
| KING BISCUIT FLOWER HOUR (June 82) Live concert | 1982 | DIR/ABC (2) | 20-30 |
| *(Live solo concert by Loverboy)* | | | |
| NBC SOURCE (Aug 82) Live concert | 1982 | NBC Radio (2) | 20-30 |
| *(Rare early concert, repeated in 1983)* | | | |
| SUPERSTAR CONCERT (Aug 84) Live concert | 1984 | Westwood One (3) | 15-25 |
| *(Box set, repeated)* | | | |
| SUPERSTAR CONCERT (Oct 86) Live concert | 1986 | Westwood One (3) | 20-30 |
| *(With Mr. Mister)* | | | |
| **Compact Discs** | | | |
| IN THE STUDIO (Mar 91) Profile of an album | 1991 | Album Network | 10-15 |
| *(Music and interviews)* | | | |
| | | | |
| **LOVETT, LYLE** | | | |
| *MCA promo color vinyl 45s $8 each* | | | |
| **45s** | | | |
| COWBOY MAN (same on both sides) | 1986 | MCA/Curb 52951 | 8 |
| *Clear vinyl* | | | |
| FARTHER DOWN THE LINE (same on both sides) | 1986 | MCA 52818 | 8 |
| *Green vinyl* | | | |
| **RADIO SHOWS** | | | |
| **Albums** | | | |
| BBC TRANSCRIPTION DISC  Live concert | 1990 | BBC Transcription | 200-300 |
| *(Very rare concert, with Darby Spillane)* | | | |
| BBC TRANSCRIPTION DISC  Live concert | 1990 | BBC Transcription | 200-300 |
| *(With Otis Grand)* | | | |
| | | | |
| **LOVICH, LENE** | | | |
| **RADIO SHOWS** | | | |
| **Albums** | | | |
| BBC COLLEGE CONCERT HOUR (May 83) | 1983 | BBC Transcription | 75-150 |
| *(Rare live concert)* | | | |
| | | | |
| **LOVIN' SPOONFUL, THE** | | | |
| *Featuring John Sebastian; Kama Sutra promo 45s $8 each; Kama Sutra, MGM and Reprise promo 45s by John Sebastian $4 each; Kama Sutra promo 45s by Zalman Yanovsky $8 each* | | | |
| **45s** | | | |
| DAYDREAM (mono/stereo) | 1976 | Kama Sutra 608 | 6 |
| *(Reissue, stock copy not known to exist)* | | | |
| **7-Inch Extended Plays** | | | |
| LOVIN' SPOONFUL, THE | 196? | Kama Sutra EK-1 | 50 |
| *(Promo-only EP with cover)* | | | |
| | | | |
| **LOWE, JIM** | | | |
| *Mercury promo 45s $6 each* | | | |
| | | | |
| **LOWE, NICK** | | | |
| *Columbia white promo label 45s $5 each* | | | |
| **12-Inch Singles** | | | |
| CRUEL TO BE KIND Lowe/Elvis Costello/Mink DeVille | 1979 | Columbia AS 443 | 25 |
| *(Promo-only 12" orange vinyl Columbia/Capitol release with three tracks from three artists)* | | | |
| HALF A BOY AND HALF A MAN (same on both sides) | 1984 | Columbia AS 1876 | 5 |
| I KNEW THE BRIDE  (same on both sides) | 1985 | Columbia CAS 2171 | 8 |
| LOVER'S JAMBOREE (same on both sides) | 1988 | Columbia CAS 2923 | 5 |
| RAGING EYES (same on both sides) | 1983 | Columbia AS 1626 | 5 |
| WITHOUT LOVE (same on both sides) | 198? | Columbia AS 921 | 8 |
| *(Nick Lowe with Johnny Cash and Dave Edmunds)* | | | |

| Title | Yr | Label, Number | NM $ |
|---|---|---|---|
| **45s** | | | |
| COOL REACTION (same on both sides) | 1983 | Columbia 03837 | 3 |
| HALF A BOY AND HALF A MAN  White promo label | 1984 | Columbia 04486 | 10 |
| *(Promo version of a rock classic)* | | | |
| I KNEW THE BRIDE  White promo label | 1985 | Columbia 05570 | 10 |
| *(Promo version of another rock classic)* | | | |
| SING THE EVERLY BROTHERS  With Dave Edmunds | 1980 | Columbia AE7 1219 | 15 |
| *(Four Everly songs, included with early copies of the Rockpile LP Seconds of Pleasure)* | | | |
| **Albums** | | | |
| AN INTERROGATION OF NICK LOWE | 1982 | Columbia AS 1400 | 25 |
| *(Interchords, music and interviews)* | | | |
| **RADIO SHOWS** | | | |
| **Albums** | | | |
| BBC LONDON WAVELENGTH (Mar 83) | 1983 | London Wavelength | 25-40 |
| *(Music and interviews)* | | | |
| BBC ROCK HOUR (June 82) | 1982 | London Wavelength | 75-150 |
| *(Live early concert)* | | | |
| BBC ROCK HOUR (Sept 84) | 1984 | London Wavelength | 75-135 |
| *(Repeat live concert)* | | | |
| BBC TRANSCRIPTION DISC Live concert | 1982 | BBC Transcription | 225-350 |
| *(Rare live concert with Noise to Go)* | | | |
| INNERVIEW (80s) Profile | 198? | Innerview | 20-30 |
| *(Music and interviews)* | | | |
| RETRO ROCK (July 83) | 1983 | Clayton Webster (2) | 50-100 |
| *(Music and interviews with some live tracks)* | | | |

## LUCAS, NICK
**Albums**

| Title | Yr | Label, Number | NM $ |
|---|---|---|---|
| PAINTING THE CLOUDS WITH SUNSHINE | 1957 | Decca 8653 | 40 |
| *(Pink promo label)* | | | |

## LULU
**Albums**

| Title | Yr | Label, Number | NM $ |
|---|---|---|---|
| MELODY FAIR | 1970 | Atco 33-330 | 30 |
| *(White label promo; no stock copies were issued in mono)* | | | |
| NEW ROUTES | 1970 | Atco 33-310 | 30 |
| *(White label promo; no stock copies were issued in mono)* | | | |

## LUMAN, BOB
*Other Warner Bros. promo 45s $15 each; Hickory promo singles $3 each; Epic promo singles $2 each; Hickory white promo label LPs $20 each*

**45s**

| Title | Yr | Label, Number | NM $ |
|---|---|---|---|
| LET'S THINK ABOUT LIVING  White and red promo label | 1960 | Warner Bros. 5172 | 25 |
| *(Promo version of this rock classic)* | | | |
| MAKE UP YOUR MIND, BABY | 1957 | Imperial 8315 | 60 |
| *(Cream colored promo label)* | | | |
| PRECIOUS | 1958 | Capitol 4059 | 20 |
| *(White promo label)* | | | |
| RED CADILLAC AND A BLACK MOUSTACHE | 1957 | Imperial 8311 | 75 |
| *(Cream colored promo label, first record)* | | | |
| RED HOT | 1957 | Imperial 8313 | 75 |
| *(Cream colored promo label)* | | | |
| TRY ME | 1958 | Capitol 3972 | 25 |
| *(White promo label)* | | | |
| **7-Inch Extended Plays** | | | |
| BOSTON ROCKER  Four-song promo EP | 1960 | Warner Bros. 5506 | 50 |
| *(White and red label, three other songs)* | | | |
| **Albums** | | | |
| LET'S THINK ABOUT LIVIN' | 1960 | Warner Bros. 1396 | 75 |
| *(White promo label)* | | | |

## LUMPKIN, HENRY
**45s**

| Title | Yr | Label, Number | NM $ |
|---|---|---|---|
| WE REALLY LOVE EACH OTHER | 1961 | Motown 1005 | 75 |
| *(White promo label)* | | | |

## LUNA
**45s**

| Title | Yr | Label, Number | NM $ |
|---|---|---|---|
| TIME/EGG NOG | 1992 | Elektra 64679 | 8 |
| *Promo only on green vinyl* | | | |

## LUSCIOUS JACKSON
**12-Inch Singles**

| Title | Yr | Label, Number | NM $ |
|---|---|---|---|
| DEEP SHAG (3 versions)/DADDY | 1994 | Capitol SPRO 79482/99 | 8 |
| *(Cream vinyl promo copy)* | | | |

## LUSH
**RADIO SHOWS**
**Compact Discs**

| Title | Yr | Label, Number | NM $ |
|---|---|---|---|
| IN CONCERT - NU ROCK (July 96) | 1996 | | 25-50 |
| *(Live concert material)* | | | |

| Title | Yr | Label, Number | NM $ |
|---|---|---|---|

**LYMON, FRANKIE**
*Includes the Teenagers (with and without Lymon); Gee white promo label 45s $25-40 each depending on year; Roulette white promo label 45s $20 each; Roulette colored promo label 45s $15 each; End promo 45s by the Teenagers $25-35 each; Roulette colored promo label 45s by the Teenagers $18 each; Decca promo 45s by Jack Hammer $15 each; Roulette and some Columbia promo 45s by Buzz Clifford $15 each*
**Albums**

| | | | |
|---|---|---|---|
| THE TEENAGERS FEATURING FRANKIE LYMON | 1957 | Gee 701 | 1,200 |
| *(White promo label)* | | | |

**LYNN, LORETTA**
*Decca pink promo label 45s $4; MCA white and red promo 45s $3; Other jukebox LLPs $18 each; Other Decca promo LPs $12 each*
**45s**

| | | | |
|---|---|---|---|
| CHRISTMAS GREETINGS  Promo picture disc | 1972 | Decca (no #) | 50 |
| *(7" picture disc also features Conway Twitty)* | | | |
| THE DARKEST DAY | 1961 | Zero 112 | 75 |
| *(Yellow promo label)* | | | |
| HEARTACHES MEET MR. BLUES | 1960 | Zero 110 | 100 |
| *(Yellow promo label)* | | | |
| I'M A HONKY TONK GIRL | 1960 | Zero 107 | 150 |
| *(First single for Loretta)* | | | |

**7-Inch Extended Plays**

| | | | |
|---|---|---|---|
| FIST CITY  Jukebox LLP | 1968 | Decca 34??? | 40 |
| *(Issued with a hard cover)* | | | |
| I LIKE 'EM COUNTRY Jukebox LLP | 1966 | Decca 34744 | 40 |
| *(Issued with a hard cover)* | | | |
| LORETTA LYNN SINGS  Jukebox LLP | 1963 | Decca 34226 | 100 |
| *(Issued with a hard cover)* | | | |
| ONE'S ON THE WAY  Jukebox LLP | 1972 | Decca 34877 (LLP 187) | 20 |
| *(Issued with a paper cover)* | | | |
| SONGS FROM THE HEART  Jukebox LLP | 1964 | Decca 34318 | 75 |
| *(Issued with a hard cover)* | | | |
| YOU AIN'T WOMAN ENOUGH  Jukebox LLP | 1964 | Decca 34418 | 50 |
| *(Issued with a hard cover)* | | | |

**Albums**

| | | | |
|---|---|---|---|
| ALLIS-CHALMERS PRESENTS LORETTA LYNN | 1978 | MCA 35013 | 40 |
| *(Promo-only Special Markets release)* | | | |
| CRISCO PRESENTS LORETTA LYNN'S COUNTRY CLASSICS | 1979 | MCA 35018 | 40 |
| *(Promo-only Special Markets release)* | | | |
| LORETTA LYNN | 1963 | Decca 4457 | 75 |
| *(Pink promo label)* | | | |
| LORETTA LYNN | 1974 | MCA L33-1934 | 40 |
| *(Promo-only compilation)* | | | |
| YOUR SQUAW IS ON THE WARPATH  Pink promo label | 1969 | Decca 75084 | 50 |
| *(Includes "Barney," omitted from later pressings)* | | | |

**RADIO SHOWS**
**Albums**

| | | | |
|---|---|---|---|
| AMERICAN EAGLE | 1982 | DIR (3) | 40-75 |
| *(Early live concert)* | | | |
| LIVE AT GILLEY'S (May 88) | 1988 | Westwood One | 25-50 |
| *(With Alabama, live concert, repeated)* | | | |
| WESTWOOD ONE PRESENTS (Apr 89) | 1989 | Westwood One | 25-50 |
| *(Live concert)* | | | |

**LYNNE, JEFF**
*Of the Electric Light Orchestra; Reprise promo CD singles $3 each*
**RADIO SHOWS**
**Albums**

| | | | |
|---|---|---|---|
| BBC TRANSCRIPTION DISC Live concert | 1973 | BBC Transcription | 300-400 |
| *(Very rare concert, with Wolf)* | | | |
| BBC TRANSCRIPTION DISC Live concert | 1974 | BBC Transcription | 400-600 |
| *(Very rare concert, with Ralph McTell)* | | | |
| OFF THE RECORD (June 90) | 1990 | Westwood One (2) | 15-25 |
| *(Music and interviews about ELO)* | | | |

**Compact Discs**

| | | | |
|---|---|---|---|
| MASTERS OF ROCK (Aug 90) | 1990 | Radio Ventures (2) | 40-75 |
| *(Music and interviews)* | | | |

**LYNYRD SKYNYRD**
*Includes listings of Rossington-Collins Band; MCA white, blue or red promo label 45s $5 each; MCA promo 45s by the Rossington-Collins Band $3 each*
**12-Inch Singles**

| | | | |
|---|---|---|---|
| GEORGIA PEACHES | 1988 | MCA 17444 | 10 |
| *(Promo-only 12" single)* | | | |
| GIMME BACK MY BULLETS | 1988 | MCA 17569 | 12 |
| *(Promo-only 12" single)* | | | |
| SWAMP MUSIC | 1988 | MCA 17488 | 10 |
| *(Promo-only 12" single)* | | | |
| TRUCK DRIVIN' MAN | 1987 | MCA 17385 | 12 |
| *(Promo-only 12" single)* | | | |

**45s**

| | | | |
|---|---|---|---|
| GIMME BACK MY BULLETS | 1977 | MCA 1966 | 25 |
| *(Promo-only release)* | | | |

**Albums**

| | | | |
|---|---|---|---|
| ONE MORE FROM THE ROAD | 1976 | MCA L33-1946 | 25 |
| *(Promo only on black vinyl)* | | | |
| ONE MORE FROM THE ROAD | 1976 | MCA L33-1946 | 50 |
| *(Promo on blue, gold, purple or red vinyl; each has the same value)* | | | |

| Title | Yr | Label, Number | NM $ |
|-------|-----|---------------|------|
| SKYNYRD'S FIRST AND...LAST | 1978 | MCA L33-1988 | 25 |
| *Promo sampler* | | | |
| **Compact Discs** | | | |
| ALL I CAN DO IS WRITE ABOUT IT | 1991 | MCA 1681 | 8 |
| *(Promo CD single)* | | | |
| BACK TO BACK | 1993 | Atlantic PRCD 5078 | 50 |
| *(Promo-only Interview disc; Travis Tritt is the interviewer)* | | | |
| BORN TO RUN | 1993 | Atlantic PRCD 5051 | 8 |
| *(Promo CD single)* | | | |
| DOUBLE TROUBLE | 1989 | MCA 17823 | 8 |
| *(Promo CD single)* | | | |
| GOOD LOVIN'S HARD TO FIND | 1993 | Atlantic PRCD 4953 | 8 |
| *(Promo CD single)* | | | |
| KEEPING THE FAITH | 1991 | Atlantic PRCD 4117 | 8 |
| *(Promo CD single)* | | | |
| LAST REBEL, THE | 1993 | Atlantic PRCD 5156 | 8 |
| *(Promo CD single)* | | | |
| PURE AND SIMPLE | 1991 | Atlantic PRCD 4240 | 8 |
| *(Promo CD single)* | | | |
| SMOKESTACK LIGHTNING | 1991 | Atlantic PRCD 3960 | 8 |
| *(Promo CD single)* | | | |
| WHITE KNUCKLE RIDE | 1997 | Columbia CSK 78284 | 8 |
| *(Promo CD single)* | | | |
| **RADIO SHOWS** | | | |
| **Albums** | | | |
| IN CONCERT Live concert | 1988 | Westwood One (2) | 40-75 |
| *(Repeated)* | | | |
| KING BISCUIT FLOWER HOUR Live concert | 1986 | DIR (2) | 40-65 |
| *(Vinyl version)* | | | |
| LEGENDS OF ROCK (Oct 87) Profile | 1987 | NBC Radio (2) | 20-30 |
| *(Music and interviews, repeated)* | | | |
| THE LYNYRD SKYNYRD STORY (Nov 82) | 1982 | NBC Source (3) | 50-75 |
| *(Music and interview, some live tracks)* | | | |
| NBC SOURCE (Oct 87) | 1987 | NBC Radio (2) | 25-40 |
| *(Music and interviews)* | | | |
| A NIGHT ON THE ROAD (June 81) Rossington-Collins Band | 1981 | ABC Radio (3) | 75-100 |
| *(Box set, mostly music and interviews)* | | | |
| PIONEERS IN MUSIC (June 86) | 1986 | NBC Radio (2) | 20-30 |
| *(With Molly Hatchet, Charlie Daniels and .38 Special)* | | | |
| SOURCE CONCERT (Mar 81) Rossington-Collins Band | 1981 | NBC Source (2) | 50-75 |
| *(Live concert)* | | | |
| **Compact Discs** | | | |
| IN THE STUDIO (Jan 89) Profile of an album | 1989 | Album Network | 10-20 |
| *(Music and interviews)* | | | |
| KING BISCUIT FLOWER HOUR (May 88) Live concert | 1988 | DIR | 50-100 |
| *(CD version)* | | | |
| KING BISCUIT FLOWER HOUR (Nov 89) Live concert | 1989 | DIR | 40-75 |
| *(Repeat concerts)* | | | |
| UP CLOSE  Profile | 1988 | Media America (2) | 30-50 |
| *(Music and interviews)* | | | |
| UP CLOSE  Profile | 1991 | Media America (2) | 30-50 |
| *(Music and interviews)* | | | |
| UP CLOSE  Profile | 1993 | Media America (2) | 25-40 |
| *(Music and interviews)* | | | |

# M

**M**
**12-Inch Singles**

| | | | |
|-------|-----|---------------|------|
| MOONIGHT AND MUZAK/WOMAN MAKE MAN | 1979 | Sire PRO-A-842 | 8 |
| THAT'S THE WAY THE MONEY GOES 1 & 2/COWBOYS AND INDIANS | 1980 | Sire PRO-A-851 | 6 |

**45s**

| | | | |
|-------|-----|---------------|------|
| POP MUZIK (Long)/(Short) | 1979 | Sire 49033 | 5 |

**MADDOX, ROSE**
*Columbia white promo label 45s $10-$15 each; Capitol promo 45s $5 each; Other promo LPs, any label, $8 each; ABC jukebox LLPs $5 each With the Maddox Brothers*
**Albums**

| | | | |
|-------|-----|---------------|------|
| ROSE MADDOX SINGS BLUEGRASS | 196? | Capitol 1799 | 75 |
| *(Blue promo label)* | | | |

**MADNESS**
*Geffen promo 45s $3 each*
**12-Inch Singles**

| | | | |
|-------|-----|---------------|------|
| ONE STEP BEYOND/MY GIRL/MADNESS | 1980 | Sire PRO-A-852 | 15 |
| THE SUN AND THE RAIN/WINGS OF A DOVE/KEEP MOVING | 1984 | Geffen PRO-A-2122 | 6 |

**RADIO SHOWS**
**Albums**

| | | | |
|-------|-----|---------------|------|
| BBC ROCK HOUR (May 83) | 1983 | London Wavelength | 30-50 |
| *(Music and interviews)* | | | |
| COLLEGE CONCERT (Oct 83) Live concert | 1983 | London Wavelength | 75-125 |
| *(Classic early concert)* | | | |
| KING BISCUIT FLOWER HOUR Live concert | 1983 | DIR/ABC (2) | 25-50 |
| *(With Robert Palmer)* | | | |

| Title | Yr | Label, Number | NM $ |
|---|---|---|---|
| NBC SOURCE (Nov 83) Live concert | 1983 | NBC Radio (2) | 75-125 |
| *(Rare early concert)* | | | |

**MADONNA**
*Other Sire promo 45s $5 each; Geffen promo 45s $6 each; Other Sire 12" promo singles $15 each (Must have the PRO- prefix)*
**12-Inch Singles**

| Title | Yr | Label, Number | NM $ |
|---|---|---|---|
| ANGEL  Long/short versions | 1985 | Sire PRO-A-2292 | 12 |
| *(6:15 and 3:40 versions, not to be confused with the stock copy that has "Into the Groove" on the flip side)* | | | |
| BEDTIME STORY CHAPTER II (Lush Vocal Mix 6:47/Luscious Dub Mix 7:38/ | 1995 | Maverick PRO-A-7600-A | 20 |
| Percapella Mix 6:31/Unconscious In The Jungle Mix 6:26) | | | |
| BORDERLINE (New Mix 6:54/Instrumental 5:41) | 1984 | Sire PRO-A-2120 | 25 |
| *(Yellow promo label, issued with picture cover)* | | | |
| BUENOS AIRES (Te Amo 12" Extended Vocal Version 7:53/ | 1997 | Maverick PRO-A-8984 | 40 |
| Te Amo Radio Version 4:09/Te Amo Instrumental 7:52/Te Amo Single Edit 5:23) | | | |
| BUENOS AIRES (Te Amo 12" Extended Vocal Version 7:53/ | 1997 | Maverick PRO-A-8984-A | 40 |
| Te Amo Radio Version 4:09/Te Amo Instrumental 7:52/Te Amo Single Edit 5:23) | | | |
| *(Same as above, but with "Advance Only" on label)* | | | |
| BURNING UP | 1983 | Sire 29715 | 20 |
| *(Gold-stamped version with numbered sticker on cover)* | | | |
| DEEPER AND DEEPER (Shep's Deep Makeover Mix 9:07/ | 1992 | Maverick PRO-A-5928 | 40 |
| Shep's Deep Bass Dub 5:00/Shep's Deeper Dub 6:08/Shep's Classic 12" 7:26/Shep's Fierce Deeper Dub 5:59/ Shep's Deep Beats 2:57/ | | | |
| David's Klub Mix 7:39/David's Love Dub 5:37/David's Deeper Dub 5:22/ + 3 more) | | | |
| *(Promo-only two-record set)* | | | |
| DON'T CRY FOR ME ARGENTINA (Miami Mix Alternate Ending 7:59/ | 1997 | Maverick PRO-A-8544 | 20 |
| Miami Spanglish Mix 6:57/Miami Mix Edit 4:29/Miami Dub Mix 6:23/Miami Mix Instrumental Version 6:55/Miami Spanglish Mix Edit 4:28) | | | |
| DON'T CRY FOR ME ARGENTINA (Miami Mix Alternate Ending 7:59/ | 1997 | Maverick PRO-A-8544-A | 25 |
| Miami Spanglish Mix 6:57/Miami Mix Edit 4:29/Miami Dub Mix 6:23/Miami Mix Instrumental Version 6:55/Miami Spanglish Mix Edit 4:28) | | | |
| *(Same as above, but with "Advance Only" on label)* | | | |
| DRESS YOU UP (12" Formal Mix 6:15/same on both sides) | 1985 | Sire PRO-A-2353 | 12 |
| EROTICA (Kenlou B-Boy Mix 6:23/Kenlou B-Boy Instrumental 5:54/Madonna's In | 1992 | Maverick PRO-A-5860 | 30 |
| My Jeep Mix 5:46/Jeep Beats 5:48/Underground Tribal Beats 3:30/Underground Club Mix 4:53/Masters At Work Dub 4:51/Bass Hit Dub 4:47/WØ 12" 6:07/ | | | |
| WØ Dub 4:53/House Instrumental 4:49) | | | |
| *(Promo-only two-record set)* | | | |
| EROTICA (LP version/Radio Edit) | 1992 | Maverick PRO-A-5665 | 15 |
| EVERYBODY (Extended/Dub) | 1982 | Sire PRO-A-1083 | 60 |
| FEVER (Murk Boys Miami Mix 7:10/Oscar G.'s Dope Dub 4:55/Murk Boys Deep | 1993 | Maverick PRO-A-6074 | 40 |
| South Mix 6:28/Back To The Dub 2 4:52/12" Instrumental 4:56/Extended 12" 6:05/T's Extended Dub A 2:56/T's Extended Dub B 5:03/ | | | |
| Hot Sweat 12"7:55/Shep's Remedy Dub 4:29/ + 2 more) | | | |
| *(Promo-only two-record set on red vinyl)* | | | |
| FROZEN (Album Version/Stereo MC's Remix/Extended Club Mix/Meltdown Mix) | 1998 | WEA (no #) | 80 |
| *(Rare test pressing with handwritten labels)* | | | |
| FROZEN (William Orbit Widescreen Mix 6:34/William Orbit Drumapella 5:15/ | 1998 | Maverick PRO-A-9254 | 50 |
| Victor Calderone Drumapella 5:09) | | | |
| HOLIDAY (New Remix 6:59/Dub 6:57)/ | 1987 | Sire PRO-A-2907 | 20 |
| OVER AND OVER (Extended Remix 7:11/Dub, 6:43) | | | |
| HUMAN NATURE (Human Club Mix 9:00/Love Is The Nature Mix 6:40) | 1995 | Maverick PRO-A-7758 | 25 |
| HUMAN NATURE (Runway Club Mix 8:18/I'm Not Your Bitch Mix 8:10/ | 1995 | Maverick PRO-A-7719 | 20 |
| Runway Club Mix Radio Edit 3:58/Bottom Heavy Dub 8:08/Howie Tee Remix 4:47/Howie Tee Clean Remix Radio Edit 4:07) | | | |
| HUMAN NATURE (Runway Club Mix 8:18/I'm Not Your Bitch Mix 8:10/Runway | 1995 | Maverick PRO-A-7719-A | 20 |
| Club Mix Radio Edit 3:58/Bottom Heavy Dub 8:08/Howie Tee Remix 4:47/Howie Tee Clean Remix Radio Edit 4:07) | | | |
| *(Same as above, but with "Advance Only" on label)* | | | |
| I'LL REMEMBER (Guerilla Beach Mix 6:17/Album Version 4:22/ | 1994 | Maverick 41355 | 15 |
| Guerilla Groove Mix 6:07/Orbit Alternative Remix 4:30) | | | |
| *(Same as stock copy, except labels say "Advance Copy - Promotion Only")* | | | |
| INTO THE GROOVE (New Remix 8:31/Dub 6:22)/ | 1987 | Sire PRO-A-2906 | 20 |
| EVERYBODY (New Remix 7:06) | | | |
| JUSTIFY MY LOVE (4:58/same on both sides) | 1990 | Sire PRO-A-4582 | 12 |
| JUSTIFY MY LOVE (Orbit Edit 4:30/Hip Hop Mix 6:30/Orbit 12" Mix 7:16/ | 1990 | Sire PRO-A-4613 | 20 |
| The Beast Within Mix 6:10) | | | |
| KEEP IT TOGETHER (12" Remix 7:50/Dub 7:00/12" Mix 6:48/Bonus Beats 3:56) | 1990 | Sire PRO-A-3791 | 12 |
| LIKE A PRAYER (12" Dance Mix 7:50/Instrumental Dub 6:11/Bass Dub 5:48/ | 1989 | Sire PRO-A-3472 | 20 |
| 12" Club Version 6:35/Dub Beats 4:40/7" remix/edit, 5:41) | | | |
| LIKE A VIRGIN (3:35/same on both sides) | 1984 | Sire PRO-A-2172 | 20 |
| LIKE A VIRGIN (Extended Remix 6:07/same on both sides) | 1984 | Sire PRO-A-2223 | 30 |
| LIVE TO TELL (4:37/5:49) | 1986 | Sire PRO-A-2470 | 12 |
| LOVE DON'T LIVE HERE ANYMORE (Ext. Journey 8:03/Hot Mix Edit 6:44/ | 1996 | Maverick PRO-A-8244 | 20 |
| Hot Mix Radio Edit 4:50/Edge Factor Dub 8:31/Early Morning Dub 10:04) | | | |
| LUCKY STAR (5:30)/HOLIDAY (6:08) | 1983 | Sire PRO-A-2069 | 30 |
| MATERIAL GIRL (3:56/same on both sides) | 1985 | Sire PRO-A-2257 | 25 |
| PAPA DON'T PREACH (4:27/3:47) | 1986 | Sire PRO-A-2517 | 15 |
| PHYSICAL ATTRACTION Promo-only version | 1983 | Sire PRO-A-???? | Unknown |
| *(Sometimes on want lists, but not known to exist on a special promo number)* | | | |
| POWER OF GOOD-BYE (Fabien's Good God Mix 8:25/Slater's Filtered Mix 6:05/ | 1998 | Maverick PRO-A-9499 | 40 |
| Slater's Super Luper Mix 8:45/Dallas Austin Low End Mix 4:33) | | | |
| RAY OF LIGHT (Album Version 5:21/Sasha's Ultra Violet Mix 10:45/ | 1998 | Maverick PRO-A-9327 | 60 |
| Victor Calderone Club Mix 9:29/William Orbit Liquid Mix 8:05) | | | |
| RAY OF LIGHT (Album Version 5:21/Sasha's Ultra Violet Mix 10:45/ | 1998 | Maverick PRO-A-9333-A | 50 |
| Victor Calderone Club Mix 9:29/William Orbit Liquid Mix 8:05) | | | |
| *("Advance Only" promo with less detailed labels than 9327)* | | | |
| RAY OF LIGHT: NEW MIXES (Sasha Twilo Mix 10:58/Sasha Strip Down Mix | 1998 | Maverick PRO-A-9359 | 40 |
| 5:00/William Orbit Ultra Violet Mix 6:59/Victor Calderone Drum Mix 5:26) | | | |
| RESCUE ME (Titanic Vocal, 8:15/Lifeboat Vocal 5:20/Lifeboat Dub 6:02/ | 1990 | Sire PRO-A-4710 | 30 |
| Houseboat Vocal 6:56/Houseboat Dub 5:23/Demanding Dub 5:20/S.O.S. Mix 6:23/Disaster Dub 3:20) | | | |
| *(Promo-only two-record set)* | | | |

| Title | Yr | Label, Number | NM $ |
|---|---|---|---|
| SECRET (Junior's Sound Factory Mix 10:16/Junior's Sound Factory Dub 7:57/Junior's Luscious Club Mix 6:19/Junior's Luscious Club Dub 6:20/Allstar Mix 5:11) | 1994 | Maverick 41772 | 8 |
| *(Same as stock copy, except labels say "Advance Copy - Promotion Only")* | | | |
| TAKE A BOW (InDaSoul Mix 4:57/Album Edit 4:31/Silky Soul Mix 4:10/InDaSoul Instrumental 4:57/Silky Soul Instrumental 4:10/Album Instrumental 5:20) | 1994 | Maverick PRO-A-7323-A | 20 |
| WHERE'S THE PARTY (Extended Remix 7:31/Dub 6:22)/ SPOTLIGHT (Extended Remix 6:24/Dub 4:49) | 1987 | Sire PRO-A-2905 | 20 |

**45s**

| Title | Yr | Label, Number | NM $ |
|---|---|---|---|
| BORDERLINE | 1984 | Sire 29354 | 50 |
| *(Price includes poster picture sleeve)* | | | |
| DRESS YOU UP | 1985 | Sire 28919 | 50 |
| *(Price includes very rare picture sleeve)* | | | |
| EVERYBODY  Mono/stereo | 1982 | Sire 29841 | 10 |
| *(Yellow promo label, her first record)* | | | |
| HOLIDAY  Mono/stereo | 1983 | Sire 29478 | 10 |
| *(Yellow promo label)* | | | |
| LIKE A PRAYER (7" Remix Edit)/LIKE A PRAYER (7" Version with Fade) | 1989 | Sire 27539 | 10 |
| PHYSICAL ATTRACTION Promo-only version | 1983 | Sire PRO-S-2023 | 20 |
| *(Yellow promo label)* | | | |
| TRUE BLUE  Blue vinyl | 1986 | Sire 28591 | 15 |
| *(Yellow promo label, price includes picture sleeve that reads "Limited edition blue vinyl pressing")* | | | |

**Albums**

| Title | Yr | Label, Number | NM $ |
|---|---|---|---|
| BEDTIME STORIES | 1994 | Maverick PRO-A-7311 | 50 |
| *(Promo-only 2-record set on pink vinyl)* | | | |
| EROTICA | 1992 | Maverick PRO-A-5904 | 50 |
| *(Promo-only 2-record set)* | | | |
| LIKE A VIRGIN  White vinyl | 1984 | Sire 25157 | 60 |
| *(Only the promo version is white vinyl, label does not identify as promo, but a gold promo stamp is on cover)* | | | |
| RAY OF LIGHT | 1998 | Maverick PRO-A-9378 | 50 |
| *(Vinyl is promo only; generic cover with sticker)* | | | |
| TRUE BLUE  Clear vinyl | 1986 | Sire 25442 | 200 |
| *(Clear vinyl, promo not identifed on label)* | | | |
| TRUE BLUE  Picture disc | 1986 | Sire 25442 | 100 |
| *(Picture disc, promo not identified on label)* | | | |

**Compact Discs**

| Title | Yr | Label, Number | NM $ |
|---|---|---|---|
| ANOTHER SUITCASE IN ANOTHER HALL | 1997 | Warner Bros. PRO-CD-8751-R | 25 |
| *(Promo-only CD single)* | | | |
| BAD GIRL | 1993 | Maverick PRO-CD-5888 | 8 |
| *(Promo-only CD single)* | | | |
| BEDTIME STORIES | 1994 | Maverick 45767-2 | 30 |
| *(Promo-only packaging of full-length album in blue velvet)* | | | |
| BEDTIME STORY  Three versions | 1995 | Maverick PRO-CD-7429 | 10 |
| *(Promo-only CD single)* | | | |
| BEDTIME STORY  Two versions | 1995 | Maverick PRO-CD-7444 | 8 |
| *(Promo-only CD single)* | | | |
| BEDTIME STORY CHAPTER II REMIXES  Two versions | 1995 | Maverick PRO-CD-7600-R | 15 |
| *(Promo-only CD single)* | | | |
| BUENOS AIRES  Three versions | 1997 | Warner Bros. PRO-CD-8984-R | 15 |
| *(Promo-only CD single)* | | | |
| CHERISH  Two versions | 1989 | Sire PRO-CD-3608 | 8 |
| *(Promo-only CD single)* | | | |
| DEEPER AND DEEPER | 1992 | Maverick PRO-CD-5896 | 8 |
| *(Promo-only CD single)* | | | |
| DON'T CRY FOR ME ARGENTINA  Four versions | 1997 | Warner Bros. PRO-CD-8544-R | 10 |
| *(Promo CD single, dance mixes)* | | | |
| DON'T CRY FOR ME ARGENTINA  Two versions | 1997 | Warner Bros. PRO-CD-8585 | 10 |
| *(Promo CD single, non-remixed ballad versions)* | | | |
| EROTIC | 1992 | Warner Books PRO-CD-5648 | 25 |
| *(Bonus CD included in the book "Sex")* | | | |
| EROTICA  Three versions | 1992 | Maverick PRO-CD-5665 | 8 |
| *(Promo-only CD single, no front insert)* | | | |
| EROTICA  Three versions | 1992 | Maverick PRO-CD-5665 | 25 |
| *(Promo-only CD single, with red tinted "toe-suck" front insert)* | | | |
| EXPRESS YOURSELF  Four versions | 1989 | Sire PRO-CD-3541 | 15 |
| *(Promo-only CD single)* | | | |
| FROZEN  Three versions | 1998 | Maverick PRO-CD-9254-R | 10 |
| *(Promo CD single, edited remixes)* | | | |
| FROZEN  Two versions | 1998 | Maverick PRO-CD-9182 | 8 |
| *(Promo CD single)* | | | |
| HANKY PANKY | 1990 | Sire PRO-CD-4304 | 8 |
| *(Promo-only CD single)* | | | |
| HUMAN NATURE  Four versions | 1995 | Maverick PRO-CD-7749-R | 10 |
| *(Promo-only CD single, different mixes)* | | | |
| HUMAN NATURE  Seven versions | 1995 | Maverick PRO-CD-7719-R | 10 |
| *(Promo-only CD single, different mixes)* | | | |
| HUMAN NATURE  Three versions | 1995 | Maverick PRO-CD-7631-R | 8 |
| *(Promo-only CD single)* | | | |
| I WANT YOU | 1995 | Maverick PRO-CD-7883-R | Unknown |
| *(Never released, though given a promo number)* | | | |
| I'LL REMEMBER | 1994 | Maverick PRO-CD-6735 | 8 |
| *(Promo-only CD single)* | | | |
| JUSTIFY MY LOVE  Five versions | 1991 | Sire PRO-CD-4613 | 10 |
| *(Promo-only CD single, different mixes)* | | | |
| JUSTIFY MY LOVE  One version | 1991 | Sire PRO-CD-4582 | 8 |
| *(Promo-only CD single)* | | | |
| KEEP IT TOGETHER  Five versions | 1989 | Sire PRO-CD-3791 | 15 |
| *(Promo-only CD single)* | | | |

| Title | Yr | Label, Number | NM $ |
|---|---|---|---|
| LIKE A PRAYER  Five versions | 1989 | Sire PRO-CD-3448 | 15 |
| *(Promo-only CD single)* | | | |
| LOVE DON'T LIVE HERE ANYMORE  Four versions | 1995 | Maverick PRO-CD-7934-R | 8 |
| *(Promo-only CD single)* | | | |
| LOVE DON'T LIVE HERE ANYMORE  Two versions | 1995 | Maverick PRO-CD-8209-R | 8 |
| *(Promo-only CD single)* | | | |
| OH FATHER | 1989 | Sire PRO-CD-3798 | 8 |
| *(Promo-only CD single)* | | | |
| ONE MORE CHANCE | 1995 | Maverick PRO-CD-7930-R | Unknown |
| *(Never released, though given a promo number)* | | | |
| POWER OF GOOD-BYE | 1998 | Maverick PRO-CD-9418 | 8 |
| *(Promo CD single)* | | | |
| RAIN  Three versions | 1993 | Maverick PRO-CD-6182 | 8 |
| *(Promo-only CD single)* | | | |
| RAY OF LIGHT | 1998 | Maverick PRO-CD-9266 | 8 |
| *(Promo CD single)* | | | |
| RAY OF LIGHT  Three versions | 1998 | Maverick PRO-CD-9327-R | 10 |
| *(Promo CD single, edited remixes)* | | | |
| RAY OF LIGHT  Two versions | 1998 | Maverick PRO-CD-9349-R | 8 |
| *(Promo CD single)* | | | |
| RESCUE ME  One version | 1991 | Sire PRO-CD-4577 | 8 |
| *(Promo-only CD single)* | | | |
| RESCUE ME  Six versions | 1991 | Sire PRO-CD-4710 | 10 |
| *(Promo-only CD single, different mixes)* | | | |
| SECRET  Eight versions | 1994 | Maverick PRO-CD-7243-R | 15 |
| *(Promo-only CD single, different mixes)* | | | |
| SECRET  Two versions | 1994 | Maverick PRO-CD-7199 | 8 |
| *(Promo-only CD single)* | | | |
| TAKE A BOW  Two versions | 1994 | Maverick PRO-CD-7277 | 8 |
| *(Promo-only CD single)* | | | |
| TAKE A BOW REMIXES  Six versions | 1994 | Maverick PRO-CD-7360-R | 15 |
| *(Promo-only CD single, different mixes)* | | | |
| THIS USED TO BE MY PLAYGROUND  Three versions | 1992 | Sire PRO-CD-5588 | 8 |
| *(Promo-only CD single)* | | | |
| VOGUE  Four versions | 1990 | Sire 21513 | 10 |
| *(First pressing, used as promo, in slide-out plastic box with cardboard sleeve)* | | | |
| WORDS AND MUSIC | 1998 | Maverick PRO-CD-9209 | 15 |
| *(Promo only, music and interviews about "Ray of Light")* | | | |
| YOU CAN DANCE | 1987 | Sire PRO-CD-2892 | 40 |
| *(Promo-only CD of radio edits from LP)* | | | |
| YOU MUST LOVE ME | 1996 | Warner Bros. PRO-CD-8472 | 8 |
| *(Promo CD single)* | | | |
| YOU'LL SEE  Four versions | 1995 | Maverick PRO-CD-8040-R | 15 |
| *(Promo-only CD single, with "Spanglish" versions)* | | | |
| YOU'LL SEE  Two versions | 1995 | Maverick PRO-CD-7900-R | 8 |
| *(Promo-only CD single)* | | | |
| **RADIO SHOWS** | | | |
| **Albums** | | | |
| BLONDE AMBITION TOUR (Aug 90) | 1990 | Westwood One (3) | 200-300 |
| *(Very rare live concert)* | | | |
| HOT ROCKS | 1988 | United Stations (2) | 40-80 |
| *(Music and interviews)* | | | |
| MUSIC OF THE 80s (Aug 84) Music and interviews | 1984 | DIR (2) | 100-150 |
| *(With Cyndi Lauper and Annie Lennox)* | | | |
| MUSIC OF THE 80s (July 85) Music and interviews | 1985 | DIR (2) | 100-150 |
| *(With Sade)* | | | |
| **Compact Discs** | | | |
| THE STORY OF MADONNA (Aug 92) Profile | 1992 | Unistar | 25-40 |
| *(Music and interviews)* | | | |

**MAESTRO, JOHNNY**
*Lead singer of the Crests*
**45s**

| | | | |
|---|---|---|---|
| BESAME BABY | 1961 | Coed 562 | 50 |
| *(White promo label)* | | | |
| HEARTBURN | 1966 | Parkway 987 | 60 |
| *(One-sided white label promo)* | | | |
| SNOW (mono/stereo) | 1971 | Buddah 289 | 10 |
| *(May be promo only)* | | | |

**MAGAZINE**
**12-Inch Singles**

| | | | |
|---|---|---|---|
| THE LIGHT POURS OUT OF ME/CUT-OUT SHAPES | 1979 | Virgin International VIDJ 1 | 15 |

**MAGGARD, CLEDUS**
**45s**

| | | | |
|---|---|---|---|
| YOVNOC | 1977 | Mercury DJ 481 | 10 |
| *(Read it backwards)* | | | |

**MAGIC TOUCH, THE**
**45s**

| | | | |
|---|---|---|---|
| HOW CAN YOU TREAT ME THIS WAY | 1953 | King 4681 | 400 |
| *(White promo label)* | | | |
| WHEN I KNEEL DOWN TO PRAY | 1953 | King 4665 | 400 |
| *(White promo label)* | | | |

| Title | Yr | Label, Number | NM $ |
|---|---|---|---|

**MAHAVISHNU ORCHESTRA**
*Columbia promo 45s $4 each*
**RADIO SHOWS**
**Compact Discs**

| | | | |
|---|---|---|---|
| KING BISCUIT FLOWER HOUR (May 88) Live concert | 1988 | DIR | 50-100 |
| *(With other artists)* | | | |

**MAHOGANY RUSH**
*Includes listings of Frank Marino; Columbia promo 45s $3 each*
**RADIO SHOWS**
**Albums**

| | | | |
|---|---|---|---|
| BBC ROCK HOUR (Feb 83) Frank Marino | 1983 | London Wavelength | 150-225 |
| *(Live concert)* | | | |
| IN CONCERT (Mar 83) Live concert | 1983 | Westwood One (2) | 75-150 |
| *(With Night Ranger)* | | | |

**MAJESTICS, THE**
**45s**

| | | | |
|---|---|---|---|
| SAY YOU/ALL FOR SOMEONE | 1965 | V.I.P. 25028 | 1,000 |
| *(Promo only; stock copies credited "The Monitors")* | | | |

**MALMSTEEN, YNGWIE**
**Compact Discs**

| | | | |
|---|---|---|---|
| ON GUITAR | 1990 | Polydor SACD 178 | 50 |
| *(Full-length CD in promo-only guitar-shaped packaging)* | | | |

**MALTAIS, GENE**
**45s**

| | | | |
|---|---|---|---|
| CRAZY BABY | 1958 | Decca 30387 | 70 |
| *(Pink promo label)* | | | |

**MAMA'S BOYS**
*Arista promo 45s $3 each*
**RADIO SHOWS**
**Albums**

| | | | |
|---|---|---|---|
| IN CONCERT (Sept 85) Live concert | 1985 | Westwood One (2) | 40-75 |
| *(With Loudness and Y & T)* | | | |

**MAMAS AND THE PAPAS, THE**
*Includes listings of the Mugwumps; The Big Three; John Phillips; Michelle Phillips; Mama Cass (Elliot); Other Dunhill white promo label 45s $10 each; Warner Bros. promo 45s by the Mugwumps $12 each; Other FM, Roulette promo singles by the Big Three $8 each; Any promo label 45s by John Phillips, Michelle Phillips or Mama Cass $5 each*
**45s**

| | | | |
|---|---|---|---|
| CALIFORNIA DREAMIN' | 1966 | Dunhill 4020 | 75 |
| *(Price is for promo record and promo-only picture sleeve)* | | | |
| CREEQUE ALLEY | 1967 | Dunhill 4083 | 50 |
| *(Record is one-sided, picture sleeve is a promo-only release)* | | | |
| CREEQUE ALLEY | 1967 | Dunhill 4083 | 40 |
| *(Two sided promo record and promo-only picture sleeve)* | | | |
| GO WHERE YOU WANNA GO | 1966 | Dunhill 4018 | 20 |
| *(First record as the Mamas & the Papas, promo-only release)* | | | |
| I CALL YOUR NAME | 197? | Goldies 45 1431 | 12 |
| *(Rare and unusual "Oldies" reissue promotional copy)* | | | |
| SAFE IN MY GARDEN | 1968 | Dunhill 4125 | 25 |
| *(One-sided promo record)* | | | |
| WHAT'S IT ALL ABOUT (June 81) Public service show | 1981 | W.I.A.A. 581 | 25 |
| *(Interviews with John Phillips, flip side is Neil Diamond)* | | | |
| WYNKIN' BLINKIN' & NOD  The Big Three | 1963 | FM 3003 | 15 |
| *(The Big Three include Cass Elliot, James Hendricks and Tim Rose)* | | | |
| **7-Inch Extended Plays** | | | |
| IF YOU CAN BELIEVE YOUR EYES AND EARS  Jukebox LLP | 1968 | Dunhill 50006 | 20 |
| *(Issued with a hard cover)* | | | |
| THE MAMAS & THE PAPAS  Jukebox LLP | 1968 | Dunhill 50010 | 20 |
| *(Issued with a hard cover)* | | | |
| THE MAMAS & THE PAPAS DELIVER  Jukebox LLP | 1968 | Dunhill 50014 | 18 |
| *(Issued with a hard cover)* | | | |
| THE MAMAS & THE PAPAS INTERVIEW | 1966 | Dunhill SPD-13 | 50 |
| *(Promotional release only)* | | | |
| PEOPLE LIKE US  Jukebox LLP | 1972 | ABC Dunhill 50106 (LLP 167) | 15 |
| *(Issued with a paper picture cover)* | | | |
| **Albums** | | | |
| IF YOU CAN BELIEVE YOUR EYES AND EARS | 1966 | Dunhill 50006 | 125 |
| *(White promo label with toilet clearly showing on the cover)* | | | |
| MYRA BRECKENRIDGE  With John Phillips | 1970 | 20th Century Fox 4210 | 300 |
| *(Promo-only soundtrack LP)* | | | |
| **RADIO SHOWS** | | | |
| **Albums** | | | |
| JOHN PHILLIPS BIRTHDAY SALUTE (Aug 90) | 1990 | Unistar | 10-15 |
| *(From Solid Gold Scrapbook, music and interviews)* | | | |

**MANCHESTER, MELISSA**
*Arista promo 45s $2 each*
**RADIO SHOWS**
**Albums**

| | | | |
|---|---|---|---|
| ABC SPECIAL (Apr 82) | 1982 | ABC Radio (2) | 25-50 |
| *(Music and interviews)* | | | |

| Title | Yr | Label, Number | NM $ |
|-------|----|--------------|------|
| NBC SPECIAL (Aug 80) | 1980 | NBC Radio (2) | 20-40 |
| *(Music and interviews)* | | | |
| STARTRACK PROFILE (June 86) | 1986 | Westwood One (2) | 40-75 |
| *(Mostly music and interviews)* | | | |

## MANCINI, HENRY
*Liberty, Coral and RCA promo 45s $2 each; Jukebox LLPs $3 each*
### 45s

| | | | |
|-------|----|--------------|------|
| MOON RIVER FOR DJS ONLY | 1966 | RCA Victor SP 45-176 | 10 |
| *(White promo label)* | | | |
| MYSTERY MOVIE THEME | 1970 | RCA SP-45-283 | 10 |
| *(Promo-only number, small "Not for Sale" under number)* | | | |
| WHAT'S IT ALL ABOUT (Nov 79) Public service show | 1979 | W.I.A.A. 498 | 20 |
| *(Flip side features Blondie)* | | | |
| WHAT'S IT ALL ABOUT (June 81) Public service show | 1981 | W.I.A.A. 580 | 10 |
| *(Flip side is Dionne Warwick)* | | | |

### 7-Inch Extended Plays

| | | | |
|-------|----|--------------|------|
| CHARADE | 196? | RCA Victor 2755 | 10 |

## MANDRELL, BARBARA
*Columbia promo 45s $2 each; ABC promo 45s $2 each; Capitol promo singles $3 each*
### 45s

| | | | |
|-------|----|--------------|------|
| FAST LANES AND COUNTRY ROADS  White label | 1985 | MCA 52737 | 12 |
| *(Yellow vinyl)* | | | |
| MEN AND TRAINS (same on both sides) | 1991 | Capitol Nashville 7PRO-79334 | 5 |
| *(Vinyl is promo only)* | | | |
| SANTA BRING MY BABY BACK HOME  White label | 1984 | MCA 1241 | 10 |
| *(Black vinyl, promo only)* | | | |
| WHAT'S IT ALL ABOUT (May 79) Public service show | 1979 | W.I.A.A. 473 | 10 |
| *(Flip side is Nicolette Larson)* | | | |
| WHAT'S IT ALL ABOUT (Sept 81) Public service show | 1981 | W.I.A.A. 594 | 25 |
| *(Flip side features The Beach Boys)* | | | |
| WHEN YOU GET TO THE HEART  White label | 1986 | MCA 52806 | 10 |
| *(Red vinyl, with the Oak Ridge Boys)* | | | |
| YOU'VE BECOME THE DREAM (same on both sides) | 1990 | Capitol Nashville 7PRO-79029 | 5 |
| *(Vinyl is promo only)* | | | |

## MANDRELL, LOUISE
*Other RCA Victor promo 45s $2 each; Other RCA Victor color vinyl 45s $8 each*
### 45s

| | | | |
|-------|----|--------------|------|
| AROUND MY HEART  Cream-colored label | 1982 | RCA 13039 | 10 |
| *(Green vinyl)* | | | |
| ROMANCE  Red label | 1982 | RCA 13373 | 12 |
| *(Green vinyl)* | | | |
| SAVE ME  Green label | 1983 | RCA 13450 | 10 |
| *(Yellow vinyl)* | | | |
| TOO HOT TO SLEEP  Yellow label | 1983 | RCA 13567 | 10 |
| *(Red vinyl)* | | | |
| WHERE THERE'S SMOKE THERE'S FIRE  Silver label | 1981 | RCA 12359 | 12 |
| *(Red vinyl, with R. C. Bannon)* | | | |

## MANGIONE, CHUCK
### 12-Inch Singles

| | | | |
|-------|----|--------------|------|
| FEELS SO GOOD (4:40) (same on both sides) | 1978 | A&M 8448 | 12 |
| LOVE WEARS NO DISGUISE/DIANA "D" | 1984 | Columbia AS 1903 | 8 |

## MANHATTAN TRANSFER
*Atlantic promo 45s $3*
### 12-Inch Singles

| | | | |
|-------|----|--------------|------|
| AMERICAN POP/WHY NOT | 1983 | Atlantic PR 560 | 6 |
| SO YOU SAY (same on both sides) | 1987 | Atlantic PR 2272 | 6 |
| SPICE OF LIFE/THE NIGHT THAT MONK RETURNED TO HEAVEN | 1983 | Atlantic PR 525 | 6 |

### 45s

| | | | |
|-------|----|--------------|------|
| CHRISTMAS SONG, THE | 1984 | Manhattan Transfer 1984 | 60 |
| *(Promo-only record with picture sleeve, B-side is blank)* | | | |
| NOTHIN' YOU CAN DO ABOUT IT (same on both sides) | 1980 | Atlantic 3756 | 5 |
| *(May be promo only)* | | | |

### RADIO SHOWS
### Albums

| | | | |
|-------|----|--------------|------|
| ROBERT W. MORGAN (Oct 81) | 1981 | Watermark | 10-20 |
| *(Music and interviews)* | | | |
| STARTRACK PROFILE (Feb 85) Live concert | 1985 | Westwood One (2) | 100-200 |
| *(Very rare live concert)* | | | |

### Compact Discs

| | | | |
|-------|----|--------------|------|
| WORLD MUSIC SERIES (May 92) | 1992 | (2) | 200-300 |
| *(Rare live performances)* | | | |

## MANHATTANS
*Columbia promo 45s $3 each*
### 12-Inch Singles

| | | | |
|-------|----|--------------|------|
| LET YOUR LOVE COME DOWN (same on both sides) | 1981 | Columbia AS 1316 | 8 |

### 45s

| | | | |
|-------|----|--------------|------|
| WHAT'S IT ALL ABOUT (Apr 77) Public service show | 1977 | W.I.A.A. 366 | 15 |
| *(Flip side features Willie Nelson)* | | | |

### Albums

| | | | |
|-------|----|--------------|------|
| THE MANHATTANS | 1980 | Columbia AS-889 | 15 |
| *(The interview special)* | | | |

| Title | Yr | Label, Number | NM $ |
|-------|-----|---------------|------|

**MANILOW, BARRY**
*Other Bell and Arista promo singles $3 each; RCA Victor promo 45s $2 each; Arista and RCA Victor promo 12" singles $5 each*

**12-Inch Singles**

| Title | Yr | Label, Number | NM $ |
|-------|-----|---------------|------|
| EN EL COPA (same on both sides) | 1978 | Arista SP-21 | 25 |
| *(Spanish version of "Copacabana")* | | | |
| WHEN OCTOBER GOES (same on both sides) | 1984 | Arista 9295 | 10 |

**45s**

| Title | Yr | Label, Number | NM $ |
|-------|-----|---------------|------|
| CLOUDBURST  White/red/black promo label | 1970 | Bell 45,422 | 20 |
| *(Flip side is the 7:17 original version of "Could It Be Magic" which was released again later and became a major hit)* | | | |
| IT'S JUST ANOTHER NEW YEAR'S EVE  Mono/stereo | 1977 | Arista SP-11 | 15 |
| *(Promo-only record issued with promo-only picture sleeve)* | | | |
| LET'S TAKE SOME TIME TO SAY GOODBYE  Mono/stereo | 1971 | Bell 45,443 | 15 |
| *(White and red promo label)* | | | |
| READY TO TAKE A CHANCE AGAIN  Black label | 1978 | Arista 0357 | 10 |
| *(Small center hole)* | | | |
| READY TO TAKE A CHANCE AGAIN  One-sided promo | 1978 | Arista SP-25 | 15 |
| *(Promo-only record issued with promo-only picture sleeve)* | | | |
| WHAT'S IT ALL ABOUT (Sept 79) Public service show | 1979 | W.I.A.A. 489 | 15 |
| *(Flip side is Firefall)* | | | |

**Compact Discs**

| Title | Yr | Label, Number | NM $ |
|-------|-----|---------------|------|
| CHRISTMAS SAMPLER | 1990 | Arista ARCD 2096 | 10 |
| *(Promo-only highlights from "Because It's Christmas")* | | | |
| EXCERPTS FROM THE COMPLETE COLLECTION | 1992 | Arista ARCD 2496 | 15 |
| *(Promo-only sampler from box set)* | | | |

**RADIO SHOWS**
**Albums**

| Title | Yr | Label, Number | NM $ |
|-------|-----|---------------|------|
| LABOR DAY SPECIAL (Sept 81) Box set | 1981 | Mutual Radio (3) | 50-100 |
| *(Music and interviews)* | | | |
| NIGHTBIRD & COMPANY (Dec 75) Various artists | 1975 | U.S. Army (2) | 25-45 |
| *(One of the four shows features Manilow, music and interviews)* | | | |
| ROBERT W. MORGAN Profile | 1976 | Watermark | 35-60 |
| *(Music and interviews)* | | | |
| STARTRACK PROFILE (Nov 85) Parts 1 and 2 | 1985 | Westwood One (4) | 75-150 |
| *(Music and interviews)* | | | |
| STARTRACK PROFILE (Nov 85) Profile | 1985 | Westwood One (2) | 40-80 |
| *(Music and interviews)* | | | |
| WORDS AND MUSIC (Nov 81) Rare show | 1981 | ABC Radio (2) | 50-100 |
| *(Music and interviews)* | | | |

**Reel-to-Reel Tapes**

| Title | Yr | Label, Number | NM $ |
|-------|-----|---------------|------|
| KING BISCUIT FLOWER HOUR (Apr 75) Live concert | 1975 | DIR/ABC (2) | 100-150 |
| *(With Linda Ronstadt, on two reels)* | | | |

**MANN, BARRY**
*Other ABC Paramount white promo label 45s $15 each; Colpix, Red Bird, Capitol, Scepter promo 45s $10 each; RCA Victor promo 45s $4 each; Other label promo 45s $3 each; Other ABC Paramount white promo label LPs $50 each*

**45s**

| Title | Yr | Label, Number | NM $ |
|-------|-----|---------------|------|
| COUNTING TEARDROPS | 1960 | ABC-Paramount 10143 | 25 |
| *(White promo label, first ABC record)* | | | |
| HAPPY BIRTHDAY, BROKEN HEART | 1961 | ABC-Paramount 10180 | 25 |
| *(White promo label)* | | | |
| WHO PUT THE BOMP | 1961 | ABC-Paramount 10237 | 25 |
| *(White promo label)* | | | |

**Albums**

| Title | Yr | Label, Number | NM $ |
|-------|-----|---------------|------|
| FLO AND EDDIE INTERVIEW BARRY MANN | 1975 | RCA Victor DJL1-1162 | 50 |
| WHO PUT THE BOMP | 1962 | ABC-Paramount 399 | 200 |
| *(White promo label)* | | | |

**MANN, HERBIE**
**12-Inch Singles**

| Title | Yr | Label, Number | NM $ |
|-------|-----|---------------|------|
| JISCO DAZZ/BODY OIL | 1979 | Atlantic DSKO 172 | 10 |

**MANN, MANFRED**
*Ascot promo 45s $18 each; Mercury white promo label 45s $12 each; Polydor promo 45s $7 each; Other Warner Bros. promo 45s $6 each; Arista promo 45s $5 each*

**12-Inch Singles**

| Title | Yr | Label, Number | NM $ |
|-------|-----|---------------|------|
| DEMOLITION MAN (same on both sides) | 1983 | Arista ADP 9110 | 8 |
| RUNNER (same on both sides) | 1983 | Arista ADP 9147 | 8 |

**45s**

| Title | Yr | Label, Number | NM $ |
|-------|-----|---------------|------|
| BLINDED BY THE LIGHT  Mono/stereo | 1976 | Warner Bros. 8252 | 10 |
| *(3:48 versions of the Springsteen classic)* | | | |
| SPIRIT (IN THE NIGHT)  Mono/stereo | 1977 | Warner Bros. 8355 | 18 |
| *(Incorrect title on label)* | | | |
| SPIRIT IN THE NIGHT  Long/short versions | 1976 | Warner Bros. 8176 | 12 |
| *(Long version 6:26, short version 3:13, first release)* | | | |
| SPIRIT IN THE NIGHT  Mono/stereo | 1977 | Warner Bros. 8355 | 10 |
| *(Correct title, both label versions are 3:20; both issues of Warner Bros. 8355 have a re-recorded vocal by Chris Thompson)* | | | |
| WHAT'S IT ALL ABOUT (Aug 77) Public service show | 1977 | W.I.A.A. 382 | 20 |
| *(Flip side is Gary Paxton)* | | | |

**7-Inch Extended Plays**

| Title | Yr | Label, Number | NM $ |
|-------|-----|---------------|------|
| NEW SONGS FROM MERCURY  Six songs, one by Manfred Mann | 1971 | Mercury DJ-115 | 12 |
| *(White promo label)* | | | |

**Albums**

| Title | Yr | Label, Number | NM $ |
|-------|-----|---------------|------|
| MANFRED MANN INTERVIEW | 1966 | United Artists 94 | 200 |
| *(Rare promo release in a plain cardboard sleeve)* | | | |

| Title | Yr | Label, Number | NM $ |
|---|---|---|---|
| **RADIO SHOWS** | | | |
| **Albums** | | | |
| BBC ROCK HOUR (Mar 81) Live concert | 1981 | London Wavelength | 60-80 |
| *(Rare early concert)* | | | |
| BBC TRANSCRIPTION DISC  Live concert | 1974 | BBC Transcription | 300-400 |
| *(Very rare radio series)* | | | |
| BBC TRANSCRIPTION DISC  Live concert | 1978 | BBC Transcription | 250-350 |
| *(Very rare concert)* | | | |
| BBC TRANSCRIPTION DISC  Live concert | 1985 | BBC Transcription | 75-150 |
| *(Paul Jones of Manfred Mann, flip is Blues Band)* | | | |
| KING BISCUIT FLOWER HOUR (Apr 81) Live concert | 1981 | DIR/ABC (2) | 75-125 |
| *(With Ry Cooder)* | | | |
| KING BISCUIT FLOWER HOUR (Aug 84) Live concert | 1984 | DIR/ABC (2) | 40-80 |
| *(With Clarence Clemons)* | | | |
| RETRO ROCK (Nov 81) Live concert | 1981 | Clayton Webster (2) | 75-100 |
| *(Rare early concert)* | | | |
| **Reel-to-Reel Tapes** | | | |
| KING BISCUIT FLOWER HOUR (Dec 76) Live concert | 1976 | DIR/ABC (2) | 75-150 |
| *(With Robin Trower, on two reels)* | | | |

## MANNHEIM STEAMROLLER

| Title | Yr | Label, Number | NM $ |
|---|---|---|---|
| **Compact Discs** | | | |
| CHRSITMAS IN THE AIRE | 1995 | American Gramaphone AG 1995-2 | 20 |
| *(Promo-only compilation of all three MS Christmas albums on two CDs)* | | | |
| **RADIO SHOWS** | | | |
| **Compact Discs** | | | |
| WORLD MUSIC SERIES (Dec 91) | 1991 | (2) | 200-300 |
| *(Rare live performances)* | | | |

## MAPHIS, JOE
*Columbia promo 45s $8-15 each; Columbia promo LPs $20 each*

| Title | Yr | Label, Number | NM $ |
|---|---|---|---|
| **Albums** | | | |
| FIRE ON THE STRINGS | 1957 | Columbia 1005 | 50 |
| *(White promo label)* | | | |
| MERLE TRAVIS & JOE MAPHIS | 1964 | Capitol T-2102 | 40 |
| *(Blue promo label)* | | | |

## MARILLION
*Other Capitol promo 45s $6 each*

| Title | Yr | Label, Number | NM $ |
|---|---|---|---|
| **45s** | | | |
| KAYLEIGH | 1985 | Capitol 5493 | 10 |
| *(White promo label)* | | | |
| **7-Inch Extended Plays** | | | |
| MARILLION | 1988 | Capitol SPRO-79521 | 18 |
| *(Four-song promo-only live EP)* | | | |
| **RADIO SHOWS** | | | |
| **Albums** | | | |
| BBC ROCK HOUR (May 84) Live concert | 1984 | London Wavelength | 50-100 |
| *(Rare early concert)* | | | |
| BBC TRANSCRIPTION DISC  Live concert | 1984 | BBC Transcription | 300-400 |
| *(Very rare live concert)* | | | |
| BBC TRANSCRIPTION DISC  Live concert | 1985 | BBC Transcription | 250-300 |
| *(Very rare radio series)* | | | |
| IN CONCERT (Oct 85) Live concert | 1985 | Westwood One (2) | 50-100 |
| *(With Go West)* | | | |
| KING BISCUIT FLOWER HOUR | 1986 | DIR (2) | 50-75 |
| *(Live concert)* | | | |

## MARLEY, BOB
*Including listings of Ziggy Marley and the Melody Makers (Members of the Marley family that recorded after Bob's death); Island promo 45s $5-8 each depending on year; Cotillion promo 45s $3 each*

| Title | Yr | Label, Number | NM $ |
|---|---|---|---|
| **12-Inch Singles** | | | |
| BUFFALO SOLDIER/BUFFALO DUB | 1983 | Island DMD 628 | 10 |
| CHANCES ARE (same on both sides) | 1981 | Cotillion PR 414 | 15 |
| MIX UP, MIX UP (LP Version) (Edit Version) | 1983 | Island DMD 668 | 10 |
| REGGAE ON BROADWAY (6:00) (3:15) | 1981 | Cotillion PR 291 | 12 |
| **45s** | | | |
| LYING IN BED  Ziggy Marley and the Melody Makers | 1986 | EMI 7PRO-9604 | 10 |
| *(Special promo-only releases)* | | | |
| **Albums** | | | |
| RASTAMAN VIBRATION | 1976 | Island ILPS 9383 | 100 |
| *(Promotional package with burlap box and press kit)* | | | |
| **RADIO SHOWS** | | | |
| **Albums** | | | |
| BBC COLLEGE ROCK CONCERT HOUR (Apr 83) Live concert | 1983 | London Wavelength | 200-300 |
| *(Very rare live concert)* | | | |
| BBC ROCK HOUR (June 81) Live concert | 1981 | London Wavelength | 200-300 |
| *(Very rare live concert)* | | | |
| BBC TRANSCRIPTION DISC Live concert | 1973 | BBC Transcription | 450-600 |
| *(Very collectible live concert)* | | | |
| **Compact Discs** | | | |
| IN CONCERT-NU ROCK (Jan 93) | 1993 | Westwood One | 100-150 |
| *(With Red Hot Chili Peppers)* | | | |
| IN CONCERT-NU ROCK (Sept 93) Ziggy Marley | 1993 | Westwood One | 50-80 |
| *(Live concert)* | | | |

| Title | Yr | Label, Number | NM $ |
|-------|----|----|------|
| ON THE EDGE (Sept 93) Ziggy Marley | 1993 | | 20-30 |
| *(Music and interviews, with the Cranberries and Blind Melon)* | | | |
| SONGS OF FREEDOM TRIBUTE (Oct 92) | 1992 | Radio Today | 50-75 |
| *(Mostly music and interviews, a few live tracks)* | | | |

### MARS, CHRIS
*Ex-Replacements*
**Albums**

| Title | Yr | Label, Number | NM $ |
|-------|----|----|------|
| HORSESHOES AND HAND GRENADES | 1992 | Smash 513 198-1 | 20 |
| *(Vinyl is promo-only)* | | | |

### MARSHALL TUCKER BAND
*Capricorn promo 45s $3 each*
**12-Inch Singles**

| Title | Yr | Label, Number | NM $ |
|-------|----|----|------|
| IT TAKES TIME (Single Version)//SING MY BLUES/CATTLE DRIVE | 1980 | Warner Bros. PRO-A-863 | 12 |
| RUNNING LIKE THE WIND (Edit)/LAST OF THE SINGING COWBOYS | 1979 | Warner Bros. PRO-A-816 | 10 |

**45s**

| Title | Yr | Label, Number | NM $ |
|-------|----|----|------|
| WHAT'S IT ALL ABOUT (Dec 78) Public service show | 1978 | W.I.A.A. 451 | 15 |
| *(Flip side features Peter, Paul & Mary)* | | | |
| WHAT'S IT ALL ABOUT (June 80) Public service show | 1980 | W.I.A.A. 526 | 15 |
| *(Flip side features the Coasters)* | | | |

**RADIO SHOWS**
**Albums**

| Title | Yr | Label, Number | NM $ |
|-------|----|----|------|
| INNERVIEW (80s) Profile | 198? | Innerview | 10-15 |
| *(Music and interviews)* | | | |
| KING BISCUIT FLOWER HOUR (Aug 80) | 1980 | DIR/ABC (2) | 50-75 |
| *(Live concert)* | | | |
| KING BISCUIT FLOWER HOUR (May 81) | 1981 | DIR/ABC (2) | 50-75 |
| *(Live concert)* | | | |
| NBC SOURCE (June 81) | 1981 | NBC Radio (2) | 50-80 |
| *(Live concert)* | | | |

**Compact Discs**

| Title | Yr | Label, Number | NM $ |
|-------|----|----|------|
| IN THE STUDIO (Oct 90) Profile of an album | 1990 | Album Network | 10-15 |
| *(Music and interviews)* | | | |
| KING BISCUIT FLOWER HOUR (Oct 88) Live concert | 1988 | DIR | 25-40 |
| *(With the New Riders of the Purple Sage)* | | | |
| SUPERSTARS (June 96) | 1996 | (2) | 50-80 |
| *(Live concert material)* | | | |

### MARTIN, DEAN
*Capitol promo 45s $3-8 each depending on year; Other Reprise and MCA promo singles $2 each; Jukebox LLPs with hard covers $5 each; Jukebox LLPs with paper covers $3 each*
**45s**

| Title | Yr | Label, Number | NM $ |
|-------|----|----|------|
| EVERYBODY LOVES SOMEBODY  White promo label | 1964 | Reprise S 190 | 12 |
| *(Small center hole)* | | | |
| SILVER BELLS | 1966 | Reprise PRO 247 | 10 |
| *(Same on both sides, promo-only Christmas single)* | | | |
| SOPHIA | 1965 | Reprise PRO 200 | 20 |
| *(Promo-only single, song never released commercially)* | | | |
| WHITE CHRISTMAS | 1966 | Reprise PRO 248 | 10 |
| *(Same on both sides, promo-only Christmas single)* | | | |

**7-Inch Extended Plays**

| Title | Yr | Label, Number | NM $ |
|-------|----|----|------|
| DREAM WITH DEAN | 1964 | Reprise 6123 | 12 |
| *(White label promo 7-inch jukebox single)* | | | |

**Albums**

| Title | Yr | Label, Number | NM $ |
|-------|----|----|------|
| DEAN MARTIN MONTH | 1966 | Reprise PRO 246 | 60 |
| *(Promo-only LP with 12 tracks)* | | | |

**RADIO SHOWS**
**16-Inch Transcriptions**

| Title | Yr | Label, Number | NM $ |
|-------|----|----|------|
| HERE'S TO VETERANS | 196? | Veterans Administration | 20-40 |
| *(Spot announcements, includes Dean Martin, Jackie Gleason and others)* | | | |
| HERE'S TO VETERANS  Program #557 | 196? | Veterans Administration | 20-40 |
| *(Music and interviews)* | | | |
| TRIBUTE TO PETER DE ROSE | 1954 | American Cancer Society | 100-200 |
| *(With songs by Dean Martin, Bing Crosby and the Ames Brothers; B-side has spot announcements by celebrities including Ted Williams and Joe DiMaggio)* | | | |

### MARTIN, GEORGE
*Producer of the Beatles 1962-70; Other United Artists promo LPs $10 each*
**45s**

| Title | Yr | Label, Number | NM $ |
|-------|----|----|------|
| ALL QUIET ON THE MERSEY FRONT | 1965 | United Artists 831 | 15 |
| *(White promo label, nothing to do with the Beatles)* | | | |
| A HARD DAY'S NIGHT | 1964 | United Artists 750 | 75 |
| *(White promo label, stock copy is very rare, worth around $100; there is a stock picture sleeve too, that is very rare, very collectible, worth around $2,000)* | | | |
| LOVE IN THE OPEN AIR  White promo label | 1966 | United Artists 50148 | 25 |
| *(From "The Family Way" written by McCartney)* | | | |
| RINGO'S THEME (THIS BOY) | 1964 | United Artists 745 | 50 |
| *(White promo label, stock picture sleeve is very rare and worth around $300)* | | | |

**Albums**

| Title | Yr | Label, Number | NM $ |
|-------|----|----|------|
| GEORGE MARTIN | 1965 | United Artists 3420 | 40 |
| *(White promo label)* | | | |
| GEORGE MARTIN PLAYS HELP | 1965 | United Artists 3448 | 50 |
| *(White promo label)* | | | |
| GEORGE MARTIN SALUTES THE BEATLE GIRLS | 1966 | United Artists 3539 | 50 |
| *(White promo label)* | | | |
| OFF THE BEATLE TRACK | 1964 | United Artists 3377 | 75 |
| *(White promo label)* | | | |

| **Title** | **Yr** | **Label, Number** | **NM $** |
|---|---|---|---|
| **RADIO SHOWS** | | | |
| **Albums** | | | |
| GEORGE MARTIN BIRTHDAY SALUTE (Jan 90) | 1990 | Unistar | 10-15 |
| *(From the "Solid Gold Scrapbook" series)* | | | |
| ROBERT W. MORGAN  Profile | 1980 | Watermark | 50-75 |
| *(Music and interviews)* | | | |
| THE HIT HEARD AROUND THE WORLD (June 69) | 1969 | U.S. Army | 25-50 |
| *(Music and interviews, George talks about "Get Back")* | | | |
| | | | |
| **MARTIN, JANIS** | | | |
| *Palette promo label 45s $15-20 each* | | | |
| **7-Inch Extended Plays** | | | |
| LOVE ME TO PIECES/TWO LONG YEARS | 1956 | RCA Victor DJ-76 | 25 |
| *(Four-song promotional EP, flip is Hank Snow)* | | | |
| | | | |
| **MARTIN, STEVE** | | | |
| *Warner Bros. promo 45s $4 each* | | | |
| **45s** | | | |
| WHAT'S IT ALL ABOUT (Apr 82) Public service show | 1982 | W.I.A.A. 620 | 15 |
| *(Flip side features Rich Little)* | | | |
| WHAT'S IT ALL ABOUT (Jan 79) Public service show | 1979 | W.I.A.A. 457 | 20 |
| *(Flip side features Meat Loaf)* | | | |
| | | | |
| **MARTINO, AL** | | | |
| *20th Century Fox promo 45s $3 each; Capitol promo 45s $2 each; Capitol jukebox LLPs $4 each* | | | |
| | | | |
| **MARVELETTES, THE** | | | |
| *Other Tamla white promo label 45s $10-15 each depending on year* | | | |
| **45s** | | | |
| YES HE IS | 1964 | Tamla 54091 | 75 |
| *(One-sided promo with different title than stock copy)* | | | |
| **7-Inch Extended Plays** | | | |
| GREATEST HITS  Jukebox LLP | 1967 | Tamla 60253 | 50 |
| *(Rare six-song jukebox LLP with a hard cover)* | | | |
| | | | |
| **MARVELS, THE** | | | |
| **45s** | | | |
| I WON'T HAVE YOU BREAKING MY HEART | 1956 | ABC-Paramount 9711 | 85 |
| *(White promo label)* | | | |
| | | | |
| **MARX, GROUCHO** | | | |
| **45s** | | | |
| HOORAY FOR CAPTAIN SPAULDING | 1952 | Decca 28182 | 25 |
| *(Pink label promo, issued concurrent with its use as theme song on "You Bet Your Life")* | | | |
| **Albums** | | | |
| AN EVENING WITH GROUCHO | 1972 | A&M 3515 | 15 |
| *(White promo label and cover, promo-only release)* | | | |
| AN EVENING WITH GROUCHO | 1972 | A&M 3515 | 12 |
| *(Picture disc special release)* | | | |
| | | | |
| **MARX, HARPO** | | | |
| **Albums** | | | |
| HARD AT WORK  White promo label | 1955 | Mercury 20363 | 75 |
| *(Harpo plays the harp)* | | | |
| | | | |
| **MARX, RICHARD** | | | |
| *Manhattan, EMI Manhattan and Capitol promo 45s and jukebox 45s $3 each* | | | |
| **Compact Discs** | | | |
| MARX | 1991 | Capitol DPRO-79942 | 12 |
| *(Promo-only sampler)* | | | |
| RICHARD MARX | 1991 | Capitol DPRO-79961 | 30 |
| *(Promo-only sampler)* | | | |
| RUSH STREET | 1992 | Capitol DPRO-79761 | 18 |
| *(Promo-only picture disc)* | | | |
| **RADIO SHOWS** | | | |
| **Albums** | | | |
| IN CONCERT  Live concert | 1987 | Westwood One (2) | 30-50 |
| *(With Bruce Hornsby)* | | | |
| IN CONCERT (Feb 87) Live concert | 1987 | Westwood One (2) | 40-75 |
| *(With Squeeze)* | | | |
| OFF THE RECORD (Feb 90) | 1990 | Westwood One (2) | 10-15 |
| *(Music and interviews)* | | | |
| POP CONCERT (July 88) | 1988 | Westwood One (2) | 20-40 |
| *(Live concert)* | | | |
| THE STORY OF RICHARD MARX (May 92) | 1992 | Unistar (2) | 10-20 |
| *(Music and interviews)* | | | |
| | | | |
| **MASEKELA, HUGH** | | | |
| **45s** | | | |
| CELEBRITY SCENE: HUGH MASEKELA | 1966 | MGM CS3-5 | 50 |
| *(Box set of five singles, price includes box, all 5 singles, jukebox title strips, bio; records are sometimes found by themselves, so they are listed separately below)* | | | |
| ALONG COMES MARY/LITTLE STAR | 1966 | MGM 13646 | 8 |
| CALIFORNIA DREAMIN'/U-DWI | 1966 | MGM 13643 | 8 |
| IF I NEEDED SOMEONE/FROM ME TO YOU | 1966 | MGM 13647 | 8 |
| NORWEGIAN WOOD/CANTALOUPE ISLAND | 1966 | MGM 13644 | 8 |
| SHE'S COMIN' MY WAY/UNHLANHLA | 1966 | MGM 13645 | 8 |

| Title | Yr | Label, Number | NM $ |
|---|---|---|---|
| **MASON DIXON** | | | |
| *Texas black vinyl promo 45s $4 each; Premier promo 45s $2 each; NLT and Capitol promo 45s $2 each* | | | |
| **45s** | | | |
| ARMADILLO COUNTRY  Blue label, red marbled vinyl | 1985 | Texas 5510 | 18 |
| *(May or may not say "DJ Copy," issued in plastic clear cover)* | | | |
| ARMADILLO COUNTRY  Blue label, red vinyl | 1985 | Texas 5510 | 10 |
| *(May or may not say "DJ Copy")* | | | |
| CIRCLE  Brown label, yellow vinyl | 1985 | Texas 5556 | 10 |
| *("DJ Copy" on label)* | | | |
| HOUSTON HEARTACHE  Blue label, blue vinyl | 1985 | Texas 5508 | 10 |
| *(May or may not say "DJ Copy")* | | | |
| ONLY A DREAM AWAY  Blue label, blue vinyl | 1985 | Texas 5558 | 10 |
| *("DJ Copy" on label)* | | | |
| **MASON, BARBARA, AND BUNNY SIGLER** | | | |
| **12-Inch Singles** | | | |
| LOCKED IN THIS POSITION (10:05)/LOVE SONG (6:14) | 1977 | Curtom PRO-A-689 | 15 |
| **MASON, DAVE** | | | |
| *More at Traffic; Blue Thumb promo 45s $4 each; Columbia promo 45s $3 each* | | | |
| **12-Inch Singles** | | | |
| DREAMS I DREAM (same on both sides) | 1987 | MCA L33-17468 | 6 |
| *(With Phoebe Snow)* | | | |
| SO HIGH (same on both sides) | 1977 | Columbia ASF 308 | 12 |
| TWO HEARTS (same on both sides) | 1988 | MCA L33-17541 | 6 |
| **RADIO SHOWS** | | | |
| **Albums** | | | |
| OFF THE RECORD (Jan 88) | 1988 | Westwood One (2) | 10-15 |
| *(Music and interviews)* | | | |
| ROBERT W. MORGAN (Feb 79) | 1979 | Watermark | 10-15 |
| *(Music and interviews)* | | | |
| WORLD OF ROCK (Apr 89) Various artists | 1989 | DIR (2) | 10-20 |
| *(Dave Mason is co-host of the show)* | | | |
| **MASON, JACKIE** | | | |
| **Albums** | | | |
| KING OF DELI RAP | 1987 | Warner Bros. PRO-S-2980 | 12 |
| *(Promo-only sampler, 11 cuts)* | | | |
| **MATHIS, JOHNNY** | | | |
| *Other Columbia promo 45s $2-5 each; Mercury promo 45s $2 each; Other Jukebox LLPs $5 each* | | | |
| **12-Inch Singles** | | | |
| SIMPLE/(Instrumental) | 1984 | Columbia AS 1867 | 7 |
| **45s** | | | |
| GIVE ME YOUR LOVE FOR CHRISTMAS  White label | 1969 | Columbia 45100 | 10 |
| *(Christmas Seal song for 1969, with special sleeve)* | | | |
| GIVE ME YOUR LOVE FOR CHRISTMAS  White label | 1969 | Columbia 45035 | 10 |
| *(Christmas Seal song for 1969, issued with blue picture sleeve)* | | | |
| WHAT WILL MY MARY SAY  White promo label | 1963 | Columbia 42666 | 15 |
| *(Red vinyl)* | | | |
| WHAT'S IT ALL ABOUT (June 77) Public service show | 1977 | W.I.A.A. 375 | 15 |
| *(Flip side features The Spinners)* | | | |
| WHAT'S IT ALL ABOUT (June 80) Public service show | 1980 | W.I.A.A. 528 | 15 |
| *(Flip side features Bob Seger)* | | | |
| **7-Inch Extended Plays** | | | |
| CLOSE TO YOU  Jukebox LLP | 1970 | Columbia 30210 | 10 |
| *(Issued with a hard cover)* | | | |
| **Compact Discs** | | | |
| YOUR PERSONAL SAMPLER | 199? | Columbia | 20 |
| *(Promo-only sampler from "The Music of Johnny Mathis: A Personal Collection" box set)* | | | |
| **RADIO SHOWS** | | | |
| **Albums** | | | |
| BIRTHDAY SALUTE TO JOHNNY MATHIS (Sept 88) | 1988 | United Stations | 10-15 |
| *(From Solid Gold Scrapbook, music and interviews)* | | | |
| MELLOW MOMENTS | 1973 | U.S. Department of Health (8) | 50-100 |
| *(Price is for all four 2-LP sets, public service programs; Johnny is host and plays his records; music and interviews)* | | | |
| **MATTEA, KATHY** | | | |
| *Mercury promo 45s $2 each; Mercury promo CD singles $3 each* | | | |
| **Compact Discs** | | | |
| LONESOME STANDARD TIME | 1992 | Mercury CDP 750-P | 50 |
| *(Promo-only two-CD set in packaging that looks like a pocket watch)* | | | |
| SPECIAL COLLECTION, A | 1995 | Mercury DMN 7040 | 25 |
| *(Promo-only sampler)* | | | |
| **RADIO SHOWS** | | | |
| **Compact Discs** | | | |
| LIVE AT THE CRAZY HORSE (June 94) | 1994 | Album Network | 50-75 |
| *(Live concert)* | | | |
| **MATTHEWS, DAVE, BAND** | | | |
| *Other RCA promo CD singles $3-5 each* | | | |
| **Compact Discs** | | | |
| ANTS MARCHING | 1995 | RCA RDJ-64350 | 8 |
| *(Promo-only CD single)* | | | |
| JIMI THING | 1995 | RCA RJC-66561 | 20 |
| *(Promo-only sampler)* | | | |

| **Title** | **Yr** | **Label, Number** | **NM $** |
|---|---|---|---|
| TYPICAL SITUATION | 1995 | RCA RDJ-64324 | 12 |
| *(Promo-only CD single)* | | | |
| **RADIO SHOWS** | | | |
| **Compact Discs** | | | |
| IN CONCERT-NU ROCK (Aug 96) | 1996 | Westwood One | 40-60 |
| *(Live concert material)* | | | |
| IN CONCERT-NU ROCK (Sept 95) | 1995 | Westwood One | 40-60 |
| *(Live concert material)* | | | |
| LIVE FROM THE HOUSE OF BLUES (Oct 95) | 1995 | (2) | 50-80 |
| *(Live concert material)* | | | |

**MAY, BRIAN**
*More at Queen*
**45s**

| STAR FLEET | 198? | Capitol SPRO-9008 | 10 |
|---|---|---|---|
| *(And Friends, promo-only number)* | | | |

**MAYALL, JOHN**
*London and Polydor promo 45s $5 each*
**12-Inch Singles**

| FASCINATIN' LOVER/INTERVIEW (22:33) | 1989 | Island PR 2595 | 12 |
|---|---|---|---|
| THE LAST TIME (same on both sides) | 1988 | Island PR 2490 | 8 |
| **RADIO SHOWS** | | | |
| **Reel-to-Reel Tapes** | | | |
| KING BISCUIT FLOWER HOUR (Aug 77) Live concert | 1977 | Westwood One | 75-100 |
| *(With Scarlet Rivera)* | | | |

**MAYFIELD, CURTIS**
*Of the Impressions; Curtom promo singles $5 each; Boardwalk promo singles $3 each*
**12-Inch Singles**

| GOT TO BE REAL/ON AND ON | 198? | Curtom 12-PO52 | 10 |
|---|---|---|---|
| I MO GIT U SUCKA/HE'S A FLY GUY | 198? | Curtom 12-PO22 | 10 |
| TELL ME, TELL ME (7:16)//HEARTBEAT/OVER THE HUMP | 1979 | RSO/Curtom 1016 | 10 |
| **45s** | | | |
| WE GOT TO HAVE PEACE  Blue label, clear vinyl | 1973 | Curtom 1968 | 25 |
| *(Rare mono/stereo clear vinyl promo release)* | | | |
| **7-Inch Extended Plays** | | | |
| BACK TO THE WORLD  Jukebox LLP | 1974 | Curtom 8015 | 18 |
| *(Issued with a hard cover)* | | | |
| SUPERFLY  Jukebox LLP | 1974 | Curtom 8014 | 20 |
| *(Issued with a hard cover)* | | | |
| **RADIO SHOWS** | | | |
| **Compact Discs** | | | |
| PEOPLE GET READY (Mar 96) | 1996 | Westwood One (2) | 20-40 |
| *(Show about tribute album, music and interviews, various artists)* | | | |

**MAZZY STAR**
**RADIO SHOWS**
**Compact Discs**

| IN CONCERT-NU ROCK (Mar 95) | 1995 | Westwood One | 40-75 |
|---|---|---|---|
| *(Live concert)* | | | |

**MC5**
*Other Elektra promo 45s $15 each; Atlantic promo 45s $10 each*
**45s**

| I CAN ONLY GIVE YOU EVERYTHING | 1966 | AMG 1000 | 50 |
|---|---|---|---|
| *(White promo label, stock copies are AMG 1001)* | | | |
| KICK OUT THE JAMS | 1969 | Elektra MC5-1 | 40 |
| *(Promo only, stock copy is Elektra 45648)* | | | |

**McAULIFF, LEON**
*Columbia promo 45s $10-20 each depending on year; Other labels promo 45s $3 each*
**Albums**

| JUST A MINUTE | 1957 | SESAC | 100 |
|---|---|---|---|
| *(For radio stations only)* | | | |
| POINTS WEST | 1957 | SESAC 1601 | 100 |
| *(For radio stations only)* | | | |

**McBRIDE AND THE RIDE**
*MCA promo CD singles $2-3 each*
**RADIO SHOWS**
**Compact Discs**

| COUNTRY CONCERT (Aug 93) | 1993 | Westwood One | 20-40 |
|---|---|---|---|
| *(Live concert)* | | | |
| COUNTRY CUTTING EDGE (Aug 93) | 1993 | Westwood One | 10-20 |
| *(Music and interviews)* | | | |

**McCANN, LES**
**12-Inch Singles**

| JUST THE WAY YOU ARE (6:31) (same on both sides) | 1978 | A&M SP-17042 | 12 |
|---|---|---|---|

**McCARTNEY, PAUL**
*Of the Beatles; Includes listings of Wings; Paul and Linda McCartney; Suzy and the Red Stripes; The Tudor Minstrels; Percy Thrillington; Sounds Sensational; Capitol purple label 45s for juke-boxes $5 each*
**12-Inch Singles**

| ANGRY | 1986 | Capitol SPRO-9797 | 25 |
|---|---|---|---|
| *(Two versions of "Angry")* | | | |

| Title | Yr | Label, Number | NM $ |
|---|---|---|---|
| COMING UP | 1980 | Columbia AS-775 | 50 |
| *(White promo label)* | | | |
| COMING UP | 1980 | Columbia AS-775 | 60 |
| *(Red promo label)* | | | |
| EBONY AND IVORY//BALLROOM DANCING/THE POUND IS SINKING | 1982 | Columbia AS 1444 | 30 |
| *(Issued with a hard cover, white vinyl record)* | | | |
| EVERY NIGHT  Various artists, four songs | 1981 | Atlantic PR-388 | 250 |
| *(One other McCartney song is "Lucille"; this 12" EP is a promo from the LP "Concerts for the People of Kampuchea")* | | | |
| GOODNIGHT TONIGHT  Wings | 1979 | Columbia 10940 | 25 |
| *(White label, two versions of the same song)* | | | |
| MAYBE I'M AMAZED  Wings | 1977 | Capitol SPRO-8574 | 75 |
| *(Promo-only 12" single)* | | | |
| NO MORE LONELY NIGHTS | 1984 | Columbia AS-1940 | 20 |
| *(White promo label, different versions)* | | | |
| NO MORE LONELY NIGHTS | 1984 | Columbia 05077 | 12 |
| *(Red promo label, different versions)* | | | |
| NO MORE LONELY NIGHTS (Special Dance Mix) (same on both sides) | 1984 | Columbia AS 1990 | 20 |
| PRESS | 1986 | Capitol SPRO-9763 | 25 |
| *(Promo label, two versions)* | | | |
| PRETTY LITTLE HEAD | 1986 | Capitol SPRO-9928 | 50 |
| *(Two versions of the song)* | | | |
| SAY SAY SAY (same on both sides) | 1983 | Columbia AS 1758 | 12 |
| *(With Michael Jackson)* | | | |
| SEASIDE WOMAN  Suzy and the Red Stripes | 1977 | Epic ASF 361 | 100 |
| *(Black vinyl, white promo label, promo only)* | | | |
| SPIES LIKE US | 1985 | Capitol SPRO-9556 | 25 |
| *(White promo label, two versions)* | | | |
| STRANGLEHOLD | 1986 | Capitol SPRO-9861 | 30 |
| *(Flip side is "Angry")* | | | |

**45s**

| Title | Yr | Label, Number | NM $ |
|---|---|---|---|
| ANOTHER DAY | 1971 | Apple PRO-6193 | 100 |
| *(Label must read "Not for Sale")* | | | |
| ANOTHER DAY | 1971 | Apple 1829 | 10 |
| *(Star on the label, not a legal promo but commonly found in radio stations)* | | | |
| ARROW THROUGH ME  Wings | 1979 | Columbia 11070 | 15 |
| *(White promo label, both sides same)* | | | |
| BAND ON THE RUN  Paul McCartney and Wings | 1974 | Apple P-1873 | 40 |
| *(Mono 3:50/stereo 5:09 versions)* | | | |
| BAND ON THE RUN  Paul McCartney and Wings | 1974 | Apple P-1873 | 100 |
| *(Mono 3:50/stereo 3:50 versions)* | | | |
| COMING UP | 1980 | Columbia 11263 | 15 |
| *(White promo label, both sides same)* | | | |
| COMING UP  Paul McCartney and Wings | 1980 | Columbia AE7 1204 | 10 |
| *("Live at Glasgow" version, one-sided free record with many copies of the LP "McCartney II")* | | | |
| COUNTRY DREAMER  Paul McCartney and Wings | 1973 | Apple PRO-6787 | 400 |
| *(Mono/stereo versions)* | | | |
| EBONY & IVORY  Paul McCartney and Stevie Wonder | 1982 | Columbia 02860 | 30 |
| *(White promo label, includes promo picture sleeve with "&")* | | | |
| EBONY AND IVORY  Paul McCartney and Stevie Wonder | 1982 | Columbia 02860 | 12 |
| *(Reddish promo label, includes promo picture sleeve)* | | | |
| FIGURE OF EIGHT | 1990 | Capitol | 100 |
| *(Test pressing for a promo-only 45 never pressed)* | | | |
| GETTING CLOSER  Wings | 1979 | Columbia 11020 | 15 |
| *(White promo label, both sides same)* | | | |
| THE GIRL IS MINE  Michael Jackson and Paul McCartney | 1982 | Epic 03288 | 25 |
| *(White promo label, edited version, not found with a stock picture sleeve)* | | | |
| THE GIRL IS MINE  Michael Jackson and Paul McCartney | 1982 | Epic 03288 | 15 |
| *(White promo label, both sides same, includes stock picture sleeve)* | | | |
| GOODNIGHT TONIGHT  Wings | 1979 | Columbia 10939 | 15 |
| *(White promo label, both sides same)* | | | |
| HELEN WHEELS  Paul McCartney and Wings | 1973 | Apple PRO-6786 | 50 |
| *(Mono/stereo versions)* | | | |
| I'VE HAD ENOUGH  Wings | 1978 | Capitol P-4594 | 25 |
| *(Mono/stereo versions)* | | | |
| JET  Paul McCartney and Wings | 1974 | Apple P-1871 | 50 |
| *(Mono/stereo versions)* | | | |
| JUNIOR'S FARM  Paul McCartney and Wings | 1974 | Apple P-1875 | 50 |
| *(Mono/stereo versions)* | | | |
| LET 'EM IN  Wings | 1976 | Capitol P-4293 | 25 |
| *(Long 5:08/short 3:43 versions)* | | | |
| LETTING GO  Wings | 1975 | Capitol P-4145 | 25 |
| *(Mono/stereo versions, label must read "Not for Sale")* | | | |
| LISTEN TO WHAT THE MAN SAID  Wings | 1975 | Capitol P-4091 | 25 |
| *(Mono/stereo, label must read "Not for Sale")* | | | |
| LIVE AND LET DIE  Radio spots | 1973 | United Artists | 750 |
| *(Very rare 7" record to promote movie)* | | | |
| LONDON TOWN  Wings | 1978 | Capitol SPRO-8908 | 25 |
| *(Mono/stereo versions)* | | | |
| LOVE IN THE OPEN AIR  Sounds Sensational | 1967 | Capitol 5957 | 100 |
| *(Green promo label, McCartney's involvement uncertain)* | | | |
| LOVE IN THE OPEN AIR  The Tudor Minstrels | 1967 | London 1012 | 200 |
| *(Orange/brown label, from "The Family Way")* | | | |
| MARY HAD A LITTLE LAMB  Wings | 1972 | Apple P-1851 | 250 |
| *(Label must read "Not for Sale")* | | | |
| MAYBE I'M AMAZED  Wings | 1976 | Capitol PRO-8570 | 35 |
| *(Mono/stereo versions)* | | | |
| MULL OF KINTYRE  Wings | 1977 | Capitol SPRO-8746 | 25 |
| *(Long 3:31/short 3:19 versions of this worldwide classic 45)* | | | |

| Title | Yr | Label, Number | NM $ |
|---|---|---|---|
| MY BRAVE FACE | 1989 | Capitol P-B-44367 | 15 |
| *(White label, same on both sides)* | | | |
| MY LOVE  Paul McCartney and Wings | 1973 | Apple P-1861 | 250 |
| *(Label must read "Not for Sale")* | | | |
| NO MORE LONELY NIGHTS | 1984 | Columbia 04581 | 12 |
| *(White promo label, includes promo sleeve)* | | | |
| ONLY LOVE REMAINS | 1986 | Capitol P-B-5672 | 10 |
| *(White promo label, both sides same, comes with stock picture sleeve worth $5)* | | | |
| PRESS | 1986 | Capitol 7PRO-9766 | 250 |
| *(Long 4:07/short 3:35 very rare record)* | | | |
| PRESS | 1986 | Capitol P-B-5597 | 10 |
| *(Promo label, both sides same, comes with a stock picture sleeve worth $5)* | | | |
| SALLY G  Paul McCartney and Wings | 1974 | Apple P-1875 | 75 |
| *(Mono/stereo versions)* | | | |
| SAY SAY SAY  Paul McCartney and Michael Jackson | 1983 | Columbia 04168 | 12 |
| *(White promo label, includes promo sleeve)* | | | |
| SEASIDE WOMAN  Suzy and the Red Stripes | 1977 | Epic 50403 | 100 |
| *(Black vinyl, orange and white promo labels)* | | | |
| SEASIDE WOMAN  Suzy and the Red Stripes | 1977 | Epic 50403 | 75 |
| *(Black vinyl, white promo label)* | | | |
| SEASIDE WOMAN  Suzy and the Red Stripes | 1977 | Epic 50403 | 50 |
| *(Red vinyl, orange and white labels)* | | | |
| SILLY LOVE SONGS  Wings | 1976 | Capitol P-4256 | 25 |
| *(Long 5:54/short 3:28 versions)* | | | |
| SO BAD | 1983 | Columbia 04296 | 12 |
| *(White promo label, includes promo sleeve)* | | | |
| SPIES LIKE US | 1985 | Capitol 7PRO-9552 | 15 |
| *(Long 4:40/short 3:46 versions)* | | | |
| STRANGLEHOLD | 1986 | Capitol P-B-5636 | 10 |
| *(White promo label, both sides same, comes with stock picture sleeve worth $5)* | | | |
| TAKE IT AWAY | 1982 | Columbia 03018 | 10 |
| *(White promo label, both sides same)* | | | |
| THIS ONE | 1989 | Capitol 7PRO-79700 | 400 |
| *(White promo label, silver paper sleeve)* | | | |
| TUG OF WAR | 1982 | Columbia 03235 | 10 |
| *(White promo label, both sides same)* | | | |
| UNCLE ALBERT/ADMIRAL HALSEY  Paul and Linda McCartney | 1971 | Apple PRO-6278 | 50 |
| *(Label must read "Not for Sale")* | | | |
| VENUS AND MARS ROCK SHOW  Wings | 1975 | Capitol P-4175 | 25 |
| *(Mono/stereo versions, label must read "Not for Sale")* | | | |
| WALKING IN THE PARK WITH ELOISE  The Country Hams | 1974 | EMI P-3977 | 40 |
| *(Paul and Linda, Floyd Cramer and Chet Atkins; a stock picture sleeve worth around $50 was issued with most copies pressed, stock and promo)* | | | |
| WATERFALLS | 1980 | Columbia 11335 | 20 |
| *(White promo label, long 4:41/short 3:22 versions)* | | | |
| WHAT'S IT ALL ABOUT (Aug 76) Public service show | 1976 | W.I.A.A. 331 | 60 |
| *(Paul and Linda interviewed, flip side is Johnny Ray)* | | | |
| WHAT'S IT ALL ABOUT (Oct 77) Public service show | 1977 | W.I.A.A. 394 | 60 |
| *(Paul and Linda interviewed, flip side is Bobby Vinton)* | | | |
| WITH A LITTLE LUCK  Wings | 1978 | Capitol SPRO-8812 | 25 |
| *(Mono/stereo versions)* | | | |
| WONDERFUL CHRISTMASTIME | 1979 | Columbia 11162 | 20 |
| *(White promo label, both sides same)* | | | |
| **7-Inch Extended Plays** | | | |
| WINGS ROCK SHOW RADIO SPOTS | 1975 | Marimax 4202 | 500 |
| *(Very rare 7" record to promote LP)* | | | |
| **Albums** | | | |
| BACK TO THE EGG | 1979 | Columbia FC 36057 | 40 |
| *(Credited to "Wings"; "Demonstration -- Not for Sale" on custom label)* | | | |
| BAND ON THE RUN INTERVIEW | 1973 | Capitol PRO-2955 | 600 |
| *(Must have a white label and plain hard cover)* | | | |
| BRUNG TO EWE BY | 1971 | Apple 6210 | 400 |
| *(Promo-only sampler from the "Ram" LP to radio stations only)* | | | |
| FAMILY WAY  Mono | 1967 | London 82007 | 150 |
| *(Promo copies of this LP were stock copies shipped with a promo sticker on the cover)* | | | |
| FAMILY WAY  Radio spots | 1967 | Warner Bros. | 300 |
| *(These radio spots are on a 10" disc)* | | | |
| GRAMMY TREASURE CHEST | 1975 | Dept. of the Treasury 75-117/8 | 15 |
| *(Various artists, includes "Band on the Run")* | | | |
| MCCARTNEY II | 1980 | Columbia 36511 | 30 |
| *(White promo label)* | | | |
| THE MCCARTNEY INTERVIEW  White promo labels | 1980 | Columbia 821 (2) | 40 |
| *(DJ copy has two records, stock copy one)* | | | |
| RAM  Paul and Linda McCartney; mono | 1971 | Apple 3375 | 3,000 |
| *(All mono copies of this LP were used as promos, however they were shipped in stereo covers)* | | | |
| SILVER PLATTER SERVICE (Mar 65) With Jack Wagner | 1965 | Capitol PRO 3143 | 400 |
| *(McCartney/Lennon interview, promo-only release, rare)* | | | |
| SOUND TRACK FIVE | 1975 | Veterans Administration 52 | 15 |
| *(Various artists, "Program No. 655" is McCartney)* | | | |
| SOUND TRACK FIVE | 1976 | Veterans Administration 55 | 15 |
| *(Various artists, "Program No. 695" is McCartney)* | | | |
| SOUND TRACK FIVE | 1976 | Veterans Administration 57 | 15 |
| *(Various artists, "Program No. 710" is McCartney and Wings)* | | | |
| TRIPPING THE LIVE FANTASTIC HIGHLIGHTS | 1990 | Capitol 594778 | 30 |
| *(Not a 3-LP set, but a Columbia House condensation, different from regular CD and cassette releases)* | | | |
| VENUS AND MARS  Wings | 1975 | Capitol 11419 | 20 |
| *(This unusual item was found in a radio station; labels are correct but LP "B" side is by Be-Bop Deluxe)* | | | |

| Title | Yr | Label, Number | NM $ |
|---|---|---|---|
| WINGS AT THE SPEED OF SOUND  Wings | 1976 | Capitol 11525 | 300 |
| (Very rare promo album) | | | |
| WINGS GREATEST | 1978 | Capitol SOO-11905 | 400 |
| (Credited to "Wings"; white label advance promo/test pressing) | | | |
| **Compact Discs** | | | |
| BIRTHDAY | 1990 | Capitol DPRO-79392 | 15 |
| (Promo-only CD single, live version) | | | |
| C'MON PEOPLE | 1993 | Capitol DPRO-79743 | 25 |
| (Promo CD single) | | | |
| FIGURE OF EIGHT | 1990 | Capitol DPRO-79871 | 10 |
| (Promo-only CD single) | | | |
| HOPE OF DELIVERANCE | 1993 | Capitol DPRO-79579 | 20 |
| (Promo CD single) | | | |
| MY BRAVE FACE | 1989 | Capitol DPRO-79590 | 10 |
| (Promo-only CD single; stock copy with three additional tracks worth many times this value) | | | |
| NEW WORLD SAMPLER | 1993 | Capitol DPRO-79671 (2) | 50 |
| (Promo-only release, 17 tracks) | | | |
| OFF THE GROUND | 1993 | Capitol DPRO-79670 | 80 |
| (Promo CD single, with no "RE1" in hub area near center hole) | | | |
| OFF THE GROUND  A.C. Edit Version | 1993 | Capitol DPRO-79782 | 80 |
| (Promo CD single) | | | |
| OFF THE GROUND  Bob Clearmountain remix | 1993 | Capitol DPRO-79670 | 20 |
| (Promo CD single, with "RE1" in hub area near center hole) | | | |
| OFF THE GROUND  Keith Cohen remix | 1993 | Capitol DPRO-79783 | 30 |
| (Promo CD single) | | | |
| OOBU JOOBU WIDE SCREEN RADIO PROGRAM #5: ECOLOGY | 1997 | MPL 27850 | 10 |
| (Limited edition, only available at Best Buy with purchase of "Flaming Pie" CD) | | | |
| OU EST LE SOLEIL | 1989 | Capitol DPRO-79836 | 20 |
| (Promo CD single) | | | |
| PAUL McCARTNEY ROCKS | 1990 | Capitol DPRO-79987 | 30 |
| (Released for radio only) | | | |
| WE GOT MARRIED | 1990 | Capitol DPRO-79979 | 15 |
| (Promo-only CD single) | | | |
| WORLD TONIGHT, THE | 1997 | Capitol DPRO 12034 | 12 |
| (Promo CD single) | | | |
| YOUNG BOY | 1997 | Capitol DPRO 12012 | 20 |
| (Promo-only CD single) | | | |
| **RADIO SHOWS** | | | |
| **Albums** | | | |
| ALBUM GREATS | 1979 | TM Special Products (2) | 30-60 |
| (Two McCartney discs of the 53-LP set) | | | |
| BBC ROCK HOUR | 1986 | London Wavelength (2) | 75-150 |
| (Music and interviews) | | | |
| BBC TRANSCRIPTION DISC | 1982 | BBC Transcription (2) | 750-1,000 |
| (Material from Tug of War) | | | |
| BBC TRANSCRIPTION DISC | 1987 | BBC Transcription (2) | 800-1,000 |
| (Music and interviews) | | | |
| BIRTHDAY SALUTE (June 90) | 1990 | Unistar | 20-35 |
| (From the "Solid Gold Scrapbook" series) | | | |
| HOT ROCKS | 1990 | Radio Today (3) | 50-75 |
| (Music and interviews) | | | |
| LEGENDS OF ROCK  Profile | 1987 | NBC Radio (2) | 30-50 |
| (Music and interviews) | | | |
| LOVE SONGS OF PAUL MCCARTNEY (Feb 87) | 1987 | United Stations (3) | 50-80 |
| (Music and interviews) | | | |
| MAN AND HIS MUSIC (July 82) | 1982 | Westwood One (2) | 100-150 |
| (Music and interviews) | | | |
| MCCARTNEY ON MCCARTNEY | 1989 | Westwood One (8) | 325-500 |
| (Music and interviews) | | | |
| MCCARTNEY-THE SOLO YEARS | 1983 | Westwood One (2) | 40-75 |
| (Music and interviews) | | | |
| NIGHTBIRD & COMPANY (Sept 76) Various artists | 1976 | Army Reserve (2) | 50-75 |
| (One of the four shows to feature Paul McCartney) | | | |
| OFF THE RECORD  Profile | 1990 | Westwood One (2) | 25-40 |
| (Music and interviews) | | | |
| PAUL MCCARTNEY SPECIAL | 1982 | Westwood One (2) | 50-100 |
| (Music and interviews) | | | |
| PAUL MCCARTNEY STORY | 1989 | United Stations (4) | 40-75 |
| (Music and interviews) | | | |
| PAUL MCCARTNEY STORY | 1990 | AT&T Showcase/Unistar (3) | 40-75 |
| (Music and interviews) | | | |
| PROFILE OF PAUL MCCARTNEY (June 86) | 1986 | United Stations | 15-25 |
| (McCartney record only from "Solid Gold Scrapbook") | | | |
| ROCK STARS (Nov 87) | 1987 | Radio International (2) | 40-75 |
| (Music and interviews) | | | |
| SOLID GOLD SCRAPBOOK (June 86) Various artists | 1986 | United Stations (5) | 20-40 |
| (One of the five discs features an hour of McCartney) | | | |
| SOURCE SPECIAL (June 82) | 1982 | NBC Source (3) | 100-150 |
| (Music and interviews, "McCartney Today") | | | |
| SOURCE SUMMER SPECIAL (Sept 82) | 1982 | NBC Source (3) | 100-150 |
| (Music and interviews) | | | |
| STARTRACK PROFILE (Dec 84) | 1984 | Westwood One (4) | 75-125 |
| (Music and interviews, parts 1 and 2) | | | |
| STARTRACK PROFILE (Oct 86) Edited version | 1986 | Westwood One (2) | 40-75 |
| ("The Solo Years" music and interviews) | | | |
| SUPERSTAR CONCERT (Sept 86) Prince's Trust | 1986 | Westwood One (3) | 50-100 |
| (Various artists, live concert, McCartney included; this concert was repeated) | | | |

| Title | Yr | Label, Number | NM $ |
|---|---|---|---|
| TICKET TO RIDE Beatles/McCartney | 198? | DIR (2) | 20-40 |
| *(Weekly shows on vinyl, price for any one volume)* | | | |
| TICKET TO RIDE (Jan 85-Dec 88) Beatles/McCartney | 1989 | DIR (414) | 4,000-5,000 |
| *(Complete set of shows, vinyl and CD. This series ran for 209 weeks and featured a Beatles-related theme weekly with a guest artist.)* | | | |
| TIMOTHY WHITE ROCK STARS (Jan 90) | 1990 | Westwood One (2) | 40-75 |
| *("20 Years" music and interviews)* | | | |
| TUG OF WAR | 1982 | Westwood One (2) | 50-100 |
| *(Music and interviews)* | | | |
| **Cassettes** | | | |
| ROCKLINE (May 89) | 1989 | | 200-300 |
| *(Music and interview, premiere of "Flowers in the Dirt")* | | | |
| **Compact Discs** | | | |
| THE BEATLE YEARS (Apr 92-Apr 93) Beatles/McCartney | 1993 | Westwood One (52) | 1,250-1,500 |
| *(First full year of the series)* | | | |
| THE BEATLE YEARS (Apr 92-present) Beatles/McCartney | 199? | Westwood One | 15-20 |
| *(Weekly series replaced Lost Lennon Tapes and has a broader focus; price for any one volume)* | | | |
| THE BEATLE YEARS (Apr 93-Apr 98) Beatles/McCartney | 199? | Westwood One (52) | 1,000-1,200 |
| *(Any subsequent full year of the series)* | | | |
| IN THE STUDIO  Profile of an album | 1990 | Album Network | 20-40 |
| *(Music and interviews)* | | | |
| IN THE STUDIO (90s) Profile of an album | 199? | Album Network (2) | 25-50 |
| *(Two-hour special, music and interviews)* | | | |
| OFF THE RECORD (Jan 93) Profile | 1993 | Westwood One | 25-40 |
| *(CD version, music and interviews)* | | | |
| OOBU JOOBU (May-Sept 95) | 1995 | (17) | 300-500 |
| *(Complete 17-week radio show of McCartney rarities, interviews with friends, and of course "Linda's Cooking Segment")* | | | |
| SUPERSTARS (July 95) | 1995 | (2) | 125-175 |
| *(Live material, includes tracks by George Harrison and Ringo Starr)* | | | |
| TICKET TO RIDE Beatles/McCartney | 198? | DIR | 15-35 |
| *(Weekly shows on CD)* | | | |
| TICKET TO RIDE (May 88-Apr 89) Beatles/McCartney | 1989 | DIR (52) | 1,500-2,000 |
| *(Complete set of CD shows)* | | | |
| UP CLOSE (June 90) Profile | 1990 | Media America (2) | 25-50 |
| *(Music and interviews)* | | | |
| UP CLOSE Profile | 1991 | Media America (2) | 25-45 |
| *(Music and interviews)* | | | |

## McCRAE, GWEN
**12-Inch Singles**

| Title | Yr | Label, Number | NM $ |
|---|---|---|---|
| KEEP THE FIRE BURNING (same on both sides) | 1982 | Atlantic PR 387 | 6 |

## McDONALD, MICHAEL
*More at the Doobie Brothers*
**12-Inch Singles**

| Title | Yr | Label, Number | NM $ |
|---|---|---|---|
| ALL WE GOT (4 versions) | 1990 | Reprise PRO-A-4395 | 10 |
| HEY GIRL (Edit) (LP Version) (Radio Remix) | 1993 | Reprise PRO-A-6538 | 8 |
| NO LOOKIN' BACK (same on both sides) | 1985 | Warner Bros. PRO-A-2325 | 8 |
| TEAR IT UP (same on both sides) | 1990 | Reprise PRO-A-4398 | 8 |
| **45s** | | | |
| DRIVIN' WHEEL | 1972 | Bell 45,259 | 8 |
| *(Stock copy may not exist)* | | | |
| WHERE DO I GO FROM HERE | 1973 | Bell 45,308 | 8 |
| *(Stock copy may not exist)* | | | |

## McDONALD, SKEETS
*Other Capitol promo 45s $5-10 each; Columbia promo 45s $3 each*
**45s**

| Title | Yr | Label, Number | NM $ |
|---|---|---|---|
| YOU OUGHTA SEE GRANDMA ROCK | 1958 | Capitol 3461 | 40 |
| *(White promo label)* | | | |
| **Albums** | | | |
| GOIN' STEADY WITH THE BLUES | 1958 | Capitol 1040 | 45 |
| *(Blue promo label)* | | | |

## McDOWELL, FRED
**Albums**

| Title | Yr | Label, Number | NM $ |
|---|---|---|---|
| I DO NOT PLAY ROCK & ROLL | 1973 | Capitol SAT-403 | 75 |
| *(Promo-only picture disc)* | | | |

## McENTIRE, REBA
*Mercury promo 45s $4 each; Other MCA promo 45s $2 each; MCA promo CD singles $3 each*
**45s**

| Title | Yr | Label, Number | NM $ |
|---|---|---|---|
| I'LL BE HOME FOR CHRISTMAS/THE CHRISTMAS GUEST | 1987 | MCA S45-17725 | 10 |
| LET THE MUSIC LIFT YOU White promo label | 1987 | MCA 52990 | 10 |
| *(Yellow vinyl)* | | | |
| ONE PROMISE TOO LATE  White promo label | 1987 | MCA 53092 | 10 |
| *(Yellow vinyl)* | | | |
| THE CHRISTMAS SONG (CHESTNUTS ROASTING ON AN OPEN FIRE)/ O HOLY NIGHT | 1987 | MCA S45-17446 | 10 |
| WHAT AM I GONNA DO ABOUT YOU  White promo label | 1986 | MCA 52922 | 10 |
| *(Blue vinyl)* | | | |
| **Compact Discs** | | | |
| MOTHER'S DAY REUNION | 1994 | | 25 |
| *(Promo-only release)* | | | |
| **RADIO SHOWS** | | | |
| **Albums** | | | |
| CHRISTMASTIME WITH REBA (Dec 88) ... and others | 1988 | Westwood One (3) | 25-35 |
| *(Music and interviews)* | | | |

| Title | Yr | Label, Number | NM $ |
|---|---|---|---|
| LIVE AT GILLEY'S (Nov 85) Live concert | 1985 | Westwood One | 25-50 |
| *(Rare early concert)* | | | |
| **Compact Discs** | | | |
| COUNTRY CONCERT (July 94) Live concert | 1994 | Westwood One | 25-50 |
| *(With Toby Keith)* | | | |
| | | | |
| **McFADDEN, BOB** | | | |
| *Also recorded as Bubi & Bob; Bob and Dor* | | | |
| **45s** | | | |
| BINGO  Bob & Dor McFadden | 1959 | Brunswick 55156 | 18 |
| *(Yellow promo label)* | | | |
| DRACULA CHA CHA | 1958 | Coral 62209 | 30 |
| *(Yellow promo label)* | | | |
| FRANKIE AND IGOR AT A ROCK AND ROLL PARTY | 1959 | Brunswick 55120 | 30 |
| *(Yellow promo label)* | | | |
| THE MUMMY  Bob & Dor McFadden | 1959 | Brunswick 55140 | 30 |
| *(Yellow promo label, stock picture sleeve worth $50)* | | | |
| THE MUMMY  Bubi & Bob | 1957 | Sphinx 1201 | 40 |
| *(White promo label)* | | | |
| | | | |
| **McFADDEN, RUTH** | | | |
| *With the Royal Tones* | | | |
| **45s** | | | |
| TWO IN LOVE | 1956 | Old Town 1020 | 75 |
| *(White promo label)* | | | |
| | | | |
| **McGRAW, TIM** | | | |
| *Curb promo CD singles $2-3 each* | | | |
| **Compact Discs** | | | |
| NOT A MOMENT TOO SOON | 1994 | Curb | 20 |
| *(Promo-only release, radio show-type program)* | | | |
| **RADIO SHOWS** | | | |
| **Compact Discs** | | | |
| COUNTRY CONCERT (Aug 94) Live concert | 1994 | Westwood One | 25-50 |
| *(With Faith Hill and Lee Roy Parnell)* | | | |
| COUNTRY CUTTING EDGE (Aug 94) Music and interviews | 1994 | Westwood One | 15-25 |
| *(Music and interviews)* | | | |
| | | | |
| **McGUINN, ROGER** | | | |
| *More at The Byrds* | | | |
| **Compact Discs** | | | |
| BACK FROM RIO | 1990 | Arista ASCD-8648 | 20 |
| *(Promo-only version with pull-out tray in cardboard box)* | | | |
| **RADIO SHOWS** | | | |
| **Albums** | | | |
| INNERVIEW (80s) Profile of McGuinn/Byrds | 198? | Innerview | 15-25 |
| *(Music and interviews)* | | | |
| OFF THE RECORD (Mar 91) Profile | 1991 | Westwood One (2) | 10-15 |
| *(Music and interviews)* | | | |
| WORLD OF ROCK (Feb 89) Various artists | 1989 | DIR (2) | 20-35 |
| *(McGuinn is a guest DJ)* | | | |
| **Compact Discs** | | | |
| KING BISCUIT FLOWER HOUR (Oct 93) | 1993 | DIR | 40-75 |
| *(Live concert)* | | | |
| KING BISCUIT FLOWER HOUR (Oct 94) | 1994 | DIR | 30-60 |
| *(Live concert)* | | | |
| LIVE AT ELECTRIC LADYLAND (July 91) | 1991 | Westwood One | 75-100 |
| *(Live concert)* | | | |
| | | | |
| **McGUIRE SISTERS, THE** | | | |
| **45s** | | | |
| CHILDREN'S HOLIDAY | 195? | Coral 98018 | 15 |
| *(Promo only, blue label)* | | | |
| **RADIO SHOWS** | | | |
| **45s** | | | |
| SINCERELY  Music in the Air | 1958 | U.S. Air Force | 15 |
| *(Promo only)* | | | |
| | | | |
| **McGUIRE, BARRY** | | | |
| *Horizon promo 45s $8 each; Other Dunhill promo 45s $6 each; Ode promo 45s $4 each* | | | |
| **45s** | | | |
| EVE OF DESTRUCTION | 1965 | Dunhill 4009 | 15 |
| *(White promo label)* | | | |
| **7-Inch Extended Plays** | | | |
| EVE OF DESTRUCTION  Jukebox LLP | 1968 | Dunhill 50003 | 25 |
| *(Issued with a hard cover)* | | | |
| THIS PRECIOUS TIME  Jukebox LLP | 1968 | Dunhill 50005 | 18 |
| *(Issued with a hard cover)* | | | |
| | | | |
| **McKENDREE SPRING** | | | |
| *Decca promo 45s $4 each* | | | |
| **45s** | | | |
| McKENDREE SPRING | 1968 | Decca 572 | 15 |
| *(Album highlights with promo picture sleeve)* | | | |

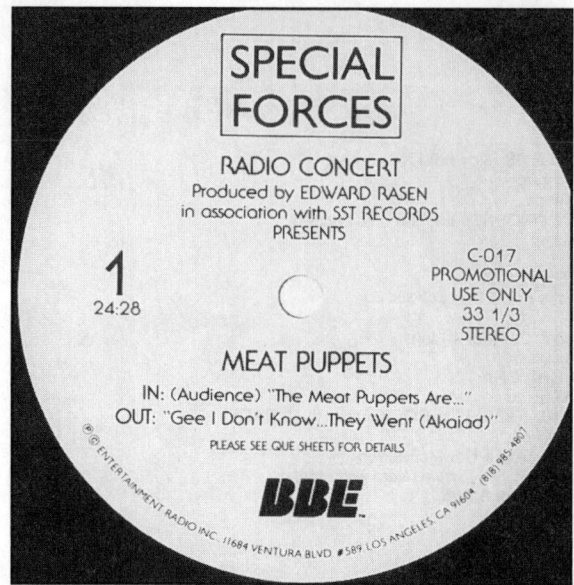

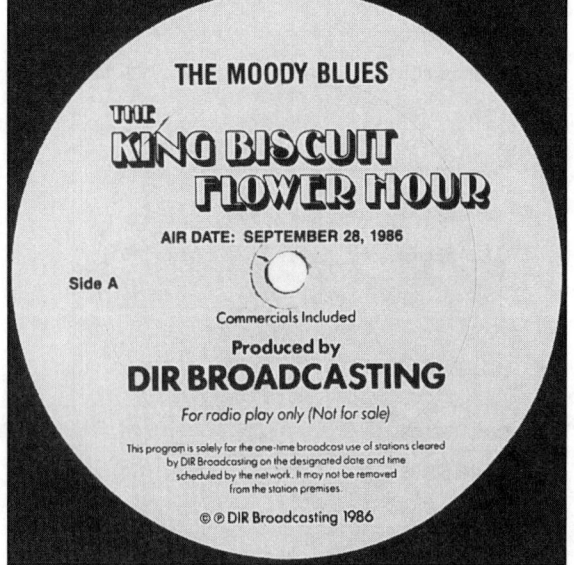

(Top left) Pre-1970 promo singles on the Motown family of labels are scarce. This one by the Marvelettes is even more interesting than most. First, it has a blank B-side; second, the title of this song was changed to "He's a Good Guy (Yes He Is)" for stock release. (Top right) The Meat Puppets, another band from the glory days of SST Records, made an appearance on the Special Forces radio show in the 1980s. (Middle row) The jacket and a label from a Moody Blues special from the mid-1980s. These "specials" are usually more rare than regular programs, as they are sold separately. (Bottom left) From the tour supporting *The Other Side of Life*, here are the Moodies on the King Biscuit Flower Hour. (Bottom right) This custom label of the New York Dolls' *In Too Much Too Soon* also appears on the stock copy.

| Title | Yr | Label, Number | NM $ |
|-------|-----|---------------|------|

**McKENNITT, LOREENA**
*Warner Bros. promo CD singles $2-3 each*
**Compact Discs**

| Title | Yr | Label, Number | NM $ |
|-------|-----|---------------|------|
| LIVE IN SAN FRANCISCO | 199? | Warner Bros. | 25 |
| *(Promo-only release)* | | | |
| MASK AND MIRROR, THE | 1994 | Warner Bros. PRO-CD-6775 | 15 |
| *(Promo-only sampler)* | | | |
| VISIT, THE | 1992 | Warner Bros. PRO-CD-5809 | 15 |
| *(Promo-only interview album)* | | | |

**McKENZIE, BOB AND DOUG**
**45s**

| Title | Yr | Label, Number | NM $ |
|-------|-----|---------------|------|
| TWELVE DAYS OF CHRISTMAS (same on both sides) | 1981 | Mercury 76133 | 10 |
| *(May be promo only)* | | | |

**McKENZIE, SCOTT**
**45s**

| Title | Yr | Label, Number | NM $ |
|-------|-----|---------------|------|
| SAN FRANCISCO | 1970 | Columbia Special Products 10010 | 10 |
| *(Unusual special-products edition)* | | | |

**McKUEN, ROD**
*Decca promo 45s $6 each; Jubilee promo 45s $5 each; Capitol, Warner Bros. promo 45s $2 each; Warner Bros. jukebox LLPs $6 each Also see Bob McFadden*
**45s**

| Title | Yr | Label, Number | NM $ |
|-------|-----|---------------|------|
| INTERVIEW  With Anita Kerr | 1968 | Warner Bros. PRO-262 | 10 |
| *(Promo-only release)* | | | |

**Albums**

| Title | Yr | Label, Number | NM $ |
|-------|-----|---------------|------|
| ALONE AFTER DARK | 1959 | Decca 8946 | 20 |
| *(White promo label)* | | | |
| ANYWHERE I WONDER | 1958 | Decca 8882 | 25 |
| *(White promo label)* | | | |
| LAZY AFTERNOON | 1956 | Liberty 3011 | 50 |
| *(White promo label)* | | | |
| SUMMER LOVE | 1958 | Decca 8714 | 100 |
| *(Pink promo label)* | | | |

**McLACHLAN, SARAH**
*Other Arista promo CD singles $3-4 each*
**Compact Discs**

| Title | Yr | Label, Number | NM $ |
|-------|-----|---------------|------|
| I WILL REMEMBER YOU | 1995 | Arista | 8 |
| *(Promo CD single)* | | | |

**RADIO SHOWS**
**Compact Discs**

| Title | Yr | Label, Number | NM $ |
|-------|-----|---------------|------|
| ALBUM NETWORK SPECIAL (Mar 95) | 1995 | Premier Entertainment | 40-75 |
| *(Live concert)* | | | |
| IN CONCERT-NU ROCK (Mar 96) | 1996 | | 50-75 |
| *(Live concert material)* | | | |

**McLAUGHLIN, JOHN**
**RADIO SHOWS**
**Albums**

| Title | Yr | Label, Number | NM $ |
|-------|-----|---------------|------|
| BBC TRANSCRIPTION DISC  Live concert | 1977 | BBC Transcription | 300-400 |
| *(Very rare live concert)* | | | |

**McLEAN, DON**
*Mediarts promo 45s $5 each; Other United Artists, Millennium, Arista and EMI promo 45s $3 each*
**45s**

| Title | Yr | Label, Number | NM $ |
|-------|-----|---------------|------|
| AMERICAN PIE  Brown promo label with star | 1971 | United Artists 50856 | 18 |
| *(Scarce promo of this classic; both sides are the same, a 4:21 version, different from that on stock copies)* | | | |
| WHAT'S IT ALL ABOUT (Feb 73) Public service show | 1973 | W.I.A.A. 163 | 25 |
| *(Flip side features Elton John)* | | | |
| WHAT'S IT ALL ABOUT (Jan/Feb 74) Public service show | 1974 | W.I.A.A. 214 | 25 |
| *(Flip side is Waylon Jennings)* | | | |

**Albums**

| Title | Yr | Label, Number | NM $ |
|-------|-----|---------------|------|
| THE RCA RADIO SERIES (VOL. 8) | 1982 | RCA Victor | 30 |
| *(Music and interviews)* | | | |

**Compact Discs**

| Title | Yr | Label, Number | NM $ |
|-------|-----|---------------|------|
| AMERICAN PIE | 1992 | Curb 099 | 8 |
| *(Promo-only single reissue to radio on the song's 20th anniversary)* | | | |

**RADIO SHOWS**
**Albums**

| Title | Yr | Label, Number | NM $ |
|-------|-----|---------------|------|
| BBC TRANSCRIPTION DISC  Live concert | 1975 | BBC Transcription | 300-400 |
| *(Very rare live concert)* | | | |
| STAR SESSIONS (Mar 82) | 1982 | (2) | 200-300 |
| *(Rare live show)* | | | |

**McTELL, RALPH**
*London promo 45s $3 each*
**Albums**

| Title | Yr | Label, Number | NM $ |
|-------|-----|---------------|------|
| BBC TRANSCRIPTION DISC  Live concert | 1974 | BBC Transcription | 400-600 |
| *(With Electric Light Orchestra)* | | | |

**McVIE, CHRISTINE**
*More at Fleetwood Mac*
**Albums**

| Title | Yr | Label, Number | NM $ |
|-------|-----|---------------|------|
| CHRISTINE MCVIE | 1984 | Warner Bros. 25059 | 15 |
| *(Promo on Quiex II vinyl)* | | | |

| Title | Yr | Label, Number | NM $ |
|---|---|---|---|

**MEAT LOAF**
*Other Epic promo 45s $5 each; RCA Victor promo 45s $3 each; MCA promo CD singles $4-6 each*
**12-Inch Singles**

| | | | |
|---|---|---|---|
| GETTING AWAY WITH MURDER (same on both sides) | 1986 | Atlantic PR 966 | 8 |
| (GIVE ME THE FUTURE WITH A) MODERN GIRL (LP Version) (7" Version) | 1984 | RCA JD-14050 | 10 |
| I'M GONNA LOVE HER FOR BOTH OF US/PEEL OUT | 1981 | Cleveland Int'l. AS 1277 | 8 |
| PARADISE BY THE DASHBOARD LIGHT (7:55)/(6:58 with play-by-play)/ (6:58 without play-by-play) | 1978 | Epic AS 477 | 20 |
| *(With "Bat Out of Hell" picture cover)* | | | |
| ROCK AND ROLL MERCENARIES (same on both sides) | 1986 | Atlantic PR 997 | 8 |
| SURF'S UP (LP Version)/(Edit)/BAD ATTITUDE | 1984 | RCA JW-14141 | 15 |

**45s**

| | | | |
|---|---|---|---|
| GETTING AWAY WITH MURDER | 198? | | 12 |
| *(Test pressing, white label)* | | | |
| PARADISE BY THE DASHBOARD LIGHT  Promo label | 1977 | Epic 50588 | 12 |
| *(Long/short versions of this rock classic)* | | | |
| WHAT'S IT ALL ABOUT  Public service show | 1978 | W.I.A.A. 457 | 20 |
| *(Flip side features Steve Martin)* | | | |
| WHAT'S IT ALL ABOUT (July 80) Public service show | 1980 | W.I.A.A. 2813 | 15 |
| *(Flip side is Marvin Gaye)* | | | |
| WHAT'S IT ALL ABOUT (July 80) Public service show | 1980 | W.I.A.A. 530 | 18 |
| *(Flip side features Marvin Gaye)* | | | |

**RADIO SHOWS**
**Albums**

| | | | |
|---|---|---|---|
| BBC ROCK HOUR (Aug 81) Live concert | 1981 | London Wavelength | 75-125 |
| *(Rare early concert)* | | | |
| BBC ROCK HOUR (Aug 81) Music and interviews | 1981 | London Wavelength | 25-40 |
| *(Jim Steinman, Meat Loaf's writer and producer)* | | | |
| IN CONCERT (80s) Live concert | 198? | Westwood One (2) | 25-50 |
| *(With Joe Satriani)* | | | |
| KING BISCUIT FLOWER HOUR (June 85) Live concert | 1985 | DIR/ABC (2) | 40-75 |
| *(With Robert Plant)* | | | |

**Compact Discs**

| | | | |
|---|---|---|---|
| ALBUM NETWORK SPECIAL (Oct 94) Live concert | 1994 | Album Network (2) | 75-150 |
| *(Again, the newer material)* | | | |
| HALLOWEEN SPECIAL (Oct 93) | 1993 | (2) | 40-75 |
| *(Music and interviews with some live material)* | | | |
| IN THE STUDIO (Aug 89) Profile of "Bat Out of Hell" | 1989 | Album Network | 20-30 |
| *(Music and interviews)* | | | |
| KING BISCUIT FLOWER HOUR (Mar 93) | 1993 | DIR | 40-75 |
| *(Live concert, repeated)* | | | |
| SUPERSTAR CONCERT (June 94) Live concert | 1994 | Westwood One (2) | 75-150 |
| *(Live music from his new material)* | | | |

**MEAT PUPPETS**
*London promo CD singles $2-3 each*
**45s**

| | | | |
|---|---|---|---|
| SAM/BALI HA'I | 1991 | London PRO 943 | 5 |
| SWIMMING GROUND/UP ON THE SUN | 1985 | SST E 39 | 6 |

**RADIO SHOWS**
**Albums**

| | | | |
|---|---|---|---|
| SPECIAL FORCES  Live concert | 1986 | Spin Magazine | 150-250 |
| *(Very rare and very special concert)* | | | |

**Compact Discs**

| | | | |
|---|---|---|---|
| IN CONCERT (Sept 94) Live concert | 1994 | Westwood One | 40-75 |
| *(Solo concert)* | | | |
| IN CONCERT-NU ROCK (Oct 94) | 1994 | Westwood One | 40-75 |
| *(Live concert)* | | | |
| ON THE EDGE (Mar 94) Music and interviews | 1994 | Westwood One | 15-25 |
| *(With the Cocteau Twins)* | | | |

**MECO**
**45s**

| | | | |
|---|---|---|---|
| THEME FROM CLOSE ENCOUNTERS (Long)/(Short) | 1978 | Millennium 608 | 5 |

**MEDALLIONAIRES**
**45s**

| | | | |
|---|---|---|---|
| MAGIC MOONLIGHT | 1958 | Mercury 71309 | 50 |
| *(White promo label)* | | | |

**MEDICINE HEAD**
**RADIO SHOWS**
**Albums**

| | | | |
|---|---|---|---|
| BBC TRANSCRIPTION DISC  Live concert | 1973 | BBC Transcription | 150-225 |
| *(With the Pretty Things)* | | | |

**MEGADETH**
*Other Capitol promo CD singles $3 each*
**45s**

| | | | |
|---|---|---|---|
| SYMPHONY OF DESTRUCTION | 1992 | Capitol S7-57798 | 10 |
| *(Capitol jukebox single with band's name misspelled "Megadeath")* | | | |

**Compact Discs**

| | | | |
|---|---|---|---|
| A TOUT LE MONDE | 1994 | Capitol DPRO-79535 | 8 |
| *(Promo-only CD single)* | | | |
| CROWN OF WORMS | 1994 | Capitol DPRO-79448 | 15 |
| *(Promo-only CD single; comes in plastic doll head)* | | | |

| Title | Yr | Label, Number | NM $ |
|---|---|---|---|
| HANGAR 18 | 1990 | Capitol DPRO-79462 | 8 |
| *(Promo CD single)* | | | |
| HOLY WARS… THE PUNISHMENT DUE | 1990 | Capitol DPRO-79292 | 8 |
| *(Promo-only CD single)* | | | |
| LIMITED EDITION! MEGADETH LIVE | 1992 | Capitol DPRO-79862 | 15 |
| *(Promo-only album)* | | | |
| MAXIMUM MEGADETH | 1991 | Capitol DPRO-79757 | 20 |
| *(Promo-only sampler)* | | | |
| MEGADETH INTERVIEW | 1992 | Capitol DPRO-79396 | 15 |
| *(Promo-only album)* | | | |
| 99 WAYS TO DIE | 1993 | Geffen 4580 | 8 |
| *(Promo-only CD single)* | | | |
| RUST IN PEACE | 1990 | Capitol CDP 7 91395 2 | 50 |
| *(Promo-only CD issued in a coffin cover)* | | | |
| SKIN O' MY TEETH | 1992 | Capitol DPRO-79363 | 8 |
| *(Promo-only CD single)* | | | |
| SYMPHONY OF DESTRUCTION | 1992 | Capitol DPRO-79339 | 8 |
| *(Promo-only CD single)* | | | |
| **RADIO SHOWS** | | | |
| **Albums** | | | |
| METALSHOP (80s) Various artists | 198? | MJI Productions (2) | 10-15 |
| *(Megadeth often was the band featured during live segments of several shows)* | | | |

## MEISNER, RANDY
*More at Eagles*

**45s**

| Title | Yr | Label, Number | NM $ |
|---|---|---|---|
| NEVER BEEN IN LOVE | 1982 | Epic | 10 |
| *(Test pressing, white label)* | | | |
| **RADIO SHOWS** | | | |
| **Albums** | | | |
| CAPTURED LIVE (May 83) | 1983 | (3) | 200-400 |
| *(Live concert material, rare show)* | | | |

## MELANIE
*Neighborhood and Buddah promo 45s $5 each (except Buddah 186 B-1 "RPM" worth $8); Portrait promo 45s $4 each; Tomato and Blanche promo 45s $3 each*

**45s**

| Title | Yr | Label, Number | NM $ |
|---|---|---|---|
| MY BEAUTIFUL PEOPLE  White promo label | 1967 | Columbia 44349 | 15 |
| *(Her first record, issued with a picture sleeve, worth an additional $25)* | | | |
| TAKE ME HOME (mono/stereo) | 1970 | Buddah 161 | 6 |
| *(May be promo only)* | | | |
| WHAT'S IT ALL ABOUT  Public service show | 197? | W.I.A.A. 115 | 18 |
| *(Flip side features Mylon)* | | | |
| WHAT'S IT ALL ABOUT (Jan 74) Public service show | 1974 | W.I.A.A. 211 | 15 |
| *(Flip side features Peter Yarrow)* | | | |
| WHY DIDN'T MY MOTHER TELL ME  White promo label | 1968 | Columbia 44524 | 10 |
| *(Also issued with a picture sleeve, worth $25)* | | | |
| **7-Inch Extended Plays** | | | |
| I'M BACK IN TOWN Jukebox LLP | 1972 | Buddah SP-2 | 20 |
| *(Issued with a hard cover)* | | | |

## MELLENCAMP, JOHN
*Also includes John Cougar; John Cougar Mellencamp; Riva promo 45s $4 each; Mercury promo 45s $3 each; Other Mercury promo CD singles $5 each*

**45s**

| Title | Yr | Label, Number | NM $ |
|---|---|---|---|
| OH PRETTY WOMAN  Johnny Cougar | 1976 | MCA 40634 | 20 |
| *(White promo label)* | | | |
| PINK HOUSES  John Cougar Mellencamp | 1983 | Riva R-215 | 20 |
| *(Promo only on pink vinyl)* | | | |
| **Albums** | | | |
| JOHN COUGAR | 1982 | Riva 219 (2) | 30 |
| *(Promo-only two-record set)* | | | |
| THE KID INSIDE | 198? | MainMan | 40 |
| *(Promo-only picture disc)* | | | |
| **Compact Discs** | | | |
| DANCE NAKED | 1994 | Mercury SACD 885 (2) | 120 |
| *(Two-CD promo in book)* | | | |
| LIMITED COLLECTOR'S EDITION | 1990 | Mercury (8) | 80 |
| *(Promo-only box set of first eight albums)* | | | |
| MR. HAPPY GO LUCKY | 1996 | Mercury (2) | 100 |
| *(Two-CD promo in book)* | | | |
| ON TOUR TOGETHER | 1994 | Mercury SACD 923 (2) | 30 |
| *(Two-CD promo; one CD has Mellencamp live tracks, the other, live tracks from the group Texas)* | | | |
| RADIO'S GREATEST HITS  17 tracks | 1993 | Mercury SACD 718 | 100 |
| *(Radio issue only)* | | | |
| WHAT IF I CAME KNOCKIN' | 1993 | Mercury CDP 965 | 8 |
| *(Promo-only CD single, not otherwise available in the U.S. as a single)* | | | |
| WHEN JESUS LEFT BIRMINGHAM | 1994 | Mercury CDP 1113 | 8 |
| *(Promo CD single)* | | | |
| WILD NIGHT  With Me'Shell Ndege'Ocello | 1994 | Mercury CDP 1230 | 8 |
| *(Promo CD single)* | | | |
| **RADIO SHOWS** | | | |
| **Albums** | | | |
| INNERVIEW  Profile | 1978 | Innerview | 10-20 |
| *(Music and interviews)* | | | |
| KING BISCUIT FLOWER HOUR (Dec 80) Live concert | 1980 | DIR/ABC (2) | 75-125 |
| *(With Gamma)* | | | |

| Title | Yr | Label, Number | NM $ |
|---|---|---|---|
| NBC SOURCE (Jan 83) Live concert | 1983 | NBC Source (2) | 75-125 |
| *(Rare early concert)* | | | |
| SOURCE SPECIAL (Oct 83) | 1983 | NBC Source (2) | 30-60 |
| *(Music and interviews)* | | | |
| SUPERGROUPS (May 83) Live concert | 1983 | DIR (3) | 75-125 |
| *(With Dexy's Midnight Runners)* | | | |
| SUPERSTAR CONCERT Live concert | 1984 | Westwood One (3) | 40-75 |
| *(Box set, repeated)* | | | |
| **Compact Discs** | | | |
| KING BISCUIT FLOWER HOUR (May 92) Live concert | 1992 | DIR | 25-50 |
| *(Mellencamp solo concert)* | | | |
| SNEAK PREVIEW (Jan 92) | 1992 | Album Network (2) | 50-100 |
| *(Mostly live tracks)* | | | |
| THE STORY OF JOHN COUGAR MELLENCAMP (Mar 92) | 1992 | Unistar | 15-25 |
| *(Music and interviews)* | | | |
| SUPERSTAR CONCERT (Sept 92) Live concert | 1992 | Westwood One (2) | 50-75 |
| *(CD format, repeated)* | | | |
| TIMOTHY WHITE SESSIONS (Nov 91) | 1991 | Westwood One (2) | 50-100 |
| *(Mostly live tracks)* | | | |
| UP CLOSE Profile | 1993 | Media America (2) | 40-75 |
| *(Mostly music and interviews)* | | | |
| **Reel-to-Reel Tapes** | | | |
| HUMAN WHEELS IN THE WINDY CITY | 1993 | Album Network (2) | 75-125 |
| *(Very rare and limited live show on two 10" reels)* | | | |

## MELLO-KINGS, THE
**45s**

| Title | Yr | Label, Number | NM $ |
|---|---|---|---|
| CHIP CHIP  The Royal Holidays | 1958 | Herald 536 | 75 |
| *(White promo label)* | | | |
| TONITE-TONITE   Mello-Tones | 1957 | Herald 502 | 80 |
| *(White promo label, original name of group)* | | | |

## MELLOW DROPS, THE
**45s**

| Title | Yr | Label, Number | NM $ |
|---|---|---|---|
| WHEN I GROW TOO OLD TO DREAM | 1954 | Imperial 5324 | 75 |
| *(Cream colored promo label)* | | | |

## MELVIN, HAROLD, AND THE BLUE NOTES
**12-Inch Singles**

| Title | Yr | Label, Number | NM $ |
|---|---|---|---|
| TODAY'S YOUR LUCKY DAY (6:20) (7:07) | 1984 | Philly World PR 751 | 8 |

## MEN AT WORK
*Columbia promo 45s $4 each; Columbia promo picture sleeves $2 each; Columbia promo 45s and sleeves by Colin James Hay $2*
Includes Colin James Hay
**12-Inch Singles**

| Title | Yr | Label, Number | NM $ |
|---|---|---|---|
| BE GOOD JOHNNY (same on both sides) | 1983 | Columbia AS 1608 | 8 |
| DR. HECKLE & MR. JIVE/UPSTAIRS AT MY HOUSE (Live)/I LIKE TO (Live) | 1983 | Columbia AS 1749 | 8 |
| EVERYTHING I NEED (same on both sides) | 1985 | Columbia CAS 2073 | 8 |
| HARD LUCK STORY/(Single Version) | 1985 | Columbia CAS 2189 | 10 |
| MARIA (same on both sides) | 1985 | Columbia CAS 2152 | 6 |
| OVERKILL (same on both sides) | 1983 | Columbia AS 1634 | 8 |
| WHO CAN IT BE NOW? (same on both sides) | 1982 | Columbia (no #) | 12 |
| **45s** | | | |
| OVERKILL  White promo label | 1983 | Columbia AE7 1633 | 12 |
| *(Includes promo-only picture sleeve not on stock copy or regular promo copy)* | | | |
| **Albums** | | | |
| CARGO (WORLD PREMIERE WEEKEND) | 1983 | Columbia A2S 1650 (2) | 15 |
| *(Promo-only two-record package of interviews and music)* | | | |
| **RADIO SHOWS** | | | |
| **Albums** | | | |
| BBC LONDON WAVELENGTH (Nov 82) | 1982 | London Wavelength | 25-40 |
| *(Music and interviews)* | | | |
| IN CONCERT (Mar 83) Live concert | 1983 | Westwood One (2) | 50-100 |
| *(Rare early concert)* | | | |
| KING BISCUIT FLOWER HOUR (Aug 84) Live concert | 1984 | DIR/ABC (2) | 35-60 |
| *(Repeated)* | | | |
| NBC SOURCE (Aug 84) | 1984 | NBC Radio (2) | 25-40 |
| *(Music and interviews)* | | | |
| SUPERSTAR CONCERT (Mar 83) Live concert | 1983 | Westwood One (3) | 50-125 |
| *(Another rare early concert)* | | | |
| **Compact Discs** | | | |
| IN THE STUDIO (90s) Profile of an album | 199? | Album Network | 20-30 |
| *(Music and interviews)* | | | |

## MEN WITHOUT HATS
*Mercury and Backstreet/MCA promo 45s $3 each; Mercury promo CDs $3 each*
**12-Inch Singles**

| Title | Yr | Label, Number | NM $ |
|---|---|---|---|
| I GOT THE MESSAGE (long)/(short) | 1983 | MCA L33-1164 | 6 |
| WHERE DO THE BOYS GO (LP) (Extended) | 1984 | MCA L33-1217 | 6 |
| **RADIO SHOWS** | | | |
| **Albums** | | | |
| RETRO ROCK (Oct 83) Live concert | 1983 | Clayton Webster | 50-75 |
| *(With A Flock of Seagulls)* | | | |

| Title | Yr | Label, Number | NM $ |
|-------|-----|---------------|------|
| **MENDES, SERGIO** | | | |
| **12-Inch Singles** | | | |
| WHAT IS THIS?/FANFARRA | 1992 | Elektra ED 5602 | 8 |
| | | | |
| **MENTAL AS ANYTHING** | | | |
| **12-Inch Singles** | | | |
| BRAIN BRAIN (Remix)/(Edit) | 1983 | A&M 17247 | 6 |
| IF YOU LEAVE ME, CAN I COME TOO? (same on both sides) | 1982 | A&M 17234 | 6 |
| | | | |
| **MERCHANT, NATALIE** | | | |
| *More at 10,000 Maniacs* | | | |
| **RADIO SHOWS** | | | |
| **Reel-to-Reel Tapes** | | | |
| COLUMBIA RADIO HOUR (June 95) | 1995 | | 100-200 |
| *(With Jeff Buckley, live material)* | | | |
| | | | |
| **MERCURY, FREDDIE** | | | |
| *More at Queen* | | | |
| **12-Inch Singles** | | | |
| LOVE KILLS (same on both sides) | 1984 | Columbia AS 1928 | 10 |
| | | | |
| **MESSINA, JIM** | | | |
| **Albums** | | | |
| MESSINA | 1981 | Warner Bros. BSK 3559 | 20 |
| *(Promo-only version on Quiex II vinyl)* | | | |
| | | | |
| **METALLICA** | | | |
| *Elektra promo 45s $4 each* | | | |
| **Compact Discs** | | | |
| AND JUSTICE FOR ALL | 1988 | Elektra PR 8099 | 10 |
| *(Promo-only CD single)* | | | |
| DON'T TREAD ON ME | 1992 | Elektra PR 8728 | 8 |
| *(Promo-only CD single)* | | | |
| ENTER SANDMAN | 1991 | Elektra PR 8421 | 8 |
| *(Promo-only CD single, different mix)* | | | |
| ENTER SANDMAN | 1991 | Elektra PR 8407 | 8 |
| *(Promo-only CD single)* | | | |
| EYE OF THE BEHOLDER | 1988 | Elektra PR 8028 | 8 |
| *(Promo-only CD single)* | | | |
| 15 PIECES OF LIVE SH*T  Box set sampler | 1993 | Elektra PR 8879 (2) | 60 |
| *(Versions exist with jewel box and cardboard sleeve; both are worth the same)* | | | |
| MANDATORY METALLICA | 1989 | Elektra PR 8020 | 150 |
| *(Version with seven tracks)* | | | |
| MANDATORY METALLICA | 1989 | Elektra PR 8071 | 125 |
| *(Version with eight tracks)* | | | |
| NOTHING ELSE MATTERS | 1992 | Elektra PR 8534 | 8 |
| *(Promo-only CD single)* | | | |
| ONE | 1988 | Elektra PR 8044 | 10 |
| *(Promo-only CD single)* | | | |
| SAD BUT TRUE | 1992 | Elektra PR 8646 | 8 |
| *(Promo-only CD single)* | | | |
| STONE COLD CRAZY | 1990 | Elektra PR 8224 | 25 |
| *(Promo-only CD single, quite rare)* | | | |
| UNFORGIVEN, THE | 1991 | Elektra PR 8479 | 8 |
| *(Promo-only CD single)* | | | |
| UNTIL IT SLEEPS | 1996 | Elektra | 10 |
| *(Promo-only CD single)* | | | |
| WHEREVER I MAY ROAM | 1992 | Elektra | 8 |
| *(Promo-only CD single)* | | | |
| **RADIO SHOWS** | | | |
| **Albums** | | | |
| METALSHOP (80s) Various artists | 198? | MJI Productions | 10-20 |
| *(Metallica was often featured on live segments of these programs)* | | | |
| | | | |
| **METRONOMES, THE** | | | |
| **45s** | | | |
| DEAR DON | | Cadence 1339 | 40 |
| *(White promo label)* | | | |
| I LOVE MY GIRL | 1957 | Cadence 1310 | 50 |
| *(White promo label)* | | | |
| | | | |
| **MICHAEL, GEORGE** | | | |
| *Includes Wham (Wham! U.K.); Other Columbia white promo label 45s by George Michael or by Wham $3 each; Columbia 12" promo singles by George Michael or Wham $6 each; Other promo CD singles $4-6 each* | | | |
| **45s** | | | |
| LAST CHRISTMAS  Wham! | 1986 | Columbia CS7 2591 | 10 |
| *(Long 6:43/short 4:24 promo-only single)* | | | |
| YOUNG GUNS  Wham! U.K. | 1982 | Columbia 03611 | 10 |
| *(Includes promo-only picture sleeve of Wham! U.K.)* | | | |
| **Compact Discs** | | | |
| DON'T LET THE SUN GO DOWN ON ME  With Elton John | 1991 | Columbia CVK 4288 | 30 |
| *(CD single and video in custom case, promo-only)* | | | |
| FAITH | 1987 | Columbia | 50 |
| *(Promo-only release of full-length album with hologram on front sleeve)* | | | |
| FASTLOVE | 1996 | Dreamworks | 8 |
| *(Promo CD single)* | | | |

| Title | Yr | Label, Number | NM $ |
|---|---|---|---|
| FIVE LIVE  George Michael with Queen | 1993 | Hollywood PRBX-10313 | 50 |
| *(Promo-only CD with VHS and press kit)* | | | |
| JESUS TO A CHILD | 1996 | Dreamworks | 8 |
| *(Promo CD single)* | | | |
| LISTEN WITHOUT PREJUDICE: AN INTERVIEW | 1990 | Columbia CSK 2226 | 12 |
| *(Promo-only release)* | | | |
| MONKEY | 1988 | Columbia CSK 1186 | 10 |
| *(Promo-only CD single)* | | | |
| SOMEBODY TO LOVE  George Michael and Queen | 1993 | Hollywood 10323 | 10 |
| *(Promo-only CD single with two tracks, not to be confused with one-track version)* | | | |

**RADIO SHOWS**
**Albums**

| Title | Yr | Label, Number | NM $ |
|---|---|---|---|
| STARTRAK PROFILE (Aug 88) | 1988 | Westwood One (2) | 75-150 |
| *(Music and interviews)* | | | |
| WESTWOOD ONE SPECIAL (80s) Live concert | 198? | Westwood One | 200-350 |
| *(From the Faith tour)* | | | |

**Compact Discs**

| Title | Yr | Label, Number | NM $ |
|---|---|---|---|
| THE GEORGE MICHAEL STORY (Apr 91) | 1991 | Unistar | 20-35 |
| *(Repeated twice in 1992)* | | | |

## MIDLER, BETTE
*Atlantic promo 45s $2 each; Atlantic promo CD singles $2-3 each*

**12-Inch Singles**

| Title | Yr | Label, Number | NM $ |
|---|---|---|---|
| BEAST OF BURDEN (same on both sides) | 1983 | Atlantic 578 | 10 |
| BIG NOISE FROM WINNETKA (same on both sides) | 1979 | Atlantic 218 | 10 |
| FAVORITE WASTE OF TIME/ONLY IN MIAMI | 1983 | Atlantic 548 | 10 |
| MARRIED MEN (7:58) (5:32) | 1979 | Atlantic DSKO 187 | 12 |
| MOONLIGHT DANCING (3 versions) | 1990 | Atlantic 1655 | 5 |

**Albums**

| Title | Yr | Label, Number | NM $ |
|---|---|---|---|
| LIVE AT LAST | 1977 | Atlantic PR-275 | 10 |
| *(Special edited version for airplay)* | | | |

**Compact Discs**

| Title | Yr | Label, Number | NM $ |
|---|---|---|---|
| BEST BETTES | 1993 | Atlantic PRCD 5154 | 20 |
| *(Promo-only sampler)* | | | |

**RADIO SHOWS**
**Albums**

| Title | Yr | Label, Number | NM $ |
|---|---|---|---|
| NBC SOURCE (June 80) | 1980 | NBC Radio (2) | 20-40 |
| *(Music and interviews)* | | | |
| ROBERT W. MORGAN (Sept 81) | 1981 | Watermark | 15-25 |
| *(Music and interviews)* | | | |

## MIDNIGHT OIL
*Columbia promo 45s $3 each; Columbia promo CD singles $3-5 each*

**12-Inch Singles**

| Title | Yr | Label, Number | NM $ |
|---|---|---|---|
| BEDS ARE BURNING (same on both sides) | 1987 | Columbia CAS 2911 | 12 |
| BEST OF BOTH WORLDS (same on both sides) | 1984 | Columbia CAS 2107 | 12 |
| BLUE SKY MINE (Food On Table Mix) (same on both sides) | 1990 | Columbia CAS 2020 | 8 |
| THE POWER AND THE PASSION/READ ABOUT IT/U.S. FORCES | 1982 | Columbia AS 1746 | 8 |

**Albums**

| Title | Yr | Label, Number | NM $ |
|---|---|---|---|
| INTERCHORDS | 1988 | Columbia | 20 |
| *(Promo-only release)* | | | |

**Compact Discs**

| Title | Yr | Label, Number | NM $ |
|---|---|---|---|
| GREEN DISC, THE | 1990 | Columbia CSK 2038 | 20 |
| *(Promo-only collection)* | | | |

**RADIO SHOWS**
**Albums**

| Title | Yr | Label, Number | NM $ |
|---|---|---|---|
| BBC COLLEGE CONCERT (Dec 83) | 1983 | London Wavelength | 25-50 |
| *(Music and interviews)* | | | |
| IN CONCERT (July 91) Live concert | 1991 | Westwood One (2) | 30-50 |
| *(With Nels Lofgren)* | | | |
| IN CONCERT (Sept 85) Live concert | 1985 | Westwood One (2) | 40-75 |
| *(With China Crisis)* | | | |
| KING BISCUIT FLOWER HOUR (Dec 81) Live concert | 1981 | DIR/ABC (2) | 50-100 |
| *(With Nils Lofgren)* | | | |
| KING BISCUIT FLOWER HOUR (June 84) Live concert | 1984 | DIR/ABC (2) | 40-75 |
| *(With Dwight Twilley)* | | | |

**Compact Discs**

| Title | Yr | Label, Number | NM $ |
|---|---|---|---|
| IN CONCERT (July 94) Live concert | 1994 | Westwood One | 25-50 |
| *(With Primal Scream)* | | | |
| IN CONCERT (June 92) Live concert | 1992 | Westwood One | 25-50 |
| *(With The Tragically Hip)* | | | |
| IN CONCERT (Nov 93) Live concert | 1993 | Westwood One | 30-60 |
| *(Solo concert)* | | | |
| IN CONCERT-NU ROCK (Aug 92) Live concert | 1992 | Westwood One (2) | 40-75 |
| *(With Suede)* | | | |
| OFF THE RECORD (June 92) Profile | 1992 | Westwood One | 10-15 |
| *(Music and interviews, repeated)* | | | |
| ON THE EDGE (Aug 93) Music and interviews | 1993 | Westwood One | 15-25 |
| *(With Catherine Wheel)* | | | |
| ON THE EDGE (July 94) Music and interviews | 1994 | Westwood One | 15-25 |
| *(With Gabriel and others)* | | | |
| ON THE EDGE (May 93) Music and interviews | 1993 | Westwood One | 15-25 |
| *(With 10,000 Maniacs)* | | | |
| ROCK AND THE ENVIRONMENT  Various artists | 1993 | (2) | 20-35 |
| *(Band member Pat Garrett is host of the show)* | | | |

| Title | Yr | Label, Number | NM $ |
|-------|-----|--------------|------|

## MIGHTY LEMON DROPS, THE
**12-Inch Singles**

| Title | Yr | Label, Number | NM $ |
|-------|-----|--------------|------|
| FALL DOWN (Remix)/INSIDE OUT (Live)/MIGHTY LEMON TALK | 1988 | Sire PRO-A-3103 | 5 |
| INSIDE OUT (12")/(7") | 1988 | Sire PRO-A-2963 | 5 |
| INTO THE HEART OF LOVE (LP)/(Edit) | 1989 | Sire PRO-A-3751 | 5 |
| MY BIGGEST THRILL (same on both sides) | 1986 | Sire PRO-A-2639 | 5 |
| OUT OF HAND (Extended)/(LP Version) | 1987 | Sire PRO-A-2791 | 5 |

## MIGHTY MIGHTY BOSSTONES, THE
**12-Inch Singles**

| Title | Yr | Label, Number | NM $ |
|-------|-----|--------------|------|
| KINDER WORDS/CHOCOLATE PUDDING/PIRATE SHIP | 1994 | Mercury 1156 | 10 |

## MIKE AND THE MECHANICS
*Mike Rutherford of Genesis, with lead singers Paul Carrack and Paul Young (Sad Café); Atlantic promo 45s $3 each; Atlantic promo 12" singles $6 each; Atlantic promo CD singles $3 each*
**Albums**

| Title | Yr | Label, Number | NM $ |
|-------|-----|--------------|------|
| MIKE ON MIKE | 1985 | Atlantic PR 820 | 20 |
| *(Promo-only music and interviews)* | | | |
| MIKE ON MIKE II | 1988 | Atlantic PR 2543 | 20 |
| *(Promo-only music and interviews)* | | | |

**RADIO SHOWS**
**Albums**

| Title | Yr | Label, Number | NM $ |
|-------|-----|--------------|------|
| KING BISCUIT FLOWER HOUR | 1986 | DIR (2) | 20-40 |
| *(Live concert)* | | | |
| OFF THE RECORD (June 89) Profile | 1989 | Westwood One (2) | 10-15 |
| *(Music and interviews)* | | | |
| WORLD OF ROCK (Apr 89) Music and interviews | 1989 | DIR (2) | 10-20 |
| *(Mike Rutherford is co-host)* | | | |

**Compact Discs**

| Title | Yr | Label, Number | NM $ |
|-------|-----|--------------|------|
| KING BISCUIT FLOWER HOUR (May 89) Live concert | 1989 | DIR | 25-40 |
| *(Repeated)* | | | |
| RADIO TODAY MIKE RUTHERFORD | 1989 | Radio International (2) | 20-30 |
| *(Music and interviews)* | | | |
| ROCK STARS MIKE RUTHERFORD | 1989 | Radio International (2) | 30-40 |
| *(Music and interviews)* | | | |

## MILES, BUDDY
**45s**

| Title | Yr | Label, Number | NM $ |
|-------|-----|--------------|------|
| CAN YOU HOLD ME (same on both sides) | 1981 | Atlantic 3852 | 4 |
| *(May be promo only)* | | | |
| SUNSHINE OF YOUR LOVE (same on both sides) | 1982 | Atlantic 4006 | 4 |
| *(May be promo only)* | | | |

## MILLER, GLENN
**45s**

| Title | Yr | Label, Number | NM $ |
|-------|-----|--------------|------|
| IN THE MOOD/AMERICAN PATROL | 1958 | United States Army HO7H-1760/1 | 40 |
| *(Promo-only "Recruiting Service" record; white label with red and blue print)* | | | |

**7-Inch Extended Plays**

| Title | Yr | Label, Number | NM $ |
|-------|-----|--------------|------|
| HIGHLIGHTS FROM THE GREAT GLENN MILLER LIMITED EDITION 1953 | 1953 | RCA Victor E3CW-3349/50 | 50 |
| *(Promo-only sampler from the limited box sets)* | | | |

**Albums**

| Title | Yr | Label, Number | NM $ |
|-------|-----|--------------|------|
| AUTHENTIC SOUND OF GLENN MILLER | 1960 | RCA Victor SP 33-90 | 40 |
| *(Released as a promo only)* | | | |

**RADIO SHOWS**
**16-Inch Transcriptions**

| Title | Yr | Label, Number | NM $ |
|-------|-----|--------------|------|
| USAF SHOWS (60s) Various artists | 196? | U.S. Air Force | 10-15 |
| *(Highlighting the music of Glenn Miller)* | | | |

**Albums**

| Title | Yr | Label, Number | NM $ |
|-------|-----|--------------|------|
| MOONLIGHT MEMORIES MILLER (Nov 86) | 1986 | Westwood One (3) | 50-75 |
| *(Thanksgiving special, music and interviews)* | | | |
| MUTUAL PRESENTS GLENN MILLER (Dec 83) | 1983 | Mutual Radio (3) | 40-75 |
| *(Music and interviews)* | | | |

## MILLER, MITCH
*Other Columbia promo 45s $2 each; Columbia compact-33 promo jukebox singles $3 each*
**45s**

| Title | Yr | Label, Number | NM $ |
|-------|-----|--------------|------|
| MARCH FROM THE RIVER KWAI | 196? | Columbia Hall of Fame 33002 | 20 |
| *(Jukebox stereo single with small hole, yellow vinyl)* | | | |
| MARCH FROM THE RIVER KWAI | 1969 | Columbia Hall of Fame 33002 | 25 |
| *(Hall of Fame series, yellow vinyl, includes stock picture sleeve, both sides same, only promo indication is sticker on label)* | | | |
| SEASON'S GREETINGS | 1959 | Columbia JZSP 48888 | 10 |
| *(Promo-only, white label)* | | | |
| SILVER BELLS | 1962 | Columbia JZSP 58221 | 10 |
| *(Promo-only, white label)* | | | |

**RADIO SHOWS**
**Albums**

| Title | Yr | Label, Number | NM $ |
|-------|-----|--------------|------|
| FOR CHRISTMAS SEALS | 1968 | Decca 201,395 | 30 |
| *(Holiday-themed show)* | | | |

## MILLER, MRS. ELVA
*Capitol promo 45s $5 each*
**45s**

| Title | Yr | Label, Number | NM $ |
|-------|-----|--------------|------|
| OPEN-END INTERVIEW | 1967 | Capitol PRO-4085 | 25 |
| *(Issued in hard cover, includes her hit "Downtown")* | | | |
| OPEN-END INTERVIEW #2 | 1967 | Capitol PRO-4186 | 25 |
| *(Issued in a hard cover, includes programming aids)* | | | |

| Title | Yr | Label, Number | NM $ |
|-------|-----|--------------|------|

**MILLER, ROGER**
**7-Inch Extended Plays**

| Title | Yr | Label, Number | NM $ |
|-------|-----|--------------|------|
| BEST OF ROGER MILLER | 196? | Mercury MEPL-9 | 15 |
| *(Jukebox LLP, small center hole)* | | | |

**MILLER, STEVE**
*Capitol promo 45s $3 each; Capitol and Polydor promo CD singles $3 each*
**12-Inch Singles**

| Title | Yr | Label, Number | NM $ |
|-------|-----|--------------|------|
| I WANNA BE LOVED (same on both sides) | 1986 | Capitol SPRO-9992 | 10 |
| *(Promo only on blue vinyl)* | | | |
| SHANGRI-LA (Extended) (7" Version) (Dub Version) | 1984 | Capitol SPRO 9252/3 | 8 |
| TRUE FINE LOVE/DANCE, DANCE, DANCE | 1976 | Capitol SPRO 9008/10 | 15 |

**Albums**

| Title | Yr | Label, Number | NM $ |
|-------|-----|--------------|------|
| GREATEST HITS 1974-1978 | 1978 | Capitol SOO-11872 | 30 |
| *(Promo only on blue vinyl)* | | | |

**RADIO SHOWS**
**Albums**

| Title | Yr | Label, Number | NM $ |
|-------|-----|--------------|------|
| HERE'S TO VETERANS | 1968 | Veterans Administration | 40-75 |
| *(Music and interviews)* | | | |
| IN CONCERT (Jan 92) Live concert | 1992 | Westwood One (2) | 15-25 |
| *(Repeated)* | | | |
| IN CONCERT (Mar 91) Live concert | 1991 | Westwood One (2) | 20-30 |
| *(With the Fabulous Thunderbirds)* | | | |
| LEGENDS OF ROCK (Jan 89) | 1989 | NBC Radio (4) | 25-40 |
| *(Music and interviews, two shows)* | | | |
| LEGENDS OF ROCK (Jan 89) | 1989 | NBC Radio (2) | 15-25 |
| *(Music and interviews)* | | | |
| OFF THE RECORD (Sept 92) Profile | 1992 | Westwood One (2) | 10-15 |
| *(Music and interview, repeated)* | | | |
| PIONEERS IN MUSIC (Dec 85) | 1985 | DIR (2) | 25-50 |
| *(Mostly music and interviews)* | | | |
| RETRO ROCK (Mar 82) | 1982 | Clayton Webster | 15-30 |
| *(Music and interviews)* | | | |
| SUPERSTAR CONCERT (Mar 90) Live concert | 1990 | Westwood One (3) | 20-35 |
| *(Repeated several times)* | | | |

**Compact Discs**

| Title | Yr | Label, Number | NM $ |
|-------|-----|--------------|------|
| IN THE STUDIO (May 89) Profile | 1989 | Album Network | 10-15 |
| *(Music and interviews)* | | | |
| KING BISCUIT FLOWER HOUR (Jan 89) Live concert | 1989 | DIR | 15-25 |
| *(Repeated)* | | | |
| SUPERSTAR CONCERT (Feb 92) Live concert | 1992 | Westwood One (2) | 25-35 |
| *(Repeated)* | | | |
| UP CLOSE  Profile | 1993 | Media America (2) | 15-25 |
| *(Music and interviews)* | | | |

**MILLER, WALTER**
**45s**

| Title | Yr | Label, Number | NM $ |
|-------|-----|--------------|------|
| EVERYBODY'S GOT A BABY BUT ME | 1959 | United Artists 104 | 40 |
| *(White promo label)* | | | |

**MILSAP, RONNIE**
*Warner Bros. promo 45s $5 each; Other RCA color vinyl promo 45s $8 each; Other RCA Victor promo 45s $2 each*
**45s**

| Title | Yr | Label, Number | NM $ |
|-------|-----|--------------|------|
| ANY DAY NOW  Orange label, blue vinyl | 1982 | RCA 13216 | 12 |
| *(Only the promo is blue vinyl)* | | | |
| DON'T YOU KNOW HOW MUCH I LOVE YOU  Brown label, yellow vinyl | 1983 | RCA 13564 | 10 |
| *(Only the promo is yellow vinyl)* | | | |
| LET'S TAKE THE LONG WAY AROUND THE WORLD Blue label, yellow vinyl | 1978 | RCA 11369 | 12 |
| *(Only the promo is yellow vinyl)* | | | |
| NO GETTIN' OVER ME Cream label, yellow vinyl | 1981 | RCA 12264 | 10 |
| *(Only the promo is yellow vinyl)* | | | |
| NOBODY LIKES SAD SONGS  Cream label, purple vinyl | 1979 | RCA 11553 | 15 |
| *(Actually purple/marble vinyl)* | | | |
| ONLY ONE LOVE IN MY LIFE Cream label, white vinyl | 1978 | RCA 11270 | 15 |
| *(Only the promo is white vinyl)* | | | |
| SANTA BARBARA  White label, blue vinyl | 1978 | RCA 11421 | 10 |
| *(Only the promo is blue vinyl)* | | | |
| SHE KEEPS THE HOME FIRES BURNING  Yellow label, green vinyl | 1985 | RCA 14034 | 10 |
| *(Only the promo is green vinyl)* | | | |
| STRANGER IN MY HOUSE  Yellow label, green vinyl | 1983 | RCA 13470 | 12 |
| *(Only the promo is green vinyl)* | | | |
| WHAT'S IT ALL ABOUT (Sept 79) Public service show | 1979 | W.I.A.A. 488 | 18 |
| *(Flip side features Styx)* | | | |
| YOUR TEARS LEAVE ME COLD | 1977 | Festival 5002 | 10 |
| *(White promo label)* | | | |

**RADIO SHOWS**
**Albums**

| Title | Yr | Label, Number | NM $ |
|-------|-----|--------------|------|
| LIVE AT GILLEY'S (May 88) Live concert | 1988 | Westwood One | 20-40 |
| *(Repeated)* | | | |
| ROBERT W. MORGAN (Dec 81) | 1981 | Watermark | 15-25 |
| *(Music and interviews)* | | | |
| SILVER EAGLE (80s) Live concert | 198? | DIR (3) | 40-75 |
| *(With George Jones)* | | | |

| Title | Yr | Label, Number | NM $ |
|---|---|---|---|
| **MINEO, SAL** | | | |
| *Other Epic promo 45s $15 each; Epic promo LPs $25 each* | | | |
| **45s** | | | |
| BABY FACE | 1958 | Epic 9287 | 20 |
| *(White promo label)* | | | |
| START MOVIN' | 1957 | Epic 9216 | 25 |
| *(White promo label, stock picture sleeve worth $40)* | | | |
| **7-Inch Extended Plays** | | | |
| SAL SINGS | 1957 | Epic 27283 | 125 |
| *(Yellow label, issued with a hard cover for Scotch brand cellophane tape)* | | | |
| | | | |
| **MINISTRY** | | | |
| **12-Inch Singles** | | | |
| STIGMATA/TONIGHT WE MURDER | 1988 | Sire PRO-A-3322 | 12 |
| | | | |
| **MINK DEVILLE** | | | |
| **12-Inch Singles** | | | |
| EACH WORD'S A BEAT OF MY HEART/ARE YOU LONELY TONIGHT | 1983 | Atlantic 551 | 8 |
| MAYBE TOMORROW (LP)/(Live) | 1981 | Atlantic 412 | 8 |
| PICK UP THE PIECES/DEMASIADO CORAZON/LILY'S DADDY | 1983 | Atlantic 598 | 8 |
| YOU BETTER MOVE ON/JUST GIVE ME ONE GOOD REASON | 1981 | Atlantic 402 | 8 |
| **RADIO SHOWS** | | | |
| **Albums** | | | |
| KING BISCUIT FLOWER HOUR (Nov 81) Live concert | 1981 | DIR/ABC (2) | 60-100 |
| *(With the Little River Band)* | | | |
| | | | |
| **MINOR THREAT** | | | |
| **Albums** | | | |
| OUT OF STEP | 1983 | Dischord 10 | 500 |
| *(Test pressing of 50; black silkscreen cover with sheep logo; paste-on back cover; blank labels; plain innersleeve with rubber stamp)* | | | |
| | | | |
| **MINUTEMEN** | | | |
| **Albums** | | | |
| EXCERPTS FROM DOUBLE NICKELS ON THE DIME | 1984 | SST PSST E28 | 25 |
| *(One-sided promo LP with etched B-side and sticker on blank cover)* | | | |
| **RADIO SHOWS** | | | |
| **Albums** | | | |
| SPIN CONCERT | 1986 | Spin Magazine (2) | 100-200 |
| *(Some music and interviews, some live material)* | | | |
| | | | |
| **MIRACLES, THE** | | | |
| *With Smokey Robinson; Other Tamla white promo label 45s $5-25 each depending on year; Other Tamla promo 45s by Smokey Robinson $3 each; Other Tamla white promo label LPs $25-40 each* | | | |
| **12-Inch Singles** | | | |
| SING FOR BROTHERHOOD (same on both sides) | 1976 | Columbia AS 283 | 15 |
| **45s** | | | |
| ALL I WANT IS YOU | 1960 | Chess 1768 | 30 |
| *(White promo label)* | | | |
| BAD GIRL | 1959 | Motown G1 | Unknown |
| *(White promo label, stock copy worth $1,000)* | | | |
| BAD GIRL | 1959 | Motown 2207 | Unknown |
| *(White promo label, stock copy worth $1,000)* | | | |
| BAD GIRL | 1959 | Chess 1734 | 50 |
| *(White promo label)* | | | |
| THE CHRISTMAS SONG  White promo label | 1963 | Tamla 009 | 200 |
| *(Promo-only release)* | | | |
| GOT A JOB  White promo label | 1958 | End 1016 | 100 |
| *(Early End label record promos are very rare)* | | | |
| HOLD ON TO YOUR LOVE  Smokey Robinson | 1985 | Motown 1828 | 10 |
| *(Price includes promo-only picture sleeve)* | | | |
| I CARE ABOUT DETROIT | 1968 | Standard Groove 13090 | 150 |
| *(With no Tamla logo on label)* | | | |
| I CARE ABOUT DETROIT | 1968 | Standard Groove 13090 | 200 |
| *(With Tamla globe logo on label)* | | | |
| I LOVE YOU SO | 1957 | Fury 1002 | 100 |
| *(White promo label)* | | | |
| MONEY  White promo label | 1958 | End 1029 | 50 |
| *(With Smokey Robinson)* | | | |
| SHOP AROUND | 1960 | Tamla 54034 | 50 |
| *(White promo label)* | | | |
| WAY OVER THERE  White promo label | 1960 | Tamla 54028 | 50 |
| *(Same song on both sides)* | | | |
| YOU CAN DEPEND ON ME | 1960 | Tamla 54028 | 400 |
| *(Stock copy worth around $200)* | | | |
| YOU'RE AN ANGEL | 1956 | Cash 1008 | 175 |
| *(White promo label)* | | | |
| **78s** | | | |
| GOT A JOB  White promo label | 1958 | End 1016 | 150 |
| *(A rare 78rpm promo, also an answer song)* | | | |
| **Albums** | | | |
| CHRISTMAS WITH THE MIRACLES | 1963 | Tamla 236 | 500 |
| *(White promo label)* | | | |
| COOKIN' WITH THE MIRACLES | 1962 | Tamla 223 | 600 |
| *(White promo label)* | | | |
| DOIN' MICKEY'S MONKEY | 1965 | Tamla 245 | 100 |
| *(White promo label)* | | | |

| Title | Yr | Label, Number | NM $ |
|-------|-----|---------------|------|
| THE FABULOUS MIRACLES | 1963 | Tamla 238 | 250 |
| *(White promo label)* | | | |
| FAVORITE CHRISTMAS SONGS | 1976 | March of Dimes | 20 |
| *(Various artists, one track by the Miracles)* | | | |
| HI! WE'RE THE MIRACLES | 1961 | Tamla 220 | 750 |
| *(White promo label)* | | | |
| I'LL TRY SOMETHING NEW | 1962 | Tamla 230 | 600 |
| *(White promo label)* | | | |
| THE MIRACLES ON STAGE | 1963 | Tamla 241 | 150 |
| *(White promo label)* | | | |
| SHOP AROUND | 1962 | Tamla 224 | 600 |
| *(White promo label)* | | | |
| **RADIO SHOWS** | | | |
| **Albums** | | | |
| STARTRACK PROFILE (Aug 88) Smokey Robinson | 1988 | Westwood One (2) | 40-75 |
| *(Mostly music and interviews)* | | | |

**MISSING PERSONS**
*Capitol promo 45s $3 each*
**12-Inch Singles**

| | | | |
|-------|-----|---------------|------|
| COLOR IN YOUR LIFE/GO AGAINST THE FLOW | 1986 | Capitol SPRO 9853 | 8 |
| DESTINATION UNKNOWN/WALKING IN L.A. | 1982 | Capitol SPRO 9837/8 | 20 |
| GIVE (Long)/(Short) | 1984 | Capitol SPRO 9081/2 | 15 |
| I CAN'T THINK ABOUT DANCING (Extended)/(LP) | 1986 | Capitol SPRO 9721 | 8 |
| RIGHT NOW (same on both sides) | 1984 | Capitol SPRO 9123 | 10 |
| SURRENDER YOUR HEART (same on both sides) | 1984 | Capitol SPRO 9187 | 6 |
| WINDOWS (same on both sides) | 1982 | Capitol SPRO 9885 | 10 |
| **RADIO SHOWS** | | | |
| **Albums** | | | |
| BBC ROCK HOUR (Oct 82) | 1982 | London Wavelength | 50-100 |
| *(Live concert)* | | | |
| CAPTURED LIVE (Oct 84) Live concert | 1984 | Westwood One (2) | 25-50 |
| *(Rare early concert)* | | | |
| KING BISCUIT FLOWER HOUR (Feb 83) Live concert | 1983 | DIR/ABC (2) | 50-100 |
| *(With Scandal)* | | | |
| KING BISCUIT FLOWER HOUR (Mar 85) Live concert | 1985 | DIR (2) | 30-50 |
| *(With John Hiatt)* | | | |
| SUPERGROUPS (May 83) Live concert | 1983 | DIR (2) | 50-100 |
| *(With Jefferson Starship)* | | | |

**MISSION, THE**
*Mercury promo CD singles $3 each; A&M promo CD singles $2 each*
**RADIO SHOWS**
**Albums**

| | | | |
|-------|-----|---------------|------|
| BBC TRANSCRIPTION DISC  Live concert | 1989 | BBC Transcription | 200-400 |
| *(Very rare live concert)* | | | |

**MR. BIG**
*Atlantic promo 45s $3 each; Atlantic promo CD singles $2-3 each*
**RADIO SHOWS**
**Albums**

| | | | |
|-------|-----|---------------|------|
| IN CONCERT (Nov 92) | 1992 | Westwood One (2) | 25-50 |
| *(With The Electric Boys)* | | | |

**MR. BUNGLE**
**45s**

| | | | |
|-------|-----|---------------|------|
| PLATYPUS/THE LEGENDARY PAPER PROJECT BY THE SECRET CHIEFS TRIO | 1995 | Warner Bros. PRO-S-7829 | 3 |
| *(Bonus 45 with LP "Disco Volante")* | | | |
| SUDDEN DEATH/BALLROOMS OF MARS | 1991 | Warner Bros. PRO-S-5452 | 25 |
| *("Soil Samples #6" on gray vinyl; B-side by the Flaming Lips)* | | | |

**MR. CLEAN**
**45s**

| | | | |
|-------|-----|---------------|------|
| MR. CLEAN | 1964 | Original Sound 40 | 50 |
| *(White promo label)* | | | |

**MR. MISTER**
*RCA Victor blue vinyl promo 45s $6 each; Other RCA Victor promo 45s $2 each; RCA promo CD singles $2 each*
**RADIO SHOWS**
**Albums**

| | | | |
|-------|-----|---------------|------|
| KING BISCUIT FLOWER HOUR (June 86) Live concert | 1986 | DIR (2) | 15-20 |
| *(Repeated)* | | | |
| SUPERSTAR CONCERT (Oct 86) Live concert | 1986 | Westwood One (3) | 20-30 |
| *(With Loverboy)* | | | |
| SUPERSTAR CONCERT (Nov 88) Live concert | 1988 | Westwood One (2) | 20-30 |
| *(With the Hooters)* | | | |
| **Compact Discs** | | | |
| KING BISCUIT FLOWER HOUR (Jan 88) Live concert | 1988 | DIR | 15-25 |
| *(Repeated)* | | | |

**MITCHELL TRIO, THE (CHAD)**
*Later featured John Denver and Michael Johnson; Kapp stereo 33 jukebox singles $8 each*
**45s**

| | | | |
|-------|-----|---------------|------|
| THE JOHN BIRCH SOCIETY | 1963 | Kapp 457 | 10 |
| *(White promo label)* | | | |

| Title | Yr | Label, Number | NM $ |
|---|---|---|---|
| LIZZIE BORDEN | 1962 | Kapp 439 | 10 |
| *(White promo label)* | | | |
| SHE LOVES YOU | 1968 | Reprise | 12 |
| *(White promo label, with John Denver and Michael Johnson)* | | | |
| **7-Inch Extended Plays** | | | |
| MIGHTY DAY ON CAMPUS | 1964 | Kapp 3262 | 12 |
| *(Jukebox LLP issued with a hard cover)* | | | |

## MITCHELL, GUY
**45s**

| Title | Yr | Label, Number | NM $ |
|---|---|---|---|
| HEARTACHES BY THE NUMBER | 196? | Columbia 30476 | 15 |
| *(Stereo jukebox single)* | | | |

## MITCHELL, JONI
*Reprise promo 45s $5 each; Asylum promo 45s $4 each; Geffen promo 45s $3 each; Geffen and Reprise promo CD singles $2-3 each*
**12-Inch Singles**

| Title | Yr | Label, Number | NM $ |
|---|---|---|---|
| GOOD FRIENDS (same on both sides) | 1985 | Geffen PRO-A-2386 | 6 |
| MY SECRET PLACE (Edit Version) (LP Version) | 1988 | Geffen PRO-A-3116 | 6 |
| SHINY TOYS (same on both sides) | 1986 | Geffen PRO-A-2441 | 6 |
| SNAKES AND LADDERS (same on both sides) | 1988 | Geffen PRO-A-3018 | 6 |
| **45s** | | | |
| WHAT'S IT ALL ABOUT (Mar 73) Public service show | 1973 | W.I.A.A. 165 | 18 |
| *(Flip side features Rare Earth)* | | | |
| **Albums** | | | |
| MUSIC AND INTERVIEW | 1985 | Geffen | 20 |
| *(Promo-only LP)* | | | |
| WILD THINGS RUN FAST SAMPLER | 1982 | Geffen PRO-A-1081 | 12 |
| *(Promo-only 4-song EP)* | | | |
| **Compact Discs** | | | |
| SPECIAL CONVERSATION, A | 1988 | Geffen PRO-CD-3076 | 15 |
| *(Promo-only interview)* | | | |
| **RADIO SHOWS** | | | |
| **Albums** | | | |
| BBC TRANSCRIPTION DISC (Jan 73) | 1973 | BBC Transcription (2) | 200-300 |
| *(One of the first worldwide syndicated shows and one of the rarest, with James Taylor)* | | | |
| INNERVIEW  Profile | 1976 | Innerview | 20-35 |
| *(Music and interviews)* | | | |

## MIZELL, HANK
**45s**

| Title | Yr | Label, Number | NM $ |
|---|---|---|---|
| JUNGLE ROCK | 1959 | King 5236 | 50 |
| *(White promo label)* | | | |

## MOBY
**12-Inch Singles**

| Title | Yr | Label, Number | NM $ |
|---|---|---|---|
| EVERYTIME YOU TOUCH ME (8 versions) | 1995 | Elektra 5725 | 25 |
| *(Promo-only two-record set)* | | | |
| HYMN (4 remixes) | 1995 | Elektra 5695 | 8 |

## MOBY GRAPE
*Other Columbia promo 45s $8 each; Reprise promo 45s $5 each; Columbia promo LPs $15-25 each*
**45s**

| Title | Yr | Label, Number | NM $ |
|---|---|---|---|
| 8:05 | 1967 | Columbia 44172 | 12 |
| *(White promo label, stock picture sleeve worth $40)* | | | |
| 8:05 | 1967 | Columbia JZSP 118976 | 25 |
| *(Yellow promo label, promo-only release)* | | | |
| FALL ON YOU | 1967 | Columbia 44170 | 15 |
| *(White promo label, stock picture sleeve worth $40)* | | | |
| HEY GRANDMA | 1967 | Columbia 44174 | 12 |
| *(White promo label, stock picture sleeve worth $40)* | | | |
| OMAHA | 1967 | Columbia 44173 | 12 |
| *(White promo label, stock picture sleeve worth $40)* | | | |
| OMAHA | 1967 | Columbia JZSP 118972 | 25 |
| *(Yellow promo label, promo-only release)* | | | |
| SITTING BY THE WINDOW | 1967 | Columbia 44171 | 12 |
| *(White promo label, stock picture sleeve worth $40)* | | | |

## MODELS, THE
**12-Inch Singles**

| Title | Yr | Label, Number | NM $ |
|---|---|---|---|
| COLD FEVER (LP)/(Extended) | 1986 | Geffen PRO-A-2521 | 8 |
| OUT OF MIND OUT OF SIGHT (long)/(short) | 1985 | Geffen PRO-A-2421 | 8 |

## MODERN ENGLISH
*Sire promo 45s $5 each*
**12-Inch Singles**

| Title | Yr | Label, Number | NM $ |
|---|---|---|---|
| INK AND PAPER (same on both sides) | 1986 | Sire PRO-A-2429 | 10 |
| SOMEONE'S CALLING (Edit)/CARRY ME DOWN (Edit) | 1983 | Sire PRO-A-2035 | 8 |
| **RADIO SHOWS** | | | |
| **Albums** | | | |
| KING BISCUIT FLOWER HOUR (May 83) Live concert | 1983 | DIR/ABC (2) | 40-75 |
| *(Early live concert)* | | | |
| SPIN CONCERT  Live concert | 1985 | BBE Radio | 40-60 |
| *(From Spin magazine)* | | | |

| Title | Yr | Label, Number | NM $ |
|---|---|---|---|
| **MOLLEEN, RONNIE** | | | |
| **45s** | | | |
| ROCKYN' UP | 1960 | King 5365 | 50 |
| *(White promo label)* | | | |
| | | | |
| **MOLLY HATCHET** | | | |
| *Epic promo 45s $4 each* | | | |
| **Albums** | | | |
| MOLLY HATCHET LIVE  2-LP box set | 1978 | Epic AS 528 (2) | 40 |
| *(Promo-only set from two stock copy LPs)* | | | |
| **RADIO SHOWS** | | | |
| **Albums** | | | |
| BBC ROCK HOUR (Feb 81) Live concert | 1981 | London Wavelength | 75-125 |
| *(With Climax Blues Band)* | | | |
| BBC TRANSCRIPTION DISC  Live concert | 1979 | BBC Transcription | 200-300 |
| *(With the Climax Blues Band)* | | | |
| CAPTURED LIVE (Mar 84) Live concert | 1984 | Westwood One (2) | 50-100 |
| *(Rare early concert)* | | | |
| IN CONCERT (Dec 84) Live concert | 1984 | Westwood One (2) | 40-80 |
| *(Repeated)* | | | |
| IN CONCERT (Jan 82) Live concert | 1982 | Westwood One (2) | 50-100 |
| *(Rare early concert)* | | | |
| INNERVIEW (80s) Profile | 1980 | Innerview | 20-30 |
| *(Music and interviews)* | | | |
| KING BISCUIT FLOWER HOUR (Feb 80) Live concert | 1980 | DIR/ABC (2) | 50-100 |
| *(Early live concert)* | | | |
| **Compact Discs** | | | |
| SUPERSTARS (June 96) | 1996 | | 40-75 |
| *(Live concert material)* | | | |
| | | | |
| **MONARCHS, THE** | | | |
| **45s** | | | |
| ANGELS IN THE SKY | 1955 | Wing 90040 | 50 |
| *(White promo label)* | | | |
| | | | |
| **MONDAY MORNING QUARTERBACK, THE** | | | |
| **45s** | | | |
| TWELVE DAYS OF CHRISTMAS (THE GAME PLAN TO BEAT MIAMI) | 1972 | Warner Bros. 7664 | 25 |
| *(White promo label, includes picture sleeve)* | | | |
| | | | |
| **MONEY, EDDIE** | | | |
| *Columbia promo singles (45 or CD) $2 each* | | | |
| **45s** | | | |
| WHAT'S IT ALL ABOUT (Mar 79) Public service show | 1979 | W.I.A.A. 466 | 25 |
| *(Flip side features Olivia Newton John)* | | | |
| **RADIO SHOWS** | | | |
| **Albums** | | | |
| HOT ROCKS (Dec 86) | 1986 | United Stations (2) | 10-15 |
| *(Music and interviews)* | | | |
| KING BISCUIT FLOWER HOUR (July 80) Live concert | 1980 | DIR/ABC (2) | 25-50 |
| *(With Warren Zevon)* | | | |
| KING BISCUIT FLOWER HOUR (Mar 81) Live concert | 1981 | DIR/ABC (2) | 25-40 |
| *(With The Cars)* | | | |
| KING BISCUIT FLOWER HOUR (Feb 84) Live concert | 1984 | DIR/ABC (2) | 10-20 |
| *(Repeated)* | | | |
| NBC SOURCE (Oct 82) | 1982 | NBC Radio (2) | 15-25 |
| *(Music and interviews)* | | | |
| OFF THE RECORD (Feb 91) Profile | 1991 | Westwood One (2) | 10-12 |
| *(Music and interviews, repeated)* | | | |
| SUPERSTAR CONCERT Live concert | 1985 | Westwood One (3) | 10-20 |
| *(Repeated)* | | | |
| WORLD OF ROCK (Apr 89) Profile | 1989 | NBC Radio (2) | 10-12 |
| *(Music and interviews)* | | | |
| **Compact Discs** | | | |
| IN THE STUDIO (Oct 92) Profile of an album | 1992 | Album Network | 10-12 |
| *(Music and interviews)* | | | |
| KING BISCUIT FLOWER HOUR Live concert | 1987 | DIR | 10-15 |
| *(Repeated)* | | | |
| OFF THE RECORD (May 92) Profile | 1992 | Westwood One | 10-15 |
| *(Music and interviews)* | | | |
| SUPERSTAR CONCERT (Sept 92) Live concert | 1992 | Westwood One (2) | 10-15 |
| *(Repeated)* | | | |
| THE STORY OF EDDIE MONEY (Apr 94) Profile | 1994 | Unistar | 10-15 |
| *(Music and interviews)* | | | |
| UP CLOSE Profile | 1989 | Media America (2) | 10-15 |
| *(Mostly music and interviews)* | | | |
| | | | |
| **MONITORS, THE** | | | |
| **45s** | | | |
| TONIGHT'S THE NIGHT | 1957 | Aladdin 3309 | 50 |
| *(White promo label)* | | | |

| **Title** | **Yr** | **Label, Number** | **NM $** |
|---|---|---|---|

**MONKEES, THE**
Includes solo listings of Micky Dolenz, Davy Jones, Michael Nesmith, Peter Tork, Tommy Boyce and Bobby Hart; Chrysalis promo 45s by Micky Dolenz $5 each; Other RCA Victor yellow promo label 45s by Michael Nesmith $6 each; Pacific Arts promo 45s by Michael Nesmith $4 each; Capitol promo 45s by Tommy Boyce $3 each; Chelsea promo 45s by Christopher Cloud (Tommy Boyce) or Bobby Hart $5 each; DCP promo 45s by Bobby Hart $20 each; Warner Bros. promo 45s by Bobby Hart $3 each; Ariola America promo 45s by Bobby Hart $2 each; A&M promo 45s by Boyce and Hart $5 each; Capitol promo 45s by Dolenz, Jones, Boyce and Hart $7 each; Warner Bros. promo 45s by the "New Monkees" (no relation) $2 each; Pacific Arts promo LPs by Michael Nesmith $20 each; A&M promo LPs by Boyce and Hart $15 each

**12-Inch Singles**

| Title | Yr | Label, Number | NM $ |
|---|---|---|---|
| CRUISIN'  Michael Nesmith | 1979 | Pacific Arts 108 | 15 |
| (Promo 12" single) | | | |

**45s**

| Title | Yr | Label, Number | NM $ |
|---|---|---|---|
| ALONG CAME LINDA  Tommy Boyce | 1961 | RCA Victor 7975 | 25 |
| (White promo label) | | | |
| BUDDY HOLLY TRIBUTE  Micky Dolenz | 1974 | Romar (ABC) 715 | 15 |
| (White promo label) | | | |
| CHANGE OF HEART  Tommy Boyce | 1962 | RCA Victor 8126 | 15 |
| (White promo label) | | | |
| CHRISTMAS IS MY TIME OF YEAR  Micky Dolenz, Davy Jones and Peter | 1976 | Christmas 700 | 20 |
| (One-sided promo record) | | | |
| COME HERE, JOANN  Tommy Boyce | 1962 | RCA Victor 8025 | 20 |
| (White promo label) | | | |
| D. W. WASHBURN | 1968 | Colgems 1023 | 30 |
| (Yellow promo label) | | | |
| DAVY JONES - MY FAVORITE MONKEE | 1966 | Colgems 101 | 250 |
| (A promo-only release, flip side is "She Hangs Out") | | | |
| DAYBREAK  Micky Dolenz | 1973 | Romar (ABC) 710 | 10 |
| (White promo label) | | | |
| DAYDREAM BELIEVER | 1967 | Colgems 1012 | 50 |
| (White promo label) | | | |
| DAYDREAM BELIEVER | 1976 | Arista 0201 | 10 |
| (White promo label) | | | |
| DON'T BE AFRAID  Tommy Boyce | 1963 | RCA Victor 8208 | 15 |
| (White promo label) | | | |
| DON'T DO IT  Micky Dolenz | 1967 | Challenge 59353 | 15 |
| (White promo label) | | | |
| DREAM GIRL  Davy Jones | 1965 | Colpix 764 | 25 |
| (White promo label) | | | |
| EASY ON YOU  Micky Dolenz | 1971 | MGM 14309 | 10 |
| (Yellow promo label) | | | |
| GIRL  Davy Jones | 1971 | Bell 45,154 | 25 |
| (White promo label) | | | |
| GIRL FROM CHELSEA  Davy Jones | 1965 | Colpix 789 | 15 |
| (White promo label) | | | |
| GIRL IN THE WINDOW  Bobby Hart | 1960 | Era 3039 | 25 |
| (White promo label) | | | |
| GIRL OF MY DREAMS  Robert Luke Harshman | 1959 | Guyden 2022 | 30 |
| (Bobby Hart, white promo label) | | | |
| GOOD CLEAN FUN | 1969 | Colgems 5005 | 25 |
| (Yellow promo label) | | | |
| HUFF PUFF  Micky Dolenz | 1967 | Challenge 59372 | 15 |
| (White promo label) | | | |
| I DON'T HAVE TO WORRY  Tommy Boyce | 1965 | MGM 13400 | 12 |
| (Yellow promo label) | | | |
| I REALLY LOVE YOU  Davy Jones | 1971 | Bell 45,136 | 15 |
| (White promo label) | | | |
| I'LL BELIEVE IN YOU  Davy Jones | 1971 | Bell 45,154 | 10 |
| (White promo label) | | | |
| I'LL REMEMBER CAROL  Tommy Boyce | 1962 | RCA Victor 8074 | 18 |
| (White promo label) | | | |
| I'M A BELIEVER | 1966 | Colgems 1002 | 50 |
| (White promo label) | | | |
| IN CASE THE WIND SHOULD BLOW  Tommy Boyce | 1966 | A&M 826 | 12 |
| (White promo label) | | | |
| LAST TRAIN TO CLARKSVILLE | 1966 | Colgems 1001 | 75 |
| (White promo label) | | | |
| LET'S GO WHERE THE ACTION IS  Tommy Boyce | 1965 | Colpix 794 | 18 |
| (White promo label) | | | |
| LISTEN TO THE BAND | 1969 | Colgems 5004 | 25 |
| (Yellow promo label) | | | |
| A LITTLE BIT ME, A LITTLE BIT YOU | 1967 | Colgems 1003 | Unknown |
| (Promo release is uncertain; was not released as a stock copy with this number) | | | |
| A LITTLE BIT ME, A LITTLE BIT YOU | 1967 | Colgems 1004 | 50 |
| (White promo label) | | | |
| LITTLE RED ROOSTER  Michael Nesmith | 1970 | RCA Victor 9853 | 10 |
| (Yellow promo label) | | | |
| LITTLE SUZY SOMETHING  Tommy Boyce | 1965 | MGM 13429 | 12 |
| (Yellow promo label) | | | |
| LOVE WHATCHA' DOIN' TO ME  Robert Harshman | 1960 | Radio 122 | 50 |
| (Bobby Hart, white promo label) | | | |
| A LOVER'S PRAYER  Micky Dolenz | 1972 | MGM 14395 | 10 |
| (Yellow promo label) | | | |
| OH MY MY | 1970 | Colgems 5011 | 30 |
| (Yellow promo label) | | | |
| PLEASANT VALLEY SUNDAY | 1967 | Colgems 1007 | 50 |
| (White promo label) | | | |
| PORPOISE SONG | 1968 | Colgems 1031 | 30 |
| (Yellow promo label) | | | |

| Title | Yr | Label, Number | NM $ |
|---|---|---|---|
| RAINY JANE  Davy Jones | 1971 | Bell 45,111 | 12 |
| *(White promo label)* | | | |
| RUBBERENE  Davy Jones | 1973 | MGM 14524 | 15 |
| *(Yellow promo label)* | | | |
| SHAKE IT  The Frosted Shake Five | 1969 | Borden's RTF 101 | 25 |
| *(Actually Tommy Boyce and Bobby Hart; blue label milk promotion 45)* | | | |
| SUNDAY, THE DAY BEFORE MONDAY Tommy Boyce | 1966 | A&M 809 | 10 |
| *(White promo label)* | | | |
| TAPIOCA TUNDRA  The Wichita Train Whistle | 1968 | Dot 17152 | 10 |
| *(Michael Nesmith involvement; white promo label)* | | | |
| TEAR DROP CITY | 1969 | Colgems 5000 | 25 |
| *(Yellow promo label)* | | | |
| TEAR DROP CITY | 1969 | Colgems SP-45-191 | 50 |
| *(Promo-only pre-issue release)* | | | |
| TEXAS MORNING Michael Nesmith | 1971 | RCA Victor SP-45-263 | 30 |
| *(Promo-only pre-issue release)* | | | |
| THAT WAS THEN, NOW IS NOW  Mickey Dolenz and Peter Tork | 1986 | Arista 9505 | 10 |
| *(Black promo label, includes picture sleeve)* | | | |
| THE NEW RECRUIT  Michael Blessing | 1965 | Colpix 787 | 100 |
| *(Michael Nesmith, white promo label)* | | | |
| UNTIL IT'S TIME FOR YOU TO GO  Michael Blessing | 1965 | Colpix 792 | 75 |
| *(Michael Nesmith, white promo label)* | | | |
| VALLERI | 1968 | Colgems 1019 | 40 |
| *(Yellow promo label)* | | | |
| WHAT ARE WE GOING TO DO  Davy Jones | 1965 | Colpix 784 | 20 |
| *(White promo label)* | | | |
| YOU'RE A LADY  Davy Jones | 1972 | MGM 14458 | 15 |
| *(Yellow promo label)* | | | |
| **7-Inch Extended Plays** | | | |
| MONKEES  Jukebox LLP | 1967 | Colgems 101 | 300 |
| *(Issued with a hard cover and title strips)* | | | |
| MONKEES (60s) Cardboard record | 196? | Colgems 1 to 5 | 25 |
| *(Four songs, Photo of group on front)* | | | |
| MONKEES (60s) Cardboard record | 196? | Colgems 1 to 5 | 25 |
| *(Four songs, Monkees logo on front)* | | | |
| MORE OF THE MONKEES  Jukebox LLP | 1967 | Colgems 102 | 300 |
| *(Issued with a hard cover and title strips)* | | | |
| **Albums** | | | |
| DAVID JONES  Davy Jones | 1965 | Colpix 493 | 40 |
| *(White promo label)* | | | |
| DAVY JONES | 1971 | Bell 6067 | 25 |
| *(White promo label)* | | | |
| MICHAEL NESMITH RADIO SPECIAL | 1979 | Pacific Arts | 40 |
| *(Music and interviews)* | | | |
| MORE OF THE MONKEES | 1967 | RCA Victor 102 | 500 |
| *(Promo-only clear vinyl for radio stations)* | | | |
| **Compact Discs** | | | |
| HEART AND SOUL | 1987 | Rhino PRCD 1 | 10 |
| *(Promo only for radio of new material for new LP)* | | | |
| SAMPLER | 1994 | Rhino PRCD 7080 | 30 |
| *(Promo-only collection of tracks from the box set, comes in guitar-shaped box)* | | | |
| **RADIO SHOWS** | | | |
| **Albums** | | | |
| HOT ROCKS (July 86) | 1986 | United Stations (2) | 60-100 |
| *(Music and interviews)* | | | |
| ROCK ROLL & REMEMBER (June 86) Various artists | 1986 | United Stations (4) | 20-40 |
| *(Dick Clark interviews Micky and Davy throughout the 4-hour show, which is dedicated to the Monkees)* | | | |
| THE IN SOUND (Sept 67) Various artists | 1967 | U.S. Army | 20-40 |
| *(One of the 5-minute shows features the Monkees, music and interviews)* | | | |
| **MONO MEN** | | | |
| **45s** | | | |
| I DON'T CARE/JEZEBEL | 1990 | Estrus ES 74 | 30 |
| *(Promos on black vinyl, no picture sleeve)* | | | |
| **MONOTONES, THE** | | | |
| **45s** | | | |
| BOOK OF LOVE | 1957 | Argo 5290 | 75 |
| *(White promo label)* | | | |
| READING THE BOOK OF LOVE | 1960 | Hull 735 | 60 |
| *(White promo label)* | | | |
| **MONROE, BILL** | | | |
| **Albums** | | | |
| KNEE DEEP IN BLUEGRASS | 1959 | Decca 8731 | 45 |
| *(Pink promo label)* | | | |
| **MONROE, MARILYN** | | | |
| **45s** | | | |
| RIVER OF NO RETURN | 1954 | RCA Victor 5745 | 50 |
| *(White promo label)* | | | |
| **78s** | | | |
| RIVER OF NO RETURN  White promo label | 1954 | RCA Victor DJ 78 | 200 |
| *(Promo only, has photo of Monroe on label)* | | | |
| RIVER OF NO RETURN  White promo label | 1954 | RCA Victor 5745 | 100 |
| *(Regular RCA promo label release)* | | | |

| Title | Yr | Label, Number | NM $ |
|---|---|---|---|
| **Albums** | | | |
| MARILYN | 1959 | 20th Fox 5000 | 150 |
| *(White promo label)* | | | |
| | | | |
| **MONROE, VAUGHN** | | | |
| **78s** | | | |
| JOLLY OLD MAN IN THE RED SUIT | 1950 | RCA Victor DJ 783 | 30 |
| *(Green colored flexible disc)* | | | |
| | | | |
| **MONSTER MAGNET** | | | |
| **45s** | | | |
| CAGE AROUND THE SUN/SUPERJUDGE | 1993 | A&M MM 1 | 10 |
| *(Sky blue vinyl)* | | | |
| MURDER/TRACTOR | 1990 | Primo Scree SCREE 2 | 25 |
| | | | |
| **MONTANA SLIM** | | | |
| *Also recorded as Wilf Carter* | | | |
| **Albums** | | | |
| I'M RAGGED BUT I'M RIGHT | 1959 | Decca 8917 | 75 |
| *(Pink promo label)* | | | |
| THE DYNAMITE TRAIL | 1960 | Decca 4092 | 75 |
| *(Pink promo label)* | | | |
| | | | |
| **MONTGOMERY, WES** | | | |
| **45s** | | | |
| BUMPIN' (Part 1)/(Part 2) | 1966 | Verve 10441 | 10 |
| BUMPIN' ON SUNSET (Part 1)/(Part 2) | 1966 | Verve 10442 | 10 |
| GOIN' OUT OF MY HEAD/TEQUILA | 1966 | Verve 10440 | 10 |
| LOVE THEME FROM "THE SANDPIPER"/QUIET THING | 1966 | Verve 10444 | 10 |
| PHOENIX LOVE THEME/CARAVAN | 1966 | Verve 10443 | 10 |
| | | | |
| **MONTGOMERYS, THE** | | | |
| **45s** | | | |
| PROMISE OF LOVE | 1961 | Amy 883 | 125 |
| *(Blue promo label)* | | | |
| | | | |
| **MONTY PYTHON** | | | |
| **Albums** | | | |
| MONTY PYTHON'S CONTRACTURAL OBLIGATION SAMPLER | 1980 | Arista SP-101 | 20 |
| *(One side is censored, the other is uncensored)* | | | |
| **Compact Discs** | | | |
| ALWAYS LOOK ON THE BRIGHT SIDE OF LIFE | 1991 | Virgin PRCD 4160 | 10 |
| *(Promo-only CD single, reissue of the famous track)* | | | |
| CD SAMPLER THINGY - LUST FOR GLORY | 1994 | Virgin DPRO-14236 | 25 |
| *(Promo-only sampler)* | | | |
| | | | |
| **MONYAKA** | | | |
| **12-Inch Singles** | | | |
| GOT THE BEAT FOR CHRISTMAS | 1985 | A&M SP-12156 | 8 |

**MOODY BLUES, THE**
*Includes listings of Justin Hayward and John Lodge and the Graeme Edge Band; Other London brownish/orange promo label 45s $6 each; London white promo label 45s $3 each; Other Deram promo label 45s $5 each; Threshold promo 45s $4 each; Other Polydor promo 45s $3 each; Any label promos by Justin Hayward and/or John Lodge $3 each; London and Threshold promo 45s by Graeme Edge Band $3 each; Polydor 12" promo singles $8 each*

| Title | Yr | Label, Number | NM $ |
|---|---|---|---|
| **12-Inch Singles** | | | |
| BLUE WORLD | 1983 | Threshold 237 | 10 |
| *(12" single)* | | | |
| GEMINI DREAM | 1981 | Threshold 174 | 12 |
| *(12" single)* | | | |
| THE OTHER SIDE OF LIFE (Edit) (LP Version) | 1986 | Polydor 431 | 8 |
| RUNNING OUT OF LOVE (same on both sides) | 1986 | Polydor 449 | 8 |
| SITTING AT THE WHEEL | 1983 | Threshold 241 | 10 |
| *(12" single)* | | | |
| **45s** | | | |
| EV'RY DAY | 1965 | London 9799 | 10 |
| *(Brownish promo label)* | | | |
| FROM THE BOTTOM OF MY HEART | 1965 | London 9764 | 15 |
| *(Brownish promo label)* | | | |
| GO NOW! | 1965 | London 9726 | 30 |
| *(Brownish promo label)* | | | |
| ISN'T LIFE STRANGE | 1972 | Threshold 67009 | 10 |
| *(Mono/stereo versions)* | | | |
| NIGHTS IN WHITE SATIN | 1968 | Deram 85023 | 15 |
| *(Brown and white promo label, with a star on the pick side)* | | | |
| QUESTION | 1970 | Threshold 67004 | 10 |
| *(Mono/stereo versions)* | | | |
| STOP! | 1966 | London 9810 | 10 |
| *(Brownish promo label)* | | | |
| THE OTHER SIDE OF LIFE | 1986 | Polydor 885 201 | 10 |
| *(Red label promo, blue vinyl)* | | | |
| **Albums** | | | |
| THE JUSTIN HAYWARD RADIO SPECIAL | 1983 | Threshold | 25 |
| *(Music and interviews)* | | | |
| OCTAVE | 1978 | London 708 | 30 |
| *(Promo-only picture disc)* | | | |

| Title | Yr | Label, Number | NM $ |
|---|---|---|---|
| OCTAVE | 1978 | London 708 | 30 |
| *(Blue marbled vinyl, promo only)* | | | |
| RAY THOMAS INTERVIEW  Ray Thomas | 1975 | Threshold 102 | 40 |
| *(Promo-only interview record)* | | | |
| SPECIAL INTERVIEW KIT | 1971 | Threshold 100 | 150 |
| *(For radio stations only, with script)* | | | |
| **Compact Discs** | | | |
| HIGHLIGHTS FROM TIME TRAVELER | 1994 | Polydor/A&M | 20 |
| *(Promo-only sampler)* | | | |
| **RADIO SHOWS** | | | |
| **Albums** | | | |
| BBC ROCK HOUR (Oct 83) | 1983 | London Wavelength | 100-150 |
| *(Live concert material)* | | | |
| BBC TRANSCRIPTION DISC  Live concert | 1987 | BBC Transcription | 400-500 |
| *(The ultimate rare Moody Blues concert)* | | | |
| CLASSIC ROCK SERIES | 1990 | Unistar (3) | 50-75 |
| *(Music and interviews)* | | | |
| DAYS OF FUTURE PAST | 1988 | Radio International (2) | 30-50 |
| *(Music and interviews, issued in picture cover)* | | | |
| HOT ROCKS | 1986 | United Stations (2) | 20-40 |
| *(Music and interviews)* | | | |
| INNERVIEW (80s) | 198? | Innerview | 15-25 |
| *(Music and interviews)* | | | |
| KING BISCUIT FLOWER HOUR (Feb 82) | 1982 | DIR (2) | 75-125 |
| *(Live concert, repeated in 1982)* | | | |
| KING BISCUIT FLOWER HOUR (Sept 86) | 1986 | DIR (2) | 50-85 |
| *(Live concert)* | | | |
| LEGENDS OF ROCK (Aug 87) Profile | 1987 | NBC Radio (4) | 25-50 |
| *(Music and interviews, two shows, parts 1 and 2)* | | | |
| LEGENDS OF ROCK (Aug 87) Profile | 1987 | NBC Radio (2) | 15-25 |
| *(Music and interviews, repeated)* | | | |
| NBC SOURCE (Apr 84) | 1984 | NBC Radio (3) | 150-225 |
| *(Rare live concert)* | | | |
| OFF THE RECORD (Aug 88) Profile | 1988 | Westwood One (2) | 25-35 |
| *(Music and interviews)* | | | |
| PIONEERS IN ROCK (Jan 86) Profile | 1986 | DIR (2) | 25-50 |
| *(Music and interviews)* | | | |
| ROCK AROUND THE WORLD | 1976 | (2) | 75-125 |
| *(Two shows, parts one and two, music and interviews)* | | | |
| ROCK CLOCK | 1987 | DIR (2) | 25-40 |
| *(Also Alice Cooper and John Waite, music and interviews)* | | | |
| SOURCE SPECIAL (Nov 83) | 1983 | NBC Radio (3) | 30-60 |
| *(Mostly music and interviews)* | | | |
| SUPERGROUPS | 1979 | ABC Radio (3) | 400-600 |
| *(Live concert issued in a picture box)* | | | |
| SUPERGROUPS (Oct 81) | 1981 | ABC Radio (3) | 100-200 |
| *(Live Mello Yello concert)* | | | |
| SUPERSTAR CONCERT (Mar 86) | 1986 | Westwood One (3) | 25-50 |
| *(Live concert)* | | | |
| SUPERSTAR CONCERT (Sept 88) | 1988 | Westwood One (3) | 25-60 |
| *(Live concert)* | | | |
| TBS SYNDICATION | 1983 | TBS | 300-500 |
| *(Rare Canadian radio show)* | | | |
| **Compact Discs** | | | |
| BBC CLASSIC TRACKS (Sept 91) | 1991 | Westwood One | 20-35 |
| *(Various live tracks)* | | | |
| IN CONCERT (Jan 93) | 1993 | Westwood One (2) | 40-80 |
| *(Live concert)* | | | |
| IN THE STUDIO (Sept 94) Profile of an album | 1994 | Album Network (2) | 20-35 |
| *(Music and interviews, parts 1 and 2)* | | | |
| IN THE STUDIO (Sept 94) Profile of an album | 1994 | Album Network | 15-25 |
| *(Music and interviews)* | | | |
| KING BISCUIT FLOWER HOUR (Aug 89) | 1989 | DIR | 50-100 |
| *(Live concert)* | | | |
| LIVE AT THE WHISKEY (Aug 93) | 1993 | Entertainment Radio | 100-200 |
| *(Rare live concert)* | | | |
| MASTERS OF ROCK (Apr 89) | 1989 | (2) | 20-30 |
| *(Music and interviews)* | | | |
| SUPERSTAR CONCERT (Nov 94) | 1994 | Westwood One (2) | 50-100 |
| *(Live concert)* | | | |
| SUPERSTAR CONCERT (Sept 93) | 1993 | Westwood One (2) | 35-75 |
| *(Live concert)* | | | |
| UP CLOSE Profile | 1988 | Media America (2) | 25-50 |
| *(Mostly music and interviews)* | | | |

**MOON, KEITH**
*Of the Who; Track promo label 45s $5 each*
**RADIO SHOWS**
**Albums**

| Title | Yr | Label, Number | NM $ |
|---|---|---|---|
| ROCK & ROLL NEVER FORGETS (May 82) | 1982 | Westwood One (5) | 40-85 |
| *(Music and interviews)* | | | |

**MOONEY, ART**
**45s**

| Title | Yr | Label, Number | NM $ |
|---|---|---|---|
| BIP BAM | 1954 | MGM 11871 | 12 |
| *(Yellow promo label)* | | | |

| Title | Yr | Label, Number | NM $ |
|---|---|---|---|
| GIANT | 1956 | MGM 12320 | 12 |
| *(Yellow promo label)* | | | |
| IS THERE A TEENAGER IN THE HOUSE | 1956 | MGM 12190 | 12 |
| *(Yellow promo label)* | | | |
| THEME FROM REBEL WITHOUT A CAUSE | 1956 | MGM 12312 | 12 |
| *(Promo single, stock picture sleeve adds $30)* | | | |
| TUTTI-FRUTTI | 1955 | MGM 12165 | 12 |
| *(Yellow promo label)* | | | |

**MOONGLOWS, THE**
*Other Chess promo 45s $50 each; RCA Victor promo 45s $8 each*
**45s**

| | | | |
|---|---|---|---|
| MOST OF ALL | 1954 | Chess 1589 | 55 |
| *(Blue/white promo label)* | | | |
| SINCERELY | 1954 | Chess 1581 | 75 |
| *(Blue/white promo label)* | | | |

**MOONLION**
**45s**

| | | | |
|---|---|---|---|
| THE LITTLE DRUMMER BOY (Airplay Version)/(Disco Version) | 1975 | P.I.P. 6513 | 4 |

**MOORE, GARY**
*Virgin promo CD singles $3-5 each*
**RADIO SHOWS**
**Albums**

| | | | |
|---|---|---|---|
| BBC ROCK HOUR (Apr 84) Live concert | 1984 | London Wavelength | 100-175 |
| *(Rare early concert)* | | | |
| BBC TRANSCRIPTION DISC  Live concert | 1984 | BBC Transcription | 300-400 |
| *(Very rare concert)* | | | |

**MOORE, HARV**
**45s**

| | | | |
|---|---|---|---|
| INTERVIEW OF THE FAB FOUR | 1964 | American Arts 20 | 250 |
| *(Very rare promo cut-in of all Beatles songs)* | | | |

**MOORE, IAN**
*Capricorn promo CD singles $2 each*
**RADIO SHOWS**
**Compact Discs**

| | | | |
|---|---|---|---|
| IN CONCERT (June 94) Live concert | 1994 | Westwood One | 20-40 |
| *(Repeated in Mar 95)* | | | |

**MOORE, MELBA**
**12-Inch Singles**

| | | | |
|---|---|---|---|
| FALLING (Single Version) (LP Version) | 1986 | Capitol SPRO-9858/9980 | 8 |
| I CAN'T BELIEVE (IT'S OVER) (Extended Version) (Edit Version) | 1985 | Capitol SPRO-9500 | 8 |
| LOVE THE ONE I'M WITH (3 versions) | 1986 | Capitol SPRO-9776 | 6 |
| LOVE THE ONE I'M WITH (5:44) (same on both sides) | 1986 | Capitol SPRO-9717 | 6 |
| LOVE'S COMIN' AT YA (7" Version) (LP Version) | 1981 | EMI America SPRO-9817 | 8 |
| MISS THING (same on both sides) | 1979 | Epic AS 660 | 8 |
| READ MY LIPS (Remix) (Extended Version) | 1985 | Capitol SPRO-9381/2 | 6 |
| READ MY LIPS (Special Mix) (Single Version) | 1985 | Capitol SPRO-9335/6 | 6 |
| WHEN YOU LOVE ME LIKE THIS (Club Mix) (Monster Groove Mix) | 1985 | Capitol SPRO-9446/7 | 8 |

**MOORE, SCOTTY**
*Elvis Presley's guitar player*
**Albums**

| | | | |
|---|---|---|---|
| GUITAR THAT CHANGED THE WORLD | 1964 | Epic 24103 | 55 |
| *(White promo label)* | | | |

**MORELLS, THE**
**RADIO SHOWS**
**Albums**

| | | | |
|---|---|---|---|
| LONDON WAVELENGTH (Feb 84) | 1984 | London Wavelength | 40-75 |
| *(Live concert)* | | | |

**MORGAN, LORRIE**
*RCA promo 45s $3 each; RCA and BNA promo CD singles $2-3 each*
**RADIO SHOWS**
**Compact Discs**

| | | | |
|---|---|---|---|
| 90'S COUNTRY (Aug 95) | 1995 | | 20-40 |
| *(Music and interviews)* | | | |

**MORISSETTE, ALANIS**
**Compact Discs**

| | | | |
|---|---|---|---|
| HAND IN MY POCKET | 1995 | Maverick | 10 |
| *(Promo-only CD single)* | | | |
| HEAD OVER FEET | 1996 | Maverick | 10 |
| *(Promo-only CD single)* | | | |
| IRONIC | 1996 | Maverick PRO-CD-8035 | 8 |
| *(Promo CD single)* | | | |
| JAGGED LITTLE PILL | 1995 | Maverick PRO-CD-7744-R | 15 |
| *(Radio-ready full-length promo LP with the profanities deleted)* | | | |
| UNINVITED | 1998 | Maverick | 15 |
| *(Promo-only CD single)* | | | |

| Title | Yr | Label, Number | NM $ |
|---|---|---|---|
| YOU LEARN | 1996 | Maverick | 10 |
| *(Promo CD single)* | | | |
| YOU OUGHTA KNOW | 1995 | Maverick PRO-CD-7732-R | 10 |
| *(Version with one edit)* | | | |
| YOU OUGHTA KNOW | 1995 | Maverick PRO-CD-7732-R | 10 |
| *(Version with two edits)* | | | |
| YOU OUGHTA KNOW | 1996 | Maverick | 20 |
| *(Live Grammy Version)* | | | |
| **RADIO SHOWS** | | | |
| **Compact Discs** | | | |
| OFF THE RECORD (Dec 95) | 1995 | Westwood One | 15-30 |
| *(Music and interviews)* | | | |

## MORMON TABERNACLE CHOIR
**45s**

| Title | Yr | Label, Number | NM $ |
|---|---|---|---|
| JOY TO THE WORLD/I HEARD THE BELLS | 1965 | Columbia JZSP 111909/10 | 10 |
| *(Green vinyl)* | | | |
| JOY TO THE WORLD/I HEARD THE BELLS | 1965 | Columbia JZSP 111909/10 | 6 |
| *(Black vinyl, yellow label)* | | | |
| JOY TO THE WORLD/I HEARD THE BELLS | 1965 | Columbia JZSP 111909/10 | 6 |
| *(Black vinyl, white label)* | | | |

## MORRIS, GARY
*Warner Bros. and RCA Victor promo singles $2 each; Universal and Capitol promo CD singles $2 each*
**RADIO SHOWS**
**Albums**

| Title | Yr | Label, Number | NM $ |
|---|---|---|---|
| THE SILVER EAGLE (80s) Live concert | 198? | DIR (3) | 20-35 |
| *(With Con Hunley)* | | | |
| WESTWOOD ONE PRESENTS (Apr 90) | 1990 | Westwood One | 10-20 |
| *(Live concert)* | | | |

## MORRISON, VAN
*Bang promo 45s $8 each; Warner Bros. promo 45s $5 each; Warner Bros. promo 12" singles $8 each; Mercury promo CD singles $3-5 each More at Them*
**12-Inch Singles**

| Title | Yr | Label, Number | NM $ |
|---|---|---|---|
| GOT TO GO BACK (same on both sides) | 1986 | Mercury 447 | 6 |
| SUMMERTIME IN ENGLAND (Edit)/HAUNTS | 1980 | Warner Bros. PRO-A-911 | 10 |
| WAVELENGTH (6:07) (3:57) | 1978 | Warner Bros. PRO-A-755 | 15 |
| **Albums** | | | |
| AN EVENING WITH VAN MORRISON | 1989 | Warner Bros. (2) | 100 |
| *(Very rare promo-only release)* | | | |
| LIVE AT THE ROXY | 1979 | Warner Bros. WBMS-102 | 50 |
| *(Part of the Warner Bros. Music Show series)* | | | |
| **Compact Discs** | | | |
| COLLECTOR'S ITEM | 1994 | Polydor | 12 |
| *(Promo-only sampler)* | | | |
| IN CELEBRATION OF VAN MORRISON'S MERCURY MUSIC | 1988 | Mercury | 80 |
| *(6-CD promo-only collection in special box)* | | | |
| VAN LIVE AT THE POINT | 1996 | Verve SACD 1234 | 20 |
| *(Promo-only sampler)* | | | |
| **RADIO SHOWS** | | | |
| **Albums** | | | |
| BBC TRANSCRIPTION DISC Live concert | 1987 | BBC Transcription | 400-600 |
| *(The ultimate Morrison concert)* | | | |
| PIONEERS IN ROCK (Jan 86) | 1986 | (2) | 40-75 |
| *(Mostly music and interviews, some live)* | | | |
| RETRO ROCK (Nov 81) Live concert | 1981 | Clayton Webster | 100-150 |
| *(Another very rare concert)* | | | |
| ROCK STARS (Mar 89) Profile | 1989 | United Stations (2) | 20-40 |
| *(Music and interviews)* | | | |
| **Compact Discs** | | | |
| BBC CLASSIC TRACKS (June 91) | 1991 | BBC Radio | 15-30 |
| *(Various live tracks)* | | | |
| BBC CLASSIC TRACKS (June 91) | 1991 | Westwood One | 25-50 |
| *(Various live tracks, repeated)* | | | |
| BBC CLASSIC TRACKS (May 93) | 1993 | Westwood One | 15-30 |
| *(Various live tracks)* | | | |
| KING BISCUIT FLOWER HOUR Live concert | 1989 | DIR | 25-50 |
| *(Repeated in 1990, 1992)* | | | |
| ROCK STARS (Mar 89) Profile | 1989 | Radio Today (2) | 25-50 |
| *(Music and interviews)* | | | |
| ST. PATRICK'S DAY SPECIAL, AN EVENING WITH VAN MORRISON (Mar 90) | 1990 | (2) | 50-75 |
| *(Mostly music and interviews)* | | | |
| TURN UP YOUR RADIO (Mar 89) | 1989 | (2) | 50-75 |
| *(Very rare live concert)* | | | |

## MORRISSEY
*More at The Smiths; Other promo CD singles $6 each*
**Compact Discs**

| Title | Yr | Label, Number | NM $ |
|---|---|---|---|
| EVERYDAY IS LIKE SUNDAY | 1988 | Sire PRO-CD-3112 | 10 |
| *(Promo CD single)* | | | |
| MORE YOU IGNORE ME, THE CLOSER I GET | 1994 | Warner Bros. PRO-CD-6624 | 10 |
| *(Promo CD single)* | | | |
| NOW MY HEART IS FULL, AN INTROSPECTIVE 1984-1994 | 1994 | Warner Bros. PRO-CD-6778 | 35 |
| *(Promo-only career retrospective)* | | | |

| Title | Yr | Label, Number | NM $ |
|---|---|---|---|
| **RADIO SHOWS** | | | |
| **Compact Discs** | | | |
| IN CONCERT - NU ROCK (Sept 95) | 1995 | | 75-100 |
| *(Live concert material)* | | | |
| IN CONCERT - NU ROCK (Sept 95) | 1995 | Westwood One | 75-100 |
| *(Live concert material)* | | | |
| | | | |
| **MORROCCOS, THE** | | | |
| **45s** | | | |
| PARDON MY TEARS | 1956 | United 188 | 100 |
| *(White promo label)* | | | |
| SAD, SAD YEARS | 1957 | United 207 | 85 |
| *(White promo label)* | | | |
| SOMEWHERE OVER THE RAINBOW | 1956 | United 193 | 50 |
| *(White promo label)* | | | |
| WHAT IS A TEENAGER'S PRAYER | 1957 | United 204 | 50 |
| *(White promo label)* | | | |
| | | | |
| **MORSE, ELLA MAE** | | | |
| **45s** | | | |
| COW COW BOOGIE | 1972 | Capitol 102 | 20 |
| *(With cardboard picture cover, special 30th Anniversary promo)* | | | |
| | | | |
| **MOSS, ROY** | | | |
| **45s** | | | |
| CORRINNE, CORINNA | 1956 | Mercury 70858 | 40 |
| *(White promo label)* | | | |
| WIGGLE WALKIN' BABY | 1956 | Fascination 1002 | 100 |
| *(Green promo label)* | | | |
| YOU'RE MY BIG BABY NOW | 1956 | Mercury 70770 | 50 |
| *(White promo label)* | | | |
| | | | |
| **MOTELS, THE** | | | |
| *Capitol promo 45s $4 each* | | | |
| **12-Inch Singles** | | | |
| REMEMBER THE NIGHTS (same on both sides) | 1983 | Capitol SPRO 9048 | 7 |
| SHAME (LP) (Extended Mix) | 1985 | Capitol SPRO 9436 | 6 |
| SHOCK (same on both sides) | 1985 | Capitol SPRO 9515 | 6 |
| TOTAL CONTROL/YOUR PLACE OR MINE | 1979 | Capitol SPRO 9267 | 10 |
| **Albums** | | | |
| ALL FOUR ONE | 1982 | Capitol ST-12177 | 15 |
| *(Promo-only high-grade vinyl pressing with different front cover)* | | | |
| POLICY   Martha Davis | 1987 | Capitol | 20 |
| *(Promo-only release)* | | | |
| **RADIO SHOWS** | | | |
| OFF THE RECORD (80s) Profile | 198? | Westwood One (2) | 10-15 |
| *(With Martha Davis, music and interviews, repeated)* | | | |
| SPOTLIGHT SPECIAL Box set | 1983 | ABC Radio (2) | 25-50 |
| *(Music and interviews)* | | | |
| SUPERSTAR CONCERT (June 86) Live concert | 1986 | Westwood One (3) | 30-50 |
| *(With The Fixx)* | | | |
| **Albums** | | | |
| BBC ROCK HOUR (May 82) Live concert | 1982 | London Wavelength | 50-100 |
| *(Rare early concert)* | | | |
| BBC ROCK HOUR (Sept 80) | 1980 | London Wavelength | 20-35 |
| *(Music and interviews)* | | | |
| INNERVIEW (80s)  Features Martha Davis | 198? | Innerview | 15-25 |
| *(Music and interviews)* | | | |
| LONDON WAVELENGTH (May 82) | 1982 | London Wavelength | 25-50 |
| *(Mostly music and interviews)* | | | |
| | | | |
| **MOTHER LOVE BONE** | | | |
| **12-Inch Singles** | | | |
| SHANGRI-LA | 1990 | Mercury PRO-900 | 20 |
| *(Promo-only single)* | | | |
| | | | |
| **MOTLEY CRUE** | | | |
| *Elektra promo 45s $4 each; Other Elektra promo 12" singles $8 each; Elektra promo CD singles $3-5 each* | | | |
| **Compact Discs** | | | |
| CRUCIAL CRUE | 1989 | Elektra PR 8116 | 50 |
| *(Promo-only sampler)* | | | |
| IN-STORE PLAY SAMPLER | 1995 | Elektra PR 8955 | 15 |
| *(Promo-only sampler)* | | | |
| QUATERNARY | 1994 | Elektra 61664 | 30 |
| *(Rare sampler, only available as a bonus by mail order after buying the "Motley Crue" LP)* | | | |
| **RADIO SHOWS** | | | |
| **Albums** | | | |
| HIGH VOLTAGE (May 89) Various artists | 1989 | Westwood One (2) | 30-50 |
| *(Live concert segment features Motley Crüe)* | | | |
| IN CONCERT  Live concert | 1986 | Westwood One (2) | 75-150 |
| *(With Black Sabbath)* | | | |
| IN CONCERT  Live concert | 1990 | Westwood One (2) | 75-125 |
| *(With Guns N' Roses)* | | | |
| IN CONCERT (Nov 84) Live concert | 1984 | Westwood One (2) | 50-100 |
| *(With Black & Blue)* | | | |

| Title | Yr | Label, Number | NM $ |
|---|---|---|---|
| INNERVIEW (80s) Profile | 198? | Innerview | 20-30 |
| *(Music and interviews)* | | | |
| KING BISCUIT FLOWER HOUR  Live concert | 1983 | DIR/ABC (2) | 50-100 |
| *(With Black Sabbath)* | | | |
| KING BISCUIT FLOWER HOUR (Dec 84) Live concert | 1984 | DIR/ABC (2) | 175-250 |
| *(With Kiss)* | | | |
| KING BISCUIT FLOWER HOUR (July 84) Live concert | 1984 | DIR/ABC (2) | 100-200 |
| *(Repeated)* | | | |
| METALSHOP (80s) Various artists | 198? | MJI Productions | 20-30 |
| *(Many shows featured Motley Crüe as the featured band during the live segment of the show)* | | | |
| OFF THE RECORD (Nov 89) Profile | 1989 | Westwood One (2) | 15-25 |
| *(Music and interviews)* | | | |
| **Compact Discs** | | | |
| IN CONCERT (Aug 93) Live concert | 1993 | Westwood One | 40-75 |
| *(Repeated)* | | | |

## MOTORHEAD
*Promo CD singles $3-5 each*
**RADIO SHOWS**
**Albums**

| | | | |
|---|---|---|---|
| IN CONCERT (Nov 83) Live concert | 1983 | Westwood One (2) | 30-50 |
| *(With Krokus)* | | | |

## MOTT THE HOOPLE
*Other Columbia promo 45s $5 each; Atlantic white promo label LPs $15 each Also see Ian Hunter*
**45s**

| | | | |
|---|---|---|---|
| ALL THE YOUNG DUDES | 1972 | Columbia 45673 | 10 |
| *(White promo label, stock picture sleeve worth $20)* | | | |

**RADIO SHOWS**
**Albums**

| | | | |
|---|---|---|---|
| BBC TRANSCRIPTION DISC  Live concert | 1980 | BBC Transcription | 300-400 |
| *(Includes Ian Hunter)* | | | |
| KING BISCUIT FLOWER HOUR (May 82) Live concert | 1982 | DIR/ABC (2) | 75-125 |
| *(With Prism)* | | | |

**Compact Discs**

| | | | |
|---|---|---|---|
| KING BISCUIT FLOWER HOUR (July 88) Live concert | 1988 | DIR | 40-75 |
| *(With Argent)* | | | |

## MOULD, BOB
**12-Inch Singles**

| | | | |
|---|---|---|---|
| SEE A LITTLE LIGHT (same on both sides) | 1989 | Virgin 2685 | 6 |
| WISHING WELL/IF YOU'RE TRUE + 4 live tracks | 1989 | Virgin 2929 | 25 |

## MOVE, THE
*Evolved into Electric Light Orchestra; Deram, A&M and Capitol promo 45s $12 each; United Artists promo 45s $4 each; A&M promo LPs $15 each, 2LP sets $25 each*
**45s**

| | | | |
|---|---|---|---|
| CHINATOWN/DOWN BY THE BAY | 1971 | MGM 14332 | 20 |
| *(Evidently not released as stock copy)* | | | |
| **7-Inch Extended Plays** | | | |
| THE MOVE | 1969 | A&M | 50 |
| *(Promo-only release)* | | | |

## MOYET, ALISON
*Columbia promo 45s $3 each; Columbia promo picture sleeves $4 each; Columbia promo CD singles $2 each*
**12-Inch Singles**

| | | | |
|---|---|---|---|
| FOR YOU ONLY (same on both sides) | 1985 | Columbia CAS 2177 | 8 |
| HOODOO (4 versions) | 1991 | Columbia CAS 4116 | 8 |
| INVISIBLE (3:56)/(5:55) | 1984 | Columbia AS 2029 | 8 |
| IS THIS LOVE (LP) (Remix) | 1986 | Columbia CAS 2679 | 6 |
| LOVE RESURRECTION (LP) (7") | 1984 | Columbia AS 2103 | 8 |

**RADIO SHOWS**
**Compact Discs**

| | | | |
|---|---|---|---|
| ON THE EDGE (Dec 92) Music and interviews | 1992 | Westwood One | 15-25 |
| *(With Shamen and the Gin Blossoms)* | | | |

## MUDHONEY
**45s**

| | | | |
|---|---|---|---|
| BLINDING SUN/KING SANDBOX | 1993 | Reprise PRO-S-6025 | 15 |
| *(Promo-only on 1970s-style Reprise brown label)* | | | |
| SUCK YOU DRY/DECEPTION PASS | 1992 | Reprise PRO-S-5740 | 15 |

## MULL, MARTIN
**45s**

| | | | |
|---|---|---|---|
| SANTA DOESN'T COP OUT ON DOPE | 1972 | Capricorn PRO 554 | 12 |
| *(Promo-only release; later came out on stock label with different number)* | | | |

## MULLICAN, MOON
*Also recorded as Moon Mullins; Other King promo 45s, 4000 series, $8 each; King promo 45s, 5000 series, $4 each; Musicor promo 45s $4 each*
**45s**

| | | | |
|---|---|---|---|
| CUSH CUSH KY-YAY | 1959 | Decca 30962 | 15 |
| *(Pink promo label)* | | | |
| JENNY LEE | 1958 | Coral 61994 | 20 |
| *(Blue promo label)* | | | |
| ROCK AND ROLL MR. BULLFROG  White promo label | 1957 | King 4915 | 20 |
| *(Includes artist bio on label)* | | | |

| Title | Yr | Label, Number | NM $ |
|---|---|---|---|
| ROCK AND ROLL RHYTHM  White promo label | 1957 | Profile 4002 | 40 |
| *(By Mickey Hawks with Moon Mullins)* | | | |
| SEVEN NIGHTS TO ROCK | 1957 | King 5172 | 15 |
| *(White promo label)* | | | |
| **78s** | | | |
| I'LL SAIL MY SHIP ALONE | 1950 | King 830 | 40 |
| *(White promo label)* | | | |
| **Albums** | | | |
| MOON OVER MULLICAN | 1958 | Coral 57235 | 200 |
| *(Blue promo label)* | | | |

**MULLINS, DEE**
**45s**

| Title | Yr | Label, Number | NM $ |
|---|---|---|---|
| REMEMBER BETHLEHEM (same on both sides) | 1970 | Plantation 68 | 5 |
| *(Green vinyl)* | | | |

**MUMFORD, GENE**
**45s**

| Title | Yr | Label, Number | NM $ |
|---|---|---|---|
| PLEASE GIVE ME ONE MORE CHANCE | 1960 | Columbia 41233 | 100 |
| *(With insert and "Introduces" paper sleeve)* | | | |

**MURPHEY, MICHAEL MARTIN**
*A&M promo 45s $3 each; Epic promo 45s $3 each; EMI promo 45s $2 each*
**45s**

| Title | Yr | Label, Number | NM $ |
|---|---|---|---|
| COLORADO CHRISTMAS/THE COWBOY'S CHRISTMAS BALL | 1987 | Warner Bros PRO-S-2869 | 6 |
| *(B-side by Nitty Gritty Dirt Band)* | | | |
| WHAT'S IT ALL ABOUT (Apr 76) Public service show | 1976 | W.I.A.A. 313 | 18 |
| *(Flip side is B. B. King)* | | | |
| **7-Inch Extended Plays** | | | |
| HEALING SPRINGS | 197? | Playback AS 69 | 20 |
| *(Promo-only sampler)* | | | |
| **RADIO SHOWS** | | | |
| **Albums** | | | |
| AMERICAN EAGLE (Nov 86) Live concert | 1986 | DIR | 15-25 |
| *(As a country singer)* | | | |
| COUNTRY SESSIONS (80s) Live concert | 198? | NBC Radio | 25-40 |
| *(As a country singer)* | | | |
| LIVE AT GILLEY'S (Sept 88) Live concert | 1988 | Westwood One | 15-25 |
| *(As a country singer)* | | | |
| WESTWOOD ONE PRESENTS (Dec 89) Live concert | 1989 | Westwood One | 15-25 |
| *(As a country singer)* | | | |

**MURPHY, JIMMY**
**45s**

| Title | Yr | Label, Number | NM $ |
|---|---|---|---|
| BABOON BOOGIE | 1956 | Columbia 21569 | 40 |
| *(White promo label)* | | | |
| HERE KITTY KITTY | 1956 | Columbia 21486 | 40 |
| *(White promo label)* | | | |
| SIXTEEN TONS OF ROCK & ROLL | 1956 | Columbia 21534 | 50 |
| *(White promo label)* | | | |

**MURPHY, PETER**
*RCA promo CD singles $2-3 each*
**RADIO SHOWS**
**Compact Discs**

| Title | Yr | Label, Number | NM $ |
|---|---|---|---|
| IN CONCERT-NU ROCK (Oct 93) | 1993 | Westwood One | 25-40 |
| *(Live concert)* | | | |

**MURRAY, ANNE**
*Capitol promo 45s $2 each*
**45s**

| Title | Yr | Label, Number | NM $ |
|---|---|---|---|
| CHRISTMAS MEDLEY | 1981 | Capitol SPRO-9723 | 10 |
| *(White promo label, this medley otherwise unreleased)* | | | |
| WHAT'S IT ALL ABOUT (Aug 75) Public service show | 1975 | W.I.A.A. 281 | 25 |
| *(Flip side features The Who)* | | | |
| WHAT'S IT ALL ABOUT (Sept 76) Public service show | 1976 | W.I.A.A. 333 | 18 |
| *(Flip side features Elton John)* | | | |
| WHAT'S IT ALL ABOUT (Dec 78) Public service show | 1978 | W.I.A.A. 454 | 10 |
| *(Flip side features Gene Cotton)* | | | |
| **RADIO SHOWS** | | | |
| **Albums** | | | |
| STARTRACK PROFILE (May 85) | 1985 | Westwood One (2) | 15-25 |
| *(Music and interviews)* | | | |

**MUSICAL YOUTH**
**12-Inch Singles**

| Title | Yr | Label, Number | NM $ |
|---|---|---|---|
| HEARTBREAKER (short)/(long) | 1983 | MCA L33-1108 | 10 |
| SHE'S TROUBLE/INCOMMUNICADO | 1983 | MCA L33-1147 | 10 |

**MY BLOODY VALENTINE**
**12-Inch Singles**

| Title | Yr | Label, Number | NM $ |
|---|---|---|---|
| SOON/GLIDER/DON'T ASK WHY/OFF YOUR FACE | 1990 | Sire PRO-A-4512 | 8 |

| Title | Yr | Label, Number | NM $ |
|---|---|---|---|
| **MYRICK, GARY, AND THE FIGURES** | | | |
| **12-Inch Singles** | | | |
| GUITAR, TALK, LOVE & DRUMS (Extended Special Version)/ | 1983 | Epic AS 1694 | 10 |
| (Short Special Version) | | | |
| *(Etched cartoon on B-side)* | | | |
| HEARTS POUND (LIKE A RHYTHM MACHINE) (same on both sides) | 1985 | Geffen PRO-A-2403 | 8 |
| WHEN ANGELS KISS/I STAND FOR LOVE | 1985 | Geffen PRO-A-2349 | 8 |
| **45s** | | | |
| LIVING IN A MOVIE/MY GIRL (IT'S SIMPLE) | 1981 | Epic AE7 1303 | 5 |
| **7-Inch Extended Plays** | | | |
| SHE TALKS IN STEREO/EVER SINCE THE WORLD BEGAN// | 1980 | Epic AE7 1207 | 8 |
| DEEP IN THE HEARTLAND/THE PARTY | | | |
| **Albums** | | | |
| LIVE SAMPLER | 1982 | Epic AS 1389 | 16 |
| *Four live tracks, including one unreleased song* | | | |
| TALKS IN STEREO | 1981 | Epic AS 912 | 40 |
| *Side one has studio tracks, side two has live versions of songs on side one* | | | |

# N

| Title | Yr | Label, Number | NM $ |
|---|---|---|---|
| **N'DOUR, YOUSSOU** | | | |
| **Compact Discs** | | | |
| EYES OPEN | 1992 | Epic ESK 4585 | 40 |
| *(Promo-only sampler)* | | | |
| **NABORS, JIM** | | | |
| **45s** | | | |
| AVE MARIA/HOW GREAT THOU ART | 1971 | Columbia AE 1028 | 6 |
| **NAKED EYES** | | | |
| **45s** | | | |
| ALWAYS SOMETHING THERE TO REMIND ME (Remix) | 1983 | EMI America SPRO 9923 | 8 |
| **NAPOLEON XIV** | | | |
| *Other Warner Bros.promo 45s $8 each; Other label promo 45s $6 each Jerry Samuels* | | | |
| **45s** | | | |
| THEY'RE COMING TO TAKE ME AWAY, HA-HAAA! | 1966 | Warner Bros. 5831 | 12 |
| *(White promo label)* | | | |
| **Albums** | | | |
| THEY'RE COMING TO TAKE ME AWAY, HA-HAAA! | 1966 | Warner Bros. 1661 | 100 |
| *(White promo label)* | | | |
| **NASH, GRAHAM** | | | |
| *More at Crosby, Stills, Nash & Young; Also see The Hollies* | | | |
| **Albums** | | | |
| SOLO IN '86 | 1986 | Atlantic PR 2806 | 15 |
| *(Promo-only sampler)* | | | |
| **NATIONAL LAMPOON** | | | |
| **45s** | | | |
| KUNG FU CHRISTMAS | 1975 | Epic AS 193 | 20 |
| *(Promo only, mono/stereo versions, with picture sleeve)* | | | |
| **7-Inch Extended Plays** | | | |
| HISTORY OF THE BEATLES | 1975 | Epic AE7 1095 | 20 |
| *(Seven-track promo)* | | | |
| **NAZARETH** | | | |
| *Other A&M promo 45s $3 each* | | | |
| **45s** | | | |
| LOVE HURTS | 1975 | | 10 |
| *(White label test pressing)* | | | |
| THIS FLIGHT TONIGHT | 1973 | A&M 1936 | 10 |
| *(White promo label)* | | | |
| WHAT'S IT ALL ABOUT (Oct 76) Public service show | 1976 | W.I.A.A. 339 | 18 |
| *(Flip is England Dan and John Ford Coley)* | | | |
| **RADIO SHOWS** | | | |
| **Albums** | | | |
| BBC ROCK HOUR (Aug 82) Live concert | 1982 | London Wavelength | 60-100 |
| *(Rare early concert)* | | | |
| BBC TRANSCRIPTION DISC  Live concert | 1973 | BBC Transcription | 200-300 |
| *(With Smith-Heckstall)* | | | |
| IN CONCERT (Oct 82) Live concert | 1982 | Westwood One (2) | 75-125 |
| *(With Toronto)* | | | |
| LONDON WAVELENGTH (Aug 82) | 1982 | London Wavelength | 30-60 |
| *(Music and interviews)* | | | |
| NBC SOURCE (Jan 84) Live concert | 1984 | NBC Radio (3) | 75-125 |
| *(Rare early concert)* | | | |

| Title | Yr | Label, Number | NM $ |
|-------|-----|---------------|------|

## NAZZ
*Featuring Todd Rundgren; Other SGC promo 45s $8 each*

**45s**

| | | | |
|-------|-----|---------------|------|
| HELLO IT'S ME | 1968 | SGC 001 | 35 |
| *(Mono, one-sided, promo label)* | | | |
| HELLO IT'S ME | 1968 | SGC 001 | 50 |
| *(Stereo, one-sided, promo label)* | | | |
| HELLO IT'S ME | 1968 | SGC 001 | 15 |
| *(Long and short versions)* | | | |
| HELLO IT'S ME | 1968 | SGC 001 | 18 |
| *(Flip side is same as the stock copy, "Open My Eyes")* | | | |
| NOT WRONG LONG | 1969 | SGC 006 | 15 |
| *(Flip side is "Under the Ice")* | | | |

**Albums**

| | | | |
|-------|-----|---------------|------|
| NAZZ NAZZ | 1969 | SGC 5002 | 80 |
| *(Promo-only mono pressing on red vinyl)* | | | |

## NDEGE'OCELLO, ME'SHELL
**12-Inch Singles**

| | | | |
|-------|-----|---------------|------|
| DRED LOC (same on both sides) | 1993 | Maverick PRO-A-6485 | 8 |
| OUTSIDE YOUR DOOR (3 versions) | 1993 | Maverick PRO-A-6852 | 8 |

**Albums**

| | | | |
|-------|-----|---------------|------|
| PLANTATION LULLABIES | 1993 | Maverick PRO-A-6622 | 20 |
| *(Promo-only U.S. vinyl release)* | | | |

**Compact Discs**

| | | | |
|-------|-----|---------------|------|
| IF THAT'S YOUR BOYFRIEND | 1993 | Maverick PRO-CD-6785 | 8 |
| *(Promo CD single)* | | | |
| LEVITICUS: FAGGOT | 1996 | Maverick | 8 |
| *(Promo CD single)* | | | |
| OUTSIDE YOUR DOOR | 1993 | Maverick PRO-CD-6852 | 8 |
| *(Promo CD single)* | | | |
| WHO IS HE AND WHAT IS HE TO YOU | 1996 | Maverick | 8 |
| *(Promo CD single)* | | | |
| WILD NIGHT  With John Mellencamp | 1994 | Mercury CDP 1230 | 8 |
| *(Promo CD single)* | | | |

## NED'S ATOMIC DUSTBIN
**12-Inch Singles**

| | | | |
|-------|-----|---------------|------|
| SATURDAY NIGHT (one-sided) | 1993 | Chaos CAS 5239 | 10 |

## NELSON, RICK(Y)
*Decca pink promo label 45s $9 each; Decca blue promo label 45s $8 each; Decca yellow promo label 45s $5 each; MCA promo 45s $3 each; Capitol promo 45s $4 each; Epic promo 45s (record only) $5 each; Decca promo LPs $20 each; United Artists promo 2LP sets $20 each; MCA promo LPs $15 each; Epic promo LPs $12 each*

**45s**

| | | | |
|-------|-----|---------------|------|
| BE-BOP BABY | 1957 | Imperial 5463 | 75 |
| *(Cream colored promo label)* | | | |
| BELIEVE WHAT YOU SAY | 1958 | Imperial 5503 | 50 |
| *(Cream colored promo label)* | | | |
| CONGRATULATIONS | 1964 | Imperial 66017 | 20 |
| *(White promo label)* | | | |
| DREAM LOVER | 1986 | Epic 06066 | 10 |
| *(Price includes promo picture sleeve)* | | | |
| I WANNA BE LOVED | 1959 | Imperial 5614 | 35 |
| *(Cream colored promo label)* | | | |
| I'M NOT AFRAID | 1960 | Imperial 5685 | 25 |
| *(Cream colored promo label)* | | | |
| IT'S UP TO YOU | 1962 | Imperial 5901 | 15 |
| *(White promo label)* | | | |
| LONESOME TOWN | 1958 | Imperial 5545 | 50 |
| *(Cream colored promo label)* | | | |
| A LONG VACATION | 1963 | Imperial 5958 | 15 |
| *(White promo label)* | | | |
| LUCKY STAR | 1964 | Imperial 66039 | 18 |
| *(White promo label)* | | | |
| NEVER BE ANYONE ELSE BUT YOU | 1959 | Imperial 5565 | 40 |
| *(Cream colored promo label)* | | | |
| OLD ENOUGH TO LOVE | 1963 | Imperial 5935 | 15 |
| *(White promo label)* | | | |
| RICK NELSON  Five stereo 33 1/3 rpm singles | 1963 | Decca 34194/5/6/7/8 | 250 |
| *(Or $50 each)* | | | |
| STOOD UP | 1957 | Imperial 5483 | 60 |
| *(Cream colored promo label)* | | | |
| SWEETER THAN YOU | 1959 | Imperial 5595 | 40 |
| *(Cream colored promo label)* | | | |
| TEEN AGE IDOL | 1962 | Imperial 5864 | 20 |
| *(White promo label)* | | | |
| THAT'S ALL | 1963 | Imperial 5910 | 15 |
| *(White promo label)* | | | |
| TIME AFTER TIME | 1963 | Imperial 5985 | 15 |
| *(White promo label)* | | | |
| TODAY'S TEARDROPS | 1964 | Imperial 66004 | 20 |
| *(White promo label on the new style label)* | | | |
| TRAVELIN' MAN | 1961 | Imperial 5741 | 25 |
| *(White promo label)* | | | |
| TRAVELIN' MAN | 1961 | Imperial 5741 | 750 |
| *(Black label, red vinyl)* | | | |

| Title | Yr | Label, Number | NM $ |
|---|---|---|---|
| A WONDER LIKE YOU | 1961 | Imperial 5770 | 25 |
| *(White promo label)* | | | |
| YOU ARE THE ONLY ONE | 1960 | Imperial 5707 | 25 |
| *(White promo label)* | | | |
| YOUNG EMOTIONS | 1960 | Imperial 5663 | 30 |
| *(Cream colored promo label)* | | | |
| YOUNG WORLD | 1962 | Imperial 5805 | 20 |
| *(White promo label)* | | | |
| **7-Inch Extended Plays** | | | |
| BEST ALWAYS  Jukebox LLP | 1966 | Decca 34319 | 75 |
| *(Issued with a hard cover)* | | | |
| RICKY | 1957 | Imperial 153 | 250 |
| *(Cream colored promo label)* | | | |
| RICKY | 1957 | Imperial 154 | 250 |
| *(Cream colored promo label)* | | | |
| RICKY | 1957 | Imperial 155 | 250 |
| *(Cream colored promo label)* | | | |
| RICKY NELSON | 1958 | Imperial 156 | 200 |
| *(Cream colored promo label)* | | | |
| RICKY NELSON | 1958 | Imperial 157 | 200 |
| *(Cream colored promo label)* | | | |
| RICKY NELSON | 1958 | Imperial 158 | 200 |
| *(Cream colored promo label)* | | | |
| RICKY SINGS AGAIN | 1959 | Imperial 159 | 175 |
| *(Cream colored promo label)* | | | |
| RICKY SINGS AGAIN | 1959 | Imperial 160 | 175 |
| *(Cream colored promo label)* | | | |
| RICKY SINGS AGAIN | 1959 | Imperial 161 | 175 |
| *(Cream colored promo label)* | | | |
| RICKY SINGS SPIRITUALS | 1960 | Imperial 165 | 200 |
| *(White promo label)* | | | |
| SONGS BY RICKY | 1959 | Imperial 162 | 150 |
| *(Cream colored promo label)* | | | |
| SONGS BY RICKY | 1959 | Imperial 163 | 150 |
| *(Cream colored promo label)* | | | |
| SONGS BY RICKY | 1959 | Imperial 164 | 150 |
| *(Cream colored promo label)* | | | |
| **Albums** | | | |
| ALBUM SEVEN BY RICK | 1962 | Imperial 9167 | 75 |
| *(White promo label)* | | | |
| BEST SELLERS | 1963 | Imperial 9218 | 60 |
| *(White promo label)* | | | |
| IT'S UP TO YOU | 1963 | Imperial 9223 | 50 |
| *(White promo label)* | | | |
| A LONG VACATION | 1963 | Imperial 9244 | 40 |
| *(White promo label)* | | | |
| MILLION SELLERS | 1963 | Imperial 9232 | 50 |
| *(White promo label)* | | | |
| MORE SONGS BY RICKY | 1960 | Imperial 12059 | 1,000 |
| *(White promo label, blue vinyl)* | | | |
| ON THE FLIP SIDE  With Joanie Sommers | 1967 | Decca 4836 | 25 |
| *(Promo label soundtrack)* | | | |
| RICK IS 21 | 1961 | Imperial 9152 | 75 |
| *(White promo label)* | | | |
| RICK NELSON SINGS FOR YOU | 1964 | Imperial 9251 | 40 |
| *(White promo label)* | | | |

## NELSON, WILLIE

*Includes duets with Waylon Jennings; Other United Artists promo 45s $5 each; Other Columbia colored vinyl promo 45s $8 each; Columbia or Epic white promo label solo or duet 45s $2 each; Columbia red promo label 45s $3 each; Columbia promo picture sleeves $2 each; Other RCA Victor colored vinyl promo 45s $8 each; RCA Victor promo 45s $2 each; Atlantic promo 45s $2 each; Columbia promo CD singles $3-5 each*

| Title | Yr | Label, Number | NM $ |
|---|---|---|---|
| **45s** | | | |
| THE DOCK OF THE BAY  Waylon and Willie | 1982 | RCA Victor 13319 | 12 |
| *(Green label, red vinyl)* | | | |
| JUST TO SATISFY YOU  Waylon and Willie | 1982 | RCA Victor 13073 | 12 |
| *(Silver label, blue vinyl)* | | | |
| MOUNTAIN DEW | 1981 | RCA Victor 12328 | 15 |
| *(Light blue label, red vinyl)* | | | |
| NIGHT LIFE | 1963 | United Artists 641 | 12 |
| *(White promo label)* | | | |
| PRETTY PAPER | 1979 | Columbia AE7 1183 | 25 |
| *(White promo label, red vinyl, only promo has colored vinyl)* | | | |
| WHAT'S IT ALL ABOUT (Apr 77) Public service show | 1977 | W.I.A.A. 366 | 15 |
| *(Flip side features the Manhattans)* | | | |
| WHITE CHRISTMAS | 1979 | Columbia AE7 1182 | 25 |
| *(White promo label, green vinyl, only promo has colored vinyl)* | | | |
| WHITE CHRISTMAS | 1983 | Columbia AE7 1775 | 10 |
| *(Promo only, black vinyl, "Pretty Paper" is B-side)* | | | |
| **7-Inch Extended Plays** | | | |
| VOTE '84  Various artists | 1984 | Ad Council 884 | 25 |
| *(10 public service commercials, one by Kristofferson and Nelson)* | | | |
| WILLIE AND FRIENDS  Demo for a radio show | 1985 | Creative 7-24 | 10 |
| *(7" record, small center hole)* | | | |
| **Albums** | | | |
| ALWAYS ON MY MIND | 1982 | Columbia 38258 | 30 |
| *(Picture disc also available as a stock copy)* | | | |

| Title | Yr | Label, Number | NM $ |
|---|---|---|---|
| AND THEN I WROTE | 1962 | Liberty 3238 | 50 |
| *(White promo label)* | | | |
| HERE'S WILLIE NELSON | 1963 | Liberty 3308 | 40 |
| *(White promo label)* | | | |
| STARDUST | 1978 | Columbia 35305 | 40 |
| *(Promo-only picture disc)* | | | |
| WILLIE NELSON AND FAMILY | 1983 | Columbia 171010 | 40 |
| *(Promo-only picture disc)* | | | |
| **RADIO SHOWS** | | | |
| **Albums** | | | |
| STORIES BEHIND THE SONGS (Nov 90) | 1990 | | 20-40 |
| *(Music and interviews)* | | | |
| WESTWOOD ONE PRESENTS (May 89) Live concert | 1989 | Westwood One | 25-50 |
| *(With Dolly Parton and Kenny Rogers)* | | | |
| WILLIE NELSON & MERLE HAGGARD (June 82) | 1982 | Mutual Radio (3) | 20-40 |
| *(Box set, music and interviews)* | | | |
| WILLIE NELSON SILVER ANNIVERSARY (Dec 86) | 1986 | United Stations (3) | 20-40 |
| *(Box set, music and interviews)* | | | |

## NERVOUS EATERS
**45s**

| Title | Yr | Label, Number | NM $ |
|---|---|---|---|
| LORETTA (mono/stereo) | 1980 | Elektra 47072 | 15 |
| NO SLEEP TONITE (mono/stereo) | 1980 | Elektra 47025 | 15 |

## NEVILLE BROTHERS, THE
**RADIO SHOWS**
**Compact Discs**

| Title | Yr | Label, Number | NM $ |
|---|---|---|---|
| LIVE FROM HOUSE OF BLUES (Feb 96) | 1996 | | 20-40 |
| *(Live concert material, with Dr. John and Rockin' Dopsie Jr.)* | | | |
| **Reel-to-Reel Tapes** | | | |
| A&M RECORDS | 1994 | A&M | 150-200 |
| *(Live concert material on two 10-inch reels)* | | | |

## NEW CHRISTY MINSTRELS, THE
*Includes listings of Randy Sparks, Barry McGuire and the New Society; Other Columbia promo 45s $2 each; RCA Victor promo 45s by the New Society $8 each; Columbia white promo label black vinyl 45s by Randy Sparks $5 each; New Horizon promo singles by Barry McGuire $6 each; Dunhill white promo label 45s by Barry McGuire $8 each; Dunhill white promo label LPs by Barry McGuire $20 each; Columbia white promo label LPs each $10 each*
**45s**

| Title | Yr | Label, Number | NM $ |
|---|---|---|---|
| CHIM CHIM CHEREE | 1965 | Columbia 43215 | 15 |
| *(Red promo label, yellow vinyl)* | | | |
| GREEN GREEN | 1963 | Columbia 42805 | 25 |
| *(White promo label, green vinyl)* | | | |
| JULIE KNOWS  Randy Sparks | 1964 | Columbia 43138 | 15 |
| *(White promo label, blue vinyl)* | | | |
| THE LOVIN' KIND  The New Society | 1965 | American Gramophone GR-3 | 25 |
| *(Promo record and picture sleeve)* | | | |
| RAMBLIN'  Five stereo jukebox singles | 1966 | Columbia 8855 | 25 |
| *(Or $5 each)* | | | |
| WE NEED A LITTLE CHRISTMAS/SLEIGH RIDE | 1966 | Columbia JZSP 116417/8 | 12 |
| *(Yellow label)* | | | |
| WE NEED A LITTLE CHRISTMAS/SLEIGH RIDE | 1966 | Columbia JZSP 116417/8 | 12 |
| *(White label)* | | | |
| **7-Inch Extended Plays** | | | |
| MERRY CHRISTMAS | 1966 | Columbia 8896 | 25 |
| *(Jukebox LLP issued with a hard cover)* | | | |

## NEW COLONY SIX
*Mercury promo 45s $6 each*
**Albums**

| Title | Yr | Label, Number | NM $ |
|---|---|---|---|
| BREAKTHROUGH | 1966 | Sentar 101 | 125 |
| *(Multi-colored promo label)* | | | |

## NEW EDITION
**45s**

| Title | Yr | Label, Number | NM $ |
|---|---|---|---|
| IT'S CHRISTMAS (ALL OVER THE WORLD) (same on both sides) | 1985 | MCA 52745 | 6 |
| *(Promo on red vinyl)* | | | |
| TEARS ON MY PILLOW | 1986 | MCA 17282 | 12 |
| *(Special promo release, with Little Anthony)* | | | |

## NEW ORDER
*Other Qwest promo 45s $4 each; Other Qwest promo CD singles $3 each*
**12-Inch Singles**

| Title | Yr | Label, Number | NM $ |
|---|---|---|---|
| BLUE MONDAY '88 (Club Mix)/ | 1988 | Qwest PRO-A-3037 | 10 |
| TOUCHED BY THE HAND OF GOD (REMIX) (Dub) | | | |
| THE PERFECT KISS (edit)/(live) | 1985 | Qwest PRO-A-2342 | 10 |
| RUINED IN A DAY (6 versions) | 1993 | Qwest PRO-A-6318 | 20 |
| SPOOKY (6 versions) | 1993 | Qwest PRO-A-6729 | 15 |
| TRUE FAITH (LP Version)/(Edit) | 1987 | Qwest PRO-A-2784 | 10 |
| WORLD (THE PRICE OF LOVE) (8 versions) | 1993 | Qwest PRO-A-6276 | 25 |
| *(Promo-only two-record set)* | | | |
| **45s** | | | |
| BIZARRE LOVE TRIANGLE (same on both sides) | 1987 | Qwest 28421 | 5 |
| FINE TIME (7" Edit)/ROUND AND ROUND (Edit) | 1989 | Qwest PRO-S-3464 | 8 |

| Title | Yr | Label, Number | NM $ |
|---|---|---|---|
| **Compact Discs** | | | |
| BLUE MONDAY 1988 | 1988 | Qwest PRO-CD-3053 | 25 |
| *(A very early, and quite rare, promo CD single)* | | | |
| IN ORDER | 1993 | Qwest PRO-CD-5970 | 20 |
| *(Promo-only sampler)* | | | |
| **RADIO SHOWS** | | | |
| **Albums** | | | |
| BBC TRANSCRIPTION DISC Live concert | 198? | BBC Transcription | 300-400 |
| *(Rare live concert)* | | | |
| BBC TRANSCRIPTION DISC Live concert | 1987 | BBC Transcription | 300-400 |
| *(Rare radio series)* | | | |
| **Compact Discs** | | | |
| IN CONCERT-NU ROCK (Feb 94) Live concert | 1994 | Westwood One | 40-80 |
| *(All new live material)* | | | |
| ON THE EDGE (May 93) Music and interviews | 1993 | Westwood One | 20-30 |
| *(With Porno for Pyros)* | | | |
| ON THE EDGE (May 94) Music and interviews | 1994 | Westwood One | 15-30 |
| *(With Frente)* | | | |

**NEW RIDERS OF THE PURPLE SAGE**
*Columbia promo 45s $4 each Features Jerry Garcia on early tracks*

| | | | |
|---|---|---|---|
| **RADIO SHOWS** | | | |
| **Compact Discs** | | | |
| KING BISCUIT FLOWER HOUR (Oct 88) Live concert | 1988 | DIR | 25-40 |
| *(With the Marshall Tucker Band)* | | | |

**NEW SEEKERS, THE**

| | | | |
|---|---|---|---|
| **45s** | | | |
| BUY THE WORLD A COKE// | 1971 | Coca-Cola (no #) | 12 |
| BRING A LITTLE SUNSHINE/IT'S THE REAL THING | | | |
| *(All three songs are Coca-Coca jingles; the A-side became "I'd Like to Teach the World to Sing")* | | | |

**NEW VAUDEVILLE BAND**

| | | | |
|---|---|---|---|
| **7-Inch Extended Plays** | | | |
| WINCHESTER CATHEDRAL  Jukebox LLP | 1966 | Fontana 752 | 15 |
| *(With picture cover)* | | | |

**NEW WORLD SYMPHONY**

| | | | |
|---|---|---|---|
| **45s** | | | |
| WONDER WOMAN | 1977 | Shady Brook 45-033 | 15 |
| *(With promo-only picture sleeve; theme from the TV series)* | | | |

**NEW YORK DOLLS**
*Featuring David Johansen;  Mercury promo 45s $8 each*

| | | | |
|---|---|---|---|
| **45s** | | | |
| PERSONALITY CRISIS (mono/stereo) | 1973 | Mercury DJ-387 | 15 |
| TRASH (mono/stereo) | 1973 | Mercury DJ-378 | 15 |
| **Albums** | | | |
| NEW YORK DOLLS | 1973 | Mercury 675 | 50 |
| *(White promo label with dolls)* | | | |
| NEW YORK DOLLS LIVE | 1978 | Mercury DJ | 50 |
| *(Live concert promo release only)* | | | |
| TOO MUCH, TOO SOON | 1974 | Mercury 1001 | 40 |
| *(White promo label with dolls)* | | | |

**NEWMAN, RANDY**
*Other Reprise and Warner Bros. promo 45s $3 each; Other Warner Bros. promo 12" singles $8 each*

| | | | |
|---|---|---|---|
| **12-Inch Singles** | | | |
| POLITICAL SCIENCE/SPYS | 1979 | Warner Bros. PRO-A-860 | 8 |
| **45s** | | | |
| GOLDEN GRIDIRON BOY | 1962 | Dot 16411 | 50 |
| *(White promo label)* | | | |
| I THINK IT'S GOING TO RAIN TODAY | 1968 | Reprise 0692 | 15 |
| *(The 45rpm version, white promo label)* | | | |
| LAST NIGHT I HAD A DREAM | 1968 | Reprise 0771 | 75 |
| *(White promo label, promo-only release)* | | | |
| **78s** | | | |
| I THINK IT'S GOING TO RAIN TODAY | 1968 | Reprise 0284 | 40 |
| *(Yes, it's a 10" promo 78rpm record!)* | | | |
| **Albums** | | | |
| RANDY NEWMAN LIVE | 1970 | Reprise | 25 |
| *(Promo-only release)* | | | |

**NEWTON, JUICE**
*Capitol promo singles with PRO- prefix $5 each; Other Capitol promo 45s $2 each; RCA Victor promo 45s $2 each; RCA colored vinyl promo 45s $5 each*

| | | | |
|---|---|---|---|
| **45s** | | | |
| FIRST TIME LOVE | 1987 | RCA 5170 | 10 |
| *(Includes promo-only picture sleeve)* | | | |
| IT'S A HEARTACHE | 1978 | | 10 |
| *(Test pressing, white label, country cover version of the Bonnie Tyler hit)* | | | |
| **Albums** | | | |
| JUICE NEWTON | 1985 | RCA Victor | 10 |
| *(Promo-only release)* | | | |

| Title | Yr | Label, Number | NM $ |
|---|---|---|---|

**RADIO SHOWS**
**Albums**

| | | | |
|---|---|---|---|
| LIVE AT GILLEY'S (July 88) | 1988 | Westwood One | 10-20 |
| *(Live concert)* | | | |
| ROBERT W. MORGAN (Jan 82) Profile | 1982 | Watermark | 10-15 |
| *(Music and interviews)* | | | |

## NEWTON, WAYNE

*Other Capitol promo 45s $2 each*
**45s**

| | | | |
|---|---|---|---|
| THE REAL THING  Promo label | 1959 | Capitol 4236 | 40 |
| *(By the Newton Brothers with Jerry and Wayne)* | | | |

## NEWTON-JOHN, OLIVIA

*Includes listings of Toomorrow; Other Uni promo 45s $8 each; MCA white promo label 45s of her hits $5 each; MCA light blue promo label 45s $4 each; MCA dark blue promo label 45s $3 each; MCA red promo label 45s $4 each; RSO promo label solo or duet 45s $3 each; Atlantic promo label duet 45s $3 each*
**10-Inch Singles**

| | | | |
|---|---|---|---|
| XANADU  With Electric Light Orchestra | 1980 | MCA 2315 | 600 |
| *(10" promo-only picture disc single)* | | | |

**45s**

| | | | |
|---|---|---|---|
| BANKS OF THE OHIO | 1971 | Uni 55304 | 10 |
| *(Multi-colored promo label)* | | | |
| DEEPER THAN THE NIGHT | 1979 | MCA 45-1810 | 50 |
| *(Promo-only picture disc)* | | | |
| IF NOT FOR YOU | 1971 | Uni 55281 | 10 |
| *(Multi-colored promo label)* | | | |
| REST YOUR LOVE ON ME  With Andy Gibb | 1979 | RSO PRO 104 | 10 |
| *(RSO record, long and short versions, white label)* | | | |
| TAKE ME HOME, COUNTRY ROADS | 1973 | MCA 40043 | 20 |
| *(Promo-only release, first MCA record)* | | | |
| WHAT IS LIFE | 1971 | Uni 55317 | 10 |
| *(Multi-colored promo label)* | | | |
| WHAT'S IT ALL ABOUT (Dec 74) Public service show | 1974 | W.I.A.A. 234/248 | 18 |
| *(Flip side is Barry White)* | | | |
| WHAT'S IT ALL ABOUT (Dec 76) Public service show | 1976 | W.I.A.A. 348 | 25 |
| *(Flip side is Dion)* | | | |
| WHAT'S IT ALL ABOUT (Mar 79) Public service show | 1979 | W.I.A.A. 466 | 25 |
| *(Flip side is Eddie Money)* | | | |
| WHAT'S IT ALL ABOUT (Nov 80) Public service show | 1980 | W.I.A.A. 550 | 25 |
| *(Flip side is Ray Charles)* | | | |
| YOU'RE MY BABY NOW  Yellow promo label | 1971 | Kirshner 5005 | 50 |
| *(Soundtrack, by Toomorrow)* | | | |

**7-Inch Extended Plays**

| | | | |
|---|---|---|---|
| LET ME BE THERE  Jukebox LLP | 1974 | MCA 34988 | 75 |
| *(Issued with a hard cover)* | | | |
| UNICEF RADIO SPOTS (81-82) Various artists | 198? | DWP 929 | 25 |
| *(20 PSA cuts, one by Olivia that is 30 seconds)* | | | |

**Albums**

| | | | |
|---|---|---|---|
| TOOMORROW | 1971 | Kirshner | 125 |
| *(Soundtrack including Olivia Newton-John)* | | | |
| TOOMORROW  White promo label | 1971 | Sire 97012 | 100 |
| *(Soundtrack including Olivia Newton-John)* | | | |

**RADIO SHOWS**
**Albums**

| | | | |
|---|---|---|---|
| NBC SOURCE (July 80) Profile | 1980 | NBC Radio (2) | 40-75 |
| *(Music and interviews)* | | | |
| ROBERT W. MORGAN  Profile | 1976 | Watermark | 50-75 |
| *(Rare, music and interviews)* | | | |
| ROBERT W. MORGAN (June 81) | 1981 | Watermark | 50-75 |
| *(Music and interviews)* | | | |
| SPOTLIGHT SPECIAL (Apr 83) Box set | 1983 | ABC Radio (2) | 75-100 |
| *(Mostly music and interviews)* | | | |
| STARTRAK PROFILE (Sept 86) Profile | 1986 | Westwood One (2) | 40-75 |
| *(Music and interviews)* | | | |
| STARTRAK PROFILE (Sept 86) Two-part profile | 1986 | Westwood One (4) | 75-150 |
| *(Music and interviews)* | | | |

## NICKS, STEVIE

*Other Modern promo 45s $3 each; Modern promo CD singles $3-5 each Of Fleetwood Mac; Includes Buckingham Nicks*
**12-Inch Singles**

| | | | |
|---|---|---|---|
| EDGE OF SEVENTEEN (Live Full Length)/(Live Edit) | 1982 | Modern PR 315 | 40 |
| I CAN'T WAIT (4 versions) | 1986 | Modern PR 925 | 15 |
| I CAN'T WAIT (Rock Mix)/IMPERIAL HOTEL | 1986 | Modern PR 868 | 20 |
| STAND BACK (full length version)/(edit) | 1983 | Modern PR 507 | 20 |
| TALK TO ME (same on both sides) | 1985 | Modern PR 807 | 12 |

**45s**

| | | | |
|---|---|---|---|
| I CAN'T WAIT | 1986 | Modern 99565 | 10 |
| *(Soft intro promo version and promo-only picture sleeve)* | | | |
| IF ANYONE FALLS | 1983 | | 15 |
| *(White label test pressing, no label name)* | | | |
| TWO KINDS OF LOVE | 1989 | | 15 |
| *(White label test pressing, no label name)* | | | |

**7-Inch Extended Plays**

| | | | |
|---|---|---|---|
| AMERICAN MUSIC CONFERENCE Various artists | 1977 | AMC 102 | 20 |
| *(Series of fourteen public service ads, two by Stevie Nicks)* | | | |

| Title | Yr | Label, Number | NM $ |
|---|---|---|---|
| **Albums** | | | |
| BUCKINGHAM NICKS  With Lindsey Buckingham | 1973 | Polydor 5058 | 75 |
| *(Rare white promo label)* | | | |
| **Compact Discs** | | | |
| ENCHANTED SAMPLER | 1998 | Modern | 20 |
| *(Promo-only collection of tracks from box set)* | | | |
| **RADIO SHOWS** | | | |
| **Albums** | | | |
| BBC ROCK HOUR | 1981 | London Wavelength | 50-75 |
| *(Music and interviews)* | | | |
| IN CONCERT | 1984 | Westwood One (2) | 60-100 |
| *(Live concert)* | | | |
| INNERVIEW  Profile | 1978 | Innerview | 25-50 |
| *(Music and interviews)* | | | |
| NBC SOURCE (Apr 83) | 1983 | NBC Radio (2) | 150-225 |
| *(Rare live concert)* | | | |
| OFF THE RECORD | 1982 | Westwood One (2) | 20-30 |
| *(Music and interviews)* | | | |
| ROCK STARS | 1989 | Radio Today (2) | 35-50 |
| *(Music and interviews)* | | | |
| STARTRACK PROFILE (June 86) | 1986 | Westwood One (2) | 40-75 |
| *(Music and interviews)* | | | |
| SUPERSTAR CONCERT (June 87) | 1987 | Westwood One (3) | 50-100 |
| *(Live concert)* | | | |
| **Compact Discs** | | | |
| IN THE STUDIO  Profile of an album | 1989 | Album Network | 25-50 |
| *(Music and interviews)* | | | |
| LIVE FROM THE WHISKEY (Aug 93) | 1993 | Westwood One | 100-200 |
| *(Live concert)* | | | |
| OFF THE RECORD (Aug 92) | 1992 | Westwood One | 20-30 |
| *(CD format version)* | | | |
| SUPERSTAR CONCERT (Jan 95) | 1995 | Westwood One (2) | 75-150 |
| *(Live concert)* | | | |
| UP CLOSE | 1989 | Media America (2) | 60-80 |
| *(Mostly music and interviews, some live tracks)* | | | |
| UP CLOSE | 1994 | Media America (2) | 50-75 |
| *(Mostly music and interviews, some live tracks)* | | | |

**NIGHT RANGER**
*MCA promo 45s $3 each; MCA promo 12" singles $5 each; MCA promo CD singles $2 each*

| Title | Yr | Label, Number | NM $ |
|---|---|---|---|
| **RADIO SHOWS** | | | |
| **Albums** | | | |
| IN CONCERT (Mar 83)  Live concert | 1983 | Westwood One (2) | 20-40 |
| *(With Frank Marino)* | | | |
| INNERVIEW (80s)  Profile | 198? | Innerview | 10-15 |
| *(Music and interviews)* | | | |
| KING BISCUIT FLOWER HOUR (Jan 85)  Live concert | 1985 | DIR (2) | 25-35 |
| *(Repeated)* | | | |
| NBC SOURCE (Apr 84)  Live concert | 1984 | NBC Radio (2) | 15-25 |
| *(This show repeated in Sept)* | | | |
| OFF THE RECORD (Jan 86)  Profile | 1986 | Westwood One (2) | 10-15 |
| *(Music and interviews, repeated)* | | | |
| SUPERSTAR CONCERT (Nov 85)  Live concert | 1985 | Westwood One (3) | 15-30 |
| *(Box set, repeated)* | | | |

**NIGHTCRAWLERS, THE**

| Title | Yr | Label, Number | NM $ |
|---|---|---|---|
| **45s** | | | |
| LITTLE BLACK EGG | 1966 | Kapp 110 | 20 |
| *(Unusual white label promo on Winners Circle Series)* | | | |

**NILE, WILLIE**

| Title | Yr | Label, Number | NM $ |
|---|---|---|---|
| **RADIO SHOWS** | | | |
| **Albums** | | | |
| KING BISCUIT FLOWER HOUR (June 81)  Live concert | 1981 | DIR/ABC (2) | 10-20 |
| *(With Greg Kihn)* | | | |
| KING BISCUIT FLOWER HOUR (May 80)  Live concert | 1980 | DIR/ABC (2) | 40-75 |
| *(With Warren Zevon)* | | | |

**NILSSON**
*Tower promo 45s $12 each; Other RCA Victor promo 45s $3 each; Polydor promo 45 $3 each*

| Title | Yr | Label, Number | NM $ |
|---|---|---|---|
| **45s** | | | |
| EXCERPTS FROM THE POINT  Four-song EP | 1971 | RCA Victor SPS-45-248 | 25 |
| *(White promo label)* | | | |
| KOJAK COLUMBO | 1975 | RCA Victor 10183 | 10 |
| *(Cream colored promo label and promo-only picture sleeve)* | | | |
| ME AND MY ARROW | 1971 | RCA Victor SPS-45-258 | 10 |
| *(Yellow promo label, promo-only release)* | | | |
| NILSSON SCHMILSSON | 1972 | RCA Victor SP | 50 |
| *($10 each, promo only)* | | | |
| **7-Inch Extended Plays** | | | |
| A LITTLE TOUCH OF SCHMILSSON IN THE NIGHT | 1973 | RCA Victor 2005 | 25 |
| *(Jukebox LLP issued in hard black and white cover)* | | | |
| **Albums** | | | |
| SCATALOGUE | 1971 | RCA Victor SPS-33-567 | 100 |
| *(Very rare, includes insert)* | | | |

| Title | Yr | Label, Number | NM $ |
|-------|-----|---------------|------|
| **RADIO SHOWS** | | | |
| **Albums** | | | |
| NIGHTBIRD & COMPANY (July 73) Various artists | 1973 | U.S. Army (2) | 20-40 |
| *(One of the four shows features Harry Nillson)* | | | |
| TOYOTA PRESENTS (70s) | 197? | Toyota (2) | 25-50 |
| *(Music and interviews)* | | | |
| | | | |
| **NINE BELOW ZERO** | | | |
| **RADIO SHOWS** | | | |
| **Albums** | | | |
| BBC TRANSCRIPTION DISC  Live concert | 1981 | BBC Transcription | 100-200 |
| *(With Toyah)* | | | |
| | | | |
| **NINE INCH NAILS** | | | |
| **12-Inch Singles** | | | |
| CLOSER TO GOD (6 versions)/ | 1994 | Nothing/TVT/Interscope 2117 | 25 |
| MEMORABILIA/MARCH OF THE F*CKHEADS/HERESY | | | |
| *(Promo-only two-record set)* | | | |
| HAPPINESS IN SLAVERY (4 versions) | 1994 | Nothing/TVT/Interscope DMD 1941 | 15 |
| **Albums** | | | |
| THE DOWNWARD SPIRAL | 1994 | Nothing/TVT/Interscope PR 5509 | 25 |
| *(Prono-only U.S. vinyl)* | | | |
| | | | |
| **999** | | | |
| **12-Inch Singles** | | | |
| MERCY MERCY/THAT'S THE WAY IT GOES/OBSESSED/TABOO | 1981 | Polydor PRO 155 | 10 |
| | | | |
| **NIRVANA** | | | |
| *DGC promo 45s $5 each* | | | |
| **12-Inch Singles** | | | |
| COME AS YOU ARE (same on both sides) | 1991 | DGC 4416 | 15 |
| HEART-SHAPED BOX/GALLONS OF RUBBIN' ALCOHOL | 1993 | DGC 4558 | 12 |
| SMELLS LIKE TEEN SPIRIT/EVEN IN HIS YOUTH/ANEURYSM | 1991 | DGC 4344 | 20 |
| *(Promo only on yellow vinyl)* | | | |
| **Compact Discs** | | | |
| ABOUT A GIRL | 1994 | DGC | 10 |
| *(Promo-only CD single from Unplugged LP)* | | | |
| ALL APOLOGIES | 1993 | DGC PROCD 4581 | 8 |
| *(Promo CD single)* | | | |
| ALL APOLOGIES | 1993 | DGC PROCD 4582 | 8 |
| *(Promo CD single, another mix)* | | | |
| ALL APOLOGIES | 1993 | DGC PROCD 4583 | 8 |
| *(Promo CD single, still another mix)* | | | |
| ALL APOLOGIES | 1993 | DGC PROCD 4618 | 8 |
| *(Promo CD single, still another mix yet)* | | | |
| COME AS YOU ARE | 1992 | DGC PROCD 4375 | 8 |
| *(Promo CD single)* | | | |
| HEART SHAPED BOX | 1993 | DGC PROCD 4545 | 8 |
| *(Promo CD single)* | | | |
| IN BLOOM | 1992 | DGC PROCD 4463 | 8 |
| *(Promo CD single)* | | | |
| LITHIUM | 1992 | DGC PROCD 4429 | 8 |
| *(Promo CD single)* | | | |
| MAN WHO SOLD THE WORLD, THE | 1995 | DGC | 10 |
| *(Promo-only CD single from Unplugged LP)* | | | |
| NEVERMIND IT'S AN INTERVIEW | 1992 | DGC PROCD-4382 | 40 |
| *(Promo-only release, music and interviews)* | | | |
| ON A PLAIN | 1992 | DGC PROCD 4354 | 10 |
| *(Promo-only CD single)* | | | |
| SMELLS LIKE TEEN SPIRIT | 1991 | DGC PROCD 4308 | 8 |
| *(Promo CD single)* | | | |
| **RADIO SHOWS** | | | |
| **Albums** | | | |
| IN CONCERT (May 92) Live concert | 1992 | Westwood One (2) | 75-125 |
| *(With Led Zeppelin)* | | | |
| IN CONCERT (Oct 92) Live concert | 1992 | Westwood One (2) | 40-75 |
| *(With Roxy Blue)* | | | |
| **Compact Discs** | | | |
| IN CONCERT (June 94) Live concert | 1994 | Westwood One | 30-50 |
| *(1991 BBC session)* | | | |
| ON THE EDGE (May 94) Music and interviews | 1994 | Westwood One | 20-30 |
| *(With Elvis Costello and others)* | | | |
| SUPERSTAR CONCERT (June 93) Live concert | 1993 | Westwood One (2) | 40-60 |
| *(With Soul Asylum)* | | | |
| | | | |
| **NITTY GRITTY DIRT BAND** | | | |
| *Recorded as The Dirt Band, mid-1970s to early 1980s; Liberty promo 45s $3 each; United Artists promo 45s $3 each; Warner Bros. promo 45s $2 each* | | | |
| **45s** | | | |
| COLORADO CHRISTMAS/THE COWBOY'S CHRISTMAS BALL | 1987 | Warner Bros PRO-S-2869 | 6 |
| *(B-side by Michael Martin Murphey)* | | | |
| WHAT'S IT ALL ABOUT (Oct 75) Public service show | 1975 | W.I.A.A. 288 | 18 |
| *(Interviews with members of the band)* | | | |
| **Albums** | | | |
| A PROGRAMMERS GUIDE TO DREAM | 1975 | United Artists 469 | 30 |
| *(Promo-only release)* | | | |

| Title | Yr | Label, Number | NM $ |
|-------|----|--------------|------|
| THE NITTY GRITTY DIRT BAND INTERVIEW | 1975 | United Artists SP-117 | 25 |
| *(Promo-only interview)* | | | |
| UNCLE CHARLIE AND HIS DOG TEDDY | 1970 | Liberty LST-7642 | 100 |
| *(Leatherette promo pack with LP, two other discs, photos, booklet)* | | | |
| **RADIO SHOWS** | | | |
| **Albums** | | | |
| ROBERT W. MORGAN (May 81) | 1981 | Watermark | 15-25 |
| *(Music and interviews)* | | | |

**NITZSCHE, JACK**
**45s**

| LONELY SURFER, THE | 1962 | Reprise 20,202 | 30 |
|-------|----|--------------|------|
| *(Does not include stock picture sleeve)* | | | |

**NIXON, MOJO, AND SKID ROPER**
**12-Inch Singles**

| I'M GONNA DIG UP HOWLIN' WOLF (same on both sides) | 1987 | Enigma 054 | 6 |
|-------|----|--------------|------|

**NO DOUBT**
**Compact Discs**

| DON'T SPEAK | 1996 | Trauma | 10 |
|-------|----|--------------|------|
| *(Promo CD single, no stock copies issued)* | | | |
| JUST A GIRL | 1996 | Trauma PRCD 6378 | 8 |
| *(Promo CD single)* | | | |
| LIVE IN LOS ANGELES | 1996 | Trauma PRCD 6667 | 20 |
| *(Promo-only sampler)* | | | |
| SPIDERWEB | 1996 | Trauma PRCD 6634 | 8 |
| *(Promo CD single)* | | | |

**NOBLES, CLIFF**
*Phil-L.A. of Soul promo 45s $3 each*
**Albums**

| THE HORSE | 1968 | Phil-L.A. of Soul 4001 | 75 |
|-------|----|--------------|------|
| *(White promo label)* | | | |

**NOEL**
**12-Inch Singles**

| CHANGE (5 versions) | 1989 | 4th & B'Way 481 | 8 |
|-------|----|--------------|------|
| OUT OF TIME (4 versions) | 1988 | 4th & B'Way 469 | 6 |

**NOLAND, TERRY**
**45s**

| EVERYONE BUT ME | 1958 | Brunswick 55069 | 20 |
|-------|----|--------------|------|
| *(Yellow promo label)* | | | |
| HYPNOTIZED  Yellow promo label | 1957 | Brunswick 55010 | 40 |
| *(Stock copies harder to find, worth a little more)* | | | |
| LONG GONE BABY | 1960 | Apt 25065 | 20 |
| *(White promo label)* | | | |
| PATTY BABY | 1957 | Brunswick 55036 | 25 |
| *(Yellow promo label)* | | | |
| PUPPY LOVE | 1958 | Brunswick 55054 | 20 |
| *(Yellow promo label)* | | | |
| TEENAGE TEARDROPS | 1959 | Brunswick 55092 | 20 |
| *(Yellow promo label)* | | | |
| THERE WAS A FUNGUS AMONG US | 1958 | Brunswick 55092 | 35 |
| *(Yellow promo label)* | | | |
| THERE WAS A FUNGUS AMONG US  Blue promo label | 1959 | Coral 62274 | 40 |
| *(Same song, different label)* | | | |
| **Albums** | | | |
| TERRY NOLAND | 1958 | Brunswick 54041 | 500 |
| *(Yellow promo label)* | | | |

**NORDINE, KEN**
**45s**

| FOREST FIRE  Public service announcements | 196? | F.P. 879 | 25 |
|-------|----|--------------|------|
| *(7-inch 33, one of eight cuts features Ken Nordine)* | | | |

**NORMAN, LARRY**
*Verve and MGM promo LPs $25 each*
**RADIO SHOWS**
**Albums**

| HERE'S TO VETERANS 110 | 196? | Veterans Administration | 50-100 |
|-------|----|--------------|------|
| *(Very rare radio show, music and interviews)* | | | |

**NOTES, THE**
**45s**

| DON'T LEAVE ME NOW | 1956 | Capitol 3332 | 65 |
|-------|----|--------------|------|
| *(White promo label)* | | | |
| TRUST IN ME | 1956 | MGM 12338 | 100 |
| *(Yellow promo label)* | | | |

**NOVA, ALDO**
*Portrait promo 45s $3 each*
**Albums**

| SPECIALLY BANDED RADIO SAMPLER | 1983 | Portrait AS 1743 | 15 |
|-------|----|--------------|------|
| *(Stock copy is not banded)* | | | |

| Title | Yr | Label, Number | NM $ |
|-------|-----|--------------|------|
| **RADIO SHOWS** | | | |
| **Albums** | | | |
| CAPTURED LIVE (June 84) | 1984 | RKO (2) | 20-40 |
| *(Live concert)* | | | |
| KING BISCUIT FLOWER HOUR (Sept 82) Live concert | 1982 | DIR (2) | 20-40 |
| *(With Prism)* | | | |
| | | | |
| **NOVAS, THE** | | | |
| **45s** | | | |
| THE CRUSHER | 1965 | Parrot 45005 | 40 |
| *(Brownish promo label)* | | | |
| | | | |
| **NOVO COMBO** | | | |
| **RADIO SHOWS** | | | |
| **Albums** | | | |
| KING BISCUIT FLOWER HOUR (Jan 82) Live concert | 1982 | DIR/ABC (2) | 40-75 |
| *(With Quarterflash)* | | | |
| NBC SOURCE (Feb 83) Live concert | 1983 | NBC Radio (3) | 30-60 |
| *(With Haircut 100)* | | | |
| | | | |
| **NRBQ** | | | |
| **45s** | | | |
| WILD WEEKEND/THIS LOVE IS TRUE | 1989 | Virgin 99161 | 4 |
| | | | |
| **NUGENT, TED** | | | |
| *Member of the Amboy Dukes; DiscReet promo 45s $8 each; Epic promo 45s $5 each; Atlantic promo 45s $3 each; Mainstream white promo label 45s by the Amboy Dukes $8 each; Epic promo LPs $12 each* | | | |
| **45s** | | | |
| TIED UP IN LOVE (same on both sides) | 1984 | Atlantic 89705 | 4 |
| *(May be promo only)* | | | |
| WHAT'S IT ALL ABOUT (Aug 81) Public service show | 1981 | W.I.A.A. 590 | 20 |
| *(Flip side is Sister Sledge)* | | | |
| **Albums** | | | |
| CALL OF THE WILD  Ted Nugent and the Amboy Dukes | 1974 | DiscReet 2181 | 20 |
| *(Brown promo label)* | | | |
| STATE OF SHOCK | 1979 | Epic AS-99-607 | 20 |
| *(Promo-only picture disc)* | | | |
| **Compact Discs** | | | |
| SLIGHTLY OUT OF CONTROL | 1993 | Legacy/Epic ESK 5036 | 20 |
| *(Sampler from box set)* | | | |
| **RADIO SHOWS** | | | |
| **Albums** | | | |
| CAPTURED LIVE (Jan 83) Live concert | 1983 | Westwood One (2) | 50-125 |
| *(Early live concert)* | | | |
| IN CONCERT Live concert | 1982 | Westwood One (2) | 25-50 |
| *(Repeated)* | | | |
| INNERVIEW (70s) Profile of Amboy Dukes | 197? | Innerview | 15-25 |
| *(Music and interviews)* | | | |
| KING BISCUIT FLOWER HOUR  Live concert | 1980 | DIR/ABC (2) | 40-80 |
| *(Early live concert)* | | | |
| KING BISCUIT FLOWER HOUR (July 84) Live concert | 1984 | DIR/ABC (2) | 50-100 |
| *(Features Danny Spanos, with Accept)* | | | |
| METALSHOP (Mar 91) Various artists | 1991 | MJI Productions | 10-20 |
| *(Live segments on some of these shows featured Ted Nugent)* | | | |
| NBC SOURCE (June 80) Live concert | 1980 | NBC Radio (2) | 50-125 |
| *(Repeated in 1982)* | | | |
| NBC SOURCE (Oct 82) Live concert | 1982 | NBC Radio (2) | 50-100 |
| *(Same show as above)* | | | |
| NIGHT ON THE ROAD (June 81) Box set | 1981 | ABC Radio (3) | 100-175 |
| *(Live concert)* | | | |
| ROCK AROUND THE WORLD (Nov 77) | 1977 | (2) | 10-20 |
| *(Music and interviews)* | | | |
| SOURCE SPECIAL (July 81) | 1981 | NBC Radio (2) | 25-50 |
| *(Music and interviews)* | | | |
| **Compact Discs** | | | |
| IN THE STUDIO (Oct 90) Profile | 1990 | Album Network | 10-20 |
| *(Music and interviews)* | | | |
| | | | |
| **NUMAN, GARY** | | | |
| *Atco or Atlantic promo 45s $5 each* | | | |
| **45s** | | | |
| REMIND ME TO SMILE | 198? | Atco 7316 | 10 |
| *(Test pressing, white label)* | | | |
| **RADIO SHOWS** | | | |
| **Albums** | | | |
| BBC COLLEGE CONCERT (Jan 83) Live concert | 1983 | London Wavelength | 20-40 |
| *(Mostly live material)* | | | |
| BBC ROCK HOUR (Sept 80) Live concert | 1980 | London Wavelength | 40-80 |
| *(Early live concert)* | | | |
| BBC TRANSCRIPTION DISC  Live concert | 1984 | BBC Transcription | 300-400 |
| *(Rare concert, rare series)* | | | |

| Title | Yr | Label, Number | NM $ |
|---|---|---|---|
| **NUTTY SQUIRRELS, THE** | | | |
| **7-Inch Extended Plays** | | | |
| SPECIAL DJ SPOTS | 1960 | Hanover DJ 1 | 50 |
| *(Four cuts, "Uh! Oh! on B-side)* | | | |
| UH! OH! /DING-DONG | 1959 | Hanover 301 | 50 |
| *(White promo label)* | | | |
| | | | |
| **NYRO, LAURA** | | | |
| *Verve/Folkways promo 45s $4 each; Columbia promo 45s $3 each* | | | |
| **45s** | | | |
| SWEET BLINDNESS | 1968 | Columbia 139152 | 10 |
| *(Yellow label promo)* | | | |
| **Albums** | | | |
| SEASON OF LIGHTS…LAURA NYRO IN CONCERT | 1977 | Columbia PC2 34331 (2) | 50 |
| *(Promo only in plain cardboard jacket; this LP was edited to one LP for release)* | | | |

# O

| Title | Yr | Label, Number | NM $ |
|---|---|---|---|
| **O'CONNOR, MARK** | | | |
| **45s** | | | |
| SLEIGH RIDE/WHITE CHRISTMAS MAKES ME BLUE | 1987 | Warner Bros PRO-S-2842 | 4 |
| *(B-side by Randy Travis)* | | | |
| | | | |
| **O'CONNOR, SINEAD** | | | |
| **12-Inch Singles** | | | |
| JERUSALEM (same on both sides) | 1988 | Ensign 1062 | 10 |
| MANDINKA (same on both sides) | 1987 | Chrysalis VAS 2967 | 10 |
| | | | |
| **O'JAYS, THE** | | | |
| **12-Inch Singles** | | | |
| HAVE YOU HAD YOUR LOVE TODAY (2 versions)/LOVIN' YOU | 1989 | EMI SPRO-04305/20 | 8 |
| MERRY CHRISTMAS BABY/THE CHRISTMAS SONG | 1991 | EMI 4853/4 | 8 |
| **Albums** | | | |
| EVERYTHING YOU ALWAYS WANTED TO HEAR BY THE O'JAYS BUT WERE AFRAID TO ASK FOR | 1975 | Philadelphia Int'l. ASZ 140 | 15 |
| | | | |
| **O'KEEFE, DANNY** | | | |
| **Albums** | | | |
| THE O'KEEFE FILE | 1977 | Warner Bros. PRO 760 | 15 |
| | | | |
| **OAK RIDGE BOYS, THE** | | | |
| *Impact 45s $6 each; Columbia promo 45s $3 each; ABC promo 45s $2 each; MCA promo 45s 1100-1200 series (promo only) $5 each; Other MCA promo 45s $2 each; MCA or RCA promo CD singles $2-3 each* | | | |
| **45s** | | | |
| COME ON IN | 1985 | MCA 52722 | 12 |
| *(White label, blue vinyl)* | | | |
| IT TAKES A LITTLE RAIN  White promo label | 1987 | MCA 53010 | 10 |
| *(Unusual one-sided record)* | | | |
| JESUS IS BORN TODAY | 1984 | MCA S45-1250 | 12 |
| *(White promo label, promo-only number)* | | | |
| JULIET | 1986 | MCA 52801 | 10 |
| *(White label, green vinyl)* | | | |
| SANTA'S SONG | 1982 | MCA S45-1154 | 12 |
| *(White promo label, promo-only number)* | | | |
| THERE'S A NEW KID IN TOWN | 1987 | MCA S45-17450 | 10 |
| *(White promo label, promo-only number)* | | | |
| THIS CRAZY LOVE | 1987 | MCA 53023 | 12 |
| *(White label, blue vinyl)* | | | |
| VOICES OF REJOICING LOVE, THE | 1986 | MCA-S45-17233 | 12 |
| *(White promo label, green vinyl, promo-only number)* | | | |
| WHEN YOU GET TO THE HEART  With Barbara Mandrell | 1986 | MCA 52806 | 10 |
| *(Red vinyl, white promo label)* | | | |
| WHEN YOU GIVE IT AWAY | 1986 | MCA 17233 | 15 |
| *(White label, green vinyl)* | | | |
| **7-Inch Extended Plays** | | | |
| MINIMUM WAGE (80s) Various artists | 198? | U.S. Department of Labot | 15 |
| *(Eleven PSA spots, two feature the Oak Ridge Boys)* | | | |
| PREVENTION OF CHILD ABUSE | 1986 | Ad Council 1285 | 20 |
| *(Eight PSA spots, all with Oak Ridge Boys, 30 and 60 second spots)* | | | |
| **Albums** | | | |
| SAIL AWAY | 1979 | MCA 51247 | 50 |
| *(Promo-only picture disc)* | | | |
| "STEP ON OUT" WORLD PREMIERE | 1985 | MCA L33-2-1276 | 25 |
| *(Promo-only interview and music LP with no script or cover)* | | | |
| **Compact Discs** | | | |
| UNSTOPPABLE STORY | 1995 | RCA | 25 |
| *(Promo-only tribute CD release)* | | | |
| **RADIO SHOWS** | | | |
| **Albums** | | | |
| LIVE AT GILLEY'S (June 87) | 1987 | Westwood One | 15-25 |
| *(Live concert, repeated)* | | | |

| Title | Yr | Label, Number | NM $ |
|---|---|---|---|
| SILVER EAGLE | 1981 | DIR (3) | 25-50 |
| *(live concert, repeated)* | | | |
| SILVER EAGLE (Sept 82) Live concert | 1982 | DIR (3) | 20-40 |
| *(With Sylvia)* | | | |
| WESTWOOD ONE PRESENTS (July 87) | 1987 | Westwood One | 25-40 |
| *(Live concert)* | | | |

## OASIS
**Compact Discs**

| | | | |
|---|---|---|---|
| CHAMPAGNE SUPERNOVA | 1996 | Epic ESK 7719 | 8 |
| *(Promo CD single)* | | | |
| DON'T LOOK BACK IN ANGER | 1994 | Epic | 10 |
| *(Promo CD single)* | | | |
| LIVE AT THE CABARET METRO | 1994 | Epic | 100 |
| *(Promo-only live show, issued in paper sleeve, scarce)* | | | |
| LIVE FOREVER | 1994 | Epic | 8 |
| *(Promo CD single)* | | | |
| MORNING GLORY | 1995 | Epic ESK 7302 | 8 |
| *(Promo CD single)* | | | |
| ROCK 'N ROLL STAR | 1994 | Epic ESK 7042 | 8 |
| *(Promo CD single)* | | | |
| SUPERSONIC | 1995 | Epic | 8 |
| *(Promo CD single)* | | | |
| WONDERWALL | 1995 | Epic ESK 7440 | 8 |
| *(Promo CD single)* | | | |

**RADIO SHOWS**
**Compact Discs**

| | | | |
|---|---|---|---|
| IN CONCERT (June 95) | 1995 | Westwood One | 30-50 |
| *(Live concert material)* | | | |
| IN CONCERT - NU ROCK (Oct 95) | 1995 | Westwood One | 30-50 |
| *(Live concert material)* | | | |
| LIVE FROM KNEBWORTH (Aug 96) | 1996 | Westwood One (2) | 50-80 |
| *(Live concert material)* | | | |
| RECORD CO. | 1994 | | 100-150 |
| *(Live material, only sent to college radio stations)* | | | |
| UP CLOSE | 1995 | Media America | 20-40 |
| *(Music and interviews)* | | | |

## OCASEK, RIC
*Lead singer of the Cars; Elektra and Geffen promo 45s $3 each; Elektra promo 12" singles $6 each*
**12-Inch Singles**

| | | | |
|---|---|---|---|
| KEEP ON LAUGHING (same on both sides) | 1986 | Geffen PRO-A-2646 | 5 |
| PROVE/CONNECT UP TO ME | 1983 | Geffen PRO-A-2002 | 5 |
| TRUE TO YOU (same on both sides) | 1986 | Geffen PRO-A-2629 | 5 |

**RADIO SHOWS**
**Albums**

| | | | |
|---|---|---|---|
| OFF THE RECORD  Profile | 1991 | Westwood One (2) | 10-20 |
| *(Music and interviews)* | | | |

## OCEAN BLUE, THE
*Sire promo CD singles $2 each*
**RADIO SHOWS**
**Compact Discs**

| | | | |
|---|---|---|---|
| IN CONCERT-NU ROCK (June 94) Live concert | 1994 | Westwood One | 40-75 |
| *(Solo concert)* | | | |

## OCHS, PHIL
*Other A&M promo 45s $10 each*
**45s**

| | | | |
|---|---|---|---|
| OUTSIDE A SMALL CIRCLE OF FRIENDS | 1967 | A&M 891 | 25 |
| *(Censored and uncensored versions)* | | | |

## OHIO PLAYERS, THE
**12-Inch Singles**

| | | | |
|---|---|---|---|
| EVERYBODY UP (9:32) (3:57) | 1979 | Arista SP-46 | 8 |
| MAGIC TRICK/GOOD LUCK CHARM | 1976 | Mercury MK-43 | 15 |

**45s**

| | | | |
|---|---|---|---|
| LOVE ROLLERCOASTER | 1975 | Mercury DJ 436 | 10 |
| *(2:52 version, light blue promo label)* | | | |

**7-Inch Extended Plays**

| | | | |
|---|---|---|---|
| SPECIAL EDITED RADIO CUTS | 1974 | Mercury 705 | 15 |
| *(Issued with promo sleeve, contains three tracks including "Skin Tight")* | | | |

## OINGO BOINGO
**12-Inch Singles**

| | | | |
|---|---|---|---|
| FLESH AND BLOOD (3 versions) | 1989 | MCA 18005 | 12 |
| JUST ANOTHER DAY (5:10)/(3:58) | 1985 | MCA 17078 | 10 |
| NOT MY SLAVE (same on both sides) | 1987 | MCA 17288 | 7 |
| PAIN (same on both sides) | 1986 | MCA 17193 | 6 |
| PRIVATE LIFE/WHOLE DAY OFF/NOTHING TO FEAR | 1982 | A&M 17203 | 10 |
| WAKE UP (IT'S 1984) (long/short) | 1983 | A&M 17240 | 8 |
| WEIRD SCIENCE (3:45) (same on both sides) | 1985 | MCA 17022 | 10 |
| WEIRD SCIENCE (6:00)/(6:38) | 1985 | MCA 17048 | 10 |
| WINNING SIDE/CINDERELLA UNDERCOVER | 1988 | MCA 17660 | 6 |

| Title | Yr | Label, Number | NM $ |
|---|---|---|---|

**45s**
WHOLE DAY OFF (stereo)/(mono) — 1982 — A&M 2504 — 4
*(Apparently, no stock copy exists)*

**OLDFIELD, MIKE**
**Albums**
HERGEST RIDGE — 1974 — Virgin VR 13-109 — 20
*(Banded for airplay)*
**Compact Discs**
VIRGIN COMPILATION, A — 1988 — Virgin PRCD 2113 — 80
*(Promo-only sampler)*

**OLENN, JOHNNY**
*Liberty promo 45s $12 each*
**Albums**
JUST ROLLIN' WITH JOHNNY OLENN — 1959 — Liberty 3029 — 400
*(Very rare white promo label, stock copy worth $300)*

**OLSSON, NIGEL**
**Albums**
DRUMMERS CAN SING TOO! — 1975 — Rocket L33-1962 — 20
*(Promo-only interview album)*

**ONO, YOKO**
*Wife of John Lennon; Other Geffen promo 45s $8 each; Polydor promo 45s $6 each*
**12-Inch Singles**
HELL IN PARADISE — 1986 — Polydor 883 445 — 30
*(Red promo label, 12" single)*
MY MAN/LET THE TEARS DRY — 1982 — Polydor 192 — 6
WALKING ON THIN ICE (3:23)/(5:58) — 1982 — Geffen PRO-A-934 — 15
WALKING ON THIN ICE (Remix)/CAPE CLEAR (2 versions) — 1986 — Polydor 883 872-1 — 12
**45s**
GREENFIELD MORNING/OPEN YOUR BOX — 1971 — Apple GM/OYB-1 — 800
*(Exactly six copies made for the personal use of Yoko Ono)*
NOW OR NEVER — 1972 — Apple P-1853 — 30
*(Add another $15 if the stock picture sleeve is included)*
RADIO PLAY — 1969 — Eva-Tone 7 — 400
*(7" flexi-disc, very rare)*
WALKING ON THIN ICE — 1981 — Geffen PRO-S-935 — 10
*(Long 5:58 and short 3:23 versions)*
WOMAN POWER — 1973 — Apple PRO-6752 — 30
*(Long 4:50 and short 3:25 versions)*
**Compact Discs**
XMAS MESSAGE FROM YOKO, A — 1991 — Rykodisc VRCD ONO — 40
*(Promo only)*
**RADIO SHOWS**
**Albums**
A PRESENT FOR YOKO (80s) — 198? — Westwood One — 25-50
*(Music and interviews)*
EVERY MAN HAS A WOMAN (Dec 84) — 1984 — MJI Broadcasting (2) — 25-50
*(A tribute to John Lennon, music and interviews)*

**ORBISON, ROY**
*Of the Teen Kings; Also see Traveling Wilburys; Other Monument promo 45s $6 each; Other MGM promo 45s $4-6 each; Mercury promo 45s $5 each; Asylum promo 45s $4 each; Virgin promo 45s by Orbison solo or duet $5 each; MGM promo LPs $30 each; Mercury promo LP $15; Later Monument promo LPs $10 each; Virgin and MCA promo CD singles $3 each*
**12-Inch Singles**
SHE'S A MYSTERY TO ME (same on both sides) — 1989 — Virgin PR 2667 — 10
YOU GOT IT (same on both sides) — 1989 — Virgin PR 2593 — 10
**45s**
ALMOST EIGHTEEN — 1959 — RCA Victor 7447 — 50
*(White promo label)*
BLUE ANGEL — 1960 — Monument 425 — 25
*(Brown/white promo label)*
CRYING — 1961 — Monument 447 — 15
*(Brown/white promo label)*
DREAM BABY — 1962 — Monument 456 — 15
*(Brown/white promo label)*
FALLING — 1963 — Monument 815 — 10
*(Brown/white promo label)*
HERE COMES THAT SONG AGAIN — 196? — Monument CSX-1 — 20
*(Promo-only release)*
I'M HURTIN' — 1960 — Monument 433 — 20
*(Brown/white promo label)*
IN DREAMS — 1963 — Monument 806 — 10
*(Brown/white promo label)*
LEAH — 1962 — Monument 467 — 10
*(Brown/white promo label)*
MGM CELEBRITY SERIES: ROY ORBISON — 1966 — MGM CS9-5 — 150
*(Five-record promo box set often used by jukebox vendors, yellow promo labels, $25 each)*
ONLY THE LONELY — 1960 — Monument 421 — 30
*(Brown/white promo label)*
PAPER BOY — 1959 — Monument 409 — 50
*(Brown/white promo label)*
RUNNING SCARED — 1961 — Monument 438 — 18
*(Brown/white promo label)*

| Title | Yr | Label, Number | NM $ |
|---|---|---|---|
| SEEMS TO ME | 1958 | RCA Victor 7381 | 50 |
| *(White promo label)* | | | |
| THE CROWD | 1962 | Monument 461 | 12 |
| *(Brown/white promo label)* | | | |
| UPTOWN | 1959 | Monument 412 | 40 |
| *(Brown/white promo label)* | | | |
| **7-Inch Extended Plays** | | | |
| THE CLASSIC ROY ORBISON Jukebox LLP | 1966 | MGM 4379 | 50 |
| *(Issued with a hard cover)* | | | |
| COKE Various artists | 1965 | Coca-Cola | 200 |
| *(Radio ads, artists include Roy Orbison)* | | | |
| IN DREAMS | 1962 | Monument 003 | 125 |
| *(Vol. 2 "Special Promotion Six-Pack" issued with a special promo paper sleeve)* | | | |
| IN DREAMS | 1962 | Monument 002 | 125 |
| *(Vol. 1 "Special Promotion Six-Pack" issued with a special promo paper sleeve)* | | | |
| MORE OF ROY ORBISON'S GREATEST HITS Jukebox LLP | 1967 | Monument 506 #2 | 50 |
| *(Issued with a hard cover)* | | | |
| ORBISONGS Jukebox LLP | 1969 | Monument 512 | 40 |
| *(Issued with a paper cover)* | | | |
| ROY ORBISON & THE TEEN KINGS | 1959 | Stars Inc. 101 | 200 |
| *(Promo-only EP shipped to fan club members)* | | | |
| ROY ORBISON'S GREATEST HITS Jukebox LLP | 1967 | Monument 506 #1 | 50 |
| *(Issued with a hard cover)* | | | |
| SWING THE JINGLE Various artists | 196? | Coca-Cola | 200 |
| *(Radio ads, price includes picture sleeve)* | | | |
| **Albums** | | | |
| A HISTORY: MONUMENT RECORD CORPORATION | 197? | Monument/CBS (2) | 25 |
| *(This promo-only release should be of interest to Orbison collectors because he was Monument's biggest star)* | | | |
| **Compact Discs** | | | |
| BLACK AND WHITE NIGHT, A | 1989 | Virgin | 40 |
| *(CD and VHS video in special promo package)* | | | |
| MYSTERY GIRL | 1989 | Virgin PRCD ROY | 25 |
| *(Special promo-only issue)* | | | |
| POLAROY | 1989 | Virgin PRCD POLAROY | 30 |
| *(Special promo-only issue of "A Black and White Night" with custom packaging)* | | | |
| **RADIO SHOWS** | | | |
| **Albums** | | | |
| HOT ROCKS | 1989 | Radio Today (2) | 50-75 |
| *(Music and interviews)* | | | |
| INTERNATIONAL FESTIVAL OF COUNTRY MUSIC (Oct 82) | 1982 | Mutual Radio (3) | 50-125 |
| *(Various artists including Orbison, live!)* | | | |
| LIVE AT GILLEY'S (80s) Live concert | 198? | Westwood One | 50-100 |
| *(Very rare and very collectible)* | | | |
| OFF THE RECORD Traveling Wilburys | 1989 | Westwood One (2) | 50-75 |
| *(Music and interviews)* | | | |
| OFF THE RECORD (Apr 89) | 1989 | Westwood One (2) | 50-80 |
| *(Music and interviews)* | | | |
| ROCK ROLL & REMEMBER Various artists | 1987 | United Stations (4) | 20-40 |
| *(Music and interview, Orbison is featured)* | | | |
| **Cassettes** | | | |
| AUSTIN ENCORE | 1994 | Radio Entertainment | 100-150 |
| *(Rare live concert on cassette)* | | | |

## ORCHESTRAL MANOEUVRES IN THE DARK (OMD)
*Epic promo 45s $4 each; Epic promo 12" singles $7 each; A&M promo CD singles $2 each; Virgin promo CD singles $3 each*

| Title | Yr | Label, Number | NM $ |
|---|---|---|---|
| **12-Inch Singles** | | | |
| ENOLA GAY/MESSAGES | 1980 | Virgin/Epic AE 1247 | 15 |
| (FOREVER) LIVE AND DIE (same on both sides) | 1986 | A&M 17428 | 10 |
| GEORGIA/SOUVENIR/SHE'S LEAVING/JOAN OF ARC | 1981 | Virgin/Epic AE 1403 | 15 |
| IF YOU LEAVE/PRETTY IN PINK | 1986 | A&M 17367 | 10 |
| *(B-side by Psychedelic Furs; promo from movie "Pretty in Pink")* | | | |
| STAND ABOVE ME (3 versions) | 1993 | Virgin 12777 | 10 |
| TELEGRAPH (LP version)/(Edit)/RADIO WAVES | 1983 | Virgin/Epic AE 1658 | 12 |
| WE LOVE YOU (7")/(Remix) | 1986 | A&M 17441 | 6 |
| **Albums** | | | |
| A CONSTRUCTIVE CONVERSATION | 1982 | Epic | 20 |
| *(Music and interviews, promo only)* | | | |
| **RADIO SHOWS** | | | |
| **Albums** | | | |
| BBC TRANSCRIPTION DISC Live concert | 1984 | BBC Transcription | 250-325 |
| *(Very rare concert)* | | | |
| **Compact Discs** | | | |
| ON THE EDGE (Aug 93) Music and interviews | 1993 | Album Network | 10-20 |
| *(With 700 Miles and Tim Finn)* | | | |

## ORIGINALS, THE

| Title | Yr | Label, Number | NM $ |
|---|---|---|---|
| **45s** | | | |
| CALL ON YOUR SIX MILLION DOLLAR MAN (mono/stereo) | 1977 | Soul 35121 | 6 |
| YOUNG TRAIN (same on both sides) | 1973 | Motown PR-1 | 200 |

## ORIOLES, THE
*With Sonny Til; Jubilee white label promo 45s $30 each*

| Title | Yr | Label, Number | NM $ |
|---|---|---|---|
| **45s** | | | |
| LONELY CHRISTMAS Sonny Til | 196? | Parker 213 | 25 |
| *(Promo label)* | | | |

| Title | Yr | Label, Number | NM $ |
|---|---|---|---|
| SECRET LOVE  Sonny Til | 196? | Parker 211 | 25 |
| *(Promo label)* | | | |
| SUGAR GIRL | 1957 | Vee Jay 244 | 50 |
| *(White promo label)* | | | |

## ORION

*Also known as Jimmy Ellis, he's the "king" of Presley sound-alikes; Sun black vinyl promo singles by Orion $5 each; Sun promo 45s by Jimmy Ellis $4 each; Sun promo EPs by Jimmy Ellis $8 each; Other Boblo promo 45s by Jimmy Ellis $5 each; Kristal promo 45s by Orion $4 each; MCA promo 45s by Jimmy Ellis $3 each*

**45s**

| Title | Yr | Label, Number | NM $ |
|---|---|---|---|
| AM I THAT EASY TO FORGET | 1980 | Sun 1156 | 10 |
| *(White promo label, yellow vinyl)* | | | |
| BORN | 1981 | Sun 1165 | 10 |
| *(White promo label, yellow vinyl)* | | | |
| HONKY TONK HEAVEN | 1981 | Sun 1175 | 10 |
| *(White promo label, yellow vinyl)* | | | |
| I'M NOT TRYING TO BE LIKE ELVIS  Jimmy Ellis | 1978 | Boblo 636 | 50 |
| *(Promo-only picture sleeve with a letter to the DJ on back)* | | | |
| IT AIN'T NO MYSTERY | 1980 | Sun 1152 | 10 |
| *(Yellow promo label, yellow vinyl)* | | | |
| ONLY A WOMAN LIKE YOU (same on both sides) | 1990 | Stargem 2465 | 5 |
| REMEMBER BETHLEHEM | 1979 | Sun 1148 | 15 |
| *(Yellow promo label, yellow vinyl)* | | | |
| ROCKABILLY REBEL | 1980 | Sun 1159 | 10 |
| *(White promo label, yellow vinyl)* | | | |
| SOME YOU WIN, SOME YOU LOSE | 1981 | Sun 1170 | 10 |
| *(White promo label, yellow vinyl)* | | | |
| TEXAS TEA | 1980 | Sun 1153 | 10 |
| *(Yellow promo label, yellow vinyl)* | | | |
| THAT'S ALL RIGHT | 1971 | Sun 1129 | 25 |
| *(First pressing, no artist listed, A lot of people then, even some now, think this was Elvis; later pressings listed artist as Jimmy Ellis)* | | | |
| THAT'S ALL RIGHT  Jimmy Ellis | 1971 | Sun 1129 | 15 |
| *("Promotion copy" on label)* | | | |
| UNCHAINED MELODY (same on both sides) | 1987 | Radioactive 18772-1 | 5 |
| **7-Inch Extended Plays** | | | |
| A STRANGER IN MY PLACE | 1980 | Sun 1152 | 40 |
| *(Promo only, six cuts of radio ads, also an insert)* | | | |
| **Albums** | | | |
| ELLIS SINGS ELVIS BY REQUEST  Jimmy Ellis | 1978 | Boblo 829 | 100 |
| *(Blue promo label)* | | | |
| ROCKABILLY | 1980 | Sun S-1021-T | 25 |
| *(Test pressing on black vinyl, by Orion, with posters and letter)* | | | |

## ORLEANS

*Includes the John Hall Band; Asylum promo singles $3 each; MCA black vinyl and Infinity promo 45s $2 each; MCA colored vinyl promo 45s $5 each*

**45s**

| Title | Yr | Label, Number | NM $ |
|---|---|---|---|
| LOVE ME AGAIN  The John Hall Band | 197? | | 10 |
| *(White label test pressing)* | | | |
| WHAT'S IT ALL ABOUT (July 79) Public service show | 1979 | W.I.A.A. 483 | 15 |
| *(Flip side features Desmond Child and Rouge)* | | | |
| WHAT'S IT ALL ABOUT (May 76) Public service show | 1976 | W.I.A.A. 315 | 12 |
| *(Flip side features Cheech and Chong)* | | | |

## ORR, BENJAMIN

*More at The Cars.*

**12-Inch Singles**

| Title | Yr | Label, Number | NM $ |
|---|---|---|---|
| TOO HOT TO STOP (same on both sides) | 1986 | Elektra 5200 | 5 |

## OSBORNE, JEFFREY

**45s**

| Title | Yr | Label, Number | NM $ |
|---|---|---|---|
| DON'T YOU GET SO MAD | 198? | A&M | 10 |
| *(White label test pressing)* | | | |

## OSBORNE, JOAN

**Compact Discs**

| Title | Yr | Label, Number | NM $ |
|---|---|---|---|
| ONE OF US | 1995 | Blue Gorilla/Mercury | 8 |
| *(Promo CD single, her biggest hit)* | | | |

**RADIO SHOWS**

**Compact Discs**

| Title | Yr | Label, Number | NM $ |
|---|---|---|---|
| IN CONCERT (May 96) | 1996 | Westwood One | 25-50 |
| *(Live concert material)* | | | |

## OSBOURNE, OZZY

*Member of Black Sabbath; Jet (CBS) promo 45s $5 each; Epic promo 45s $4 each; RCA promo 45s, duet, $3 each*

**7-Inch Extended Plays**

| Title | Yr | Label, Number | NM $ |
|---|---|---|---|
| MR. CROWLEY LIVE | 1981 | Epic 37640 | 25 |
| *(Picture disc shipped to radio stations)* | | | |
| **Albums** | | | |
| DIARY OF A MADMAN | 1981 | JET AS-99-1372 | 25 |
| *(Promo-only picture disc)* | | | |
| **Compact Discs** | | | |
| LIVE AND LOUD SAMPLER | 1993 | Epic ZSK 5247 | 20 |
| *(Promo-only release, four tracks)* | | | |
| NO MORE TEARS DEMO SESSIONS | 1992 | Epic ZSK 4643 | 120 |
| *(Very rare promo, early versions of songs from "No More Tears" LP)* | | | |

| Title | Yr | Label, Number | NM $ |
|---|---|---|---|
| **RADIO SHOWS** | | | |
| **Albums** | | | |
| CAPTURED LIVE  Black Sabbath | 1983 | RKO (3) | 75-150 |
| *(Live concert)* | | | |
| CAPTURED LIVE (July 84) | 1984 | RKO (4) | 100-175 |
| *(Live shows, part one and two)* | | | |
| CAPTURED LIVE (July 84) | 1984 | RKO (2) | 50-100 |
| *(Live show)* | | | |
| CAPTURED LIVE (Oct 84) | 1984 | RKO (2) | 100-175 |
| *(Live concert with Randy Rhoads)* | | | |
| IN CONCERT  Black Sabbath | 1986 | Westwood One (2) | 75-150 |
| *(Live concert, repeated)* | | | |
| INNERVIEW (80s) Profile | 198? | Innerview | 15-25 |
| *(Music and interviews)* | | | |
| KING BISCUIT FLOWER HOUR (Sept 81) | 1981 | DIR/ABC (2) | 150-225 |
| *(Live concert with Whitford Holmes and Randy Rhoads)* | | | |
| KING BISCUIT FLOWER HOUR (May 82) | 1982 | DIR/ABC (2) | 200-300 |
| *(Live concert with Randy Rhoads)* | | | |
| METALSHOP (Feb 92) Various artists | 1992 | MJI Productions | 30-40 |
| *(Live segment on some of these shows features Osbourne)* | | | |
| NBC SOURCE (July 82) | 1982 | NBC Radio (2) | 175-250 |
| *(Live concert with Randy Rhoads)* | | | |
| OFF THE RECORD (Feb 89) | 1989 | Westwood One (2) | 15-25 |
| *(Music and interviews)* | | | |
| RETRO ROCK  Black Sabbath | 1983 | Clayton Webster | 40-75 |
| *(Mostly live material)* | | | |
| SUPERGROUPS (Aug 83) Live concert | 1983 | Westwood One (3) | 225-350 |
| *(Includes Randy Rhodes)* | | | |
| WORLD OF ROCK (May 89) Various artists | 1989 | DIR (2) | 15-25 |
| *(Ozzy is guest DJ, music and interviews)* | | | |
| **Compact Discs** | | | |
| GLOBAL SATELLITE | 1993 | Global Satellite (3) | 75-125 |
| *(Music and interviews)* | | | |
| LET THE MADNESS CONTINUE | 1993 | (3) | 75-125 |
| *(Music and interviews)* | | | |
| UP CLOSE  Profile | 1993 | Media America (2) | 30-50 |
| *(Mostly music and interviews)* | | | |
| | | | |
| **OSIBISA** | | | |
| **RADIO SHOWS** | | | |
| **Albums** | | | |
| BBC TRANSCRIPTION DISC | 1971 | BBC Transcription | 200-300 |
| *(Live concert)* | | | |

**OSMONDS, THE**

*Featuring Donny Osmond; Includes solo acts; Other MGM promo 45s, group or solo $3 each; Polygram promo 45s, group or solo $2 each; Barnaby promo 45s by Osmonds $5 each; EMI promo 45s by Osmonds $2 each; Other RCA Victor color vinyl promo 45s by Marie Osmond $8 each; RCA Victor promo 45s by Marie Osmond $2 each; Capitol promo 45s by Marie Osmond $2 each*

| Title | Yr | Label, Number | NM $ |
|---|---|---|---|
| **12-Inch Singles** | | | |
| MY LOVE IS A FIRE (3 versions) Donny Osmond | 1990 | Capitol SPRO-79419 | 8 |
| **45s** | | | |
| BE MY LITTLE BABY BUMBLE BEE  The Osmond Brothers | 1963 | MGM 13162 | 10 |
| *(Yellow promo label)* | | | |
| HOLD ON (same on both sides)  Donny Osmond | 1989 | Capitol 7PRO-79683 | 5 |
| *(Vinyl is promo only)* | | | |
| I CAN'T STOP  The Osmond Brothers | 1967 | Uni 55276 | 10 |
| *(Promo copy with a star on the label)* | | | |
| I'LL BE GOOD TO YOU (same on both sides)  Donny Osmond | 1990 | Capitol 7PRO-79913 | 5 |
| *(Vinyl is promo only)* | | | |
| LET ME BE THE FIRST (same on both sides)  Marie Osmond | 1990 | Capitol 7PRO-79??? | 5 |
| *(Vinyl is promo only)* | | | |
| LET ME IN | 1973 | MGM 14617 | 15 |
| *(White label promo, includes sleeve with tour dates)* | | | |
| MISTER SANDMAN  The Osmond Brothers | 1964 | MGM 13281 | 25 |
| *(Yellow promo label, add another $30 if the stock picture sleeve is included)* | | | |
| SACRED EMOTION (same on both sides)  Donny Osmond | 1989 | Capitol 7PRO-79608 | 12 |
| *(Includes promo-only picture sleeve)* | | | |
| SLOWLY BUT SURELY (same on both sides) Marie Osmond | 1989 | Capitol 7PRO-79808 | 5 |
| *(Vinyl is promo only)* | | | |
| THEME FROM TRAVELS OF JAMIE MCPHEETERS  The Osmond Brothers | 1963 | MGM 13174 | 18 |
| *(Yellow promo label, TV soundtrack)* | | | |
| WHAT'S IT ALL ABOUT (May/June 75) Public service show, Donny Osmond | 1975 | W.I.A.A. 267 | 12 |
| *(Flip side features Roy Clark)* | | | |
| WHO'S COUNTING  Marie Osmond | 1984 | RCA  13680 | 10 |
| *(Red promo label, green vinyl)* | | | |

**OTIS, JOHNNY**

*Member of the Peacocks; Head of The Johnny Otis Show; Savoy white promo label 45s $75 each; Mercury white promo label 78s $75 each; Mercury white promo label 45s $50 each; Other Capitol promo 45s $20 each; Other King promo 45s $25 each; Epic promo LPs $30 each; Savoy promo double-LPs $15 each*

| Title | Yr | Label, Number | NM $ |
|---|---|---|---|
| **45s** | | | |
| DANDY'S BOOGIE  The Peacocks | 1957 | Peacock 1675 | 40 |
| *(Colored promo label)* | | | |
| HUM DING A LING | 1957 | Capitol 3799 | 35 |
| *(Pink promo label)* | | | |

| Title | Yr | Label, Number | NM $ |
|---|---|---|---|
| IT'S TOO SOON TO KNOW | 1957 | Capitol 3802 | 35 |
| *(Pink promo label)* | | | |
| JOHNNY OTIS SHOW | 1957 | Capitol PRO | 200 |
| *(Set of four Capitol promo singles 3799, 3800, 3801, 3802 with a special cover)* | | | |
| MA | 1957 | Capitol 3800 | 35 |
| *(Pink promo label)* | | | |
| ROCK ME, BABY  The Peacocks | 1952 | Peacock 1625 | 75 |
| *(Colored promo label)* | | | |
| SHAKE IT  The Peacocks | 1954 | Peacock 1636 | 50 |
| *(Colored promo label)* | | | |
| TELL ME SO | 1957 | Capitol 3801 | 35 |
| *(Pink promo label)* | | | |
| WILLIE AND THE HAND JIVE | 1958 | Capitol 3966 | 25 |
| *(White promo label)* | | | |
| YOU GOT ME CRYING  The Peacocks | 1955 | Peacock 1648 | 50 |
| *(Colored promo label)* | | | |
| **7-Inch Extended Plays** | | | |
| NEW RELEASES  Various artists | 1958 | Capitol PRO-511 | 40 |
| *(Orange promo label, includes one Otis song)* | | | |
| **Albums** | | | |
| THE JOHNNY OTIS SHOW | 1958 | Capitol 940 | 175 |
| *(Blue promo label)* | | | |
| **RADIO SHOWS** | | | |
| **Albums** | | | |
| BBC TRANSCRIPTION DISC | 1972 | BBC Transcription | 150-250 |
| *(Live concert)* | | | |

## OUTLAWS

*Arista promo 45s $2 each*

**Albums**

| Title | Yr | Label, Number | NM $ |
|---|---|---|---|
| OUTLAWS  Music and interviews | 1979 | Arista SP-?? | 15 |
| *(Promo-only release)* | | | |
| **RADIO SHOWS** | | | |
| **Albums** | | | |
| IN CONCERT (Feb 82) | 1982 | Westwood One (2) | 75-125 |
| *(Live concert)* | | | |
| IN CONCERT (Feb 86) | 1986 | Westwood One (2) | 25-50 |
| *(With Joe Walsh)* | | | |
| KING BISCUIT FLOWER HOUR (July 82) Live concert | 1982 | DIR/ABC (2) | 20-40 |
| *(With Johnny and the Distractions)* | | | |
| NBC SOURCE (Jan 81) | 1981 | NBC Radio (2) | 40-80 |
| *(Live concert)* | | | |
| RETRO ROCK (Jan 82) | 1982 | Clayton Webster | 40-75 |
| *(Live concert)* | | | |

## OWEN, JIM

**45s**

| Title | Yr | Label, Number | NM $ |
|---|---|---|---|
| BOGALUSA (same on both sides) | 1982 | Sun 1179 | 4 |
| *(No stock copies issued)* | | | |

## OWENS, BUCK

*Other Capitol promo 45s $2-6 each depending on year; Warner Bros. promo 45s $2 each; Other jukebox LLPs $8 each; Other Capitol promo LPs $25 each*
*Also recorded as Corky Jones*

**45s**

| Title | Yr | Label, Number | NM $ |
|---|---|---|---|
| ACT NATURALLY  With Ringo Starr | 1989 | Capitol 44409 | 25 |
| *(White promo label)* | | | |
| GONNA HAVE LOVE (same on both sides) | 1989 | Capitol 7PRO-79805 | 10 |
| *(Vinyl is promo only)* | | | |
| GOOSE ROCK  Yellow promo label | 1953 | MGM 11579 | 75 |
| *(Owens' first recording, plays guitar)* | | | |
| I KNOW WHAT IT MEANS  Yellow promo label | 1957 | Capitol 3824 | 25 |
| *(First Capitol single)* | | | |
| SWEET THING | 1958 | Capitol 3957 | 25 |
| *(Both sides are rockabilly)* | | | |
| **7-Inch Extended Plays** | | | |
| CARNEGIE HALL CONCERT  Jukebox LLP | 1966 | Capitol 2556 | 10 |
| *(Issued with a hard cover)* | | | |
| OPEN UP YOUR HEART  Jukebox LLP | 1967 | Capitol 2640 | 10 |
| *(Issued with a hard cover)* | | | |
| ROLL OUT THE RED CARPET  Jukebox LLP | 1966 | Capitol 2443 | 10 |
| *(Issued with a hard cover)* | | | |
| **Albums** | | | |
| BUCK OWENS MINUTE MASTERS | 1966 | Capitol 2980 | 50 |
| *(White promo label edited versions, promo-only release)* | | | |
| **Compact Discs** | | | |
| ACT NATURALLY  With Ringo Starr | 1989 | Capitol DPRO-79765 | 100 |
| *(Rare CD single, two tracks)* | | | |

## OXO

**12-Inch Singles**

| Title | Yr | Label, Number | NM $ |
|---|---|---|---|
| WHIRLY GIRL/MY RIDE | 1983 | Geffen PRO-A-2015 | 5 |

| Title | Yr | Label, Number | NM $ |
|-------|-----|---------------|------|

**OZRIC TENTACLES**
**Compact Discs**

| STRANGETUDE | 1990 | I.R.S. | 20 |

*(Promo full-length CD)*

# P

**P.M. DAWN**
**Albums**

| THE BLISS ALBUM | 1993 | Gee Street 6768 | 20 |

*(Promo-only vinyl edition)*

**PABLO CRUISE**
*A&M promo 45s $3 each; Any other A&M promo 12" singles $6 each; A&M promo LPs $5 each*
**12-Inch Singles**

| COOL LOVE/THIS TIME | 1981 | A&M SP-17161 | 8 |
| DON'T WANT TO LIVE WITHOUT IT (DISCO VERSION) (same on both sides) | 1978 | A&M SP-17050 | 10 |
| I WANT YOU TONIGHT (LP Version)/(Edit) | 1979 | A&M SP-17105 | 8 |
| WILL YOU, WON'T YOU (LP Version)/(Edit) | 1983 | A&M SP-17244 | 8 |

**45s**

| PART OF THE GAME (mono/stereo) | 1980 | A&M 2217 | 5 |

*(No stock copies known)*
**RADIO SHOWS**
**Albums**

| ROBERT W. MORGAN (Mar 79) | 1979 | Watermark | 15-25 |

*(Music and interviews)*

**PACIFIC GAS & ELECTRIC**
**45s**

| RAKE, THE/WORK YOUR SHOW | 1970 | Columbia AE 22 | 15 |

*(Promo-only number)*

**PAGANS, THE**
**45s**

| (US AND ) ALL OUR FRIENDS ARE SO MESSED UP/HEART OF STONE | 1988 | Treehouse PR 01 | 10 |

*(Black vinyl promo)*

| (US AND ) ALL OUR FRIENDS ARE SO MESSED UP/HEART OF STONE | 1988 | Treehouse PR 01 | 25 |

*(Clear vinyl promo)*

**PAGE, GENE**
**12-Inch Singles**

| CLOSE ENCOUNTERS OF THE THIRD KIND (6:00) (3:38) | 1978 | Arista SP-13 | 10 |
| WILD CHERRY (6:00) (same on both sides) | 1976 | Atlantic DSKO 69 | 12 |

**PAGE, JIMMY**
*Member of the Yardbirds, Cartoone, Led Zeppelin, The Firm;  Geffen promo CD singles $6 each*
**45s**

| MR. POOR MAN  Cartoone | 1969 | Atlantic 2598 | 10 |

*(Atlantic promo label)*

| REFLECTIONS ON A COMMON THEME  Cartoone | 1970 | Atlantic 2630 | 10 |

*(Atlantic promo label)*
**Compact Discs**

| CONVERSATIONS WITH PLANT & PAGE | 1995 | Atlantic PRCD 5987 | 40 |

*(Promo-only interview disc)*

| OUTRIDER   Special promo-only package | 1988 | Geffen | 100 |

*(Includes CD, videotape, cassette, poster in lunch box-type package)*

| OUTRIDER: AN INTERVIEW WITH JIMMY PAGE | 1988 | Geffen PRO-CD-3099 | 20 |

*(Record company promo sent to radio)*

| SONGWRITING LEGACY Plant & Page | 1996 | Atlantic PRCD 6094 | 50 |

*(Promotional sampler from Miller Genuine Draft)*

| SONGWRITING LEGACY Plant & Page | 1996 | Atlantic PRCD 6095 | 40 |

*(Promotional sampler, 12 tracks)*

| SONGWRITING LEGACY Plant & Page | 1996 | Atlantic | 30 |

*(Promotional sampler, 10 tracks)*
**RADIO SHOWS**
**Albums**

| HIGH VOLTAGE Various artists | 1989 | Westwood One (2) | 40-75 |

*(Live segment of the show features Jimmy Page)*

| LEGENDS OF ROCK | 1989 | NBC Radio (2) | 20-40 |

*(Music and interviews)*

| METALSHOP (Feb 85)  With The Firm | 1985 | MJI Productions (2) | 20-40 |

*(Various artists, special segment features Page and The Firm)*

| OFF THE RECORD (Apr 85) The Firm | 1985 | Westwood One (2) | 15-25 |

*(Repeated)*

| OFF THE RECORD (June 88) | 1988 | Westwood One (2) | 15-25 |

*(Music and interviews)*

| OFF THE RECORD (June 88) | 1988 | Westwood One (4) | 30-40 |

*(Music and interviews, two shows)*

| Title | Yr | Label, Number | NM $ |
|---|---|---|---|
| SUPERSTAR CONCERT | 1988 | Westwood One (3) | 50-100 |
| (Box set, live concert) | | | |
| SUPERSTAR CONCERT  The Firm | 1985 | Westwood One (3) | 40-80 |
| (Box set, live concert) | | | |
| **Compact Discs** | | | |
| OFF THE RECORD (Sept 93) Coverdale/Page | 1993 | Westwood One | 20-30 |
| (Music and interviews) | | | |
| UP CLOSE | 1988 | Media America (2) | 50-100 |
| (Music and interview with some live) | | | |
| **Reel-to-Reel Tapes** | | | |
| WORLD PREMIERE (Mar 93) Coverdale/Page | 1993 | | 40-80 |
| (Music and interviews) | | | |

## PAGE, PATTI

Mercury promo 45s and 78s $3-8 each; Columbia promo 45s $2 each; Sun colored vinyl promo 45s $3 each

| **45s** | | | |
|---|---|---|---|
| HAPPY BIRTHDAY, JESUS (A CHILD'S PRAYER)/CHRISTMAS BELLS | 1965 | Columbia JZSP 111907/8 | 8 |
| (Black vinyl) | | | |
| HAPPY BIRTHDAY, JESUS (A CHILD'S PRAYER)/CHRISTMAS BELLS | 1965 | Columbia JZSP 111907/8 | 10 |
| (Green vinyl) | | | |
| TENNESSEE WALTZ | 197? | Plantation 208 | 10 |
| (Re-recording on green vinyl) | | | |
| **RADIO SHOWS** | | | |
| **16-Inch Transcriptions** | | | |
| MARCH OF DIMES  Various artists | 1958 | March of Dimes | 25-40 |
| (Patti Page is host, music and interviews) | | | |

## PALMER, ROBERT

Member of Vinegar Joe; Member of Power Station; Island promo 45s $4 each (including 99597 with small center hole); Capitol and Manhattan promo 45s $3 each; MCA promo 45s $3 each; MCA promo 12" singles $6 each; Island and EMI promo CD singles $2-4 each

| **12-Inch Singles** | | | |
|---|---|---|---|
| ADDICTED TO LOVE (6:01) (same on both sides) | 1986 | Island PR 827 | 8 |
| DISCIPLINE OF LOVE (6:44) (3:20) | 1985 | Island PR 791 | 6 |
| HYPERACTIVE (same on both sides) | 1986 | Island PR 879 | 6 |
| I DIDN'T MEAN TO TURN YOU ON (3 versions)/ADDICTED TO LOVE | 1986 | Island PR 969 | 10 |
| I DIDN'T MEAN TO TURN YOU ON (same on both sides) | 1986 | Island PR 891 | 6 |
| JOHNNY AND MARY | 1980 | Island PRO-A-906 | 8 |
| (B-side is blank) | | | |
| LOOKING FOR CLUES (same on both sides) | 1980 | Island PRO-A-922 | 8 |
| MERCY MERCY ME (THE ECOLOGY)-I WANT YOU (4 versions) | 1991 | EMI SPRO 4739/45 | 8 |
| MORE THAN EVER (LP Version)/(Live) | 1988 | EMI Manhattan SPRO 04192 | 6 |
| PRIDE (3 versions) | 1983 | Island PR 678 | 8 |
| SIMPLY IRRESISTIBLE (same on both sides) | 1988 | EMI Manhattan SPRO 04074 | 6 |
| SWEET LIES (same on both sides) | 1988 | Island 2236 | 6 |
| YOU ARE IN MY SYSTEM (6:06) (2:57) | 1983 | Island PR 635 | 6 |
| **45s** | | | |
| RIPTIDE | 1986 | Island PR 980 | 10 |
| (Promo only single release) | | | |
| TELL ME I'M NOT DREAMING (LP)/(12" Edit) | 1989 | EMI 7PRO-04311 | 5 |
| (Vinyl is promo only) | | | |
| WHAT'S IT ALL ABOUT (Jan 80) Public service show | 1980 | W.I.A.A. 506 | 18 |
| (With Jethro Tull) | | | |
| **Albums** | | | |
| LIVE IN BOSTON | 1979 | Warner Bros. WBMS-111 | 30 |
| (Part of "The Warner Bros. Music Show") | | | |
| SECRETS | 1979 | Island PRO-819 | 20 |
| (Promo-only picture disc) | | | |
| **RADIO SHOWS** | | | |
| **Albums** | | | |
| BBC TRANSCRIPTION DISC | 1983 | BBC Transcription | 75-125 |
| (Live concert, Island material) | | | |
| BBC TRANSCRIPTION DISC  Vinegar Joe | 1973 | BBC Transcription | 300-400 |
| (Live concert with Karavan) | | | |
| KING BISCUIT FLOWER HOUR (Mar 80) Live concert | 1980 | DIR/ABC (2) | 50-100 |
| (With Talking Heads) | | | |
| KING BISCUIT FLOWER HOUR Live concert | 1983 | DIR/ABC (2) | 25-50 |
| (With Madness) | | | |
| LEGENDS OF ROCK (June 89) | 1989 | NBC Radio (2) | 20-35 |
| (Music and interviews) | | | |
| OFF THE RECORD (80s) | 198? | Westwood One (2) | 10-20 |
| (Music and interviews, repeated) | | | |
| SOURCE SPECIAL | 1980 | NBC Radio (2) | 20-35 |
| (Music and interviews) | | | |
| SUPERSTAR CONCERT | 1986 | Westwood One (3) | 25-50 |
| (Live concert) | | | |
| SUPERSTAR CONCERT (80s) The Power Station | 198? | Westwood One (3) | 25-50 |
| (Live concert) | | | |
| **Compact Discs** | | | |
| BBC CLASSIC TRACKS (Feb 91) | 1991 | Westwood One | 10-15 |
| (Classic live tracks) | | | |
| KING BISCUIT FLOWER HOUR (Apr 88) Live concert | 1988 | DIR | 25-50 |
| (Repeated) | | | |
| UP CLOSE Profile | 1988 | Media America (2) | 25-50 |
| (Music and interviews with some live tracks) | | | |

| Title | Yr | Label, Number | NM $ |
|---|---|---|---|

**PALMS, THE**
**45s**

| | | | |
|---|---|---|---|
| EDNA | 1957 | United 208 | 75 |
| *(White promo label)* | | | |

**PARKER, GRAHAM**
*Mercury and Arista promo 45s $4-8 each; Mercury and other Arista promo 12" singles $10 each*
**12-Inch Singles**

| | | | |
|---|---|---|---|
| DON'T LET IT BREAK YOU DOWN (same on both sides) | 1988 | RCA 8685-1 | 6 |
| LOCAL GIRLS/I WANT YOU BACK (ALIVE) | 1979 | Arista SP-54 | 6 |
| MERCURY POISONING (one-sided) | 1979 | Arista SP-41 | 12 |
| *(Gray vinyl with custom labels)* | | | |
| MERCURY POISONING/I WANT YOU BACK (ALIVE) | 1979 | Arista SP-65 | 12 |
| THE PINK PARKER | 1977 | Mercury MK-28 | 30 |
| *(Pink vinyl, promo-only release, not to be confused with 7-inch stock copies on pink vinyl)* | | | |
| START A FIRE (LP version)/(Edit) | 1988 | RCA 8336-1 | 6 |
| TEMPORARY BEAUTY/NO MORE EXCUSES (Instrumental) | 1982 | Arista SP-118 | 7 |
| WAKE UP (NEXT TO YOU) (Long Version)/(Short Version) | 1984 | Elektra ED 5040 | 5 |
| THE WEEKEND'S TOO SHORT (same on both sides) | 1985 | Elektra ED 5078 | 5 |
| YOU CAN'T TAKE LOVE FOR GRANTED (2 versions) | 1983 | Arista 9098 | 6 |
| YOU HIT THE SPOT (LP)/(Extended) | 1982 | Arista SP-130 | 6 |

**45s**

| | | | |
|---|---|---|---|
| HOLD BACK THE NIGHT (same on both sides) | 1977 | Mercury DJ-491 | 12 |
| STICK TO ME (same on both sides) | 1977 | Mercury DJ-531 | 12 |

**Albums**

| | | | |
|---|---|---|---|
| LIVE SPARKS | 1979 | Arista SP-63 | 25 |
| *(Promo-only release)* | | | |

**RADIO SHOWS**
**Albums**

| | | | |
|---|---|---|---|
| BBC ROCK HOUR (May 82) | 1982 | London Wavelength | 40-75 |
| *(Live concert)* | | | |
| BBC TRANSCRIPTION DISC  Live concert | 1982 | BBC Transcription | 200-300 |
| *(Very rare concert)* | | | |
| IN CONCERT (May 85) Live concert | 1985 | Westwood One (2) | 40-75 |
| *(With Little River Band)* | | | |
| IN CONCERT Live concert | 1988 | Westwood One (2) | 25-50 |
| *(Graham Parker solo concert)* | | | |
| INNERVIEW (80s) Profile | 198? | Innerview | 20-30 |
| *(Music and interviews)* | | | |
| KING BISCUIT FLOWER HOUR (July 82) Live concert | 1982 | DIR/ABC (2) | 75-125 |
| *(With Sparks)* | | | |
| KING BISCUIT FLOWER HOUR (Feb 84) Live concert | 1984 | DIR/ABC (2) | 25-50 |
| *(With Bryan Adams)* | | | |
| KING BISCUIT FLOWER HOUR (July 85) Live concert | 1985 | DIR (2) | 50-100 |
| *(With Roxy Music)* | | | |
| LONDON WAVELENGTH (June 82) | 1982 | London Wavelength | 20-40 |
| *(Music and interviews)* | | | |

**Compact Discs**

| | | | |
|---|---|---|---|
| LIVE FROM HOUSE OF BLUES (Jan 96) | 1996 | (2) | 50-80 |
| *(Live concert material, with Junior Wells)* | | | |

**PARKER, RAY**
*Arista promo 45s $3 each; MCA promo CD singles $2 each*
**RADIO SHOWS**
**Albums**

| | | | |
|---|---|---|---|
| STARTRACK PROFILES (Sept 85) | 1985 | Westwood One (2) | 15-25 |
| *(Music and interviews)* | | | |

**PARSONS, ALAN, PROJECT**
*Arista and 20th Century promo 45s $3 each*
**Albums**

| | | | |
|---|---|---|---|
| AUDIO GUIDE TO THE ALAN PARSONS PROJECT | 1979 | Arista SP-68 (6) | 50 |
| *(Box set, promo only, Parsons' work includes Beatles tracks)* | | | |
| COMPLETE AUDIO GUIDE TO THE ALAN PARSONS PROJECT | 1980 | Arista SP-140 (8) | 80 |
| *(Box set, extended version, also includes Beatles tracks)* | | | |
| VULTURE CULTURE | 1985 | Arista ALPD 8263 | 25 |
| *(Promo-only picture disc)* | | | |

**RADIO SHOWS**
**Albums**

| | | | |
|---|---|---|---|
| BBC TRANSCRIPTION DISC  Profile | 198? | BBC Transcription (2) | 200-300 |
| *(With the Who, music and interviews)* | | | |
| INNERVIEW (80s) Profile | 198? | Innerview | 20-30 |
| *(Music and interviews)* | | | |
| LEGENDS OF ROCK (Apr 87) Profile | 1987 | NBC Radio (2) | 20-30 |
| *(Music and interviews)* | | | |
| SOURCE SPECIAL (Jan 83) | 1983 | NBC Radio (3) | 30-60 |
| *(Mostly music and interviews)* | | | |

**Compact Discs**

| | | | |
|---|---|---|---|
| IN THE STUDIO (Sept 93) Profile of an album | 1993 | Album Network | 15-25 |
| *(Music and interviews)* | | | |

**PARTON, DOLLY**
*Monument promo 45s $8 each; Other RCA Victor color vinyl promo 45s $8 each; Other RCA Victor promo 45s $3 each; Other Columbia promo 45s $2 each; Other Columbia promo CD singles $4-6 each*
**45s**

| | | | |
|---|---|---|---|
| HARD CANDY CHRISTMAS  Pink label, red vinyl | 1982 | RCA 13361 | 12 |
| *(Only the promo is colored vinyl)* | | | |

| Title | Yr | Label, Number | NM $ |
|---|---|---|---|
| HE'S ALIVE | 1989 | Columbia (no #) | 10 |
| *(White label, only title and artist listed)* | | | |
| HE'S ALIVE  7-inch red promo label | 1989 | Columbia CS7-01929 | 12 |
| *(Small center hole)* | | | |
| MEDLEY: WINTER WONDERLAND/SLEIGH RIDE (same on both sides) | 1984 | RCA JK-13944 | 4 |
| 9 TO 5  Pink label, blue vinyl | 1980 | RCA 12133 | 20 |
| *(Only the promo is colored vinyl)* | | | |
| POTENTIAL NEW BOYFRIEND  Brown/yellow label, yellow vinyl | 1983 | RCA 13514 | 15 |
| *(Long 3:35 and short 3:15 versions)* | | | |
| POTENTIAL NEW BOYFRIEND  Light purple label, blue vinyl | 1983 | RCA 13514 | 15 |
| *(Long 3:35 and short 3:15 versions)* | | | |
| SAVE THE LAST DANCE FOR ME  Pink label, green vinyl | 1983 | RCA 13703 | 15 |
| *(Only the promo is colored vinyl)* | | | |
| SINGLE WOMEN  Pink label, red vinyl | 1982 | RCA 13057 | 12 |
| *(Only the promo is colored vinyl)* | | | |
| STARTING OVER AGAIN  Green label, green vinyl | 1980 | RCA 11926 | 12 |
| *(Only the promo is colored vinyl)* | | | |
| WHAT'S IT ALL ABOUT (Sept 77) Public service show | 1977 | W.I.A.A. 389 | 15 |
| *(Flip side features B. J. Thomas)* | | | |
| **7-Inch Extended Plays** | | | |
| BALLY (80s)  EP cover for Bally | 198? | Bally (no #) | 50 |
| *(Very rare hard EP sleeve for 7" record, with photo of Dolly standing by a Bally pinball machine called "Dolly Parton")* | | | |
| PORTER WAYNE AND DOLLY REBECCA  With Porter Wagoner | 1970 | RCA Victor 4305 | 40 |
| *(Jukebox LLP issued with a hard cover; oddly, the sleeve opening is at the left)* | | | |
| **Albums** | | | |
| AS LONG AS I LOVE | 1970 | Monument 18136 | 25 |
| *(White promo label)* | | | |
| HBO PRESENTS DOLLY PARTON  Picture disc | 1983 | RCA Victor 812 | 25 |
| *(Promo-only release)* | | | |
| HELLO I'M DOLLY | 1967 | Monument 8085 | 50 |
| *(White promo label)* | | | |
| THE WORLD OF DOLLY | 1972 | Monument 31913 | 20 |
| *(White promo label)* | | | |
| **Compact Discs** | | | |
| HOME FOR CHRISTMAS | 1990 | Columbia CSK 2159 | 15 |
| *(Promo-only radio show to promote her first solo Christmas album)* | | | |
| SLOW DANCING WITH THE MOON | 1992 | Columbia CSK 53199 | 20 |
| *(Promo-only issue in cardboard digipak)* | | | |
| WHY'D YOU COME IN HERE LOOKIN' LIKE THAT | 1989 | Columbia CSK 1588 | 8 |
| *(Promo CD single)* | | | |
| **RADIO SHOWS** | | | |
| **Albums** | | | |
| DOLLY & DON  With Don Williams | 1983 | Mutual Radio (3) | 20-30 |
| *(Music and interviews)* | | | |
| WESTWOOD ONE PRESENTS (May 89) | 1989 | Westwood One | 25-50 |
| *(With Kenny Rogers and Willie Nelson)* | | | |

**PATTON, JIMMY**
**45s**

| Title | Yr | Label, Number | NM $ |
|---|---|---|---|
| OKIE'S IN THE POKIE | 1961 | Sims 117 | 75 |
| *(White promo label)* | | | |

**PAUL, HENRY, BAND**
**RADIO SHOWS**
**Albums**

| Title | Yr | Label, Number | NM $ |
|---|---|---|---|
| KING BISCUIT FLOWER HOUR (Aug 80) Live concert | 1980 | DIR/ABC (2) | 40-75 |
| *(With Point Blank)* | | | |
| KING BISCUIT FLOWER HOUR (Dec 81) Live concert | 1981 | DIR/ABC (2) | 40-75 |
| *(With Nils Lofgren)* | | | |

**PAVAROTTI, LUCIANO**
**Compact Discs**

| Title | Yr | Label, Number | NM $ |
|---|---|---|---|
| SONGBOOK | 1991 | London PAV 1 | 20 |
| *(Promo-only sampler)* | | | |

**PAXTON, GARY**
*Capitol, Liberty and Garpax promo 45s $20 each; MGM, RCA Victor and Private Stock promo 45s $5 each Was the Hollywood Argyles*
**45s**

| Title | Yr | Label, Number | NM $ |
|---|---|---|---|
| WHAT'S IT ALL ABOUT (Aug 77) Public service show | 1977 | W.I.A.A. 381 | 20 |
| *(Flip side is Manfred Mann)* | | | |
| WHAT'S IT ALL ABOUT (Aug 81) Public service show | 1981 | W.I.A.A. 588 | 18 |
| *(Flip side features Journey)* | | | |

**PAXTON, TOM**
*Elektra promo singles $3 each; Reprise promo LPs $8 each*
**RADIO SHOWS**
**Albums**

| Title | Yr | Label, Number | NM $ |
|---|---|---|---|
| BBC TRANSCRIPTION DISC  Live concert | 1972 | BBC Transcription | 200-300 |
| *(Very rare live concert)* | | | |

**PAYCHECK, JOHNNY**
*Epic, Little Darlin' and Cutlass promo 45s $3 each*
**45s**

| Title | Yr | Label, Number | NM $ |
|---|---|---|---|
| MY KIND OF LOVE  Jimmy Dallas | 1960 | Decca 31133 | 15 |
| *(Pink promo label)* | | | |

| Title | Yr | Label, Number | NM $ |
|---|---|---|---|
| TAKE THIS JOB AND SHOVE IT | 1977 | Epic 50469 | 8 |
| *(White promo label, mono/stereo, by far his biggest hit single)* | | | |
| **RADIO SHOWS** | | | |
| **Albums** | | | |
| COUNTRY SESSIONS (80s) | 198? | Westwood One | 10-15 |
| *(This show was repeated)* | | | |
| LIVE AT GILLEY'S (July 84) Live concert | 1984 | Westwood One | 20-30 |
| *(Repeated)* | | | |
| | | | |
| **PAYNE, FREDA** | | | |
| **12-Inch Singles** | | | |
| HAPPY DAYS ARE HERE AGAIN-HAPPY MUSIC | 1978 | Capitol SPRO-8922/3 | 15 |
| RED HOT (7:01) (same on both sides) | 1979 | Capitol SPRO-9219 | 10 |
| | | | |
| **PAYOLA$** | | | |
| **RADIO SHOWS** | | | |
| **Albums** | | | |
| KING BISCUIT FLOWER HOUR (Nov 83) Live concert | 1983 | DIR/ABC (2) | 25-50 |
| *(With the Eric Martin Band)* | | | |
| | | | |
| **PEACHES AND HERB** | | | |
| **12-Inch Singles** | | | |
| FREEWAY (6:03) (same on both sides) | 1981 | Polydor PRO 165 | 12 |
| | | | |
| **PEARL HARBOUR AND THE EXPLOSIONS** | | | |
| **12-Inch Singles** | | | |
| YOU GOT IT/DRIVIN'/BUSY B SIDE | 1979 | Warner Bros. PRO-A-843 | 6 |
| | | | |
| **PEARL JAM** | | | |
| **45s** | | | |
| ANGEL/RAMBLINGS | 1993 | Epic ZS7 5610 | 40 |
| *(Third annual fan club single, with picture sleeve)* | | | |
| LET ME SLEEP (CHRISTMAS TIME)/RAMBLINGS | 1991 | Epic Associated ZS7 4354 | 50 |
| *(First fan club single, small hole, plays at 33 1/3 RPM)* | | | |
| WHO KILLED RUDOLPH | 1992 | Epic ZS7 4906 | 40 |
| *(Second annual fan club single, with "Sonic Reducer" and "Ramblings Continued")* | | | |
| **Compact Discs** | | | |
| ALIVE | 1991 | Epic ZSK 4041 | 15 |
| *(With three tracks and front insert)* | | | |
| ALIVE | 1991 | Epic ZSK 4146 | 10 |
| *(With one track and no front insert)* | | | |
| BOOTLEG #2 -- CHECKPOINT CHARLIE | 1996 | 98-Rock Radio (2) | 50 |
| *(Berlin concert, issued as radio giveaway by Tampa, Fla. station)* | | | |
| CULTIVATE THE TOUR | 1992 | Epic ZSK 4285 | 25 |
| *(Promo-only sampler, has three tracks including live version of "Alive")* | | | |
| EVEN FLOW | 1992 | Epic ZSK 4496 | 10 |
| *(Promo-only CD single)* | | | |
| FOX THEATRE, ATLANTA, GEORGIA 4/3/94 | 1994 | KROQ Radio (2) | 50 |
| *(Promo only, released by Los Angeles radio station KROQ)* | | | |
| FOX THEATRE, ATLANTA, GEORGIA 4/3/94 | 1994 | Z-100 Radio (2) | 50 |
| *(Promo only, released by New York radio station Z-100)* | | | |
| FOX THEATRE, ATLANTA, GEORGIA 4/3/94 | 1994 | WBCN Radio (2) | 50 |
| *(Promo only, released by radio station WBCN)* | | | |
| GIVEN TO FLY | 1998 | Epic ESK 3946 | 10 |
| *(Promo CD single)* | | | |
| GO | 1993 | Epic ZSK 5487 | 10 |
| *(Promo-only CD single)* | | | |
| HAIL, HAIL | 1996 | Epic ESK 8772 | 10 |
| *(Promo CD single)* | | | |
| IMMORTALITY | 1995 | Epic ESK 7113 | 10 |
| *(Promo CD single)* | | | |
| IN HIDING | 1998 | Epic (no #) | 20 |
| *(Promo-only CD single)* | | | |
| JEREMY | 1992 | Epic ZSK 4606 | 10 |
| *(Promo-only CD single)* | | | |
| NOT FOR YOU | 1995 | Epic ESK 6858 | 10 |
| *(Promo-only CD single)* | | | |
| OFF HE GOES | 1996 | Epic ESK 9221 | 10 |
| *(Promo CD single)* | | | |
| PEARL JAM LIVE  Recorded at Spartan Stadium | 1995 | KOME Radio (2) | 40 |
| *(Offered as a giveaway by KOME Radio, San Jose, California)* | | | |
| SELF-POLLUTION RADIO | 1995 | Z-100 Radio (4) | 100 |
| *(Four-CD set issued as giveaway by Z-100 New York)* | | | |
| SOLDIER FIELD LIVE | 1995 | Q101 Radio (2) | 40 |
| *(Offered as a giveaway by Q-101 Radio, Chicago)* | | | |
| TRANSMISSIONS FROM SELF-POLLUTION RADIO | 1995 | Q101 Radio | 30 |
| *(Highlight CD from Self-Pollution Radio, given away by Q101 Chicago)* | | | |
| WHO YOU ARE | 1996 | Epic ESK 8397 | 10 |
| *(Promo CD single)* | | | |
| WISHLIST | 1998 | Epic ESK 41068 | 10 |
| *(Promo CD single)* | | | |
| YIELD | 1997 | Epic ESK 3936 | 20 |
| *(Advance promo of album of the same name, no front insert)* | | | |

| Title | Yr | Label, Number | NM $ |
|---|---|---|---|
| **RADIO SHOWS** | | | |
| **Compact Discs** | | | |
| IN CONCERT (Aug 94) Live concert | 1994 | Westwood One | 40-75 |
| *(New material)* | | | |
| IN CONCERT (Sept 93) Live concert | 1993 | Westwood One | 25-50 |
| *(Repeated)* | | | |
| IN CONCERT-NU ROCK (Sept 94) Live concert | 1994 | Westwood One | 40-75 |
| *(Same show as above)* | | | |
| OFF THE RECORD (Apr 92) Music and interviews | 1992 | Westwood One | 10-20 |
| *(With Social Distortion)* | | | |
| ON THE EDGE (Jan 93) Music and interviews | 1993 | Westwood One | 25-40 |
| *(With Neneh Cherry and EMF)* | | | |
| ON THE EDGE (Oct 93) Music and interviews | 1993 | Westwood One | 25-35 |
| *(With Big Country and The Breeders)* | | | |
| SUPERSTAR CONCERT (Mar 93) Live concert | 1993 | Westwood One (2) | 30-60 |
| *(Repeated)* | | | |

**PEEL, DAVID**

| Title | Yr | Label, Number | NM $ |
|---|---|---|---|
| **45s** | | | |
| F IS NOT A DIRTY WORD/THE BALLAD OF NEW YORK CITY | 1972 | Apple PRO-6498/9 | 120 |
| HIPPIE FROM NEW YORK CITY/THE BALLAD OF NEW YORK CITY | 1972 | Apple PRO-6545/6 | 120 |

**PENGUINS, THE**

*Other Mercury promo 45s $40 each*

| Title | Yr | Label, Number | NM $ |
|---|---|---|---|
| **45s** | | | |
| A CHRISTMAS PRAYER | 1955 | Mercury 70762 | 60 |
| *(White promo label)* | | | |
| MEMORIES OF EL MONTE | 1963 | Original Sound 27 | 100 |
| *(Written by Frank Zappa)* | | | |
| PLEDGE OF LOVE | 1957 | Atlantic 1132 | 50 |
| *(White promo label)* | | | |

**PENN, MICHAEL**

*RCA promo 45s $3 each; RCA promo CD singles $2 each*

| Title | Yr | Label, Number | NM $ |
|---|---|---|---|
| **RADIO SHOWS** | | | |
| **Albums** | | | |
| IN CONCERT (Dec 92) Live concert | 1992 | Westwood One (2) | 25-50 |
| *(With the Zoo/Fleetwood Mac)* | | | |
| IN CONCERT (Nov 90) Live concert | 1990 | Westwood One (2) | 25-40 |
| *(With John Hiatt)* | | | |
| **Compact Discs** | | | |
| KING BISCUIT FLOWER HOUR (Oct 92) Live concert | 1992 | DIR | 20-40 |
| *(With The Kinks)* | | | |

**PEPPERS, THE**

| Title | Yr | Label, Number | NM $ |
|---|---|---|---|
| **45s** | | | |
| HOLD ON | 1954 | Chess 1577 | 100 |
| *(White promo label)* | | | |

**PERE UBU**

| Title | Yr | Label, Number | NM $ |
|---|---|---|---|
| **12-Inch Singles** | | | |
| BREATHE/BANG THE DRUM/OVER MY HEAD/UNIVERSAL VIBRATION | 1989 | Fontana PRO 747 | 10 |

**PERKINS, CARL**

*None of the Sun material was pressed on custom promos; Other Columbia promo 45s through 42753 $15 each; Columbia promo 45s 44723 and after $5 each; Decca promo 45s $12 each; Dollie promo 45s $8 each; Mercury and Jet (UA) promo 45s $3 each; America/Smash promo 45s $4 each*

| Title | Yr | Label, Number | NM $ |
|---|---|---|---|
| **45s** | | | |
| HOLLYWOOD CITY | 1962 | Columbia 42405 | 20 |
| *(White promo label, stock picture sleeve worth $75)* | | | |
| LEVI JACKET | 1958 | Columbia 41207 | 20 |
| *(White promo label)* | | | |
| LOW CLASS | 197? | Mercury DJ-420 | 10 |
| *(Special promo number)* | | | |
| PINK PEDAL PUSHERS | 1958 | Columbia 41131 | 25 |
| *(White promo label, stock picture sleeve is worth $75)* | | | |
| SISTER TWISTER | 1962 | Columbia 42514 | 20 |
| *(White promo label, stock picture sleeve worth $200)* | | | |
| **7-Inch Extended Plays** | | | |
| DIG THIS Various artists | 1970 | Columbia AS 3 | 15 |
| *(One cut by Carl Perkins and NRBQ, issued with paper sleeve)* | | | |
| THE SURVIVORS Various artists | 1982 | Columbia AE7 1505 | 25 |
| *(White promo label, one cut by Perkins, issued in a paper picture sleeve)* | | | |
| **Albums** | | | |
| BOPPIN' THE BLUES  With NRBQ | 1970 | Columbia 9981 | 25 |
| *(White promo label)* | | | |
| BROWN EYED HANDSOME MAN | 1972 | Harmony 31179 | 20 |
| *(White promo label)* | | | |
| CARL PERKINS | 1972 | Harmony 31185 | 20 |
| *(White promo label)* | | | |
| CARL PERKINS GREATEST HITS | 1969 | Columbia 9833 | 25 |
| *(White promo label)* | | | |
| MY KIND OF COUNTRY | 1973 | Mercury 691 | 15 |
| *(White promo label)* | | | |
| OL' BLUE SUEDE'S BACK | 1978 | Jet (UA) 856 | 15 |
| *(White promo label)* | | | |

| **Title** | **Yr** | **Label, Number** | **NM $** |
|---|---|---|---|
| ON TOP | 1969 | Columbia 9931 | 25 |
| *(White promo label)* | | | |
| THE GREATEST HITS OF CARL PERKINS | 1972 | Harmony 31192 | 20 |
| *(White promo label)* | | | |
| WHOLE LOTTA SHAKIN' | 1958 | Columbia CL 1234 | 400 |
| *(Red promo label)* | | | |
| WHOLE LOTTA SHAKIN' | 1958 | Columbia CL 1234 | 800 |
| *(White promo label)* | | | |
| **RADIO SHOWS** | | | |
| **Albums** | | | |
| AMERICAN EAGLE LIVE  Various artists | 1983 | Westwood One (3) | 40-75 |
| *(Includes Carl Perkins in concert)* | | | |

## PERLE, ADAM, AND WESLEY CROW
**45s**

| | | | |
|---|---|---|---|
| A SILENT NIGHT/HAPPINESS IS A SAD, SAD SONG | 1972 | Atco 6916 | 5 |

## PET SHOP BOYS
*EMI and EMI Manhattan promo 45s $4 each;Other EMI promo 12" singles $10 each; EMI promo CD singles $6-8 each*
**12-Inch Singles**

| | | | |
|---|---|---|---|
| ALWAYS ON MY MIND (5 versions)/DO I HAVE TO | 1988 | EMI Manhattan SPRO 04051 | 16 |
| HOW CAN YOU EXPECT TO BE TAKEN SERIOUSLY (5 versions) | 1991 | EMI SPRO 04727 | 10 |
| I'M NOT SCARED/I WANT A DOG | 1988 | EMI Manhattan SPRO 04231/2 | 15 |
| ONE MORE CHANCE (LP)/(Remix) | 1984 | Bobcat 05019 | 20 |
| *Promo stamp on generic black jacket* | | | |
| OPPORTUNITIES (LET'S MAKE LOTS OF MONEY) (same on both sides) | 1985 | EMI America SPRO 9669 | 20 |
| SO HARD (4 mixes) | 1990 | EMI SPRO 04690 | 10 |
| SUBURBIA (2 versions) | 1986 | EMI America SPRO 9925 | 10 |
| WEST END GIRLS | 1984 | Bobcat (CBS) 05019 | 40 |
| *(Rare early mix, later a major hit on EMI)* | | | |
| WHAT HAVE I DONE TO DESERVE THIS (2 mixes)/RENT/I WANT A DOG | 1988 | EMI Manhattan SPRO 04013/4 | 25 |
| **Albums** | | | |
| SPECIAL LIMITED EDITION: INTROSPECTIVE CLUB MIXES | 1988 | EMI Manhattan 04233 | 40 |
| *(Promo-only set of three 12" records of remixes)* | | | |
| **Compact Discs** | | | |
| ALWAYS ON MY MIND | 1988 | EMI Manhattan DPRO-04058 | 15 |
| *(Their first promo CD single in the U.S.)* | | | |

## PETER AND GORDON
**45s**

| | | | |
|---|---|---|---|
| WRONG FROM THE START | 196? | Capitol Creative Products SP-51 | 25 |
| *(Frito-Lay giveaway, with special sleeve with "#51" printed on it; B-side by the Lettermen)* | | | |

## PETER, PAUL AND MARY
*Other Warner Bros. promo 45s $4 each; Warner Bros. promo solo 45s $3 each; Benson label promo 45s by Noel Paul Stookey $5 each; Warner promo LPs by PPM $10-15 each; Warner promo LPs by solo PPM $8 each*
**45s**

| | | | |
|---|---|---|---|
| A'SOALIN' | 196? | Warner Bros. (no #) | 25 |
| *(Green and white label, mono/stereo, includes lyric booklet)* | | | |
| IF YOU LOVE YOUR COUNTRY | 1968 | (No label or #) | 25 |
| *(Promo-only record for the campaign of Eugene McCarthy for President of the United States)* | | | |
| MORNING TRAIN | 1965 | Warner Bros. PRO 149 | 15 |
| *(Red/white label, small center hole, stereo single)* | | | |
| QUIT YOUR LOW DOWN WAYS | 1966 | Warner Bros. S 155 | 15 |
| *(Red/white label, small center hole, stereo single)* | | | |
| WHAT'S IT ALL ABOUT (Dec 78) Public service show | 1978 | W.I.A.A. 451 | 15 |
| *(Interviews with Mary Travers and Yarrow, flip is Marshall Tucker Band)* | | | |
| WHAT'S IT ALL ABOUT (Jan 74) Public service show | 1974 | W.I.A.A. 212 | 15 |
| *(Interviews with Peter Yarrow, flip side is Melanie)* | | | |
| WHAT'S IT ALL ABOUT (Dec 81) Public service show | 1981 | W.I.A.A. 603 | 25 |
| *(Flip side features Blondie)* | | | |
| **7-Inch Extended Plays** | | | |
| ALBUM 1700 | 1967 | Warner Bros. PRO 265 | 25 |
| *(White promo label, four songs, for radio)* | | | |
| IN THE WIND | 1963 | Warner Bros. S 1507 | 25 |
| *(Promo only, small center hole, six songs, no sleeve)* | | | |
| LATE AGAIN | 1968 | Warner Bros. 1751 | 25 |
| *(Jukebox LLP issued with a hard cover)* | | | |
| MOVING | 1962 | Warner Bros. S 1473 | 25 |
| *(Promo only, small center hole, six songs, no sleeve)* | | | |
| **RADIO SHOWS** | | | |
| **Albums** | | | |
| FOR CHRISTMAS SEALS  Various artists | 1965 | Decca 200,545 | 25-50 |
| *(5-minute shows including one by PPM and one by Barbra Streisand)* | | | |
| FOR CHRISTMAS SEALS  With Lorne Greene | 1965 | Decca 200,540 | 50-100 |
| *(Very rare 15-minute PPM show, music and interviews)* | | | |

## PETERS, BERNADETTE
**45s**

| | | | |
|---|---|---|---|
| PEARL'S A SINGER | 1980 | MCA S45-1883 | 10 |
| *(Promo-only number)* | | | |

## PETERSON, RAY
*RCA Victor promo 45s $5 each; MGM promo 45s $4 each; Uni promo 45s $3 each*
**Albums**

| | | | |
|---|---|---|---|
| THE OTHER SIDE OF RAY PETERSON | 1965 | MGM 4277 | 15 |
| *(Yellow promo label)* | | | |

| Title | Yr | Label, Number | NM $ |
|-------|----|----|------|
| THE VERY BEST OF RAY PETERSON | 1964 | MGM 4250 | 20 |
| *(Yellow promo label)* | | | |

## PETTY, NORMAN, TRIO

*Other Columbia promo 45s by Norman Petty Trio and/or Vi Petty $8 each; Other ABC Paramount, "X" (RCA), Felsted, Nor-Va-Jac promos $5 each Produced Buddy Holly's recordings*

**45s**

| | | | |
|-------|----|----|------|
| THE FIRST KISS  With Vi Petty | 1957 | Columbia 40929 | 10 |
| *(No Holly guitar on this one)* | | | |
| HEY, PUNKIN'  The Bowman Brothers with Norman Petty | 1958 | Columbia 41176 | 40 |
| *(White promo label)* | | | |
| IT'S BEEN A LONG LONG TIME | 1956 | ABC-Paramount 9787 | 10 |
| *(Before Buddy Holly recorded)* | | | |
| MOOD INDIGO | 1955 | "X" 0040 | 10 |
| *(Before Buddy Holly recorded)* | | | |
| MOONDREAMS | 1957 | Columbia 41039 | 50 |
| *(White promo label, Buddy Holly on guitar)* | | | |

**Albums**

| | | | |
|-------|----|----|------|
| MOONDREAMS | 1958 | Columbia 1092 | 300 |
| *(White promo label, Buddy Holly plays guitar on one track, "Moondreams")* | | | |

**RADIO SHOWS**

**Albums**

| | | | |
|-------|----|----|------|
| BUDDY HOLLY | 1987 | Creative Radio (2) | 40-75 |
| *(Music and interviews, Norman Petty involvement)* | | | |
| BUDDY HOLLY SPECIAL WITH HOST JIM PEWTER | 198? | Creative Radio (4) | 50-100 |
| *(With Norman Petty involvement)* | | | |
| ROYALTY OF ROCK  Profile of Buddy Holly | 1982 | RKO | 30-50 |
| *(Music and interviews, Norman Petty involvement)* | | | |
| A TRIBUTE TO BUDDY HOLLY  With Jerry Naylor | 1985 | Creative Radio (2) | 40-75 |
| *(Music and interviews, Norman Petty involvement)* | | | |

## PETTY, TOM, AND THE HEARTBREAKERS

*Includes Mudcrutch; Also see Traveling Wilburys; Shelter (ABC) promo 45s $4 each; Other MCA promo 45s $3 each; MCA promo 12" singles $8 each; Other Shelter (ABC) promo LPs $12 each; Other promo CD singles $3-5 each*

**45s**

| | | | |
|-------|----|----|------|
| BREAKDOWN (Mono)/(Stereo) | 1976 | Shelter 62006 | 10 |
| CHANGE OF HEART  Red vinyl | 1982 | Backstreet 52181 | 10 |
| *(White promo label, red vinyl, some stock copies also are red vinyl)* | | | |
| DEPOT STREET  Mudcrutch | 1975 | Shelter (MCA) 40357 | 20 |
| *(White promo label, stock copy worth much more)* | | | |

**Albums**

| | | | |
|-------|----|----|------|
| OFFICIAL LIVE 'LEG | 1976 | Shelter 12677 | 40 |
| *(One-sided promo-only release)* | | | |
| PACK UP THE PLANTATION | 1985 | MCA | 15 |
| *(Promo-only sampler)* | | | |
| YOU'RE GONNA GET IT | 1978 | Shelter 52029 | 25 |
| *(Red vinyl promo-only release)* | | | |

**Compact Discs**

| | | | |
|-------|----|----|------|
| AMERICAN GIRL | 1994 | MCA 3008 | 8 |
| *(Promo CD single, re-release from Greatest Hits CD)* | | | |
| WALLS | 1996 | Warner Bros. | 8 |
| *(Promo CD single)* | | | |
| YOU DON'T KNOW HOW IT FEELS | 1994 | Warner Bros. PRO-CD-7250 | 8 |
| *(Promo CD single with revised lyric "let's hit another joint," not otherwise available)* | | | |
| YOU DON'T KNOW HOW IT FEELS | 1994 | Warner Bros. PRO-CD-7222 | 8 |
| *(Promo CD single with original lyric "let's roll another joint")* | | | |
| YOU WRECK ME | 1994 | Warner Bros. PRO-CD-7226 | 8 |
| *(Promo-only CD single)* | | | |

**RADIO SHOWS**

**Albums**

| | | | |
|-------|----|----|------|
| INNERVIEW (80s) Profile | 198? | Innerview | 15-25 |
| *(Music and interviews)* | | | |
| INSIDE TOM PETTY (June 81) | 1981 | DIR (3) | 20-40 |
| *(Music and interviews)* | | | |
| KING BISCUIT FLOWER HOUR (Apr 85) Live concert | 1985 | DIR (2) | 25-40 |
| *(With George Thorogood)* | | | |
| LEGENDS OF ROCK (Mar 88) Profile | 1988 | NBC Radio (2) | 20-35 |
| *(Mostly music and interviews)* | | | |
| LEUKEMIA CONCERT (Nov 81) Various artists | 1981 | (3) | 40-75 |
| *(Tom Petty is the headliner in this all-star concert)* | | | |
| LIVE FROM CENTRAL PARK | 1993 | TBS Syndications | 75-125 |
| *(Live concert for Canadian broadcast)* | | | |
| NBC SOURCE (Mar 83) | 1983 | NBC Source (3) | 25-50 |
| *(Mostly music and interviews, some live tracks)* | | | |
| OFF THE RECORD (May 89) Profile | 1989 | Westwood One (2) | 15-25 |
| *(Music and interviews)* | | | |
| ROCK AROUND THE WORLD (Feb 78) Live concert | 1978 | | 75-125 |
| *(With Sammy Hagar)* | | | |
| SUPERSTAR CONCERT | 1987 | Westwood One (3) | 30-60 |
| *(Box set, live concert, repeated)* | | | |
| SUPERSTAR CONCERT  With Bob Dylan | 1987 | Westwood One (3) | 75-150 |
| *(Box set, live concert, repeated)* | | | |
| WORLD OF ROCK (June 89) Various artists | 1989 | DIR (2) | 15-25 |
| *(Music and interviews, Tom Petty is guest DJ)* | | | |

**Compact Discs**

| | | | |
|-------|----|----|------|
| AMERICAN REBELS (Sept 90) | 1990 | Global Satellite (3) | 40-60 |
| *(Music and interviews)* | | | |

| **Title** | **Yr** | **Label, Number** | **NM $** |
|---|---|---|---|
| BBC CLASSIC TRACKS (Oct 93) | 1993 | Westwood One | 25-45 |
| *(Various live tracks)* | | | |
| IN THE STUDIO (Aug 91) Profile of an album | 1991 | Album Network | 15-25 |
| *(Music and interviews)* | | | |
| INTO THE GREAT WIDE OPEN | 1991 | Album Network | 10-15 |
| *(Music and interviews)* | | | |
| KING BISCUIT FLOWER HOUR (June 91) Live concert | 1991 | DIR | 25-50 |
| *(Repeated several times)* | | | |
| KING BISCUIT FLOWER HOUR (Oct 92) Live concert | 1992 | DIR | 25-50 |
| *(With Tom Cochrane)* | | | |
| SUPERSTAR CONCERT (Mar 93) | 1993 | Westwood One (2) | 25-40 |
| *(Live concert)* | | | |
| SUPERSTAR CONCERT (Mar 94) | 1994 | Westwood One (2) | 20-35 |
| *(Live concert with Mary Jane)* | | | |
| UP CLOSE  Profile | 1989 | Media America (2) | 20-40 |
| *(Music and interviews)* | | | |
| UP CLOSE  Profile | 1995 | Media America (2) | 20-40 |
| *(Mostly music and interviews)* | | | |
| WESTWOOD ONE SPECIAL (Dec 94) | 1994 | Westwood One | 20-35 |
| *(Music and interviews)* | | | |
| WILDFLOWER WEEKEND | 1994 | Westwood One | 15-25 |
| *(Music and interviews)* | | | |

**PHILADELPHIA BRASS ENSEMBLE, THE**
**45s**

| WE WISH YOU A MERRY CHRISTMAS/DECK THE HALLS | 1967 | Columbia JZSP 135463/7 | 6 |
|---|---|---|---|

**PHILLIPS, ESTHER**
**12-Inch Singles**

| OO-OOP-OO-OOP (Long Version)/(Edit) | 1979 | Mercury 90 | 12 |
|---|---|---|---|
| OUR DAY WILL COME (same on both sides) | 1979 | Mercury 101 | 12 |

**PHILLIPS, PHIL**
*Mercury white promo label 45s $8 each*

**PIANO RED**
*RCA Victor promo 45s $8 each*

**PICKETT, BOBBY "BORIS"**
*Garpax promo 45s $25 each; RCA Victor, Parrot and Metromedia promo 45s $10 each*
**45s**

| MONSTER MAN JAM | 1970 | White Whale 363 | 25 |
|---|---|---|---|
| *(White promo label, promo-only release)* | | | |

**PICKETT, WILSON**
**45s**

| SALES STIMULATOR | 1966 | Rowe/AMI 1012 | 15 |
|---|---|---|---|
| *(Red vinyl jukebox-related promo)* | | | |

**PIERCE, WEBB**
*Other Decca promo 45s $5-8 each*
**45s**

| HIDEAWAY HEART  Five 7-inch 33 1/3 rpm singles | 1962 | Decca 34014/5/6/7/8 | 40 |
|---|---|---|---|
| *(Singles pack for jukebox vendors, $8 each)* | | | |
| I'VE GOT A NEW HEARTACHE  Five 7-inch 33 1/3 rpm singles | 1962 | Decca 34138 | 40 |
| *(Singles pack for jukebox vendors, $8 each)* | | | |

**7-Inch Extended Plays**

| WEBB PIERCE SINGS  Promo only | 195? | SESAC AD 33 | 50 |
|---|---|---|---|

**Albums**

| JUST IMAGINATION | 1957 | Decca 8728 | 40 |
|---|---|---|---|
| *(Pink promo label)* | | | |
| THE ONE AND ONLY WEBB PIERCE | 1959 | King 648 | 40 |
| THAT WONDERING BOY | 1956 | Decca 8295 | 50 |
| *(Pink promo label)* | | | |
| WEBB PIERCE | 1955 | Decca 8129 | 50 |
| *(Pink promo label)* | | | |
| THE WEBB PIERCE STORY | 1964 | Decca 181 (2) | 40 |
| *(White promo labels)* | | | |

**RADIO SHOWS**
**16-Inch Transcriptions**

| COUNTRY STYLE USA | 1955 | Public service show | 60 |
|---|---|---|---|
| *(Music and interviews)* | | | |

**PINK FLOYD**
*Includes Roger Waters and David Gilmour; Other Columbia promo 45s $8 each (including promo picture sleeve); Columbia promo 45s by Roger Waters or David Gilmour $6 each (including promo picture sleeve); Other Columbia promo 12" singles by Roger Waters or David Gilmour $8 each*
**12-Inch Singles**

| LEARNING TO FLY (Edit)/ (LP) | 1987 | Columbia CAS 2775 | 12 |
|---|---|---|---|
| MONEY/ANOTHER BRICK IN THE WALL, PART 2 | 1981 | Columbia AS 1334 | 25 |
| *(Pink vinyl)* | | | |
| ON THE TURNING AWAY (7" Edit)/(Live) | 1987 | Columbia CAS 2878 | 12 |
| PROS AND CONS OF HITCH HIKING  Roger Waters | 1984 | Columbia AS 1864 | 15 |
| *(Five tracks from the album on a promo-only release)* | | | |
| RUN LIKE HELL | 1980 | Columbia AS-777 | 20 |
| *(Promo-only 12" single)* | | | |

| Title | Yr | Label, Number | NM $ |
|-------|-----|---------------|------|
| WHEN THE TIGERS BROKE FREE | 1982 | Columbia AS-1541 | 12 |
| (Promo-only 12" single) | | | |
| YOUR POSSIBLE PASTS/THE FINAL CUT | 1982 | Columbia AS 1635 | 12 |
| **45s** | | | |
| ANOTHER BRICK IN THE WALL | 1979 | Columbia 11187 | 20 |
| (White label version of this great classic) | | | |
| ARNOLD LAYNE | 1967 | Tower 333 | 150 |
| (White promo label, picture sleeve worth over $750) | | | |
| COMFORTABLY NUMB | 1980 | Columbia 11311 | 15 |
| (Long and short versions) | | | |
| FREE FOUR | 1972 | Harvest P-3391 | 20 |
| (Flip side is "Stay") | | | |
| THE GNOME | 1968 | Tower 378 | 150 |
| (White promo label) | | | |
| JULIA DREAM | 1968 | Tower 426 | 150 |
| (White promo label) | | | |
| MONEY | 1973 | Harvest P-3609 | 20 |
| (Unedited version with "Bullshit") | | | |
| MONEY | 1973 | Harvest PRO-6682 | 15 |
| (Stereo/mono versions, both with "Bull-" and the rest of the word deleted, flip side is PRO-6669, with insert explaining this promo) | | | |
| NOT NOW JOHN | 1983 | Columbia AE7-1653 | 25 |
| (Red promo stereo single with small center hole) | | | |
| ONE OF THESE DAYS | 1971 | Harvest P-3240 | 25 |
| (Flip side is "Fearless," P-3240) | | | |
| ONE OF THESE DAYS | 1971 | Harvest PRO-6378 | 50 |
| (Flip side is "Fearless," PRO-6370) | | | |
| ONE OF THESE DAYS | 1971 | Harvest PRO-6378 | 25 |
| (Same song on both sides) | | | |
| REMEMBER A DAY | 1968 | Tower 440 | 200 |
| (White promo label) | | | |
| RUN LIKE HELL | 1980 | Columbia 11265 | 10 |
| (White promo label) | | | |
| SEE EMILY PLAY | 1967 | Tower 356 | 150 |
| (White promo label, picture sleeve worth over $600) | | | |
| US AND THEM | 1974 | Harvest P-3832 | 20 |
| (Stereo and mono versions) | | | |
| WELCOME TO THE MACHINE | 1975 | Columbia 10248 | 20 |
| (White promo label) | | | |
| WHEN THE TIGERS BROKE FREE | 1982 | Columbia 03142 | 15 |
| (White promo label, price includes cardboard fold-out picture sleeve) | | | |
| **7-Inch Extended Plays** | | | |
| DARK SIDE OF THE MOON | 1973 | Harvest 6746/7 | 250 |
| (Promo-only EP, silver promo paper sleeve) | | | |
| **Albums** | | | |
| ANIMALS | 1977 | Columbia AP-1 | 150 |
| (White promo label and promo cover, includes insert) | | | |
| ANIMALS | 1977 | Columbia JC 33474 | 100 |
| ("Demonstration Not for Sale" on label; also has insert) | | | |
| FINAL CUT | 1983 | Columbia AS-1636 | 25 |
| (Banded for radio play) | | | |
| MORE | 1968 | Tower 5169 | 125 |
| (White promo label, movie soundtrack) | | | |
| OFF THE WALL | 1983 | Columbia | 100 |
| (Edited for radio play, promo cover) | | | |
| PINK FLOYD TOUR '75 | 1975 | Capitol SPRO-8116 | 80 |
| (Promo-only release) | | | |
| PIPER AT THE GATES OF DAWN | 1967 | Tower T-5093 | 250 |
| (White promo label) | | | |
| RADIO KAOS   Roger Waters | 1987 | Columbia CAS 2722 | 15 |
| (Red promo label and promo cover) | | | |
| SAUCERFUL OF SECRETS | 1968 | Tower 5131 | 150 |
| (White promo label) | | | |
| WISH YOU WERE HERE | 1975 | Columbia AS ??? | 250 |
| (White cover, record banded for airplay) | | | |
| WISH YOU WERE HERE | 1975 | Columbia PC 33453 | 300 |
| (Blue cover with photo and title on jacket; unbanded record) | | | |
| **Compact Discs** | | | |
| BBC CLASSIC TRACKS: FAMILY TREE (Dec 95) | 1995 | Westwood One | 30-60 |
| (Live material) | | | |
| CD FULL OF SECRETS (RARITIES VOL. 10) | 1992 | On the Radio | 50 |
| (Promo-only CD sampler for radio, 17 tracks) | | | |
| COMFORTABLY NUMB | 1988 | Columbia CSK 1375 | 25 |
| (Promo-only CD single from "Delicate Sound of Thunder") | | | |
| DARK SIDE OF THE MOON | 1993 | Capitol 81479 | 100 |
| (Press kit containing CD, photo, press release and three slides, all in box) | | | |
| HIGH HOPES | 1994 | Columbia | 10 |
| (Promo-only CD single) | | | |
| KEEP TALKING | 1994 | Columbia CSK 6007 | 10 |
| (Promo-only CD single) | | | |
| LEARNING TO FLY | 1987 | Columbia CSK 2775 | 30 |
| (Orange disc, promo-only release) | | | |
| LIMITED EDITION INTERVIEW DISC | 1994 | Columbia CSK 6060 | 40 |
| (Promo-only interview for radio) | | | |
| MOMENTARY LOSS OF REASON TOUR CD | 1988 | Columbia CSK 1100 | 30 |
| (Promo-only CD sampler for radio) | | | |
| SELECTIONS FROM THE BOX | 1992 | Columbia CSK 4848 | 20 |
| (Sampler from "Shine On") | | | |

(Top left) Jimmy Page makes an appearance on the Up Close radio show. This show usually is dated (except for a year) only on the accompanying cue sheets and not on the disc itself. (Top right) Pearl Jam's fan club sends out a special 7-inch single every year near the end of the year. This was the first one, from 1991, and it actually had a unique Christmas tune on it. (Middle row and bottom left) Three radio shows featuring another popular classic rock group, Pink Floyd. (Bottom right) A rare early stereo promo from Mercury Records, this one features the Platters and their hit version of "Harbor Lights."

| Title | Yr | Label, Number | NM $ |
|---|---|---|---|
| TAKE IT BACK | 1994 | Columbia CSK 6069 | 10 |
| *(Promo CD single)* | | | |
| THE WALL IN BERLIN  Pink Floyd/Roger Waters | 199? | Mercury (2) | 75 |
| *(Promo-only CD box set with video and tour book enclosed)* | | | |

**RADIO SHOWS**
**Albums**

| Title | Yr | Label, Number | NM $ |
|---|---|---|---|
| BBC ROCK HOUR (Apr 81) | 1981 | London Wavelength | 100-150 |
| *(Live concert)* | | | |
| BBC ROCK HOUR (July 81)  Nick Mason | 1981 | London Wavelength | 50-75 |
| *(Mostly music and interviews)* | | | |
| BBC ROCK HOUR (July 81)  Roger Waters | 1981 | London Wavelength | 50-75 |
| *(Mostly music and interviews)* | | | |
| BBC ROCK HOUR (May 84) Live concert | 1984 | London Wavelength | 100-200 |
| *(With King Crimson)* | | | |
| BBC TRANSCRIPTION DISC  Live concert | 1970 | BBC Transcription | 400-600 |
| *(The ultimate Pink Floyd show)* | | | |
| BBC TRANSCRIPTION DISC  Live concert | 1973 | BBC Transcription | 400-600 |
| *(Just as rare as the first one)* | | | |
| BBC TRANSCRIPTION DISC  Live concert | 1976 | BBC Transcription | 400-600 |
| *(Anybody in the world have all three?)* | | | |
| THE GILMOUR CONCERT (Nov 86) David Gilmour | 1986 | DIR (3) | 50-90 |
| *(Live concert)* | | | |
| IN CONCERT | 1986 | Westwood One (2) | 100-150 |
| *(Live concert, BBC sessions, repeated)* | | | |
| IN CONCERT (Mar 85) David Gilmour | 1985 | Westwood One (2) | 150-250 |
| *(Live concert, repeated)* | | | |
| IN CONCERT (Nov 87) Roger Waters | 1987 | Westwood One (2) | 125-200 |
| *(Live concert, repeated)* | | | |
| INNERVIEW  David Gilmour | 198? | Innerview (2) | 40-75 |
| *(Different shows, in two parts)* | | | |
| INNERVIEW  David Gilmour | 198? | Innerview | 25-30 |
| *(Music and interviews, any one of the six shows)* | | | |
| INNERVIEW  David Gilmour | 198? | Innerview (4) | 50-100 |
| *(Music and interviews, in four parts)* | | | |
| INNERVIEW  Nick Mason | 1976 | Innerview | 25-50 |
| *(Music and interviews)* | | | |
| INNERVIEW  Roger Waters | 198? | Innerview | 25-40 |
| *(Music and interviews, any one of the six shows)* | | | |
| INNERVIEW  Roger Waters | 198? | Innerview (4) | 100-150 |
| *(Music and interviews, in four parts)* | | | |
| INNERVIEW  Roger Waters | 198? | Innerview (2) | 40-75 |
| *(Different shows, in two parts)* | | | |
| KING BISCUIT FLOWER HOUR | 1987 | DIR (2) | 50 |
| *(David Gilmour with Townshend, Hynde and friends)* | | | |
| LEGENDS OF ROCK | 1987 | NBC Radio (4) | 40-75 |
| *(Music and interviews, two shows)* | | | |
| LEGENDS OF ROCK | 1987 | NBC Radio (2) | 25-40 |
| *(Music and interviews, repeated)* | | | |
| NBC SOURCE (Apr 84) Roger Waters and David Gilmour | 1984 | NBC Radio | 40-65 |
| *(Music and interviews)* | | | |
| OFF THE RECORD  David Gilmour | 1984 | Westwood One (2) | 25-50 |
| *(Music and interviews, repeated)* | | | |
| OFF THE RECORD (Mar 85) Roger Waters | 1985 | Westwood One (2) | 25-50 |
| *(Music and interviews, repeated)* | | | |
| ROCK STARS  Roger Waters | 1987 | Radio Today (2) | 50-85 |
| *(Music and interviews with some live tracks)* | | | |
| ROYALTY OF ROCK | 1982 | RKO | 30-50 |
| *(Music and interviews, repeated in 1983)* | | | |
| SHADES OF PINK (Sept 84) | 1984 | NBC Radio (6) | 100-200 |
| *(Music and interviews)* | | | |
| SUPERSTAR CONCERT  Various artists | 1986 | Westwood One (3) | 50 |
| *(David Gilmour live with Townshend, Pretenders and Lennox)* | | | |
| WESTWOOD ONE PRESENTS (Mar 89) Roger Waters | 1989 | Westwood One | 75-125 |
| *(Live concert with Henry Lee Summer)* | | | |

**Compact Discs**

| Title | Yr | Label, Number | NM $ |
|---|---|---|---|
| BBC CLASSIC TRACKS (Oct 92) | 1992 | Westwood One | 50-75 |
| *(Live tracks)* | | | |
| CLASSIC CD (Apr 90) | 1990 | (2) | 100-175 |
| *(Profiles "Dark Side of the Moon")* | | | |
| ECHOES, A HISTORY OF PINK FLOYD (Sept 95) | 1995 | Westwood One (6) | 150-250 |
| *(Music and interviews with many archival and live tracks)* | | | |
| IN THE STUDIO (Aug 88) | 1988 | Album Network | 25-50 |
| *(Profiles "Dark Side of the Moon"; repeated)* | | | |
| IN THE STUDIO (July 89) | 1989 | Album Network (2) | 75-125 |
| *(Profiles "The Wall")* | | | |
| IN THE STUDIO | 199? | Album Network (2) | 75-125 |
| *(Profiles "The Division Bell")* | | | |
| IN THE STUDIO (90s) | 199? | Album Network | 75-100 |
| *(Profiles "Wish You Were Here")* | | | |
| IN THE STUDIO (Dec 92) | 1992 | Album Network (2) | 75-125 |
| *(Profiles "Shine On")* | | | |
| KING BISCUIT FLOWER HOUR | 1987 | DIR | 100 |
| *(David Gilmour with Townshend, Hynde and friends)* | | | |
| OFF THE RECORD (Oct 92) Roger Waters | 1992 | Westwood One | 25-50 |
| *(Music and interviews)* | | | |
| SHOW GOES ON (July 94) | 1994 | Westwood One (3) | 100-175 |
| *(Mostly music and interview, some live tracks)* | | | |

| Title | Yr | Label, Number | NM $ |
|---|---|---|---|
| SUPERSTAR CONCERT (Feb 90) | 1990 | Westwood One (2) | 50-100 |
| *(Live concert, repeated)* | | | |
| SUPERSTAR CONCERT (May 94) | 1994 | Westwood One (2) | 75-125 |
| *(Live concert, retrospective)* | | | |
| SUPERSTARS (June 95) | 1995 | (2) | 100-150 |
| *(Live concert material)* | | | |
| 25TH ANNIVERSARY (May 92) | 1992 | Westwood One (6) | 200-350 |
| *(Music and interview, very rare)* | | | |
| UP CLOSE  Profile | 1987 | MCA Radio (2) | 100-175 |
| *(Music and interview with some live tracks, the debut of this series)* | | | |
| UP CLOSE  Profile | 1989 | Media America (2) | 75-150 |
| *(Music and interview with some live tracks)* | | | |
| UP CLOSE  Profile | 1995 | Media America (4) | 125-175 |
| *(Music and interview with some live tracks)* | | | |
| UP CLOSE  Profile of Roger Waters | 1993 | Media America (2) | 75-150 |
| *(Music and interview with some live tracks)* | | | |
| WISH YOU WERE HERE | 1991 | Global Satellite (3) | 100-200 |
| *(Music and interviews)* | | | |

## PISCOPO, JOE
**12-Inch Singles**

| Title | Yr | Label, Number | NM $ |
|---|---|---|---|
| HONEYMOONERS RAP (Original)/(Captain Video Version) | 1985 | Columbia CAS 2092 | 8 |

## PITNEY, GENE
*Musicor promo 45s $5-8 each; Epic promo 45s $4 each*

## PIXIES
**12-Inch Singles**

| Title | Yr | Label, Number | NM $ |
|---|---|---|---|
| HERE COMES YOUR MAN (same on both sides) | 1989 | Elektra ED 5386 | 6 |
| VELOURIA/MAKE BELIEVE/I'VE BEEN WAITING FOR YOU/THE THING | 1990 | Elektra ED 5476 | 10 |

**Albums**

| Title | Yr | Label, Number | NM $ |
|---|---|---|---|
| DOOLITTLE | 1989 | Elektra 60856 | 12 |
| *(Promo-only on audiophile vinyl)* | | | |
| LIVE | 1989 | Elektra/4AD PR-8127 | 50 |
| *(Promo-only seven-song live collection of mostly songs from their pre-Elektra days)* | | | |

## PLAIDS, THE
**45s**

| Title | Yr | Label, Number | NM $ |
|---|---|---|---|
| HUNGRY FOR YOUR LOVE | 1958 | Liberty 55167 | 125 |
| *(White promo label, stock copy worth over $400)* | | | |

## PLANET P (PROJECT)
*MCA promo 45s by Tony Carey $3 each Tony Carey*

**45s**

| Title | Yr | Label, Number | NM $ |
|---|---|---|---|
| WHAT I SEE | 1984 | MCA 52515 | 10 |
| *(Pink vinyl, MCA colored label promo, clear sleeve)* | | | |

**7-Inch Extended Plays**

| Title | Yr | Label, Number | NM $ |
|---|---|---|---|
| BEHIND THE BARRIER | 1984 | MCA 1227 | 12 |
| *(Pink vinyl, white promo label, pink cover)* | | | |

**Albums**

| Title | Yr | Label, Number | NM $ |
|---|---|---|---|
| PLANET P PROJECT | 1984 | MCA 8019 (2) | 20 |
| *(Double pink vinyl stock discs, the cover is promo stamped)* | | | |

**RADIO SHOWS**
**Albums**

| Title | Yr | Label, Number | NM $ |
|---|---|---|---|
| KING BISCUIT FLOWER HOUR (June 84) Live concert | 1984 | DIR/ABC (2) | 60-80 |
| *(Tony Carey, with Blue Oyster Cult)* | | | |

## PLANT, ROBERT
*Lead singer of Listen, Led Zeppelin and the Honeydrippers; Atlantic, Swan Song and Es Paranza promo label 45s $5 each; Es Paranza promo 45s by the Honeydrippers $6 each*

**12-Inch Singles**

| Title | Yr | Label, Number | NM $ |
|---|---|---|---|
| BIG LOG | 1983 | Atlantic PR 518 | 15 |
| *(Promo-only 12" single w/two songs on flip)* | | | |
| ROCKIN' AT MIDNIGHT  The Honeydrippers | 1984 | Es Paranza PR 648 | 15 |
| *(Long 5:57 and short 3:02 versions)* | | | |
| ROCKIN' AT MIDNIGHT  The Honeydrippers | 1984 | Es Paranza PR 671 | 18 |
| *(Same version 5:57 on both sides)* | | | |
| TOO LOUD | 1985 | Es Paranza PR 762 | 10 |
| *(Both sides are the same on this promo-only 12-incher)* | | | |

**45s**

| Title | Yr | Label, Number | NM $ |
|---|---|---|---|
| ROCKIN' AT MIDNIGHT  The Honeydrippers | 1984 | Es Paranza 99686 | 10 |
| *(Long 5:57 and short 3:02 versions)* | | | |
| WHAT'S IT ALL ABOUT (Feb 82) Public service show | 1982 | W.I.A.A. 613 | 30 |
| *(Interviews with Robert Plant, flip is Supertramp)* | | | |
| WHAT'S IT ALL ABOUT (Jan 81) Public service show | 1981 | W.I.A.A. 557 | 30 |
| *(Interviews with Robert Plant, flip is Larry Gatlin)* | | | |
| YOU BETTER RUN  Listen | 1967 | Columbia 43967 | 100 |
| *(White promo label)* | | | |

**Albums**

| Title | Yr | Label, Number | NM $ |
|---|---|---|---|
| NON-STOP GO | 1988 | Es Paranza PR 2244 (2) | 25 |
| *(Music and interviews, promo only)* | | | |
| PICTURES AT ELEVEN | 1982 | Atlantic PR | 15 |
| *(Music and interviews)* | | | |

**Compact Discs**

| Title | Yr | Label, Number | NM $ |
|---|---|---|---|
| CONVERSATIONS WITH PLANT & PAGE | 1995 | Atlantic PRCD 5987 | 40 |
| *(Promo-only interview disc)* | | | |

| Title | Yr | Label, Number | NM $ |
|---|---|---|---|
| SONGWRITING LEGACY Plant & Page | 1996 | Atlantic PRCD 6094 | 50 |
| *(Promotional sampler from Miller Genuine Draft)* | | | |
| SONGWRITING LEGACY Plant & Page | 1996 | Atlantic PRCD 6095 | 40 |
| *(Promotional sampler, 12 tracks)* | | | |
| SONGWRITING LEGACY Plant & Page | 1996 | Atlantic | 30 |
| *(Promotional sampler, 10 tracks)* | | | |
| **RADIO SHOWS** | | | |
| **Albums** | | | |
| BBC ROCK HOUR (Dec 83) | 1983 | London Wavelength | 25-40 |
| *(Music and interviews)* | | | |
| BIG LOG (Feb 84) | 1984 | DIR | 10 |
| *(King Biscuit Flower Hour special single version release from the concert)* | | | |
| HIGH VOLTAGE Various artists | 1989 | Westwood One (2) | 35-65 |
| *(Live concert segment of the show features Robert Plant)* | | | |
| INNERVIEW | 1978 | Sound Communications | 75-100 |
| *(Music and interviews)* | | | |
| INSIDE TRACKS (Aug 83) with others | 1983 | RKO | 20-40 |
| *(With Phil Collins, music and interviews)* | | | |
| KING BISCUIT FLOWER HOUR (Feb 84) | 1984 | DIR/ABC (2) | 50-100 |
| *(Live concert, includes Side 4, "Big Log")* | | | |
| KING BISCUIT FLOWER HOUR (Feb 84) | 1984 | DIR/ABC | 10 |
| *(Price is for the "Big Log" disc only)* | | | |
| KING BISCUIT FLOWER HOUR (Mar 86) | 1986 | DIR (2) | 25-50 |
| *(Live concert)* | | | |
| LEGENDS OF ROCK | 1987 | NBC Radio (2) | 20-40 |
| *(Music and interviews)* | | | |
| LEGENDS OF ROCK | 1987 | NBC Radio (4) | 25-50 |
| *(Music and interviews, two shows)* | | | |
| OFF THE RECORD | 1983 | Westwood One (2) | 15-25 |
| *(Music and interviews)* | | | |
| OFF THE RECORD | 1983 | Westwood One (4) | 25-35 |
| *(Music and interviews, two shows)* | | | |
| ROBERT PLANT | 1984 | London Wavelength (2) | 50-100 |
| *(Music and interviews, black labels)* | | | |
| ROBERT PLANT STORY | 1990 | Unistar (3) | 30-50 |
| *(Music and interviews)* | | | |
| SOURCE CHRISTMAS SPECIAL (Dec 83) | 1983 | NBC Source (6) | 100-150 |
| *(Mostly music and interviews)* | | | |
| SOURCE SPECIAL | 1982 | NBC Source (6) | 100-150 |
| *(Mostly music and interviews)* | | | |
| SOURCE SPECIAL | 1983 | NBC Source (2) | 30-50 |
| *(Music and interviews)* | | | |
| SOURCE SPECIAL  Various artists | 1982 | NBC Source (2) | 25-50 |
| *(Music and interviews w/Plant, Stones, Elton, Ozzy)* | | | |
| SUPERSTAR CONCERT (Feb 91) | 1991 | Westwood One (3) | 40-75 |
| *(With Van Halen and Neil Young)* | | | |
| SUPERSTAR CONCERT (June 86) | 1986 | Westwood One (3) | 40-75 |
| *(Live concert)* | | | |
| **Compact Discs** | | | |
| IN THE STUDIO | 1988 | Album Network | 15-25 |
| *(Profile of an album, music and interviews)* | | | |
| IN THE STUDIO | 1990 | Album Network | 10-25 |
| *(World premiere of "Manic," music and interviews)* | | | |
| KING BISCUIT FLOWER HOUR (Mar 90) | 1990 | DIR | 40-80 |
| *(Live concert)* | | | |
| SUPERSTAR CONCERT (Mar 95) | 1995 | Westwood One (2) | 40-75 |
| *(Live concert)* | | | |
| SUPERSTAR CONCERT (Sept 93) | 1993 | Westwood One (2) | 40-75 |
| *(Live concert)* | | | |
| UP CLOSE | 1989 | Media America (2) | 40-80 |
| *(Mostly music and interviews, some live tracks)* | | | |
| UP CLOSE | 1989 | Media America (4) | 75-150 |
| *(Same show as above, two parts)* | | | |
| UP CLOSE | 1993 | Media America (3) | 50-100 |
| *(Edited version of the above shows)* | | | |

## PLATTERS, THE

*Includes listings of Tony Williams; Other Mercury promo 45s through 71383 $20 each; Mercury promo 45s 71427-72359 $10 each; Musicor promo 45s $8 each; Other Mercury or Wing white promo label LPs $50 each; Musicor promo LPs $20 each; Reprise and Philips promo LPs by Tony Williams $15 each*

**45s**

| Title | Yr | Label, Number | NM $ |
|---|---|---|---|
| CHRISTMAS WITH THE PLATTERS  Stereo compact 33s | 1963 | Mercury 7097 | 250 |
| *(Five records in the set, $50 each; blue labels, small center hole, for jukebox use)* | | | |
| GIVE THANKS | 1953 | Federal 12153 | 300 |
| *(White promo label)* | | | |
| I NEED YOU ALL THE TIME | 1954 | Federal 12164 | 250 |
| *(White promo label)* | | | |
| ONLY YOU  Original version | 1955 | Federal 12244 | 250 |
| *(White promo label)* | | | |
| ONLY YOU  Hit version | 1955 | Mercury 70633 | 60 |
| *(White promo label)* | | | |
| PLATTERAMA MEDLEY | 1982 | Mercury 76160 | 10 |
| *(Same on both sides, multi-colored label)* | | | |
| ROSES OF PICARDY | 1954 | Federal 12181 | 250 |
| *(White promo label)* | | | |
| TAKE ME BACK | 1954 | Federal 12204 | 75 |
| *(White promo label)* | | | |
| TELL THE WORLD | 1954 | Federal 12188 | 75 |
| *(White promo label)* | | | |

| Title | Yr | Label, Number | NM $ |
|---|---|---|---|
| TELL THE WORLD | 1955 | Federal 12250 | 60 |
| *(White promo label)* | | | |
| WHAT'S IT ALL ABOUT (Sept 81) Public service show | 1981 | W.I.A.A. 592 | 25 |
| *(Interview with Buck Ram, flip side is Harry Chapin)* | | | |
| WHAT'S IT ALL ABOUT (Sept 82) Public service show | 1982 | W.I.A.A. 640 | 25 |
| *(Interview with members of the group, flip is Count Basie)* | | | |
| **7-Inch Extended Plays** | | | |
| ONLY YOU  Forest fire prevention PSA spots | 1984 | U.S. Dept. of Agriculture | 50 |
| *(PSA commercials, eight ads, features Platters and includes a spot by Ted Nugent)* | | | |
| THE PLATTERS | 1959 | Mercury MEP-64 | 250 |
| *(White promo label, no sleeve, promo release only)* | | | |
| **Albums** | | | |
| CHRISTMAS WITH THE PLATTERS | 1963 | Mercury 20841 | 75 |
| *(White promo label)* | | | |
| FLYING PLATTERS | 1957 | Mercury 20298 | 75 |
| *(White promo label)* | | | |
| FLYING PLATTERS AROUND THE WORLD | 1957 | Mercury 20366 | 75 |
| *(White promo label)* | | | |
| A GIRL IS A GIRL IS A GIRL  Tony Williams | 1959 | Mercury 20454 | 50 |
| *(White promo label)* | | | |
| THE PLATTERS | 1956 | Mercury 20146 | 150 |
| *(White promo label)* | | | |
| THE PLATTERS, VOLUME 2 | 1956 | Mercury 20216 | 100 |
| *(White promo label)* | | | |

## PLIMSOULS, THE
**12-Inch Singles**

| Title | Yr | Label, Number | NM $ |
|---|---|---|---|
| A MILLION MILES AWAY/THE OLDEST STORY/MAGIC TOUCH | 1983 | Geffen PRO-A-2068 | 12 |

## POCO
*Epic, MCA, ABC and RCA promo 45s $3 each; RCA promo CD singles $3-5 each*
**12-Inch Singles**

| Title | Yr | Label, Number | NM $ |
|---|---|---|---|
| CALL IT LOVE (Edit)/(LP) | 1989 | RCA 9039-1-RAB | 6 |
| UNDER THE GUN (same on both sides) | 1980 | MCA 2314 | 8 |
| **45s** | | | |
| BREAK OF HEARTS (same on both sides) | 1983 | Atlantic 89851 | 3 |
| *(May be promo only)* | | | |
| SAVE A CORNER OF YOUR HEART (same on both sides) | 1984 | Atlantic 89629 | 3 |
| *(May be promo only)* | | | |
| WHAT'S IT ALL ABOUT (Jan 76) Public service show | 1976 | W.I.A.A. 299 | 12 |
| *(Flip side is Roger Whittaker)* | | | |
| WHAT'S IT ALL ABOUT (June 79) Public service show | 1979 | W.I.A.A. 476 | 18 |
| *(Flip side is Judy Collins)* | | | |
| **RADIO SHOWS** | | | |
| **Albums** | | | |
| ROBERT W. MORGAN (June 80) | 1980 | Watermark | 15-25 |
| *(Music and interviews)* | | | |
| **Compact Discs** | | | |
| KING BISCUIT FLOWER HOUR (Oct 88) Live concert | 1988 | DIR | 25-40 |
| *(With Foghat)* | | | |

## POGUES, THE
**12-Inch Singles**

| Title | Yr | Label, Number | NM $ |
|---|---|---|---|
| YEAH YEAH YEAH YEAH YEAH (2 versions)/THE LIMERICK RAKA | 1988 | Island 2607 | 7 |

## POI DOG PONDERING
**12-Inch Singles**

| Title | Yr | Label, Number | NM $ |
|---|---|---|---|
| LIVING WITH THE DREAMING BODY/FACT OF LIFE | 1989 | Columbia CAS 1777 | 6 |
| U LI LA LU/BURY ME DEEP | 1990 | Columbia CAS 1995 | 8 |
| *(One-sided 12-inch with etched B-side)* | | | |
| **45s** | | | |
| BIG BEAUTIFUL SPOON/SUGARBUSH CUSHMAN | 1990 | Columbia CS7 2000 | 8 |
| **Albums** | | | |
| INTERCHORDS | 1989 | Columbia CAS 1856 | 20 |
| *(Promo-only interview and music)* | | | |

## POINDEXTER, BUSTER
**45s**

| Title | Yr | Label, Number | NM $ |
|---|---|---|---|
| ZAT YOU SANTA CLAUS | 1987 | RCA 6893-7-RAB | 15 |
| *(Promo-only, yellow label)* | | | |

## POINT BLANK
*MCA promo 45s $3 each*
**RADIO SHOWS**
**Albums**

| Title | Yr | Label, Number | NM $ |
|---|---|---|---|
| BBC ROCK HOUR (July 81) Live concert | 1981 | London Wavelength | 50-100 |
| KING BISCUIT FLOWER HOUR (July 80) Live concert | 1980 | DIR/ABC (2) | 40-75 |
| *(With the Henry Paul Band)* | | | |
| KING BISCUIT FLOWER HOUR (July 81) Live concert | 1981 | DIR/ABC (2) | 100-200 |
| *(With Steppenwolf)* | | | |

## POINTER SISTERS, THE
*Blue Thumb promo 45s $4 each; Planet and RCA promo 45s $3 each*
**12-Inch Singles**

| Title | Yr | Label, Number | NM $ |
|---|---|---|---|
| COME AND GET YOUR LOVE + 3 | 1979 | Planet 11406 | 12 |

| Title | Yr | Label, Number | NM $ |
|---|---|---|---|
| FIRE/HAPPINESS | 1979 | Planet 11407 | 12 |
| *(Red vinyl promo)* | | | |
| FRIEND'S ADVICE (Don't Take It) (5 versions) | 1990 | Motown L33-17922 | 8 |
| GOLDMINE (2 versions)/SEXUAL POWER | 1986 | RCA 5774-1-RDAC | 6 |
| HAPPINESS (same on both sides) | 1979 | Planet 11403 | 8 |
| I'M SO EXCITED | 1982 | Planet JD-13328 | 10 |
| *(One-sided promo)* | | | |
| I'M SO EXCITED (same on both sides) | 1984 | Planet JR-13858 | 10 |
| MERCURY RISING (3 versions) | 1986 | RCA 6491-1-RDAC | 6 |
| **45s** | | | |
| WHAT'S IT ALL ABOUT  Public service show | 1974 | W.I.A.A. 245 | 20 |
| *(Flip side features The 5th Dimension)* | | | |
| WHAT'S IT ALL ABOUT (July 75) Public service show | 1975 | W.I.A.A. 273 | 25 |
| *(Flip side features "Tommy" by The Who)* | | | |
| WHAT'S IT ALL ABOUT (Mar 79) Public service show | 1979 | W.I.A.A. 464 | 15 |
| *(Flip side features Glen Campbell)* | | | |
| WHAT'S IT ALL ABOUT (Sept 81) Public service show | 1981 | W.I.A.A. 595 | 15 |
| *(Flip side features Lou Rawls)* | | | |
| WHAT'S IT ALL ABOUT (Apr 82) Public service show | 1982 | W.I.A.A. 623 | 18 |
| *(Flip side features Journey)* | | | |
| **RADIO SHOWS** | | | |
| **Albums** | | | |
| STARTRACK PROFILE (Mar 86) | 1986 | Westwood One (2) | 20-40 |
| *(Music and interviews)* | | | |

**POINTER, BONNIE**
Other Motown promo 45s $4 each

| **45s** | | | |
|---|---|---|---|
| FREE ME FROM MY FREEDOM | 1978 | Motown 1451 | 15 |
| *(Red vinyl, white promo label)* | | | |

**POISON**
*Capitol promo 45s $4 each; Capitol promo CD singles $3 each*
**RADIO SHOWS**
**Albums**

| METALSHOP (Dec 91) Various artists | 1991 | MJI Broadcasting (2) | 15-25 |
|---|---|---|---|
| *(Live segments of this show feature Poison)* | | | |

**POLICE, THE**
*Includes listings of solo members; More at Sting; Other A&M promo 45s $5 each; Other test pressing 45s $15 each (these are not rare for A&M label artists); A&M and MCA promo 45s by Stewart Copeland, Andy Summers and Sting $3 each; A&M promo 12" singles by Police or solos $6 each; A&M white promo label LPs by Police or solos $10 each*
**12-Inch Singles**

| DON'T STAND SO CLOSE TO ME | 1981 | A&M | 100 |
|---|---|---|---|
| *(Promo picture disc)* | | | |
| DON'T STAND SO CLOSE TO ME '86 (same on both sides) | 1986 | A&M SP-17432 | 7 |
| EVERY BREATH YOU TAKE | 1983 | A&M 17230 | 10 |
| *(Promo 12" single)* | | | |
| I BURN FOR YOU | 1982 | A&M 17216 | 10 |
| *(Promo 12" single)* | | | |
| MESSAGE IN A BOTTLE | 1979 | A&M 17122 | 20 |
| *(Promo 12" single, studio and live versions)* | | | |
| ONE WORLD | 1981 | A&M 17173 | 10 |
| *(Promo 12" single)* | | | |
| SPIRITS IN THE MATERIAL WORLD/SECRET JOURNEY | 1981 | A&M SP-17182 | 12 |
| VOICES INSIDE MY HEAD | 1979 | A&M 17137 | 10 |
| *(Promo 12" single)* | | | |
| WALKING ON THE MOON (same on both sides) | 1986 | A&M SP-17449 | 8 |
| **45s** | | | |
| EVERY BREATH YOU TAKE | 1983 | Monarch | 15 |
| *(White label test pressing)* | | | |
| EVERY LITTLE THING SHE DOES IS MAGIC | 1981 | | 15 |
| *(White label test pressing)* | | | |
| KING OF PAIN | 1983 | Monarch | 15 |
| *(White label test pressing)* | | | |
| MESSAGE IN A BOTTLE | 1979 | A&M PRO-4400 | 15 |
| *(Promo star-shaped picture disc)* | | | |
| THE POLICE FILE | 1985 | A&M (no #) | 50 |
| *Boxed set of five "A&M Memories" singles released to radio. Price is mostly for the box.* | | | |
| ROXANNE | 1979 | A&M 2096 | 10 |
| *(White promo label)* | | | |
| ROXANNE | 1979 | A&M 2096 | 15 |
| *(Badge-shaped promo picture disc)* | | | |
| SPIRITS IN THE MATERIAL WORLD | 1981 | | 15 |
| *(White label test pressing)* | | | |
| SYNCHRONICITY II | 1983 | | 15 |
| *(White label test pressing)* | | | |
| WHAT'S IT ALL ABOUT (Apr 80) Public service show | 1980 | W.I.A.A. 520 | 25 |
| *(Flip side is Rupert Holmes)* | | | |
| WHAT'S IT ALL ABOUT (May 81) Public service show | 1981 | W.I.A.A. 578 | 20 |
| *(Flip side features Jethro Tull)* | | | |
| WHAT'S IT ALL ABOUT (Apr 82) Public service show | 1982 | W.I.A.A. 622 | 25 |
| *(Flip side features Hall & Oates)* | | | |
| WRAPPED AROUND YOUR FINGER | 1983 | | 15 |
| *(White label test pressing)* | | | |
| **Albums** | | | |
| GHOST IN THE MACHINE | 1981 | A&M SP-3730 | 1,000 |
| *(Special prototype picture disc that lights up when placed on a turntable)* | | | |

| Title | Yr | Label, Number | NM $ |
|---|---|---|---|
| ZENYATTA MONDATTA | 1980 | A&M NR 19 | 40 |
| *(Nautilus half-speed master for in-store play)* | | | |
| **Compact Discs** | | | |
| DON'T STAND SO CLOSE TO ME '86 | 1986 | A&M 17435 | 25 |
| *(The first U.S. promo CD single by anyone)* | | | |
| LIVE! | 1995 | A&M | 30 |
| *(Promo-only sampler from 2-CD set)* | | | |
| ROXANNE '97 | 1997 | A&M | 12 |
| *(Promo CD single of the Puff Daddy remix)* | | | |
| SELECTIONS FROM MESSAGE IN A BOX | 1993 | A&M | 20 |
| *(Promo-only sampler from box set)* | | | |
| **RADIO SHOWS** | | | |
| **Albums** | | | |
| BBC COLLEGE CONCERT (Feb 83) | 1983 | London Wavelength | 50-100 |
| *(Live concert)* | | | |
| BBC ROCK HOUR (Dec 81) | 1981 | London Wavelength | 50-100 |
| *(Live concert, repeated)* | | | |
| BBC ROCK HOUR (Feb 81) | 1981 | London Wavelength | 60-110 |
| *(Live concert)* | | | |
| BBC TRANSCRIPTION DISC | 1978 | BBC Transcription | 400-500 |
| *(Classic and very rare live concert)* | | | |
| BBC TRANSCRIPTION DISC | 1979 | BBC Transcription | 400-500 |
| *(Repeat show)* | | | |
| DECADE AND BEYOND (May 88) Profile | 1988 | Unistar (3) | 25-35 |
| *(Music and interviews)* | | | |
| IN CONCERT | 1988 | Westwood One (2) | 30-50 |
| *(Live concert, with Dire Straits)* | | | |
| INNERVIEW (80s) | 198? | Innerview | 20-30 |
| *(Music and early interviews)* | | | |
| INSIDE TRACK (Nov 82) | 1982 | RKO (3) | 50-100 |
| *(Mostly live concert)* | | | |
| LEGENDS OF ROCK | 1987 | NBC Radio (2) | 20-30 |
| *(Music and interviews)* | | | |
| LEGENDS OF ROCK | 1987 | NBC Radio (4) | 40-60 |
| *(Music and interviews, two shows)* | | | |
| NBC SOURCE (July 84) | 1984 | NBC Radio (4) | 75-125 |
| *(Box set, music and interview with some live tracks)* | | | |
| OFF THE RECORD (Sept 86) Sting | 1986 | Westwood One (2) | 15-25 |
| *(Music and interviews, repeated)* | | | |
| PENTHOUSE/OMNI COLLEGE ROCK CONCERT (Oct 83) | 1983 | London Wavelength | 75-150 |
| *(Rare early live concert)* | | | |
| THE POLICE TAPES (Mar 81) | 1981 | DIR (3) | 75-135 |
| *(Live concert, from the Supergroups series)* | | | |
| RETRO ROCK (Mar 82) | 1982 | Clayton Webster | 60-125 |
| *(Rare early live concert)* | | | |
| ROCK CLOCK  Various artists | 1987 | DIR (2) | 30-50 |
| *(Live material from the Police, Huey Lewis and J. Geils Band)* | | | |
| SELF-PORTRAIT (Jan 85) | 1985 | NBC Radio (6) | 125-200 |
| *(Box set, music and interviews)* | | | |
| STARTRACK PROFILE (Dec 83) | 1983 | Westwood One (2) | 20-40 |
| *(Music and interviews)* | | | |
| THEN AND NOW (Nov 86) | 1986 | DIR (3) | 75-125 |
| *(Live concert)* | | | |
| **Compact Discs** | | | |
| BBC CLASSIC TRACKS (May 91) | 1991 | Westwood One | 25-50 |
| *(Various classic live tracks)* | | | |
| IN CONCERT (Apr 94) | 1994 | Westwood One | 40-75 |
| *(Live concert)* | | | |
| IN CONCERT (Mar 94) | 1994 | Westwood One | 50-75 |
| *(Live concert with the Spin Doctors)* | | | |
| IN THE STUDIO (Dec 90) | 1990 | Album Network | 10-20 |
| *(Profile of an album, music and interviews)* | | | |
| MASTERS OF ROCK  Sting | 1989 | Radio Ventures | 20-40 |
| *(Music and interviews)* | | | |
| MASTERS OF ROCK (Oct 87) Sting and the Police | 1987 | Radio Ventures | 20-40 |
| *(Music and interviews)* | | | |
| MESSAGE IN A BOX  The Police and Sting | 1993 | Media America (3) | 50-100 |
| *(Music and interviews)* | | | |
| OFF THE RECORD (Aug 93) Sting | 1993 | Westwood One | 15-25 |
| *(Music and interviews, repeated)* | | | |
| OFF THE RECORD (Sept 93) | 1993 | Westwood One | 15-25 |
| *(Music and interviews, repeated)* | | | |
| ON THE EDGE (Dec 93) | 1993 | Westwood One | 15-25 |
| *(Music and interviews, with Wonderstuff) See Sting* | | | |
| ON THE EDGE (Sept 93) Sting | 1993 | Westwood One | 15-25 |
| *(Music and interviews, with Lenny Kravitz)* | | | |
| OUTLANDOS TO SYNCHRO | 1996 | Radio Today | 30-60 |
| *(Music and interviews)* | | | |
| SUPERSTAR CONCERT (Jan 92) Sting | 1992 | Westwood One (2) | 40-75 |
| *(Live concert, repeated)* | | | |
| SUPERSTAR CONCERT (Mar 93) | 1993 | Westwood One (2) | 40-80 |
| *(Live concert, repeated)* | | | |
| TIMOTHY WHITE SESSIONS (Apr 91) Sting | 1991 | Westwood One (2) | 60-125 |
| *(Live tracks, music and interviews)* | | | |
| TIMOTHY WHITE SESSIONS (July 93) Sting | 1993 | Westwood One (2) | 75-150 |
| *(Live tracks, music and interviews)* | | | |
| UP CLOSE | 1989 | Media America (2) | 40-60 |
| *(Mostly music and interviews)* | | | |

| Title | Yr | Label, Number | NM $ |
|---|---|---|---|
| UP CLOSE Sting | 1988 | Media America (2) | 40-60 |
| *(Mostly music and interviews)* | | | |
| UP CLOSE Sting | 1991 | Media America (2) | 40-60 |
| *(Music and interviews)* | | | |
| UP CLOSE Sting | 1995 | Media America (2) | 40-75 |
| *(Mostly music and interviews)* | | | |
| **Reel-to-Reel Tapes** | | | |
| STUDIO JAM (June 79) | 1979 | (2) | 600-900 |
| *(Live material, a rare early live show)* | | | |

**POLYROCK**
**RADIO SHOWS**
**Albums**

| | | | |
|---|---|---|---|
| BBC COLLEGE CONCERT (Oct 83) | 1983 | London Wavelength | 20-35 |
| *(Live concert)* | | | |

**PONTY, JEAN-LUC**
**12-Inch Singles**

| | | | |
|---|---|---|---|
| AS (3:15) (5:45) | 1982 | Atlantic PR 420 | 6 |
| FAR FROM BEATEN PATHS (3:50) (5:58) | 1983 | Atlantic PR 524 | 6 |
| INFINITE PURSUIT (same on both sides) | 1985 | Atlantic PR 809 | 6 |
| OPEN MIND (Edit) (Extended) | 1984 | Atlantic PR 801 | 6 |

**POP WILL EAT ITSELF**
**12-Inch Singles**

| | | | |
|---|---|---|---|
| CAN U DIG IT? (LP)/ (7" English Mix) | 1989 | RCA 9009 | 10 |

**POSIES, THE**
*DGC promo CD singles $2-4 each*
**RADIO SHOWS**
**Compact Discs**

| | | | |
|---|---|---|---|
| IN CONCERT-NU ROCK (Oct 93) | 1993 | Westwood One | 40-65 |
| *(Live concert)* | | | |

**POSTER CHILDREN**
**45s**

| | | | |
|---|---|---|---|
| HE'S MY STAR//CHILDLIKE AND EVERGREEN/SOMEONE ELSE'S SONG | 1995 | Warner Bros. PRO-S-???? | 7 |
| *("Soil Samples #19" promo on white vinyl; B-side by Wilco)* | | | |

**POWER STATION, THE**
**12-Inch Singles**

| | | | |
|---|---|---|---|
| SOME LIKE IT HOT (LP)/(7" Mix) | 1985 | Capitol SPRO-9344 | 10 |

**PREFAB SPROUT**
**12-Inch Singles**

| | | | |
|---|---|---|---|
| FARON (2 versions)/APPETITE | 1985 | Epic AS 2236 | 5 |
| THE GOLDEN CALF (Remix)/(LP version) | 1988 | Epic EAS 01020 | 5 |

**PRELUDE**
**45s**

| | | | |
|---|---|---|---|
| CHRISTMAS MESSAGE (same on both sides) | 1974 | Island IXPI 1 | 10 |

**PRELUDES, THE**
**45s**

| | | | |
|---|---|---|---|
| VANISHING ANGEL | 1958 | Cub 9005 | 60 |
| *(Red/white promo label)* | | | |

**PRESIDENTS OF THE UNITED STATES OF AMERICA, THE**
**RADIO SHOWS**
**Compact Discs**

| | | | |
|---|---|---|---|
| SPIN SESSIONS (Dec 96) | 1996 | Spin Magazine (2) | 30-50 |
| *(Live concert material)* | | | |

**PRESLEY, ELVIS**
**12-Inch Singles**

| | | | |
|---|---|---|---|
| LITTLE SISTER | 1983 | RCA EP-0517 | 150 |
| *(White promo label, promo only, the only Presley 12" single)* | | | |
| **16-Inch Transcriptions** | | | |
| MARCH OF DIMES  Public service interviews | 1956 | March of Dimes 0657 | 2,500 |
| *(16" 33rpm disc, interviews and songs by six artists including Presley)* | | | |
| MARCH OF DIMES  Public service spots | 1956 | March of Dimes 0653 | 2,500 |
| *(16" 33rpm disc, spots by 20 artists including one by Presley)* | | | |
| **45s** | | | |
| AIN'T THAT LOVING YOU, BABY | 1964 | RCA Victor 8440 | 50 |
| *(White promo label, stock picture sleeve $30)* | | | |
| ALL SHOOK UP | 1964 | RCA Victor 0618 | 100 |
| *(White promo label, stock picture sleeve $250)* | | | |
| ALWAYS ON MY MIND  Purple vinyl | 1985 | RCA 14090 | 20 |
| *(Only the promo is purple vinyl)* | | | |
| AMAZING WORLD OF SHORTWAVE LISTENING | 1957 | Hall'cters 4434 | 75 |
| *(Contains excerpts from several Presley songs)* | | | |
| AN AMERICAN TRILOGY | 1972 | RCA Victor 0672 | 30 |
| *(Yellow promo label, stock picture sleeve $30)* | | | |
| ARE YOU SINCERE | 1979 | RCA 11533 | 10 |
| *(Cream colored promo label)* | | | |

| **Title** | **Yr** | **Label, Number** | **NM $** |
|---|---|---|---|
| BABY, LET'S PLAY HOUSE  Gold vinyl | 1984 | RCA 13875 | 200 |
| *(Yellow vinyl special release)* | | | |
| BABY, LET'S PLAY HOUSE  Picture sleeve | 1984 | RCA 13875 | 40 |
| *(Picture sleeve for the special record above)* | | | |
| BIG BOSS MAN | 1967 | RCA Victor 9341 | 50 |
| *(White promo label, stock picture sleeve $30)* | | | |
| BLUE CHRISTMAS | 1957 | RCA Victor 0808 | 1,500 |
| *(Promo-only release for radio)* | | | |
| BLUE CHRISTMAS | 1965 | RCA Victor 0647 | 40 |
| *(White promo label, stock picture sleeve $40)* | | | |
| BLUE CHRISTMAS | 1964 | RCA Victor 0720 | 50 |
| *(White promo label, stock picture sleeve $75)* | | | |
| BLUE SUEDE SHOES  Blue vinyl | 1985 | RCA 13929 | 20 |
| *(Stock copy is also blue vinyl)* | | | |
| THE BOSOM OF ABRAHAM | 1972 | RCA Victor 0651 | 50 |
| *(Yellow promo label, stock picture sleeve $100)* | | | |
| BRINGIN' IT BACK | 1975 | RCA Victor 10401 | 12 |
| *(Cream colored promo label, stock picture sleeve $10)* | | | |
| BURNING LOVE | 1972 | RCA Victor 0769 | 15 |
| *(Yellow promo label, stock picture sleeve $15)* | | | |
| CLEAN UP YOUR OWN BACK YARD | 1969 | RCA Victor 9747 | 30 |
| *(Yellow promo label, stock picture sleeve $25)* | | | |
| CRYING IN THE CHAPEL | 1965 | RCA Victor 0643 | 40 |
| *(White promo label, stock picture sleeve $20)* | | | |
| DO THE CLAM | 1965 | RCA Victor 8500 | 50 |
| *(White promo label, stock picture sleeve $30)* | | | |
| DON'T | 1958 | RCA Victor SP45-76 | 750 |
| *(Promo-only release)* | | | |
| DON'T  Picture sleeve | 1958 | RCA Victor SP45-76 | 2,000 |
| *(Promo picture sleeve for the above)* | | | |
| DON'T CRY DADDY | 1969 | RCA Victor 9768 | 30 |
| *(Yellow promo label, stock picture sleeve $15)* | | | |
| EASY QUESTION | 1965 | RCA Victor 8585 | 50 |
| *(White promo label, stock picture sleeve $30)* | | | |
| THE ELVIS MEDLEY  Black vinyl | 1982 | RCA 13351 | 10 |
| *(Cream colored promo label)* | | | |
| THE ELVIS MEDLEY  Gold vinyl | 1982 | RCA 13351 | 300 |
| *(Gold label, colored vinyl promo only)* | | | |
| FOR THE HEART | 1976 | RCA Victor 10601 | 12 |
| *(Cream colored promo label, stock picture sleeve $10)* | | | |
| FRANKIE AND JOHNNY | 1966 | RCA Victor 8780 | 50 |
| *(White promo label, stock picture sleeve $40)* | | | |
| GOOD ROCKIN' TONIGHT | 1964 | RCA Victor 0602 | 100 |
| *(White promo label, stock picture sleeve $250)* | | | |
| GUITAR MAN | 1968 | RCA Victor 9425 | 40 |
| *(Yellow promo label, stock picture sleeve $30)* | | | |
| GUITAR MAN  Black vinyl | 1981 | RCA 12158 | 10 |
| *(Cream colored promo label)* | | | |
| GUITAR MAN  Red vinyl | 1981 | RCA 12158 | 300 |
| *(Promo-only release to radio stations)* | | | |
| HEARTBREAK HOTEL | 1964 | RCA Victor 0605 | 100 |
| *(White promo label, stock picture sleeve $250)* | | | |
| HEARTBREAK HOTEL | 1988 | RCA 8760-7-RA1 | 25 |
| *(Promo number, opaque vinyl)* | | | |
| HOUND DOG | 1964 | RCA Victor 0608 | 100 |
| *(White promo label, stock picture sleeve $250)* | | | |
| HOW GREAT THOU ART | 1969 | RCA Victor 0130 | 50 |
| *(Yellow promo label, stock picture sleeve $150)* | | | |
| HOW GREAT THOU ART | 1969 | RCA Victor SP 162 | 150 |
| *(White promo-only label, for radio)* | | | |
| HOW GREAT THOU ART  Picture sleeve | 1969 | RCA Victor SP 162 | 200 |
| *(Promo-only picture sleeve for the above record)* | | | |
| I REALLY DON'T WANT TO KNOW | 1970 | RCA Victor 9960 | 20 |
| *(Yellow promo label, stock picture sleeve $15)* | | | |
| I WANT YOU, I NEED YOU, I LOVE YOU | 1956 | No number (RCA Victor 6540) | 1,500 |
| *(Promo-only "This is His Life" picture sleeve, comes with stock records at radio stations)* | | | |
| I WAS THE ONE  Black vinyl | 1983 | RCA 13500 | 10 |
| *(Cream colored promo label)* | | | |
| I WAS THE ONE  Gold vinyl | 1983 | RCA 13500 | 300 |
| *(Bright yellow label, colored vinyl is promo only)* | | | |
| I'LL BE BACK  One-sided single | 1966 | RCA Victor 4-834-115 | 8,000 |
| *(One-sided promo with designation "For Special Academy Consideration Only")* | | | |
| I'M LEAVIN' | 1971 | RCA Victor 9998 | 20 |
| *(Yellow promo label, stock picture sleeve $25)* | | | |
| I'M YOURS | 1965 | RCA Victor 8657 | 50 |
| *(White promo label, stock picture sleeve $40)* | | | |
| I'VE GOT A THING ABOUT YOU BABY | 1974 | RCA Victor 0196 | 15 |
| *(Cream colored promo label, stock picture sleeve $10)* | | | |
| I'VE LOST YOU | 1970 | RCA Victor 9873 | 20 |
| *(Yellow promo label, stock picture sleeve $15)* | | | |
| IF EVERY DAY WAS LIKE CHRISTMAS | 1966 | RCA Victor 8950 | 50 |
| *(White promo label, stock picture sleeve $100)* | | | |
| IF I CAN DREAM | 1968 | RCA Victor 9670 | 30 |
| *(Yellow promo label, stock picture sleeve $15)* | | | |
| IF I CAN DREAM  Picture sleeve | 1968 | RCA Victor 9670 | 300 |
| *(Experimental cardboard singles sleeve)* | | | |
| IF YOU TALK IN YOUR SLEEP | 1974 | RCA Victor 0280 | 15 |
| *(Cream colored promo label, stock picture sleeve $15)* | | | |

| Title | Yr | Label, Number | NM $ |
|---|---|---|---|
| THE IMPOSSIBLE DREAM  Gold vinyl | 1982 | RCA 13302 | 50 |
| *(Not a regular promo release, this was a giveaway item)* | | | |
| THE IMPOSSIBLE DREAM  Picture sleeve | 1982 | RCA 13302 | 50 |
| *(Picture sleeve for the giveaway record listed above)* | | | |
| IN THE GHETTO | 1969 | RCA Victor 9741 | 30 |
| *(Yellow promo label, stock picture sleeve $20)* | | | |
| INDESCRIBABLY BLUE | 1967 | RCA Victor 9056 | 50 |
| *(White promo label, stock picture sleeve $40)* | | | |
| IT'S NOW OR NEVER  Green promo label | 1961 | U.S. Air Force 125 | 250 |
| *(Public service five-minute program includes host)* | | | |
| IT'S ONLY LOVE | 1971 | RCA Victor 1017 | 20 |
| *(Yellow promo label, stock picture sleeve $20)* | | | |
| JOSHUA FIT THE BATTLE | 1966 | RCA Victor 0651 | 50 |
| *(White promo label, stock picture sleeve $150)* | | | |
| JUDY | 1967 | RCA Victor 9287 | 50 |
| *(White promo label, stock picture sleeve $75)* | | | |
| KENTUCKY RAIN | 1970 | RCA Victor 9791 | 25 |
| *(Yellow promo label, stock picture sleeve $15)* | | | |
| THE KING IS DEAD | 1978 | Evatone 52578 | 125 |
| *(Plastic soundsheet)* | | | |
| KING OF THE WHOLE WIDE WORLD | 1962 | RCA Victor SP-45-118 | 200 |
| *(Promo only for radio stations)* | | | |
| KING OF THE WHOLE WIDE WORLD Title sleeve | 1962 | RCA Victor SP-45-118 | 300 |
| *(Promo-only sleeve for the record above)* | | | |
| KING OF THE WHOLE WIDE WORLD/KING CREOLE | 1997 | RCA DME1-1803 | 400 |
| *(Test pressings of above on green, blue, white and clear vinyl; value is for any of them)* | | | |
| KISS ME QUICK | 1964 | RCA Victor 0639 | 50 |
| *(White promo label, stock picture sleeve $50)* | | | |
| LET ME BE THERE | 1976 | RCA 10951 | 200 |
| *(Cream colored promo label, special publisher's release)* | | | |
| LET YOURSELF GO | 1968 | RCA Victor 9547 | 40 |
| *(Yellow promo label, stock picture sleeve $30)* | | | |
| LIFE | 1971 | RCA Victor 9985 | 25 |
| *(Yellow promo label, stock picture sleeve $20)* | | | |
| A LITTLE LESS CONVERSATION | 1968 | RCA Victor 9610 | 40 |
| *(Yellow promo label, stock picture sleeve $30)* | | | |
| LITTLE SISTER  Black vinyl | 1983 | RCA 13547 | 10 |
| *(Cream colored promo label)* | | | |
| LITTLE SISTER  Blue vinyl | 1983 | RCA 13547 | 300 |
| *(Blue label, colored vinyl is promo only)* | | | |
| LONG LEGGED GIRL | 1967 | RCA Victor 9115 | 50 |
| *(White promo label, stock picture sleeve $40)* | | | |
| LOVE LETTERS | 1966 | RCA Victor 8870 | 50 |
| *(White promo label, stock picture sleeve $30)* | | | |
| LOVIN' ARMS  Black vinyl | 1981 | RCA 12205 | 10 |
| *(Cream colored promo label)* | | | |
| LOVIN' ARMS  Green vinyl | 1981 | RCA 12205 | 300 |
| *(Yellow promo label, colored vinyl, promo only)* | | | |
| MEMORIES | 1969 | RCA Victor 9731 | 30 |
| *(Yellow promo label, stock picture sleeve $25)* | | | |
| MERRY CHRISTMAS BABY | 1971 | RCA Victor 0572 | 30 |
| *(Yellow promo label, stock picture sleeve $50)* | | | |
| MERRY CHRISTMAS BABY  Green vinyl | 1985 | RCA 14237 | 15 |
| *(There is a green vinyl and black vinyl stock copy)* | | | |
| MILKY WHITE WAY | 1966 | RCA Victor 0652 | 50 |
| *(White promo label, stock picture sleeve $100)* | | | |
| MOODY BLUE | 1976 | RCA 10857 | 12 |
| *(Cream colored promo label, stock picture sleeve $10)* | | | |
| MOODY BLUE  Promo-only blue vinyl | 1976 | RCA 10857 | 1,250 |
| *(Very limited, for RCA employees)* | | | |
| MOODY BLUE  Promo-only gold vinyl | 1976 | RCA 10857 | 1,250 |
| *(Very limited, for RCA employees)* | | | |
| MOODY BLUE  Promo-only green vinyl | 1976 | RCA 10857 | 1,250 |
| *(Very limited, for RCA employees)* | | | |
| MOODY BLUE  Promo-only multi-color swirl vinyl | 1976 | RCA 10857 | 2,000 |
| *(Very limited, for RCA employees)* | | | |
| MOODY BLUE  Promo-only red vinyl | 1976 | RCA 10857 | 1,250 |
| *(Very limited, for RCA employees)* | | | |
| MOODY BLUE  Promo-only swirl vinyl | 1976 | RCA 10857 | 1,500 |
| *(Very limited, for RCA employees)* | | | |
| MOODY BLUE  Promo-only white vinyl | 1976 | RCA 10857 | 1,250 |
| *(Very limited, for RCA employees)* | | | |
| MY BOY | 1975 | RCA Victor 10191 | 15 |
| *(Cream colored promo label, stock picture sleeve $10)* | | | |
| MY WAY | 1977 | RCA 11165 | 10 |
| *(Cream colored promo label)* | | | |
| MYSTERY TRAIN | 1955 | RCA Victor 6357 | 500 |
| *(White promo label; the only "Record Prevue" issued in the U.S., though some exist on Canadian releases)* | | | |
| OLD SHEP  White label | 1956 | RCA Victor CR 15 | 1,000 |
| *(Promo-only one-sided record for radio stations)* | | | |
| PROMISED LAND | 1974 | RCA Victor 10074 | 15 |
| *(Cream colored promo label, stock picture sleeve $20)* | | | |
| RAISED ON ROCK | 1973 | RCA Victor 0088 | 15 |
| *(Cream colored promo label, stock picture sleeve $25)* | | | |
| ROUSTABOUT | 1964 | RCA Victor SP-139 | 300 |
| *(White promo label, promo only)* | | | |
| ROUSTABOUT  Theater ads | 1964 | Paramount Pictures 2414 | 1,000 |
| *(Promo-only release for selected theatres)* | | | |

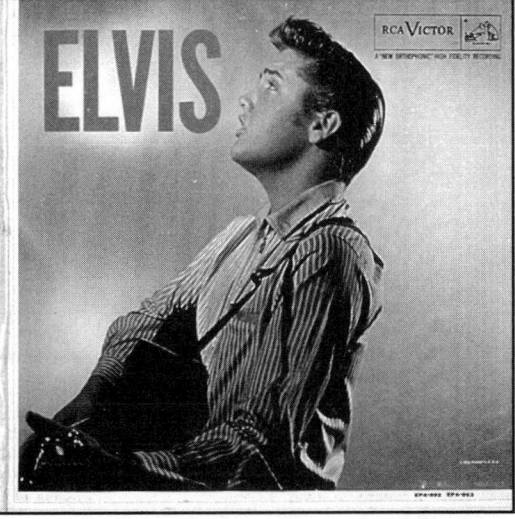
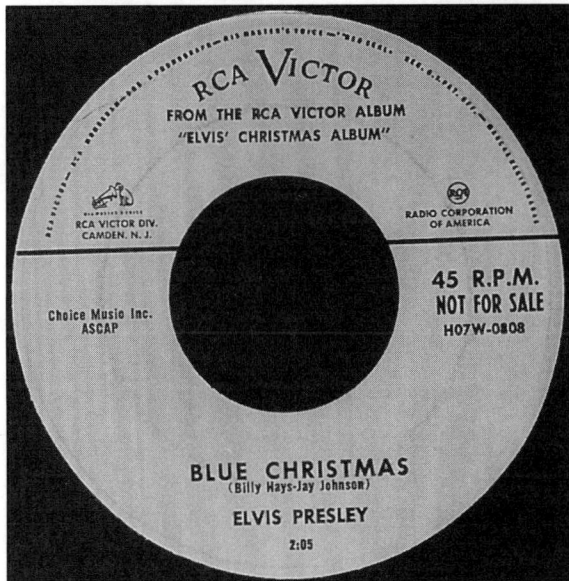

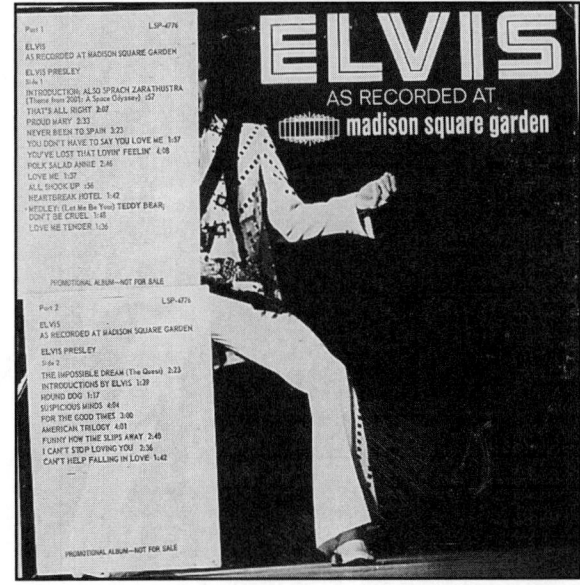

Elvis Presley is the king of collectible promos. Almost any promotional record by or relating to the King is highly collectible, and here are several examples. (Top row) This promo-only item paired a Jaye P. Morgan extended-play record with an Elvis EP record; the idea was to show that the Morgan EP was worthy of sales even though it had sold a fraction of the Elvis EP.  A nice copy of this has sold for close to $10,000! (Middle left) The first American 45 rpm pressing of  "Blue Christmas" was on this rare promo that fetches four figures in nice condition. (Middle right) The extremely rare title sleeve for the extremely rare promo 45 of "Don't" backed with "Wear My Ring Around Your Neck," another four-figure item. (Bottom left) From 1967, here is a rare Elvis radio show produced by his record company. (Bottom right) Promotional copies of *Elvis As Recorded At Madison Square Garden* include thorough notes pasted on the cover.

| Title | Yr | Label, Number | NM $ |
|---|---|---|---|
| SEPARATE WAYS | 1972 | RCA Victor 0815 | 15 |
| *(Yellow promo label, stock picture sleeve $15)* | | | |
| SPINOUT | 1966 | RCA Victor 8941 | 50 |
| *(White promo label, stock picture sleeve $40)* | | | |
| STEAMROLLER BLUES | 1973 | RCA Victor 0910 | 15 |
| *(Cream colored promo label, stock picture sleeve $10)* | | | |
| SUCH A NIGHT | 1964 | RCA Victor 8400 | 5,000 |
| *(White promo label, the rarest Presley promo)* | | | |
| SURRENDER  Green promo label | 1961 | U.S. Air Force 159 | 250 |
| *(Public service five-minute program includes host)* | | | |
| SUSPICIOUS MINDS | 1969 | RCA Victor 9764 | 30 |
| *(Yellow promo label, stock picture sleeve $20)* | | | |
| T-R-O-U-B-L-E | 1975 | RCA Victor 10278 | 15 |
| *(Cream colored promo label, stock picture sleeve $10)* | | | |
| TEDDY BEAR | 1978 | RCA 11320 | 10 |
| *(Cream colored promo label)* | | | |
| TELL ME WHY | 1965 | RCA Victor 8740 | 50 |
| *(White promo label, stock picture sleeve $30)* | | | |
| THAT'S ALL RIGHT | 1964 | RCA Victor 0601 | 100 |
| *(White promo label, stock picture sleeve $250)* | | | |
| THERE GOES MY EVERYTHING | 1982 | RCA 13058 | 10 |
| *(Cream colored promo label)* | | | |
| THERE GOES MY EVERYTHING | 1982 | RCA 13302 | 10 |
| *(Cream colored promo label)* | | | |
| THERE'S A HONKY TONK ANGEL | 1979 | RCA 11679 | 10 |
| *(Cream colored promo label)* | | | |
| TV GUIDE PRESENTS ELVIS PRESLEY | 1956 | RCA Victor 8705 | 1,750 |
| *(White promo label, includes two paper inserts)* | | | |
| TV GUIDE PRESENTS ELVIS PRESLEY | 1956 | RCA Victor 8705 | 1,500 |
| *(Blue promo label, no inserts)* | | | |
| U.S. MALE | 1968 | RCA Victor 9465 | 40 |
| *(Yellow promo label, stock picture sleeve $30)* | | | |
| UNCHAINED MELODY | 1978 | RCA 11212 | 10 |
| *(Cream colored promo label)* | | | |
| UNTIL IT'S TIME FOR YOU TO GO | 1972 | RCA Victor 0619 | 15 |
| *(Yellow promo label, stock picture sleeve $20)* | | | |
| WAY DOWN | 1977 | RCA 10998 | 10 |
| *(Cream colored promo label, stock picture sleeve $10)* | | | |
| WAY DOWN | 1977 | RCA 10998 | 150 |
| *(White promo label, stock picture sleeve $10)* | | | |
| WE CALL ON HIM | 1968 | RCA Victor 9600 | 40 |
| *(Yellow promo label, stock picture sleeve $150)* | | | |
| WHAT'S IT ALL ABOUT  Public service show | 1977 | W.I.A.A. 78 | 50 |
| *(Music profile plus interview; featured song is "Life")* | | | |
| WHAT'S IT ALL ABOUT  Public service show | 1980 | W.I.A.A. 555/556 | 75 |
| *(Parts 1 and 2, profile and interview)* | | | |
| WHAT'S IT ALL ABOUT  Public service show | 1980 | W.I.A.A. 633/634 | 75 |
| *(Parts 1 and 2, profile and interview)* | | | |
| WHERE DID THEY GO, LORD? | 1971 | RCA Victor 9980 | 25 |
| *(Yellow promo label, stock picture sleeve $25)* | | | |
| THE WONDER OF YOU | 1970 | RCA Victor 9835 | 25 |
| *(Yellow promo label, stock picture sleeve $15)* | | | |
| WOODEN HEART | 1965 | RCA Victor 0650 | 30 |
| *(White promo label, stock picture sleeve $25)* | | | |
| YOU DON'T HAVE TO SAY YOU LOVE ME | 1970 | RCA Victor 9916 | 20 |
| *(Yellow promo label, stock picture sleeve $15)* | | | |

**7-Inch Extended Plays**

| Title | Yr | Label, Number | NM $ |
|---|---|---|---|
| ALOHA FROM HAWAII VIA SATELLITE  Jukebox LLP | 1973 | RCA Victor 2006 | 100 |
| *(Issued with a hard cover)* | | | |
| CHRONOLOGY OF AMERICAN MUSIC  Demo disc EP | 197? | | 40 |
| *(One-second excerpts from all #1 singles, 1955-72, including Elvis)* | | | |
| DEALER'S PREVUE  Custom envelope | 1956 | RCA Victor 7-2 | 300 |
| *(Also known as RCA Victor SDS-39)* | | | |
| DEALER'S PREVUE  White promo label | 1956 | RCA Victor 7-2 | 600 |
| *(Two cuts by Presley)* | | | |
| EASY COME, EASY GO  White promo label | 1967 | RCA Victor 4387 | 100 |
| *(Only white promo label EP of a stock release, no cover)* | | | |
| THE ELVIS HOUR  Demo disc EP | 1986 | Creative Radio | 40 |
| *(7" sample of promo radio show, there are two versions, same value)* | | | |
| ELVIS PRESLEY | 1956 | RCA Victor 1254 (2) | 3,000 |
| *(Paper picture sleeve; "Most talked about new personality," used promotionally to send stock copies of the EP to radio stations; records are stock copies; 90% of the value is for the sleeve)* | | | |
| ELVIS PRESLEY  Free with Elvis record changer | 1956 | RCA Victor SPD-23 (3) | 4,000 |
| *(This is a 3-record set, as opposed to the 2-record set above)* | | | |
| ELVIS PRESLEY  Free with Elvis record player | 1956 | RCA Victor SPD-22 (2) | 1,000 |
| *("Elvis" on front cover in dark pink color)* | | | |
| ELVIS PRESLEY  Free with Elvis record player | 1956 | RCA Victor SPD-22 (2) | 1,500 |
| *("Elvis" on front cover in light pink color)* | | | |
| ELVIS PRESLEY/JAYE P. MORGAN | 1956 | RCA Victor 992/689 (2) | 6,000 |
| *(Promotional item for record stores for in-store play; records inside the sleeve are stock copy, 95% of the value is for the cover)* | | | |
| EP BOX SET  10-EP box set | 1956 | RCA Victor 15 (10) | 1,500 |
| *(One of the ten EPs is by Presley, price is for the whole box set, which is a promo release of 10 stock copy EPs)* | | | |
| EP BOX SET  Elvis disc from set | 1956 | RCA Victor 9089 | 875 |
| *(Harder to find black label)* | | | |
| EP BOX SET  Elvis disc from set | 1956 | RCA Victor 9089 | 750 |
| *(Gray label)* | | | |
| FOLLOW THAT DREAM  Black label | 1962 | RCA Victor 4368 | 200 |
| *(Promo version for radio, songs' timings on label)* | | | |

| Title | Yr | Label, Number | NM $ |
|---|---|---|---|
| FOLLOW THAT DREAM  Paper sleeve | 1962 | RCA Victor 4368 | 200 |
| *(Paper sleeve used on stock EPs for jukebox vendors)* | | | |
| GREAT COUNTRY/WESTERN HITS  10-EP box set | 1956 | RCA Victor 26 (10) | 850 |
| *(Price is for the whole set, of which there is one Presley disc)* | | | |
| GREAT COUNTRY/WESTERN HITS  Elvis disc from set | 1956 | RCA Victor 9141 | 200 |
| *(Black label)* | | | |
| LOVE ME TENDER / ANY WAY YOU WANT ME | 1956 | RCA Victor DJ-7 | 300 |
| *(Promo only, white label, both songs on same side, two songs by Jean Chapel on the flip side)* | | | |
| PERFECT FOR PARTIES  Black promo label | 1956 | RCA Victor 7-37 | 100 |
| *(With horizontal lines)* | | | |
| PERFECT FOR PARTIES  Black promo label | 1956 | RCA Victor 7-37 | 100 |
| *(Without horizontal line)* | | | |
| PERFECT FOR PARTIES  Promo picture sleeve | 1956 | RCA Victor 7-37 | 100 |
| *(Paper picture sleeve for either above record)* | | | |
| RCA FAMILY RECORD CENTER  Promo label | 1962 | RCA Victor 121 | 1,000 |
| *(Excerpts from several songs including Presley, promo-only sampler)* | | | |
| SAMPLER  Black promo label | 1957 | RCA Victor 61 | 1,000 |
| *(Promo only with one excerpt of a Presley song)* | | | |
| SAVE-ON-RECORDS  Paper sleeve | 1956 | RCA Victor 7-27 | 400 |
| *(Promo-only paper sleeve for the record above)* | | | |
| SAVE-ON-RECORDS  Promo label | 1956 | RCA Victor 7-27 | 150 |
| *(Sampler including Presley and other RCA artists)* | | | |
| SOUND OF LEADERSHIP  8-EP box set | 1956 | RCA Victor 19 (8) | 1,500 |
| *(One of the eight EPs is by Presley; price is for the whole box set)* | | | |
| SOUND OF LEADERSHIP  Elvis disc from set | 1956 | RCA Victor 9113 | 750 |
| *(Promo-only release)* | | | |
| THAT'S THE WAY IT IS  Seven movie ads | 1972 | MGM WLC-448 | 2,500 |
| *(The rarest, only from MGM, and last of the movie ad discs)* | | | |
| TOO MUCH / PLAYING FOR KEEPS | 1957 | RCA Victor DJ-56 | 300 |
| *(Promo only, white label, both songs on same side, two songs by Dinah Shore on the flip side)* | | | |
| TUPPERWARE'S HIT PARADE  Sampler | 1973 | Tupperware 11973 | 50 |
| *(Tupperware sales tool, includes Presley song)* | | | |
| **78s** | | | |
| DON'T BE CRUEL | 1956 | RCA Victor 6604 | 400 |
| *(White promo label; there are some doubts about the authenticity of Elvis 78 rpm promos)* | | | |
| ELVIS PRESLEY SPEAKS-IN-PERSON  Flexi-disc | 1956 | Rainbow | 250 |
| *(Price is for the flexi-disc AND magazine)* | | | |
| ELVIS PRESLEY SPEAKS-IN-PERSON  Flexi-disc | 1956 | Rainbow | 150 |
| *(Price is for the flexi-disc only)* | | | |
| JAILHOUSE ROCK | 1957 | RCA Victor 7035 | 400 |
| *(White promo label; there are some doubts about the authenticity of Elvis 78 rpm promos)* | | | |
| MYSTERY TRAIN | 1955 | RCA Victor 6357 | 400 |
| *(White promo label; there are some doubts about the authenticity of Elvis 78 rpm promos)* | | | |
| THE TRUTH ABOUT ME  Flexi-disc | 1956 | Rainbow 1404 | 175 |
| *(Price is for flexi-disc AND "Teen Parade" magazine)* | | | |
| THE TRUTH ABOUT ME  Flexi-disc | 1956 | Rainbow 1404 | 100 |
| *(Flexi-disc only, from the "Teen Parade" magazine)* | | | |
| THE TRUTH ABOUT ME  Flexi-disc | 1956 | Rainbow | 250 |
| *(Price is for flexi-disc AND magazine)* | | | |
| THE TRUTH ABOUT ME  Flexi-disc | 1956 | Rainbow | 150 |
| *(Price is for the flexi-disc only)* | | | |
| **Albums** | | | |
| (SP-33-10) (Aug 58) Various artists | 1958 | RCA Victor SP-33-10 | 750 |
| *(Promo-only sampler including Presley)* | | | |
| (SP-33-27) (Aug 59) Various artists | 1959 | RCA Victor SP-33-27 | 650 |
| *(Promo-only sampler of 13 artists including Presley)* | | | |
| (SP-33-4) (July 56) Various artists | 1956 | RCA Victor SP-33-4 | 800 |
| *(Promo-only sampler of 21 artists including Presley)* | | | |
| (SP-33-54) (Oct 59) Various artists | 1959 | RCA Victor SP-33-54 | 500 |
| *(Promo-only sampler including Presley)* | | | |
| (SP-33-59) (Feb 59) Various artists | 1959 | RCA Victor SP-33-59 | 450 |
| *(Promo-only sampler including Presley)* | | | |
| (SP-33-66) (Dec 59) Paper sleeve | 1959 | RCA Victor SP-33-66 | 500 |
| *(Promo-only paper sleeve for record above, Santa is pictured at a console)* | | | |
| (SP-33-66) (Dec 59) Various artists | 1959 | RCA Victor SP-33-66 | 500 |
| *(Promo-only Christmas sampler including Presley cut)* | | | |
| (SPS-33-141)  Various artists | 1962 | RCA Victor SPS-33-141 | 400 |
| *(Promo-only sampler including Presley)* | | | |
| (SPS-33-191)  Various artists | 1962 | RCA Victor SPS-33-191 | 400 |
| *(Promo-only sampler including Presley)* | | | |
| (SPS-33-219) (Oct 63) Various artists | 1963 | RCA Victor 33-219 | 400 |
| *(Promo-only sampler including Presley)* | | | |
| (SPS-33-247) (Dec 63) Various artists | 1963 | RCA Victor 33-247 | 400 |
| *(Promo-only sampler including Presley)* | | | |
| (SPS-33-272) (Oct 64) Various artists | 1964 | RCA Victor 33-272 | 400 |
| *(Promo-only sampler including Presley)* | | | |
| (SPS-33-331) (Apr 65) Various artists | 1965 | RCA Victor 33-331 | 400 |
| *(Promo-only sampler including Presley)* | | | |
| (SPS-33-347) (Aug 65) Various artists | 1965 | RCA Victor 33-347 | 400 |
| *(Promo-only sampler including Presley)* | | | |
| (SPS-33-403) (Apr 66) Various artists | 1966 | RCA Victor 33-403 | 400 |
| *(Promo-only sampler including Presley)* | | | |
| (SPS-33-96) (Oct 60) Various artists | 1960 | RCA Victor SPS-33-96 | 400 |
| *(Promo-only sampler including Presley)* | | | |
| AGE OF ROCK  Various artists | 1969 | EMR 8 | 60 |
| *(Various artists LP features three songs by Presley)* | | | |
| ALOHA FROM HAWAII | 1973 | RCA Victor 6089 (2) | 2,500 |
| *("Chicken of the Sea" sticker on the cover, special promo for employees of Stokely-Van Camp's)* | | | |

| Title | Yr | Label, Number | NM $ |
|---|---|---|---|
| ALOHA FROM HAWAII | 1973 | RCA Victor 6089 (2) | 150 |
| (Orange label, cover has timing strip, record is stock copy, sent to radio stations) | | | |
| AUDIO SELF-PORTRAIT | 1985 | RCA Victor 0835 | 50 |
| (White promo label, includes interviews) | | | |
| BLUE HAWAII  Movie ads | 1961 | Paramount 1796 | 750 |
| (Four ads on one-sided promo record for radio advertising) | | | |
| E-Z COUNTRY PROGRAMMING #2  Various artists | 1956 | RCA Victor 0108 | 300 |
| (Promo-only 10-inch sampler including Presley) | | | |
| E-Z POP PROGRAMMING #5  Various artists | 1956 | RCA Victor 9681 | 300 |
| (Promo-only 10-inch sampler including Presley) | | | |
| E-Z PROGRAMMING #3  Various artists | 1956 | RCA Victor 0199 | 250 |
| (Promo-only 10-inch sampler including Presley) | | | |
| E-Z PROGRAMMING #6  Various artists | 1956 | RCA Victor 0197 | 250 |
| (Promo-only 10-inch sampler including Presley) | | | |
| ELVIS ARON PRESLEY  Promo edit | 1980 | RCA Victor 3729 | 150 |
| (In-store sampler) | | | |
| ELVIS ARON PRESLEY  Promo edit | 1980 | RCA Victor 3780 | 200 |
| (Radio station sampler) | | | |
| ELVIS ARON PRESLEY  Promo edit | 1980 | RCA Victor (no #) | 300 |
| (For radio stations) | | | |
| ELVIS AS RECORDED AT MADISON SQUARE GARDEN | 1972 | RCA Victor SPS 571 | 300 |
| ("Radio Station Banded Special Version"; came in plain white cover with stickers) | | | |
| ELVIS AS RECORDED AT MADISON SQUARE GARDEN | 1972 | RCA Victor LSP 4776 | 150 |
| (Orange label, timing strip on cover, record is stock copy, sent to radio stations) | | | |
| ELVIS COMMEMORATIVE ALBUM  Gold vinyl | 1978 | RCA Victor 0056 | 15-20 |
| (TV marketing offer) | | | |
| ELVIS NOW | 1972 | RCA Victor 4671 | 150 |
| (Orange label, cover has timing strip, record is stock copy, sent to radio stations) | | | |
| EPIC OF THE 70s  Various artists | 1976 | Century 21 (6) | 125 |
| (This set includes at least one Presley song) | | | |
| FELTON JARVIS TALKS ABOUT ELVIS | 1981 | RCA Victor 1981 | 100 |
| (Issued in a plain jacket with scripts) | | | |
| GIRLS! GIRLS! GIRLS!  Movie ads | 1962 | Paramount 2014 | 750 |
| (Four ads on one-sided promo record for radio advertising) | | | |
| HE TOUCHED ME | 1972 | RCA Victor 4690 | 150 |
| (Orange label, cover has timing strip, record is stock copy, sent to radio stations) | | | |
| INTERNATIONAL HOTEL PRESENTS ELVIS | 1969 | RCA 4088 & 4155 | 2,500 |
| (Two LPs plus misc. items specially boxed, price is mostly for box, the records are not rare) | | | |
| INTERNATIONAL HOTEL PRESENTS ELVIS | 1970 | RCA Victor 6020 | 2,500 |
| (LP and 45rpm plus misc. items specially boxed, price is mostly for box and 45rpm record, the LP is not rare) | | | |
| JAILHOUSE ROCK  Interview, red vinyl | 1957 | MGM 12-232 | 500 |
| (Radio interview with Leiber and Stoller) | | | |
| KID GALAHAD  Movie ads | 1962 | Paramount 1964 | 750 |
| (Four ads on one-sided promo record for radio advertising) | | | |
| LET'S BE FRIENDS  Gold vinyl | 1975 | PICKWICK 2408 | 350 |
| (Special release gold vinyl for record VIPs in promotion) | | | |
| MOODY BLUE  Gold vinyl | 1977 | RCA Victor 2428 | 1,500 |
| (Experimental) | | | |
| MOODY BLUE  Green vinyl | 1977 | RCA Victor 2428 | 1,500 |
| (Experimental) | | | |
| MOODY BLUE  Purple/white vinyl | 1977 | RCA Victor 2428 | 2,000 |
| (Experimental issues, only a few copies made) | | | |
| MOODY BLUE  Red vinyl | 1977 | RCA Victor 2428 | 1,500 |
| (Experimental) | | | |
| MOODY BLUE  Red/white vinyl | 1977 | RCA Victor 2428 | 2,000 |
| (Experimental) | | | |
| MOODY BLUE  White vinyl | 1977 | RCA Victor 2428 | 1,500 |
| (Experimental) | | | |
| MOODY BLUE  Yellow/white vinyl | 1977 | RCA Victor 2428 | 2,000 |
| (Experimental) | | | |
| OUR MEMORIES OF ELVIS  "Pure Elvis" | 1979 | RCA Victor 3455 | 500 |
| (White promo label, same songs on each side, one side with overdubs) | | | |
| RCA VICTROLA SPOTS  Radio ads | 1956 | RCA Victor 401 | 500 |
| (Promo-only one-sided disc advertising phonographs plus the SPD-22, SPD-23 giveaway record EPs) | | | |
| RECORDED LIVE ON STAGE IN MEMPHIS | 1974 | RCA Victor DJL1-0606 | 300 |
| (No mention of promo, is banded for DJs and includes DJL-prefix on label number) | | | |
| ROBERT W. SARNOFF - 25 YEARS OF LEADERSHIP | 1973 | RCA Victor 0001 | 250 |
| (Various RCA artists, four Presley songs) | | | |
| SHELBY SINGLETON PRESENTS SONGS FOR THE 70s | 1969 | Shelby Singleton 1 (2) | 150 |
| (White promo label records plus 66-page booklet, for radio stations) | | | |
| SPECIAL CHRISTMAS PROGRAMMING  White promo label | 1967 | RCA Victor 5697 | 1,500 |
| (Promo only for radio stations, price includes inserts) | | | |
| SPECIAL PALM SUNDAY PROGRAMMING  Promo-only label | 1967 | RCA Victor 461 | 1,500 |
| (For radio stations, price is for record and programming booklet) | | | |

**Compact Discs**

| Title | Yr | Label, Number | NM $ |
|---|---|---|---|
| ELVIS AT HIS ROMANTIC BEST | 1991 | RCA Special Products DPC1-0984 | 15 |
| (Only available through Avon distributors) | | | |
| HONEYMOON COMPANION | 1992 | RCA 66124 | 50 |
| (Promo-only CD, contains Elvis' versions of songs re-done by others on the "Honeymoon in Vegas" soundtrack) | | | |
| INTERVIEW RADIO SPECIAL | 1992 | RCA 66121 | 50 |
| (Promo-only CD, music and interview) | | | |
| MY HAPPINESS | 1990 | RCA 2654-2-RDJ | 50 |
| (Promo-only CD release) | | | |
| OUT OF THE BOX | 1992 | RCA 62328 | 50 |
| (Promo-only CD release from 1950s box set, 4 tracks) | | | |
| OUT OF THE BOX: 6 FROM THE 60s | 1993 | RCA 62624 | 25 |
| (Promo-only sampler from 1960s box set) | | | |

| Title | Yr | Label, Number | NM $ |
|-------|-----|---------------|------|
| OUT OF THE BOX: 6 FROM THE 70s | 1995 | RCA 66765 | 25 |
| *(Promo-only sampler from 1970s box set)* | | | |
| SELECTIONS FROM AMAZING GRACE | 1994 | RCA | 40 |
| *(Promo-only sampler from gospel-music box set)* | | | |
| SHAKE, RATTLE & ROLL  18 tracks | 1992 | RCA 6382-2-RDJ | 100 |
| *(Promo-only CD release)* | | | |
| **RADIO SHOWS** | | | |
| **Albums** | | | |
| BILLBOARD SOUND OF '77 (Dec 77) Box set | 1977 | Billboard Magazine (5) | 75-125 |
| *(Country version of the countdown of top records of the year)* | | | |
| BILLBOARD SOUND OF '77 (Dec 77) Box set | 1977 | Billboard Magazine (5) | 75-125 |
| *(Rock version of countdown, both shows feature Presley tribute)* | | | |
| BILLBOARD'S OFFICIAL TOP 40 PRESLEY HITS (May 87) | 1987 | United Stations (3) | 50-100 |
| *(All the Presley hits ranked by Billboard Magazine)* | | | |
| CHRISTMAS WITH ELVIS (Dec 87) | 1987 | Creative Radio | 20-40 |
| *(Music and interviews)* | | | |
| COUNTRY CROSSROADS (May 82) Show 21-82 | 1982 | Southern Baptist | 100-150 |
| *(Includes Presley song and interview from Louisiana Hayride)* | | | |
| COUNTRY CROSSROADS (Aug 83) Show 32-83 | 1983 | Southern Baptist | 30-60 |
| *(Includes Presley song)* | | | |
| COUNTRY EXPRESS (WITH GENE PRICE) | 1975 | U.S. Air Force (8) | 10-20 |
| *(Price is for each of the four 2-LP sets that feature Presley songs)* | | | |
| COUNTRY SESSIONS  Show 122 | 1983 | Country Sessions | 40-75 |
| *(Various artists, includes two Presley songs)* | | | |
| COUNTRY SESSIONS  Show 126 | 1983 | Country Sessions | 100-200 |
| *(Elvis Tribute)* | | | |
| EARTH NEWS (Aug 77) Daily news shows | 1977 | Earth News | 150-250 |
| *(The whole week dedicated to Presley)* | | | |
| ELVIS MEMORIES (Jan 79) Box set | 1979 | ABC Radio 1003 (3) | 250-400 |
| *(Price includes scripts, programming booklet and box)* | | | |
| ELVIS PRESLEY BIRTHDAY TRIBUTE | 1989 | United Stations (4) | 100-200 |
| *(Various artists salute Elvis)* | | | |
| ELVIS PRESLEY HOUR, THE | 1987 | Creative Radio | 60-100 |
| *(Weekly radio show, price for any one of at least 38 volumes)* | | | |
| ELVIS PRESLEY STORY | 1975 | Watermark (13) | 400-750 |
| *(Price includes manual, labels have pink letters)* | | | |
| ELVIS PRESLEY STORY | 1975 | Watermark (13) | 350-650 |
| *(Price includes manual, labels have blue letters)* | | | |
| ELVIS REMEMBERED | 1978 | Creative Radio (3) | 150-225 |
| *(Music and interviews, price includes scripts)* | | | |
| ELVIS' 10TH ANNIVERSARY RADIO TRIBUTE (Jan 87) | 1987 | Creative Radio (6) | 150-250 |
| *(Price includes scripts)* | | | |
| ELVIS, A THREE HOUR SPECIAL | 1977 | Drake-Chenault (3) | 125-250 |
| *(Tribute to Elvis Presley)* | | | |
| 50TH ANNIVERSARY SPECIAL (Jan 85) | 1985 | Creative Radio (6) | 175-250 |
| *(Price includes scripts)* | | | |
| 50TH ANNIVERSARY SPECIAL (Jan 85) | 1985 | Creative Radio (3) | 75-125 |
| *(Creative shows are designed to air any time during the year)* | | | |
| FRANTIC FIFTIES | 197? | Mutual Radio | 50-100 |
| *(Music and interviews, includes Presley)* | | | |
| A GOLDEN CELEBRATION  Box set | 1984 | Westwood One (3) | 100-175 |
| *(Price includes cue sheets and box)* | | | |
| LEGEND OF A KING | 1980 | Associated Broadcasters | 40-75 |
| *(White promo label sent to radio stations)* | | | |
| LEGEND OF A KING | 1985 | Associated Broadcasters (3) | 100-175 |
| *(Radio show, NOT a box set)* | | | |
| LEGEND OF A KING | 1985 | Associated Broadcasters (3) | 150-225 |
| *(Radio show version that IS a box set)* | | | |
| LEGEND OF A KING | 1986 | Associated Broadcasters (3) | 150-225 |
| *(Radio show version, box set)* | | | |
| LOUISIANA HAYRIDE | 1976 | La. Hayride 8454 | 300-500 |
| *(Yellow label, for radio stations, various artists)* | | | |
| LOUISIANA HAYRIDE | 1981 | La. Hayride 8454 | 125-250 |
| *(Gold label repeat of the show above)* | | | |
| LOUISIANA HAYRIDE | 1984 | (RCA Victor) 3061 | 125-250 |
| *(White promo label advance from RCA, non white label version worth around $12)* | | | |
| MEMORIES OF ELVIS (Jan 87) | 1987 | Creative Radio (3) | 75-125 |
| *(Music and interviews)* | | | |
| MEMORIES OF ELVIS | 1989 | United Stations (4) | 75-125 |
| *(Music and interviews)* | | | |
| MICHELOB PRESENTS HIGHLIGHTS | 1978 | ABC Radio | 125-200 |
| *(Advance material from "Elvis Memories" radio show)* | | | |
| ON THE RECORD  Top news of '77 | 1977 | Caedmon 1572 | 25-40 |
| *(Available to radio stations from United Press International)* | | | |
| REFLECTIONS OF ELVIS | 1977 | Diamond P (3) | 200-350 |
| *(Tribute to Elvis Presley)* | | | |
| ROCK, ROLL & REMEMBER  With Dick Clark | 1977 | United Stations (6) | 50-100 |
| *(Special "Presley Remembered" show of the weekly series)* | | | |
| SOUNDS OF SOLID COUNTRY  Box set | 198? | U.S. Marine Corps (7) | 15-25 |
| *(Price is for any 7-LP box set that contains at least one Presley cut)* | | | |
| SOUNDS OF SOLID GOLD  Box set | 198? | U.S. Marine Corps (7) | 15-25 |
| *(Price is for any 7-LP box set that contains at least one Presley cut)* | | | |
| SOUNDS OF SOLID GOLD  Box set | 198? | U.S. Marine Corps (7) | 40-75 |
| *(Price is for Vol. 51, which includes three sides of Presley exclusive)* | | | |
| STILL THE KING (Aug 87) | 1987 | Westwood One (4) | 75-125 |
| *(Red label, Presley tribute radio show)* | | | |
| STILL THE KING (Aug 88) Repeat | 1988 | Westwood One (4) | 75-125 |
| *(Presley tribute radio show)* | | | |

| Title | Yr | Label, Number | NM $ |
|---|---|---|---|
| THE WORLD OF ELVIS PRESLEY (Jan 85-Dec 85) Complete set | 1985 | NBC Radio (30) | 1,000-1,500 |
| *(Only a few collectors claim a complete set of these weekly shows)* | | | |
| THE WORLD OF ELVIS PRESLEY | 1985 | NBC Radio | 25-50 |
| *(Price is for any one of the 30 shows above)* | | | |
| WORLD OF SOUND  Top news of '77 | 1977 | AP 1977 | 25-50 |
| *(Available to radio stations from Associated Press)* | | | |
| **Compact Discs** | | | |
| BBC TRANSCRIPTION DISC | 1993 | BBC Transcription | 600-800 |
| *(With Sid Vicious)* | | | |
| BIOGRAPHY | 1994 | Entertainment Radio (3) | 50-100 |
| *(Music and interviews)* | | | |
| LEGEND OF A KING (90s) | 199? | Associated Broadcasters (2) | 75-150 |
| *(CD version of the show)* | | | |
| SIXTIES LEGENDS (May 92) | 1992 | Unistar (2) | 40-75 |
| *(Music and interviews)* | | | |
| TICKET TO RIDE (Aug 88) | 1988 | DIR | 25-50 |
| *(This one show "The Beatles Meet the King")* | | | |

## PRESTON, BILLY

*MGM and Capitol promo 45s $4 each; A&M promo singles $3 each; Motown promo 45s $2 each; A&M and Buddah promo LPs $5 each*

**12-Inch Singles**

| Title | Yr | Label, Number | NM $ |
|---|---|---|---|
| GIVE IT UP HOT/SOCK-IT, ROCKET | 1979 | Motown PR-64 | 12 |
| **45s** | | | |
| MY SWEET LORD  Star on label | 1970 | Apple 1826 | 10 |
| *(Apple 1826 is the number on the error Ringo "Beaucoup" sleeve)* | | | |
| THAT'S THE WAY GOD PLANNED IT | 1969 | Apple 1808 | 60 |
| *(Same song on both sides)* | | | |
| THAT'S THE WAY GOD PLANNED IT  Four-inch flexidisc | 1969 | Americom 433 | 150 |
| *(Very rare)* | | | |
| WHAT'S IT ALL ABOUT (Feb 80) Public service show | 1980 | W.I.A.A. 511 | 15 |
| *(Flip side is Alicia Bridges)* | | | |
| WHAT'S IT ALL ABOUT (Jan 82) Public service show | 1982 | W.I.A.A. 610 | 15 |
| *(Flip side is Gino Vannelli)* | | | |
| **RADIO SHOWS** | | | |
| **Albums** | | | |
| ROBERT W. MORGAN (Jan 81) | 1981 | Watermark | 20-40 |
| *(Music and interviews)* | | | |
| TOYOTA PRESENTS (70s) | 197? | Toyota (2) | 25-50 |
| *(Music and interviews)* | | | |

## PRESTON, JOHNNY

*Mercury white promo label 45s $15 each; Imperial promo 45s $12 each; ABC promo 45s $5 each*

**Albums**

| Title | Yr | Label, Number | NM $ |
|---|---|---|---|
| COME ROCK WITH ME | 1961 | Mercury 20609 | 100 |
| *(White promo label)* | | | |
| RUNNING BEAR | 1960 | Mercury 20592 | 150 |
| *(White promo label)* | | | |

## PRESTOS, THE

**45s**

| Title | Yr | Label, Number | NM $ |
|---|---|---|---|
| TILL WE MEET AGAIN | 1955 | Mercury 70747 | 50 |
| *(White promo label)* | | | |

## PRETENDERS

*Sire promo 45s $4 each; Sire/Reprise promo CD singles $3 each*

**12-Inch Singles**

| Title | Yr | Label, Number | NM $ |
|---|---|---|---|
| BACK ON THE CHAIN GANG/MY CITY WAS GONE | 1982 | Sire PRO-A-1085 | 8 |
| HYMN TO HER (Edit)/(LP Version) | 1986 | Sire PRO-A-2732 | 7 |
| MIDDLE OF THE ROAD/2000 MILES | 1983 | Sire PRO-A-2106 | 6 |
| ROOM FULL OF MIRRORS (same on both sides) | 1986 | Sire PRO-A-2627 | 6 |
| SHOW ME/TIME THE AVENGER | 1984 | Sire PRO-A-2128 | 7 |
| THIN LINE BETWEEN LOVE AND HATE/THUMBELINA | 1984 | Sire PRO-A-2154 | 7 |
| TRADITION OF LOVE (long)/(edit) | 1986 | Sire PRO-A-2677 | 6 |
| WINDOWS OF THE WORLD/1969 | 1988 | Polydor 632 | 8 |
| **45s** | | | |
| MESSAGE OF LOVE/TALK OF THE TOWN | 1981 | Sire PRO-S-942 | 10 |
| **Albums** | | | |
| GET CLOSE INTERVIEW | 1987 | Warner Bros. WBMS-142 | 20 |
| *(Part of "The Warner Bros. Music Show" series)* | | | |
| LEARNING TO CRAWL | 1983 | Sire 23980 | 12 |
| *(Promo-only Quiex II pressing)* | | | |
| **RADIO SHOWS** | | | |
| **Albums** | | | |
| BBC TRANSCRIPTION DISC  Live concert | 1982 | BBC Transcription | 200-300 |
| *(Very rare concert)* | | | |
| KING BISCUIT FLOWER HOUR  Live concert | 1987 | DIR (2) | 40-75 |
| *(Repeated)* | | | |
| KING BISCUIT FLOWER HOUR (Feb 81) Live concert | 1981 | DIR/ABC (2) | 60-100 |
| *(With Jim Carroll)* | | | |
| OFF THE RECORD (80s) Profile | 198? | Westwood One (2) | 15-25 |
| *(Music and interviews)* | | | |
| PIONEERS IN MUSIC Profile | 1987 | DIR (2) | 20-40 |
| *(With Heart)* | | | |
| RETRO ROCK (Apr 84) Live concert | 1984 | Clayton Webster (2) | 75-125 |
| *(Rare early material)* | | | |

| Title | Yr | Label, Number | NM $ |
|-------|-----|---------------|------|
| SOURCE CONCERT | 1981 | NBC Source (2) | 40-75 |
| *(Mostly live material)* | | | |
| SUPERSTAR CONCERT  Live concert | 1986 | Westwood One (3) | 35-60 |
| *(Box set, repeated several times)* | | | |
| **Compact Discs** | | | |
| BBC CLASSIC TRACKS (Jan 94) | 1994 | Westwood One | 15-30 |
| *(Various live tracks)* | | | |
| IN CONCERT (Apr 94) Live concert | 1994 | Westwood One | 30-60 |
| *(Repeated)* | | | |
| IN CONCERT (Nov 94) Live concert) | 1994 | Westwood One | 30-60 |
| *(With Green Day)* | | | |
| IN CONCERT-NU ROCK (June 94) Live concert | 1994 | Westwood One | 30-60 |
| *(New material, repeated)* | | | |
| KING BISCUIT FLOWER HOUR (Jan 94) Live concert | 1994 | DIR | 25-40 |
| *(Repeated)* | | | |
| OFF THE RECORD (Sept 94) Profile | 1994 | Westwood One | 15-25 |
| *(Music and interviews)* | | | |
| ON THE EDGE (Aug 94) | 1994 | Westwood One | 15-25 |
| *(Music and interviews)* | | | |
| ROCK STARS (Aug 90) Profile | 1990 | Radio International (2) | 25-40 |
| *(Music and interviews)* | | | |
| SUPERSTAR CONCERT (Mar 94) Live concert | 1994 | Westwood One (2) | 40-75 |
| *(Repeated)* | | | |
| UP CLOSE Profile | 1994 | Media America (2) | 25-50 |
| *(Mostly music and interviews with some live tracks)* | | | |
| **Reel-to-Reel Tapes** | | | |
| LINE ONE (May 87) | 1987 | | 20-30 |
| *(Music and interviews on one 7" reel)* | | | |

## PRETTY POISON
**12-Inch Singles**

| | | | |
|-------|-----|---------------|------|
| CATCH ME (I'M FALLING) (4 versions) | 1987 | Virgin 1080 | 8 |
| CATCH ME (I'M FALLING) (SPANISH ULTIMIX) (same on both sides) | 1987 | Virgin 1100 | 6 |
| NIGHTIME (4 versions) | 1988 | Virgin 1143 | 5 |
| NIGHTIME (4 versions) | 1988 | Virgin 1190 | 6 |
| WHEN I LOOK INTO YOUR EYES (3 versions) | 1988 | Virgin 1204 | 5 |

## PRETTY THINGS, THE
*Fontana white promo label 45s $12 each; Rare Earth promo 45s $10 each; Swan Song promo 45s $5 each; Other Rare Earth, Warner Bros. and Swan Song promo LPs $5 each*

**45s**

| | | | |
|-------|-----|---------------|------|
| TALKIN' ABOUT THE GOOD TIMES | 1968 | Laurie 3458 | 25 |
| *(Laurie red/white advance copy)* | | | |
| **Albums** | | | |
| PARACHUTE | 1970 | Rare Earth 515 | 20 |
| *(Red/white promo label)* | | | |
| S. F. SORROW | 1969 | Rare Earth 506 | 25 |
| *(Red/white promo label)* | | | |
| THE PRETTY THINGS | 1966 | Fontana 27544 | 125 |
| *(White promo label)* | | | |
| THE VINTAGE YEARS | 1976 | Sire 3713 (2) | 20 |
| *(White promo labels)* | | | |

**RADIO SHOWS**
**Albums**

| | | | |
|-------|-----|---------------|------|
| BBC TRANSCRIPTION DISC  Live concert | 1973 | BBC Transcription | 150-250 |
| *(With Medicine Head)* | | | |
| NIGHTBIRD & COMPANY (July 75) Various artists | 1975 | U.S. Army Reserve (2) | 15-30 |
| *(One of the four shows features the Pretty Things, shows are music and interviews)* | | | |

## PREVIN, ANDRE
**45s**

| | | | |
|-------|-----|---------------|------|
| GOD REST YE MERRY, GENTLEMEN/LET NO WALLS DIVIDE | 1961 | Columbia JZSP 55071/0 | 12 |
| *(B-side by Doris Day)* | | | |

## PRICE, LLOYD
*Specialty white promo label 45s $50 each; Other KRC white promo label 45s $25 each; Other promo 78s $50 each; Other ABC-Paramount promo 45s $10-15 each; Double-L, Monument and Scepter promo 45s $4 each; ABC Paramount white promo label EPs $100 each; ABC Paramount jukebox LLPs $50 each; Other ABC Paramount, Double-L and Monument promo LPs $10 each*

**45s**

| | | | |
|-------|-----|---------------|------|
| THE CHICKEN AND THE BOP | 1958 | KRC 301 | 50 |
| *(White promo label)* | | | |
| JUST BECAUSE | 1957 | KRC 300 | 75 |
| *(White promo label)* | | | |
| STAGGER LEE | 1958 | ABC-Paramount 9972 | 30 |
| *(White promo label)* | | | |
| **78s** | | | |
| STAGGER LEE | 1958 | ABC-Paramount 9972 | 250 |
| *(White promo label)* | | | |
| **Albums** | | | |
| COOKIN' WITH LLOYD PRICE | 1961 | ABC-Paramount 382 | 25 |
| *(White promo label)* | | | |
| LLOYD PRICE SINGS THE MILLION SELLERS | 1961 | ABC-Paramount 366 | 25 |
| *(White promo label)* | | | |
| MR. PERSONALITY | 1959 | ABC-Paramount 297 | 75 |
| *(White promo label)* | | | |
| MR. PERSONALITY SINGS THE BLUES | 1960 | ABC-Paramount 315 | 50 |
| *(White promo label)* | | | |

| **Title** | **Yr** | **Label, Number** | **NM $** |
|---|---|---|---|
| MR. PERSONALITY'S 15 HITS | 1960 | ABC-Paramount 324 | 35 |
| *(White promo label)* | | | |
| THE EXCITING LLOYD PRICE | 1959 | ABC-Paramount 277 | 150 |
| *(White promo label)* | | | |
| THE FANTASTIC LLOYD PRICE | 1960 | ABC-Paramount 346 | 25 |
| *(White promo label)* | | | |

## PRICE, RAY

*Columbia promo 45s, 21000 series $8 each; Columbia 33-single (Jukebox) singles $5 each; Columbia promo 45s, 40000, 41000 series $5 each; Other Columbia promo 45s $3 each; Dot and Dimension promo 45s $2 each; Columbia LLPs (Jukebox EPs) with hard covers $8 each*

**45s**

| | | | |
|---|---|---|---|
| DANNY BOY  Green vinyl | 1965 | Columbia 44042 | 15 |
| *(This promo record is commonly found with a stock picture sleeve worth an additional $5)* | | | |
| MAKE THE WORLD GO AWAY  Red vinyl | 1963 | Columbia 42827 | 15 |
| *(Price includes special insert/paper sleeve/letter)* | | | |

## PRICE, WALTER

**45s**

| | | | |
|---|---|---|---|
| JUNIOR JUMPED IN | 1955 | TNT 8005 | 100 |
| *(White promo label)* | | | |
| SIX WEEKS OF MISERY | 1955 | TNT 8006 | 75 |
| *(White promo label)* | | | |
| THIS IS ALL | 1955 | TNT 8009 | 50 |
| *(White promo label)* | | | |

## PRIDE, CHARLEY

*RCA Victor promo 45s by Country Charley Pride $4 each; Other RCA Victor color vinyl promo 45s $8 each; Other RCA Victor promo 45s $2 each; 16th Avenue (Capitol) promo 45s $2 each; RCA Victor LLPs (Jukebox EPs) with hard covers $8 each; RCA Victor LLPs (Jukebox EPs) with paper covers $4 each*

**45s**

| | | | |
|---|---|---|---|
| DOWN ON THE FARM | 1985 | RCA Victor 14045 | 10 |
| *(Green label, blue vinyl)* | | | |
| I DON'T THINK SHE'S IN LOVE ANYMORE | 1982 | RCA Victor 13096 | 10 |
| *(Yellow label, red vinyl)* | | | |
| MORE AND MORE | 1983 | RCA Victor 13451 | 10 |
| *(Orange label, green vinyl)* | | | |
| NIGHT GAMES | 1983 | RCA Victor 13542 | 10 |
| *(Orange label, red vinyl)* | | | |
| WHAT'S IT ALL ABOUT (July 77) Public service show | 1977 | W.I.A.A. 378 | 25 |
| *(The flip side features the Kinks)* | | | |
| YOU'RE SO GOOD WHEN YOU'RE BAD | 1982 | RCA Victor 13293 | 10 |
| *(Orange label, red vinyl)* | | | |

**7-Inch Extended Plays**

| | | | |
|---|---|---|---|
| IN CONCERT WITH HOST CHARLEY PRIDE  Various artists | 1975 | RCA JF-10287 | 12 |
| *(White promo label, five songs featuring RCA's top artists)* | | | |

**RADIO SHOWS**

**Albums**

| | | | |
|---|---|---|---|
| SILVER EAGLE Live concert | 1981 | DIR (3) | 20-35 |
| *(Repeated)* | | | |

## PRIMA, LOUIS

*Other Capitol and Dot promos $4 each; Other Capitol promo LPs $20 each*

**45s**

| | | | |
|---|---|---|---|
| TIGER RAG | 1958 | Capitol PRO 680 | 12 |
| *(Blue promo label, promo-only release)* | | | |

**Albums**

| | | | |
|---|---|---|---|
| THE WILDEST SHOW AT TAHOE  With Keely Smith | 1958 | Capitol 908 | 25 |
| *(Yellow promo label)* | | | |

## PRIMAL SCREAM

*Sire promo CD singles $3-5 each*

**12-Inch Singles**

| | | | |
|---|---|---|---|
| COME TOGETHER (3 versions)/LOADED (3 versions) + 2 | 1990 | Sire PRO-A-4513 | 8 |

**RADIO SHOWS**

**Compact Discs**

| | | | |
|---|---|---|---|
| IN CONCERT-NU ROCK (July 94) | 1994 | Westwood One | 30-60 |
| *(Live concert)* | | | |

## PRIMITIVE RADIO GODS

**Compact Discs**

| | | | |
|---|---|---|---|
| STANDING OUTSIDE A BROKEN PHONE BOOTH WITH MONEY IN MY HAND | 1996 | Columbia | 8 |
| *(Promo-only CD single, no commercial single issued)* | | | |

## PRINCE

*Also known as The Artist or a goofy male-female glyph; Other Warner Bros./Paisley Park promo 45s $4-8 each; Other Warner Bros./Paisley Park promo 12" singles $8-10 each; Warner/Reprise promo 45s by the following music related artists $4 each: Taja Sevelle, Krush Groove All Stars, Morris Day and/or The Time, Sheila E., The Family, Madhouse 6, Apollonia 6, Vanity 6; Columbia promo 45s and picture sleeves by these artists $3 each: Andre Cymone, Wendy & Lisa; A&M promo 45s by Jesse Johnson/Johnson's Revue $4 each; Promo 12" singles by any of the above related artists $6-8 each*

**12-Inch Singles**

| | | | |
|---|---|---|---|
| AMERICA (same on both sides) | 1985 | Paisley Park PRO-A-2300 | 15 |
| BATDANCE (4 versions) | 1989 | Warner Bros. PRO-A-3702 | 10 |
| BATDANCE (LP Version)/(edit) | 1989 | Warner Bros. PRO-A-3579 | 10 |
| CONTROVERSY (2 versions) | 1981 | Warner Bros. PRO-A-980 | 50 |
| DAMN U (same on both sides) | 1992 | Paisley Park PRO-A-5890 | 12 |
| DELIRIOUS (2 versions) | 1983 | Warner Bros. PRO-A-2080 | 30 |
| DIAMONDS AND PEARLS (LP)/(Edit) | 1991 | Paisley Park PRO-A-5148 | 15 |

March 28, 1981

**SUPER GROUPS**

SIDE C

**THE POLICE TAPES**

STARRING THE POLICE

D.I.R. Broadcasting Corp.
℗ & © 1981

SIRE®

PRETENDERS
PRODUCED BY
CHRIS THOMAS
RECORDED BY
BILL PRICE
A REAL
RECORD

PROMO-
TION
NOT
FOR SALE

PRO-S-942
SIDE 1
3:24

From the Sire
Mini Album
MINI 3563
PRETENDERS

Al Gallico
Music Corp.
BMI

**MESSAGE OF LOVE**
(Chrissie Hynde)
℗ 1981 Real Records
℗ 1981 Sire Records Company

Sire Records, Inc. Marketed by Warner Bros. Records Inc. Made in U.S.A.

COPYRIGHT RECORD MADE IN ENGLAND BY THE BRITISH BROADCASTING CORPORATION

**TCS BBC**

**BBC TRANSCRIPTION SERVICES**

STEREO/SQ       SIDE 1
L.P. 33⅓ rpm
DUR. 25'00"   135128—SQ

Use expires 31.7.78 unless contracted otherwise. Annual subscription permits continued use for duration of contract.

STEREO POP SPECIAL—66 (i)
**POP SPECTACULAR**
featuring
**PROCOL HARUM**
In Concert
CN 2023/SQ
© BBC 1974

REPRODUCTION RESTRICTED TO BROADCASTING STATIONS AUTHORISED BY THE BBC

**THE SOURCE**

NBC Radio's Young Adult Network

STEREO
33 1/3 RPM
NBC 82-52

1.

**THE SOURCE CHRISTMAS COUNTDOWN**

**QUARTERFLASH CONCERT**

**THE ROBERT W. MORGAN SPECIAL OF THE WEEK**

STEREO       SIDE 1

Program No. SWB-814-1
Air Date 10/3-4/81

**COMMERCIALS INCLUDED**

THIS RADIO PROGRAM IS RESTRICTED TO RADIO STATION BROADCAST ONLY, SUBJECT TO LICENSING AGREEMENT WITH WATERMARK, INC., 10700 VENTURA BLVD, STUDIO CITY, CALIFORNIA 91604. ALL RIGHTS RESERVED BY WATERMARK, INC. ANY OTHER USE EXPRESSLY PROHIBITED. ©℗ 1981 WATERMARK, INC.

**W** Watermark

**QUEEN**

**QUEEN**

A Queen-Roy Thomas Baker Production

All songs
published by
Queen Music Ltd./
Beechwood Music Corp. BMI

℗ 1978 by Elektra Records

**JAZZ**

6E-166-A
STEREO
PRC

Side One
**MUSTAPHA**
(May)
**FAT BOTTOMED GIRLS**
(May)
**JEALOUSY**
(Mercury)
**BICYCLE RACE**
(Mercury)
**IF YOU CAN'T BEAT THEM**
(Deacon)
**LET ME ENTERTAIN YOU**
(Mercury)

**PROMOTION COPY NOT FOR SALE**

(Top left) A sought-after Police radio show is "The Police Tapes," part of the Super Groups series from 1981. This was about the time they were having their first massive hit singles. (Top right) There were no official singles released from the album *Pretenders II*. But this promo-only 45 did come out, with the two biggest airplay hits on one 7-inch. "Message of Love" was Side 1 and "Talk of the Town" was Side 2. (Middle left) Another rare BBC Transcription Disc, Procol Harum makes a rare radio-show appearance here. (Middle right) Quarterflash was around long enough to appear on a radio show for The Source, the NBC service to younger-skewing stations. (Bottom left) Robert W. Morgan was a popular Los Angeles DJ and also the voice of the countdown on the TV show "Solid Gold." He also had a radio show called the "Special of the Week." This episode features Queen. (Bottom right) This promo label for Queen's *Jazz* album is identical to the stock copy except for those all-important words "Promotion Copy Not for Sale."

| Title | Yr | Label, Number | NM $ |
|---|---|---|---|
| DIRTY MIND (same on both sides) | 1980 | Warner Bros. PRO-A-929 | 60 |
| DO ME, BABY/PRIVATE JOY | 1982 | Warner Bros. PRO-A-1035 | 75 |
| GETT OFF | 1991 | Paisley Park 7 | 500 |
| *(Promo-only one-sided 10:00 version)* | | | |
| GETT OFF (6 versions) | 1991 | Paisley Park PRO-A-4977 | 15 |
| GOLD (3 mixes)/ROCK 'N' ROLL IS ALIVE! (AND IT LIVES IN MINNEEAPOLIS) | 1995 | Warner Bros. PRO-A-7941 | 20 |
| *(Gold vinyl)* | | | |
| GOTTA STOP MESSIN' ABOUT | 1981 | Warner Bros. PRO-A-937 | 80 |
| *(Price includes an insert)* | | | |
| GOTTA STOP (MESSIN' ABOUT) (same on both sides) | 1981 | Warner Bros. PRO-A-938 | 60 |
| HEAD/SISTER/PARTY UP | 1980 | Warner Bros. PRO-A-915 | 80 |
| HEAD/WHEN U WERE MINE/UPTOWN//GOTTA STOP (MESSIN' ABOUT) + 1 | 1981 | Warner Bros. PRO-A-937 | 80 |
| I COULD NEVER TAKE THE PLACE OF YOUR MAN (LP)/(Fade) | 1987 | Paisley Park PRO-A-2770 | 18 |
| I HATE U (LP)/(Edit) | 1995 | Warner Bros. PRO-A-7594 | 15 |
| I WANNA BE YOUR LOVER (same on both sides) | 1979 | Warner Bros. PRO-A-832 | 75 |
| I WISH U HEAVEN (same on both sides) | 1988 | Paisley Park PRO-A-3283 | 12 |
| I WOULD DIE 4 U (same on both sides) | 1984 | Warner Bros. PRO-A-2233 | 20 |
| IF I WAS YOUR GIRLFRIEND (same on both sides) | 1987 | Paisley Park PRO-A-2758 | 12 |
| INSATIABLE (LP)/(Edit) | 1991 | Paisley Park PRO-A-5141 | 15 |
| KISS (Extended Version) (same on both sides) | 1986 | Paisley Park PRO-A-2458 | 15 |
| LET'S GO CRAZY (LP version)/(Edit) | 1984 | Warner Bros. PRO-A-2173 | 30 |
| LET'S GO CRAZY (7:35)/ (4:40) | 1984 | Warner Bros. PRO-A-2182 | 40 |
| LET'S PRETEND WE'RE MARRIED/D.M.S.R./AUTOMATIC | 1982 | Warner Bros. PRO-A-1082 | 50 |
| LET'S WORK (Dance Remix)/(7" Version) | 1982 | Warner Bros. PRO-A-1002 | 75 |
| LETITGO (LP)/(Edit) | 1994 | Warner Bros. PRO-A-7000 | 15 |
| LITTLE RED CORVETTE (Dance Mix)/(LP Version) | 1983 | Warner Bros. PRO-A-2001 | 40 |
| MONEY DON'T MATTER 2 NIGHT (LP)/(Edit) | 1992 | Paisley Park PRO-A-5298 | 15 |
| MOUNTAINS (LP)/(10:03) | 1986 | Paisley Park PRO-A-2476 | 18 |
| MY NAME IS PRINCE (LP)/(Edit) | 1992 | Paisley Park PRO-A-5770 | 15 |
| NEW POWER GENERATION (same on both sides) | 1990 | Paisley Park PRO-A-4515 | 10 |
| NEW POWER GENERATION (FUNKY WEAPON REMIX) (same on both sides) | 1990 | Paisley Park PRO-A-4578 | 10 |
| 1999 (Edit)/(LP Version) | 1982 | Warner Bros. PRO-A-1070 | 60 |
| 1999/FREE/AUTOMATIC | 1983 | Warner Bros. PRO-A-2042 | 50 |
| NOTHING COMPARES 2 U (LP)/(Edit) | 1993 | Paisley Park PRO-A-5994 | 12 |
| PARTYMAN (same on both sides) | 1989 | Warner Bros. PRO-A-3705 | 8 |
| PINK CASHMERE (3 versions) | 1993 | Paisley Park PRO-A-5993 | 25 |
| *(With picture cover; deduct 40% if missing)* | | | |
| POP LIFE (same on both sides) | 1985 | Paisley Park PRO-A-2331 | 15 |
| PURPLE MEDLEY (3:34)/(11:03) | 1995 | Warner Bros. PRO-A-7481 | 25 |
| PURPLE RAIN (LP version)/(Edit) | 1984 | Warner Bros. PRO-A-2192 | 40 |
| *(Purple vinyl)* | | | |
| RASPBERRY BERET (same on both sides) | 1985 | Paisley Park PRO-A-2313 | 15 |
| SEXY MF (same on both sides) | 1992 | Paisley Park PRO-A-5570 | 12 |
| SIGN "O" THE TIMES (LP)/(Edit) | 1987 | Paisley Park PRO-A-2687 | 10 |
| SOFT AND WET (same on both sides) | 1978 | Warner Bros. PRO-A-781 | 100 |
| STILL WAITING (same on both sides) | 1980 | Warner Bros. PRO-A-870 | 60 |
| TAKE ME WITH U (same on both sides) | 1985 | Warner Bros. PRO-A-2263 | 30 |
| THIEVES IN THE TEMPLE (same on both sides) | 1990 | Paisley Park PRO-A-4345 | 10 |
| U GOT THE LOOK (same on both sides) | 1987 | Paisley Park PRO-A-2771 | 15 |
| UPTOWN (4:09)/(5:29) | 1980 | Warner Bros. PRO-A-904 | 60 |
| WHEN DOVES CRY (Long)/(Short) | 1984 | Warner Bros. PRO-A-2139 | 25 |
| WHEN YOU WERE MINE (same on both sides) | 1980 | Warner Bros. PRO-A-916 | 60 |
| WHY YOU WANNA TREAT ME SO BAD?/BAMBI | 1979 | Warner Bros. PRO-A-848 | 75 |

**45s**

| Title | Yr | Label, Number | NM $ |
|---|---|---|---|
| CONTROVERSY (same on both sides) | 1981 | Warner Bros. 49808 | 10 |
| CRAZAY | 1986 | A&M | 500 |
| *(Label is blank white in an A&M sleeve; three copies of this test pressing were made in Minneapolis by Prince as a cover to the newly released Jesse Johnson single, which is A&M 2878. This test pressing must have in the trail-off "AM-02904-AES2.")* | | | |
| DELIRIOUS | 1983 | Warner Bros. 29503 | 60 |
| *(Price includes stock picture sleeve, a rare fold-out poster)* | | | |
| DIRTY MIND (same on both sides) | 1980 | Warner Bros. 49638 | 10 |
| DO ME, BABY (same on both sides) | 1982 | Warner Bros. 29942 | 10 |
| I WANNA BE YOUR LOVER (mono/stereo) | 1979 | Warner Bros. 49050 | 15 |
| JUST AS LONG AS WE'RE TOGETHER (mono/stereo) | 1978 | Warner Bros. 8713 | 15 |
| LET'S WORK (same on both sides) | 1982 | Warner Bros. 50002 | 10 |
| MY LOVE IS FOREVER (mono/stereo) | 1979 | Warner Bros. 49050 | 15 |
| 1999 | 1982 | Warner Bros. 29896 | 15 |
| *(Price includes stock picture sleeve)* | | | |
| PURPLE RAIN | 1984 | Warner Bros. 29174 | 10 |
| *(Purple vinyl, white/purple promo label)* | | | |
| SOFT AND WET (mono/stereo) | 1978 | Warner Bros. 8619 | 20 |
| STILL WAITING (mono/stereo) | 1980 | Warner Bros. 49226 | 12 |
| UPTOWN (mono/stereo) | 1980 | Warner Bros. 49559 | 10 |
| WHEN DOVES CRY (same on both sides) | 1984 | Warner Bros. 29286 | 10 |
| WHY YOU WANNA TREAT ME SO BAD (mono/stereo) | 1980 | Warner Bros. 49178 | 15 |

**Albums**

| Title | Yr | Label, Number | NM $ |
|---|---|---|---|
| BLACK ALBUM | 1987 | Paisley Park 25677DJ (2) | 6,000 |
| *(Only this promo version is double-LP, 45rpm)* | | | |
| BLACK ALBUM | 1994 | Warner Bros. PRO-A-7330 | 50 |
| *(Promo-only release of CD/cassette of the same name)* | | | |
| COME | 1994 | Warner Bros. PRO-A-7270 | 35 |
| *(Promo-only release of CD/cassette of the same name)* | | | |
| THE GOLD EXPERIENCE | 1995 | Warner Bros. PRO-A-7835 | 100 |
| *(Promo-only release of CD/cassette of the same name, on two gold vinyl LPs with numbered gold foil jacket)* | | | |

| Title | Yr | Label, Number | NM $ |
|---|---|---|---|
| LOVESEXY | 1988 | Paisley Park 25720DJ | 16 |
| *(Gold stamped and stickered cover – no UPC – with promo labels)* | | | |
| PURPLE RAIN  Purple vinyl | 1984 | Warner Bros. 25110 | 40 |
| *(Only the promo is purple vinyl)* | | | |
| **Compact Discs** | | | |
| ALPHABET ST. | 1988 | Paisley Park PRO-CD-3079 | 8 |
| *(Promo CD single)* | | | |
| ARMS OF ORION, THE | 1989 | Warner Bros. PRO-CD-3787 | 8 |
| *(Promo CD single)* | | | |
| BATDANCE | 1989 | Warner Bros. PRO-CD-3574 | 8 |
| *(Promo CD single)* | | | |
| BETCHA BY GOLLY, WOW | 1996 | EMI/NPG | 12 |
| *(Promo CD single, not commercially released as a single)* | | | |
| BLACK ALBUM | 1994 | Warner Bros. | 40 |
| *(Special DJ copy of the newly released version)* | | | |
| CREAM | 1991 | Paisley Park PRO-CD-4985 | 8 |
| *(Promo CD single)* | | | |
| DAMN U | 1992 | Paisley Park PRO-CD-5890 | 8 |
| *(Promo CD single)* | | | |
| DIAMONDS AND PEARLS | 1991 | Paisley Park 25379-2-DJ | 40 |
| *(Promo-only CD picture disc)* | | | |
| DIAMONDS AND PEARLS | 1991 | Paisley Park PRO-CD-5148 | 8 |
| *(Promo CD single)* | | | |
| FUTURE, THE | 1989 | Warner Bros. PRO-CD-3597 | 12 |
| *(Promo CD single, not commercially released as a single)* | | | |
| GETT OFF | 1991 | Paisley Park PRO-CD-4977 | 8 |
| *(Promo CD single)* | | | |
| GLAM SLAM | 1988 | Paisley Park PRO-CD-3181 | 8 |
| *(Promo CD single)* | | | |
| GOLD | 1995 | Warner Bros. PRO-CD-7941-R | 8 |
| *(Promo CD single)* | | | |
| GRAFFITI BRIDGE | 1990 | Paisley Park 27493-2-DJ | 40 |
| *(Promo-only CD picture disc)* | | | |
| I HATE U | 1995 | Warner Bros. PRO-CD-7793-R | 8 |
| *(Promo CD single)* | | | |
| I WISH U HEAVEN | 1988 | Paisley Park PRO-CD-3242 | 8 |
| *(Promo CD single)* | | | |
| IF I WAS YOUR GIRLFRIEND | 1987 | Paisley Park PRO-CD-2747 | 8 |
| *(Promo CD single)* | | | |
| INSATIABLE | 1991 | Paisley Park PRO-CD-5141 | 8 |
| *(Promo CD single)* | | | |
| THE JAMS (90s)  Gold box | 199? | Warner Bros. | 40 |
| *(Promo-only CD release, 18 tracks)* | | | |
| LETITGO | 1994 | Warner Bros. PRO-CD-7000 | 8 |
| *(Promo CD single)* | | | |
| MONEY DON'T MATTER 2 NIGHT | 1992 | Paisley Park PRO-CD-5298 | 8 |
| *(Promo CD single)* | | | |
| MORNING PAPERS, THE | 1992 | Paisley Park PRO-CD-5985 | 8 |
| *(Promo CD single)* | | | |
| MOST BEAUTIFUL GIRL IN THE WORLD, THE | 1994 | Bellmark/NPG 72516 | 40 |
| *(Promo CD single in 6x12 folder)* | | | |
| MOST BEAUTIFUL GIRL IN THE WORLD, THE | 1994 | Bellmark/NPG 72516 | 12 |
| *(Promo CD single without folder)* | | | |
| MY NAME IS PRINCE | 1992 | Paisley Park PRO-CD-5770 | 8 |
| *(Promo CD single)* | | | |
| NEW POWER GENERATION | 1990 | Paisley Park PRO-CD-4515 | 8 |
| *(Promo CD single)* | | | |
| NEW POWER GENERATION | 1990 | Paisley Park PRO-CD-4578 | 8 |
| *(Promo CD single, second version)* | | | |
| NOTHING COMPARES 2 U | 1993 | Paisley Park PRO-CD-5994 | 10 |
| *(Promo CD single, not commercially released as a single)* | | | |
| PARTYMAN | 1989 | Warner Bros. PRO-CD-3705 | 8 |
| *(Promo CD single)* | | | |
| PEACH | 1993 | Paisley Park PRO-CD-5992 | 8 |
| *(Promo CD single)* | | | |
| PINK CASHMERE | 1993 | Paisley Park PRO-CD-5993 | 8 |
| *(Promo CD single)* | | | |
| PURPLE MEDLEY | 1994 | Warner Bros. | 10 |
| *(Promo CD single)* | | | |
| SCANDALOUS | 1989 | Warner Bros. PRO-CD-3704 | 8 |
| *(Promo CD single)* | | | |
| 7 | 1992 | Paisley Park PRO-CD-5581 | 8 |
| *(Promo CD single, first version)* | | | |
| 7 | 1992 | Paisley Park PRO-CD-5981 | 8 |
| *(Promo CD single, second version)* | | | |
| SPACE | 1994 | Warner Bros. PRO-CD-7241-R | 8 |
| *(Promo CD single)* | | | |
| THIEVES IN THE TEMPLE | 1990 | Paisley Park PRO-CD-4345 | 8 |
| *(Promo CD single)* | | | |
| WILLING AND ABLE | 1992 | Paisley Park PRO-CD-5301 | 8 |
| *(Promo CD single)* | | | |
| **RADIO SHOWS** | | | |
| **Albums** | | | |
| HOT ROCKS | 1987 | United Stations (2) | 50-100 |
| *(Music and interviews)* | | | |
| MILLER SOUND EXPRESS (Jan 87) Sheila E. | 1987 | Miller Beer (2) | 200-300 |
| *(Live concert, Prince does a duet with Sheila E. on the song "A Love Bizarre")* | | | |

| Title | Yr | Label, Number | NM $ |
|---|---|---|---|
| PRINCE AND THE PURPLE PERFORMANCE | 1986 | (2) | 500-800 |
| *(Music and interviews, purple vinyl)* | | | |
| SUPERJAM '87 (June 87)  Prince and others | 1987 | Superjam '87 (2) | 25-50 |
| *(Make-believe concert made from limited concert footage)* | | | |

**PRINE, JOHN**
*Atlantic and Asylum promo 45s $3 each*
**RADIO SHOWS**
**Albums**

| | | | |
|---|---|---|---|
| BBC TRANSCRIPTION DISC  Live concert | 1973 | BBC Transcription | 100-200 |
| *(With Claire Hamill)* | | | |

**PRISM**
*Capitol promo 45s $3 each*
**RADIO SHOWS**
**Albums**

| | | | |
|---|---|---|---|
| BBC ROCK HOUR (Mar 82) | 1982 | London Wavelength | 20-30 |
| *(Music and interviews)* | | | |
| IN CONCERT (July 82) Live concert | 1982 | Westwood One (2) | 40-75 |
| *(With Quarterflash)* | | | |
| KING BISCUIT FLOWER HOUR (Oct 82) Live concert | 1982 | DIR/ABC (2) | 40-75 |
| *(With Aldo Nova)* | | | |

**Compact Discs**

| | | | |
|---|---|---|---|
| KING BISCUIT FLOWER HOUR (July 88) Live concert | 1988 | DIR | 40-75 |
| *(With Mott The Hoople)* | | | |

**PROCLAIMERS, THE**
*Chrysalis promo CD singles $3-5 each*
**RADIO SHOWS**
**Compact Discs**

| | | | |
|---|---|---|---|
| ON THE EDGE (May 94) Music and interviews | 1994 | Westwood One | 20-35 |
| *(With Stone Temple Pilots)* | | | |

**PROCOL HARUM**
*A&M promo 45s $6 each; Other Chrysalis promo 45s $5 each; Warner Bros. promo 45s $4 each*
**45s**

| | | | |
|---|---|---|---|
| BRINGING HOME THE BACON | 1973 | Chrysalis 2011 | 10 |
| *(4:21 and 3:20 versions)* | | | |
| FIRES OF LONDON | 1973 | Chrysalis PRO-562 | 12 |
| *(Promo-only release)* | | | |
| GRAND HOTEL | 1973 | Chrysalis 2013 | 10 |
| *(6:10 and 4:18 versions)* | | | |

**Albums**

| | | | |
|---|---|---|---|
| PROCOL HARUM LIVES | 197? | A&M SP-8503 | 300 |
| *(Promo-only box set with press kit, photos, keychain and interview LP)* | | | |
| PROCOL HARUM LIVES | 197? | A&M SP-8503 | 50 |
| *(Interview LP alone)* | | | |

**RADIO SHOWS**
**Albums**

| | | | |
|---|---|---|---|
| BBC TRANSCRIPTION DISC  Live concert | 1974 | BBC Transcription | 200-300 |
| *(With Trower and Coyne)* | | | |
| BBC TRANSCRIPTION DISC  Live concert | 1974 | BBC Transcription | 300-400 |
| *(Procol Harum alone; very rare radio series)* | | | |
| BBC TRANSCRIPTION DISC  Live concert | 1978 | BBC Transcription | 300-400 |
| *(Very rare concert)* | | | |
| IN CONCERT (Sept 91) Live concert | 1991 | Westwood One (2) | 50-80 |
| *(With Jethro Tull)* | | | |
| RETRO ROCK (June 82) Live concert | 1982 | Clayton Webster (2) | 100-150 |
| *(Rare early concert)* | | | |

**Compact Discs**

| | | | |
|---|---|---|---|
| BBC CLASSIC TRACKS (July 93) | 1993 | Westwood One | 15-25 |
| *(Various classic tracks)* | | | |
| IN THE STUDIO Profile of an album | 1991 | Album Network (2) | 15-25 |
| *(Two-part show, "Turning Back the Pages" and "Prodigal Stranger")* | | | |
| KING BISCUIT FLOWER HOUR (June 88) Live concert | 1988 | DIR | 40-75 |
| *(Repeated)* | | | |
| KING BISCUIT FLOWER HOUR (Mar 91) Live concert | 1991 | DIR | 40-75 |
| *(With Jethro Tull)* | | | |

**PRODIGY**
**Albums**

| | | | |
|---|---|---|---|
| THE FAT OF THE LAND | 1997 | Maverick PRO-A-8929 | 30 |
| *(Promo-only U.S. vinyl in generic white sleeve)* | | | |

**PSEUDO ECHO**
*RCA promo 45s $3 each*
**12-Inch Singles**

| | | | |
|---|---|---|---|
| LIVING IN A DREAM (same on both sides) | 1986 | RCA 5799 | 6 |

**RADIO SHOWS**
**Albums**

| | | | |
|---|---|---|---|
| IN CONCERT (July 87) Live concert | 1987 | Westwood One (2) | 30-60 |
| *(With Wang Chung)* | | | |

| Title | Yr | Label, Number | NM $ |
|-------|-----|---------------|------|
| **PSYCHEDELIC FURS** | | | |
| *Columbia promo 45s $4 each; Columbia promo picture sleeves $2 each; Columbia promo CD singles $2 each* | | | |
| **12-Inch Singles** | | | |
| ANGELS DON'T CRY (LP version)/(7" Remix) | 1987 | Columbia CAS 02829 | 6 |
| THE GHOST IN YOU (Edit)/(LP Version) | 1984 | Columbia AS 1839 | 8 |
| HEARTBREAK BEAT (LP version)/(7" version) | 1986 | Columbia CAS 2538 | 6 |
| HERE COMES COWBOY (Remix Edit)/(LP Version) | 1984 | Columbia AS 1908 | 8 |
| LOVE MY WAY/FOREVER NOW/PRESIDENT GAS/ANGELS | 1980 | Columbia AS 1538 | 20 |
| PRETTY IN PINK/IF YOU LEAVE | 1986 | A&M 17367 | 10 |
| *(B-side by Orchestral Manoeuvres in the Dark; promo from movie "Pretty in Pink")* | | | |
| WE LOVE YOU/SISTER EUROPE | 1980 | Columbia AS 879 | 8 |
| **Albums** | | | |
| INTERCHORDS | 1981 | Columbia AS 1296 | 25 |
| INTERCHORDS WITH RICHARD BUTLER | 1988 | Columbia CAS 01310 | 20 |
| RICHARD BUTLER INTERVIEW | 1987 | Columbia CAS 2719 | 15 |
| **RADIO SHOWS** | | | |
| **Albums** | | | |
| BBC COLLEGE CONCERT HOUR  Live concert | 1982 | London Wavelength | 50-100 |
| *(Early live concert)* | | | |
| BBC ROCK HOUR (Aug 84) Live concert | 1984 | London Wavelength | 50-100 |
| *(Early live concert)* | | | |
| BBC TRANSCRIPTION DISC  Live concert | 1982 | BBC Transcription | 250-375 |
| *(Very rare concert)* | | | |
| BBC TRANSCRIPTION DISC  Live concert | 1984 | BBC Transcription | 175-250 |
| *(Repeat concert)* | | | |
| BBC TRANSCRIPTION DISC  Live concert | 1992 | BBC Transcription | 200-325 |
| *(Very rare radio series)* | | | |
| IN CONCERT (May 83) Live concert | 1983 | Westwood One (2) | 40-75 |
| *(With Greg Kihn)* | | | |
| KING BISCUIT FLOWER HOUR (Jan 83) Live concert | 1983 | DIR/ABC (2) | 40-80 |
| *(With the Fixx)* | | | |
| **Compact Discs** | | | |
| IN CONCERT (Feb 93) Live concert | 1993 | Westwood One | 40-75 |
| *(With L7)* | | | |
| | | | |
| **PUBLIC ENEMY** | | | |
| **12-Inch Singles** | | | |
| BROTHERS GONNA WORK IT OUT (4 mixes)/ | 1990 | Def Jam CAS 2082 | 12 |
| ANTI-NIGGER MACHINE (censored) | | | |
| GIVE IT UP (3 versions)/BEDLAM (Clean)/BEDLAM (Instrumental) | 1994 | Def Jam SE-2 | 15 |
| LIVIN' IN A ZOO (4 versions) | 1992 | MCA 2586 | 10 |
| | | | |
| **PUBLIC IMAGE LTD.** | | | |
| **12-Inch Singles** | | | |
| BODY (Remix)/(7" version) | 1988 | Virgin 2247 | 8 |
| DISAPPOINTED (3 versions) | 1989 | Virgin 2709 | 10 |
| HAPPY (3 versions) | 1989 | Virgin 1406 | 6 |
| RISE (3 versions) | 1986 | Elektra ED 5129 | 8 |
| SEATTLE (12" Mix)/BODY (12" Mix) | 1987 | Virgin 1120 | 8 |
| | | | |
| **PUCKETT, GARY, AND THE UNION GAP** | | | |
| *Columbia promo 45s $12 each* | | | |
| **RADIO SHOWS** | | | |
| **Albums** | | | |
| VOICES OF VISTA (70s) | 197? | VISTA 221130 | 40-75 |
| *(Music and interviews, Gary Puckett is host)* | | | |
| | | | |
| **PULLEN, DWIGHT** | | | |
| **45s** | | | |
| SUNGLASSES AFTER DARK | 1958 | Carlton 455 | 100 |
| *(Green promo label)* | | | |
| | | | |
| **PULLEN, WHITEY** | | | |
| **45s** | | | |
| LET'S ALL GO WILD TONIGHT | 195? | Sage 294 | 40 |
| *(Black promo label)* | | | |
| WALK MY WAY BACK HOME | 195? | Sage 274 | 40 |
| *(Black promo label)* | | | |
| | | | |
| **PULLENS, VERN** | | | |
| **45s** | | | |
| BOP CRAZY BABY | 1958 | Spade 1927 | 200 |
| *(Spade promo label)* | | | |
| | | | |
| **PYRAMIDS, THE** | | | |
| *Cub and Vee Jay promo 45s $20 each* | | | |

| Title | Yr | Label, Number | NM $ |
|-------|-----|---------------|------|

# Q

**QUAILS, THE**
*With Bill Robinson*
**45s**

| Title | Yr | Label, Number | NM $ |
|-------|-----|---------------|------|
| I KNOW SHE'S GONE | 1954 | DeLuxe 6047 | 125 |
| *(White promo label)* | | | |
| A LITTLE BIT OF LOVE | 1954 | DeLuxe 6057 | 100 |
| *(White promo label)* | | | |
| LONELY STAR | 1954 | DeLuxe 6030 | 150 |
| *(White promo label)* | | | |
| LOVE OF MY LIFE | 1955 | DeLuxe 6074 | 75 |
| *(White promo label)* | | | |
| THE THINGS SHE USED TO DO | 1955 | DeLuxe 6085 | 50 |
| *(White promo label)* | | | |
| WHY DO I WAIT | 1954 | DeLuxe 6059 | 100 |
| *(White promo label)* | | | |

**QUAILTONES, THE**
**45s**

| Title | Yr | Label, Number | NM $ |
|-------|-----|---------------|------|
| TEARS OF LOVE | 1955 | Josie 779 | 75 |
| *(White promo label)* | | | |

**QUARTERFLASH**
*Geffen promo 45s $3 each*
**45s**

| Title | Yr | Label, Number | NM $ |
|-------|-----|---------------|------|
| FIND ANOTHER FOOL | 1981 | Geffen PRO-S-1012 | 10 |
| *(Remix longer 4:34 version)* | | | |
| WHAT'S IT ALL ABOUT (Mar 82) Public service show | 1982 | W.I.A.A. 615 | 25 |
| *(Flip side features The Go-Go's)* | | | |

**RADIO SHOWS**
**Albums**

| Title | Yr | Label, Number | NM $ |
|-------|-----|---------------|------|
| IN CONCERT (July 82) Live concert | 1982 | Westwood One (2) | 40-75 |
| *(With Prism)* | | | |
| IN CONCERT (Mar 82) Live concert | 1982 | Westwood One (2) | 40-75 |
| *(With Ian Hunter)* | | | |
| IN CONCERT (Oct 83) Live concert | 1983 | Westwood One (2) | 40-75 |
| *(Repeated)* | | | |
| KING BISCUIT FLOWER HOUR (Jan 82) Live concert | 1982 | DIR/ABC (2) | 40-75 |
| *(With Novo Combo)* | | | |
| NBC SOURCE (Dec 82) Live concert | 1982 | NBC Radio (2) | 25-50 |
| *(Early material)* | | | |
| SUPERGROUPS Live concert | 1982 | DIR (3) | 100-200 |
| *(With Yes)* | | | |
| SUPERSTAR CONCERT (Aug 83) Live concert | 1983 | Westwood One (3) | 40-75 |
| *(Box set, repeated)* | | | |

**QUATRO, SUZI**
*Other Bell promo 45s $5 each; Arista promo 45s $4 each; Dreamland promo 45s $3 each; RSO duet promo 45s $2 each; RSO and Dreamland promo LPs $8 each*
**45s**

| Title | Yr | Label, Number | NM $ |
|-------|-----|---------------|------|
| ALL SHOOK UP | 1974 | Bell 45,477 | 10 |
| *(White promo label)* | | | |
| CAN THE CAN | 1974 | Bell 45,416 | 12 |
| *(Promo version of another European smash)* | | | |
| DEVIL GATE DRIVE | 1974 | Bell 45,609 | 10 |
| *(White promo label)* | | | |
| 48 CRASH | 1974 | Bell 45,401 | 15 |
| *(White promo label version of a big European hit)* | | | |
| ROLLING STONE | 1972 | Rak 4512 | 12 |
| *("Radio station copy")* | | | |
| WHAT'S IT ALL ABOUT (July 79) Public service show | 1979 | W.I.A.A. 480 | 25 |
| *(Flip side features Eric Clapton)* | | | |

**Albums**

| Title | Yr | Label, Number | NM $ |
|-------|-----|---------------|------|
| QUATRO | 1974 | Bell 1313 | 20 |
| *(White promo label)* | | | |
| SUZI QUATRO | 1974 | Bell 1302 | 25 |
| *(White promo label)* | | | |
| YOUR MAMA WON'T LIKE ME | 1975 | Arista 4035 | 15 |
| *(White promo label)* | | | |

**QUEEN**
*Includes listings of Freddie Mercury, Roger Taylor and Brian May and Friends; also includes Smile, Larry Lurex (Freddie Mercury); Other Elektra white promo label 45s $5 each; Other Capitol white promo label 45s $5 each; Other Capitol promo 45s by Brian May and Friends $4 each; Elektra promo 45s by Roger Taylor $5 each; Other Elektra and Capitol promo 12" singles, group or solo, $8 each; Other Elektra white promo label LPs $10 each*
**12-Inch Singles**

| Title | Yr | Label, Number | NM $ |
|-------|-----|---------------|------|
| ANOTHER ONE BITES THE DUST | 1980 | Elektra 11461 | 15 |
| *(White promo label 12" single)* | | | |
| BICYCLE RACE | 1978 | Elektra 11401 | 15 |
| *(White promo label 12" single)* | | | |
| BODY LANGUAGE | 1982 | Elektra | 10 |
| *(White promo label 12" single)* | | | |
| CALLING ALL GIRLS | 1982 | Elektra | 10 |
| *(White promo label 12" single)* | | | |

| Title | Yr | Label, Number | NM $ |
|---|---|---|---|
| FLASH'S THEME | 1980 | Elektra 11481 | 15 |
| *(White promo label 12" single)* | | | |
| HAMMER TO FALL | 1984 | Capitol SPRO-9271 | 15 |
| *(Black promo label with title cover)* | | | |
| A KIND OF MAGIC (4:30) (6:30) | 1986 | Capitol SPRO-9714/5 | 15 |
| LOVE KILLS  Freddie Mercury | 1984 | Columbia AS-1928 | 15 |
| *(Red promo label with picture cover)* | | | |
| STAYING POWER | 1982 | Elektra 06754 | 10 |
| *(White promo label 12" single)* | | | |
| **45s** | | | |
| BOHEMIAN RHAPSODY | 1975 | Elektra 45297 | 15 |
| *(White promo label, different flip side)* | | | |
| BREAKTHRU | 1989 | Capitol 7PRO-79685 | 50 |
| *(White promo label, both sides same)* | | | |
| EARTH  Smile | 1968 | Mercury 72977 | 250 |
| *(Promo only, first record for the pre-Queen group)* | | | |
| GREAT PRETENDER  Freddie Mercury | 1987 | Capitol 5696 | 20 |
| *(White promo label, no label name or artist name on the labels)* | | | |
| HAMMER TO FALL | 1984 | Capitol 5424 | 10 |
| *(White promo label, "special new mix")* | | | |
| I CAN HEAR MUSIC  Larry Lurex | 1973 | Anthem 204 | 150 |
| *(Same song on both sides)* | | | |
| I WANT TO BREAK FREE | 1984 | Capitol 7PRO-9114 | 12 |
| *(White promo label, long 4:21/short 3:59 versions)* | | | |
| I WANT TO BREAK FREE | 1984 | Capitol 7PRO-9114 | 15 |
| *(Same as above, except no title of song or name of group on label)* | | | |
| I WAS BORN TO LOVE YOU  Freddie Mercury | 1985 | Columbia 04869 | 12 |
| *(White promo label, price includes promo picture sleeve)* | | | |
| KEEP YOURSELF ALIVE | 1973 | Elektra 45863 | 25 |
| *(Their first U.S. single, stereo/mono version, white label)* | | | |
| KEEP YOURSELF ALIVE | 1975 | Elektra 45268 | 15 |
| *(White promo label, stereo/mono versions, 6-30-75 in trailoff)* | | | |
| KILLER QUEEN | 1974 | Elektra 45226 | 15 |
| *(White promo label, stereo/mono versions, 11-13-74 in trailoff)* | | | |
| KIND OF MAGIC | 1986 | Capitol 5590 | 10 |
| *(White promo label, this version includes a stock picture sleeve and insert info/postcard)* | | | |
| LIAR | 1974 | Elektra 45884 | 25 |
| *(White promo label, stereo/mono versions, 2-1-74 in trailoff)* | | | |
| LIVING ON MY OWN  Freddie Mercury | 1985 | Columbia 05455 | 10 |
| *(White promo label)* | | | |
| LOVE KILLS  Freddie Mercury | 1984 | Columbia 04606 | 12 |
| *(White promo label, price includes promo picture sleeve)* | | | |
| ONE VISION | 1985 | Capitol 7PRO-9546/7 | 12 |
| *(White promo label, long 4:00/short 3:46 versions)* | | | |
| PAIN IS SO CLOSE TO PLEASURE | 1986 | Capitol 5633 | 10 |
| *(White promo label)* | | | |
| PRINCES OF THE UNIVERSE | 1986 | Capitol 5568 | 10 |
| *(White promo label)* | | | |
| SEVEN SEAS OF RHYE | 1974 | Elektra 45891 | 25 |
| *(White promo label, stereo/mono versions, 5-23-74 in trailoff)* | | | |
| **Albums** | | | |
| JAZZ | 1978 | Elektra 166 | 15 |
| *(Black promo label)* | | | |
| NEWS OF THE WORLD | 1977 | Elektra 6E-112 | 150 |
| *(White label promo with oversize cover and press kit)* | | | |
| NIGHT AT THE OPERA | 1975 | Elektra 1053 | 25 |
| *(White promo label)* | | | |
| QUEEN | 1973 | Elektra 75064 | 50 |
| *(White promo label, "Queen" is embossed in gold on the cover)* | | | |
| QUEEN II | 1974 | Elektra 75082 | 50 |
| *(White promo label)* | | | |
| SHEER HEART ATTACK | 1974 | Elektra 7E-1026 | 50 |
| *(White label promo)* | | | |
| **Compact Discs** | | | |
| BOHEMIAN RHAPSODY | 1992 | Hollywood | 12 |
| *(Promo CD single, reissue of 1975-76 hit)* | | | |
| BREAKTHRU | 1989 | Capitol DPRO-79720 | 8 |
| *(Promo CD single, one version)* | | | |
| BREAKTHRU | 1989 | Capitol DPRO-79746 | 15 |
| *(Three versions)* | | | |
| CLASSIC QUEEN | 1989 | Capitol DPRO-79591 | 50 |
| *(Promo-only greatest hits CD, 14 tracks)* | | | |
| FIVE LIVE  George Michael with Queen | 1993 | Hollywood PRBX-10313 | 50 |
| *(Promo-only CD with VHS and press kit)* | | | |
| HEADLONG | 1991 | Hollywood PRCD 8262 | 8 |
| *(Promo CD single)* | | | |
| HEAVEN FOR EVERYONE | 1995 | Hollywood | 8 |
| *(Promo CD single)* | | | |
| I CAN'T LIVE WITHOUT YOU | 1991 | Hollywood PRCD 8319 | 8 |
| *(Promo CD single)* | | | |
| INNUENDO | 1991 | Hollywood | 12 |
| *(Promo CD single)* | | | |
| ONE YEAR OF LOVE | 1992 | Hollywood 10196 | 8 |
| *(Promo CD single)* | | | |
| QUEEN TALKS | 1992 | Hollywood PRCD 8674 | 20 |
| *(Promo-only interview disc)* | | | |

| Title | Yr | Label, Number | NM $ |
|---|---|---|---|
| ROCKS, VOLUME ONE | 1990 | Hollywood PRCD 8263 | 20 |
| *(Promo-only collection)* | | | |
| ROCKS, VOLUME TWO | 1991 | Hollywood PRCD 8296 | 15 |
| *(Promo-only collection)* | | | |
| ROCKS, VOLUME THREE | 1991 | Hollywood PRCD 8297 | 15 |
| *(Promo-only collection)* | | | |
| ROCKS, VOLUME FOUR | 1991 | Hollywood PRCD 8298 | 15 |
| *(Promo-only collection)* | | | |
| ROCKS, VOLUMES 1-4 | 1991 | Hollywood (4) | 250 |
| *(Promo-only CD set in custom box)* | | | |
| SCANDAL | 1989 | Capitol DPRO-79785 | 10 |
| *(Promo CD single)* | | | |
| THESE ARE THE DAYS OF OUR LIVES | 1991 | Hollywood PRCD 8390 | 8 |
| *(Promo CD single)* | | | |
| THESE ARE THE DAYS OF OUR LIVES | 1992 | Hollywood 10061 | 8 |
| *(Promo CD single, reserive)* | | | |
| TOO MUCH LOVE WILL KILL YOU | 1995 | Hollywood 10546 | 8 |
| *(Promo CD single)* | | | |
| WE ARE THE CHAMPIONS | 1991 | Hollywood PRCD 8347 | 20 |
| *(Promo-only CD single, Desert Storm-related, with overdubbed President George Bush pronouncements)* | | | |
| WE ARE THE CHAMPIONS | 1992 | Hollywood | 8 |
| *(Promo CD single, reissue of 1977-78 hit)* | | | |

**RADIO SHOWS**
**Albums**

| Title | Yr | Label, Number | NM $ |
|---|---|---|---|
| BBC ROCK HOUR (Feb 82) Live concert | 1982 | London Wavelength | 150-225 |
| *(Rare early concert)* | | | |
| BBC ROCK HOUR (Mar 84) Live concert | 1984 | London Wavelength | 100-200 |
| *(Repeated show)* | | | |
| BBC TRANSCRIPTION DISC Live concert | 1975 | BBC Transcription | 650-800 |
| *(The ultimate Queen concert)* | | | |
| BBC TRANSCRIPTION DISC Live concert | 1976 | BBC Transcription | 650-800 |
| *(An ultimate show by any artist)* | | | |
| IN CONCERT (Feb 91) | 1991 | Westwood One (2) | 100-150 |
| *(Live concert with Badfinger)* | | | |
| IN CONCERT (Dec 91) | 1991 | Westwood One (2) | 75-125 |
| *(Live concert, repeated)* | | | |
| IN CONCERT (Apr 92) | 1992 | Westwood One (2) | 75-100 |
| *(Live concert with Electric Light Orchestra)* | | | |
| IN CONCERT (June 93) Brian May | 1993 | Westwood One (2) | 40-75 |
| *(Live concert by Brian May)* | | | |
| OFF THE RECORD | 1982 | Westwood One (4) | 25-40 |
| *(Music and interviews, two parts)* | | | |
| OFF THE RECORD | 1982 | Westwood One (2) | 15-25 |
| *(Music and interviews)* | | | |
| OFF THE RECORD (Feb 91) | 1991 | Westwood One (2) | 20-25 |
| *(Music and interviews)* | | | |
| PIONEERS IN MUSIC (Jan 86) | 1986 | DIR (2) | 25-50 |
| *(Music and interviews)* | | | |
| ROBERT W. MORGAN (Oct 81) Profile | 1981 | Watermark | 25-50 |
| *(Music and interviews)* | | | |
| SUPERSTAR CONCERT (Aug 86) | 1986 | Westwood One (3) | 50-100 |
| *(Live concert, box set)* | | | |
| SUPERSTAR CONCERT (May 92) | 1992 | Westwood One (3) | 75-100 |
| *(Live concert, box set)* | | | |
| WORLD OF ROCK (Sept 89) Brian May | 1989 | DIR (2) | 15-30 |
| *(Music and interviews, May is co-host)* | | | |

**Compact Discs**

| Title | Yr | Label, Number | NM $ |
|---|---|---|---|
| BBC CLASSIC TRACKS (Aug 91) | 1991 | Westwood One | 35-60 |
| *(Classic live tracks)* | | | |
| BBC CLASSIC TRACKS (Mar 93) | 1993 | Westwood One | 25-50 |
| *(Classic live tracks)* | | | |
| IN THE STUDIO (90s) Profile of an album | 199? | Album Network | 15-25 |
| *(Music and interviews)* | | | |
| KING BISCUIT FLOWER HOUR (Aug 88) | 1988 | DIR | 50-100 |
| *(Live concert, with Kansas)* | | | |
| KING BISCUIT FLOWER HOUR (Mar 91) Various artists | 1991 | DIR | 40-75 |
| *(Live concert with Queen, Steppenwolf and Scorpions)* | | | |
| OFF THE RECORD (June 93) | 1993 | Westwood One | 20-30 |
| *(Music and interviews)* | | | |
| SUPERSTAR CONCERT (Apr 94) | 1994 | Westwood One (2) | 75-125 |
| *(Live concert)* | | | |
| UP CLOSE (Mar 92) | 1992 | Media America (2) | 30-60 |
| *(Music and interviews)* | | | |

**QUEENSRYCHE**
*Other EMI promo 45s $4 each; Other EMI promo CD singles $6 each*
**45s**

| Title | Yr | Label, Number | NM $ |
|---|---|---|---|
| I DON'T BELIEVE IN LOVE | 1989 | EMI 7PRO-04345 | 10 |
| *(Promo-only 7-inch vinyl, no stock copies issued)* | | | |
| SILENT LUCIDITY | 1992 | EMI 57752 | 10 |
| *("For Jukeboxes Only!" on label, though it was sold to the public)* | | | |

**Albums**

| Title | Yr | Label, Number | NM $ |
|---|---|---|---|
| OPERATION MINDCRIME | 1988 | EMI SPRO-1436 | 50 |
| *(Promo-only picture disc)* | | | |
| SPEAKING IN DIGITAL | 1989 | EMI SPRO 9869 | 40 |
| *(Promo-only interview release)* | | | |

| Title | Yr | Label, Number | NM $ |
|---|---|---|---|
| THE WARNING | 1984 | EMI America ST-17134 | 40 |
| *("High Quality Vinyl" pressing)* | | | |
| **Compact Discs** | | | |
| BREAKING THE SILENCE | 1988 | Manhattan DPRO-04049 | 20 |
| *(An early promo CD single)* | | | |
| I DON'T BELIEVE IN LOVE | 1989 | EMI DPRO-04344 | 20 |
| *(Promo-only CD single)* | | | |
| REVOLUTION CALLING | 1988 | Manhattan DPRO-04142 | 20 |
| *(Promo-only CD single)* | | | |
| ROAD TO THE PROMISED LAND | 1995 | EMI DPRO-19985 | 50 |
| *(Promo-only sampler)* | | | |
| THE SOUND OF BUILDING EMPIRES (90s) | 199? | EMI | 25 |
| *(Promo-only release, five tracks)* | | | |
| **RADIO SHOWS** | | | |
| **Albums** | | | |
| KING BISCUIT FLOWER HOUR | 1983 | DIR/ABC (2) | 50-100 |
| *(Live concert)* | | | |
| **Reel-to-Reel Tapes** | | | |
| PROMISED LAND | 1994 | World Premiere | 40-75 |
| *(Music and interviews on a 10" reel)* | | | |

## QUIET RIOT
*Pasha (CBS) label promo 45s $3 each; Pasha (CBS) label promo picture sleeves $3 each*

| | | | |
|---|---|---|---|
| **RADIO SHOWS** | | | |
| **Albums** | | | |
| IN CONCERT (June 83) Live concert | 1983 | Westwood One (2) | 40-75 |
| *(With Krokus)* | | | |
| IN CONCERT (Sept 83) Live concert | 1983 | Westwood One (2) | 40-75 |
| *(Solo concert, repeated)* | | | |
| INNERVIEW (80s) Profile | | | |
| KING BISCUIT FLOWER HOUR (July 83) Live concert | 1983 | DIR/ABC (2) | 40-75 |
| *(With Zebra)* | | | |

# R

## R.A.D.D. (ROCKERS AGAINST DRUNK DRIVING)

| | | | |
|---|---|---|---|
| **Compact Discs** | | | |
| AUDIO MESSAGE PROJECT  Radio ads | 1987 | R.A.D.D. | 60 |
| *(Ninety-two radio public service ads; features Elton John, Bob Geldof, CSN & Y, Rolling Stones and others, for radio stations only)* | | | |

## R.E.M.

| | | | |
|---|---|---|---|
| **12-Inch Singles** | | | |
| (DON'T GO BACK TO) ROCKVILLE (Edit)/CATAPULT (Live) | 1984 | I.R.S. 70982 | 25 |
| AGES OF YOU  (same on both sides) | 1987 | I.R.S. 70416 | 8 |
| DRIVER 8 | 1985 | I.R.S. 17034 | 25 |
| *(Promo 12" single, flip side is a live version)* | | | |
| FALL ON ME (same on both sides) | 1986 | I.R.S. L33-17159 | 25 |
| FINEST WORKSONG (same on both sides) | 1988 | I.R.S. L33-17510 | 15 |
| I BELIEVE/TOYS IN THE ATTIC | 1986 | I.R.S. L33-17199 | 18 |
| IT'S THE END OF THE WORLD AS WE KNOW IT (AND I FEEL FINE)/ | 1987 | I.R.S. L33-17430 | 20 |
| DISTURBANCE HEROIN HOUSE (Live) | | | |
| LIFE AND HOW TO LIVE IT/BANDWAGON/CRAZY | 1985 | I.R.S. L33-17060 | 25 |
| THE ONE I LOVE (same on both sides) | 1987 | I.R.S. L33-17384 | 20 |
| ORANGE CRUSH (same on both sides) | 1988 | Warner Bros. PRO-A-3306 | 20 |
| *(Orange vinyl, custom labels)* | | | |
| RADIO SONG (Tower of Luv Bug Mix)/(Monster Remix) | 1991 | Warner Bros. PRO-A-5263 | 25 |
| SUPERMAN | 1986 | I.R.S. 17200 | 15 |
| *(Promo 12" single)* | | | |
| **45s** | | | |
| CAN'T GET THERE FROM HERE | 1985 | I.R.S. 52642 | 12 |
| *(Price includes stock picture sleeve)* | | | |
| DRIVER 8 | 1985 | I.R.S. 52678 | 12 |
| *(Price includes stock picture sleeve)* | | | |
| FALL ON ME | 1986 | I.R.S. 52883 | 10 |
| *(Price includes stock picture sleeve)* | | | |
| RADIO FREE EUROPE | 1983 | I.R.S. 9916 | 25 |
| *(Both sides are the same)* | | | |
| ROCKVILLE | 1984 | I.R.S. 9931 | 12 |
| *(Price includes stock picture sleeve)* | | | |
| S. CENTRAL RAIN | 1984 | I.R.S. 9927 | 15 |
| *(Price includes stock picture sleeve)* | | | |
| SUPERMAN | 1986 | I.R.S. 52971 | 10 |
| *(Price includes stock picture sleeve)* | | | |
| **Albums** | | | |
| SHOULD WE TALK ABOUT THE WEATHER? | 1988 | Warner Bros. PRO-A-3377 | 40 |
| *(Promo-only interviews and music)* | | | |
| WINTER WARNERLAND  Various artists | 1988 | Warner Bros. PRO-A-3328 | 25 |
| *(Promo-only holiday sampler, one red vinyl record, one green, includes one R.E.M. track, "Deck the Halls")* | | | |
| **Compact Discs** | | | |
| AOR RADIO STAPLE | 1988 | I.R.S. 7 | 75 |
| *(Promo-only CD for radio)* | | | |

| Title | Yr | Label, Number | NM $ |
|---|---|---|---|
| BANG AND BLAME | 1994 | Warner Bros. PRO-CD-7271-R | 8 |
| *(Promo CD single)* | | | |
| BITTERSWEET ME | 1996 | Warner Bros. PRO-CD-8462 | 8 |
| *(Promo CD single, first issue)* | | | |
| BITTERSWEET ME | 1996 | Warner Bros. PRO-CD-8476 | 8 |
| *(Promo CD single, second issue)* | | | |
| CRUSH WITH EYELINER | 1995 | Warner Bros. PRO-CD-7455-R | 8 |
| *(Promo CD single)* | | | |
| DAYSLEEPER | 1998 | Warner Bros. | 12 |
| *(Promo CD single)* | | | |
| DRIVE | 1992 | Warner Bros. PRO-CD-5700 | 8 |
| *(Promo CD single)* | | | |
| E-BOW THE LETTER | 1996 | Warner Bros. PRO-CD-8400 | 8 |
| *(Promo CD single)* | | | |
| ELECTROLITE | 1997 | Warner Bros. PRO-CD-8575 | 10 |
| *(Promo CD single)* | | | |
| EVERYBODY HURTS | 1993 | Warner Bros. PRO-CD-5900 | 8 |
| *(Promo CD single)* | | | |
| GET UP | 1989 | Warner Bros. PRO-CD-3716 | 15 |
| *(Promo CD single, includes two live tracks)* | | | |
| I DON'T SLEEP, I DREAM | 1995 | Warner Bros. PRO-CD-7532-R | 10 |
| *(Promo-only CD single, not released commercially in U.S.)* | | | |
| I TOOK YOUR NAME | 1995 | Warner Bros. PRO-CD-7894-R | 10 |
| *(Promo-only CD single, not released commercially in U.S.)* | | | |
| IGNORELAND | 1992 | Warner Bros. PRO-CD-5844 | 8 |
| *(Promo-only CD single, not released commercially in U.S.)* | | | |
| IT'S THE END OF THE WORLD AS WE KNOW IT | 1987 | I.R.S. 17476 | 100 |
| *(A very early promo CD single)* | | | |
| LOSING MY RELIGION | 1991 | Warner Bros. PRO-CD-4881 | 10 |
| *(Promo-only CD single, live acoustic version)* | | | |
| LOSING MY RELIGION | 1991 | Warner Bros. PRO-CD-4707 | 8 |
| *(Promo CD single)* | | | |
| MAN ON THE MOON | 1992 | Warner Bros. PRO-CD-5894 | 8 |
| *(Promo CD single)* | | | |
| MAN ON THE MOON | 1994 | Warner Bros. PRO-CD-6828-R | 15 |
| *(Promo-only CD single with four tracks)* | | | |
| MUSIC FROM TOURFILM | 1990 | Warner Bros. PRO-CDV-4460 | 25 |
| *(Promo-only CD with five live tracks from video)* | | | |
| NEAR WILD HEAVEN | 1991 | Warner Bros. PRO-CD-5058 | 8 |
| *(Promo-only CD single, not released commercially in U.S.)* | | | |
| ORANGE CRUSH | 1988 | Warner Bros. PRO-CD-3306 | 20 |
| *(Promo-only CD single, not released commercially in U.S.)* | | | |
| POP SONG 89 | 1989 | Warner Bros. PRO-CD-3357 | 10 |
| *(Promo CD single)* | | | |
| RADIO SONG | 1991 | Warner Bros. PRO-CD-4808 | 8 |
| *(Promo CD single)* | | | |
| SHINY HAPPY PEOPLE | 1991 | Warner Bros. PRO-CD-4888 | 8 |
| *(Promo CD single)* | | | |
| SHINY HAPPY PEOPLE | 1991 | Warner Bros. PRO-CD-5060 | 10 |
| *(Promo CD single, three new mixes)* | | | |
| SIDEWINDER SLEEPS TONITE, THE | 1993 | Warner Bros. PRO-CD-5903 | 8 |
| *(Promo CD single)* | | | |
| SONGS THAT ARE LIVE | 1995 | Warner Bros. PRO-CD-7888 | 20 |
| *(Promo-only four-song sampler, all live tracks)* | | | |
| STAND | 1988 | Warner Bros. PRO-CD-3353 | 8 |
| *(Promo CD single)* | | | |
| STAR 69 | 1995 | Warner Bros. PRO-CD-7402 | 8 |
| *(Promo CD single, first issue)* | | | |
| STAR 69 | 1995 | Warner Bros. PRO-CD-7442-R | 8 |
| *(Promo CD single, second issue)* | | | |
| STRANGE CURRENCIES | 1995 | Warner Bros. PRO-CD-7510 | 8 |
| *(Promo CD single)* | | | |
| TEXARKANA | 1991 | Warner Bros. PRO-CD-4826 | 8 |
| *(Promo-only CD single, not released commercially in U.S.)* | | | |
| TONGUE | 1995 | Warner Bros. PRO-CD-7875-R | 8 |
| *(Promo CD single)* | | | |
| TURN YOU INSIDE-OUT | 1989 | Warner Bros. PRO-CD-3448 | 10 |
| *(Promo-only CD single, not released commercially in U.S.)* | | | |
| WAKE-UP BOMB, THE | 1997 | Warner Bros. PRO-CD-8584 | 10 |
| *(Promo CD single)* | | | |
| WHAT'S THE FREQUENCY, KENNETH? | 1994 | Warner Bros. PRO-CD-7155 | 8 |
| *(Promo CD single)* | | | |
| **RADIO SHOWS** | | | |
| **Albums** | | | |
| BBC TRANSCRIPTION DISC  Live concert | 1984 | BBC Transcription | 700-1,000 |
| *(The ultimate live concert)* | | | |
| IN CONCERT (Nov 86) Live concert | 1986 | Westwood One (2) | 125-200 |
| *(With Alarm)* | | | |
| IN CONCERT (Apr 90) Live concert | 1990 | Westwood One (2) | 150-225 |
| *(Repeated)* | | | |
| NBC SOURCE (July 84) Live concert | 1984 | NBC Radio (2) | 750-1,000 |
| *(One of the most collectible shows ever!)* | | | |
| OFF THE RECORD (Feb 89) Profile | 1989 | Westwood One (2) | 25-50 |
| *(Music and interviews)* | | | |
| ROCK STARS (Mar 89) Music and interviews | 1989 | Radio International (2) | 100-150 |
| *("Green Tour" material)* | | | |

| Title | Yr | Label, Number | NM $ |
|---|---|---|---|
| SUPERSTAR CONCERT (Apr 89) Live concert | 1989 | Westwood One (3) | 150-225 |
| *(Repeated again July 89)* | | | |
| TIMOTHY WHITE SESSIONS (80s) Live concert | 198? | Westwood One (2) | 150-225 |
| *(Also a very collectible show)* | | | |
| **Compact Discs** | | | |
| IN CONCERT (July 95) Live concert | 1995 | Westwood One (2) | 50-100 |
| *(With 22 live tracks)* | | | |
| IN CONCERT-NU ROCK (Mar 93) Live concert | 1993 | Westwood One | 75-125 |
| *(With the Pixies)* | | | |
| IN CONCERT-NU ROCK (Oct 94) Live concert | 1994 | Westwood One | 50-100 |
| *(With Frente)* | | | |
| OFF THE RECORD (Apr 93) Profile | 1993 | Westwood One | 30-50 |
| *(Music and interviews)* | | | |
| OFF THE RECORD (May 95) | 1995 | Westwood One (3) | 30-50 |
| *(Music and interviews, with Soul Asylum and Blues Traveler)* | | | |
| ON THE EDGE (Nov 92) Music and interviews | 1992 | Westwood One | 20-30 |
| *(With Grant Lee Buffalo)* | | | |
| ON THE EDGE (Nov 93) Music and interviews | 1993 | Westwood One | 10-20 |
| *(With k.d. lang)* | | | |
| ON THE EDGE (Nov 94) Music and interviews | 1994 | Westwood One | 20-30 |
| *(With two live tracks)* | | | |
| ON THE EDGE (July 95) Music and interviews | 1995 | Westwood One | 20-40 |
| *(With Chris Isaak)* | | | |
| UP CLOSE  Profile | 1989 | Media America (2) | 200-325 |
| *(Includes some live tracks)* | | | |
| UP CLOSE  Profile | 1991 | Media America (2) | 60-100 |
| *(Music and interviews, one unreleased track)* | | | |
| UP CLOSE  Profile | 1992 | Media America (2) | 30-60 |
| *(Mostly music and interviews)* | | | |
| UP CLOSE  Profile | 1996 | Media America (3) | 80-120 |
| *(Music and interviews)* | | | |
| WESTWOOD ONE SPECIAL (July 95) | 1995 | Westwood One (4) | 150-200 |

**RABBITT, EDDIE**
*Date promo 45s $8 each; Other Elektra and RCA Victor promo 45s $2 each*
**45s**

| Title | Yr | Label, Number | NM $ |
|---|---|---|---|
| SIX NIGHTS AND SEVEN DAYS | 1964 | 20th Fox 474 | 20 |
| *(His first 45, black and gold label)* | | | |
| SONG OF IRELAND | 1978 | Elektra 378 | 15 |
| *(Green vinyl, green promo label, promo only, small center hole)* | | | |

**RACHEL AND THE REVOLVERS**
**45s**

| Title | Yr | Label, Number | NM $ |
|---|---|---|---|
| THE REVOLUTION  White promo label | 1962 | Dot 16392 | 300 |
| *(Produced by Brian Wilson)* | | | |

**RADHA KRISHNA TEMPLE**
**45s**

| Title | Yr | Label, Number | NM $ |
|---|---|---|---|
| GOVINDA (Edit)/GOVINDA | 1970 | Apple SPRO-5067/8 | 40 |
| GOVINDA/GOVINDA JAI JAI | 1970 | Apple PRO-5013/4 | 25 |
| *(With an edit of the A-side)* | | | |

**RADIATORS, THE**
**Compact Discs**

| Title | Yr | Label, Number | NM $ |
|---|---|---|---|
| LAW OF THE FISH | 1989 | Epic ESK 2809 | 15 |
| *(Promo-only sampler)* | | | |

**RADIO SHOWS**
**Compact Discs**

| Title | Yr | Label, Number | NM $ |
|---|---|---|---|
| KING BISCUIT FLOWER HOUR (Nov 88) | 1988 | DIR | 10-20 |
| *(Live concert)* | | | |
| LIVE FROM HOUSE OF BLUES (Jan 96) | 1996 | (2) | 40-75 |
| *(Live concert material, with Jorma Kaukonen)* | | | |
| ON THE EDGE (Sept 93) Music and interviews | 1993 | Westwood One | 25-35 |
| *(With Blondie)* | | | |

**RADIO HEART**
**12-Inch Singles**

| Title | Yr | Label, Number | NM $ |
|---|---|---|---|
| RADIO HEART (3 versions) | 1987 | Critique 1068 | 5 |

**RADIOHEAD**
*Capitol promo CD singles $4 each*
**RADIO SHOWS**
**Compact Discs**

| Title | Yr | Label, Number | NM $ |
|---|---|---|---|
| IN CONCERT-NU ROCK (Nov 93) | 1993 | Westwood One | 40-75 |
| *(Live concert)* | | | |

**RAFFERTY, GERRY**
*Of Stealers Wheel; A&M promo 45s by Stealers Wheel $3 each; Other United Artists promo 45s $3 each*
**45s**

| Title | Yr | Label, Number | NM $ |
|---|---|---|---|
| BAKER STREET | 1978 | United Artists 1192 | 10 |
| *(Mono/stereo 4:08 versions)* | | | |

| Title | Yr | Label, Number | NM $ |
|---|---|---|---|
| **RADIO SHOWS** | | | |
| **Albums** | | | |
| ROBERT W. MORGAN (Mar 81) | 1981 | Watermark | 20-30 |
| *(Music and interviews)* | | | |

**RAINBOW**

*Mercury promo 45s $5 each*

**45s**

| Title | Yr | Label, Number | NM $ |
|---|---|---|---|
| STONE COLD | 1982 | Mercury 76146 | 12 |
| *(Blue vinyl promo)* | | | |
| **RADIO SHOWS** | | | |
| **Albums** | | | |
| CAPTURED LIVE | 1983 | RKO (3) | 100-200 |
| *(Live concert, repeated)* | | | |
| CAPTURED LIVE (Feb 84) | 1984 | RKO (4) | 150-250 |
| *(Live concert, repeated)* | | | |
| CAPTURED LIVE (Aug 84) | 1984 | RKO (2) | 75-125 |
| *(Live concert)* | | | |
| KING BISCUIT FLOWER HOUR | 1981 | DIR/ABC (2) | 125-200 |
| *(Live concert)* | | | |
| KING BISCUIT FLOWER HOUR (Feb 82) | 1982 | DIR/ABC (2) | 75-125 |
| *(Live concert with Pat Travers)* | | | |
| KING BISCUIT FLOWER HOUR (Jan 83) | 1983 | DIR/ABC (2) | 100-200 |
| *(Live concert, repeated May 83)* | | | |
| KING BISCUIT FLOWER HOUR (Feb 86) | 1986 | DIR (2) | 100-175 |
| *(Live concert, repeated)* | | | |
| KING BISCUIT FLOWER HOUR (Oct 86) | 1986 | DIR (2) | 75-150 |
| *(Live concert, repeated)* | | | |
| OFF THE RECORD  Profile | 1982 | Westwood One (2) | 20-40 |
| *(Music and interviews)* | | | |
| RETRO ROCK | 1983 | Clayton Webster (2) | 50-100 |
| *(Rare early concert)* | | | |
| SUPERGROUPS | 1983 | Westwood One (3) | 100-200 |
| *(Live concert)* | | | |

**RAINSFORD, WILLIE**

**45s**

| Title | Yr | Label, Number | NM $ |
|---|---|---|---|
| CHRISTMAS SHOES/THERE'LL BE RAIN, DEAR THIS CHRISTMAS | 197? | Candy 1035 | 4 |

**RAINWATER, MARVIN**

*Other MGM promo 78s $10 each; Other MGM promo 45s $8 each; United Artists promo 45s $4 each; Kajac promo 45s $5 each*

**45s**

| Title | Yr | Label, Number | NM $ |
|---|---|---|---|
| BABY, DON'T GO | 1957 | MGM 12609 | 10 |
| *(Yellow promo label)* | | | |
| BOO HOO | 196? | Warwick 666 | 25 |
| *(White promo label)* | | | |
| DEM LOW DOWN BLUES | 1955 | MGM 12152 | 12 |
| *(Yellow promo label)* | | | |
| ESPECIALLY FOR FRIENDS  White promo label | 1955 | (no label) MR 1-A | 75 |
| *(An MGM promo-only tribute to Hank Williams including dialogue and three songs with "Hearts Hall of Fame")* | | | |
| GONNA FIND ME A BLUEBIRD | 1956 | MGM 12412 | 12 |
| *(Yellow promo label)* | | | |
| HALF BREED | 1959 | MGM 12803 | 10 |
| *(Yellow promo label)* | | | |
| HOT AND COLD | 1956 | MGM 12240 | 30 |
| *(Yellow promo label)* | | | |
| I DIG YOU BABY | 1958 | MGM 12665 | 10 |
| *(Yellow promo label)* | | | |
| I GOTTA GO GET MY BABY | 1956 | Coral 61342 | 15 |
| *(Blue promo label)* | | | |
| LUCKY STAR | 1957 | MGM 12586 | 12 |
| *(Yellow promo label)* | | | |
| THE MAJESTY OF LOVE  With Connie Francis | 1957 | MGM 12555 | 15 |
| *(Yellow promo label)* | | | |
| MY BRAND OF BLUES | 1957 | MGM 12511 | 12 |
| *(Yellow promo label)* | | | |
| NOTHIN' NEEDS NOTHIN' | 1958 | MGM 12701 | 10 |
| *(Yellow promo label)* | | | |
| STICKS AND STONES | 1955 | MGM 12071 | 15 |
| *(Yellow promo label)* | | | |
| TENNESSEE HOUN' DOG YODEL | 1955 | MGM 12090 | 15 |
| *(Yellow promo label)* | | | |
| TWO FOOLS IN LOVE  Marv and Patty | 1958 | MGM 12625 | 10 |
| *(Yellow promo label)* | | | |
| **78s** | | | |
| DEM LOW DOWN BLUES | 1955 | MGM 12152 | 15 |
| *(Yellow promo label)* | | | |
| GONNA FIND ME A BLUEBIRD | 1956 | MGM 12412 | 18 |
| *(Yellow promo label)* | | | |
| HOT AND COLD | 1956 | MGM 12240 | 40 |
| *(Yellow promo label)* | | | |
| STICKS AND STONES | 1955 | MGM 12071 | 20 |
| *(Yellow promo label)* | | | |
| TENNESSEE HOUN' DOG YODEL | 1955 | MGM 12090 | 18 |
| *(Yellow promo label)* | | | |

| Title | Yr | Label, Number | NM $ |
|---|---|---|---|
| **Albums** | | | |
| GONNA FIND ME A BLUEBIRD | 1962 | MGM 4046 | 75 |
| *(Yellow promo label)* | | | |
| MARVIN RAINWATER SINGS WITH A HEART | 1958 | MGM 3721 | 100 |
| *(Yellow promo label)* | | | |
| SONGS BY MARVIN RAINWATER | 1957 | MGM 3534 | 125 |
| *(Yellow promo label)* | | | |

## RAITT, BONNIE
*Other Warner Bros. and Capitol promo 45s $3 each; Capitol and Arista promo CD singles $3 each*

| Title | Yr | Label, Number | NM $ |
|---|---|---|---|
| **12-Inch Singles** | | | |
| CRIMES OF PASSION (same on both sides) | 1986 | Warner Bros. PRO-A-2655 | 6 |
| ME AND THE BOYS (same on both sides) | 1982 | Warner Bros. PRO-A-1030 | 12 |
| NO WAY TO TREAT A LADY (same on both sides) | 1986 | Warner Bros. PRO-A-2536 | 6 |
| WHO BUT A FOOL (same on both sides) | 1986 | Warner Bros. PRO-A-2613 | 6 |
| **45s** | | | |
| HAVE A HEART (same on both sides) | 1990 | Capitol 7PRO-79940 | 5 |
| *(Vinyl is promo only)* | | | |
| **Albums** | | | |
| NINE LIVES | 1986 | Warner Bros. WBMS-143 | 25 |
| *(Part of "The Warner Bros. Music Show," music and interviews)* | | | |
| **RADIO SHOWS** | | | |
| **Albums** | | | |
| OFF THE RECORD (Apr 82) | 1982 | Westwood One (2) | 25-40 |
| *(Music and interviews)* | | | |
| OFF THE RECORD (Mar 90) | 1990 | Westwood One (2) | 15-25 |
| *(Music and interviews)* | | | |
| RETRO ROCK (Dec 81) Live concert | 1981 | Clayton Webster | 75-125 |
| *(Rare early material)* | | | |
| **Compact Discs** | | | |
| KING BISCUIT FLOWER HOUR Live concert | 1990 | DIR | 30-60 |
| *(Repeated)* | | | |
| KING BISCUIT FLOWER HOUR (Mar 92) Live concert | 1992 | DIR | 25-50 |
| *(With Paul Simon)* | | | |
| OFF THE RECORD (June 94) | 1994 | Westwood One | 15-25 |
| *(Music and interviews)* | | | |

## RAMONES, THE
*Other Sire promo 45s $8 each; Other Sire promo 12" singles $8 each; Other Sire promo LPs $15 each; Sire and Radioactive promo CD singles $4-6 each*

| Title | Yr | Label, Number | NM $ |
|---|---|---|---|
| **12-Inch Singles** | | | |
| HOWLING AT THE MOON/CHASING THE NIGHT | 1984 | Sire PRO-A-2219 | 10 |
| I WANNA BE SEDATED | 1988 | Sire PRO-A-3193 | 20 |
| *(Promo-only 12" single)* | | | |
| I WANNA LIVE | 1987 | Sire PRO-A-2816 | 12 |
| *(Promo-only 12" single)* | | | |
| PET SEMATARY | 1988 | Sire 22911 | 10 |
| *(Promo 12" single)* | | | |
| ROAD TO RUIN | 1978 | Sire PRO-A-756 | 18 |
| *(Promo-only 12" single)* | | | |
| ROCK 'N' ROLL HIGH SCHOOL | 1979 | Sire PRO-A-805 | 20 |
| *(Promo-only 12" single)* | | | |
| **45s** | | | |
| BLITZKRIEG BOP | 1976 | Sire 725 | 50 |
| *("Bop" in mono, flip is " Havana Affair"; stock copy worth slightly more)* | | | |
| BLITZKRIEG BOP | 1976 | Sire 725 | 40 |
| *(This version has "Bop" on both sides, stereo/mono)* | | | |
| DO YOU WANNA DANCE? | 1978 | Sire 1017 | 15 |
| *(Price includes stock picture sleeve, yellow promo label)* | | | |
| DON'T COME CLOSE | 1978 | Sire 1025 | 18 |
| *(Price includes stock picture sleeve, yellow promo label, stereo/mono versions)* | | | |
| I WANNA BE SEDATED | 1988 | Sire 27663 | 20 |
| *(Price includes stock picture sleeve worth $15, yellow promo label, long 5:12/short 2:29 versions)* | | | |
| I WANNA BE YOUR BOYFRIEND | 1976 | Sire 734 | 20 |
| *(Price includes stock picture sleeve, yellow promo label, "Boyfriend" is in mono)* | | | |
| ROCK 'N' ROLL HIGH SCHOOL | 1979 | Sire 1051 | 15 |
| *(Price includes stock picture sleeve, yellow promo label, stereo/mono versions)* | | | |
| ROCKAWAY BEACH | 1977 | Sire 1008 | 15 |
| *(Price includes stock picture sleeve, yellow promo label)* | | | |
| SHEENA IS A PUNK ROCKER | 1977 | Sire 746 | 20 |
| *(Price includes stock picture sleeve with 746 number, yellow promo label)* | | | |
| SHEENA IS A PUNK ROCKER | 1977 | Sire 1006 | 20 |
| *(Price includes stock picture sleeve with 1006 number, yellow promo label)* | | | |
| SWALLOW MY PRIDE | 1976 | Sire 738 | 15 |
| *(Price includes stock picture sleeve, yellow promo label)* | | | |
| **7-Inch Extended Plays** | | | |
| ROCK 'N' ROLL HIGH SCHOOL Movie ads | 1979 | New World Pictures | 75 |
| *(30-second, 60-second radio ads for the movie)* | | | |
| **Albums** | | | |
| PLEASANT DREAMS | 1981 | Sire PRO-A-966 | 25 |
| *(Promo-only 12" EP sampler)* | | | |
| RAMONES | 1976 | Sire 7520 | 40 |
| *(Yellow promo label)* | | | |
| RAMONES | 1977 | Sire 6020 | 20 |
| *(Yellow promo label, reissue of Sire 7520)* | | | |

| Title | Yr | Label, Number | NM $ |
|---|---|---|---|
| RAMONES ARE HERE THERE AND EVERYWHERE | 1983 | Sire | 30 |
| *(Sampler from Sire Records)* | | | |
| RAMONES LEAVE HOME | 1977 | Sire 7528 | 40 |
| *(Yellow promo label)* | | | |
| RAMONES LEAVE HOME | 1977 | Sire 6031 | 20 |
| *(Yellow promo label, reissue of Sire 7528)* | | | |
| ROAD TO RUIN RADIO SAMPLER | 1978 | Sire PRO-A-756 | 25 |
| ROCK 'N' ROLL HIGH SCHOOL RADIO SAMPLER | 1979 | Sire PRO-A-605 | 25 |
| ROCKET TO RUSSIA | 1977 | Sire 6042 | 20 |
| *(Yellow promo label)* | | | |
| **RADIO SHOWS** | | | |
| **Albums** | | | |
| ROCK AROUND THE WORLD (Sept 76) Live concert | 1976 | RATW | 150-225 |
| *(Very rare show, with Velez)* | | | |
| **Compact Discs** | | | |
| IN CONCERT-NU ROCK (Jan 93) Live concert | 1993 | Westwood One | 75-125 |
| *(With Dramarama)* | | | |
| **Reel-to-Reel Tapes** | | | |
| IN CONCERT-NU ROCK (Jan 93) Live concert | 1993 | Westwood One | 100-200 |
| *(Reel-to-reel with Dramarama)* | | | |

## RANDOLPH, BOOTS
**7-Inch Extended Plays**

| Title | Yr | Label, Number | NM $ |
|---|---|---|---|
| SLEIGH RIDE/RUDOLPH THE RED-NOSED REINDEER// WHITE CHRISTMAS/I'LL BE HOME FOR CHRISTMAS | 1969 | Monument SMN-361 | 15 |

## RARE EARTH
*Rare Earth (label) promo 45s (black vinyl) $3 each*
**45s**

| Title | Yr | Label, Number | NM $ |
|---|---|---|---|
| HEY BIG BROTHER | 1972 | Rare Earth 5038 | 15 |
| *(Red vinyl promo, white and orange label)* | | | |
| WHAT'D I SAY | 1973 | Rare Earth 960 S 01 | 25 |
| *(Red vinyl, white promo label, mono/stereo)* | | | |
| WHAT'S IT ALL ABOUT (July 76) Public service show | 1976 | W.I.A.A. 326 | 15 |
| *(Flip side is Seals & Crofts)* | | | |
| WHAT'S IT ALL ABOUT (Mar 73) Public service show | 1973 | W.I.A.A. 165 | 18 |
| *(Flip side features Joni Mitchell)* | | | |

## RASCALS, THE
*Atlantic promo 45s $5 each; Other Atlantic promo LPs $18 each Also known as The Young Rascals*
**45s**

| Title | Yr | Label, Number | NM $ |
|---|---|---|---|
| IT'S WONDERFUL | 1967 | Atlantic 2463 | 15 |
| *(Edited version with two bands for radio play)* | | | |
| **7-Inch Extended Plays** | | | |
| ONCE UPON A DREAM | 1968 | Atlantic 1005 | 40 |
| *(Promo-only release)* | | | |
| ONCE UPON A DREAM  Jukebox LLP | 1968 | Atlantic 8169 | 25 |
| *(Issued with a cover)* | | | |
| THE YOUNG RASCALS  Jukebox LLP | 1968 | Atlantic LLP 190 | 30 |
| *(Issued with a cover)* | | | |
| **Albums** | | | |
| FREEDOM SUITE | 1969 | Atlantic 901 (2) | 35 |
| *(Two white promo label discs)* | | | |
| FREEDOM SUITE  Sampler | 1969 | Atlantic 137 | 50 |
| *(Promo-only single-LP sampler for in-store use)* | | | |
| SONGS FROM THE RASCALS (70s) | 197? | Wes Farrell Organization 1002 | 25 |
| *(Promo only, black promo label and special cover)* | | | |

## RATIONALS, THE
**45s**

| Title | Yr | Label, Number | NM $ |
|---|---|---|---|
| FEELIN' LOST/RESPECT | 1966 | A-Square 103/4 | 30 |

## RAVEN, EDDY
**45s**

| Title | Yr | Label, Number | NM $ |
|---|---|---|---|
| BLUE CHRISTMAS/WHITE CHRISTMAS | 1981 | Elektra 47233 | 5 |
| *(B-side by Mel Tillis)* | | | |

## RAVENS, THE
*With Jimmy Ricks*
**45s**

| Title | Yr | Label, Number | NM $ |
|---|---|---|---|
| COME A LITTLE BIT CLOSER | 1953 | Mercury 70119 | 75 |
| *(White promo label)* | | | |
| DON'T MENTION MY NAME | 1952 | Mercury 70060 | 100 |
| *(White promo label)* | | | |
| GOING HOME  Jimmy Ricks | 1954 | Mercury 70330 | 50 |
| *(White promo label)* | | | |
| LOVE IS NO DREAM | 1954 | Mercury 70413 | 75 |
| *(White promo label)* | | | |
| OLD MAN RIVER | 1954 | Mercury 70554 | 50 |
| *(White promo label)* | | | |
| SEPTEMBER SONG | 1954 | Mercury 70307 | 60 |
| *(White promo label)* | | | |
| A SIMPLE PRAYER | 1956 | Argo 5261 | 40 |
| *(White promo label)* | | | |

| Title | Yr | Label, Number | NM $ |
|---|---|---|---|
| WHITE CHRISTMAS | 1954 | Savoy 1540 | 40 |
| (White promo label) | | | |
| WHITE CHRISTMAS | 1954 | Mercury 70505 | 60 |
| (White promo label) | | | |
| WHO'LL BE THE FOOL | 1953 | Mercury 70213 | 75 |
| (White promo label) | | | |
| WITHOUT A SONG | 1953 | Mercury 70240 | 50 |
| (White promo label) | | | |
| **Albums** | | | |
| JIMMY RICKS | 1961 | Signature SM-1032 | 200 |

## RAY, JOHNNIE
**45s**

| Title | Yr | Label, Number | NM $ |
|---|---|---|---|
| WHAT'S IT ALL ABOUT (Dec 77) Public service show | 1977 | W.I.A.A. | 10 |
| (B-side is Dr. Hook) | | | |

## RE-FLEX
**12-Inch Singles**

| Title | Yr | Label, Number | NM $ |
|---|---|---|---|
| HURT (6:45)/(9:30) | 1983 | Capitol SPRO 9120/1 | 8 |
| HURT (same on both sides) | 1983 | Capitol SPRO 9122 | 8 |
| HURT (5:35)/(6:45) | 1983 | Capitol SPRO 9127/8 | 8 |
| THE POLITICS OF DANCING (single)/(LP) | 1983 | Capitol SPRO 9033/4 | 20 |
| PRAYING TO THE BEAT (same on both sides) | 1983 | Capitol SPRO 9083 | 8 |
| **Albums** | | | |
| THE POLITICS OF DANCING | 1983 | Capitol ST-12314 | 15 |
| (High-grade vinyl edition with sticker on cover) | | | |

## REAL LIFE
**12-Inch Singles**

| Title | Yr | Label, Number | NM $ |
|---|---|---|---|
| BABIES (3 versions) | 1986 | MCA Curb 17176 | 8 |
| CATCH ME I'M FALLING/OPENHEARTED/HEARTLAND | 1984 | MCA Curb L33-1166 | 8 |
| FACE TO FACE (Rock Edit)/FACE TO FACE (Dance Mix) | 1985 | MCA Curb 17058 | 7 |
| SEND ME AN ANGEL/CATCH ME I'M FALLING | 1984 | MCA Curb L33-1169 | 10 |

## RECORDS, THE
**12-Inch Singles**

| Title | Yr | Label, Number | NM $ |
|---|---|---|---|
| RUMOUR SETS THE WOODS ALIGHT/HEARTS IN HER EYES | 1980 | Virgin PR 365 | 8 |
| STARRY EYES/PAINT HER FACE/ANOTHER STAR | 1989 | Virgin PR 337 | 15 |

## RED HOT CHILI PEPPERS
*EMI promo CD singles $6 each; Other Warner Bros. promo CD singles $4-6 each*
**12-Inch Singles**

| Title | Yr | Label, Number | NM $ |
|---|---|---|---|
| BEHIND THE SUN/SPECIAL SECRET SONG | 1987 | EMI America SPRO 04002 | 8 |
| FIGHT LIKE A BRAVE (same on both sides) | 1988 | EMI Manhattan SPRO 79147 | 7 |
| GIVE IT AWAY (3 versions) | 1991 | Warner Bros. PRO-A-5182 | 12 |
| HIGHER GROUND (2 versions) | 1989 | EMI SPRO 04387 | 10 |
| HIGHER GROUND (3 mixes)/IF YOU WANT ME TO STAY (2 versions) | 1992 | EMI SPRO 04896 | 15 |
| JUNGLE MAN/NEVERMIND/STRANDED | 1986 | EMI America SPRO 9466 | 8 |
| SHOW ME YOUR SOUL (same on both sides) | 1990 | EMI SPRO 04542 | 10 |
| STONE COLD BUSH/FIRE/NOBODY WEIRD LIKE ME + 1 | 1989 | EMI SPRO 04385 | 15 |
| TASTE THE PAIN/CASTLES (Live)/SPECIAL SECRET SAUCE (Live)/F.U. (Live) | 1989 | EMI SPRO 04504 | 20 |
| **Albums** | | | |
| BLOOD SUGAR SEX MAGIK | 1991 | Warner Bros. PRO-A-5170 | 40 |
| ("Radio-ready" version of LP, this is the only U.S. vinyl release of this band's biggest album) | | | |
| **Compact Discs** | | | |
| BLOOD SUGAR SEX MAGIK SANITIZED | 1991 | Warner Bros. PRO-CD-5170 | 20 |
| (Radio-ready version of their biggest hit album) | | | |
| UNDER THE BRIDGE | 1991 | Warner Bros. PRO-CD-5255 | 8 |
| (Promo CD single, their biggest hit) | | | |
| UPLIFT MOFO PARTY PLAN SAMPLER | 1987 | EMI America DPRO-31492 | 20 |
| (Promo-only EP) | | | |
| **RADIO SHOWS** | | | |
| **Compact Discs** | | | |
| IN CONCERT-NU ROCK (Jan 93) Live concert | 1993 | Westwood One | 100-150 |
| (With Bob Marley) | | | |
| LIVE FROM THE PIT (May 96) | 1996 | (2) | 65 |
| (Live concert material) | | | |
| ON THE EDGE (Oct 93) Music and interviews | 1993 | Westwood One | 25-35 |
| (With Squeeze) | | | |

## RED RIDER
*Capitol promo 45s $4 each*
**RADIO SHOWS**
**Albums**

| Title | Yr | Label, Number | NM $ |
|---|---|---|---|
| BBC ROCK HOUR (Nov 81) | 1981 | London Wavelength | 20-25 |
| (Live concert) | | | |
| IN CONCERT (June 83) | 1983 | Westwood One (2) | 30-50 |
| (With Fastway) | | | |

| Title | Yr | Label, Number | NM $ |
|-------|-----|---------------|------|
| **RED ROCKERS** | | | |
| **RADIO SHOWS** | | | |
| **Albums** | | | |
| BBC COLLEGE CONCERT (Oct 83) | 1983 | London Wavelength | 30-60 |
| *(Live concert)* | | | |
| KING BISCUIT FLOWER HOUR (July 83) | 1983 | DIR/ABC (2) | 25-50 |
| *(With Members)* | | | |
| KING BISCUIT FLOWER HOUR (Nov 83) | 1983 | DIR/ABC (2) | 50-100 |
| *(With Stevie Ray Vaughan)* | | | |
| RETRO ROCK (Aug 83) | 1983 | Clayton Webster | 25-50 |
| *(Live concert)* | | | |
| | | | |
| **REDDING, OTIS** | | | |
| *Volt promo 45s $10 each; Atco promo 45s $8 each* | | | |
| **Compact Discs** | | | |
| DEFINITIVE OTIS REDDING SAMPLER | 1993 | Rhino | 20 |
| *(Promo collection from box set)* | | | |
| | | | |
| **REDDY, HELEN** | | | |
| *Capitol promo 45s $2 each* | | | |
| **45s** | | | |
| ONE WAY TICKET | 1968 | Fontana 1611 | 12 |
| *(Her first American release, scarcer on stock copy)* | | | |
| WHAT'S IT ALL ABOUT (Dec 75) Public service show | 1975 | W.I.A.A. 294 | 10 |
| *(Flip side features Kris Kristofferson)* | | | |
| | | | |
| **REED, JERRY** | | | |
| *Other Capitol promo 45s $8 each; Columbia promo 45s $10 each; Other RCA Victor colored vinyl promo 45s $8 each; RCA Victor promo 45s $3 each* | | | |
| **45s** | | | |
| THE BIRD | 1982 | RCA 13355 | 15 |
| *(Blue vinyl, cream colored promo label)* | | | |
| CHRISTMAS TIME'S A-COMING (same on both sides) | 1983 | RCA JK-13666 | 5 |
| DOWN ON THE CORNER | 1982 | RCA 13422 | 10 |
| *(Green vinyl, gold promo label)* | | | |
| GOOD OLE BOYS | 1983 | RCA 13527 | 10 |
| *(Green vinyl, orange promo label)* | | | |
| HIGH BALLIN'  Movie ads | 1978 | American International | 25 |
| *(One-sided movie ads, two tracks)* | | | |
| I'M A LOVER, NOT A FIGHTER | 1957 | Capitol 3381 | 10 |
| *(White promo label)* | | | |
| IF THE LORD'S WILLING AND THE CREEKS DON'T RISE | 1957 | Capitol 3294 | 10 |
| *(White promo label)* | | | |
| IT'S HIGH TIME | 1958 | Capitol 3657 | 12 |
| *(White promo label)* | | | |
| THE LINE IN GASOLINE | 1979 | RCA 11638 | 10 |
| *(Red vinyl, red promo label)* | | | |
| LITTLE LOVIN' LISA | 1957 | NRC 5008 | 12 |
| *(White promo label)* | | | |
| THE MAN WITH THE GOLDEN THUMB | 1982 | RCA 13081 | 10 |
| *(Green vinyl, gold promo label)* | | | |
| ROCKIN' IN BAGHDAD | 1959 | Capitol 3731 | 20 |
| *(Yellow promo label)* | | | |
| YOU'RE BRAGGIN' BOY | 1957 | Capitol 3592 | 15 |
| *(White promo label)* | | | |
| YOUR MONEY MAKES YOU PURTY | 1960 | Capitol 3992 | 12 |
| *(White promo label)* | | | |
| **7-Inch Extended Plays** | | | |
| SMOKEY AND THE BANDIT | 1977 | MCA 1961 | 12 |
| *(Four songs from the soundtrack including one by Jerry Reed, issued with a promo hard cover)* | | | |
| SMOKEY THE BEAR  PSA spots | 1982 | US Dept. of Agriculture | 25 |
| *(Eight PSA commercials, one by Reed, issued with a hard cover)* | | | |
| TOO YOUNG TO BE BLUE | 1959 | Capitol PRO 527 | 20 |
| *(Promo-only release)* | | | |
| | | | |
| **REED, LOU** | | | |
| *Also see Velvet Underground; RCA Victor promo 45s $5 each; Sire promo CD singles $3 each* | | | |
| **12-Inch Singles** | | | |
| DIRTY BLVD. (Radio Edit)/(LP Version) | 1988 | Sire PRO-A-3359 | 8 |
| DISCO MYSTIC/I WANNA BOOGIE WITH YOU | 1979 | Arista SP-56 | 10 |
| HOT HIPS (same on both sides) | 1985 | Arista 9375 | 10 |
| HOW DO YOU SPEAK TO AN ANGEL/KEEP AWAY/ | 1980 | Arista SP-84 | 15 |
| THE POWER OF POSITIVE DRINKING/STANDING ON CEREMONY | | | |
| I LOVE YOU, SUZANNE (same on both sides) | 1984 | RCA JR-13849 | 7 |
| MY LOVE IS CHEMICAL (same on both sides) | 1985 | Atlantic 819 | 7 |
| NO MONEY DOWN (same on both sides) | 1986 | RCA Victor JR-14343 | 12 |
| *(Green vinyl)* | | | |
| SEPTEMBER SONG (LP)/(7" Version) | 1986 | A&M 17352 | 6 |
| STREET HASSLE (stereo)/(mono) | 1978 | Arista SP-14 | 10 |
| SOUL MAN (same on both sides)  With Sam Moore | 1986 | A&M 17434 | 6 |
| VIDEO VIOLENCE (same on both sides) | 1986 | RCA Victor JR-14420 | 8 |
| WALK ON THE WILD SIDE/CONEY ISLAND BABY/SATELLITE OF LOVE | 1978 | Arista SP-36 | 10 |
| **45s** | | | |
| OSTRICH, THE   The Primitives | 1964 | Pickwick 1001 | 250 |
| *(Stock copy is rarer, worth over $300)* | | | |

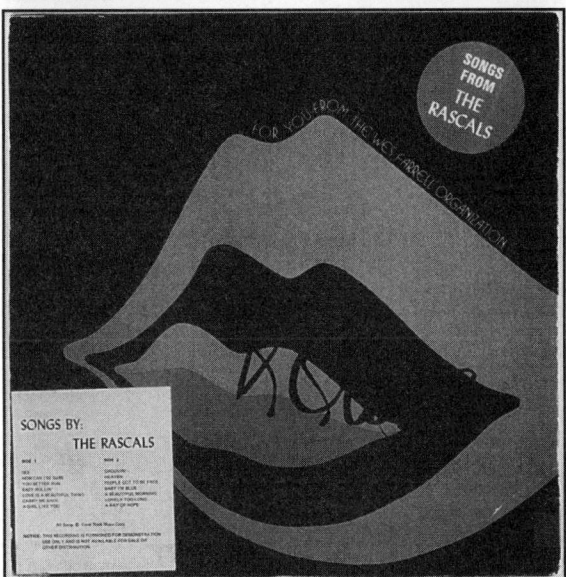

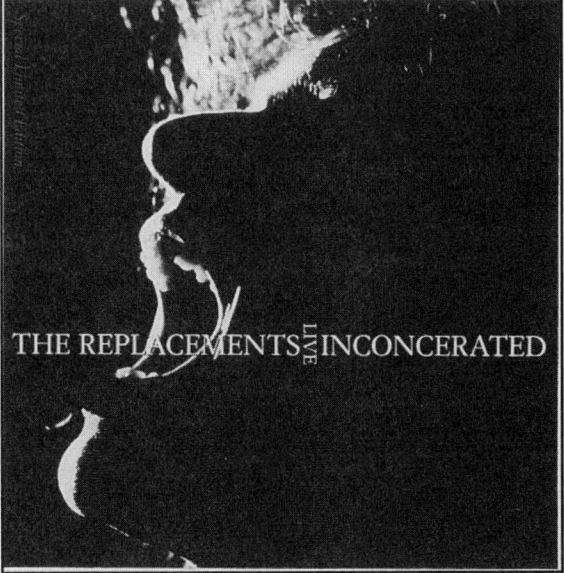

(Top left) R.E.M.'s collector base looks for anything related to the group, including this Up Close appearance from 1989. (Top right) Capitol Records released a few dozen, and perhaps as many as a hundred, promo-only 45s from 1989 through 1991. All of these are very limited, and some are quite sought after. Here's one by Bonnie Raitt. (Middle row) The cover and record label for *Songs By the Rascals* (or *Songs From the Rascals* – the front cover has both titles!), a promo-only publisher's sample from the Wes Farrell Organization. (Bottom row) The cover and disc from The Replacements' promo-only live recording, *Inconcerated.*

| Title | Yr | Label, Number | NM $ |
|---|---|---|---|
| **Albums** | | | |
| THE BLUE MASK | 1982 | Direct Disk (no #) | 150 |
| *(Only exists on test pressings; no stock copies made)* | | | |
| BLUE MASK INTERVIEW ALBUM | 1980 | RCA Victor 4267 | 20 |
| *(Music and interviews)* | | | |
| THE BLUE MASK SAMPLER | 1982 | RCA Victor DJL1-4345 | 12 |
| *(Three-song EP released to radio)* | | | |
| LOU REED | 1982 | RCA Victor | 25 |
| *(Promo only, music and interviews)* | | | |
| SPECIAL RADIO SERIES, VOL. XVII | 1980 | RCA Victor DJL1-4266 | 25 |
| *(Promo-only with insert)* | | | |
| **Compact Discs** | | | |
| MAGIC AND LOSS | 1992 | Sire | 150 |
| *(Promo-only release in metal case, only 500 pressed)* | | | |
| ROCK AND ROLL LIFE, A | 1989 | Sire PRO-CD-3358 (2) | 40 |
| *(Music and interviews, promo only)* | | | |
| SELECTIONS FROM BETWEEN THOUGHT AND EXPRESSION | 1992 | RCA RDJ-62284 | 15 |
| *(Promo-only sampler from box set)* | | | |
| **RADIO SHOWS** | | | |
| **Albums** | | | |
| KING BISCUIT FLOWER HOUR  Live concert | 1984 | DIR (2) | 150-225 |
| *(Lou Reed and Bruce Cockburn)* | | | |
| KING BISCUIT FLOWER HOUR (Sept 86) | 1986 | DIR (2) | 100-150 |
| *(Live solo concert)* | | | |
| KING BISCUIT FLOWER HOUR (Jan 87) Live concert | 1987 | DIR (2) | 75-125 |
| *(Lou Reed and Iggy Pop)* | | | |
| OFF THE RECORD | 1989 | Westwood One (2) | 20-35 |
| *(Music and interviews)* | | | |
| RETRO ROCK (July 82) Live concert | 1982 | Clayton Webster (2) | 50-100 |
| *(Mostly live concert)* | | | |
| **Compact Discs** | | | |
| IN THE STUDIO (June 89) | 1989 | | 15-25 |
| *(Profile of "Rock and Roll Animal" LP)* | | | |
| KING BISCUIT FLOWER HOUR (June 90) Live concert | 1990 | DIR | 40-75 |
| *(With Talking Heads)* | | | |
| KING BISCUIT FLOWER HOUR (Mar 92) | 1992 | DIR | 25-50 |
| *(Live concert)* | | | |

## REED, PAUL, AND CHORUS

| | | | |
|---|---|---|---|
| **45s** | | | |
| THAT MAN OVER THERE/THE BIG CLOWN BALLOONS | 1963 | Columbia JZSP 76341/0 | 8 |
| *B-side by "Orchestra and Chorus"; both from the play "Here's Love"* | | | |

## REEVES, JIM

*Other RCA Victor promo 45s to 8000 $8 each; Other RCA Victor promo 45s to 9500 $5 each; Other RCA Victor promo 45s after 9500 $3 each; MCA promo 45s duet with Patsy Cline $3 each*

| | | | |
|---|---|---|---|
| **45s** | | | |
| DIAMONDS BY THE DOZEN  Set of five stereo singles | 1963 | RCA Victor 2668-1 to 5 | 125 |
| *(Or $25 each for the five jukebox singles)* | | | |
| I LOVE YOU   With Ginny Wright | 1954 | Fabor 101A | 100 |
| *(Black promo label)* | | | |
| I'M HURTIN' INSIDE | 1955 | RCA Victor 6200 | 40 |
| *(White label promo, includes a promo-only "Introduction by Jim Reeves" to the song)* | | | |
| A STRANGER'S JUST A FRIEND | 1961 | RCA Victor SP-45-143 | 40 |
| *(Promo-only release, white promo label)* | | | |
| A TOUCH OF VELVET  Set of five stereo singles | 1962 | RCA Victor 2487-1 to 5 | 150 |
| *(Or $30 each for the five jukebox singles)* | | | |
| **7-Inch Extended Plays** | | | |
| AM I LOSING YOU/WAITIN' FOR A TRAIN | 1957 | RCA Victor DJ-42 | 30 |
| *(Both songs on same side, flip side is Dave Rich)* | | | |
| THE BEST OF JIM REEVES | 1966 | RCA Victor 2890 | 25 |
| *(Jukebox LLP, issued with a hard cover)* | | | |
| THE BEST OF JIM REEVES II | 1966 | RCA Victor 3482 | 25 |
| *(Jukebox LLP, issued with a hard cover)* | | | |
| THE BLUE SIDE OF LONESOME | 1967 | RCA Victor 3793 | 25 |
| *(Jukebox LLP, issued with a hard cover that opens from left and is blank on back )* | | | |
| JIM REEVES | 1974 | RCA Victor 10133 | 10 |
| *(Cream colored promo label, no EP cover)* | | | |
| THE JIM REEVES WAY | 1965 | RCA Victor 2968 | 25 |
| *(Jukebox LLP, issued with a hard cover)* | | | |
| MOONLIGHT AND ROSES | 1964 | RCA Victor 2854 | 50 |
| *(Nipper on the cover, jukebox LLP)* | | | |
| MOONLIGHT AND ROSES | 197? | RCA Victor 2854 | 25 |
| *(Later pressing, no Nipper on cover; both versions of the above EP issued with a hard cover)* | | | |
| **Albums** | | | |
| SOMETHING SPECIAL - FOR DISC JOCKEYS | 196? | RCA Victor 33-479 | 125 |
| *(White promo-only label sampler with special cover)* | | | |
| **RADIO SHOWS** | | | |
| **16-Inch Transcriptions** | | | |
| COUNTRY MUSIC TIME (60s) Various artists | 196? | U.S. Army | 50-100 |
| *(Music and interviews, host is Jim Reeves)* | | | |
| LEATHERNECK JAMBOREE (50s) Various artists | 195? | | 100-150 |
| *(Music and interviews, host is Jim Reeves)* | | | |
| **Albums** | | | |
| BBC TRANSCRIPTION DISC  Music and interviews | 1982 | BBC Transcription (7) | 650-800 |
| *(Seven record set, all Jim Reeves)* | | | |

| Title | Yr | Label, Number | NM $ |
|---|---|---|---|
| COUNTRY CROSSROADS (July 82)  Tribute | 1982 | Southern Baptist | 25-50 |
| *(Music and interviews)* | | | |

**REEVES, RONNA**
*Mercury promo CD singles $2-3 each*
**Compact Discs**

| | | | |
|---|---|---|---|
| MY HEART WASN'T IN IT | 1996 | River North 4564 | 15 |
| *(Heart-shaped promo-only CD single, the first shaped CD promo made in the U.S.)* | | | |

**REGALS, THE**
**45s**

| | | | |
|---|---|---|---|
| RUN PRETTY BABY | 1956 | Aladdin 3266 | 75 |
| *(White promo label)* | | | |

**REGENCY CHOIR, THE**
**45s**

| | | | |
|---|---|---|---|
| THE BELLS OF CHRISTMAS/THREE WISE MEN, WISE MEN THREE | 1966 | Columbia JZSP 116425/6 | 10 |

**RELF, KEITH**
*Of the Yardbirds*
**45s**

| | | | |
|---|---|---|---|
| MR. ZERO/KNOWING | 1966 | Epic 10044 | 150 |
| *(Promo on red vinyl… Reportedly, two promos were released for this single; the second, a different mix, was accompanied by a note telling the radio people not to play the first one, but to use the second one instead. This has not been confirmed)* | | | |
| SHAPES IN MY MIND/BLUE SANDS | 1966 | Epic 10110 | 150 |
| *(Promo on red vinyl)* | | | |

**REMAINS, THE**
*Other Epic promo 45s $20-30 each*
**45s**

| | | | |
|---|---|---|---|
| DIDDY WAH DIDDY/ONCE BEFORE | 1966 | Epic 10001 | 150 |
| *(Promo on red vinyl)* | | | |
| I CAN'T GET AWAY  Red vinyl | 1966 | Epic 9872 | 75 |
| *(Only the promo version is red vinyl)* | | | |
| I CAN'T GET AWAY  Picture sleeve | 1966 | Epic 9872 | 75 |
| *(Promo-only picture sleeve)* | | | |

**REMBRANDTS, THE**
*Other promo CD singles $2-3 each*
**Compact Discs**

| | | | |
|---|---|---|---|
| I'LL BE THERE FOR YOU | 1995 | EastWest | 8 |
| *(Promo-only CD single, their biggest airplay hit)* | | | |
| L.P. | 1995 | EastWest | 18 |
| *(Promo-only issue of CD in 12-inch vinyl-sized package)* | | | |
| REMBRANDTS, THE | 1990 | Atco | 15 |
| *(Promo-only issue of CD in cardboard picture frame)* | | | |

**REN AND STIMPY**
**Compact Discs**

| | | | |
|---|---|---|---|
| LITTLE CROCK O' CHRISTMAS | 1993 | Sony Wonder LSK 5608 | 18 |
| *(Promo-only sampler)* | | | |
| LITTLE EEDIOT | 1993 | Sony Wonder LSK 5473 (2) | 25 |
| *(Promo-only sampler and interview)* | | | |

**RENAISSANCE**
*Sire promo 45s $6 each; I.R.S. promo 45s $4 each*
**RADIO SHOWS**
**Albums**

| | | | |
|---|---|---|---|
| ALISON STEELE (70s) Various artists | 197? | | 10-20 |
| *(Includes Renaissance, music and interviews)* | | | |
| BBC TRANSCRIPTION DISC | 1978 | London Wavelength | 300-400 |
| *(Rare live concert)* | | | |
| ROCK AROUND THE WORLD (June 76) | 1976 | RATW | 50-100 |
| *(Live concert)* | | | |

**REO SPEEDWAGON**
*Other Epic promo 45s $3 each; Epic promo picture sleeves $2 each; Epic promo CD singles $2-3 each*
**12-Inch Singles**

| | | | |
|---|---|---|---|
| GOTTA FEEL MORE (3 versions) | 1985 | Epic EAS 2091 | 8 |
| KEEP THE FIRE BURNIN' (same on both sides) | 1982 | Epic AE 1489 | 6 |
| RIDIN' THE STORM OUT (mono/stereo) | 1977 | Epic AE 314 | 10 |

**45s**

| | | | |
|---|---|---|---|
| ROLL WITH THE CHANGES White promo labels | 1978 | Epic 50545 | 10 |
| *(Long 3:49 and short 2:50 versions)* | | | |
| WHAT'S IT ALL ABOUT (Apr 81) Public service show | 1981 | W.I.A.A. 571 | 15 |
| *(Flip side features Jerry Jeff Walker)* | | | |
| WHAT'S IT ALL ABOUT (Oct 82) Public service show | 1982 | W.I.A.A. 644 | 25 |
| *(Flip side features The Who)* | | | |

**7-Inch Extended Plays**

| | | | |
|---|---|---|---|
| PLAYBACK Various artists | 197? | Playback (CBS) AS7 1033 | 15 |
| *(Includes one REO song, "157 Riverside Drive"; also issued with a paper Playback sleeve)* | | | |

**Albums**

| | | | |
|---|---|---|---|
| LIVE AGAIN | 1978 | Epic AS-410 | 20 |
| *(Promo-only release)* | | | |

| Title | Yr | Label, Number | NM $ |
|---|---|---|---|
| NINE LIVES | 1979 | Epic AS-643 | 20 |
| *(Promo-only release)* | | | |
| **RADIO SHOWS** | | | |
| **Albums** | | | |
| BBC ROCK HOUR (Nov 82) | 1982 | London Wavelength | 10-20 |
| *(Music and interviews)* | | | |
| IN CONCERT (Nov 82) | 1982 | Westwood One (2) | 15-20 |
| *(Live concert)* | | | |
| LIVE AS WE KNOW IT | 1987 | Westwood One | 15-25 |
| *(Limited release)* | | | |
| NBC SOURCE (May 81) | 1981 | NBC Radio (2) | 15-25 |
| *(Live concert)* | | | |
| OFF THE RECORD (80s) Profile | 198? | Westwood One (2) | 10-15 |
| *(Music and interviews)* | | | |
| SUPERSTAR CONCERT (Jan 85) Live concert | 1985 | Westwood One (3) | 20-30 |
| *(Box set, repeated)* | | | |
| **Compact Discs** | | | |
| IN THE STUDIO (June 91) Profile of an album | 1991 | Album Network | 10-15 |
| *(Music and interviews)* | | | |

## REPLACEMENTS, THE
**12-Inch Singles**

| Title | Yr | Label, Number | NM $ |
|---|---|---|---|
| ALEX CHILTON (same on both sides) | 1987 | Sire PRO-A-2761 | 12 |
| CAN'T HARDLY WAIT (Remix)/(LP Version) | 1987 | Sire PRO-A-2863 | 8 |
| I'LL BE YOU (same on both sides) | 1989 | Sire PRO-A-3419 | 10 |
| KISS ME ON THE BUS (same on both sides) | 1985 | Sire PRO-A-2412 | 12 |
| THE LEDGE (same on both sides) | 1987 | Sire PRO-A-2727 | 6 |
| **Albums** | | | |
| DON'T SELL OR BUY...IT'S CRAP | 1991 | Sire PRO-A-4632 | 30 |
| *(Promo-only 5-track sampler)* | | | |
| AN INTERVIEW WITH PAUL WESTERBERG | 1987 | Warner Bros. WBMS-148 | 40 |
| **Compact Discs** | | | |
| DON'T BUY OR SELL...IT'S CRAP | 1991 | Sire PRO-CD-4632 | 25 |
| *(Promo-only compilation)* | | | |
| INCONCERATED | 1989 | Sire PRO-CD-3633 | 20 |
| *(Promo-only live collection)* | | | |

## RESIDENTS, THE
**Albums**

| Title | Yr | Label, Number | NM $ |
|---|---|---|---|
| FREAK SHOW | 1991 | OP 011 | 50 |
| *(Promo-only black vinyl pressing; 400 made)* | | | |
| PLEASE DO NOT STEAL IT! | 1979 | Ralph DJ 7901 | 25 |
| *(Promo-only sampler)* | | | |
| **Compact Discs** | | | |
| LOUISIANA LICK | 199? | East Side Digital 3 | 15 |
| UNCLE WILLIE'S HIGHLY OPINIONATED GUIDE TO THE RESIDENTS | 1993 | Ralph RZ 9302 | 15 |
| *(Sampler of excerpts contained in book of the same name)* | | | |

## REUNION
*Joey Levine (the voice of many Buddah bubblegum hits; Other RCA Victor promo 45s $3 each; A&M promo 45s $2 each)*

**45s**

| Title | Yr | Label, Number | NM $ |
|---|---|---|---|
| LIFE IS A ROCK | 1974 | RCA Victor 10056 | 12 |
| *(Cream colored promo label, yellow vinyl)* | | | |
| LIFE IS A ROCK  Regional versions | 1974 | RCA Victor | 20 |
| *(Custom versions for some radio stations that contained the call letters; one we know about, from Philadelphia, has the lyric "Life is a rock, but 'FIL rolled me"; we don't know whether these are on record, cassette or reel-to-reel)* | | | |

## REVERE, PAUL, AND THE RAIDERS
*Also known as The Unknowns and The Brotherhood;  Other Columbia white promo label 45s $8-10 each; 20th Century promo 45s $6 each; Columbia promo 45s by Freddy Weller $3 each; Columbia promo 45s by Mark Lindsay $3 each; Jerden promo 45s by Jim Valley $5 each; Dunhill promo 45s by Jim Valley $4 each; Other Columbia white promo label LPs $15 each; Columbia promo LPs by Lindsay or Weller $8 each*

**45s**

| Title | Yr | Label, Number | NM $ |
|---|---|---|---|
| ALL NIGHT LONG | 1962 | Gardena 124 | 25 |
| *(White promo label)* | | | |
| BEATNICK STICKS | 1960 | Gardena 106 | 40 |
| *(White promo label) An earlier stock label version on Apex is worth over $150)* | | | |
| DON'T LET GO  The Brotherhood | 1969 | RCA Victor 0216 | 10 |
| *(White promo label, members include Smitty, Drake and Fang)* | | | |
| GOOD THING | 1966 | Columbia 43907 | 50 |
| *(White promo label, red vinyl, only the promo is colored vinyl)* | | | |
| THE GREAT AIRPLANE STRIKE | 1966 | Columbia 43810 | 50 |
| *(White promo label, red vinyl, only the promo is colored vinyl)* | | | |
| HUNGRY | 1966 | Columbia 43678 | 50 |
| *(White promo label, red vinyl, only the promo is colored vinyl)* | | | |
| JUMP OUT THE WINDOW  The Brotherhood | 1968 | RCA Victor 9621 | 25 |
| *(White promo label, price includes stock picture sleeve)* | | | |
| JUST LIKE ME | 1965 | Columbia 43461 | 50 |
| *(White promo label, red vinyl, only the promo is colored vinyl)* | | | |
| KICKS | 1966 | Columbia 43556 | 50 |
| *(White promo label, red vinyl, only the promo is colored vinyl)* | | | |
| LIKE, BLUEGRASS | 1962 | Gardena 127 | 30 |
| *(White promo label)* | | | |
| LIKE, CHARLESTON | 1961 | Gardena 118 | 25 |
| *(White promo label)* | | | |

| Title | Yr | Label, Number | NM $ |
|---|---|---|---|
| LIKE, LONG HAIR | 1961 | Gardena 116 | 30 |
| *(White promo label)* | | | |
| LOUIE LOUIE | 1963 | Columbia 42814 | 25 |
| *(White promo label, stock single is much rarer, worth $50; an earlier label version on Sande is worth over $200)* | | | |
| MELODY FOR AN UNKNOWN GIRL  The Unknowns | 1967 | Parrot 307 | 25 |
| *(Brownish promo label, Allison, Lindsay and Steve Alaimo, written by Paul Revere)* | | | |
| PAUL REVERE INTERVIEWS THE RAIDERS | 1967 | Teen Scoop (no #) | 50 |
| *(Cardboard picture disc from the magazine)* | | | |
| PAUL REVERE'S RIDE | 1961 | Gardena 115 | 40 |
| *(White promo label)* | | | |
| SHAKE IT UP. PART 1 | 1962 | Gardena 131 | 30 |
| *(White promo label)* | | | |
| SO FINE | 1962 | Jerden 807 | 30 |
| *(White promo label)* | | | |
| SS 396 | 1965 | Columbia CSP-262 | 25 |
| *(Flip side is "Corvair Baby")* | | | |
| SS 396 | 1967 | Columbia CSP-466 | 35 |
| *(Flip side is by the Cyrkle, price includes picture sleeve from Columbia Special Products)* | | | |
| STEPPIN' OUT | 1965 | Columbia 43375 | 50 |
| *(White promo label, red vinyl, only the promo is colored vinyl)* | | | |
| TALL COOL ONE | 1962 | Gardena 137 | 50 |
| *(White promo label)* | | | |
| WHAT'S IT ALL ABOUT  Public service show | 1972 | W.I.A.A. 112 | 20 |
| *(Interviews with Freddy Weller and Mark Lindsay)* | | | |
| **7-Inch Extended Plays** | | | |
| IN THE BEGINNING | 1967 | Jerden 7004 | 75 |
| *(Jukebox LLP issued with a hard cover)* | | | |
| THE JUDGE  Seven-track LLP with picture cover | 1969 | Columbia Special Products | 1,500 |
| *(Label resembles a '69 Pontiac Rally II, record and cover are very rare)* | | | |
| SOMETHING HAPPENING | 1968 | Columbia 9665 | 40 |
| *(Jukebox LLP issued with a hard cover)* | | | |
| **Albums** | | | |
| CHRISTMAS PAST AND PRESENT | 1967 | Columbia 2755 | 40 |
| *(White promo label)* | | | |
| HERE THEY COME | 1965 | Columbia 2307 | 50 |
| *(White promo label)* | | | |
| JUST LIKE US! | 1966 | Columbia 2451 | 35 |
| *(White promo label)* | | | |
| MIDNIGHT RIDE | 1966 | Columbia 2508 | 30 |
| *(White promo label)* | | | |
| PINK PUZZ | 1969 | Columbia (no #) | Unknown |
| *(Produced by Mark Lindsay as promo only, released commercially as "Alias Pink Puzz")* | | | |
| THE SPIRIT OF '67 | 1967 | Columbia 2595 | 25 |
| *(White promo label)* | | | |

## RHYTHM ACES, THE
**45s**

| Title | Yr | Label, Number | NM $ |
|---|---|---|---|
| I WONDER WHY | 1955 | Vee Jay 124 | 150 |
| *(White promo label)* | | | |
| THAT'S MY SUGAR | 1955 | Vee Jay 160 | 75 |
| *(White promo label)* | | | |
| WHISPER TO ME | 1955 | Vee Jay 138 | 100 |
| *(White promo label)* | | | |
| WHISPER TO ME | 1956 | Vee Jay 212 | 75 |
| *(White promo label)* | | | |

## RHYTHM HERITAGE
**45s**

| Title | Yr | Label, Number | NM $ |
|---|---|---|---|
| HOLDIN' OUT FOR YOU LOVE (mono/stereo) | 1978 | ABC 12334 | 4 |
| *(May be promo only)* | | | |
| THEME FROM S.W.A.T. | 1975 | Special Discotheque Release SPDJ-25 | 20 |
| *(An ABC record with no label name, contains 4:07 version)* | | | |

## RIA AND THE REASONS
**45s**

| Title | Yr | Label, Number | NM $ |
|---|---|---|---|
| MEMORIES LINGER ON | 1964 | Amy 888 | 75 |
| *(Blue vinyl, blue promo label)* | | | |

## RICH, CHARLIE
*Phillips International promo 45s $15 each; Smash promo 45s $8 each; Epic promo 45s $2 each; Epic promo AS and AE7 EPs $5 each; RCA Victor promo 45s (1960s) $8 each; RCA Victor promo 45s (1970s) $2 each; Sun white promo label LPs $6 each*
**45s**

| Title | Yr | Label, Number | NM $ |
|---|---|---|---|
| THE GRASS IS ALWAYS GREENER | 196? | Groove 0020 | 20 |
| *(Promo label, stock picture sleeve adds $10 to value)* | | | |
| **7-Inch Extended Plays** | | | |
| CHARLIE RICH | 1976 | Epic AE7 1099 | 15 |
| *(Promo-only release, 4 songs, with picture cover)* | | | |
| YOUR PLACE IS HERE WITH ME | 1974 | Epic AS 96 | 15 |
| *(Promo-only release)* | | | |
| **Albums** | | | |
| CHARLIE RICH | 1973 | Epic AS 50 | 30 |
| *(Promo-only compilation)* | | | |
| EVERYTHING YOU ALWAYS WANTED TO HEAR BY CHARLIE RICH BUT WERE AFRAID TO ASK FOR | 1976 | Epic AS-139 | 20 |
| *(Promo-only greatest hits album)* | | | |

| Title | Yr | Label, Number | NM $ |
|-------|-----|---------------|------|

## RICHARD, CLIFF

*Other Epic white promo label 45s $10 each; Uni yellow/red promo label 45s $10 each; Warner Bros. promo 45s $6 each; Monument promo 45s $3 each; Sire promo 45s $6 each; Rocket (MCA) promo 45s $4 each; Rocket (RCA) promo 45s $5 each; EMI green promo label 45s $4 each; EMI gray promo label 45s $3 each*

**12-Inch Singles**

| Title | Yr | Label, Number | NM $ |
|-------|-----|---------------|------|
| NEVER SAY DIE | 1983 | EMI 7813 | 10 |
| *(12" single for radio)* | | | |
| WE DON'T TALK ANYMORE | 1979 | EMI SPRO-9252 | 12 |
| *(Promo-only 12" single)* | | | |

**45s**

| Title | Yr | Label, Number | NM $ |
|-------|-----|---------------|------|
| BACHELOR BOY | 1964 | Epic 9691 | 15 |
| *(White promo label)* | | | |
| CATCH ME, I'M FALLING | 1961 | ABC-Paramount 10175 | 25 |
| *(White promo label)* | | | |
| FALL IN LOVE WITH YOU | 1960 | ABC-Paramount 10109 | 25 |
| *(White promo label)* | | | |
| I DON'T WANNA LOVE YOU | 1964 | Epic 9737 | 15 |
| *(White promo label)* | | | |
| I'M THE ONLY ONE | 1964 | Epic 9670 | 20 |
| *(White promo label)* | | | |
| IT'S ALL IN THE GAME | 1963 | Epic 9633 | 20 |
| *(White promo label)* | | | |
| IT'S WONDERFUL TO BE YOUNG | 1962 | Dot 16399 | 18 |
| *(White promo label)* | | | |
| LIVIN' LOVIN' DOLL | 1959 | Capitol 4154 | 50 |
| *(Red promo label)* | | | |
| LIVING DOLL | 1959 | ABC-Paramount 10042 | 35 |
| *(White promo label)* | | | |
| LUCKY LIPS | 1963 | Epic 9597 | 25 |
| *(White promo label)* | | | |
| MISTLETOE AND WINE | 1997 | EMI S7-19767 | 5 |
| *("For Jukeboxes Only!" issue, its only U.S. release to date)* | | | |
| MOVE IT | 1959 | Capitol 4096 | 50 |
| *(Red promo label)* | | | |
| PLEASE DON'T TEASE | 1960 | ABC-Paramount 10136 | 25 |
| *(White promo label)* | | | |
| THEME FOR A DREAM | 1961 | ABC-Paramount 10195 | 30 |
| *(White promo label)* | | | |
| TRAVELIN' LIGHT | 1959 | ABC-Paramount 10066 | 30 |
| *(White promo label)* | | | |
| VOICE IN THE WILDERNESS, A | 1960 | ABC-Paramount 10093 | 25 |
| *(White promo label)* | | | |
| THE YOUNG ONES | 1962 | Big Top 3101 | 25 |
| *(White promo label, mega UK hit)* | | | |

**7-Inch Extended Plays**

| Title | Yr | Label, Number | NM $ |
|-------|-----|---------------|------|
| IT'S ALL IN THE GAME  Jukebox LLP | 1968 | Epic 26089 | 40 |
| *(Issued with a hard cover)* | | | |
| TWO A PENNY  Soundtrack | 1968 | World Wide Pictures PR-1 | 25 |
| *(33rpm 7", small center hole, no cover)* | | | |
| TWO A PENNY  Soundtrack | 1968 | Light 101 | 25 |
| *(Released in a "mailer" type hard cover)* | | | |
| TWO A PENNY  Soundtrack | 1968 | Uni 001 | 25 |
| *(All of the above soundtrack EPs released to radio)* | | | |

**Albums**

| Title | Yr | Label, Number | NM $ |
|-------|-----|---------------|------|
| CLIFF RICHARD IN SPAIN | 1964 | Epic 24115 | 50 |
| *(White promo label)* | | | |
| CLIFF SINGS | 1960 | ABC-Paramount 321 | 150 |
| *(White promo label)* | | | |
| FINDERS KEEPERS  Acetate version | 197? | (no label) | 200 |
| *(Pressed at the Knickerbocker plant, this is otherwise unreleased in the USA)* | | | |
| IT'S ALL IN THE GAME | 1964 | Epic 24089 | 50 |
| *(White promo label)* | | | |
| LISTEN TO CLIFF | 1961 | ABC-Paramount 391 | 100 |
| *(White promo label)* | | | |
| SUMMER HOLIDAY | 1963 | Epic 24063 | 75 |
| *(White promo label)* | | | |
| SWINGER'S PARADISE | 1965 | Epic 24145 | 50 |
| *(White promo label)* | | | |
| TWO A PENNY | 1971 | Uni 1086/1087 | 50 |
| *(Many copies rushed to radio stations)* | | | |
| TWO A PENNY  Movie ads | 1971 | World Wide Pictures | 200 |
| *(Thirteen spots for radio, one side for broadcast, the other side not for broadcast)* | | | |

**Compact Discs**

| Title | Yr | Label, Number | NM $ |
|-------|-----|---------------|------|
| I STILL BELIEVE IN YOU | 1993 | EMI | 10 |
| *(Promo-only CD single, one of his very few U.S. releases in recent years)* | | | |

## RADIO SHOWS

**Albums**

| Title | Yr | Label, Number | NM $ |
|-------|-----|---------------|------|
| BBC TRANSCRIPTION DISC  Live concert | 1978 | BBC Transcription | 200-300 |
| *(In the UK, he is the King)* | | | |
| BBC TRANSCRIPTION DISC  Live concert | 1980 | BBC Transcription | 200-300 |
| *(Worth more in the UK)* | | | |
| NATIONAL MUSIC SURVEY (May 25, 1985) Various artists | 1985 | Mutual Radio (4) | 25-40 |
| *(This show, hosted by Dick Clark, features Cliff Richard interviews and music)* | | | |
| ROBERT W. MORGAN (May 81) | 1981 | Watermark | 50-100 |
| *(Rare music and interview show)* | | | |

| Title | Yr | Label, Number | NM $ |
|---|---|---|---|
| **RICHIE, LIONEL** | | | |
| **45s** | | | |
| SAY YOU, SAY ME | 1985 | (No label) 1819 | 15 |
| *(With special sleeve, "Finally Cleared by ASCAP")* | | | |
| | | | |
| **RICHMAN, JONATHAN, AND THE MODERN LOVERS** | | | |
| *Beserkley promo 45s $5 each* | | | |
| **RADIO SHOWS** | | | |
| **Albums** | | | |
| PENTHOUSE/OMNI COLLEGE ROCK CONCERT (Nov 83) | 1983 | London Wavelength | 40-75 |
| *(Live concert)* | | | |
| | | | |
| **RIGHT SAID FRED** | | | |
| **12-Inch Singles** | | | |
| I'M TOO SEXY (6 versions) | 1991 | Charisma 1743 | 15 |
| | | | |
| **RIGHTEOUS BROTHERS, THE** | | | |
| *Bill Medley and Bobby Hatfield; Other Moonglow white promo label 45s $10 each; Other Philles promo 45s $10 each; Other Verve blue and yellow promo label 45s $6 each; Capitol/Haven promo 45s $3 each; Verve yellow promo label 45s by Bobby Hatfield $4 each; Other RCA Victor promo 45s by Bill Medley $2 each; Verve yellow or blue promo label LPs $15 each* | | | |
| **45s** | | | |
| BRING YOUR LOVE TO ME | 1964 | Moonglow 234 | 18 |
| *(White promo label)* | | | |
| FANNIE MAE | 1965 | Moonglow 238 | 15 |
| *(White promo label)* | | | |
| GOTTA TELL YOU HOW I FEEL | 1963 | Moonglow 221 | 25 |
| *(White promo label)* | | | |
| I STILL DO  Bill Medley | 1984 | RCA Victor 13753 | 12 |
| *(Gold label, yellow vinyl)* | | | |
| IS THERE ANYTHING I CAN DO  Bill Medley | 1985 | RCA Victor 14021 | 10 |
| *(Green label, red vinyl)* | | | |
| JUST ONCE IN MY LIFE | 1965 | Philles 127 | 15 |
| *(White promo label)* | | | |
| KO KO JO | 1963 | Moonglow 224 | 20 |
| *(White promo label)* | | | |
| LITTLE LATIN LUPE LU  Black vinyl | 1963 | Moonglow 215 | 25 |
| *(White promo label)* | | | |
| LITTLE LATIN LUPE LU  Red vinyl | 1963 | Moonglow 215 | 50 |
| *(Only the promo is red vinyl)* | | | |
| MY BABE | 1963 | Moonglow 223 | 20 |
| *(White promo label)* | | | |
| THE RIGHTEOUS BROTHERS  Box set of five jukebox 45s | 1967 | Verve CS 8-5 | 75 |
| *(Price is for all five singles plus the box, records all have blue promo labels and are numbered from 10520 to 10524)* | | | |
| THIS LITTLE GIRL OF MINE | 1965 | Moonglow 235 | 15 |
| *(White promo label)* | | | |
| TILL YOUR MEMORY'S GONE  Bill Medley | 1983 | RCA Victor 13692 | 12 |
| *(Silver label, blue vinyl)* | | | |
| TRY TO FIND ANOTHER MAN | 1964 | Moonglow 231 | 18 |
| *(White promo label)* | | | |
| WOMEN IN LOVE  Bill Medley | 1985 | RCA Victor 14081 | 10 |
| *(Blue label, green vinyl)* | | | |
| YOU'VE LOST THAT LOVIN' FEELIN' | 1964 | Philles 124 | 15 |
| *(White promo label)* | | | |
| **7-Inch Extended Plays** | | | |
| THE RIGHTEOUS BROTHERS GREATEST HITS | 1967 | Moonglow 1004 | 40 |
| *(Jukebox LLP, issued with a hard cover)* | | | |
| **RADIO SHOWS** | | | |
| **Albums** | | | |
| FOR CHRISTMAS SEALS  Various artists | 1968 | Decca Custom 201-176 | 50 |
| *(One PSA show includes the Righteous Brothers, music and interviews)* | | | |
| | | | |
| **RILEY, BILLY** | | | |
| **45s** | | | |
| IS THAT ALL TO THE BALL | 1958 | Brunswick 55085 | 50 |
| *(Yellow promo label)* | | | |
| | | | |
| **RILEY, JEANNIE C.** | | | |
| *Other Plantation promo 45s $3 each* | | | |
| **45s** | | | |
| HARPER VALLEY P.T.A.  Reissue | 1978 | Plantation 173 | 10 |
| *(Green vinyl, white promo label, stock copy is also green vinyl and has a picture sleeve)* | | | |
| MY MAN | 1970 | Plantation 65 | 10 |
| *(Green vinyl promo, stereo/mono)* | | | |
| OH, SINGER | 1971 | Plantation 72 | 10 |
| *(Green vinyl promo)* | | | |
| THE LION'S CLUB | 1972 | Plantation 85 | 10 |
| *(Green vinyl promo)* | | | |
| **7-Inch Extended Plays** | | | |
| HARPER VALLEY P.T.A.  Jukebox LLP | 1970 | Plantation | 18 |
| *(Issued with a hard cover)* | | | |
| **Albums** | | | |
| FOR CHRISTMAS SEALS | 1969 | Decca Custom | 25 |
| *(Eight cuts, one by Jeannie C. Riley)* | | | |

| Title | Yr | Label, Number | NM $ |
|---|---|---|---|

**RINCON SURFSIDE BAND, THE**
*Steve Barri and Phil Sloan*
**7-Inch Extended Plays**

| | | | |
|---|---|---|---|
| THE RINCON SURFSIDE BAND | 196? | Dunhill D-1 | 75 |

*(Promo-only EP issued with a paper sleeve)*

**RIP CHORDS, THE**
*Other Columbia promo 45s $10 each; Columbia promo LPs $25 each*
**45s**

| | | | |
|---|---|---|---|
| GONE | 1963 | Columbia 42812 | 100 |
| *(Price is for blue vinyl promo record and promo only picture sleeve)* | | | |
| HERE I STAND | 1963 | Columbia 42687 | 100 |
| *(Price is for green vinyl promo record and promo only picture sleeve)* | | | |
| HEY, LITTLE COBRA | 1963 | Columbia 42921 | 50 |
| *(Yellow vinyl, white promo label)* | | | |
| THREE WINDOW COUPE | 1964 | Columbia 43035 | 50 |
| *(Red vinyl, white promo label)* | | | |

**RITTER, TEX**
*Capitol promo 45s $5 each*
**Albums**

| | | | |
|---|---|---|---|
| SONGS FROM THE WESTERN SCREEN | 1958 | Capitol 971 | 40 |
| *(Promo label)* | | | |

**RIVERS, BOB, COMEDY CORP**
**45s**

| | | | |
|---|---|---|---|
| I'M DRESSING UP LIKE SANTA (WHEN I GET OUT ON PAROLE) | 1987 | Critique PR 2135 | 5 |
| WRECK THE MALLS | 1987 | Critique PR 2119 | 5 |
| *(Promo only, white label)* | | | |

**RIVERS, JOHNNY**
*Capitol promo label 45s $15-20 each; Imperial white promo label 45s $15 each; Imperial cream colored promo label 45s $8; Imperial black promo label 45s $6 each; Soul City promo 45s $5 each; Big Tree promo 45s $3 each; Atlantic promo 45s $3 each; Other Imperial white promo label LPs $15 each*
**45s**

| | | | |
|---|---|---|---|
| ANSWER ME, MY LOVE | 1959 | Cub 9058 | 25 |
| *(Reddish promo label)* | | | |
| ANSWER ME, MY LOVE | 1964 | MGM 13266 | 15 |
| *(Yellow promo label)* | | | |
| BABY COME BACK | 1958 | Gone 5026 | 25 |
| *(White promo label)* | | | |
| CALL ME | 1960 | Era 3037 | 25 |
| *(Green and white promo label)* | | | |
| EVERY DAY | 1959 | Cub 9047 | 25 |
| *(Reddish promo label)* | | | |
| HELP ME RHONDA | 1975 | Epic 50121 | 15 |
| *(With promotional "Epic Records Welcomes Johnny Rivers" sleeve)* | | | |
| KNOCK THREE TIMES | 1961 | Chancellor 1070 | 20 |
| *(White promo label)* | | | |
| KNOCK THREE TIMES | 1964 | United Artists 741 | 10 |
| *(White promo label)* | | | |
| SALES STIMULATOR "PLAY ME"  Red vinyl | 1966 | Rowe AMI 1008-B | 15 |
| *(About 30 seconds long, flip side is Boots Randolph)* | | | |
| THAT'S MY BABE | 1964 | Coral 62425 | 15 |
| *(Blue promo label)* | | | |
| TO BE LOVED | 1962 | Chancellor 1108 | 20 |
| *(White promo label)* | | | |
| TO BE LOVED | 1964 | United Artists 769 | 10 |
| *(White promo label)* | | | |
| WHAT'S IT ALL ABOUT  Public service show | 1972 | W.I.A.A. 148 | 15 |
| *(Music and interviews)* | | | |
| YOU'RE THE ONE | 1959 | Guyden 2003 | 25 |
| *(Promo label)* | | | |
| YOU'RE THE ONE | 1964 | Guyden 2110 | 18 |
| *(Promo label)* | | | |

**7-Inch Extended Plays**

| | | | |
|---|---|---|---|
| AT THE WHISKEY A-GO-GO Jukebox LLP | 1967 | Imperial 2264 | 25 |
| *(Issued with a hard cover)* | | | |
| HERE WE A-GO-GO AGAIN  Jukebox LLP | 1967 | Imperial 2274 | 25 |
| *(Issued with a hard cover)* | | | |
| JOHNNY RIVERS ROCKS THE FOLK Jukebox LLP | 1967 | Imperial 2293 | 25 |
| *(Issued with a hard cover)* | | | |
| REALIZATION  Radio spots | 1968 | Imperial JRC-1 | 25 |
| *(Promotion device from the label)* | | | |
| SPECIAL INTERVIEW WITH JOHNNY RIVERS | 1969 | Imperial JRC-372 | 20 |
| *(Promotion device from the label)* | | | |
| A TOUCH OF GOLD  Radio spots | 1969 | Imperial SP-9 | 25 |
| *(Promotion device from the label)* | | | |
| VOTER REGISTRATION SPOTS | 1972 | United Artists SP-77 | 25 |
| *(Public service ads from the label)* | | | |

**Albums**

| | | | |
|---|---|---|---|
| FOR CHRISTMAS SEALS | 1969 | Decca Custom | 25 |
| *(Eight cuts, one by Johnny Rivers)* | | | |
| HERE WE A-GO-GO AGAIN | 1964 | Imperial 9274 | 25 |
| *(White promo label)* | | | |

(Top left) Cliff Richard made a rare appearance on a U.S. radio show with this 1981 broadcast of the Robert W. Morgan Special of the Week. (Top right) Around the time of his solo album *Talk Is Cheap,* Up Close featured the Rolling Stone by himself. (Middle row) On his very first record, Carlton Records couldn't make up its mind how it wanted to bill its new signing. So "That Crazy Feeling" was sent to radio stations with some copies billed "Kenneth Rogers" and other billed "Kenny Rogers." (Bottom left) A rarely-seen soundtrack promo on the Jolly Rogers label, Kenny's vanity label distributed by MGM in the mid-1970s. (Bottom right) Popular Philadelphia artist Bobby Rydell recorded this promo-only song paying tribute to Atlantic City, N.J.'s Steel Pier.

| Title | Yr | Label, Number | NM $ |
|---|---|---|---|
| JOHNNY RIVERS AT THE WHISKEY A-GO-GO | 1964 | Imperial 9264 | 50 |
| *(White promo label)* | | | |
| JOHNNY RIVERS IN ACTION | 1965 | Imperial 9280 | 20 |
| *(White promo label)* | | | |
| **RADIO SHOWS** | | | |
| **Albums** | | | |
| ROBERT W. MORGAN | 1978 | Watermark | 25-50 |
| *(Music and interviews)* | | | |

## RIVIERAS, THE
*Two different groups; Coed promo 45s $18 each; Riviera promo 45s $10 each*

## RIVINGTONS, THE
**45s**

| Title | Yr | Label, Number | NM $ |
|---|---|---|---|
| PAPA-OOM-MOW-MOW (same on both sides) | 1982 | Liberty 1484 | 6 |
| *(Reissue; promo only)* | | | |

## ROBBINS, MARTY
*Other Columbia white promo label 78s $12 each; Columbia Hall of Fame white promo label 45s $8 each; Columbia Hall of Fame red promo label 45s $4 each; Other Columbia promo 45s from 41589 to 42701 $8 each; Columbia promo 45s after 42781 $5 each; Warner/Viva promo 45s $3 each; MCA promo 45s $3 each; Audiograph promo 45s duets $2 each; Other Columbia white promo label LPs $15 each*

**45s**

| Title | Yr | Label, Number | NM $ |
|---|---|---|---|
| AIN'T I THE LUCKY ONE | 1959 | Columbia 41282 | 18 |
| *(White promo label)* | | | |
| CAP AND GOWN | 1959 | Columbia 41408 | 12 |
| *(White promo label)* | | | |
| A CASTLE IN THE SKY | 1953 | Columbia 21111 | 35 |
| *(White promo label)* | | | |
| DON'T MAKE ME ASHAMED | 1953 | Columbia 21176 | 25 |
| *(White promo label)* | | | |
| EL PASO | 1959 | Columbia 41511 | 10 |
| *(White promo label, stock picture sleeve is worth an additional $25)* | | | |
| HANGING TREE, THE | 1959 | Columbia 41325 | 15 |
| *(White promo label, stock picture sleeve is worth an additional $40)* | | | |
| I COULDN'T KEEP FROM CRYING | 1953 | Columbia 21075 | 35 |
| *(White promo label)* | | | |
| I'LL GO ON ALONE | 1953 | Columbia 21011 | 40 |
| *(White promo label)* | | | |
| I'M TOO BIG TO CRY | 1954 | Columbia 21291 | 25 |
| *(White promo label)* | | | |
| IT LOOKS LIKE I'M JUST IN YOUR WAY | 1955 | Columbia 21414 | 18 |
| *(White promo label)* | | | |
| IT'S A PITY WHAT MONEY CAN DO | 1954 | Columbia 21324 | 25 |
| *(White promo label)* | | | |
| JOLIE GIRL  Stereo/mono versions | 1970 | Columbia 45215 | 10 |
| *(Rare brown and blue/yellow promo labels)* | | | |
| JUST MARRIED | 1958 | Columbia 41143 | 18 |
| *(White promo label)* | | | |
| KNEE DEEP IN THE BLUES | 1957 | Columbia 40815 | 30 |
| *(White promo label)* | | | |
| LONG TALL SALLY | 1956 | Columbia 40679 | 50 |
| *(White promo label)* | | | |
| MAYBELLENE | 1955 | Columbia 21446 | 50 |
| *(White promo label)* | | | |
| MY ISLAND OF GOLDEN DREAMS | 1954 | Columbia 21213 | 25 |
| *(White promo label)* | | | |
| PRAY FOR ME MOTHER OF MINE | 1955 | Columbia 21388 | 20 |
| *(White promo label)* | | | |
| PRETTY MAMA | 1955 | Columbia 21461 | 50 |
| *(White promo label)* | | | |
| RESPECTFULLY, MISS BROOKS | 1956 | Columbia 40706 | 40 |
| *(White promo label)* | | | |
| SHE WAS ONLY SEVENTEEN | 1958 | Columbia 41208 | 15 |
| *(White promo label, stock picture sleeve is worth an additional $40)* | | | |
| SING ME SOMETHING SENTIMENTAL | 1953 | Columbia 21145 | 30 |
| *(White promo label)* | | | |
| SINGING THE BLUES | 1956 | Columbia 21545 | 30 |
| *(White promo label)* | | | |
| STORY OF MY LIFE, THE | 1957 | Columbia 41013 | 20 |
| *(White promo label, stock picture sleeve is worth an additional $40)* | | | |
| TEEN-AGE DREAM | 1957 | Columbia 40969 | 25 |
| *(White promo label)* | | | |
| TENNESSEE TODDY | 1955 | Columbia 21477 | 50 |
| *(White promo label)* | | | |
| THAT'S ALL RIGHT | 1954 | Columbia 21351 | 50 |
| *(White promo label)* | | | |
| A WHITE SPORT COAT | 1957 | Columbia 40864 | 30 |
| *(White promo label, stock picture sleeve is worth an additional $50)* | | | |

**78s**

| Title | Yr | Label, Number | NM $ |
|---|---|---|---|
| KNEE DEEP IN THE BLUES | 1957 | Columbia 40815 | 25 |
| *(Columbia promo label)* | | | |
| LONG TALL SALLY | 1956 | Columbia 40679 | 60 |
| *(Columbia promo label)* | | | |
| MAYBELLENE | 1955 | Columbia 21446 | 60 |
| *(Columbia promo label)* | | | |

| Title | Yr | Label, Number | NM $ |
|---|---|---|---|
| PRETTY MAMA | 1955 | Columbia 21461 | 60 |
| (Columbia promo label) | | | |
| RESPECTFULLY, MISS BROOKS | 1956 | Columbia 40706 | 25 |
| (Columbia promo label) | | | |
| SINGING THE BLUES | 1956 | Columbia 21545 | 25 |
| (Columbia promo label) | | | |
| TENNESSEE TODDY | 1955 | Columbia 21477 | 60 |
| (Columbia promo label) | | | |
| THAT'S ALL RIGHT | 1954 | Columbia 21351 | 75 |
| (Columbia promo label) | | | |
| A WHITE SPORT COAT | 1957 | Columbia 40864 | 25 |
| (Columbia promo label) | | | |
| **Albums** | | | |
| ALAMO, THE | 1961 | Columbia 1799 | 40 |
| (White promo label) | | | |
| BEND IN THE RIVER | 1968 | Columbia 445 | 30 |
| (Special release from Columbia Record Club) | | | |
| CHRISTMAS WITH MARTY ROBBINS | 1967 | Columbia 2735 | 40 |
| (White promo label) | | | |
| GUNFIGHTER BALLADS & TRAIL SONGS | 1959 | Columbia 1599 | 75 |
| (Columbia promo label) | | | |
| MARTY AFTER MIDNIGHT | 1962 | Columbia 1801 | 75 |
| (White promo label) | | | |
| MARTY ROBBINS | 1958 | Columbia 1189 | 100 |
| (Columbia promo label) | | | |
| MARTY'S GREATEST HITS | 1958 | Columbia 1325 | 50 |
| (Columbia promo label) | | | |
| MORE GUNFIGHTER BALLADS & TRAIL SONGS | 1960 | Columbia 1713 | 60 |
| (White promo label) | | | |
| SONG OF ROBBINS, THE | 1957 | Columbia 976 | 150 |
| (Columbia promo label) | | | |
| SONG OF THE ISLANDS | 1957 | Columbia 1087 | 125 |
| (Columbia promo label) | | | |
| **RADIO SHOWS** | | | |
| COUNTRY COOKIN' (Nov 76) Various artists | 1976 | U.S. Army Reserve | 40-75 |
| (One of the four shows features Marty, music and interviews) | | | |
| INTERNATIONAL FESTIVAL OF COUNTRY MUSIC (Oct 82) | 1982 | Mutual Radio | 100-200 |
| (Robbins live on nine songs) | | | |
| SILVER EAGLE, THE (Aug 82) Live concert | 1982 | DIR | 100-150 |
| (With Floyd Cramer) | | | |
| **16-Inch Transcriptions** | | | |
| LEATHERNECK JAMBOREE (50s) | 195? | Public Service | 75-150 |
| (Music and interviews) | | | |
| U. S. ARMY BAND (50s) Various artists | 195? | U.S. Army | 50-75 |
| (Music and interviews, Marty Robbins is host) | | | |
| **Albums** | | | |
| AUTHORIZED RADIO BIOGRAPHY, THE | 1984 | Trailor Communications Tech (4) | 80-120 |
| (Music and interviews) | | | |
| COUNTRY SESSIONS (70s)  Profile | 197? | NBC Radio | 40-75 |
| (Music and interviews) | | | |
| GRAND OL' OPRY | 1961 | WSM Radio | 40-75 |
| (Music and interviews) | | | |
| HERE'S TO VETERANS (60s) | 196? | Veterans Administration | 75-150 |
| (Music and interviews, Marty is host) | | | |
| HOOTENAVY (60s) Public service show | 196? | U. S. Navy | 50-100 |
| (Music and interviews) | | | |

## ROBINS, THE

| Title | Yr | Label, Number | NM $ |
|---|---|---|---|
| **45s** | | | |
| ALL NIGHT BABY | 1953 | RCA Victor 5271 | 300 |
| (White promo label) | | | |
| DON'T STOP NOW | 1953 | RCA Victor 5564 | 175 |
| (White promo label) | | | |
| A FOOL SUCH AS I | 1953 | RCA Victor 5175 | 500 |
| (White promo label) | | | |
| HOW WOULD YOU KNOW | 1953 | RCA Victor 5434 | 250 |
| (White promo label) | | | |
| JUST LIKE THAT | 1960 | Arvee 5001 | 25 |
| (White promo label) | | | |
| LIVE WIRE SUZIE | 1960 | Arvee 5013 | 20 |
| (White promo label) | | | |
| MY BABY DONE TOLD ME | 1953 | RCA Victor 5486 | 200 |
| (White promo label) | | | |
| SMOKEY JOE'S CAFE | 1956 | Atco 6059 | 75 |
| (White promo label) | | | |
| TEN DAYS IN JAIL | 1953 | RCA Victor 5489 | 175 |
| (White promo label) | | | |
| WE LOVED | 1961 | Gone 5101 | 25 |
| (White promo label) | | | |
| **78s** | | | |
| ALL NIGHT BABY | 1953 | RCA Victor 5271 | 200 |
| (White promo label) | | | |
| DON'T STOP NOW | 1953 | RCA Victor 5564 | 150 |
| (White promo label) | | | |
| A FOOL SUCH AS I | 1953 | RCA Victor 5175 | 350 |
| (White promo label) | | | |

| Title | Yr | Label, Number | NM $ |
|---|---|---|---|
| HOW WOULD YOU KNOW | 1953 | RCA Victor 5434 | 200 |
| *(White promo label)* | | | |
| MY BABY DONE TOLD ME | 1953 | RCA Victor 5486 | 150 |
| *(White promo label)* | | | |
| TEN DAYS IN JAIL | 1953 | RCA Victor 5489 | 150 |
| *(White promo label)* | | | |

**ROBINSON, BILL**
**45s**

| | | | |
|---|---|---|---|
| HEAVEN IS THE PLACE | 1955 | DeLuxe 6059 | 75 |
| *(White promo label)* | | | |
| I KNOW SHE'S GONE | 1954 | DeLuxe 6047 | 75 |
| *(White promo label)* | | | |
| LONELY STAR | 1954 | DeLuxe 6030 | 100 |
| *(White promo label)* | | | |
| OH SUGAR | 1955 | DeLuxe 6074 | 75 |
| *(White promo label)* | | | |
| SOMEWHERE SOMEBODY CARES | 1955 | DeLuxe 6057 | 75 |
| *(White promo label)* | | | |

**ROBINSON, SMOKEY**
**12-Inch Singles**

| | | | |
|---|---|---|---|
| (IT'S THE) SAME OLD LOVE (3 versions) | 1990 | Motown L33-17828 | 6 |
| AND I DON'T LOVE YOU (7:10)/(Dub) | 1984 | Tamla 145 | 8 |
| EVERYTHING YOU TOUCH (3 versions)/IT'S THE SAME OLD FEELING | 1990 | Motown L33-18141 | 6 |
| TELL ME TOMORROW/RIGHT IN THE MIDDLE (vocal) (instrumental) | 1982 | Motown PR-92 | 10 |
| *(B-side by Bettye Lavette)* | | | |

**45s**

| | | | |
|---|---|---|---|
| HOLD ON TO YOUR LOVE | 1985 | Motown 1828 | 10 |
| *(White label, includes picture sleeve)* | | | |
| LOVE DON'T GIVE NO REASON | 1987 | Motown 1925 | 10 |
| *(White label, includes picture sleeve)* | | | |
| WHY YOU WANNA SEE | 198? | Monarch | 15 |
| *(White label test pressing)* | | | |

**Albums**

| | | | |
|---|---|---|---|
| MOTOWN SUPERSTAR INTERVIEW | 1986 | Motown PR-179 | 15 |
| *(Promo-only release)* | | | |

**ROBINSON, TOM, BAND**
**12-Inch Singles**

| | | | |
|---|---|---|---|
| WAR BABY/ATMOSPHERICS/LISTEN TO THE RADIO/ RIKKI DON'T LOSE THAT NUMBER | 1984 | Geffen PRO-A-2209 | 6 |

**ROBISON, CARSON**
**45s**

| | | | |
|---|---|---|---|
| ROCKIN' AND ROLLIN' WITH GRANDMA | 1957 | MGM 12266 | 40 |
| *(Yellow promo label)* | | | |

**ROCKETS, THE**
*RSO promo 45s $2 each*
**RADIO SHOWS**
**Albums**

| | | | |
|---|---|---|---|
| IN CONCERT (Feb 82) Live concert | 1982 | Westwood One (2) | 20-30 |
| *(With Loverboy)* | | | |
| KING BISCUIT FLOWER HOUR (June 80) Live concert | 1980 | DIR/ABC (2) | 25-50 |
| *(With Pat Benatar)* | | | |
| KING BISCUIT FLOWER HOUR (Mar 80) Live concert | 1980 | DIR/ABC (2) | 40-75 |
| *(With The Cars)* | | | |

**ROCKPILE**
*Includes Dave Edmunds and Nick Lowe; Columbia promo 45s $3 each*
**RADIO SHOWS**
**Albums**

| | | | |
|---|---|---|---|
| BBC ROCK HOUR (Mar 81) | 1981 | London Wavelength | 40-75 |
| *(Music and interviews)* | | | |
| KING BISCUIT FLOWER HOUR (Sept 81) Live concert | 1981 | DIR/ABC (2) | 40-75 |
| *(With Greg Kihn)* | | | |

**ROCKY FELLERS, THE**
**45s**

| | | | |
|---|---|---|---|
| SANTA SANTA/SANTA'S GROVE | 1963 | Scepter 1245 | 12 |
| *(Promo reissue with new B-side, all-white label with no black oval)* | | | |
| SANTA SANTA (same on both sides) | 196? | Scepter 1245 | 8 |
| *(Promo reissue; white label with mid-1960s Scepter Records black oval logo)* | | | |

**RODGERS, JIMMIE**
*Roulette promo 45s $12 each; Other Dot promo 45s $4 each; A&M promo 45s $3 each*
**45s**

| | | | |
|---|---|---|---|
| IT'S OVER | 1966 | Dot 16861 | 20 |
| *(Blue vinyl, white promo label)* | | | |

**7-Inch Extended Plays**

| | | | |
|---|---|---|---|
| JIMMIE RODGERS | 196? | Roulette 303 | 40 |
| *(White label promo)* | | | |

| Title | Yr | Label, Number | NM $ |
|---|---|---|---|
| **RODGERS, PAUL** | | | |
| *Lead singer of Bad Company and The Firm* | | | |
| **RADIO SHOWS** | | | |
| **Albums** | | | |
| OFF THE RECORD (May 93) | 1993 | Westwood One (2) | 10-15 |
| *(Music and interviews)* | | | |
| **Compact Discs** | | | |
| ELECTRIC LADYLAND (Apr 93) | 1993 | Album Network | 40-75 |
| *(Live concert)* | | | |
| IN CONCERT (Aug 94) | 1994 | Westwood One | 30-50 |
| *(Live concert)* | | | |
| IN CONCERT (Nov 95) | 1995 | Westwood One (2) | 40-75 |
| *(Live concert material)* | | | |
| SUPERSTAR CONCERT (Jan 94) | 1994 | Westwood One (2) | 30-60 |
| *(Live concert)* | | | |
| | | | |
| **ROE, TOMMY** | | | |
| *Other ABC Paramount white promo label 45s $5 each; ABC white promo label 45s $4 each; MGM/South promo 45s $3 each; Monument and Warner promo 45s $2 each; ABC Paramount promo 45s by the Roemans $15 each; ABC promo LPs $10 each* | | | |
| **45s** | | | |
| EVERYBODY | 1963 | ABC-Paramount 10478 | 15 |
| *(White promo label)* | | | |
| SHEILA | 1962 | ABC-Paramount 10329 | 20 |
| *(White promo label)* | | | |
| WHAT'S IT ALL ABOUT (Mar 77) Public service show | 1977 | W.I.A.A. 360 | 18 |
| *(Flip side is Hall & Oates)* | | | |
| **Albums** | | | |
| IT'S NOW WINTER'S DAY | 1967 | ABC-Paramount 594 | 15 |
| *(White promo label)* | | | |
| SHEILA | 1962 | ABC-Paramount 432 | 50 |
| *(White promo label)* | | | |
| SOMETHING FOR EVERYBODY | 1964 | ABC-Paramount 467 | 25 |
| *(White promo label)* | | | |
| SWEET PEA | 1966 | ABC-Paramount 575 | 20 |
| *(White promo label)* | | | |
| | | | |
| **ROGERS, KENNY** | | | |
| *Includes The First Edition; Jolly Roger (MGM) promo 45s $4 each; Reprise promo 45s $3 each; United Artists and RCA promo 45s $2 each; Reprise LPs $5 each; Reprise promo CD singles $2-3 each* | | | |
| **45s** | | | |
| BURIED TREASURE (same on both sides) | 1984 | RCA JK-13713 | 5 |
| CHRISTMAS EVERYDAY | 1981 | Liberty 4065-2 | 10 |
| *(Promo only, standard label)* | | | |
| COWARD OF THE COUNTY | 1979 | United Artists | 15 |
| *(White label test pressing)* | | | |
| HERE'S THAT RAINY DAY | 1966 | Mercury 72545 | 25 |
| *(White promo label)* | | | |
| I'VE GOT A LOT TO LEARN | 1958 | Carlton 468 | 50 |
| *(Promo-only release)* | | | |
| JOLE BLON | 1959 | KEN-LEE 102 | 30 |
| *(Promo-only release)* | | | |
| LOVE OR SOMETHING LIKE IT | 1978 | United Artists | 15 |
| *(White label test pressing)* | | | |
| MAYBE | 1989 | Reprise PRO-S-3904 | 10 |
| *(Promo-only number, with Holly Dunn)* | | | |
| THAT CRAZY FEELING | 1958 | Carlton 454 | 70 |
| *(Promo-only release, blue label, "Kenneth Rogers")* | | | |
| THAT CRAZY FEELING | 1958 | Carlton 454 | 50 |
| *(Promo-only release, blue label, "Kenny Rogers")* | | | |
| WHAT'S IT ALL ABOUT (July 79) Public service show | 1979 | W.I.A.A. 477 | 18 |
| *(Flip side features Ray Charles)* | | | |
| **Albums** | | | |
| GAMBLER, THE | 1979 | United Artists 934 | 50 |
| *(Promo-only picture disc)* | | | |
| HBO PRESENTS KENNY ROGERS | 1983 | Liberty 8344 | 35 |
| *(Promo-only picture disc)* | | | |
| SALES HYPE  With Ken Kragen | 1974 | | 20 |
| *(With the First Edition)* | | | |
| **RADIO SHOWS** | | | |
| **Albums** | | | |
| ROYALTY OF ROCK (80s) Music and interviews | 198? | (2) | 20-40 |
| *(With Neil Diamond)* | | | |
| WESTWOOD ONE PRESENTS (May 89) Music and interviews | 1989 | Westwood One (2) | 25-50 |
| *(With Dolly Parton and Willie Nelson)* | | | |
| | | | |
| **ROGERS, WELDON** | | | |
| **45s** | | | |
| SO LONG, GOOD LUCK AND GOODBYE | 1957 | Imperial 5451 | 100 |
| *(Flip side is "Trying to Get to You" which is actually Roy Orbison, a mixup of master tapes at the studio)* | | | |
| | | | |
| **ROGUES, THE** | | | |
| *Bruce Johnston and Terry Melcher* | | | |
| **45s** | | | |
| C'MON LET'S GO | 1965 | Columbia 43253 | 15 |
| *(White promo label)* | | | |

| Title | Yr | Label, Number | NM $ |
|---|---|---|---|
| EVERYDAY | 1964 | Columbia 43190 | 15 |
| *(White promo label)* | | | |

## ROLLING CREW, THE
**45s**

| | | | |
|---|---|---|---|
| HOME ON ALCATRAZ | 1955 | Aladdin 3301 | 75 |
| *(White promo label)* | | | |

## ROLLING STONES, THE

*Includes listings of Mick Jagger, Keith Richards and other solo acts, and Willie and the Poor Boys; EMI promo 45s by Bowie/Jagger $5 each; Atlantic promo 45s by Bette Midler and Mick Jagger $4 each; Warner Bros. promo 45s by Ron Wood $5 each; Epic promo 45s by Jacksons/Mick Jagger $5 each; Epic promo picture sleeves by Jacksons/Mick Jagger $5 each; EMI promo 45s by Peter Tosh (Rolling Stones label) $3 each*

**12-Inch Singles**

| Title | Yr | Label, Number | NM $ |
|---|---|---|---|
| BEAST OF BURDEN  Bette Midler | 1983 | Atlantic PR-573 | 10 |
| *(Promo 12" single, Mick Jagger appears)* | | | |
| EMOTIONAL RESCUE | 1980 | Rolling Stones PR-367 | 25 |
| *(Promo 12" single)* | | | |
| HARLEM SHUFFLE (same on both sides?) | 1986 | Rolling Stones CAS 2275 | 12 |
| *(Promo 12" single with picture cover)* | | | |
| HOT STUFF | 1976 | Rolling Stones PR-70 | 75 |
| *(Promo-only 12" single, black/blue vinyl)* | | | |
| IF I WAS A DANCER | 1981 | Rolling Stones DMD 253 | 20 |
| *(Promo-only 12" single)* | | | |
| JE SUIS UN ROCK STAR  Bill Wyman | 1981 | A&M 12041 | 15 |
| *(Promo 12" single with picture cover)* | | | |
| JUST ANOTHER NIGHT  Mick Jagger | 1985 | Columbia | 12 |
| *(Red promo label, 12" single with promo picture sleeve)* | | | |
| LUCKY IN LOVE  Mick Jagger | 1985 | Columbia 2060 | 12 |
| *(Red promo label, 12" single with promo picture cover)* | | | |
| MISS YOU | 1978 | Rolling Stones PR-119 | 15 |
| *(Promo 12" single)* | | | |
| MISS YOU/HOT STUFF | 1979 | Rolling Stones DSKO 174 | 20 |
| MIXED EMOTIONS | 1989 | Rolling Stones CAS 1765 | 20 |
| *(Promo-only 12" single)* | | | |
| ONE HIT (TO THE BODY) (London Mix 7:00) (Edit) (LP Version) | 1986 | Rolling Stones CAS 2340 | 15 |
| *(Promo 12" single with promo picture cover)* | | | |
| RUTHLESS PEOPLE Mick Jagger | 1986 | Epic 05931 | 12 |
| *(Promo 12" single)* | | | |
| SEXDRIVE | 1991 | Rolling Stones CAS 4051 | 20 |
| *(Promo-only 12" single, with cover)* | | | |
| SHE WAS HOT/THINK I'M GOING MAD | 1983 | Rolling Stones PR 574 | 25 |
| START ME UP | 1981 | Rolling Stones PR-397 | 25 |
| *(Promo 12" single with picture cover)* | | | |
| TOO MUCH BLOOD | 1984 | Rolling Stones PR-692 | 20 |
| *(Promo-only 12" single)* | | | |
| UNDERCOVER OF THE NIGHT | 1983 | Rolling Stones 685 | 25 |
| *(White promo label 12" single)* | | | |
| UNDERCOVER OF THE NIGHT | 1983 | Rolling Stones 685 | 15 |
| *(Yellow promo label 12" single)* | | | |

**45s**

| Title | Yr | Label, Number | NM $ |
|---|---|---|---|
| 19TH NERVOUS BREAKDOWN | 1966 | London 9823 | 50 |
| *(Brown/orange promo label)* | | | |
| AIN'T TOO PROUD TO BEG | 1974 | Rolling Stones 19302 | 15 |
| *(All blue and all white promo labels, stereo/mono)* | | | |
| ANGIE | 1973 | Rolling Stones 19105 | 20 |
| *(All blue and all white promo labels, stereo/mono)* | | | |
| APACHE WOMAN  Bill Wyman | 1975 | Rolling Stones 19303 | 15 |
| *(All blue and all white promo labels, stereo/mono)* | | | |
| AS TEARS GO BY | 1965 | London 9808 | 50 |
| *(Brown/orange promo label)* | | | |
| BABY PLEASE DON'T GO  Willie and the Poor Boys | 1985 | Passport 7928 | 10 |
| *(Group includes Bill Wyman, Charlie Watts, Paul Rodgers and Jimmy Page; cream colored promo label, price includes stock picture sleeve)* | | | |
| BEAST OF BURDEN | 1978 | Rolling Stones 19309 | 15 |
| *(Blue promo labels, long 4:24/short 3:30 versions)* | | | |
| BEFORE THEY MAKE ME RUN | 1978 | Rolling Stones PR-316 | 50 |
| *(Promo-only record and picture sleeve)* | | | |
| BROWN SUGAR | 1971 | Atco 19100 | 100 |
| *(First promo pressing on Atco instead of Rolling Stones label, both owned by Atlantic)* | | | |
| BROWN SUGAR | 1971 | Rolling Stones 19100 | 25 |
| *(Stereo/mono versions)* | | | |
| BUK-IN-HAMM PALACE  Peter Tosh | 1979 | Rolling Stones 20000 | 10 |
| *(Long 4:29/short 3:45 versions)* | | | |
| DANDELION | 1967 | London 905 | 50 |
| *(Brown/orange promo label)* | | | |
| DON'T LOOK BACK  Peter Tosh | 1978 | Rolling Stones 19308 | 20 |
| *(Price includes stock picture sleeve with Mick and Peter, all blue and all white promo labels with "The Rolling Stones" at top of label, stereo and mono versions)* | | | |
| DOO DOO DOO DOO DOO (HEARTBREAKER) | 1973 | Rolling Stones 19109 | 20 |
| *(All blue and all white promo labels, stereo/mono)* | | | |
| EMOTIONAL RESCUE | 1980 | Rolling Stones 20001 | 10 |
| *(Blue promo labels, long 5:38/short 4:18 versions)* | | | |
| FAR AWAY EYES | 1978 | Rolling Stones 19307 | 150 |
| *(Both sides same, 3:45 versions, rare)* | | | |
| FOOL TO CRY | 1976 | Rolling Stones 19304 | 15 |
| *(Both sides same, 3:59 versions)* | | | |
| GET OFF OF MY CLOUD | 1965 | London 9792 | 50 |
| *(Brown/orange promo label)* | | | |

| Title | Yr | Label, Number | NM $ |
|---|---|---|---|
| GOING TO A GO-GO | 1982 | Rolling Stones 21301 | 10 |
| *(All blue and all white promo labels, live version)* | | | |
| HAPPY | 1972 | Rolling Stones 19104 | 25 |
| *(All blue and all white promo labels, stereo/mono)* | | | |
| HARLEM SHUFFLE | 1986 | Columbia 05802 | 12 |
| *(Both sides same, price includes promo picture sleeve, yellow label)* | | | |
| HAVE YOU SEEN YOUR MOTHER, BABY, STANDING IN THE SHADOW? | 1966 | London 903 | 50 |
| *(Brown/orange promo label)* | | | |
| HEART OF STONE | 1965 | London 9725 | 50 |
| *(Brown/orange promo label)* | | | |
| HONKY TONK WOMEN | 1969 | London 910 | 30 |
| *(Brown/orange promo label)* | | | |
| HOT STUFF | 1976 | Rolling Stones 19304 | 15 |
| *(Both sides same, 5:21 versions)* | | | |
| HOT STUFF | 1976 | Rolling Stones 19304 | 15 |
| *(Long 5:21/short 3:26 versions)* | | | |
| HOT STUFF | 1976 | Rolling Stones 19304 | 30 |
| *(Both sides same, 3:26 versions)* | | | |
| I DON'T KNOW WHY | 1975 | Abkco 4701 | 15 |
| *(Blue promo label)* | | | |
| I WANNA BE YOUR MAN/STONED | 1964 | London 9641 | 600 |
| *(Black, purple and white promo label, stock copy is much more valuable)* | | | |
| IN ANOTHER LAND  Bill Wyman | 1967 | London 907 | 40 |
| *(Brown/orange promo label; credited to Bill Wyman even though it appears on the group LP "Their Satanic Majesties Request")* | | | |
| IT'S ALL OVER NOW | 1964 | London 9687 | 50 |
| *(Brown/orange promo label)* | | | |
| IT'S ONLY ROCK N' ROLL | 1974 | Rolling Stones 19301 | 15 |
| *(All blue and all white promo labels, stereo/mono)* | | | |
| JUMPIN' JACK FLASH | 1968 | London 908 | 50 |
| *(Brown/orange promo label)* | | | |
| JUMPIN' JACK FLASH  Aretha Franklin | 1986 | Arista 9528 | 10 |
| *(Black promo label, clear vinyl, stock picture sleeve w/Aretha and Keith Richards included in price)* | | | |
| JUST ANOTHER NIGHT  Mick Jagger | 1985 | Columbia 04743 | 10 |
| *(Price includes promo picture sleeve)* | | | |
| LAST TIME, THE | 1965 | London 9741 | 75 |
| *(Brown/orange promo label)* | | | |
| LET'S WORK  Mick Jagger | 1987 | Columbia 07306 | 15 |
| *(Price includes picture sleeve)* | | | |
| LUCKY IN LOVE  Mick Jagger | 1985 | Columbia 04893 | 12 |
| *(White promo label with promo picture sleeve)* | | | |
| MAKE NO MISTAKE  Keith Richards | 1988 | Virgin 99240 | 10 |
| *(White promo label, price includes stock picture sleeve)* | | | |
| MISS YOU | 1978 | Rolling Stones 19307 | 15 |
| *(Both sides same, 3:31 versions)* | | | |
| MISS YOU | 1978 | Rolling Stones 19307 | 10 |
| *("Far Away Eyes" on the flip side)* | | | |
| MISS YOU | 1984 | Rolling Stones 99724 | 40 |
| *(Both sides same, 3:33 versions)* | | | |
| MISS YOU | 1984 | Rolling Stones 99724 | 10 |
| *(Flip side is "Too Tough," stock copy worth significantly more)* | | | |
| MOTHERS LITTLE HELPER | 1966 | London 902 | 50 |
| *(Brown/orange promo label)* | | | |
| NOT FADE AWAY | 1964 | London 9657 | 125 |
| *(Black, purple and white promo copy)* | | | |
| ONE HIT (TO THE BODY) | 1986 | Columbia 05906 | 10 |
| *(Both sides same, price includes promo sleeve)* | | | |
| OUT OF TIME | 1975 | Abkco 4702 | 15 |
| *(Blue promo label)* | | | |
| PAINT IT, BLACK | 1966 | London 901 | 50 |
| *(Brown/orange promo label)* | | | |
| RUBY TUESDAY | 1967 | London 904 | 50 |
| *(Brown/orange promo label)* | | | |
| RUN RUDOLPH RUN  Keith Richards | 1978 | Rolling Stones 19311 | 15 |
| *(All blue and all white promo labels, stereo/mono)* | | | |
| RUTHLESS PEOPLE Mick Jagger | 1986 | Epic 06211 | 10 |
| *(White promo label)* | | | |
| SATISFACTION | 1965 | London 9766 | 50 |
| *(Brown/orange promo label)* | | | |
| SAY YOU WILL  Mick Jagger | 1987 | Columbia 07703 | 20 |
| *(Price includes picture sleeve)* | | | |
| SHATTERED | 1978 | Rolling Stones 19310 | 12 |
| *(Blue promo labels, long 3:46/short 2:44 versions)* | | | |
| SHE WAS HOT | 1983 | Rolling Stones 99788 | 10 |
| *(Flip side is "Think I'm Going Mad")* | | | |
| SHE WAS HOT | 1983 | Rolling Stones 99788 | 25 |
| *(Long 4:40/short 3:59 versions)* | | | |
| SHE'S A RAINBOW | 1967 | London 906 | 50 |
| *(Brown/orange promo label)* | | | |
| SHE'S SO COLD | 1980 | Rolling Stones 21001 | 15 |
| *(Blue promo labels, "cleaned-up version" and "God Damn version")* | | | |
| START ME UP | 1981 | Rolling Stones 21003 | 10 |
| *(All blue and all white promo labels)* | | | |
| STREET FIGHTING MAN | 1968 | London 909 | 50 |
| *(Brown/orange promo label)* | | | |
| TAKE IT SO HARD  Keith Richards | 1988 | Virgin 99297 | 10 |
| *(White promo label, price includes stock picture sleeve)* | | | |

| Title | Yr | Label, Number | NM $ |
|---|---|---|---|
| TELL ME | 1964 | London 9682 | 75 |
| (Black and white promo label) | | | |
| THESE ARMS OF MINE  Willie and the Poor Boys | 1985 | Passport 7929 | 10 |
| (Cream colored promo label, stock picture sleeve included in price) | | | |
| THROWAWAY  Mick Jagger | 1987 | Columbia 07653 | 10 |
| (White promo label) | | | |
| TIME IS ON MY SIDE | 1964 | London 9708 | 50 |
| (Brown/orange promo label) | | | |
| TIME IS ON MY SIDE | 1982 | Rolling Stones 99978 | 10 |
| (Both sides same, blue promo label, live version) | | | |
| TIME WAITS FOR NO ONE | 1974 | Rolling Stones 228 | 75 |
| (Price is for record and picture sleeve, promo only) | | | |
| TUMBLING DICE | 1972 | Rolling Stones 19103 | 25 |
| (Long/short versions) | | | |
| UNDERCOVER OF THE NIGHT | 1983 | Rolling Stones 99813 | 10 |
| (Album version 4:31/edited version 3:59) | | | |
| WAITING ON A FRIEND | 1981 | Rolling Stones 21004 | 10 |
| (All blue and all white promo labels) | | | |
| WHAT'S IT ALL ABOUT  Public service show | 1976 | W.I.A.A. 1790 | 35 |
| (Flip side is the Beach Boys) | | | |
| WHAT'S IT ALL ABOUT (Feb 78) Public service show | 1978 | W.I.A.A. 411 | 25 |
| (Flip side is George Benson) | | | |
| WHAT'S IT ALL ABOUT  Public service show | 1980 | W.I.A.A. 218 | 30 |
| (Flip side is Janis Ian) | | | |
| WHAT'S IT ALL ABOUT  Public service show | 1980 | W.I.A.A. 3024 | 30 |
| (Flip side is Chicago) | | | |
| WHAT'S IT ALL ABOUT (Oct 82) Public service show | 1982 | W.I.A.A. 645 | 40 |
| (Flip side is Bob Dylan) | | | |
| WHITE LIGHTNIN'  Bill Wyman | 1974 | Rolling Stones 19111 | 15 |
| (All blue and all white promo labels, stereo/mono) | | | |
| WILD HORSES | 1971 | Rolling Stones 19101 | 35 |
| (Long stereo 5:41/short stereo 3:25 versions, blue promo label) | | | |
| WILD HORSES | 1971 | Rolling Stones 19101 | 25 |
| (Long mono 5:38/short mono 3:25 versions, white promo label) | | | |

**7-Inch Extended Plays**

| Title | Yr | Label, Number | NM $ |
|---|---|---|---|
| 12 X 5  Jukebox LLP | 1968 | London 23 | 400 |
| (Issued with hard cover and title strips) | | | |
| DECEMBER'S CHILDREN  Jukebox LLP | 1968 | London 43 | 400 |
| (Issued with hard cover and title strips) | | | |
| EXILE ON MAIN STREET  Jukebox LLP | 1973 | Atlantic 22900 (LLP 199) | 200 |
| (Issued with paper cover and title strips) | | | |
| GOAT'S HEAD SOUP  Jukebox LLP | 1973 | Atlantic | 125 |
| (Issued with paper cover and title strips) | | | |
| OUT OF OUR HEADS  Jukebox LLP | 1968 | London 37 | 400 |
| (Issued with hard cover and title strips) | | | |
| ROLLING STONES NOW  Jukebox LLP | 1968 | London 34 | 400 |
| (Issued with hard cover and title strips) | | | |
| THEIR SATANIC MAJESTIES REQUEST  Jukebox LLP | 1968 | London 54 | 450 |
| (Issued with non-3D hard cover and title strips) | | | |

**Albums**

| Title | Yr | Label, Number | NM $ |
|---|---|---|---|
| ENGLAND'S NEWEST HIT MAKERS -- THE ROLLING STONES | 1964 | London LL 3375 | 3,000 |
| White label promo | | | |
| INTERVIEW WITH MICK JAGGER BY TOM DONAHUE | 1971 | Rolling Stones 164 | 150 |
| (Yellow promo label) | | | |
| INTERVIEW WITH MICK JAGGER BY TOM DONAHUE | 1971 | Rolling Stones 164 | 200 |
| (White promo label) | | | |
| JAMMING WITH EDWARD  Jagger/Richards/Watts/Ry Cooder/Nicky Hopkins | 1972 | Rolling Stones 39100 | 75 |
| (White promo label) | | | |
| PERFORMANCE  Mick Jagger | 1970 | Warner Bros. 2554 | 40 |
| (White promo label soundtrack) | | | |
| PROMOTIONAL ALBUM, THE | 1969 | London RSD-1 | 1,000 |
| (Promo-only release) | | | |
| ROAD AHEAD, THE  Various artists | 1980 | DIR TRA-12 | 40 |
| (Sponsored by Honda, promo-only sampler of live tracks from "King Biscuit Flower Hour" concerts, special cover) | | | |
| ROLLING STONES (LOVE YOU LIVE) Picture disc | 1977 | Rolling Stones PR-287 | 150 |
| (Promo-only "Brown Sugar" EP picture disc) | | | |
| ROLLING STONES (LOVE YOU LIVE) White promo label | 1977 | Rolling Stones PR-287 | 100 |
| (Promo-only "Brown Sugar" EP for radio stations) | | | |
| SONGS OF THE ROLLING STONES | 1975 | Abkco MPD-1 | 300 |
| (Cover has group in a field) | | | |
| SONGS OF THE ROLLING STONES | 1975 | Abkco MPD-1 | 1,500 |
| (Orange cover, sampler for radio, must have MPD prefix) | | | |
| STICKY FINGERS | 1971 | Rolling Stones 59100 | 300 |
| (White promo label, mono) | | | |
| STICKY FINGERS | 1971 | Rolling Stones 59100 | 250 |
| (White promo label, stereo) | | | |
| THROUGH THE PAST, DARKLY | 1969 | London NPS-3 | 4,000 |
| (Picture disc, has LP graphics from either "Big Hits" or a Ten Years After LP) | | | |

**Compact Discs**

| Title | Yr | Label, Number | NM $ |
|---|---|---|---|
| 1964-1971: A SELECTION OF NO. 1 SINGLES | 1994 | Abkco | 150 |
| (Promo-only sampler) | | | |
| ALMOST HEAR YOU SIGH | 1990 | Rolling Stones CSK 73093 | 25 |
| (Promo-only CD single) | | | |
| ANYBODY SEEN MY BABY | 1997 | Virgin | 15 |
| (Promo-only CD single; no commercial single in U.S.) | | | |
| DESERT ISLAND SURVIVAL KIT | 1994 | Abkco 1848 | 50 |
| (Promo-only record-store sampler) | | | |

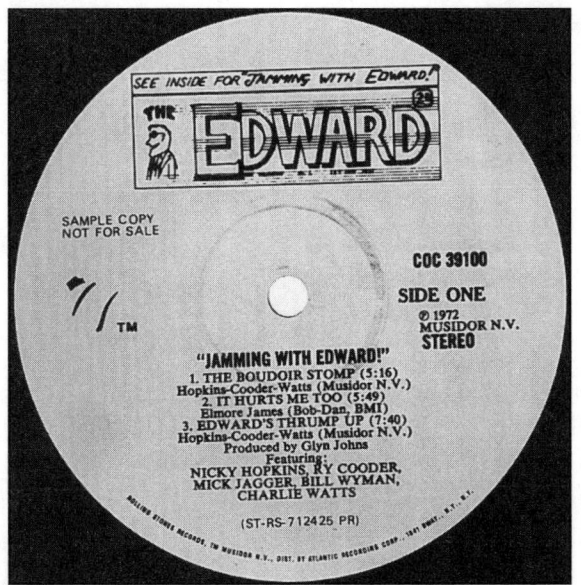

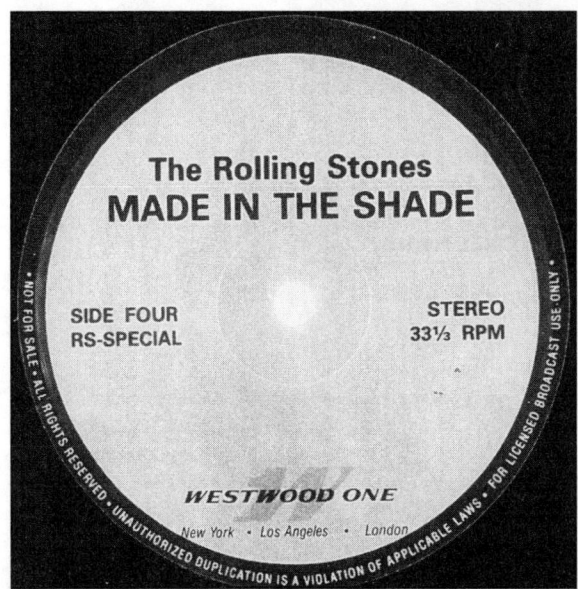

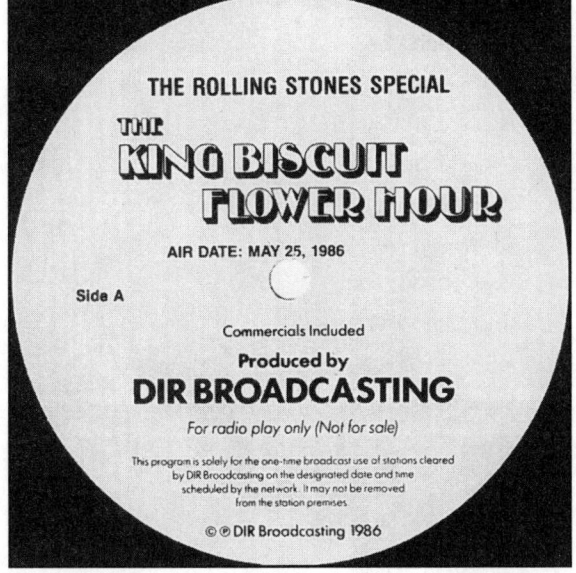

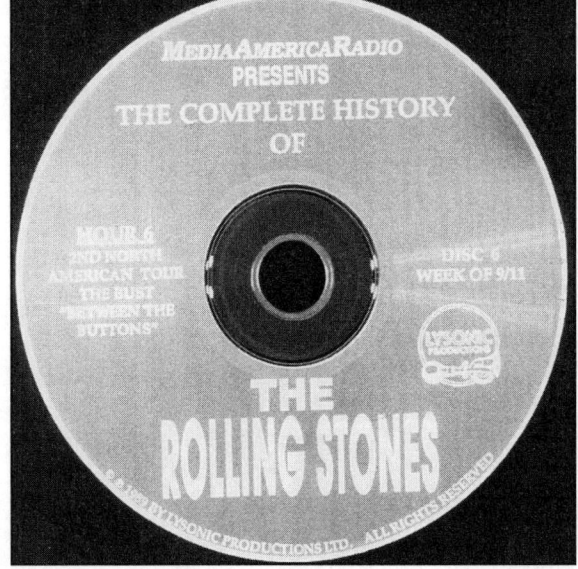

Many collectible promos feature the Rolling Stones, and here are some examples. (Top left) The semi-official *Jamming with Edward*, which features three of the five Stones, is tough to find on stock copy and even tougher as a promo. (Top right) As the Stones are one of the top classic rock acts, special radio shows occur early and often. Here's a part of a Westwood One special called "Made in the Shade." (Middle left) From the tour that eventually gave us the album *Still Life*, here's a Stones appearance on the Super Groups program. (Middle right) Anything to celebrate: This was the King Biscuit Flower Hour's 21st anniversary tribute to the Stones' first tour. (Bottom left) Another special Stones show from the KBFH for the Memorial Day weekend of 1986. (Bottom right) This part of "The Complete History of the Rolling Stones" is from a multi-CD series that aired in 1989 at the time of *Steel Wheels*. Multiple record or disc sets of Stones history are extremely rare and highly collectible, even by many who don't normally collect radio shows.

| Title | Yr | Label, Number | NM $ |
|---|---|---|---|
| DON'T TEAR ME UP  Mick Jagger | 1993 | Atlantic PRCD 5015 | 8 |
| *(Promo-only CD single)* | | | |
| EILEEN  Keith Richards | 1992 | Virgin DPRO-12770 | 8 |
| *(Promo-only CD single)* | | | |
| FLASHPOINT & COLLECTIBLES | 1991 | Columbia C2K 47880 (2) | 50 |
| *(Limited edition, not a promo, in a leather package)* | | | |
| HIGHWIRE | 1991 | Rolling Stones CSK 73742 | 10 |
| *(Promo-only CD single)* | | | |
| I GO WILD | 1995 | Virgin | 15 |
| *(Promo CD single)* | | | |
| INTERVIEW, THE | 1990 | Rolling Stones CSK 1910 | 40 |
| *(Promo-only release)* | | | |
| KEITH IN A CAN (TALK IS CHEAP) Keith Richards | 1988 | Virgin 9047C (3) | 35 |
| *(Three 3" promo CDs)* | | | |
| LIKE A ROLLING STONE | 1995 | Virgin DPRO-11044 | 10 |
| *(Promo-only CD single; no commercial single in U.S.)* | | | |
| LIVE AT THE HOLLYWOOD PALLADIUM  Keith Richards | 1991 | Virgin 50303 | 40 |
| *(Promo-only release, issued with a VHS video, 10,000 pressed)* | | | |
| LIVE AT THE MAX | 1994 | Polygram Video SACD 1004 | 80 |
| *(Promo sampler from the IMAX movie)* | | | |
| LOVE IS STRONG | 1994 | Virgin DPRO-14180 | 10 |
| *(Promo CD single)* | | | |
| MAKING OF SYMPHONIC MUSIC OF THE ROLLING STONES | 1994 | RCA SSP RCD-2 | 20 |
| *(Promo only, music and interviews)* | | | |
| MIXED EMOTIONS | 1989 | Rolling Stones CSK 1755 | 20 |
| *(Promo-only CD single)* | | | |
| NINETEEN GREATEST RADIO HITS | 1991 | Century 21 | 125 |
| *(Promo-only radio release)* | | | |
| OUT OF TEARS | 1994 | Virgin | 20 |
| *(Promo CD single)* | | | |
| RARITIES ON COMPACT DISC VOL. 16 | 1993 | Westwood One | 50 |
| *(Promo, distributed to radio, tracks not generally found on CD in U.S.)* | | | |
| RARITIES ON COMPACT DISC VOL. 20 | 1993 | Westwood One | 50 |
| *(Promo, distributed to radio, more tracks not generally found on CD in U.S.)* | | | |
| ROCK AND A HARD PLACE | 1989 | Rolling Stones CSK 73057 | 15 |
| *(Promo-only CD single)* | | | |
| SAINT OF ME | 1998 | Virgin | 12 |
| *(Promo CD single)* | | | |
| SAY AHH! | 1990 | Rolling Stones CSK 1827 | 75 |
| *(Promo-only release, 17 tracks)* | | | |
| SEXDRIVE | 1991 | Rolling Stones CSK 73789 | 10 |
| *(Promo-only CD single)* | | | |
| SINGLES COLLECTION, THE | 1989 | Abkco 121831 | 40 |
| *(Promo-only release, 6 tracks)* | | | |
| SPARKS WILL FLY | 1994 | Virgin | 20 |
| *(Promo-only CD single; no commercial single in U.S.)* | | | |
| STEEL WHEELS | 1989 | Rolling Stones CSK 1952 | 100 |
| *(Promo-only release in steel can, note promo number)* | | | |
| STONES ON CD: A RADIO SAMPLER | 1986 | Rolling Stones CSK 2498 | 150 |
| *(Promo-only release)* | | | |
| SWEET THING  Mick Jagger | 1993 | Atlantic PRCD 4939 | 8 |
| *(Promo-only CD single, different mix)* | | | |
| SYMPHONIC MUSIC OF THE ROLLING STONES | 1994 | RCA SSP RCD-1 | 20 |
| *(Promo-only sampler)* | | | |
| TAKE IT SO HARD  Keith Richards | 1988 | Virgin PRCD 2396 | 12 |
| *(Promo-only CD single)* | | | |
| TERRIFYING | 1990 | Rolling Stones | 25 |
| *(Promo-only CD single)* | | | |
| TOGETHER AND SOLO | 199? | (3) | 60 |
| *(Promo-only release)* | | | |
| TOO GREAT TO MAKE YOU WAIT | 1992 | Columbia CSK 4004 | 75 |
| *(Promo-only release, five tracks)* | | | |
| VOODOO LOUNGE: A SAMPLER | 1994 | Virgin DPRO-14158 | 40 |
| *(Promo-only sampler)* | | | |
| WANDERING SPIRIT Mick Jagger | 1993 | Atlantic 5002 (2) | 50 |
| *(Music and interviews, 35 segments)* | | | |
| WICKED AS IT SEEMS  Keith Richards | 1992 | Virgin DPRO-12715 | 8 |
| *(Promo-only CD single)* | | | |
| WILD HORSES | 1996 | Virgin DPRO-11075 | 10 |
| *(Promo-only CD single; no commercial single in U.S.)* | | | |
| WIRED ALL NIGHT  Mick Jagger | 1993 | Atlantic PRCD 5020 | 8 |
| *(Promo-only CD single)* | | | |
| YOU DON'T MOVE ME  Keith Richards | 1988 | Virgin PRCD 2557 | 12 |
| *(Promo-only CD release)* | | | |
| YOU GOT ME ROCKING | 1995 | Virgin | 10 |
| *(Promo CD single)* | | | |
| **RADIO SHOWS** | | | |
| **Albums** | | | |
| ALBUM GREATS | 1979 | TM Special Products (7) | 100-150 |
| *(From the 53-LP set, price is for the seven Stones discs)* | | | |
| BBC ROCK HOUR (80s) | 198? | London Wavelength | 30-60 |
| *(Music and interviews)* | | | |
| BBC TRANSCRIPTION DISC ROLLING STONES | 1984 | BBC Transcription (2) | 500-700 |
| *(Music and interviews profile)* | | | |
| BEST OF THE SUPERGROUPS (July 82) Various artists | 1982 | DIR/ABC (3) | 40-100 |
| *(Live concert, includes Stones tracks)* | | | |

| Title | Yr | Label, Number | NM $ |
|---|---|---|---|
| BRITISH INVASION SERIES (June 16-18) | 198? | United Stations (2) | 50-100 |
| *(Part of an ongoing radio series)* | | | |
| BRITISH INVASION SERIES (Aug. 25-27) | 198? | United Stations (2) | 50-100 |
| *(Part of an ongoing radio series)* | | | |
| CONTINUOUS HISTORY OF ROCK & ROLL (Jan 82) | 1982 | Rolling Stone (2) | 30-60 |
| *(Music and interviews)* | | | |
| CONTINUOUS HISTORY OF ROCK & ROLL (Jan 82) | 1982 | Rolling Stone (4) | 50-100 |
| *(Produced by Rolling Stone magazine, two 2-LP sets)* | | | |
| CRAWDADDY RADIO INTERVIEW | 1976 | Crawdaddy Magazine | 100-150 |
| *(One-sided promo-only release for radio)* | | | |
| EARTH NEWS RADIO | 1981 | Earth News | 15-30 |
| *(Daily features, interviews Jagger and Richards)* | | | |
| HOT ROCKS  Mick Jagger | 1986 | United Stations (2) | 40-75 |
| *(Music and interviews)* | | | |
| INSIDE TRACK  Keith Richards | 1982 | RKO (4) | 25-50 |
| *(Music and interviews)* | | | |
| INSIDE TRACK  Keith Richards | 1983 | RKO (2) | 25-50 |
| *(Music and interviews)* | | | |
| INSIDE TRACK (Apr 82)  Keith Richards, Van Zant | 1982 | RKO (3) | 50-80 |
| *(Music and interviews)* | | | |
| INSIDE TRACK (June 83) Mick Jagger, David Lee Roth | 1983 | RKO (3) | 50-100 |
| *(Music and interviews)* | | | |
| INSIDE TRACK (Mar 82)  With David Lee Roth | 1982 | RKO (2) | 40-75 |
| *(Music and interviews)* | | | |
| INSIDE TRACK (Mar 82) Jagger/Richards/Wyman | 1982 | RKO (3) | 50-80 |
| *(Music and interviews)* | | | |
| KING BISCUIT FLOWER HOUR (Apr 80) | 1980 | DIR/ABC (2) | 75-125 |
| *(Error, Elvis Costello listed as artist, live concert by the Stones)* | | | |
| KING BISCUIT FLOWER HOUR (July 80) | 1980 | DIR/ABC (2) | 75-125 |
| *(Live concert)* | | | |
| KING BISCUIT FLOWER HOUR (June 85) | 1985 | DIR (2) | 75-125 |
| *(Live "21st Anniversary Show" concert)* | | | |
| KING BISCUIT FLOWER HOUR (July 85)  Willie and the Poor Boys | 1985 | DIR (2) | 50-100 |
| *(Live concert)* | | | |
| KING BISCUIT FLOWER HOUR (May 86) | 1986 | DIR (2) | 75-125 |
| *(Live concert)* | | | |
| LEGENDS OF ROCK (Mar 87) | 1987 | NBC Radio (4) | 25-50 |
| *(Music and interviews, two parts)* | | | |
| LEGENDS OF ROCK (Mar 87) | 1987 | NBC Radio (2) | 15-30 |
| *(Music and interviews)* | | | |
| LEGENDS OF ROCK (Mar 88) | 1988 | NBC Radio (2) | 30-60 |
| *(Music and interviews, some live tracks)* | | | |
| LEGENDS OF ROCK (Mar 89) Keith Richards | 1989 | NBC Radio (2) | 40-75 |
| *(Music and interviews)* | | | |
| MADE IN THE SHADE (Nov 85) | 1985 | Westwood One (4) | 50-100 |
| *(Music and interviews)* | | | |
| MICK JAGGER SPECIAL | 1982 | London Wavelength | 40-75 |
| *(Music and interviews)* | | | |
| MICK JAGGER UNDERCOVER | 1984 | NBC Source | 40-75 |
| *(Music and interviews)* | | | |
| NBC RADIO (Dec 85) | 1985 | NBC Radio | 20-40 |
| *(Music and interviews)* | | | |
| NBC SOURCE  Mick Jagger | 1983 | NBC Radio | 75-125 |
| *(Music and interviews, promo photo cover)* | | | |
| NBC SOURCE (Jan 83) Mick Jagger | 1983 | NBC Radio (3) | 40-75 |
| *(Music and interviews)* | | | |
| NIGHTBIRD & COMPANY  Various artists/Bill Wyman | 1975 | U.S. Army Reserve (2) | 40-75 |
| *(Wyman is host of one show, plays Rolling Stones hits)* | | | |
| OFF THE RECORD | 1982 | Westwood One (2) | 30-60 |
| *(Music and interviews)* | | | |
| OFF THE RECORD | 1982 | Westwood One (4) | 50-125 |
| *(Music and interviews, two shows)* | | | |
| OFF THE RECORD  Keith Richards | 1982 | Westwood One (4) | 40-100 |
| *(Music and interviews, two shows)* | | | |
| OFF THE RECORD  Keith Richards | 1982 | Westwood One (2) | 25-50 |
| *(Music and interviews)* | | | |
| OFF THE RECORD (Apr 89) Keith Richards | 1989 | Westwood One (2) | 25-50 |
| *(Music and interviews)* | | | |
| OFF THE RECORD (Aug 80) Five Stones and others | 1980 | Westwood One (2) | 20-40 |
| *(Music and interviews)* | | | |
| PROFILES IN ROCK (Jan 80) | 1980 | Watermark | 20-40 |
| *(Music and interviews)* | | | |
| RADIO CONTROL (Nov 87) Mick Jagger | 1987 | DIR (2) | 200-300 |
| *(Mostly music and interviews, rare show)* | | | |
| ROCK & RELIGION (Jan 81) Anti-Stones show | 1981 | | 250-350 |
| *(Music and interviews)* | | | |
| ROCK AND ROLL NEVER FORGETS | 1982 | Westwood One (5) | 75-150 |
| *(Music and interviews)* | | | |
| ROCK AND ROLL NEVER FORGETS (July 84) Brian Jones | 1984 | Westwood One (5) | 125-200 |
| *(Music and interviews)* | | | |
| ROLLING STONES AT THE BEEB | 1983 | London Wavelength (3) | 200-325 |
| *(Music and interviews, box set)* | | | |
| ROLLING STONES PAST & PRESENT (Sept 83) | 1983 | Mutual Radio (12) | 600-850 |
| *(Music and interviews, box set, one of the most sought-after Stones items)* | | | |
| ROLLING STONES STORY (Sept 89) | 1989 | Unistar (3) | 25-40 |
| *(Music and interviews)* | | | |

| Title | Yr | Label, Number | NM $ |
|---|---|---|---|
| ROYALTY OF ROCK | 1982 | (2) | 25-50 |
| (Music and interviews) | | | |
| ROYALTY OF ROCK | 1983 | (2) | 25-40 |
| (Music and interviews) | | | |
| SATISFACTION (Jan 83) | 1983 | Clayton Webster (2) | 75-150 |
| (Music and interviews) | | | |
| SATISFACTION - A TRIBUTE | 1981 | TS-81-1143 | 75-150 |
| (Music and interviews) | | | |
| SILVER ANNIVERSARY SPECIAL | 1988 | United Stations (4) | 100-175 |
| (Career retrospective, music and interviews) | | | |
| SOLID GOLD SCRAPBOOK  Jagger/Stones | 1986 | United Stations (5) | 25-40 |
| (Of the 5-record set only one record features the Stones) | | | |
| SONIC WORKSHOP (Sept 82) | 1982 | (12) | 400-500 |
| (Music and interviews; Canadian version of sought-after Mutual Radio 12-LP box set show) | | | |
| SPECIAL (Aug 86) | 1986 | (4) | 40-75 |
| (Music and interviews) | | | |
| SPOTLIGHT SPECIAL (Mar 83) | 1983 | ABC Radio (2) | 75-150 |
| (Music and interviews, box set) | | | |
| SUPERGROUPS (Oct 81) | 1981 | DIR/ABC (3) | 150-200 |
| (Live concert) | | | |
| SUPERSTAR CONCERT | 1982 | Westwood One (3) | 100-150 |
| (Live concert, box set) | | | |
| TIME IS ON OUR SIDE (Nov 85) | 1985 | Westwood One (8) | 100-175 |
| (Music and interviews) | | | |
| **Compact Discs** | | | |
| 30 YEARS OF THE ROLLING STONES (May 93) | 1993 | Westwood One (6) | 175-250 |
| (Music and Interviews and many live tracks) | | | |
| BBC CLASSIC TRACKS (Dec 90) | 1990 | Westwood One | 75-125 |
| (Live tracks) | | | |
| BBC CLASSIC TRACKS (Sept 91) | 1991 | Westwood One | 60-90 |
| (Live tracks) | | | |
| BBC CLASSIC TRACKS (Dec 91) | 1991 | Westwood One | 50-75 |
| (Live tracks) | | | |
| BBC CLASSIC TRACKS (Mar 93) | 1993 | Westwood One | 30-60 |
| (Live tracks, repeated June 93) | | | |
| BBC CLASSIC TRACKS (Jan 94) | 1994 | Westwood One | 25-45 |
| (Live tracks) | | | |
| BBC CLASSIC TRACKS (Nov 94) | 1994 | Westwood One | 35-50 |
| (Live tracks from new tour) | | | |
| COMPLETE HISTORY OF THE ROLLING STONES | 1990 | Media America (16) | 480 |
| (Sixteen weekly single-CD one-hour shows) | | | |
| COMPLETE HISTORY OF THE ROLLING STONES | 1990 | Media America (20) | 600-750 |
| (Complete series set with pilot) | | | |
| COMPLETE HISTORY OF THE ROLLING STONES | 1994 | Media America (21) | 1,000-1,200 |
| (Updated version, music and interviews) | | | |
| COMPLETE HISTORY OF THE ROLLING STONES (Nov 89) | 1989 | Media America (4) | 125 |
| (Pilot show for the series) | | | |
| GLOBAL SATELLITE (May 93) | 1993 | Global Network (2) | 200-275 |
| (Music and interviews, rare show) | | | |
| IN THE STUDIO (90s) | 199? | Album Network | 30-60 |
| (Music and interview, profile of an album) | | | |
| KING BISCUIT FLOWER HOUR (June 88)  Mick Jagger | 1988 | DIR (2) | 125-200 |
| (Live concert, "Under Radio Control") | | | |
| KING BISCUIT FLOWER HOUR (Nov 88) | 1988 | DIR | 200-300 |
| (Live concert) | | | |
| KING BISCUIT FLOWER HOUR (Sept 87) | 1987 | DIR | 250-300 |
| (Live concert, the very rare silver CD) | | | |
| KING BISCUIT FLOWER HOUR (Sept 89) | 1989 | DIR | 100-175 |
| (Live concert) | | | |
| KING BISCUIT FLOWER HOUR (Dec 90) | 1990 | DIR | 50-75 |
| (Live concert, repeated several times) | | | |
| KING BISCUIT FLOWER HOUR (June 95) | 1995 | DIR | 50-75 |
| (Live concert) | | | |
| LIVE AT ELECTRIC LADYLAND (Nov 92)  Ron Wood | 1992 | Westwood One | 100-200 |
| (Live concert) | | | |
| LIVE AT THE VOODOO LOUNGE (Sept 94) | 1994 | Westwood One (6) | 350-500 |
| (Music and interviews with some live tracks) | | | |
| MASTERS OF ROCK (Sept 90) | 1990 | Radio Ventures (2) | 100-200 |
| (Mostly music and interviews) | | | |
| OFF THE RECORD (Sept 94) | 1994 | Westwood One | 25-40 |
| (Music and interviews, Voodoo Lounge) | | | |
| OFF THE RECORD (Oct 94) | 1994 | Westwood One | 25-40 |
| (Continuation of above show) | | | |
| OFF THE RECORD (Nov 94) | 1994 | Westwood One | 25-40 |
| (Continuation of above show) | | | |
| OFF THE RECORD (June 95) | 1995 | Westwood One | 25-40 |
| (With the Toadies and Charlie Sexton) | | | |
| OFF THE RECORD (July 95) | 1995 | Westwood One | 25-40 |
| (Music and interviews) | | | |
| ON TOUR SPECIAL (Feb 95)  Keith Richards | 1995 | Album Network | 125-250 |
| (Live concert) | | | |
| ROCK AND ROLL GREATS (May 92) | 1992 | | 40-75 |
| (Music and interviews) | | | |
| ROLLING STONES 25TH ANNIVERSARY SPECIAL (Nov 89) | 1989 | ABC Radio (4) | 200-325 |
| (Music and interviews) | | | |
| SUPERSTARS | 1995 | (2) | 200-250 |
| (Live concert material) | | | |

| Title | Yr | Label, Number | NM $ |
|---|---|---|---|
| SUPERSTARS | 1996 | (2) | 125-175 |
| *(Live concert material)* | | | |
| TIME IS ON OUR SIDE (May 93) | 1993 | Westwood One (6) | 175-250 |
| *(Music and interviews)* | | | |
| TIMOTHY WHITE SESSIONS (Jan 93)  Keith Richards | 1993 | Westwood One (2) | 100-200 |
| *(Live tracks, music and interviews)* | | | |
| UP CLOSE | 1990 | Media America (2) | 75-125 |
| *(Mostly music and interviews)* | | | |
| UP CLOSE | 1991 | Media America (4) | 125-225 |
| *(Mostly music and interviews)* | | | |
| UP CLOSE  Mick Jagger | 1993 | Media America (2) | 80-140 |
| *(Mostly music and interviews)* | | | |
| UP CLOSE  Keith Richards | 1988 | Media America (4) | 275-400 |
| *(Mostly music and interviews)* | | | |
| UP CLOSE  Keith Richards | 1988 | Media America (2) | 100-200 |
| *(Part of the above show)* | | | |
| UP CLOSE  Keith Richards | 1993 | Media America (3) | 100-200 |
| *(Mostly music and interviews)* | | | |
| WORLD'S GREATEST ROCK AND ROLL BAND (May 91) | 1991 | Unistar | 50-85 |
| *(Music and interviews)* | | | |
| **Reel-to-Reel Tapes** | | | |
| KING BISCUIT FLOWER HOUR (June 78) | 1978 | DIR/ABC (2) | 125-200 |
| *(Live concert on two reels with Peter Tosh)* | | | |
| KING BISCUIT FLOWER HOUR (Apr 79) | 1979 | DIR/ABC (2) | 100-150 |
| *(Live concert on two reels)* | | | |
| KING BISCUIT FLOWER HOUR (Apr 80) | 1980 | DIR/ABC (2) | 90-150 |
| *(Error, Elvis Costello listed as artist, live concert by the Stones on reel tapes)* | | | |

## ROMAN, DICK
**45s**

| Title | Yr | Label, Number | NM $ |
|---|---|---|---|
| CHRISTMAS VILLAGE/CLIMB EVERY MOUNTAIN | 19?? | Harmon 1011 | 3 |

## ROMANTICS, THE
*Nemperor promo 45s $3 each*
**12-Inch Singles**

| Title | Yr | Label, Number | NM $ |
|---|---|---|---|
| NATIONAL BREAKOUT/21 AND OVER | 1980 | Nemperor AS 870 | 10 |
| ONE IN A MILLION/OPEN UP YOUR DOOR/ROCK YOU UP | 1983 | Nemperor AS 1814 | 10 |
| SHE'S HOT/BOP/LOOK AT HER/CAN'T GET OVER YOU | 1981 | Nemperor AS 1330 | 10 |
| TEST OF TIME (same on both sides) | 1985 | Nemperor AS 2168 | 5 |

**RADIO SHOWS**
**Albums**

| Title | Yr | Label, Number | NM $ |
|---|---|---|---|
| IN CONCERT (July 84) Live concert | 1984 | Westwood One | 30-60 |
| *(Repeated)* | | | |
| KING BISCUIT FLOWER HOUR  Live concert | 1982 | DIR/ABC (2) | 25-40 |
| *(With Nick Heywood)* | | | |
| KING BISCUIT FLOWER HOUR (Feb 82) Live concert | 1982 | DIR/ABC (2) | 100-200 |
| *(With Joan Jett)* | | | |
| KING BISCUIT FLOWER HOUR (May 84) Live concert | 1984 | DIR/ABC (2) | 30-60 |
| *(Repeated)* | | | |

## ROMEOS, THE
**45s**

| Title | Yr | Label, Number | NM $ |
|---|---|---|---|
| JINGLE BELLS JAM/SERIOUSLY AFFECTED | | Columbia AE7 1222 | 8 |

## RONETTES, THE
*With Ronnie Spector; Other Philles promo label 45s $20 each; Buddah promo label 45s $8 each*
**45s**

| Title | Yr | Label, Number | NM $ |
|---|---|---|---|
| BABY, I LOVE YOU | 1963 | Philles 118 | 40 |
| *(White promo label)* | | | |
| BREAKIN' UP | 1964 | Philles 120 | 30 |
| *(White promo label)* | | | |
| DO I LOVE YOU? | 1964 | Philles 121 | 30 |
| *(White promo label)* | | | |
| GOOD GIRLS | 1962 | May 138 | 60 |
| *(Promo label)* | | | |
| HE DID IT | 1964 | Dimension 1046 | 75 |
| *(Blue promo label)* | | | |
| I'M GONNA QUIT WHILE I'M AHEAD | 1962 | Colpix 646 | 50 |
| *(White promo label)* | | | |
| SILHOUETTES | 1962 | May 114 | 75 |
| *(Promo label)* | | | |
| WALKIN' IN THE RAIN | 1964 | Philles 123 | 30 |
| *(White promo label)* | | | |
| **Albums** | | | |
| A CHRISTMAS GIFT FOR YOU  Various artists | 1963 | Philles 4005 | 750 |
| *(White promo label)* | | | |
| PRESENTING THE FABULOUS RONETTES | 1965 | Philles 4006 | 500 |
| *(Rare white promo label)* | | | |
| THE RONETTES, FEATURING VERONICA | 1965 | Colpix 486 | 1,000 |
| *(White promo label)* | | | |

## RONNY AND THE DAYTONAS
**45s**

| Title | Yr | Label, Number | NM $ |
|---|---|---|---|
| 4-CAST SHE'LL LOVE ME AGAIN | 1968 | Show Biz 21207 | 20 |
| *(One-sided promo)* | | | |

| Title | Yr | Label, Number | NM $ |
|---|---|---|---|

## RONSON, MICK
**7-Inch Extended Plays**

| | | | |
|---|---|---|---|
| SLAUGHTER ON 10TH AVENUE/GROWING UP AND I'M FINE// ALL CUT UP ON YOU/ANDY WARHOL | 1974 | RCA Victor DJEO-0259 | 12 |
| *Promo-only EP with B-side by Dana Gillespie* | | | |

## RONSTADT, LINDA
*Capitol promo 45s $3-5 each; Asylum promo 45s $3 each; ;Elektra promo CD singles $2-3 each*

**12-Inch Singles**

| | | | |
|---|---|---|---|
| BLUE BAYOU/LAGO AZUL | 1977 | Asylum AS 11431 | 30 |
| *(Blue vinyl)* | | | |
| LIVING LIKE A FOOL (same on both sides) | 1977 | Capitol ST-1003 | 40 |
| *(Red vinyl; yellow "SM" label with Capitol tower)* | | | |
| LIVING LIKE A FOOL (same on both sides) | 1977 | Capitol ST-1003 | 30 |
| *(Red vinyl; yellow label, "Capitol" in red at bottom)* | | | |
| WHAT'S NEW (same on both sides) | 1983 | Asylum 4935 | 8 |

**45s**

| | | | |
|---|---|---|---|
| LAGO AZUL | 1977 | Asylum 45464 | 10 |
| *(White promo label, "Blue Bayou" in Spanish)* | | | |
| SO FINE | 1966 | Sidewalk 937 | 100 |
| *(Promo label)* | | | |
| SPUN GOLD HITS KIT  Five reissue singles | 1980 | Asylum | 40 |
| *(Price includes all five singles plus box; most of the value is in the box, as records were available separately for years)* | | | |
| WHAT'S IT ALL ABOUT (May 75) Public service show | 1975 | W.I.A.A. 265 | 18 |
| *(Flip side features Fanny)* | | | |
| WHAT'S NEW | 1983 | Asylum | 10 |
| *(White label test pressing)* | | | |
| YOU'RE NO GOOD | 1974 | Capitol | 15 |
| *(White label test pressing)* | | | |

**Compact Discs**

| | | | |
|---|---|---|---|
| SONY DIGITAL MASTERS SERIES | 199? | Sony/Elektra | 40 |
| *(Promo-only sampler)* | | | |

**RADIO SHOWS**

**Albums**

| | | | |
|---|---|---|---|
| DIR SPECIAL (July 82)  With James Taylor and Paul Simon | 1982 | DIR (3) | 100-200 |
| *(Rare live concert)* | | | |
| RHYMES, RHYTHM & ROMANCE (May 90) | 1990 | Westwood One (2) | 20-40 |
| *(Music and interviews)* | | | |
| ROYALTY OF ROCK | 1982 | Watermark | 20-35 |
| *(Music and interviews)* | | | |

## ROOFTOP SINGERS, THE
**45s**

| | | | |
|---|---|---|---|
| WALK RIGHT IN | 1962 | Vanguard (no #) | 20 |
| *(With promo-only title sleeve, "From the Company That Gave You...")* | | | |

## ROSS, DIANA
*Other Motown white promo label 45s (including duets) $4; RCA Victor cream colored promo label 45s $3 each; RCA Victor white promo label 45s $4 each; Columbia promo duet 45s $3 each; Columbia promo picture sleeve duets $3 each*

**12-Inch Singles**

| | | | |
|---|---|---|---|
| BOTTOM LINE (4 versions) | 1989 | Motown L33-18048 | 7 |
| CHAIN REACTION (6:52) (same on both sides) | 1985 | RCA JR-14267 | 8 |
| EATEN ALIVE/(Instrumental) | 1985 | RCA JD-14183 | 8 |
| IT'S MY HOUSE//NO ONE GETS THE PRIZE/THE BOSS | 1979 | Motown PR 54 | 15 |
| LOVE HANGOVER '89 (5 versions) | 1989 | Motown L33-17770 | 8 |
| PARADISE (3 versions) | 1989 | Motown L33-17909 | 8 |
| THIS HOUSE (4:20) (5:34) | 1989 | Motown L33-17963 | 8 |
| WHAT YOU GAVE ME (6:06) (same on both sides) | 1978 | Motown PR 42 | 15 |
| WORKIN' OVERTIME (6 versions) | 1989 | Motown L33-17827 | 8 |

**45s**

| | | | |
|---|---|---|---|
| AIN'T NO MOUNTAIN HIGH ENOUGH | 1970 | Motown 1169 | 25 |
| *(White promo label, red vinyl, edited 3:15 versions)* | | | |
| DREAMING OF YOU  With Lionel Richie | 1981 | (no label) PR 571 | 10 |
| *(White promo label, Polygram pressing)* | | | |
| EASE ON DOWN THE ROAD  With Michael Jackson | 1978 | MCA/Motown 40947 | 10 |
| *(White promo label, price includes stock picture sleeve)* | | | |
| ENDLESS LOVE | 1981 | RCA Victor 13013 | 25 |
| *(Black promo label, white vinyl, long 4:55 and short 3:47 versions)* | | | |
| LADY SINGS THE BLUES  Radio spots | 1972 | Paramount Pictures | 150 |
| *(Cream colored label, five tracks, one-sided)* | | | |
| MAHOGANY  Radio spots | 1976 | Paramount Pictures | 125 |
| *(Yellow label, six tracks, one-sided record)* | | | |
| MAHOGANY/LADY SINGS THE BLUES  Radio spots | 1976 | Paramount Pictures | 125 |
| *(Yellow label, four tracks, 30 and 60 seconds each, one-sided, movie spots are from both movies)* | | | |
| MY OLD PIANO | 1980 | Motown 1531 | 10 |
| *(Price includes promo-only picture sleeve)* | | | |
| POPS, WE LOVE YOU  Various artists | 1978 | Motown 1455 | 15 |
| *(White promo label, green vinyl, artists are Diana Ross, Marvin Gaye, Smokey Robinson and Stevie Wonder)* | | | |
| REACH OUT I'LL BE THERE | 1971 | Motown 1184 | 25 |
| *(White promo label, red vinyl)* | | | |
| THEME FROM MAHOGANY | 1975 | Motown 1377 | 20 |
| *(White promo label, yellow vinyl)* | | | |
| WHAT'S IT ALL ABOUT (Mar 80) Public service show | 1980 | W.I.A.A. 515 | 20 |
| *(Flip side features Randy Vanwarmer)* | | | |

| Title | Yr | Label, Number | NM $ |
|---|---|---|---|

**Albums**
THE BOSS — 1979 — Motown 923 — 30
*(White promo label, gold vinyl)*
**RADIO SHOWS**
**Albums**
ROYALTY OF ROCK Music and interviews — 1983 — (2) — 40-75
*(With Barbra Streisand)*

## ROSSINGTON-COLLINS BAND
*MCA promo 45s $3 each Formed from the ashes of Lynyrd Skynyrd*
**Albums**
A CONVERSATION WITH ROSSINGTON-COLLINS BAND — 1980 — MCA — 10
*(Promo-only release)*
**RADIO SHOWS**
**Albums**
IN CONCERT (Jan 82) Live concert — 1982 — Westwood One (2) — 50-100
*(With the Henry Paul Band)*
IN CONCERT (June 82) Live concert — 1982 — Westwood One (2) — 40-75
A NIGHT ON THE ROAD — 1981 — ABC Radio (3) — 40-75
*(Music and interviews)*
**Reel-to-Reel Tapes**
KING BISCUIT FLOWER HOUR (Aug 78) Various artists — 1978 — DIR/ABC (2) — 50-100
*(Superjam in two reels)*

## ROTH, DAVID LEE
*Formerly of Van Halen; Warner Bros. promo 45s $3 each; Warner Bros. promo 12" singles $7 each*
**RADIO SHOWS**
**Albums**
INSIDE TRACK (June 83) With Joan Jett and Mick Jagger — 1983 — RKO (2) — 40-75
*(Music and interviews)*
MEMORIAL DAY PARTY (May 84) Box set — 1984 — NBC Source (6) — 50-100
*(Van Halen material, David Lee Roth is the host)*
OFF THE RECORD — 1991 — Westwood One (2) — 15-25
*(Music and interviews)*
PROFILE 86 (Apr 86) — 1986 — NBC Radio (2) — 25-40
*(A profile of David Lee Roth with Van Halen material included)*
SUPERSTAR CONCERT (Dec 86) — 1986 — Westwood One (3) — 50-100
*(Live concert with Van Halen)*
**Compact Discs**
UP CLOSE — 1988 — Media America (2) — 25-50
*(Music and interviews)*
UP CLOSE — 1990 — Media America (2) — 45-75
*(Music and interviews)*
UP CLOSE — 1994 — Media America (2) — 25-50
*(Music and interviews)*

## ROWLAND, DAVE, AND SUGAR
**45s**
WINTER WONDERLAND/RUDOLPH THE RED-NOSED REINDEER — 1981 — Elektra 47234 — 8
*B-side by Mel and Nancy (Tillis and Sinatra)*

## ROXETTE
*Other EMI promo 45s $3 each; Other EMI promo CD singles $3-5 each*
**45s**
LISTEN TO YOUR HEART (same on both sides) — 1989 — EMI 7PRO-04409 — 8
*(Vinyl originally was promo only)*
**Compact Discs**
DANGEROUS — 1989 — EMI — 10
*(White disc with LP and 12" versions)*
DANGEROUS — 1989 — EMI DPRO-4445 — 10
*(Yellow disc with LP and two "club" versions)*
IT MUST HAVE BEEN LOVE — 1990 — EMI DPRO-4515 — 10
*(Pink and white disc, single and LP versions)*
LISTEN TO YOUR HEART — 1989 — EMI DPRO-4399 — 10
*(Black disc, edit and LP versions, many copies have round sticker on front of jewel box)*
LISTEN TO YOUR HEART — 1989 — EMI DPRO-04417 — 10
*(Red disc with LP version and two remixes. Infamous as the first No. 1 record not to be available on 45 since 1950, though a 45 was released a year later)*
**RADIO SHOWS**
**Albums**
THE STORY OF ROXETTE (Sept 91) — 1991 — Unistar (2) — 15-25
*(Music and interviews)*

## ROXY MUSIC
*Other Atco promo 45s $4 each; Any label promo 45s by Bryan Ferry $3 each Featuring Bryan Ferry*
**12-Inch Singles**
MORE THAN THIS/AVALON — 1982 — Warner Bros. PRO-A-2033 — 10
TAKE A CHANCE WITH ME (2 versions)/MORE THAN THIS/AVALON — 1982 — Warner Bros. PRO-A-1056 — 12
**45s**
JEALOUS GUY — 1981 — Atco 7329 — 10
*(USA promo of a worldwide John Lennon classic, long 6:10 and short 3:40 versions)*
LOVE IS THE DRUG — 1975 — Atco — 15
*(White label test pressing)*
LOVE IS THE DRUG — 1975 — Atco 7042 — 10
*(Long 3:58 and short 3:00 versions)*

| Title | Yr | Label, Number | NM $ |
|---|---|---|---|
| WHAT'S IT ALL ABOUT (July 79) Public service show | 1979 | W.I.A.A. 482 | 18 |
| *(Flip side features Hoyt Axton)* | | | |
| **RADIO SHOWS** | | | |
| **Albums** | | | |
| BBC COLLEGE CONCERT HOUR (July 83) | 1983 | London Wavelength | 60-100 |
| *(Live concert)* | | | |
| BBC ROCK HOUR  Bryan Ferry | 1983 | London Wavelength | 25-40 |
| *(Music and interviews)* | | | |
| BBC ROCK HOUR (July 83) | 1983 | London Wavelength | 60-100 |
| *(Live concert)* | | | |
| BBC TRANSCRIPTION DISC | 1972 | BBC Transcription | 100-150 |
| *(Live concert with Atomic Rooster)* | | | |
| BBC TRANSCRIPTION DISC | 1974 | BBC Transcription | 300-400 |
| *(Live concert with Roxy Music)* | | | |
| IN CONCERT (Oct 92) Live concert | 1992 | Westwood One (2) | 30-50 |
| *(With Blue and Nirvana)* | | | |
| INSIDE TRACK (Sept 83) | 1983 | RKO (3) | 25-40 |
| *(With David Byrne and Ray Davies)* | | | |
| KING BISCUIT FLOWER HOUR (Aug 83) | 1983 | DIR/ABC (2) | 60-120 |
| *(Live concert)* | | | |
| KING BISCUIT FLOWER HOUR (July 85) | 1985 | DIR (2) | 50-100 |
| *(Live concert with Graham Parker)* | | | |
| KING BISCUIT FLOWER HOUR (Sept 80) | 1980 | DIR/ABC (2) | 75-125 |
| *(Live concert)* | | | |
| NIGHTBIRD & COMPANY (Aug 74) Various artists | 1974 | U.S. Army Reserve (2) | 25-40 |
| *(Bryan Ferry is host of one show, Buffy Sainte-Marie is host of another)* | | | |
| ROCK CLOCK  With others | 1987 | DIR (2) | 25-50 |
| *(Mostly music and interviews)* | | | |
| SOURCE CONCERT (Aug 83) | 1983 | NBC Radio (2) | 75-125 |
| *(Live concert)* | | | |
| **Compact Discs** | | | |
| BBC CLASSIC TRACKS (Dec 91) | 1991 | Westwood One | 20-35 |
| *(Classic live tracks)* | | | |
| IN CONCERT-NU ROCK (Mar 95) Bryan Ferry/Roxy Music | 1995 | Westwood One | 40-75 |
| *(Live concert)* | | | |
| KING BISCUIT FLOWER HOUR (Feb 88) | 1988 | DIR | 40-75 |
| *(Repeated several times)* | | | |

**ROYAL TONES, THE**
*Other Old Town promo 45s $30 each*
**45s**

| Title | Yr | Label, Number | NM $ |
|---|---|---|---|
| CRAZY LOVE | 1956 | Old Town 1018 | 75 |
| *(White promo label)* | | | |
| LATIN LOVE | 1956 | Old Town 1028 | 50 |
| *(White promo label)* | | | |

**ROYAL, BILLY JOE**
**45s**

| Title | Yr | Label, Number | NM $ |
|---|---|---|---|
| ANCHORS AWEIGH (mono/stereo) | 1979 | Private Stock 45,212 | 5 |
| DOWN IN THE BOONDOCKS (same on both sides) | 1965 | Columbia 43305 | 40 |
| *(Red vinyl promo)* | | | |

**ROYALS, THE**
**45s**

| Title | Yr | Label, Number | NM $ |
|---|---|---|---|
| GIVE IT UP/THAT WOMAN | 1954 | Federal 12177 | 100 |
| *(Evidently, some promos exist crediting The Royals; stock copies credit "The Midnighters")* | | | |

**RTZ**
*Giant promo CD singles $2-3 each*
**RADIO SHOWS**
**Albums**

| Title | Yr | Label, Number | NM $ |
|---|---|---|---|
| IN CONCERT Live concert | 1991 | Westwood One (2) | 30-60 |
| *(With the BoDeans)* | | | |

**RUBINOOS, THE**
*Other Beserkley white label promo 45s $5 each; Warner Bros. promo 45s $4 each; Warner Bros. white promo label LPs $10 each*
**45s**

| Title | Yr | Label, Number | NM $ |
|---|---|---|---|
| HOLD ME | 1979 | Beserkley 5750 | 10 |
| *(Black promo label)* | | | |
| I THINK WE'RE ALONE NOW | 1976 | Beserkley 5741 | 12 |
| *(Black/yellow promo label, price includes stock picture sleeve)* | | | |
| NOTHING A LITTLE LOVE WON'T CURE | 1977 | Columbia | 15 |
| *(White label test pressing)* | | | |
| NOTHING A LITTLE LOVE WON'T CURE | 1977 | Beserkley 5810 | 10 |
| *(White promo label)* | | | |
| **7-Inch Extended Plays** | | | |
| GREAT IDEAS FROM BESERKLEY  Various artists | 1977 | Beserkley | 12 |
| *(White promo label, small center hole, promo paper sleeve, includes "Rock & Roll is Dead" by The Rubinoos)* | | | |

**RUBY**
**10-Inch Singles**

| Title | Yr | Label, Number | NM $ |
|---|---|---|---|
| PARAFFIN (4 mixes) | 1996 | Work 30S 7512 | 6 |
| *(On red vinyl in plastic sleeve)* | | | |

AMPEX RECORDS

RUNT
Todd Rundgren

A10105A
Side 1

D. J. COPY
NOT FOR SALE

33⅓ RPM
STEREO

1. BROKE DOWN AND BUSTED        4:32
2. BELIEVE IN ME                2:04
3. WE GOT TO GET YOU A WOMAN    2:52
4. WHO'S THAT MAN               2:59
5. ONCE BURNED                  2:09
6. DEVIL'S BITE                 3:53

ALL SONGS WRITTEN BY TODD RUNDGREN
EARMARK MUSIC/BMI

AMPEX RECORDS, 555 MADISON AVENUE, NEW YORK CITY 10022 — MADE IN U.S.A.

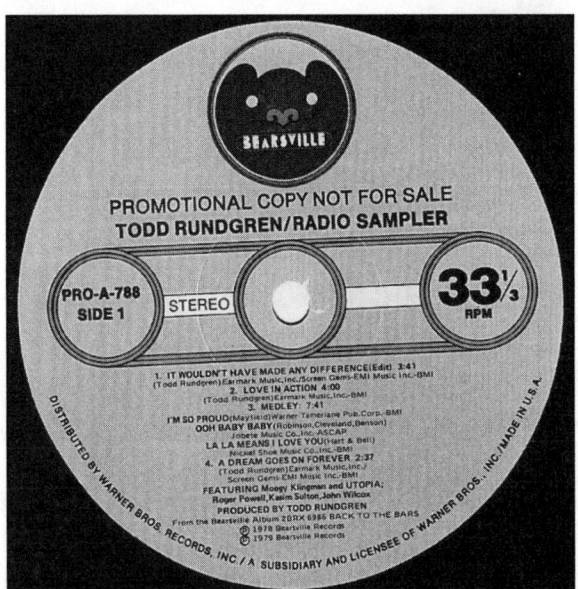

BEARSVILLE

PROMOTIONAL COPY NOT FOR SALE
TODD RUNDGREN/RADIO SAMPLER

PRO-A-788
SIDE 1      STEREO      33⅓ RPM

1. IT WOULDN'T HAVE MADE ANY DIFFERENCE(Edit) 3:41
(Todd Rundgren)Earmark Music,Inc/Screen Gems-EMI Music Inc-BMI
2. LOVE IN ACTION 4:00
(Todd Rundgren)Earmark Music,Inc-BMI
3. MEDLEY: 7:41
I'M SO PROUD(Mayfield)Warner Tamerlane Pub.Corp.-BMI
OOH BABY BABY (Robinson, Cleveland, Benson)
Jobete Music Co.,Inc-ASCAP
LA LA MEANS I LOVE YOU(Hart & Bell)
Nickel Shoe Music Co.,Inc-BMI
4. A DREAM GOES ON FOREVER 2:37
(Todd Rundgren)Earmark Music,Inc./
Screen Gems-EMI Music Inc-BMI
FEATURING Moogy Klingman and UTOPIA;
Roger Powell,Kasim Sulton,John Wilcox
PRODUCED BY TODD RUNDGREN
℗ 1978 Bearsville Records
℗ 1979 Bearsville Records
From the Bearsville Album 2BDX 6986 BACK TO THE BARS

DISTRIBUTED BY WARNER BROS. RECORDS, INC./ A SUBSIDIARY AND LICENSEE OF WARNER BROS., INC. MADE IN U.S.A.

TODD RUNDGREN

THE
KING BISCUIT FLOWER HOUR

AIR DATE: DECEMBER 15, 1985

Side A

Commercials Included

abc rock radio network

Produced by D.I.R. Broadcasting
For radio play only (Not for sale)

This program is solely for the one-time broadcast use of stations cleared
by the ABC Radio Networks on the designated date and time
scheduled by the networks. It may not be removed
from the station premises.

© ℗ D.I.R. Broadcasting
1985

THE SOURCE

NBC Radio's Young Adult Network

STEREO
33 1/3 RPM
NBC 83-53

1

THE SOURCE CHRISTMAS COUNTDOWN

RUSH

BROADCAST DATE: DECEMBER 12 through 24, 1983

Executive Producer  Denny Somach
Producer  Sean McKay

BEST OF THE BISCUIT
RUSH

THE
KING BISCUIT
FLOWER HOUR

AIR DATE: AUGUST 3, 1986

Side B

Commercials Included

Produced by
DIR BROADCASTING

For radio play only (Not for sale)

This program is solely for the one-time broadcast use of stations cleared
by DIR Broadcasting on the designated date and time
scheduled by the network. It may not be removed
from the station premises.

© ℗ DIR Broadcasting 1986

THE KING BISCUIT FLOWER HOUR

DIR RADIO NETWORK

RUSH
Produced by
DIR BROADCASTING
For radio play only (Not for sale)

(Top left) Todd Rundgren's first solo album was called *Runt* and appeared on the short-lived Ampex label. Here's a rare white label promo copy. (Top right) The *Radio Sampler* was a promo-only abridgment of Rundgren's two-LP live set *Back to the Bars*. (Middle left) Rundgren also made appearances on the King Biscuit Flower Hour; this one aired in late 1985. (Middle right) Rush, another popular classic rock band, is often on radio shows. Here's a segment of The Source Christmas Countdown from 1983. (Bottom row) And here are two King Biscuit Flower Hour concerts by Geddy Lee & Co. The first one is a "Best of the Biscuit" show; by 1986 DIR had dropped the special logo for the best-of shows. The second is an early KBFH on CD.

| Title | Yr | Label, Number | NM $ |
|---|---|---|---|

**RUFUS**
*ABC promo 45s $3 each; Warner Bros. promo 45s $2 each; MCA promo 45s $2 each*
**Albums**

| | | | |
|---|---|---|---|
| STREET PLAYER | 1979 | ABC 1049 | 18 |
| *(Promo-only picture disc)* | | | |

**RUGBYS, THE**
*Other Amazon promo 45s $3 each*
**45s**

| | | | |
|---|---|---|---|
| YOU, I | 1969 | Amazon 1 | 20 |
| *(Blue vinyl, white promo label)* | | | |

**RUNAWAYS, THE**
*Other Mercury promo 45s $8 each Features Joan Jett, Lita Ford, Cherie and Marie Currie*
**45s**

| | | | |
|---|---|---|---|
| CHERRY BOMB | 1976 | Mercury 73819 | 15 |
| *(Song later recorded by Joan Jett)* | | | |
| HEARTBEAT | 1977 | Mercury 73890 | 10 |
| *(Blue promo label)* | | | |

**RADIO SHOWS**
**Albums**

| | | | |
|---|---|---|---|
| IN CONCERT (Feb 85) Lita Ford | 1985 | Westwood One (2) | 100-200 |
| *(With Survivor)* | | | |
| INSIDE TRACK (June 83) Joan Jett/Mick Jagger/David Lee Roth | 1983 | RKO (2) | 75-125 |
| *(Mostly music and interviews)* | | | |
| KING BISCUIT FLOWER HOUR (Feb 82) Joan Jett | 1982 | DIR/ABC (2) | 100-200 |
| *(Live concert with the Romantics)* | | | |
| SUPERGROUPS (Aug 82) | 1982 | DIR (3) | 200-350 |
| *(Rare live concert)* | | | |

**RUNDGREN, TODD**
*Includes Runt, Nazz, Utopia; Other Bearsville promo 45s $5-8 each; Warner Bros./Curb promo duet 45s $3 each (with Shaun Cassidy); Warner Bros. promo 45s $5 each; Columbia promo duet 45s $3 each (with Bonnie Tyler); Bearsville promo 45s by Utopia $4 each; Passport promo 45s by Utopia $3-5 each; Network (Elektra) promo 45s by Utopia $3 each; Other Bearsville and Warner Bros. promo 12" singles by Todd Rundgren and/or Utopia $12 each; Network white promo label LPs by Utopia $10 each (Including 60183 with bonus promo disc)*
**12-Inch Singles**

| | | | |
|---|---|---|---|
| DAY JOB (LP Version) (Radio Version) (Dub) | 1993 | Forward 7008 | 15 |
| SOMETHING TO FALL BACK ON | 1985 | Warner Bros. PRO-A-2371 | 10 |
| *(Promo-only 12" single with picture cover)* | | | |
| WE GOTTA GET YOU A WOMAN  Runt | 1970 | Ampex 31001 | 25 |
| *(Promo 12" single)* | | | |

**45s**

| | | | |
|---|---|---|---|
| BE NICE TO ME  Runt | 1971 | Bearsville 31002 | 10 |
| *(White promo label, stereo/mono versions)* | | | |
| HELLO IT'S ME  Nazz | 1968 | SGC 001 | 15 |
| *(Long/short versions)* | | | |
| HELLO IT'S ME  Nazz | 1968 | SGC 001 | 18 |
| *(Flip side is "Open My Eyes")* | | | |
| HELLO IT'S ME  Nazz | 1968 | SGC 001 | 35 |
| *(One-sided mono version)* | | | |
| HELLO IT'S ME  Nazz | 1968 | SGC 001 | 50 |
| *(One-sided stereo version)* | | | |
| I SAW THE LIGHT | 1972 | Bearsville 0003 | 12 |
| *(Stereo/mono versions, black vinyl)* | | | |
| I SAW THE LIGHT | 1972 | Bearsville 0003 | 25 |
| *(Stereo/mono versions, blue vinyl)* | | | |
| JUST ONE VICTORY | 1973 | Bearsville PRO-562 | 18 |
| *(Brown label, promo-only release)* | | | |
| KICKS  Nazz | 1970 | SGC 009 | 25 |
| *("Magic Me" on the flip)* | | | |
| A LONG TIME, A LONG WAY TO GO  Runt | 1971 | Bearsville 31004 | 10 |
| *(White promo label, stereo/mono versions)* | | | |
| NOT WRONG LONG  Nazz | 1969 | SGC 006 | 25 |
| *(There is a stock picture sleeve worth $25)* | | | |
| SOME PEOPLE  Nazz | 1970 | SGC 009 | 12 |
| *("Magic Me" on the flip)* | | | |
| WE GOTTA GET YOU A WOMAN  Runt | 1970 | Ampex 31001 | 10 |
| *(White promo label)* | | | |
| WOLFMAN JACK | 1974 | Bearsville 0301 | 15 |
| *(Brown promo label)* | | | |

**7-Inch Extended Plays**

| | | | |
|---|---|---|---|
| SOMETHING/ANYTHING? | 1972 | Bearsville 2066 (LLP 236) | 40 |
| *(Jukebox LLP with paper cover)* | | | |
| UTOPIA  Utopia | 1980 | Bearsville PRO-908 | 18 |
| *(Promo-only EP of five tracks issued with title cover)* | | | |

**Albums**

| | | | |
|---|---|---|---|
| ANOTHER LIVE  Utopia | 1975 | Bearsville 6961 | 18 |
| *(Brown promo label)* | | | |
| BANDED RADIO INTERVIEW | 1974 | Bearsville PRO 597 | 100 |
| *(For radio only)* | | | |
| NAZZ NAZZ  Nazz, red vinyl | 1969 | SGC 5002 | 50 |
| *(Used as a promo, not a legal promo but there is a "Promotional copy-not for sale" sticker on the cover)* | | | |
| RUNT  Runt | 1970 | Ampex 10105 | 150 |
| *(White promo label)* | | | |
| SOMETHING/ANYTHING? | 1972 | Bearsville 2066 (2) | 300 |
| *(One disc red vinyl, the other blue vinyl)* | | | |

| Title | Yr | Label, Number | NM $ |
|-------|-----|---------------|------|
| THE BALLAD OF TODD RUNDGREN  Runt | 1971 | Ampex 10106 | 100 |
| *(White promo label)* | | | |
| TODD RUNDGREN RADIO SAMPLER | 1979 | Bearsville PRO-A-788 | 50 |
| *(Highlights of "Back to the Bars" plus interview of Todd by Patti Smith)* | | | |
| TODD RUNDGREN RADIO SHOW | 1973 | Bearsville PRO 524 | 150 |
| *(Released for radio, not a syndicated show)* | | | |
| TODD RUNDGREN'S UTOPIA  Utopia | 1974 | Bearsville 6954 | 20 |
| *(White promo label)* | | | |

**RADIO SHOWS**
**Albums**

| Title | Yr | Label, Number | NM $ |
|-------|-----|---------------|------|
| BBC ROCK HOUR (Sept 82) | 1982 | London Wavelength | 100-200 |
| *(Live concert)* | | | |
| BBC TRANSCRIPTION DISC | 1975 | BBC Transcription | 600-700 |
| *(Live concert)* | | | |
| BBC TRANSCRIPTION DISC  Utopia | 1977 | BBC Transcription | 600-750 |
| *(Live concert)* | | | |
| DR. DEMENTO | 1988 | DIR (2) | 25-50 |
| *(Todd is guest co-host, music and interviews)* | | | |
| IN CONCERT (Aug 89) | 1989 | Westwood One (2) | 175-250 |
| *(Rare live concert)* | | | |
| KING BISCUIT FLOWER HOUR (Apr 80)  Utopia | 1980 | DIR/ABC (2) | 75-150 |
| *(Live concert, with Squeeze)* | | | |
| KING BISCUIT FLOWER HOUR (Apr 81) | 1981 | DIR/ABC (2) | 100-175 |
| *(Live concert, repeated in 1983)* | | | |
| KING BISCUIT FLOWER HOUR (Dec 85) | 1985 | DIR (2) | 100-150 |
| *(Live concert)* | | | |
| KING BISCUIT FLOWER HOUR (May 84)  Utopia | 1984 | DIR (2) | 100-150 |
| *(Live concert)* | | | |
| MUSIC SPECIAL | 1985 | | 20-40 |
| *(Music and interviews)* | | | |
| ROBERT KLEIN SHOW | 1982 | Robert Klein (2) | 30-60 |
| *(Music and interviews)* | | | |
| ROBERT W. MORGAN | 1979 | Watermark | 50-100 |
| *(Profile, music and interviews)* | | | |
| ROCK AROUND THE WORLD | 1985 | RATR | 40-75 |
| *(Music and interviews)* | | | |
| ROLLING STONE CONTINUOUS HISTORY | 1982 | Rolling Stone (2) | 30-60 |
| *(Part of a series, music and interviews)* | | | |
| SOURCE CONCERT (Jan 80)  Utopia | 1980 | NBC Radio (2) | 150-250 |
| *(Rare live concert)* | | | |
| WORLD OF ROCK (July 89) | 1989 | DIR (2) | 25-40 |
| *(Todd is guest co-host, music and interviews)* | | | |

**Compact Discs**

| Title | Yr | Label, Number | NM $ |
|-------|-----|---------------|------|
| DIFFERENCE, THE (Jan 95-present) Various artists | 199? | Unistar (2) | 40-75 |
| *(Weekly music and interview shows with some rare live tracks, Todd Rundgren is host; price for any one show)* | | | |
| IN THE STUDIO (90s) | 199? | Album Network | 25-50 |
| *(Profile of an album, music and interviews)* | | | |
| IN THE STUDIO (90s) Utopia | 199? | Album Network | 20-40 |
| *(Profile of an album, music and interviews)* | | | |
| KING BISCUIT FLOWER HOUR (May 92) | 1992 | DIR | 75-125 |
| *(Live concert, repeated)* | | | |

**Reel-to-Reel Tapes**

| Title | Yr | Label, Number | NM $ |
|-------|-----|---------------|------|
| KING BISCUIT FLOWER HOUR (70s) Rundgren/Utopia | 197? | DIR/ABC (2) | 150-250 |
| *(Live concert)* | | | |

## RUSH

Mercury promo 76000 series 45s $8 each; Mercury promo 76134 (Bob and Doug McKenzie) 45s $6 each; Other Mercury black promo label 45s $5 each (mostly long/short versions promo 45s); Other Mercury promo 12" singles $10 each

**12-Inch Singles**

| Title | Yr | Label, Number | NM $ |
|-------|-----|---------------|------|
| BATTLESCAR | 1981 | Mercury 159 | 15 |
| *(Promo-only 12" single, flip side by Max Webster)* | | | |
| THE BIG MONEY | 1985 | Mercury PRO-382 | 12 |
| *(Promo 12" single)* | | | |
| BODY ELECTRIC | 1984 | Mercury PRO-290 | 18 |
| *(Promo-only 12" single)* | | | |
| DISTANT EARLY WARNING | 1984 | Mercury PRO-276 | 25 |
| *(Promo-only 12" single)* | | | |
| ENTRE NOUS | 1981 | Mercury 137 | 18 |
| *(Promo-only 12" single, long and short versions)* | | | |
| FORCE TEN (same on both sides) | 1987 | Mercury 532 | 12 |
| MYSTIC RHYTHMS | 1985 | Mercury PRO-400 | 18 |
| *(Promo 12" single)* | | | |
| PASSAGE TO BANGKOK | 1981 | Mercury | 20 |
| *(Promo-only 12" single)* | | | |
| SPIRIT OF THE RADIO | 1979 | Mercury 125 | 75 |
| *(Promo-only 12" single issued with a picture cover)* | | | |
| TAKE OFF  Bob and Doug McKenzie | 1981 | Mercury 184 | 20 |
| *(Promo-only 12" single, Geddy Lee sings, flip side is "The Twelve Days of Christmas" by Bob and Doug McKenzie)* | | | |
| THE TREES | 1977 | Mercury 75 | 75 |
| *(Promo-only 12" single issued with a picture cover)* | | | |

**45s**

| Title | Yr | Label, Number | NM $ |
|-------|-----|---------------|------|
| BASTILLE DAY | 1976 | Mercury 73737 | 15 |
| *(Blue with buildings promo label)* | | | |
| CLOSER TO THE HEART | 1977 | Mercury 73958 | 10 |
| *(Blue with buildings promo label)* | | | |

| Title | Yr | Label, Number | NM $ |
|---|---|---|---|
| FINDING MY WAY | 1974 | Mercury 406 | 40 |
| *(Blue label promo-only release)* | | | |
| FLY BY NIGHT | 1975 | Mercury 73681 | 15 |
| *(Blue with buildings promo label)* | | | |
| FLY BY NIGHT | 1978 | Mercury 73990 | 10 |
| *(Blue with buildings promo label)* | | | |
| FLY BY NIGHT/IN THE MOOD | 1976 | Mercury 73873 | 12 |
| *(Blue with buildings promo label)* | | | |
| LESSONS | 1976 | Mercury 73803 | 12 |
| *(Blue with buildings promo label)* | | | |
| MAKING MEMORIES | 1977 | Mercury 73912 | 12 |
| *(Blue with buildings promo label)* | | | |
| RED SECTOR A | 1984 | Mercury PRO-319 | 30 |
| *(Black label promo-only release, red vinyl)* | | | |
| THE TREES | 1978 | Mercury 74051 | 10 |
| *(Blue with buildings promo label)* | | | |
| **Albums** | | | |
| EVERYTHING YOUR LISTENER EVER WANTED TO HEAR BY RUSH | 1975 | Mercury MK-32 | 100 |
| RUSH 'N ROULETTE | 1982 | Mercury LP | 30 |
| *(Promo-only sampler for radio)* | | | |
| **Compact Discs** | | | |
| BRAVADO | 1992 | Atlantic PRCD 4580 | 15 |
| *(Promo-only CD single)* | | | |
| DOUBLE AGENT | 1994 | Atlantic PRCD 5431 | 8 |
| *(Promo-only CD single)* | | | |
| DREAMLINE | 1991 | Atlantic PRCD 4120 | 8 |
| *(Promo-only CD single)* | | | |
| DRIVEN | 1996 | Atlantic PRCD 8009 | 10 |
| *(Promo-only CD single)* | | | |
| GHOST OF A CHANCE | 1991 | Atlantic PRCD 4458 | 20 |
| *(Promo-only CD single)* | | | |
| NOBODY'S HERO | 1994 | Atlantic PRCD 5497 | 8 |
| *(Promo-only CD single, reservice)* | | | |
| NOBODY'S HERO | 1994 | Atlantic PRCD 5430 | 8 |
| *(Promo-only CD single)* | | | |
| PASS, THE | 1989 | Atlantic PR 3165 | 10 |
| *(Promo-only CD single)* | | | |
| PROFILED | 1989 | Atlantic PRCD 3200 | 40 |
| *(Music and interviews)* | | | |
| ROLL THE BONES | 1991 | Atlantic PRCD 4260 | 25 |
| *(Promo-only CD single)* | | | |
| SHOW DON'T TELL | 1989 | Atlantic PR 3125 | 8 |
| *(Promo-only CD single, second version)* | | | |
| SHOW DON'T TELL | 1989 | Atlantic PR 3082 | 8 |
| *(Promo-only CD single)* | | | |
| STICK IT OUT | 1993 | Atlantic PRCD 5314 | 8 |
| *(Promo-only CD single)* | | | |
| SUPERCONDUCTOR | 1989 | Atlantic PR 3331 | 30 |
| *(Promo-only CD single)* | | | |
| TEST FOR ECHO | 1996 | Atlantic PRCD 6853 | 12 |
| *(Promo-only CD single)* | | | |
| TEST FOR ECHO | 1996 | Atlantic PRCD 6885 | 15 |
| *(Promo-only CD single)* | | | |
| TIME STAND STILL | 1987 | Mercury CDP 05 | 10 |
| *(Promo-only CD single)* | | | |
| WHERE'S MY THING? | 1991 | Atlantic PRCD 4126 | 50 |
| *(Promo-only CD single)* | | | |
| **RADIO SHOWS** | | | |
| **Albums** | | | |
| INNERVIEW (80s)  Geddy Lee | 198? | Innerview | 25-40 |
| *(Music and interviews)* | | | |
| INNERVIEW (80s)  Neal Peart | 198? | Innerview | 20-35 |
| *(Music and interviews)* | | | |
| KING BISCUIT FLOWER HOUR (Apr 86) | 1986 | DIR (2) | 100-150 |
| *(Live concert)* | | | |
| KING BISCUIT FLOWER HOUR (Oct 81)  With Ian Hunter | 1981 | DIR/ABC (2) | 150-200 |
| *(Live concert)* | | | |
| KING BISCUIT FLOWER HOUR (Sept 83)  With Squeeze | 1983 | DIR/ABC (2) | 125-175 |
| *(Live concert)* | | | |
| LEGENDS OF ROCK (May 87) | 1987 | NBC Radio (2) | 20-35 |
| *(Music and interviews)* | | | |
| LEGENDS OF ROCK (May 87) | 1987 | NBC Radio (4) | 40-60 |
| *(Two shows, parts 1 and 2, music and interviews)* | | | |
| LEGENDS OF ROCK (July 88) | 1988 | NBC Radio (2) | 40-60 |
| *(Music and interviews and live tracks)* | | | |
| METALSHOP (80s) Geddy Lee | 198? | MJI Radio | 20-35 |
| *(Some of these shows featured live tracks by Lee)* | | | |
| NBC PROFILE '86 (May 86) | 1986 | NBC Radio (2) | 25-50 |
| *(Music and interviews)* | | | |
| NBC SOURCE  "The Rush Profile" | 198? | NBC Radio (3) | 100-150 |
| *(Music and interviews)* | | | |
| NBC SOURCE  "The Rush Special" | 198? | NBC Radio (3) | 100-150 |
| *(Music and interviews)* | | | |
| NBC SOURCE  "Total Access Rush" | 198? | NBC Radio | 75-125 |
| *(Music and interviews)* | | | |
| NBC SOURCE (Mar 80) | 1980 | NBC Radio (2) | 175-250 |
| *(Live concert)* | | | |

| Title | Yr | Label, Number | NM $ |
|-------|-----|---------------|------|
| NBC SOURCE (Dec 83) | 1983 | NBC Radio (3) | 100-150 |
| *(Mostly music and interviews)* | | | |
| OFF THE RECORD | 1981 | Westwood One (2) | 20-40 |
| *(Music and interviews, repeated)* | | | |
| SUPERGROUPS (Oct 83)  With Black Sabbath | 1983 | DIR/ABC (3) | 175-250 |
| *(Live concerts)* | | | |
| WORLD OF ROCK (Jan 90) Geddy Lee | 1990 | DIR (2) | 20-35 |
| *(Lee is a co-host, music and interviews)* | | | |
| **Compact Discs** | | | |
| IN THE STUDIO (90s) | 199? | Album Network | 20-35 |
| *(Profile of an album, music and interviews)* | | | |
| KING BISCUIT FLOWER HOUR (Dec 87) | 1987 | DIR | 200-350 |
| *(Live concert, silver CD, recalled from broadcast)* | | | |
| KING BISCUIT FLOWER HOUR (Dec 93) | 1993 | DIR | 40-60 |
| *(Live concert, repeated)* | | | |
| KING BISCUIT FLOWER HOUR (Jan 95) | 1995 | DIR | 25-50 |
| *(Live concert)* | | | |
| OFF THE RECORD (Dec 93) | 1993 | Westwood One | 25-40 |
| *(Music and interviews, repeated)* | | | |
| OFF THE RECORD (Nov 93) | 1993 | Westwood One | 25-40 |
| *("Counterparts" CD)* | | | |
| OFF THE RECORD (Apr 94) | 1994 | Westwood One | 25-50 |
| *(Music and interviews)* | | | |
| ROCK STARS (Dec 89) | 1989 | Radio Today (2) | 100-200 |
| *(Music and interviews)* | | | |
| SPIRIT OF RUSH (July 91) | 1991 | Global Satellite (3) | 200-300 |
| *(Music and interviews)* | | | |
| UP CLOSE | 1990 | Media America (2) | 45-80 |
| *(Mostly music and interviews)* | | | |
| UP CLOSE | 1994 | Media America (3) | 75-125 |
| *(Mostly music and interviews)* | | | |
| **Reel-to-Reel Tapes** | | | |
| COUNTERPARTS | 1993 | Album Network (2) | 100-150 |
| *(Music and interviews on two 10" reels)* | | | |
| WORLD PREMIERE: TEST FOR ECHO | 1996 | Album Network (2) | 100-150 |
| *(Music and interviews)* | | | |

## RUSSELL, LEON

*Shelter promo 45s $4 each From the Asylum Choir and Dave & Lee*

| Title | Yr | Label, Number | NM $ |
|-------|-----|---------------|------|
| **45s** | | | |
| MISTY | 1967 | A&M 734 | 12 |
| *(White promo label)* | | | |
| TALKING ABOUT THE YOUNG | 1963 | Dot 16771 | 15 |
| *(White promo label, promo-only release)* | | | |

## RUTLES, THE

*Warner Bros. promo 45s $5 each*

| Title | Yr | Label, Number | NM $ |
|-------|-----|---------------|------|
| **Albums** | | | |
| MEET THE RUTLES | 1978 | Warner Bros. PRO-A-723 | 30 |
| *(Gold vinyl promo release)* | | | |

## RYDELL, BOBBY

*Cameo promo 45s $10 each; Capitol promo 45s $4 each*

| Title | Yr | Label, Number | NM $ |
|-------|-----|---------------|------|
| **45s** | | | |
| STEEL PIER | 1963 | Cameo (no #) | 25 |
| *(One-sided "Steel Pier Promotion")* | | | |
| WHAT ARE YOU DOING NEW YEAR'S EVE?  With Chubby Checker | 1962 | Cameo 13E | 40 |
| *(Promo-only on red/black Cameo label, blank B-side, probably a publisher's demo)* | | | |
| **7-Inch Extended Plays** | | | |
| SOMEBODY LOVES YOU  Jukebox LLP | 1965 | Capitol 2281 | 15 |
| *(Issued with a hard cover)* | | | |
| **Albums** | | | |
| FOR CHRISTMAS SEALS | 1969 | Decca 202,202 | 25 |
| *(Eight cuts, one by Rydell)* | | | |

| Title | Yr | Label, Number | NM $ |
|---|---|---|---|

# S

## SADE
*Portrait promo 45s $3 each; Portrait promo picture sleeves $3 each; Epic promo CD singles $2-3 each*

**12-Inch Singles**

| Title | Yr | Label, Number | NM $ |
|---|---|---|---|
| LOVE IS STRONGER THAN PRIDE (same on both sides) | 1988 | Epic EAS 01499 | 8 |
| NEVER AS GOOD AS THE FIRST TIME (2 mixes)/KEEP HANGIN' ON | 1986 | Portrait AS 2293 | 8 |
| NO ORDINARY LOVE (3 versions)/PARADISE (Remix) | 1992 | Epic EAS 04876 | 15 |
| PARADISE (extended)/(7" Mix) | 1988 | Epic EAS 01121 | 8 |

**Compact Discs**

| Title | Yr | Label, Number | NM $ |
|---|---|---|---|
| INTERVIEW DELUXE | 1992 | Epic ESK 4877 | 12 |

*(Promo-only interview disc)*

## SADLER, BARRY
*Other RCA Victor promo 45s $5 each; King of Music promo label 45s $3 each*

**45s**

| Title | Yr | Label, Number | NM $ |
|---|---|---|---|
| THE BALLAD OF THE GREEN BERETS White label | 1966 | RCA Victor 8739 | 10 |

*(Promo copy of a mega-hit)*

**7-Inch Extended Plays**

| Title | Yr | Label, Number | NM $ |
|---|---|---|---|
| BALLADS OF THE GREEN BERETS Jukebox LLP | 1966 | RCA Victor 3547 | 25 |

*(Issued with a hard cover)*

## SAGA
**RADIO SHOWS**
**Albums**

| Title | Yr | Label, Number | NM $ |
|---|---|---|---|
| CAPTURED LIVE (Apr 84) Live concert | 1984 | RKO Radio (2) | 50-100 |
| *(Repeated)* | | | |
| KING BISCUIT FLOWER HOUR (Feb 83) | 1983 | DIR/ABC (2) | 40-75 |
| *(Live concert)* | | | |
| KING BISCUIT FLOWER HOUR (Sept 84) Live concert | 1984 | DIR/ABC (2) | 20-40 |
| *(With Honeymoon Suite)* | | | |
| KING BISCUIT FLOWER HOUR (Sept 85) Live concert | 1985 | DIR (2) | 20-40 |
| *(With April Wine)* | | | |

## SAGER, CAROLE BAYER
*Boardwalk promo 45s $2 each*

**Albums**

| Title | Yr | Label, Number | NM $ |
|---|---|---|---|
| CAROLE BAYER SAGER RADIO SPECIAL | 1981 | Boardwalk 002 | 10 |

*(Music and interview show with Burt Bacharach)*

## SAHM, DOUG
*Atlantic promo 45s $6 each; Dot and Warner Bros. promo 45s $5 each*

**45s**

| Title | Yr | Label, Number | NM $ |
|---|---|---|---|
| BABY, TELL ME Gold vinyl | 1960 | Harlem 108 | 100 |
| *(Harlem promo label, only the promo is gold vinyl)* | | | |
| BABY, WHAT'S ON YOUR MIND Red vinyl | 1961 | Renner 215 | 100 |
| *(Renner promo label, only the promo is red vinyl)* | | | |
| JUST BECAUSE | 1962 | Renner 226 | 50 |
| *(Renner promo label)* | | | |
| LITTLE ANGEL | 1963 | Renner 232 | 40 |
| *(Renner promo label)* | | | |
| LUCKY ME | 1963 | Renner 240 | 40 |
| *(Renner promo label)* | | | |
| MAKES NO DIFFERENCE Red vinyl | 1961 | Renner 212 | 100 |
| *(Renner promo label, only the promo is red vinyl)* | | | |
| MR. KOOL | 1964 | Renner 247 | 40 |
| *(Renner promo label)* | | | |
| SLOWDOWN Black vinyl | 1960 | Harlem 113 | 40 |
| *(Harlem promo label)* | | | |
| WHY WHY WHY Black vinyl | 1960 | Harlem 107 | 150 |
| *(Harlem promo label)* | | | |

## SAINTS, THE
**12-Inch Singles**

| Title | Yr | Label, Number | NM $ |
|---|---|---|---|
| JUST LIKE FIRE WOULD (same on both sides) | 1987 | TVT 2111 | 10 |

## SALSOUL ORCHESTRA, THE
**12-Inch Singles**

| Title | Yr | Label, Number | NM $ |
|---|---|---|---|
| DECK THE HALLS (7:29)/THE SALSOUL CHRISTMAS SUITE (7:59) | 1981 | Salsoul 358 | 12 |

## SALT-N-PEPA
**12-Inch Singles**

| Title | Yr | Label, Number | NM $ |
|---|---|---|---|
| HE'S GAMIN' ON YA (3 versions) | 1991 | Soul 2127 | 6 |

## SAM THE SHAM AND THE PHARAOHS
*Other MGM promo 45s $5 each; Atlantic promo 45s by Sam Samudio $4 each*

**45s**

| Title | Yr | Label, Number | NM $ |
|---|---|---|---|
| WOOLY BULLY | 1965 | MGM 13322 | 12 |
| *(Yellow promo copy)* | | | |
| WOOLY BULLY Purple/red vinyl | 1965 | MGM 13322 | Unknown |
| *(No value for this record has ever been seen)* | | | |

| Title | Yr | Label, Number | NM $ |
|---|---|---|---|

## SAMBORA, RICHIE
*Mercury promo CD singles $2 each; More at Bon Jovi*
**RADIO SHOWS**
**Albums**

| | | | |
|---|---|---|---|
| IN CONCERT (Mar 82) | 1982 | Westwood One | 50-100 |

*(Live concert)*

## SANBORN, DAVID
**RADIO SHOWS**
**Compact Discs**

| | | | |
|---|---|---|---|
| DAVID SANBORN HOUR (91-92) Music and interviews | 199? | (2) | 10-15 |

*(Price per show, jazz oriented)*

## SANDS, TOMMY
*Other Capitol promo 45s $8 each; ABC Paramount promo 45s $5 each; Imperial promo 45s $4 each; Liberty promo 45s $3 each; Other Capitol promo LPs $25 each*
**45s**

| | | | |
|---|---|---|---|
| AFTER THE SENIOR PROM | 1958 | Capitol 3985 | 12 |
| *(White promo label, stock picture sleeve is worth $30)* | | | |
| BLUE RIBBON BABY Tommy Sands and the Raiders | 1958 | Capitol 4036 | 25 |
| *(White promo label)* | | | |
| GOIN' STEADY | 1957 | Capitol 3723 | 25 |
| *(White promo label)* | | | |
| I'LL BE SEEING YOU | 1959 | Capitol 4259 | 12 |
| *(Blue promo label, stock picture sleeve is worth $30)* | | | |
| LET ME BE LOVED | 1958 | Capitol 3743 | 15 |
| *(White promo label)* | | | |
| LET'S GET TOGETHER With Annette | 1961 | Buena Vista 802 | 25 |
| *(White promo label, stock picture sleeve worth an additional $25)* | | | |
| THE OLD OAKEN BUCKET | 1960 | Capitol 4407 | 12 |
| *(Red promo label)* | | | |
| RING-A-DING-A-DING | 1957 | Capitol 3690 | 30 |
| *(White promo label)* | | | |
| ROSES SPEAK LOUDER THAN WORDS | 1953 | RCA Victor 5510 | 40 |
| *(White promo label)* | | | |
| SING BOY, SING | 1958 | Capitol 3867 | 18 |
| *(White promo label)* | | | |
| SINNER MAN | 1959 | Capitol 4231 | 15 |
| *(Blue promo label)* | | | |
| A SWINGIN' ROMANCE | 1958 | Capitol 3810 | 15 |
| *(White promo label)* | | | |
| TEEN AGE CRUSH | 1957 | Capitol 3639 | 35 |
| *(White promo label)* | | | |
| TEENAGE DOLL | 1958 | Capitol 3953 | 15 |
| *(White promo label)* | | | |
| THAT'S LOVE | 1959 | Capitol 4366 | 10 |
| *(Red promo label)* | | | |
| TOO YOUNG TO GO STEADY | 1957 | Capitol T-848 | 50 |
| *(White promo label, promo-only release, LP number)* | | | |
| THE WORRYIN' KIND | 1958 | Capitol 4082 | 12 |
| *(Capitol promo label)* | | | |
| YOU HOLD THE FUTURE | 1959 | Capitol 4316 | 12 |
| *(Red promo label)* | | | |

**7-Inch Extended Plays**

| | | | |
|---|---|---|---|
| LET ME BE LOVED Various artists | 1959 | Capitol PRO-396 | 25 |
| *(Four cuts, one by Tommy Sands, blue promo-only label)* | | | |
| SANDS AT THE SANDS | 1960 | Capitol PRO-1541 | 75 |
| *(Capitol "Artist of the Month" series, promo-only release, blue label)* | | | |
| STEADY DATE | 1957 | Capitol PRO-351 | 125 |
| *(Yellow promo label, promo-only EP, not to be confused with the stock copy hard cover EPs that were released in 1957, of which no promo versions were pressed)* | | | |
| THIS THING CALLED LOVE | 1959 | Capitol 1123 | 125 |
| *(This is a promo version of the EP series 1123, yellow promo label. Very rarely did Capitol issue promo versions of their EPs in the late 50s.)* | | | |

**78s**

| | | | |
|---|---|---|---|
| RING-A-DING-A-DING | 1957 | Capitol 3690 | 75 |
| *(White promo label)* | | | |
| ROSES SPEAK LOUDER THAN WORDS | 1953 | RCA Victor 5510 | 50 |
| *(White promo label)* | | | |
| TEEN AGE CRUSH | 1957 | Capitol 3639 | 40 |
| *(White promo label)* | | | |

**Albums**

| | | | |
|---|---|---|---|
| SANDS STORM | 1959 | Capitol 1081 | 50 |
| *(Yellow promo label)* | | | |
| SING BOY, SING | 1958 | Capitol 929 | 75 |
| *(Yellow promo label, soundtrack)* | | | |
| STEADY DATE | 1957 | Capitol 848 | 100 |
| *(Yellow promo label)* | | | |
| TEENAGE ROCK | 1959 | Capitol 1109 | 60 |
| *(Yellow promo label)* | | | |

## SANTANA
*Other Columbia promo 45s $4 each; Columbia promo picture sleeves $3 each; Other Columbia promo 12" singles $8 each; Other Columbia promo LPs $10 each*
**12-Inch Singles**

| | | | |
|---|---|---|---|
| I'M THE ONE WHO LOVES YOU (same on both sides) | 1985 | Columbia CAS 2068 | 6 |
| LOVE THEME FROM SPARTACUS/SONG FOR MY BROTHER/SWAPAN TARI | 1980 | Columbia AS 842 | 12 |
| ONE CHAIN (DON'T MAKE NO PRISON) (Long) (Short) (both on each side) | 1978 | Columbia AS 585 | 8 |
| SAY IT AGAIN (same on both sides) | 1985 | Columbia AS 1998 | 6 |
| SENSITIVE KIND (Studio)/(Live) | 1981 | Columbia AS 1266 | 10 |
| SHE'S NOT THERE (4:08) (2:58) (stereo/mono) | 1977 | Columbia AS 383 | 15 |

| Title | Yr | Label, Number | NM $ |
|---|---|---|---|
| VERACRUZ (same on both sides) | 1987 | Columbia CAS 2630 | 6 |
| WELL ALL RIGHT (short) (long) | 1978 | Columbia AS 517 | 12 |
| WINNING/E PAPA NE | 1981 | Columbia AS 937 | 8 |
| **45s** | | | |
| JUST IN TIME TO SEE THE SUN | 1971 | Columbia AE7 1064 | 12 |
| *(Promo-only release)* | | | |
| **7-Inch Extended Plays** | | | |
| SANTANA 3 Jukebox LLP | 1971 | Columbia 30595 | 25 |
| *(Issued with a hard cover)* | | | |
| WELCOME Jukebox LLP | 1973 | Columbia 32445 | 25 |
| *(Issued with a hard cover)* | | | |
| **Albums** | | | |
| SANTANA | 1969 | Columbia 9781 | 15 |
| *(White promo label)* | | | |
| THE SOLO GUITAR OF DEVADIP CARLOS SANTANA | 1979 | Columbia AS 573 | 15 |
| **Compact Discs** | | | |
| MOTHER EARTH TOUR | 1990 | Columbia CSK 2099 | 25 |
| *(Promo-only release, 15 tracks)* | | | |
| **RADIO SHOWS** | | | |
| **Albums** | | | |
| BBC ROCK HOUR (Sept 82) | 1982 | London Wavelength | 20-40 |
| *(Music and interviews)* | | | |
| KING BISCUIT FLOWER HOUR (Feb 83) | 1983 | DIR/ABC (2) | 75-125 |
| *(Live concert)* | | | |
| KING BISCUIT FLOWER HOUR (Feb 87) | 1987 | DIR/ABC (2) | 50-100 |
| *(Live concert with Crosby, Stills & Nash)* | | | |
| LEGENDS OF ROCK (May 87) | 1987 | NBC Radio (2) | 15-25 |
| *(Music and interviews)* | | | |
| NBC SOURCE (Dec 79) | 1979 | NBC Source (2) | 125-200 |
| *(Rare live concert)* | | | |
| ROBERT W. MORGAN (Oct 81) | 1981 | Watermark | 20-30 |
| *(Music and interviews)* | | | |
| SANTANA CONCERT ENCORE (Oct 81) | 1981 | NBC Source (2) | 50-100 |
| *(Mostly music and interviews)* | | | |
| **Compact Discs** | | | |
| CARLOS SANTANA MEMORIAL DAY TRIBUTE CONCERT | 199? | MJI Broadcasting (2) | 125-175 |
| *(Live material, with Buddy Guy, Bob Weir and Kirk Hammett of Metallica)* | | | |
| IN THE STUDIO Profile of an album | 1988 | Album Network | 20-35 |
| *(Music and interviews)* | | | |
| KING BISCUIT FLOWER HOUR (June 93) With Warren Hayes | 1993 | DIR | 25-40 |
| *(Live concert)* | | | |
| KING BISCUIT FLOWER HOUR (Oct 88) | 1988 | DIR | 25-50 |
| *(Live concert, repeated)* | | | |
| LIVE FROM HOUSE OF BLUES | 1993 | (2) | 20-40 |
| *(Live concert material)* | | | |
| OFF THE RECORD (Nov 93) | 1993 | Westwood One (2) | 20-35 |
| *(Music and interviews)* | | | |
| SUPERSTAR CONCERT (July 92) | 1992 | Westwood One (2) | 25-50 |
| *(Live concert)* | | | |
| UP CLOSE Profile | 1994 | Media America (2) | 25-35 |
| *(Music and interviews)* | | | |
| UP CLOSE (Oct 88) Profile | 1988 | Media America (2) | 25-40 |
| *(Music and interviews)* | | | |

## SATINTONES, THE
*Featuring Chico Leverette*

| Title | Yr | Label, Number | NM $ |
|---|---|---|---|
| **45s** | | | |
| I KNOW HOW IT FEELS | 1961 | Motown 1010 | 200 |
| *(White promo label)* | | | |
| I'LL NEVER LOVE AGAIN Chico Leverette | 1960 | Tamla 54024 | 300 |
| *(White promo label)* | | | |
| MOTOR CITY | 1960 | Tamla 54026 | 400 |
| *(White promo label)* | | | |
| MY BELOVED | 1960 | Motown 1000 | 250 |
| *(Very rare white promo label)* | | | |
| TOMORROW AND ALWAYS | 1961 | Motown 1006 | 200 |
| *(Very rare white promo label)* | | | |
| ZING WENT THE STRINGS OF MY HEART | 1962 | Motown 1020 | 400 |
| *(White promo label)* | | | |

## SATRIANI, JOE
*Relativity promo CD singles $5-7 each*

| Title | Yr | Label, Number | NM $ |
|---|---|---|---|
| **RADIO SHOWS** | | | |
| **Albums** | | | |
| OFF THE RECORD (Nov 92) | 1992 | Westwood One (2) | 15-25 |
| *(Music and interview, with Sass Jordan)* | | | |
| **Compact Discs** | | | |
| IN CONCERT (Oct 93) Live concert | 1993 | Westwood One (2) | 40-75 |
| *(With Meat Loaf)* | | | |
| IN CONCERT (Sept 94) | 1994 | Westwood One (2) | 40-60 |
| *(Live concert)* | | | |
| KING BISCUIT FLOWER HOUR (Jul 88) | 1988 | DIR | 25-50 |
| *(Live concert)* | | | |
| OFF THE RECORD (Oct 93) | 1993 | Westwood One | 15-30 |
| *(Music and interviews)* | | | |

| Title | Yr | Label, Number | NM $ |
|---|---|---|---|
| **SAWYER BROWN** | | | |
| *Other Capitol promo 45s $2 each; Curb promo CD singles $2-4 each* | | | |
| **45s** | | | |
| DIRT ROAD, THE | 1991 | Curb/Capitol 7PRO-79050 | 12 |
| *(Promo-only release)* | | | |
| MAMA'S LITTLE BABY LOVES ME | 1991 | Curb/Capitol 7PRO-79653 | 10 |
| *(Promo-only release)* | | | |
| ONE LESS PONY | 1991 | Curb/Capitol 7PRO-79432 | 10 |
| *(Promo-only release)* | | | |
| PUTTIN' THE DARK BACK INTO THE NIGHT | 1990 | Capitol 7PRO-79040 | 10 |
| *(Promo-only release)* | | | |
| WALK, THE | 1991 | Curb/Capitol 7PRO-79750 | 10 |
| *(Promo-only release)* | | | |
| WHEN LOVE COMES CALLIN' | 1990 | Curb/Capitol 7PRO-79231 | 10 |
| *(Promo-only release)* | | | |
| **Compact Discs** | | | |
| SAWYER BROWN/BOY HOWDY | 1994 | Curb | 25 |
| *(Radio only sampler release)* | | | |
| **RADIO SHOWS** | | | |
| **Albums** | | | |
| AMERICAN EAGLE (Aug 86) | 1986 | DIR | 20-30 |
| *(Live concert)* | | | |
| WESTWOOD ONE PRESENTS (Feb 90) | 1990 | Westwood One | 15-25 |
| *(Live concert)* | | | |
| **Cassettes** | | | |
| AUSTIN ENCORE With Tanya Tucker | 1990 | Entertainment Radio | 15-25 |
| *(Mostly music and interviews)* | | | |
| **SAXON, EDDIE, AND THE PARAMOUNTS** | | | |
| **45s** | | | |
| BLUES NO MORE | 1962 | Empress 106 | 200 |
| *(Single-sided promo)* | | | |
| **SAYER, LEO** | | | |
| *Warner Bros. promo 45s $3 each* | | | |
| **12-Inch Singles** | | | |
| THUNDER IN MY HEART (Disco Version) (same on both sides) | 1977 | Warner Bros. PRO-A-699 | 8 |
| **45s** | | | |
| WHAT'S IT ALL ABOUT (Feb 79) Public service show | 1979 | W.I.A.A. 462 | 10 |
| *(Flip side features Paul Williams)* | | | |
| WHAT'S IT ALL ABOUT (June 75) Public service show | 1975 | W.I.A.A. 270 | 12 |
| *(Other side is Phoebe Snow)* | | | |
| WHAT'S IT ALL ABOUT (May 77) Public service show | 1977 | W.I.A.A. 370 | 18 |
| *(Other side features Vince Gill and Pure Prairie League)* | | | |
| **RADIO SHOWS** | | | |
| **Albums** | | | |
| LIVE (80s) Live concert | 198? | DIR (3) | 100-175 |
| *(With Christopher Cross)* | | | |
| ROBERT W. MORGAN | 1981 | Watermark | 10-20 |
| *(Music and interviews)* | | | |
| **SCAFFOLD** | | | |
| *With Mike McGear (Paul McCartney's brother)* | | | |
| **45s** | | | |
| CHARITY BUBBLES | 1968 | Bell | 30 |
| *(White/red promo label)* | | | |
| DO YOU REMEMBER? | 1968 | Bell 724 | 12 |
| *(White/red promo label)* | | | |
| LEAVE IT Mike McGear | 1974 | Warner Bros. 8037 | 15 |
| *(Produced by Paul McCartney)* | | | |
| LILY THE PINK | 1968 | Bell 747 | 18 |
| *(White/red promo label, UK megahit!)* | | | |
| LIVERPOOL LOU | 1968 | Warner Bros. 8001 | 10 |
| *(Warner promo label)* | | | |
| THANK U VERY MUCH | 1968 | Bell 701 | 18 |
| *(White/red promo label)* | | | |
| **SCAGGS, BOZ** | | | |
| *Columbia promo 45s $3 each; Columbia promo picture sleeves $2 each; Columbia and Virgin promo CD singles $2-3 each* | | | |
| **12-Inch Singles** | | | |
| HARD TIMES (same on both sides) | 1977 | Columbia AS 380 | 8 |
| **Albums** | | | |
| THE BOZ SCAGGS SAMPLER | 1976 | Columbia AS-203 | 20 |
| *(Promo-only release)* | | | |
| KSAN LIVE CONCERT | 1974 | Columbia A2S-71-4 (2) | 50 |
| *(Promo-only release)* | | | |
| **RADIO SHOWS** | | | |
| **Albums** | | | |
| ROBERT W. MORGAN (Dec 80) | 1980 | Watermark | 10-15 |
| *(Music and interviews)* | | | |
| **SCANDAL** | | | |
| *Columbia promo 45s $3 each; Columbia promo picture sleeves $3 each* | | | |
| **RADIO SHOWS** | | | |
| **Albums** | | | |
| IN CONCERT (Dec 85) Live concert | 1985 | Westwood One (2) | 30-60 |
| *(With Jon Butcher Axis)* | | | |

| Title | Yr | Label, Number | NM $ |
|---|---|---|---|
| KING BISCUIT FLOWER HOUR (Feb 83) Live concert | 1983 | DIR/ABC (2) | 50-100 |
| *(With Missing Persons)* | | | |
| KING BISCUIT FLOWER HOUR (Nov 84) | 1984 | DIR/ABC (2) | 30-60 |
| *(Live concert)* | | | |
| KING BISCUIT FLOWER HOUR (Mar 85) Live concert | 1985 | DIR (2) | 100-150 |
| *(With Bruce Cockburn)* | | | |

**SCHILLING, PETER**
**12-Inch Singles**

| | | | |
|---|---|---|---|
| CHILL OF THE NIGHT (same on both sides) | 1985 | Elektra ED 5054 | 7 |
| THE NOAH PLAN/DIE WUSTE LEBT | 1983 | Elektra ED 4951 | 8 |

**SCHNEIDER, FRED**
*Of the B-52's*
**12-Inch Singles**

| | | | |
|---|---|---|---|
| MONSTER/BOONGA | 1984 | Warner Bros. PRO-A-2224 | 10 |

**SCHUMACHER, CHRISTINE, SINGS WITH THE SUPREMES**
**45s**

| | | | |
|---|---|---|---|
| MOTHER YOU, SMOTHER YOU (same on both sides) | 1968 | Motown L294-MO5 | 300 |
| *(Schumacher won a "Record a Record with the Supremes" contest on WKNR of Detroit; this is the rare result)* | | | |

**SCHUMANN, WALTER**
**45s**

| | | | |
|---|---|---|---|
| CHRISTMAS CHOPSTICKS/PEARLS ON VELVET | 1955 | RCA Victor LPM-1141/LPT-6702 | 12 |
| *(B-side by Glenn Miller; promo-only record using the numbers of the LPs from which the songs were taken)* | | | |

**SCORPIONS**
*Mercury promo 45s $4 each; Other Mercury promo CD singles $4-6 each*
**12-Inch Singles**

| | | | |
|---|---|---|---|
| BIG CITY NIGHTS (Edit) (LP)/NO ONE LIKE YOU (Live) | 1985 | Mercury 359 | 8 |
| I'M LEAVING YOU (Long) (Short) | 1984 | Mercury 833 | 8 |
| LOVING YOU SUNDAY MORNING/NO ONE LIKE YOU | 1985 | Mercury 378 | 8 |
| ROCK YOU LIKE A HURRICANE (same on both sides) | 1984 | Mercury 265 | 10 |
| YOU GIVE ME ALL I NEED (same on both sides) | 1982 | Mercury MK 212 | 8 |

**Compact Discs**

| | | | |
|---|---|---|---|
| WIND OF CHANGE | 1991 | Mercury CDP 423 | 8 |
| *(Promo CD single of their biggest U.S. hit)* | | | |

**RADIO SHOWS**
**Albums**

| | | | |
|---|---|---|---|
| INNERVIEW (70s) Profile | 197? | Innerview | 15-25 |
| *(Music and interviews)* | | | |
| KING BISCUIT FLOWER HOUR | 1980 | DIR/ABC (2) | 40-75 |
| *(Live concert)* | | | |
| KING BISCUIT FLOWER HOUR (July 82) Live concert | 1982 | DIR/ABC (2) | 50-100 |
| *(With Black Sabbath)* | | | |
| SUPERSTAR CONCERT (Oct 90) Live concert | 1990 | Westwood One (3) | 40-75 |
| *(Box set, repeated)* | | | |

**Compact Discs**

| | | | |
|---|---|---|---|
| ALBUM NETWORK SPECIAL (Jun 96) | 1996 | Album Network (2) | 50-75 |
| *(Music and interviews)* | | | |
| KING BISCUIT FLOWER HOUR (Mar 91) Live concert | 1991 | DIR | 40-75 |
| *(With Queen and Steppenwolf)* | | | |
| UP CLOSE Profile | 1994 | Media America (2) | 30-50 |
| *(Music and interviews)* | | | |

**Reel-to-Reel Tapes**

| | | | |
|---|---|---|---|
| ALBUM NETWORK (Oct 93) Live concert | 1993 | Album Network | 75-125 |
| *("Live from Germany" on two 10" reels)* | | | |

**SCOTT, JACK**
*Includes the Chantones (his backing vocal group; )Capitol promo 45s $25 each; Capitol promo 45s by the Chantones $30 each; Dot promo 45s $6 each; Curb (MCA) promo 45s $4 each*
**45s**

| | | | |
|---|---|---|---|
| BABY, SHE'S GONE | 1957 | ABC-Paramount 9818 | 80 |
| *(White promo label)* | | | |
| BEFORE THE BIRD FLIES | 1966 | ABC-Paramount 10843 | 25 |
| *(White promo label)* | | | |
| BURNING BRIDGES | 1960 | Top Rank 2041 | 25 |
| *(White promo label, stock picture sleeve worth $50)* | | | |
| DON'T HUSH THE LAUGHTER | 1965 | RCA Victor 8724 | 12 |
| *(White promo label)* | | | |
| DON'T OPEN THAT DOOR The Chantones | 1960 | Top Rank 2066 | 35 |
| *(White promo label)* | | | |
| GO WILD, LITTLE SADIE | 1960 | Guaranteed 211 | 25 |
| *(White promo label)* | | | |
| GOODBYE, BABY | 1958 | Carlton 493 | 35 |
| *(Carlton promo label, stock picture sleeve is worth an additional $50)* | | | |
| I DON'T BELIEVE IN TEA LEAVES | 1965 | RCA Victor 8505 | 15 |
| *(White promo label)* | | | |
| I KNEW YOU FIRST | 1964 | Groove 0031 | 18 |
| *(White promo label)* | | | |
| I NEVER FELT LIKE THIS | 1959 | Carlton 504 | 30 |
| *(Carlton promo label)* | | | |
| IS THERE SOMETHING ON YOUR MIND | 1960 | Top Rank 2093 | 25 |
| *(White promo label, stock picture sleeve worth $50)* | | | |
| IT ONLY HAPPENED YESTERDAY | 1960 | Top Rank 2055 | 25 |
| *(White promo label)* | | | |

| Title | Yr | Label, Number | NM $ |
|---|---|---|---|
| IT WAS JUST A SUMMER LOVE The Chantones | 1958 | Carlton 485 | 40 |
| *(Red promo label)* | | | |
| JINGLE BELL SLIDE | 1963 | Groove 0027 | 25 |
| *(White promo label)* | | | |
| LOOKING FOR LINDA | 1965 | RCA Victor 8685 | 12 |
| *(White promo label)* | | | |
| MY SPECIAL ANGEL | 1967 | Jubilee 5606 | 25 |
| *(White promo label)* | | | |
| MY TRUE LOVE | 1958 | Carlton 462 | 50 |
| *(Red promo label)* | | | |
| PATSY | 1960 | Top Rank 2075 | 25 |
| *(White promo label)* | | | |
| TALL TALES | 1964 | Groove 0049 | 18 |
| *(White promo label)* | | | |
| THERE COMES A TIME | 1959 | Carlton 519 | 25 |
| *(Carlton promo label)* | | | |
| THOU SHALT NOT STEAL | 1964 | Groove 0042 | 15 |
| *(White promo label)* | | | |
| TWO TIMIN' WOMAN | 1957 | ABC-Paramount 9860 | 75 |
| *(White promo label)* | | | |
| THE WAY I WALK | 1959 | Carlton 514 | 30 |
| *(Carlton promo label)* | | | |
| WHAT A WONDERFUL NIGHT OUT | 1964 | Groove 0037 | 20 |
| *(White promo label)* | | | |
| WHAT AM I LIVING FOR? | 1960 | Guaranteed 209 | 25 |
| *(White promo label)* | | | |
| WHAT IN THE WORLD'S COME OVER YOU | 1960 | Top Rank 2028 | 25 |
| *(White promo label)* | | | |
| WITH YOUR LOVE | 1958 | Carlton 483 | 40 |
| *(Red promo label, stock picture sleeve is worth an additional $50)* | | | |
| **Albums** | | | |
| SOUL STIRRING Black and yellow label | 196? | SESAC 4201 | 175 |
| *(Promo only released to radio stations)* | | | |

**SCOTT, TOM**
**12-Inch Singles**

| | | | |
|---|---|---|---|
| GOT TO GET OUT OF NEW YORK/AEROBIA | 1983 | Atlantic 703 | 6 |
| SO WHITE AND SO FUNKY (same on both sides) | 1981 | Columbia AS 1249 | 6 |

**SCOTT-HERON, GIL**
*Arista promo 45s $5 each*
**RADIO SHOWS**
**Albums**

| | | | |
|---|---|---|---|
| BBC TRANSCRIPTION DISC | 1986 | BBC Transcription | 100-175 |
| *(Live concert)* | | | |

**SCREAMING BLUE MESSIAHS**
**12-Inch Singles**

| | | | |
|---|---|---|---|
| BIKINI RED (same on both sides) | 1987 | Elektra ED 5282 | 6 |
| *(Red vinyl)* | | | |
| I WANNA BE A FLINTSTONE (same on both sides) | 1987 | Elektra ED 5262 | 6 |
| SMASH THE MARKET PLACE (same on both sides) | 1986 | Elektra ED 5173 | 6 |
| WILD BLUE YONDER (Short)/(Long) | 1986 | Elektra ED 5150 | 6 |
| **Albums** | | | |
| BIKINI RED | 1987 | Elektra 60755 | 12 |
| *(Promo-only pressing on audiophile vinyl)* | | | |
| TOTALLY RELIGIOUS | 1989 | Elektra 60859 | 12 |
| *(Promo-only pressing on audiophile vinyl)* | | | |

**SCREAMING TREES**
**12-Inch Singles**

| | | | |
|---|---|---|---|
| SOMETHING ABOUT TODAY/THIS PERFECT DAY/NEW DAY YESTERDAY | 1991 | Epic EAS 3092 | 8 |

**SCRITTI POLITTI**
**12-Inch Singles**

| | | | |
|---|---|---|---|
| PERFECT WAY (Remix)/(7") | 1985 | Warner Bros. PRO-A-2397 | 7 |
| **45s** | | | |
| PERFECT WAY/PERFECT WAY | 1985 | Sire 28949 | 12 |
| *(Independent Project limited edition promo)* | | | |

**SEA LEVEL**
**RADIO SHOWS**
**Albums**

| | | | |
|---|---|---|---|
| BBC ROCK HOUR (Nov 80) | 1980 | London Wavelength | 50-75 |
| *(Live concert)* | | | |

**SEAL**
*Other Sire promo CD singles $3-5 each*
**12-Inch Singles**

| | | | |
|---|---|---|---|
| PRAYER FOR THE DYING (3 versions) | 1994 | Sire PRO-A-7057 | 20 |
| **Compact Discs** | | | |
| KISS FROM A ROSE | 1995 | Sire PRO-CD-7190-R | 8 |
| *(Promo CD single of his biggest U.S. hit, short version)* | | | |

| Title | Yr | Label, Number | NM $ |
|---|---|---|---|
| **RADIO SHOWS** | | | |
| **Compact Discs** | | | |
| IN CONCERT-NU ROCK (Dec 95) | 1995 | Westwood One | 40-60 |
| *(Live concert material)* | | | |

**SEALS AND CROFTS**
*T.A. promo 45s $5 each; Warner Bros. promo 45s $3 each; Challenge promo 45s by Jimmy Seals $12 each*

| Title | Yr | Label, Number | NM $ |
|---|---|---|---|
| **12-Inch Singles** | | | |
| YOU'RE THE LOVE (5:22) (stereo/mono) | 1978 | Warner Bros. PRO-A-722 | 15 |
| **45s** | | | |
| WHAT'S IT ALL ABOUT Public service show | 1972 | W.I.A.A. 208 | 18 |
| *(Flip side features Three Dog Night)* | | | |
| WHAT'S IT ALL ABOUT (July 76) Public service show | 1976 | W.I.A.A. 325 | 15 |
| *(Flip side features Rare Earth)* | | | |
| **7-Inch Extended Plays** | | | |
| SEALS & CROFTS Jukebox LLP | 1974 | Warner Bros. 2761 (LLP 248) | 12 |
| *(Issued with a paper cover)* | | | |
| **RADIO SHOWS** | | | |
| **Albums** | | | |
| HERE'S TO VETERANS (70s) | 197? | Veterans Administration | 30-50 |
| *(Music and interviews)* | | | |
| ROBERT W. MORGAN Profile | 1976 | Watermark | 25-40 |
| *(Music and interviews)* | | | |

**SEARCHERS, THE**

| Title | Yr | Label, Number | NM $ |
|---|---|---|---|
| **Albums** | | | |
| HEAR! HEAR! | 1964 | Mercury MG-20914 | 50 |
| *(White label promo)* | | | |

**SEDAKA, NEIL**
*Other RCA Victor promo 45s $6-8 each; RCA Victor stereo singles $50 each (used in jukeboxes); SGC promo 45s $8 each; Rocket (MCA) promo 45s $4 each; Elektra promo duet 45s $3 each*

| Title | Yr | Label, Number | NM $ |
|---|---|---|---|
| **45s** | | | |
| BEAUTIFUL YOU | 1971 | Kirshner SP-370 | 10 |
| *(Yellow promo label)* | | | |
| CALENDAR GIRL | 1960 | RCA Victor 7829 | 12 |
| *(White promo label)* | | | |
| CIRCULATE Various artists | 1961 | RCA Victor SPS-33-99 | 25 |
| *(Sampler compact-33 EP issued with paper cover and one song by Neil Sedaka, "Circulate")* | | | |
| THE DIARY | 1958 | RCA Victor 7408 | 25 |
| *(White promo label)* | | | |
| I GO APE | 1958 | RCA Victor 7473 | 20 |
| *(White promo label)* | | | |
| I'M A SONG | 1971 | Kirshner SPS-291 | 10 |
| *(Yellow promo label)* | | | |
| LAURA LEE | 1958 | Decca 30520 | 75 |
| *(Green promo label)* | | | |
| LITTLE DEVIL | 1961 | RCA Victor 7874 | 10 |
| *(White promo label)* | | | |
| OH, CAROL | 1959 | RCA Victor 7595 | 15 |
| *(White promo label)* | | | |
| PREVENT BLINDNESS Various artists | 1980 | Ad Council 1080 | 25 |
| *(16 tracks of ads, one of the four 60-second ads is by Neil Sedaka)* | | | |
| RING-A-ROCKIN' | 1958 | Guyden 2004 | 60 |
| *(White promo label, earlier Legion stock single is worth around $100)* | | | |
| STAIRWAY TO HEAVEN | 1959 | RCA Victor 7709 | 15 |
| *(White promo label)* | | | |
| SUPERBIRD | 1971 | Kirshner SP-313 | 10 |
| *(Yellow promo label)* | | | |
| SWEET LITTLE YOU | 1961 | RCA Victor 7922 | 10 |
| *(White promo label)* | | | |
| WHAT'S IT ALL ABOUT (Sept 75) Public service show | 1975 | W.I.A.A. 284 | 18 |
| *(Flip side features the Bee Gees)* | | | |
| WHAT'S IT ALL ABOUT (July 76) Public service show | 1976 | W.I.A.A. 324 | 15 |
| *(Flip side is Head East)* | | | |
| YOU GOTTA LEARN YOUR RHYTHM & BLUES | 1959 | RCA Victor 7530 | 18 |
| *(White promo label)* | | | |
| YOU MEAN EVERYTHING TO ME | 1960 | RCA Victor 7781 | 12 |
| *(White promo label)* | | | |
| **Reel-to-Reel Tapes** | | | |
| TUNE INTO THE POWER OF RADIO (80s) Various artists | 198? | Radio Advertising Board | 25 |
| *(Eight tracks of radio promos, one by Sedaka, on a 5" reel)* | | | |
| **RADIO SHOWS** | | | |
| **Albums** | | | |
| ALISON STEELE (80s) Various artists | 198? | | 30-50 |
| *(Interview feature)* | | | |
| NBC SPECIAL (Dec 80) | 1980 | NBC Radio (2) | 30-50 |
| *(Music and interviews)* | | | |

**SEEDS, THE**
*GNP Crescendo promo 45s $15 each*

| Title | Yr | Label, Number | NM $ |
|---|---|---|---|
| **45s** | | | |
| BAD PART OF TOWN | 1969 | MGM 14163 | 20 |
| *(Yellow promo label)* | | | |
| DID HE DIE? | 1969 | MGM 14190 | 20 |
| *(Yellow promo label)* | | | |

| Title | Yr | Label, Number | NM $ |
|-------|-----|---------------|------|

**SEEGER, PETE**
*Other Columbia promo 45s $4 each; Columbia promo LPs $20 each*
**45s**

| Title | Yr | Label, Number | NM $ |
|-------|-----|---------------|------|
| LITTLE BOXES | 1964 | Columbia 42940 | 10 |
| *(White promo label)* | | | |
| OLD DEVIL TIME | 197? | Columbia AE 22 | 15 |
| *(White promo label)* | | | |
| WAIST DEEP IN THE BIG MUDDY | 1969 | Columbia 44273 | 10 |
| *(White promo label)* | | | |

**SEEKERS, THE**
**45s**

| Title | Yr | Label, Number | NM $ |
|-------|-----|---------------|------|
| ISLAND OF DREAMS | 1966 | Capitol Creative Products 50 | 25 |
| *(Frito-Lay giveaway, B-side by Lou Rawls, includes custom Frito-Lay sleeve)* | | | |

**7-Inch Extended Plays**

| Title | Yr | Label, Number | NM $ |
|-------|-----|---------------|------|
| GEORGY GIRL Jukebox LLP | 1967 | Capitol 2431 | 15 |
| *(Issued with hard cover)* | | | |

**SEGER, BOB**
*Other Capitol promo 45s by Bob Seger System $8 each; Other Capitol white promo label 45s $3 each; Palladium promo 45s $10 each (Pressed in Detroit by Motown); Palladium (Reprise) promo 45s $8 each; MCA promo 45s $4 each; Other Capitol promo 12" singles $8 each (All are promo-only releases)*

**12-Inch Singles**

| Title | Yr | Label, Number | NM $ |
|-------|-----|---------------|------|
| THE AFTERMATH (remix)/(LP) | 1986 | Capitol SPRO-9736 | 6 |
| AMERICAN STORM (Edit)/(LP) | 1986 | Capitol SPRO-9641/2 | 6 |
| IT'S YOU (45 remix)/THE AFTERMATH (remix) | 1986 | Capitol SPRO-9778 | 6 |
| LIKE A ROCK (Edit)/(LP) | 1986 | Capitol SPRO-9705 | 8 |
| MIAMI (Extended)/(LP) | 1986 | Capitol SPRO-9866/74 | 6 |
| OLD TIME ROCK AND ROLL/SUNSPOT BABY | 1979 | Capitol SPRO-9085/6 | 15 |
| TRYIN' TO LIVE MY LIFE WITHOUT YOU (3:00)/(3:46) | 1981 | Capitol SPRO-9687/8 | 10 |
| WE'VE GOT TONITE (single)/(LP) | 1978 | Capitol SPRO-8987 | 12 |

**45s**

| Title | Yr | Label, Number | NM $ |
|-------|-----|---------------|------|
| 2 + 2 = ? | 1968 | Capitol 2143 | 12 |
| *(Light green promo label)* | | | |
| EAST SIDE STORY | 1966 | Cameo 438 | 30 |
| *(Red promo label)* | | | |
| GET OUT OF DENVER | 1974 | Palladium (Reprise) 1205 | 12 |
| *(Reprise promo label)* | | | |
| HEAVY MUSIC | 1967 | Cameo 494 | 18 |
| *(Red/yellow promo label)* | | | |
| LIKE A ROCK | 1986 | Capitol PRO-9698 | 12 |
| *(Long 5:53/short 4:36 versions, promo-only release)* | | | |
| MIDNIGHT RIDER | 1974 | Reprise PRO 571 | 15 |
| *(Promo-only release)* | | | |
| PERSECUTION SMITH | 1966 | Cameo 465 | 25 |
| *(Red promo label)* | | | |
| RAMBLIN' GAMBLIN' MAN | 1968 | Capitol 2297 | 10 |
| *(Light green promo label)* | | | |
| ROLL ME AWAY | 1983 | Capitol SPRO-9945 | 10 |
| *(Promo-only version release)* | | | |
| ROSALIE | 1973 | Reprise 1143 | 12 |
| *(White promo label)* | | | |
| SHAME ON THE MOON | 1982 | Capitol SPRO-9878 | 10 |
| *(Promo-only version release)* | | | |
| SOCK IT TO ME, SANTA | 1966 | Cameo 444 | 35 |
| Last Heard *(Red promo label)* | | | |
| TRAVELIN' MAN | 1975 | Capitol 8433 | 10 |
| *(Promo-only release)* | | | |
| TURN ON YOUR LOVE LIGHT | 1972 | Reprise 1117 | 12 |
| *(White promo label)* | | | |
| VAGRANT WINTER | 1967 | Cameo 473 | 25 |
| *(Red/yellow promo label)* | | | |
| WE'VE GOT TONITE | 1978 | Capitol 4653 | 10 |
| *(Silver vinyl, only the promo is silver vinyl)* | | | |
| WHAT'S IT ALL ABOUT (Jan 79) Public service show | 1979 | W.I.A.A. 455 | 25 |
| *(Flip side features Boston)* | | | |
| WHAT'S IT ALL ABOUT (June 80) Public service show | 1980 | W.I.A.A. 528 | 15 |
| *(Flip side features Johnny Mathis)* | | | |
| WHAT'S IT ALL ABOUT (May 77) Public service show | 1977 | W.I.A.A. 368 | 15 |
| *(Flip side features Clive Davis, Arista label boss)* | | | |
| WHAT'S IT ALL ABOUT (Oct 75) Public service show | 1975 | W.I.A.A. 285 | 15 |
| *(Flip side features Lobo)* | | | |

**Albums**

| Title | Yr | Label, Number | NM $ |
|-------|-----|---------------|------|
| LIVE BULLET | 1976 | Capitol SPRO-8433 | 25 |
| *(Promo-only release)* | | | |
| NIGHT MOVES Picture disc | 1978 | Capitol | 40 |
| *(Special promo-only picture disc)* | | | |

**RADIO SHOWS**
**Albums**

| Title | Yr | Label, Number | NM $ |
|-------|-----|---------------|------|
| OFF THE RECORD | 1983 | Westwood One (4) | 20-40 |
| *(Two shows, music and interviews)* | | | |
| OFF THE RECORD | 1983 | Westwood One (2) | 15-20 |
| *(Music and interviews)* | | | |
| PIONEERS IN MUSIC (Feb 86) | 1986 | (2) | 25-50 |
| *(Mostly music and interviews)* | | | |
| PROFILE '86 (Aug 86) | 1986 | NBC Radio (2) | 15-30 |
| *(Music and interviews)* | | | |

| Title | Yr | Label, Number | NM $ |
|-------|-----|---------------|------|
| PROFILES IN ROCK (June 80) | 1980 | Watermark | 20-35 |
| *(Music and interviews)* | | | |
| RETRO ROCK (Jan 82) | 1982 | Clayton Webster (2) | 75-125 |
| *(Early live concert)* | | | |
| STARTRACK PROFILE (Jan 85) | 1985 | Westwood One (2) | 30-60 |
| *(Mostly music and interviews)* | | | |
| THE STORY OF BOB SEGER (Nov 91) Profile | 1991 | Unistar (2) | 15-25 |
| *(Music and interviews)* | | | |
| **Compact Discs** | | | |
| ALBUM NETWORK-WORLD PREMIERE (Aug 91) | 1991 | Album Network | 15-25 |
| *(Music and interviews for "The Fire Inside" LP)* | | | |
| IN THE STUDIO (May 93) Profile of an album | 1993 | Album Network | 15-25 |
| *(Music and interviews)* | | | |
| TIMOTHY WHITE SESSIONS (Dec 91) | 1991 | Westwood One (2) | 50-100 |
| *(Music and interview and live tracks)* | | | |
| WESTWOOD ONE SPECIAL (Nov 94) | 1994 | Westwood One | 20-40 |
| *(Music and interviews)* | | | |

**SELENA**
*Other EMI Latin promo CD singles $4-6 each*

| | | | |
|-------|-----|---------------|------|
| **Compact Discs** | | | |
| BOY LIKE THAT, A | 1995 | RCA RDJ-68463 | 8 |
| *(Promo-only CD single)* | | | |
| LAST DANCE | 1997 | EMI Latin DPRO-11947 | 10 |
| *(Promo-only CD single)* | | | |

**SELF, RONNIE**

| | | | |
|-------|-----|---------------|------|
| **45s** | | | |
| PRETTY BAD BLUES | 1956 | ABC-Paramount 9714 | 50 |
| *(White promo label)* | | | |
| SWEET LOVE | 1956 | ABC-Paramount 9768 | 40 |
| *(White promo label)* | | | |
| YOU'RE SO RIGHT FOR ME | 1958 | Columbia 41241 | 50 |
| *(White promo label)* | | | |

**SEMISONIC**

| | | | |
|-------|-----|---------------|------|
| **Compact Discs** | | | |
| CLOSING TIME | 1998 | MCA | 8 |
| *(Promo-only CD single, not released commercially)* | | | |

**SETZER, BRIAN**
*More at Stray Cats.*

| | | | |
|-------|-----|---------------|------|
| **12-Inch Singles** | | | |
| BOULEVARD OF BROKEN DREAMS (same on both sides) | 1986 | EMI America SPRO 9865 | 12 |
| THE KNIFE FEELS LIKE JUSTICE (same on both sides) | 1985 | EMI America SPRO-9576 | 16 |
| REBELENE (same on both sides) | 1988 | EMI Manhattan 04109 | 12 |

**SEX PISTOLS**
*Featuring Johnny Rotten; More at Public Image Ltd.*

| | | | |
|-------|-----|---------------|------|
| **45s** | | | |
| PRETTY VACANT | 1978 | Warner Bros. 8516 | 20 |
| *(Warner promo label, stock picture sleeve is worth an additional $25)* | | | |
| **RADIO SHOWS** | | | |
| **Albums** | | | |
| INSIDE TRACK (June 83) Johnny Rotten and others | 1983 | RKO (2) | 75-125 |
| *(Music and interviews, with Joan Jett and Pete Townshend)* | | | |
| **Compact Discs** | | | |
| REWIND '96 (Dec 96) | 1996 | (3) | 40-60 |
| *(Various artists, includes live Sex Pistols track)* | | | |
| UNDER THE BIG BLACK SUN (May 96) Various artists | 1996 | (3) | 45 |
| *(Music and interviews)* | | | |

**SHA NA NA**
*Any other promo 45s $4 each*

| | | | |
|-------|-----|---------------|------|
| **45s** | | | |
| IN THE STILL OF THE NIGHT (mono/stereo) | 1973 | Kama Sutra 578 | 15 |
| *(As "Eddie and the Evergreens"; may be promo only)* | | | |
| **Albums** | | | |
| JOY PRESENTS SHA NA NA | 1977 | Buddah PG-1 | 12 |
| *(Promo-only album released by Joy soap)* | | | |

**SHADES, THE**

| | | | |
|-------|-----|---------------|------|
| **45s** | | | |
| DEAR LORI | 1959 | Aladdin 3453 | 50 |
| *(White promo label)* | | | |

**SHANGRI-LAS, THE**
*Scepter promo 45s $35 each; Red Bird promo 45s $25 each; Mercury promo 45s $15 each*

**SHANNON, DEL**
*Other Big Top promo singles $15 each; Other Amy blue promo label 45s $12 each; Other Liberty promo 45s $10 each; ABC Dunhill promo 45s $12 each; Warner Bros. promo 45s $5 each; Network promo 45s $4 each; Other Liberty promo LPs $15 each*

| | | | |
|-------|-----|---------------|------|
| **45s** | | | |
| CRY BABY CRY | 1975 | Island 038 | 10 |
| *(Both sides are the same)* | | | |

| Title | Yr | Label, Number | NM $ |
|---|---|---|---|
| FROM ME TO YOU | 1963 | Big Top 3152 | 75 |
| *(White promo label, first U.S. release of a song written by the Beatles)* | | | |
| HATS OFF TO LARRY | 1961 | Big Top 3075 | 25 |
| *(White promo label)* | | | |
| HEY! LITTLE GIRL | 1961 | Big Top 3091 | 15 |
| *(White promo label)* | | | |
| I CAN'T BELIEVE MY EARS | 1965 | Amy 947 | 30 |
| *(Stock copy is very rare, promo has blue label)* | | | |
| MARY JANE | 1964 | Amy 897 | 30 |
| *(Blue promo label)* | | | |
| RESTLESS | 1975 | Island 021-B | 10 |
| *(Unusual B-side/B-side release)* | | | |
| RUNAWAY | 1961 | Big Top 3067 | 50 |
| *(White promo label)* | | | |
| SO LONG BABY | 1961 | Big Top 3083 | 20 |
| *(White promo label)* | | | |
| TELL HER NO | 1975 | Island 021-A | 10 |
| *(White promo label, A-side/A-side release)* | | | |
| UNDER MY THUMB | 1966 | Liberty 55904 | 30 |
| *(Cream colored promo label, Rolling Stones song)* | | | |
| **Albums** | | | |
| 1,661 SECONDS OF DEL SHANNON | 1965 | Amy 8006 | 60 |
| *(White promo label)* | | | |
| ARMED FORCES RADIO & TELEVISION SERVICE | 1963 | Department of Defense | 40 |
| *(Includes "From Me to You" among others by other artists)* | | | |
| DEL SHANNON SINGS HANK WILLIAMS | 1965 | Amy 8004 | 75 |
| *(White promo label)* | | | |
| HANDY MAN | 1964 | Amy 8003 | 75 |
| *(White promo label)* | | | |
| THIS IS MY BAG | 1966 | Liberty 3453 | 30 |
| *(White promo label)* | | | |
| THE VINTAGE YEARS | 1975 | Sire 3708 (2) | 25 |
| *(White promo labels)* | | | |

## SHARKEY, FEARGAL
**12-Inch Singles**

| | | | |
|---|---|---|---|
| IF THIS IS LOVE (same on both sides) | 1988 | Virgin 2260 | 5 |

## SHARPS, THE
*Jamie promo 45s $25 each*
**45s**

| | | | |
|---|---|---|---|
| WHAT WILL I GAIN | 1957 | Aladdin 3401 | 40 |
| *(White promo label, stock copy that is purple vinyl is worth over $400)* | | | |

**7-Inch Extended Plays**

| | | | |
|---|---|---|---|
| THE SHARPS | 1957 | Vik VDJ-6 | 175 |
| *(Yellow promo label, flip side features two songs by The Heartbreakers)* | | | |

## SHAW, MARLENA
**12-Inch Singles**

| | | | |
|---|---|---|---|
| I WANT TO KNOW (same on both sides) | 1988 | Polydor PRO 628 | 8 |

## SHEILA E.
*Paisley Park promo 45s $2 each; Promo CD singles $2-3 each*
**Compact Discs**

| | | | |
|---|---|---|---|
| SEX CYMBAL | 1991 | Warner Bros. 26255-2-DJ | 25 |
| *(Promo-only package of full-length CD; comes in round container with booklet and miniature cymbal)* | | | |

## SHELLS, THE
**45s**

| | | | |
|---|---|---|---|
| PLEADING NO MORE | 1958 | Johnson 106 | 50 |
| *(White promo label)* | | | |
| PRETTY LITTLE GIRL | 1958 | End 1022 | 50 |
| *(White promo label)* | | | |

## SHERMAN, ALLAN
*Warner Bros. promo 45s $4 each; Other RCA Victor promo 45s $3 each*
**45s**

| | | | |
|---|---|---|---|
| BEETHOVEN'S FIFTH CHA-CHA-CHA | 1970 | RCA Victor SP-45-140 | 10 |
| *(White promo label)* | | | |
| **Albums** | | | |
| ALLAN SHERMAN AND YOU | 1970 | RCA Victor SP-33-310 | 15 |
| *(Promo-only open-ended interview album)* | | | |

## SHERMAN, BOBBY
*Other Metromedia promo 45s $4 each; Janus promo singles $3 each; Metromedia white promo label LPs $10 each*
**45s**

| | | | |
|---|---|---|---|
| ANYTHING YOUR LITTLE HEART DESIRES | 1965 | Parkway 967 | 12 |
| *(White promo label, stock picture sleeve worth $25)* | | | |
| BOBBY SHERMAN Cardboard records | 197? | Metromedia 1-5 | 15 |
| *(Five different discs, each with one song, blue photo label)* | | | |
| BOBBY SHERMAN Cardboard records | 197? | Metromedia 1-5 | 15 |
| *(Five different discs, each with one song, red photo label)* | | | |
| COLD GIRL | 1967 | Epic 10181 | 12 |
| *(White promo label, stock picture sleeve worth $12)* | | | |
| HAPPINESS IS One-sided | 1965 | Cameo 403 | 20 |
| *(White promo label)* | | | |

| Title | Yr | Label, Number | NM $ |
|-------|-----|--------------|------|
| HEY, LITTLE GIRL | 1965 | Decca 31779 | 15 |
| *(Decca promo label)* | | | |
| I WANNA BE BOBBY'S GIRL Patti | 1970 | Metromedia 189 | 15 |
| *(White promo label, stock picture sleeve with Bobby Sherman's picture on the cover, worth $15)* | | | |
| I WANT TO HEAR IT FROM HER | 1964 | Dot 16566 | 20 |
| *(White promo label)* | | | |
| I'LL NEVER TELL YOU | 1969 | Condor 1002 | 10 |
| *(White promo label)* | | | |
| IT HURTS ME | 1965 | Decca 31741 | 15 |
| *(Decca promo label, stock picture sleeve worth $50)* | | | |
| YOU MAKE ME HAPPY | 1964 | Decca 31672 | 15 |
| *(Decca promo label)* | | | |
| **Albums** | | | |
| BOBBY SHERMAN Special products album | 197? | Metromedia PMS 501 | 18 |
| *(Yellow promo label, special gatefold cover, promo-only release)* | | | |

## SHIRELLES, THE
*Scepter white promo label 45s thru 1211 $20 each; Other Scepter white promo label 45s $10 each; Bell blue promo label 45s $8 each (Shirley & the Shirelles); United Artists promo 45s $6 each; RCA Victor promo 45s $4 each (Featuring Shirley Alston)*

| **45s** | | | |
|---------|-----|--------------|------|
| I GOT THE MESSAGE | 1958 | Decca 30761 | 30 |
| *(Decca promo label)* | | | |
| I MET HIM ON A SUNDAY | 1958 | Decca 30588 | 30 |
| *(Green promo label)* | | | |
| MY LOVE IS A CHARM | 1958 | Decca 30669 | 30 |
| *(Decca promo label)* | | | |

## SHIRLEY AND LEE
*Aladdin and Warwick promo 45s $15 each*

## SHOCKED, MICHELLE
| **12-Inch Singles** | | | |
|---------------------|-----|--------------|------|
| ANCHORAGE (same on both sides) | 1988 | Mercury 618 | 6 |
| ON THE GREENER SIDE/MUST BE LUFF | 1989 | Mercury 757 | 10 |
| WHEN I GROW UP/MEMORIES OF EAST TEXAS/ JAMBOREE QUEEN/STRAWBERRY JAM | 1988 | Mercury PRO 701 | 15 |
| **Albums** | | | |
| LIVE | 1990 | Mercury PRO 797 | 20 |
| *(Five-song mini-LP for radio stations with custom jacket)* | | | |

## SHOES
| **12-Inch Singles** | | | |
|---------------------|-----|--------------|------|
| I DON'T WANNA HEAR IT/NOW AND THEN | 1979 | Elektra 11440 | 15 |
| **Albums** | | | |
| SHOES ON ICE -- LIVE | 1982 | Elektra AS 11570 | 40 |
| *(Promo-only 7-song live record; issued in generic jacket)* | | | |

## SHOOTING STAR
*Virgin promo 45s $4 each; Enigma promo CD singles $2-3 each*

| **12-Inch Singles** | | | |
|---------------------|-----|--------------|------|
| HEAT OF THE NIGHT (same on both sides) | 1985 | Geffen PRO-A-2351 | 8 |
| SUMMER SUN (same on both sides) | 1985 | Geffen PRO-A-2335 | 8 |
| TAKE IT/GET READY BOY | 1984 | Pasha AS 1877 | 8 |
| WINNER/TRAIN ROLLS ON | 1983 | Epic AS 1739 | 8 |
| **RADIO SHOWS** | | | |
| **Albums** | | | |
| NBC SOURCE (Aug 82) | 1982 | NBC Radio (2) | 30-60 |
| *(Live concert)* | | | |

## SHRIEKBACK
*Any promo CD single $2-3 each*

| **RADIO SHOWS** | | | |
|-----------------|-----|--------------|------|
| **Albums** | | | |
| BBC TRANSCRIPTION DISC Live concert | 1985 | BBC Transcription | 200-300 |
| *(With Killing Joke)* | | | |

## SHUFFLERS, THE
| **45s** | | | |
|---------|-----|--------------|------|
| AIN'T NOTHIN' WRONG WITH THAT | 1954 | Okeh 7040 | 75 |
| *(White promo label)* | | | |

## SIGUE SIGUE SPUTNIK
| **12-Inch Singles** | | | |
|---------------------|-----|--------------|------|
| LOVE MISSILE F 1-11 (single version)/(extended version) | 1986 | Manhattan SPRO 9677/8 | 12 |

## SILL, JUDEE
| **RADIO SHOWS** | | | |
|-----------------|-----|--------------|------|
| **Albums** | | | |
| BBC TRANSCRIPTION DISC Live concert | 197? | BBC Transcription | 50-125 |
| *(With Harding and York, possibly the least collectible show in the BBC Transcription series)* | | | |

## SILLY SURFERS, THE
*Gary Usher*

| **45s** | | | |
|---------|-----|--------------|------|
| HON-DA-BEACH The Wheel-Men | 1964 | Warner Bros. 5480 | 75 |
| *(White promo label)* | | | |

| Title | Yr | Label, Number | NM $ |
|---|---|---|---|
| THREE SURFER BOYS White promo label | 1963 | Dot 16158 | 250 |
| *(Gary Usher with the Honeys)* | | | |

**Albums**

| Title | Yr | Label, Number | NM $ |
|---|---|---|---|
| SOUNDS OF THE SILLY SURFERS | 1965 | Mercury 20977 | 40 |
| *(White promo label)* | | | |

## SILVER CONVENTION
**12-Inch Singles**

| Title | Yr | Label, Number | NM $ |
|---|---|---|---|
| HOLLYWOOD MUSIC/(B-side unknown) | 1976 | Midsong Int'l. JD-11027 | 15 |
| SPEND THE NIGHT WITH ME (9:27)/MISSION TO VENUS (8:45) | 1978 | Midsong Int'l. L33-1977 | 15 |

## SILVERCHAIR
**45s**

| Title | Yr | Label, Number | NM $ |
|---|---|---|---|
| FREAK//PUNK SONG II/NEW RACE | 1997 | Epic ES7 9355 | 10 |
| *(Includes picture sleeve)* | | | |

## SILVERSTEIN, SHEL
**Albums**

| Title | Yr | Label, Number | NM $ |
|---|---|---|---|
| SELECTED CUTS FROM SONGS AND STORIES | 1978 | Parachute 20512 | 20 |
| *(Promo-only EP)* | | | |

## SIMON AND GARFUNKEL

*Includes solo work of Paul Simon and Art Garfunkel; also includes Tom & Jerry, Jerry Landis, Paul Kane, Greg Harrison, True Taylor and Tico & the Triumphs as well as Artie Garr; Other Columbia promo 45s thru 44785 $8 each; Other Columbia promo 45s after 44785 $5 each; Other Columbia promo 45s by Paul Simon $3 each; Columbia promo 45s by Art Garfunkel $3 each; Warner Bros. promo 45s by Paul Simon $4 each; Warner Bros. promo 45s by Paul Simon $2 each; Warner Bros. promo 45s duets w/Paul Simon $3 each; Other Warner Bros. 12" promo singles by Paul Simon $8 each; Other Columbia white promo label LPs $25 each*

**12-Inch Singles**

| Title | Yr | Label, Number | NM $ |
|---|---|---|---|
| ALLERGIES (LP) (7" Version) Paul Simon | 1983 | Warner Bros. PRO-A-2100 | 8 |
| THE BOY IN THE BUBBLE (LP Version) (Extended) Paul Simon | 1987 | Warner Bros. PRO-A-2652 | 6 |
| GRACELAND (LP Version) (Edit) Paul Simon | 1986 | Warner Bros. PRO-A-2610 | 6 |
| LATE IN THE EVENING Paul Simon | 1980 | Warner Bros. PRO-A-889 | 10 |
| *(Promo-only 12" single)* | | | |
| THE OBVIOUS CHILD (THE SINGLE) (same on both sides) Paul Simon | 1990 | Warner Bros. PRO-A-4480 | 8 |

**45s**

| Title | Yr | Label, Number | NM $ |
|---|---|---|---|
| 7 O'CLOCK NEWS-SILENT NIGHT (same on both sides) | 1966 | Columbia JZSP 116469 | 25 |
| *(Promo-only Christmas release for radio stations)* | | | |
| AMERICA | 1972 | Columbia AE-43 | 15 |
| *(Blue promo label, promo only)* | | | |
| AMERICAN TUNE Paul Simon | 1973 | Columbia AE7 1105 | 15 |
| *(Promo-only record and picture sleeve included in the price listed)* | | | |
| ANNA BELLE Jerry Landis | 1959 | MGM 12822 | 40 |
| *(Yellow promo label, stock copy worth more)* | | | |
| BABY DRIVER | 1969 | Columbia 44785 | 20 |
| *(Mono and stereo versions, "Special Rush Reservice" on label)* | | | |
| BABY TALK Tom & Jerry | 1959 | Big 621 | 75 |
| *(White promo label, the existence of this is in question)* | | | |
| BOXER, THE | 1969 | Columbia 44785 | 10 |
| *(White label with large "A")* | | | |
| CARDS OF LOVE Tico & the Triumphs | 1963 | Amy 876 | 225 |
| *(Blue/green promo label, stock copy is higher)* | | | |
| CRY, LITTLE BOY, CRY Tico & the Triumphs | 1962 | Amy 860 | 125 |
| *(Blue/green promo label, stock copy worth more)* | | | |
| DANGLING CONVERSATION, THE | 1966 | Columbia 43728 | 50 |
| *(Red vinyl, white promo label)* | | | |
| DREAM ALONE Artie Garr | 1959 | Warwick 515 | 50 |
| *(White promo label)* | | | |
| EXPRESS TRAIN Tico & the Triumphs | 1962 | Amy 845 | 150 |
| *(Blue/green promo label, stock copy worth more)* | | | |
| HAVING YOU AROUND Dana Valery with Paul Simon | 1967 | Columbia 44004 | 18 |
| *(White promo label)* | | | |
| HE WAS MY BROTHER Paul Kane | 1964 | Tribute 128 | 50 |
| *(The original has NO mention of Paul Simon on the label)* | | | |
| HEY SCHOOLGIRL Tom & Jerry | 1957 | Big 613 | 75 |
| *(White promo label; Writers on both sides of this record are identified as A. Garfunkel and P. Simon)* | | | |
| HEY SCHOOLGIRL Tom & Jerry | 1958 | King 5167 | 100 |
| *(White promo label)* | | | |
| HOMEWARD BOUND | 1966 | Columbia 43511 | 50 |
| *(Red vinyl, white promo label)* | | | |
| HOMEWARD BOUND | 1966 | Columbia 43511 | 15 |
| *(White promo label, black vinyl)* | | | |
| I AM A ROCK | 1966 | Columbia 43617 | 50 |
| *(Red vinyl, white promo label)* | | | |
| I AM A ROCK | 1966 | Columbia 43617 | 15 |
| *(White promo label, black vinyl)* | | | |
| I'D LIKE TO BE Jerry Landis | 1960 | Warwick 588 | 50 |
| *(White promo label, "Just A Boy" on flip)* | | | |
| I'M LONELY Jerry Landis | 1961 | Canadian American 130 | 100 |
| *(White promo label, stock copy worth more)* | | | |
| I'M LONESOME Tom & Jerry | 1959 | Ember 1094 | 50 |
| *(White promo label)* | | | |
| THE LONE TEEN RANGER Jerry Landis | 1962 | Amy 875 | 75 |
| *(Blue/green promo label reads "Advance Copy")* | | | |
| MOTORCYCLE Tico & the Triumphs | 1961 | Madison 169 | 200 |
| *(Brown promo label, stock copy worth more)* | | | |
| MOTORCYCLE Tico & the Triumphs | 1962 | Amy 835 | 150 |
| *(Blue/green promo label, stock copy worth more)* | | | |

| Title | Yr | Label, Number | NM $ |
|---|---|---|---|
| OUR SONG Tom & Jerry | 1958 | Big 616 | 75 |
| (White promo label, Writers of "Our Song" are identified as Tommy Graph and Jerry Landis) | | | |
| PLAY ME A SAD SONG Jerry Landis | 1961 | Warwick 616 | 50 |
| (White promo label) | | | |
| PRIVATE WORLD Artie Garr | 1960 | Octavia 8002 | 35 |
| (Octavia promo label) | | | |
| SAVE THE CHILDREN Various artists | 1987 | DWP 126 | 25 |
| (20 PSA ads including one 30-second by Paul Simon) | | | |
| SHY Jerry Landis | 1960 | Warwick 552 | 50 |
| (White promo label, "Just A Boy" on flip) | | | |
| THE SOUNDS OF SILENCE | 1965 | Columbia 43396 | 100 |
| (Red vinyl, white promo label, this is the acoustic version and rock-enhanced version) | | | |
| THE SOUNDS OF SILENCE | 1965 | Columbia 43396 | 18 |
| (White promo label, black vinyl) | | | |
| STRANDED IN A LIMOUSINE Paul Simon | 1977 | Columbia AE7 1158 | 10 |
| (Promo-only release) | | | |
| SURRENDER, PLEASE SURRENDER Tom & Jerry | 1962 | ABC-Paramount 10363 | 40 |
| (White promo label) | | | |
| THAT'S MY STORY Art Garfunkel & Paul Simon | 1966 | ABC-Paramount 10788 | 25 |
| (White promo label) | | | |
| THAT'S MY STORY Tom & Jerry | 1958 | Hunt 319 | 60 |
| (Hunt promo label) | | | |
| THAT'S MY STORY Tom & Jerry | 1958 | Big 618 | 75 |
| (White promo label; Writers of both sides are identified as Tommy Graph and Jerry Landis) | | | |
| TRUE OR FALSE True Taylor | 1958 | Big 614 | 100 |
| (White promo label, stock copy is higher) | | | |
| WHAT'S IT ALL ABOUT Public service show | 1981 | W.I.A.A. 535 | 25 |
| (Interviews with Paul Simon, flip is Foreigner) | | | |
| WHAT'S IT ALL ABOUT (July 81) Public service show | 1981 | W.I.A.A. 583 | 25 |
| (Interviews with Paul Simon, flip is Pat Benatar, which on the label is spelled "Benatur") | | | |
| **7-Inch Extended Plays** | | | |
| BOOKENDS | 1968 | Columbia 9529 | 40 |
| (Blue/white label, jukebox LLP issued with a hard cover) | | | |
| BRIDGE OVER TROUBLED WATER | 1970 | Columbia 9914 | 35 |
| (Red label, jukebox LLP issued with a hard cover) | | | |
| PARSLEY, SAGE, ROSEMARY & THYME | 1968 | Columbia 70007 | 50 |
| (Blue/white label, jukebox LLP issued with a hard cover) | | | |
| **Albums** | | | |
| THE EARLY SONGS OF PAUL SIMON | 1972 | E.B. Marks | 200 |
| (Promo-only LP released by the publisher) | | | |
| GRACELAND INTERVIEW SHOW Paul Simon | 1986 | Warner Bros. WBMS-140 (2) | 25 |
| (Music and interviews, promo-only release) | | | |
| THE GRADUATE Soundtrack | 1968 | Columbia 3180 | 25 |
| (White promo label) | | | |
| HEARTS AND BONES Paul Simon | 1983 | Warner Bros. 23942 | 20 |
| (Must have "Quiex II vinyl" sticker on cover) | | | |
| THE SONGS OF PAUL SIMON | 197? | De Shufflin DMG 1 | 50 |
| (Promo-only collection of songs by Simon and other artists, "A Collection of Hits") | | | |
| STILL CRAZY AFTER ALL THESE YEARS Paul Simon | 1975 | Columbia 33540 | 25 |
| ("Advance Promotion Not For Sale," issued in plain cover) | | | |
| **Compact Discs** | | | |
| 1964-1993 SAMPLER Paul Simon | 1993 | Warner Bros. PRO-CD-6577 | 20 |
| (Promo-only collection from box set) | | | |
| CONCERT IN CENTRAL PARK SAMPLER Paul Simon | 1991 | Warner Bros. PRO-CD-5220 | 15 |
| (Radio-only highlights from the 2-CD set) | | | |
| RHYTHM OF THE SAINTS, THE Paul Simon | 1990 | Warner Bros. 26098-2-DJ | 20 |
| (Promo-only packaging; box wrapped in twine, comes with either a miniature drum or miniature bead, no difference in value) | | | |
| WORDS + MUSIC Paul Simon | 1997 | Warner Bros. PRO-CD-9034 | 20 |
| (Music and interviews about "Songs from the Capeman," promo only) | | | |
| **RADIO SHOWS** | | | |
| **Albums** | | | |
| BBC TRANSCRIPTION DISC Live concert | 1975 | BBC Transcription | 800-1,000 |
| (One of the hobby's most collectible and rare radio shows/concerts) | | | |
| DIR SPECIAL (July 82) Live concert | 1982 | DIR (3) | 100-200 |
| (With James Taylor, Linda Ronstadt) | | | |
| HOT ROCKS Paul Simon | 1986 | United Stations (2) | 25-40 |
| (Music and interviews) | | | |
| KING BISCUIT FLOWER HOUR (Nov 80) Live concert | 1980 | DIR/ABC (2) | 40-60 |
| (With Jack Bruce) | | | |
| OFF THE RECORD (Aug 91) Paul Simon | 1991 | Westwood One (2) | 20-35 |
| (Music and interviews) | | | |
| PIONEERS IN MUSIC (Oct 86) Paul Simon and others | 1986 | DIR (2) | 20-35 |
| (Music and interviews, also Steven Stills and Loggins & Messina) | | | |
| PROFILE (Nov 90) Art Garfunkel | 1990 | Unistar | 10-15 |
| (Music and interviews, from Solid Gold Scrapbook) | | | |
| PROFILE (Oct 86) Paul Simon | 1986 | United Stations | 10-20 |
| (Music and interviews, from Solid Gold Scrapbook) | | | |
| ROBERT KLEIN RADIO SHOW (Feb 81) Paul Simon | 1981 | RKRS-16 (2) | 30-50 |
| (Music and interviews, with Phoebe Snow) | | | |
| ROCK, ROLL & REMEMBER (Aug 87) Various artists | 1987 | United Stations (4) | 25-30 |
| (Host Dick Clark has several interviews with Simon and Garfunkel during this 4-hour oldies show) | | | |
| SCOTT MUNI'S WORLD OF ROCK (Oct 88) Paul Simon | 1988 | DIR (4) | 50-75 |
| (Music and interview) | | | |
| STARTRACK PROFILE Paul Simon | 1986 | Westwood One (2) | 25-40 |
| (Music and interviews, repeated Nov 88) | | | |
| STARTRACK PROFILE Paul Simon | 1986 | Westwood One (4) | 40-75 |
| (Two shows, music and interviews) | | | |

| Title | Yr | Label, Number | NM $ |
|---|---|---|---|
| TIMOTHY WHITE'S ROCK STARS (Oct 90) Paul Simon | 1990 | Westwood One (2) | 50-75 |
| *(Music and interview)* | | | |
| **Compact Discs** | | | |
| A CONVERSATION WITH PAUL SIMON (Dec 90) | 1990 | (2) | 15-25 |
| *(Music and interviews)* | | | |
| IN THE STUDIO (90s) | 199? | Album Network | 15-25 |
| *(Profile of an album)* | | | |
| IN THE STUDIO (90s) Paul Simon | 199? | Album Network | 15-20 |
| *(Profile of an album)* | | | |
| KING BISCUIT FLOWER HOUR (Mar 92) | 1992 | DIR | 20-40 |
| *(With Bonnie Riatt)* | | | |
| SIXTIES LEGENDS (Apr 92) | 1992 | Unistar (2) | 20-40 |
| *(Music and interviews)* | | | |

## SIMON, CARLY
*Elektra promo 45s $4 each; Warner Bros. and Epic promo 45s $3 each; Arista promo singles $2 each; Any promo CD singles $2-3 each*

| Title | Yr | Label, Number | NM $ |
|---|---|---|---|
| **12-Inch Singles** | | | |
| TRANQUILLO (same on both sides) | 1978 | Elektra 11399 | 10 |
| **45s** | | | |
| WHAT'S IT ALL ABOUT (Oct 78) Public service show | 1978 | W.I.A.A. 533 | 15 |
| *(Paul Davis on flip side)* | | | |
| WHAT'S IT ALL ABOUT Public service show | 1972 | W.I.A.A. 134 | 15 |
| *(The Royal Scots Dragoon Guard and Judy Collins on flip)* | | | |
| **Compact Discs** | | | |
| CLOUDS IN MY COFFEE 1965-1995 | 1995 | Arista | 20 |
| *(Promo-only sampler from box set)* | | | |
| **RADIO SHOWS** | | | |
| **Albums** | | | |
| INNERVIEW (80s) Profile | 198? | Innerview | 15-25 |
| *(Music and interviews)* | | | |
| ROBERT W. MORGAN (Jan 81) | 1981 | Watermark | 20-40 |
| *(Music and interviews)* | | | |
| STARTRACK PROFILE (Jan 87) | 1987 | Westwood One (2) | 20-40 |
| *(Music and interviews)* | | | |

## SIMON, JOE

| Title | Yr | Label, Number | NM $ |
|---|---|---|---|
| **12-Inch Singles** | | | |
| LOVE VIBRATION (same on both sides) | 1978 | Spring 057 | 12 |
| ONE STEP AT A TIME (5:33) (3:39) | 1977 | Spring 025 | 15 |

## SIMPLE MINDS
*A&M promo 45s $3 each; A&M promo 12" singles $8 each; A&M and Virgin promo CD singles $3-4 each*

| Title | Yr | Label, Number | NM $ |
|---|---|---|---|
| **12-Inch Singles** | | | |
| ALIVE & KICKING (Live)/DON'T YOU (FORGET ABOUT ME) (Live)/ | 1988 | A&M 17480 | 8 |
| PROMISED YOU A MIRACLE (Live) | | | |
| ALL THE THINGS SHE SAID (same on both sides) | 1986 | A&M 17371 | 8 |
| HYPNOTISED (4 versions) | 1995 | Virgin 12726 | 8 |
| PROMISED YOU A MIRACLE (Long)/(Short) | 1982 | A&M 17223 | 10 |
| SANCTIFY YOURSELF (same on both sides) | 1985 | A&M 17363 | 8 |
| SPEED YOUR LOVE TO ME/WATERFRONT | 1984 | A&M 17277 | 10 |
| THIS IS YOUR LAND (Edit)/(LP)/SATURDAY GIRL/YEAR OF THE DRAGON | 1989 | A&M 17728 | 8 |
| **45s** | | | |
| ALL THE THINGS SHE SAID | 1986 | A&M | 12 |
| *(White label test pressing)* | | | |
| SOMEONE, SOMEWHERE IN SUMMERTIME (same on both sides) | 1983 | A&M 2556 | 4 |
| *(No stock copy was issued)* | | | |
| **Compact Discs** | | | |
| REAL LIFE | 1991 | A&M 75021 5352 2 (2) | 25 |
| *(Promo-only 3-CD set)* | | | |
| **RADIO SHOWS** | | | |
| **Albums** | | | |
| BBC COLLEGE CONCERT (Apr 83) | 1983 | London Wavelength | 40-75 |
| *(Mostly music and interviews)* | | | |
| SUPERSTAR CONCERT Live concert | 1986 | Westwood One (3) | 30-50 |
| *(Box set, repeated)* | | | |
| SUPERSTAR CONCERT (May 87) Live concert | 1987 | Westwood One (3) | 30-50 |
| *(With the Fixx)* | | | |
| SUPERSTAR CONCERT (June 89) Live concert | 1989 | Westwood One (3) | 40-75 |
| *(With Dire Straits)* | | | |
| **Compact Discs** | | | |
| ALBUM NETWORK | 1995 | Album Network (2) | 50-100 |
| *(Live concert)* | | | |
| ALBUM NETWORK (Apr 95) | 1995 | (2) | 60-100 |
| *(Live concert material)* | | | |
| UP CLOSE | 1995 | Media America (2) | 20-40 |
| *(Music and interviews)* | | | |

## SIMPLY RED
*Elektra promo 45s $3 each*

| Title | Yr | Label, Number | NM $ |
|---|---|---|---|
| **12-Inch Singles** | | | |
| COME TO MY AID (2 mixes)/GRANMA'S HANDS | 1985 | Elektra ED 5112 | 8 |
| IF YOU DON'T KNOW ME BY NOW (same on both sides) | 1989 | Elektra ED 5378 | 8 |
| INFIDELITY (LP)/(Stretch Mix) | 1987 | Elektra 5227 | 5 |
| IT'S ONLY LOVE (Valentine Mix)/(Edit of Mix) | 1989 | Elektra 5358 | 5 |
| MAYBE SOMEDAY ... (same on both sides) | 1987 | Elektra 5247 | 5 |
| MONEY'S TOO TIGHT (TO MENTION) (3 versions) | 1985 | Elektra 5088 | 10 |

| Title | Yr | Label, Number | NM $ |
|---|---|---|---|
| THE RIGHT THING (3 versions) | 1987 | Elektra 5210 | 6 |
| SOMETHING GOT ME STARTED (3 mixes) | 1991 | EastWest 1738 | 10 |
| SUFFER (Edit) (same on both sides) | 1987 | Elektra 5268 | 6 |
| YOU'VE GOT IT (same on both sides) | 1989 | Elektra 5407 | 7 |
| **Albums** | | | |
| SIMPLY RED INTERVIEW | 1989 | Elektra ED 5236 | 30 |
| *(Nelson George interviews Mick Hucknall and Lamont Dozier; promo-only)* | | | |
| **RADIO SHOWS** | | | |
| **Albums** | | | |
| STARTRACK PROFILE (80s) | 198? | Westwood One (4) | 40-75 |
| *(Two parts, music and interviews)* | | | |
| STARTRACK PROFILE (80s) | 198? | Westwood One (2) | 25-40 |
| *(Music and interviews)* | | | |

## SIMPSONS, THE

**Compact Discs**

| Title | Yr | Label, Number | NM $ |
|---|---|---|---|
| DEEP, DEEP TROUBLE | 1990 | Geffen PRO-CD-4208 | 10 |
| *(Promo CD single)* | | | |
| DO THE BARTMAN | 1990 | Geffen PRO-CD-4170 | 15 |
| *(Promo-only CD single with cartoon book)* | | | |
| GOD BLESS THE CHILD | 1990 | Geffen PRO-CD-4218 | 10 |
| *(Promo-only CD single)* | | | |

## SINATRA, FRANK

*Columbia promo 78s $15-20 each; Columbia promo 45s $12 each; Capitol white label promo 45s $5 each; Capitol yellow label promo 45s $4 each; Other Reprise promo 45s $4 each; Qwest promo 45s $3 each; Other Capitol or Reprise jukebox LLPs $8-10 each*

**12-Inch Singles**

| Title | Yr | Label, Number | NM $ |
|---|---|---|---|
| MACK THE KNIFE (Remix 4:50) (same on both sides) | 1984 | Qwest PRO-A-2216 | 12 |
| NIGHT AND DAY/EVERYBODY OUGHT TO BE IN LOVE | 1977 | Reprise PRO-A-674 | 80 |
| THEME FROM NEW YORK, NEW YORK (same on both sides) | 1980 | Reprise PRO-A-865 | 50 |
| **45s** | | | |
| ALL THE WAY | 1958 | Capitol PRO 596 | 400 |
| *(Rare promo with sleeve quoting Sinatra, Jimmy Van Heusen and Sammy Cahn)* | | | |
| CALIFORNIA/AMERICA THE BEAUTIFUL | 1963 | Reprise 20,157 | 250 |
| *(No stock copies isssued)* | | | |
| CALIFORNIA/AMERICA THE BEAUTIFUL | 1978 | Reprise 20,178 | 200 |
| *(Private pressing of 1,000 for Sinatra's personal use)* | | | |
| CALL ME IRRESPONSIBLE/COME BLOW YOUR HORN | 1963 | Reprise 20,151 | 100 |
| COME BACK TO ME | 1966 | Reprise PRO 406 | 15 |
| *(White label promo-only release)* | | | |
| FRANK SINATRA READS FROM GUNGA DIN | 1966 | Reprise 0493 | 300 |
| *(Promo-only release)* | | | |
| HIGH HOPES | 1959 | Capitol F4214/38 | 400 |
| *(Odd promo with sleeve, has Sinatra's version on one side, Jonah Jones' version on the other)* | | | |
| HIGH HOPES | 1960 | Capitol 4214 | 400 |
| *(With promo-only sleeve that has Sinatra's photo in the "G" of "High"; contains red label promo with silver print)* | | | |
| HIGH HOPES WITH JACK KENNEDY | 1960 | (no label) KB-2077 | 300 |
| *(Promo only for campaign)* | | | |
| HIGH SOCIETY INTERVIEW | 1956 | Capitol PRO 2811 | 50 |
| *("Disc Jockey Interview Record"; promo only)* | | | |
| HUCKLE BUCK, THE | 1949 | Columbia 1-222 | 50 |
| *(White promo label Microgroove 33 1/3 rpm 7-inch single; other titles may exist with white promo labels, which would be worth about the same)* | | | |
| IT'S TIME FOR YOU | 1987 | (no label) U-21863 | 50 |
| *(Promo-only 45, Chrysler commercial)* | | | |
| JEALOUS LOVER | 1955 | Capitol 3552 | 25 |
| *(Yellow promo label with Frank's photo)* | | | |
| MISTLETOE AND HOLLY | 1957 | Capitol F3900 | 20 |
| *(Light blue promo label)* | | | |
| MISTLETOE AND HOLLY "The Christmas Seal Song" | 1960 | Capitol PRO 1708 | 100 |
| *(Includes Sinatra's spoken intro; white label)* | | | |
| ON A CLEAR DAY | 196? | Reprise PRO 406 | 25 |
| RING-A-DING-DING | 1961 | Cal-Neva Lodge 101 | 250 |
| *(Promo-only record and picture sleeve)* | | | |
| SPECIAL MESSAGE TO YOU FROM FRANK SINATRA | 196? | Reprise 45-3DM-XX-2 | 400 |
| *(Spoken-word record sent to stores)* | | | |
| SPECIAL MESSAGE TO YOU FROM FRANK SINATRA | 1961 | Reprise 45-KBM-XX-1 | 150 |
| *(Spoken-word record sent to distributors)* | | | |
| WHITE CHRISTMAS | 1966 | Columbia JZSP 116427 | 50 |
| *(White promo label, promo only)* | | | |
| **7-Inch Extended Plays** | | | |
| CAN-CAN | 1960 | Capirol PRO 1549/50 | 400 |
| *(Three Sinatra tracks on promo-only EP, with picture sleeve)* | | | |
| CAPITOL RECORD: A SOUVENIR OF THE CAPITOL TOWER | 1956 | Capitol PRO 254/5 | 200 |
| *(Promo-only giveaway to visitors to the Capitol Tower; includes sleeve; has two tracks with Sinatra involvement)* | | | |
| FRANCIS A. & EDWARD K. With Duke Ellington | 1968 | Reprise 1024 | 15 |
| *(Jukebox LLP, issued with a hard cover)* | | | |
| GREATEST HITS VOL. 1 | 1968 | Reprise 1025 | 10 |
| *(Jukebox LLP, issued with a hard cover)* | | | |
| GREATEST HITS VOL. 2 | 1968 | Reprise 1034 (LLP 191) | 10 |
| *(Jukebox LLP, issued with a paper cover)* | | | |
| MY WAY | 1968 | Reprise 1029 | 10 |
| *(Jukebox LLP, issued with a paper sleeve)* | | | |
| PAL JOEY | 1957 | Capitol PRO 434/5 | 200 |
| *(Promo-only EP; contains two Sinatra songs)* | | | |
| SHORT PLAYING CHRISTMAS FAVORITES | 195? | Capitol PRO 4470/1 | 150 |
| *(Promo-only snippets of Christmas songs, including one by Sinatra)* | | | |

| Title | Yr | Label, Number | NM $ |
|---|---|---|---|
| SINATRA'S SINATRA | 1968 | Reprise 1010 | 15 |
| (Jukebox LLP, issued with a hard cover) | | | |
| SOFTLY AS I LEAVE YOU | 1968 | Reprise 1013 | 10 |
| (Jukebox LLP, issued with a hard cover) | | | |
| THE WORLD WE KNEW | 1968 | Reprise 1022 | 12 |
| (Jukebox LLP, issued with a hard cover) | | | |
| THIS IS SINATRA | 196? | Capitol 789 | 25 |
| (Duophonic, issued with hard cover that reads "For Coin Operated Phonographs Only") | | | |
| TRIPLE HIT PREVIEW FOR BILLBOARD READERS | 1956 | Capitol PRO 304/5 | 250 |
| (Promo-only six-track EP, two Sinatra tracks; sent to Billboard subscribers) | | | |
| **78s** | | | |
| OH LOOK AT ME NOW Frank Sinatra with Tommy Dorsey | 1982 | RCA YN-13247 | 100 |
| (Promo-only release, one-sided single, only 1,000 made) | | | |
| **Albums** | | | |
| A MAN AND HIS MUSIC | 1965 | Reprise PRO-3004 | 125 |
| (Promo-only LP for TV sponsor use) | | | |
| A MAN AND HIS MUSIC, PART II | 1966 | Reprise 5004 | 200 |
| (Promotional album for use by Budweiser) | | | |
| THE ESSENTIAL FRANK SINATRA | 1967 | Columbia 42 (3) | 150 |
| (White promo labels) | | | |
| FRANK SINATRA MINUTE MASTERS | 1965 | Capitol PRO-2974/5 | 40 |
| (Edited version of 20 songs) | | | |
| I SING THE SONGS | 1976 | Reprise 5409 | 50 |
| SELECTIONS FROM SINATRA, THE GREAT YEARS | 1962 | Capitol PRO-2163/4/5/6 | 40 |
| SINATRA JOBIM | 1969 | Reprise 1028 | 5,000 |
| (Only test pressings and a few 8-tracks exist) | | | |
| SONGBOOK, VOL. 1 | 1971 | Reprise 5230 | 50 |
| SONGBOOK, VOL. 2 | 1972 | Reprise 5267 | 100 |
| THE VOICE: THE COLUMBIA YEARS SAMPLER | 1986 | Columbia CAS 2475 | 40 |
| **Compact Discs** | | | |
| CAPITOL YEARS, THE | 1990 | Capitol DPRO-79375 | 15 |
| (Promo sampler from 3-CD box set) | | | |
| COMPLETE FRANK SINATRA SAMPLER, THE | 1993 | Columbia CSK 5224 | 18 |
| (Promo sampler from box set) | | | |
| COMPLETE REPRISE STUDIO RECORDINGS SAMPLER, THE | 1995 | Reprise FAS 80 | 150 |
| (Incredibly rare sampler from leather-bound box) | | | |
| DUETS II | 1996 | Capitol Studio DPRO-79500 | 20 |
| (Gold "Reference CD," similar to a test pressing) | | | |
| FLY ME TO THE MOON | 1991 | Reprise PRO-CD-4753 | 8 |
| (Promo-only CD single from "Sinatra Reprise") | | | |
| I'VE GOT A CRUSH ON YOU With Barbra Streisand | 1993 | Capitol DPRO-79316 | 18 |
| (Promo-only release, two tracks) | | | |
| I'VE GOT YOU UNDER MY SKIN With Bono | 1993 | Capitol DPRO-79305 | 8 |
| (Promo only CD single from "Duets") | | | |
| IT WAS A VERY GOOD YEAR | 1990 | Reprise PRO-CD-4653 | 8 |
| (Promo-only CD single) | | | |
| IT WAS A VERY GOOD YEAR | 1992 | Reprise PRO-CD-5937 | 8 |
| (Promo-only CD single) | | | |
| MY WAY | 1995 | Reprise | 10 |
| (Promo-only CD single) | | | |
| SELECTIONS FROM THE REPRISE COLLECTION | 1990 | Reprise PRO-CD-4510 | 15 |
| (Promo-only sampler from box set) | | | |
| SINATRA'S 80TH BIRTHDAY: CELEBRITY TRIBUTES | 1995 | Capitol DPRO-11154 | 15 |
| (Others salute Sinatra, promo only) | | | |
| **RADIO SHOWS** | | | |
| **16-Inch Transcriptions** | | | |
| TREASURY DEPARTMENT (50s) | 195? | U.S. Dept. of the Treasury | 40-75 |
| (Music and interviews) | | | |
| **Albums** | | | |
| HERE'S TO VETERANS (50s, 60s) | 196? | Veterans Administration | 20-35 |
| (Music and interviews) | | | |
| SOUNDS OF SINATRA Host: Sid Mark | 198? | Orange Productions (2) | 25-50 |
| (Weekly music and interviews, price for any vinyl show 1987-93) | | | |
| WESTWOOD ONE SPECIAL (80s) | 198? | Westwood One (3) | 100-200 |
| (Music and interviews, with live tracks) | | | |
| **Compact Discs** | | | |
| DUETS: THE RADIO SPECIAL | 1993 | (3) | 50-75 |
| (Music and interviews) | | | |
| SOUNDS OF SINATRA (Jan 94-present) | 199? | Orange Productions (2) | 50-75 |
| (Hosted by Sid Mark, weekly program, often with alternate and unreleased versions, price for any one show on CD) | | | |

## SINATRA, NANCY

Private Stock promo 45s $4 each; Reprise promo 45s through 0407 $8 each; Other Reprise promo 45s after 0432 $5 each; RCA Victor promo 45s $3 each; Elektra promo 45s $2 each; Reprise white promo label LPs $10 each

| Title | Yr | Label, Number | NM $ |
|---|---|---|---|
| **45s** | | | |
| RUDOLPH THE RED-NOSED REINDEER | 1981 | Elektra 47234 | 8 |
| (As "Mel (Tillis) and Nancy"; B-side by Dave Rowland and Sugar) | | | |
| THESE BOOTS ARE MADE FOR WALKIN' | 1965 | Reprise 0432 | 10 |
| (White promo label) | | | |
| **7-Inch Extended Plays** | | | |
| BOOTS | 1968 | Reprise 6202 | 20 |
| (Jukebox LLP, issued with a hard cover) | | | |
| COUNTRY MY WAY | 1968 | Reprise 6251 | 12 |
| (Jukebox LLP, issued with a hard cover) | | | |
| HOW DOES THAT GRAB YOU DARLIN' | 1968 | Reprise 6207 | 15 |
| (Jukebox LLP, issued with a hard cover) | | | |
| MOVIN' WITH NANCY | 1968 | Reprise 6277 | 10 |
| (Jukebox LLP, issued with a hard cover) | | | |

(Top left) This Santana concert on The Source was different because it actually lists the live tracks on the label! Most of the time, the track listings were only on the enclosed cue sheets. (Top right) By the time of this Joe Satriani concert in 1989, the King Biscuit Flower Hour had its fanciest logo since the early 1980s. (Middle left) Another unusual radio subject was Leo Sayer, the focus of this Star Sessions show from 1982. (Middle right) In 1972, there was almost no one more popular in England than Slade, and this BBC transcription catches the band in its full glory. (Bottom left) One of the last King Biscuit Flower Hour shows on vinyl was this Bruce Springsteen program for airing during Fourth of July weekend. (Bottom right) Another act more popular in the UK than in the US is Status Quo, which was featured on this BBC exclusive in the 1970s.

| Title | Yr | Label, Number | NM $ |
|-------|-----|---------------|------|
| NANCY IN LONDON | 1968 | Reprise 6221 | 12 |
| (Jukebox LLP, issued with a hard cover) | | | |
| SUGAR | 1968 | Reprise 6239 | 12 |
| (Jukebox LLP, issued with a hard cover) | | | |

**SINCEROS, THE**
**12-Inch Singles**

| | | | |
|-------|-----|---------------|------|
| DISAPPEARING/MEMORY LANE/BARCELONA | 1981 | Columbia AS 970 | 6 |

**SINGING DOGS, THE, DON CHARLES PRESENTS**
**45s**

| | | | |
|-------|-----|---------------|------|
| PEARL'S JINGLE BELLS/CAESAR'S PAT-A-CAKE/ | 1955 | RCA Victor F2NW-7846/7 | 40 |
| KING'S THREE BLIND MICE//DOLLY'S OH! SUSANNA (FAST)/ DOLLY'S OH! SUSANNA (SLOW) | | | |
| (Banded version for radio use; "Jingle Bells" is 1:15) | | | |

**SINGING NUN, THE**
Philips promo 45s $3 each; Other Philips promo LPs $6 each
**Albums**

| | | | |
|-------|-----|---------------|------|
| THE SINGING NUN STORY | 1963 | Philips PHM-3 | 15 |
| (Philips red label promo-only documentary of the number one pop hit "The Singing Nun") | | | |

**SIOUXSIE AND THE BANSHEES**
Geffen promo 45s $4 each; Geffen promo CD singles $3-5 each
**12-Inch Singles**

| | | | |
|-------|-----|---------------|------|
| CITIES IN DUST (Remix)/(LP Version) | 1986 | Geffen PRO-A-2478 | 20 |
| DEAR PRUDENCE/DAZZLE | 1984 | Geffen PRO-A-2114 | 20 |
| FEAR (OF THE UNKNOWN) (6 versions) | 1991 | Geffen 4361 | 12 |
| FEAR (OF THE UNKNOWN) (Techno-Vertigo Mix)/(Dub) | 1991 | Geffen 4368 | 10 |
| KISS THEM FOR ME (4 versions) | 1991 | Geffen 4281 | 10 |
| THE PASSENGER (3 versions) | 1987 | Geffen PRO-A-2731 | 15 |
| PEEK-A-BOO (3 versions) | 1988 | Geffen PRO-A-3195 | 10 |
| THIS WHEEL'S ON FIRE (7")/(LP Version) | 1987 | Geffen PRO-A-2648 | 8 |

**Albums**

| | | | |
|-------|-----|---------------|------|
| SIOUXSIE & THE BANSHEES | 1986 | Geffen | 20 |
| (Promo-only sampler album) | | | |

**RADIO SHOWS**
**Albums**

| | | | |
|-------|-----|---------------|------|
| BBC TRANSCRIPTION DISC Live concert | 1981 | BBC Transcription | 175-350 |
| (With Gillan) | | | |

**SISCO, BOBBY**
**45s**

| | | | |
|-------|-----|---------------|------|
| GO GO GO | 1955 | Chess 1650 | 75 |
| (Red/white promo label) | | | |

**SISTER DOUBLE HAPPINESS**
**Albums**

| | | | |
|-------|-----|---------------|------|
| HEART AND MIND | 1991 | Reprise PRO-A-5010 | 40 |
| (Available as stock copy on cassette and CD only) | | | |

**SISTER SLEDGE**
Cotillion promo 45s $3 each
**12-Inch Singles**

| | | | |
|-------|-----|---------------|------|
| AS (same on both sides) | 1977 | Atlantic DSKO 97 | 15 |
| B.Y.O.B. (BRING YOUR OWN BODY) (6:43) (3:50) | 1983 | Cotillion 645 | 6 |
| DANCING ON THE JAGGED EDGE/(Dub) | 1985 | Atlantic 868 | 6 |
| FRANKIE (Club Mix) (Dub Mix)/HOLD OUT POPPY | 1985 | Atlantic 850 | 6 |
| HE'S JUST A RUNAWAY (6:05) (3:57) | 1981 | Cotillion 277 | 8 |
| HERE TO STAY (2 mixes)/MAKE A WISH | 1986 | Atlantic 979 | 6 |
| (B-side by Joe Cruz) | | | |
| REACH YOUR PEAK (5:26) (same on both sides) | 1980 | Cotillion 229 | 8 |

**45s**

| | | | |
|-------|-----|---------------|------|
| WHAT'S IT ALL ABOUT (Aug 81) Public service show | 1981 | W.I.A.A. 590 | 20 |
| (Flip side features Ted Nugent) | | | |

**SISTERS OF MERCY**
**12-Inch Singles**

| | | | |
|-------|-----|---------------|------|
| DOMINION/DOMINION MOTHER RUSSIA | 1987 | Elektra 5294 | 8 |
| LUCRETIA MY REFLECTION (3 versions) | 1987 | Elektra ED 5321 | 10 |
| THIS CORROSION (2 mixes) | 1987 | Elektra ED 5263 | 10 |

**SKAGGS, RICKY**
**45s**

| | | | |
|-------|-----|---------------|------|
| CHILDREN GO | 1983 | Sugar Hill/Epic AE7 1802 | 10 |
| (White label, promo-only, same on both sides) | | | |

**SKAGGS, RICKY, AND JAMES TAYLOR**
**45s**

| | | | |
|-------|-----|---------------|------|
| NEW STAR SHINING (same on both sides) | 1986 | Epic AE7 2569 | 8 |
| (Includes promo-only picture sleeve) | | | |

**SKELTON, RED**
**45s**

| | | | |
|-------|-----|---------------|------|
| THE LITTLE CHRISTMAS TREE (Part 1)/(Part 2) | 195? | Columbia J-1973 | 12 |

| Title | Yr | Label, Number | NM $ |
|-------|----|--------------|------|

**SKID ROW**
*Atlantic promo 45s $3 each; Atlantic promo CD singles $3-5 each*
**RADIO SHOWS**
**Albums**

| | | | |
|-------|----|--------------|------|
| HI VOLTAGE (Oct 89) Various artists | 1989 | Westwood One (2) | 20-40 |
| *(Live segment features Skid Row in concert)* | | | |
| IN CONCERT (Feb 90) | 1990 | Westwood One (2) | 25-50 |
| *(Live concert)* | | | |

**SKINNER, JIMMIE**
*Mercury promo 45s $3 each*
**Albums**

| | | | |
|-------|----|--------------|------|
| SONGS THAT MADE THE JUKEBOX PLAY | 1957 | Mercury 20352 | 50 |
| *(White promo label)* | | | |

**SKYLAR, NORM**
**45s**

| | | | |
|-------|----|--------------|------|
| ROCK AND ROLL BLUES | 1957 | Crest 1044 | 60 |
| *(White promo label)* | | | |

**SKYLINERS, THE**
**45s**

| | | | |
|-------|----|--------------|------|
| SINCE I FELL FOR YOU/I'D DIE | 1963 | Motown 1046 | 2,000 |
| *(Record never got beyond the test pressing stage; only two known copies)* | | | |
| THE DOOR IS STILL OPEN | 1961 | Colpix 188 | 45 |
| *(White promo label)* | | | |

**SLADE**
*Other Warner Bros. promo 45s $6 each; CBS Associated promo 45s $4 each (U.S. hits were on this label)*
**45s**

| | | | |
|-------|----|--------------|------|
| COZ I LOVE YOU | 1971 | Cotillion 44139 | 25 |
| *(White or blue promo label, most copies have no promo markings, but stock copies are red-orange)* | | | |
| CUM ON FEEL THE NOIZE | 1973 | Polydor 15069 | 15 |
| *(Stereo/mono, one side red label, other side white label)* | | | |
| CUZ I LOVE YOU | 1972 | Polydor 15044 | 18 |
| *(Stereo/mono, one side red label, other side white label)* | | | |
| GET DOWN AND GET WITH IT | 1971 | Cotillion 44128 | 30 |
| *(White or blue promo label, most copies have no promo markings, but stock copies are red-orange)* | | | |
| GUDBUY T' JANE | 1972 | Polydor 15060 | 15 |
| *(Stereo/mono, one side red label, other side white label)* | | | |
| LOOK WUT YOU DUN | 1972 | Cotillion 44150 | 20 |
| *(White or blue promo label, most copies have no promo markings, but stock copies are red-orange)* | | | |
| LOOK WUT YOU DUN | 1972 | Polydor 15041 | 18 |
| *(Stereo/mono, one side red label, other side white label)* | | | |
| MAMA WEER ALL CRAZEE NOW | 1972 | Polydor 15053 | 15 |
| *(Stereo/mono, one side red label, other side white label)* | | | |
| MERRY XMAS EVERYBODY | 1973 | Warner Bros. 7758 | 15 |
| *(The group's biggest UK/worldwide hit)* | | | |
| SKWEEZE ME, PLEEZE ME | 1973 | Reprise 1182 | 15 |
| *(White promo label, another UK classic)* | | | |
| TAKE ME BAK 'OME | 1972 | Polydor 15046 | 15 |
| *(Stereo/mono, one side red label, other side white label)* | | | |

**Albums**

| | | | |
|-------|----|--------------|------|
| BALLZY Ambrose Slade | 1969 | Fontana 67598 | 50 |
| *(White promo label)* | | | |
| PLAY IT LOUD | 1971 | Cotillion 9035 | 25 |
| *(White promo label)* | | | |
| SLADE ALIVE! | 1972 | Polydor 5508 | 20 |
| *(White promo label)* | | | |
| SLADEST | 1973 | Reprise 2173 | 18 |
| *(White promo label)* | | | |
| SLAYED | 1973 | Polydor 5524 | 20 |
| *(White promo label)* | | | |

**RADIO SHOWS**
**Albums**

| | | | |
|-------|----|--------------|------|
| BBC ROCK HOUR (May 84) | 1984 | London Wavelength | 20-40 |
| *(Music and interviews)* | | | |
| BBC TRANSCRIPTION DISC Live concert | 1977 | BBC Transcription | 300-400 |
| *(Very rare concert)* | | | |

**Compact Discs**

| | | | |
|-------|----|--------------|------|
| KING BISCUIT FLOWER HOUR (Mar 88) Live concert | 1988 | DIR | 40-75 |
| *(With J. Geils Band)* | | | |

**SLASH**
*From Guns N' Roses*
**RADIO SHOWS**
**Compact Discs**

| | | | |
|-------|----|--------------|------|
| HARD EDGE OF ROCK | 1991 | (3) | 100-200 |
| *(Live concert)* | | | |

**SLAUGHTER**
*Other Chrysalis promo CD singles $3 each*
**Compact Discs**

| | | | |
|-------|----|--------------|------|
| UP ALL NIGHT | 1990 | Chrysalis DPRO 6107 | 8 |
| *(Promo CD single)* | | | |

| Title | Yr | Label, Number | NM $ |
|-------|-----|---------------|------|

**RADIO SHOWS**
**Compact Discs**

| | | | |
|-------|-----|---------------|------|
| LIVE FROM ELECRTIC LADYLAND (Mar 91) | 1991 | Westwood One | 20-40 |
| *(Live concert)* | | | |

**SLAYER**
*Def American promo CD singles $3-5 each*
**Compact Discs**

| | | | |
|-------|-----|---------------|------|
| LIVE | 1992 | Def American | 30 |
| *(Promo-only release)* | | | |

**SLEDGE, PERCY**
**12-Inch Singles**

| | | | |
|-------|-----|---------------|------|
| WHEN SHE'S TOUCHING ME (same on both sides) | 1977 | Capricorn PRO 672 | 12 |

**SLICK, GRACE**
*Also see Jefferson Airplane*
**12-Inch Singles**

| | | | |
|-------|-----|---------------|------|
| ALL THE MACHINES (Long)/(Short) | 1984 | RCA Victor JD-13708 | 6 |

**45s**

| | | | |
|-------|-----|---------------|------|
| WHAT'S IT ALL ABOUT (Aug 80) Public service show | 1980 | W.I.A.A. 1802/537 | 15 |
| *(Heart is on flip side)* | | | |

**Albums**

| | | | |
|-------|-----|---------------|------|
| RCA SPECIAL RADIO SERIES | 1981 | RCA Victor DJL1-3923 | 20 |
| WELCOME TO THE WRECKING BALL INTERVIEW | 1981 | RCA Victor DJL1-3922 | 20 |

**RADIO SHOWS**
**Albums**

| | | | |
|-------|-----|---------------|------|
| ROBERT W. MORGAN | 198? | Watermark | 20-40 |
| *(Music and interview)* | | | |

**SLY AND THE FAMILY STONE**
*Other Epic white promo label 45s $5 each; Warner Bros. promo 45s $3 each; Other Epic white promo label LPs $18 each*
**45s**

| | | | |
|-------|-----|---------------|------|
| HIGHER | 1967 | Epic 10229 | 10 |
| *(White promo label, their first major-label release)* | | | |

**7-Inch Extended Plays**

| | | | |
|-------|-----|---------------|------|
| SLY & THE FAMILY STONE Jukebox LLP | 1968 | Epic 26397 | 25 |
| *(Issued with a hard cover)* | | | |

**Albums**

| | | | |
|-------|-----|---------------|------|
| EVERYTHING YOU WANTED TO HEAR BY SLY AND THE FAMILY STONE BUT WERE AFRAID TO ASK FOR | 1976 | Epic AS-264 | 25 |
| *(From the Epic promo-only greatest hits LP series)* | | | |

**SLY FOX**
**12-Inch Singles**

| | | | |
|-------|-----|---------------|------|
| LET'S GO ALL THE WAY (3 versions) | 1985 | Capitol SPRO 9643/4 | 6 |

**SMASHING PUMPKINS**
**Compact Discs**

| | | | |
|-------|-----|---------------|------|
| AEROPLANE FLIES HIGH SAMPLER | 1996 | Virgin | 25 |
| *(Promo-only sampler from box set)* | | | |
| AVA ADORE | 1998 | Virgin | 12 |
| *(Promo CD single)* | | | |
| BULLET WITH BUTTERFLY WINGS | 1995 | Virgin DPRO-11040 | 10 |
| *(Promo CD single)* | | | |
| DISARM | 1993 | Virgin DPRO-14196 | 10 |
| *(Promo-only CD single)* | | | |
| EARPHORIA | 1994 | Virgin | 50 |
| *(Promo-only sampler)* | | | |
| LANDSLIDE | 1994 | Virgin | 15 |
| *(Promo-only CD single)* | | | |
| 1979 | 1995 | Virgin DPRO-11072 | 10 |
| *(Promo CD single)* | | | |
| 1979 | 1995 | Virgin DPRO-11089 | 10 |
| *(Promo CD single, second version)* | | | |
| ROCKET | 1993 | Virgin DPRO-14143 | 10 |
| *(Promo-only CD single)* | | | |
| TODAY | 1993 | Virgin DPRO-14103 | 10 |
| *(Promo-only CD single)* | | | |

**RADIO SHOWS**
**Compact Discs**

| | | | |
|-------|-----|---------------|------|
| IN CONCERT-NU ROCK (Aug 94) | 1994 | Westwood One | 50-85 |
| *(Live concert, repeated)* | | | |
| IN CONCERT-NU ROCK (Jan 94) | 1994 | Westwood One | 50-80 |
| *(Live concert, repeated)* | | | |
| OFF THE RECORD | 1996 | Westwood One | 25-45 |
| *(Music and interviews)* | | | |
| ON THE EDGE (May 94) Music and interviews | 1994 | Westwood One | 15-30 |
| *(With New Order and Frente)* | | | |
| ON THE EDGE (Oct 94) Music and interviews | 1994 | Westwood One | 15-25 |
| *(With Gin Blossoms and Oasis)* | | | |
| UP CLOSE | 1995 | Media America | 25-45 |
| *(Music and interviews)* | | | |

| Title | Yr | Label, Number | NM $ |
|---|---|---|---|
| **SMITH, JIMMY** | | | |
| **45s** | | | |
| THE CAT/BASIN STREET BLUES | 1967 | Verve 10503 | 10 |
| CAT IN A TREE (Part 1)/(Part 2) | 1967 | Verve 10506 | 10 |
| GOT MY MOJO WORKING (Part 1)/(Part 2) | 1967 | Verve 10504 | 10 |
| I'M YOUR HOOCHIE COOCHIE MAN (Part 1)/(Part 2) | 1967 | Verve 10505 | 10 |
| WALK ON THE WILD SIDE (Part 1)/(Part 2) | 1967 | Verve 10502 | 10 |
| | | | |
| **SMITH, PATTI** | | | |
| *Other Arista promo 45s $5 each* | | | |
| **12-Inch Singles** | | | |
| FREDERICK Live/studio versions | 1977 | Arista SP-62 | 15 |
| *(Promo-only 12" single)* | | | |
| **45s** | | | |
| ASK THE ANGELS | 1975 | Arista SP-4 | 15 |
| *(Promo-only release)* | | | |
| HEY JOE | 1977 | Sire 1009 | 12 |
| *(Yellow promo label, stock picture sleeve worth $12)* | | | |
| PISSING IN THE RIVER (mono/stereo) | 1976 | Arista SP-2 | 25 |
| **Compact Discs** | | | |
| CD SAMPLER | 1988 | Arista 9683 | 40 |
| *(Six classic cuts, promo-only CD for radio)* | | | |
| SELECTED SONGS | 1996 | Arista | 25 |
| *(Promo-only sampler from the "Masters" box set)* | | | |
| **RADIO SHOWS** | | | |
| **Reel-to-Reel Tapes** | | | |
| KING BISCUIT FLOWER HOUR (Feb 76) Live concert | 1976 | DIR/ABC (2) | 100-150 |
| *(With Steven Stills, on two 10" reels)* | | | |
| KING BISCUIT FLOWER HOUR (May 78) Live concert | 1978 | DIR/ABC (2) | 100-150 |
| *(With Ian Dury, on two 10" reels)* | | | |
| | | | |
| **SMITH, WARREN** | | | |
| **Albums** | | | |
| THE FIRST COUNTRY COLLECTION | 1958 | Liberty 7199 | 45 |
| *(White promo label)* | | | |
| | | | |
| **SMITHEREENS, THE** | | | |
| *Other Enigma promo 45s $5 each; Capitol and RCA promo CD singles $3-5 each* | | | |
| **12-Inch Singles** | | | |
| BEHIND THE WALL OF SLEEP (same on both sides) | 1986 | Enigma EPRO 14 | 8 |
| BEHIND THE WALL OF SLEEP/(two more songs) | 1986 | Enigma EPRO 21 | 8 |
| BLOOD AND ROSES | 1986 | Enigma PRO-5 | 12 |
| *(Promo-only 12" single)* | | | |
| BLOOD AND ROSES (same on both sides) | 1986 | Enigma EPRO 5 | 10 |
| HOUSE WE USED TO LIVE IN (same on both sides) | 1988 | Capitol/Enigma SPRO-79335 | 6 |
| IN A LONELY PLACE (same on both sides) | 1986 | Enigma EPRO 22 | 8 |
| ONLY A MEMORY (same on both sides) | 1988 | Capitol SPRO-79276 | 8 |
| TIME AND TIME AGAIN (same on both sides) | 1986 | Enigma EPRO 26 | 8 |
| **45s** | | | |
| A GIRL LIKE YOU | 1989 | Capitol 7PRO 79842 | 15 |
| *(Promo-only release)* | | | |
| HOUSE WE USED TO LIVE IN | 1988 | Capitol PB-44174 | 10 |
| *(Promo record without picture sleeve; stock copies and picture sleeves are extremely rare and may be worth over $100 each)* | | | |
| SICK OF SEATTLE + 2 | 1993 | RCA 62803 | 7.5 |
| **Albums** | | | |
| LIVE AT THE ROXY -- SPECIAL FORCES RADIO CONCERT | 1986 | Enigma (no #) | 40 |
| **Compact Discs** | | | |
| BLOWN TO SMITHEREENS | 1991 | Capitol DPRO-79107 | 20 |
| *(Promo-only collection, later released in similar form as a stock copy)* | | | |
| **RADIO SHOWS** | | | |
| **Albums** | | | |
| IN CONCERT | 1987 | Westwood One (2) | 60-100 |
| *(Live concert)* | | | |
| IN CONCERT (May 89) Live concert | 1989 | Westwood One (2) | 50-80 |
| *(With the Jeff Healey Band)* | | | |
| LIVE AT THE ROXY (90s) Live concert | 199? | Entertainment Radio | 100-150 |
| *(Very rare live concert)* | | | |
| SPECIAL FORCES (SPIN CONCERT) | 1986 | BBE 016 | 75-150 |
| *(Very rare live concert)* | | | |
| **Compact Discs** | | | |
| ALBUM NETWORK (July 94) | 1994 | Album Network | 60-100 |
| *(Live concert)* | | | |
| IN CONCERT (Sept 94) | 1994 | Westwood One | 50-75 |
| *(Live concert)* | | | |
| | | | |
| **SMITHS, THE** | | | |
| *Sire promo 45s $8 each; Sire promo 12" singles $12 each Also see Morrissey* | | | |
| **12-Inch Singles** | | | |
| GIRLFRIEND IN A COMA (same on both sides) | 1987 | Sire PRO-A-2843 | 20 |
| STOP ME IF YOU'VE HEARD THIS ONE BEFORE (same on both sides) | 1987 | Sire PRO-A-2893 | 15 |
| **Albums** | | | |
| THE WARNER BROS. MUSIC SHOW | 1985 | Warner Bros. WBMS-130 | 14 |
| *One side: The Smiths; the other side: The Blasters* | | | |

| Title | Yr | Label, Number | NM $ |
|-------|-----|--------------|------|

**RADIO SHOWS**
**Albums**

| | | | |
|-------|-----|--------------|------|
| BBC TRANSCRIPTION DISC Live concert | 1987 | BBC Transcription | 450-600 |

*(Should prove to be one of the great concert collectibles of 80s music)*

**Compact Discs**

| | | | |
|-------|-----|--------------|------|
| IN CONCERT-NU ROCK (Sept 93) | 1993 | Westwood One (2) | 100-150 |

*(Live concert)*

**SMOKING POPES**
**45s**

| | | | |
|-------|-----|--------------|------|
| PURE IMAGINATION/O HOLY NIGHT | 1996 | Capitol 7PRO-11335/6 | 8 |

*(Promo-only with plastic sleeve and paper insert; 1,000 printed)*

**SMOTHERS BROTHERS, THE**
**Albums**

| | | | |
|-------|-----|--------------|------|
| BEST OF THE SMOTHERS BROTHERS | 1964 | Mercury MGDJ-20 | 40 |
| IT'S BROTHERS SMOTHERS MONTH | 1964 | Mercury MGDJ-25 | 40 |

**SNOW, HANK**

*RCA Victor promo 78s $20 each; RCA Victor white promo label 45s to 5698 $12 each; Other RCA Victor white promo label 45s $3-5 each; RCA Victor green promo label 45s $3 each; RCA Victor compact 33 singles $15 each*

**7-Inch Extended Plays**

| | | | |
|-------|-----|--------------|------|
| MORE HANK SNOW SOUVENIRS Jukebox LLP | 1964 | RCA Victor 2812 | 40 |

*(Issued with a hard cover)*

| | | | |
|-------|-----|--------------|------|
| POP SHOPPER Various artists | 195? | RCA Victor SPC-7-13 | 15 |

*(3-EP set, Hank Snow appears)*

**Albums**

| | | | |
|-------|-----|--------------|------|
| SHOP AT THE STORE One record from set | 1958 | RCA Thesaurus | 150 |

*(Radio jingles, two cuts by Snow :06 and :09, from the RCA Victor sound effects library; the above two are discs 1A and 6A from the "Shop at the Store with the Mike on the Door" series and each disc has a light brown titled and numbered sleeve)*

| | | | |
|-------|-----|--------------|------|
| SHOP AT THE STORE One record from set | 1958 | RCA Thesaurus 5119 | 150 |

*(Radio jingle, one 30-second cut by Snow, from the RCA Victor sound effects library)*

**RADIO SHOWS**
**16-Inch Transcriptions**

| | | | |
|-------|-----|--------------|------|
| COUNTRY STYLE USA | 1955 | Public Service | 40-75 |

*(Hank is host of this 15-minute show, music and interviews)*

| | | | |
|-------|-----|--------------|------|
| NAVY HOEDOWN (50s) | 195? | U.S. Navy | 40-75 |

*(Music and interviews, various guests)*

| | | | |
|-------|-----|--------------|------|
| U. S. ARMY BAND (50s) | 195? | U.S. Army | 40-75 |

*(Music and interviews, with various guests)*

**Albums**

| | | | |
|-------|-----|--------------|------|
| GRAND OL' OPRY | 1963 | WSM Radio | 50 |

*(Music and interviews)*

| | | | |
|-------|-----|--------------|------|
| THE LIVING LEGEND | 1978 | RCA Victor DPL2-0134 (2) | 100 |

*(RCA Special Products release)*

**SNOW, PHOEBE**

*Any promo 45s $2 each; Any promo CD singles $2 each*

**12-Inch Singles**

| | | | |
|-------|-----|--------------|------|
| IF I CAN JUST GET THROUGH THE NIGHT (same on both sides) | 1989 | Elektra ED 5370 | 6 |
| SOMETHING REAL (same on both sides) | 1989 | Elektra ED 5383 | 6 |

**45s**

| | | | |
|-------|-----|--------------|------|
| WHAT'S IT ALL ABOUT (70s) Public service show | 197? | W.I.A.A. | 12 |

*(Interview)*

**RADIO SHOWS**
**Albums**

| | | | |
|-------|-----|--------------|------|
| INNERVIEW (70s) Profile | 197? | Innerview | 10-15 |

*(Music and interviews)*

**SOCIAL DISTORTION**
**12-Inch Singles**

| | | | |
|-------|-----|--------------|------|
| BAD LUCK (same on both sides) | 1992 | Epic EAS 4348 | 15 |
| RING OF FIRE/LONESOME TRAIN | 1990 | Epic EAS 2120 | 15 |

**45s**

| | | | |
|-------|-----|--------------|------|
| COLD FEELINGS/BAD LUCK (Live Acoustic) | 1992 | Epic ES7 4568 | 4 |

**SOFT CELL**

*Other Sire promo 45s $3 each*

**12-Inch Singles**

| | | | |
|-------|-----|--------------|------|
| LOVING YOU, HATING ME (2 versions)/HEAT | 1983 | Sire PRO-A-1096 | 12 |
| WHAT!/INSECURE ME | 1982 | Sire PRO-A-1037 | 15 |

**45s**

| | | | |
|-------|-----|--------------|------|
| LOVING YOU HATING ME (mono/stereo) | 1983 | Sire 29812 | 3 |
| TAINTED LOVE/WHERE DID OUR LOVE GO | 1981 | Sire PRO-S-1028 | 12 |

*(Promo-only version, long 4:10/short 3:58)*

**SOHO**
**12-Inch Singles**

| | | | |
|-------|-----|--------------|------|
| FREAKY (6 mixes) | 1990 | Atco 1637 | 7 |
| RADIO SOUL GROOVE (4 versions) | 1991 | Atco 1896 | 6 |
| RIDE (6 versions) | 1991 | Atco 1842 | 8 |

**SOLITAIRES, THE**
**45s**

| | | | |
|-------|-----|--------------|------|
| BLUE VALENTINE | 1954 | Old Town 1000 | 500 |

*(White promo label, black vinyl)*

| Title | Yr | Label, Number | NM $ |
|---|---|---|---|
| CHANCES I'VE TAKEN | 1954 | Old Town 1008 | 250 |
| *(White promo label)* | | | |
| GIVE ME ONE MORE CHANCE | 1956 | Old Town 1032 | 75 |
| *(White promo label)* | | | |
| I DON'T STAND A GHOST OF A CHANCE | 1955 | Old Town 1010 | 250 |
| *(White promo label)* | | | |
| I REALLY LOVE YOU SO | 1957 | Old Town 1044 | 50 |
| *(White promo label)* | | | |
| MAGIC ROSE | 1955 | Old Town 1015 | 80 |
| *(White promo label)* | | | |
| PLEASE REMEMBER MY HEART | 1954 | Old Town 1006 | 250 |
| *(White promo label)* | | | |
| THE HONEYMOON | 1956 | Old Town 1019 | 75 |
| *(White promo label)* | | | |
| THE WEDDING | 1955 | Old Town 1014 | 100 |
| *(White promo label)* | | | |
| WALKING ALONE | 1957 | Old Town 1034 | 75 |
| *(White promo label)* | | | |
| WHAT DID SHE SAY | 1955 | Old Town 1012 | 200 |
| *(White promo label)* | | | |
| YOU'VE SINNED | 1956 | Old Town 1026 | 75 |
| *(White promo label)* | | | |

**SOLOTONES, THE**
**45s**

| PORK AND BEANS | 1955 | Excello 2060 | 75 |
|---|---|---|---|
| *(Blue/white promo label)* | | | |

**SONIC YOUTH**
*Geffen promo CD singles $4-6 each*
**12-Inch Singles**

| CANDLE (Edit)/HEY JONI (Live)/FLOWER (Live)/GHOST BITCH (Live) | 1989 | Enigma EPRO 182 | 25 |
|---|---|---|---|
| DISAPPEAR (3 versions) | 1991 | DGC 4172 | 8 |
| KOOL THING (LP)/(8-track demo) | 1990 | DGC 4123 | 12 |

**45s**

| GOO | 1990 | DGC 106610 | 10 |
|---|---|---|---|
| *(Promo flexi-disc with backing card)* | | | |

**Compact Discs**

| SCREAMING FIELDS OF SONIC LOVE | 1994 | DGC 4577 | 20 |
|---|---|---|---|
| *(Promo-only collection)* | | | |
| SUPERSTAR | 1994 | A&M 8324 | 8 |
| *(Promo-only CD single from the "If I Were a Carpenter" tribute album)* | | | |

**RADIO SHOWS**
**Compact Discs**

| IN CONCERT-NU ROCK (Apr 94) | 1994 | Westwood One | 40-75 |
|---|---|---|---|
| *(Live concert)* | | | |
| ON THE EDGE (Sept 94) Music and interviews | 1994 | Westwood One | 20-30 |
| *(With They Might Be Giants)* | | | |

**SONICS, THE**
**45s**

| AS I LIVE ON | 1955 | Groove 0112 | 150 |
|---|---|---|---|
| *(White promo label)* | | | |

**SONNY AND CHER**
*Includes Caesar & Cleo and Sonny Bono; More at Cher; Other Atco promo 45s $6-8 each; Kapp promo 45s $4 each; MCA promo 45s $3 each; Atco promo 45s by Sonny Bono $4 each; MCA promo 45s by Sonny Bono $2 each*
**45s**

| BABY DON'T GO | 1965 | Reprise 0309 | 25 |
|---|---|---|---|
| *(White promo label)* | | | |
| BABY DON'T GO | 1965 | Reprise 0392 | 15 |
| *(White promo label)* | | | |
| I GOT YOU, BABE | 1965 | Atco 6359 | 10 |
| *(All white promo label)* | | | |
| JUST YOU | 1965 | Atco 6345 | 12 |
| *(White promo label)* | | | |
| THE LETTER | 1965 | Vault 916 | 12 |
| *(White promo label, stock picture sleeve worth $50)* | | | |
| THE LETTER Caesar and Cleo | 1965 | Vault 909 | 15 |
| *(White promo label)* | | | |
| WHAT'S IT ALL ABOUT (Nov 82) Public service show | 1982 | W.I.A.A. 647 | 15 |
| *(Cher talks about Sonny & Cher, flip is Roberta Flack)* | | | |

**7-Inch Extended Plays**

| ALL I EVER NEED IS YOU | 1972 | Kapp 34875 (LLP 184) | 15 |
|---|---|---|---|
| *(Issued with a paper cover)* | | | |
| BABY DON'T GO | 1968 | Reprise 6177 | 50 |
| *(Issued with a hard cover)* | | | |

**Albums**

| BABY DON'T GO | 1965 | Reprise 6177 | 50 |
|---|---|---|---|
| *(White promo label)* | | | |

**SONS OF THE PIONEERS**
*Any label promo 78s $10 each; Other RCA Victor promo 45s $5 each; Decca promo 45s $4 each; Granite promo 45s $3 each*
**45s**

| TENNESSEE ROCK AND ROLL | 1954 | RCA Victor 6123 | 10 |
|---|---|---|---|
| *(White promo label)* | | | |

| Title | Yr | Label, Number | NM $ |
|---|---|---|---|
| **7-Inch Extended Plays** | | | |
| OUR MEN OUT WEST Jukebox LLP | 1963 | RCA Victor 2603 | 40 |
| *(Jukebox LLP, price includes hard cover and title strips)* | | | |
| **RADIO SHOWS** | | | |
| **Albums** | | | |
| HERE'S TO VETERANS (60s) | 196? | Veterans Administration | 40 |
| *(Music and interviews)* | | | |
| HOOTENAVY | 1965 | U.S. Navy | 50 |
| *(With Marian Hall, music and interviews)* | | | |
| NAVY HOEDOWN | 1966 | U.S. Navy | 45 |
| *(Ralph Emery MC, music and interviews)* | | | |
| | | | |
| **SOUL ASYLUM** | | | |
| *A&M promo 45s $5 each; Other A&M and Columbia promo CD singles $3-4 each* | | | |
| **12-Inch Singles** | | | |
| EASY STREET/ONE WAY CONVERSATION | 1991 | A&M 75021 7410 1 | 10 |
| SOMETHING OUT OF NOTHING/FREAKS (Live)/ | 1990 | A&M 75021 7503 1 | 20 |
| TO SIR WITH LOVE (Live)/MARIONETTE | | | |
| SOMETIME TO RETURN (same on both sides) | 1988 | A&M 17552 | 6 |
| SPINNING/ALL THE KING'S FRIENDS | 1990 | A&M 75021 7401 1 | 6 |
| STANDING IN THE DOORWAY | 1988 | A&M 17610 | 40 |
| *(Promo-only 12" single with title cover)* | | | |
| **Albums** | | | |
| HANG TIME | 1988 | A&M 5197 | 20 |
| *(White promo label)* | | | |
| **Compact Discs** | | | |
| RUNAWAY TRAIN | 1992 | Columbia CSK 5016 | 8 |
| *(Promo CD single, their biggest hit)* | | | |
| SOMETHING OUT OF NOTHING | 1990 | A&M 75021 7498 2 | 10 |
| *(Promo CD single)* | | | |
| **RADIO SHOWS** | | | |
| **Albums** | | | |
| OFF THE RECORD (May 93) Profile | 1993 | Westwood One (2) | 20-30 |
| *(Music and interviews, with Living Colour)* | | | |
| **Compact Discs** | | | |
| IN CONCERT (Sept 93) | 1993 | Westwood One (2) | 40-60 |
| *(Live concert)* | | | |
| IN CONCERT (July 94) Live concert | 1994 | Westwood One | 30-60 |
| *(With Big Head Todd and the Monsters)* | | | |
| IN CONCERT (Jan 95) | 1995 | Westwood One | 25-50 |
| *(Live concert)* | | | |
| IN CONCERT-NU ROCK (June 93) | 1993 | Westwood One | 30-60 |
| *(Live concert)* | | | |
| ON THE EDGE (Aug 93) Music and interviews | 1993 | Westwood One | 15-25 |
| *(With Bjork and Lisa Germano)* | | | |
| SUPERSTAR CONCERT (June 93) Live concert | 1993 | Westwood One (2) | 40-60 |
| *(With Nirvana)* | | | |
| **Reel-to-Reel Tapes** | | | |
| MTV UNPLUGGED | 1994 | | 40-80 |
| *(Live concert with Stone Temple Pilots on 10" reel)* | | | |
| | | | |
| **SOUNDGARDEN** | | | |
| *A&M promo CD singles $4-6 each* | | | |
| **12-Inch Singles** | | | |
| HANDS ALL OVER (same on both sides) | 1989 | A&M SP-17896 | 20 |
| JESUS CHRIST POSE/DRAWING FLIES | 1992 | A&M 75021 7290 1 | 8 |
| LOUD LOVE (same on both sides) | 1989 | A&M SP-17933 | 20 |
| RUSTY CAGE (2 versions)/GIRL U WANT/SHOW ME/INTO THE VOID | 1991 | A&M 75021 7338 1 | 15 |
| **Albums** | | | |
| LOUDER THAN LIVE | 1990 | A&M SP-17951 | 50 |
| *(Promo-only live album on blue vinyl)* | | | |
| **Compact Discs** | | | |
| FORESHOCKS | 1994 | A&M 31454 8053 2 | 80 |
| *(Promo-only sampler)* | | | |
| LOUDER THAN LIVE | 1991 | A&M 17951 | 40 |
| *(Promo-only release, eight live tracks)* | | | |
| SUPERINTERVIEW | 1994 | A&M 31454 8056 2 | 25 |
| *(Promo-only interview disc)* | | | |
| **RADIO SHOWS** | | | |
| **Compact Discs** | | | |
| OFF THE RECORD (July 94) Profile | 1994 | Westwood One | 15-25 |
| *(Music and interviews)* | | | |
| ON THE EDGE (Feb 94) Music and interviews | 1994 | Westwood One | 20-35 |
| *(With Nick Haywood and James)* | | | |
| ON THE EDGE (July 94) Music and interviews | 1994 | Westwood One | 20-40 |
| *(With Buffalo Tom and Sheryl Crow)* | | | |
| | | | |
| **SOUP DRAGONS** | | | |
| **12-Inch Singles** | | | |
| BACKWARDS DOG (3 versions) | 1989 | Big Life 897 | 8 |
| MAJESTIC HEAD (same on both sides) | 1988 | Sire PRO-A-2965 | 12 |
| | | | |
| **SOUTHER, J.D.** | | | |
| *Asylum promo 45s $3 each; Columbia promo 45s $3 each* | | | |
| **12-Inch Singles** | | | |
| BAD NEWS/HOMEBY DOWN/GO AHEAD | 1984 | Warner Bros. PRO-A-2140 | 6 |

| Title | Yr | Label, Number | NM $ |
|---|---|---|---|
| **RADIO SHOWS** | | | |
| **Albums** | | | |
| ROCK AROUND THE WORLD (Oct 76) Live concert | 1976 | RATW | 125-250 |
| *(With Ian Matthews)* | | | |

**SOUTHSIDE JOHNNY AND THE ASBURY JUKES**
**12-Inch Singles**

| | | | |
|---|---|---|---|
| GET YOUR BODY ON THE JOB (same on both sides) | 1983 | Mirage 683 | 6 |
| LOVE IS THE DRUG (same on both sides) | 1983 | Mirage 652 | 6 |
| TELL ME (same on both sides) | 1986 | Atlantic 954 | 6 |
| TRASH IT UP (Remix)/MS. PARK AVE. | 1983 | Mirage 666 | 6 |
| WALK AWAY RENEE (same on both sides) | 1986 | Atlantic 907 | 6 |

**SOVINE, RED**
**Albums**

| | | | |
|---|---|---|---|
| RED SOVINE | 1957 | MGM 3465 | 50 |
| *(Yellow promo label)* | | | |

**SPADES, THE**
*Liberty promo 45s $10 each*

**SPANDAU BALLET**
*Chrysalis promo 45s $3 each*
**12-Inch Singles**

| | | | |
|---|---|---|---|
| HOW MANY LIES (same on both sides) | 1986 | Epic EAS 02664 | 7 |
| LIFELINE (same on both sides) | 1983 | Chrysalis AS 1630 | 6 |
| **RADIO SHOWS** | | | |
| **Albums** | | | |
| BBC ROCK HOUR (July 83) | 1983 | London Wavelength | 40-75 |
| *(Music and interviews)* | | | |

**SPANIELS, THE**
*Other Vee Jay promo 45s $40 each*
**45s**

| | | | |
|---|---|---|---|
| DEAR HEART | 1956 | Vee Jay 189 | 50 |
| *(White promo label)* | | | |
| FALSE LOVE | 1956 | Vee Jay 178 | 50 |
| *(White promo label)* | | | |
| SINCE I FELL FOR YOU | 1956 | Vee Jay 202 | 50 |
| *(White promo label)* | | | |
| YOU PAINTED PICTURES | 1955 | Vee Jay 154 | 50 |
| *(White promo label)* | | | |

**SPANKY AND OUR GANG**
*Other Mercury promo 45s $3 each; Mercury promo LPs $8 each*
**7-Inch Extended Plays**

| | | | |
|---|---|---|---|
| LIKE TO GET TO KNOW YOU | 1968 | Mercury MEP-90 | 10 |
| *(Four song promo-only EP)* | | | |

**SPANN, OTIS**
**45s**

| | | | |
|---|---|---|---|
| IT MUST HAVE BEEN THE DEVIL | 1955 | Checker 807 | 200 |
| *(White promo label)* | | | |

**SPARKS**
*Other Island promo 45s $5 each; Atlantic promo 45s $3 each; Elektra promo 45s $5 each; Curb promo 45s $3 each; Morocco promo 45s $3 each*
**12-Inch Singles**

| | | | |
|---|---|---|---|
| BEAT THE CLOCK (7:44)/TRYOUTS FOR THE HUMAN RACE (7:54) | 1979 | Elektra 11412 | 10 |
| I PREDICT (6:19) (2:55) | 1982 | Atlantic 325 | 10 |
| MUSIC THAT YOU CAN DANCE TO (same on both sides) | 1986 | MCA Curb L33-17143 | 6 |
| PROGRESS (Extended Club)/SPARKS IN THE DARK (Extended Club)/ | 1984 | Atlantic 753 | 6 |
| WITH ALL MY MIGHT | | | |
| TRYOUTS FOR THE HUMAN RACE (7:54) (4:00) | 1979 | Elektra 11412 | 12 |
| **45s** | | | |
| ACHOO | 1974 | Island 023 | 10 |
| *(White promo label, the promo copy does not have "The Wedding of Jacqueline Kennedy to Russell Mael" on the flip side)* | | | |
| OVER THE SUMMER | 1977 | Columbia 10579 | 10 |
| *(White promo label)* | | | |
| TALENT IS AN ASSET | 1974 | Island 009 | 10 |
| *(White promo label)* | | | |
| THIS TOWN AIN'T BIG ENOUGH FOR THE BOTH OF US | 1974 | Island 001 | 10 |
| *(White promo label)* | | | |
| WONDER GIRL | 1972 | Bearsville 0006 | 12 |
| *(White promo label, yes there was a stock copy)* | | | |
| **RADIO SHOWS** | | | |
| **Albums** | | | |
| BBC ROCK HOUR (June 82) | 1982 | London Wavelength | 75-125 |
| *(Live concert)* | | | |
| BBC ROCK HOUR (June 83) | 1983 | London Wavelength | 80-150 |
| *(Live concert)* | | | |
| IN CONCERT (July 83) Live concert | 1983 | Westwood One (2) | 50-100 |
| *(With Marshall Crenshaw)* | | | |
| KING BISCUIT FLOWER HOUR (July 82) Live concert | 1982 | DIR/ABC (2) | 75-125 |
| *(With Graham Parker)* | | | |

| Title | Yr | Label, Number | NM $ |
|---|---|---|---|

**SPARROW ARTISTS**
**45s**
THE CHRISTMAS STORY/CHRISTMAS ID'S — 1987 — Sparrow SGL CMAS — 4
(Artists on this disc: Michael Card, Scott Wesley Brown, Margaret Becker, Steve Camp, Richard Souther, Steven Curtis Chapman, Geoff Moore, Rick Florian of White Heart, Deniece Williams, Steve Green and Billy Smiley of White Heart)

**SPARROW, THE**
*Early Steppenwolf*
**45s**
GREEN BOTTLE LOVER — 1967 — Columbia 43960 — 25
(White promo label)
TOMORROW'S SHIP — 1966 — Columbia 43755 — 100
(White promo label record and promo-only "Introducing" picture sleeve included in price)

**SPECIALS, THE**
*Chrysalis promo 45s (U.S.) $5 each*
**RADIO SHOWS**
**Albums**
BBC COLLEGE CONCERT (Apr 83) — 1983 — London Wavelength — 40-75
(Music and interviews)

**SPECTOR, PHIL**
*Imperial promo 45s by the Teddy Bears $25 each Member of the Teddy Bears; One of the great producers*
**45s**
I REALLY DO The Spectors Three — 1959 — Trey 3001 — 30
(Brown/white promo label, stock picture sleeve worth $60)
PHIL SPECTOR'S CHRISTMAS MEDLEY (same on both sides) — 1981 — Pavillion AE7 1354 — 15
(Promo-only sampler from the Pavillion reissue of Phil Spector's Christmas Album)
THANKS FOR GIVING ME THE RIGHT TIME! (same on both sides) — 1965 — Philles (no #) — 1,000
(Has Phil's picture on label; actually plays "Ebb Tide" by the Righteous Brothers)
**Albums**
A CHRISTMAS GIFT FOR YOU Various artists — 1963 — Philles 4005 — 1,000
(White promo label)
THE PHIL SPECTOR SPECTACULAR Various artists — 1969 — Philles PHLP-100 — 2,500
(Yellow promo label)
TODAY'S HITS Various artists — 1963 — Philles 4004 — 1,250
(White promo label)
**Compact Discs**
BACK TO MONO — 1991 — Phil Spector/Abkco 711831 — 15
(Promo-only sampler from box set)
CHRISTMAS GIFT FOR YOU, A — 1991 — Phil Spector/Abkco 711832 — 10
(Promo-only sampler from Christmas album)

**SPECTOR, RONNIE**
*Also see The Ronettes; Warner Bros. promo 45s $12 each; Columbia promo 45s $5 each; Columbia promo picture sleeves $4 each*
**12-Inch Singles**
SAY GOODBYE TO HOLLYWOOD/BABY PLEASE DON'T GO — 1977 — Epic ASF 350 — 40
WHO CAN SLEEP (same on both sides) — 1987 — Columbia CAS 2701 — 8
YOU'D BE GOOD FOR ME (same on both sides) — 197? — Tom Cat JD-10380 — 30
(Promo only on red vinyl)
**45s**
SAY GOODBYE TO HOLLYWOOD — 1977 — Cleveland Int'l. 50374 — 35
(Price includes promo picture sleeve, features Bruce Springsteen and The E Street Band)
TRY SOME, BUY SOME — 1971 — Apple P-1832 — 25
(Apple promo label must have the "P" prefix)
YOU'LL BE GOOD FOR ME — 1975 — Tom Cat 10380 — 20
(Blue vinyl promo)

**SPENCER, JEREMY**
*Also see Fleetwood Mac*
**45s**
TRAVELIN' (same on both sides) — 1979 — Atlantic 3624 — 5
(May be promo-only)

**SPIN DOCTORS**
*Epic promo CD singles $3-4 each*
**Compact Discs**
POCKET FULL OF KRYPTONITE — 1991 — Epic Associated — 25
(Promo package with CD, cassette and press kit in green bag)
**RADIO SHOWS**
**Compact Discs**
IN CONCERT (Aug 93) Live concert — 1993 — Westwood One (2) — 40-75
(With Blind Melon)
IN CONCERT (Mar 94) Live concert — 1994 — Westwood One — 50-75
(With the Police)
IN CONCERT (Aug 94) — 1994 — Westwood One — 30-60
(Live concert)
IN CONCERT (Feb 95) — 1995 — Westwood One — 25-50
(Live concert)
IN CONCERT-NU ROCK (Aug 94) — 1994 — Westwood One — 30-60
(Live concert)
UP CLOSE Profile — 1994 — Media America (2) — 20-40
(Music and interviews)

| Title | Yr | Label, Number | NM $ |
|-------|-----|---------------|------|

**SPINAL TAP**
*Enigma promo 45s $5 each; MCA promo CD singles $3 each*
**RADIO SHOWS**
**Albums**

| | | | |
|-------|-----|---------------|------|
| METALSHOP (80s) Various artists | 198? | MJI Broadcasting | 20-35 |
| *(Live segment performed by Spinal Tap)* | | | |

**SPINNERS, THE**
*Other Motown promo 45s $8 each; V.I.P. promo 45s $5 each; Atlantic promo 45s $3 each; Motown white promo label LPs $20 each*
**45s**

| | | | |
|-------|-----|---------------|------|
| I'LL ALWAYS LOVE YOU | 1965 | Motown 1078 | 18 |
| *(White promo label)* | | | |
| LOVE CONNECTION (same on both sides) | 1981 | Atlantic 3882 | 5 |
| *(May be promo only)* | | | |
| WHAT'S IT ALL ABOUT (Apr 79) Public service show | 1979 | W.I.A.A. 468 | 25 |
| *(Flip side is Elton John)* | | | |
| WHAT'S IT ALL ABOUT (June 77) Public service show | 1977 | W.I.A.A. 376 | 15 |
| *(Flip side features Johnny Mathis)* | | | |

**7-Inch Extended Plays**

| | | | |
|-------|-----|---------------|------|
| SPINNERS Jukebox LLP | 1973 | Atlantic 7256 (LLP 216) | 20 |
| *(Issued in a paper cover)* | | | |

**SPIRIT**
**12-Inch Singles**

| | | | |
|-------|-----|---------------|------|
| I GOT A LINE ON YOU (Edit)/BLACK SATIN NIGHTS | 1984 | Mercury 301 | 6 |

**SPLIT ENZ**
*A&M promo 45s $3 each*
**12-Inch Singles**

| | | | |
|-------|-----|---------------|------|
| MESSAGE TO MY GIRL/I GOT YOU | 1987 | A&M 17483 | 8 |
| SIX MONTHS IN A LEAKY BOAT/HELLO SANDY ALLEN/ | 1982 | A&M 17192 | 8 |
| NEVER CEASES TO AMAZE | | | |

**45s**

| | | | |
|-------|-----|---------------|------|
| DIRTY CREATURE (same on both sides) | 1982 | A&M 2430 | 5 |
| MERRY CHRISTMAS FROM SPLIT ENZ | 1982 | Fan Club (no #) | 10 |
| *(Green vinyl for members of fan club)* | | | |

**RADIO SHOWS**
**Albums**

| | | | |
|-------|-----|---------------|------|
| BBC ROCK HOUR (Dec 80) | 1980 | Westwood One | 40-75 |
| *(Live concert)* | | | |

**SPOTLIGHTERS, THE**
**45s**

| | | | |
|-------|-----|---------------|------|
| PLEASE BE MY GIRLFRIEND | 1958 | Aladdin 3436 | 100 |
| *(White promo label)* | | | |
| THIS IS MY STORY | 1958 | Aladdin 3441 | 75 |
| *(White promo label)* | | | |

**SPRING**
**Albums**

| | | | |
|-------|-----|---------------|------|
| SPRING | 1972 | United Artists UAS-5571 | 100 |
| *(Special promo package in 12x12 folder; includes LP, press kit and a packet of seeds)* | | | |

**SPRINGFIELD, DUSTY**
*Atlantic promo 45s $3 each; Philips promo 45s by The Springfields or solo $4 each Of The Springfields (folk group)*
**12-Inch Singles**

| | | | |
|-------|-----|---------------|------|
| DONNEZ-MOI/I AM CURIOUS + 1 | 1982 | Casablanca 20245 | 15 |
| THAT'S THE KIND OF LOVE I'VE GOT FOR YOU (7:06) (same on both sides) | 1978 | United Artists SP-178 | 20 |

**7-Inch Extended Plays**

| | | | |
|-------|-----|---------------|------|
| THE LOOK OF LOVE | 1968 | Philips 2700 | 25 |
| *(Issued with a hard cover)* | | | |

**SPRINGFIELD, RICK**
*Capitol promo singles $4 each; Columbia promo 45s $4 each; Chelsea promo singles $4 each; RCA promo 45s $3 each*
**12-Inch Singles**

| | | | |
|-------|-----|---------------|------|
| AFFAIR OF THE HEART (Long) (Short) | 1983 | RCA JD-13509 | 8 |
| BOP 'TIL YOU DROP (same on both sides) | 1984 | RCA JR-13882 | 8 |
| CELEBRATE YOUTH (same on both sides) | 1985 | RCA JR-14051 | 6 |
| DON'T WALK AWAY (3:38) (4:00) | 1984 | RCA JD-13815 | 8 |
| HUMAN TOUCH (same on both sides) | 1983 | RCA JR-13577 | 8 |
| LOVE SOMEBODY (same on both sides) | 1984 | RCA JR-13747 | 8 |
| STATE OF THE HEART (Special Rock Radio Edited Version) | 1985 | RCA JR-14119 | 8 |

**45s**

| | | | |
|-------|-----|---------------|------|
| BRUCE | 1984 | Mercury 880 405-7 | 10 |
| *(Black promo label, includes letter explaining the song)* | | | |

**RADIO SHOWS**
**Albums**

| | | | |
|-------|-----|---------------|------|
| ROBERT W. MORGAN (Feb 82) | 1982 | Watermark | 10-15 |
| *(Music and interviews)* | | | |
| SOURCE CONCERT (July 83) | 1983 | NBC Radio (2) | 50-75 |
| *(Live concert)* | | | |
| STARTRACK Profile (Aug 85) | 1985 | Westwood One (2) | 30-50 |
| *(Music and interviews)* | | | |

| Title | Yr | Label, Number | NM $ |
|-------|----|--------------|------|
| **SPRINGSTEEN, BRUCE** | | | |
| **12-Inch Singles** | | | |
| BORN IN THE U.S.A. | 1984 | Columbia AS-1959 | 20 |
| *(Promo-only 12" single)* | | | |
| BRILLIANT DISGUISE (same on both sides) | 1987 | Columbia CAS 2806 | 15 |
| DANCING IN THE DARK | 1984 | Columbia AS-1862 | 20 |
| *(Promo-only 12" single with black/white promo picture cover)* | | | |
| DANCING IN THE DARK | 1984 | Columbia 05028 | 25 |
| *(Promo 12" single with color picture cover)* | | | |
| DEVIL WITH A BLUE DRESS MEDLEY/BEFORE THE DELUGE | 1979 | Asylum 11442 | 40 |
| *(B-side by Jackson Browne)* | | | |
| FADE AWAY | 1981 | Columbia AS-928 | 50 |
| *(Promo-only 12" single, with black generic cover and sticker to identify title/artist)* | | | |
| FIRE | 1987 | Columbia CAS-2636 | 25 |
| *(Red promo-only 12" single with/without intro versions, with promo-only picture cover)* | | | |
| GLORY DAYS (same on both sides) | 1985 | Columbia AS 2082 | 20 |
| *(Red label, black and white cover)* | | | |
| GLORY DAYS | 1985 | Columbia CAS-2083 | 25 |
| *(Promo-only 12" single with promo picture cover)* | | | |
| I'M GOIN' DOWN | 1985 | Columbia CAS-2147 | 20 |
| *(Promo-only 12" single with promo picture cover)* | | | |
| I'M ON FIRE | 1985 | Columbia AS-2007 | 20 |
| *(Promo-only 12" single with promo picture cover)* | | | |
| MY HOMETOWN | 1985 | Columbia CAS-2233 | 20 |
| *(Promo-only 12" single with a promo picture cover)* | | | |
| SANTA CLAUS IS COMIN' TO TOWN | 1981 | Columbia AS-1329 | 40 |
| *(Promo-only 12" single)* | | | |
| **45s** | | | |
| BADLANDS | 1978 | Columbia 10801 | 20 |
| *(White promo label, mono/stereo)* | | | |
| BLINDED BY THE LIGHT | 1973 | Playback 45 | 250 |
| *(Blue promo label, 33 1/3 rpm single with small center hole, 5:05, flip side is by Andy Pratt, price includes generic paper Playback sleeve)* | | | |
| BLINDED BY THE LIGHT | 1973 | Columbia 45805 | 60 |
| *(White promo label, mono/stereo; Some of the promo copies included the stock picture sleeve, worth $150)* | | | |
| BORN IN THE U.S.A. | 1984 | Columbia 04680 | 18 |
| *(White promo label, price includes promo picture sleeve)* | | | |
| BORN TO RUN | 1975 | Columbia 10209 | 50 |
| *(White promo label, mono/stereo)* | | | |
| BRILLIANT DISGUISE | 1987 | Columbia 07595 | 12 |
| *(White promo label, price includes picture sleeve)* | | | |
| CIRCUS SONG | 1973 | Playback 52 | 300 |
| *(Blue label, most sought after of the Playbacks, includes generic Playback sleeve)* | | | |
| COVER ME | 1984 | Columbia 04561 | 18 |
| *(White promo label, price includes promo picture sleeve)* | | | |
| DANCING IN THE DARK | 1984 | Columbia 04463 | 18 |
| *(White promo label, price includes promo picture sleeve)* | | | |
| FADE AWAY | 1981 | Columbia 11431 | 12 |
| *(White promo label, mono/stereo)* | | | |
| FIRE | 1987 | Columbia 2639 | 25 |
| *(White promo label, with spoken intro 2:58; without spoken intro 2:49, price includes promo picture sleeve)* | | | |
| GLORY DAYS | 1985 | Columbia 04924 | 18 |
| *(White promo label, price includes promo picture sleeve)* | | | |
| HUNGRY HEART | 1980 | Columbia 11391 | 15 |
| *(White promo label, mono/stereo)* | | | |
| I'M GOIN' DOWN | 1985 | Columbia 05603 | 18 |
| *(White promo label, price includes promo picture sleeve)* | | | |
| I'M ON FIRE | 1985 | Columbia 04772 | 18 |
| *(White promo label, price includes promo picture sleeve)* | | | |
| MEDLEY | 1979 | Asylum 11442 | 300 |
| *(Asylum promo label, from "No Nukes" LP, songs are "Devil with the Blue Dress," "Good Golly Miss Molly" and "Jenny Take A Ride")* | | | |
| MEDLEY | 1979 | Asylum 11442 | 100 |
| *(45 rpm version of above)* | | | |
| MY HOMETOWN | 1985 | Columbia 05728 | 18 |
| *(White promo label, price includes promo picture sleeve)* | | | |
| ONE STEP UP | 1988 | Columbia 07726 | 15 |
| *(White promo label, price includes picture sleeve)* | | | |
| PROVE IT ALL NIGHT | 1978 | Columbia 10763 | 25 |
| *(White promo label, mono/stereo)* | | | |
| ROSALITA | 1974 | Columbia AE7 1088 | 300 |
| *(White promo label, promo-only release, also includes "Spirit In the Night" and "Growin' Up")* | | | |
| ROSALITA | 1973 | Playback 66 | 250 |
| *(Blue label, Side 2, flip side has songs by the Hollies and Johnny Winter)* | | | |
| ROSALITA | 1973 | Playback 66 | 300 |
| *(White promo label, rarer than the blue label)* | | | |
| SANTA CLAUS IS COMIN' TO TOWN | 1981 | Columbia AE7-1332 | 30 |
| *(Promo-only record and promo-only picture sleeve)* | | | |
| SAY GOODBYE TO HOLLYWOOD Ronnie Spector | 1977 | Cleveland Int'l. 50374 | 30 |
| *(White/orange promo labels, promo picture sleeve included in price, Bruce and E Street Band play on the record and appear on the picture sleeve)* | | | |
| SPIRIT IN THE NIGHT | 1973 | Columbia 45864 | 50 |
| *(White promo label, mono/stereo; stock copy worth many times this value)* | | | |
| TENTH AVENUE FREEZE-OUT | 1976 | Columbia 10274 | 35 |
| *(White promo label, mono/stereo)* | | | |
| TUNNEL OF LOVE | 1987 | Columbia 07663 | 12 |
| *(White promo label, price includes picture sleeve)* | | | |
| WAR | 1986 | Columbia 2257 | 25 |
| *(White promo label, with spoken intro 5:10; without spoken intro 3:15, price includes promo picture sleeve)* | | | |

| Title | Yr | Label, Number | NM $ |
|-------|----|---------------|------|
| **Albums** | | | |
| AS REQUESTED AROUND THE WORLD | 1981 | Columbia AS-978 | 50 |
| *(White promo label, promo-only release)* | | | |
| BORN TO RUN | 1975 | Columbia PC 33795 | 100 |
| *(White label promo)* | | | |
| BORN TO RUN | 1975 | Columbia PC 33795 | 1,200 |
| *(Test pressing with "Bruce Springsteen -- Born to Run" in script print. Also includes mailing envelope, letter from CBS and orange patch)* | | | |
| BRUCE SPRINGSTEEN | 1985 | Columbia AS 1957 | 30 |
| *(Five-song mini-LP with five B-sides of singles from Born in the U.S.A.)* | | | |
| BRUCE SPRINGSTEEN | 1987 | Columbia AS 1957 | 20 |
| *(Five-song mini-LP with five B-sides of singles from Born in the U.S.A.; second pressings say so on the label)* | | | |
| BRUCE SPRINGSTEEN AND THE E STREET BAND: LIVE 1975-1985 | 1986 | Columbia 40558 (5) | 40 |
| *(Box set, price is for cover with promo stamp)* | | | |
| BRUCE SPRINGSTEEN AND THE E STREET BAND: LIVE 1975-1985 | 1986 | Columbia AS 2543 | 30 |
| *(Sampler from 5-LP live set)* | | | |
| DARKNESS ON THE EDGE OF TOWN | 1978 | Columbia 35318 | 125 |
| *(Promo-only picture disc sent to DJs)* | | | |
| DARKNESS ON THE EDGE OF TOWN | 1978 | Columbia JC 35318 | 100 |
| *(White label promo)* | | | |
| EXCITING HIGHLIGHTS FROM Various artists | 1981 | Columbia AS-902 | 60 |
| *(Half-speed master, extended range white label promo-only LP with one Springsteen song, "Thunder Road" and promo cover)* | | | |
| GREETINGS FROM ASBURY PARK, N.J. | 1973 | Columbia KC 31903 | 200 |
| *(Promotional copy with timing strip and "Bruce Springsteen Fact Sheet" attached to back cover; authentic fact sheets are on glossy stock)* | | | |
| THE RIVER | 1980 | Columbia PC2 36854 | 75 |
| *(White label promo, with photocopied letter from CBS)* | | | |
| THE RIVER | 1980 | Columbia PC2 36854 | 40 |
| *(White label promo, without letter)* | | | |
| **Compact Discs** | | | |
| ALL THAT HEAVEN WILL ALLOW | 1990 | Columbia | 40 |
| *(Promo-only 5-track CD release)* | | | |
| BETTER DAYS | 1992 | Columbia CSK 74274 | 10 |
| *(Promo CD single, released as B-side of "Human Touch")* | | | |
| DEAD MAN WALKIN' | 1995 | Columbia CSK 7905 | 12 |
| *(Promo-only CD single)* | | | |
| 57 CHANNELS (AND NOTHIN' ON) | 1992 | Columbia CSK 4670 | 10 |
| *(Promo CD single with remixes)* | | | |
| 57 CHANNELS (AND NOTHIN' ON) | 1992 | Columbia CSK 4599 | 10 |
| *(Promo CD single)* | | | |
| GHOST OF TOM JOAD, THE | 1995 | Columbia CSK 7626 | 10 |
| *(Promo-only CD single)* | | | |
| GREATEST HITS With gatefold cover | 1995 | Columbia ACK 67060 | 40 |
| *(Promo-only version for radio)* | | | |
| HUMAN TOUCH | 1992 | Columbia CSK 74273 | 10 |
| *(Promo CD single, edit and full-length versions)* | | | |
| LEAP OF FAITH | 1992 | Columbia CSK 4703 | 12 |
| *(Promo-only CD single)* | | | |
| MURDER INCORPORATED | 1995 | Columbia CSK 6947 | 15 |
| *(Promo-only CD single)* | | | |
| ONE STEP UP | 1988 | Columbia CSK 1031 | 50 |
| *(Early promo-only CD single)* | | | |
| SECRET GARDEN | 1995 | Columbia CSK 6942 | 10 |
| *(Promo CD single)* | | | |
| SECRET GARDEN | 1997 | Columbia | 20 |
| *(Promo CD single, "The Jerry Maguire Mix" with snippets of dialogue from the movie, not released commercially)* | | | |
| STREETS OF PHILADELPHIA | 1994 | Columbia CSK 5664 | 10 |
| *(Promo CD single)* | | | |
| TUNNEL OF LOVE EXPRESS TOUR | 1988 | Columbia CSK 1046 | 40 |
| *(Promo-only release with five tracks)* | | | |
| TUNNEL OF LOVE EXPRESS TOUR CONTINUED | 1988 | Columbia CSK 1108 | 50 |
| *(Promo-only collection, follow-up to first one)* | | | |
| **RADIO SHOWS** | | | |
| **Albums** | | | |
| ALBUM GREATS | 1979 | TM Special Products | 20-40 |
| *(Music and interviews, one disc from the set)* | | | |
| BORN IN THE U.S.A. | 1985 | Westwood One (3) | 100-150 |
| *(Music and interviews, white labels)* | | | |
| CONVERSATION WITH BRUCE SPRINGSTEEN | 1984 | Westwood One (3) | 100-150 |
| *(Music and interviews, red labels)* | | | |
| CONVERSATION WITH BRUCE SPRINGSTEEN | 1985 | Westwood One (3) | 100-150 |
| *(Music and interviews, red labels)* | | | |
| COUNTDOWN TO CHRISTMAS (Dec 85) | 1985 | NBC Radio | 40-75 |
| *(Music and interviews)* | | | |
| HOT ROCKS | 1988 | United Stations (2) | 50-80 |
| *(Music and interviews)* | | | |
| KING BISCUIT FLOWER HOUR (July 87) | 1987 | DIR (2) | 75-150 |
| *(July 4th special, Bruce Springsteen tribute)* | | | |
| ROYALTY OF ROCK | 1982 | | 20-40 |
| *(Music and interviews)* | | | |
| SPRINGSTEEN RADIO SPECIAL (June 88) | 1988 | (4) | 75-125 |
| *(Mostly music and interviews)* | | | |
| STORY OF BRUCE SPRINGSTEEN | 1987 | United Stations (3) | 100-150 |
| *(Music and interviews)* | | | |
| **Compact Discs** | | | |
| THE BRUCE SPRINGSTEEN STORY (Apr 92) | 1992 | Unistar | 40-75 |
| *(Music and interviews)* | | | |
| SHOWCASE OF ROCK (Apr 92) | 1992 | (3) | 150-250 |
| *(Music and interviews)* | | | |

| Title | Yr | Label, Number | NM $ |
|---|---|---|---|
| THE STORY OF BRUCE SPRINGSTEEN (Apr 93) | 1993 | Unistar (3) | 75-150 |
| *(Music and interviews, "Showcase of Rock")* | | | |
| **Reel-to-Reel Tapes** | | | |
| COLUMBIA RECORDS RADIO HOUR (Dec 95) | 1995 | (2) | 400-600 |
| *(Includes live set plus interview by Bob Costas)* | | | |

## SQUEEZE
*A&M promo 45s $4 each; Other A&M and Reprise promo CD singles $3 each*

| Title | Yr | Label, Number | NM $ |
|---|---|---|---|
| **12-Inch Singles** | | | |
| HITS OF THE YEAR/BY YOUR TIME/LAST TIME FOREVER | 1985 | A&M 17349 | 8 |
| HOURGLASS (same on both sides) | 1987 | A&M 17489 | 8 |
| TEMPTED/IS THAT LOVE/MESSED AROUND | 1981 | A&M 17158 | 8 |
| **45s** | | | |
| TAKE ME, I'M YOURS (mono)/(stereo) | 1978 | A&M 2033 | 4 |
| *Label credit: U.K. Squeeze* | | | |
| **Albums** | | | |
| U. K. SQUEEZE | 1978 | A&M 4687 | 20 |
| *(Red vinyl, white promo label)* | | | |
| **Compact Discs** | | | |
| PLAY | 1991 | Reprise 26644-2-DJ | 30 |
| *(Promo-only picture disc with seeds and flowerpot)* | | | |
| THREE FROM BABYLON AND ON | 1987 | A&M 17490 | 15 |
| *(Rare promo-only 3-inch CD)* | | | |
| **RADIO SHOWS** | | | |
| **Albums** | | | |
| BBC COLLEGE CONCERT (Nov 83) | 1983 | London Wavelength | 40-60 |
| *(Live concert)* | | | |
| BBC ROCK HOUR (Nov 84) Live concert | 1984 | London Wavelength | 50-100 |
| *(Includes the music of Difford & Tilbrook)* | | | |
| BBC TRANSCRIPTION DISC Live concert | 1981 | BBC Transcription | 200-300 |
| *(Very rare radio show)* | | | |
| BBC TRANSCRIPTION DISC Live concert | 1986 | BBC Transcription | 175-225 |
| *(Also very rare)* | | | |
| IN CONCERT (Nov 85) Live concert | 1985 | Westwood One (2) | 40-75 |
| *(With John Parr)* | | | |
| IN CONCERT (Feb 87) Live concert | 1987 | Westwood One (2) | 40-75 |
| *(With Richard Marx)* | | | |
| KING BISCUIT FLOWER HOUR (Apr 80) Live concert | 1980 | DIR/ABC (2) | 75-125 |
| *(With Todd Rundgren and Utopia)* | | | |
| KING BISCUIT FLOWER HOUR (Sept 83) Live concert | 1983 | DIR/ABC (2) | 75-125 |
| *(With Rush)* | | | |
| LONDON WAVELENGTH CONCERT (Dec 83) | 1983 | London Wavelength | 75-125 |
| *(Live concert)* | | | |
| RETRO ROCK (Oct 82) | 1982 | Clayton Webster | 40-75 |
| *(Live concert)* | | | |
| WORLD OF ROCK (Nov 89) Various artists | 1989 | DIR (2) | 15-25 |
| *(Members of the group serve as co-hosts, music and interviews)* | | | |
| **Compact Discs** | | | |
| IN CONCERT-NU ROCK (Apr 94) Live concert | 1994 | Westwood One | 40-75 |
| *(With Counting Crows)* | | | |
| KING BISCUIT FLOWER HOUR (Feb 88) Live concert | 1988 | DIR | 40-75 |
| *(With Crowded House)* | | | |
| KING BISCUIT FLOWER HOUR (Dec 89) Live concert | 1989 | DIR | 20-40 |
| *(With Paul Carrack)* | | | |
| ON THE EDGE (Oct 93) Music and interviews | 1993 | Westwood One | 25-35 |
| *(Includes Red Hot Chili Peppers)* | | | |

## SQUIER, BILLY
*Capitol promo 45s $3 each; Capitol promo CD singles $2 each*

| Title | Yr | Label, Number | NM $ |
|---|---|---|---|
| **45s** | | | |
| CHRISTMAS IS THE TIME TO SAY I LOVE YOU/WHITE CHRISTMAS | 1983 | Capitol SPRO 9870 | 8 |
| *(Has the same picture sleeve as B-5303)* | | | |
| DON'T SAY YOU LOVE ME (same on both sides) | 1989 | Capitol 7PRO-79694 | 10 |
| *(Vinyl is promo only)* | | | |
| **Compact Discs** | | | |
| HEAR, THEN AND NOW | 1989 | Capitol DPRO-79769 | 15 |
| *(Promo-only compilation)* | | | |
| **RADIO SHOWS** | | | |
| **Albums** | | | |
| BBC ROCK HOUR (Dec 81) | 1981 | London Wavelength | 40-75 |
| *(With Steve Hackett)* | | | |
| DESERT ISLAND DISCS (June 91) | 1991 | | 15-25 |
| *(Music and interviews)* | | | |
| IN CONCERT (Jan 91) Live concert | 1991 | Westwood One (2) | 30-60 |
| *(With Robin Trower)* | | | |
| KING BISCUIT FLOWER HOUR (Nov 83) | 1983 | DIR/ABC (2) | 20-40 |
| *(Live concert)* | | | |
| NBC SOURCE (Oct 82) | 1982 | NBC Radio (3) | 15-25 |
| *(Music and interviews)* | | | |
| OFF THE RECORD (Dec 86) | 1986 | Westwood One (2) | 10-15 |
| *(Music and interviews)* | | | |
| SUPERGROUPS (July 82) | 1982 | DIR (3) | 40-75 |
| *(With Triumph)* | | | |
| **Compact Discs** | | | |
| IN THE STUDIO (July 89) | 1989 | Westwood One | 15-25 |
| *(Profile of an LP, music and interviews)* | | | |
| KING BISCUIT FLOWER HOUR (Oct 89) | 1989 | DIR | 20-35 |
| *(Live concert, with Aerosmith)* | | | |

| Title | Yr | Label, Number | NM $ |
|---|---|---|---|
| **SQUIRES, THE** | | | |
| **45s** | | | |
| DREAMY EYES | 1958 | Aladdin 3360 | 45 |
| *(White promo label)* | | | |
| LET'S GIVE LOVE A TRY | 1954 | Combo 35 | 200 |
| *(White promo label)* | | | |
| OH DARLING | 1954 | Combo 42 | 150 |
| *(White promo label)* | | | |
| **STAFFORD, JIM** | | | |
| **45s** | | | |
| WHAT'S IT ALL ABOUT (Nov 76) Public service show | 1976 | W.I.A.A. 345 | 15 |
| *(Captain and Tennille on flip side)* | | | |
| **STAFFORD, JO** | | | |
| **45s** | | | |
| CHRISTMAS IS THE SEASON/MERRY CHRISTMAS | 1964 | Capitol PRO 2756 | 10 |
| **78s** | | | |
| ST. LOUIS BLUES | 1952 | RR 22270 | 20 |
| *(Special giveaway for Snowy Bleach and Glass Wax)* | | | |
| **STANDELLS** | | | |
| *Liberty promo 45s $25 each; Vee Jay promo 45s $20 each; MGM promo 45s $15 each; Other Tower promo 45s $30 each* | | | |
| **45s** | | | |
| DIRTY WATER | 1966 | Tower 185 | 40 |
| *(White promo label)* | | | |
| SOMETIMES GOOD GUYS DON'T WEAR WHITE | 1966 | Tower 257 | 40 |
| *(White promo label)* | | | |
| WHY PICK ON ME? | 1966 | Tower 282 | 40 |
| *(White promo label)* | | | |
| **Albums** | | | |
| DIRTY WATER | 1966 | Tower 5027 | 45 |
| *(White promo label)* | | | |
| WHY PICK ON ME | 1967 | Tower 5044 | 40 |
| *(White promo label)* | | | |
| **STANLEY BROTHERS, THE** | | | |
| *King & Mercury promo 45s $5 each* | | | |
| **Albums** | | | |
| COUNTRY PICKIN' AND SINGIN' | 1958 | Mercury 20349 | 40 |
| *(White promo label)* | | | |
| **STANLEY, MICHAEL, BAND** | | | |
| *Epic promo 45s $4 each; EMI promo 45s $3 each* | | | |
| **RADIO SHOWS** | | | |
| **Albums** | | | |
| KING BISCUIT FLOWER HOUR (Oct 81) Live concert | 1981 | DIR/ABC (2) | 50-80 |
| *(With Icehouse)* | | | |
| NBC SOURCE (Nov 83) | 1983 | NBC Radio (2) | 40-75 |
| *(Live concert)* | | | |
| **STANSFIELD, LISA** | | | |
| **12-Inch Singles** | | | |
| MAKE IT RIGHT (4 versions) | 1994 | Giant PRO-A-7240 | 8 |
| **STAPLES, MAVIS** | | | |
| **12-Inch Singles** | | | |
| MELODY COOL (Edit) (LP) | 1990 | Paisley Park PRO-A-4397 | 8 |
| SHOW ME HOW IT WORKS (same on both sides) | 1986 | Warner Bros. PRO-A-2444 | 6 |
| THE VOICE (same on both sides) | 1993 | Paisley Park PRO-A-5991 | 10 |
| **45s** | | | |
| CHRISTMAS VACATION (same on both sides) | 1989 | Warner Bros. PRO-S-3878 | 5 |
| **STARETTES** | | | |
| **45s** | | | |
| FIFI THE CHRISTMAS FAWN/LITTLE CHRISTMAS BELLS | 1962 | Venett 101 | 12 |
| **STARFIRES, THE** | | | |
| *With Steve Ellis* | | | |
| **45s** | | | |
| WALKING AROUND | 1965 | Century 22355 | 40 |
| *(Test press only, later release on Decima a different mix, worth $25)* | | | |
| **Albums** | | | |
| STEVE ELLIS SONGBOOK | 1967 | IGL 105 | 225 |
| *(Less than 100 copies, used as promos)* | | | |
| **STARLAND VOCAL BAND** | | | |
| *Windsong promo 45s $2 each* | | | |
| **45s** | | | |
| WHAT'S IT ALL ABOUT (Jan 77) Public service show | 1977 | W.I.A.A. 353 | 10 |
| *(Flip side features Perry Botkin Jr.)* | | | |

| Title | Yr | Label, Number | NM $ |
|---|---|---|---|
| **STARR, ANDY** | | | |
| **45s** | | | |
| NO ROOM FOR YOUR KIND | 1957 | MGM 12421 | 50 |
| *(Yellow promo label)* | | | |
| ROCKIN' ROLLIN' STONE | 1956 | MGM 12263 | 60 |
| *(Yellow promo label)* | | | |
| ROUND AND ROUND | 1957 | MGM 12364 | 50 |
| *(Yellow promo label)* | | | |
| SHE'S A-GOIN' JESSIE | 1956 | MGM 12315 | 50 |
| *(Yellow promo label)* | | | |
| **STARR, EDWIN** | | | |
| *Gordy promo 45s $6 each; Other Soul promo 45s $4 each* | | | |
| **12-Inch Singles** | | | |
| REAL LIVE #10 (stereo/mono) | 1981 | 20th Century TCD-128 | 10 |
| TELL A STAR (same on both sides) | 1980 | 20th Century TCD-107 | 10 |
| **45s** | | | |
| SCOTT'S ON SWINGERS (S.O.S.)/I HAVE FAITH IN YOU | 1966 | Ric-Tic 109X | 50 |
| WHO IS THE LEADER OF THE PEOPLE | 1972 | Soul 35100 | 15 |
| *(Blue vinyl, white promo label)* | | | |
| **STARR, FRANK** | | | |
| **45s** | | | |
| DIG THEM SQUEEKY SHOES | 1955 | Lin 1009 | 125 |
| *(White promo label)* | | | |
| **STARR, KAY** | | | |
| **45s** | | | |
| ROCK AND ROLL WALTZ | 1956 | U.S. Army Recruiting 0714 | 15 |
| *(Special promo version)* | | | |
| **STARR, RINGO** | | | |
| *Also see The Beatles; The Right Stuff jukebox colored vinyl 45s $5 each* | | | |
| **12-Inch Singles** | | | |
| DROWNING IN THE SEA OF LOVE | 1977 | Atlantic DSKO-93 | 30 |
| *(Promo 12" single)* | | | |
| **45s** | | | |
| ACT NATURALLY With Buck Owens | 1989 | Capitol 44409 | 25 |
| *(White promo label)* | | | |
| BACK OFF BOOGALOO | 1972 | Apple 1849 | 150 |
| *(White promo label, stock picture sleeve worth $15)* | | | |
| BEAUCOUPS OF BLUES | 1970 | Apple 2969 | 15 |
| *(Star on the label, not a promo but used as one)* | | | |
| A DOSE OF ROCK 'N' ROLL | 1976 | Atlantic 3361 | 50 |
| *(Long with intro/short without intro, blue labels)* | | | |
| A DOSE OF ROCK 'N' ROLL | 1976 | Atlantic 3361 | 15 |
| *(Long/short versions, red/white labels)* | | | |
| A DOSE OF ROCK 'N' ROLL | 1976 | Atlantic 3361 | 75 |
| *(Long/short versions, white promo labels)* | | | |
| DROWNING IN THE SEA OF LOVE | 1977 | Atlantic 3412 | 15 |
| *(Long/short versions, blue labels)* | | | |
| HEART ON MY SLEEVE | 1978 | Portrait 70018 | 15 |
| *(Stereo/mono white promo label versions)* | | | |
| HEY BABY | 1976 | Atlantic 3371 | 15 |
| *(Red/white and blue labels)* | | | |
| HEY BABY | 1976 | Atlantic 3371 | 175 |
| *(One-sided record, blue label)* | | | |
| HEY BABY | 1976 | Atlantic 3371 | 75 |
| *(White promo labels)* | | | |
| IT DON'T COME EASY | 1971 | Apple 1831 | 10 |
| *(Star on label, stock picture sleeve worth $25)* | | | |
| IT'S ALL DOWN TO GOODNIGHT VIENNA | 1975 | Apple P-1882 | 40 |
| *(Mono/stereo versions)* | | | |
| LIPSTICK TRACES | 1978 | Portrait 70015 | 15 |
| *(Stereo/mono white promo label versions)* | | | |
| NO NO SONG | 1975 | Apple P-1880 | 30 |
| *(Mono version)* | | | |
| NO NO SONG | 1975 | Apple P-1880 | 30 |
| *(Stereo version)* | | | |
| OH MY MY | 1974 | Apple P-1872 | 50 |
| *(Mono 3:15/stereo 3:39 versions)* | | | |
| ONLY YOU | 1974 | Apple P-1876 | 40 |
| *(Mono versions)* | | | |
| OO-WEE | 1975 | Apple P-1882 | 70 |
| *(Mono/stereo versions)* | | | |
| PHOTOGRAPH | 1973 | Apple P-1865 | 50 |
| *(Same song on both sides)* | | | |
| PRIVATE PROPERTY | 1982 | Boardwalk 134 | 10 |
| *(Mono/stereo versions)* | | | |
| WHAT'S IT ALL ABOUT (June 82) Public service show | 1982 | W.I.A.A. 627 | 25 |
| *(Flip side features B. B. King)* | | | |
| WHAT'S IT ALL ABOUT (Mar 81) Public service show | 1981 | W.I.A.A. 567 | 25 |
| *(Flip side features Robin Williams)* | | | |
| WINGS | 1977 | Atlantic 3429 | 15 |
| *(Stereo/mono red/white and blue labels)* | | | |
| WINGS | 1977 | Atlantic 3429 | 75 |
| *(White promo labels)* | | | |

| Title | Yr | Label, Number | NM $ |
|-------|----|--------------|----|
| WRACK MY BRAIN | 1981 | Boardwalk 130 | 10 |
| *(Mono/stereo versions)* | | | |
| YOU'RE SIXTEEN | 1973 | Apple P-1870 | 50 |
| *(Mono/stereo versions)* | | | |
| **Albums** | | | |
| BAD BOY | 1978 | Portrait 35378 | 30 |
| *(White promo label, "Demonstration," regular cover)* | | | |
| BAD BOY | 1978 | Portrait 35378 | 100 |
| *(White promo label, "Advance Promotion" and issued in a plain white sleeve)* | | | |
| THE MAGIC CHRISTIAN Various artists | 1970 | Commonwealth United 6004 | 50 |
| *(White promo label)* | | | |
| RINGO | 1973 | Apple 3413 | 200 |
| *(The only way to identify this LP as promo, "Six O'Clock" is 5:26 both on the label and when played)* | | | |
| RINGO THE 4TH | 1977 | Atlantic 19108 | 30 |
| *("DJ only" in trail-off area)* | | | |
| RINGO'S ROTOGRAVURE | 1976 | Atlantic 18193 | 30 |
| *(Only way to identify is "DJ only" etched in trail-off)* | | | |
| **Compact Discs** | | | |
| ACT NATURALLY With Buck Owens | 1989 | Capitol DPRO-79765 | 100 |
| *(Promo-only CD release, two tracks)* | | | |
| 4-STARR COLLECTION | 1995 | Private Issue | 50 |
| *(Promo CD given to some Discover Card Private Issue cardholders)* | | | |
| LA DE DA | 1998 | Mercury MECP 419 | 20 |
| *(Promo-only CD single)* | | | |
| STOP AND SMELL THE ROSES/OLD WAVE | 1994 | The Right Stuff | 80 |
| *(Sampler from re-release of these two albums)* | | | |
| **RADIO SHOWS** | | | |
| **Albums** | | | |
| LEGENDS OF ROCK | 1987 | NBC Radio (2) | 40-75 |
| *(Music and interviews)* | | | |
| RINGO'S YELLOW SUBMARINE Eight box sets | 1984 | ABC Watermark (25) | 500-750 |
| *(Seven sets have 3LP, one set has 4LP)* | | | |
| RINGO'S YELLOW SUBMARINE Five box sets | 1985 | ABC Watermark (15) | 350-500 |
| *(Each box set has 3LP, series is a profile of the Beatles)* | | | |
| **Compact Discs** | | | |
| UP CLOSE | 1992 | (2) | 60-150 |
| *(Music and interviews)* | | | |
| **Reel-to-Reel Tapes** | | | |
| CONVERSATION | 1977 | DIR | 175-250 |
| *(Music and interviews on four 7" reels)* | | | |

## STARSHIP
*More at Jefferson Airplane*

| Title | Yr | Label, Number | NM $ |
|-------|----|--------------|----|
| **45s** | | | |
| WE BUILT THIS CITY (Short)/(Long) | 1985 | Grunt JK-14170 | 8 |
| WE BUILT THIS CITY (Special Non-DJ Rock Radio Version) | 1985 | Grunt JB-14200 | 10 |

## STARZ
*Other Capitol promo 45s $4 each*

| Title | Yr | Label, Number | NM $ |
|-------|----|--------------|----|
| **45s** | | | |
| CHERRY BABY | 1977 | Capitol 4399 | 10 |
| *(Yellow vinyl, black/yellow promo label)* | | | |
| SING IT, SHOUT IT | 1977 | Capitol 4434 | 10 |
| *(Yellow vinyl, black/yellow promo label)* | | | |
| **Albums** | | | |
| LIVE IN LOUISVILLE | 1978 | Capitol SPRO-8857 | 30 |
| *(Black vinyl, promo-only release)* | | | |
| VIOLATION | 1977 | Capitol 11617 | 25 |
| *(Yellow vinyl, only the promo is colored)* | | | |

## STATLER BROTHERS, THE
*Other Columbia promo 45s $4 each; Mercury promo 45s $2 each*

| Title | Yr | Label, Number | NM $ |
|-------|----|--------------|----|
| **45s** | | | |
| ATLANTA BLUE | 1984 | Mercury 818 700 | 10 |
| *(Blue vinyl, black promo label)* | | | |
| FLOWERS ON THE WALL | 1966 | Columbia 43315 | 18 |
| *(Red vinyl, white promo label)* | | | |
| **7-Inch Extended Plays** | | | |
| STATLER BROTHERS CHRISTMAS CARD | 1978 | Mercury DJ-577 | 10 |
| *(Promo-only 33 1/3 rpm 4-song EP, small center hole; issued with a paper cover)* | | | |

## STATON, CANDI

| Title | Yr | Label, Number | NM $ |
|-------|----|--------------|----|
| **12-Inch Singles** | | | |
| CHANCE (5:34)/ROCK (7:16) | 1979 | Warner Bros. PRO-A-827 | 12 |
| HONEST I DO LOVE YOU (6:31) (same on both sides) | 1978 | Warner Bros. PRO-A-772 | 12 |
| LOOKING FOR LOVE (same on both sides) | 1980 | Warner Bros. PRO-A-867 | 12 |

## STATUES, THE

| Title | Yr | Label, Number | NM $ |
|-------|----|--------------|----|
| **45s** | | | |
| WHITE CHRISTMAS/GET OFF MY ROOF | 197? | Holiday 1026 | 12 |
| *(B-side by Jerry and the Landsliders)* | | | |

## STATUS QUO
*Other Cadet Concept promo 45s $8 each; A&M promo 45s $4 each*

| Title | Yr | Label, Number | NM $ |
|-------|----|--------------|----|
| **45s** | | | |
| PICTURES OF MATCHSTICK MEN | 1968 | Cadet Concept 7001 | 10 |
| *(Whitish label, same as stock copy but is identified as "DJ Copy")* | | | |

| Title | Yr | Label, Number | NM $ |
|---|---|---|---|
| **RADIO SHOWS** | | | |
| **Albums** | | | |
| BBC TRANSCRIPTION DISC | 1973 | BBC Transcription | 400-600 |
| (Live concert) | | | |
| BBC TRANSCRIPTION DISC | 1976 | BBC Transcription | 300-400 |
| (Live concert) | | | |
| BBC TRANSCRIPTION DISC | 1982 | BBC Transcription | 300-400 |
| (Live concert) | | | |
| | | | |
| **STEEL BREEZE** | | | |
| *RCA Victor promo 45s $3 each* | | | |
| **RADIO SHOWS** | | | |
| **Albums** | | | |
| IN CONCERT (Dec 82) | 1982 | Westwood One (2) | 75-150 |
| (Live concert) | | | |
| **Compact Discs** | | | |
| IN THE STUDIO (90s) Profile of an album | 199? | Album Network | 15-25 |
| (Music and interviews) | | | |
| | | | |
| **STEELY DAN** | | | |
| *Donald Fagen and Walter Becker; Other ABC promo 45s $4 each; MCA promo 45s $3 each; Warner Bros. promo 45s by Donald Fagen $4 each* | | | |
| **12-Inch Singles** | | | |
| AJA (same on both sides) | 1977 | ABC SPDJ-26 | 20 |
| DEACON BLUES (same on both sides) | 1978 | ABC SPDJ-32 | 20 |
| HERE AT THE WESTERN WORLD (same on both sides) | 1978 | ABC SPDJ-47 | 15 |
| JOSIE (same on both sides) | 1978 | ABC SPDJ-36 | 20 |
| **45s** | | | |
| DALLAS | 1972 | ABC 11323 | 10 |
| (White promo label, first record, stock copy much rarer) | | | |
| EAST SAINT LOUIS TOODLE-OO | 1974 | ABC DJ-20 | 15 |
| (One-sided promo-only release) | | | |
| **7-Inch Extended Plays** | | | |
| COUNTDOWN TO ECSTASY Jukebox LLP | 1973 | ABC LLP 225 | 20 |
| (Issued with a paper picture cover) | | | |
| PRETZEL LOGIC Jukebox LLP | 1974 | ABC LLP 255 | 30 |
| (Quadraphonic; Issued with a paper picture cover) | | | |
| **Compact Discs** | | | |
| ALIVE IN AMERICA | 1995 | Giant | 15 |
| (Promo sampler from album of the same name) | | | |
| **RADIO SHOWS** | | | |
| **Albums** | | | |
| CAPTURED LIVE (Oct 84) Donald Fagen | 1984 | RKO (2) | 75-150 |
| (Live concert) | | | |
| LEGENDS OF ROCK (Nov 87) | 1987 | NBC Radio (2) | 20-40 |
| (Music and interviews) | | | |
| NIGHTBIRD & COMPANY (May 73) Various artists | 1973 | U.S. Army Reserve (2) | 25-40 |
| (Donald Fagen is host of one of the three shows; music and interviews) | | | |
| **Compact Discs** | | | |
| IN THE STUDIO (Nov 89) Profile of an album | 1989 | Album Network | 15-25 |
| (Music and interviews) | | | |
| OFF THE RECORD (Feb 94) | 1994 | Westwood One | 20-30 |
| (Music and interviews) | | | |
| OFF THE RECORD (Feb 95) Walter Becker | 1995 | Westwood One | 15-25 |
| (Music and interviews) | | | |
| **Reel-to-Reel Tapes** | | | |
| ALBUM NETWORK Donald Fagen/Steely Dan | 1994 | Album Network | 40-75 |
| (Mostly music and interviews on a 10" reel) | | | |
| | | | |
| **STEINMAN, JIM** | | | |
| *Writer-producer for Meat Loaf and others; Epic promo 45s $4 each* | | | |
| **45s** | | | |
| ROCK AND ROLL DREAMS COME THROUGH | 1981 | Cleveland Int'l. AE7 1232 | 10 |
| (Small center hole, with picture sleeve, originally came taped to the back cover of the "Bad for Good" LP) | | | |
| **RADIO SHOWS** | | | |
| **Albums** | | | |
| BBC ROCK HOUR (Aug 81) | 1981 | London Wavelength | 20-40 |
| (Music and interviews) | | | |
| | | | |
| **STEPPENWOLF** | | | |
| *With John Kay and Nick St. Nicholas; Includes the Sparrow; Other ABC Dunhill promo 45s $5 each; ABC promo 45s $3 each; Mums (CBS) promo label 45s $4 each; Allegiance promo 45s $4 each; ABC Dunhill promo 45s by John Kay $3 each; ABC Dunhill white promo label LPs $15-20 each* | | | |
| **45s** | | | |
| BORN TO BE WILD | 1968 | ABC Dunhill 4138 | 10 |
| (White promo label) | | | |
| A GIRL I KNOW | 1968 | ABC Dunhill 4109 | 10 |
| (White promo label) | | | |
| GREEN BOTTLE LOVER The Sparrow | 1967 | Columbia 43960 | 25 |
| (White promo label) | | | |
| ROCK ME | 1969 | Dunhill | 20 |
| (White label test pressing) | | | |
| SNOWBLIND FRIEND | 1971 | ABC Dunhill 4269 | 10 |
| (White promo label, classic track) | | | |
| SOOKIE SOOKIE | 1968 | ABC Dunhill 4123 | 10 |
| (White promo label) | | | |
| SOOKIE SOOKIE | 1968 | ABC Dunhill 4161 | 12 |
| (White promo label, flip side is "Magic Carpet Ride," Sookie was the original "A" side) | | | |

| Title | Yr | Label, Number | NM $ |
|-------|----|----|------|
| TOMORROW'S SHIP The Sparrow | 1966 | Columbia 43755 | 100 |
| *(White promo label record and promo-only picture sleeve)* | | | |
| **7-Inch Extended Plays** | | | |
| STEPPENWOLF THE SECOND Jukebox LLP | 1968 | ABC Dunhill 50037 | 40 |
| *(Black Dunhill label, issued in a hard cover)* | | | |
| **RADIO SHOWS** | | | |
| **Albums** | | | |
| IN CONCERT (Oct 87) Live concert | 1987 | Westwood One (2) | 75-125 |
| *(With Stevie Ray Vaughan)* | | | |
| KING BISCUIT FLOWER HOUR (July 81) Live concert | 1981 | DIR/ABC (2) | 100-200 |
| *(With Point Blank)* | | | |
| NIGHTBIRD & COMPANY (Feb 75) Various artists | 1975 | U.S. Army Reserve (2) | 20-35 |
| *(John Kay is host of one of the four shows, music and interviews)* | | | |
| RETRO ROCK (June 82) Live concert | 1982 | Clayton Webster | 100-200 |
| *(With John Kay)* | | | |
| **Compact Discs** | | | |
| IN THE STUDIO (Oct 91) Profile of an album | 1991 | Album Network | 15-25 |
| *(Music and interviews)* | | | |
| KING BISCUIT FLOWER HOUR (Mar 91) Live concert | 1991 | DIR | 40-75 |
| *(With Queen and Scorpions)* | | | |

## STEREOLAB
**45s**

| Title | Yr | Label, Number | NM $ |
|-------|----|----|------|
| JENNY ONIOLINE PT. 1/GOLDEN BALL | 1993 | Elektra 64615 | 20 |
| *(Clear vinyl in Elektra sleeve)* | | | |

## STEVENS, APRIL
*Other Imperial, King, Atco, Verve and A&M promo 45s $3 each*
**45s**

| Title | Yr | Label, Number | NM $ |
|-------|----|----|------|
| TEACH ME TIGER | 1959 | Imperial 5626 | 18 |
| *(Cream colored promo label)* | | | |

## STEVENS, CAT
*Deram promo 45s $8 each; A&M promo 45s $3 each; A&M promo LPs $8 each*
**12-Inch Singles**

| Title | Yr | Label, Number | NM $ |
|-------|----|----|------|
| WAS DOG A DOUGHNUT (Remix) (same on both sides) | 1977 | A&M 8440 | 15 |
| **45s** | | | |
| FATHER AND SON (same on both sides) | 1985 | A&M 2711 | 10 |
| *(No stock copies issued)* | | | |
| WHAT'S IT ALL ABOUT (Feb 74) Public service show | 1974 | W.I.A.A. 219 | 18 |
| *(Flip side is the Rock 'N' Roll Revival with Freddie Cannon, Little Richard and others)* | | | |
| **7-Inch Extended Plays** | | | |
| FOREIGNER Jukebox LLP | 1973 | A&M 4391 (LLP 227) | 20 |
| *(Issued with a paper picture cover)* | | | |
| TEASER AND THE FIRECAT Jukebox LLP | 1972 | A&M | 15 |
| *(With cardboard picture cover)* | | | |

## STEVENS, RAY
*Also recorded as the Henhouse Five Plus Too; Other Mercury promo 45s (60s) $8 each; Mercury Celebrity Series white promo label 45s $7 each; Monument promo 45s $5 each; Barnaby promo 45s $4 each; Warner Bros. promo 45s $3 each; Mercury promo 45s (80s) $3 each; Other RCA promo 45s $3 each; Other MCA promo 45s $4 each; Curb (MCA) promo 45s $2 each; Monument or Barnaby promo LPs $15 each*
**45s**

| Title | Yr | Label, Number | NM $ |
|-------|----|----|------|
| THE BALLAD OF THE BLUE CYCLONE | 1985 | MCA 52771 | 10 |
| *(Blue vinyl, white promo label)* | | | |
| BUTCH BARBARIAN | 1963 | Mercury DJ-66 | 50 |
| *(Promo record and promo picture sleeve)* | | | |
| CAN HE LOVE YOU HALF AS MUCH AS I | 1987 | MCA 53007 | 10 |
| *(Blue vinyl, white promo label)* | | | |
| CAT PANTS | 1958 | Capitol 4030 | 25 |
| *(White promo label)* | | | |
| CHICKIE CHICKIE WAH WAH | 1958 | Capitol 3967 | 25 |
| *(White promo label)* | | | |
| THE CLOWN | 1958 | Capitol 4101 | 20 |
| *(White promo label)* | | | |
| FIND YOURSELF A STAR Various artists | 1976 | U.S.A.F. RAD-74 | 25 |
| *(Twelve U.S.A.F. ads, two by Ray Stevens, 30- and 60-second, issued with a hard cover)* | | | |
| FIVE MORE STEPS | 1957 | Prep 122 | 25 |
| *(White promo label)* | | | |
| HAPPY BLUE YEAR | 1960 | NRC 063 | 20 |
| *(White promo label)* | | | |
| HELP ME MAKE IT THROUGH THE NIGHT (same on both sides) | 1991 | Capitol 7PRO-79430 | 5 |
| *(Vinyl is promo only)* | | | |
| HIGH SCHOOL YEARBOOK | 1950 | NRC 031 | 25 |
| *(White promo label)* | | | |
| JEREMIAH PEABODY'S POLYUNSATURATED QUICK DISSOLVING FAST ACTING PLEASANT TASTING GREEN AND PURPLE PILLS | 1961 | Mercury 71843 | 15 |
| *(White promo label, stock picture sleeve worth $25)* | | | |
| MY HEART CRIES FOR YOU | 1960 | NRC 042 | 20 |
| *(White promo label)* | | | |
| NIGHT GAMES | 1980 | RCA Victor 12069 | 12 |
| *(Blue vinyl, silver promo label)* | | | |
| 1980 INTERNATIONAL FAN FAIR Various artists | 1980 | CMA (CBS) no # | 25 |
| *(Seventeen PSA ads, Ray Stevens does one 30-second)* | | | |
| ONE MORE LAST CHANCE | 1981 | RCA Victor 12170 | 12 |
| *(Blue vinyl, silver promo label)* | | | |
| PART OF THE TIME | 1957 | Prep 102 | 30 |
| *(White promo label)* | | | |

(Top left) Another of the Retro Rock programs with the stickers, this one features the Stray Cats. (Top right) Donna Summer is rarely featured on syndicated radio shows, but here she is on this Words and Music program from 1982. (Middle row) Two early American releases by the band that became T. Rex. It was still Tyrannosaurus Rex when *A Beard of Stars* came out on Blue Thumb, and the A&M reissue of *Prophets, Seers and Sages/The Angels of the Ages* used the old name to illustrate that these were not current recordings. (Bottom left) Getting them while they were hot, the King Biscuit Flower Hour had Tears for Fears on its September 15, 1985 show, while *Songs from the Big Chair* was still high on the charts. (Bottom right) The Spin Radio Concert series, this one featuring early 10,000 Maniacs, had some of its cue markings on the record, unusual for radio shows.

| Title | Yr | Label, Number | NM $ |
|---|---|---|---|
| RANG TANG DING DONG | 1957 | Prep 108 | 25 |
| *(White promo label)* | | | |
| SANTA CLAUS IS WATCHING YOU | 1985 | MCA 52738 | 15 |
| *(Red vinyl, green promo label)* | | | |
| SAVE THE CHILDREN Various artists | 1987 | DWP 126 | 25 |
| *(Twenty PSA ads, Ray Stevens does one 30-second, issued with paper picture sleeve)* | | | |
| SERGEANT PRESTON OF THE YUKON | 1960 | NRC 057 | 25 |
| *(White promo label)* | | | |
| SHRINER'S CONVENTION | 1980 | RCA Victor 11911 | 15 |
| *(Red vinyl, white promo label, long 5:33 and short 4:10 versions)* | | | |
| SOUTHERN AIR | 1986 | MCA 52906 | 10 |
| *(Red vinyl, white promo label)* | | | |
| THERE'S A STAR SPANGLED BANNER | 1989 | MCA S45-17981 | 10 |
| *(White promo label, black vinyl, promo-only release)* | | | |
| WHAT'S IT ALL ABOUT (Dec 75) Public service show | 1975 | W.I.A.A. 295 | 20 |
| *(The flip features the 5th Dimension)* | | | |
| WHAT'S IT ALL ABOUT (Jan 75) Public service show | 1975 | W.I.A.A. 250 | 20 |
| *(Flip side features Gladys Knight & the Pips)* | | | |
| WRITTEN DOWN IN MY HEART | 1981 | RCA Victor 13038 | 12 |
| *(Yellow vinyl, yellow promo label)* | | | |
| **Albums** | | | |
| THE BEST OF RAY STEVENS | 1968 | Mercury 61272 | 30 |
| *(White promo label)* | | | |
| 1,837 SECONDS OF HUMOR | 1962 | Mercury 60732 | 50 |
| *(White promo label)* | | | |
| THIS IS RAY STEVENS | 1963 | Mercury 20828 | 30 |
| *(White promo label)* | | | |
| **Compact Discs** | | | |
| BREAKFAST WITH RAY STEVENS | 1993 | Curb 1058 | 15 |
| *(Promo-only sampler in LP-size sleeve)* | | | |
| CHRISTMAS THROUGH A DIFFERENT WINDOW | 1997 | MCA 70004A | 15 |
| *(Advance copy, so labeled on disc and back cover, not issued with booklet)* | | | |
| **RADIO SHOWS** | | | |
| **Albums** | | | |
| COUNTRY MUSIC TIME (70s) | 197? | U.S. Air Force | 20-40 |
| *(Music and interviews)* | | | |
| HERE'S TO VETERANS (60s) The Ray Stevens Show | 196? | Veterans Administration | 25-50 |
| *(Music and interviews)* | | | |

**STEVENS, SHAKIN'**

*Other Epic promo 45s $4 each*

**12-Inch Singles**

| | | | |
|---|---|---|---|
| I CRY JUST A LITTLE BIT/(Instrumental) | 1983 | Epic AS 1863 | 10 |
| **45s** | | | |
| I CRY JUST A LITTLE BIT | 1983 | Epic AE7 1866 | 10 |
| *(Promo-only single, white label)* | | | |

**STEWART, AL**

*Janus promo 45s $4 each; Arista promo 45s $3 each*

**45s**

| | | | |
|---|---|---|---|
| WHAT'S IT ALL ABOUT (May 80) Public service show | 1980 | W.I.A.A. 523 | 20 |
| *(Flip side features Burt Cummings of the Guess Who)* | | | |
| WHAT'S IT ALL ABOUT (Sept 77) Public service show | 1977 | W.I.A.A. 388 | 20 |
| *(Flip side features Peter, Paul & Mary)* | | | |
| **Albums** | | | |
| THE EARLY YEARS | 1977 | Janus 7026 | 30 |
| *(Promo-only condensation of 2-LP set with rubber-stamp cover)* | | | |
| THE LIVE RADIO CONCERT | 1980 | Arista SP-40 | 40 |
| *(Released for radio only)* | | | |
| **RADIO SHOWS** | | | |
| **Albums** | | | |
| BBC ROCK HOUR (Dec 80) | 1980 | London Wavelength | 75-125 |
| *(Live concert)* | | | |
| ROBERT W. MORGAN (Mar 80) | 1980 | Watermark | 10-15 |
| *(Music and interviews)* | | | |
| ROCK AROUND THE WORLD (Nov 76) | 1976 | RATW | 50-100 |
| *(Live concert)* | | | |
| **Compact Discs** | | | |
| IN THE STUDIO (Oct 88) Profile of an album | 1988 | Album Network | 15-25 |
| *(Music and interviews)* | | | |

**STEWART, JOHN**

*Also see The Kingston Trio; Other RCA promo 45s $4 each; Capitol, Reprise and RSO promo 45s $3 each; Allegiance promo 45s $2 each; Any promo LP $8*

**45s**

| | | | |
|---|---|---|---|
| LADY AND THE OUTLAW | 196? | Capitol PRO-4904 | 10 |
| *(Promo only number)* | | | |
| MARSHALL WIND | 197? | Capitol SPRO 6024 | 10 |
| *(Promo only number)* | | | |
| SURVIVORS | 1975 | RCA Victor 10268 | 15 |
| *(Long/short versions, picture sleeve is promo only)* | | | |
| **RADIO SHOWS** | | | |
| **Albums** | | | |
| ROBERT W. MORGAN (Dec 80) Profile | 1980 | Watermark | 25-50 |
| *(Music and interview)* | | | |

| Title | Yr | Label, Number | NM $ |
|---|---|---|---|

**STEWART, ROD**

*From Faces, Python Lee Jackson and Jeff Beck Group; Other Mercury promo 45s to 73412 $8 each; Mercury promo 45s after 73412 $5 each; Other Warner Bros. promo 45s $4 each; Other Warner Bros. promo 45s by the Faces $5 each; Other Warner Bros. 12" promo singles $8 each; Warner Bros. promo CD singles $3 each*

**12-Inch Singles**

| Title | Yr | Label, Number | NM $ |
|---|---|---|---|
| ANOTHER HEARTACHE | 1986 | Warner Bros. PRO-A-2559 | 10 |
| *(Promo-only 12" single)* | | | |
| BABY JANE | 1983 | Warner Bros. PRO-A-2032 | 10 |
| *(Promo-only 12" single)* | | | |
| DANCIN' ALONE/GHETTO BLASTER/WHAT AM I GONNA DO | 1983 | Warner Bros. PRO-A-2063 | 6 |
| EVERY BEAT OF MY HEART | 1986 | Warner Bros. PRO-A-2618 | 10 |
| *(Promo-only 12" single)* | | | |
| GUESS I'LL ALWAYS LOVE YOU (same on both sides) | 1982 | Warner Bros. PRO-A-1078 | 10 |
| HOT LEGS | 1978 | Warner Bros. | 15 |
| *(Promo-only 12" single)* | | | |
| INFATUATION | 1984 | Warner Bros. PRO-A-2148 | 10 |
| *(Promo-only 12" single)* | | | |
| THE KILLING OF GEORGIE | 1977 | Warner Bros. PRO-A-680 | 35 |
| *(Promo-only 12" single, blue vinyl)* | | | |
| LOVE TOUCH (same on both sides) | 1986 | Warner Bros. PRO-A-2505 | 6 |
| A NIGHT LIKE THIS (same on both sides) | 1986 | Warner Bros. PRO-A-2538 | 5 |
| PASSION | 1981 | Warner Bros. PRO-A-921 | 12 |
| *(Promo-only 12" single, long/short versions)* | | | |
| SOME GUYS HAVE ALL THE LUCK | 1984 | Warner Bros. PRO-A-2184 | 10 |
| *(Promo-only 12" single)* | | | |
| TWISTIN' THE NIGHT AWAY | 1987 | Geffen PRO-A-2787 | 12 |
| *(Promo-only 12" single)* | | | |
| YOUNG TURKS | 1982 | Warner Bros. PRO-A-989 | 12 |
| *(Promo-only 12" single, long/short versions, title cover)* | | | |

**45s**

| Title | Yr | Label, Number | NM $ |
|---|---|---|---|
| CINDY INCIDENTALLY Faces | 1973 | Warner Bros. 7681 | 18 |
| *(Price includes promo-only picture sleeve)* | | | |
| CLOUD NINE Python Lee Jackson | 1972 | GNP Crescendo 462 | 10 |
| *(White promo label, Rod Stewart identified on label)* | | | |
| COUNTRY COMFORT | 1971 | Mercury DJ-318 | 15 |
| *(White promo label, stock copies on Mercury 73196)* | | | |
| GOOD MORNING, LITTLE SCHOOL GIRL | 1965 | Press 9722 | 40 |
| *(Brownish promo label)* | | | |
| HI HO SILVER LINING Jeff Beck Group | 1967 | Epic 10157 | 18 |
| *(White promo label)* | | | |
| IN A BROKEN DREAM Python Lee Jackson | 1972 | GNP Crescendo 449 | 10 |
| *(White promo label, long 3:37/short 3:00 versions, Rod Stewart is not identified on the label)* | | | |
| IT'S ALL OVER NOW | 1970 | Mercury DJ-252 | 15 |
| *(White/red labels, mono/stereo versions, promo only)* | | | |
| JAILHOUSE ROCK Jeff Beck Group | 1969 | Epic 10484 | 12 |
| *(White promo label)* | | | |
| THE KILLING OF GEORGIE | 1977 | Warner Bros. 8396 | 10 |
| *(Promo version, 6:31 mono/stereo versions)* | | | |
| MY WAY OF GIVING | 1970 | Mercury DJ-313 | 12 |
| *(White promo label, stock copies on Mercury 73175)* | | | |
| OH! NO NOT MY BABY | 1973 | Mercury DJ-385 | 12 |
| *(White promo label, stock copies on Mercury 73426)* | | | |
| ONLY A HOBO | 1970 | Mercury DJ-275 | 12 |
| *(White promo label, stock copies on Mercury 73115)* | | | |
| SHAKE | 1977 | Private Stock 45,130 | 10 |
| *(Gray promo label)* | | | |
| TALLY MAN Jeff Beck Group | 1967 | Epic 10218 | 18 |
| *(White promo label)* | | | |
| WHAT'S IT ALL ABOUT (Dec 79) Public service show | 1979 | W.I.A.A. 501 | 18 |
| *(Interviews with Carmine Appice, Stewart's drummer, flip side features the Doobie Brothers)* | | | |

**7-Inch Extended Plays**

| Title | Yr | Label, Number | NM $ |
|---|---|---|---|
| BY POPULAR REQUEST | 1970 | Mercury MEPL-3 | 25 |
| *(White label promo-only release)* | | | |
| TOMMY Various artists | 1972 | Ode EP-10 | 25 |
| *(Promo-only release, Rod Stewart sings "Pinball Wizard")* | | | |
| TWISTING THE NIGHT AWAY | 1972 | Mercury MEPL-28 | 25 |
| *(White promo label only release)* | | | |

**Albums**

| Title | Yr | Label, Number | NM $ |
|---|---|---|---|
| A NOD IS AS GOOD AS A WINK Faces | 1971 | Warner Bros. 2574 | 18 |
| *(White promo label)* | | | |
| ABSOLUTELY LIVE | 1982 | Warner Bros. 23743 (2) | 25 |
| *(Promo only on Quiex II vinyl)* | | | |
| EVERY PICTURE TELLS A STORY | 1971 | Mercury 609 | 25 |
| *(White promo label)* | | | |
| FIRST STEP Small Faces | 1970 | Warner Bros. PRO | 400 |
| *(Price includes a badge, cutouts, press kit, photos and other stuff in a box)* | | | |
| FIRST STEP Small Faces | 1970 | Warner Bros. 1851 | 25 |
| *(White promo label version of the stock LP; later stock copies credit this to "Faces")* | | | |
| GASOLINE ALLEY | 1970 | Mercury 61264 | 30 |
| *(White promo label)* | | | |
| LONG PLAYER Faces | 1971 | Warner Bros. 1892 | 20 |
| *(White promo label)* | | | |
| NEVER A DULL MOMENT | 1972 | Mercury 646 | 25 |
| *(White promo label)* | | | |
| OOH LA LA Faces | 1973 | Warner Bros. 2665 | 15 |
| *(White promo label)* | | | |
| THE ROD STEWART ALBUM | 1969 | Mercury 61237 | 40 |
| *(White promo label)* | | | |

| Title | Yr | Label, Number | NM $ |
|-------|-----|---------------|------|
| **Compact Discs** | | | |
| YOUR SONG | 1991 | Polydor CDP 669 | 8 |
| *(Promo-only CD single from the "Two Rooms" tribute album)* | | | |
| **RADIO SHOWS** | | | |
| **Albums** | | | |
| BBC CONCERT Rod Stewart/Faces | 1982 | London Wavelength | 25-50 |
| *(Live concert)* | | | |
| BBC ROCK HOUR | 1981 | London Wavelength | 20-30 |
| *(Music and interviews)* | | | |
| BBC TRANSCRIPTION DISC Faces | 1972 | BBC Transcription | 150-250 |
| *(With Rory Gallagher)* | | | |
| BBC TRANSCRIPTION DISC Faces | 1973 | BBC Transcription | 200-350 |
| *(Rare live concert)* | | | |
| BBC TRANSCRIPTION DISC (Mar 76) Faces | 1976 | BBC Transcription | 750-1,000 |
| *(Flip side is live concert by Led Zeppelin)* | | | |
| BBC TRANSCRIPTION DISC Faces | 1976 | BBC Transcription | 200-300 |
| *(Live concert)* | | | |
| BBC TRANSCRIPTION DISC | 1977 | BBC Transcription | 200-300 |
| *(Live concert)* | | | |
| CAPTURED LIVE (Oct 84) | 1984 | RKO (2) | 30-60 |
| *(Live concert)* | | | |
| IN CONCERT | 1983 | Westwood One (2) | 40-75 |
| *(Live concert)* | | | |
| IN CONCERT Faces | 1987 | Westwood One (2) | 30-60 |
| *(BBC Classic live concert)* | | | |
| IN CONCERT (June 91) Faces | 1991 | Westwood One (2) | 25-50 |
| *(Live concert)* | | | |
| KING BISCUIT FLOWER HOUR (Aug 86) | 1986 | DIR (2) | 40-75 |
| *(Live concert, repeated)* | | | |
| LEGENDS OF ROCK Jeff Beck | 1987 | NBC Radio (2) | 20-40 |
| *(Music and interviews)* | | | |
| LEGENDS OF ROCK (Apr 89) | 1989 | NBC Radio (2) | 20-35 |
| *(Music and interviews)* | | | |
| MELLO YELLO PRESENTS (May 82) Live concert | 1982 | DIR (3) | 30-60 |
| *(One original disc, two replacements)* | | | |
| MELLO YELLO PRESENTS (May 82) Live concert | 1982 | DIR (5) | 40-75 |
| *(Three original discs, two replacements, letter of explanation and scripts)* | | | |
| NIGHTBIRD & COMPANY (June 75) Various artists | 1975 | U.S. Army Reserve (2) | 20-35 |
| *(Rod Stewart is host of one of the four shows, music and interviews)* | | | |
| OFF THE RECORD | 1982 | Westwood One (2) | 20-30 |
| *(Music and interviews)* | | | |
| PIONEERS IN MUSIC (May 86) With Freddie Mercury, Jim Morrison | 1986 | DIR (2) | 20-35 |
| *(Mostly music and interviews)* | | | |
| ROBERT W. MORGAN (Dec 81) | 1981 | Watermark | 20-40 |
| *(Music and interviews)* | | | |
| ROD STEWART STORY | 1989 | United Stations (2) | 20-35 |
| *(Music and interviews)* | | | |
| SOURCE SPECIAL | 1982 | NBC Source (3) | 20-40 |
| *(Music and interviews)* | | | |
| SPOTLIGHT SPECIAL | 1982 | ABC Radio (2) | 20-40 |
| *(Music and interviews)* | | | |
| SUPERSTAR CONCERT | 1989 | Westwood One (3) | 40-75 |
| *(Box set, live concert)* | | | |
| SUPERSTAR CONCERT (Oct 90) | 1990 | Westwood One (3) | 35-60 |
| *(Box set, live concert)* | | | |
| SUPERSTAR CONCERT (Apr 93) Faces | 1993 | Westwood One (3) | 25-50 |
| *(Box set, live concert)* | | | |
| UP CLOSE | 1988 | Media America (2) | 30-60 |
| *(Mostly music and interviews)* | | | |
| WEEKLY SPECIAL | 1990 | Unistar (2) | 25-40 |
| *(Music and interviews)* | | | |
| WORLD OF ROCK | 1989 | DIR (4) | 25-50 |
| *(Rod Stewart is co-host, music and interviews)* | | | |
| **Compact Discs** | | | |
| BBC CLASSIC TRACKS (Jan 93) | 1993 | Westwood One | 20-35 |
| *(Various live tracks; other shows in this series worth about the same)* | | | |
| KING BISCUIT FLOWER HOUR (July 88) | 1988 | DIR | 35-60 |
| *(Live concert, repeated)* | | | |
| KING BISCUIT FLOWER HOUR (Aug 92) | 1992 | DIR | 20-40 |
| *(Live concert, repeated)* | | | |
| MASTERS OF ROCK | 1989 | Radio Ventures | 20-40 |
| *(Music and interviews)* | | | |
| SOME GUYS HAVE ALL THE LUCK (May 96) | 1996 | Westwood One (3) | 25-40 |
| *(Music and interviews)* | | | |
| SUPERSTAR CONCERT (May 94) | 1994 | Westwood One (2) | 40-75 |
| *(Live concert)* | | | |
| SUPERSTAR CONCERT (Feb 95) | 1995 | Westwood One (2) | 30-60 |
| *(Live concert)* | | | |
| **Reel-to-Reel Tapes** | | | |
| KING BISCUIT FLOWER HOUR (Apr 78) | 1978 | DIR/ABC (4) | 125-225 |
| *(Two-hour live concert on four reels)* | | | |
| | | | |
| **STILLS, STEPHEN** | | | |
| *More at Crosby, Stills, Nash and Young* | | | |
| **12-Inch Singles** | | | |
| CAN'T LET GO (same on both sides) | 1984 | Atlantic PR 650 | 6 |
| STRANGER (same on both sides) | 1984 | Atlantic PR 623 | 6 |

| Title | Yr | Label, Number | NM $ |
|---|---|---|---|
| **STING** | | | |
| *Ex-member of The Police; A&M promo 45s $3 each; A&M promo CD singles $4-6 each* | | | |
| **12-Inch Singles** | | | |
| BE STILL MY BEATING HEART (2 versions) | 1987 | A&M 17526 | 6 |
| FORTRESS AROUND YOUR HEART/CONSIDER ME GONE (Live) | 1985 | A&M 17339 | 6 |
| I BURN FOR YOU/ONLY YOU | 1982 | A&M 17216 | 10 |
| IF YOU LOVE SOMEBODY SET THEM FREE (same on both sides) | 1985 | A&M 17324 | 6 |
| WHEN WE DANCE (3 versions)/ | 1994 | A&M 31458 8380 1 | 25 |
| IF YOU LOVE SOMEBODY SET THEM FREE (8 versions)/DEMOLITION MAN | | | |
| **45s** | | | |
| THEY DANCE ALONE | 1987 | A&M 1242 | 10 |
| *(7:16 version, small center hole, plays at 33 1/3 rpm)* | | | |
| **Compact Discs** | | | |
| NUGGETS FROM FIELDS OF GOLD | 1993 | A&M | 25 |
| *(Sampler from greatest-hits collection)* | | | |
| SOUL CAGES, THE | 1991 | A&M | 60 |
| *(Promo-only packaging; comes in a linen cloth with twine)* | | | |
| **RADIO SHOWS** | | | |
| **Albums** | | | |
| OFF THE RECORD (Sept 86) | 1986 | Westwood One (2) | 15-25 |
| *(Music and interviews)* | | | |
| **Compact Discs** | | | |
| LIVE FROM HOUSTON, TEXAS (Sept 96) | 1996 | Westwood One (2) | 50-80 |
| *(Live concert material)* | | | |
| MASTERS OF ROCK (Oct 87) With the Police | 1987 | Radio Ventures | 20-40 |
| *(Music and interviews)* | | | |
| MERCURY FALLING | 1996 | (3) | 25-40 |
| *(Music and interviews, introducing the album of the same name)* | | | |
| MESSAGE IN A BOTTLE With the Police | 1993 | Media America (3) | 50-100 |
| *(Music and interviews)* | | | |
| OFF THE RECORD (Aug 93) | 1993 | Westwood One | 15-25 |
| *(CD version of the show)* | | | |
| ON THE EDGE (Sept 93) Music and interviews | 1993 | Westwood One | 15-25 |
| *(With Lenny Kravitz)* | | | |
| SUPERSTAR CONCERT (Jan 92) | 1992 | Westwood One (2) | 40-75 |
| *(Live concert)* | | | |
| TIMOTHY WHITE SESSIONS (Apr 91) | 1991 | Westwood One (2) | 60-125 |
| *(Live tracks, music and interviews)* | | | |
| TIMOTHY WHITE SESSIONS (July 93) | 1993 | Westwood One (2) | 75-150 |
| *(Live tracks, music and interviews)* | | | |
| UP CLOSE | 1988 | Media America (2) | 40-60 |
| *(Mostly music and interviews)* | | | |
| UP CLOSE | 1991 | Media America (2) | 40-60 |
| *(Mostly music and interviews)* | | | |
| UP CLOSE | 1995 | Media America (2) | 40-75 |
| *(Mostly music and interviews)* | | | |
| | | | |
| **STIVELL, ALAN** | | | |
| **RADIO SHOWS** | | | |
| **Albums** | | | |
| BBC TRANSCRIPTION DISC Live concert | 1973 | BBC Transcription | 85-160 |
| *(With Andrews and Cooper)* | | | |
| | | | |
| **STONE CITY BAND** | | | |
| **45s** | | | |
| ALL DAY AND ALL OF THE NIGHT (mono/stereo) | 1981 | Gordy 7195 | 4 |
| *(May be promo only)* | | | |
| | | | |
| **STONE TEMPLE PILOTS** | | | |
| *There has never been a stock U.S. single by this band, thus the promo CD singles are quite collectible* | | | |
| **Compact Discs** | | | |
| ART SCHOOL GIRL | 1997 | Atlantic PRCD 8140 | 8 |
| *(Promo-only CD single)* | | | |
| BIG BANG BABY | 1996 | Atlantic PRCD 6691 | 8 |
| *(Promo-only CD single)* | | | |
| BIG EMPTY | 1994 | Atlantic | 10 |
| *(Promo-only CD single)* | | | |
| CREEP | 1993 | Atlantic PRCD 5328 | 10 |
| *(Promo-only CD single, new versions)* | | | |
| CREEP | 1993 | Atlantic PRCD 5339 | 10 |
| *(Promo-only CD single)* | | | |
| DANCING DAYS | 1995 | Atlantic PRCD 6223 | 10 |
| *(Promo-only CD single)* | | | |
| INTERSTATE LOVE SONG | 1994 | Atlantic PRCD 5824 | 10 |
| *(Promo-only CD single)* | | | |
| LADY PICTURE SHOW | 1996 | Atlantic PRCD 6881 | 8 |
| *(Promo-only CD single)* | | | |
| PLUSH | 1993 | Atlantic PRCD 4982 | 10 |
| *(Promo-only CD single, includes edit and LP version)* | | | |
| PRETTY PENNY | 1994 | Atlantic PRCD 6102 | 10 |
| *(Promo-only CD single)* | | | |
| SEX TYPE THING | 1992 | Atlantic PRCD 4785 | 10 |
| *(Promo-only CD single)* | | | |
| TRIPPIN' ON A HOLE IN A PAPER HEART | 1996 | Atlantic PRCD 6693 | 8 |
| *(Promo-only CD single)* | | | |
| TUMBLE IN THE ROUGH | 1996 | Atlantic PRCD 7038 | 8 |
| *(Promo-only CD single)* | | | |

| Title | Yr | Label, Number | NM $ |
|---|---|---|---|
| UNGLUED | 1994 | Atlantic PRCD 6024 | 10 |
| (Promo-only CD single) | | | |
| VASOLINE | 1994 | Atlantic PRCD 5672 | 10 |
| (Promo-only CD single) | | | |
| WICKED GARDEN | 1993 | Atlantic PRCD 5141 | 10 |
| (Promo-only CD single) | | | |
| **RADIO SHOWS** | | | |
| **Compact Discs** | | | |
| IN CONCERT (Dec 93) | 1993 | Westwood One | 30-60 |
| (Live concert) | | | |
| IN CONCERT (May 94) | 1994 | Westwood One | 25-50 |
| (Live concert) | | | |
| IN CONCERT (Jan 95) | 1995 | Westwood One | 25-40 |
| (Live concert) | | | |
| IN CONCERT-NU ROCK (Jan 94) | 1994 | Westwood One | 30-60 |
| (Live concert) | | | |
| IN CONCERT-NU ROCK (Feb 95) | 1995 | Westwood One | 25-40 |
| (Live concert) | | | |
| ON THE EDGE (May 93) Music and interviews | 1993 | Westwood One | 15-25 |
| (With Star and Isaac) | | | |
| ON THE EDGE (May 94) Music and interviews | 1994 | Westwood One | 20-35 |
| (With the Proclaimers) | | | |
| **Reel-to-Reel Tapes** | | | |
| MTV UNPLUGGED Live concert | 1994 | | 40-80 |
| (Concert with Soul Asylum on a 10" reel) | | | |

**STONE THE CROWS**
**RADIO SHOWS**
**Albums**

| Title | Yr | Label, Number | NM $ |
|---|---|---|---|
| BBC TRANSCRIPTION DISC | 1972 | BBC Transcription | 200-300 |
| (Live concert) | | | |

**STONE, DOUG**
*Epic promo 45s $3 each; Epic promo CD singles $3 each*
**RADIO SHOWS**
**Compact Discs**

| Title | Yr | Label, Number | NM $ |
|---|---|---|---|
| LIVE FROM CRAZY HORSE | 1993 | Westwood One (2) | 20-40 |
| (Live concert) | | | |
| WESTWOOD ONE SPECIAL (Feb 94) | 1994 | Westwood One (2) | 15-25 |
| (Music and interviews) | | | |

**STOOKEY, PAUL**
**45s**

| Title | Yr | Label, Number | NM $ |
|---|---|---|---|
| FOR CHRISTMAS (same on both sides) | 198? | Benson 5616 | 4 |
| (As "Noel Paul Stookey and the Bodyworks Band") | | | |

**STRAIT, GEORGE**
*MCA promo CD singles $3-4 each*
**45s**

| Title | Yr | Label, Number | NM $ |
|---|---|---|---|
| FOR CHRIST'S SAKE, IT'S CHRISTMAS | 1987 | MCA S45-17451 | 15 |
| (Promo only on white vinyl) | | | |
| MERRY CHRISTMAS STRAIT TO YOU | 1986 | MCA S45-17234 | 20 |
| (Promo only, white label, red vinyl) | | | |
| **Compact Discs** | | | |
| SELECTIONS FROM STRAIT OUT OF THE BOX | 1995 | MCA | 20 |
| (Promo-only sampler from box set) | | | |
| TENTH ANNIVERSARY LIMITED EDITION | 1991 | MCA 10204 | 30 |
| (Promo-only CD in round wooden box) | | | |

**STRANGERS, THE**
**45s**

| Title | Yr | Label, Number | NM $ |
|---|---|---|---|
| BLUE FLOWERS | 1954 | King 4709 | 300 |
| (White promo label) | | | |
| DREAMS COME TRUE | 1955 | King 4766 | 175 |
| (White promo label) | | | |
| DROP DOWN TO MY PLACE | 1954 | King 4745 | 200 |
| (White promo label) | | | |
| HOPING YOU'LL UNDERSTAND | 1954 | King 4722 | 250 |
| (White promo label) | | | |
| MY FRIENDS | 1954 | King 4697 | 300 |
| (White promo label) | | | |
| WITHOUT A FRIEND | 1955 | King 4821 | 200 |
| (White promo label) | | | |

**STRANGLERS, THE**
*Epic promo CD singles $2-3 each*
**12-Inch Singles**

| Title | Yr | Label, Number | NM $ |
|---|---|---|---|
| ALL DAY AND ALL OF THE NIGHT (Short)/(Long) | 1988 | Epic EAS 1022 | 6 |
| ALWAYS THE SUN (3 mixes) | 1986 | Epic EAS 02573 | 6 |
| DREAMTIME/SHAKIN' LIKE A LEAF (Jelly Mix) | 1986 | Epic EAS 02711 | 6 |
| SOMEONE LIKE YOU/MOTORBIKE/SOMETHING | 1990 | Epic EAS 2160 | 10 |
| SWEET SMELL OF SUCCESS (4 versions)/INSTEAD OF THIS/POISONALITY | 1990 | Epic EAS 2067 | 12 |
| **45s** | | | |
| HANGING AROUND/GRIP (GET A GRIP ON YOURSELF)/ | 1977 | A&M 1973 | 10 |
| SOMETHING BETTER CHANGE/STRAIGHTEN OUT | | | |
| (With pink and white marbled vinyl; "totally safe" promo versions, includes picture sleeve) | | | |

| Title | Yr | Label, Number | NM $ |
|---|---|---|---|
| **RADIO SHOWS** | | | |
| **Albums** | | | |
| BBC ROCK HOUR (Nov 80) | 1980 | London Wavelength | 100-200 |
| *(Live concert)* | | | |
| BBC TRANSCRIPTION DISC | 1982 | BBC Transcription | 350-425 |
| *(Rare live concert)* | | | |
| BBC TRANSCRIPTION DISC | 1985 | BBC Transcription | 300-400 |
| *(Live concert)* | | | |

## STRATTON, BERT
**45s**

| TINY CHRISTMAS HEART (same on both sides) | 1986 | Gallery II 008 | 3 |
|---|---|---|---|

## STRAWBERRY ALARM CLOCK
*Uni promo 45s $5 each*

## STRAWBS, THE
*A&M promo 45s $4 each*
**45s**

| WHERE IS THIS DREAM OF YOUR YOUTH (mono/stereo) | 1971 | A&M 1242 | 6 |
|---|---|---|---|
| *(No stock copies known)* | | | |
| **RADIO SHOWS** | | | |
| **Albums** | | | |
| BBC TRANSCRIPTION DISC | 1973 | BBC Transcription | 125-225 |
| *(Live concert)* | | | |
| BBC TRANSCRIPTION DISC | 1974 | BBC Transcription | 100-200 |
| *(Live concert)* | | | |
| BBC TRANSCRIPTION DISC | 1978 | BBC Transcription | 100-200 |
| *(Live concert)* | | | |

## STRAY CATS
*Featuring Brian Setzer; Became Phantom, Rocker and Slick after Setzer went solo; EMI promo 45s $5 each; EMI promo 45s by Brian Setzer $4 each; EMI promo 45s by Phantom, Rocker and Slick $3 each*

| **12-Inch Singles** | | | |
|---|---|---|---|
| RECKLESS | 1986 | EMI SPRO-9868 | 15 |
| *(Promo-only 12" single)* | | | |
| SEXY + 17 | 1983 | EMI SPRO-9959 | 12 |
| *(Long 3:28/short 3:13 versions on a promo-only 12" single issued with a promo picture cover)* | | | |
| **45s** | | | |
| SEXY + 17 | 1983 | EMI | 12 |
| *(White label test pressing)* | | | |
| **Albums** | | | |
| STRAY CATS | 1981 | EMI SPRO-9793 | 20 |
| *(Promo-only 12" EP, four songs including "Stray Cat Strut" and "Rock This Town," issued with a title cover)* | | | |
| **RADIO SHOWS** | | | |
| **Albums** | | | |
| CAPTURED LIVE (Oct 84) | 1984 | RKO (2) | 75-125 |
| *(Live concert)* | | | |
| IN CONCERT (Nov 83) | 1983 | Westwood One (2) | 75-125 |
| *(Live concert)* | | | |
| KING BISCUIT FLOWER HOUR (Jan 83) | 1983 | DIR/ABC (2) | 75-150 |
| *(Live concert)* | | | |
| KING BISCUIT FLOWER HOUR (Dec 85) Phantom, Rocker and Slick | 1985 | DIR (2) | 25-50 |
| *(Live concert)* | | | |
| KING BISCUIT FLOWER HOUR (June 86) Brian Setzer | 1986 | DIR (2) | 75-125 |
| *(Live concert)* | | | |
| NBC SOURCE (Dec 82) | 1982 | NBC Radio (2) | 100-150 |
| *(Rare early live concert)* | | | |
| NBC SOURCE (Mar 83) | 1983 | NBC Radio (2) | 100-150 |
| *(Live concert)* | | | |
| NBC SOURCE (Dec 83) | 1983 | NBC Radio (2) | 50-100 |
| *(Music and interviews, some live tracks)* | | | |
| NBC SOURCE (Dec 84) | 1984 | NBC Radio (2) | 40-80 |
| *(Music and interviews)* | | | |
| OFF THE RECORD (July 83) | 1983 | Westwood One (2) | 25-50 |
| *(Music and interviews)* | | | |
| RETRO ROCK (Sept 83) | 1983 | Clayton Webster (2) | 75-125 |
| *(Live concert)* | | | |
| ROCKIN' AND TALKIN' Brian Setzer; George Thorogood | 1988 | | 20-30 |
| *(Music and interviews)* | | | |
| SUPERGROUPS (July 83) With .38 Special | 1983 | DIR (3) | 200-300 |
| *(Very rare live concert)* | | | |
| SUPERSTAR CONCERT (Aug 83) | 1983 | Westwood One (3) | 50-100 |
| *(Live concert, box set)* | | | |
| **Compact Discs** | | | |
| KING BISCUIT FLOWER HOUR (Apr 89) | 1989 | DIR | 50-100 |
| *(Live concert)* | | | |
| ON THE EDGE Brian Setzer | 1994 | Album Network | 20-35 |
| *(Music and interviews)* | | | |

## STREISAND, BARBRA
*Other Columbia promo 45s $4 each; Arista promo 45s $5 each; Columbia promo picture sleeves $4 each; Other Columbia white promo label LPs $15-20 each; Columbia promo CD singles $4-6 each*

| **45s** | | | |
|---|---|---|---|
| ENOUGH IS ENOUGH | 1979 | Columbia | 20 |
| *(White label test pressing with alternate title, released as "No More Tears [Enough Is Enough]")* | | | |

| Title | Yr | Label, Number | NM $ |
|---|---|---|---|
| GOTTA MOVE | 1966 | Columbia JZSP 115999 | 20 |
| *(White promo label, promo-only release)* | | | |
| SECOND HAND ROSE | 1965 | Columbia 43469 | 25 |
| *(Red vinyl, white promo label)* | | | |
| SLEEP IN HEAVENLY PEACE | 1966 | Columbia JZSP 116534 | 20 |
| *(Regular promo with promo-only picture sleeve; stock sleeve is completely different)* | | | |
| SLEEP IN HEAVENLY PEACE | 1966 | Columbia ZSS 116927 | 18 |
| *(White promo label, promo-only release)* | | | |
| WHY DID I CHOOSE YOU | 1964 | Columbia 43248 | 25 |
| *(Blue vinyl, white promo label)* | | | |
| **7-Inch Extended Plays** | | | |
| STONEY END Jukebox LLP | 1971 | Columbia 30378 | 30 |
| *(Red label, issued with a hard picture cover)* | | | |
| **Albums** | | | |
| COLOR ME BARBRA | 1966 | Columbia 2478 | 200 |
| *(Red vinyl, mono version)* | | | |
| COLOR ME BARBRA | 1966 | Columbia 9278 | 200 |
| *(Red vinyl, stereo version)* | | | |
| FAVORITE CHRISTMAS SONGS | 1978 | Columbia | 15 |
| *(Five-song sampler with one Streisand track)* | | | |
| THE LEGEND OF BARBRA STREISAND | 1983 | Columbia 1779 (2) | 30 |
| *(White promo label, interviews and music)* | | | |
| THE SECOND BARBRA STREISAND ALBUM | 1963 | Columbia 2054 | 200 |
| *(Blue vinyl, mono version)* | | | |
| THE SECOND BARBRA STREISAND ALBUM | 1963 | Columbia 8854 | 200 |
| *(Blue vinyl, stereo version)* | | | |
| YENTL | 1983 | Columbia AS-1891 | 40 |
| *(Promo-only picture disc)* | | | |
| **Compact Discs** | | | |
| I'VE GOT A CRUSH ON YOU With Frank Sinatra | 1993 | Capitol DPRO-79316 | 18 |
| *(Promo-only release, two tracks)* | | | |
| ONE VOICE | 1988 | Columbia | 40 |
| *(3" promo-only CD release)* | | | |
| ORDINARY MIRACLE TOUR CD '94 With inserts | 1994 | Columbia CSK 6120 | 30 |
| *(Greatest hits album with one live track, promo only release)* | | | |
| SELECTIONS FROM JUST FOR THE RECORD | 1991 | Columbia CSK 4196 | 15 |
| *(Promo-only sampler from box set, 12 tracks)* | | | |
| SELECTIONS FROM JUST FOR THE RECORD | 1991 | Columbia CSK 4200 | 15 |
| *(Promo-only sampler from box set, 12 tracks, all different than on CSK 4196)* | | | |
| **RADIO SHOWS** | | | |
| **Albums** | | | |
| LEGEND OF BARBRA STREISAND, THE (Nov 83) | 1983 | (3) | 150-225 |
| *(Music and interviews, rare show)* | | | |
| ROYALTY OF ROCK With Diana Ross | 1983 | | 40-75 |
| *(Music and interviews)* | | | |
| WESTWOOD ONE PRESENTS | 1983 | Westwood One | 40-75 |
| *(Music and interviews)* | | | |

**STRING DRIVEN THING**
**RADIO SHOWS**
**Albums**

| Title | Yr | Label, Number | NM $ |
|---|---|---|---|
| BBC TRANSCRIPTION DISC Live concert | 1973 | BBC Transcription | 100-175 |
| *(With Solid Gold Cadillac)* | | | |

**STRUMMER, JOE**
*More at The Clash.*
**12-Inch Singles**

| Title | Yr | Label, Number | NM $ |
|---|---|---|---|
| FILIBUSTERO (3 versions) | 1987 | Virgin 1125 | 6 |
| TRASH CITY (same on both sides) | 1988 | Epic EAS 01103 | 5 |

**STYLE COUNCIL, THE**
*Featuring Paul Weller; More at The Jam; Geffen promo 45s $3 each*
**12-Inch Singles**

| Title | Yr | Label, Number | NM $ |
|---|---|---|---|
| HAVE YOU EVER HAD IT BLUE (2 mixes) | 1986 | EMI America SPRO-9690 | 6 |
| INTERNATIONALISTS/WALLS COME TUMBLING | 1984 | Geffen PRO-A-2319 | 6 |
| LONG HOT SUMMER (same on both sides) | 1983 | Polydor 241 | 6 |
| (WHEN YOU) CALL ME (same on both sides) | 1986 | Geffen PRO-A-2490 | 6 |

**45s**

| Title | Yr | Label, Number | NM $ |
|---|---|---|---|
| HOW SHE THREW IT ALL AWAY (Edit) (same on both sides) | 1988 | Polydor PRO 617-7 | 4 |

**RADIO SHOWS**
**Albums**

| Title | Yr | Label, Number | NM $ |
|---|---|---|---|
| BBC TRANSCRIPTION DISC | 1984 | BBC Transcription | 250-350 |
| *(Very rare live concert)* | | | |
| BBC TRANSCRIPTION DISC | 1985 | BBC Transcription | 250-350 |
| *(Live concert)* | | | |

**STYX**
*Wooden Nickel (RCA) white promo label 45s $5 each; Wooden Nickel (RCA) brown promo label 45s $4 each; A&M promo 45s $3 each; A&M promo 45s by Tommy Shaw or Dennis DeYoung $2 each; Other A&M promo CD singles $3 each*
**12-Inch Singles**

| Title | Yr | Label, Number | NM $ |
|---|---|---|---|
| THE GRAND ILLUSION (same on both sides) | 1977 | A&M SP-17021 | 15 |

**45s**

| Title | Yr | Label, Number | NM $ |
|---|---|---|---|
| DESERT MOON Dennis DeYoung | 1984 | A&M | 12 |
| *(White label test pressing)* | | | |
| LIGHT UP | 1975 | A&M | 12 |
| *(Special radio version 3:14)* | | | |

| Title | Yr | Label, Number | NM $ |
|-------|----|----|----|
| MR. ROBOTO | 1983 | A&M | 12 |
| *(White label test pressing)* | | | |
| MUSIC TIME | 198? | A&M | 12 |
| *(White label test pressing)* | | | |
| WHAT'S IT ALL ABOUT (Apr 78) Public service show | 1978 | W.I.A.A. 416 | 15 |
| *(Flip side features Andrew Gold)* | | | |
| WHAT'S IT ALL ABOUT (Aug 79) Public service show | 1979 | W.I.A.A. 487 | 18 |
| *(Flip side features Ronnie Milsap)* | | | |
| **Albums** | | | |
| A&M RADIO SPECIAL | 1977 | A&M 8431 (2) | 25 |
| *(Music and interviews)* | | | |
| A&M RADIO SPECIAL | 1977 | A&M 17053 (3) | 40 |
| *(Music and interviews in a black/silver box)* | | | |
| STYX RADIO SAMPLER | 1978 | A&M 17222 (2) | 25 |
| *(Promo-only release)* | | | |
| THE GRAND ILLUSION | 1976 | A&M 17021 | 15 |
| *(Album sampler from record company)* | | | |
| **Compact Discs** | | | |
| RADIO MADE HITS | 1991 | A&M 75021 7465 2 | 20 |
| *(Promo-only sampler)* | | | |
| SHOW ME THE WAY | 1991 | A&M | Unknown |
| *(Promo CD single; this is the "Desert Storm" version with snippets of speeches interspersed. Some stations received this from satellite uplinks, though a promo may exist)* | | | |
| **RADIO SHOWS** | | | |
| **Albums** | | | |
| INNERVIEW (70s) | 197? | Innerview | 20-25 |
| *(Music and interviews)* | | | |
| INNERVIEW (80s) Tommy Shaw | 198? | Innerview | 15-25 |
| *(Music and interviews)* | | | |
| OFF THE RECORD (70s) | 197? | Westwood One (2) | 25-40 |
| *(Music and interviews, short-lived blue/white labels)* | | | |
| PROFILES IN ROCK (July 80) | 1980 | Watermark | 15-25 |
| *(Music and interviews)* | | | |
| ROBERT W. MORGAN (Sept 80) | 1980 | Watermark | 15-25 |
| *(Music and interviews)* | | | |
| SOURCE SPECIAL (Dec 81) | 1981 | NBC Radio (2) | 20-40 |
| *(Music and interviews)* | | | |
| STARTRACK PROFILE | 1985 | Westwood One (2) | 20-30 |
| *(Music and interviews)* | | | |
| SUPERSTAR CONCERT (Sept 84) | 1984 | Westwood One (2) | 40-75 |
| *(Live concert, repeated)* | | | |
| WORLD OF ROCK (Mar 89) Dennis DeYoung | 1989 | DIR (2) | 15-25 |
| *(DeYoung is co-host for music and interviews)* | | | |
| **Compact Discs** | | | |
| IN THE STUDIO (Sept 93) Profile of an album | 1993 | Album Network | 15-25 |
| *(Music and interviews)* | | | |
| **Reel-to-Reel Tapes** | | | |
| KING BISCUIT FLOWER HOUR (Mar 76) Live concert | 1976 | DIR/ABC (2) | 100-150 |
| *(With Deep Purple, on two reels)* | | | |

## SUDDENLY, TAMMY!
**45s**

| Title | Yr | Label, Number | NM $ |
|-------|----|----|----|
| WHOLE LOTTA GIRL/MY HAT//HARD LESSON/LONG WAY DOWN | 1995 | Warner Bros. PRO-S-7589 | 5 |
| *("Soil X Samples" 20; yellow vinyl)* | | | |

## SUGAR HILL GANG
**45s**

| Title | Yr | Label, Number | NM $ |
|-------|----|----|----|
| RAPPER'S DELIGHT (4:55)/ (6:30) | 1979 | Sugar Hill 752 | 20 |

## SUGARCUBES, THE
**12-Inch Singles**

| Title | Yr | Label, Number | NM $ |
|-------|----|----|----|
| BIRTHDAY (LP)/(Icelandic Version) | 1988 | Elektra 5306 | 6 |
| COLD SWEAT (remix)/(edit) | 1988 | Elektra ED 5322 | 6 |
| LEASH CALLED LOVE (3 versions) | 199? | Elektra 5627 | 10 |
| MOTORCRASH (same on both sides) | 1989 | Elektra ED 5337 | 8 |
| MOTORCRASH (same on both sides) | 1988 | Elektra 5341 | 6 |
| PLANET (LP)/(Somersault Version)/(Icelandic Version) | 1989 | Elektra ED 5433 | 8 |
| REGINA (same on both sides) | 1989 | Elektra 5406 | 6 |
| **Albums** | | | |
| HERE TODAY, TOMORROW, NEXT WEEK! | 1989 | Elektra 60860 | 15 |
| *(White label promo on audiophile vinyl)* | | | |
| LIFE'S TOO GOOD | 1988 | Elektra 60801 | 15 |
| *(White label promo on audiophile vinyl)* | | | |

## SUICIDAL TENDENCIES
**12-Inch Singles**

| Title | Yr | Label, Number | NM $ |
|-------|----|----|----|
| SURF AND SLAM/PLEDGE YOUR ALLEGIANCE | 1988 | Epic AS 1386 | 12 |

## SULLIVAN, ED, PRESENTS
**45s**

| Title | Yr | Label, Number | NM $ |
|-------|----|----|----|
| RUDOLPH, THE RED-NOSED REINDEER/THE LITTLE DRUMMER BOY// JINGLE BELLS/O HOLY NIGHT | 1968 | Columbia JZSP 135543/4 | 6 |

## SUMMER, DONNA
*Oasis promo 45s $5 each; Other Casablanca promo 45s $4 each; Mercury and Geffen promo 45s $3 each; Other promo 12" singles $8 each; Any label promo CD singles $2-3 each*

**12-Inch Singles**

| Title | Yr | Label, Number | NM $ |
|-------|----|----|----|
| ALL SYSTEMS GO (Dance Mix)/FASCINATION | 1987 | Geffen PRO-A-3036 | 8 |

| Title | Yr | Label, Number | NM $ |
|---|---|---|---|
| BREAKAWAY (Extended Mix) (Power Radio Mix) /I DON'T WANNA GET HURT (12" Mix) | 1989 | Atlantic DMD 1431 | 7 |
| COLD LOVE/LOOKING UP/WHO DO YOU THINK YOU'RE FOOLIN' | 1980 | Geffen PRO-A-925 | 8 |
| DINNER WITH GERSHWIN (7:43) (same on both sides) | 1987 | Geffen PRO-A-2802 | 10 |
| HOT STUFF (Long) | 1979 | Casablanca NBD 20159 | 12 |
| *(B-side is blank)* | | | |
| LOVE IS IN CONTROL (Edit) (LP) | 1982 | Geffen PRO-A-1041 | 12 |
| *(Promo only on Quiex II vinyl)* | | | |
| LOVE TO LOVE YOU BABY (16:49)/FLASH LIGHT (10:43) | 1994 | Casablanca PRO 1148 | 20 |
| *(B-side by Parliament; promo-only reissue)* | | | |
| LOVE'S ABOUT TO CHANGE MY HEART (5 versions) | 1989 | Atlantic 1382 | 8 |
| RUMOUR HAS IT/I LOVE YOU | 1978 | Casablanca NBD 20112 | 12 |
| *(B-side is blank, both tracks are on Side 1)* | | | |
| THERE GOES MY BABY (same on both sides) | 1984 | Geffen PRO-A-2180 | 6 |
| UNCONDITIONAL LOVE (Club Mix)/(Instrumental) | 1983 | Mercury PRO 226-1 | 6 |
| WALK AWAY (7:15) | 1979 | Casablanca NBD 20226 | 10 |
| *B-side is blank* | | | |
| THE WANDERER (stereo/mono) | 1980 | Geffen PRO-A-910 | 12 |
| WHEN LOVE CRIES (4 versions) | 1991 | Atlantic 1709 | 6 |
| WITH YOUR LOVE | 1978 | Casablanca 101 | 10 |
| *(Promo-only release)* | | | |
| WORK THAT MAGIC (4:34) (6:20) (5:00)/LET THERE BE PEACE | 1991 | Atlantic 1758 | 7 |
| **45s** | | | |
| CAN'T WE JUST SIT DOWN | 1977 | Casablanca 884 | 10 |
| *(Casablanca promo label)* | | | |
| COULD IT BE MAGIC | 1976 | Oasis 405 | 10 |
| *(Promo label)* | | | |
| COULD IT BE MAGIC | 1976 | Casablanca 405 | 12 |
| *(Promo label)* | | | |
| **Albums** | | | |
| CATS WITHOUT CLAWS | 1984 | Geffen GHS 24040 | 15 |
| *(Promo only on Quiex II vinyl)* | | | |
| **RADIO SHOWS** | | | |
| **Albums** | | | |
| NBC SOURCE (Feb 84) | 1984 | NBC Radio (2) | 50-100 |
| *(Live concert)* | | | |
| WORDS AND MUSIC (Oct 82) | 1982 | DIR (3) | 100-150 |
| *(Rare live concert)* | | | |

## SUMMERS, ANDY
*More at The Police*

| Title | Yr | Label, Number | NM $ |
|---|---|---|---|
| **12-Inch Singles** | | | |
| I ADVANCE MASKED (same on both sides) | 1982 | A&M 17219 | 10 |
| **45s** | | | |
| I ADVANCE MASKED (same on both sides) | 1982 | A&M 2513 | 4 |
| *(With Robert Fripp; no stock copy was issued)* | | | |
| **Albums** | | | |
| SPEAK OUT INTERVIEW | 1982 | A&M SP-17299 | 25 |
| *(Issued in generic cover with sticker)* | | | |

## SUMMERS, GENE

| Title | Yr | Label, Number | NM $ |
|---|---|---|---|
| **45s** | | | |
| GOODBYE PRISCILLA (BYE BYE BLUE BABY) | 1977 | Teardrop 3405 | 12 |
| *(Single-sided promo copies have erroneous subtitle)* | | | |

## SUN, JOE

| Title | Yr | Label, Number | NM $ |
|---|---|---|---|
| **45s** | | | |
| SILENT NIGHT/OH HOLY NIGHT | 1981 | Elektra 47232 | 5 |
| *(B-side by Helen Cornelius)* | | | |

## SUNBEAMS, THE

| Title | Yr | Label, Number | NM $ |
|---|---|---|---|
| **45s** | | | |
| TELL ME WHY | 1955 | Herald 451 | 60 |
| *(White promo label)* | | | |

## SUNDIALS, THE

| Title | Yr | Label, Number | NM $ |
|---|---|---|---|
| **45s** | | | |
| CHAPEL OF LOVE | 1962 | Guyden 2065 | 50 |
| *(White promo label)* | | | |

## SUNSETS, THE
*Challenge promo 45s $25 each*

## SUPER STOCKS, THE

| Title | Yr | Label, Number | NM $ |
|---|---|---|---|
| **45s** | | | |
| MIDNIGHT RUN | 1964 | Capitol PRO-2642 | 25 |
| *(Promo-only release)* | | | |
| **Albums** | | | |
| HOT ROD RALLY | 1963 | Capitol 1997 | 50 |
| *(Black/blue promo label)* | | | |
| SCHOOL IS A DRAG | 1964 | Capitol 2190 | 75 |
| *(Black/blue promo label)* | | | |
| SURF ROUTE 101 | 1964 | Capitol 2113 | 75 |
| *(Black/blue promo label)* | | | |
| THUNDER ROAD | 1964 | Capitol 2060 | 75 |
| *(Black/blue promo label)* | | | |

| Title | Yr | Label, Number | NM $ |
|---|---|---|---|
| **SUPERTRAMP** | | | |
| *A&M promo 45s $3 each; A&M promo 45s by Roger Hodgson $2 each Featuring Roger Hodgson* | | | |
| **12-Inch Singles** | | | |
| CANNONBALL (Edit) (Single Version) (Direct-to-Disc Version) | 1985 | A&M SP-17320 | 10 |
| **45s** | | | |
| IT'S RAINING AGAIN | 1982 | A&M | 12 |
| *(White label test pressing)* | | | |
| MY KIND OF LADY | 1983 | A&M | 12 |
| *(White label test pressing)* | | | |
| WHAT'S IT ALL ABOUT (Feb 82) Public service show | 1982 | W.I.A.A. 614 | 30 |
| *(Flip side features Robert Plant/Led Zeppelin)* | | | |
| WHAT'S IT ALL ABOUT (Sept 79) Public service show | 1979 | W.I.A.A. 491 | 20 |
| *(Flip side features Count Basie)* | | | |
| **Albums** | | | |
| BREAKFAST IN AMERICA | 1979 | A&M 3730 | 300 |
| *(Picture disc used for LP promotion)* | | | |
| **RADIO SHOWS** | | | |
| **Albums** | | | |
| BBC ROCK HOUR (Oct 80) | 1980 | London Wavelength | 20-35 |
| *(Music and interviews)* | | | |
| BBC TRANSCRIPTION DISC | 1975 | BBC Transcription | 125-250 |
| *(Very rare live concert)* | | | |
| IN CONCERT | 1987 | Westwood One (2) | 35-65 |
| *(Live concert)* | | | |
| OFF THE RECORD Roger Hodgson | 1985 | Westwood One (2) | 15-25 |
| *(Music and interviews)* | | | |
| PIONEERS IN MUSIC (Feb 86) | 1986 | DIR (2) | 20-40 |
| *(Mostly music and interviews)* | | | |
| PROFILES IN ROCK (Feb 80) | 1980 | Watermark | 25-40 |
| *(Music and interviews)* | | | |
| ROBERT W. MORGAN (May 81) | 1981 | Watermark | 25-35 |
| *(Music and interviews)* | | | |
| SELF PORTRAIT (Feb 85) | 1985 | NBC Source (4) | 75-125 |
| *(Live concert, photo box)* | | | |
| STARTRACK PROFILE | 1986 | Westwood One (2) | 20-30 |
| *(Music and interviews)* | | | |
| SUPERGROUPS | 1982 | DIR (3) | 75-125 |
| *(Live concert)* | | | |
| SUPERSTAR CONCERT | 1985 | Westwood One (3) | 25-50 |
| *(Live concert, repeated)* | | | |
| THE SUPERTRAMP SPECIAL (Dec 80) | 1980 | NBC Source (2) | 40-75 |
| *(Mostly live concert)* | | | |
| **Compact Discs** | | | |
| BBC CLASSIC TRACKS (Nov 93) | 1993 | Westwood One | 20-30 |
| *(Various live tracks)* | | | |
| IN CONCERT (Dec 90) | 1990 | Westwood One | 25-50 |
| *(Live concert)* | | | |
| IN CONCERT (Mar 92) | 1992 | Westwood One (2) | 40-75 |
| *(Live concert)* | | | |
| IN THE STUDIO (90s) Profile of an album | 199? | Album Network | 15-25 |
| *(Music and interviews)* | | | |
| SUPERSTARS (Sept 95) | 1995 | Westwood One (2) | 25-40 |
| *(Live concert)* | | | |
| **Reel-to-Reel Tapes** | | | |
| KING BISCUIT FLOWER HOUR (Feb 78) Live concert | 1978 | DIR/ABC | 75-125 |
| *(With Foreigner on two reels)* | | | |
| | | | |
| **SUPREMES, THE** | | | |
| *Includes records as Diana Ross & the Supremes; Other Motown promo 45s through 1085 $15 each; Other Motown promo 45s 1089 and after $10 each; Motown promo 45s duets with other groups $8 each; Other Motown white promo label LPs $25 each* | | | |
| **45s** | | | |
| A BREATH TAKING, FIRST SIGHT SOUL SHAKING, ONE NIGHT LOVE MAKING, NEXT DAY HEART BREAKING GUY | 1963 | Motown 1044 | 40 |
| *(White promo label, later shortened to "A Breath Taking Guy")* | | | |
| BUTTERED POPCORN | 1961 | Tamla 54045 | 60 |
| *(White promo label)* | | | |
| CHILDREN'S CHRISTMAS SONG/TWINKLE, TWINKLE LITTLE ME | 1965 | Motown 1085 | 25 |
| *(Promo only on red vinyl)* | | | |
| I WANT A GUY | 1961 | Tamla 54038 | 150 |
| *(White promo label, stock copy worth $100)* | | | |
| LET ME GO THE RIGHT WAY | 1962 | Motown 1034 | 50 |
| *(White promo label)* | | | |
| MEDLEY OF HITS | 1980 | Motown PR-69 | 15 |
| *(Promo-only white label release)* | | | |
| MY HEART CAN'T TAKE IT ANYMORE | 1962 | Motown 1040 | 40 |
| *(White promo label)* | | | |
| NO MATTER WHAT SIGN YOU ARE | 1969 | Motown 1148 | 75 |
| *(Red vinyl, white promo label)* | | | |
| THE ONLY TIME I'M HAPPY | 1965 | Geo. Alexander 1079 | 125 |
| *(Special products release includes interview on the flip side, promo only)* | | | |
| THINGS ARE CHANGING (same on both sides) | 1965 | EEOC (# unknown) | 150 |
| YOUR HEART BELONGS TO ME | 1962 | Motown 1027 | 50 |
| *(White promo label, stock picture sleeve $100)* | | | |
| **7-Inch Extended Plays** | | | |
| A' GO-GO Jukebox LLP | 1966 | Motown 60649 | 25 |
| *(Issued with a hard cover)* | | | |

| Title | Yr | Label, Number | NM $ |
|---|---|---|---|
| A BIT OF LIVERPOOL Jukebox LLP | 1968 | Motown 623 | 25 |
| *(Issued with a hard cover)* | | | |
| COLLECTION-VOL. 5 Various artists | 1968 | Motown 60651 | 12 |
| *(Jukebox LLP, includes two songs by the Supremes)* | | | |
| COUNTRY, WESTERN & POP Jukebox LLP | 1968 | Motown 625 | 25 |
| *(Issued with a hard cover)* | | | |
| DR. GOLDFOOT & THE BIKINI MACHINE | 1966 | American International | 150 |
| *(Movie ads for the movie featuring the Supremes)* | | | |
| I HEAR A SYMPHONY Jukebox LLP | 1965 | Motown 643 | 25 |
| *(Issued with a hard cover)* | | | |
| THE MAGNIFICENT 7 Supremes/Four Tops | 1970 | Motown 60717 (LLP 134) | 18 |
| *(Jukebox LLP, issued with a paper sleeve)* | | | |
| MEET THE SUPREMES Jukebox LLP | 1968 | Motown 606 | 35 |
| *(Issued with a hard cover)* | | | |
| MERRY CHRISTMAS Jukebox LLP | 1968 | Motown 638 | 40 |
| *(Issued with a hard cover)* | | | |
| MORE HITS BY THE SUPREMES Jukebox LLP | 1968 | Motown 627 | 25 |
| *(Issued with a hard cover)* | | | |
| THE SUPREMES AT THE COPA Jukebox LLP | 1968 | Motown 636 | 25 |
| *(Issued with a hard cover)* | | | |
| SUPREMES SING HOLLAND-DOZIER-HOLLAND Jukebox LLP | 1967 | Motown 60650 | 25 |
| *(Issued with a hard cover)* | | | |
| THINGS GO BETTER WITH COKE With others | 1968 | Coca-Cola | 100 |
| *(German pressing, used in USA, also with Ray Charles and Dave Dee, Dozy, Beaky Mick & Tich; picture sleeve has picture of D-D-D-B-M & T)* | | | |
| WE REMEMBER SAM COOKE Jukebox LLP | 1968 | Motown 629 | 25 |
| *(Issued with a hard cover)* | | | |
| WHERE DID OUR LOVE GO Jukebox LLP | 1968 | Motown 621 | 30 |
| *(Issued with a hard cover)* | | | |
| **Albums** | | | |
| ANTHOLOGY | 1974 | Motown 794 (3) | 40 |
| *(White promo labels)* | | | |
| TOUCH INTERVIEW | 1971 | Motown PR-102 | 25 |
| **RADIO SHOWS** | | | |
| **Albums** | | | |
| ROCK, ROLL & REMEMBER (Jan 86) | 1986 | United Stations (4) | 20-40 |
| *(Supremes tribute show includes interviews with Diana Ross and Mary Wilson with Dick Clark)* | | | |
| ROYALTY OF ROCK Diana Ross and Barbra Streisand | 1983 | RKO | 40-75 |
| *(Music and interviews)* | | | |
| **Compact Discs** | | | |
| SIXTIES LEGENDS (July 92) | 1992 | Unistar (2) | 25-50 |
| *(Music and interviews)* | | | |

## SURFARIS, THE

Decca promo 45s $15 each; Other Dot promo 45s $10 each; MCA promo 45s $4 each

| **45s** | | | |
|---|---|---|---|
| SURFER JOE | 1965 | Dot 16757 | 40 |
| *(White promo label)* | | | |
| WIPE OUT | 1963 | Universal | 60 |
| *(Promo label)* | | | |
| WIPE OUT | 1966 | Dot 144 | 100 |
| *(Red vinyl promo reissue)* | | | |
| WIPE OUT (same on both sides) | 1966 | Dot 144 | 150 |
| *(Red vinyl; error pressing with "Surfer Joe" on both sides)* | | | |
| **7-Inch Extended Plays** | | | |
| HIT CITY '65 Jukebox LLP | 1965 | Decca 34292 | 50 |
| *(Issued with a hard cover)* | | | |
| IT AIN'T ME BABE Jukebox LLP | 1968 | Decca 34293 | 50 |
| *(Issued with a hard cover)* | | | |

## SURVIVOR

Scotti Brothers promo 45s $3 each; Scotti Brothers promo picture sleeve $4; Epic promo 45s by Jim Peterik $3 each; Warner Bros. and Parrot promo 45s by The Ides of March $6 each

| **Albums** | | | |
|---|---|---|---|
| SNEAK PREVIEW | 1983 | | 25 |
| *(Music and interviews)* | | | |
| **RADIO SHOWS** | | | |
| **Albums** | | | |
| IN CONCERT (Feb 85) Live concert | 1985 | Westwood One (2) | 100-200 |
| *(With Lita Ford)* | | | |
| SUPERSTAR CONCERT (July 85) Live concert | 1985 | Westwood One (3) | 40-75 |
| *(With John Waite)* | | | |
| SUPERSTAR CONCERT (Sept 83) | 1983 | Westwood One (3) | 50-100 |
| *(Live concert, box set)* | | | |

## SUTHERLAND BROTHERS, THE
**RADIO SHOWS**
**Albums**

| | | | |
|---|---|---|---|
| BBC TRANSCRIPTION DISC Live concert | 1973 | BBC Transcription | 100-200 |
| *(With T. J. White)* | | | |

## SUZY AND THE RED STRIPES

*See Paul McCartney*

## SWALLOWS, THE

*Federal promo 45s $25 each*

| Title | Yr | Label, Number | NM $ |
|---|---|---|---|
| **SWANS, THE** | | | |
| **45s** | | | |
| BOY WITH THE BEATLE HAIR, THE | 1964 | Cameo 302 | 50 |
| *(White label promo, one of the first Beatles novelties)* | | | |
| | | | |
| **SWANSON, BRAD, AND HIS WHISPERING ORGAN SOUND** | | | |
| **45s** | | | |
| RUDOLPH THE RED NOSE REINDEER/JINGLE BELLS | 19?? | Thunderbird 525 | 6 |
| | | | |
| **SWEATT, AL** | | | |
| **45s** | | | |
| LET'S PAINT THE TOWN RED | 195? | Keen 289 | 65 |
| | | | |
| **SWEET INSPIRATIONS, THE** | | | |
| **12-Inch Singles** | | | |
| BLACK SUNDAY PARTS 1 AND 2 (same on both sides) | 1977 | Caribou ASD 333 | 15 |
| LOVE IS ON THE WAY (6:10)/(Instrumental) | 1979 | RSO 304 | 12 |
| | | | |
| **SWEET TEENS, THE** | | | |
| **45s** | | | |
| YOUR CANDY KISSES | 1958 | Federal 12334 | 50 |
| *(White promo label)* | | | |
| | | | |
| **SWEET, MATTHEW** | | | |
| *A&M promo CD singles $4 each; Other Zoo promo CD singles $3 each* | | | |
| **12-Inch Singles** | | | |
| SAVE TIME FOR ME (same on both sides) | 1986 | Columbia CAS 2484 | 5 |
| VERTIGO (2 versions)/YOU GOTTA/SILENT CITY | 1989 | A&M 17691 | 6 |
| **Compact Discs** | | | |
| GIRLFRIEND | 1991 | Zoo 1414 | 8 |
| *(Promo CD single)* | | | |
| GOODFRIEND: ANOTHER TAKE ON GIRLFRIEND | 1992 | Zoo 17098 | 25 |
| *(Promo-only sampler, includes demo versions of several songs)* | | | |
| I'VE BEEN WAITING | 1992 | Zoo 17070 | 8 |
| *(Promo CD single)* | | | |
| **RADIO SHOWS** | | | |
| **Compact Discs** | | | |
| IN CONCERT-NU ROCK (Mar 94) | 1994 | Westwood One | 40-80 |
| *(Live concert)* | | | |
| ON THE EDGE (Oct 93) Music and interviews | 1993 | Westwood One | 20-35 |
| *(With Ocean Blue)* | | | |
| | | | |
| **SWEET, RACHEL** | | | |
| **12-Inch Singles** | | | |
| (THEME FROM) HAIRSPRAY (same on both sides) | 1988 | MCA 17513 | 6 |
| | | | |
| **SWEET, THE** | | | |
| *Bell white promo label 45s $6 each; Capitol promo 45s $3 each* | | | |
| **45s** | | | |
| ALL YOU'LL EVER GET FROM ME | 1969 | Paramount 0044 | 18 |
| *(White promo label, first record)* | | | |
| IT'S LONELY OUT THERE | 1973 | 20th Century 2033 | 12 |
| *(Blue promo label)* | | | |
| **Albums** | | | |
| CUT ABOVE THE REST | 1979 | Capitol PRO-11929 | 50 |
| *Special promo box contains record, cassette, 8-track, photo, bio* | | | |
| FOR A.O.R. RADIO ONLY | 1976 | Capitol SPRO-8371/2 | 25 |
| SHORT AND SWEET | 1978 | Capitol SPRO-8849 | 30 |
| | | | |
| **SWIMMING POOL Q'S, THE** | | | |
| **12-Inch Singles** | | | |
| THE COMMON YEARS (same on both sides) | 1989 | Capitol SPRO-79552 | 5 |
| MORE THAN ONE HEAVEN (Remix) (same on both sides) | 1986 | A&M 17399 | 5 |
| NOW I'M TALKING ABOUT NOW (same on both sides) | 1986 | A&M 17369 | 5 |
| | | | |
| **SWING OUT SISTER** | | | |
| **12-Inch Singles** | | | |
| SURRENDER (Stuffed Gun Mix)/(Popstand Mix) | 1986 | Mercury PRO 588 | 6 |
| TWILIGHT WORLD (4 versions) | 1986 | Mercury PRO 560 | 6 |
| | | | |
| **SWINGIN' MEDALLIONS** | | | |
| **45s** | | | |
| DOUBLE SHOT | 1966 | Smash 2022 | 20 |
| *(White promo label)* | | | |
| | | | |
| **SWINGIN' TIGERS** | | | |
| **45s** | | | |
| SNAKE WALK | 1960 | Tamla 54024 | 75 |
| *(White promo label)* | | | |
| | | | |
| **SWINGING BLUE JEANS, THE** | | | |
| *Imperial white promo label 45s $10 each* | | | |
| **Albums** | | | |
| HIPPY HIPPY SHAKE | 1964 | Imperial 9261 | 75 |
| *(White promo label)* | | | |

| Title | Yr | Label, Number | NM $ |
|-------|-----|---------------|------|
| **SWINGING PHILLIES, THE** | | | |
| **45s** | | | |
| L-O-V-E | 1958 | DeLuxe 6171 | 60 |
| *(White promo label)* | | | |
| | | | |
| **SYCAMORES, THE** | | | |
| **45s** | | | |
| I'LL BE WAITING | 1955 | Groove 0121 | 150 |
| *(White promo label)* | | | |
| | | | |
| **SYLVAIN SYLVAIN** | | | |
| **Albums** | | | |
| RCA SPECIAL RADIO SERIES XII | 1981 | RCA Victor DJL1-4062 | 15 |
| *(Promo-only interviews and music)* | | | |
| | | | |
| **SYLVIAN, DAVID** | | | |
| **12-Inch Singles** | | | |
| DARSHAN (3 versions) | 1994 | Virgin 14125 | 12 |
| **Albums** | | | |
| INK IN THE WELL -- A CONVERSATION | 1987 | Virgin 2167 | 20 |
| *(Promo-only interview album)* | | | |
| | | | |
| **SYNERGY** | | | |
| **12-Inch Singles** | | | |
| PHOBOS AND DEIMOS GO TO MARS (Edit) (LP) | 1978 | Passport SP-30 | 15 |
| REDSTONE/METROPOLITAN THEME | 1987 | Audion 12204 | 12 |
| | | | |
| **SYREETA** | | | |
| **12-Inch Singles** | | | |
| QUICK SLICK/OUT OF THE BOX | 1981 | Motown PR 90 | 10 |

# T

| Title | Yr | Label, Number | NM $ |
|-------|-----|---------------|------|
| **T'PAU** | | | |
| **12-Inch Singles** | | | |
| BRIDGE OF SIGHS (AOR Remix) (same on both sides) | 1987 | Virgin 2092 | 8 |
| HEART AND SOUL (2 versions)/ON THE WING | 1987 | Virgin 1046 | 10 |
| HEART AND SOUL (Edit) (same on both sides) | 1987 | Virgin PR 2001 | 10 |
| | | | |
| **T. REX** | | | |
| *Also known as Tyrannosaurus Rex; Blue Thumb promo 45s $8 each; Reprise promo 45s $6 each; Casablanca promo 45s $4 each; Reprise promo LPs $25 each* | | | |
| **45s** | | | |
| CHILD STAR Tyrannosaurus Rex | 1968 | A&M 995 | 15 |
| *(White promo label)* | | | |
| HOT LOVE | 1970 | Reprise 1006 | 10 |
| *(4:50 version, later re-released on Reprise 1170)* | | | |
| RIDE A WHITE SWAN Tyrannosaurus Rex | 1971 | Blue Thumb 6115/6116 | 12 |
| *(Promo single with "Bonus" on the label)* | | | |
| **Albums** | | | |
| A BEARD OF STARS Tyrannosaurus Rex | 1970 | Blue Thumb 18 | 25 |
| *(White promo label)* | | | |
| AN INTERVIEW WITH MARC BOLAN | 1971 | Reprise PRO 511 | 100 |
| *(White promo label)* | | | |
| TYRANNOSAURUS REX | 1972 | A&M 3514 (2) | 35 |
| *(White promo labels)* | | | |
| UNICORN Tyrannosaurus Rex | 1969 | Blue Thumb 7 | 30 |
| *(White promo label)* | | | |
| **Compact Discs** | | | |
| T. REX SAMPLER | 1991 | Relativity | 20 |
| *(Promo-only collection)* | | | |
| **RADIO SHOWS** | | | |
| **Albums** | | | |
| IN CONCERT | 1981 | Westwood One (2) | 150-225 |
| *(Live concert)* | | | |
| RETRO ROCK (Aug 82) | 1982 | Clayton Webster (2) | 175-250 |
| *(With Blues Project)* | | | |
| | | | |
| **T.C. ATLANTIC** | | | |
| **45s** | | | |
| LOVE IS JUST | 1969 | London 338 | 18 |
| *(Brownish promo label)* | | | |
| TWENTY YEARS AGO | 1969 | London 330 | 30 |
| *(Brownish promo label)* | | | |
| | | | |
| **TALK TALK** | | | |
| *EMI America promo 45s $3 each* | | | |
| **12-Inch Singles** | | | |
| LIFE'S WHAT YOU MAKE IT (same on both sides) | 1985 | EMI America SPRO 9580 | 8 |
| LIVING IN ANOTHER WORLD (4 versions)/TALK TALK (Remix) | 1991 | EMI SPRO 04735/51 | 10 |
| LIVING IN ANOTHER WORLD (Edit)/(LP) | 1986 | EMI America SPRO 9651/2 | 7 |
| SUCH A SHAME (extended)/(single)/(dub) | 1984 | EMI America SPRO 9155/6 | 8 |

| Title | Yr | Label, Number | NM $ |
|---|---|---|---|
| **RADIO SHOWS** | | | |
| **Albums** | | | |
| BBC TRANSCRIPTION DISC | 1986 | BBC Transcription | 300-400 |
| *(Very rare live concert)* | | | |
| IN CONCERT (Nov 84) Live concert | 1984 | Westwood One (2) | 50-100 |
| *(With Alarm)* | | | |

## TALKING HEADS

*With David Byrne; Other Sire promo 45s $5 each; Other Sire promo 12" singles $6 each; Sire promo 12" singles by Jerry Harrison $6 each; Sire promo CD singles $3-5 each*

| Title | Yr | Label, Number | NM $ |
|---|---|---|---|
| **12-Inch Singles** | | | |
| AND SHE WAS (same on both sides) | 1985 | Sire PRO-A-2348 | 6 |
| BLIND (Extended Remix) (same on both sides) | 1988 | Sire PRO-A-3182 | 5 |
| BURNING DOWN THE HOUSE (same on both sides) | 1983 | Sire PRO-A-2057 | 8 |
| BURNING DOWN THE HOUSE/PULL UP THE ROOTS/ | | | |
| SLIPPERY PEOPLE (Cassette Version) | 1983 | Sire PRO-A-2046 | 8 |
| CROSSEYED AND PAINLESS (long)/(short) | 1980 | Sire PRO-A-903 | 16 |
| LIFE DURING WARTIME/I ZIMBRA/AIR | 1979 | Sire PRO-A-846 | 16 |
| LOVE FOR SALE (same on both sides) | 1986 | Sire PRO-A-2638 | 5 |
| (NOTHING BUT) FLOWERS (Radio Edit)/(LP Version) | 1988 | Sire PRO-A-2947 | 5 |
| ONCE IN A LIFETIME (Edit) (same on both sides) | 1984 | Sire PRO-A-2207 | 6 |
| PUZZLIN' EVIDENCE (same on both sides) | 1986 | Sire PRO-A-2593 | 8 |
| ROAD TO NOWHERE (LP version)/(Edit) | 1985 | Sire PRO-A-2305 | 6 |
| STAY UP LATE (same on both sides) | 1985 | Sire PRO-A-2376 | 6 |
| THIS MUST BE THE PLACE (NAIVE MELODY) (LP)/(Edit) | 1983 | Sire PRO-A-2101 | 8 |
| WILD WILD LIFE (same on both sides) | 1986 | Sire PRO-A-2556 | 6 |
| **45s** | | | |
| LOVE GOES TO BUILDING ON FIRE | 1977 | Sire SAA-737 | 10 |
| *(Yellow promo label, stock picture sleeve worth $15)* | | | |
| PSYCHO KILLER | 1977 | Sire 1013 | 10 |
| *(Yellow promo label, stock picture sleeve worth $12)* | | | |
| UH OH, LOVE COMES TO TOWN | 1977 | Sire 1002 | 10 |
| *(Yellow promo label, stock picture sleeve worth $15)* | | | |
| UH OH, LOVE COMES TO TOWN | 1977 | Sire PRO-696 | 15 |
| *(Yellow promo label, promo-only release)* | | | |
| **Albums** | | | |
| PSYCHO KILLER/LIFE DURING WARTIME/ | 1982 | Sire PRO-A-1033 | 15 |
| TAKE ME TO THE RIVER/HOUSES IN MOTION | | | |
| *(Promo-only 4-song sampler)* | | | |
| SPEAKING IN TONGUES | 1983 | Warner Bros. 23771 | 40 |
| *(Promotional, clear vinyl, issued in an "oversize" album sleeve/plastic box, also; early stock copies also came this way)* | | | |
| TALKING HEADS | 1980 | Sire PRO-A-930 | 15 |
| *Promo-only 4-song sampler from "Remain in Light"* | | | |
| THE WARNER BROS. MUSIC SHOW -- TALKING HEADS LIVE ON TOUR | 1979 | Warner Bros. WBMS-104 | 25 |
| *(Promo-only radio show; has been counterfeited)* | | | |
| **RADIO SHOWS** | | | |
| **Albums** | | | |
| THE INSIDE TRACK (Nov 84) U2 and David Byrne | 1984 | DIR (3) | 100-175 |
| *(Mostly music and interviews)* | | | |
| KING BISCUIT FLOWER HOUR (Mar 80) | 1980 | DIR/ABC (2) | 50-100 |
| *(Live concert with Robert Palmer)* | | | |
| OFF THE RECORD (Aug 85) David Byrne | 1985 | Westwood One (2) | 20-30 |
| *(Music and interviews)* | | | |
| ROBERT KLEIN (Feb 81) | 1981 | (2) | 15-25 |
| *(Music and interviews, with Traffic)* | | | |
| SUPERSTAR CONCERT (Dec 90) | 1990 | Westwood One (3) | 25-40 |
| *(Live concert, repeated)* | | | |
| TIMOTHY WHITE SESSIONS (Apr 88) | 1988 | Westwood One (2) | 25-40 |
| *(Music and interviews)* | | | |
| TIMOTHY WHITE SESSIONS (Dec 88) David Byrne | 1988 | Westwood One (2) | 20-35 |
| *(Music and interviews)* | | | |
| **Compact Discs** | | | |
| IN THE STUDIO (June 90) Profile of an album | 1990 | Album Network | 15-25 |
| *(Music and interviews)* | | | |
| KING BISCUIT FLOWER HOUR (June 90) | 1990 | DIR | 40-75 |
| *(Live concert)* | | | |

## TALL, TOM

| Title | Yr | Label, Number | NM $ |
|---|---|---|---|
| **45s** | | | |
| STACK-A-RECORDS | 196? | Crest 1038 | 40 |
| *(White promo label)* | | | |

## TANGERINE DREAM

*Virgin promo 45s $8-10 each; MCA promo 45s $8 each; Elektra promo 12" singles $10 each*

| Title | Yr | Label, Number | NM $ |
|---|---|---|---|
| **45s** | | | |
| MOONLIGHT (PART 2) (mono/stereo) | 1977 | Virgin 9516 | 10 |
| MOONLIGHT/CHEROKEE LANE | 1977 | Virgin 9516 | 10 |
| MOONLIGHT/DESERT DREAM | 1977 | Virgin 9516 | 10 |
| **Compact Discs** | | | |
| TANGENTS 1973-1983 BOX SET SAMPLER | 1995 | Virgin | 25 |
| *(Promo-only collection)* | | | |

## TANGIERS, THE

*Also see Hollywood Flames*

| Title | Yr | Label, Number | NM $ |
|---|---|---|---|
| **45s** | | | |
| TABARIN | 1955 | Decca 29603 | 50 |
| *(Pink promo label)* | | | |

| **Title** | **Yr** | **Label, Number** | **NM $** |
|---|---|---|---|
| **TAUPIN, BERNIE** | | | |
| **Albums** | | | |
| INTERVIEW ALBUM | 1987 | RCA 6420-1-RAB | 20 |
| | | | |
| **TAVARES** | | | |
| **12-Inch Singles** | | | |
| STRAIGHT FROM THE HEART (7:23) (same on both sides) | 1979 | Capitol SPRO-9087 | 12 |
| | | | |
| **TAYLOR, ANDY** | | | |
| *More at Duran Duran* | | | |
| **12-Inch Singles** | | | |
| DEAD ON THE MONEY (same on both sides) | 1988 | Capitol SPRO-79463 | 8 |
| DON'T LET ME DIE YOUNG (same on both sides) | 1987 | MCA 17318 | 8 |
| I MIGHT LIE (3:58)/(4:53) | 1987 | MCA 17307 | 8 |
| I MIGHT LIE (same on both sides) | 1987 | MCA 17247 | 6 |
| TAKE IT EASY (same on both sides) | 1986 | Atlantic PR 896 | 8 |
| TAKE IT EASY (2 versions)/ANGEL EYES | 1986 | Atlantic PR 955 | 7 |
| | | | |
| **TAYLOR, EARL** | | | |
| **Albums** | | | |
| BLUEGRASS TAYLOR-MADE | 1963 | Capitol 2090 | 50 |
| *(Blue promo label)* | | | |
| | | | |
| **TAYLOR, JAMES** | | | |
| *Warner Bros. promo 45s $5 each; Columbia promo 45s $3 each; Columbia promo picture sleeves $2 each; Columbia promo CD singles $3 each* | | | |
| **12-Inch Singles** | | | |
| HANDY MAN (mono/stereo) | 1977 | Columbia ASF 358 | 15 |
| SUMMER'S HERE/HARD TIMES | 1981 | Columbia AS 1240 | 8 |
| **45s** | | | |
| CAROLINA ON MY MIND/SOMETHING'S WRONG | 1970 | Apple 1805 | 30 |
| *(Promo with error in title on A-side; actual title is "Carolina In My Mind")* | | | |
| KNOCKING 'ROUND THE ZOO  With the Original Flying Machine | 1971 | Euphoria 201 | 10 |
| *(Multi-colored promo label; the Flying Machine that did "Smile a Little Smile for Me" is no relation whatsoever)* | | | |
| MUD SLIDE SLIM AND THE BLUE HORIZON | 1971 | Warner Bros. PRO-483 | 40 |
| *(Radio ads, plays at 33 1/3 rpm)* | | | |
| NEW STAR SHINING  With Ricky Skaggs | 1986 | Epic ES7 2569 | 8 |
| *(With promo-only picture sleeve)* | | | |
| SWEET BABY JAMES | 1970 | Warner Bros. PRO-379 | 40 |
| *(Radio ads, plays at 33 1/3 rpm)* | | | |
| **7-Inch Extended Plays** | | | |
| MUD SLIDE SLIM AND THE BLUE HORIZON | 1971 | Warner Bros. 2561 (LLP 150) | 25 |
| *(Jukebox LLP, issued with a paper sleeve)* | | | |
| **RADIO SHOWS** | | | |
| **Albums** | | | |
| BBC TRANSCRIPTION DISC (Jan 73) Live concert | 1973 | BBC Transcription | 200-300 |
| *(With Joni Mitchell)* | | | |
| RETRO ROCK (Dec 81) | 1981 | Clayton Webster (2) | 100-175 |
| *(Live concert)* | | | |
| STARTRACK Profile (Feb 87) | 1987 | Westwood One (2) | 30-60 |
| *(Music and interviews)* | | | |
| TIMOTHY WHITE SESSIONS (Feb 88) | 1988 | Westwood One (3) | 25-50 |
| *(Music and interviews)* | | | |
| **Reel-to-Reel Tapes** | | | |
| ALBUM NETWORK SPECIAL | 1994 | Album Network (2) | 100-175 |
| *(Live concert on two 10" reels)* | | | |
| | | | |
| **TAYLOR, JOHN** | | | |
| *More at Duran Duran* | | | |
| **12-Inch Singles** | | | |
| I DO WHAT I DO... (same on both sides) | 1986 | Capitol SPRO-9653 | 10 |
| | | | |
| **TAYLOR, JOHNNIE** | | | |
| **45s** | | | |
| GOD IS STANDING BY/GOD IS AMAZING | 1977 | Columbia AE7 1153 | 8 |
| *(B-side by Deniece Williams; promo with "Suggested Christmas Programming" on label)* | | | |
| | | | |
| **TCHAIKOVSKY, BRAM** | | | |
| **12-Inch Singles** | | | |
| LADY FROM THE USA (same on both sides) | 1979 | Polydor PRO 109 | 5 |
| SHALL WE DANCE/MIRACLE CURE | 1981 | Arista SP-104 | 8 |
| | | | |
| **TEARDROP EXPLODES, THE** | | | |
| **12-Inch Singles** | | | |
| WHEN I DREAM/HA HA I'M DROWNING/REWARD | 1980 | Mercury 172 | 20 |
| **RADIO SHOWS** | | | |
| **Albums** | | | |
| BBC COLLEGE CONCERT HOUR (Nov 82) | 1982 | London Wavelength | 25-50 |
| *(Live concert)* | | | |
| BBC TRANSCRIPTION DISC  Live concert | 1981 | BBC Transcription | 250-350 |
| *(Very rare live concert)* | | | |
| | | | |
| **TEARS FOR FEARS** | | | |
| *Mercury promo 45s $3 each; Other Mercury promo 12" singles $8 each; Fontana and Epic promo CD singles $3-5 each* | | | |
| **12-Inch Singles** | | | |
| EVERYBODY WANTS TO RULE THE WORLD (same on both sides) | 1985 | Mercury PRO 340-1 | 8 |
| HEAD OVER HEELS (Live)/BROKEN-HEAD-BROKEN (Live) | 1985 | Mercury PRO 393-1 | 15 |
| HEAD OVER HEELS (Remix 45 Version)/ | 1985 | Mercury 374 | 8 |

| Title | Yr | Label, Number | NM $ |
|-------|-----|--------------|------|
| BROKEN-HEAD-BROKEN | | | |
| MAD WORLD (same on both sides) | 1983 | Mercury 238 | 12 |
| MOTHERS TALK (same on both sides) | 1986 | Mercury 410 | 6 |
| PALE SHELTER (same on both sides) | 1983 | Mercury 234 | 8 |
| SHOUT (Edit)/(LP version) | 1985 | Mercury PRO 363-1 | 12 |
| **45s** | | | |
| HEAD OVER HEELS (Live) (same on both sides) | 1985 | Mercury PRO 392-7 DJ | 10 |
| **Albums** | | | |
| NOW PLAYING-SELECTED CUTS | 1985 | Polygram Select 1 | 25 |
| (Made in Canada for the U.S., sampler LP) | | | |
| **RADIO SHOWS** | | | |
| **Albums** | | | |
| BBC ROCK HOUR (June 83) | 1983 | London Wavelength | 75-125 |
| (Rare live concert) | | | |
| BBC TRANSCRIPTION DISC Live concert | 1983 | BBC Transcription | 300-400 |
| (Very rare radio series) | | | |
| HOT ROCKS | 1986 | United Stations (2) | 25-40 |
| (Music and interviews) | | | |
| IN CONCERT (July 90) | 1990 | Westwood One (2) | 30-60 |
| (Live concert) | | | |
| IN CONCERT (June 91) Live concert | 1991 | Westwood One (2) | 25-50 |
| (With Toy Matinee) | | | |
| KING BISCUIT FLOWER HOUR (Dec 85) Live concert | 1985 | DIR (2) | 50-100 |
| (With the Thompson Twins) | | | |
| KING BISCUIT FLOWER HOUR (Sept 85) | 1985 | DIR/ABC (2) | 50-100 |
| (Rare live concert) | | | |
| PENTHOUSE/OMNI COLLEGE ROCK CONCERT (Sept 83) | 1983 | London Wavelength | 40-75 |
| (Rare live concert) | | | |
| SUPERSTAR CONCERT (Oct 85) Live concert | 1985 | Westwood One (3) | 40-75 |
| (With the Hooters) | | | |
| SUPERSTAR CONCERT  Live concert | 1986 | Westwood One (3) | 45-80 |
| (Box set, repeated) | | | |

**TEDDY BEARS, THE**
*With Phil Spector; Imperial promo 45s $25 each*
**Albums**

| THE TEDDY BEARS SING | 1959 | Imperial 9067 | 500 |
|-------|-----|--------------|------|
| (White promo label) | | | |

**TEENAGERS, THE**
*More at Frankie Lymon*
**45s**

| CAN YOU TELL ME | 1960 | End 1076 | 40 |
|-------|-----|--------------|------|
| (White promo label) | | | |
| FLIP FLOP | 1957 | Gee 1046 | 40 |
| (White promo label) | | | |
| MY BROKEN HEART | 1958 | Roulette 4086 | 75 |
| (Multi-colored promo label) | | | |
| TONIGHT'S THE NIGHT | 1960 | End 1071 | 60 |
| (White promo label) | | | |
| WHAT'S ON YOUR MIND | 1961 | Columbia 42054 | 30 |
| (White promo label) | | | |

**TELEVISION**
**45s**

| AIN'T THAT NOTHIN' (mono/stereo) | 1978 | Elektra 45516 | 25 |
|-------|-----|--------------|------|
| (Radically different recording than on LP; unknown whether this also appears on stock copy) | | | |
| **Albums** | | | |
| TELEVISION | 1992 | Capitol SPRO-79456 | 20 |
| (Promo-only vinyl release; stock copies on CD and cassette only) | | | |

**TEMPEST**
**RADIO SHOWS**
**Albums**

| BBC TRANSCRIPTION DISC | 1973 | BBC Transcription | 75-150 |
|-------|-----|--------------|------|
| (Live concert) | | | |

**TEMPLE OF THE DOG**
**12-Inch Singles**

| PUSHIN' FORWARD BACK/HUNGER STRIKE/YOUR SAVIOR | 1991 | A&M 75021 7533 1 | 15 |
|-------|-----|--------------|------|

**TEMPOS, THE**
*Kapp promo 45s $18 each*

**TEMPTATIONS, THE**
*Includes listings of Eddie Kendricks; Other Gordy white promo label 45s through 7057 $12 each; Other Gordy promo 45s $8 each; Motown promo 45s $3 each; Motown promo picture sleeves $4 each; Motown promo 45s by David Ruffin $5 each; RCA Victor promo 45s by Ruffin and "Kendrick" $3 each; Gordy promo LPs $30 each; Gordy 3-LP promo sets $25 each*
**12-Inch Singles**

| ALL I WANT FROM YOU (Club Mix)/(Debbie Favorite Mix) | 1989 | Motown L33-17880 | 8 |
|-------|-----|--------------|------|
| A FINE MESS (same on both sides) | 1986 | Motown 180 | 6 |
| GET READY 1990 (4 versions) | 1990 | Motown 1132 | 8 |
| HOOPS ON FIRE (3 versions) | 1992 | Motown 3746310251 | 8 |
| THE JONES (4 versions) | 1991 | Motown 1604 | 8 |
| ONE STEP AT A TIME (3 versions) | 1990 | Motown L33-18206 | 8 |
| SOUL TO SOUL (3 versions) | 1990 | Motown L33-18149 | 8 |

| Title | Yr | Label, Number | NM $ |
|---|---|---|---|
| **45s** | | | |
| CAN I  Eddie Kendricks | 1971 | Tamla 54210 | 30 |
| *(Blue vinyl, white promo label, long 6:05/short 3:10 versions)* | | | |
| CHECK YOURSELF | 1961 | Miracle 12 | 50 |
| *(Promo label)* | | | |
| DREAM COME TRUE | 1962 | Gordy 7001 | 40 |
| *(White promo label)* | | | |
| FAREWELL MY LOVE | 1963 | Gordy 7020 | 25 |
| *(White promo label)* | | | |
| FINE MESS, A | 1986 | Motown | 10 |
| *(With promo-only picture sleeve)* | | | |
| FUNKY MUSIC SHO NUFF TURNS ME ON | 1971 | Gordy 7119 | 25 |
| *(Red vinyl, white promo label)* | | | |
| I WANT A LOVE I CAN SEE | 1963 | Gordy 7015 | 30 |
| *(White promo label)* | | | |
| IT'S SO HARD FOR ME TO SAY GOODBYE  Eddie Kendricks | 1971 | Tamla 54203 | 25 |
| *(Red vinyl, white promo label)* | | | |
| OH MOTHER OF MINE | 1961 | Miracle 5 | 75 |
| *(Promo label)* | | | |
| PARADISE | 1962 | Gordy 7010 | 35 |
| *(White promo label)* | | | |
| RUDOLPH, THE RED-NOSED REINDEER | 1968 | Gordy 7082 | 25 |
| *(Red vinyl, white promo label)* | | | |
| WHAT'S IT ALL ABOUT  Public service show | 1973 | W.I.A.A. 225 | 20 |
| *(Interviews with Mel Franklin, flip side is B.J. Thomas)* | | | |
| **RADIO SHOWS** | | | |
| **Albums** | | | |
| SUPER JAM (Sept 91) Live concert | 1991 | (3) | 100-200 |
| *(With the Four Tops)* | | | |

## 10CC

*Lol Creme, Kevin Godley, Graham Gouldman and Eric Stewart; Also recorded as Hotlegs; Other UK promo 45s $8 each; Other Mercury promo 45s $4 each; Polydor promo 45s $4 each; Other Warner Bros. promo 45s $3 each; Mirage (Atlantic) promo 45s by Godley and Creme $3 each; Polydor promo 45s by Godley and Creme $3 each*

| Title | Yr | Label, Number | NM $ |
|---|---|---|---|
| **45s** | | | |
| ART FOR ART'S SAKE | 1975 | Mercury 441 | 12 |
| *(Price includes stock picture sleeve)* | | | |
| FIVE O'CLOCK IN THE MORNING  Creme & Godley | 1977 | Mercury DJ-526 | 10 |
| *(Promo-only release)* | | | |
| GOOD MORNING JUDGE | 1977 | Mercury DJ-507 | 10 |
| *(Promo-only release)* | | | |
| NEANDERTHAL MAN  Hotlegs | 1970 | Capitol P-2886 | 18 |
| *(Red/orange promo label)* | | | |
| THE POWER OF LOVE | 1982 | Warner Bros. PRO-S-1058 | 10 |
| *(Mono/stereo, promo release only)* | | | |
| RUBBER BULLETS | 1973 | UK 49015 | 12 |
| *(Blue promo label)* | | | |
| RUN BABY RUN   Hotlegs | 1970 | Capitol 3043 | 15 |
| *(Red/orange promo label)* | | | |
| THE WALL STREET SHUFFLE | 1974 | UK 49023 | 10 |
| *(Blue promo label)* | | | |
| WHAT'S SO GREAT ABOUT UK RECORDS  Various artists | 1972 | UK 101 | 18 |
| *(Bits from UK label artists including "Donna" by 10cc; included in price is a promo-only sleeve)* | | | |

## 10,000 MANIACS

*Elektra promo CD singles $3-5 each*

| Title | Yr | Label, Number | NM $ |
|---|---|---|---|
| **12-Inch Singles** | | | |
| DON'T TALK (LP)/(Edit) | 1987 | Elektra ED 5258 | 6 |
| EAT FOR TWO (same on both sides) | 1989 | Elektra ED 5399 | 5 |
| LIKE THE WEATHER (same on both sides) | 1987 | Elektra ED 5278 | 6 |
| MY MOTHER THE WAR (same on both sides) | 1990 | Elektra ED 5499 | 6 |
| PEACE TRAIN (same on both sides) | 1987 | Elektra ED 5239 | 5 |
| TROUBLE ME (same on both sides) | 1989 | Elektra ED 5376 | 8 |
| WHAT'S THE MATTER HERE (LP version)/(Edit) | 1987 | Elektra ED 5312 | 5 |
| YOU HAPPY PUPPET (same on both sides) | 1989 | Elektra ED 5416 | 5 |
| **Albums** | | | |
| BLIND MAN'S ZOO | 1989 | Elektra 60815 | 15 |
| *(Promo-only audiophile pressing; white promo labels)* | | | |
| IN MY TRIBE | 1987 | Elektra 60738 | 12 |
| *(Promo-only audiophile pressing)* | | | |
| INTERVIEW | 1987 | Elektra 5270 | 25 |
| *(Lenny Kaye interviews Natalie Merchant; promo only)* | | | |
| **RADIO SHOWS** | | | |
| **Albums** | | | |
| SPIN CONCERT | 1986 | Spin Magazine | 40-75 |
| *(Live concert)* | | | |
| **Compact Discs** | | | |
| IN CONCERT (May 94) | 1994 | Westwood One | 75-125 |
| *(Live concert)* | | | |
| IN CONCERT-NU ROCK (May 94) | 1994 | Westwood One | 75-125 |
| *(Live concert)* | | | |
| ON THE EDGE (May 93) Music and interviews | 1993 | Westwood One | 15-25 |
| *(With Midnight Oil)* | | | |
| UP CLOSE  Profile | 1994 | Media America (2) | 30-60 |
| *(Mostly music and interviews)* | | | |

| Title | Yr | Label, Number | NM $ |
|---|---|---|---|

**TEN YEARS AFTER**
*Deram promo 45s $6 each; Columbia promo 45s $4 each*
**RADIO SHOWS**
**Albums**

| | | | |
|---|---|---|---|
| WORLD OF ROCK (Sept 89) Music and interviews | 1989 | DIR (2) | 15-25 |
| *(Members of Ten Years After co-host the show)* | | | |

**Compact Discs**

| | | | |
|---|---|---|---|
| IN THE STUDIO  Profile of an album | 1989 | Album Network | 15-25 |
| *(Music and interviews)* | | | |
| KING BISCUIT FLOWER HOUR (June 88) | 1988 | DIR | 25-50 |
| *(Live concert, with Edgar Winter)* | | | |

**TENDERFOOTS, THE**
**45s**

| | | | |
|---|---|---|---|
| SINDY | 1955 | Federal 12228 | 150 |
| *(White promo label)* | | | |
| THOSE GOLDEN BELLS | 1955 | Federal 12225 | 75 |
| *(White promo label)* | | | |

**TESLA**
*Other Geffen promo CD singles $3-5 each*
**Compact Discs**

| | | | |
|---|---|---|---|
| ELECTRIC, ACOUSTIC AND PSYCHOTIC | 1992 | Geffen 4411 | 25 |
| *(Promo-only sampler)* | | | |
| SIGNS | 1990 | Geffen PRO-CD-4178 | 8 |
| *(Promo-only CD single in cardboard sleeve, their biggest hit)* | | | |

**TEX, JOE**
**45s**

| | | | |
|---|---|---|---|
| KING THADDEUS (mono/stereo) | 1971 | Dial 1006 | 7 |
| *(May be promo only)* | | | |

**THARP, CHUCK**
**45s**

| | | | |
|---|---|---|---|
| I DON'T KNOW | 1958 | Kapp 248 | 45 |
| *(White promo label)* | | | |

**THAT PETROL EMOTION**
**12-Inch Singles**

| | | | |
|---|---|---|---|
| ABANDON/HEY VENUS/SENSITIZE/GROOVE CHECK | 1989 | Virgin 1516 | 8 |
| BIG DECISION (Extended)/(Edit) | 1987 | Polydor 514 | 5 |
| BIG DECISION (3 versions) | 1987 | Polydor 528 | 5 |
| GROOVE CHECK (same on both sides) | 1988 | Virgin 1290 | 5 |

**THE THE**
*Epic promo CD singles $3-5 each*
**12-Inch Singles**

| | | | |
|---|---|---|---|
| HEARTLAND (2 versions)/SLOW TRAIN TO DAWN (2 versions) | 1986 | Epic EAS 2690 | 12 |
| INFECTED (LP)/(Remix) | 1986 | Epic EAS 2567 | 12 |
| JEALOUS OF YOUTH (2 versions)/BEYOND LOVE | 1990 | Epic EAS 01958 | 10 |
| KINGDOM OF RAIN/FLESH & BONES/ | 1989 | Epic EAS 01895 | 12 |
| NATURE OF VIRTUE/WAITIN' FOR THE UPTURN | | | |
| THIS IS THE DAY (Long)/(Short) | 1983 | Epic AS 1873 | 15 |
| UNCERTAIN SMILE (Long Version Edit)/(Short Version Edit) | 1982 | Sire PRO-A-1005 | 25 |

**45s**

| | | | |
|---|---|---|---|
| HEARTLAND/SLOW TRAIN TO DAWN | 1987 | Epic ES7 02718 | 8 |

**Compact Discs**

| | | | |
|---|---|---|---|
| THE THE VS. HANK | 1995 | Sony/550 BSK 6968 | 20 |
| *(Promo-only sampler)* | | | |

**RADIO SHOWS**
**Compact Discs**

| | | | |
|---|---|---|---|
| IN CONCERT-NU ROCK (June 93) | 1993 | Westwood One | 30-60 |
| *(Live concert)* | | | |

**THEY MIGHT BE GIANTS**
*Elektra promo CD singles $2-3 each*
**12-Inch Singles**

| | | | |
|---|---|---|---|
| ANA NG (same on both sides) | 1988 | Bar None 130 | 8 |
| BIRDHOUSE IN YOUR SOUL (same on both sides) | 1989 | Elektra 5427 | 6 |
| THEY'LL NEED A CRANE (same on both sides) | 1989 | Bar None 167 | 8 |
| TWISTING (same on both sides) | 1990 | Elektra 5453 | 6 |
| TWISTING/JAMES K. POLK/ANT | 1990 | Elektra 5458 | 8 |
| YOUR RACIST FRIEND (same on both sides) | 1990 | Elektra ED 5496 | 8 |

**RADIO SHOWS**
**Compact Discs**

| | | | |
|---|---|---|---|
| ALBUM NETWORK SPECIAL (June 93) | 1993 | Album Network | 40-75 |
| *(Live concert)* | | | |
| ON THE EDGE (Sept 94) Music and interviews | 1994 | Westwood One | 20-30 |
| *(With Sonic Youth)* | | | |

**THIN LIZZY**
*Other London promo 45s $5 each; Vertigo (Mercury) promo 45s $4 each; Mercury promo 45s $3 each; Warner Bros. promo 45s $3 each; Other Mercury and Warner Bros. promo 12" singles $8 each*
**12-Inch Singles**

| | | | |
|---|---|---|---|
| COWBOY SONG/THE BOYS ARE BACK IN TOWN/ROSALIE | 1978 | Warner Bros. PRO-A-754 | 20 |

**45s**

| | | | |
|---|---|---|---|
| DANCING IN THE MOONLIGHT | 1977 | Mercury DJ-509 | 10 |
| *(Promo-only number)* | | | |

| Title | Yr | Label, Number | NM $ |
|-------|----|----|----|
| ROCKY | 1973 | London DJ-475 | 10 |
| *(Promo-only release)* | | | |
| **RADIO SHOWS** | | | |
| **Albums** | | | |
| BBC ROCK HOUR (Apr 83) | 1983 | London Wavelength | 75-125 |
| *(Live concert)* | | | |
| BBC TRANSCRIPTION DISC | 1983 | BBC Transcription | 450-600 |
| *(Rare live concert)* | | | |
| BBC TRANSCRIPTION DISC  Live concert | 1973 | BBC Transcription | 700-800 |
| *(With Badfinger)* | | | |
| IN CONCERT (Mar 86) Live concert | 1986 | Westwood One (2) | 75-100 |
| *(With Def Leppard)* | | | |
| IN CONCERT (Mar 88) Live concert | 1988 | Westwood One (2) | 75-100 |
| *(With Def Leppard)* | | | |
| KING BISCUIT FLOWER HOUR (Feb 81) Live concert | 1981 | DIR/ABC (2) | 50-100 |
| *(With Dire Straits)* | | | |
| **Compact Discs** | | | |
| BBC CLASSIC TRACKS (Aug 91) | 1991 | Westwood One | 40-75 |
| *(Various classic live tracks)* | | | |
| KING BISCUIT FLOWER HOUR (Sept 88) Live concert | 1988 | DIR | 25-50 |
| *(With Aerosmith)* | | | |
| **Reel-to-Reel Tapes** | | | |
| KING BISCUIT FLOWER HOUR (Sept 76) Live concert | 1976 | DIR/ABC (2) | 100-150 |
| *(With Emmylou Harris)* | | | |

**THIRD WORLD**
*Island promo 45s $4 each; Mercury promo CD singles $2 each*

| **RADIO SHOWS** | | | |
|-------|----|----|----|
| **Albums** | | | |
| BBC ROCK HOUR | 1982 | London Wavelength | 30-60 |
| *(Live concert)* | | | |

**THIRTEENTH FLOOR ELEVATORS, THE**
*Originally The Spades*

| **45s** | | | |
|-------|----|----|----|
| YOU'RE GONNA MISS ME | 1966 | Zero 10002 | 200 |
| *(By the Spades)* | | | |
| YOU'RE GONNA MISS ME  White promo label | 1966 | Hanna-Barbera 492 | 50 |
| *(White promo label)* | | | |
| **Albums** | | | |
| BULL OF THE WOODS | 1967 | International Artists 9 | 100 |
| *(White promo label)* | | | |
| EASTER EVERYWHERE | 1966 | International Artists 5 | 100 |
| *(White promo label)* | | | |
| LIVE | 1967 | International Artists 8 | 100 |
| *(White promo label)* | | | |
| THE PSYCHEDELIC SOUND OF... | 1966 | International Artists 1 | 175 |
| *(White promo label)* | | | |

**38 SPECIAL**
*A&M promo 45s $3 each; Capitol promo 45s $3 each; A&M and Capitol promo 12" singles $6 each; Other A&M promo CD singles $2 each*

| **7-Inch Extended Plays** | | | |
|-------|----|----|----|
| FLASHBACK LIVE | 1987 | A&M 39101 | 10 |
| *(Four-song EP, bonus with early pressings of Flashback LP)* | | | |
| **Compact Discs** | | | |
| LIKE NO OTHER NIGHT | 1986 | A&M 17378 | 15 |
| *(One of the first promo CD releases)* | | | |
| **RADIO SHOWS** | | | |
| **Albums** | | | |
| CAPTURED LIVE | 1983 | RKO (2) | 25-50 |
| *(Live concert)* | | | |
| CAPTURED LIVE (Apr 84) | 1984 | RKO (2) | 30-60 |
| *(Live concert)* | | | |
| OFF THE RECORD | 1989 | Westwood One (2) | 15-25 |
| *(Music and interviews)* | | | |
| SUPERGROUPS (July 83) Live concert | 1983 | DIR (3) | 200-300 |
| *(With the Stray Cats)* | | | |
| SUPERSTAR CONCERT | 1989 | Westwood One (2) | 20-35 |
| *(Live concert)* | | | |
| **Compact Discs** | | | |
| BBC CLASSIC TRACKS (June 94) | 1994 | Westwood One | 15-25 |
| *(Various classic live tracks)* | | | |
| IN THE STUDIO (June 91) | 1991 | Album Network | 15-25 |
| *(Profile of an album, music and interviews)* | | | |
| LIVE AT ELECTRIC LADYLAND (Aug 91) | 1991 | Westwood One | 30-60 |
| *(Live concert, repeated in 1993)* | | | |
| OFF THE RECORD (Aug 93) | 1993 | Westwood One | 15-25 |
| *(Music and interviews)* | | | |
| UP CLOSE  Profile | 1989 | Media America (2) | 25-40 |
| *(Mostly music and interviews)* | | | |
| UP CLOSE  Profile | 1991 | Media America (2) | 20-35 |
| *(Mostly music and interviews)* | | | |

**THOMAS, B.J.**
*Hickory promo 45s $10 each; Scepter promo 45s $4 each; MCA promo 45s $3 each; Cleveland Int'l. promo 45s $2 each*

| **45s** | | | |
|-------|----|----|----|
| WHAT'S IT ALL ABOUT (Oct 77) Public service show | 1977 | W.I.A.A. 390 | 15 |
| *(Flip side is Dolly Parton)* | | | |

| Title | Yr | Label, Number | NM $ |
|-------|-----|---------------|------|

**THOMAS, KID**
**45s**
THE SPELL — 1957 — Federal 12298 — 50
*(White promo label)*

**THOMAS, RAY**
*Also see The Moody Blues*
**Albums**
RAY THOMAS DISCUSSES THE RECORDING OF HIS FIRST SOLO ALBUM FROM MIGHTY OAKS — 1975 — Threshold THSX-102 — 50

**THOMAS, TIMMY**
**12-Inch Singles**
GOTTA GIVE A LITTLE LOVE (5:26) (4:35) — 1984 — Gold Mountain 81203 — 8

**THOMPSON TWINS**
*Arista promo 45s $3 each; Other Arista promo 12" singles $7 each; Arista and Warner Bros. promo CD singles $3 each*
**12-Inch Singles**
BOMBERS IN THE SKY (4 versions) — 1989 — Warner Bros. PRO-A-3901 — 6
COME INSIDE (8 versions) — 1991 — Warner Bros. PRO-A-4941 — 12
*(Two 12-inch singles in promo-only gatefold sleeve)*
GROOVE ON (5 versions) — 1991 — Warner Bros. PRO-A-5207 — 8
YOU TAKE ME UP (same on both sides) — 1984 — Arista 9245 — 8
**Albums**
INTERVIEW SAMPLER — 1987 — Arista ADP 9586 — 20
*One side of interviews, the other of music; promo only*
**RADIO SHOWS**
**Albums**
BBC COLLEGE CONCERT (Sept 83) — 1983 — London Wavelength — 25-50
*(Live concert)*
IN CONCERT (Aug 83) — 1983 — Westwood One (2) — 20-40
*(Live concert with the Fixx)*
INNERVIEW — 1986 — Innerview — 15-20
*(Music and interviews)*
KING BISCUIT FLOWER HOUR (Dec 85) Live concert — 1985 — DIR (2) — 50-100
*(With Tears for Fears)*

**THOMPSON, HANK**
*Other Capitol white promo label 45s $5-8 each; Tower promo 45s $4 each; Dot promo 45s $3 each; Churchill promo 45s $3 each; Other Capitol jukebox LLPs $8 each; Capitol blue promo label LPs $30-40 each*
**45s**
AT THE GOLDEN NUGGET  Set of five stereo singles — 1961 — Capitol 1-5 1632 — 40
*(Or $8 each)*
ROCKIN' IN THE CONGO — 1958 — Capitol 3623 — 10
*(White promo label)*
SQUAWS ALONG THE YUKON — 1958 — Capitol 4017 — 10
*(White promo label)*
**7-Inch Extended Plays**
BREAKIN' IN ANOTHER HEART   Jukebox LLP — 1965 — Capitol 2274 — 12
*(Issued with a hard cover)*
**Albums**
COUNTRY BLUES — 1968 — Tower 5120 — 25
*(White promo label)*
HANK — 1957 — Capitol 816 — 75
*(Yellow promo label)*
HANK THOMPSON FAVORITES — 1957 — Capitol 911 — 75
*(Yellow promo label)*
HANK THOMPSON'S DANCE RANCH — 1957 — Capitol 975 — 50
*(Yellow promo label)*
NEW RECORDINGS OF HANK THOMPSON FAVORITES — 1956 — Capitol 729 — 75
*(Yellow promo label)*
NORTH OF THE RIO GRANDE — 1956 — Capitol 618 — 100
*(Yellow promo label)*
SONGS OF THE BRAZOS VALLEY — 1956 — Capitol 418 — 125
*(Yellow promo label)*

**THOMPSON, SUE**
*Mercury promo 45s $8 each; Decca promo 45s $6 each; Hickory promo 45s $4 each; Hickory promo LPs $20-25 each; Wing (Mercury) promo LPs $25 each*
**7-Inch Extended Plays**
TWO OF A KIND — 1962 — Hickory 107 — 25
*(Six songs on a 7" EP, black promo label and small center hole)*

**THOROGOOD, GEORGE**
*EMI promo 45s $4 each; EMI and Capitol promo CD singles $3 each*
**12-Inch Singles**
ROCK AND ROLL CHRISTMAS/NEW YEAR'S EVE PARTY — 1983 — EMI America SPRO-9293/4 — 8
*(Promo only on red vinyl)*
**Compact Discs**
BONE-A-FIDE BADNESS — 1990 — EMI DPRO-4715 — 20
*(Promo-only sampler)*
**RADIO SHOWS**
**Albums**
CAPTURED LIVE — 1983 — RKO (2) — 40-75
*(Live concert)*
DESERT ISLAND DISCS (July 91) — 1991 — — 10-15
*(Music and interviews)*
IN CONCERT — 1981 — Westwood One (2) — 40-75
*(Live concert)*

| Title | Yr | Label, Number | NM $ |
|---|---|---|---|
| IN CONCERT (Nov 82) Live concert *(With Billy Idol)* | 1982 | Westwood One (2) | 25-40 |
| IN CONCERT (Apr 85) *(Live concert)* | 1985 | Westwood One (2) | 35-60 |
| IN CONCERT (July 93) *(Live concert)* | 1993 | Westwood One (2) | 20-35 |
| KING BISCUIT FLOWER HOUR (Feb 82) Live concert *(With Bryan Adams)* | 1982 | DIR/ABC (2) | 25-50 |
| KING BISCUIT FLOWER HOUR (Apr 85) Live concert *(With Tom Petty)* | 1985 | DIR (2) | 25-40 |
| KING BISCUIT FLOWER HOUR (Aug 85) Live concert *(With Stevie Ray Vaughan)* | 1985 | DIR (2) | 40-80 |
| KING BISCUIT FLOWER HOUR (Jan 87) *(Live concert)* | 1987 | DIR (2) | 25-40 |
| OFF THE RECORD *(Music and interviews, repeated)* | 1986 | Westwood One (2) | 10-15 |
| RETRO ROCK (May 82) *(Live concert)* | 1982 | Clayton Webster (2) | 25-40 |
| ROCKIN' AND TALKIN'  With Brian Setzer *(Music and interviews)* | 1988 | | 20-30 |

**Compact Discs**

| Title | Yr | Label, Number | NM $ |
|---|---|---|---|
| IN CONCERT (Mar 94) *(Live concert)* | 1994 | Westwood One (2) | 25-50 |
| IN THE STUDIO (90s) Profile of an album *(Music and interviews)* | 199? | Album Network | 15-25 |
| KING BISCUIT FLOWER HOUR (Apr 88) *(Live concert, repeated)* | 1988 | DIR | 25-40 |
| KING BISCUIT FLOWER HOUR (Mar 89) *(Live concert)* | 1989 | DIR | 20-40 |
| KING BISCUIT FLOWER HOUR (Sept 90) Live concert *(With Little Caesar)* | 1990 | DIR | 20-30 |
| KING BISCUIT FLOWER HOUR (June 93) *(Live concert)* | 1993 | DIR | 15-25 |
| LIVE AT ELECTRIC LADYLAND (July 93) *(Live concert)* | 1993 | Album Network | 30-60 |
| SUPERSTAR CONCERT (Nov 92) *(Live concert, repeated)* | 1992 | Westwood One (2) | 20-35 |
| UP CLOSE Profile *(Mostly music and interviews)* | 1992 | Media America (2) | 20-30 |

## THREE CHUCKLES, THE

*With Teddy Randazzo; Also recorded as The Kartunes; "X" (RCA Victor) promo 45s by the Three Chuckles $30 each; Vik (RCA Victor) promo 45s by the Three Chuckles $20 each; Vik promo 45s by Teddy Randazzo $18 each; ABC Paramount promo 45s by Teddy Randazzo $15 each; DCP promo 45s by Teddy Randazzo $5 each*

**45s**

| Title | Yr | Label, Number | NM $ |
|---|---|---|---|
| DEDICATED TO LOVE  The Kartunes *(Yellow promo label)* | 1958 | MGM 12680 | 35 |
| RAINDROPS  The Kartunes *(Yellow promo label)* | 1957 | MGM 12598 | 40 |

**7-Inch Extended Plays**

| Title | Yr | Label, Number | NM $ |
|---|---|---|---|
| VIK SAMPLER  Various artists *(Yellow promo label EP, promo only, one song by the Three Chuckles, "Won't You Give Me A Chance")* | 1955 | VIK VDJ-4 | 50 |

**Albums**

| Title | Yr | Label, Number | NM $ |
|---|---|---|---|
| JOURNEY TO LOVE  Teddy Randazzo *(White promo label)* | 1961 | ABC-Paramount 352 | 40 |
| TEDDY RANDAZZO TWISTS  Teddy Randazzo *(White promo label)* | 1962 | ABC-Paramount 421 | 25 |

## THREE DOG NIGHT

*Includes Danny Hutton and Cory Wells; Other ABC Dunhill promo 45s $5 each; HBR (Hanna-Barbera) and MGM promo 45s by Danny Hutton $8 each; ABC Dunhill white promo label LPs $12 each*

**45s**

| Title | Yr | Label, Number | NM $ |
|---|---|---|---|
| NOBODY *(Promo record and promo-only picture sleeve)* | 1968 | ABC Dunhill 4168 | 50 |
| 'TIL THE WORLD ENDS *(White label test pressing)* | 1975 | ABC | 12 |
| WHAT'S IT ALL ABOUT Public service show *(With Cory Wells and Danny Hutton, flip is Seals & Crofts)* | 1972 | W.I.A.A. 208 | 18 |
| WHAT'S IT ALL ABOUT (June 76) Public service show *(Interviews with Danny Hutton, flip is ELO)* | 1976 | W.I.A.A. 322 | 25 |

**7-Inch Extended Plays**

| Title | Yr | Label, Number | NM $ |
|---|---|---|---|
| CYAN *(Jukebox LLP, issued with a paper cover)* | 1973 | ABC Dunhill 50158 (LLP 231 | 15 |
| HARMONY *(Jukebox LLP, issued with a paper cover)* | 1972 | ABC Dunhill 50108 (LLP 164) | 15 |

## 311
**RADIO SHOWS**
**Compact Discs**

| Title | Yr | Label, Number | NM $ |
|---|---|---|---|
| LIVE FROM THE PIT (Nov 96) *(Live concert material)* | 1996 | | 30-50 |

## THREE STOOGES, THE
**Albums**

| Title | Yr | Label, Number | NM $ |
|---|---|---|---|
| THE NONSENSE SONGBOOK *(Blue promo label)* | 1959 | Coral 57289 | 50 |

## THROWING MUSES
**12-Inch Singles**

| Title | Yr | Label, Number | NM $ |
|---|---|---|---|
| DIZZY (Too Many Words Mix)/(Too Many Notes Mix) | 1989 | Sire PRO-A-3395 | 6 |

THE SOURCE

NBC Radio's Young Adult Network

STEREO
33 1/3 RPM
NBC 82-49

1.

THE SOURCE CHRISTMAS COUNTDOWN

TRIUMPH CONCERT

M-G-M
SPECIAL DISC
JOCKEY RECORD

Not For Sale
MGM RECORDS
A DIVISION OF METRO-GOLDWYN-MAYER INC.
MADE IN U.S.A.
CONWAY TWITTY
STEREO
Side 1

GAS 110
MGS 2204

1. THE STORY OF MY LOVE—2:14
(Twitty-Nance) Marielle Music—BMI
2. LONELY BLUE BOY—2:12
(F. Wiseman-B. Wiseman)
Anne-Rachel Music & May Music—ASCAP
3. DANNY BOY—2:41
(Weatherly) Bossey & Hawkes, Inc.—ASCAP
4. MAKE ME KNOW YOU'RE MINE—2:20
(Schroeder-Hill)
Charles N. Daniels, Inc. & Moorpark Music—ASCAP
5. IT'S ONLY MAKE BELIEVE—2:10
(Twitty-Nance) Marielle Music—BMI
6. IS A BLUE BIRD BLUE—2:37
(Penn) Travis Music & Spar Music—BMI

ROCK STARS

U2

STEREO
33⅓ RPM

1

AIRDATE: MAY 18, 1987 – MAY 25, 1987

RADIO TODAY
ENTERTAINMENT

WESTWOOD ONE RADIO NETWORKS

THE RISE AND RISE OF U2

STEREO

SIDE 1

NOT FOR SALE • ALL RIGHTS RESERVED • UNAUTHORIZED DUPLICATION IS A VIOLATION OF APPLICABLE LAWS • FOR LICENSED BROADCAST USE ONLY

March 8, 1981

UFO/PAT TRAVERS

KBFH

SIDE A

33 1/3 RPM

FLOWER HOUR

D.I.R. Broadcasting Corp.

℗©1980

VIBRATIONS

FROM THE

UNITED STATES AIR FORCE

33⅓ RPM
STEREO

SIDE 1
71746

PROGRAM 1
URIAH HEEP
5:00 TO SPIRAL
15:00 TO TOTAL SHOW
APRIL, 1973
SERIES #9

PUBLIC SERVICE PROGRAMS
NOT FOR COMMERCIAL USE

(Top left) Another in the Source Christmas Countdown series, this one featured the briefly popular band Triumph. (Top right) Here's a Conway Twitty promo LP from 1970, a compilation of material he recorded for MGM in the late 1950s and early 1960s, before he became a successful country singer. (Middle left) U2 finally became big stars with the release of *The Joshua Tree* in 1987. It didn't take long for the radio shows to notice; U2 was featured on this Rock Stars program in May of that year. (Middle right) Part of a special show that Westwood One created in the late 1980s, *The Rise and Rise of U2* traces the band's career through *Rattle and Hum*. (Bottom left) Another example of a King Biscuit Flower Hour with two mid-line artists, this one had UFO and Pat Travers on a 1981 program. (Bottom right) Here's an unusual program from 1973: A British band, Uriah Heep, is on a public service program for the United States Air Force.

| Title | Yr | Label, Number | NM $ |
|---|---|---|---|
| THE RIVER (same on both sides) | 1988 | Sire PRO-A-3070 | 6 |
| SAVING GRACE/KRISTIN HERSH INTERVIEW | 1988 | Sire PRO-A-3157 | 8 |

## THUNDERBIRDS, THE
### 45s
| | | | |
|---|---|---|---|
| BABY, LET'S PLAY HOUSE | 1955 | DeLuxe 6075 | 50 |
| *(White promo label)* | | | |

## 'TIL TUESDAY
*Epic promo 45s $3 each*
### 12-Inch Singles
| | | | |
|---|---|---|---|
| COMING UP CLOSE (Long)/(Short) | 1986 | Epic AS 2577 | 6 |
| LOOKING OVER MY SHOULDER (long) (short) | 1985 | Epic AS 2104 | 8 |
| LOVE IN A VACUUM (Long)/(Remix) | 1985 | Epic EAS 2210 | 8 |
| RIP IN HEAVEN (same on both sides) | 1989 | Epic EAS 01492 | 5 |
| WHAT ABOUT LOVE (one-sided) | 1986 | Epic AS 2470 | 5 |

### Compact Discs
| | | | |
|---|---|---|---|
| COMING UP CLOSE | 1991 | Epic | Unknown |
| *(Special "Desert Storm" version with overdubbed speeches; unknown if this was distributed only via satellite or there were CDs or cassettes involved)* | | | |

### RADIO SHOWS
### Albums
| | | | |
|---|---|---|---|
| KING BISCUIT FLOWER HOUR (Jan 87) Live concert | 1987 | DIR (2) | 40-80 |

## TIL, SONNY
*Also see The Orioles*
### 45s
| | | | |
|---|---|---|---|
| WHAT ARE YOU DOING NEW YEAR'S EVE | 1971 | RCA SPS-45-247 | 12 |
| *(Promo-only, yellow label)* | | | |

## TILLIS, MEL
*Other Columbia white promo label 45s $5-8 each; Kapp promo 45s $4 each; MGM promo 45s $3 each; Elektra promo 45s $2 each; MCA promo 45s $2 each*
### 45s
| | | | |
|---|---|---|---|
| HEARTS OF STONE | 1957 | Columbia 41026 | 20 |
| *(White promo label)* | | | |
| HEARTS OF STONE | 1961 | Columbia 41986 | 15 |
| *(White promo label)* | | | |
| HEARTS OF STONE | 1961 | Columbia 41986 | 25 |
| *(Compact 33 single, small hole)* | | | |
| IT TAKES A WORRIED MAN TO SING A WORRIED SONG | 1957 | Columbia 40845 | 10 |
| *(White promo label)* | | | |
| JUKEBOX MAN | 1957 | Columbia 40944 | 15 |
| *(White promo label)* | | | |
| RUDOLPH THE RED-NOSED REINDEER/WINTER WONDERLAND | 1981 | Elektra 47234 | 8 |
| *(As "Mel and Nancy" (Sinatra); B-side by Dave Rowland and Sugar)* | | | |
| TEENAGE WEDDING | 1958 | Columbia 41115 | 20 |
| *(White promo label)* | | | |
| THERE'S NO TURNING BACK | 1977 | KFC (MCA) 001 | 10 |
| *(Songwriter promotion from KFC)* | | | |
| WHITE CHRISTMAS/BLUE CHRISTMAS | 1981 | Elektra 47233 | 5 |
| *(B-side by Eddy Raven)* | | | |

### Albums
| | | | |
|---|---|---|---|
| HEART OVER MIND | 1962 | Columbia 1724 | 40 |
| *(Columbia promo label)* | | | |

### RADIO SHOWS
### Albums
| | | | |
|---|---|---|---|
| SILVER EAGLE (Feb 82) | 1982 | DIR (3) | 25-50 |
| *(Live concert)* | | | |
| SILVER EAGLE (May 87) | 1987 | DIR (3) | 15-25 |
| *(Live concert)* | | | |
| WESTWOOD ONE PRESENTS (Apr 90) | 1990 | Westwood One | 15-25 |
| *(Mostly live material)* | | | |

### Cassettes
| | | | |
|---|---|---|---|
| AUSTIN ENTERTAINMENT | 1990 | Radio Entertainment | 15-25 |
| *(Live with the Geesinslaws, on cassette)* | | | |

## TILLOTSON, JOHNNY
*Cadence promo 45s $10-15 each; MGM promo 45s $8 each; Buddah promo 45s $5 each; Columbia and United Artists promo 45s $3 each; Passport promo 45s $3 each; MGM promo LPs $12 each; Other label promo LPs $8 each*
### 7-Inch Extended Plays
| | | | |
|---|---|---|---|
| THIS IS JOHNNY TILLOTSON   Jukebox LLP | 1964 | Cadence LLP-331 | 30 |
| *(Issued with a hard cover)* | | | |
| WORDS AND MUSIC BY JOHNNY TILLOTSON | 1964 | Cadence LLP-332 | 30 |
| *(Issued with a hard cover)* | | | |

## TIMBUK 3
### 12-Inch Singles
| | | | |
|---|---|---|---|
| ALL I WANT FOR CHRISTMAS/MEDLEY: BLUE CHRISTMAS-I WANT YOU x 3 | 1987 | I.R.S. L33-17427 | 15 |
| THE FUTURE'S SO BRIGHT, I GOTTA WEAR SHADES (same on both sides) | 1986 | I.R.S. 17183 | 8 |
| HAIRSTYLES AND ATTITUDES (same on both sides) | 1985 | I.R.S. 17285 | 5 |
| LIFE IS HARD (same on both sides) | 1986 | I.R.S. 17236 | 5 |
| RECKLESS DRIVER (same on both sides) | 1988 | I.R.S. 17631 | 6 |
| REV. JACK AND HIS ROAMIN' CADILLAC CHURCH (same on both sides) | 1988 | I.R.S. 17540 | 5 |

## TIN HUEY
### 12-Inch Singles
| | | | |
|---|---|---|---|
| I'M A BELIEVER/HUMP DAY | 1979 | Warner Bros. PRO 806 | 8 |

| Title | Yr | Label, Number | NM $ |
|---|---|---|---|
| **TIN MACHINE** | | | |
| *More at David Bowie* | | | |
| **12-Inch Singles** | | | |
| HEAVEN'S IN HERE (LP)/(Edit) | 1989 | EMI SPRO 04374 | 15 |
| UNDER THE GOD (same on both sides) | 1989 | EMI SPRO 04282 | 15 |
| **TINY TIM** | | | |
| *Reprise white promo label 45s $6 each; NLT promo 45s $3 each; Reprise promo LPs $15 each* | | | |
| **45s** | | | |
| COMIC STRIP MAN | 1982 | Solid Brass 101 | 10 |
| *(Promo record and promo-only picture sleeve, and yes, this record is disco!)* | | | |
| **TODD, JOHNNY** | | | |
| **45s** | | | |
| PINK CADILLAC | 1956 | Modern 1003 | 50 |
| *(White promo label)* | | | |
| **TOKENS, THE** | | | |
| *RCA Victor promo 45s (After 1988) $4 each; B.T. Puppy promo 45s $8 each; Warner Bros. promo 45s $6 each; Buddah promo 45s $4 each; Bell, Atco and Kirshner promo 45s $3 each* | | | |
| **45s** | | | |
| TONIGHT I FELL IN LOVE | 1961 | Warwick 615 | 40 |
| *(White promo label)* | | | |
| WHEN THE SUMMER IS THROUGH | 1961 | RCA Victor 37-7925 | 75 |
| *(Compact 33 single for jukebox use, must have the"37" prefix)* | | | |
| **TOM TOM CLUB** | | | |
| **12-Inch Singles** | | | |
| GENIUS OF LOVE/LORELEI | 1981 | Sire PRO-A-996 | 10 |
| PLEASURE OF LOVE/(Instrumental) | 1983 | Sire PRO-A-2096 | 7 |
| **Albums** | | | |
| WORDY RAPPING WITH THE TOM TOM CLUB | 1986 | Warner Bros. WBMS-120 | 25 |
| *(Part of "The Warner Bros. Music Show"; promo only)* | | | |
| **TOMLIN, LILY** | | | |
| *Polydor promo 45s $3 each* | | | |
| **7-Inch Extended Plays** | | | |
| LILY TOMLIN ON STAGE | 1977 | Arista SP-10 | 10 |
| *(Four cuts, promo-only record and picture sleeve)* | | | |
| MODERN SCREAM | 1975 | Polydor PRO-003 | 10 |
| *(Seven cuts, 7" record, promo-only record and picture sleeve)* | | | |
| OPEN-END INTERVIEW | 1976 | Polydor 007 | 10 |
| *(7" record, back is blank)* | | | |
| **TOMMY TUTONE** | | | |
| *Columbia promo 45s $4 each* | | | |
| **Albums** | | | |
| TOMMY TUTONE | 1982 | Columbia AS 1461 | 18 |
| *(Three tracks from "Tommy Tutone-2" and the same three tracks live; promo-only)* | | | |
| **RADIO SHOWS** | | | |
| **Albums** | | | |
| CAPTURED LIVE (May 84) | 1984 | RKO (2) | 40-75 |
| *(Live concert)* | | | |
| IN CONCERT (May 82) Live concert | 1982 | Westwood One (2) | 40-75 |
| *(With Krokus)* | | | |
| **TOMPALL AND THE GLASER BROTHERS** | | | |
| **45s** | | | |
| SILVER BELLS/PLEASE COME HOME FOR CHRISTMAS | 1981 | Elektra 47230 | 5 |
| *(B-side by Johnny Lee)* | | | |
| **TOO MUCH JOY** | | | |
| **12-Inch Singles** | | | |
| THAT'S A LIE (Remix)/SEASONS IN THE SUN/IF I WAS A MEKON | 1990 | Giant PRO-A-4352 | 8 |
| **7-Inch Extended Plays** | | | |
| RAP LIKE MINE/G.I. JESUS//NO GOOD FOR YOU (LIVE)/LUCIFER CHICKEN | 1991 | Warner Bros. PRO-S-5034 | 15 |
| *("Soil X Samples 5"; clear yellow vinyl, purple label; B-side by Sister Double Happiness)* | | | |
| **TORME, MEL** | | | |
| **45s** | | | |
| EVERY DAY'S A HOLIDAY/ONE LITTLE SNOWFLAKE | 1964 | Columbia 43167 | 15 |
| *(Promo only on green vinyl)* | | | |
| **TORONTO** | | | |
| **RADIO SHOWS** | | | |
| **Albums** | | | |
| IN CONCERT (Jan 83) Live concert | 1983 | Westwood One (2) | 40-75 |
| *(With Bryan Adams)* | | | |
| IN CONCERT (Oct 82) Live concert | 1982 | Westwood One (2) | 75-150 |
| *(With Nazareth)* | | | |
| **TOSH, PETER** | | | |
| *EMI promo 45s $5 each; Columbia promo 45s $4 each; Columbia promo 12" singles $8 each More at the Rolling Stones* | | | |
| **45s** | | | |
| BUK-IN-HAMM PALACE | 1979 | Rolling Stones 20000 | 15 |
| DON'T LOOK BACK  With Mick Jagger | 1978 | Rolling Stones 19308 | 15 |
| *(With "The Rolling Stones" at top of label)* | | | |

| Title | Yr | Label, Number | NM $ |
|-------|-----|---------------|------|
| **RADIO SHOWS** | | | |
| **Albums** | | | |
| BBC COLLEGE CONCERT | 1983 | London Wavelength | 175-250 |
| *(Very rare live concert)* | | | |
| BBC COLLEGE CONCERT (Jan 84) | 1984 | London Wavelength | 175-275 |
| *(Live concert)* | | | |
| **Reel-to-Reel Tapes** | | | |
| KING BISCUIT FLOWER HOUR (June 78) Live concert | 1978 | DIR | 100-200 |
| *(Peter Tosh and the Rolling Stones on two 10" reels)* | | | |

## TOTO

*Recorded with Frank Farian as the Farian Corporation; Columbia promo 45s $3 each; Columbia promo picture sleeves $2 each; Columbia promo 12" singles $6 each; Atco promo 45s by Farian Corporation $6 each ("Stairway to Heaven"); Atco promo 12" singles by Farian Corporation $8 each ("Stairway to Heaven")*

| Title | Yr | Label, Number | NM $ |
|-------|-----|---------------|------|
| **Albums** | | | |
| TOTO IV | 1981 | Columbia 37928 | 18 |
| *(Promo-only picture disc)* | | | |
| TOTO IV | 1981 | Columbia 47928 | 25 |
| *(Promo-only half-speed master recording)* | | | |
| TURN BACK | 1979 | Columbia 36813 | 18 |
| *(Promo-only picture disc)* | | | |
| **RADIO SHOWS** | | | |
| **Albums** | | | |
| ABC RADIO (May 83) | 1983 | ABC Radio (2) | 50-100 |
| *(Live concert)* | | | |
| STARTRACK Profile (Oct 86) | 1986 | Westwood One (2) | 30-60 |
| *(Music and interviews)* | | | |

## TOWNSHEND, PETE

*Atco and Atlantic promo 45s $4 each Of The Who; Includes Angie*

| Title | Yr | Label, Number | NM $ |
|-------|-----|---------------|------|
| **12-Inch Singles** | | | |
| FACE THE FACE (long and short)/HIDING OUT | 1985 | Atco PR 804 | 15 |
| SECONDHAND LOVE (same on both sides) | 1985 | Atco PR 863 | 8 |
| **45s** | | | |
| PEPPERMINT LUMP   Angie | 1979 | Epic 50793 | 25 |
| *(White promo label record and promo-only picture sleeve, different from stock picture sleeve)* | | | |
| WHAT'S IT ALL ABOUT  Public service show | 1979 | W.I.A.A. | 25 |
| *(Flip side features Paul Williams)* | | | |
| WHAT'S IT ALL ABOUT (Aug 75) Public service show | 1975 | W.I.A.A. 281 | 25 |
| *(Flip side features Anne Murray)* | | | |
| WHAT'S IT ALL ABOUT (July 75) Public service show | 1975 | W.I.A.A. 274 | 25 |
| *(Flip side features the Pointer Sisters)* | | | |
| WHAT'S IT ALL ABOUT (Mar 80) Public service show | 1980 | W.I.A.A. 517 | 30 |
| *(Flip side features James Brown)* | | | |
| WHAT'S IT ALL ABOUT (Oct 80) Public service show | 1980 | W.I.A.A. 643 | 25 |
| *(Flip side features REO)* | | | |
| **Albums** | | | |
| PETE TOWNSHEND TALKS TO AND ABOUT THUNDERCLAP NEWMAN | 1970 | Track PR-A-160 | 100 |
| *One-sided promo-only interview record* | | | |
| **Compact Discs** | | | |
| PSYCHODERELICT | 1993 | Atlantic PRCD 5103 (2) | 40 |
| *(Promo-only CD release)* | | | |
| **RADIO SHOWS** | | | |
| **Albums** | | | |
| INNERVIEW (70s) | 197? | Innerview | 20-30 |
| *(Music and interviews)* | | | |
| INSIDE TRACK (Oct 82) | 1982 | DIR (2) | 25-50 |
| *(Music and interviews with live tracks)* | | | |
| INSIDE TRACK (June 83) | 1983 | DIR (2) | 75-125 |
| *(Music and interviews with live tracks, with Joan Jett and Johnny Rotten)* | | | |
| KING BISCUIT FLOWER HOUR (Dec 79) | 1979 | DIR/ABC (2) | 75-150 |
| *(Live concert, rare on vinyl)* | | | |
| KING BISCUIT FLOWER HOUR | 1986 | DIR (4) | 50-100 |
| *(Live concert, two shows)* | | | |
| KING BISCUIT FLOWER HOUR | 1986 | DIR (2) | 30-60 |
| *(Live concert)* | | | |
| OFF THE RECORD | 1985 | Westwood One (2) | 20-35 |
| *(Music and interviews)* | | | |
| PROFILES IN ROCK (May 80) | 1980 | Innerview (2) | 20-40 |
| *(Music and interviews)* | | | |
| SUPERSTAR CONCERT | 1987 | Westwood One (3) | 30-60 |
| *(Live concert box set)* | | | |
| SUPERSTAR CONCERT (June 88) | 1988 | Westwood One (3) | 30-60 |
| *(Live concert box set)* | | | |
| **Compact Discs** | | | |
| KING BISCUIT FLOWER HOUR | 1987 | DIR | 40-75 |
| *(Live concert)* | | | |
| KING BISCUIT FLOWER HOUR (Dec 88) With Roger Daltrey | 1988 | DIR | 40-75 |
| *(Live concert)* | | | |
| UP CLOSE | 1989 | Media America (2) | 40-65 |
| *(Music and interviews)* | | | |
| UP CLOSE | 1993 | Media America (2) | 40-65 |
| *(Music and interviews)* | | | |
| **Reel-to-Reel Tapes** | | | |
| KING BISCUIT FLOWER HOUR (Dec 79) | 1979 | DIR/ABC (2) | 75-125 |
| *(Live concert on two reels)* | | | |

| Title | Yr | Label, Number | NM $ |
|---|---|---|---|

**TRACTORS, THE**
*Arista promo CD singles $5 each*
**RADIO SHOWS**
**Compact Discs**

| Title | Yr | Label, Number | NM $ |
|---|---|---|---|
| COUNTRY EDGE (Jan 95) | 1995 | Westwood One | 10-15 |

*(Music and interviews)*

**TRAFFIC**
*Dave Mason, Jim Capaldi and Steve Winwood; Other United Artists promo 45s $8 each; Island promo 45s $5 each; Asylum promo 45s $8 each; Island promo 45s by Steve Winwood $5 each; Virgin promo 45s by Steve Winwood $3 each; Island or Atlantic promo 45s by Jim Capaldi $3 each; Blue Thumb promo 45s by Dave Mason $5 each; Columbia promo 45s by Dave Mason $3 each; Virgin or Island promo 12" singles by Steve Winwood $6 each; Island promo 12" singles by Jim Capaldi $5 each*
**12-Inch Singles**

| Title | Yr | Label, Number | NM $ |
|---|---|---|---|
| NIGHT TRAIN   U2 on flip side | 1980 | Island PRO-A-940 | 40 |

**45s**

| Title | Yr | Label, Number | NM $ |
|---|---|---|---|
| HOLE IN MY SHOE | 1967 | United Artists 50218 | 10 |

*(White promo label, stock picture sleeve worth $25)*

| Title | Yr | Label, Number | NM $ |
|---|---|---|---|
| PAPER SUN | 1967 | United Artists 50195 | 12 |

*(White promo label)*
**Compact Discs**

| Title | Yr | Label, Number | NM $ |
|---|---|---|---|
| TRAFFIC CONTROL | 1988 | Island 2300 | 35 |

*(Eleven tracks, promo-only CD release)*

| Title | Yr | Label, Number | NM $ |
|---|---|---|---|
| TRAFFIC REPORT | 1987 | Island 2158 | 40 |

*(Thirteen tracks, promo-only CD release)*
**RADIO SHOWS**
**Albums**

| Title | Yr | Label, Number | NM $ |
|---|---|---|---|
| BBC ROCK HOUR (Apr 81) | 1981 | London Wavelength | 40-75 |
| *(Live concert)* | | | |
| BBC TRANSCRIPTION DISC  Live show | 1973 | BBC Transcription | 225-350 |
| *(Featuring Steve Winwood)* | | | |
| DESERT ISLAND DISCS (Oct 92) Steve Winwood | 1992 | | 10-20 |
| *(Music and interviews)* | | | |
| HOT ROCKS | 1989 | United Stations (4) | 25-50 |
| *(Music and interviews, two shows)* | | | |
| IN CONCERT (Dec 86) | 1986 | Westwood One (2) | 30-60 |
| *(Live concert)* | | | |
| IN CONCERT (Oct 91) | 1991 | Westwood One (2) | 40-60 |
| *(Live concert)* | | | |
| JIM CAPALDI/STEVE WINWOOD SPECIAL (Apr 83) | 1983 | NBC Source (3) | 25-50 |
| *(Mostly music and interviews)* | | | |
| LEGENDS OF ROCK  Dave Mason | 1987 | NBC Radio (2) | 25-40 |
| *(Music and interviews)* | | | |
| LEGENDS OF ROCK (Apr 87) Steve Winwood | 1987 | NBC Radio (4) | 30-45 |
| *(Music and interviews, two shows)* | | | |
| LEGENDS OF ROCK (Apr 87) Steve Winwood | 1987 | NBC Radio (2) | 25-40 |
| *(Music and interviews, repeated)* | | | |
| LEGENDS OF ROCK (July 88) | 1988 | NBC Radio (2) | 25-45 |
| *(Music and interviews)* | | | |
| OFF THE RECORD  Steve Winwood | 1986 | Westwood One (2) | 15-25 |
| *(Music and interviews)* | | | |
| OFF THE RECORD (Sept 87)  Steve Winwood | 1987 | Westwood One (2) | 20-25 |
| *(Music and interviews, repeated)* | | | |
| RADIO TODAY (Aug 88) Steve Winwood | 1988 | (2) | 20-35 |
| *(Music and interviews)* | | | |
| ROBERT KLEIN (Feb 81) Music and interviews | 1981 | (2) | 15-25 |
| *(With Talking Heads)* | | | |
| ROCK STARS (Apr 88) Steve Winwood | 1988 | (2) | 10-20 |
| *(Music and interviews)* | | | |
| THE STEVE WINWOOD SPECIAL (Dec 81) Steve Winwood | 1981 | NBC Source (2) | 20-40 |
| *(Music and interviews)* | | | |
| SUPERSTAR CONCERT | 1987 | Westwood One (3) | 25-50 |
| *(Live concert, box set, repeated)* | | | |
| SUPERSTAR CONCERT  Steve Winwood | 1987 | Westwood One (3) | 25-50 |
| *(Live concert, box set, repeated)* | | | |

**Compact Discs**

| Title | Yr | Label, Number | NM $ |
|---|---|---|---|
| BBC CLASSIC TRACKS | 1993 | Westwood One | 10-20 |
| *(Various live tracks)* | | | |
| IN CONCERT (July 92) | 1992 | Westwood One (2) | 25-50 |
| *(Live concert, repeated)* | | | |
| IN CONCERT (July 93) | 1993 | Westwood One | 25-40 |
| *(Live concert)* | | | |
| IN THE STUDIO (Nov 90) | 1990 | Album Network | 15-25 |
| *(Profile of an album)* | | | |
| OFF THE RECORD (July 93) | 1993 | Westwood One | 15-25 |
| *(Music and interviews)* | | | |
| SUPERSTAR CONCERT (June 94) | 1994 | Westwood One (2) | 20-35 |
| *(Live concert, repeated)* | | | |
| TIMOTHY WHITE SESSIONS (July 90) Steve Winwood | 1990 | Westwood One | 30-60 |
| *(Music and interviews from "The One and Only")* | | | |
| UP CLOSE  Steve Winwood | 1989 | Media America (4) | 50-80 |
| *(Mostly music and interviews, two shows)* | | | |
| UP CLOSE  Steve Winwood | 1989 | Media America (2) | 20-40 |
| *(Mostly music and interviews)* | | | |

**Reel-to-Reel Tapes**

| Title | Yr | Label, Number | NM $ |
|---|---|---|---|
| ALBUM NETWORK (Apr 94) | 1994 | Album Network | 20-35 |

*(Music and interviews for "Far from Home" on one 10" reel)*

**TRAITS, THE**
**45s**

| Title | Yr | Label, Number | NM $ |
|---|---|---|---|
| GOT MY MOJO WORKING/WOE WOE | 1962 | Renner 229 | 40 |

*(Promo only on colored vinyl)*

| Title | Yr | Label, Number | NM $ |
|---|---|---|---|
| **TRAMMELL, BOBBY LEE** | | | |
| **45s** | | | |
| SHIRLEY LEE | 1957 | Fabor 4038 | 40 |
| *(Black promo label)* | | | |
| SHIRLEY LEE | 1958 | ABC-Paramount 9890 | 40 |
| *(White promo label)* | | | |
| | | | |
| **TRAMMPS, THE** | | | |
| **12-Inch Singles** | | | |
| HARD ROCK AND DISCO (same on both sides) | 1980 | Atlantic PR 224 | 12 |
| LOOKING FOR YOU/MELLOW OUT | 1980 | Atlantic PR 251 | 12 |
| THE NIGHT THE LIGHTS WENT OUT (same on both sides) | 1977 | Atlantic PR 102 | 12 |
| SOUL BONES/LOVE MAGNET | 1978 | Atlantic PR 139 | 12 |
| TEASER/LIFE INSURANCE POLICY | 1979 | Atlantic PR 170 | 12 |
| | | | |
| **TRANSLATOR** | | | |
| **RADIO SHOWS** | | | |
| **Albums** | | | |
| BBC COLLEGE CONCERT (Nov 82) | 1982 | London Wavelength | 100-175 |
| *(Live concert)* | | | |
| | | | |
| **TRANSVISION VAMP** | | | |
| **12-Inch Singles** | | | |
| (I JUST WANNA) BE WITH U (4 versions) | 1991 | MCA 1523 | 7 |
| I WANT YOUR LOVE (extended) (7" version) | 1988 | Uni 10009 | 12 |
| IF LOOKS COULD KILL (4 versions) | 1991 | MCA 2051 | 7 |
| | | | |
| **TRAPEZE** | | | |
| **45s** | | | |
| BLACK CLOUD (mono/stereo) | 1971 | Threshold 67005 | 10 |
| | | | |
| **TRASH** | | | |
| **45s** | | | |
| ROAD TO NOWHERE  Star on label | 1969 | Apple 1804 | 40 |
| *(Stock copy used as a promo)* | | | |
| | | | |
| **TRASHMEN, THE** | | | |
| *Other Garrett promo 45s $20 each* | | | |
| **45s** | | | |
| DANCING WITH SANTA | 1966 | Garrett 4013 | 45 |
| *(White promo label)* | | | |
| SURFIN' BIRD | 1963 | Garrett 3962 | 40 |
| *(White promo label)* | | | |
| WHOA DAD | 1965 | Garrett 4012 | 25 |
| *(White promo label)* | | | |
| | | | |
| **TRAVELING WILBURYS** | | | |
| *Roy Orbison (on the 1st LP), Bob Dylan, Jeff Lynne (ELO), Tom Petty and George Harrison* | | | |
| **45s** | | | |
| END OF THE LINE | 1988 | Wilbury 27637 | 20 |
| *(Brown Warner promo label)* | | | |
| HANDLE WITH CARE | 1988 | Wilbury 27732 | 15 |
| *(Brown Warner promo label)* | | | |
| **Compact Discs** | | | |
| END OF THE LINE | 1988 | Wilbury PRO-CD-3364 | 20 |
| *(Promo-only CD single)* | | | |
| HANDLE WITH CARE | 1988 | Wilbury PRO-CD-3258 | 25 |
| *(Promo-only CD single)* | | | |
| INSIDE OUT | 1991 | Wilbury PRO-CD-4652 | 12 |
| *(Promo-only CD single)* | | | |
| LAST NIGHT | 1988 | Wilbury PRO-CD-3337 | 20 |
| *(Promo-only CD single)* | | | |
| SHE'S MY BABY | 1990 | Wilbury PRO-CD-4518 | 12 |
| *(Promo-only CD single)* | | | |
| TRAVELING WILBURYS VOL. 1 | 1988 | Wilbury 25796-2-DJ | 40 |
| *(Promo picture disc)* | | | |
| TRAVELING WILBURYS VOL. 3 | 1990 | Wilbury 26324-2-DJ | 30 |
| *("Promotion only. Not for sale" on CD)* | | | |
| WILBURY TWIST | 1991 | Wilbury PRO-CD-4642 | 12 |
| *(Promo-only CD single)* | | | |
| **RADIO SHOWS** | | | |
| **Albums** | | | |
| OFF THE RECORD (Jan 89) | 1989 | Westwood One (2) | 40-75 |
| *(Music and interviews)* | | | |
| OFF THE RECORD  Roy Orbison/Traveling Wilburys | 1989 | Westwood One (2) | 50-75 |
| *(Music and interviews)* | | | |
| OFF THE RECORD (Dec 90) | 1990 | Westwood One (2) | 40-65 |
| *(Music and interviews)* | | | |
| OFF THE RECORD (Mar 91) | 1991 | Westwood One (2) | 35-65 |
| *(Music and interviews)* | | | |
| **Compact Discs** | | | |
| CLASSIC CD-THE TRAVELING WILBURYS (July 90) | 1990 | WWI/Source (2) | 100-175 |
| *(Music and interviews)* | | | |
| IN THE STUDIO | 1990 | Album Network | 40-75 |
| *(Profile of the Traveling Wilburys Vol. 1 LP, music and interviews)* | | | |

| Title | Yr | Label, Number | NM $ |
|---|---|---|---|
| **Reel-to-Reel Tapes** | | | |
| OFF THE RECORD (Jan 89) | 1989 | Westwood One | 40-75 |
| *(10" reel version of the show)* | | | |
| | | | |
| **TRAVERS, PAT** | | | |
| *Polydor promo singles $3 each* | | | |
| **Albums** | | | |
| PAT TRAVERS YOU MISSED, THE | 1979 | Polydor PRO 043 | 20 |
| *(Red vinyl, mini-album)* | | | |
| **RADIO SHOWS** | | | |
| **Albums** | | | |
| IN CONCERT (Dec 82) Live concert | 1982 | Westwood One (2) | 100-150 |
| *(With Kansas)* | | | |
| KING BISCUIT FLOWER HOUR (Dec 82) Live concert | 1982 | DIR/ABC (2) | 50-100 |
| *(With Van Zant)* | | | |
| KING BISCUIT FLOWER HOUR (Feb 82) Live concert | 1982 | DIR/ABC (2) | 75-125 |
| *(With Rainbow)* | | | |
| KING BISCUIT FLOWER HOUR (June 84) Live concert | 1984 | DIR/ABC (2) | 85-150 |
| *(With Accept)* | | | |
| KING BISCUIT FLOWER HOUR (Mar 81) Live concert | 1981 | DIR/ABC (2) | 50-100 |
| *(With UFO)* | | | |
| NBC SOURCE (Jan 83) | 1983 | NBC Radio (2) | 75-125 |
| *(Rare live concert)* | | | |
| NBC SOURCE (May 81) | 1981 | NBC Radio (2) | 40-75 |
| *(Live concert)* | | | |
| SOURCE CONCERT (Aug 80) | 1980 | NBC Radio (2) | 40-75 |
| *(Live concert)* | | | |
| | | | |
| **TRAVIS, MERLE** | | | |
| *Capitol white promo label 45s $5-10 each* | | | |
| **Albums** | | | |
| BACK HOME | 1957 | Capitol 891 | 75 |
| *(Yellow promo label)* | | | |
| MERLE TRAVIS & JOE MAPHIS | 1964 | Capitol 2102 | 50 |
| *(Blue promo label)* | | | |
| THE MERLE TRAVIS GUITAR | 1956 | Capitol 650 | 100 |
| *(Yellow promo label)* | | | |
| WALKIN' THE STRINGS | 1960 | Capitol 1391 | 50 |
| *(Blue promo label)* | | | |
| | | | |
| **TRAVIS, RANDY** | | | |
| *Other Paula promo 45s $10 each; Warner Bros. promo 45s $2 each; Warner Bros. promo CD singles $3 each; Dreamworks promo CD singles $2 each* | | | |
| **45s** | | | |
| SHE'S MY WOMAN  "Randy Traywick" | 1978 | Paula 431 | 15 |
| *(Red promo label, beware of 1990 reissues)* | | | |
| WHITE CHRISTMAS MAKES ME BLUE/SLEIGH RIDE | 1987 | Warner Bros PRO-S-2842 | 4 |
| *(B-side by Mark O'Connor)* | | | |
| **Compact Discs** | | | |
| HE OPENED THE DOOR | 1992 | Warner Bros. PRO-CD-5675 (2) | 60 |
| *(2-CD set in package shaped like a barn)* | | | |
| STRAIGHT TALK WITH RANDY TRAVIS | 1993 | Warner Bros. PRO-CD-6363 | 20 |
| *(Promo-only interview disc)* | | | |
| | | | |
| **TRAVOLTA, JOEY** | | | |
| **45s** | | | |
| I DON'T WANT TO GO | 197? | Millennium | 15 |
| *(White label test pressing with insert)* | | | |
| | | | |
| **TRAVOLTA, JOHN** | | | |
| **45s** | | | |
| LET HER IN | 1976 | Midland Int'l. 10623 | 10 |
| *(Includes promo-only picture sleeve, no "RE" on sleeve)* | | | |
| | | | |
| **TREMELOES, THE** | | | |
| *Featuring Brian Poole; Epic promo 45s $8 each; Date promo 45s by Brian Poole $8 each; Monument promo 45s by Brian Poole $4 each; Epic white promo label LPs $15-18 each* | | | |
| **45s** | | | |
| SILENCE IS GOLDEN | 1967 | Epic 10184 | 125 |
| *(Red vinyl, flip side is by the Hollies, price includes promo-only picture sleeve)* | | | |
| **7-Inch Extended Plays** | | | |
| EVEN THE BAD TIMES ARE GOOD | 1967 | Epic 24326 | 25 |
| *(Jukebox LLP, issued with a hard cover)* | | | |
| THE TREMELOES | 1968 | Epic 26388 | 25 |
| *(Jukebox LLP, issued with a hard cover)* | | | |
| | | | |
| **TREVOR, VAN** | | | |
| **45s** | | | |
| CHRISTMAS IN THE COUNTRY/PSA ANNOUNCEMENTS | 1966 | Band Box 373 | 10 |
| | | | |
| **TRIBBLE, MARK** | | | |
| **45s** | | | |
| THE YEAR I SAW SANTA CLAUS (same on both sides) | 1987 | Paloma 92787 | 3 |
| | | | |
| **TRIP SHAKESPEARE** | | | |
| **12-Inch Singles** | | | |
| CRANE, THE | 199? | A&M | 10 |
| *(Promo-only 12" single)* | | | |

| Title | Yr | Label, Number | NM $ |
|---|---|---|---|

**TRITT, TRAVIS**
*Warner Bros. promo 45s $3 each; Other Warner Bros. promo CD singles $3 each*
**Compact Discs**

| | | | |
|---|---|---|---|
| WINTER WONDERLAND | 1992 | Warner Bros. PRO-CD-5767 | 8 |
| *(Promo-only CD single)* | | | |

**RADIO SHOWS**
**Compact Discs**

| | | | |
|---|---|---|---|
| COUNTRY CONCERT SERIES (Aug 93) | 1993 | Westwood One | 40-75 |
| *(Live concert)* | | | |

**TRIUMPH**
*With Mike Levine; Other MCA promo 45s $3 each; Other MCA promo 12" singles $5 each*
**12-Inch Singles**

| | | | |
|---|---|---|---|
| SPELLBOUND | 1984 | MCA 1240 | 12 |
| *(Promo-only 12" single with 10 introductions by members of the group)* | | | |

**45s**

| | | | |
|---|---|---|---|
| FOLLOW YOUR HEART | 1984 | MCA 52540 | 10 |
| *(Red vinyl, white label)* | | | |

**RADIO SHOWS**
**Albums**

| | | | |
|---|---|---|---|
| CAPTURED LIVE (Mar 84) | 1984 | RKO (2) | 50-100 |
| *(Live concert)* | | | |
| CAPTURED LIVE (Apr 84) | 1984 | RKO (4) | 75-125 |
| *(Live concert)* | | | |
| CAPTURED LIVE (Aug 84) | 1984 | RKO (2) | 45-90 |
| *(Live concert)* | | | |
| INNERVIEW | 1985 | Innerview | 15-25 |
| *(Music and interviews)* | | | |
| INNERVIEW (80s) Mike Levine | 198? | Innerview | 15-25 |
| *(Music and interviews)* | | | |
| KING BISCUIT FLOWER HOUR (July 80) Live concert | 1980 | DIR/ABC (2) | 75-125 |
| *(With Blackfoot)* | | | |
| KING BISCUIT FLOWER HOUR (Oct 85) Live concert | 1985 | DIR (2) | 25-50 |
| *(Live concert)* | | | |
| NBC SOURCE (Dec 82) | 1982 | NBC Radio (2) | 50-100 |
| *(Live concert)* | | | |
| OFF THE RECORD | 1985 | Westwood One (2) | 15-25 |
| *(Music and interviews)* | | | |
| SOURCE CONCERT (Dec 82) | 1982 | NBC Radio (2) | 40-75 |
| *(Live concert)* | | | |
| SOURCE CONCERT (Jan 82) | 1982 | NBC Radio (2) | 30-60 |
| *(Live concert)* | | | |
| SUPERGROUPS (July 82) Live concert | 1982 | DIR (3) | 40-75 |
| *(With Billy Squier)* | | | |
| WESTWOOD ONE PRESENTS (80s) | 198? | Westwood One | 20-40 |
| *(Live concert, the Tour Show)* | | | |

**Compact Discs**

| | | | |
|---|---|---|---|
| KING BISCUIT FLOWER HOUR (Feb 93) Live concert | 1993 | DIR | 40-75 |
| *(Live concert with Dada)* | | | |

**TROGGS, THE**
*Atco promo 45s $10 each; Fontana promo 45s $8 each; Page One and Bell promo 45s $5 each; Pye and Private Stock promo 45s $4 each; Fontana promo LPs $25 each; Sire 2LP promo $20 each*
**7-Inch Extended Plays**

| | | | |
|---|---|---|---|
| LIVE AT MAX'S | 1980 | Max's Kansas City | 15 |
| *(Four-song promo-only EP from the LP)* | | | |

**Albums**

| | | | |
|---|---|---|---|
| WILD THING | 1966 | Atco 193 | 50 |
| *(White promo label)* | | | |

**TROWER, ROBIN**
*Chrysalis promo 45s $4 each*
**12-Inch Singles**

| | | | |
|---|---|---|---|
| CAROLINE (same on both sides) | 1987 | GNP Crescendo PRO-3 | 8 |
| LOVE WON'T WAIT FOREVER (same on both sides) | 1988 | Atlantic PR 2374 | 6 |
| NO TIME (same on both sides) | 1987 | GNP Crescendo PRO-2 | 8 |
| SECRET DOORS (same on both sides) | 1986 | GNP Crescendo PRO-1 | 8 |
| SHATTERED (LP version)/(Live Version) | 1988 | Atlantic PR 2251 | 8 |

**RADIO SHOWS**
**Albums**

| | | | |
|---|---|---|---|
| BBC ROCK HOUR (Jan 82) | 1982 | London Wavelength | 40-75 |
| *(Live concert)* | | | |
| BBC TRANSCRIPTION DISC  Live concert | 1974 | BBC Transcription | 150-300 |
| *(With Kevin Coyne)* | | | |
| IN CONCERT (Jan 91) Live concert | 1991 | Westwood One (2) | 30-60 |
| *(With Billy Squier)* | | | |
| INNERVIEW (80s) | 198? | Innerview | 15-25 |
| *(Music and interviews)* | | | |

**Compact Discs**

| | | | |
|---|---|---|---|
| IN THE STUDIO (Feb 93) Profile of an album | 1993 | Album Network | 15-25 |
| *(Music and interviews)* | | | |
| KING BISCUIT FLOWER HOUR (July 88) | 1988 | DIR | 20-40 |
| *(Live concert, with Johnny Winter)* | | | |

**Reel-to-Reel Tapes**

| | | | |
|---|---|---|---|
| KING BISCUIT FLOWER HOUR (Dec 76) Live concert | 1976 | DIR/ABC (2) | 75-150 |
| *(With Manfred Mann, on two reels)* | | | |
| KING BISCUIT FLOWER HOUR (July 76) Live concert | 1976 | DIR/ABC (2) | 75-100 |
| *(With Chicago, on two reels)* | | | |

| Title | Yr | Label, Number | NM $ |
|---|---|---|---|

## TUBB, ERNEST
*Decca promo 78s $10-15 each; Decca pink promo label 45s before 30300 $8 each; Decca green promo label 45s $6 each; Decca blue promo label 45s $4 each; Decca pink or yellow promo label 45s after 30700 $3 each; First Generation promo 45s $3 each (Mostly duets); Other Decca jukebox LLPs $8 each; Other Decca promo LPs $15-20 each (Including duets with Loretta Lynn)*

**45s**

| | | | |
|---|---|---|---|
| ERNEST TUBB'S GOLDEN FAVORITES   Jukebox singles | 1961 | Decca 38303/38307 | 40 |
| *(Set of five 33 1/3 rpm singles, $8 each)* | | | |

**7-Inch Extended Plays**

| | | | |
|---|---|---|---|
| MY PICK OF THE HITS   Jukebox LLP | 1965 | Decca 34329 | 15 |
| *(Issued with a hard cover)* | | | |

**Albums**

| | | | |
|---|---|---|---|
| THE DADDY OF 'EM ALL | 1956 | Decca 8553 | 60 |
| *(Pink promo label)* | | | |
| ERNEST TUBB FAVORITES | 1956 | Decca 8291 | 75 |
| *(Pink promo label)* | | | |
| THE IMPORTANCE OF BEING ERNEST | 1959 | Decca 8834 | 50 |
| *(Pink promo label)* | | | |

**RADIO SHOWS**
**16-Inch Transcriptions**

| | | | |
|---|---|---|---|
| LEATHERNECK JAMBOREE (50s) | 195? | Public Service | 40-75 |
| *(Music and interviews)* | | | |
| NAVY HOEDOWN (50s) | 195? | U.S. Navy | 25-50 |
| *(Music and interviews)* | | | |
| U. S. ARMY BAND (50s) | 195? | U.S. Army | 25-50 |
| *(Music and interviews)* | | | |

**Albums**

| | | | |
|---|---|---|---|
| GRAND OL' OPRY | 1962 | WSM Radio | 25-50 |
| *(Music and interviews)* | | | |
| HOOTENAVY (60s) | 196? | U.S. Navy | 30-60 |
| *(Music and interviews)* | | | |

## TUBB, JUSTIN
*Groove white promo label 45s $8 each; Decca pink promo label 45s $6 each; Challenge white promo label 45s $6 each*

**Albums**

| | | | |
|---|---|---|---|
| COUNTRY BOY IN LOVE | 1957 | Decca 2559 | 40 |
| *(Pink promo label)* | | | |

## TUBES, THE
*A&M promo 45s $6 each; Capitol promo 45s $4 each; Capitol promo 45s by Fee Waybill $3 each; Other A&M and Capitol promo 12" singles $8 each; A&M promo LPs $12 each*

**12-Inch Singles**

| | | | |
|---|---|---|---|
| GONNA GET IT NEXT TIME (same on both sides) | 1982 | Capitol SPRO 9728 | 6 |
| PIECE BY PIECE (same on both sides) | 198? | Capitol SPRO 9332 | 6 |
| PRIME TIME/NO WAY OUT | 1979 | A&M 17068 | 8 |

**45s**

| | | | |
|---|---|---|---|
| SPORTS FANS (same on both sides) | 1982 | Capitol SPRO-9740 | 5 |

**Albums**

| | | | |
|---|---|---|---|
| FIRST CLEAN TUBES ALBUM, THE | 1978 | A&M 17012 | 25 |
| *(Promo release only, white cover with sticker)* | | | |

**RADIO SHOWS**
**Albums**

| | | | |
|---|---|---|---|
| BBC LONDON WAVELENGTH (Aug 81) | 1981 | London Wavelength | 25-40 |
| *(Mostly music and interviews)* | | | |
| BBC ROCK HOUR (Aug 81) | 1981 | London Wavelength | 50-100 |
| *(Live concert)* | | | |
| BBC TRANSCRIPTION DISC | 1981 | BBC Transcription | 200-300 |
| *(Very rare live concert)* | | | |
| IN CONCERT (Feb 84) | 1984 | Westwood One (2) | 40-75 |
| *(Live concert)* | | | |
| IN CONCERT (July 84) | 1984 | Westwood One (2) | 35-75 |
| *(Live concert)* | | | |
| INNERVIEW (80s) | 198? | Innerview | 15-25 |
| *(Music and interviews)* | | | |
| INNERVIEW (80s) Fee Waybill | 198? | Innerview | 15-25 |
| *(Music and interviews)* | | | |
| RETRO ROCK (Oct 84) | 1984 | Clayton Webster (2) | 30-60 |
| *(Music and interview with some live tracks)* | | | |
| SOURCE CONCERT (Sept 81) | 1981 | NBC Radio (2) | 25-50 |
| *(Mostly music and interviews)* | | | |

**Compact Discs**

| | | | |
|---|---|---|---|
| KING BISCUIT FLOWER HOUR (Aug 91) | 1991 | DIR | 40-75 |
| *(Live concert)* | | | |

## TUCKER, TANYA
*Columbia promo 45s $4 each; MCA and Arista promo 45s $3 each; Capitol promo 45s (PB prefix) $2 each; Other Capitol promo 45s (7PRO prefix) $5 each; Capitol/Liberty promo CD singles $3 each*

**45s**

| | | | |
|---|---|---|---|
| DOWN TO MY LAST TEARDROP (same on both sides) | 1991 | Capitol Nashville 7PRO-79711 | 5 |
| *(Vinyl is promo only)* | | | |
| IT WON'T BE ME (same on both sides) | 1990 | Capitol Nashville 7PRO-79338 | 5 |
| *(Vinyl is promo only)* | | | |
| OH WHAT IT DID TO ME (same on both sides) | 1991 | Capitol Nashville 7PRO-79535 | 5 |
| *(Vinyl is promo only)* | | | |

**RADIO SHOWS**
**Cassettes**

| | | | |
|---|---|---|---|
| AUSTIN ENCORE (90s)  Live concert | 199? | Entertainment Radio | 15-25 |
| *(With Sawyer Brown)* | | | |

| Title | Yr | Label, Number | NM $ |
|---|---|---|---|
| **Compact Discs** | | | |
| '90s COUNTRY (Dec 95) | 1995 | | 15-30 |
| *(Music and interviews, may be repeat of May 95 show)* | | | |
| '90s COUNTRY (May 95) | 1995 | | 15-30 |
| *(Music and interviews)* | | | |

**TUNEMASTERS, THE**

| | | | |
|---|---|---|---|
| **45s** | | | |
| I'VE LIED | 1957 | End 1011 | 75 |
| *(White promo label)* | | | |

**TURNER, IKE AND TINA**

*More at Tina Turner; Kent promo 45s $15 each; Warner Bros. promo 45s $10 each; Philles white promo label 45s $15 each; Blue Thumb white promo label 45s $8 each; Liberty promo 45s $6 each; United Artists promo 45s $4 each*

| | | | |
|---|---|---|---|
| **45s** | | | |
| I'VE BEEN LOVING YOU TOO LONG | 1973 | United Artists 2303 | 18 |
| *(Promo only, small center hole, 8:35 version, two songs on the other side)* | | | |
| **Albums** | | | |
| IKE & TINA TURNER'S GREATEST HITS | 1969 | Warner Bros. 1810 | 25 |
| *(White promo label)* | | | |
| RIVER DEEP-MOUNTAIN HIGH  No cover | 1966 | Philles 4011 | 10,000 |
| *(Yellow/black promo label, only a few copies known, no cover went to print, finally reissued on A&M in 1969)* | | | |
| RIVER DEEP-MOUNTAIN HIGH  Reissue of Philles 4011 | 1969 | A&M 4178 | 25 |
| *(White promo label)* | | | |
| THE IKE & TINA TURNER SHOW LIVE | 1965 | Warner Bros. 1579 | 30 |
| *(White promo label)* | | | |

**TURNER, JOE LYNN**
**RADIO SHOWS**

| | | | |
|---|---|---|---|
| **Albums** | | | |
| IN CONCERT (Mar 86) | 1986 | Westwood One (2) | 40-75 |
| *(Live concert)* | | | |

**TURNER, TINA**

*Other Capitol promo 45s $3 each; A&M promo 45s with Bryan Adams $3 each; Duck promo 45s with Eric Clapton $4 each; Other Capitol promo 12" singles $8 each*

| | | | |
|---|---|---|---|
| **12-Inch Singles** | | | |
| AFTERGLOW (4 versions) | 1987 | Capitol SPRO-79168/92 | 6 |
| BACK WHERE YOU STARTED (same on both sides) | 198? | Capitol SPRO-9826 | 6 |
| BETTER BE GOOD TO ME (LIVE) (same on both sides) | 1984 | Capitol SPRO-9264 | 10 |
| ONE OF THE LIVING (Club Version)/(Single Version) | 1985 | Capitol SPRO-9493/4 | 10 |
| OVERNIGHT SENSATION (same on both sides) | 1987 | Capitol SPRO-9867 | 6 |
| WE DON'T NEED ANOTHER HERO//(Instrumental) | 1985 | Capitol SPRO-9425/6 | 6 |
| WHAT'S LOVE GOT TO DO WITH IT (Extended) (same on both sides) | 1984 | Capitol SPRO-9196 | 12 |
| **45s** | | | |
| ACID QUEEN/PINBALL WIZARD | 1975 | Polydor PRO-002 | 40 |
| *(B-side by Elton John; promo-only)* | | | |
| TYPICAL MALE | 1986 | Capitol P-5615 | 12 |
| *(Special release, handwritten label print, issued in a clear plastic cover)* | | | |
| **RADIO SHOWS** | | | |
| **Albums** | | | |
| IN CONCERT (July 84) | 1984 | Westwood One | 200-350 |
| *(Very rare live concert)* | | | |

**TURRENTINE, STANLEY**

| | | | |
|---|---|---|---|
| **12-Inch Singles** | | | |
| BOOGIE ON REGGAE WOMAN (2 versions)/CREEPIN' | 1987 | Blue Note SPRO-79031 | 6 |
| DEJA VU (mono/stereo) | 1980 | Elektra 11472 | 10 |

**TURTLES, THE**

*Including Flo & Eddie;  Other White Whale promo 45s $8 each; Other Reprise promo 45s by Flo & Eddie $5 each; Columbia promo 45s by Flo & Eddie $4 each; Reprise and Columbia promo LPs by Flo & Eddie $12 each*

| | | | |
|---|---|---|---|
| **45s** | | | |
| FEEL OLDER NOW  Flo & Eddie | 1972 | Reprise 112 | 12 |
| *(Promo-only release)* | | | |
| FLO & EDDIE MEET THE WOLFMAN   Flo & Eddie | 1975 | Reprise PRO-564 | 15 |
| *(White promo label, promo only, issued in a hard picture cover)* | | | |
| GUIDE FOR THE MARRIED MAN | 1967 | White Whale 251 | 35 |
| *(Blue promo label, very rare on stock copy)* | | | |
| **7-Inch Extended Plays** | | | |
| FLO & EDDIE  Flo & Eddie | 1973 | Reprise PRO-564 | 25 |
| *(Radio ads for the album)* | | | |
| THE FLUORESCENT LEECH & EDDIE   Flo & Eddie | 1972 | Reprise PRO-333 | 25 |
| *(Radio ads for the album)* | | | |

**TWAIN, SHANIA**

*Mercury Nashville promo CD singles $5 each*

**TWILLEY, DWIGHT**

*Shelter and EMI promo 45s $3 each*

| | | | |
|---|---|---|---|
| **12-Inch Singles** | | | |
| LITTLE BIT OF LOVE (Edit)/(LP) | 1984 | EMI America SPRO-9104 | 8 |
| SEXUAL (same on both sides) | 1986 | CBS Associated ZAS 2360 | 10 |
| SOMEBODY TO LOVE/MONEY | 1979 | Arista SP-79 | 12 |
| **RADIO SHOWS** | | | |
| **Albums** | | | |
| KING BISCUIT FLOWER HOUR (June 82) Live concert | 1982 | DIR/ABC (2) | 60-100 |
| *(With Dave Edmunds)* | | | |

| Title | Yr | Label, Number | NM $ |
|---|---|---|---|
| KING BISCUIT FLOWER HOUR (June 84) Live concert | 1984 | DIR/ABC (2) | 40-75 |
| (With Midnight Oil) | | | |
| KING BISCUIT FLOWER HOUR  Live concert | 1985 | DIR (2) | 25-35 |
| (With Los Lobos) | | | |
| ROCK AROUND THE WORLD (Nov 76) Live concert | 1976 | RATW | 50-100 |
| (With the Little River Band) | | | |

**TWISTED SISTER**
*Atlantic promo 45s $4 each; Atlantic promo 12" singles $6 each*
**RADIO SHOWS**
**Albums**

| Title | Yr | Label, Number | NM $ |
|---|---|---|---|
| IN CONCERT (Aug 84) Live concert | 1984 | Westwood One (2) | 50-125 |
| (With Stevie Ray Vaughan) | | | |
| IN CONCERT (Jan 85) Live concert | 1985 | Westwood One (2) | 175-250 |
| (With Kiss) | | | |
| KING BISCUIT FLOWER HOUR | 1983 | DIR/ABC (2) | 20-40 |
| (Live concert) | | | |
| KING BISCUIT FLOWER HOUR (Feb 85) Live concert | 1985 | DIR (2) | 40-60 |
| (With Dio) | | | |
| KING BISCUIT FLOWER HOUR (Oct 84) Live concert | 1984 | DIR/ABC (2) | 30-50 |
| (With Kick Axe) | | | |
| NBC SOURCE (Aug 84) Live concert | 1984 | NBC Radio (2) | 15-25 |
| (With Ratt) | | | |

**TWITTY, CONWAY**
*Other MGM yellow promo label 45s $8 each; MGM white promo label 45s $5 each; Decca yellow promo label 45s $4 each; Other MCA promo 45s $3 each; Elektra promo 45s $3 each; Warner Bros. promo 45s $2 each; Other Decca jukebox LLPs with hard covers $25 each; Other Decca jukebox LLPs with soft covers $15 each; Metro promo LPs $15 each; Decca promo LPs $10 each (Including duets)*
**45s**

| Title | Yr | Label, Number | NM $ |
|---|---|---|---|
| DANNY BOY | 1959 | MGM 12826 | 15 |
| (Yellow promo label) | | | |
| DON'T CRY JONI | 1975 | MCA 40407 | 10 |
| (White promo label, long 4:21 and short 3:05 versions) | | | |
| DOUBLE TALK BABY | 1957 | Mercury 71384 | 50 |
| (White promo label) | | | |
| HELLO DARLIN' | 1975 | MCA 60180 | 10 |
| (White promo label includes Russian version) | | | |
| HEY, LITTLE LUCY! | 1959 | MGM 12785 | 20 |
| (Yellow promo label) | | | |
| I NEED YOUR LOVIN' | 1957 | Mercury 71086 | 50 |
| (White promo label) | | | |
| I WANT TO KNOW YOU BEFORE WE MAKE LOVE | 1987 | MCA 53134 | 10 |
| (Blue vinyl, white promo label) | | | |
| IT'S ONLY MAKE BELIEVE | 1958 | MGM 12677 | 35 |
| (Yellow promo label) | | | |
| JULIA | 1987 | MCA 53034 | 12 |
| (Red vinyl, white promo label) | | | |
| LONELY BLUE BOY | 1959 | MGM 12857 | 12 |
| (Yellow promo label) | | | |
| LONELY BLUE BOY  Set of five stereo singles | 1960 | MGM SB-5 400-410 | 200 |
| (Small center hole, for jukeboxes, $40 each) | | | |
| MONA LISA | 1959 | MGM 12804 | 18 |
| (Yellow promo label) | | | |
| SEASON'S GREETINGS  With Loretta Lynn | 1972 | (Decca) 7211281 | 75 |
| (Promo-only picture disc, no label mentioned on disc but pressed by Decca) | | | |
| SHAKE IT UP | 1957 | Mercury 71148 | 40 |
| (White promo label) | | | |
| THE STORY OF MY LIFE | 1959 | MGM 12748 | 25 |
| (Yellow promo label) | | | |
| WHAT AM I LIVING FOR? | 1960 | MGM 12886 | 10 |
| (Yellow promo label) | | | |
| **7-Inch Extended Plays** | | | |
| FIFTEEN YEARS AGO | 1970 | Decca 75248 | 15 |
| (Jukebox LLP, issued with a soft cover) | | | |
| LOOK INTO MY TEARDROPS | 1966 | Decca 34437 | 25 |
| (Jukebox LLP, issued with a hard cover) | | | |
| **Albums** | | | |
| 20 GREAT HITS BY CONWAY TWITTY | 1972 | MGM 4884 (2) | 25 |
| (White promo labels) | | | |
| CLINGING TO A SAVING HAND/STEAL AWAY | 1973 | MCA 376 | 25 |
| (White label promo copy, rare album) | | | |
| CONWAY TWITTY | 1970 | MGM 110 | 20 |
| (Yellow promo label, Golden Archive series) | | | |
| CONWAY TWITTY SINGS | 1959 | MGM 3744 | 150 |
| (Yellow promo label) | | | |
| THE CONWAY TWITTY TOUCH | 1961 | MGM 3943 | 50 |
| (Yellow promo label) | | | |
| HIT THE ROAD | 1964 | MGM 4217 | 40 |
| (Yellow or white promo label) | | | |
| LONELY BLUE BOY | 1960 | MGM 3818 | 75 |
| (Yellow promo label) | | | |
| PORTRAIT OF A FOOL | 1962 | MGM 4019 | 50 |
| (Yellow promo label) | | | |
| R & B '63 | 1963 | MGM 4089 | 50 |
| (Yellow promo label) | | | |
| THE ROCK & ROLL STORY | 1961 | MGM 3907 | 75 |
| (Yellow promo label) | | | |
| SATURDAY NIGHT WITH CONWAY TWITTY | 1959 | MGM 3786 | 100 |
| (Yellow promo label) | | | |

| Title | Yr | Label, Number | NM $ |
|---|---|---|---|

**RADIO SHOWS**
**Albums**
THEN AND NOW — 1972 — Opryland 12636 (6) — 100-150
*(Music and interviews)*

**TYLER, BONNIE**
*Chrysalis promo 45s $4 each; RCA promo 45s $3 each; Columbia promo 45s $3 each; Columbia promo picture sleeves $3 each*
**45s**
IF I SING YOU A LOVE SONG — 197? — RCA 11349 — 15
*(With promo-only picture sleeve)*

# U

## U2
**10-Inch Singles**
LEMON (Bad Yard Dub)/(Serious Def Dub) — 1993 — Island PR12 6804 — 50
*(Promo-only 10-inch single on yellow vinyl)*
**12-Inch Singles**
ALL I WANT IS YOU/UNCHAINED MELODY/EVERLASTING LOVE — 1989 — Island DMD 1349 — 12
ANGEL OF HARLEM/A ROOM AT THE HEARTBREAK HOTEL/ — 1988 — Island PR 1269 — 10
LOVE RESCUE ME (Live)
BAD (Live) (same on both sides) — 1985 — Island PR 774 — 75
DESIRE (2:59) (5:58)/HALLELUJAH HERE SHE COMES — 1988 — Island DMD 1258 — 15
DESIRE (same on both sides) — 1988 — Island 2499 — 10
DISCOTHEQUE — 1997 — Island PR12 7398 — 20
*(Promo 12" single, 2 club mixes)*
I WILL FOLLOW/NIGHT TRAIN — 1980 — Island PRO-A2-940 RE-1 — 70
*(B-side by Steve Winwood)*
NEW YEAR'S DAY (same on both sides) — 1983 — Island DMD 604 — 15
*(Contains a slightly longer version than on LP)*
NUMB (same on both sides) — 1993 — Island PR12 6784 — 40
*(No label name on label)*
(PRIDE) IN THE NAME OF LOVE (same on both sides) — 1984 — Island PR 635 — 15
*(With title parentheses in the wrong place as above)*
A SORT OF HOMECOMING (same on both sides) — 1984 — Island PR 701 — 15
STARING AT THE SUN — 1997 — Island PR12 7463 — 20
*(Promo-only 12" single, 3 versions)*
TWO HEARTS BEAT AS ONE (5:57)//(Album Version) (Edit) — 1983 — Island DMD 643 — 25
WHEN LOVE COMES TO TOWN (7:30) (3:30)/ — 1989 — Island DMD 1310 — 15
GOD PART II/DANCING BAREFOOT
WHEN LOVE COMES TO TOWN (same on both sides) — 1989 — Island 1324 — 15
WIRE — 1984 — Island PR 675 — 30
*(Promo-only 12" single)*
WITH OR WITHOUT YOU — 1987 — Island PR 1021 — 20
*(Promo-only 12" single)*
**45s**
ALL I WANT IS YOU — 1989 — Island 99199 — 10
*(White promo label)*
ANGEL OF HARLEM — 1988 — Island 99254 — 10
*(White promo label)*
DESIRE — 1988 — Island 99250 — 10
*(White promo label)*
I STILL HAVEN'T FOUND WHAT I'M LOOKING FOR — 1987 — Island 99430 — 10
*(White promo label)*
I WILL FOLLOW — 1983 — Island PR 564 — 30
*(Promo-only special remix for radio, live 3:36 version, issued with a printer insert from Island Records)*
I WILL FOLLOW — 1980 — Island 49716 — 75
*(Promo record, mono/stereo, and special poster picture sleeve issued with the promo record)*
I WILL FOLLOW — 1983 — Island 99789 — 15
*(Blue promo label)*
IN GOD'S COUNTRY — 1987 — Island 99385 — 10
*(White promo label)*
NEW MUSICAL EXPRESS  Various artists — 1985 — NME GIV 1B — 25
*(Pressed in UK for use in US, one U2 song, "Wire"; promo-only EP given away with purchase of NME magazine)*
NEW YEAR'S DAY — 1983 — Island 99915 — 18
*(Blue promo label)*
PRIDE (IN THE NAME OF LOVE) — 1984 — Island 99704 — 15
*(Blue promo label)*
TWO HEARTS BEAT AS ONE — 1983 — Island 99861 — 18
*(Blue promo label, stock picture sleeve worth $18)*
WHEN LOVE COMES TO TOWN — 1989 — Island 99225 — 10
*(White promo label)*
WHERE THE STREETS HAVE NO NAME — 1987 — Island 99408 — 10
*(White promo label)*
WITH OR WITHOUT YOU — 1987 — Island 99453 — 10
*(White promo label)*
**Albums**
THEIR WORDS AND MUSIC — 1987 — Island 2049 — 40
*(Music and interviews from the Joshua Tree)*
TWO SIDES LIVE (Mar 81) — 1981 — Warner Bros. WBMS-117 — 175
*(Live concert special promo-only release)*
VOICES OF SUN CITY  Various artists — 1985 — Manhattan — 20
*(Includes an interview with Bono)*

| **Title** | **Yr** | **Label, Number** | **NM $** |
|---|---|---|---|
| **Compact Discs** | | | |
| ALL I WANT IS YOU | 1989 | Island PR 2770 | 15 |
| *(Promo CD single)* | | | |
| ANGEL OF HARLEM | 1988 | Island PR 2559 | 20 |
| *(Promo CD single)* | | | |
| BOSNIA  Passengers | 1995 | Island | 40 |
| *(Promo-only package with CD single and video)* | | | |
| DESIRE | 1988 | Island PR 2500 | 40 |
| *(Promo CD single)* | | | |
| DISCOTHEQUE | 1997 | Island PRCD 7316 | 10 |
| *(Promo CD single)* | | | |
| EVEN BETTER THAN THE REAL THING | 1992 | Island PRCD 6735 | 10 |
| *(Promo CD single, 6 mixes)* | | | |
| FLY, THE | 1991 | Island PRCD 6680 | 10 |
| *(Promo CD single)* | | | |
| GOD PART II | 1989 | Island PR 2677 | 50 |
| *(Promo-only CD release, six tracks)* | | | |
| HOLD ME, THRILL ME, KISS ME, KILL ME | 1995 | Atlantic/Island PRCD 6237 | 15 |
| *(Promo CD single, 2 versions)* | | | |
| HOLD ME, THRILL ME, KISS ME, KILL ME | 1995 | Atlantic/Island PRCD 6266 | 15 |
| *(Promo CD single, 2 more versions)* | | | |
| I'VE GOT YOU UNDER MY SKIN  Frank Sinatra with Bono | 1993 | Capitol DPRO-79305 | 8 |
| *(Promo only CD single from Sinatra's "Duets")* | | | |
| IF GOD WILL SEND HIS ANGELS | 1997 | Island PRCD 7749 | 12 |
| *(Promo CD single with "research hook")* | | | |
| IN THE NAME OF THE FATHER  Bono | 1994 | Island | 10 |
| *(Promo CD single)* | | | |
| LAST NIGHT ON EARTH | 1997 | Island PRCD 7517 | 10 |
| *(Promo CD single)* | | | |
| LEMON | 1993 | Island PRCD 6800 | 15 |
| *(Promo CD single, 4 mixes)* | | | |
| MISS SARAJEVO  Passengers | 1995 | Island PRCD 7131 | 10 |
| *(Promo-only CD single, with Luciano Pavarotti)* | | | |
| MYSTERIOUS WAYS | 1991 | Island PRCD 6698 | 10 |
| *(Promo CD single)* | | | |
| MYSTERIOUS WAYS | 1991 | Island PRCD 6701 | 10 |
| *(Promo CD single, two different mixes)* | | | |
| NUMB | 1993 | Island PRCD 6785 | 15 |
| *(Promo CD single, includes Perfecto Mix)* | | | |
| NUMB | 1993 | Island PRCD 6795 | 15 |
| *(Promo CD single, 2 different versions than on 6785)* | | | |
| ONE | 1991 | Island PRCD 6706 | 10 |
| *(Promo CD single)* | | | |
| ORIGINAL SOUNDCHATS  Passengers | 1995 | Island OST 2 | 100 |
| *(Promo-only two-CD set)* | | | |
| PLEASE | 1997 | Island PRCD 7673 | 12 |
| *(Promo CD single, 3 versions)* | | | |
| PLEASE | 1997 | Island PRCD 7679 | 12 |
| *(Promo CD single, 2 single versions)* | | | |
| STARING AT THE SUN | 1997 | Island PRCD 7445 | 10 |
| *(Promo CD single)* | | | |
| STAY (FARAWAY, SO CLOSE!) | 1993 | Island PRCD 6806 | 10 |
| *(Promo CD single, edit version)* | | | |
| SWEETEST THING | 1998 | Island PRCD 7961 | 15 |
| *(Promo CD single)* | | | |
| THEME FROM MISSION IMPOSSIBLE  Adam Clayton and Larry Mullen | 1996 | Mother PRCD 7180 | 12 |
| *(Promo CD single)* | | | |
| UNTIL THE END OF THE WORLD | 1991 | Island PRCD 6704 | 10 |
| *(Promo CD single)* | | | |
| WHEN LOVE COMES TO TOWN | 1989 | Island PR 2659 | 15 |
| *(Promo CD single)* | | | |
| WHERE THE STREETS HAVE NO NAME | 1987 | Island PR 2104 | 40 |
| *(An early promo CD single)* | | | |
| WHO'S GONNA RIDE YOUR WILD HORSES | 1992 | Island PRCD 6745 | 10 |
| *(Promo CD single, radio edit)* | | | |
| WHO'S GONNA RIDE YOUR WILD HORSES | 1992 | Island PRCD 6744 | 15 |
| *(Promo CD single, 2 versions)* | | | |
| ZOOROPA | 1993 | Island PRCD 6792 | 10 |
| *(Promo CD single, edit version)* | | | |
| **RADIO SHOWS** | | | |
| **Albums** | | | |
| BBC COLLEGE CONCERT HOUR (Mar 83) | 1983 | London Wavelength | 75-125 |
| *(Live concert)* | | | |
| BBC LONDON WAVELENGTH (Mar 84) | 1984 | London Wavelength | 100-150 |
| *(Live concert)* | | | |
| BBC ROCK HOUR (Mar 83) | 1983 | London Wavelength | 75-125 |
| *(Live concert)* | | | |
| BBC ROCK HOUR (Mar 84) | 1984 | London Wavelength | 100-150 |
| *(Early live concert)* | | | |
| BBC TRANSCRIPTION DISC | 1983 | BBC Transcription | 600-750 |
| *(Very rare live concert)* | | | |
| DIR SPECIAL (Dec 87) Live concert | 1987 | DIR | 200-350 |
| *("Rock on the Road")* | | | |
| IN CONCERT | 1982 | Westwood One | 150-250 |
| *(Live concert)* | | | |
| INNERVIEW | 1984 | Clayton Webster | 25-50 |
| *(Music and interviews)* | | | |
| KING BISCUIT FLOWER HOUR | 1983 | DIR/ABC (2) | 100-200 |
| *(Live concert)* | | | |

| Title | Yr | Label, Number | NM $ |
|---|---|---|---|
| KING BISCUIT FLOWER HOUR (June 84) *(Live concert)* | 1984 | DIR/ABC (2) | 100-150 |
| KING BISCUIT FLOWER HOUR (Nov 86) *(Live concert)* | 1986 | DIR (2) | 100-200 |
| PIONEERS IN MUSIC  U2 and others *(Music and interviews with Boomtown Rats and Van Morrison)* | 1986 | DIR (2) | 40-75 |
| ROCK CLOCK Various artists *(Live tracks from three artists including U2)* | 1987 | DIR (2) | 40-75 |
| ROCK STARS (May 87) *(Music and interview with some live tracks)* | 1987 | Radio Today (2) | 75-150 |
| SOURCE BEST OF THE NEW TOURS  Various artists *(Music and interviews, includes U2)* | 1984 | NBC Radio (3) | 25-50 |
| SOURCE CONCERT (Mar 84) *(Live concert)* | 1984 | NBC Radio (2) | 175-225 |
| SOURCE NEW MUSIC PROFILE  Various artists *(Music and interviews, includes U2)* | 1983 | NBC Radio (3) | 25-50 |
| SUPERGROUPS (Aug 83)  With Judas Priest *(Live concert)* | 1983 | DIR (3) | 75-150 |
| SUPERSTAR CONCERT (Sept 85) *(Live concert box set)* | 1985 | Westwood One (3) | 175-250 |
| SUPERSTAR CONCERT *(Live concert box set)* | 1986 | Westwood One (3) | 150-250 |
| THE INSIDE TRACK (Nov 84)  With David Byrne *(Mostly music and interviews)* | 1984 | DIR (3) | 100-175 |
| THE RISE AND RISE OF U2 *(Music and interviews)* | 1988 | Westwood One (3) | 150-250 |
| WAR IS DECLARED (July 83) *(Very rare box set)* | 1983 | NBC Radio 83-27 (3) | 200-325 |
| **Compact Discs** | | | |
| ALBUM NETWORK SPECIAL (Dec 93) *(Music and interviews)* | 1993 | Album Network (2) | 75-125 |
| BBC CLASSIC TRACKS (June 91) *(Various live classic tracks)* | 1991 | Westwood One | 75-125 |
| BBC CLASSIC TRACKS (June 92) *(Various live classic tracks)* | 1992 | Westwood One | 40-80 |
| BBC CLASSIC TRACKS (Mar 93) *(Various live classic tracks)* | 1993 | Westwood One | 30-60 |
| IN CONCERT-NU ROCK (Nov 92) *(Live concert)* | 1992 | Westwood One | 150-250 |
| IN THE STUDIO (Dec 92) Profile of an album *(Music and interviews on "Achtung Baby")* | 1992 | Album Network | 40-75 |
| LIVE FROM DUBLIN (Sept 93) *(Very rare live concert, fewer than 100 copies made)* | 1993 | Westwood One (3) | 300-400 |
| LIVE FROM SYDNEY (May 94) *(Live concert)* | 1994 | (2) | 75-125 |
| RADIO TRANSMIT (Nov 92) *(Music and interviews, some live tracks, released for alternative radio)* | 1992 | Album Network | 100-150 |
| SUPERSTAR CONCERT (Nov 94) *(Live concert)* | 1994 | Westwood One (2) | 75-125 |
| WESTWOOD ONE SPECIAL (May 94) *(Music, interviews and live tracks featured)* | 1994 | Westwood One (2) | 100-200 |
| ZOO TV *(Music and interviews)* | 1992 | Album Network (2) | 75-125 |
| ZOORADIO (Aug 93)  Bono and The Edge *(Music and interviews)* | 1993 | Westwood One (2) | 75-125 |
| ZOOROPA (Sept 93) Bono and The Edge *(Music and interviews)* | 1993 | Westwood One (2) | 75-125 |
| **Reel-to-Reel Tapes** | | | |
| IN CONCERT-NU ROCK (Nov 92) *(Live concert on two 10" reels)* | 1992 | Westwood One | 200-300 |
| THE FINAL BROADCAST (Nov 92) *(Live concert issued on two 10" reels)* | 1992 | | 300-400 |

**UB40**

*A&M promo 45s $4 each; A&M and Virgin promo CD singles $3 each*

**12-Inch Singles**

| Title | Yr | Label, Number | NM $ |
|---|---|---|---|
| CHERRY OH BABY (LIVE IN MOSCOW) (same on both sides) | 1986 | A&M 17487 | 8 |
| DON'T BREAK MY HEART (LP)/(Remix) | 1985 | A&M 17350 | 8 |
| RAT IN THE KITCHEN (LP)/(Single) | 1986 | A&M 17440 | 8 |
| SING OUR OWN SONG (Long)/(Short) | 1986 | A&M 17424 | 8 |

**RADIO SHOWS**

**Albums**

| Title | Yr | Label, Number | NM $ |
|---|---|---|---|
| BBC COLLEGE CONCERT HOUR (Nov 82) *(Music and interviews)* | 1982 | London Wavelength | 25-40 |
| BBC TRANSCRIPTION DISC *(Live concert)* | 1981 | BBC Transcription | 150-200 |
| BBC TRANSCRIPTION DISC *(Live concert)* | 1982 | BBC Transcription | 125-200 |
| PENTHOUSE/OMNI COLLEGE CONCERT *(Music and interviews)* | 1984 | London Wavelength | 25-40 |
| SOURCE CONCERT (May 84) *(Live concert with Paul Young)* | 1984 | NBC Radio (2) | 40-75 |

**Compact Discs**

| Title | Yr | Label, Number | NM $ |
|---|---|---|---|
| ON THE EDGE (June 93) Music and interviews *(With Emotional Fish and Sun-60)* | 1993 | Westwood One | 20-30 |

| Title | Yr | Label, Number | NM $ |
|---|---|---|---|
| **UFO** | | | |
| *Other Chrysalis promo 45s $4 each* | | | |
| **12-Inch Singles** | | | |
| LONELY HEART (same on both sides) | 1981 | Chrysalis 28 | 8 |
| NIGHT RUN/BLUE | 1986 | Chrysalis VAS 2363 | 12 |
| **45s** | | | |
| TOO HOT TO HANDLE | 1977 | Chrysalis 2157 | 15 |
| *(Red vinyl, white promo label, stock picture sleeve worth additional $10)* | | | |
| **RADIO SHOWS** | | | |
| **Albums** | | | |
| BBC ROCK HOUR (Apr 82) | 1982 | London Wavelength | 50-100 |
| *(Live concert)* | | | |
| KING BISCUIT FLOWER HOUR (Aug 82) Live concert | 1982 | DIR/ABC (2) | 50-75 |
| *(With Foreigner)* | | | |
| KING BISCUIT FLOWER HOUR (Mar 81) Live concert | 1981 | DIR/ABC (2) | 50-100 |
| *(With Pat Travers)* | | | |
| **UGLY KID JOE** | | | |
| *Stardog/Mercury promo CD singles $3 each* | | | |
| **ULTRAVOX** | | | |
| *More at Midge Ure* | | | |
| **12-Inch Singles** | | | |
| HYMN (2 versions)/REAP THE WILD WIND | 1983 | Chrysalis AS 1662 | 8 |
| LOVE'S GREAT ADVENTURE/ONE SMALL DAY (Edit) | 1985 | Chrysalis VAS 2028 | 7 |
| ONE SMALL DAY (same on both sides) | 1984 | Chrysalis VAS 1840 | 6 |
| REAP THE WILD WIND/HOSANNA | 1982 | Chrysalis CHS 51 PDJ | 15 |
| SLEEPWALK (same on both sides) | 1980 | Chrysalis CHS-22-PDJ | 10 |
| THE VOICE (same on both sides) | 1981 | Chrysalis CHS 35 PDJ | 8 |
| **RADIO SHOWS** | | | |
| **Albums** | | | |
| KING BISCUIT FLOWER HOUR (May 83) Live concert | 1983 | DIR/ABC (2) | 40-80 |
| *(With ABC)* | | | |
| **UNBELIEVABLE UGLIES, THE** | | | |
| *Includes Bob Eveslage* | | | |
| **45s** | | | |
| KEEP HER SATISFIED | 1967 | Soma 1451 | 75 |
| *(White promo label, less than 100 copies pressed)* | | | |
| WINGS | 1969 | No label (Sound 80) | 100 |
| *(Raw unused version, 30 copies pressed)* | | | |
| YOU'RE THE ONLY ONE  Bob Eveslage | 1988 | Clowd 8804 | 75 |
| *(Red/white promo label, six promo copies exist)* | | | |
| **UNCLE TUPELO** | | | |
| **Compact Discs** | | | |
| LONG CUT, THE, AND FIVE LIVE | 1994 | Sire PRO-CD-6727 | 20 |
| *(Promo-only sampler)* | | | |
| **UNDERTONES, THE** | | | |
| **Compact Discs** | | | |
| BEST OF THE UNDERTONES (90s) | 1994 | Rykodisc | 25 |
| *(Promo-only CD issued with a book)* | | | |
| **RADIO SHOWS** | | | |
| **Albums** | | | |
| BBC TRANSCRIPTION DISC Live concert | 1980 | BBC Transcription | 100-200 |
| *(With Wreckless Eric)* | | | |
| COLLEGE CONCERT (May 83) | 1983 | London Wavelength | 40-80 |
| *(Live concert)* | | | |
| **UNDISPUTED TRUTH, THE** | | | |
| **45s** | | | |
| PAPA WAS A ROLLIN' STONE | 1972 | Gordy 7117 | 15 |
| *(Red vinyl, white promo label, became a hit by the Temptations)* | | | |
| **UNFORGIVEN, THE** | | | |
| **RADIO SHOWS** | | | |
| **Albums** | | | |
| INNERVIEW (80s) | 198? | Innerview | 15-25 |
| *(Music and interviews)* | | | |
| **URE, MIDGE** | | | |
| *More at Ultravox* | | | |
| **12-Inch Singles** | | | |
| IF I WAS (Edit)/(LP version) | 1985 | Chrysalis VAS 2257 | 7 |
| JUST FOR YOU (same on both sides) | 1989 | Chrysalis SPRO 23387 | 6 |
| **URIAH HEEP** | | | |
| *Other Mercury promo 45s $3 each; Warner Bros. promo 45s $3 each* | | | |
| **45s** | | | |
| GYPSY | 1971 | Mercury DJ-262 | 10 |
| *(Red promo label)* | | | |
| WHAT'S IT ALL ABOUT (Aug 76) Public service show | 1976 | W.I.A.A. 328 | 20 |
| *(Flip side features Foghat)* | | | |
| **7-Inch Extended Plays** | | | |
| SWEET FREEDOM  Jukebox LLP | 1972 | Warner Bros. 2724 (LLP 230) | 15 |
| *(Issued with a paper cover)* | | | |

| Title | Yr | Label, Number | NM $ |
|---|---|---|---|
| **USHER, GARY** | | | |
| **45s** | | | |
| HON-DA-BEACH  The Wheel Men | 1964 | Warner Bros. 5480 | 75 |
| *(White promo label)* | | | |
| THREE SURFER BOYS  With the Honeys | 1963 | Dot 16158 | 250 |
| *(White promo label)* | | | |
| | | | |
| **UTOPIANS, THE** | | | |
| **45s** | | | |
| ALONG MY LONELY WAY | 1961 | Imperial 5876 | 250 |
| *(Cream colored promo label)* | | | |

# V

| Title | Yr | Label, Number | NM $ |
|---|---|---|---|
| **VAL-TONES, THE** | | | |
| **45s** | | | |
| TENDER DARLING | 1955 | DeLuxe 6084 | 50 |
| *(White promo label)* | | | |
| | | | |
| **VALE, JERRY** | | | |
| *Other Columbia promo 45s $2 each; Columbia Hall of Fame promo 45s $3 each* | | | |
| **45s** | | | |
| BLUE CHRISTMAS (same on both sides) | 1965 | Columbia JZSP 111776 | 10 |
| HAVE YOU LOOKED INTO YOUR HEART | 1965 | Columbia 43181 | 10 |
| *(Red vinyl, white promo label)* | | | |
| SILENT NIGHT, HOLY NIGHT/OH HOLY NIGHT | 1963 | Columbia JZSP 79175/6 | |
| **7-Inch Extended Plays** | | | |
| MISSION SUNDAY  Radio ads | 1974 | SPF (no #) | 10 |
| *(Three PSA spots for Mission Sunday, issued with a paper picture sleeve)* | | | |
| | | | |
| **VALENS, RITCHIE** | | | |
| *Del-Fi promo 12" singles (from the 1980s) $6 each Also recorded as Arvee Allens* | | | |
| **45s** | | | |
| FAST FREIGHT  Arvee Allens | 1959 | Del-Fi 4111 | 50 |
| *(White promo label)* | | | |
| LITTLE GIRL | 1959 | Del-Fi 4117 | 35 |
| *(White promo label)* | | | |
| THAT'S MY LITTLE SUZIE | 1959 | Del-Fi 4114 | 35 |
| *(White promo label)* | | | |
| **7-Inch Extended Plays** | | | |
| RICHIE VALENS | 1959 | Del-Fi 1 | 300 |
| *(Promo-only EP release)* | | | |
| **Albums** | | | |
| RICHIE VALENS | 1970 | MGM 117 | 50 |
| *(Yellow promo label)* | | | |
| | | | |
| **VALLI, FRANKIE** | | | |
| *More at The Four Seasons* | | | |
| **45s** | | | |
| CIRCLES IN THE SAND | 196? | Philips DJP-66 | 10 |
| *(Promo-only number)* | | | |
| I GO APE  Frankie Tyler | 195? | Okeh 7103 | 60 |
| *(White promo label)* | | | |
| WHAT'S IT ALL ABOUT (Dec 80) Public service show | 1980 | W.I.A.A. 553 | 25 |
| *(Flip side is Cher)* | | | |
| WHAT'S IT ALL ABOUT (Dec 81) Public service show | 1981 | W.I.A.A. 608 | 25 |
| *(Flip side is Grace Slick)* | | | |
| | | | |
| **VALTONES, THE** | | | |
| **45s** | | | |
| HAVE YOU EVER MET AN ANGEL | 1956 | Gee 1004 | 250 |
| *(White promo label)* | | | |
| | | | |
| **VAN DYKES, THE** | | | |
| **45s** | | | |
| COME ON, BABY | 1958 | Decca 30762 | 40 |
| *(Pink promo label)* | | | |
| | | | |
| **VAN HALEN** | | | |
| *Also includes David Lee Roth, Sammy Hagar, HSAS Band; Other Warner Bros. promo 45s $3 each; Other Geffen promo 45s by Sammy Hagar $3 each; Warner Bros. promo 45s by David Lee Roth $4 each; Warner Bros. promo CD singles $3-5 each* | | | |
| **45s** | | | |
| AIN'T TALKIN' 'BOUT LOVE | 1978 | Warner Bros. 8707 | 10 |
| *(Light brown promo label)* | | | |
| DANCE THE NIGHT AWAY | 1979 | Warner Bros. 8823 | 10 |
| *(Light brown promo label)* | | | |
| HOT FOR TEACHER | 1984 | Warner Bros. 29199 | 12 |
| *(Promo record in a special clear plastic gatefold cover with photo, early stock copies also came in this package)* | | | |
| JAMIE'S CRYIN' | 1978 | Warner Bros. 8631 | 10 |
| *(Light brown promo label)* | | | |
| TWO SIDES OF LOVE  Sammy Hagar | 1984 | Geffen 29246 | 12 |
| *(Red vinyl, gray promo label)* | | | |
| YOU REALLY GOT ME | 1978 | Warner Bros. 8515 | 10 |
| *(Tree lined promo label)* | | | |

| Title | Yr | Label, Number | NM $ |
|---|---|---|---|
| **Albums** | | | |
| 1984 | 1984 | Warner Bros. 23985 | 25 |
| *(Promo on Quiex II vinyl)* | | | |
| LOONEY TUNES | 1978 | Warner Bros. PRO 705 | 40 |
| *(Promo-only EP on red vinyl)* | | | |
| **Compact Discs** | | | |
| BEST OF VAN HALEN | 1996 | Warner Bros. 46332-2-DJ | 40 |
| *(Promo-only packaging; silver foil package in black case)* | | | |
| **RADIO SHOWS** | | | |
| **Albums** | | | |
| BBC ROCK HOUR (Mar 82) Sammy Hagar | 1982 | London Wavelength | 15-25 |
| *(Music and interviews)* | | | |
| IN CONCERT HSAS Band | 1984 | Westwood One (2) | 20-40 |
| *(Live concert)* | | | |
| IN CONCERT Sammy Hagar | 1982 | Westwood One (2) | 25-50 |
| *(Live concert)* | | | |
| INSIDE TRACK (Mar 82) With Mick Jagger | 1982 | RKO (2) | 40-75 |
| *(Music and interviews)* | | | |
| INSIDE TRACK Eddie Van Halen, David Lee Roth | 1983 | RKO (3) | 40-75 |
| *(Music and interviews)* | | | |
| INSIDE TRACK (June 83) With Mick Jagger | 1983 | RKO (3) | 50-100 |
| *(Music and interviews)* | | | |
| LEGENDS OF ROCK | 1988 | NBC Radio (2) | 25-40 |
| *(Music and interviews)* | | | |
| MEMORIAL DAY PARTY (May 84) | 1984 | NBC Source (6) | 50-100 |
| *(Live concert; music and interviews)* | | | |
| OFF THE RECORD David Lee Roth | 1991 | Westwood One (2) | 15-25 |
| *(Music and interviews)* | | | |
| PROFILE '86 David Lee Roth | 1986 | NBC Radio (2) | 25-40 |
| *(Music and interviews)* | | | |
| SPECIAL ENCORE (May 83) | 1983 | NBC Source (3) | 25-50 |
| *(Music and interviews)* | | | |
| SUPERSTAR CONCERT (Dec 86) Van Halen/David Lee Roth | 1986 | Westwood One (3) | 50-100 |
| *(Live concert)* | | | |
| SUPERSTAR CONCERT Van Halen/Sammy Hagar | 1987 | Westwood One (3) | 30-60 |
| *(Live concert)* | | | |
| THANKSGIVING SPECIAL (Nov 84) | 1984 | NBC Source | 30-60 |
| *(Mostly music and interviews)* | | | |
| VAN HALEN HOLIDAY SPECTACULAR (Dec 83) | 1983 | NBC Source (3) | 50-100 |
| *(Rare box set concert)* | | | |
| **Compact Discs** | | | |
| ALBUM NETWORK SPECIAL (Oct 96) | 1996 | Album Network (2) | 100-150 |
| *(Live concert material)* | | | |
| IN CONCERT (Feb 95) Sammy Hagar | 1995 | Westwood One | 25-50 |
| *(Live concert)* | | | |
| IN THE STUDIO | 1988 | Album Network | 15-25 |
| *(Profile of an album, music and interviews)* | | | |
| OFF THE RECORD (Jan 94) | 1994 | Westwood One | 15-30 |
| *(Music and interviews)* | | | |
| OFF THE RECORD (Apr 94) David Lee Roth | 1994 | Westwood One | 10-20 |
| *(Music and interviews)* | | | |
| OFF THE RECORD (Mar 95) | 1995 | Westwood One | 15-20 |
| *(Music and interviews)* | | | |
| SUPERSTAR CONCERT (Feb 91) With others | 1991 | Westwood One (2) | 40-75 |
| *(Live concert with Robert Plant and Neil Young)* | | | |
| SUPERSTAR CONCERT (May 93) | 1993 | Westwood One (2) | 25-50 |
| *(Live concert)* | | | |
| SUPERSTAR CONCERT (Mar 94) | 1994 | Westwood One (2) | 30-60 |
| *(Live concert)* | | | |
| SUPERSTAR CONCERT (Aug 94) | 1994 | Westwood One (2) | 25-40 |
| *(Live concert)* | | | |
| SUPERSTAR CONERT (Mar 95) | 1995 | Westwood One (2) | 30-60 |
| *(Live concert)* | | | |
| UP CLOSE David Lee Roth | 1988 | Media America (2) | 25-50 |
| *(Mostly music and interviews)* | | | |
| UP CLOSE David Lee Roth | 1990 | Media America (3) | 45-75 |
| *(Music, interviews and live tracks)* | | | |
| UP CLOSE David Lee Roth | 1994 | Media America (2) | 25-50 |
| *(Mostly music and interviews)* | | | |
| UP CLOSE | 1995 | Media America (2) | 40-75 |
| *(Mostly music and interviews)* | | | |
| WESTWOOD ONE SPECIAL (Aug 93) | 1993 | Westwood One (3) | 50-100 |
| *(From "Standing on Top of the World")* | | | |
| **Reel-to-Reel Tapes** | | | |
| ALBUM NETWORK | 1994 | Premier Radio (2) | 40-75 |
| *(Special on two 10" reels)* | | | |

## VAN ZANT
### RADIO SHOWS

| Title | Yr | Label, Number | NM $ |
|---|---|---|---|
| **Albums** | | | |
| BBC ROCK HOUR (Aug 81) Live concert | 1981 | London Wavelength | 30-60 |
| *(With Mother's Finest)* | | | |
| IN CONCERT (June 82) Live concert | 1982 | Westwood One (2) | 40-75 |
| *(With Rossington Collins Band)* | | | |
| INSIDE TRACK (Apr 83) | 1983 | RKO (2) | 25-50 |
| *(Music and interviews, with Keith Richards)* | | | |
| KING BISCUIT FLOWER HOUR (Aug 81) Live concert | 1981 | DIR/ABC (2) | 40-75 |
| *(With Blackfoot)* | | | |

| Title | Yr | Label, Number | NM $ |
|-------|-----|---------------|------|
| KING BISCUIT FLOWER HOUR (June 82) Live concert | 1982 | DIR/ABC (2) | 50-100 |
| (With Pat Travers) | | | |
| KING BISCUIT FLOWER HOUR (June 85) Live concert | 1985 | DIR (2) | 40-75 |

## VANDENBERG
*Mercury promo 45s $4 each*
**RADIO SHOWS**
**Albums**

| | | | |
|-------|-----|---------------|------|
| IN CONCERT (Apr 83) Live concert | 1983 | Westwood One (2) | 30-50 |
| (With Blue Oyster Cult) | | | |

## VANDROSS, LUTHER
*Epic promo 45s $3 each; Epic promo picture sleeves $3 each; Epic promo CD singles $2-3 each*
**Compact Discs**

| | | | |
|-------|-----|---------------|------|
| COMMEMORATIVE NARM SAMPLER | 1993 | Epic ESM 5068 | 25 |
| (Promo-only for the National Association of Record Merchandisers; actually a mini-disc, not a regular CD) | | | |

**RADIO SHOWS**
**Albums**

| | | | |
|-------|-----|---------------|------|
| MILLER CONCERT (90s) Live concert | 199? | Miller Beer (4) | 150-250 |
| (Very rare concert, in two weekly parts) | | | |

## VANGELIS
*Polydor and RCA Victor promo 45s $3 each*
**Albums**

| | | | |
|-------|-----|---------------|------|
| THE VANGELIS RADIO SPECIAL | 1976 | RCA Victor DJL1-1849 | 200 |
| (Promo only, music and interviews) | | | |

## VANILLA FUDGE
*Atco promo 45s $8 each; Other Atco white promo label LPs $15 each*
**Albums**

| | | | |
|-------|-----|---------------|------|
| THE BEAT GOES ON | 1968 | Atco 237 | 30 |
| (White promo label) | | | |
| RENAISSANCE | 1968 | Atco 224 | 25 |
| (White promo label) | | | |
| VANILLA FUDGE | 1967 | Atco 224 | 50 |
| (White promo label) | | | |

**RADIO SHOWS**
**Albums**

| | | | |
|-------|-----|---------------|------|
| DESERT ISLAND DISCS (June 91) | 1991 | Westwood One | 20-35 |
| (Music and interviews) | | | |

## VANNELLI, GINO
*A&M and Arista promo 45s $3 each; Other A&M promo LPs $6 each*
**12-Inch Singles**

| | | | |
|-------|-----|---------------|------|
| BLACK CARS (Dance Mix) (LP Version) | 1985 | HME ZAS 2059 | 8 |
| WILD HORSES (same on both sides) | 1987 | CBS Associated ZAS 2663 | 8 |

**45s**

| | | | |
|-------|-----|---------------|------|
| WHAT'S IT ALL ABOUT (Jan 82) Public service show | 1982 | W.I.A.A. 610 | 15 |
| (Flip side features Billy Preston) | | | |

**Albums**

| | | | |
|-------|-----|---------------|------|
| BROTHER TO BROTHER RADIO SPECIAL | 1979 | A&M 17054 | 10 |
| (Promo only, music and interviews) | | | |

## VAPORS, THE
*United Artists and Liberty promo 45s $5*
**RADIO SHOWS**
**Albums**

| | | | |
|-------|-----|---------------|------|
| BBC ROCK HOUR (May 81) | 1981 | London Wavelength | 40-75 |
| (Live concert) | | | |

## VARIETEERS, THE
**45s**

| | | | |
|-------|-----|---------------|------|
| CALL MY GAL MISS JONES | 1954 | Hickory 1025 | 150 |
| (Yellow promo label) | | | |
| DEEP BLUES | 1953 | Hickory 1004 | 125 |
| (White promo label) | | | |
| IF YOU AND I COULD BE SWEETHEARTS | 1953 | Hickory 1014 | 250 |
| (White promo label) | | | |

## VAUGHAN, SARAH
*Mercury white promo label 45s $5-10 each*
**45s**

| | | | |
|-------|-----|---------------|------|
| FOOL ON THE HILL (same on both sides) | 1981 | Atlantic 3835 | 5 |
| (May be promo only) | | | |

**7-Inch Extended Plays**

| | | | |
|-------|-----|---------------|------|
| GREAT SONGS FROM HIT SHOWS | 1958 | Mercury 18A | 15 |
| (Promo-only EP with promo cover) | | | |

## VAUGHAN, STEVIE RAY
*Epic promo 45s $4 each; Other Epic promo 12" singles $10 each; Other Epic promo CD singles $6 each*
**12-Inch Singles**

| | | | |
|-------|-----|---------------|------|
| WILLIE THE WIMP | 1986 | Epic | 25 |
| (Promo-only 12-inch single with title cover) | | | |

| Title | Yr | Label, Number | NM $ |
|---|---|---|---|
| **Albums** | | | |
| INTERCHORDS | 1988 | Epic | 30 |
| *(Music and interviews)* | | | |
| **Compact Discs** | | | |
| FIRE MEETS FURY | 1989 | Epic ESK 1901 | 50 |
| *(Promo-only CD release with cover shaped like a Fender guitar)* | | | |
| IN THE BEGINNING | 1992 | Epic ESK 4822 | 25 |
| *(Promo-only CD release)* | | | |
| INTERCHORDS | 1992 | Epic ESK 4418 | 20 |
| *(Reissue of 1988 vinyl promo)* | | | |
| LITTLE WING | 1992 | Epic ESK 4435 | 10 |
| *(Promo CD single)* | | | |
| MADE IN TEXAS RADIO HOUR (Sept 95) | 1995 | | 75-125 |
| *(Tribute to Stevie Ray from various friends, distributed only to radio stations in Texas)* | | | |
| OCTOBER 3, 1954-AUGUST 27, 1990 | 1990 | Epic ESK 2221 | 40 |
| *(Promo-only sampler)* | | | |
| TIMOTHY WHITE SESSIONS (Aug 96) | 1996 | (2) | 100-150 |
| *("In Step with Stevie Ray Vaughan," rerun of 1990 vinyl show)* | | | |
| WALL OF DENIAL | 199? | Epic | 25 |
| *(Promo-only release with four tracks)* | | | |
| **RADIO SHOWS** | | | |
| **Albums** | | | |
| IN CONCERT (Aug 84) Live concert | 1984 | Westwood One (2) | 75-125 |
| *(With Twisted Sister)* | | | |
| IN CONCERT (Jan 87) Live concert | 1987 | Westwood One (2) | 100-175 |
| *(With Lone Justice)* | | | |
| IN CONCERT (Oct 87) Live concert | 1987 | Westwood One (2) | 75-125 |
| *(With Steppenwolf)* | | | |
| KING BISCUIT FLOWER HOUR (Nov 83) Live concert | 1983 | DIR/ABC (2) | 50-100 |
| *(With the Red Rockers)* | | | |
| KING BISCUIT FLOWER HOUR (Dec 84) Live concert | 1984 | DIR/ABC (2) | 75-125 |
| *(With Jon Butcher Axis)* | | | |
| KING BISCUIT FLOWER HOUR (Aug 85) Live concert | 1985 | DIR (2) | 50-100 |
| *(With George Thorogood)* | | | |
| KING BISCUIT FLOWER HOUR (Mar 87) Live concert | 1987 | DIR (2) | 50-100 |
| *(With the Fabulous Thunderbirds)* | | | |
| OFF THE RECORD (Jan 90) | 1990 | Westwood One (2) | 15-25 |
| *(Music and interviews)* | | | |
| SUPERSTAR CONCERT (Sept 90) | 1990 | Westwood One (3) | 30-60 |
| *(Live concert, box set, repeated)* | | | |
| TIMOTHY WHITE ROCK STARS (Mar 90) | 1990 | Westwood One (2) | 100-150 |
| *(Rare live concert)* | | | |
| **Compact Discs** | | | |
| IN THE STUDIO (June 93) Profile of an album | 1993 | Album Network (2) | 50-100 |
| *(Double shows, "Best of Vaughan")* | | | |
| KING BISCUIT FLOWER HOUR (Jan 89) | 1989 | DIR | 40-75 |
| *(Live concert)* | | | |
| KING BISCUIT FLOWER HOUR (Apr 90) | 1990 | DIR | 40-80 |
| *(Live concert)* | | | |
| KING BISCUIT FLOWER HOUR (June 93) | 1993 | DIR | 40-60 |
| *(Live concert)* | | | |
| ROCK STARS (Mar 90) | 1990 | Radio Today (2) | 100-150 |
| *(Rare live concert)* | | | |
| SUPERSTAR CONCERT (Apr 93) | 1993 | Westwood One (2) | 40-80 |
| *(Live concert, repeated)* | | | |
| TIMOTHY WHITE SESSIONS (Sept 90) | 1990 | Westwood One (2) | 45-90 |
| *(Music and interviews)* | | | |
| UP CLOSE Profile | 1991 | Media America (2) | 50-100 |
| *(Music and interviews with some live tracks)* | | | |

## VAUGHN, BILLY

**45s**

| Title | Yr | Label, Number | NM $ |
|---|---|---|---|
| WHEELS | 1961 | Dot 1530 | 12 |
| *(Stereo 33 rpm 7" single, small center hole)* | | | |

## VEE, BOBBY

*Also recorded as Robert Thomas Velline; Other Liberty promo 45s $8-10 each; United Artists promo 45s by Robert Thomas Velline $8 each; United Artists promo 45s by Bobby Vee $6 each; Shady Brook white promo label 45s $5 each (Disco records); Other Liberty promo label LPs $20-25 each*

**45s**

| Title | Yr | Label, Number | NM $ |
|---|---|---|---|
| BE TRUE TO YOURSELF | 1963 | Liberty 55581 | 10 |
| *(Cream colored promo label)* | | | |
| CHARMS | 1963 | Liberty 55530 | 12 |
| *(Cream colored promo label)* | | | |
| CHRISTMAS VACATION | 1962 | Liberty 55517 | 35 |
| *(Cream colored promo label)* | | | |
| COME BACK WHEN YOU GROW UP | 1967 | Liberty 55964 | 150 |
| *(Stereo 7" single with small center hole)* | | | |
| DEVIL OR ANGEL | 1960 | Liberty 55270 | 25 |
| *(White promo label)* | | | |
| ELECTRIC TRAINS AND YOU | 1970 | Liberty 56149 | 12 |
| *(Black promo label, Christmas song)* | | | |
| FAKER, FAKER  The Eligibles | 1959 | Capitol 4265 | 25 |
| *(Red promo label, they later recorded with Bobby Vee)* | | | |
| HOW MANY TEARS | 1961 | Liberty 55325 | 25 |
| *(Cream colored promo label)* | | | |
| HOW MANY TEARS | 1961 | Liberty 3331 | 50 |
| *(Compact 33 single, common for jukeboxes)* | | | |

| Title | Yr | Label, Number | NM $ |
|---|---|---|---|
| MIND READER/CARD SHARK  The Strangers | 1963 | Liberty 55550 | 50 |
| *(Cream colored promo label, without Bobby, with his brother Bill)* | | | |
| NEVER LOVE A ROBIN | 1963 | Liberty 55636 | 10 |
| *(Cream colored promo label)* | | | |
| THE NIGHT HAS A THOUSAND EYES | 1962 | Liberty 55521 | 15 |
| *(Cream colored promo label)* | | | |
| ONE LAST KISS | 1960 | Liberty 55251 | 30 |
| *(Liberty promo label)* | | | |
| PLEASE DON'T ASK ABOUT BARBARA | 1962 | Liberty 55419 | 20 |
| *(Cream colored promo label)* | | | |
| PUNISH HER | 1962 | Liberty 55479 | 25 |
| *(Cream colored promo label)* | | | |
| RUBBER BALL | 1960 | Liberty 55287 | 25 |
| *(White promo label)* | | | |
| RUN TO HIM | 1961 | Liberty 55388 | 25 |
| *(Cream colored promo label)* | | | |
| SHARING YOU | 1962 | Liberty 55451 | 18 |
| *(Cream colored promo label)* | | | |
| STAYIN' IN | 1961 | Liberty 55296 | 25 |
| *(White promo label)* | | | |
| STRANGER IN YOUR ARMS | 1964 | Liberty 55654 | 10 |
| *(Cream colored promo label)* | | | |
| SUZIE BABY | 1959 | Liberty 55208 | 75 |
| *(White promo label)* | | | |
| TAKE GOOD CARE OF MY BABY | 1961 | Liberty 55354 | 30 |
| *(Cream colored promo label)* | | | |
| TOY SOLDIER  The Strangers | 1962 | Liberty 55481 | 50 |
| *(Cream colored promo label, without Bobby, with his brother Bill)* | | | |
| WHAT DO YOU WANT? | 1960 | Liberty 55234 | 75 |
| *(White promo label, very hard to find)* | | | |
| WHERE IS SHE?  With the Eligibles | 1964 | Liberty 55726 | 15 |
| *(Cream colored promo label)* | | | |
| **7-Inch Extended Plays** | | | |
| ROBERT THOMAS VELLINE | 1972 | United Artists 85 | 40 |
| *(Promo-only interview record)* | | | |
| **Albums** | | | |
| BOBBY VEE | 1960 | Liberty 3181 | 60 |
| *(White promo label, audition record)* | | | |
| BOBBY VEE MEETS THE CRICKETS | 1962 | Liberty 3228 | 50 |
| *(White promo label, audition record)* | | | |
| BOBBY VEE MEETS THE VENTURES | 1963 | Liberty 3289 | 75 |
| *(White promo label)* | | | |
| A BOBBY VEE RECORDING SESSION | 1962 | Liberty 3232 | 35 |
| *(White promo label, audition record)* | | | |
| BOBBY VEE SINGS HITS OF THE ROCKIN' 50'S | 1961 | Liberty 3205 | 40 |
| *(White promo label, audition record)* | | | |
| BOBBY VEE SINGS YOUR FAVORITES | 1960 | Liberty 3165 | 75 |
| *(White promo label, audition record)* | | | |
| BOBBY VEE WITH STRINGS AND THINGS | 1961 | Liberty 3186 | 50 |
| *(White promo label, audition record)* | | | |
| BOBBY VEE'S GOLDEN GREATS | 1962 | Liberty 3245 | 30 |
| *(White promo label, audition record)* | | | |
| MERRY CHRISTMAS FROM BOBBY VEE | 1962 | Liberty 3267 | 50 |
| *(White promo label, audition record)* | | | |
| TAKE GOOD CARE OF MY BABY | 1961 | Liberty 3211 | 40 |
| *(White promo label, audition record)* | | | |
| TEENSVILLE!  Various artists | 1961 | Liberty 5503 | 25 |
| *(White promo label, audition record, Bobby Vee sings three songs, "$1.49 special price" sticker on cover)* | | | |
| **RADIO SHOWS** | | | |
| **Albums** | | | |
| ROCK, ROLL & REMEMBER (80s) Various artists | 198? | United Stations (4) | 25 |
| *(Four-hour oldies show with Dick Clark features many Bobby Vee interviews and music segments; several episodes of this show feature Bobby Vee)* | | | |

## VEGA, SUZANNE
*Other A&M promo 45s $3 each; A&M promo 12" singles $8 each; A&M promo CD singles $3 each*

| | | | |
|---|---|---|---|
| **45s** | | | |
| GYPSY | 1987 | A&M 2988 | 50 |
| *(Promo record and promo-only sleeve)* | | | |
| **Albums** | | | |
| RADIO SPECIAL | 1987 | A&M 17472 | 25 |
| *(Music and interviews)* | | | |
| **RADIO SHOWS** | | | |
| **Compact Discs** | | | |
| IN CONCERT-NU ROCK | 1994 | Westwood One | 50-100 |
| *(Live concert)* | | | |
| KING BISCUIT FLOWER HOUR | 1987 | DIR | 75-150 |
| *(Live concert)* | | | |

## VELVET UNDERGROUND, THE
*Includes Lou Reed, Jades, Primitives, Nico*

| | | | |
|---|---|---|---|
| **12-Inch Singles** | | | |
| FOGGY NOTION | 1985 | Polydor 349 | 15 |
| *(Promo-only 12" single)* | | | |
| **45s** | | | |
| ALL TOMORROW'S PARTIES  With Nico | 1966 | Verve 10427 | 7,500 |
| *(Light blue promo label, most of the listed value is for the promo picture sleeve; only a few copies known. The promo record only is worth $150)* | | | |
| LOOP | 1966 | Aspen Magazine | 200 |
| *(Flexi-disc from a magazine)* | | | |

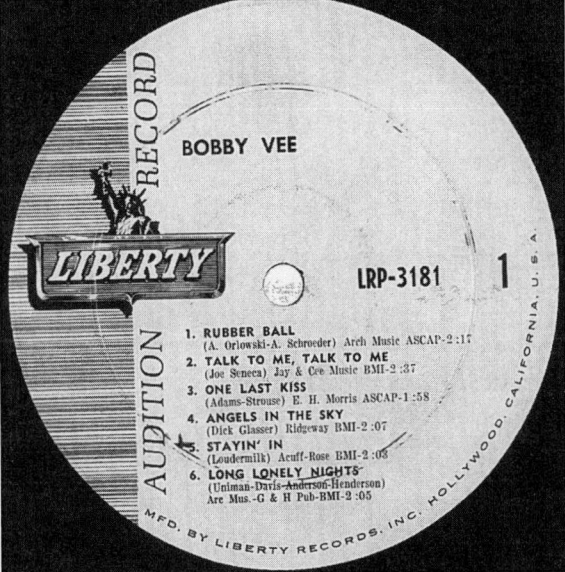

(Top row) It may seem odd today, but on Stevie Ray Vaughan's early appearances on the King Biscuit Flower Hour, he was billed under other acts. The 1985 show also featured George Thorogood, and in 1987, he was featured with his brother Jimmie's band, The Fabulous Thunderbirds. (Middle row) Here are the cover and label of a rare promo album, Bobby Vee's second. Notice that the front cover has no promo markings on it whatsoever; you have to look at the label to discover it's a promo! (Bottom left) Suzanne Vega got onto the King Biscuit Flower Hour in 1987, in the wake of her biggest hit single, "Luka." (Bottom right) Not as rare as promos on Verve, but still tough to find, here is a Mercury promo of a post-breakup Velvet Underground live album.

| Title | Yr | Label, Number | NM $ |
|---|---|---|---|
| THE OSTRICH  The Primitives | 1964 | Pickwick 1001 | 100 |
| *(Black promo label)* | | | |
| SUNDAY MORNING  With Nico | 1966 | Verve 10466 | 250 |
| *(Light blue promo label)* | | | |
| VELVET UNDERGROUND RADIO SPOT | 1969 | MGM 1 | 2,500 |
| *(Radio spots with promo-only picture sleeve)* | | | |
| WHAT GOES ON? | 1969 | MGM 14057 | 200 |
| *(MGM promo-only release)* | | | |
| WHITE LIGHT, WHITE HEAT | 1968 | Verve 10560 | 250 |
| *(Light blue promo label, flip side is "Here She Comes Now")* | | | |
| WHITE LIGHT, WHITE HEAT | 1968 | Verve 10560 | 300 |
| *(Light blue promo label, flip side is "I Heard Her Call My Name" )* | | | |
| WHO LOVES THE SUN? | 1971 | Cotillion 44107 | 200 |
| *(White promo label)* | | | |
| **Albums** | | | |
| CHELSEA GIRL  Nico | 1967 | Verve 5032 | 50 |
| *(Yellow promo label)* | | | |
| DESERT SHORE  Nico | 1972 | Reprise 6424 | 25 |
| *(White promo label)* | | | |
| LIVE 1969 | 1972 | Mercury 7504 (2) | 40 |
| *(White promo labels)* | | | |
| LIVE AT MAX'S KANSAS CITY | 1972 | Cotillion 9500 | 75 |
| *(White promo label)* | | | |
| LOADED | 1970 | Cotillion SD 9034 | 75 |
| *(White promo label)* | | | |
| THE MARBLE INDEX  Nico | 1968 | Elektra 74029 | 25 |
| *(White promo label)* | | | |
| THE VELVET UNDERGROUND | 1969 | MGM SE-4617 | 250 |
| *(Yellow promo label)* | | | |
| THE VELVET UNDERGROUND AND NICO | 1967 | Verve 5008 | 300 |
| *(Yellow promo label)* | | | |
| WHITE LIGHT, WHITE HEAT | 1967 | Verve 5046 | 300 |
| *(White promo label)* | | | |
| WHITE LIGHT, WHITE HEAT | 1967 | Verve 5046 | 250 |
| *(Yellow promo label)* | | | |

## VELVETONES, THE

**45s**

| Title | Yr | Label, Number | NM $ |
|---|---|---|---|
| GLORY OF LOVE | 1957 | Aladdin 3372 | 150 |
| *(White promo label)* | | | |
| HOW I MISS YOU | 1964 | Columbia 43031 | 250 |
| *(White promo label)* | | | |
| I FOUND MY LOVE | 1957 | Aladdin 3391 | 150 |
| *(White promo label)* | | | |
| MY EVERY THOUGHT | 1959 | Aladdin 3463 | 100 |
| *(White promo label)* | | | |

## VENTURES, THE

*Other Dolton cream colored promo label 45s $8-10 each; Other Liberty promo 45s $4 each; United Artists promo 45s $3 each; Dolton and Liberty white promo label LPs $25 each; United Artists promo LPs $15 each*

**45s**

| Title | Yr | Label, Number | NM $ |
|---|---|---|---|
| BLUE MOON | 1961 | Dolton 47 | 15 |
| *(Dolton promo label)* | | | |
| DELILAH | 1970 | Liberty 56213 | 25 |
| *(One-sided promo-only release)* | | | |
| LULLABY OF THE LEAVES | 1961 | Dolton 41 | 25 |
| *(Dolton promo label)* | | | |
| PERFIDIA | 1960 | Dolton 28 | 25 |
| *(White promo label)* | | | |
| RAM-BUNK-SHUSH | 1961 | Dolton 32 | 25 |
| *(White promo label)* | | | |
| RUDOLF THE RED-NOSED REINDEER/DEPRESSION | 1994 | EMI SPRO 19949 | 10 |
| *(B-side by Johnny and the Dwellers, with sleeve)* | | | |
| SILVER CITY | 1961 | Dolton 44 | 20 |
| *(Dolton promo label)* | | | |
| WALK DON'T RUN | 1960 | Dolton 25 | 30 |
| *(White promo label)* | | | |
| **7-Inch Extended Plays** | | | |
| THE HORSE | 1967 | Liberty TV-1 | 40 |
| *(Radio spots from the record label)* | | | |

## VERLAINE, TOM

**12-Inch Singles**

| Title | Yr | Label, Number | NM $ |
|---|---|---|---|
| A TOWN CALLED WALKER/MARQUEE MOON (LIVE) | 1987 | I.R.S. 17369 | 10 |

## VERVE PIPE, THE

*RCA promo CD singles $3 each*

**RADIO SHOWS**

**Compact Discs**

| Title | Yr | Label, Number | NM $ |
|---|---|---|---|
| ALBUM NETWORK SPECIAL (Oct 96) | 1996 | | 25-50 |
| *(Live concert material)* | | | |

## VETTES, THE

*Bruce Johnston*

**45s**

| Title | Yr | Label, Number | NM $ |
|---|---|---|---|
| LITTLE FORD RAGTOP | 1963 | MGM 13186 | 25 |
| *(Yellow promo label)* | | | |

| Title | Yr | Label, Number | NM $ |
|---|---|---|---|
| **VICE-ROYS, THE** | | | |
| **45s** | | | |
| PLEASE, BABY, PLEASE | 1955 | Aladdin 3273 | 75 |
| (White promo label) | | | |
| | | | |
| **VICIOUS, SID** | | | |
| *Of the Sex Pistols* | | | |
| **RADIO SHOWS** | | | |
| **Albums** | | | |
| BBC TRANSCRIPTION DISC | 1993 | BBC Transcription | 600-900 |
| (With Elvis Presley) | | | |
| | | | |
| **VILLAGE PEOPLE** | | | |
| *Casablanca promo 45s $3 each; Other Casablanca promo 12" singles $6 each* | | | |
| **12-Inch Singles** | | | |
| IN THE NAVY | 1979 | Casablanca 20155 | 10 |
| (Promo 12" single 6:21 version issued with a hard promo cover) | | | |
| Y.M.C.A. | 1978 | Casablanca 20144 | 15 |
| (Promo 12" single 6:47 version with "Macho Man" the 5:18 version) | | | |
| **RADIO SHOWS** | | | |
| **Albums** | | | |
| ROBERT W. MORGAN (80s) Profile | 198? | Watermark | 40-75 |
| (Music and interviews) | | | |
| | | | |
| **VINCENT, GENE** | | | |
| *And His Blue Caps* | | | |
| **45s** | | | |
| B-I-BICKEY-BI-BO-BO-GO | 1957 | Capitol 3678 | 25 |
| (Capitol promo label) | | | |
| BABY BLUE | 1958 | Capitol 3959 | 40 |
| (White promo label) | | | |
| BE-BOP-A-LULA | 1956 | Capitol 3450 | 75 |
| (Yellow promo label) | | | |
| BIRD DOGGIN' | 1966 | Challenge 59337 | 25 |
| (White promo label) | | | |
| BLUEJEAN BOP | 1956 | Capitol 3558 | 30 |
| (Yellow promo label) | | | |
| BORN TO BE A ROLLING STONE | 1967 | Challenge 59365 | 25 |
| (White promo label) | | | |
| CRAZY LEGS | 1957 | Capitol 3617 | 25 |
| (Capitol promo label) | | | |
| DANCE TO THE BOP | 1957 | Capitol 3839 | 25 |
| (White promo label) | | | |
| THE DAY THE WORLD TURNED BLUE | 1971 | Kama Sutra 518 | 10 |
| (Colored promo label) | | | |
| GIT IT | 1958 | Capitol 4051 | 40 |
| (White promo label) | | | |
| LONELY STREET | 1966 | Challenge 59347 | 25 |
| (White promo label) | | | |
| LOTTA LOVIN' | 1957 | Capitol 3763 | 25 |
| (Capitol promo label) | | | |
| LUCKY STAR | 1961 | Capitol 4665 | 30 |
| (Red promo label) | | | |
| MISTER LONELINESS | 1961 | Capitol 4525 | 30 |
| (Red promo label) | | | |
| PISTOL PACKIN' MAMA | 1960 | Capitol 4442 | 45 |
| (Red promo label) | | | |
| RACE WITH THE DEVIL | 1956 | Capitol 3530 | 40 |
| (Yellow promo label) | | | |
| RIGHT NOW | 1959 | Capitol 4237 | 50 |
| (Capitol promo label, stock picture sleeve is one of the most in demand of collectors, worth over $2,000) | | | |
| SAY MAMA | 1959 | Capitol 4105 | 40 |
| (White promo label) | | | |
| SUNSHINE | 1971 | Kama Sutra 514 | 12 |
| (Colored promo label) | | | |
| WALKIN' HOME FROM SCHOOL | 1958 | Capitol 3874 | 30 |
| (White promo label) | | | |
| WHO'S PUSHIN' YOUR SWING? | 1959 | Capitol 4153 | 50 |
| (Capitol promo label) | | | |
| WILD CAT | 1960 | Capitol 4313 | 50 |
| (Red promo label) | | | |
| YES, I LOVE YOU BABY | 1958 | Capitol 4010 | 40 |
| (White promo label) | | | |
| **7-Inch Extended Plays** | | | |
| DANCE TO THE BOP | 1958 | Capitol PRO 438 | 400 |
| (Released as a promo only with no EP sleeve) | | | |
| HOT ROD GANG | 1958 | Capitol PRO-985 | 600 |
| (Must have the "P" prefix to be the promo version; the stock copy is very rare and is Capitol EAP 1-985.) | | | |
| **78s** | | | |
| B-I-BICKEY-BI-BO-BO-GO | 1957 | Capitol 3678 | 250 |
| (Capitol promo label) | | | |
| BE-BOP-A-LULA | 1956 | Capitol 3450 | 250 |
| (Capitol promo label) | | | |
| BLUEJEAN BOP | 1956 | Capitol 3558 | 150 |
| (Capitol promo label) | | | |
| CRAZY LEGS | 1957 | Capitol 3617 | 150 |
| (Capitol promo label) | | | |

| Title | Yr | Label, Number | NM $ |
|-------|----|----|------|
| LOTTA LOVIN' | 1957 | Capitol 3763 | 300 |
| (Capitol promo label) | | | |
| RACE WITH THE DEVIL | 1956 | Capitol 3530 | 200 |
| (Capitol promo label) | | | |
| **Albums** | | | |
| BLUEJEAN BOP | 1957 | Capitol 764 | 400 |
| (Yellow promo label) | | | |
| CRAZY TIMES | 1960 | Capitol 1342 | 300 |
| (Blue promo label) | | | |
| GENE VINCENT & HIS BLUE CAPS | 1957 | Capitol 811 | 350 |
| (Yellow promo label) | | | |
| A GENE VINCENT RECORD DATE | 1958 | Capitol 1059 | 300 |
| (Blue promo label) | | | |
| GENE VINCENT ROCKS & THE BLUE CAPS ROLL | 1958 | Capitol 970 | 300 |
| (Yellow promo label) | | | |
| SOUNDS LIKE GENE VINCENT | 1959 | Capitol 1207 | 300 |
| (Blue promo label) | | | |

## VINCENT, VINNIE, INVASION
**45s**

| ARE YOU READY TO ROCK | 1986 | Chrysalis VS7 42447-1 | 12 |
|-------|----|----|------|
| (Pink vinyl, small hole, with promo sleeve) | | | |

## VINEGAR JOE
*See Robert Palmer*
**RADIO SHOWS**
**Albums**

| BBC TRANSCRIPTION DISC | 1973 | BBC Transcription | 300-400 |
|-------|----|----|------|
| (Live concert) | | | |

## VINTON, BOBBY
*Other Epic promo 45s $2-4 each; ABC promo 45s $3 each; Tapestry promo 45s $2 each; Epic white promo label LPs $12-15 each*
**45s**

| BLUE ON BLUE | 1963 | Epic 9593 | 25 |
|-------|----|----|------|
| (Blue vinyl, white promo label) | | | |
| CLINGING VINE | 1964 | Epic 9705 | 25 |
| (Red vinyl, white promo label) | | | |
| CORRINA, CORRINA | 1961 | Epic 9440 | 12 |
| (White promo label) | | | |
| HIP-SWINGING, HIGH STEPPING DRUM MAJORETTE | 1962 | Epic 9469 | 12 |
| (White promo label) | | | |
| I LOVE YOU THE WAY YOU ARE | 1962 | Diamond 121 | 20 |
| (Green/black promo label) | | | |
| MR. LONELY | 1964 | Epic 9730 | 25 |
| (Red vinyl, white promo label, black print, same song on each side) | | | |
| MR. LONELY | 1964 | Epic 9730 | 30 |
| (Red vinyl, red print, flip is "Dearest Santa") | | | |
| NEVER ENDING SONG OF LOVE | 1974 | ABC SPDJ-21 | 10 |
| (White promo label, for jukeboxes only) | | | |
| ROSES ARE RED | 1962 | Epic 9509 | 10 |
| (White promo label, stock picture sleeve worth $15) | | | |
| SATIN PILLOWS | 1965 | Epic 9869 | 25 |
| (Red vinyl, white promo label) | | | |
| THE SHEIK | 1960 | Alpine 59 | 30 |
| (White promo label) | | | |
| TORNADO | 1961 | Epic 9417 | 10 |
| (White promo label) | | | |
| WHAT'S IT ALL ABOUT (July 75) Public service show | 1975 | W.I.A.A. 271 | 20 |
| (Elton John on the flip side) | | | |
| WHAT'S IT ALL ABOUT (Sept 82) Public service show | 1982 | W.I.A.A. 638 | 12 |
| (Flip side features Paul Williams) | | | |
| YOU'LL NEVER FORGET | 1959 | Alpine 50 | 40 |
| (White promo label) | | | |
| **7-Inch Extended Plays** | | | |
| DANCING AT THE HOP | 1961 | Epic ZEP 51016/7 | 30 |
| (Promo-only EP with six tracks from first LP) | | | |
| MELODIES OF LOVE | 1974 | ABC PRO-851 (LLP 271) | 10 |
| (Jukebox LLP issued with a paper cover) | | | |
| MERRY CHRISTMAS | 1964 | Epic 7215 | 15 |
| (White promo label, issued with a paper gatefold picture cover) | | | |
| PLEASE LOVE ME FOREVER | 1971 | Epic 26341 | 10 |
| (Jukebox LLP issued with a soft cover) | | | |
| SEALED WITH A KISS | 1970 | Epic 31642 | 12 |
| (Jukebox LLP issued with a hard cover) | | | |

## VIOLENT FEMMES
*Any promo CD single $4-6 each*
**12-Inch Singles**

| CHILDREN OF THE REVOLUTION (edit) (LP) | 1986 | Warner Bros. PRO-A-2422 | 20 |
|-------|----|----|------|
| CHILDREN OF THE REVOLUTION (edit) (LP) | 1986 | Slash PRO-A-2422 | 6 |
| NIGHTMARES/WORLD WE'RE LIVING IN | 1989 | Slash PRO-A-3411 | 10 |
| **Albums** | | | |
| 3 ON 3 | 1989 | Warner Bros. PRO-A-3519 | 25 |
| (Promo-only music and interviews) | | | |

| Title | Yr | Label, Number | NM $ |
|-------|-----|---------------|------|

**RADIO SHOWS**
**Albums**

| IN CONCERT-NU ROCK (Sept 94) | 1994 | Westwood One | 50-75 |
|---|---|---|---|

*(Live concert)*

**VISAGE**
**12-Inch Singles**

| DAMNED DON'T CRY/HORSEMAN/NIGHT TRAIN | 1982 | Polydor 178 | 10 |
|---|---|---|---|
| NIGHT TRAIN (2 versions)/I'M STILL SEARCHING | 1982 | Polydor 521 | 10 |

**VIXEN**
*Other EMI/Manhattan promo CD singles $3-5 each*
**Compact Discs**

| HOW MUCH LOVE | 1990 | EMI DPRO-4541 | 10 |
|---|---|---|---|

*(Promo CD single in case with flashing lights)*

| REV IT UP | 1990 | EMI CDP 92923 (2) | 40 |
|---|---|---|---|

*(Promo-only package has two copies of the CD in a rubber tire)*

**VOCAL TONES/VOCALTONES, THE**
**45s**

| DARLING | 1956 | Apollo 492 | 75 |
|---|---|---|---|

*(White promo label)*

| MY GIRL | 1955 | Apollo 488 | 75 |
|---|---|---|---|

*(White promo label)*

| MY VERSION OF LOVE | 1956 | Apollo 497 | 75 |
|---|---|---|---|

*(White promo label)*

**VOGUES, THE**
*Co and Ce promo 45s $8 each; Reprise promo 45s $4 each*
**45s**

| PLEASE MR. SUN | 1966 | Co & Ce 240 | 20 |
|---|---|---|---|

*(White label promo, B side blank)*
**7-Inch Extended Plays**

| MEMORIES   Jukebox LLP | 1970 | Reprise 6347 | 10 |
|---|---|---|---|

*(Issued with a paper cover)*

**VOLZ, GREG X.**
**45s**

| HARK THE HERALD ANGELS SING | 1987 | (no label) 20738 | 4 |
|---|---|---|---|

# W

**WADE, ADAM**
*Coed promo 45s $12 each; Epic promo 45s $8 each; Epic promo LPs $15 each*

**WAILERS, THE**
**45s**

| HOT LOVE | 1954 | Columbia 40288 | 100 |
|---|---|---|---|

*(White promo label)*

**WAITE, JOHN**
*EMI promo 45s $3 each More at The Babys*
**RADIO SHOWS**
**Albums**

| KING BISCUIT FLOWER HOUR (Aug 85) Live concert | 1985 | DIR (2) | 25-50 |
|---|---|---|---|

*(With "X")*

| OFF THE RECORD (80s) | 198? | Westwood One (2) | 10-20 |
|---|---|---|---|

*(Music and interviews)*

| ROCK CLOCK   Various live tracks | 1987 | DIR (2) | 25-40 |
|---|---|---|---|

*(With Moody Blues and Alice Cooper)*

| SUPERSTAR CONCERT (July 85) Live concert | 1985 | Westwood One (3) | 40-75 |
|---|---|---|---|

*(With Survivor)*

| SUPERSTAR CONCERT (Nov 85) Live concert | 1985 | Westwood One (3) | 25-50 |
|---|---|---|---|

*(With the Fixx)*

**WAITRESSES, THE**
**12-Inch Singles**

| BREAD AND BUTTER (Remix)/(Dub) | 1983 | Polydor PRO 196 | 7 |
|---|---|---|---|
| BRUISEOLOGY/MAKE THE WEATHER | 1983 | Polydor 203 | 7 |
| I KNOW WHAT BOYS LIKE/NO GUILT | 1982 | Polydor PRO 179 | 8 |

**45s**

| CHRISTMAS WRAPPING (same on both sides) | 1981 | Polydor PRO ??? | 20 |
|---|---|---|---|

*(Stock copy does not exist on Polydor)*
**Albums**

| BRUISEOLOGY | 1983 | Polydor 810 980-1 | 25 |
|---|---|---|---|

*(Promo only on purpleish vinyl)*

**WALKER, JERRY JEFF**
*Atco and MCA promo 45s $3 each*
**45s**

| WHAT'S IT ALL ABOUT (Apr 81) Public service show | 1981 | W.I.A.A. 572 | 15 |
|---|---|---|---|

*(REO Speedwagon on flip side)*

| Title | Yr | Label, Number | NM $ |
|---|---|---|---|
| **Albums** | | | |
| FIVE YEARS GONE  White promo label | 1969 | Atco 297 | 30 |
| **RADIO SHOWS** | | | |
| **Albums** | | | |
| AMERICAN EAGLE | 1981 | DIR (3) | 50-100 |
| *(Live concert)* | | | |
| COUNTRY COOKIN' (Jan 76) Various artists | 1976 | U.S. Army Reserve (2) | 25-50 |
| *(Walker is host of a music and interview show)* | | | |
| LIVE AT GILLEY'S (Feb 85) | 1985 | Westwood One | 50-100 |
| *(Live concert)* | | | |

### WALKER, WAYNE
**45s**

| Title | Yr | Label, Number | NM $ |
|---|---|---|---|
| ALL I CAN DO IS CRY | 195? | ABC-Paramount 9735 | 40 |
| *(White promo label)* | | | |

### WALL OF VOODOO
*IRS promo 45s $5 each Featuring Stan Ridgway*
**12-Inch Singles**

| Title | Yr | Label, Number | NM $ |
|---|---|---|---|
| CAMOUFLAGE  Stan Ridgway | 1986 | MCA 17142 | 10 |
| *(Promo-only 12" single with picture cover)* | | | |
| FAR SIDE OF CRAZY (same on both sides) | 1985 | I.R.S. 17051 | 6 |
| **45s** | | | |
| MEXICAN RADIO (Stereo)/(Mono) | 1982 | I.R.S. 70963 | 4 |
| *(Promo-only number)* | | | |
| **RADIO SHOWS** | | | |
| **Albums** | | | |
| BBC COLLEGE CONCERT HOUR (Feb 83) | 1983 | London Wavelength | 25-50 |
| *(Live concert)* | | | |

### WALSH, JOE
*Of the James Gang and the Eagles; ABC promo 45s $4 each; Asylum promo 45s $3 each*
**12-Inch Singles**

| Title | Yr | Label, Number | NM $ |
|---|---|---|---|
| GOOD MAN DOWN (same on both sides) | 1985 | Warner Bros. PRO-A-2340 | 5 |
| MALIBU (same on both sides) | 1985 | Warner Bros. PRO-A-2833 | 5 |
| RADIO SONG (same on both sides) | 1985 | Warner Bros. PRO-A-2756 | 5 |
| SPACE AGE WHIZ KIDS (same on both sides) | 1983 | Warner Bros. PRO-A-2038 | 6 |
| TURN TO STONE (same on both sides) | 1978 | ABC SPDJ-46 | 20 |
| **RADIO SHOWS** | | | |
| **Albums** | | | |
| IN CONCERT (Dec 86) Live concert | 1986 | Westwood One (2) | 25-50 |
| *(With the Outlaws)* | | | |
| KING BISCUIT FLOWER HOUR (Nov 81) | 1981 | DIR/ABC (2) | 40-75 |
| *(Live concert)* | | | |
| KING BISCUIT FLOWER HOUR (Apr 82) | 1982 | DIR/ABC (2) | 40-60 |
| *(Live concert, repeated)* | | | |
| KING BISCUIT FLOWER HOUR | 1985 | DIR (2) | 25-50 |
| *(Live concert, repeated)* | | | |
| LEGENDS OF ROCK (Oct 88) | 1988 | NBC Radio (2) | 20-35 |
| *(Music and interviews)* | | | |
| NBC SOURCE (July 83) | 1983 | NBC Radio (2) | 20-40 |
| *(Mostly music and interviews)* | | | |
| OFF THE RECORD | 1991 | Westwood One (2) | 10-20 |
| *(Music and interviews)* | | | |
| SOURCE CONCERT (Dec 83) | 1983 | NBC Radio (2) | 40-75 |
| *(Live concert)* | | | |
| SUPERSTAR CONCERT (Jan 92) | 1992 | Westwood One (3) | 25-50 |
| *(Live concert, box set, repeated)* | | | |
| **Compact Discs** | | | |
| BBC CLASSIC TRACKS (July 94) | 1994 | Westwood One | 15-25 |
| *(Various live classic tracks)* | | | |
| IN CONCERT (Aug 94) | 1994 | Westwood One | 20-40 |
| *(Live concert, repeated)* | | | |
| IN THE STUDIO (90s) Profile of an album | 199? | Album Network | 15-25 |
| *(Music and interviews)* | | | |
| KING BISCUIT FLOWER HOUR (July 88) | 1988 | DIR | 20-40 |
| *(Live concert, repeated)* | | | |

### WANG CHUNG
*Geffen promo 45s $3 each; Other Geffen promo 12" singles $6 each*
**12-Inch Singles**

| Title | Yr | Label, Number | NM $ |
|---|---|---|---|
| CHINA/TI NA NA | 1982 | Arista SP-143 | 10 |
| *(As "Huang Chung")* | | | |
| DANCE HALL DAYS/TO LIVE AND DIE IN L.A. (edit) | 1986 | Geffen PRO-A-2582 | 12 |
| EVERYBODY HAVE FUN TONIGHT (edit) | | | |
| DON'T BE MY ENEMY (LP)/(Edit Remix) | 1984 | Geffen PRO-A-2205 | 6 |
| DON'T LET GO/WAIT/DANCE HALL DAYS | 1983 | Geffen PRO-A-2108 | 6 |
| EVERYBODY HAVE FUN TONIGHT (2 mixes) | 1986 | Geffen PRO-A-2581 | 10 |
| EVERYBODY HAVE FUN TONIGHT (4 mixes) | 1986 | Geffen PRO-A-2589 | 8 |
| EYES ON THE GIRL (same on both sides) | 1986 | Geffen PRO-A-2630 | 5 |
| WAIT (LP)/(Edit) | 1984 | Geffen PRO-A-2152 | 10 |
| **45s** | | | |
| HOLD BACK THE TEARS (same on both sides) | 1983 | Arista 1012 | 8 |
| *(As "Huang Chung"; stock copy appears not to exist)* | | | |

| Title | Yr | Label, Number | NM $ |
|-------|-----|---------------|------|
| **RADIO SHOWS** | | | |
| **Albums** | | | |
| BBC ROCK HOUR (Apr 84) | 1984 | London Wavelength | 30-60 |
| *(Music and interviews)* | | | |
| IN CONCERT (June 84) Live concert | 1984 | Westwood One (2) | 20-40 |
| *(With Greg Kihn Band)* | | | |
| IN CONCERT  Live concert | 1987 | Westwood One (2) | 30-60 |
| *(With Pseudo Echo)* | | | |
| | | | |
| **WAR** | | | |
| *United Artists, MCA and RCA promo 45s $3 each* | | | |
| **12-Inch Singles** | | | |
| JUST BECAUSE (same on both sides) | 1982 | RCA JD-13323 | 8 |
| YOUNGBLOOD (LIVIN' IN THE STREETS) (9:07)/KEEP ON DOIN' | 1978 | United Artists SP-184 | 15 |
| **45s** | | | |
| BABY, IT'S COLD OUTSIDE (same on both sides) | 1982 | RCA JH-13426 | 5 |
| **Albums** | | | |
| RADIO FREE WAR | 1974 | United Artists 103 | 25 |
| *(Blue vinyl, promo-only release)* | | | |
| **Compact Discs** | | | |
| COLLECTOR'S EDITION | 1994 | Rhino | 75 |
| *(Promo-only box set of eight War CDs)* | | | |
| | | | |
| **WARD, BURT** | | | |
| *Robin from the Batman TV series* | | | |
| **45s** | | | |
| BOY WONDER, I LOVE YOU | 1967 | MGM 13632 | 100 |
| *(Yellow promo copy, written and produced by Frank Zappa)* | | | |
| | | | |
| **WARINER, STEVE** | | | |
| *RCA, MCA and Arista promo 45s $3 each; MCA, Arista and Capitol Nashville promo CDs $2 each* | | | |
| **45s** | | | |
| ON CHRISTMAS MORNING | 1990 | MCA S45-1164 | 10 |
| *(White label promo, no stock copies made)* | | | |
| **Compact Discs** | | | |
| GOTTA DRIVE | 1993 | Arista 2638 | 30 |
| *(Promo-only interview disc, Garth Brooks is the host)* | | | |
| | | | |
| **WARING, FRED, AND THE PENNSYLVANIANS** | | | |
| **78s** | | | |
| FO FUM FI FEE | 195? | Decca | 15 |
| *(7-inch 78 rpm, made for Le Sueur Peas for Green Giant's 20th anniversary)* | | | |
| | | | |
| **WARMEST SPRING, THE** | | | |
| **45s** | | | |
| YOUNGER GIRL | 1966 | Parkway 985 | 20 |
| *(One-sided white label promo)* | | | |
| | | | |
| **WARRANT** | | | |
| *Columbia promo 45s $3 each; Columbia promo CD singles $2-3 each* | | | |
| **RADIO SHOWS** | | | |
| **Albums** | | | |
| IN CONCERT (Mar 91) Live concert | 1991 | Westwood One (2) | 20-40 |
| *(With Bonham)* | | | |
| | | | |
| **WARWICK, DIONNE** | | | |
| *Scepter promo 45s $4 each; Warner Bros. and Arista promo 45s $2 each* | | | |
| **12-Inch Singles** | | | |
| GOT A DATE (7:04) (4:07) | 1983 | Arista ADP 9145 | 8 |
| **45s** | | | |
| WHAT'S IT ALL ABOUT (Apr 80) Public service show | 1980 | W.I.A.A. 522 | 15 |
| *(The Dirt Band on flip side)* | | | |
| WHAT'S IT ALL ABOUT (June 81) Public service show | 1981 | W.I.A.A. 580 | 10 |
| *(Flip side features Henry Mancini)* | | | |
| **7-Inch Extended Plays** | | | |
| DIONNE WARWICK  Jukebox LLP | 196? | Scepter 568 | 15 |
| *(With picture cover)* | | | |
| MAKE WAY FOR DIONNE WARWICK  Jukebox LLP | 196? | Scepter 523 | 15 |
| *(With picture cover)* | | | |
| UNITED NEGRO COLLEGE FUND | 197? | UNCF 181 | 10 |
| *(Six cuts, all with Dionne Warwick)* | | | |
| **Albums** | | | |
| MARCH IS DIONNE WARWICK MONTH | 1968 | Scepter 200 | 25 |
| *(Red promo-only label, special cover)* | | | |
| **RADIO SHOWS** | | | |
| **Albums** | | | |
| ABC RADIO | 1980 | ABC Radio (2) | 20-35 |
| *(Music and interviews)* | | | |
| IN CONCERT (July 86) | 1986 | Westwood One (2) | 30-60 |
| *(Live concert)* | | | |
| NBC SOURCE (May 81) | 1981 | NBC Radio (2) | 20-35 |
| *(Music and interviews)* | | | |

| Title | Yr | Label, Number | NM $ |
|---|---|---|---|
| STARTRACK Profile (Apr 85) | 1985 | Westwood One (2) | 20-35 |
| *(Music and interviews)* | | | |
| WESTWOOD ONE PRESENTS (Aug 90) | 1990 | Westwood One (2) | 20-30 |
| *(Music and interviews)* | | | |

## WAS (NOT WAS)
**12-Inch Singles**

| | | | |
|---|---|---|---|
| OUT COME THE FREAKS (Extended)/(Dub) | 1981 | Island PRO 961 | 8 |
| TELL ME THAT I'M DREAMING (2 versions) | 1981 | Island PRO 1000 | 6 |
| WHITE PEOPLE CAN'T DANCE (same on both sides) | 1989 | 4th & B'Way PRO 493 | 8 |

**Albums**

| | | | |
|---|---|---|---|
| SHAKE YOUR HEAD + 3 | 1983 | Geffen PRO-A-2079 | 12 |
| *(Promo-only sampler from Born to Laugh at Tornadoes)* | | | |

## WASHINGTON, DINAH
*Mercury promo 45s $8 each*

## WATERBOYS, THE
**12-Inch Singles**

| | | | |
|---|---|---|---|
| CHURCH NOT MADE WITH HANDS (Edit)  (same on both sides) | 1984 | Island 661 | 8 |
| DON'T BANG THE DRUM  (same on both sides) | 1985 | Island 840 | 6 |

## WATERS, MUDDY
**Albums**

| | | | |
|---|---|---|---|
| THE BEST OF MUDDY WATERS | 1957 | Chess LP-1427 | 1,500 |
| *(White label promo)* | | | |
| MUDDY WATERS SINGS BIG BILL | 1960 | Chess LP-1444 | 1,000 |
| *(White label promo)* | | | |

## WATERS, ROGER
*More at Pink Floyd*
**Compact Discs**

| | | | |
|---|---|---|---|
| ANOTHER BRICK IN THE WALL | 1990 | Mercury CDP 342 | 25 |
| *(Promo CD single in a foam brick)* | | | |
| BRAVERY OF BEING OUT OF RANGE | 1992 | Columbia CSK 4830 | 8 |
| *(Promo CD single)* | | | |
| HEY YOU | 1990 | Mercury CDP 349 | 8 |
| *(Promo CD single)* | | | |
| THE WALL BERLIN | 1990 | Columbia CSK 2126 | 40 |
| *(Promo-only compilation of Pink Floyd studio tracks to capitalize on the Berlin performance of The Wall)* | | | |
| THE WALL LIVE IN BERLIN (PIECES FROM THE WALL) | 1990 | Mercury CDP 318 | 12 |
| *(Promo-only sampler from live album)* | | | |
| THREE WISHES | 1992 | Columbia CSK 4941 | 8 |
| *(Promo CD single)* | | | |
| TIDE IS TURNING | 1990 | Mercury CDP 367 | 8 |
| *(Promo CD single)* | | | |
| WHAT GOD WANTS | 1992 | Columbia CSK 4607 | 8 |
| *(Promo CD single)* | | | |

## WAYNE, DICK, AND THE SATELLITES
**45s**

| | | | |
|---|---|---|---|
| I KNOW THERE IS A SANTA CLAUS/TEARS COME EASY TO MY EYES | 198? | Hart-Van 16011 | 4 |

## WE FIVE
**45s**

| | | | |
|---|---|---|---|
| MY FAVORITE THINGS | 1965 | A&M XMAS-1 | 12 |
| *(Promo-only Christmas release)* | | | |

## WEIRDOS
**Albums**

| | | | |
|---|---|---|---|
| MESSAGE FROM THE UNDERWORLD | 198? | Out of Darkness OTD 001 | 40 |
| *(Promo-only release)* | | | |

## WELCH, BOB
*Also see Fleetwood Mac; Capitol promo 45s $3 each*
**Albums**

| | | | |
|---|---|---|---|
| FRENCH KISS | 1979 | Capitol 11663 | 18 |
| *(Promo-only picture disc)* | | | |

## WELK, LAWRENCE
*Decca and Coral promo 45s $8 each; Dot promo 45s $6 each; Brunswick promo 45s by the Lennon Sisters $4 each; Other Brunswick and Coral promo 45s by Larry Hooper $6 each; Thesaurus (RCA) EPs $8 each; Dot jukebox LLPs $5 each; Any label promo LPs $5 each*
**45s**

| | | | |
|---|---|---|---|
| CHRISTMAS CAROLS | 195? | Coral 98054 | 10 |
| *(Promo only release on this number)* | | | |
| CHRISTMAS MUSIC FOR YOUR HOLIDAY PLEASURE | 1958 | | 12 |
| *(Cardboard record, plays at 33 1/3 rpm, given out by Dodge dealers)* | | | |
| ON THE ALAMO   Music in the Air | 1957 | U.S. Air Force | 10 |
| *(Five-minute public service show)* | | | |
| ROGER BOOM  Larry Hooper | 1956 | Coral 61763 | 15 |
| *(Blue promo label)* | | | |

| Title | Yr | Label, Number | NM $ |
|---|---|---|---|
| **RADIO SHOWS** | | | |
| **16-Inch Transcriptions** | | | |
| THE LAWRENCE WELK SHOW (50s) | 195? | U.S. Navy | 20-30 |
| *(Weekly series, ran "forever")* | | | |
| **Albums** | | | |
| LAWRENCE WELK (60s-70s) | 196? | U.S. Navy (2) | 15-25 |
| *(Double record cover, also ran for a long time)* | | | |
| THE LAWRENCE WELK CHRISTMAS PROGRAM | 1955 | Thesaurus (RCA) 1975 | 15-30 |
| *(Part of the radio station Thesaurus Library)* | | | |
| THE LAWRENCE WELK SHOW (50s-60s) | 195? | U.S. Navy | 10-20 |
| *(The 12" version)* | | | |
| | | | |
| **WELLINGTON, RUSTY** | | | |
| **45s** | | | |
| ROCKING CHAIR ON THE MOON | 1958 | MGM 12581 | 50 |
| *(Yellow promo label)* | | | |
| | | | |
| **WELLS, KITTY** | | | |
| *Decca pink promo label 45s $5-8 each; Decca yellow promo label 45s $3 each; Other Decca jukebox LLPs $10-20 each; Other Decca promo LPs $10-15 each* | | | |
| **45s** | | | |
| CHRISTMAS DAY WITH KITTY WELLS | 1962 | Decca 34185/6/7/8/9 | 40 |
| *(Five jukebox 33 1/3 rpm singles, $8 each)* | | | |
| KITTY'S CHOICE | 1959 | Decca 38110/1/2/3/4 | 40 |
| *(Five jukebox 33 1/3 rpm singles, $8 each)* | | | |
| SEASONS OF MY HEART | 1960 | Decca 38215/6/7/8/9 | 40 |
| *(Five jukebox 33 1/3 rpm singles, $8 each)* | | | |
| **7-Inch Extended Plays** | | | |
| COUNTRY MUSIC TIME  Jukebox LLP | 1966 | Decca 34255 | 30 |
| *(Issued with a hard cover)* | | | |
| KITTY WELLS SHOWCASE  Jukebox LLP | 1968 | Decca 734535 | 25 |
| *(Issued with a hard cover)* | | | |
| SONGS MADE FAMOUS BY JIM REEVES   Jukebox LLP | 1966 | Decca 34362 | 30 |
| *(Issued with a hard cover)* | | | |
| THE KITTY WELLS SHOW  Jukebox LLP | 1966 | Decca 34181 | 40 |
| *(Issued with a hard cover)* | | | |
| **Albums** | | | |
| AFTER DARK | 1959 | Decca 8888 | 40 |
| *(Pink promo label)* | | | |
| DUST ON THE BIBLE | 1959 | Decca 8858 | 50 |
| *(Pink promo label)* | | | |
| KITTY WELLS' COUNTRY HIT PARADE | 1956 | Decca 8293 | 75 |
| *(Decca promo label)* | | | |
| KITTY WELLS' GOLDEN FAVORITES | 1961 | Decca 4108 | 30 |
| *(Decca promo label)* | | | |
| THE KITTY WELLS STORY | 1963 | Decca 174 (2) | 25 |
| *(White promo labels)* | | | |
| WINNER OF YOUR HEART | 1956 | Decca 8552 | 60 |
| *(Pink promo label)* | | | |
| **RADIO SHOWS** | | | |
| **Albums** | | | |
| HERE'S TO VETS (60s)  Public service show | 196? | Veterans Administration | 20-40 |
| *(Music and interviews)* | | | |
| | | | |
| **WELLS, MARY** | | | |
| *Other Motown promo 45s $20 each; 20th Century promo 45s $8 each; Atco, Jubilee and Epic promo 45s $4 each* | | | |
| **45s** | | | |
| BYE BYE BABY | 1961 | Motown 1003 | 40 |
| *(White promo label)* | | | |
| **7-Inch Extended Plays** | | | |
| MARY WELLS GREATEST HITS  Jukebox LLP | 1964 | Motown 60616 | 75 |
| *(Very rare, issued with a hard cover)* | | | |
| **Albums** | | | |
| I'M THE ONE WHO REALLY LOVES YOU | 1962 | Motown 605 | 100 |
| *(White promo label)* | | | |
| MARY WELLS | 1961 | Motown 600 | 150 |
| *(White promo label)* | | | |
| SERVIN' UP SOME SOUL | 1968 | Jubilee 8018 | 30 |
| *(White label promo)* | | | |
| | | | |
| **WEST, KEITH** | | | |
| **45s** | | | |
| EXCERPT FROM A TEENAGE OPERA | 1968 | New Voice 825 | 12 |
| *(White promo label)* | | | |
| | | | |
| **WEST, LESLIE** | | | |
| **7-Inch Extended Plays** | | | |
| HONEY/DEAR PRUDENCE//GET IT UP/THE SETTING SUN | 1975 | Phantom JF-10424 | 10 |
| | | | |
| **WET WET WET** | | | |
| *London promo CD singles $3 each* | | | |
| **12-Inch Singles** | | | |
| WISHING I WAS LUCKY  (same on both sides) | 1987 | Uni L33-10000 | 5 |

| Title | Yr | Label, Number | NM $ |
|-------|-----|---------------|------|
| **RADIO SHOWS** | | | |
| **Albums** | | | |
| BBC TRANSCRIPTION DISC | 1987 | BBC Transcription | 100-175 |
| *(Live concert)* | | | |
| | | | |
| **WET WILLIE** | | | |
| *Capricorn promo 45s $5 each; Epic promo 45s $3 each* | | | |
| **Albums** | | | |
| MANORISMS | 1978 | Epic 428 | 10 |
| *(Promo-only release)* | | | |
| | | | |
| **WHAM!** | | | |
| *More at George Michael* | | | |
| **12-Inch Singles** | | | |
| CARELESS WHISPER (same on both sides) | 1984 | Columbia AS 1980 | 15 |
| *(As "Wham! featuring George Michael")* | | | |
| FREEDOM (LP)/(Single Remix) | 1985 | Columbia CAS 2122 | 25 |
| **45s** | | | |
| LAST CHRISTMAS | 1986 | Columbia CS7 2591 | 12 |
| *(White promo label, 6:43 and 4:24 versions)* | | | |
| | | | |
| **WHEN IN ROME** | | | |
| **12-Inch Singles** | | | |
| HEAVEN KNOWS (8:00)/(Dub)/WHATEVER THE WEATHER | 1988 | Virgin 1270 | 6 |
| SIGHT OF YOUR TEARS (5 mixes) | 1988 | Virgin DMD 1319 | 6 |
| | | | |
| **WHIRLWINDS, THE** | | | |
| **45s** | | | |
| HEARTBEATS | 1963 | Philips 40139 | 50 |
| *(White promo label)* | | | |
| | | | |
| **WHISPERS, THE** | | | |
| **12-Inch Singles** | | | |
| CONTAGIOUS (LP Version) (Edit Version)/KEEP YOUR LOVE AROUND | 1984 | Solar ED 5017 | 8 |
| SOME KINDA LOVER (same on both sides) | 1984 | Solar ED 5036 | 8 |
| **45s** | | | |
| INNOCENT (7" Edit)/(Club Edit) | 1990 | Capitol 7PRO-79170/215 | 8 |
| *(Vinyl is promo only)* | | | |
| | | | |
| **WHITE LION** | | | |
| *Atlantic promo 45s $4 each; Atlantic promo CD singles $3 each* | | | |
| **RADIO SHOWS** | | | |
| **Albums** | | | |
| HIGH VOLTAGE (Feb 89) Various artists | 1989 | Westwood One (2) | 25-40 |
| *(Live segment of the show features White Lion)* | | | |
| IN CONCERT (Apr 88) Live concert | 1988 | Westwood One (2) | 50-100 |
| *(With Guns N' Roses)* | | | |
| IN CONCERT (Mar 89) Live concert | 1989 | Westwood One (2) | 25-50 |
| *(With Bad Company)* | | | |
| | | | |
| **WHITE ZOMBIE** | | | |
| *Geffen promo CD singles $4-6 each* | | | |
| **RADIO SHOWS** | | | |
| **Compact Discs** | | | |
| LIVE FROM THE PIT (Nov 95) | 1995 | Global Satellite (2) | 30-60 |
| *(Live concert material)* | | | |
| | | | |
| **WHITE, BARRY** | | | |
| *20th Century promo 45s $3 each; A&M promo CD singles $3 each* | | | |
| **12-Inch Singles** | | | |
| CHANGE (4:22) (7:04) | 1982 | Unlimited Gold AS 1509 | 10 |
| I BELIEVE IN LOVE (3:26) (8:01) | 1980 | Unlimited Gold AS 864 | 10 |
| I WANNA DO IT GOOD TO YA (5 versions) | 1989 | A&M 18026 | 6 |
| PRACTICE WHAT YOU PREACH (7 versions) | 1994 | A&M 31458 8375 1 | 8 |
| **45s** | | | |
| WHAT'S IT ALL ABOUT (Sept 74) Public service show | 1974 | W.I.A.A. 223 | 15 |
| *(Olivia Newton-John on flip side)* | | | |
| WHAT'S IT ALL ABOUT (Dec 74) Public service show | 1974 | W.I.A.A. 235 | 18 |
| *(Interviews)* | | | |
| WHAT'S IT ALL ABOUT (Nov 76) Public service show | 1976 | W.I.A.A. 343 | 20 |
| *(Flip side features Donovan)* | | | |
| | | | |
| **WHITE, TONY JOE** | | | |
| *Monument promo 45s $4 each* | | | |
| **RADIO SHOWS** | | | |
| **Albums** | | | |
| BBC TRANSCRIPTION DISC  Live concert | 1973 | BBC Transcription | 100-200 |
| *(With the Sutherland Brothers)* | | | |

| Title | Yr | Label, Number | NM $ |
|---|---|---|---|
| **WHITESNAKE** | | | |

*Mirage promo 45s $4 each; Geffen promo 45s $3 each; Geffen promo CD singles $3 each*

**45s**

| Title | Yr | Label, Number | NM $ |
|---|---|---|---|
| AIN'T NO LOVE IN THE HEART OF THE CITY (same on both sides) | 1981 | Mirage 3794 | 5 |
| *(May be promo only)* | | | |
| **Compact Discs** | | | |
| SNAKE BITES | 1990 | Geffen PRO-CD-3846 | 20 |
| *(Promo-only greatest-hits collection)* | | | |
| **RADIO SHOWS** | | | |
| **Albums** | | | |
| BBC ROCK HOUR (Jan 81) | 1981 | London Wavelength | 75-125 |
| *(Live concert)* | | | |
| BBC ROCK HOUR (June 83) Live concert | 1983 | London Wavelength | 60-100 |
| *(With Deep Purple)* | | | |
| BBC ROCK HOUR (June 84) Live concert | 1984 | London Wavelength | 60-100 |
| *(With Deep Purple)* | | | |
| BBC TRANSCRIPTION DISC | 1979 | BBC Transcription | 250-325 |
| *(Live concert)* | | | |
| BBC TRANSCRIPTION DISC | 1980 | BBC Transcription | 250-325 |
| *(Live concert)* | | | |
| IN CONCERT (Mar 85) Live concert | 1985 | Westwood One (2) | 75-125 |
| *(With Dokken)* | | | |
| IN CONCERT (Oct 84) Live concert | 1984 | Westwood One (2) | 75-150 |
| *(With Lita Ford)* | | | |
| OFF THE RECORD (Mar 90) | 1990 | Westwood One (2) | 15-25 |
| *(Music and interviews)* | | | |
| **Compact Discs** | | | |
| MASTERS OF ROCK (Feb 90) | 1990 | Westwood One (2) | 25-50 |
| *(Music and interviews)* | | | |
| | | | |
| **WHITLEY, KEITH** | | | |

*RCA promo 45s $3 each*

**Compact Discs**

| Title | Yr | Label, Number | NM $ |
|---|---|---|---|
| THE SINGLES | 1995 | BNA | 20 |
| *(Promo-only collection)* | | | |
| WHEN YOU SAY NOTHING AT ALL | 1995 | BNA | 10 |
| *(Promo-only CD single, electronically created duet with Alison Krauss)* | | | |
| | | | |
| **WHITMAN, SLIM** | | | |

*Other Imperial cream colored promo label 45s $10-15 each; Imperial white promo label 45s $5 each; Epic promo 45s $3 each*

**45s**

| Title | Yr | Label, Number | NM $ |
|---|---|---|---|
| BIRMINGHAM JAIL | 1953 | RCA Victor 5557 | 50 |
| *(White promo label)* | | | |
| CURTAIN OF TEARS | 1954 | Imperial 8308 | 200 |
| *(Red vinyl, cream colored promo label)* | | | |
| I'LL NEVER STOP LOVING YOU | 1954 | Imperial 8298 | 25 |
| *(Cream colored promo label)* | | | |
| MY LOVE IS GROWING STALE | 1953 | Imperial 8134 | 25 |
| *(Cream colored promo label)* | | | |
| PLEASE PAINT A ROSE ON THE GARDEN WALL | 1954 | RCA Victor 5742 | 50 |
| *(White promo label)* | | | |
| ROLL ON SILVERY MOON | 1953 | Imperial 8290 | 25 |
| *(Cream colored promo label)* | | | |
| THERE'S A RAINBOW IN EVERY TEARDROP | 1953 | RCA Victor 5431 | 50 |
| *(White promo label)* | | | |
| **7-Inch Extended Plays** | | | |
| AMERICA'S FAVORITE FOLK ARTIST | 1954 | Imperial 106 | 100 |
| *(Cream colored promo label)* | | | |
| COUNTRY SONGS   Jukebox LLP | 1964 | Imperial 42268 | 40 |
| *(Issued with a hard cover)* | | | |
| MORE THAN YESTERDAY  Jukebox LLP | 1965 | Imperial 42303 | 40 |
| *(Issued with a hard cover)* | | | |
| SLIM WHITMAN | 1956 | Imperial 135 | 50 |
| *(Cream colored promo label, also known as "North Wind")* | | | |
| SLIM WHITMAN | 1956 | Imperial 137 | 50 |
| *(Cream colored promo label)* | | | |
| SLIM WHITMAN SINGING | 1954 | Imperial 130 | 75 |
| *(Cream colored promo label)* | | | |
| SONGS BY SLIM WHITMAN | 1956 | Imperial 131 | 75 |
| *(Cream colored promo label, also known as "When I Grow Too Old To Dream")* | | | |
| SONGS BY SLIM WHITMAN | 1956 | Imperial 132 | 60 |
| *(Cream colored promo label, also known as "When My Blue Moon Turns To Gold Again")* | | | |
| SONGS BY SLIM WHITMAN | 1956 | Imperial 133 | 60 |
| *(Cream colored promo label, also known as "Darlin' Don't Cry")* | | | |
| SONGS BY SLIM WHITMAN | 1956 | Imperial 134 | 50 |
| *(Cream colored promo label, also known as "An Amateur In Love")* | | | |
| SONGS BY SLIM WHITMAN | 1956 | Imperial 136 | 40 |
| *(Cream colored promo label, also known as "Roll On Silvery Moon")* | | | |
| **78s** | | | |
| BIRMINGHAM JAIL | 1953 | RCA Victor 5557 | 50 |
| *(White promo label)* | | | |
| PLEASE PAINT A ROSE ON THE GARDEN WALL | 1954 | RCA Victor 5742 | 50 |
| *(White promo label)* | | | |
| THERE'S A RAINBOW IN EVERY TEARDROP | 1953 | RCA Victor 5431 | 50 |
| *(White promo label)* | | | |

| Title | Yr | Label, Number | NM $ |
|---|---|---|---|
| **Albums** | | | |
| SLIM WHITMAN FAVORITES | 1956 | Imperial 9003 | 125 |
| *(White promo label, Imperial at top)* | | | |
| SLIM WHITMAN SINGS | 1957 | Imperial 9026 | 100 |
| *(White promo label, Imperial at top)* | | | |
| SLIM WHITMAN SINGS | 1958 | Imperial 9056 | 75 |
| *(White promo label, Imperial at top)* | | | |
| SLIM WHITMAN SINGS | 1959 | Imperial 9064 | 75 |
| *(White promo label, Imperial at top)* | | | |

## WHITTAKER, ROGER

| Title | Yr | Label, Number | NM $ |
|---|---|---|---|
| **45s** | | | |
| TOO BEAUTIFUL TO CRY/TOGETHER | 1982 | RCA JB-13379 | 5 |

## WHO, THE

Also includes The High Numbers, Pete Townshend, Roger Daltrey, Keith Moon; Other Decca promo 45s $8 each; Other Track (Decca/MCA) 45s $6 each; MCA promo 45s $5-8 each; Warner Bros. promo 45s $4 each; MCA pink promo label 45s by Pete Townshend and Ronnie Lane $5 each; MCA white promo label 45s by Townshend and Lane $4 each; Atco promo 45s by Pete Townshend $5 each; Polydor red promo label 45s by Pete Townshend $6 each; Track (MCA) white promo label 45s by Roger Daltrey $4 each; MCA maroon promo label 45s by Roger Daltrey $5 each; MCA blue promo label 45s by Roger Daltrey $4 each; MCA white promo label 45s by Roger Daltrey $3 each; Polydor red promo label 45s by Roger Daltrey $6 each; Polydor white promo label 45s by Roger Daltrey $4 each; Atlantic promo 45s by Roger Daltrey $3 each; Atco promo 45s by John Entwistle $4 each; Atco promo-only 12" singles by Pete Townshend $8 each; Atlantic promo-only 12" singles by Roger Daltrey $8 each (PR 982 includes an insert)

| Title | Yr | Label, Number | NM $ |
|---|---|---|---|
| **12-Inch Singles** | | | |
| ATHENA | 1982 | Warner Bros. PRO-A-1065 | 10 |
| *(Promo-only 12" single issued with title cover)* | | | |
| EMINENCE FRONT | 1982 | Warner Bros. PRO-A-1087 | 10 |
| *(Promo-only 12" single, long/short versions issued with a title cover)* | | | |
| I DON'T EVEN KNOW MYSELF | 1985 | MCA 17072 | 10 |
| *(Promo-only 3-song 12" single, issued with a title cover)* | | | |
| ONE OF THE BOYS  Roger Daltrey | 1977 | MCA 1962 | 15 |
| *(Promo-only 12" single has Steve Gibbons on the flip and is issued with a title cover)* | | | |
| TWIST AND SHOUT | 1984 | MCA 1257 | 12 |
| *(Promo-only 3-song 12" single)* | | | |
| YOU BETTER YOU BET | 1981 | Warner Bros. PRO-A-938 | 12 |
| *(Promo-only 12" single, long/short versions issued with a title cover)* | | | |
| **45s** | | | |
| ANYWAY, ANYWHERE, ANYHOW | 1965 | Decca 31801 | 60 |
| *(Pink promo label, stock copy of this title is rarer than the promo and worth a little more)* | | | |
| CALL ME LIGHTNING | 1968 | Decca 32288 | 12 |
| *(Decca promo label)* | | | |
| DON'T WORRY BABY  Keith Moon | 1975 | Track 40316 | 18 |
| *(White promo label)* | | | |
| GIVING IT ALL AWAY  Roger Daltrey | 1972 | Track (MCA) 40053 | 10 |
| *(White promo label, top 10 in UK)* | | | |
| HAD ENOUGH | 1978 | MCA 1809 | 15 |
| *(Promo-only release)* | | | |
| HAPPY JACK | 1967 | Decca 32114 | 15 |
| *(Pink promo label, stock picture sleeve worth $30)* | | | |
| I CAN SEE FOR MILES | 1967 | Decca 32206 | 12 |
| *(Decca promo label)* | | | |
| I CAN'T EXPLAIN | 1965 | Decca 31725 | 75 |
| *(Pink promo label)* | | | |
| I'M THE FACE  The High Numbers | 1980 | Mercury DJ-570 | 15 |
| *(Promo-only record and sleeve, U.S. reissue of the British Fontana label release of 1964)* | | | |
| IN MY LIFE  Keith Moon | 1975 | Track 40433 | 15 |
| *(White promo label)* | | | |
| THE KIDS ARE ALRIGHT  Movie ads | 1979 | New World 3426 | 200 |
| *(One-sided record)* | | | |
| LONG LIVE ROCK | 1979 | MCA 41053 | 50 |
| *(Promo picture disc advertising one of six sponsors)* | | | |
| MADE IN JAPAN   John Entwistle | 1972 | Track 40066 | 10 |
| *(White promo label)* | | | |
| MAGIC BUS | 1968 | Decca 32362 | 12 |
| *(Decca promo label)* | | | |
| MY GENERATION | 1965 | Decca 31877 | 30 |
| *(Pink promo label)* | | | |
| MY GENERATION/PINBALL WIZARD | 1969 | Eva-Tone | 20 |
| *(Soundsheet, plays at 33 1/3 rpm)* | | | |
| MY SIZE  John Entwistle | 1971 | Decca 32896 | 10 |
| *(Yellow promo label)* | | | |
| PEPPERMINT LUMP  Angie | 1979 | Epic 50793 | 25 |
| *(White promo label record and promo-only picture sleeve; there is a stock picture sleeve)* | | | |
| PICTURES OF LILY | 1967 | Decca 32156 | 12 |
| *(Decca promo label)* | | | |
| PINBALL WIZARD | 1969 | Decca 32465 | 12 |
| *(Decca promo label, stock picture sleeve worth $25)* | | | |
| POSTCARD | 1974 | Track 40330 | 18 |
| *(White promo label, stock copy is rarer)* | | | |
| THE RELAY | 1972 | Track (Decca) 33041 | 12 |
| *(Silver promo label)* | | | |
| SEE ME, FEEL ME | 1970 | Decca 32729 | 15 |
| *(Special promo release)* | | | |
| THE SEEKER | 1970 | Decca 32670 | 10 |
| *(Decca promo label)* | | | |
| SOLID GOLD  Keith Moon | 1975 | Track 40387 | 15 |
| *(White promo label)* | | | |

| Title | Yr | Label, Number | NM $ |
|---|---|---|---|
| SQUEEZE BOX | 1975 | MCA 40475 | 45 |
| *(White promo record and promo-only picture sleeve)* | | | |
| SUBSTITUTE | 1966 | Atco 6409 | 75 |
| *(All white promo label)* | | | |
| SUBSTITUTE | 1967 | Atco 6509 | 50 |
| *(White promo label)* | | | |
| SUBSTITUTE | 1970 | Decca 32737 | 500 |
| *(Promo-only record with stock picture sleeve)* | | | |
| SUMMERTIME BLUES | 1970 | Decca 32708 | 10 |
| *(Yellow promo label)* | | | |
| TOMMY | 1970 | Decca 73410/1/2/3 | 175 |
| *(Box set of four promo 45s from "Tommy" with gold promo labels and insert; individually, 45s are $30 each)* | | | |
| WE'RE NOT GONNA TAKE IT | 1969 | Decca 32519 | 12 |
| *(Decca promo label)* | | | |
| WHAT'S IT ALL ABOUT (July 75) Public service show | 1975 | W.I.A.A. 274 | 25 |
| *(Interviews with Townshend and Daltrey, flip side is the Pointer Sisters)* | | | |
| WHAT'S IT ALL ABOUT (Aug 75) Public service show | 1975 | W.I.A.A. 281 | 25 |
| *(Interviews from "Tommy" include Elton John, flip is Anne Murray)* | | | |
| WHAT'S IT ALL ABOUT  Public service show | 1979 | W.I.A.A. | 25 |
| *(Flip side features Paul Williams)* | | | |
| WHAT'S IT ALL ABOUT (Mar 80) Public service show | 1980 | W.I.A.A. 517 | 30 |
| *(Interviews with Pete Townshend, flip side features rare show from James Brown)* | | | |
| WHAT'S IT ALL ABOUT (Oct 82) Public service show | 1982 | W.I.A.A. 644 | 25 |
| *(Pete Townshend, flip side features REO Speedwagon)* | | | |
| WHO ARE YOU | 1978 | MCA 40948 | 12 |
| *(White promo label, long 6:11/short 3:22 versions)* | | | |
| WON'T GET FOOLED AGAIN | 1971 | Decca 32856 | 10 |
| *(Yellow promo label)* | | | |
| **7-Inch Extended Plays** | | | |
| CONCERTS FOR THE PEOPLE OF KAMPUCHEA | 1981 | Atlantic PR-388 | 75 |
| *(Various artists including McCartney and the Who)* | | | |
| MY GENERATION/PINBALL WIZARD | 1982 | Eva-Tone 62382 | 50 |
| *(Promo-only flexi-disc released by St. Martin's Press)* | | | |
| TOMMY  Movie ads | 1975 | Columbia | 200 |
| *(Several tracks)* | | | |
| TOMMY  Various artists | 1972 | Ode EP-10 | 25 |
| *(Promo EP with four songs, one by Roger Daltrey, "I'm Free")* | | | |
| **Albums** | | | |
| FILLING IN THE GAPS | 1981 | Warner Bros. WBMS-116 (2) | 80 |
| *(With drawing on cover)* | | | |
| FILLING IN THE GAPS | 1981 | Warner Bros. WBMS-116 (2) | 50 |
| *(With generic "Warner Bros. Music Show" cover)* | | | |
| HAPPY JACK | 1967 | Decca 4892 | 200 |
| *(White promo label, mono)* | | | |
| HAPPY JACK | 1967 | Decca DL 74892 | 150 |
| *(White promo label, stereo)* | | | |
| INTERVIEW WITH PETE TOWNSHEND AND THUNDERCLAP NEWMAN | 1970 | Track (MCA) PR-160 | 100 |
| *(One-sided promo-only release)* | | | |
| IT'S HARD | 1982 | Warner Bros. 23731 | 30 |
| *("Quiex II vinyl" sticker on cover)* | | | |
| LIVE AT LEEDS | 1970 | Decca 79175 | 100 |
| *(White promo label)* | | | |
| MAGIC BUS -- THE WHO ON TOUR | 1968 | Decca DL 5064 | 200 |
| *(Mono White label promo; no stock copies were released in mono)* | | | |
| MAGIC BUS – THE WHO ON TOUR | 1968 | Decca 75064 | 150 |
| *(White promo label, stereo)* | | | |
| QUADROPHENIA | 1979 | Polydor 6235 (2) | 50 |
| *(White promo labels)* | | | |
| TOMMY | 1969 | Decca 7205 (2) | 250 |
| *(White promo labels version of a classic LP)* | | | |
| THE WHO/ THE STRAWBERRY ALARM CLOCK | 1970 | Decca 734568 | 150 |
| *(Rare LP available only from Philco Electronics)* | | | |
| WHO ARE YOU | 1978 | MCA 3050 | 25 |
| *(White promo label)* | | | |
| WHO ARE YOU | 1978 | MCA L33-1987 | 25 |
| *(White promo label with sticker "Who Are You Edited for Broadcast" on cover)* | | | |
| THE WHO SELL OUT | 1967 | Decca DL 4950 | 200 |
| *(White promo label, mono, with songs in the same order as the stock copy)* | | | |
| THE WHO SELL OUT | 1967 | Decca 4950 | 200 |
| *(White promo label, mono, all the commercials are on one side of the LP)* | | | |
| THE WHO SELL OUT | 1967 | Decca DL 74950 | 250 |
| *(White promo label, stereo, with songs in the same order as the stock copy)* | | | |
| THE WHO SELL OUT | 1967 | Decca DL 74950 | 400 |
| *(White promo label, stereo, all the commercials are on one side of the LP)* | | | |
| WHO SING MY GENERATION, THE | 1966 | Decca 4664 | 250 |
| *(White promo label, mono)* | | | |
| WHO SING MY GENERATION, THE | 1966 | Decca DL 74664 | 200 |
| *(White promo label, stereo)* | | | |
| **Compact Discs** | | | |
| BETCHA CAN'T PICK JUST ONE | 1990 | MCA 17721 | 30 |
| *(Promo-only sampler)* | | | |
| JOIN TOGETHER | 1990 | MCA 18258 | 8 |
| *(Promo-only CD single from live album)* | | | |
| SATURDAY NIGHT'S ALRIGHT (FOR FIGHTING) | 1990 | Polydor CDP 586 | 8 |
| *(Promo-only CD single from "Two Rooms," an Elton John-Bernie Taupin tribute album)* | | | |
| 30 YEARS OF MAXIMUM ROCK & ROLL | 1994 | MCA 3082 | 25 |
| *(Promo-only CD release with 15 tracks, sampler from box set)* | | | |

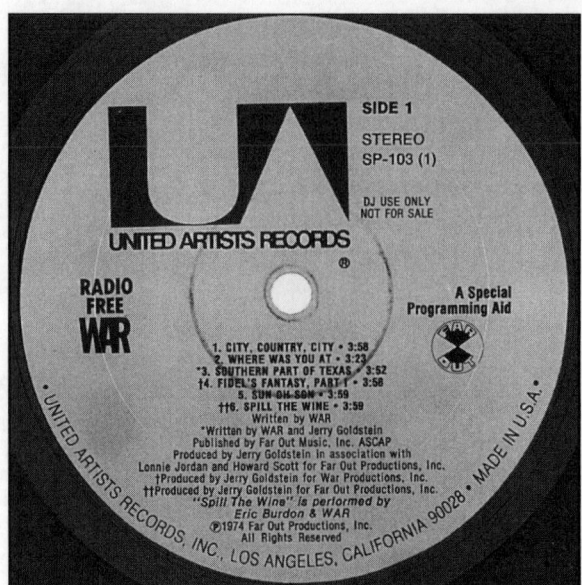

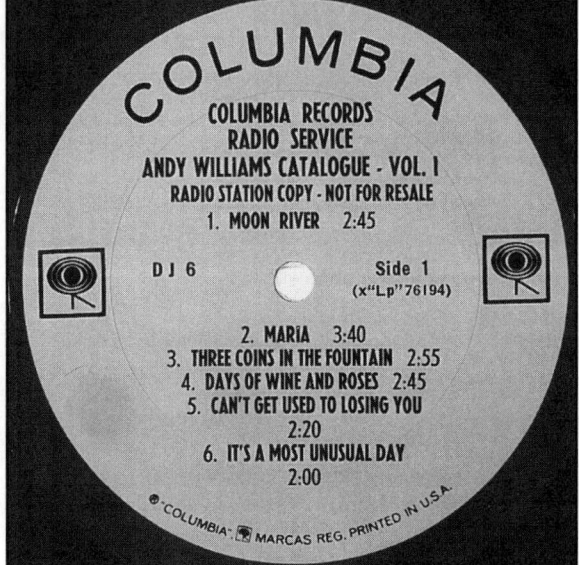

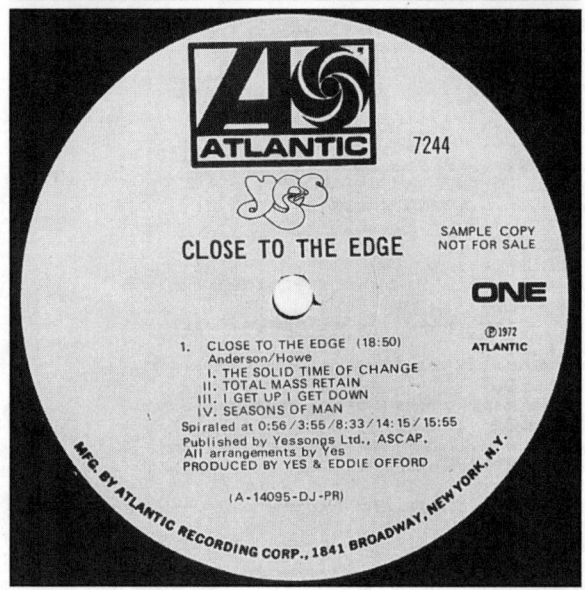

(Top row) The cover and label for *Radio Free War,* the sought-after blue vinyl radio-only sampler that predated a regular greatest-hits set by two years. (Middle row) Two interesting promo-only LPs from the Andy Williams catalog. At left is an album released to radio by SESAC, a music licensing firm; on the right is a collection of hits from Columbia that was meant only for radio station use. (Bottom left) Anyone else remember Y&T? Well, they were popular enough to warrant an appearance on the King Biscuit Flower Hour on Sept. 22, 1985. (Bottom right) One of the rare items in the Yes catalog, here is a mono copy of *Close to the Edge* on which the side-long title track is broken into segments for easier airplay. How do we know it's mono? The "SD" is missing from the catalog number 7244, and so is the word "Stereo" at the left.

| Title | Yr | Label, Number | NM $ |
|---|---|---|---|
| 30TH ANNIVERSARY SAMPLER | 1993 | MCA 2592 | 25 |
| *(Promo-only collection)* | | | |
| **RADIO SHOWS** | | | |
| **Albums** | | | |
| BBC TRANSCRIPTION DISC  Live concert | 1982 | BBC Transcription | 200-300 |
| *(With the Alan Parsons Project)* | | | |
| BBC TRANSCRIPTION DISC  Live concert | 1985 | BBC Transcription | 150-250 |
| *(With Culture Club)* | | | |
| COUNTDOWN TO CHRISTMAS (Dec 85) | 1985 | NBC Radio | 20-35 |
| *(Mostly music and interviews)* | | | |
| DIR SPECIAL-WHODUNIT (Dec 82) | 1982 | DIR (5) | 100-200 |
| *(Picture box set, live concert)* | | | |
| IN CONCERT (Feb 89) | 1989 | Westwood One (2) | 40-75 |
| *(Live concert)* | | | |
| THE IN SOUND (May 67) | 1967 | U.S. Army | 20-30 |
| *(Five-minute show music and interviews)* | | | |
| THE IN SOUND (Nov 67) | 1967 | U.S. Army | 20-25 |
| *(Five-minute show music and interviews)* | | | |
| INNERVIEW (70s) | 197? | Innerview (2) | 25-50 |
| *(Two shows, the "Headphone Experience")* | | | |
| INNERVIEW (70s) Pete Townshend | 197? | Innerview | 20-30 |
| *(Music and interviews)* | | | |
| INSIDE TRACK  Pete Townshend | 1982 | DIR (2) | 25-50 |
| *(Music and interviews with live tracks)* | | | |
| INSIDE TRACK (Oct 82) | 1982 | DIR (3) | 30-60 |
| *(Music and interviews with live tracks)* | | | |
| INSIDE TRACK (June 83)  Pete Townshend | 1983 | DIR (2) | 75-125 |
| *(Music and interviews with live tracks, with Joan Jett and Johnny Rotten)* | | | |
| IT'S HARD TO SAY GOODBYE (Dec 82) | 1982 | Westwood One (5) | 100-150 |
| *(Picture box set, music and interviews)* | | | |
| KING BISCUIT FLOWER HOUR (Dec 79)  Pete Townshend | 1979 | DIR/ABC (2) | 75-150 |
| *(Live concert, rare on vinyl)* | | | |
| KING BISCUIT FLOWER HOUR | 1983 | DIR/ABC (2) | 40-75 |
| *(Live concert, repeated)* | | | |
| KING BISCUIT FLOWER HOUR  Pete Townshend | 1986 | DIR (4) | 50-100 |
| *(Live concert, two weekly shows)* | | | |
| KING BISCUIT FLOWER HOUR  Pete Townshend | 1986 | DIR (2) | 30-60 |
| *(Live concert, repeated)* | | | |
| KING BISCUIT FLOWER HOUR  Roger Daltrey | 1986 | DIR (4) | 50-100 |
| *(Live concert, two weekly shows)* | | | |
| KING BISCUIT FLOWER HOUR  Roger Daltrey | 1986 | DIR (2) | 30-60 |
| *(Live concert, repeated)* | | | |
| KING BISCUIT FLOWER HOUR (Apr 86) | 1986 | DIR (3) | 40-75 |
| *(Unusual 3-LP live Biscuit concert)* | | | |
| LEGENDS OF ROCK (Nov 87) | 1987 | NBC Radio (4) | 40-75 |
| *(Music and interviews, two shows)* | | | |
| LEGENDS OF ROCK (Nov 87) | 1987 | NBC Radio (2) | 20-35 |
| *(Music and interviews)* | | | |
| MASTERS OF ROCK (Oct 81) | 1981 | | 20-30 |
| *(Music and interviews)* | | | |
| MASTERS OF ROCK (May 89) | 1989 | (4) | 40-75 |
| *(Music and interviews)* | | | |
| NIGHTBIRD & COMPANY (Apr 75) Various artists | 1975 | U.S. Army Reserve (2) | 25-50 |
| *(One of the 15-minute shows features the Who as co-host; music and interviews)* | | | |
| OFF THE RECORD | 1984 | Westwood One (4) | 40-75 |
| *(Music and interviews, two shows)* | | | |
| OFF THE RECORD | 1984 | Westwood One (2) | 20-35 |
| *(Music and interviews)* | | | |
| OFF THE RECORD  Roger Daltrey | 1984 | Westwood One (2) | 20-35 |
| *(Music and interviews)* | | | |
| OFF THE RECORD  Pete Townshend | 1985 | Westwood One (2) | 20-35 |
| *(Music and interviews)* | | | |
| OFF THE RECORD (July 89) | 1989 | Westwood One (2) | 25-40 |
| *(25th anniversary celebration)* | | | |
| PROFILES IN ROCK (May 80) Pete Townshend | 1980 | Watermark (2) | 20-40 |
| *(Music and interviews)* | | | |
| RETRO ROCK | 1984 | Clayton Webster (2) | 20-40 |
| *(Music and interviews with live tracks)* | | | |
| ROCK & ROLL NEVER FORGETS | 1984 | Westwood One (5) | 75-125 |
| *(Music and interviews)* | | | |
| SILVER ANNIVERSARY SPECIAL | 1989 | United Stations (3) | 75-125 |
| *(Music and interviews)* | | | |
| SOUNDS LIKE THE NAVY (Mar 75) Keith Moon | 1975 | U.S. Navy (2) | 50-100 |
| *(Very rare music and interview series that features Keith Moon as host of all four shows with music of the Who)* | | | |
| SOURCE SPECIAL (Dec 83) | 1983 | NBC Radio (3) | 25-50 |
| *(Music and interviews, live tracks)* | | | |
| SUPERSTAR CONCERT  Pete Townshend, David Gilmour and others | 1987 | Westwood One (3) | 30-60 |
| *(Live concert, repeated)* | | | |
| SUPERSTAR CONCERT (June 88)  Pete Tonwshend | 1988 | Westwood One (3) | 30-60 |
| *(Live concert box set, repeated)* | | | |
| SUPERSTAR CONCERT (Oct 89) | 1989 | Westwood One (3) | 30-60 |
| *(Live concert box set, repeated)* | | | |
| SUPERSTAR CONCERT (July 90) | 1990 | Westwood One (3) | 30-65 |
| *(Live concert, "Kids Are Alright" tour)* | | | |
| SUPERSTAR CONCERT | 1990 | Westwood One (3) | 40-75 |
| *(Live concert, "Tommy concert" repeated July 91)* | | | |

| Title | Yr | Label, Number | NM $ |
|---|---|---|---|
| 25 YEARS OF THE WHO (July 88) | 1988 | ABC Radio (5) | 50-100 |
| *(Mostly music and interviews)* | | | |
| THE WHO SPECIAL (Dec 82) | 1982 | London Wavelength | 20-40 |
| *(Music and interviews)* | | | |
| **Compact Discs** | | | |
| CLASSIC CD (June 90) | 1990 | (2) | 50-100 |
| *(Music and interviews about "Who's Next")* | | | |
| CLASSIC TRACKS (June 90) | 1990 | Westwood One (2) | 40-75 |
| *(Various classic live tracks)* | | | |
| CLASSIC TRACKS (Mar 91) | 1991 | Westwood One | 20-40 |
| *(Various classic live tracks)* | | | |
| 4TH OF JULY SPECIAL (July 90) | 1990 | Media America (3) | 40-75 |
| *(Mostly music and interviews)* | | | |
| IN THE STUDIO (90s) | 199? | Album Network | 15-25 |
| *(Profile of an album, music and interviews)* | | | |
| IN THE STUDIO (May 93) | 1993 | Album Network (2) | 25-50 |
| *(Profile of the "Tommy" LP, two shows)* | | | |
| KING BISCUIT FLOWER HOUR  Pete Townshend | 1987 | DIR | 40-75 |
| *(Live concert, repeated)* | | | |
| KING BISCUIT FLOWER HOUR Pete Townshend and Roger Daltrey | 1988 | DIR | 40-75 |
| *(Live concert, repeated)* | | | |
| KING BISCUIT FLOWER HOUR | 1988 | DIR | 40-75 |
| *(Live concert, repeated)* | | | |
| KING BISCUIT FLOWER HOUR  Roger Daltrey | 1989 | DIR | 35-75 |
| *(Live concert, repeated)* | | | |
| MAXIMUM R&B (July 95) | 1995 | Westwood One (4) | 75-125 |
| *(Music and interviews, career overview)* | | | |
| OFF THE RECORD (May 94) | 1994 | Westwood One | 20-30 |
| *(Music and interviews)* | | | |
| OFF THE RECORD (Sept 95) | 1995 | Westwood One | 20-30 |
| *(Music and interviews)* | | | |
| ONE ON ONE (Apr 93) | 1993 | | 30-60 |
| *(Music and interviews)* | | | |
| SUPERSTAR CONCERT (Apr 92) | 1992 | Westwood One (2) | 30-65 |
| *(Live concert)* | | | |
| SUPERSTARS (Oct 96) | 1996 | (2) | 75-125 |
| *(Live concert material, full performance of "Tommy")* | | | |
| SUPERSTARS (Nov 96) | 1996 | (2) | 75-125 |
| *(Live concert material, full performance of "Quadrophenia")* | | | |
| TOMMY 25TH ANNIVERSARY SPECIAL (Mar 93) | 1993 | (2) | 50-100 |
| *(Music and interviews about "Tommy")* | | | |
| UP CLOSE | 1989 | Media America (2) | 40-75 |
| *(Mostly music and interviews)* | | | |
| UP CLOSE   Pete Townshend | 1989 | Media America (2) | 40-65 |
| *(Music and interviews)* | | | |
| UP CLOSE   Pete Townshend | 1993 | Media America (3) | 40-65 |
| *(Music and interviews)* | | | |
| UP CLOSE | 1994 | Media America (3) | 40-75 |
| *(Mostly music and interviews)* | | | |
| **Reel-to-Reel Tapes** | | | |
| KING BISCUIT FLOWER HOUR (Mar 74) | 1974 | DIR/ABC (2) | 75-150 |
| *(Live concert on two reels)* | | | |
| KING BISCUIT FLOWER HOUR (July 79) | 1979 | DIR/ABC (2) | 75-125 |
| *(Live concert on two reels)* | | | |
| KING BISCUIT FLOWER HOUR (Dec 79)  Pete Townshend | 1979 | DIR/ABC (2) | 75-125 |
| *(Live concert on two reels)* | | | |

## WILBURN BROTHERS, THE

*Decca promo 45s $3 each*

**7-Inch Extended Plays**

| | | | |
|---|---|---|---|
| THE WILBURN BROTHERS  Jukebox LLP | 1966 | Decca LLP | 50 |
| *(Price includes hard cover and title strips)* | | | |

**Albums**

| | | | |
|---|---|---|---|
| THE WILBURN BROTHERS | 1966 | Decca 4721 | 65 |
| *(Pink promo label)* | | | |

## WILCO

**45s**

| | | | |
|---|---|---|---|
| CHILDLIKE AND EVERGREEN/SOMEONE ELSE'S SONG//HE'S MY STAR | 1995 | Warner Bros. PRO-S-???? | 7 |
| *("Soil Samples #19" promo on white vinyl; B-side by Poster Children)* | | | |

## WILD CHERRY

**45s**

| | | | |
|---|---|---|---|
| GET DOWN (mono/stereo) | 1973 | United Artists XW217 | 5 |
| *(Stock copy not known to exist)* | | | |

## WILD SWANS, THE

**Albums**

| | | | |
|---|---|---|---|
| MUSIC AND INTERVIEWS FROM LIVERPOOL | 1988 | Sire PRO-A-3062 | 12 |
| *(Promo-only album)* | | | |

| Title | Yr | Label, Number | NM $ |
|---|---|---|---|

**WILDWOODS, THE**
*See Five Satins*
**45s**

| | | | |
|---|---|---|---|
| WHEN THE SWALLOWS COME BACK TO CAPISTRANO | 1959 | Caprice 101 | 75 |
| *(White promo label)* | | | |

**WILLIAMS, ANDY**
*Cadence white promo label 45s $8-10 each; Columbia promo 45s $3 each; Columbia 33rpm singles $5 each; Columbia jukebox LLPs $6 each*
**45s**

| | | | |
|---|---|---|---|
| AWAY IN A MANGER | 1963 | Columbia JZSP 76322 | 12 |
| *(Promo-only "Special Album Excerpt")* | | | |
| CAMP FIRE GIRLS  Various artists | 1965 | CFG (Decca) 8986 | 18 |
| *(Public service ads including one by Andy Williams)* | | | |
| CAN'T GET USED TO LOSING YOU | 1963 | Columbia 42674 | 10 |
| *(Red vinyl, white promo label)* | | | |
| THE CHRISTMAS SONG | 1963 | Columbia 42894 | 12 |
| *(Green vinyl, white promo label)* | | | |
| HAVE YOURSELF A MERRY LITTLE CHRISTMAS | 1963 | Columbia JZSP 111911 | 12 |
| *(Green vinyl, promo-only white label release)* | | | |
| HAVE YOURSELF A MERRY LITTLE CHRISTMAS | 1966 | Columbia JZSP 111911 | 10 |
| *(Black vinyl, white promo label)* | | | |
| HAVE YOURSELF A MERRY LITTLE CHRISTMAS | 1967 | Columbia JZSP 111911 | 10 |
| *(Black vinyl, yellow promo label)* | | | |
| HOLIDAY GREETINGS VOICE TRACKS  Various artists | 1963 | Columbia JZSP 111921 | 15 |
| *(Green vinyl, radio only promos from Jimmy Dean, Jerry Vale, Patti Page and Andy Williams)* | | | |
| IT'S THE MOST WONDERFUL TIME OF THE YEAR | 1964 | Columbia JZSP 79169 | 12 |
| *(First release on 45, promo only)* | | | |
| IT'S THE MOST WONDERFUL TIME OF THE YEAR | 1968 | Columbia 44709 | 15 |
| *(Christmas Seals record for 1968, with spoken intro and promo-only picture sleeve)* | | | |
| IT'S THE MOST WONDERFUL TIME OF THE YEAR | 1976 | Columbia AE7 1108 | 10 |
| *(Promo-only record and promo-only picture sleeve)* | | | |
| WHITE CHRISTMAS | 1963 | Columbia JZSP 71508 | 18 |
| *(Green vinyl, white promo label, with promo-only sleeve consisting of a letter)* | | | |
| WRONG FOR EACH OTHER | 1964 | Columbia 43015 | 10 |
| *(Yellow vinyl, white promo label)* | | | |
| YOU CAN'T BUY HAPPINESS | 1954 | "X" (RCA) 0036 | 15 |
| *(White promo label)* | | | |

**7-Inch Extended Plays**

| | | | |
|---|---|---|---|
| EXCERPTS FROM TO YOU SWEETHEART ALOHA | 1961 | Cadence DJ-903 | 15 |
| *(White promo label, four songs, no cover)* | | | |
| EXCERPTS FROM TWO TIME WINNERS | 1960 | Cadence DJ-902 | 15 |
| *(White promo label, four songs, no cover)* | | | |
| GREAT SONGS OF JIMMY McHUGH (70s) With Tony Bennett | 197? | (no label) | 10 |
| *(33rpm, small center hole, four songs, paper sleeve, released as a promo only)* | | | |
| MERRY CHRISTMAS FROM ANDY WILLIAMS | 1967 | Columbia Special Products CSM 639 | 15 |
| *(With picture sleeve, plays at 33 1/3 rpm, special promo for Fireman's Fund American insurance)* | | | |

**Albums**

| | | | |
|---|---|---|---|
| ANDY & COMPANY | 1969 | Columbia Special Products  CSS 966 | 15 |
| *(Available only at Woolworth's)* | | | |
| ANDY WILLIAMS CATALOGUE - VOL. 1 (70s) | 197? | Columbia DJ 6 | 75 |
| *(Blue vinyl, promo only, special sleeve)* | | | |
| SKITCH HENDERSON FEATURING ANDY WILLIAMS (60s) | 196? | SESAC 1451 | 50 |
| *(Promo-only album)* | | | |

**WILLIAMS, DENIECE**
**12-Inch Singles**

| | | | |
|---|---|---|---|
| LET'S HEAR IT FOR THE BOY (6:00) (3:34) | 1984 | Columbia AS 1838 | 15 |
| NEVER SAY NEVER (3 versions) | 1987 | Columbia CAS 2688 | 6 |

**45s**

| | | | |
|---|---|---|---|
| GOD IS AMAZING/GOD IS STANDING BY | 1977 | Columbia AE7 1153 | 8 |
| *(B-side by Johnnie Taylor; promo with "Suggested Christmas Programming" on label)* | | | |

**WILLIAMS, DON**
*JMI promo 45s $4 each; All other label 45s $2 each; Columbia promo 45s by Pozo Seco Singers $5 each Lead singer with the Pozo Seco Singers*
**45s**

| | | | |
|---|---|---|---|
| A SPECIAL MESSAGE FROM DON WILLIAMS | 1982 | MCA S45-1763 | 12 |
| *(Promo-only short dialog release)* | | | |

**Albums**

| | | | |
|---|---|---|---|
| EXPRESSIONS | 1978 | ABC 44 | 18 |
| *(Promo-only picture disc)* | | | |

**RADIO SHOWS**
**Albums**

| | | | |
|---|---|---|---|
| AMERICAN EAGLE (Jan 87) Live concert | 1987 | DIR (3) | 75-125 |
| *(With Emmylou Harris)* | | | |
| DOLLY & DON (Music and interviews) | 1983 | Mutual Radio (3) | 20-30 |
| *(With Dolly Parton)* | | | |
| INTERNATIONAL FESTIVAL OF COUNTRY MUSIC (Oct 82) | 1982 | Mutual Radio (3) | 20-40 |
| *(Williams, Boxcar Willie, Razzy Bailey and others)* | | | |

**WILLIAMS, HANK**
*Also known as Luke the Drifter; Other yellow promo label 78s $12-15 each; Other MGM yellow promo label 45s $10-20 each; MGM white promo label 45s $5 each; Decca promo 78s by Audrey Williams $18 each; Decca promo 45s by Audrey Williams $15 each; Other promo LPs $15-25 each*
**45s**

| | | | |
|---|---|---|---|
| A HOME IN HEAVEN  Hank and Audrey Williams | 1956 | MGM 12394 | 18 |
| *(Yellow promo label)* | | | |

| Title | Yr | Label, Number | NM $ |
|---|---|---|---|
| LITTLE BOSEPHUS  Audrey Williams | 1955 | MGM 12082 | 50 |
| *(Yellow promo label, song about six-year-old Hank Jr., whose name appears on the label on this 1955 record)* | | | |
| **7-Inch Extended Plays** | | | |
| THE LEGEND LIVES ON   Jukebox LLP | 1966 | MGM 4377 | 40 |
| *(Issued with a hard cover)* | | | |
| THE VERY BEST OF HANK WILLIAMS  Jukebox LLP | 1965 | MGM 4168 | 50 |
| *(Issued with a hard cover)* | | | |
| **78s** | | | |
| BABY, WE'RE REALLY IN LOVE | 1951 | MGM 11100 | 25 |
| *(Yellow promo label)* | | | |
| COLD COLD HEART | 1951 | MGM 10904 | 25 |
| *(Yellow promo label)* | | | |
| CRAZY HEART | 1951 | MGM 11054 | 25 |
| *(Yellow promo label)* | | | |
| HALF AS MUCH | 1952 | MGM 11202 | 25 |
| *(Yellow promo label)* | | | |
| HELP ME UNDERSTAND  Audrey Williams | 1950 | Decca 46275 | 25 |
| *(Decca promo label)* | | | |
| HELP ME UNDERSTAND  Luke the Drifter | 1950 | MGM 10806 | 50 |
| *(Yellow promo label)* | | | |
| HEY, GOOD LOOKIN' | 1951 | MGM 11000 | 25 |
| *(Yellow promo label)* | | | |
| A HOME IN HEAVEN  Hank and Audrey Williams | 1956 | MGM 12394 | 25 |
| *(Yellow promo label)* | | | |
| HONKY TONK BLUES | 1952 | MGM 11160 | 25 |
| *(Yellow promo label)* | | | |
| I CAN'T HELP IT | 1951 | MGM 10961 | 25 |
| *(Yellow promo label)* | | | |
| I JUST DON'T LIKE THIS KIND OF LIVIN' | 1950 | MGM 10609 | 50 |
| I'LL NEVER GET OUT OF THIS WORLD ALIVE | 1952 | MGM 11366 | 30 |
| *(Yellow promo label, this was his current record at the time of his death)* | | | |
| IF YOU SEE MY BABY  Audrey Williams | 1951 | MGM 11083 | 20 |
| *(Yellow promo label)* | | | |
| JAMBALAYA | 1952 | MGM 11283 | 20 |
| *(Yellow promo label)* | | | |
| KAW-LIGA | 1953 | MGM 11416 | 20 |
| *(Yellow promo label)* | | | |
| LITTLE BOSEPHUS  Audrey Williams | 1955 | MGM 12082 | 60 |
| *(Yellow promo label)* | | | |
| MOANIN' THE BLUES | 1951 | MGM 10832 | 35 |
| *(Yellow promo label)* | | | |
| MY SON CALLS ANOTHER MAN DADDY | 1950 | MGM 10645 | 50 |
| *(Yellow promo label)* | | | |
| TAKE THESE CHAINS FROM MY HEART | 1953 | MGM 11479 | 18 |
| *(Yellow promo label)* | | | |
| THEY'LL NEVER TAKE HER LOVE FROM ME | 1950 | MGM 10760 | 40 |
| *(Yellow promo label)* | | | |
| WHY DON'T YOU LOVE ME | 1950 | MGM 10696 | 50 |
| *(Yellow promo label)* | | | |
| YOU WIN AGAIN | 1952 | MGM 11318 | 25 |
| *(Yellow promo label)* | | | |
| **Albums** | | | |
| HANK WILLIAMS AS LUKE THE DRIFTER | 1955 | MGM 3267 | 150 |
| *(Yellow promo label)* | | | |
| HANK WILLIAMS MEMORIAL ALBUM | 1955 | MGM 3272 | 125 |
| *(Yellow promo label)* | | | |
| HONKY TONKIN' | 1957 | MGM 3412 | 125 |
| *(Yellow promo label)* | | | |
| I SAW THE LIGHT | 1956 | MGM 3331 | 150 |
| *(Yellow promo label)* | | | |
| THE IMMORTAL HANK WILLIAMS | 1958 | MGM 3605 | 125 |
| *(Yellow promo label)* | | | |
| MOANIN' THE BLUES | 1956 | MGM 3330 | 125 |
| *(Yellow promo label)* | | | |
| RAMBLIN' MAN | 1955 | MGM 3219 | 150 |
| *(Yellow promo label)* | | | |
| REFLECTIONS BY THOSE WHO LOVED HIM  Box set | 1975 | MGM PRO 912 (3) | 250 |
| *(White promo labels, various artists, with Hank Williams Jr.)* | | | |
| SAMPLER OF MGM ALBUMS  Various artists | 1956 | MGM DJ-2 | 40 |
| *(Includes one Hank Williams song, "I'm A Long Gone Daddy")* | | | |
| SING ME A SONG | 1957 | MGM 3560 | 125 |
| *(Yellow promo label)* | | | |
| THE UNFORGETTABLE HANK WILLIAMS | 1959 | MGM 3733 | 125 |
| *(Yellow promo label)* | | | |

## WILLIAMS, HANK, JR.

Also recorded as Luke the Drifter, Jr. and Bocephus; MGM yellow promo label 45s $6 each (Including Luke the Drifter, Jr.); MGM white promo label 45s $5 each; Elektra promo 45s $3 each; Other Warner Bros. promo 45s $2 each; MGM yellow or white promo LPs $10 each; Other Warner Bros., Capricorn or Curb promo CD singles $3 each

| Title | Yr | Label, Number | NM $ |
|---|---|---|---|
| **12-Inch Singles** | | | |
| MY NAME IS BOCEPHUS (same on both sides) | 1987 | Warner Bros. PRO-A-2662 | 8 |
| WOMAN ON THE RUN (same on both sides) | 1983 | Warner Bros. PRO-A-2088 | 8 |
| **45s** | | | |
| ALL MY ROWDY FRIENDS (ARE HERE ON MONDAY NIGHT) | 1989 | Warner Bros. PRO-S-3838 | 15 |
| *(Promo-only release of the Monday Night Football theme, later reissued on CD/cassette/LP as "All My Rowdy Friends Are Coming Over for Monday Night Football" and later still as "Monday Night Football Boogie")* | | | |

| Title | Yr | Label, Number | NM $ |
|---|---|---|---|
| DON'T GIVE US A REASON | 1990 | No label (Warner Bros.) PRO-S-4492 | 10 |
| *(White label promo-only release)* | | | |
| LITTLE DRUMMER BOY/THE CHRISTMAS SONG | 1981 | Elektra 47231 | 8 |
| *(B-side by Sonny Curtis)* | | | |
| THE LAST PICTURE SHOW  Movie ads | 1971 | Columbia Pictures | 75 |
| *(Four 60-second spots, yellow promo label)* | | | |
| **7-Inch Extended Plays** | | | |
| BALLADS OF THE HILLS & PLAINS  Jukebox LLP | 1965 | MGM 4316 | 40 |
| *(Issued with a hard cover)* | | | |
| **Albums** | | | |
| THE HANK WILLIAMS, JR., INTERVIEW | 1983 | Warner Bros. PRO-A-2092 | 25 |
| **Compact Discs** | | | |
| MONDAY NIGHT FOOTBALL BOOGIE | 1991 | Warner Bros. PRO-CD-5109 | 10 |
| *(The Monday Night Football theme, third different title for this famous theme)* | | | |
| **RADIO SHOWS** | | | |
| **Albums** | | | |
| COUNTRY MUSIC TIME (70s) | 197? | U.S. Air Force | 15-25 |
| *(White label, music and interviews)* | | | |
| COUNTRY MUSIC TIME (80s) | 198? | U.S. Air Force | 15-25 |
| *(Blue label, music and interviews)* | | | |
| COUNTRY SESSIONS | 1981 | Country Sessions | 25-40 |
| *(Mostly music and interviews)* | | | |
| LIVE AT GILLEY'S (Aug 88) | 1988 | Westwood One | 30-60 |
| *(Live concert, repeated)* | | | |
| THE SILVER EAGLE | 1981 | DIR (3) | 40-75 |
| *(Live concert, repeated several times)* | | | |

**WILLIAMS, LARRY**
*Specialty and Okeh promo 45s $15 each*

**WILLIAMS, LEE**

| **45s** | | | |
|---|---|---|---|
| I'M SO IN LOVE | 1960 | King 5409 | 100 |
| *(White promo label)* | | | |

**WILLIAMS, MAURICE**
*And the Zodiacs*

| **45s** | | | |
|---|---|---|---|
| STAY | 1960 | Herald 552 | 12 |
| *(White promo label)* | | | |

**WILLIS, CHUCK**
*Atlantic promo 45s $15 each; Epic promo 45s $8 each*

| **Albums** | | | |
|---|---|---|---|
| CHUCK WILLIS WAILS THE BLUES | 1958 | Epic 3425 | 200 |
| *(White promo label)* | | | |
| I REMEMBER CHUCK WILLIS | 1963 | Atlantic 8079 | 75 |
| *(White promo label)* | | | |
| A TRIBUTE TO CHUCK WILLIS | 1960 | Epic 3728 | 175 |
| *(White promo label)* | | | |

**WILLIS, HAL**

| **45s** | | | |
|---|---|---|---|
| BOP-A-DEE, BOP-A-DOO | 1957 | Atlantic 1114 | 175 |
| *(White promo label)* | | | |

**WILLS, BOB**
*MGM promo 45s $10 each; Decca promo 45s $6 each*

| **7-Inch Extended Plays** | | | |
|---|---|---|---|
| FOR THE LAST TIME | 1974 | United Artists SP-102 | 15 |
| *(Four-song promo only, yellow label, issued with a promo paper picture sleeve)* | | | |

**WILSON, BRIAN**
*Of the Beach Boys, The Timers*

| **45s** | | | |
|---|---|---|---|
| LET'S GO TO HEAVEN IN MY CAR | 1987 | Sire 28350 | 10 |
| *(Yellow promo label)* | | | |
| LOVE AND MERCY | 1988 | Sire 27814 | 10 |
| *(Yellow promo label)* | | | |
| MELT AWAY | 1988 | Sire 27694 | 15 |
| *(Yellow promo label)* | | | |
| NIGHT TIME | 1988 | Sire 27787 | 100 |
| *(Yellow promo label, promo-only release, price includes picture sleeve)* | | | |
| NO-GO SHOWBOAT  The Timers | 1963 | Reprise 0231 | 50 |
| *(White promo label)* | | | |
| **Albums** | | | |
| SILVER PLATTER SERVICE (Oct 64) | 1964 | Capitol 3123 | 75-100 |
| *(Includes music and interview with Jack Wagner)* | | | |
| SILVER PLATTER SERVICE (Sept 67) | 1967 | Capitol 3266 | 75-100 |
| *(Includes music and interviews with Jack Wagner)* | | | |
| SILVER PLATTER SHOW (Dec 64) The Beach Boys | 1964 | Capitol 3133 | 150-250 |
| *(Special music and interview Christmas show)* | | | |
| WORDS AND MUSIC | 1988 | Sire PRO-A-3248 | 25 |
| *Promo-only music and interview* | | | |

| Title | Yr | Label, Number | NM $ |
|---|---|---|---|
| **Cassettes** | | | |
| IN MY CAR  Special cassette remix | 1989 | (No label or number) | 100 |
| *(Listed on cassette as "The Beach Boys," but it is Wilson solo; only 150 copies were made and the price includes letter from Brian Wilson)* | | | |
| **Compact Discs** | | | |
| LOVE AND MERCY | 1988 | Sire PRO-CD-3168 | 10 |
| *(Promo CD single)* | | | |
| MELT AWAY | 1988 | Sire PRO-CD-3303 | 10 |
| *(Promo CD single)* | | | |
| NIGHT TIME | 1988 | Sire PRO-CD-3200 | 10 |
| *(Promo CD single)* | | | |
| WORDS AND MUSIC | 1990 | Sire PRO-CD-3248 | 25 |
| *(Music and interview promo-only CD release)* | | | |
| YOUR IMAGINATION | 1998 | Giant | 10 |
| *(Promo CD single)* | | | |
| **RADIO SHOWS** | | | |
| **Albums** | | | |
| THE CRAWDADDY BRIAN WILSON INTERVIEW | 1977 | Crawdaddy | 100-150 |
| *(Promo-only interview record)* | | | |

**WILSON, JACKIE**
*Brunswick promo 45s through 55166 $20 each; Brunswick promo 45s after 55167 $5-15 each*

**WILSON, PEANUTS**

| Title | Yr | Label, Number | NM $ |
|---|---|---|---|
| **45s** | | | |
| CAST IRON ARM | 1958 | Brunswick 55039 | 125 |
| *(Features Buddy Holly on guitar)* | | | |

**WILSON, RON**

| Title | Yr | Label, Number | NM $ |
|---|---|---|---|
| **45s** | | | |
| I'LL KEEP ON LOVIN' YOU | 1968 | Columbia 44636 | 50 |
| *(White promo label)* | | | |

**WINCHESTER, JESSE**
*Bearsville promo 45s $3 each*

| Title | Yr | Label, Number | NM $ |
|---|---|---|---|
| **Albums** | | | |
| THE JESSE WINCHESTER RADIO SHOW | 1976 | Bearsville PRO 560 | 40 |
| LIVE AT THE BIJOU CAFÉ | 1977 | Bearsville PRO-693 | 40 |
| *(Promo only, live music and interviews)* | | | |

**WINGER**
*Atlantic promo 45s $3 each; Atlantic promo CD singles $2-3 each*

| Title | Yr | Label, Number | NM $ |
|---|---|---|---|
| **RADIO SHOWS** | | | |
| **Albums** | | | |
| HIGH VOLTAGE (Apr 89) Various artists | 1989 | Westwood One (2) | 20-40 |
| *(Live segment features Winger)* | | | |
| OFF THE RECORD | 1990 | Westwood One (2) | 15-25 |
| *(Music and interviews)* | | | |
| SUPERSTAR CONCERT (May 91) | 1991 | Westwood One (3) | 40-60 |
| *(With the Black Crowes)* | | | |

**WINTER, EDGAR**
*Epic promo 45s $5 each; Blue Sky promo 45s $3 each; Body Rock promo 45s $3 each; Epic promo LPs $15 each Includes Edgar Winter's White Trash*

| Title | Yr | Label, Number | NM $ |
|---|---|---|---|
| **45s** | | | |
| WHAT'S IT ALL ABOUT (Sept 73) Public service show | 1973 | W.I.A.A. 191 | 25 |
| *(Interviews)* | | | |
| **Albums** | | | |
| JOHNNY & EDGAR WINTER DISCUSS… | 1976 | Blue Sky ASZ-242 | 25 |
| *(White promo label, special cover, interviews)* | | | |
| **RADIO SHOWS** | | | |
| **Albums** | | | |
| PIONEERS IN MUSIC (Dec 85)  Johnny & Edgar Winter | 1985 | DIR (2) | 25-50 |
| *(Mostly music and interviews)* | | | |
| **Compact Discs** | | | |
| IN THE STUDIO EDGAR WINTER | 1990 | Album Network | 15-25 |
| *(Profile of an album, music and interviews)* | | | |
| KING BISCUIT FLOWER HOUR (June 88) Johnny & Edgar Winter | 1988 | DIR | 40-75 |
| *(Live concert, repeated)* | | | |
| KING BISCUIT FLOWER HOUR (Apr 91) Live concert | 1991 | DIR | 25-50 |
| *(With Blues Traveler)* | | | |
| KING BISCUIT FLOWER HOUR (Feb 93) | 1993 | DIR | 30-60 |
| *(Live concert)* | | | |

**WINTER, JOHNNY**
*Columbia promo 45s $4 each*

| Title | Yr | Label, Number | NM $ |
|---|---|---|---|
| **Albums** | | | |
| JOHNNY & EDGAR WINTER DISCUSS … | 1976 | Blue Sky ASZ-242 | 25 |
| *(White promo label, special cover, interviews)* | | | |
| PROGRESSIVE BLUES EXPERIMENT | 1968 | Sonobeat 1002 | 400 |
| *(Issued with a plain white cover)* | | | |
| **RADIO SHOWS** | | | |
| **Albums** | | | |
| PIONEERS IN MUSIC (Dec 85) Johnny & Edgar Winter | 1985 | DIR (2) | 25-50 |
| *(Music and interviews)* | | | |

| Title | Yr | Label, Number | NM $ |
|---|---|---|---|
| RETRO ROCK (Jan 82) JOHNNY WINTER | 1982 | Clayton Webster | 100-175 |
| *(Rare live concert)* | | | |
| **Compact Discs** | | | |
| KING BISCUIT FLOWER HOUR (Apr 91) Live concert | 1991 | DIR | 25-50 |
| *(With Blues Traveler)* | | | |
| KING BISCUIT FLOWER HOUR (June 88) Johnny & Edgar Winter | 1988 | DIR | 40-75 |
| *(Live concert, repeated)* | | | |

## WINWOOD, STEVE
*Also see Traffic; Island promo 45s $3 each; Virgin promo CD singles $3 each*

| Title | Yr | Label, Number | NM $ |
|---|---|---|---|
| **12-Inch Singles** | | | |
| FREEDOM OVERSPILL (Edit) (LP Version) | 1986 | Island PRO-A-2562 | 6 |
| HEARTS ON FIRE (Remix) (LP Version) | 1988 | Virgin 2637 | 6 |
| STILL IN THE GAME (same on both sides) | 1982 | Island PRO-A-1054 | 8 |
| TALKING BACK TO THE NIGHT (same on both sides) | 1987 | Island PRO-A-2908 | 6 |
| **Compact Discs** | | | |
| HIGHLIGHTS FROM THE FINER THINGS BOX SET | 1995 | Island PRCD 6842 | 25 |
| *(With press kit, promo-only sampler)* | | | |
| REFUGEES OF THE HEART | 1990 | Virgin PRCD STEVE | 20 |
| *(Promo-only version, full-length in pouch)* | | | |
| **RADIO SHOWS** | | | |
| **Albums** | | | |
| DESERT ISLAND DISCS (Oct 92) | 1992 | Westwood One | 10-20 |
| *(Music and interviews)* | | | |
| LEGENDS OF ROCK (Apr 87) | 1987 | NBC Radio (2) | 25-40 |
| *(Music and interviews)* | | | |
| LEGENDS OF ROCK (Apr 87) | 1987 | NBC Radio (4) | 30-45 |
| *(Music and interviews)* | | | |
| OFF THE RECORD (Sept 87) | 1987 | Westwood One (2) | 20-25 |
| *(Music and interviews)* | | | |
| OFF THE RECORD | 1988 | Westwood One (2) | 15-25 |
| *(Music and interviews)* | | | |
| OFF THE RECORD (July 93)  With Traffic | 1993 | Westwood One (2) | 15-25 |
| *(Music and interviews)* | | | |
| RADIO TODAY (Aug 88) | 1988 | Radio International (2) | 20-35 |
| *(Music and interviews)* | | | |
| ROCK STARS (Apr 88) | 1988 | Radio International (2) | 10-20 |
| *(Music and interviews)* | | | |
| SUPERSTAR CONCERT | 1987 | Westwood One (3) | 25-50 |
| *(Live concert)* | | | |
| THE STEVE WINWOOD SPECIAL (Dec 81) | 1981 | NBC Source (3) | 20-40 |
| *(Music and interviews)* | | | |
| **Compact Discs** | | | |
| BBC CLASSIC TRACKS (July 93) | 1993 | Westwood One | 10-20 |
| *(Classic live tracks)* | | | |
| SUPERSTAR CONCERT (June 94) With Traffic | 1994 | Westwood One (2) | 20-35 |
| *(Music and interviews)* | | | |
| TIMOTHY WHITE SESSIONS (July 90) | 1990 | Westwood One (2) | 30-60 |
| *(Music and interviews)* | | | |
| UP CLOSE | 1989 | Media America (4) | 50-80 |
| *(Mostly music and interviews)* | | | |
| UP CLOSE | 1989 | Media America (2) | 20-40 |
| *(Mostly music and interviews)* | | | |

## WIRE

| Title | Yr | Label, Number | NM $ |
|---|---|---|---|
| **12-Inch Singles** | | | |
| IN VIVO (3 versions) | 1989 | Enigma EPRO 215 | 10 |

## WISHBONE ASH
*Decca promo 45s $4 each*

| Title | Yr | Label, Number | NM $ |
|---|---|---|---|
| **Albums** | | | |
| AN EVENING PROGRAM WITH WISHBONE ASH | 1972 | Decca 71919 | 30 |
| *(Promo-only release)* | | | |
| LIVE FROM MEMPHIS | 1972 | Decca 71922 | 40 |
| *(Promo-only release)* | | | |
| **RADIO SHOWS** | | | |
| **Albums** | | | |
| BBC ROCK HOUR (Jan 82) | 1982 | London Wavelength | 40-75 |
| *(Live concert)* | | | |
| BBC TRANSCRIPTION DISC | 1971 | BBC Transcription | 200-300 |
| *(Very rare live concert)* | | | |

## WITHERS, BILL

| Title | Yr | Label, Number | NM $ |
|---|---|---|---|
| **12-Inch Singles** | | | |
| SOMETHING THAT TURNS YOU ON (same on both sides) | 1985 | Columbia CAS 2112 | 8 |

## WOLF, PETER
*EMI promo 45s $3 each; EMI promo 12" singles $6 each Lead singer of the J. Geils Band*

| Title | Yr | Label, Number | NM $ |
|---|---|---|---|
| **Compact Discs** | | | |
| HOUSE OF BLUES (June 94) | 1994 | (2) | 20-40 |
| *(Live concert)* | | | |
| ROCK STARS (Apr 90) | 1990 | Radio International (2) | 10-20 |
| *(Music and interviews)* | | | |

| Title | Yr | Label, Number | NM $ |
|---|---|---|---|
| **WOLFE, RICHARD, CHILDREN'S CHORUS** | | | |
| **45s** | | | |
| A MERRY CHRISTMAS WISH/A MERRY CHRISTMAS SONG! | 1970 | RCA Victor SPS-45-279 | 6 |
| *(B-side by Living Strings and Living Voices)* | | | |
| | | | |
| **WOLFGANG PRESS, THE** | | | |
| **12-Inch Singles** | | | |
| GOING SOUTH (2 versions)/11 YEARS/EXECUTIONER | 1994 | Warner Bros. PRO-A-7174 | 8 |
| | | | |
| **WOMACK, BOBBY** | | | |
| **12-Inch Singles** | | | |
| GYPSY WOMAN/WHATEVER HAPPENED TO THE TIMES? (2 versions) | 1986 | MCA L33-17104 | 8 |
| SAVE THE CHILDREN (3 versions) | 1989 | Solar ZAS 1923 | 8 |
| **45s** | | | |
| HARRY HIPPIE (mono/stereo) | 1972 | United Artists 50988 | 8 |
| *(Apparently, no stock copy exists on this number)* | | | |
| | | | |
| **WONDER, STEVIE** | | | |
| *Also recorded as Eivets Rednow; Other Tamla promo 45s $5-10 each; Tamla all-white label 1808 test pressings $8 each; Tamla promo picture sleeves $4 each; Tamla EP from "Key of Life" LP $5 each; Gordy promo 45s by Eivets Rednow $6 each; Other white promo label LPs $20-30 each* | | | |
| **12-Inch Singles** | | | |
| DO I DO (LP)/(Instrumental)//FRONT LINE (LP) (Instrumental) | 1982 | Tamla 98/99 | 15 |
| *Two-record promo set* | | | |
| FOR YOUR LOVE (4 versions) | 1995 | Motown 374631261 | 8 |
| FUN DAY (8 versions) | 1991 | Motown 1690 | 8 |
| FUN DAY (Edit) (LP) (Instrumental) | 1991 | Motown 1602 | 8 |
| GOTTA HAVE YOU (3 versions) | 1991 | Motown 1093 | 8 |
| KEEP OUR LOVE ALIVE/(Instrumental) | 1990 | Motown 1065 | 7 |
| LAND OF LA LA (8:40)/(Instrumental) | 1986 | Tamla PR 186 | 6 |
| LOVE LIGHT IN FLIGHT (Remix) (Instrumental) | 1984 | Motown PR 161 | 6 |
| WITH EACH BEAT OF MY HEART (LP) (Edit) (Instrumental) | 1987 | Motown L33-17755 | 6 |
| **45s** | | | |
| I CALL IT PRETTY MUSIC | 1962 | Tamla 54061 | 20 |
| *(White promo label, stock picture sleeve worth $50)* | | | |
| I JUST CALLED TO SAY I LOVE YOU | 1984 | Motown 1745 | 50 |
| *(White promo label with extremely rare promo picture sleeve; a tiny handful of these sleeves can be found with stock copies)* | | | |
| NEVER DREAMED YOU'D LEAVE IN SUMMER | 1970 | Tamla 54202 | 20 |
| *(Red vinyl, white promo label)* | | | |
| OVERJOYED | 1986 | Tamla 1832 | 8 |
| *(White promo label with promo picture sleeve)* | | | |
| A PLACE IN THE SUN | 1966 | Tamla 54139 | 25 |
| *(Red vinyl, white promo label)* | | | |
| WHAT'S IT ALL ABOUT (May 81) Public service show | 1981 | W.I.A.A. 574 | 15 |
| *(Flip side features Judy Collins)* | | | |
| **7-Inch Extended Plays** | | | |
| SOMETHING'S EXTRA, A | 1975 | Tamla 340 EP | 5 |
| *(Bonus 7-inch 33 1/3 EP with large hole, issued with "Songs in the Key of Life" LP but often found separately in the secondary market)* | | | |
| **Albums** | | | |
| CONVERSATION PEACE | 1995 | Motown 31453 0238-1 (2) | 25 |
| *(Vinyl is promo only; white cover with custom sticker)* | | | |
| JAZZ SOUL OF STEVIE WONDER | 1963 | Tamla 233 | 50 |
| *(White promo label)* | | | |
| JOURNEY THROUGH THE SECRET LIFE OF PLANTS | 1979 | Tamla PR-61 | 18 |
| *(Promo-only edited version of the multi-LP)* | | | |
| LITTLE STEVIE WONDER THE 12-YEAR-OLD GENIUS | 1963 | Tamla 240 | 40 |
| *(White promo label)* | | | |
| SOMEDAY AT CHRISTMAS | 1967 | Tamla 281 | 50 |
| *(White promo label)* | | | |
| TRIBUTE TO UNCLE RAY | 1963 | Tamla 232 | 75 |
| *(White promo label)* | | | |
| **RADIO SHOWS** | | | |
| **Albums** | | | |
| INNERVIEW (70s) Profile | 197? | Innerview (2) | 25-40 |
| *(Music and interviews, two weekly shows)* | | | |
| STEVIE WONDER (July 83) | 1983 | Mutual Radio (3) | 25-50 |
| *(Box set, music and interviews)* | | | |
| | | | |
| **WOOD, BOBBY** | | | |
| **45s** | | | |
| EVERYBODY'S SEARCHIN'/HUMAN EMOTIONS | 1961 | Sun 369 | 600 |
| *(No stock copies known; should one be discovered, it would be worth much more)* | | | |
| | | | |
| **WOOD, ROY** | | | |
| **Albums** | | | |
| BOULDERS FOLDER | 1973 | United Artists (# unknown) | 40 |
| *(Promo version of United Artists 168 in 13x13 folder with press kit and postcards)* | | | |
| | | | |
| **WOODY, DON** | | | |
| **45s** | | | |
| YOU'RE BARKING UP THE WRONG TREE | 1958 | Decca 30277 | 40 |
| *(Pink promo label)* | | | |

| Title | Yr | Label, Number | NM $ |
|-------|-----|--------------|------|

**WOOLEY, SHEB**
*Also recorded as Ben Colder; Other MGM yellow promo label 45s $5 each; MGM white promo label 45s $3 each; Sunbird promo 45s $2 each; MGM yellow and white promo label 45s by Ben Colder $4-5 each; Other MGM yellow promo label LPs $18 each; MGM yellow promo label LPs by Ben Colder $8 each*

**45s**

| Title | Yr | Label, Number | NM $ |
|-------|-----|--------------|------|
| THE PURPLE PEOPLE EATER | 1958 | MGM 12651 | 25 |
| *(Yellow promo label)* | | | |
| SANTA AND THE PURPLE PEOPLE EATER | 1958 | MGM 12733 | 18 |
| *(Yellow promo label)* | | | |
| **Albums** | | | |
| SHEB WOOLEY | 1956 | MGM 3299 | 125 |
| *(Yellow promo label)* | | | |

**WORLD PARTY**

**12-Inch Singles**

| Title | Yr | Label, Number | NM $ |
|-------|-----|--------------|------|
| ALL COME TRUE (same on both sides) | 1987 | Chrysalis VAS 2708 | 5 |
| PRIVATE REVOLUTION (same on both sides) | 1987 | Chrysalis VAS 2657 | 5 |
| SHIP OF FOOLS (same on both sides) | 1986 | Chrysalis VAS 2482 | 5 |

**WRAY, LINK**
*Cadence promo 45s $12 each; Epic promo 45s $8 each; Swan promo 45s $5 each Also recorded as Lucky Wray*

**Albums**

| Title | Yr | Label, Number | NM $ |
|-------|-----|--------------|------|
| LINK WRAY & THE WRAYMEN | 1960 | Epic 3661 | 60 |
| *(White promo label)* | | | |

**WRIGHT, GARY**
*A&M promo 45s by Gary Wright or Spooky Tooth $5 each; Warner Bros. promo 45s $3 each; Cypress and Reprise promo CD singles $3 each Of Spooky Tooth*

**45s**

| Title | Yr | Label, Number | NM $ |
|-------|-----|--------------|------|
| WHAT'S IT ALL ABOUT (June 77) Public service show | 1977 | W.I.A.A. 374 | 12 |
| *(Flip side features Brick)* | | | |
| WHAT'S IT ALL ABOUT (Nov 73) Public service show | 1973 | W.I.A.A. 201 | 15 |
| *(Interviews)* | | | |
| **RADIO SHOWS** | | | |
| **Compact Discs** | | | |
| IN THE STUDIO (90s) Profile of an album | 199? | Album Network | 15-25 |
| *(Music and interviews)* | | | |

**WYNETTE, TAMMY**
*Other Epic promo 45s $2-3 each; Columbia promo 45s $2 each; Epic white promo label LPs $8 each*

**45s**

| Title | Yr | Label, Number | NM $ |
|-------|-----|--------------|------|
| THE WONDERS YOU PERFORM | 1971 | Epic TW 1 | 15 |
| *(Pink vinyl, white promo label, "Bonus Record")* | | | |
| WHITE CHRISTMAS | 1973 | Epic AS 60 | 15 |
| *(Promo-only record and promo-only picture sleeve)* | | | |
| **7-Inch Extended Plays** | | | |
| THE FIRST LADY   Jukebox LLP | 1971 | Epic 30213 | 15 |
| *(Issued with a hard cover)* | | | |
| TAMMY WYNETTE   Jukebox LLP | 1973 | Epic 30658 | 15 |
| *(Issued with a hard cover)* | | | |
| **Compact Discs** | | | |
| STAND BY YOUR MAN | 1998 | Epic | 8 |
| *(Promo-only CD single, 30th anniversary re-release to radio)* | | | |
| **RADIO SHOWS** | | | |
| **Albums** | | | |
| AMERICAN EAGLE (Jan 87) Live concert | 1987 | DIR (3) | 50-100 |
| *(With George Jones)* | | | |
| LIVE FROM GILLEY'S (Mar 84) Live concert | 1984 | Westwood One | 20-30 |
| *(Repeated Nov 84)* | | | |
| SILVER EAGLE (Apr 82) Live concert | 1982 | DIR (3) | 25-50 |
| *(Repeated Feb 83 and Mar 85)* | | | |
| WESTWOOD ONE PRESENTS (Nov 89) | 1989 | Westwood One | 25-50 |
| *(Live concert)* | | | |

# X

**X**
*Elektra promo 45s $4 each; Any promo CD singles $3-4 each*

**12-Inch Singles**

| Title | Yr | Label, Number | NM $ |
|-------|-----|--------------|------|
| 4TH OF JULY (same on both sides) | 1987 | Elektra ED 5232 | 8 |
| AROUND MY HEART (Edit)/(LP) | 1985 | Elektra ED 5106 | 6 |
| BREATHLESS/RIDING WITH MARY | 1983 | Elektra 4912 | 10 |
| BURNING HOUSE OF LOVE (same on both sides) | 1985 | Elektra 5068 | 8 |
| DEVIL DOLL/NEW WORLD/BURNING HOUSE OF LOVE | 1988 | Elektra ED 5305 | 6 |
| SEE HOW WE ARE (same on both sides) | 1987 | Elektra 5248 | 6 |
| TRUE LOVE PART II (3 versions) | 1983 | Elektra 4943 | 8 |
| **45s** | | | |
| BURNING HOUSE OF LOVE (edit) (same on both sides) | 1985 | Elektra 69626 | 4 |
| WILD THING/WILD THING, PART 2 | 1988 | Curb 10538 | 30 |
| *(Does not exist as stock copy)* | | | |

| Title | Yr | Label, Number | NM $ |
|---|---|---|---|
| **RADIO SHOWS** | | | |
| **Albums** | | | |
| BBC COLLEGE CONCERT (Nov 83) | 1983 | London Wavelength | 20-35 |
| *(Music and interviews with John Doe and Billy Zoom)* | | | |
| IN CONCERT (Dec 85) Live concert | 1985 | Westwood One (2) | 50-100 |
| *(Very rare concert with Alarm)* | | | |
| KING BISCUIT FLOWER HOUR (Aug 85) Live concert | 1985 | DIR (2) | 25-50 |
| *(Rare concert with John Waite)* | | | |
| **Compact Discs** | | | |
| IN CONCERT-NU ROCK (Jan 94) | 1994 | Westwood One | 30-60 |
| *(Live concert)* | | | |
| | | | |
| **XTC** | | | |
| *Virgin promo 45s $5 each; Geffen promo 45s $4 each* | | | |
| **12-Inch Singles** | | | |
| ALL YOU PRETTY GIRLS/WAKE UP/SHAKE YOU DONKEY UP | 1984 | Geffen PRO-A-2214 | 15 |
| BALL & CHAIN/SENSES WORKING OVERTIME | 1982 | Epic AS 1405 | 12 |
| GREAT FIRE/LOVE ON A FARMBOY'S WAGES/FUNK POP A ROLL | 1983 | Geffen PRO-A-2117 | 12 |
| KING FOR A DAY (3 mixes)/TOYS/DESERT ISLAND | 1989 | Geffen PRO-A-3522 | 8 |
| **45s** | | | |
| LIMELIGHT//DAY IN DAY OUT/CHAIN OF COMMAND | 1979 | Virgin PR 344 | 6 |
| *(7-inch 33 1/3 record with small center hole; included in first 15,000 copies of album 13134)* | | | |
| MAKING PLANS FOR NIGEL (mono/stereo) | 1980 | Virgin 67009 | 3 |
| TEN FEET TALL (mono/stereo) | 1980 | Virgin 67004 | 3 |
| **Albums** | | | |
| WARNER MUSIC | 1986 | Warner Bros. | 30 |
| *(Promo-only release)* | | | |
| **Compact Discs** | | | |
| NAC SAMPLER | 1993 | Geffen 4398 | 10 |
| *(Promo-only sampler)* | | | |
| RADIOS IN MOTION: A HISTORY OF XTC | 1992 | Geffen 4897 | 12 |
| *(Promo-only sampler)* | | | |
| THIS IS NOT THE NEW ALBUM | 1992 | Geffen 4396 | 10 |
| *(Promo-only sampler)* | | | |
| **RADIO SHOWS** | | | |
| **Albums** | | | |
| BBC COLLEGE CONCERT HOUR (Mar 81) | 1981 | London Wavelength | 100-175 |
| *(Live concert)* | | | |
| BBC TRANSCRIPTION DISC  Live concert | 1978 | BBC Transcription | 200-300 |
| *(With Frankie Miller)* | | | |
| BBC TRANSCRIPTION DISC | 1981 | BBC Transcription | 300-400 |
| *(Live concert)* | | | |

# Y

**YANKOVIC, "WEIRD AL"**
*T.K. promo 45s $5 each; Rock 'N' Roll (CBS) promo 45s $4 each; Other Scotti Brothers promo CD singles $4-6 each*

| Title | Yr | Label, Number | NM $ |
|---|---|---|---|
| **12-Inch Singles** | | | |
| EAT IT (same on both sides) | 1984 | Rock N Roll 1830 | 10 |
| I LOST ON JEOPARDY/MR. POPEIL | 1985 | Rock N Roll 1887 | 10 |
| LIVING WITH A HERNIA (same on both sides) | 1986 | Rock N Roll 2536 | 10 |
| **45s** | | | |
| MY BOLOGNA | 1979 | Capitol P-4816 | 10 |
| *(White promo label, his version of My Sharona)* | | | |
| **Compact Discs** | | | |
| BEDROCK ANTHEM | 1993 | Scotti Brothers 75378 | 8 |
| *(Promo-only CD single)* | | | |
| SMELLS LIKE NIRVANA | 1992 | Scotti Brothers 75314 | 8 |
| *(Promo-only CD single)* | | | |
| **RADIO SHOWS** | | | |
| **Albums** | | | |
| THE HOT ONES (May 84) | 1984 | RKO | 20-30 |
| *(Music and interviews)* | | | |
| KING BISCUIT FLOWER HOUR (Apr 84) Live concert | 1984 | DIR/ABC (2) | 75-125 |
| *(With Jason & the Scorchers)* | | | |

**YARDBIRDS, THE**
*Among the members were Jeff Beck, Eric Clapton, Jimmy Page and Keith Relf; Relf recorded with Renaissance and Armageddon; A&M and Elektra promo 45s by Renaissance and Armageddon $4 each*

| Title | Yr | Label, Number | NM $ |
|---|---|---|---|
| **45s** | | | |
| FOR YOUR LOVE | 1965 | Epic 9790 | 40 |
| *(White promo label)* | | | |
| GOODNIGHT, SWEET JOSEPHINE | 1968 | Epic 10303 | 75 |
| *(White promo label, rare record)* | | | |
| HA HA SAID THE CLOWN | 1967 | Epic 10204 | 25 |
| *(White promo label)* | | | |
| HAPPENINGS TEN YEARS TIME AGO | 1966 | Epic 10094 | 30 |
| *(White promo label, stock picture sleeve worth $30)* | | | |
| HEART FULL OF SOUL | 1965 | Epic 9823 | 40 |
| *(White promo label, stock picture sleeve worth $50)* | | | |
| I WISH YOU COULD | 1964 | Epic 9709 | 50 |
| *(White promo label, wrong title, song released as "I Wish You Would")* | | | |

| Title | Yr | Label, Number | NM $ |
|---|---|---|---|
| I WISH YOU COULD | 1964 | Epic 9709 | 600 |
| (Promo-only picture sleeve) | | | |
| I'M A MAN | 1965 | Epic 9857 | 40 |
| (White promo label) | | | |
| I'M A MAN | 197? | Epic 2247 | 18 |
| (White promo label "Memory Lane") | | | |
| LITTLE GAMES | 1967 | Epic 10156 | 25 |
| (White promo label) | | | |
| OVER UNDER SIDEWAYS DOWN | 1966 | Epic 10035 | 35 |
| (White promo label, stock picture sleeve worth $40) | | | |
| SHAPES OF THINGS | 1966 | Epic 10006 | 40 |
| (White promo label) | | | |
| SHAPES OF THINGS | 1966 | Epic 9891 | 40 |
| (White promo label) | | | |
| TEN LITTLE INDIANS | 1967 | Epic 10248 | 25 |
| (White promo label) | | | |
| **7-Inch Extended Plays** | | | |
| SHAKE-OUT  Various artists | 1967 | Columbia CSM 468 | 50 |
| (Four songs, hard cover, one by Yardbirds, "My Girl Sloopy") | | | |
| **Albums** | | | |
| ARMAGEDDON  Armageddon | 1975 | A&M 4513 | 25 |
| (White promo label) | | | |
| FOR YOUR LOVE | 1965 | Epic 24167 | 400 |
| (White promo label) | | | |
| HAVING A RAVE UP | 1965 | Epic 24177 | 400 |
| (White promo label) | | | |
| LITTLE GAMES | 1967 | Epic 24313 | 300 |
| (White promo label) | | | |
| LIVE YARDBIRDS FEATURING JIMMY PAGE | 1971 | Epic 30615 | 75 |
| (White promo label) | | | |
| OVER UNDER SIDEWAYS DOWN | 1966 | Epic 24210 | 400 |
| (White promo label) | | | |
| RENAISSANCE  Renaissance | 1970 | Elektra 74068 | 20 |
| (White promo label) | | | |
| YARDBIRDS FEATURING PERFORMANCES BY CLAPTON, BECK & PAGE | 1970 | Epic 30135 (2) | 150 |
| (White promo labels) | | | |
| YARDBIRDS' GREAT HITS | 1977 | Epic 34491 | 40 |
| (White promo label) | | | |
| YARDBIRDS' GREATEST HITS | 1966 | Epic 24246 | 300 |
| (White promo label) | | | |
| **RADIO SHOWS** | | | |
| **Albums** | | | |
| RETRO ROCK (Sept 81) | 1981 | Clayton Webster (2) | 125-200 |
| (Music and interviews with some live tracks) | | | |
| RETRO ROCK (Sept 82) | 1982 | Clayton Webster (2) | 100-200 |
| (Music and interviews with some live tracks) | | | |
| **Compact Discs** | | | |
| BBC CLASSIC TRACKS (Sept 91) | 1991 | Westwood One | 30-40 |
| (Various classic live tracks) | | | |
| BBC CLASSIC TRACKS (Sept 93) | 1993 | Westwood One | 25-35 |
| (Various classic live tracks) | | | |

## YAZ

With Alison Moyet; Band known as Yazoo outside the U.S.; Sire promo 45s $4 each; Sire promo 12" singles $8 each; Columbia promo 45s by Alison Moyet $4 each; Columbia promo picture sleeves by Alison Moyet $3 each

| | | | |
|---|---|---|---|
| **RADIO SHOWS** | | | |
| **Albums** | | | |
| BBC COLLEGE CONCERT HOUR (Feb 83) | 1983 | London Wavelength | 150-250 |
| (Very rare live concert) | | | |
| BBC TRANSCRIPTION DISC  Yazoo | 1983 | BBC Transcription | 250-375 |
| (Very rare live concert) | | | |

## YEARWOOD, TRISHA

MCA promo CD singles $3 each

| | | | |
|---|---|---|---|
| **RADIO SHOWS** | | | |
| **Compact Discs** | | | |
| COUNTRY CONCERT (June 93) | 1983 | Westwood One | 40-75 |
| (Live concert) | | | |
| 90's COUNTRY (Apr 95) | 1995 | | 15-30 |
| (Music and interviews) | | | |
| 90's COUNTRY (Dec 95) | 1995 | | 15-30 |
| (Music and interviews) | | | |
| SWEETEST GIFT, THE (Dec 94) | 1994 | (3) | 20-40 |
| (Christmas special based on release of the same name) | | | |

## YELLO

| | | | |
|---|---|---|---|
| **12-Inch Singles** | | | |
| I LOVE YOU (3 versions) | 1983 | Elektra EAOR 4920 | 10 |
| PUMPING VELVET/NO MORE WORDS/LOST AGAIN/BOSTICH | 1983 | Elektra 4941 | 10 |
| THE RACE (4 versions)/I LOVE YOU | 1989 | Mercury PRO 744-1 | 12 |
| TIED UP (4 versions) | 1988 | Mercury PRO 768-1 | 8 |
| TREMENDOUS PAIN (4 mixes) | 1995 | 4th & B'Way PR12 607 | 10 |
| (Black vinyl) | | | |
| TREMENDOUS PAIN (4 versions) | 1995 | 4th & B'Way PR12 609 | 10 |
| Yellow vinyl | | | |
| UNBELIEVABLE (6 versions) | 1990 | Elektra 5487 | 8 |
| VICIOUS GAMES (3 versions) | 1985 | Elektra ED 5039 | 10 |

| Title | Yr | Label, Number | NM $ |
|---|---|---|---|

**YES**

*Also includes GTR, ABWH, Jon Anderson and Rick Wakeman; Other Atlantic promo 45s $5-8 each; Atco promo 45s $4 each; Other Atco promo 12" singles $8 each; A&M promo 45s by Rick Wakeman $4 each; Polydor promo 45s by Jon (Anderson) and Vangelis $5 each; Arista promo 45s by GTR $3 each; Arista promo 12" singles by GTR $6 each; A&M promo LPs by Rick Wakeman $10 each; Arista promo CD singles $6 each*

**12-Inch Singles**

| Title | Yr | Label, Number | NM $ |
|---|---|---|---|
| HOLD ON (Edit)/(LP Version) | 1985 | Atco PR 796 | 12 |
| LEAVE IT (3 versions) | 1984 | Atco PR 587 | 8 |
| LOVE WILL FIND A WAY (Edit)/(LP Version) | 1987 | Atco PR 2088 | 12 |
| OWNER OF A LONELY HEART (Edit)/(LP Version) | 1983 | Atco PR 529 | 12 |
| RHYTHM OF LOVE (3 versions) | 1987 | Atco PR 1133 | 10 |

**45s**

| Title | Yr | Label, Number | NM $ |
|---|---|---|---|
| EASIER SAID THAN DONE  Jon Anderson | 1985 | No label (Elektra) 69580 | 10 |
| *(Green vinyl, white promo label)* | | | |
| ROUNDABOUT | 1972 | Atlantic 2854 | 100 |
| *(Yellow vinyl, red promo label, mono/stereo versions)* | | | |
| ROUNDABOUT | 1981 | Atlantic PR 415 | 10 |
| *(White promo label, small center hole, 7:23 version, recorded live, issued in a plain white sleeve, included with early copies of "Classic Yes")* | | | |

**Albums**

| Title | Yr | Label, Number | NM $ |
|---|---|---|---|
| CLOSE TO THE EDGE | 1972 | Atlantic 7244 | 50 |
| *(White label mono copies banded for airplay)* | | | |
| RELAYER | 1975 | Atlantic SD 18122 | 20 |
| *(Promo copies banded for airplay)* | | | |
| TALES FROM TOPOGRAPHIC OCEANS | 1974 | Atlantic SD2-908 (2) | 50 |
| *(Special banded copy for radio, includes a sticker on the cover)* | | | |
| YES MUSIC: AN EVENING WITH JON ANDERSON | 1977 | Atlantic PR 285 | 50 |
| YES SOLO LP SAMPLER | 1976 | Atlantic PR 260 | 25 |

**Compact Discs**

| Title | Yr | Label, Number | NM $ |
|---|---|---|---|
| LOVE WILL FIND A WAY | 1987 | Atco PR 2088 | 8 |
| *(Early promo-only CD single, LP and edit versions)* | | | |
| RHYTHM OF LOVE | 1987 | Atco PR 2089 | 8 |
| *(Early promo-only CD single)* | | | |
| YES YEARS SAMPLER | 1991 | Atco PRCD 4009 | 30 |
| *(Sample from box set, in scale model of actual box used for the release)* | | | |

**RADIO SHOWS**

**Albums**

| Title | Yr | Label, Number | NM $ |
|---|---|---|---|
| ALISON STEELE (70s)  Yes, Anderson, Wakeman | 197? | Tea House | 15-25 |
| *(Short interviews)* | | | |
| BBC TRANSCRIPTION DISC  Rick Wakeman | 1976 | BBC Transcription | 750-1,250 |
| *(One of the most collectible discs in the series, with the English Rock Ensemble, live concert)* | | | |
| CAPTURED LIVE (Sept 84) | 1984 | RKO (4) | 150-225 |
| *(Live concert, designer box set)* | | | |
| IN CONCERT | 1989 | Westwood One (2) | 50-100 |
| *(Live concert)* | | | |
| KING BISCUIT FLOWER HOUR (Sept 82) Jon Anderson | 1982 | DIR/ABC (2) | 300-400 |
| *(Very rare live concert, with Animotion)* | | | |
| KING BISCUIT FLOWER HOUR (Aug 86) GTR | 1986 | DIR (3) | 75-150 |
| *(Live concert)* | | | |
| KING BISCUIT FLOWER HOUR (Oct 86) GTR | 1986 | DIR (2) | 50-100 |
| *(Repeat and edited live concert show)* | | | |
| LEGENDS OF ROCK (Jan 88) | 1988 | NBC Radio (2) | 25-35 |
| *(Music and interviews)* | | | |
| LEGENDS OF ROCK (Jan 88) | 1988 | NBC Radio (4) | 35-60 |
| *(Music and interviews with some live tracks)* | | | |
| LEGENDS OF ROCK (Mar 87) | 1987 | NBC Radio (2) | 25-35 |
| *(Music and interviews)* | | | |
| LEGENDS OF ROCK (Mar 87) | 1987 | NBC Radio (4) | 30-60 |
| *(Music and interviews, two weeks)* | | | |
| NBC SOURCE (Jan 84) | 1984 | NBC Radio (3) | 30-60 |
| *(Mostly music and interviews, 90215 LP)* | | | |
| NIGHTBIRD & COMPANY (Aug 74) Various artists | 1974 | U.S. Army Reserve (2) | 40-75 |
| *(Rick Wakeman is host of one of the shows)* | | | |
| NIGHTBIRD & COMPANY (Sept 77) Various artists | 1977 | U.S. Army Reserve (2) | 40-75 |
| *(Rick Wakeman is host of one of the shows)* | | | |
| OFF THE RECORD (Dec 87) | 1987 | Westwood One (2) | 20-30 |
| *(Music and interviews)* | | | |
| PIONEERS IN MUSIC | 1986 | DIR (2) | 25-40 |
| *(Music and interviews)* | | | |
| THE PRE-CONCERT SPECIAL | 1984 | (3) | 100-175 |
| *(Live concert)* | | | |
| ROCK STARS | 1988 | Radio Today (2) | 20-40 |
| *(Music and interviews)* | | | |
| SUPERGROUPS  With Quarterflash | 1982 | DIR (3) | 100-200 |
| *(Live concert)* | | | |
| SUPERSTAR CONCERT  Various artists | 1988 | Westwood One (3) | 40-75 |
| *(Live concert)* | | | |
| SUPERSTAR CONCERT (Sept 91) | 1991 | Westwood One (3) | 75-125 |
| *(Live concert)* | | | |
| SUPERSTAR CONCERT | 1992 | Westwood One (3) | 30-60 |
| *(Live concert, repeated)* | | | |
| UP CLOSE | 1987 | MCA Radio (2) | 25-50 |
| *(Mostly music and interviews, some live tracks)* | | | |
| THE YES SPECIAL (June 80) | 1980 | NBC Radio (3) | 40-75 |
| *(Mostly music and interviews)* | | | |

**Compact Discs**

| Title | Yr | Label, Number | NM $ |
|---|---|---|---|
| IN THE STUDIO | 1989 | Album Network | 15-25 |
| *(Profile of an album, music and interviews)* | | | |
| KING BISCUIT FLOWER HOUR (Mar 88) | 1988 | DIR | 40-75 |
| *(Live concert)* | | | |

| Title | Yr | Label, Number | NM $ |
|---|---|---|---|
| KING BISCUIT FLOWER HOUR (June 89) | 1989 | DIR (2) | 75-150 |
| (Live concert, two shows, repeated Aug 91) | | | |
| KING BISCUIT FLOWER HOUR (Sept 91) | 1991 | DIR | 30-60 |
| (Live concert) | | | |
| MASTERS OF ROCK  Anderson Bruford Wakeman Howe | 1989 | Radio Ventures | 25-35 |
| (Music and interviews) | | | |
| UP CLOSE | 1994 | MCA Radio (3) | 75-125 |
| (Music and interviews and live tracks) | | | |
| UP CLOSE  Anderson Bruford Wakeman Howe | 1989 | MCA Radio (2) | 25-50 |
| (Music and interviews) | | | |
| THE YES STORY (May 94) | 1994 | Westwood One (3) | 50-100 |
| (Music and interviews with live tracks) | | | |
| YESSTORY (May 94) | 1994 | Unistar (3) | 40-75 |
| (Music and interviews) | | | |
| **Reel-to-Reel Tapes** | | | |
| TALK LISTENING PARTY (Apr 94) | 1994 | Album Network | 40-80 |
| (Music and interviews) | | | |

## YOAKAM, DWIGHT
*Reprise promo CD singles $3-5 each*
**12-Inch Singles**

| | | | |
|---|---|---|---|
| LONG WHITE CADILLAC (Edit)/(FM) | 1989 | Reprise PRO-A-3799 | 8 |
| **45s** | | | |
| THIS DRINKIN' WILL KILL ME (LIVE)/MINER'S PRAYER (LIVE) | 1985 | Warner Bros. PRO-S-2424 | 8 |
| **Compact Discs** | | | |
| SUSPICIOUS MINDS | 1993 | Epic ESK 74753 | 10 |
| (Promo CD single, his remake of the Elvis song, from "Honeymoon in Vegas") | | | |
| **RADIO SHOWS** | | | |
| **Compact Discs** | | | |
| 90's COUNTRY (Dec 95) | 1995 | 15-25 | |
| (Music and interviews) | | | |

## YORK, PETER'S, PERCUSSION BAND
**RADIO SHOWS**
**Albums**

| | | | |
|---|---|---|---|
| BBC TRANSCRIPTION DISC | 1973 | BBC Transcription | 75-125 |
| (Live concert) | | | |

## YOU AM I
**45s**

| | | | |
|---|---|---|---|
| COOL HAND LUKE/EMBARRASSED | 1995 | Warner Bros. PRO-S-7699 | 5 |
| ("Soil X Samples" 21; blue vinyl) | | | |

## YOUNG, ANN
**45s**

| | | | |
|---|---|---|---|
| SOUVENIRS OF CHRISTMAS/ONCE A FOOL | 19?? | Class 805 | 5 |
| (B-side by Bobby Grabeau) | | | |

## YOUNG, CATHY
*And the Innocents; Also recorded as Washer Windshield*
**45s**

| | | | |
|---|---|---|---|
| KATHY YOUNG FINDS THE INNOCENTS GUILTY | 1961 | Indigo (NO #) | 125 |
| (Indigo promo label, price includes picture sleeve) | | | |
| A THOUSAND STARS | 196? | Port 3025 | 40 |
| (White promo label) | | | |
| **Albums** | | | |
| INNOCENTLY YOURS | 1961 | Indigo 503 | 150 |
| (Indigo promo label) | | | |
| THE SOUND OF CATHY YOUNG | 1961 | Indigo 504 | 100 |
| (Indigo promo label) | | | |

## YOUNG, FARON
*Capitol promo 45s $5-10 each; Mercury promo 45s $3 each; Mercury compact 33 singles (jukebox) $8 each; Other jukebox LLPs $8 each; Other Capitol or Mercury promo LPs $10 each*
**7-Inch Extended Plays**

| | | | |
|---|---|---|---|
| AND NOW | 1955 | SESAC AD 1 | 40 |
| (Promo-only release) | | | |
| COUNTRY DANCE FAVORITES  Jukebox LLP | 1964 | Mercury 60931 | 12 |
| (Issued with a hard cover) | | | |
| **Albums** | | | |
| FARON YOUNG CHURCH SONGS | 1955 | SESAC | 50 |
| (Yellow and black label, promo-only release) | | | |
| FARON YOUNG SINGS ON STAGE FOR MARY CARTER PAINTS | 196? | Mary Carter 1000 | 40 |
| (Promo-only LP from Mary Carter Paints) | | | |
| SWEETHEARTS OR STRANGERS | 1957 | Capitol 778 | 50 |
| (Yellow promo label) | | | |
| THE OBJECT OF MY AFFECTION | 1958 | Capitol 1004 | 35 |
| (Yellow promo label) | | | |
| THIS IS FARON YOUNG | 1959 | Capitol 1096 | 25 |
| (Yellow promo label) | | | |

## YOUNG, GEORGE
**45s**

| | | | |
|---|---|---|---|
| CAN'T STOP ME | 1958 | Mercury 71259 | 40 |
| (White promo label) | | | |

| Title | Yr | Label, Number | NM $ |
|---|---|---|---|

**YOUNG, JESSE COLIN**
*Of the Youngbloods*
**RADIO SHOWS**
**Albums**

| Title | Yr | Label, Number | NM $ |
|---|---|---|---|
| IN CONCERT (Mar 83) Live concert | 1983 | Westwood One (2) | 150-250 |
| *(Rare concert, with Karla Bonoff)* | | | |
| ROCK AROUND THE WORLD (Apr 77) | 1977 | RATW | 100-175 |
| *(Live concert)* | | | |

**YOUNG, NEIL**
*Of Crosby, Stills, Nash & Young and Buffalo Springfield; Other Reprise promo 45s 1209 and earlier $15 each; Other Reprise white promo label 45s $5-8 each; Columbia promo 45s duets $3 each; Geffen promo 45s $4 each; Other Reprise white promo label LPs $20 each*
**12-Inch Singles**

| Title | Yr | Label, Number | NM $ |
|---|---|---|---|
| BUFFALO STOMP | 1980 | Backstreet (MCA) 1878 | 40 |
| *(Promo-only 12" single)* | | | |
| GET BACK TO THE COUNTRY (Long)/(Short) | 1985 | Geffen PRO-A-2373 | 10 |
| HAWKS AND DOVES | 1980 | Reprise PRO-901 | 18 |
| *(Blue vinyl promo-only 12" single)* | | | |
| PEOPLE ON THE STREET (same on both sides) | 1986 | Geffen PRO-A-2623 | 10 |
| TOO LONELY (REMIX EDIT) (same on both sides) | 1987 | Geffen PRO-A-2811 | 10 |
| WEIGHT OF THE WORLD (same on both sides) | 1986 | Geffen PRO-A-2528 | 10 |

**45s**

| Title | Yr | Label, Number | NM $ |
|---|---|---|---|
| COMES A TIME | 1978 | Reprise 1395 | 250 |
| *(Promo-only picture disc)* | | | |
| DOWN BY THE RIVER | 1969 | Reprise 0836 | 20 |
| *(White promo label)* | | | |
| EVERYBODY KNOWS THIS IS NOWHERE | 1969 | Reprise 0819 | 300 |
| *(First pressing acoustic version)* | | | |
| EVERYBODY KNOWS THIS IS NOWHERE | 1969 | Reprise 0819 | 20 |
| *(Second pressing rock version, RE-1 in the trailoff area)* | | | |
| THE LONER | 1968 | Reprise 0785 | 40 |
| *(White promo label)* | | | |
| OH, LONESOME ME | 1969 | Reprise 0898 | 18 |
| *(White promo label)* | | | |
| ROCKIN' IN THE FREE WORLD (same on both sides) | 1989 | Reprise 22776 | 10 |
| SOUTHERN PACIFIC | 1980 | Reprise 49895 | 300 |
| *(Promo-only picture disc)* | | | |
| SOUTHERN PACIFIC | 1980 | Reprise 49895 | 200 |
| *(Promo-only green vinyl)* | | | |
| WALK ON | 1974 | Reprise 1209 | 18 |
| *(Small center hole)* | | | |
| WALK ON | 1974 | Reprise 1209 | 10 |
| *(Large center hole)* | | | |

**7-Inch Extended Plays**

| Title | Yr | Label, Number | NM $ |
|---|---|---|---|
| AFTER THE GOLD RUSH  Radio ads | 1970 | Reprise PRO-424 | 200 |
| *(Promo-only record company spots for LP)* | | | |
| EVERYBODY KNOWS THIS IS NOWHERE  Radio ads | 1969 | Reprise PRO-334 | 250 |
| *(Promo-only record company spots for LP)* | | | |
| HARVEST  Jukebox LLP | 1972 | Reprise LLP 183 | 40 |
| *(Issued with a paper cover)* | | | |
| NEIL YOUNG  Radio ads | 1968 | Reprise PRO-314 | 250 |
| *(Promo-only record company spots for LP)* | | | |

**Albums**

| Title | Yr | Label, Number | NM $ |
|---|---|---|---|
| AFTER THE GOLD RUSH | 1970 | Reprise 6383 | 50 |
| *(White promo label)* | | | |
| DECADE | 1977 | Reprise 3RS 2257 (3) | 500 |
| *(Test pressing; "Campaigner" contains extra verse deleted from the final version)* | | | |
| EVERYBODY KNOWS THIS IS NOWHERE | 1969 | Reprise 6349 | 50 |
| *(White promo label)* | | | |
| JOURNEY THROUGH THE PAST | 1972 | Reprise 6480 (2) | 50 |
| *(White promo labels)* | | | |
| ODE TO THE WIND | 1978 | Reprise MSK 2266 | 1,000 |
| *(Test pressing; plain white jacket with inserts; Title changed to "Comes A Time" for commercial release)* | | | |
| TIME FADES AWAY | 1973 | Reprise MS 2151 | 200 |
| *(With a cardboard inner sleeve, withdrawn after the earliest pressing)* | | | |
| TIME FADES AWAY | 1973 | Reprise M 2151 | 100 |
| *(Special mono pressing for radio stations)* | | | |
| TRANS | 1982 | Geffen GHS 2018 | 15 |
| *(Promo on Quiex II audiophile vinyl)* | | | |
| THE WARNER BROS. MUSIC SHOW | 1979 | Warner Bros. WBMS-107 | 50 |
| *(Promo-only interview album)* | | | |

**Compact Discs**

| Title | Yr | Label, Number | NM $ |
|---|---|---|---|
| ALL ALONG THE WATCHTOWER | 1994 | Columbia CSK 5493 | 8 |
| *(Promo-only CD single)* | | | |
| ARC: THE SINGLE | 1991 | Reprise PRO-CD-5232 | 8 |
| *(Promo-only CD single)* | | | |
| BIG TIME | 1996 | Reprise PRO-CD-8289 | 10 |
| *(Promo-only CD single)* | | | |
| CHANGE YOUR MIND | 1994 | Reprise PRO-CD-7118 | 8 |
| *(Promo-only CD single, edit and full-length versions)* | | | |
| COMPLEX SESSIONS, THE | 1994 | Reprise PRO-CD-7342 | 15 |
| *(Promo-only four-track collection)* | | | |
| CRIME IN THE CITY | 1990 | Reprise PRO-CD-3952 | 8 |
| *(Promo-only CD single)* | | | |
| DOWNTOWN | 1995 | Reprise PRO-CD-7646 | 8 |
| *(Promo-only CD single)* | | | |
| FREEDOM | 1990 | Reprise 25899 | 30 |
| *(Promo-only picture disc CD)* | | | |

| Title | Yr | Label, Number | NM $ |
|-------|-----|---------------|------|
| FROM HANK TO HENDRIX | 1993 | Reprise PRO-CD-6244 | 10 |
| *(Promo-only CD single)* | | | |
| HARVEST MOON | 1992 | Reprise PRO-CD-5811 | 8 |
| *(Promo CD single, 3 versions)* | | | |
| INCA QUEEN | 1986 | Geffen PRO-CD-2796 | 12 |
| *(Early promo-only CD single)* | | | |
| LONG MAY YOU RUN | 1993 | Reprise PRO-CD-6292 | 10 |
| *(Promo-only CD single, from "Unplugged", 1 version)* | | | |
| LONG MAY YOU RUN | 1993 | Reprise PRO-CD-6337 | 10 |
| *(Promo-only CD single, from "Unplugged", 2 versions)* | | | |
| LOVE TO BURN | 1991 | Reprise PRO-CD-4669 | 8 |
| *(Promo-only CD single)* | | | |
| LUCKY THIRTEEN ALBUM SAMPLER | 1993 | Geffen NYCD 1 | 20 |
| *(Promo-only collection)* | | | |
| MANSION ON THE HILL | 1990 | Reprise PRO-CD-4448 | 12 |
| *(Promo-only CD single)* | | | |
| MR. SOUL | 1993 | Reprise PRO-CD-6294 | 8 |
| *(Promo-only CD single, from "Unplugged")* | | | |
| MY HEART | 1994 | Reprise PRO-CD-7110 | 12 |
| *(Promo-only CD single)* | | | |
| NEEDLE AND THE DAMAGE DONE, THE | 1993 | Reprise PRO-CD-6319 | 8 |
| *(Promo-only CD single, from "Unplugged")* | | | |
| NO MORE | 1989 | Reprise PRO-CD-3864 | 10 |
| *(Promo-only CD single)* | | | |
| OVER AND OVER | 1991 | Reprise PRO-CD-4576 | 8 |
| *(Promo-only CD single)* | | | |
| PEACE AND LOVE | 1995 | Reprise PRO-CD-7623 | 8 |
| *(Promo-only CD single)* | | | |
| PIECE OF CRAP | 1994 | Reprise PRO-CD-7105 | 8 |
| *(Promo-only CD single)* | | | |
| PRIME OF LIFE | 1995 | Reprise PRO-CD-7274-R | 8 |
| *(Promo-only CD single)* | | | |
| ROCKIN' IN THE FREE WORLD | 1989 | Reprise PRO-CD-3729 | 8 |
| *(Promo-only CD single)* | | | |
| SLEEPS WITH ANGELS | 1994 | Reprise PRO-CD-7136 | 15 |
| *(Promo version of album)* | | | |
| SLEEPS WITH ANGELS | 1994 | Reprise PRO-CD-7460 | 8 |
| *(Promo-only CD single)* | | | |
| TEN MEN WORKIN' | 1988 | Reprise PRO-CD-3073 | 10 |
| *(Early promo-only CD single)* | | | |
| THEME FROM DEAD MAN | 1996 | Vapor PRO-CD-8142 | 10 |
| *(Promo-only CD single)* | | | |
| THIS NOTE'S FOR YOU | 1988 | Reprise PRO-CD-3091 | 25 |
| *(Promo-only CD single, includes live version)* | | | |
| THROW YOUR HATRED DOWN | 1995 | Reprise PRO-CD-7761 | 8 |
| *(Promo-only CD single)* | | | |
| UNKNOWN LEGEND | 1993 | Reprise PRO-CD-5960 | 8 |
| *(Promo-only CD single)* | | | |
| WAR OF MAN | 1993 | Reprise PRO-CD-5864 | 8 |
| *(Promo-only CD single)* | | | |
| **RADIO SHOWS** | | | |
| **Albums** | | | |
| OFF THE RECORD (Jan 93) | 1993 | Westwood One (2) | 20-35 |
| *(Music and interviews)* | | | |
| ROCK STARS (July 88) | 1988 | Radio Today (2) | 30-60 |
| *(Music and interviews)* | | | |
| SUPERSTAR CONCERT (Feb 87) | 1987 | Westwood One (3) | 75-125 |
| *(Live concert, box set)* | | | |
| SUPERSTAR CONCERT (July 90) | 1990 | Westwood One (3) | 50-100 |
| *(Live concert, box set)* | | | |
| SUPERSTAR CONCERT (Feb 91) | 1991 | Westwood One (3) | 40-75 |
| *(Live concert with Van Halen and Robert Plant)* | | | |
| **Compact Discs** | | | |
| IN THE STUDIO (90s) Profile of an album | 199? | Album Network | 15-25 |
| *(Music and interviews)* | | | |
| OFF THE RECORD (Jan 95) | 1995 | Westwood One | 25-35 |
| *(Music and interviews)* | | | |
| OFF THE RECORD (July 95) | 1995 | | 15-30 |
| *(With Goo Goo Dolls and Sugar Ray, music and interviews)* | | | |
| RARITIES ON COMPACT DISC (July 94) | 1994 | On the Radio | 20-35 |
| *(Various tracks, some live)* | | | |
| SUPERSTAR CONCERT (Dec 93) | 1993 | Westwood One (2) | 50-100 |
| *(Live concert, repeated)* | | | |
| SUPERSTARS (July 95) | 1995 | (2) | 50-100 |
| *(Live material, collection of early 1990s tracks)* | | | |

## YOUNG, PAUL
*Columbia promo 45s $3 each; Columbia promo picture sleeves $2 each*
**RADIO SHOWS**
**Albums**

| Title | Yr | Label, Number | NM $ |
|-------|-----|---------------|------|
| BBC ROCK HOUR (Feb 84) Live concert | 1984 | London Wavelength | 20-40 |
| *(With Howard Jones)* | | | |
| IN CONCERT (Oct 85) Live concert | 1985 | Westwood One (2) | 25-40 |
| *(With Eddie & the Tide)* | | | |
| SOURCE CONCERT (May 84) Live concert | 1984 | NBC Radio (3) | 40-75 |
| *(With UB40)* | | | |

| Title | Yr | Label, Number | NM $ |
|---|---|---|---|

# Z

## ZACK, EDDIE
*Other Columbia promo 45s $20-30 each*
**45s**

| Title | Yr | Label, Number | NM $ |
|---|---|---|---|
| ROCKY ROAD BLUES | 1955 | Columbia 21387 | 45 |

*(White promo label)*

## ZAPPA, FRANK
*Includes The Mothers of Invention and Ruben & The Jets; Reprise (Bizarre), other DiscReet and Warner promo LPs $20-35 each; Zappa and Barking Pumpkin promo LPs $25 each*

**12-Inch Singles**

| Title | Yr | Label, Number | NM $ |
|---|---|---|---|
| DANCIN' FOOL | 1979 | Zappa 83 | 20 |
| *(Promo-only 12" single)* | | | |
| I DON'T WANNA GET DRAFTED | 1980 | Zappa 1001 | 30 |
| *(Promo 12" single with picture cover)* | | | |
| JOE'S GARAGE | 1979 | Zappa 107 | 40 |
| *(Promo-only 12" single with title cover)* | | | |
| VALLEY GIRL | 1982 | Barking Pumpkin AS 1485 | 30 |
| *(Promo 12" single with picture cover)* | | | |

**45s**

| Title | Yr | Label, Number | NM $ |
|---|---|---|---|
| BOY WONDER I LOVE YOU  Burt Ward | 1967 | MGM 13632 | 125 |
| *(Yellow promo label, produced, written and backing vocals by Zappa, stock copy worth more)* | | | |
| CHARLENE  Ruben & the Jets | 1973 | Mercury 73411 | 10 |
| *(White promo label)* | | | |
| CLETUS AWREETUS-AWRIGHTUS  The Mothers of Invention | 1972 | Reprise 1127 | 30 |
| *(White promo label)* | | | |
| DANCIN' FOOL | 1979 | Zappa 10 | 10 |
| *(White promo label)* | | | |
| DISCO BOY | 1976 | Warner Bros. 8342 | 20 |
| *(Green promo label)* | | | |
| DON'T EAT THE YELLOW SNOW | 1974 | DiscReet 1312 | 20 |
| *(Yellow promo label, mono/stereo versions)* | | | |
| FIND HER FINER | 1976 | Warner Bros. 8296 | 20 |
| *(White promo label)* | | | |
| GOBLIN GIRL | 1981 | Barking Pumpkin AS 1328 | 15 |
| *(Purple promo label, small center hole 33 1/3 rpm)* | | | |
| HOW COULD I BE SUCH A FOOL  The Mothers of Invention | 1966 | Verve 10418 | 125 |
| *(Blue promo label, stock copy worth more)* | | | |
| I DON'T WANNA GET DRAFTED | 1980 | Zappa 1001 | 10 |
| *(White promo label)* | | | |
| I'M THE SLIME  The Mothers of Invention | 1973 | DiscReet 1180 | 30 |
| *(White promo label)* | | | |
| IF I COULD BE YOUR LOVE AGAIN  Ruben & the Jets | 1973 | Mercury 73381 | 10 |
| *(White promo label)* | | | |
| JELLY ROLL GUM DROP/ANY WAY THE WIND BLOWS | 1968 | Verve 10632 | 75 |
| *(As "Ruben & The Jets:; yellow promo label)* | | | |
| JELLY ROLL GUM DROP/DESERI | 1968 | Verve 10632 | 75 |
| *(As "Ruben & The Jets:; yellow promo label)* | | | |
| JESSIE LEE | 196? | Original Sound 40 | 75 |
| *(White promo label)* | | | |
| MAGIC FINGERS  The Mothers of Invention | 1971 | United Artists 50857 | 35 |
| *(White promo label)* | | | |
| MOTHER PEOPLE  The Mothers of Invention | 1967 | Verve 10570 | 100 |
| *(Blue promo label, stock copy worth more)* | | | |
| MY GUITAR  The Mothers of Invention | 1969 | Reprise 0840 | 40 |
| *(White promo label)* | | | |
| PEACHES EN REGALIA  The Mothers of Invention | 1970 | Reprise 0889 | 40 |
| *(White promo label)* | | | |
| TEARS BEGAN TO FALL  The Mothers of Invention | 1971 | Reprise 1052 | 40 |
| *(White promo label)* | | | |
| TELL ME YOU LOVE ME  The Mothers of Invention | 1970 | Reprise 0967 | 40 |
| *(White promo label)* | | | |
| TROUBLE COMIN' EVERY DAY  The Mothers of Invention | 1966 | Verve 10458 | 100 |
| *(Blue promo label, stock copy worth more)* | | | |
| VALLEY GIRL | 1982 | Barking Pumpkin AS 1490 | 25 |
| *(Purple promo label, price includes promo-only picture sleeve featuring Frank and Moon Zappa, long 4:58/short 3:47 versions)* | | | |
| WHAT'S IT ALL ABOUT (Nov 80) Public service show | 1980 | W.I.A.A. 548 | 40 |
| *(Flip side features David Bowie)* | | | |
| WHY DON'T YOU DO ME RIGHT  The Mothers of Invention | 1967 | Verve 10513 | 100 |
| *(Blue promo label, stock copy worth more)* | | | |
| WPLJ  The Mothers of Invention | 1970 | Reprise 0892 | 40 |
| *(White promo label)* | | | |

**7-Inch Extended Plays**

| Title | Yr | Label, Number | NM $ |
|---|---|---|---|
| 200 MOTELS  Radio ads | 1971 | United Artists | 400 |
| *(Radio spots from the record company for LP)* | | | |
| HOT RATS  Radio ads | 1970 | Reprise PRO-336 | 400 |
| *(Radio spots from the record company for LP)* | | | |
| UNCLE MEAT  Radio ads | 1969 | Reprise PRO-332 | 400 |
| *(Radio spots from the record company for LP)* | | | |
| WEASELS RIPPED MY FLESH  Radio ads | 1970 | Reprise PRO-420 | 400 |
| *(Radio spots from the record company for LP)* | | | |

**Albums**

| Title | Yr | Label, Number | NM $ |
|---|---|---|---|
| ... OF THE MOTHERS  The Mothers of Invention | 1969 | Verve 5074 | 100 |
| *(Yellow promo label)* | | | |
| ABSOLUTELY FREE  The Mothers of Invention | 1967 | Verve 5013 | 150 |
| *(Yellow promo label)* | | | |
| CLEAN CUTS FROM SHEIK YERBOUTI | 1979 | Zappa 78 | 30 |
| *(Seven-song EP from the LP)* | | | |

| Title | Yr | Label, Number | NM $ |
|---|---|---|---|
| CRUISIN' WITH RUBEN AND THE JETS  The Mothers of Invention | 1968 | Verve 5055 | 150 |
| *(Yellow promo label)* | | | |
| FREAK OUT  The Mothers of Invention | 1966 | Verve 5005 (2) | 125 |
| *(White promo label)* | | | |
| FREAK OUT  The Mothers of Invention | 1966 | Verve 5005 (2) | 250 |
| *(Yellow promo label)* | | | |
| JOE'S GARAGE | 1979 | Zappa 129 | 30 |
| *(Six-song EP, different from the two-song 12" single)* | | | |
| LATHER | 1977 | Columbia (no #) | 750 |
| *(Test pressing only; parts of this LP are on DSK 2291, 2292 and 2294; released as a whole only after Zappa's death, with vinyl only coming out in Japan)* | | | |
| LUMPY GRAVY  The Mothers of Invention | 1968 | Verve 8741 | 150 |
| *(Yellow promo label)* | | | |
| MOTHERMANIA  The Mothers of Invention | 1969 | Verve 5068 | 100 |
| *(Yellow promo label)* | | | |
| THE MOTHERS OF INVENTION | 1970 | MGM 122 | 75 |
| *(Yellow promo label)* | | | |
| SAVE THE CHILDREN Various artists | 1983 | DWP-943 | 30 |
| *(Twenty PSA spots including one 30-second by Moon Unit Zappa)* | | | |
| THING FISH | 1984 | Barking Pumpkin SPRO-9261 | 30 |
| *(Six-song EP with incorrect cover for two songs)* | | | |
| TINSEL TOWN REBELLION | 1981 | Barking Pumpkin AS-995 | 20 |
| *(Promo-only five-song EP)* | | | |
| WE'RE ONLY IN IT FOR THE MONEY  The Mothers of Invention | 1968 | Verve 5045 | 150 |
| *(Yellow promo label)* | | | |
| THE WORST OF THE MOTHERS | 1971 | MGM 4754 | 75 |
| *(Yellow promo label)* | | | |
| YOU ARE WHAT YOU IS SPECIAL CLEAN CUTS EDITION | 1981 | Barking Pumpkin AS 1294 | 20 |
| ZAPPA IN NEW YORK | 1978 | DiscReet 2290 | 400 |
| *(Promo copy with cover and record that includes "Punky's Whips")* | | | |
| ZAPPA IN NEW YORK | 1978 | DiscReet 2290 | 150 |
| *(Promo copy that has "Punky's Whips" listed on the cover, not on the record)* | | | |
| ZAPPED  The Mothers of Invention | 1969 | Warner Bros. PRO-368 | 40 |
| *(Promo-only release with collage cover)* | | | |
| ZAPPED  The Mothers of Invention | 1969 | Warner Bros. PRO-368 | 30 |
| *(Promo-only release with Zappa cover)* | | | |
| **Compact Discs** | | | |
| IN-STORE PLAY CD (CLEAN AMERICAN VERSION) | 1995 | Rykodisc 0501 | 50 |
| *(Promo-only sampler)* | | | |
| KILL UGLY RADIO | 1995 | Rykodisc 0502 | 25 |
| *(Promo-only sampler)* | | | |
| KILL UGLY RADIO SOME MORE | 1995 | Rykodisc 0503 | 25 |
| *(Promo-only sampler)* | | | |
| YOU CAN'T DO THAT ON THE RADIO ANYMORE | 1990 | Rykodisc 9003 | 60 |
| *(Promo-only sampler from past LPs, black cardboard cover with Frank's picture on the disc)* | | | |
| **RADIO SHOWS** | | | |
| **Albums** | | | |
| ALISON'S TEA HOUSE (70s) Various artists | 197? | Chelsea Productions | 25-50 |
| *(Two of the ten 3-minute shows feature interviews with Frank Zappa and with Kiss)* | | | |
| DOCTOR DEMENTO  Various artists | 1988 | Westwood One (2) | 40-75 |
| *(Zappa is co-host of the show)* | | | |
| KING BISCUIT FLOWER HOUR (June 81) | 1981 | DIR/ABC (2) | 750-900 |
| *(Live concert from Munich, West Germany)* | | | |
| PROFILES IN ROCK | 1980 | Watermark | 40-80 |
| *(Music and interviews)* | | | |
| ROBERT KLEIN HOUR (Sept 79) | 1979 | Watermark (2) | 100-150 |
| *(Live concert with Genya Raven)* | | | |
| **Compact Discs** | | | |
| DOCTOR DEMENTO (Jan 94) Various artists | 1994 | Westwood One | 75-150 |
| *(Zappa tribute show, music and interviews)* | | | |
| **Reel-to-Reel Tapes** | | | |
| KING BISCUIT FLOWER HOUR (Apr 78) | 1978 | DIR/ABC (2) | 300-425 |
| *(Live concert on two 7" reels)* | | | |

## ZEBRA
**RADIO SHOWS**
**Albums**

| Title | Yr | Label, Number | NM $ |
|---|---|---|---|
| CAPTURED LIVE (Mar 84) | 1984 | RKO (2) | 40-75 |
| *(Live concert)* | | | |
| KING BISCUIT FLOWER HOUR (Feb 85) Live concert | 1985 | DIR (2) | 20-40 |
| *(With Autograph)* | | | |
| KING BISCUIT FLOWER HOUR (July 83) Live concert | 1983 | DIR/ABC (2) | 40-75 |
| *(With Quiet Riot)* | | | |
| SOURCE CONCERT (June 83) | 1983 | NBC Radio (2) | 20-35 |
| *(Music and interviews, with Kix)* | | | |
| SOURCE CONCERT (Nov 83) Live concert | 1983 | NBC Radio (3) | 30-50 |
| *(With Golden Earring)* | | | |

## ZEBULONS, THE
**45s**

| Title | Yr | Label, Number | NM $ |
|---|---|---|---|
| FALLING WATER | 1960 | Cub 9069 | 50 |
| *(Red/white promo label)* | | | |

## ZENTNER, SI
**45s**

| Title | Yr | Label, Number | NM $ |
|---|---|---|---|
| THE GOULASH (SHUFFLIN' BLUES) | 1962 | Liberty 55420 | 15 |
| *(One-sided promo-only release)* | | | |

| Title | Yr | Label, Number | NM $ |
|---|---|---|---|

**ZEVON, WARREN**
*Asylum promo 45s $3 each; Other Virgin and Giant CD singles $3 each*
**12-Inch Singles**

| Title | Yr | Label, Number | NM $ |
|---|---|---|---|
| BOOM BOOM MANCINI (same on both sides) | 1987 | Virgin 2133 | 6 |
| DETOX MANSION/LEAVE MY MONKEY ALONE | 1987 | Virgin 2062 | 6 |
| LEAVE MY MONKEY ALONE (10:31) (5:45) (5:51) | 1987 | Virgin 1053 | 8 |
| WEREWOLVES OF LONDON | 1978 | Asylum AS 11386 | 20 |

**Compact Discs**

| Title | Yr | Label, Number | NM $ |
|---|---|---|---|
| RECONSIDER ME | 1987 | Virgin PR 2216 | 15 |

*(Early promo CD single)*
**RADIO SHOWS**
**Albums**

| Title | Yr | Label, Number | NM $ |
|---|---|---|---|
| KING BISCUIT FLOWER HOUR (July 80) Live concert | 1980 | DIR/ABC (2) | 25-50 |
| *(With Eddie Money)* | | | |
| KING BISCUIT FLOWER HOUR (May 80) Live concert | 1980 | DIR/ABC (2) | 40-75 |
| *(With Willie Nile)* | | | |

**Compact Discs**

| Title | Yr | Label, Number | NM $ |
|---|---|---|---|
| IN THE STUDIO (90s) | 1990 | Album Network | 10-20 |
| *(Profile of an album, music and interviews)* | | | |
| KING BISCUIT FLOWER HOUR  Live concert | 1990 | DIR | 40-75 |
| *(With John Lennon)* | | | |

**ZZ TOP**
*Originally the Moving Sidewalks; London promo 45s $6 each; Warner Bros. promo 45s $4 each; Other Warner Bros. promo 12" singles $8 each; Warner Bros. and RCA promo CD singles $4-6 each*
**12-Inch Singles**

| Title | Yr | Label, Number | NM $ |
|---|---|---|---|
| CHEAP SUNGLASSES (LP Version)/(Live Version) | 1979 | Warner Bros. PRO-A-877 | 20 |
| DELIRIOUS (same on both sides) | 1985 | Warner Bros. PRO-A-2432 | 6 |
| LEGS (DANCE MIX) (same on both sides) | 1983 | Warner Bros. PRO-A-2146 | 12 |
| SLEEPING BAG (same on both sides) | 1985 | Warner Bros. PRO-A-2365 | 6 |
| STAGES (same on both sides) | 1985 | Warner Bros. PRO-A-2407 | 6 |
| TV DINNERS (same on both sides) | 1983 | Warner Bros. PRO-A-2094 | 12 |
| VELCRO FLY (same on both sides) | 1985 | Warner Bros. PRO-A-2529 | 6 |
| VIVA LAS VEGAS (5:11) (8:36) | 1992 | Warner Bros. PRO-A-5483 | 10 |

**Albums**

| Title | Yr | Label, Number | NM $ |
|---|---|---|---|
| TAKIN' TEXAS TO THE PEOPLE | 1976 | London 1001 | 50 |
| *(Promo-only release)* | | | |

**Compact Discs**

| Title | Yr | Label, Number | NM $ |
|---|---|---|---|
| ANTENNA | 1994 | RCA RDJ-62732 | 40 |
| *(Promo edition in leather case, disc is layered in brass)* | | | |
| RECYCLER | 1990 | Warner Bros. 26548-2-DJ | 30 |
| *(Promo edition in case with metal binding)* | | | |
| TASTE OF THE ZZ TOP SIX-PACK, A | 1987 | Warner Bros. PRO-CD-2875 | 25 |
| *(Promo-only sampler)* | | | |

**RADIO SHOWS**
**Albums**

| Title | Yr | Label, Number | NM $ |
|---|---|---|---|
| COUNTDOWN TO CHRISTMAS (Dec 85) | 1985 | NBC Radio | 20-40 |
| *(Music and interviews)* | | | |
| INNERVIEW (80s) | 198? | Innerview | 10-20 |
| *(Music and interviews)* | | | |
| KING BISCUIT FLOWER HOUR (Aug 82) | 1982 | DIR/ABC (2) | 100-200 |
| *(Live concert with Krokus)* | | | |
| TRIBUTE TO MUDDY WATERS (Apr 89) | 1989 | | 20-40 |
| *(Music and interviews)* | | | |
| WESTWOOD ONE PRESENTS (90s) | 199? | Westwood One (2) | 30-60 |
| *(Music and interviews for the LP "Electric Mudd")* | | | |
| WORLD PREMIERE | 1990 | Album Network | 10-20 |
| *(For LP "Recycler," music and interviews)* | | | |

**Compact Discs**

| Title | Yr | Label, Number | NM $ |
|---|---|---|---|
| IN THE STUDIO (Dec 94) | 1994 | Album Network (2) | 20-40 |
| *(Two shows, music and interviews)* | | | |
| IN THE STUDIO (Mar 93) | 1993 | Album Network | 10-20 |
| *(Profile of an album, music and interviews)* | | | |
| KING BISCUIT FLOWER HOUR (Apr 90) | 1990 | DIR | 40-75 |
| *(Live concert, repeated)* | | | |
| MEMORIAL DAY SPECIAL (May 90) | 1990 | Westwood One (3) | 50-125 |
| *(Music and interviews)* | | | |
| OFF THE RECORD (Mar 94) | 1994 | Westwood One | 15-25 |
| *(Music and interviews, repeated)* | | | |
| UP CLOSE | 1996 | (2) | 40-75 |
| *(Music and interviews)* | | | |

| Title | Yr | Label, Number | NM $ |
|---|---|---|---|
| **SOUNDTRACKS** | | | |
| **45s** | | | |
| DUEL OF THE TITANS | 196? | | 50 |
| (Radio ads featuring Steve Reeves) | | | |
| PSYCHO | 196? | | 50 |
| (Promo-only record with ads promoting the movie) | | | |
| SATURDAY NIGHT LIVE | 1976 | Arista SP-3 | 20 |
| (Promo-only sampler 45 from the LP) | | | |
| **7-Inch Extended Plays** | | | |
| HOT ROD GANG  Promo label | 1958 | Capitol PRO 985 | 750 |
| (Promo-only release for radio stations) | | | |
| PETER PAN | 196? | RCA Victor PR-136 | 20 |
| (Small center hole, cardboard cover, special products issue) | | | |
| SUMMER MAGIC | 1963 | Alcoa Wrap 701 | 25 |
| (Giveaway from Alcoa Wrap; with Hayley Mills, Burl Ives and Eddie Hodges) | | | |
| **Albums** | | | |
| ALEXANDER THE GREAT | 1956 | Mercury 20148 | 125 |
| (White promo label) | | | |
| THE BIRD WITH THE CRYSTAL PLUMAGE | 1970 | Capitol 642 | 40 |
| (Promo label) | | | |
| CERTAIN SMILE, A  Stereo | 1958 | Columbia 8068 | 75 |
| (White promo label) | | | |
| COBWEB, THE | 1957 | MGM 3501 | 50 |
| (Yellow promo label) | | | |
| DIARY OF ANNE FRANK, THE | 1959 | 20th Century Fox 3012 | 40 |
| (White promo label) | | | |
| DOG OF FLANDERS | 1959 | 20th Century Fox 3026 | 50 |
| (White promo label) | | | |
| DRANGO | 1957 | Liberty 3036 | 75 |
| (White promo label) | | | |
| EDGE OF THE CITY | 1957 | MGM 3501 | 50 |
| (Yellow promo label) | | | |
| FRANCIS OF ASSISI | 1961 | 20th Century Fox 3053 | 50 |
| (White promo label) | | | |
| GOD'S LITTLE ACRE | 1958 | United Artists 4002 | 50 |
| (White promo label) | | | |
| GOLDEN COACH | 1954 | MGM 3111 | 65 |
| (Yellow promo label) | | | |
| GREATEST STORY EVER TOLD | 196? | United Artists 5120 | 100 |
| (White promo label) | | | |
| GREENWICH VILLAGE USA | 1960 | 20th Century Fox 105-25 (2) | 40 |
| (White promo label) | | | |
| HIGH TOR  Television soundtrack | 1956 | Decca 8272 | 100 |
| (Pink promo label) | | | |
| HOT ROD RUMBLE | 1957 | Liberty 3048 | 60 |
| (White promo label) | | | |
| JAMBOREE  White promo label, promo-only release | 1957 | Warner Bros. | 5,000 |
| (Various artists rock & roll soundtrack has no label number. Only 500 were pressed, all promos.) | | | |
| JOHN PAUL JONES | 1959 | Warner Bros. 1293 | 50 |
| (White promo label) | | | |
| KINGS GO FORTH | 1958 | Capitol 1063 | 60 |
| (Blue promo label) | | | |
| LOST CONTINENT, THE | 1957 | MGM 3635 | 85 |
| (Yellow promo label) | | | |
| MAN WHO SHOT LIBERTY VALANCE, THE | 1962 | Paramount SP-1890 | 40 |
| (Radio station spots for the movie) | | | |
| MEN OF WAR | 1957 | Imperial 9032 | 50 |
| (White promo label) | | | |
| MYRA BRECKENRIDGE | 1970 | 20th Fox 4210 | 500 |
| (White promo label) | | | |
| MYSTERIOUS ISLAND | 196? | | 30 |
| (Radio ad spots for the movie) | | | |
| NUN'S STORY, THE | 1959 | Warner Bros. 1306 | 65 |
| (White promo label) | | | |
| PARADE | 1960 | Kapp 7005 | 75 |
| (Kapp promo label) | | | |
| ROOTS OF HEAVEN | 1958 | 20th Century Fox 3005 | 125 |
| (White promo label) | | | |
| SANDHOG | 1954 | Vanguard 9001 | 75 |
| (White promo label) | | | |
| SEVEN COME ELEVEN | 1961 | Columbia 5740 | 40 |
| (Columbia promo label) | | | |
| 7TH VOYAGE OF SINBAD | 1959 | Colpix 504 | 75 |
| (White promo label) | | | |
| TENDER IS THE NIGHT | 1962 | 20th Century Fox 3054 | 75 |
| (White promo label) | | | |
| YOJIMBO | 1962 | MGM 4096 | 150 |
| (Yellow promo label) | | | |

| Title | Yr | Label, Number | NM $ |
|-------|-----|---------------|------|

**VARIOUS ARTISTS**

**10-Inch Singles**

WOODSTOCK Movie ads — 1970 — Warner Bros. — 400
*(33 1/3 rpm 10" disc with 60-second radio ads for the movie)*

**45s**

BRITISH INVASION  7" promo disc — 1983 — NSBA — 10
*(Issued in a file folder)*

BUBBLE UP (COCA-COLA)  With Stan Freberg — 1965 — Coca-Cola 2227 — 75
*(Issued with a cover, pressed by Capitol)*

CHRONOLOGY OF AMERICAN MUSIC  Demo disc — 1973 — More Music Productions — 40
*(One side of this 33 1/3 rpm demo disc features one-second clips from each record to hit #1 on the Billboard Hot 100 from 1955-72)*

COCA-COLA JINGLE A GO-GO — 1962 — Coca-Cola Vol. 1 — 75
*(With small center hole)*

COCA-COLA JINGLE A GO-GO — 1962 — Coca-Cola Vol. 2 — 200
*(With small center hole, artists are Ray Charles and the Everly Brothers)*

COCA-COLA JINGLE A GO-GO — 1963 — Coca-Cola Vol. 1 — 200
*(With small center hole, artists include the Four Seasons)*

COCA-COLA JINGLE A GO-GO — 1963 — Coca-Cola Vol. 2 — 50
*(With small center hole)*

**7-Inch Extended Plays**

SWING THE JINGLE  Price includes picture sleeve — 1966 — Coca-Cola — 100
*(This 45rpm includes the Drifters, Lou Bravos, Lesley Gore and Roy Orbison)*

TELEVISION'S GREATEST HITS VALENTINE — 1987 — TVT (no number) — 20
*(Promo-only 7-inch sampler, red vinyl, contains "romantic" tracks from the album "Television's Greatest Hits")*

THINGS GO BETTER WITH COKE  Mail-in offer — 1967 — Coke GMBH 105 112 — 100
*(Artists: Supremes, Ray Charles, Petula Clark and Dave Dee Dozy Beaky Mick & Tich; pressed in Germany for U.S. use)*

**Albums**

CONCERTS FOR THE PEOPLE OF KAMPUCHEA  Four-song sampler — 1981 — Atlantic PR 388 — 75
*(Promo-only EP includes "Every Night" by Paul McCartney, "Sister Disco" by the Who, "Little Sister" by Rockpile with Robert Plant, and "Lucille" by Rockestra)*

CRUISIN'  Promo-only sampler — 1973 — Increase — 50
*(This 6-track LP was sent to radio stations with no cover)*

IMPERIAL SAMPLER  White promo label — 1954 — Imperial DJ LP-1 — 50
*(10-inch LP, Includes music of Torok, Mark, Sanders & Henslee)*

SWING THE JINGLE  The Four Seasons — 196? — Coca-Cola — 400
*(Six tracks, price includes special cover)*

TODAY'S HITS — 1963 — Philles 4004 — 400
*(With the Ronettes, Crystals, Bob B. Soxx and Alley Cats)*

**Compact Discs**

WESTWOOD ONE SAMPLER (90s) Various artists — 199? — Westwood One — 40
*(Promo-only sampler from Westwood One syndicated live concert)*

**RADIO SHOWS**

**Albums**

1986 GRAMMY AWARDS (Feb 86) Music and interviews — 1986 — MJI Broadcasting (2) — 20-35
*(Hosted by Phil Collins)*

20 YEARS OF BRITISH ROCK (June 83) Part 1 — 1983 — NBC Source (5) — 75-125
*(Spencer Davis is host of this profile of UK rock, photo box set cover, music and interviews)*

20 YEARS OF BRITISH ROCK (June 83) Part 2 — 1983 — NBC Source (5) — 75-125
*(Davis is host, box set includes photo cover, music and interviews)*

4TH OF JULY SUMMER BEACH PARTY (July 84) — 1984 — United Stations (3) — 40
*(Beach Boys, Jan & Dean and the Motels)*

60 OF THE 60S (July 87) — 1987 — DIR — 20-40
*(The top 60 hits of the 60s, music and interviews)*

60S AT THE BEEB (July 87) Various artists — 1987 — Westwood One — 100-175
*(BBC Concert performances from Beatles, Stones, Who and others, all live UK tracks)*

70 OF THE 70S (May 87) — 1987 — DIR — 20-40
*(One time special, 70 top hits of the 70s, music and interviews)*

A.R.M.S. CONCERT  Ronnie Lane and friends — 1981 — DIR/ABC (3) — 75-100
*(Live concert)*

AIR FORCE COUNTRY (74-76) Public service ads — 197? — U. S. Air Force — 10-20
*(Various artists)*

ALBUM GREATS  Beatles discs only — 1979 — TM Special Products (6) — 150-250
*(Music and interviews)*

ALBUM GREATS  Bowie disc only — 1979 — TM Special Products — 20-40
*(Music and interviews)*

ALBUM GREATS  Dylan disc only — 1979 — TM Special Products — 20-40
*(Music and interviews)*

ALBUM GREATS  Elton John discs only — 1979 — TM Special Products (2) — 20-40
*(Music and interviews)*

ALBUM GREATS  John Lennon disc only — 1979 — TM Special Products — 20-40
*(Music and interviews)*

ALBUM GREATS  Led Zeppelin discs only — 1979 — TM Special Products (2) — 30-60
*(Music and interviews)*

ALBUM GREATS  Paul McCartney discs only — 1979 — TM Special Products (2) — 30-60
*(Music and interviews)*

ALBUM GREATS  Rolling Stones discs only — 1979 — TM Special Products (7) — 100-150
*(Music and interviews)*

ALBUM GREATS  Springsteen disc only — 1979 — TM Special Products — 20-40
*(Music and interviews)*

ALBUM GREATS  The entire 48-hour show — 1979 — TM Special Products (53) — 500-1,000
*(Highlights from best selling LPs)*

AMERICAN COUNTRY COUNTDOWN  Average show — 198? — Westwood One (4) — 5-10

AMERICAN COUNTRY COUNTDOWN  Year-end shows — 198? — Westwood One (8) — 10-25

AMERICAN TOP 40  Box sets from 1973, first shows on records — 1973 — Watermark (3) — 15-50
*(Music and interviews)*

AMERICAN TOP 40 (73-85) Year-end countdowns — 19?? — Watermark (8) — 40-75
*(Music and interviews)*

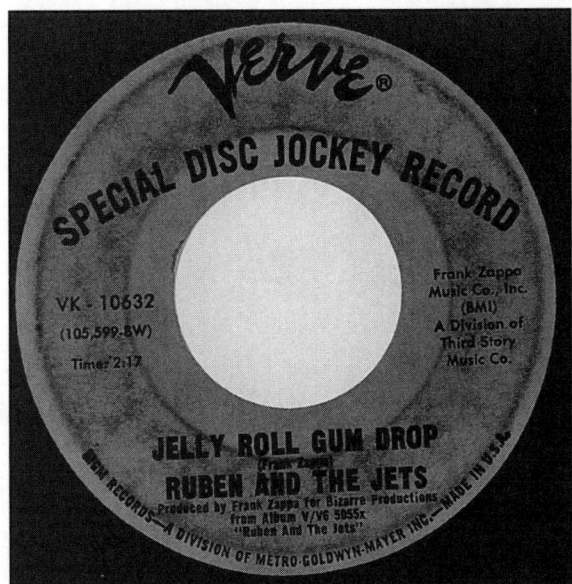

(Top left) A rare Verve promo from Frank Zappa, he confounded his fans by releasing this single under the name of the fictitious band on the album *Cruisin' with Ruben and the Jets*. (Top right) Zappa made his only appearance on the King Biscuit Flower Hour on this June 28, 1981 broadcast. A truly rare Zappa collectible, it fetches in the high three figures among Zappa collectors. (Middle left) A segment from the "Isle of Dreams Festival," a fictitious "concert" created using edited live tapes from prior Westwood One programs and hosted by Eric Clapton. (Middle right) A generic episode of the King Biscuit Flower Hour. Until the recent release of a series of highlight CDs, the only way you could get these live performances, other than on bootleg or by taping them from the radio, was by hunting down the original broadcast. (Bottom left) This is the sixth CD of another truly rare item, a radio show honoring the 1967 Monterey Pop Festival that featured much unreleased material. (Bottom right) SATCON I was a fictional worldwide live-via-satellite concert that aired over an entire weekend in 1980. [The editor even recalls hearing this on the radio and was fooled into thinking it was really happening as it aired!]

| Title | Yr | Label, Number | NM $ |
|-------|-----|---------------|------|
| AMERICAN TOP 40 (1974-Sept 78) | 197? | Watermark (3) | 10-15 |
| *(Three-hour shows, hosted by Casey Kasem or guest host)* | | | |
| AMERICAN TOP 40 (July 81) Special Beatles show | 1981 | Watermark (4) | 40-80 |
| *(Music and interviews)* | | | |
| AMERICAN TOP 40 (Oct 78-1988) | 198? | Watermark (4) | 12-18 |
| *(Four-hour shows, hosted by Casey Kasem or guest host)* | | | |
| ATLANTIC'S 40TH ANNIVERSARY SHOW | 1988 | Westwood One (2) | 20-30 |
| *(Music and interviews)* | | | |
| ATLANTIC'S 40TH ANNIVERSARY SHOW | 1989 | Atlantic (3) | 30-40 |
| *(Music and interviews)* | | | |
| AXEMAN COMETH (July 89) Live BBC w/major artists | 1989 | BBC Shows (9) | 50-100 |
| *(Various live tracks)* | | | |
| BILLBOARD MAGAZINE | 1979 | Billboard Magazine (5) | 40 |
| *(Music and interviews)* | | | |
| BILLBOARD'S 1978 YEARBOOK (Dec 78) | 1978 | Billboard Magazine (5) | 60 |
| *(Music and interviews)* | | | |
| BRITISH INVASION | 1988 | DB Productions (12) | 50-100 |
| *(Also available on CD)* | | | |
| BRITISH INVASION  "From Britain with Love" | 1984 | DIR (24) | 150-200 |
| *(Box set with colored vinyl records)* | | | |
| BRITISH INVASION  "From Britain with Love" | 1985 | DIR (24) | 125-200 |
| *(Box set, records are black vinyl)* | | | |
| BRITISH INVASION  "From Britain with Love" | 1987 | DIR (13) | 75-100 |
| *(All reissues of the original DIR show)* | | | |
| BRITISH INVASION  Entire show and promo kits | 1983 | NSBA (24) | 200-350 |
| *(Yellow labels)* | | | |
| BRITISH INVASION  Promo kit box set | 1983 | NSBA (2) | 50 |
| *(Two discs, one is blue vinyl, the other clear vinyl)* | | | |
| BRITISH INVASION  Promo spot kit disc | 1983 | NSBA | 25 |
| *(Yellow label)* | | | |
| CASEY'S TOP 40 (1988-early 1990s) | 199? | (4) | 10-15 |
| *(Casey Kasem's new countdown show after leaving American Top 40; vinyl editions)* | | | |
| CHRONOLOGY OF AMERICAN MUSIC  Complete show | 1973 | More Music Productions | 100 |
| *(Features the #1 Billboard Hot 100 records from 1955-72)* | | | |
| CONCERT FOR THE COLONIES (July 86) Live material | 1986 | Westwood One (8) | 150-300 |
| *(Great BBC concerts of major UK groups edited into one concert that sounds convincing)* | | | |
| CONCERT OVER AMERICA (Sept 88) Live material | 1988 | CBS RadioRadio (6) | 50-75 |
| *(Concert created in the studio)* | | | |
| CONTINUOUS HISTORY OF ROCK AND ROLL | 1983 | Drake-Chenault (65) | 250-400 |
| *(Issued as 13 box sets, day long show)* | | | |
| COUNTDOWN AMERICA | 198? | RKO Radio (4) | 8-12 |
| *(Average for any of the weekly shows in this series)* | | | |
| COUNTDOWN AMERICA (Dec 83)  Two 4-LP weekly shows | 1983 | RKO Radio (8) | 30-50 |
| *(The Top 83 hits of '83)* | | | |
| COUNTDOWN AMERICA (Dec 84)  Two 4-LP weekly shows | 1984 | RKO Radio (8) | 30-50 |
| *(The Top 84 hits of '84)* | | | |
| CROSSROADS Seasonal rock profiles | 1988 | Global/ABC (6) | 50-75 |
| *(Music and interviews)* | | | |
| CRUISIN' AMERICA (88-90) | 198? | (3) | 10-15 |
| *(Music and interviews weekly with Cousin Brucie, 86 shows were on LPs)* | | | |
| FARM AID (SUPERSTAR CONCERT) (80s-90s) | 199? | Westwood One (3) | 40-75 |
| *(Annual benefit concert for farmers under the direction of Willie Nelson)* | | | |
| GREAT AMERICAN SUMMER (June 83) | 1983 | CBS RadioRadio (6) | 30-60 |
| *(Music and interviews)* | | | |
| GREAT CONCERT MOMENTS (July 89) | 1989 | United Stations (4) | 25-40 |
| *(Music and interviews)* | | | |
| GREATEST MOMENTS IN ROCK (Aug 86) Box set | 1986 | NBC Radio (6) | 30-60 |
| *(Benefit concert profile includes Woodstock)* | | | |
| HISTORY OF COUNTRY MUSIC (June 82) | 1982 | Drake-Chenault (52) | 100-200 |
| *(52-hour documentary with scripts)* | | | |
| HISTORY OF ROCK & ROLL: SILVER ANNIVERSARY EDITION | 1981 | Drake-Chenault (51) | 400-700 |
| *(Weekly radio show)* | | | |
| HIT MEN OF ROCK (Dec 86) | 1986 | Barnett-Robbins | 20-30 |
| *(Profiles Roth, Julian Lennon, Gabriel, Jagger, Phil Collins, Sting and others, music and interviews)* | | | |
| HITSVILLE USA | 1985 | London Wavelength (12) | 150-300 |
| *(This version of "Story of Motown" was produced in USA for BBC/England)* | | | |
| HONOR ROLL OF ROCK & ROLL | 198? | CBS RadioRadio (6) | 35-50 |
| *(Six hours, 25 top artists of the rock era, music and interviews)* | | | |
| ISLE OF DREAMS   Hosted by Eric Clapton | 1985 | Westwood One (18) | 150-250 |
| *(12-hour "concert," edited tapes of prior Westwood One broadcasts to create the effect of a superstar live festival)* | | | |
| ISLE OF DREAMS   Hosted by Eric Clapton | 1987 | Westwood One (18) | 125-200 |
| *(Repeat of the above)* | | | |
| ISLE OF DREAMS   Hosted by Eric Clapton | 1989 | Westwood One (9) | 75-125 |
| *(Edited version)* | | | |
| JOURNEY | 1987 | Radio International | 20-30 |
| *(Issued with cover, features 60s-early 70s groups)* | | | |
| KING BISCUIT FLOWER HOUR  Live concerts, syndicated, for other editions look under the artist in question | | | |
| KING BISCUIT FLOWER HOUR (Summer) On tour | 198? | ABC/DIR (2) | 20-40 |
| *(Average price)* | | | |
| KING BISCUIT FLOWER HOUR (Dec) Year-enders | 198? | ABC/DIR (2) | 20-40 |
| *(Average price)* | | | |
| KING BISCUIT FLOWER HOUR (Apr 85) 500th show | 1985 | ABC/DIR (2) | 40-75 |
| *(Parts 1 and 2 feature highlights of last 499 shows, including John Lennon and Bruce Springsteen)* | | | |
| KING BISCUIT FLOWER HOUR (Apr 85) 500th show | 1985 | ABC/DIR (4) | 50-125 |
| *(Price is for both 2LP weekly parts of this 500th show)* | | | |
| KING BISCUIT FLOWER HOUR (July 85) July 4th special | 1985 | ABC/DIR (3) | 20-50 |
| *(Sometimes DIR would issue a 3LP)* | | | |

| Title | Yr | Label, Number | NM $ |
|---|---|---|---|
| KING BISCUIT FLOWER HOUR (Oct 85) Halloween special | 1985 | ABC/DIR (2) | 20-40 |
| (Various artists) | | | |
| KING BISCUIT FLOWER HOUR (Apr 86) Reason to Rock | 1986 | DIR (2) | 30-60 |
| (Includes cuts from Live Aid and other charity events) | | | |
| KING BISCUIT FLOWER HOUR (Feb 87) Anti-crack | 1987 | DIR (4) | 50-100 |
| (Includes CSNY and Allman Brothers and others, two 2-LP weekly sets) | | | |
| KING BISCUIT FLOWER HOUR (May 87) Memorial Day concert | 1987 | DIR (2) | 20-45 |
| (Foreigner in concert) | | | |
| LOLLAPALOOZA: OFF THE RECORD (Aug 92) | 1992 | Westwood One (2) | 10-15 |
| (Music and interviews about the concert series) | | | |
| LOVE AND A WHOLE LOT MORE  12-hour special | 1980 | TM Special Products (12) | 30-60 |
| (Music and interviews) | | | |
| MONTEREY POP - THE RADIO CONCERT (May 88) | 1988 | Radio Express (9) | 400-600 |
| (Nine-hour concert on vinyl, very limited) | | | |
| MOSCOW PEACE FEST (IN CONCERT) (Mar 90) | 1990 | Westwood One (2) | 30-50 |
| (Edited version of the above concert) | | | |
| MOSCOW PEACE FEST (SUPERSTAR CONCERT) (Feb 90) | 1990 | Westwood One (3) | 40-60 |
| (Live concert, box set) | | | |
| THE MOTOWN STORY | 1983 | Motown | 100-200 |
| (Box set, profile of the label) | | | |
| THE MOTOWN STORY VOL. 1 | 1983 | Motown 121 (7) | 50-100 |
| (Box set, hosted by Lionel Richie, white promo labels) | | | |
| THE MOTOWN STORY  VOL.1 AND VOL. 2 | 1983 | Motown 121/122 (8) | 60-100 |
| (Same as above with additional LP) | | | |
| MUNI-TRIBUTE TO LONDON (May 85) | 1985 | Westwood One (4) | 20-30 |
| (Scott Muni is host, music and interviews) | | | |
| REMEMBERING THE 70S | 198? | Radio Works (12) | 40-75 |
| (Music and interviews that highlight the 70s) | | | |
| RETRO ROCK (Aug 84) | 1984 | Clayton Webster (4) | 40-75 |
| (Same show as "Woodstock Spirit") | | | |
| ROCK AND ROLL VALENTINE (Feb 81) | 1981 | ABC Radio (18) | 50-100 |
| (Twelve-hour special with music by John Lennon, Elton John and others) | | | |
| ROCK FOR AMNESTY (June 87) | 1987 | Westwood One (5) | 60-125 |
| (Live benefit concert with major artists) | | | |
| ROCK IN THE YULETIDE (Dec 87) | 1987 | Westwood One (2) | 40-75 |
| (Music and interviews, previews "A Very Special Christmas," a benefit LP for Special Olympics) | | | |
| ROCK INTO SUMMER (May 88) Box set | 1988 | NBC Radio (9) | 25-50 |
| (Music and interviews) | | | |
| ROCK OF YOUR LIFE | 1986 | NBC Radio (30) | 200-300 |
| (Same show as above, edited to 20 hours, price includes poster) | | | |
| ROCK OF YOUR LIFE   History of rock music | 1985 | NBC Radio (45) | 250-500 |
| (Music and interviews, four label varieties within the set) | | | |
| ROCK OLDIES SHOW (June 88) Dick Bartley | 1988 | Westwood One (5) | 25-40 |
| (Music and interviews, oldies countdown show) | | | |
| ROCK SALUTES MOTOWN | 1986 | NBC Radio | 40-80 |
| (Phil Collins is host) | | | |
| ROCK SCOPE (70s) | 197? | Sangre Productions (8) | 75-100 |
| (Four 2-LP monthly sets, titled Stairway to Heaven) | | | |
| ROCK SCOPE (70s) | 197? | Sangre Productions (2) | 25-50 |
| (Music and interviews, on the Doors) | | | |
| ROCK SCOPE (70s) | 197? | Sangre Productions (2) | 25-50 |
| (Music and interviews, on the Beatles) | | | |
| ROCK, ROLL & REMEMBER (Sept 77) Dick Clark | 1977 | United Stations (6) | 75-150 |
| (Special "Elvis Remembered" version of the show, music and interviews) | | | |
| ROLLING STONE 20TH ANNIVERSARY SALUTE (Mar 87) | 1987 | Westwood One (2) | 25-50 |
| (Part one, orange labels) | | | |
| ROLLING STONE 20TH ANNIVERSARY SALUTE (June 87) | 1987 | Westwood One (3) | 25-50 |
| (Part two, purple labels) | | | |
| ROLLING STONE 20TH ANNIVERSARY SALUTE (Sept 87) | 1987 | Westwood One (3) | 25-50 |
| (Part three, yellow labels) | | | |
| ROLLING STONE 20TH ANNIVERSARY SALUTE (Oct 87) | 1987 | Westwood One (2) | 25-40 |
| (Music and interviews) | | | |
| ROLLING STONE 20TH ANNIVERSARY SALUTE (Mar-Oct 87) | 1987 | Westwood One (10) | 75-150 |
| (Complete set in four releases, magazine tribute, all shows are music and interviews) | | | |
| ROYALTY OF ROCK (Jan 83) Various artists | 1983 | RKO Radio (50) | 200-300 |
| (Music and interviews) | | | |
| SATCON I  Various artists | 1980 | Drake-Chenault (48) | 1,500-2,500 |
| (Live concert material from major artists, very rare as a complete 48-record set) | | | |
| SOLID GOLD SCRAPBOOK (Aug 86) Box set | 1986 | United Stations (5) | 20-40 |
| (One of five discs is a Woodstock profile) | | | |
| SOLID GOLD SCRAPBOOK 1963-1982 | 1985 | RKO Radio (20) | 50-125 |
| (Top 10 singles of each year with trivia and news) | | | |
| SOUND OF '77 (Dec 77)  Country version, Elvis tribute | 1977 | Billboard Magazine (5) | 75 |
| (Music and interviews) | | | |
| SOUND OF '77 (Dec 77)  Rock version, Elvis tribute | 1977 | Billboard Magazine (5) | 60 |
| (Music and interviews) | | | |
| SOUNDS OF SOLID GOLD  Ex-Beatles Vol. 47 | 1984 | U.S. Marine Corps (7) | 25-60 |
| (One of the seven discs is "Ex-Beatles" show) | | | |
| SOUNDS OF SOLID GOLD  Solo Beatles Vol. 49 | 1984 | U.S. Marine Corps (7) | 25-50 |
| (Some of the shows are that of solo Beatles) | | | |
| SOUNDS OF SOLID GOLD  Solo Beatles Vol. 50 | 1985 | U.S. Marine Corps (7) | 40-75 |
| (Includes shows that are solo Beatles) | | | |
| SOUNDS OF SOLID GOLD  Presley shows Vol. 51 | 1985 | U.S. Marine Corps (7) | 40-75 |
| (Three sides, shows are exclusively Elvis Presley) | | | |
| SOUNDS OF SOLID GOLD (Through June 85) | 1985 | U.S. Marine Corps (7) | 20-40 |
| (Any show, "Solid Gold" or "Solid Gold Country" that includes Elvis Presley cut) | | | |
| SPECIAL FORCES  Meat Puppets | 1986 | BBE Radio | 40-75 |
| (Live concert) | | | |

| Title | Yr | Label, Number | NM $ |
|---|---|---|---|
| SPECIAL FORCES  The Smithereens | 1986 | BBE Radio | 75-150 |
| *(Live concert, issued with promo-only black/white hard picture cover)* | | | |
| SPIN CONCERT  10,000 Maniacs | 1985 | BBE Radio | 40-75 |
| *(Live concert)* | | | |
| SPIN CONCERT  Circle Jerks | 1985 | BBE Radio (2) | 40-75 |
| *(Live concert)* | | | |
| SPIN CONCERT  Fine Young Cannibals | 1986 | BBE Radio | 50-75 |
| *(Live concert, issued with promo-only black/white hard picture cover)* | | | |
| SPIN CONCERT  Husker Du | 1986 | BBE Radio (2) | 100-200 |
| *(Live concert)* | | | |
| SPIN CONCERT  Jesus and Mary Chain | 1987 | BBE Radio (2) | 50-100 |
| *(Live concert)* | | | |
| SPIN CONCERT  Modern English | 1986 | BBE Radio | 40-75 |
| *(Live concert)* | | | |
| SPIN RADIO UNDERGROUND  Various artists | 1985 | BBE Radio (2) | 25-50 |
| *(Live tracks, shows 001-007, each show is composed of various artists of the college music scene)* | | | |
| STORY OF COUNTRY MUSIC (80s) Various artists | 198? | TM Special Products (48) | 125-250 |
| *(Music and interviews)* | | | |
| SUPERSTAR CONCERT  Box set, Amnesty Fund | 1988 | Westwood One (3) | 40-75 |
| *(Live concert)* | | | |
| TOP 30 ARTISTS OF ALL TIME (Nov 82) | 1982 | Mutual Radio (3) | 20-40 |
| *(One song each from top 30 acts ranked by Dick Clark, box set)* | | | |
| US FESTIVAL | 1983 | Westwood One (18) | 200 |
| *(Live concert from Devore, California with Bowie, Clash, U2, Van Halen and others)* | | | |
| WOODSTOCK REUNION (Aug 84) | 1984 | NBC Source (3) | 40-75 |
| *(Concert and interviews)* | | | |
| WOODSTOCK SPIRIT (Aug 84) | 1984 | Clayton Webster (4) | 40-75 |
| *(Two 2-LP sets, part 1 and part 2)* | | | |
| **Compact Discs** | | | |
| 60s AT THE BEEB Various artists | 1990 | Westwood One (6) | 100-200 |
| *(CD version of the same show)* | | | |
| AMERICAN TOP 40 (1988-95) | 198? | ABC/Watermark (4) | 8-12 |
| *(Four-hour shows, hosted by Shadoe Stevens or guest host, some early volumes may have been on vinyl, same value)* | | | |
| AMERICAN TOP 40 (Mar 98-present) | 1998 | AMFM Radio (4) | 8-12 |
| *(Revival of AT40, hosted by Casey Kasem, available with several different types of music)* | | | |
| AMERICANS ON THE BEEB (July 94) | 1994 | BBC Classic Tracks | 20-25 |
| *(Includes Allmans, Alice Cooper, Meat Loaf and Turtles)* | | | |
| BBC CLASSIC TRACKS (Aug 94) | 1994 | Westwood One | 15-25 |
| *(Live classic tracks)* | | | |
| BRITISH INVASION | 1988 | DB Productions (10) | 75-100 |
| *(Radio stations had their choice of vinyl or CD)* | | | |
| BRITISH INVASION  Twelve designer CDs | 1990 | DB Productions (12) | 100-200 |
| *(Not the same program as the NSBA production)* | | | |
| CASEY'S TOP 20 (90s) | 199? | (2) | 8-12 |
| *(Shorter version of Casey's Top 40, price for any one weekly show)* | | | |
| CASEY'S TOP 40 (Early 1990s-1998) | 199? | (4) | 10-15 |
| *(Compact disc editions)* | | | |
| CLASSIC TRACKS (Feb 94) Profile | 1994 | Westwood One | 20-40 |
| *(In general, profile of the British Invasion)* | | | |
| CONTINUOUS HISTORY OF ROCK AND ROLL | 1989 | Drake-Chenault (50) | 250-500 |
| *(Easier to find than the 13-box set vinyl version)* | | | |
| CROSSROADS | 1988 | Global Satellite (4) | 50-75 |
| *(Music and interviews)* | | | |
| CRUISIN' AMERICA (88-90) | 199? | (3) | 10-15 |
| *(Music and interviews weekly with Cousin Brucie, 22 shows were on CDs)* | | | |
| GLASTONBURY FESTIVAL (July 95) | 1995 | Westwood One (9) | 200-300 |
| *(Highlights of the festival, live concert material)* | | | |
| GUITAR LEGENDS (Mar 92) Seville, Spain live concert | 1992 | (3) | 150-250 |
| *(With Dylan, Richards, McGuinn, Walsh, Robertson, Brian May, Waters, B.B. King and Albert Collins)* | | | |
| HISTORY OF ROCK & ROLL | 1989 | ABC Radio (52) | 600-1,000 |
| *(Issued in 15 box sets)* | | | |
| HISTORY OF ROCK & ROLL | 1994 | ABC Radio (52) | 900-1,750 |
| *(Issued in a special notebook)* | | | |
| KING BISCUIT FLOWER HOUR (Dec) Year-enders | 199? | DIR | 20-40 |
| *(Average price)* | | | |
| KING BISCUIT FLOWER HOUR (May 88) | 1988 | DIR (4) | 75-250 |
| *(This "15th Anniversary Celebration" was a one-time special carried by fewer stations than the regular weekly Biscuit)* | | | |
| KING BISCUIT FLOWER HOUR (May 88) "KB #1" | 1988 | DIR | 50-125 |
| *(This is a repeat on CD of the first Biscuit show from 1973)* | | | |
| MADE IN AMERICA (July 92) | 1992 | (12) | 25-50 |
| *(Music and interviews, includes some Elvis Presley material)* | | | |
| MASTERS OF ROCK  Value for most common artists | 199? | Radio Ventures | 40 |
| *(Higher priced artists listed with artists)* | | | |
| MONTEREY POP - THE RADIO CONCERT (May 88) | 1988 | Radio Express (9) | 600-850 |
| *(On nine compact discs, very limited on CD)* | | | |
| NUMBER ONE GOODTIME OLDIES (MAY 91) Charlie Tuna | 1991 | Westwood One (12) | 50-100 |
| *(Music and interviews)* | | | |
| POLYGRAM BRINGS YOU THE RICHNESS OF BLACK MUSIC | 1990 | Polygram (7) | 40 |
| *(Promo-only series)* | | | |
| PROFILED  Music and interviews | 199? | | 15-25 |
| *(Average value for any edition of this series)* | | | |
| READING FESTIVAL (Mar 96) | 1996 | Westwood One (3) | 95 |
| *(With Hole, Smashing Pumpkins, Foo Fighters, White Zombie, Beck)* | | | |
| ROAD TO SAUGHERTIES (Aug 94) | 1994 | Media America (3) | 40-75 |
| *(Live performances of the newer artists, Woodstock '94 related)* | | | |
| ROCK IN RIO (Jan 91) | 1991 | Westwood One (2) | 20-40 |
| *(Live concert from Brazil)* | | | |

| Title | Yr | Label, Number | NM $ |
|---|---|---|---|
| ROCK OF YOUR LIFE  Edited version | 1989 | NBC Radio | 150-200 |
| *(No poster)* | | | |
| SOUL OF THE 60s (July 89)  With Dick Bartley | 1989 | Westwood One (10) | 40-75 |
| *(Music and interviews)* | | | |
| TOP 25 ROCK ALBUMS (Nov 89) | 1989 | DIR (6) | 40-75 |
| *(Thanksgiving special, music and interviews)* | | | |
| WOODSTOCK (Aug 89) "Summer of '69" | 1989 | Media America (4) | 40-75 |
| *(Music and interviews)* | | | |
| WOODSTOCK (Aug 94) | 1994 | Media America (4) | 40-75 |
| *(Live performances)* | | | |
| WOODSTOCK ANNIVERSARY SPECIAL (Aug 84) | 1984 | (3) | 40-75 |
| *(Music and interviews and live tracks)* | | | |
| WOODSTOCK MINUTES (Aug 89) | 1989 | Media America (5) | 40-75 |
| *(Series of 1-minute shows to run 12 weeks, featuring the 20th anniversary and top stars of Woodstock)* | | | |
| WOODSTOCK MINUTES (Aug 94) | 1994 | Media America (5) | 25-50 |
| *(Update series)* | | | |
| WOODSTOCK REVISITED (Aug 89) | 1989 | Media America (3) | 25-50 |
| *(Also known as "Where Are They Now")* | | | |
| WOODSTOCK REVISITED (Aug 94) | 1994 | Media America (3) | 50-100 |
| *(Unreleased live tracks included)* | | | |
| WOODSTOCK ROCK BLOCKS (Aug 94) | 1994 | Westwood One (5) | 50-100 |
| *(Live performances)* | | | |
| WOODSTOCK '94: BEST OF THE REST (Sept 94) | 1994 | Media America (4) | 125-250 |
| *(More material from Woodstock '94 not broadcast earlier)* | | | |
| **Reel-to-Reel Tapes** | | | |
| AMERICAN TOP 40 (July 70) | 1970 | Watermark | 100-150 |
| *(The very first show, aired July 4, 1970, hosted by Casey Kasem)* | | | |
| AMERICAN TOP 40 (1970-73) | 197? | Watermark | 30-50 |
| *(Early shows distributed on reel-to-reel tape)* | | | |
| KING BISCUIT FLOWER HOUR  Debut show | 1973 | DIR (2) | 250-400 |
| *(With Bruce Springsteen, Blood, Sweat & Tears, and Mahavishnu Orchestra)* | | | |
| WOODSTOCK '94 (Aug 94) | 1994 | Media America (11) | 300-500 |
| *(Same material as on the live satellite feed of the concert, distributed to stations without a satellite uplink)* | | | |